Middle School Accelerated Grade 7

Edward B. Burger
Juli K. Dixon
Timothy D. Kanold
Matthew R. Larson
Steven J. Leinwand
Martha E. Sandoval-Martinez

Printed in the U.S.A.

ISBN 978-0-544-24796-3

15 0877 25 24 23 22 21

4500819080 E F G

Authors

Edward B. Burger, Ph.D., is the President of Southwestern University, a former Francis Christopher Oakley Third Century Professor of Mathematics at Williams College and a former vice provost at Baylor University. He has authored or coauthored more than sixty-five articles, books, and video series; delivered over five hundred addresses and workshops throughout the world; and made more than fifty radio and television appearances. He is a Fellow of the American Mathematical Society as well as having earned many national honors, including the Robert Foster Cherry Award for Great Teaching in 2010. In 2012, Microsoft Education named him a "Global Hero in Education."

Juli K. Dixon, Ph.D., is a Professor of Mathematics Education at the University of Central Florida. She has taught mathematics in urban schools at the elementary, middle, secondary, and post-secondary levels. She is an active researcher and speaker with numerous publications and conference presentations. Key areas of focus are deepening teachers' content knowledge and communicating and justifying mathematical ideas. She is a past chair of the NCTM Student Explorations in Mathematics Editorial Panel and member of the Board of Directors for the Association of Mathematics Teacher Educators.

Timothy D. Kanold, Ph.D., is an award-winning international educator, author, and consultant. He is a former superintendent and director of mathematics and science at Adlai E. Stevenson High School District 125 in Lincolnshire, Illinois. He is a past president of the National Council of Supervisors of Mathematics (NCSM) and the Council for the Presidential Awardees of Mathematics (CPAM). He has served on several writing and leadership commissions for NCTM during the past decade. He presents motivational professional development seminars with a focus on developing professional learning communities (PLC's) to improve the teaching, assessing, and learning of students. He has recently authored nationally recognized articles, books, and textbooks for mathematics education and school leadership, including *What Every Principal Needs to Know about the Teaching and Learning of Mathematics*.

Matthew R. Larson, Ph.D., is the K-12 mathematics curriculum specialist for the Lincoln Public Schools and served on the Board of Directors for the National Council of Teachers of Mathematics from 2010-2013. He is a past chair of NCTM's Research Committee and was a member of NCTM's Task Force on Linking Research and Practice. He is the author of several books on implementing the Common Core Standards for Mathematics. He has taught mathematics at the secondary and college levels and held an appointment as an honorary visiting associate professor at Teachers College, Columbia University.

Steven J. Leinwand is a Principal Research Analyst at the American Institutes for Research (AIR) in Washington, D.C., and has over 30 years in leadership positions in mathematics education. He is past president of the National Council of Supervisors of Mathematics and served on the NCTM Board of Directors. He is the author of numerous articles, books, and textbooks and has made countless presentations with topics including student achievement, reasoning, effective assessment, and successful implementation of standards.

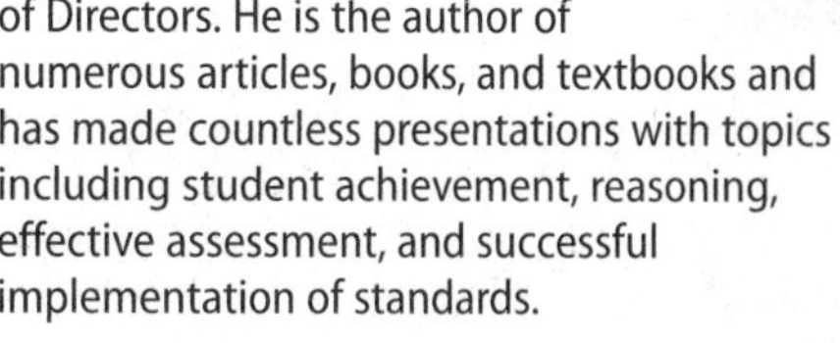

Martha E. Sandoval-Martinez is a mathematics instructor at El Camino College in Torrance, California. She was previously a Math Specialist at the University of California at Davis and former instructor at Santa Ana College, Marymount College, and California State University, Long Beach. In her current and former positions, she has worked extensively to improve fundamental pre-algebra and algebra skills in students who have historically struggled with mathematics.

California Consulting Reviewers

Elizabeth Jiménez, CEO
GEMAS Consulting
Pomona, CA

Erin Bostick Mason, MA.Ed.
Adjunct Faculty
Dept. of Language, Literature and Culture
College of Education, California State University
San Bernardino, CA

Jill Kerper Mora, Ed.D.
Associate Professor Emerita
School of Teacher Education
San Diego State University
San Diego, CA

California Advisory Board

Ashley A. Downing
Eagle Peak Middle School
Ukiah Unified School District
Redwood Valley, CA

Robert Kaplinsky
Teacher Specialist, Mathematics
Downey Unified School District
Downey, CA

Peggy M. Mendez
Charles Wagner Elementary School
Placentia, CA

Melissa Samson
Kraemer Middle School
Placentia, CA

Lori With
BMS Math Teacher
Benicia Middle School
Benicia, CA

UNIT 1 CALIFORNIA

The Number System

MODULE 1 Adding and Subtracting Integers

MODULE 2 Multiplying and Dividing Integers

MODULE 3 Rational Numbers

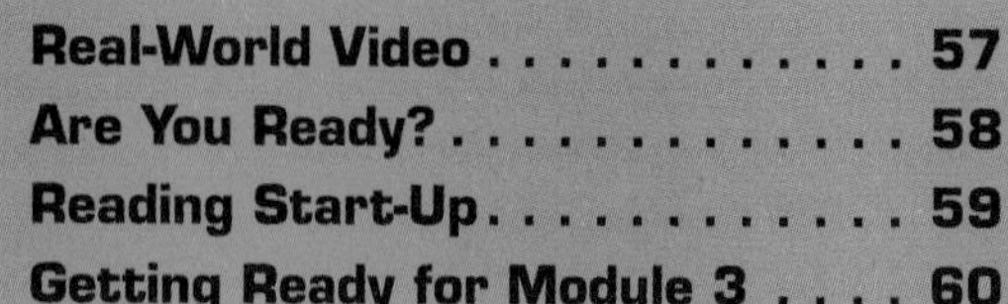

CA CC

UNIT 2 CALIFORNIA

Ratios and Proportional Relationships

MODULE 4 Ratios and Proportionality

MODULE 5 Proportions and Percent

Expressions, Equations, and Inequalities

Expressions and Equations

Inequalities

UNIT 4 CALIFORNIA

Geometry

MODULE 8 Modeling Geometric Figures

MODULE 9 Circumference, Area, and Volume

Statistics

MODULE 10 Analyzing and Comparing Data

MODULE 11 Random Samples and Populations

UNIT 6

CALIFORNIA

Probability

MODULE 12 Experimental Probability

MODULE 13 Theoretical Probability and Simulations

Real Numbers, Exponents and Scientific Notation

MODULE 14 Real Numbers

CA CC

MODULE 15 Exponents and Scientific Notation

CA CC

UNIT 8 Linear Relationships and Equations

MODULE 16 Proportional Relationships

CA CC

MODULE 17 Nonproportional Relationships

CA CC

MODULE 18 Solving Linear Equations

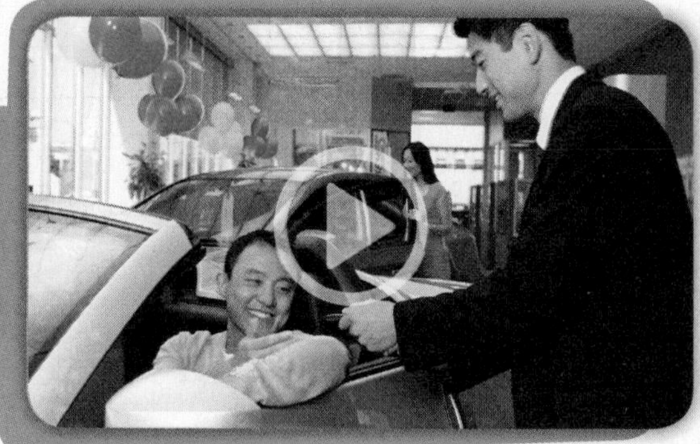

CA CC

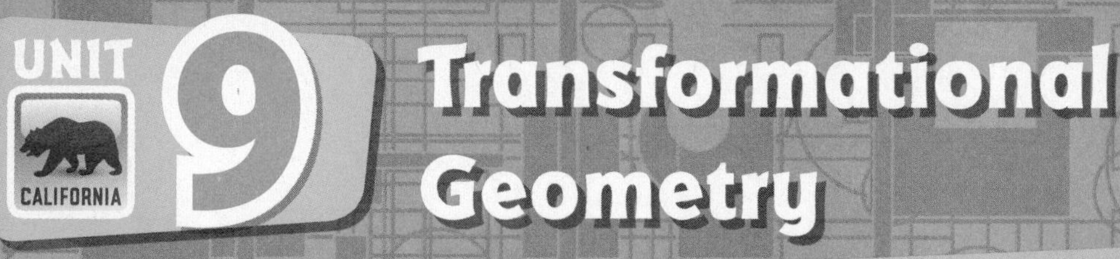

UNIT 9 Transformational Geometry

MODULE 19 Transformations and Congruence

MODULE 20 Transformations and Similarity

UNIT 10 Measurement Geometry

MODULE 21 Angle Relationships in Parallel Lines and Triangles

CA CC

MODULE 22 Volume

CA CC

APPENDIX

The Pythagorean Theorem

California Common Core Standards for Mathematics

Correlations for *HMH California Go Math* Accelerated Grade 7

Standard	Descriptor	Taught	Reinforced
7.RP RATIOS AND PROPORTIONAL RELATIONSHIPS			
Analyze proportional relationships and use them to solve real-world and mathematical problems.			
7.RP.1	Compute unit rates associated with ratios of fractions, including ratios of lengths, areas and other quantities measured in like or different units.	SE: 117–120	SE: 121–122, 135–136
7.RP.2	Recognize and represent proportional relationships between quantities.	SE: 123–126, 129–132; *See also parts a–d below.*	SE: 127–128, 133–134, 135–136; *See also parts a–d below.*
7.RP.2a	Decide whether two quantities are in a proportional relationship, e.g., by testing for equivalent ratios in a table or graphing on a coordinate plane and observing whether the graph is a straight line through the origin.	SE: 123–124, 126, 129–130, 132	SE: 127–128, 133–134, 135–136
7.RP.2b	Identify the constant of proportionality (unit rate) in tables, graphs, equations, diagrams, and verbal descriptions of proportional relationships.	SE: 123–126, 129–130	SE: 127–128, 133–134, 135–136
7.RP.2c	Represent proportional relationships by equations.	SE: 125–126, 131–132, 319	SE: 127–128, 133–134, 135–136, 321, 330
7.RP.2d	Explain what a point (x, y) on the graph of a proportional relationship means in terms of the situation, with special attention to the points $(0, 0)$ and $(1, r)$ where r is the unit rate.	SE: 129–130	SE: 133
7.RP.3	Use proportional relationships to solve multistep ratio and percent problems.	SE: 141–144, 147–150, 153–156	SE: 145–146, 151–152, 157–158, 159–160

Standard	Descriptor	Taught	Reinforced
7.NS THE NUMBER SYSTEM			
Apply and extend previous understandings of operations with fractions to add, subtract, multiply, and divide rational numbers.			
7.NS.1	Apply and extend previous understandings of addition and subtraction to add and subtract rational numbers; represent addition and subtraction on a horizontal or vertical number line diagram.	SE: 7–10, 13–16, 19–22, 25, 75–79; *See also parts a–d that follow.*	SE: 11–12, 17–18, 23–24, 30, 31–32, 80–82, 101–102; *See also parts a–d that follow.*
7.NS.1a	Describe situations in which opposite quantities combine to make 0.	SE: 13, 15, 16, 70, 72	SE: 17, 74
7.NS.1b	Understand $p + q$ as the number located a distance $\lvert q \rvert$ from p, in the positive or negative direction depending on whether q is positive or negative. Show that a number and its opposite have a sum of 0 (are additive inverses). Interpret sums of rational numbers by describing real-world contexts.	SE: 8, 13–16, 67–70, 72	SE: 11–12, 17–18, 31–32, 73–74, 102
7.NS.1c	Understand subtraction of rational numbers as adding the additive inverse, $p - q = p + (-q)$. Show that the distance between two rational numbers on the number line is the absolute value of their difference, and apply this principle in real-world contexts.	SE: 20–22, 77–79	SE: 23–24, 31–32, 80–82, 101–102
7.NS.1d	Apply properties of operations as strategies to add and subtract rational numbers.	SE: 9, 26, 70–72	SE: 12, 29, 73–74
7.NS.2	Apply and extend previous understandings of multiplication and division and of fractions to multiply and divide rational numbers.	SE: 37–40, 43–46, 83–86, 89, 92; *See also parts a–d below.*	SE: 41–42, 47–48, 55–56, 87–88, 93–94, 101–102; *See also parts a–d below.*
7.NS.2a	Understand that multiplication is extended from fractions to rational numbers by requiring that operations continue to satisfy the properties of operations, particularly the distributive property, leading to products such as $(-1)(-1) = 1$ and the rules for multiplying signed numbers. Interpret products of rational numbers by describing real-world contexts.	SE: 37–38, 49, 52, 83–84, 86	SE: 42, 53–54, 55–56, 87–88, 101
7.NS.2b	Understand that integers can be divided, provided that the divisor is not zero, and every quotient of integers (with non-zero divisor) is a rational number. If p and q are integers, then $-\left(\frac{p}{q}\right) = \frac{(-p)}{q} = \frac{p}{(-q)}$. Interpret quotients of rational numbers by describing real-world contexts.	SE: 44, 46, 61, 64, 89–90, 92	SE: 48, 66, 93–94, 101

Standard	Descriptor	Taught	Reinforced
7.NS.2c	Apply properties of operations as strategies to multiply and divide rational numbers.	SE: 49, 52, 85–86, 91–92	SE: 53, 55–56, 87–88, 93–94, 101–102
7.NS.2d	Convert a rational number to a decimal using long division; know that the decimal form of a rational number terminates in 0s or eventually repeats.	SE: 61–64	SE: 65–66, 101–102
7.NS.3	Solve real-world and mathematical problems involving the four operations with rational numbers.	SE: 25–28, 43–46, 50–52, 71–72, 95–98	SE: 29–30, 31–32, 47–48, 53–54, 55–56, 73–74, 99–100, 101–102
7.EE EXPRESSIONS AND EQUATIONS			
Use properties of operations to generate equivalent expressions.			
7.EE.1	Apply properties of operations as strategies to add, subtract, factor, and expand linear expressions with rational coefficients.	SE: 173–176	SE: 177–178, 197–198
7.EE.2	Understand that rewriting an expression in different forms in a problem context can shed light on the problem and how the quantities in it are related.	SE: 147–150, 173–176	SE: 151–152, 159–160, 177–178, 197–198
Solve real-life and mathematical problems using numerical and algebraic expressions and equations.			
7.EE.3	Solve multi-step real-life and mathematical problems posed with positive and negative rational numbers in any form (whole numbers, fractions, and decimals), using tools strategically. Apply properties of operations to calculate with numbers in any form; convert between forms as appropriate; and assess the reasonableness of answers using mental computation and estimation strategies.	SE: 26–28, 50–52, 95–98, 153–156	SE: 29–30, 31–32, 53–54, 55–56, 99–100, 101–102, 157–158
7.EE.4	Use variables to represent quantities in a real-world or mathematical problem, and construct simple equations and inequalities to solve problems by reasoning about the quantities.	SE: 179–182, 185–188, 191, 207–208, 211–214; *See also parts a and b below.*	SE: 183–184, 189–190, 194, 195–196, 197–198, 209–210, 215–216, 223–224; *See also parts a and b below.*

Standard	Descriptor	Taught	Reinforced
7.EE.4a	Solve word problems leading to equations of the form $px + q = r$ and $p(x + q) = r$, where p, q, and r are specific rational numbers. Solve equations of these forms fluently. Compare an algebraic solution to an arithmetic solution, identifying the sequence of the operations used in each approach.	SE: 191–194	SE: 195–196, 197–198
7.EE.4b	Solve word problems leading to inequalities of the form $px + q > r$ or $px + q < r$, where p, q, and r are specific rational numbers. Graph the solution set of the inequality and interpret it in the context of the problem.	SE: 203–208, 217–220	SE: 209–210, 221–222, 223–224
7.G GEOMETRY			
Draw, construct, and describe geometrical figures and describe the relationships between them.			
7.G.1	Solve problems involving scale drawings of geometric figures, including computing actual lengths and areas from a scale drawing and reproducing a scale drawing at a different scale.	SE: 237–240	SE: 241–242, 259–260
7.G.2	Draw (freehand, with ruler and protractor, and with technology) geometric shapes with given conditions. Focus on constructing triangles from three measures of angles or sides, noticing when the conditions determine a unique triangle, more than one triangle, or no triangle.	SE: 243–245	SE: 245–246, 259–260
7.G.3	Describe the two-dimensional figures that result from slicing three-dimensional figures, as in plane sections of right rectangular prisms and right rectangular pyramids.	SE: 247–249	SE: 249–250, 259–260
Solve real-life and mathematical problems involving angle measure, area, surface area, and volume.			
7.G.4	Know the formulas for the area and circumference of a circle and use them to solve problems; give an informal derivation of the relationship between the circumference and area of a circle.	SE: 265–268, 271–274	SE: 269–270, 275–276, 295–296
7.G.5	Use facts about supplementary, complementary, vertical, and adjacent angles in a multi-step problem to write and solve simple equations for an unknown angle in a figure.	SE: 251–256	SE: 257–258, 259–260
7.G.6	Solve real-world and mathematical problems involving area, volume and surface area of two- and three-dimensional objects composed of triangles, quadrilaterals, polygons, cubes, and right prisms.	SE: 277–280, 283–286, 289–292	SE: 281–282, 287–288, 293–294, 295–296

Standard	Descriptor	Taught	Reinforced
7.SP STATISTICS AND PROBABILITY			
Use random sampling to draw inferences about a population.			
7.SP.1	Understand that statistics can be used to gain information about a population by examining a sample of the population; generalizations about a population from a sample are valid only if the sample is representative of that population. Understand that random sampling tends to produce representative samples and support valid inferences.	SE: 335–338, 341–344	SE: 339–340, 345–346, 353–354
7.SP.2	Use data from a random sample to draw inferences about a population with an unknown characteristic of interest. Generate multiple samples (or simulated samples) of the same size to gauge the variation in estimates or predictions.	SE: 341, 347–350	SE: 345–346, 351–352, 353–354
Draw informal comparative inferences about two populations.			
7.SP.3	Informally assess the degree of visual overlap of two numerical data distributions with similar variabilities, measuring the difference between the centers by expressing it as a multiple of a measure of variability.	SE: 312, 314, 318, 320, 323–324, 326	SE: 315–316, 321–322, 327–328, 329–330
7.SP.4	Use measures of center and measures of variability for numerical data from random samples to draw informal comparative inferences about two populations.	SE: 311, 313–314, 317, 319–320, 325–326	SE: 315–316, 321–322, 327–328, 329–330

Standard	Descriptor	Taught	Reinforced
Investigate chance processes and develop, use, and evaluate probability models.			
7.SP.5	Understand that the probability of a chance event is a number between 0 and 1 that expresses the likelihood of the event occurring. Larger numbers indicate greater likelihood. A probability near 0 indicates an unlikely event, a probability around $\frac{1}{2}$ indicates an event that is neither unlikely nor likely, and a probability near 1 indicates a likely event.	SE: 367–369, 371–372	SE: 373–374
7.SP.6	Approximate the probability of a chance event by collecting data on the chance process that produces it and observing its long-run relative frequency, and predict the approximate relative frequency given the probability.	SE: 375, 377–378, 387–390, 401–402, 411–414	SE: 379–380, 391–392, 415–416
7.SP.7	Develop a probability model and use it to find probabilities of events. Compare probabilities from a model to observed frequencies; if the agreement is not good, explain possible sources of the discrepancy.	SE: 401–402; *See also parts a and b below.*	SE: 403–404; *See also parts a and b below.*
7.SP.7a	Develop a uniform probability model by assigning equal probability to all outcomes, and use the model to determine probabilities of events.	SE: 369–372, 399–400, 413–414	SE: 373–374, 393–394, 403–404, 415–416, 423–424
7.SP.7b	Develop a probability model (which may not be uniform) by observing frequencies in data generated from a chance process.	SE: 375–377, 378	SE: 379–380, 393–394
7.SP.8	Find probabilities of compound events using organized lists, tables, tree diagrams, and simulation.	SE: 381–384, 405–408, 418–420; *See also parts a–c below.*	SE: 385–386, 393–394, 409–410, 421–422, 423–424; *See also parts a–c below.*
7.SP.8a	Understand that, just as with simple events, the probability of a compound event is the fraction of outcomes in the sample space for which the compound event occurs.	SE: 381–384, 405, 408	SE: 385–386, 393–394, 409–410, 423–424
7.SP.8b	Represent sample spaces for compound events using methods such as organized lists, tables and tree diagrams. For an event described in everyday language (e.g., "rolling double sixes"), identify the outcomes in the sample space which compose the event.	SE: 381–384, 406–408	SE: 385–386, 393–394, 409–410
7.SP.8c	Design and use a simulation to generate frequencies for compound events.	SE: 383–384, 417–420	SE: 386, 421–422, 423–424

Standard	Descriptor	Taught	Reinforced
8.NS THE NUMBER SYSTEM			
Know that there are numbers that are not rational, and approximate them by rational numbers.			
8.NS.1	Know that numbers that are not rational are called irrational. Understand informally that every number has a decimal expansion; for rational numbers show that the decimal expansion repeats eventually, and convert a decimal expansion which repeats eventually into a rational number.	SE: 437–439, 442, 445–447, 448	SE: 443–444, 449–450, 457, 458
8.NS.2	Use rational approximations of irrational numbers to compare the size of irrational numbers, locate them approximately on a number line diagram, and estimate the value of expressions (e.g., π^2).	SE: 440–442, 451–453, 454	SE: 444, 455–456, 457, 458
8.EE EXPRESSIONS AND EQUATIONS			
Work with radicals and integer exponents.			
8.EE.1	Know and apply the properties of integer exponents to generate equivalent numerical expressions.	SE: 463, 467	SE: 469–470, 489, 490
8.EE.2	Use square root and cube root symbols to represent solutions to equations of the form $x^2 = p$ and $x^3 = p$, where p is a positive rational number. Evaluate square roots of small perfect squares and cube roots of small perfect cubes. Know that $\sqrt{2}$ is irrational.	SE: 439–441, 442	SE: 443–444, 457, 458
8.EE.3	Use numbers expressed in the form of a single digit times an integer power of 10 to estimate very large or very small quantities, and to express how many times as much one is than the other.	SE: 471–473, 474, 477–479	SE: 475–476, 481–482, 489, 490
8.EE.4	Perform operations with numbers expressed in scientific notation, including problems where both decimal and scientific notation are used. Use scientific notation and choose units of appropriate size for measurements of very large or very small quantities (e.g., use millimeters per year for seafloor spreading). Interpret scientific notation that has been generated by technology.	SE: 483–485, 486	SE: 487–488, 489, 490

Standard	Descriptor	Taught	Reinforced
Understand the connections between proportional relationships, lines, and linear equations.			
8.EE.5	Graph proportional relationships, interpreting the unit rate as the slope of the graph. Compare two different proportional relationships represented in different ways.	SE: 515–517, 518	SE: 519–520, 521, 522
8.EE.6	Use similar triangles to explain why the slope m is the same between any two distinct points on a non-vertical line in the coordinate plane; derive the equation $y = mx$ for a line through the origin and the equation $y = mx + b$ for a line intercepting the vertical axis at b.	SE: 503–505, 506, 533, 535, 536, 684–685	SE: 507–508, 521, 522, 538, 553, 554, 688
Analyze and solve linear equations and pairs of simultaneous linear equations.			
8.EE.7	Solve linear equations in one variable.	SE: 559–561, 562, 565–567, 568, 675, 678, 683–684, 686; *See also parts a and b below.*	SE: 563–564, 569–570, 583, 584, 679–680, 687–688; *See also parts a and b below.*
8.EE.7a	Give examples of linear equations in one variable with one solution, infinitely many solutions, or no solutions. Show which of these possibilities is the case by successively transforming the given equation into simpler forms, until an equivalent equation of the form $x = a$, $a = a$, or $a = b$ results (where a and b are different numbers).	SE: 577–579, 580	SE: 581–582, 583, 584
8.EE.7b	Solve linear equations with rational number coefficients, including equations whose solutions require expanding expressions using the distributive property and collecting like terms.	SE: 559–561, 565–567, 568, 571–573, 574, 677, 678	SE: 563–564, 569–570, 575–576, 583, 584, 679–680

Standard	Descriptor	Taught	Reinforced
8.F FUNCTIONS			
Define, evaluate, and compare functions.			
8.F.2	Compare properties of two functions each represented in a different way (algebraically, graphically, numerically in tables, or by verbal descriptions).	SE: 517, 518, 548–550	SE: 519–520, 552, 553, 554
8.F.3	Interpret the equation $y = mx + b$ as defining a linear function, whose graph is a straight line; give examples of functions that are not linear.	SE: 527–529, 530, 539–541, 542, 545, 549	SE: 531–532, 543–544, 551, 553, 554
Use functions to model relationships between quantities.			
8.F.4	Construct a function to model a linear relationship between two quantities. Determine the rate of change and initial value of the function from a description of a relationship or from two (x, y) values, including reading these from a table or from a graph. Interpret the rate of change and initial value of a linear function in terms of the situation it models, and in terms of its graph or a table of values.	SE: 509–511, 512, 515, 518, 534, 536, 540–541, 542, 546–547, 549	SE: 508, 513–514, 519, 521, 522, 537–538, 543–544, 551–552, 553, 554

Standard	Descriptor	Taught	Reinforced
8.G GEOMETRY			
Understand congruence and similarity using physical models, transparencies, or geometry software.			
8.G.1a	Verify experimentally the properties of rotations, reflections, and translations: Lines are taken to lines, and line segments to line segments of the same length.	SE: 599–601, 602, 605–607, 608, 611–613, 614	SE: 603–604, 609–610, 615–616, 629, 630
8.G.1b	Verify experimentally the properties of rotations, reflections, and translations: Angles are taken to angles of the same measure.	SE: 599–601, 602, 605–607, 608, 611–613, 614	SE: 603–604, 609–610, 615–616, 629, 630
8.G.1c	Verify experimentally the properties of rotations, reflections, and translations: Parallel lines are taken to parallel lines.	SE: 599–601, 602, 605–607, 608, 611–613, 614	SE: 603–604, 609–610, 615–616, 629, 630
8.G.2	Understand that a two-dimensional figure is congruent to another if the second can be obtained from the first by a sequence of rotations, reflections, and translations; given two congruent figures, describe a sequence that exhibits the congruence between them.	SE: 623–625, 626	SE: 627–628, 629, 630
8.G.3	Describe the effect of dilations, translations, rotations, and reflections on two-dimensional figures using coordinates.	SE: 601–602, 607–608, 613–614, 617–620, 636–637, 638, 641–643, 644	SE: 603–604, 609–610, 615–616, 621–622, 639–640, 645–646, 653, 654
8.G.4	Understand that a two-dimensional figure is similar to another if the second can be obtained from the first by a sequence of rotations, reflections, translations, and dilations; given two similar two-dimensional figures, describe a sequence that exhibits the similarity between them.	SE: 635–636, 637–638, 647–649, 650	SE: 639–640, 651–652, 653, 654
8.G.5	Use informal arguments to establish facts about the angle sum and exterior angle of triangles, about the angles created when parallel lines are cut by a transversal, and the angle-angle criterion for similarity of triangles.	SE: 667–670, 673–675, 676, 678, 681–682	SE: 671–672, 679–680, 687–688, 689, 690
Understand and apply the Pythagorean Theorem.			
8.G.6	Explain a proof of the Pythagorean Theorem and its converse.	SE: AL1–AL4, AL7–AL10	SE: AL5–AL6, AL11–AL12
8.G.7	Apply the Pythagorean Theorem to determine unknown side lengths in right triangles in real-world and mathematical problems in two and three dimensions.	SE: AL1–AL4	SE: AL5–AL6
8.G.8	Apply the Pythagorean Theorem to find the distance between two points in a coordinate system.	SE: AL13–AL16	SE: AL17–AL18

Standard	Descriptor	Taught	Reinforced
Solve real-world and mathematical problems involving volume of cylinders, cones, and spheres.			
8.G.9	Know the formulas for the volumes of cones, cylinders, and spheres and use them to solve real-world and mathematical problems.	SE: 695–697, 698, 701–703, 704, 707–709, 710	SE: 699–700, 705–706, 711–712, 713, 714

Standard	Descriptor	Citations
MP MATHEMATICAL PRACTICES STANDARDS		*The mathematical practices standards are integrated throughout the book. See, for example, the citations below.*
MP.1	**Make sense of problems and persevere in solving them.**	SE: 100, 155, 222, 282, 348, 389, 444, 552, 564, 573, 581, 628, 711
MP.2	**Reason abstractly and quantitatively.**	SE: 94, 149, 218, 273, 323–324, 392, 444, 470, 512, 535, 543, 560–564, 576, 674–675
MP.3	**Construct viable arguments and critique the reasoning of others.**	SE: 18, 134, 210, 258, 316, 404, 450, 532, 570, 622, 672, 706
MP.4	**Model with mathematics.**	SE: 12, 122, 193, 270, 346, 386, 505, 566–567, 683–684, 709
MP.5	**Use appropriate tools strategically.**	SE: 100, 147, 191, 243–246, 347, 422, 452, 485, 559, 605, 635, 667–668, 673, 695
MP.6	**Attend to precision.**	SE: 62, 128, 190, 250, 322, 380, 488, 538, 576, 672, 700
MP.7	**Look for and make use of structure.**	SE: 97, 146, 175, 283, 325, 410, 440–441, 463–466, 477, 570, 617–620
MP.8	**Look for and express regularity in repeated reasoning.**	SE: 61, 152, 203–204, 265, 290, 407, 438, 463–466, 477, 539, 559, 617–620

Succeeding with HMH California Go Math

Actively participate in your learning with your write-in Student Edition. Explore concepts, take notes, answer questions, and complete your homework right in your textbook!

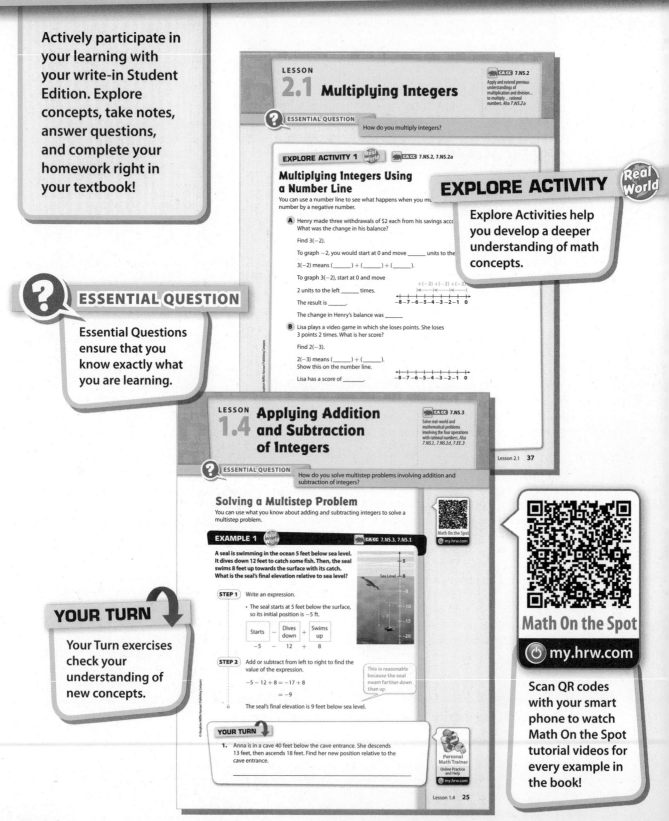

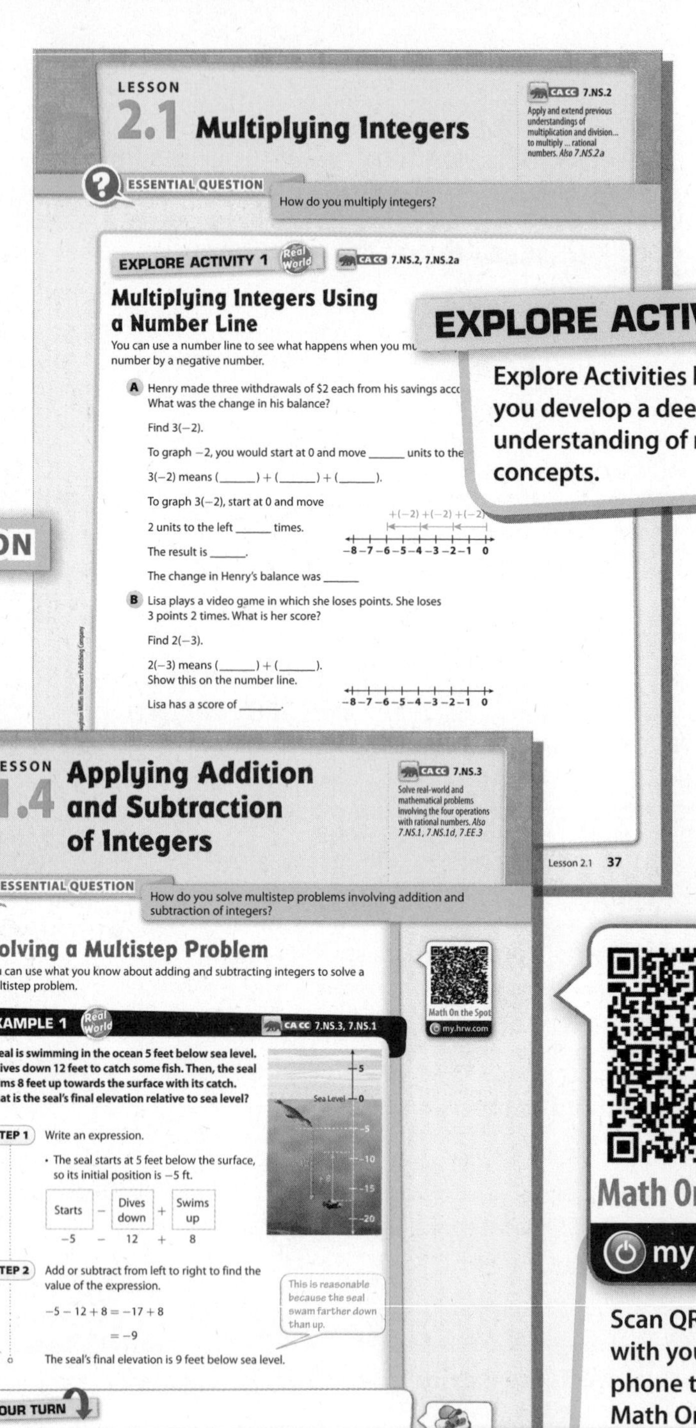

EXPLORE ACTIVITY Real World

Explore Activities help you develop a deeper understanding of math concepts.

ESSENTIAL QUESTION

Essential Questions ensure that you know exactly what you are learning.

YOUR TURN

Your Turn exercises check your understanding of new concepts.

Math On the Spot

my.hrw.com

Scan QR codes with your smart phone to watch Math On the Spot tutorial videos for every example in the book!

Unit Project CA CC 7.RP.1, 7.RP.2, 7.RP.2a, 7.RP.2b, 7.RP.2c

To Infinity (Almost)...and Beyond!

For a science project, Orlando decided to make a scale model of the solar system using a scale of 1 inch = 10,000 miles. That would make Earth a sphere about the size of a golf ball.

He quickly discovered that he would need a lot more ... ol could possibly give him. Create a ... the scaled-down sizes and ... d need to use for his model ... on should include each

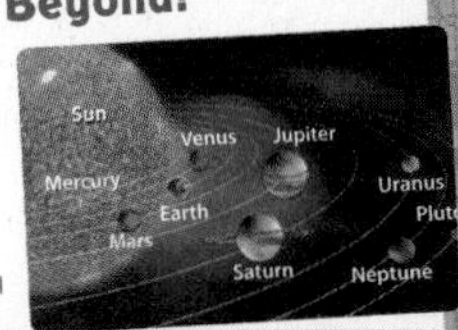

Unit Project

Apply new skills and concepts to solve real-world problems in Unit Projects and Math in Careers Activities.

MATH IN CAREERS | ACTIVITY

Architect Edith is an architect. She is currently ... old warehouse to house a new fitness center. O... feet long. Edith plans to increase the length of t... ensure that there is a minimum of 1 electrical o... along the wall. What is the length of the new w... outlets she should include in her plan for that v...

164 Unit 2

Reading Start-Up

Visualize Vocabulary

Use the ✔ words to complete the graphic. You can put more than one word in each bubble.

$\frac{2}{4}=\frac{3}{6}$ | 36% | Uses of Ratios | $\frac{12 \text{ inches}}{1 \text{ foot}}$ | 6 to 1

Vocabulary

Review Words

- constant (*constante*)
- ✔ conversion factor (*factor de conversión*)
- ✔ equivalent ratios (*razones equivalentes*)
- ✔ percent (*porcentaje*)
- rate (*tasa*)
- ✔ ratio (*razón*)

Understand Vocabulary

Match the term on the left to the definition on the right.

1. rate of change — A. Statement that two rates or ratios are equivalent.
2. proportion — B. A rate that describes how one quantity changes in relation to another quantity.
3. unit rate — C. Rate in which the second quantity is one unit.

Active Reading

Three-Panel Flip Chart Before beginning the module, create a three-panel flip chart to help you organize what you learn. Label each flap ... om this module. ... te important ideas ... d formulas under

Module 4 115

Reading Start-Up

Get vocabulary, language, and note-taking support throughout the book.

UNIT 2 MIXED REVIEW
Assessment Readiness

1. The regular prices of sandals at a shoe store are marked down by 15%. Look at each sale price and determine whether it is a 15% markdown to the nearest cent.

Select Yes or No.

A. regular price: \$24.30; sale price: \$20.66 ○ Yes ○ No
B. regular price: \$55.80; sale price: \$40.80 ○ Yes ○ No
C. regular price: \$66.50; sale price: \$56.53 ○ Yes ○ No

2. The graph shows the relationship between the number of gold beads and the number of black beads on the bracelets that Kassie makes.

Choose True or False for each statement.

A. The relationship has a constant rate of change. ○ True ○ False
B. The relationship can be represented by $y = 4x$. ○ True ○ False
C. The point (1, 4) indicates a unit rate of 4 gold beads per black bead. ○ True ○ False

3. Last year, 20,820 people attended a kite festival. This year, 19,779 people attended it. If attendance continues to decrease by the same percent each year, how many people can be expected to attend the kite festival next ye... Explain your reasoning.

4. David and Brad are competing in a 20-mile bicycle race. David rides 6.2 ... in $\frac{1}{4}$ hour. Brad rides 11.9 miles in $\frac{1}{2}$ hour. If both riders continue at the sa... average speed, who will finish first? Explain how you know.

Performance Tasks

★5. On Monday, Anya r... pages in $\frac{3}{4}$ hour. Did ... Monday to Tuesday? Justify your ans...

★★6. The table shows the relationship between the cost of a T-shirt to a store and the retail price that the store charges for T-shirts after a markup.

6.00	7.50
7.00	8.75
8.00	10.00
9.00	11.25

a. Graph the relationship in the table.
b. Is the relationship proportional? Explain how you know.
c. Write an equation that represents the relationship.
d. Predict the retail price that the store will charge for a T-shirt that costs the store \$9.50. Justify your reasoning.

★★★7. The table shows how much simple interest a \$1,000 deposit in a savings account at Joyner Bank will earn over time. The graph shows how much simple interest a \$750 deposit will earn at Ross Bank over time. Evan has \$600 that he plans to deposit in a savings account for 6 years. Which bank should he choose? Use mathematics to justify your reasoning.

Ross Bank: \$750 Deposit

Assessment Readiness

Prepare for new high-stakes tests with SBAC aligned practice items and Performance Tasks.

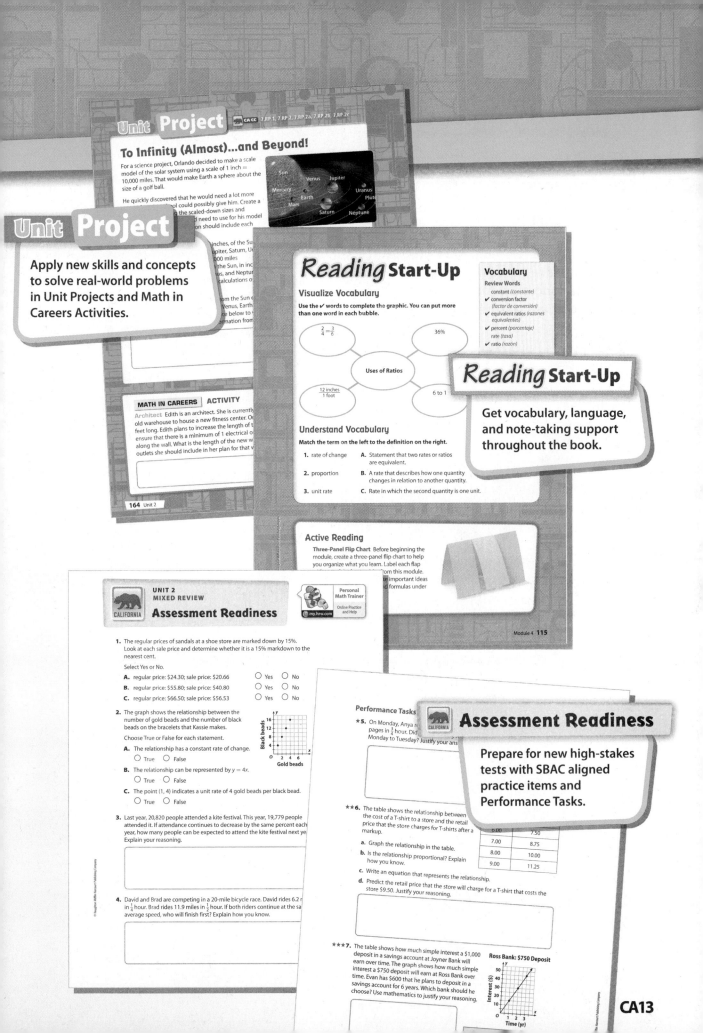

GO DIGITAL
my.hrw.com

Enhance Your Learning!

The eStudent Edition provides additional multimedia resources to enhance your learning. You can write in answers, take notes, watch videos, explore concepts with virtual manipulatives, and get homework help!

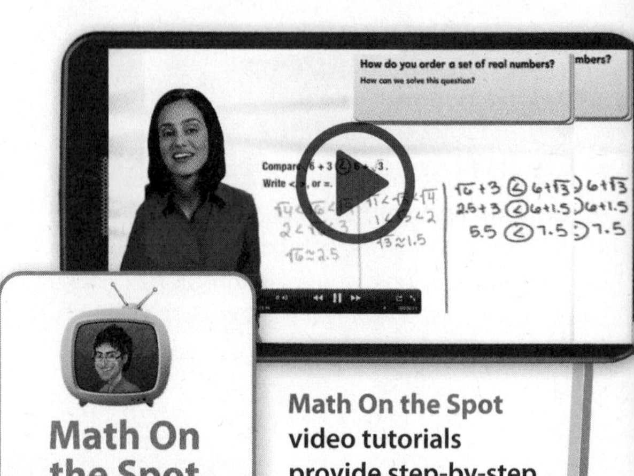

Math On the Spot

my.hrw.com

Math On the Spot video tutorials provide step-by-step instruction of the math concepts covered in each example.

my.hrw.com

Real-World Videos show you how specific math topics can be used in all kinds of situations.

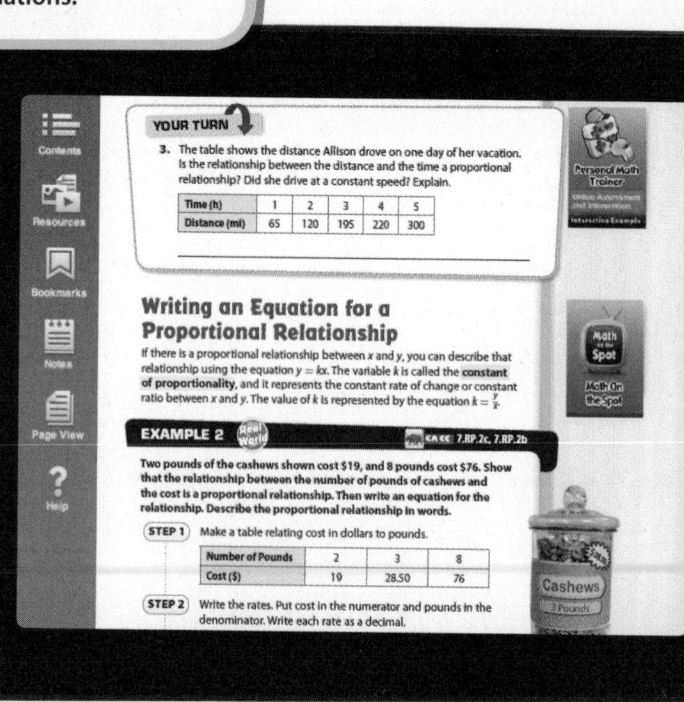

YOUR TURN
3. The table shows the distance Allison drove on one day of her vacation. Is the relationship between the distance and the time a proportional relationship? Did she drive at a constant speed? Explain.
Writing an Equation for a Proportional Relationship
EXAMPLE 2
Cashews

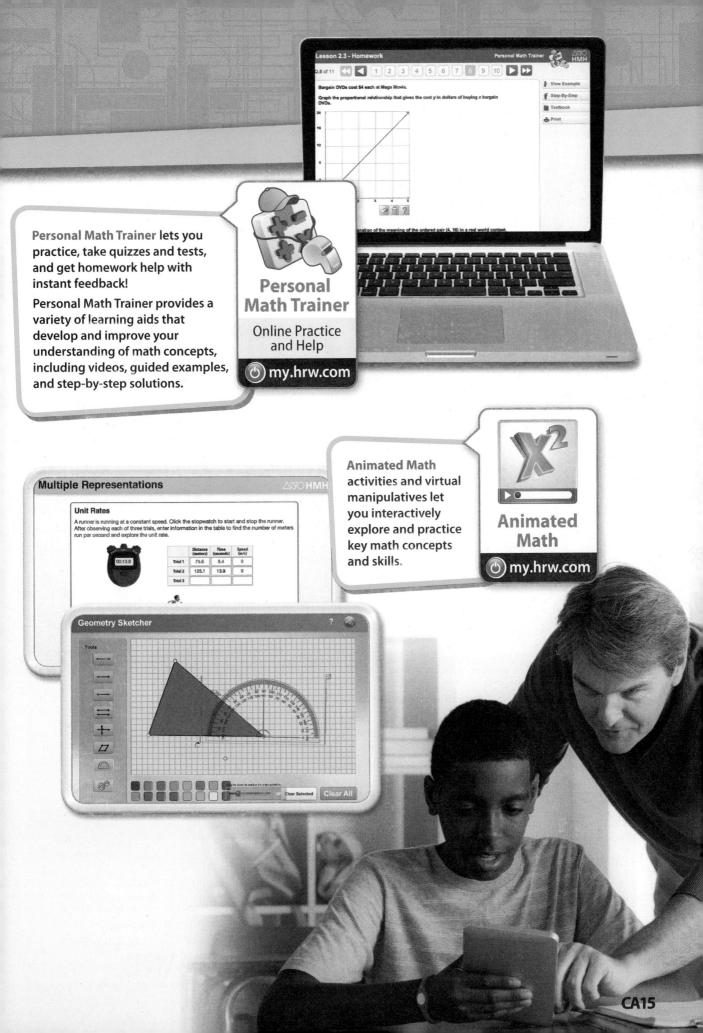

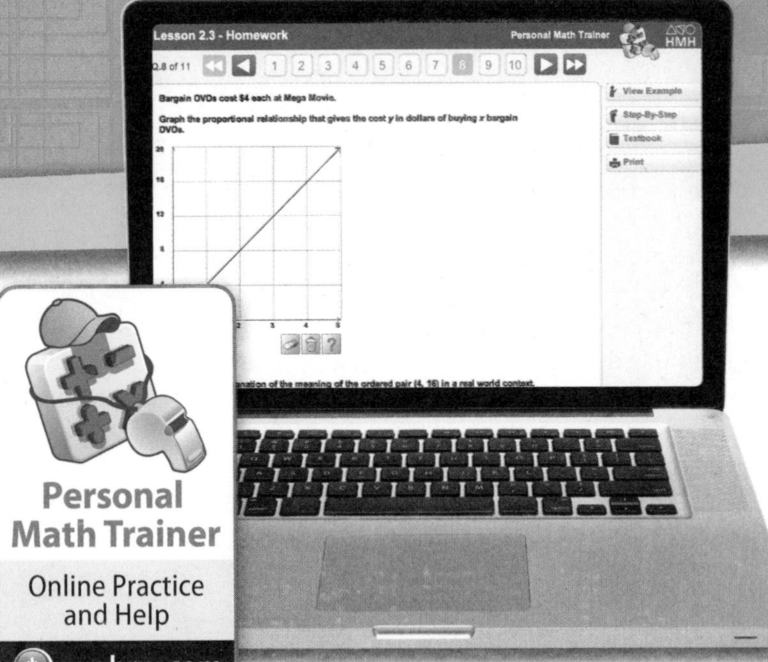

Personal Math Trainer lets you practice, take quizzes and tests, and get homework help with instant feedback!

Personal Math Trainer provides a variety of learning aids that develop and improve your understanding of math concepts, including videos, guided examples, and step-by-step solutions.

Personal Math Trainer
Online Practice and Help
my.hrw.com

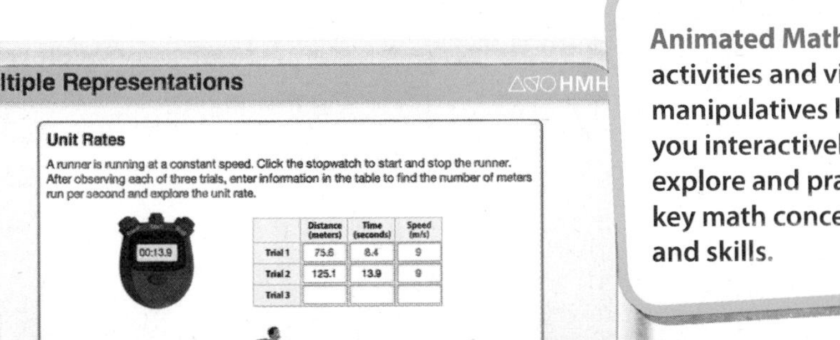

Animated Math activities and virtual manipulatives let you interactively explore and practice key math concepts and skills.

Animated Math
my.hrw.com

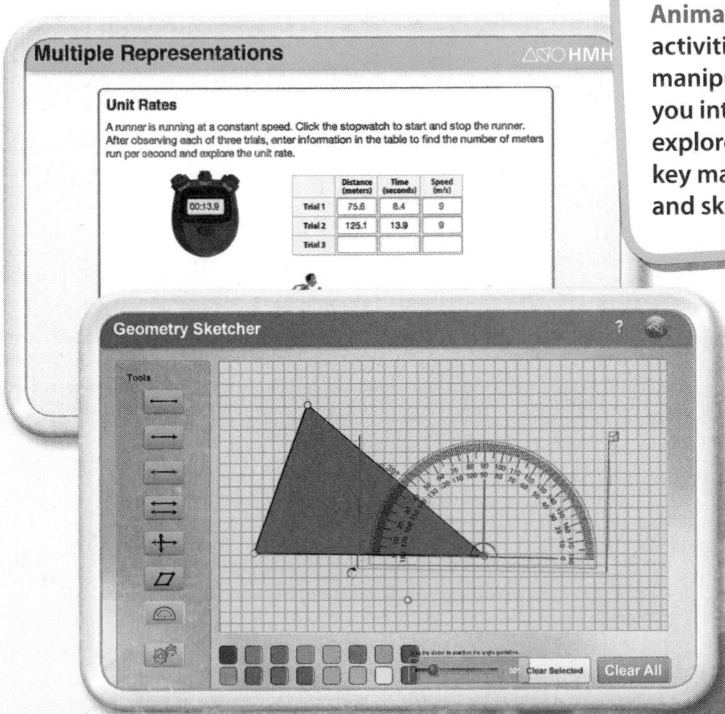

Standards for Mathematical Practice

The topics described in the Standards for Mathematical Content will vary from year to year. However, the *way* in which you learn, study, and think about mathematics will not. The Standards for Mathematical Practice describe skills that you will use in all of your math courses. These pages show some features of your book that will help you gain these skills and use them to master this year's topics.

MP.1 Make sense of problems and persevere in solving them.

Mathematically proficient students start by explaining to themselves the meaning of a problem… They analyze givens, constraints, relationships, and goals. They make conjectures about the form… of the solution and plan a solution pathway…

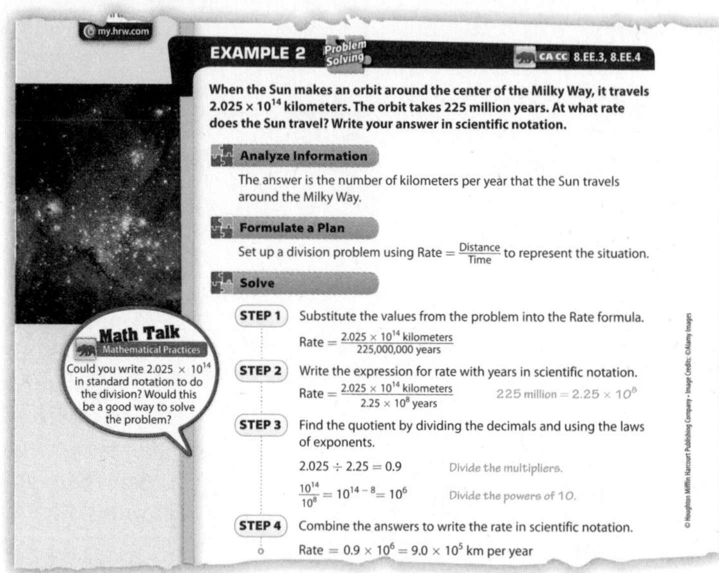
my.hrw.com

EXAMPLE 2 Problem Solving CA CC 8.EE.3, 8.EE.4

When the Sun makes an orbit around the center of the Milky Way, it travels 2.025×10^{14} kilometers. The orbit takes 225 million years. At what rate does the Sun travel? Write your answer in scientific notation.

Analyze Information

The answer is the number of kilometers per year that the Sun travels around the Milky Way.

Formulate a Plan

Set up a division problem using Rate $= \frac{\text{Distance}}{\text{Time}}$ to represent the situation.

Solve

STEP 1 Substitute the values from the problem into the Rate formula.

Rate $= \frac{2.025 \times 10^{14} \text{ kilometers}}{225{,}000{,}000 \text{ years}}$

STEP 2 Write the expression for rate with years in scientific notation.

Rate $= \frac{2.025 \times 10^{14} \text{ kilometers}}{2.25 \times 10^{8} \text{ years}}$ 225 million $= 2.25 \times 10^8$

STEP 3 Find the quotient by dividing the decimals and using the laws of exponents.

$2.025 \div 2.25 = 0.9$ Divide the multipliers.

$\frac{10^{14}}{10^8} = 10^{14-8} = 10^6$ Divide the powers of 10.

STEP 4 Combine the answers to write the rate in scientific notation.

Rate $= 0.9 \times 10^6 = 9.0 \times 10^5$ km per year

Math Talk — Mathematical Practices: Could you write 2.025×10^{14} in standard notation to do the division? Would this be a good way to solve the problem?

Problem-solving examples and exercises lead students through problem solving steps.

MP.2 Reason abstractly and quantitatively.

Mathematically proficient students… bring two complementary abilities to bear on problems…: the ability to decontextualize—to abstract a given situation and represent it symbolically… and the ability to contextualize, to pause… in order to probe into the referents for the symbols involved.

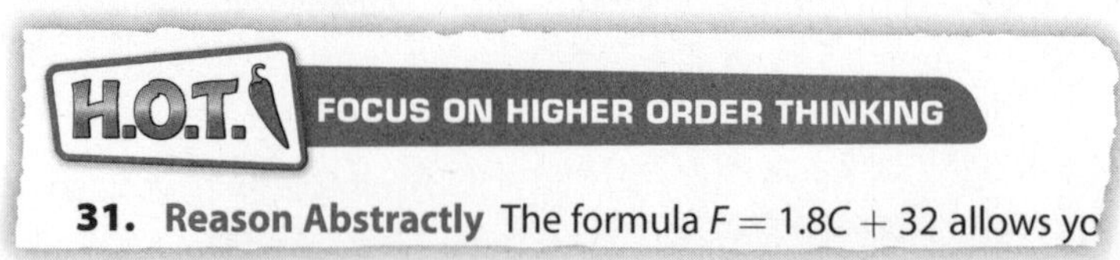
H.O.T. FOCUS ON HIGHER ORDER THINKING

31. Reason Abstractly The formula $F = 1.8C + 32$ allows yo

Focus on Higher Order Thinking exercises in every lesson and a **Project** in every unit require you to use logical reasoning, represent situations symbolically, use mathematical models to solve problems, and state your answers in terms of a problem context.

MP.3 Construct viable arguments and critique the reasoning of others.

Mathematically proficient students… justify their conclusions, [and]… distinguish correct… reasoning from that which is flawed.

Reflect
3. Critique Reasoning David considered moving even closer to workplace. He claims that if he had done so, the percent of de

Essential Question Check-in and **Reflect** in every lesson ask you to evaluate statements, explain relationships, apply mathematical principles, make conjectures, construct arguments, and justify your reasoning.

MP.4 Model with mathematics.

Mathematically proficient students can apply… mathematics… to… problems… in everyday life, society, and the workplace.

EXAMPLE 2 Real World

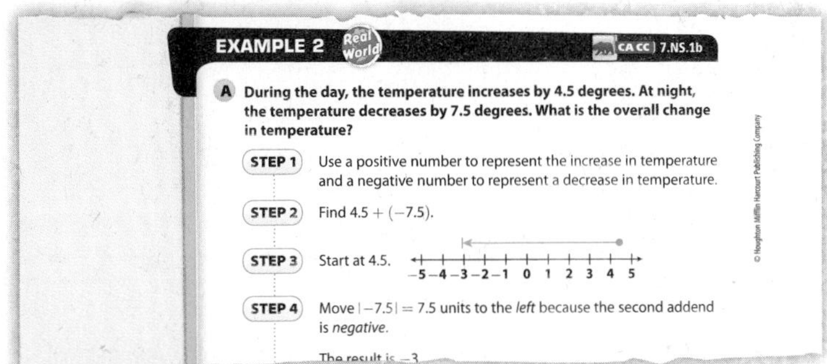

EXAMPLE 2 Real World
CA CC 7.NS.1b
A During the day, the temperature increases by 4.5 degrees. At night, the temperature decreases by 7.5 degrees. What is the overall change in temperature?
STEP 1 Use a positive number to represent the increase in temperature and a negative number to represent a decrease in temperature.
STEP 2 Find 4.5 + (−7.5).
STEP 3 Start at 4.5.
−5 −4 −3 −2 −1 0 1 2 3 4 5
STEP 4 Move |−7.5| = 7.5 units to the left because the second addend is negative.

Real-world examples and **mathematical modeling** apply mathematics to other disciplines and real-world contexts such as science and business.

MP.5 Use appropriate tools strategically.

Mathematically proficient students consider the available tools when solving a… problem… [and] are… able to use technological tools to explore and deepen their understanding…

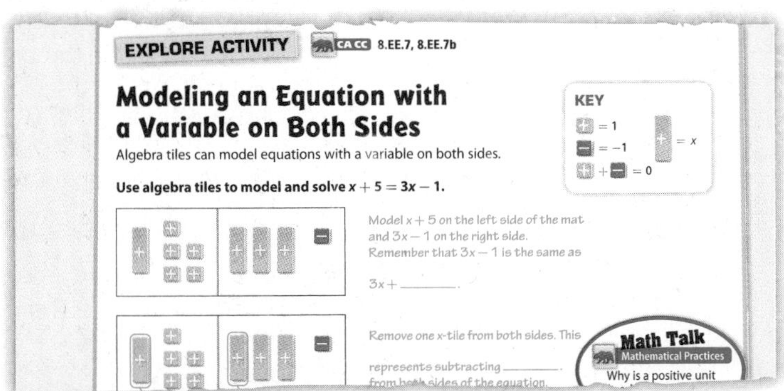

EXPLORE ACTIVITY
CA CC 8.EE.7, 8.EE.7b
Modeling an Equation with a Variable on Both Sides
Algebra tiles can model equations with a variable on both sides.
KEY
= 1
= −1
+ = 0
= x
Use algebra tiles to model and solve x + 5 = 3x − 1.
Model x + 5 on the left side of the mat and 3x − 1 on the right side. Remember that 3x − 1 is the same as
3x +
Remove one x-tile from both sides. This
represents subtracting
Math Talk
Mathematical Practices
Why is a positive unit

Exploration Activities in lessons use concrete and technological tools, such as manipulatives or graphing calculators, to explore mathematical concepts.

MP.6 Attend to precision.

Mathematically proficient students… communicate precisely… with others and in their own reasoning… [They] give carefully formulated explanations…

19. Communicate Mathematical Ideas Explain how you can fir height of a cylinder if you know the diameter and the volum an example with your explana

Key Vocabulary

slope *(pendiente)*
A measure of the steepness of a line on a graph; the rise divided by the run.

Precision refers not only to the correctness of calculations but also to the proper use of mathematical language and symbols. **Communicate Mathematical Ideas** exercises and **Key Vocabulary** highlighted for each module and unit help you learn and use the language of math to communicate mathematics precisely.

MP.7 Look for and make use of structure.

Mathematically proficient students… look closely to discern a pattern or structure… They can also step back for an overview and shift perspectives.

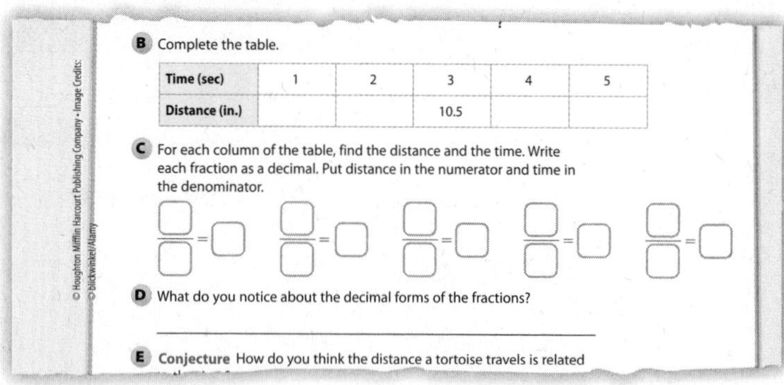

B Complete the table.

Time (sec)	1	2	3	4	5
Distance (in.)			10.5		

C For each column of the table, find the distance and the time. Write each fraction as a decimal. Put distance in the numerator and time in the denominator.

D What do you notice about the decimal forms of the fractions?

E **Conjecture** How do you think the distance a tortoise travels is related

Throughout the lessons, you will observe regularity in mathematical structures in order to make generalizations and make connections between related problems. For example, you can learn to recognize proportional relationships.

MP.8 Look for and express regularity in repeated reasoning.

Mathematically proficient students… look both for general methods and for shortcuts… [and] maintain oversight of the process, while attending to the details.

25. Look for a Pattern Find the next three terms in the pattern -11, … . Then describe the pattern.

27. Look for a Pattern Leroi and Sylvia both put $100 in a Leroi decides he will put in an additional $10 each wee put in an additional 10% of the amount in the account

a. Who has more money after the first additional dep

27. Look for a Pattern Solve $x + 1 > 10$, $x + 11 > 20$, and $x + 2$ Describe a pattern. Then use the pattern to predict the solut $x + 9{,}991 > 10{,}000$.

You will look for repeated calculations and mathematical patterns in examples and exercises. Recognizing patterns can help you make generalizations and obtain a better understanding of the underlying mathematics.

MATHEMATICS 1 PART 1

Review Test

1. Suppose you have developed a scale that indicates the brightness of sunlight. Each category in the table is 5 times brighter than the category above it. For example, a day that is dazzling is 5 times brighter than a day that is radiant. How many times brighter is a dazzling day than a dim day?

Sunlight Intensity	
Category	**Brightness**
Dim	2
Illuminated	3
Radiant	4
Dazzling	5

____

2. Patricia paid $584 for 8 nights at a hotel. Find the unit rate.

____

3. Valerie sold 6 tickets to the school play and Mark sold 16 tickets. What is the ratio of the number of tickets Valerie sold to the number of tickets Mark sold?

____

4. Grant and Pedro are comparing their stocks for the week. On Monday, their results were opposites. Explain how you would graph their results for Monday if Grant lost $4.

____

____

____

____

5. The fuel for a chain saw is a mix of oil and gasoline. The label says to mix 5 ounces of oil with 15 gallons of gasoline. How much oil would you use if you had 45 gallons of gasoline?

____

6. A stack of blocks is 12.3 inches tall. If there are 10 blocks stacked one on top of the other, how tall is each block?

____

7. Which temperature is warmest: 16 °F, −16 °F, −21 °F, or 21 °F?

____

8. Each student needs a pencil and an eraser to take a test. If pencils come 8 in a box and erasers come 12 in a bag, what is the least number of boxes and the least number of bags needed for 24 students to each have a pencil and an eraser?

____

____

9. Find the quotient $7\frac{1}{6} \div \frac{5}{9}$.

____

10. Find the product 4.7×4.75.

____

11. Carla is building a table out of boards that are 4.25 inches wide. She wants the table to be at least 36 inches wide. What is the least number of boards she can use?

____

12. How many centimeters are there in 740.2 millimeters?

____

13. Jada is making lasagna and pizzas for a large party. Her lasagna recipe calls for $1\frac{1}{4}$ cups of tomato paste, and her pizza recipe uses $\frac{1}{2}$ cup of tomato paste per pizza. She will double her lasagna recipe and make 5 pizzas. Write and evaluate an expression for how many $\frac{3}{4}$-cup cans of tomato paste she will need in all.

____

14. Explain how you can use multiplication to find the quotient $\frac{3}{5} \div \frac{3}{15}$. Then evaluate the expression.

____

____

____

15. You are working as an assistant to a chef. The chef has 8 cups of berries and will use $\frac{2}{3}$ cup of berries for each dessert he makes. How many desserts can he make?

____

____

____

Performance Task

16. School A has 216 students and 12 classrooms. School B has 104 students and 4 classrooms.

Part A: What is the ratio of students to classrooms at School A?

Part B: What is the ratio of students to classrooms at School B?

Part C: How many students would have to transfer from School B to School A for the ratios of students to classrooms at both schools to be the same? Explain your reasoning.

____

____

____

____

____

____

____

____

____

____

____

____

____

____

MATHEMATICS 1 PART 2

Review Test

1. Kahlil is recording a beat for a song that he is working on. He wants the length of the beat to be more than 17 seconds long. His friend tells him the beat needs to be 9 seconds longer than that to match the lyrics he has written.

Write an inequality to represent the beat's length. Give three possible beat lengths that satisfy the inequality.

____

2. Write an expression for the missing value in the table.

Tom's Age	Kim's Age
11	14
12	15
13	16
a	?

____

3. A plant's height is 1.6 times its age. Write an equation for the situation, where h is the plant's height and y is the plant's age.

____

4. A driveway is 162 feet long, 6 feet wide, and 4 inches deep. How many cubic feet of concrete will be required for the driveway?

____

5. Write the phrase as an algebraic expression. 6 less than a number times 11

____

6. Wilson bought gift cards for some lawyers and their assistants. Each lawyer got a gift card worth $\$\ell$. Each assistant got a gift card worth $\$a$. There are 14 lawyers. Each lawyer has 3 assistants. The expression for the total cost of the gift cards is $14\ell + 42a$. Write an expression that is equivalent to the given expression.

____

7. At the beginning of the year, Jason had \$80 in his savings account. Each month, he added \$15 to his account. Write an expression for the amount of money in Jason's savings account each month. Then use the expression to find the amount of money in his account at the end of the year.

Month	January	February	March	m
Amount	\$95	\$110	\$125	\$?

____

8. In a fish tank, $\frac{6}{7}$ of the fish have a red stripe on them. If 18 of the fish have red stripes, how many total fish are in the tank?

____

____

9. Solve the equation $s + 2.8 = 6.59$.

____

____

10. Which question is a statistical question? Select Yes or No.

A. How long is lunch period at your school?

○ Yes ○ No

B. How old is the oldest student in your class?

○ Yes ○ No

C. How many classrooms are there in the buildings of your school?

○ Yes ○ No

D. What are the ages of all the people in your class?

○ Yes ○ No

11. In a box-and-whisker plot, the *interquartile range* is a measure of the spread of the middle half of the data. Find the interquartile range for the data set: 10, 3, 7, 6, 9, 12, 13.

____

____

12. Mike was in charge of collecting contributions for the Food Bank. He received contributions of \$50, \$80, \$60, \$50, and \$90. Find the mean and median of the contributions.

____

____

13. Which expression is equivalent to the expression $11y - 5$? Select Yes or No.

A. $\frac{1}{8}(88y - 40)$ ○ Yes ○ No

B. $\frac{1}{2}(22y - 10)$ ○ Yes ○ No

C. $3(33y - 15)$ ○ Yes ○ No

D. $5 - 11y$ ○ Yes ○ No

14. It costs \$9 to go to Pete's Pottery Place to make your own bowls for \$3 per bowl. Natalie goes to Pete's Pottery Place and makes b bowls. She decides to make bowls 5 days this month so she can sell them at a crafts fair.

Part A: Write an expression that will represent Natalie's total cost for this month.

Part B: If she makes 4 bowls each time she goes to Pete's Pottery Place, what will her total cost be?

____

____

15. To find the mileage, or how many miles per gallon a car can travel, you can use the expression $\frac{m}{g}$, where m is the distance in miles and g is the number of gallons of gas used. Find the mileage for a car that travels 576 miles on 18 gallons of gas.

____

Performance Task

16. ***Part A:*** Is $x = 6$ a solution of the equation $8x + 8 = 56$? Explain.

Part B: Suppose the solution $x = 6$ increases to $x = 9$, and the left side of the equation stays the same. How would the right side need to change if the solution is now $x = 9$?

____

____

____

____

____

____

____

____

ACCELERATED GRADE 7 PART 1

Benchmark Test

1. What are the actual dimensions of the Books section?

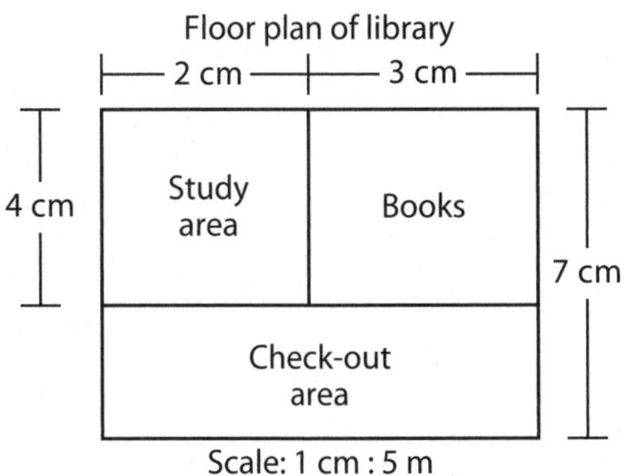

2. For a history fair, a school is building a circular wooden stage. Find the area of the stage if the radius of the stage is 4 meters. Use 3.14 for π.

3. Tell whether the data sets show a direct variation. If so, identify the constant of variation.

Number of Baskets	Cost
3	$12
5	$20
6	$24
8	$32
15	$60

4. Find m$\angle ABC$.

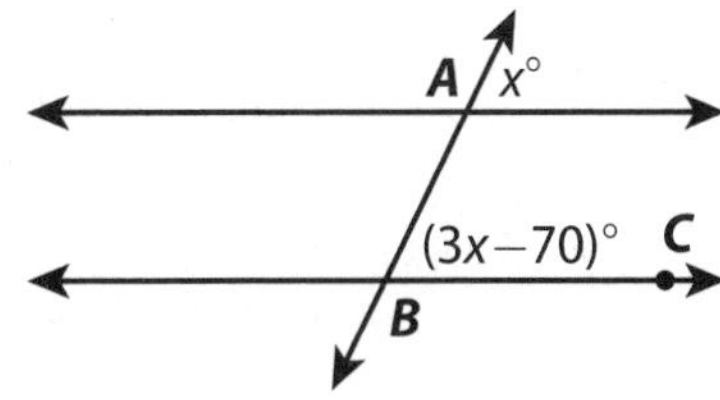

5. Ralph is an electrician. He charges an initial fee of $24, plus $24 per hour. If Ralph earned $144 on a job, how long did the job take?

6. Find the volume of the cylinder. Use 3.14 for π. Round your answer to the nearest tenth.

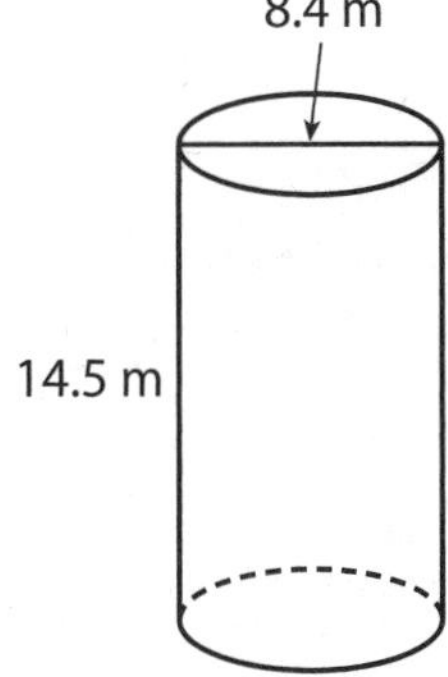

7. Find the unit price for each offer to determine which is the better buy: 6 paperback books for $19.00 or 8 paperback books for $26.00.

8. Write an equation that models the situation and find its solution.

It's going to be Lindsay's birthday soon, and her friends Chris, Mikhail, Wolfgang, and Adrian have contributed equal amounts of money to buy her a present. They have \$27.00 to spend altogether. Determine how much each contributed.

____

9. A vacation cabin has a water storage tank. In the first month (30 days) of the vacation season, the amount of water in the tank changed by an average of −36 gallons per day. At the end of the month, the tank contained 1,340 gallons of water. How much water was in the tank originally?

____

10. An experiment consists of rolling two fair number cubes. What is the probability that the sum of the two numbers will be 4? Express your answer as a fraction in simplest form.

____

11. A manufacturer inspects a sample of 500 smartphones and finds that 496 of them have no defects. The manufacturer sent a shipment of 2,000 smartphones to a distributor. Predict the number of smartphones in the shipment that are likely to have no defects.

____

12. One winter day, the temperature increased from a low of −5 °F to a high of 40 °F. By how many degrees did the temperature change?

____

13. A United States senator from Maine wants to find out the opinion of Maine voters on issues concerning education. The office of the senator sends out a survey to state residents who have contacted the senator in the past year. Is this sampling method random? Explain.

____

____

____

14. Using the following data, identify the errors in the box plot.

17, 13, 10, 15, 16, 12, 13, 20, 18

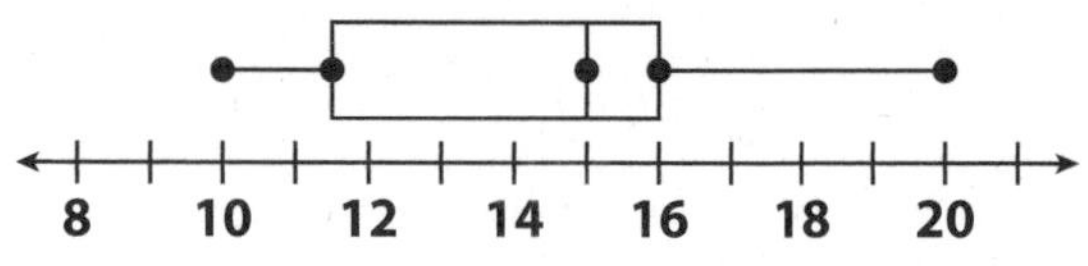

____

____

____

Performance Task

15. The number of goals scored by a soccer team in each of its first 10 games is shown below.

2, 6, 1, 2, 4, 1, 3, 2, 0, 4

Part A: Find the mean number of goals scored.

Part B: Find the mean absolute deviation (MAD) of the number of goals scored.

Part C: A second team in the same division scores a mean of 3.2 goals in its first 10 games, with the same MAD as the team above. Compare the difference in the teams' mean number of goals with the MAD in the number of goals scored.

____

____

____

ACCELERATED GRADE 7 PART 2

Benchmark Test

1. In the gift shop of the History of Flight museum, Elisa bought a kit to make a model of a jet airplane. The actual plane is 21 feet long with a wingspan of 17.5 feet. If the finished model will be 12 inches long, what will the wingspan be?

____

2. Find the angle measures in the isosceles triangle.

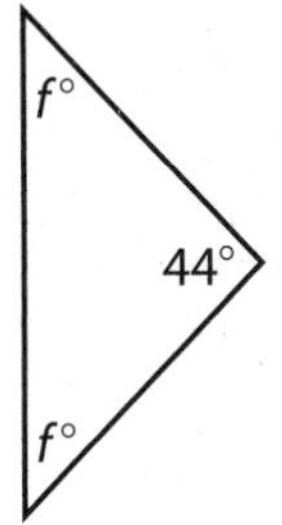

____

3. A passenger plane travels at about 7.97×10^2 feet per second. The plane takes 1.11×10^4 seconds to reach its destination.

About how far must the plane travel to reach its destination? Write your answer in scientific notation.

____

4. Approximate $\sqrt{158}$ to the nearest hundredth.

____

5. Identify $\sqrt{\frac{169}{64}}$ as *rational* or *irrational*. Explain your reasoning.

____

6. Which of the following is a congruence transformation? Select Yes or No.

A. A reflection over the *x*-axis.

○ Yes ○ No

B. A dilation with scale factor 0.5.

○ Yes ○ No

C. A translation 1 unit left.

○ Yes ○ No

D. A dilation with scale factor 1.

○ Yes ○ No

7. A bicyclist heads east at 19 km/h. After she has traveled 24.2 kilometers, another cyclist sets out in the same direction going 30 km/h. About how long will it take the second cyclist to catch up to the first cyclist?

____

8. Which of the following ratios forms a proportion? Select Yes or No.

A. $\frac{3}{7} \stackrel{?}{=} \frac{9}{21}$ ○ Yes ○ No

B. $\frac{24}{56} \stackrel{?}{=} \frac{3}{7}$ ○ Yes ○ No

C. $\frac{3}{7} \stackrel{?}{=} \frac{9}{28}$ ○ Yes ○ No

D. $\frac{3}{7} \stackrel{?}{=} \frac{12}{28}$ ○ Yes ○ No

9. Angles *B* and *F* are corresponding angles formed by a transversal intersecting two parallel lines. Angle *B* has a measure of 44°. What is the measure of Angle *F*?

____

10. What transformation preserves similarity between the preimage and image, but does not preserve congruence?

____

____

11. An artist is creating a large conical sculpture for a park. The cone has a height of 16 m and a diameter of 25 m. Find the volume of the sculpture to the nearest hundredth.

____

12. A cylindrical barrel has a radius of 7.6 ft and a height of 10.8 ft. Tripling which dimension(s) will triple the volume of the barrel? Select Yes or No.

A. height ◯ Yes ◯ No

B. radius ◯ Yes ◯ No

C. diameter ◯ Yes ◯ No

13. A square mosaic is made of small glass squares. If there are 196 small squares in the mosaic, how many are along an edge?

____

14. Iris wants to buy two necklaces, one for her sister and one for herself. The necklace for her sister costs $42.00, and the necklace for herself costs $28.00. The sales tax on the purchases is 8%. Find the total cost of Iris's purchases, including sales tax. If necessary, round your answer to the nearest cent.

____

15. Dilate the figure by a scale factor of 0.5 with the origin as the center of dilation.

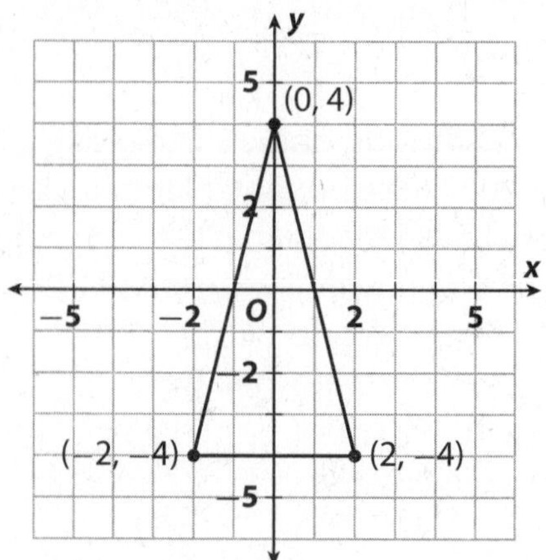

Performance Task

16. A company makes a paperweight in the shape of a hemisphere. The paperweight is made of an alloy of different metals. The area of the flat base is 28.26 square centimeters.

a. What is the volume of the paperweight in cubic centimeters? Use 3.14 for π. Explain how you arrive at your answer.

____

____

____

____

b. The paperweight weighs about 14 ounces. What is the density of the alloy used to make the paperweight in ounces per cubic centimeter?

____

c. How many cubic centimeters of the alloy would weigh exactly 1 ounce?

____

UNIT 1

The Number System

MODULE 1

Adding and Subtracting Integers

CA CC 7.NS.1, 7.NS.1b, 7.NS.1c, 7.NS.1d, 7.NS.3, 7.EE.3

MODULE 2

Multiplying and Dividing Integers

CA CC 7.NS.2, 7.NS.2a, 7.NS.2b, 7.NS.2c, 7.NS.3, 7.EE.3

MODULE 3

Rational Numbers

CA CC 7.NS.1, 7.NS.1a, 7.NS.1b, 7.NS.1c, 7.NS.1d, 7.NS.2, 7.NS.2a, 7.NS.2b, 7.NS.2c, 7.NS.2d, 7.NS.3, 7.EE.3

MATH IN CAREERS

Urban Planner An urban planner creates plans for urban, suburban, and rural communities and makes recommendations about locations for infrastructure, such as buildings, roads, and sewer and water pipes. Urban planners perform cost-benefit analysis of projects, use measurement and geometry when they design the layout of infrastructure, and use statistics and mathematical models to predict the growth and future needs of a population.

If you are interested in a career as an urban planner, you should study these mathematical subjects:

- Algebra
- Geometry
- Trigonometry
- Statistics

Research other careers that require using measurement, geometry, and mathematical modeling.

ACTIVITY At the end of the unit, check out how **urban planners** use math.

Unit Project Preview

It's Okay to Be Negative!

In the Unit Project at the end of this unit you will do research to find real-world examples of negative rational numbers. Then you will write four problems involving the numbers you find. To successfully complete the Unit Project you'll need to master these skills:

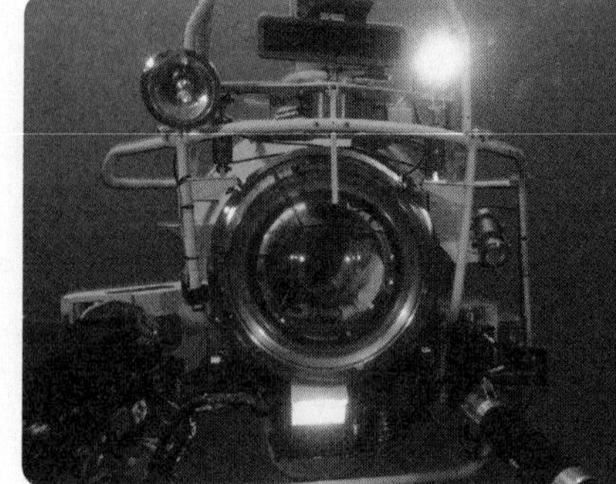

- Add rational numbers.
- Subtract rational numbers.
- Multiply rational numbers.
- Divide rational numbers.

1. Name some real-world situations that could involve negative numbers.

____

____

2. Write (but do not solve) a problem involving these facts: The low temperatures for four consecutive days were $-15\,°F$, $-12\,°F$, $-17\,°F$, and $-9\,°C$.

____

____

Tracking Your Learning Progression

This unit addresses important California Common Core Standards in the Critical Areas of applying understanding of operations to rational numbers and solving problems involving algebraic expressions.

Domain 7.NS The Number System

Cluster Apply and extend previous understandings of operations with fractions to add, subtract, multiply, and divide rational numbers.

The unit also supports additional standards.

Domain 7.EE Expressions and Equations

Cluster Solve real-life and mathematical problems using numerical and algebraic expressions and equations.

Adding and Subtracting Integers

ESSENTIAL QUESTION

How can you use addition and subtraction of integers to solve real-world problems?

LESSON 1.1
Adding Integers with the Same Sign
CA CC 7.NS.1, 7.NS.1b, 7.NS.1d

LESSON 1.2
Adding Integers with Different Signs
CA CC 7.NS.1, 7.NS.1b

LESSON 1.3
Subtracting Integers
CA CC 7.NS.1, 7.NS.1c

LESSON 1.4
Applying Addition and Subtraction of Integers
CA CC 7.NS.1, 7.NS.1d, 7.NS.3, 7.EE.3

Real-World Video

my.hrw.com

Death Valley contains the lowest point in North America, elevation −282 feet. The top of Mt. McKinley, elevation 20,320 feet, is the highest point in North America. To find the difference between these elevations, you can subtract integers.

GO DIGITAL
my.hrw.com

my.hrw.com

Go digital with your write-in student edition, accessible on any device.

Math On the Spot

Scan with your smart phone to jump directly to the online edition, video tutor, and more.

Animated Math

Interactively explore key concepts to see how math works.

Personal Math Trainer

Get immediate feedback and help as you work through practice sets.

Are YOU Ready?

Complete these exercises to review skills you will need for this module.

Understand Integers

EXAMPLE A diver descended 20 meters.

Decide whether the integer is positive or negative:
descended → negative

−20

Write the integer.

Write an integer to represent each situation.

1. an elevator ride down 27 stories ______

2. a $700 profit ______

3. 46 degrees below zero ______

4. a gain of 12 yards ______

Whole Number Operations

EXAMPLE 245 − 28

$$\begin{array}{r} \overset{3\ 15}{2\not{4}\not{5}} \\ -\ 28 \\ \hline 217 \end{array}$$

245 − 28 = 217

Think:
8 > 5
Regroup 1 ten as 10 ones.
1 ten + 5 ones = 15 ones
Subtract: 15 − 8 = 7

Find the sum or difference.

5. $\begin{array}{r} 183 \\ +\ 78 \\ \hline \end{array}$

6. $\begin{array}{r} 677 \\ -288 \\ \hline \end{array}$

7. $\begin{array}{r} 1{,}188 \\ +\ 902 \\ \hline \end{array}$

8. $\begin{array}{r} 2{,}647 \\ -1{,}885 \\ \hline \end{array}$

Locate Points on a Number Line

EXAMPLE

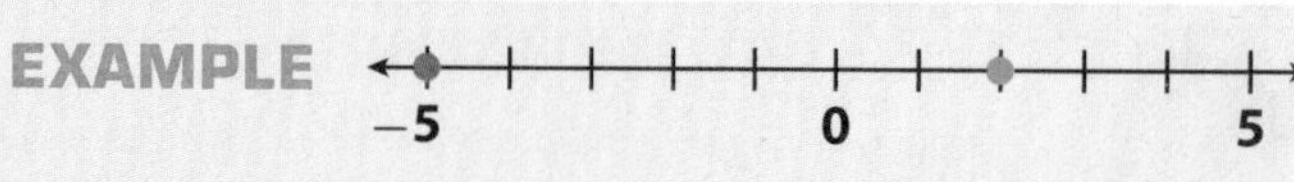

Graph +2 by starting at 0 and counting 2 units to the *right*.
Graph −5 by starting at 0 and counting 5 units to the *left*.

Graph each number on the number line.

9. 7 **10.** −4 **11.** −9 **12.** 4

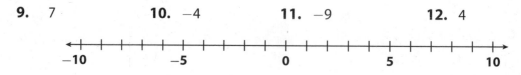

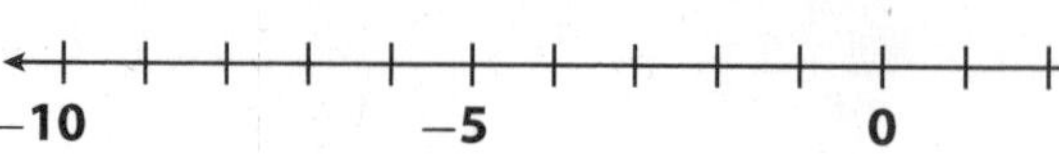

Reading Start-Up

Visualize Vocabulary

Use the ✔ words to fill in the ovals on the graphic. You may put more than one word in each oval.

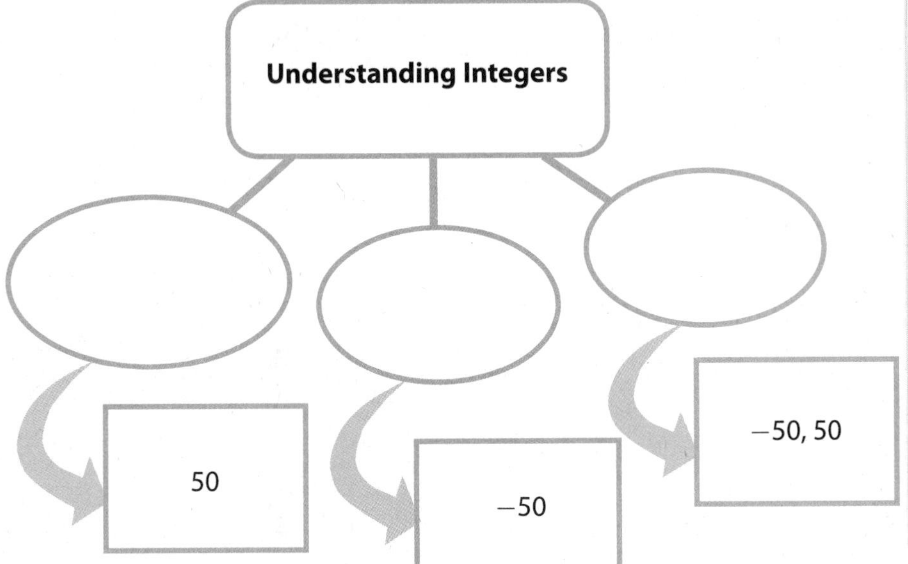

Vocabulary

Review Words

difference *(diferencia)*

integers *(enteros)*

✔ negative number *(número negativo)*

✔ opposites *(opuestos)*

✔ positive number *(número positivo)*

sum *(suma)*

✔ whole number *(número entero)*

Preview Words

absolute value *(valor absoluto)*

additive inverse *(inverso aditivo)*

expression *(expresión)*

model *(modelo)*

Understand Vocabulary

Complete the sentences using the preview words.

1. The ____________________ of a number gives its distance from zero.

2. The sum of a number and its ____________________ is zero.

Active Reading

Booklet Before beginning the module, create a booklet to help you learn the concepts in this module. Write the main idea of each lesson on each page of the booklet. As you study each lesson, write important details that support the main idea, such as vocabulary and processes. Refer to your finished booklet as you work on assignments and study for tests.

GETTING READY FOR

Adding and Subtracting Integers

Understanding the standards and the vocabulary terms in the standards will help you know exactly what you are expected to learn in this module.

CA CC 7.NS.1

Apply and extend previous understandings of addition and subtraction to add and subtract rational numbers; represent addition and subtraction on a horizontal or vertical number line diagram.

Key Vocabulary

additive inverse *(inverso aditivo)*
The opposite of a number.

What It Means to You

You will learn how to use models to add and subtract integers with the same sign and with different signs.

EXAMPLE 7.NS.1

You will learn how to use models to add and subtract integers with the same sign and with different signs.

$4 + (-7)$

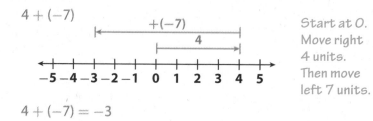

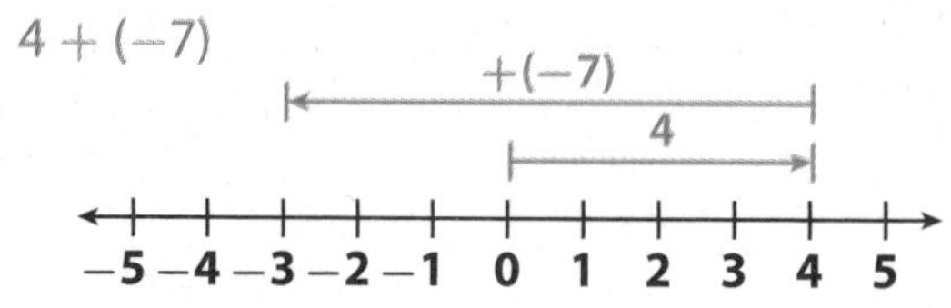

Start at 0. Move right 4 units. Then move left 7 units.

$4 + (-7) = -3$

CA CC 7.NS.1c

Understand subtraction of rational numbers as adding the additive inverse, $p - q = p + (-q)$. Show that the distance between two rational numbers on the number line is the absolute value of their difference, and apply this principle in real-world contexts.

Key Vocabulary

integer *(entero)*
A member of the set of whole numbers and their opposites.

What It Means to You

You will learn that subtracting an integer is the same as adding its additive inverse.

EXAMPLE 7.NS.1c

Find the difference between 3,000 °F and −250 °F, the temperatures the space shuttle must endure.

$3{,}000 - (-250)$

$3{,}000 + 250 = 3{,}250$

The difference in temperatures the shuttle must endure is 3,250 °F.

Visit **my.hrw.com** to see all **CA Common Core Standards** explained.

my.hrw.com

LESSON 1.1

Adding Integers with the Same Sign

CA CC 7.NS.1

Apply and extend previous understandings of addition and subtraction to add and subtract rational numbers; represent addition and subtraction on a horizontal or vertical number line diagram. *Also 7.NS.1b, 7.NS.1d*

ESSENTIAL QUESTION

How do you add integers with the same sign?

EXPLORE ACTIVITY 1

Modeling Sums of Integers with the Same Sign

You can use colored counters to add positive integers and to add negative integers.

(light counter) = 1
(dark counter) = −1

Model with two-color counters.

A $3 + 4$

How many counters are there in total? ________

What is the sum and how do you find it?

____

____

B $-5 + (-3)$

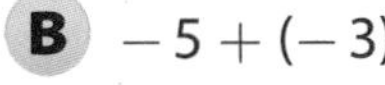

Math Talk
Mathematical Practices
What does the color of each row of counters represent?

How many counters are there in total? ________

Since the counters are negative integers, what is the sum? ________

Reflect

1. **Communicate Mathematical Ideas** When adding two numbers with the same sign, what sign do you use for the sum?

____

EXPLORE ACTIVITY 2

CA CC 7.NS.1, 7.NS.1b

Adding on a Number Line

Just as you can add positive integers on a number line, you can add negative integers.

The temperature was 2 °F below zero. The temperature drops by 5 °F. What is the temperature now?

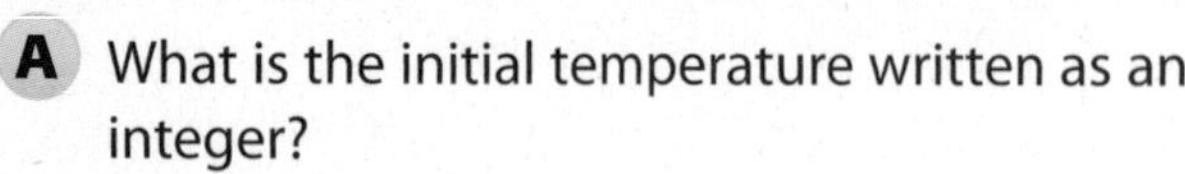

A What is the initial temperature written as an integer?

____

B Mark the initial temperature on the number line.

C A drop in temperature of 5° is like adding −5° to the temperature.

Count on the number line to find the final temperature. Mark the temperature now on the number line.

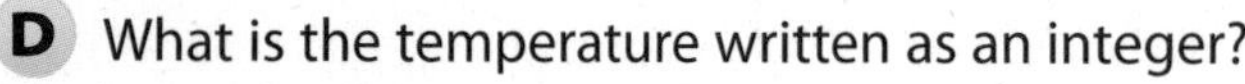

D What is the temperature written as an integer?

____

The temperature is _______________ **above / below** zero.

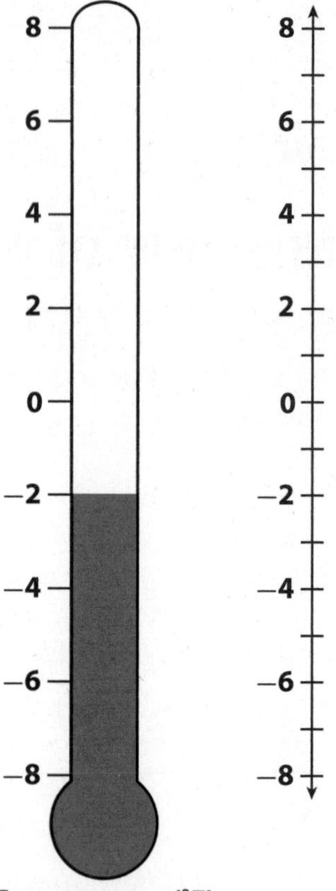

Reflect

2. **What If?** Suppose the temperature is −1 °F and drops by 3 °F. Explain how to use the number line to find the new temperature.

____

____

3. **Communicate Mathematical Ideas** How would using a number line to find the sum 2 + 5 be different from using a number line to find the sum −2 + (−5)?

____

____

4. **Analyze Relationships** What are two other negative integers that have the same sum as −2 and −5?

____

Adding Integers with a Common Sign

To add integers with the same sign, add the absolute values of the integers and use the sign of the integers for the sum.

CA CC 7.NS.1, 7.NS.1d

Add $-7 + (-6)$.   *The signs of both integers are the same.*

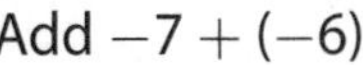

Find the absolute values.

$|-7| = 7 \quad |-6| = 6$ *The absolute value is always positive or zero.*

Find the sum of the absolute values: $7 + 6 = 13$

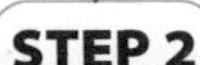

Use the sign of the integers to write the sum.

$-7 + (-6) = -13$ *The sign of each integer is negative.*

Math Talk
Mathematical Practices

Can you use the same procedure you use to find the sum of two negative integers to find the sum of two *positive* numbers? Explain.

Reflect

5. **Communicate Mathematical Ideas** Does the Commutative Property of Addition apply when you add two negative integers? Explain.

____

____

6. **Critical Thinking** Choose any two negative integers. Is the sum of the integers less than or greater than the value of either of the integers? Will this be true no matter which integers you choose? Explain.

____

____

____

____

Find each sum.

7. $-8 + (-1) =$ ______

8. $-3 + (-7) =$ ______

9. $-48 + (-12) =$ ______

10. $-32 + (-38) =$ ______

11. $109 + 191 =$ ______

12. $-40 + (-105) =$ ______

13. $-150 + (-1500) =$ ______

14. $-200 + (-800) =$ ______

Guided Practice

Find each sum. (Explore Activity 1)

1. $-5 + (-1)$

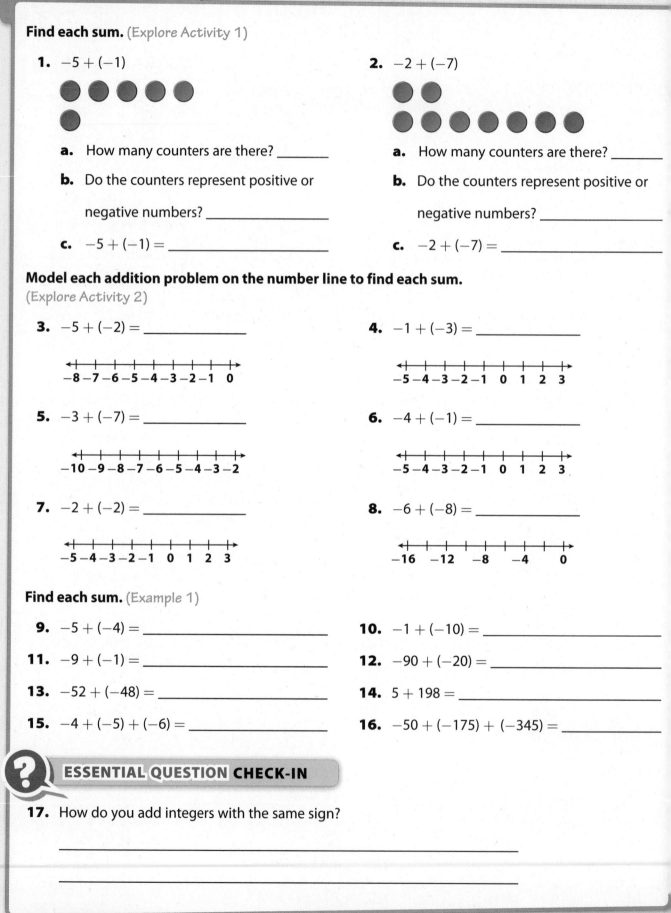

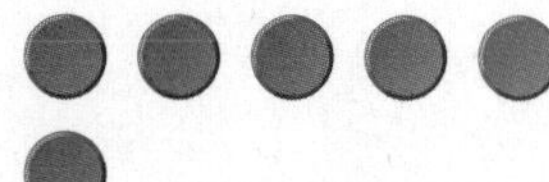

a. How many counters are there? ______

b. Do the counters represent positive or negative numbers? ______

c. $-5 + (-1) =$ ______

2. $-2 + (-7)$

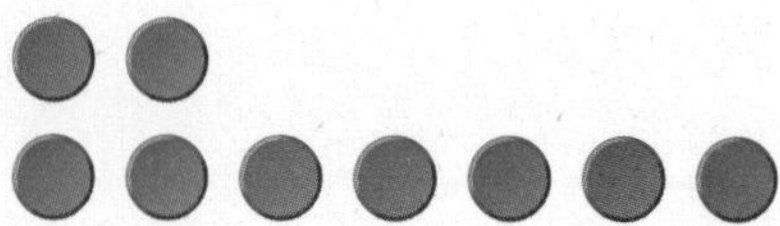

a. How many counters are there? ______

b. Do the counters represent positive or negative numbers? ______

c. $-2 + (-7) =$ ______

Model each addition problem on the number line to find each sum. (Explore Activity 2)

3. $-5 + (-2) =$ ______

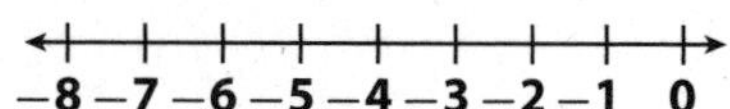

4. $-1 + (-3) =$ ______

−5 −4 −3 −2 −1 0 1 2 3

5. $-3 + (-7) =$ ______

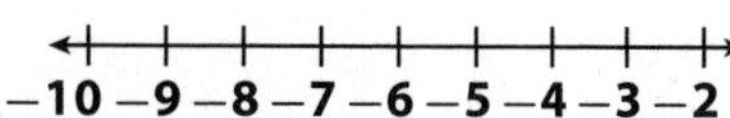

6. $-4 + (-1) =$ ______

−5 −4 −3 −2 −1 0 1 2 3

7. $-2 + (-2) =$ ______

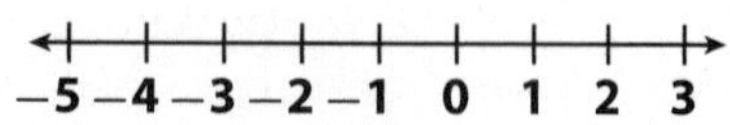

8. $-6 + (-8) =$ ______

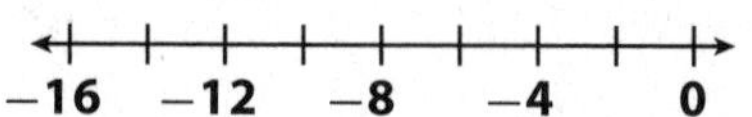

Find each sum. (Example 1)

9. $-5 + (-4) =$ ______

10. $-1 + (-10) =$ ______

11. $-9 + (-1) =$ ______

12. $-90 + (-20) =$ ______

13. $-52 + (-48) =$ ______

14. $5 + 198 =$ ______

15. $-4 + (-5) + (-6) =$ ______

16. $-50 + (-175) + (-345) =$ ______

ESSENTIAL QUESTION CHECK-IN

17. How do you add integers with the same sign?

______

______

Name ______________________ Class ______________ Date ______________

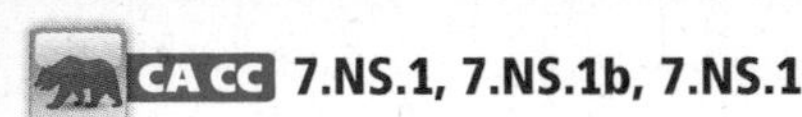

CA CC 7.NS.1, 7.NS.1b, 7.NS.1d

18. Represent Real-World Problems Jane and Sarah both dive down from the surface of a pool. Jane first dives down 5 feet, and then dives down 3 more feet. Sarah first dives down 3 feet, and then dives down 5 more feet.

a. Multiple Representations Use the number line to model the equation $-5 + (-3) = -3 + (-5)$.

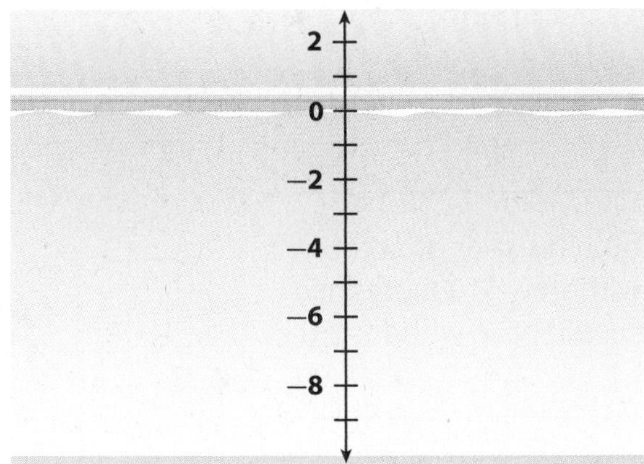

b. Does the order in which you add two integers with the same sign affect the sum? Explain.

____

____

19. A golfer has the following scores for a 4-day tournament.

Day	1	2	3	4
Score	−3	−1	−5	−2

What was the golfer's total score for the tournament?

____

20. A football team loses 3 yards on one play and 6 yards on another play. Write a sum of negative integers to represent this situation. Find the sum and explain how it is related to the problem.

____

____

21. When the quarterback is sacked, the team loses yards. In one game, the quarterback was sacked four times. What was the total sack yardage?

Sack	1	2	3	4
Sack yardage	−14	−5	−12	−23

____

22. Multistep The temperature in Jonestown and Cooperville was the same at 1:00. By 2:00, the temperature in Jonestown dropped 10 degrees, and the temperature in Cooperville dropped 6 degrees. By 3:00, the temperature in Jonestown dropped 8 more degrees, and the temperature in Cooperville dropped 2 more degrees.

a. Write an equation that models the change to the temperature in Jonestown since 1:00.

____

b. Write an equation that models the change to the temperature in Cooperville since 1:00.

____

c. Where was it colder at 3:00, in Jonestown or Cooperville?

____

23. Represent Real-World Problems Julio is playing a trivia game. On his first turn, he lost 100 points. On his second turn, he lost 75 points. On his third turn, he lost 85 points. Write a sum of three negative integers that models the change to Julio's score after his first three turns.

____

FOCUS ON HIGHER ORDER THINKING

Work Area

24. Multistep On Monday, Jan made withdrawals of \$25, \$45, and \$75 from her savings account. On the same day, her twin sister Julie made withdrawals of \$35, \$55, and \$65 from *her* savings account.

a. Write a sum of negative integers to show Jan's withdrawals on Monday. Find the total amount Jan withdrew.

____

b. Write a sum of negative integers to show Julie's withdrawals on Monday. Find the total amount Julie withdrew.

____

c. Julie and Jan's brother also withdrew money from his savings account on Monday. He made three withdrawals and withdrew \$10 more than Julie did. What are three possible amounts he could have withdrawn?

____

25. Communicate Mathematical Ideas Why might you want to use the Commutative Property to change the order of the integers in the following sum before adding?

$$-80 + (-173) + (-20)$$

____

____

26. Critique Reasoning The absolute value of the sum of two different integers with the same sign is 8. Pat says there are three pairs of integers that match this description. Do you agree? Explain.

____

____

____

____

____

LESSON 1.2

Adding Integers with Different Signs

CA CC 7.NS.1

Apply and extend previous understandings of addition and subtraction to add and subtract rational numbers; represent addition and subtraction on a horizontal or vertical number line diagram. *Also 7.NS.1b*

ESSENTIAL QUESTION

How do you add integers with different signs?

EXPLORE ACTIVITY 1

Adding on a Number Line

To find the sum of integers with the same sign, such as $3 + 2$, you can start at 3 and move $|2| = 2$ units in the positive direction.

$3 + 2 = 5$

−3 −2 −1 0 1 2 3 4 5

The sum of $3 + 2$ is the number that is $|2|$ units from 3 in the positive direction.

To find the sum of integers with different signs, such as $3 + (-2)$, you can start at 3 and move $|-2| = 2$ units in the negative direction.

$3 + (-2) = 1$

−3 −2 −1 0 1 2 3 4 5

The sum of $3 + (-2)$ is the number that is $|-2|$ units from 3 in the negative direction.

Model each sum on a number line.

A Model $4 + (-3)$.

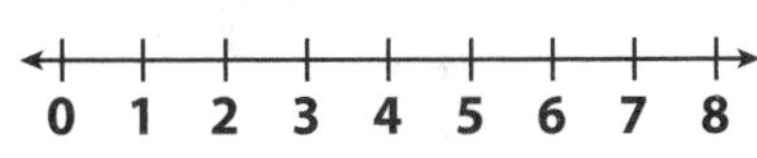

Start at 4. Move 3 units to the left, or in the negative direction.

$4 + (-3) =$ ____________

B Model $-7 + 5$.

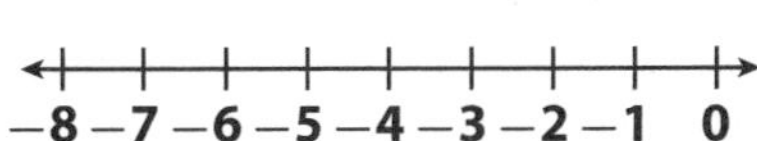

Start at ____________. Move 5 units to the ____________,

or in the ____________ direction. $-7 + 5 =$ ____________

C Model $6 + (-6)$.

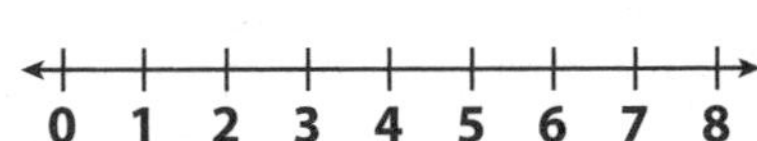

Start at ____________. Move ____________ units to

the ____________, or in the ____________ direction.

$6 + (-6) =$ ____________

Reflect

1. **Make a Prediction** Predict the sum of $-2 + 2$. Explain your prediction and check it using the number line.

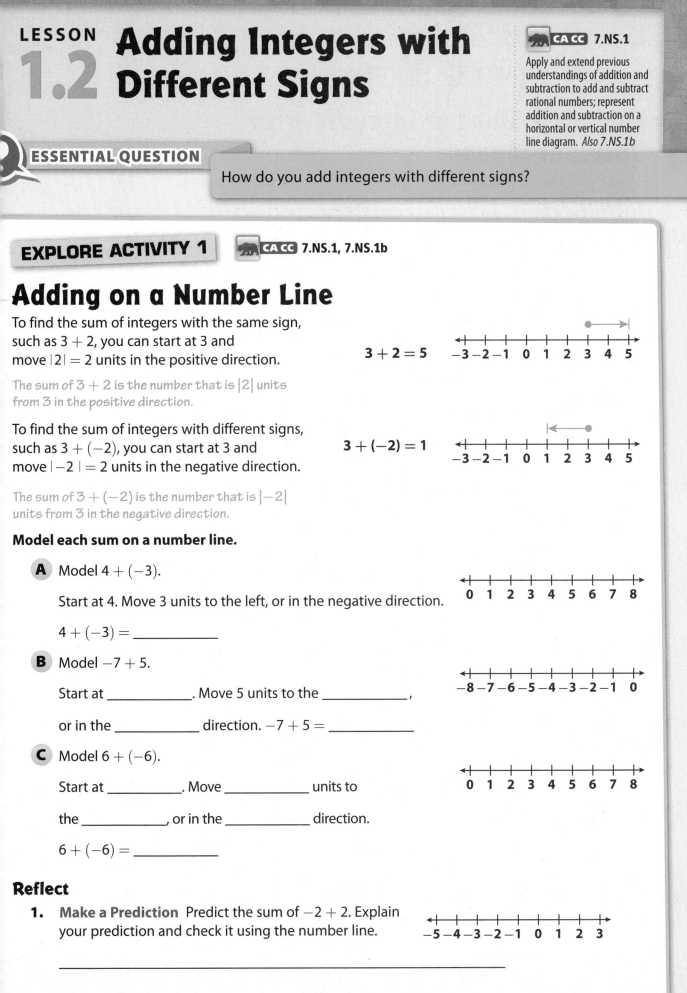

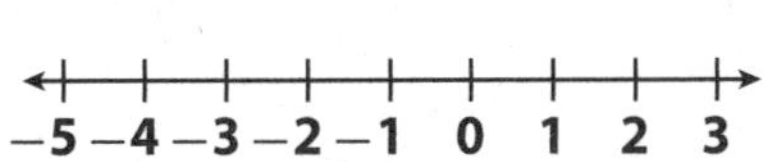

____

EXPLORE ACTIVITY 2 

Modeling Sums of Integers with Different Signs

You can use colored counters to model adding integers with different signs. When you add a positive integer (yellow counter) and a negative integer (red counter), the result is 0. One red and one yellow counter form a *zero pair*.

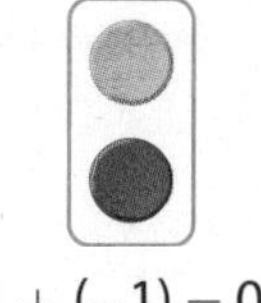

$1 + (-1) = 0$

Model and find each sum using counters. Part A is modeled for you. For Part B, follow the steps to model and find the sum using counters.

A Model $3 + (-2)$.

Start with 3 positive counters to represent 3.

Add 2 negative counters to represent adding -2.

Form zero pairs.

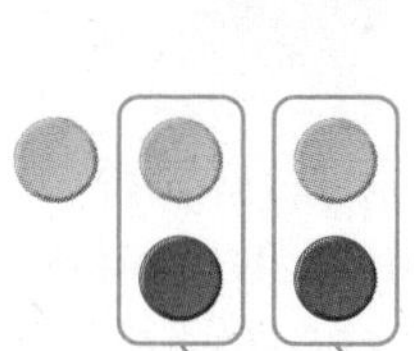

The value of a zero pair is 0. Adding or subtracting 0 to any number does not change its value.

What is left when you remove the zero pairs?

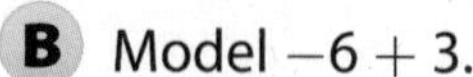 counter

Find the sum: $3 + (-2) =$ ____________

B Model $-6 + 3$.

Start with ____________ counters to represent ____________.

Add ____________ counters to represent adding ____________.

Form zero pairs.

What is left when you remove the zero pairs?

____________ counters

Find the sum: $-6 + 3 =$ ____________

Reflect

2. **Make a Prediction** Kyle models a sum of two integers. He uses more negative (red) counters than positive (yellow) counters. What do you predict about the sign of the sum? Explain.

____

____

____

EXPLORE ACTIVITY 2 *(cont'd)*

Model and find each sum using counters.

3. $5 + (-1)$ ________ **4.** $4 + (-6)$ ________

5. $1 + (-7)$ ________ **6.** $3 + (-4)$ ________

Adding Integers

You have learned how to add integers with the same signs and how to add integers with different signs. The table below summarizes the rules for adding integers.

Adding Integers		Examples
Same signs	Add the absolute values of the integers. Use the common sign for the sum.	$3 + 5 = 8$ $-2 + (-7) = -9$
Different signs	Subtract the lesser absolute value from the greater absolute value. Use the sign of the integer with the greater absolute value for the sum.	$3 + (-5) = -2$ $-10 + 1 = -9$
A number and its opposite	The sum is 0. The opposite of any number is called its **additive inverse.**	$4 + (-4) = 0$ $-11 + 11 = 0$

EXAMPLE 1

Find each sum.

A $-11 + 6$

$|-11| - |6| = 5$ *Subtract the lesser absolute value from the greater.*

$-11 + 6 = -5$ *Use the sign of the number with the greater absolute value.*

B $(-37) + 37$

$(-37) + 37 = 0$ *The sum of a number and its opposite is 0.*

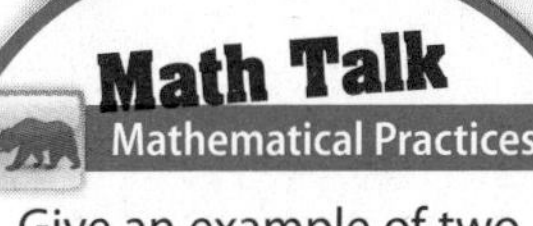

Give an example of two integers with different signs whose sum is a positive number. How did you choose the integers?

Find each sum.

7. $-51 + 23 =$ ________ **8.** $10 + (-18) =$ ________

9. $13 + (-13) =$ ________ **10.** $25 + (-26) =$ ________

Guided Practice

Use a number line to find each sum. (Explore Activity 1)

1. $9 + (-3) =$ ______

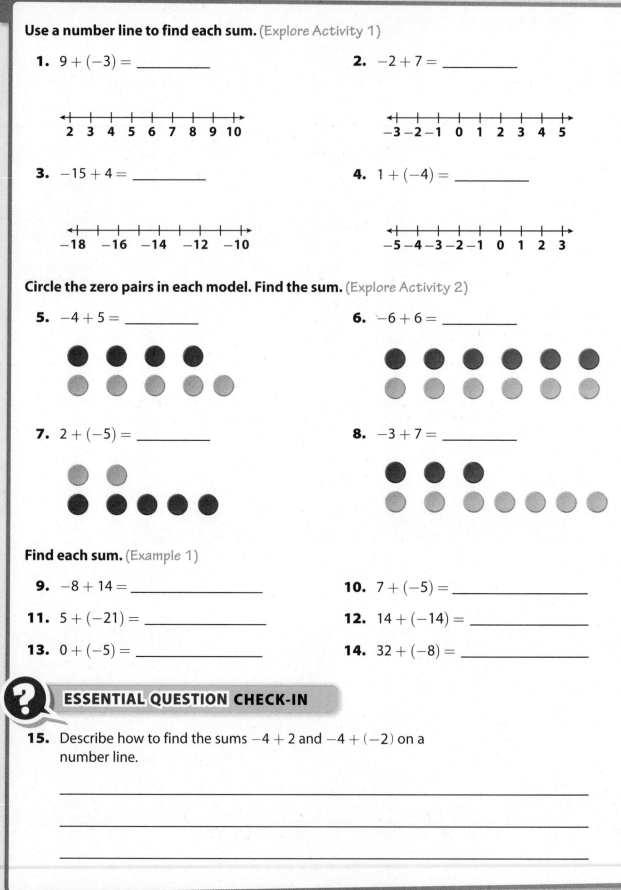

2 3 4 5 6 7 8 9 10

2. $-2 + 7 =$ ______

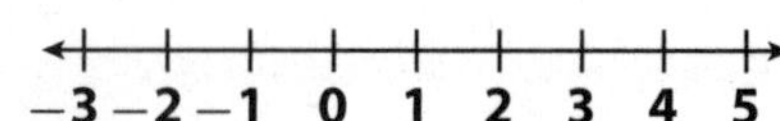

3. $-15 + 4 =$ ______

−18 −16 −14 −12 −10

4. $1 + (-4) =$ ______

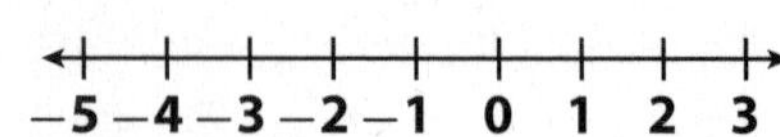

Circle the zero pairs in each model. Find the sum. (Explore Activity 2)

5. $-4 + 5 =$ ______

6. $-6 + 6 =$ ______

7. $2 + (-5) =$ ______

8. $-3 + 7 =$ ______

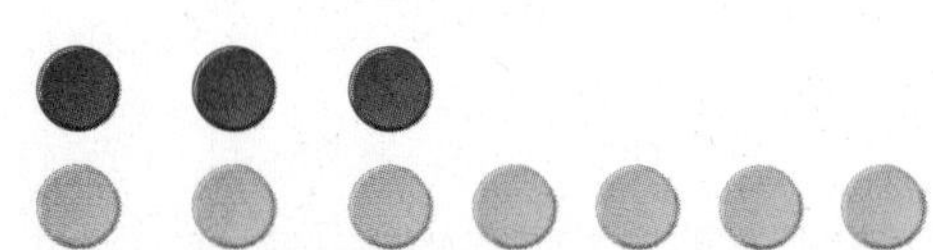

Find each sum. (Example 1)

9. $-8 + 14 =$ ______

10. $7 + (-5) =$ ______

11. $5 + (-21) =$ ______

12. $14 + (-14) =$ ______

13. $0 + (-5) =$ ______

14. $32 + (-8) =$ ______

ESSENTIAL QUESTION CHECK-IN

15. Describe how to find the sums $-4 + 2$ and $-4 + (-2)$ on a number line.

______

______

______

Name ______________________ Class ______________ Date ______________

1.2 Independent Practice

Find each sum.

16. $-15 + 71 =$ ______________

17. $-53 + 45 =$ ______________

18. $-79 + 79 =$ ______________

19. $-25 + 50 =$ ______________

20. $18 + (-32) =$ ______________

21. $5 + (-100) =$ ______________

22. $-12 + 8 + 7 =$ ______________

23. $-8 + (-2) + 3 =$ ______________

24. $15 + (-15) + 200 =$ ______________

25. $-500 + (-600) + 1200 =$ ______________

26. A football team gained 9 yards on one play and then lost 22 yards on the next. Write a sum of integers to find the overall change in field position. Explain your answer.

____

27. A soccer team is having a car wash. The team spent \$55 on supplies. They earned \$275, including tips. The team's profit is the amount the team made after paying for supplies. Write a sum of integers that represents the team's profit.

____

28. As shown in the illustration, Alexa had a negative balance in her checking account before depositing a \$47.00 check. What is the new balance of Alexa's checking account?

____

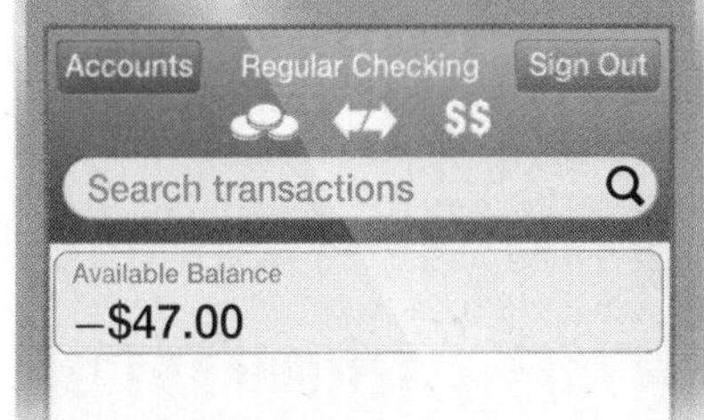

29. The sum of two integers with different signs is 8. Give two possible integers that fit this description.

____

30. **Multistep** Bart and Sam played a game in which each player earns or loses points in each turn. A player's total score after two turns is the sum of his points earned or lost. The player with the greater score after two turns wins. Bart earned 123 points and lost 180 points. Sam earned 185 points and lost 255 points. Which person won the game? Explain.

____

____

____

H.O.T. FOCUS ON HIGHER ORDER THINKING

Work Area

31. Critical Thinking Explain how you could use a number line to show that $-4 + 3$ and $3 + (-4)$ have the same value. Which property of addition states that these sums are equivalent?

32. Represent Real-World Problems Jim is standing beside a pool. He drops a weight from 4 feet above the surface of the water in the pool. The weight travels a total distance of 12 feet down before landing on the bottom of the pool. Explain how you can write a sum of integers to find the depth of the water.

33. Communicate Mathematical Ideas Use counters to model two integers with different signs whose sum is positive. Explain how you know the sum is positive.

34. Analyze Relationships You know that the sum of -5 and another integer is a positive integer. What can you conclude about the sign of the other integer? What can you conclude about the value of the other integer? Explain.

LESSON 1.3 Subtracting Integers

Understand subtraction of rational numbers as adding the additive inverse, $p - q = p + (-q)$. Show that the distance between two rational numbers on the number line is the absolute value of their difference, and apply this principle in real-world contexts. *Also 7.NS.1*

How do you subtract integers?

EXPLORE ACTIVITY 1

Modeling Integer Subtraction

You can use counters to find the difference of two integers. In some cases, you may need to add zero pairs.

$1 + (-1) = 0$

Model and find each difference using counters.

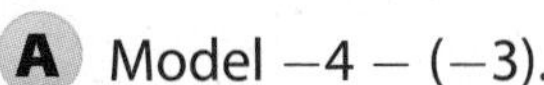

A Model $-4 - (-3)$.

Start with 4 negative counters to represent -4.

Take away 3 negative counters to represent subtracting -3.

What is left? ______________________

Find the difference: $-4 - (-3) =$ _____

B Model $6 - (-3)$.

Start with 6 positive counters to represent 6.

You need to take away 3 negative counters, so add 3 zero pairs.

Take away 3 negative counters to represent subtracting -3.

What is left? ______________________

Find the difference: $6 - (-3) =$ _____

C Model $-2 - (-5)$.

Start with ______________ counters.

You need to take away ______________ counters, so add _____ zero pairs.

Take away ______________ counters.

What is left? ______________________

Find the difference: $-2 - (-5) =$ _____

EXPLORE ACTIVITY 1 *(cont'd)*

Reflect

1. **Communicate Mathematical Ideas** Suppose you want to model the difference $-4 - 7$. Do you need to add zero pairs? If so, why? How many should you add? What is the difference?

____

____

____

EXPLORE ACTIVITY 2 CA CC 7.NS.1, 7.NS.1c

Subtracting on a Number Line

To model the difference $5 - 3$ on a number line, you start at 5 and move 3 units to the left. Notice that you model the sum $5 + (-3)$ in the same way. Subtracting 3 is the same as adding its opposite, -3.

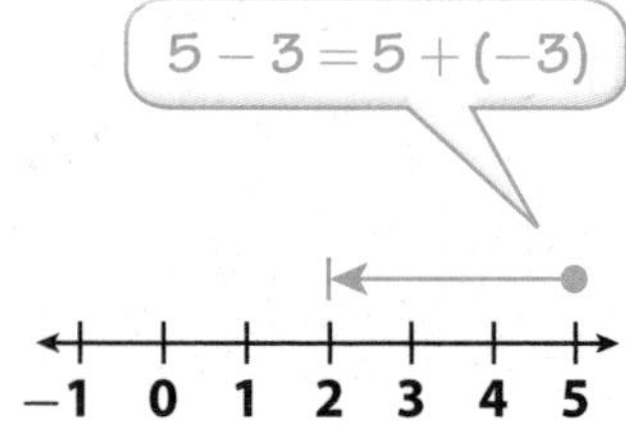

You can use the fact that subtracting a number is the same as adding its opposite to find a difference of two integers.

Find each difference on a number line.

A Find $-1 - 5$ on a number line.

Rewrite subtraction as addition of the opposite.

$-1 - 5 = -1 +$ _____

Start at _____ and move _____ units to the left.

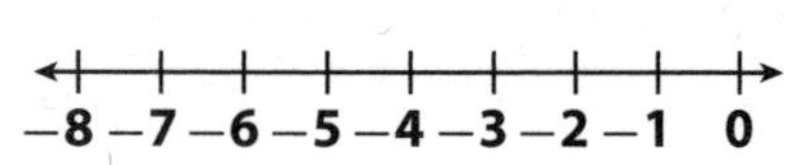

The difference is _____

B Find $-7 - (-3)$.

Rewrite subtraction as addition of the opposite.

$-7 - (-3) = -7 +$ _____

Start at _____ and move _____ units to the _______.

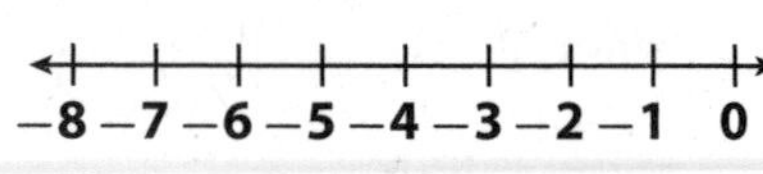

The difference is _____

EXPLORE ACTIVITY 2 *(cont'd)*

Reflect

2. **Communicate Mathematical Ideas** Describe how to find $5 - (-8)$ on a number line. If you found the difference using counters, would you get the same result? Explain.

____

____

____

____

____

Subtracting Integers by Adding the Opposite

You can use the fact that subtracting an integer is the same as adding its opposite to solve problems.

Math On the Spot
my.hrw.com

EXAMPLE 1 

The temperature on Monday was -5 °C. By Tuesday the temperature rose to -2 °C. Find the change in temperature.

Animated Math
my.hrw.com

Write a subtraction expression.

final temperature − Monday's temperature = change in temperature

$-2\ °C - (-5\ °C)$

Find the difference.

$-2 - (-5) = -2 + 5$ — *To subtract -5, add its opposite, 5.*

$-2 + 5 = 3$ — *Use the rule for adding integers.*

The temperature increased by 3 °C.

Why does it make sense that the change in temperature is a positive number?

Reflect

3. **What If?** In Example 1, the temperature rose by 3 °C. Suppose it fell from -2 °C to -10 °C. Predict whether the change in temperature would be positive or negative. Then subtract to find the change.

____

____

YOUR TURN

Find each difference.

4. $-7 - 2 =$ ______

5. $-1 - (-3) =$ ______

6. $3 - 5 =$ ______

7. $-8 - (-4) =$ ______

Guided Practice

Explain how to find each difference using counters. (Explore Activity 1)

1. $5 - 8 =$ ______

______

______

______

______

2. $-5 - (-3) =$ ______

______

______

______

______

Use a number line to find each difference. (Explore Activity 2)

3. $-4 - 5 = -4 +$ ______ $=$ ______

−9 −8 −7 −6 −5 −4 −3 −2 −1 0

4. $1 - 4 = 1 +$ ______ $=$ ______

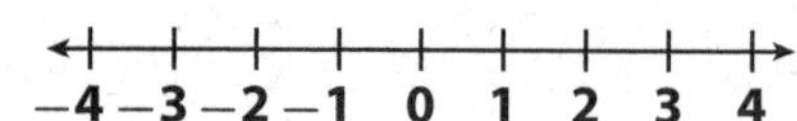

Solve. (Example 1)

5. $8 - 11 =$ ______

6. $-3 - (-5) =$ ______

7. $15 - 21 =$ ______

8. $-17 - 1 =$ ______

9. $0 - (-5) =$ ______

10. $1 - (-18) =$ ______

11. $15 - 1 =$ ______

12. $-3 - (-45) =$ ______

13. $19 - (-19) =$ ______

14. $-87 - (-87) =$ ______

ESSENTIAL QUESTION CHECK-IN

15. How do you subtract an integer from another integer without using a number line or counters? Give an example.

______

______

Name ____________________ Class ____________________ Date ____________________

1.3 Independent Practice

CA CC 7.NS.1, 7.NS.1c

16. Theo had a balance of −$4 in his savings account. After making a deposit, he has $25 in his account. What is the overall change to his account?

____

17. As shown, Suzi starts her hike at an elevation below sea level. When she reaches the end of the hike, she is still below sea level at −127 feet. What was the change in elevation from the beginning of Suzi's hike to the end of the hike?

____

18. The record high January temperature in Austin, Texas, is 90 °F. The record low January temperature is −2 °F. Find the difference between the high and low temperatures.

____

19. Cheyenne is playing a board game. Her score was −275 at the start of her turn, and at the end of her turn her score was −425. What was the change in Cheyenne's score from the start of her turn to the end of her turn?

____

20. A scientist conducts three experiments in which she records the temperature of some gases that are being heated. The table shows the initial temperature and the final temperature for each gas.

Gas	Initial Temperature	Final Temperature
A	−21 °C	−8 °C
B	−12 °C	12 °C
C	−19 °C	−15 °C

a. Write a difference of integers to find the overall temperature change for each gas.

Gas A: _______________

____

Gas B: _______________

____

Gas C: _______________

____

b. **What If?** Suppose the scientist performs an experiment in which she cools the three gases. Will the changes in temperature be positive or negative for this experiment? Why?

____

____

____

____

____

____

21. **Analyze Relationships** For two months, Nell feeds her cat Diet Chow brand cat food. Then for the next two months, she feeds her cat Kitty Diet brand cat food. The table shows the cat's change in weight over 4 months.

	Cat's Weight Change (oz)
Diet Chow, Month 1	−8
Diet Chow, Month 2	−18
Kitty Diet, Month 3	3
Kitty Diet, Month 4	−19

Which brand of cat food resulted in the greatest weight loss for Nell's cat? Explain.

____

____

FOCUS ON HIGHER ORDER THINKING

Work Area

22. **Represent Real-World Problems** Write and solve a word problem that can be modeled by the difference −4 − 10.

____

____

____

23. **Explain the Error** When Tom found the difference −11 − (−4), he got −15. What might Tom have done wrong?

____

____

____

24. **Draw Conclusions** When you subtract one negative integer from another, will your answer be greater than or less than the integer you started with? Explain your reasoning and give an example.

____

____

____

____

25. **Look for a Pattern** Find the next three terms in the pattern 9, 4, −1, −6, −11, … . Then describe the pattern.

____

LESSON 1.4

Applying Addition and Subtraction of Integers

Solve real-world and mathematical problems involving the four operations with rational numbers. *Also 7.NS.1, 7.NS.1d, 7.EE.3*

ESSENTIAL QUESTION

How do you solve multistep problems involving addition and subtraction of integers?

Solving a Multistep Problem

You can use what you know about adding and subtracting integers to solve a multistep problem.

EXAMPLE 1

CA CC 7.NS.3, 7.NS.1

A seal is swimming in the ocean 5 feet below sea level. It dives down 12 feet to catch some fish. Then, the seal swims 8 feet up towards the surface with its catch. What is the seal's final elevation relative to sea level?

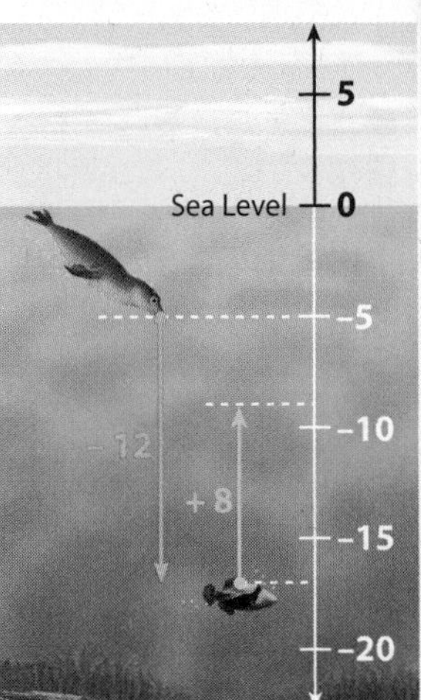

STEP 1 Write an expression.

- The seal starts at 5 feet below the surface, so its initial position is -5 ft.

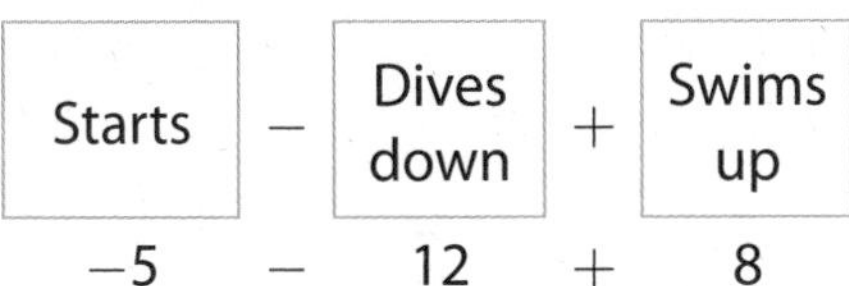

STEP 2 Add or subtract from left to right to find the value of the expression.

$$-5 - 12 + 8 = -17 + 8$$

$$= -9$$

This is reasonable because the seal swam farther down than up.

The seal's final elevation is 9 feet below sea level.

YOUR TURN

1. Anna is in a cave 40 feet below the cave entrance. She descends 13 feet, then ascends 18 feet. Find her new position relative to the cave entrance.

____

Applying Properties to Solve Problems

You can use properties of addition to solve problems involving integers.

EXAMPLE 2

CA CC 7.NS.1d, 7.NS.3, 7.EE.3

Irene has a checking account. On Monday she writes a $160 check for groceries. Then she deposits $125. Finally she writes another check for $40. What was the total change in the amount in Irene's account?

My Notes

Analyze Information

When Irene deposits money, she adds that amount to the account. When she writes a check, that money is deducted from the account.

Formulate a Plan

Use a positive integer for the amount Irene added to the account. Use negative integers for the checks she wrote. Find the sum.

$-160 + 125 + (-40)$

Solve

Add the amounts to find the total change in the account. Use properties of addition to simplify calculations.

$-160 + 125 + (-40) = -160 + (-40) + 125$ Commutative Property

$= -200 + 125$ Associative Property

$= -75$

The amount in the account decreased by $75.

Justify and Evaluate

Irene's account has $75 less than it did before Monday. This is reasonable because she wrote checks for $200 but only deposited $125.

Reflect

2. **Communicative Mathematical Ideas** Describe a different way to find the change in Irene's account.

____

____

YOUR TURN

3. Alex wrote checks on Tuesday for $35 and $45. He also made a deposit in his checking account of $180. Find the overall change in the amount in his checking account.

____

Comparing Values of Expressions

Sometimes you may want to compare values obtained by adding and subtracting integers.

EXAMPLE 3   CA CC 7.NS.3, 7.EE.3

The Tigers, a football team, must gain 10 yards in the next four plays to keep possession of the ball. The Tigers lose 12 yards, gain 5 yards, lose 8 yards, and gain 14 yards. Do the Tigers maintain possession of the ball?

 **Analyze Information**

When the team gains yards, add that distance.

When the team loses yards, subtract that distance.

If the total change in yards is greater than or equal to 10, the team keeps possession of the ball.

 **Formulate a Plan**

$-12 + 5 - 8 + 14$

 **Solve**

$-12 + 5 - 8 + 14$

$-12 + 5 + (-8) + 14$ *To subtract, add the opposite.*

$-12 + (-8) + 5 + 14$ *Commutative Property*

$(-12 + (-8)) + (5 + 14)$ *Associative Property*

$-20 + 19 = -1$

$-1 < 10$ *Compare to 10 yards.*

The Tigers gained less than 10 yards, so they do not maintain possession.

 **Justify and Evaluate**

The football team gained 19 yards and lost 20 yards for a total of -1 yard.

Math Talk
Mathematical Practices

What does it mean that the football team had a total of -1 yard over four plays?

4. Jim and Carla are scuba diving. Jim started out 10 feet below the surface. He descended 18 feet, rose 5 feet, and descended 12 more feet. Then he rested. Carla started out at the surface. She descended 20 feet, rose 5 feet, and descended another 18 feet. Then she rested. Which person rested at a greater depth? Explain.

____

____

Guided Practice

Write an expression. Then find the value of the expression. (Examples 1, 2, 3)

1. Tomas works as an underwater photographer. He starts at a position that is 15 feet below sea level. He rises 9 feet, then descends 12 feet to take a photo of a coral reef. Write and evaluate an expression to find his position relative to sea level when he took the photo.

____

2. The temperature on a winter night was −23 °F. The temperature rose by 5 °F when the sun came up. When the sun set again, the temperature dropped by 7 °F. Write and evaluate an expression to find the temperature after the sun set.

____

3. Jose earned 50 points in a video game. He lost 40 points, earned 87 points, then lost 30 more points. Write and evaluate an expression to find his final score in the video game.

____

Find the value of each expression. (Example 2)

4. $-6 + 15 + 15 =$ _______________
5. $9 - 4 - 17 =$ _______________
6. $50 - 42 + 10 =$ _______________
7. $6 + 13 + 7 - 5 =$ _______________
8. $65 + 43 - 11 =$ _______________
9. $-35 - 14 + 45 + 31 =$ _______________

Determine which expression has a greater value. (Example 3)

10. $-12 + 6 - 4$ or $-34 - 3 + 39$

____

11. $21 - 3 + 8$ or $-14 + 31 - 6$

____

ESSENTIAL QUESTION CHECK-IN

12. Explain how you can find the value of the expression $-5 + 12 + 10 - 7$.

____

____

Name ______________________ Class ______________ Date ______________

1.4 Independent Practice

7.NS.1, 7.NS.1d, 7.NS.3, 7.EE.3

13. **Sports** Cameron is playing 9 holes of golf. He needs to score a total of at most 15 over par on the last four holes to beat his best golf score. On the last four holes, he scores 5 over par, 1 under par, 6 over par, and 1 under par.

a. Write and find the value of an expression that gives Cameron's score for 4 holes of golf.

____

b. Is Cameron's score on the last four holes over or under par?

____

c. Did Cameron beat his best golf score?

____

14. Herman is standing on a ladder that is partly in a hole. He starts out on a rung that is 6 feet under ground, climbs up 14 feet, then climbs down 11 feet. What is Herman's final position, relative to ground level?

____

15. **Explain the Error** Jerome tries to find the value of the expression $3 - 6 + 5$ by first applying the Commutative Property. He rewrites the expression as $3 - 5 + 6$. Explain what is wrong with Jerome's approach.

____

____

____

____

____

16. Lee and Barry play a trivia game in which questions are worth different numbers of points. If a question is answered correctly, a player earns points. If a question is answered incorrectly, the player loses points. Lee currently has -350 points.

a. Before the game ends, Lee answers a 275-point question correctly, a 70-point question correctly, and a 50-point question incorrectly. Write and find the value of an expression to find Lee's final score.

____

b. Barry's final score is 45. Which player had the greater final score?

____

17. **Multistep** Rob collects data about how many customers enter and leave a store every hour. He records a positive number for customers entering the store each hour and a negative number for customers leaving the store each hour.

	Entering	Leaving
1:00 to 2:00	30	−12
2:00 to 3:00	14	−8
3:00 to 4:00	18	−30

a. During which hour did more customers leave than arrive?

____

b. There were 75 customers in the store at 1:00. The store must be emptied of customers when it closes at 5:00. How many customers must leave the store between 4:00 and 5:00?

____

The table shows the changes in the values of two friends' savings accounts since the previous month.

	June	July	August
Carla	−18	22	−53
Leta	−17	−22	18

18. Carla had $100 in her account in May. How much money does she have in her account in August? ______

19. Leta had $45 in her account in May. How much money does she have in her account in August? ______

20. **Analyze Relationships** Whose account had the greatest decrease in value from May to August? ______

Work Area

FOCUS ON HIGHER ORDER THINKING

21. **Represent Real-World Problems** Write and solve a word problem that matches the diagram shown.

−9 −8 −7 −6 −5 −4 −3 −2 −1 0

______

______

______

22. **Critical Thinking** Mary has $10 in savings. She owes her parents $50. She does some chores and her parents pay her $12. She also gets $25 for her birthday from her grandmother. Does Mary have enough money to pay her parents what she owes them? If not, how much more money does she need? Explain.

______

______

23. **Draw Conclusions** An expression involves subtracting two numbers from a positive number. Under what circumstances will the value of the expression be negative? Give an example.

______

______

______

______

MODULE QUIZ

Ready to Go On?

1.1 Adding Integers with the Same Sign

Add.

1. $-8 + (-6)$ ______ **2.** $-4 + (-7)$ ______ **3.** $-9 + (-12)$ ______

1.2 Adding Integers with Different Signs

Add.

4. $5 + (-2)$ ______ **5.** $-8 + 4$ ______ **6.** $15 + (-8)$ ______

1.3 Subtracting Integers

Subtract.

7. $2 - 9$ ______ **8.** $-3 - (-4)$ ______ **9.** $11 - (-12)$ ______

1.4 Applying Addition and Subtraction of Integers

10. A bus makes a stop at 2:30, letting off 15 people and letting on 9. The bus makes another stop ten minutes later to let off 4 more people. How many more or fewer people are on the bus after the second stop compared to the number of people on the bus before the 2:30 stop?

______

11. Cate and Elena were playing a card game. The stack of cards in the middle had 24 cards in it to begin with. Cate added 8 cards to the stack. Elena then took 12 cards from the stack. Finally, Cate took 9 cards from the stack. How many cards were left in the stack? ______

ESSENTIAL QUESTION

12. Write and solve a word problem that can be modeled by addition of two negative integers.

______

______

______

MODULE 1
MIXED REVIEW

Assessment Readiness

1. Look at each expression. Does it have the same value as $-6 - 4$?

Select Yes or No for expressions A–C.

A. $-6 + (-4)$ ○ Yes ○ No
B. $-4 + (-6)$ ○ Yes ○ No
C. $6 + (-4)$ ○ Yes ○ No

2. Choose True or False for A–C.

A. $x = 4$ is the solution for $x + 4 = 0$. ○ True ○ False
B. $x = 24$ is the solution for $\frac{x}{3} = 8$. ○ True ○ False
C. $x = 6$ is the solution for $6x = 1$ ○ True ○ False

3. At 3:00 a.m., the temperature is –5 °F. Between 3:00 a.m. and 6:00 a.m., the temperature drops by 12 °F. Between 6:00 a.m. and 9:00 a.m., the temperature rises by 4 °F. What is the temperature at 9:00 a.m.? Explain how you solved this problem.

4. Sherri and Darren are playing a board game. The table shows the number of points each player scores in 3 rounds. If the player with the greater total score wins, who is the winner? Explain how you know.

Round	Sherri's Points	Darren's Points
1	35	−10
2	−20	15
3	−5	15

Multiplying and Dividing Integers

ESSENTIAL QUESTION

How can you use multiplication and division of integers to solve real-world problems?

LESSON 2.1

Multiplying Integers

7.NS.2, 7.NS.2a

LESSON 2.2

Dividing Integers

7.NS.2, 7.NS.2b, 7.NS.3

LESSON 2.3

Applying Integer Operations

CA CC 7.NS.2a, 7.NS.2c, 7.NS.3, 7.EE.3

Real-World Video

The giant panda is an endangered animal. For some endangered species, the population has made a steady decline. This can be represented by multiplying integers with different signs.

my.hrw.com

GO DIGITAL
my.hrw.com

my.hrw.com

Go digital with your write-in student edition, accessible on any device.

Math On the Spot

Scan with your smart phone to jump directly to the online edition, video tutor, and more.

Animated Math

Interactively explore key concepts to see how math works.

Personal Math Trainer

Get immediate feedback and help as you work through practice sets.

Are YOU Ready?

Complete these exercises to review skills you will need for this module.

Personal Math Trainer

Online Practice and Help

Multiplication Facts

EXAMPLES $7 \times 9 = \blacksquare$

$7 \times 9 = 63$ — Use patterns. When you multiply 9 by a number 1 through 9, the digits of the product add up to 9. $6 + 3 = 9$

$12 \times 10 = \blacksquare$

$12 \times 10 = 120$ — Products of 10 end in 0.

Multiply.

1. 9×3 ______ **2.** 7×10 ______ **3.** 9×8 ______ **4.** 15×10 ______

5. 6×9 ______ **6.** 10×23 ______ **7.** 9×9 ______ **8.** 10×20 ______

Division Facts

EXAMPLE $48 \div 6 = \blacksquare$ — Think: 6 times what number equals 48?

$6 \times 8 = 48$

$48 \div 6 = 8$ — So, $48 \div 6 = 8$

Divide.

9. $54 \div 9$ ______ **10.** $42 \div 6$ ______ **11.** $24 \div 3$ ______ **12.** $64 \div 8$ ______

13. $90 \div 10$ ______ **14.** $56 \div 7$ ______ **15.** $81 \div 9$ ______ **16.** $110 \div 11$ ______

Order of Operations

EXAMPLE $32 - 2(10 - 7)^2$

$32 - 2(3)^2$ — To evaluate, first operate within parentheses.

$32 - 2(9)$ — Next, simplify exponents.

$32 - 18$ — Then multiply and divide from left to right.

14 — Finally add and subtract from left to right.

Evaluate each expression.

17. $12 + 8 \div 2$ ______ **18.** $15 - (4 + 3) \times 2$ ______ **19.** $18 - (8 - 5)^2$ ______

20. $6 + 7 \times 3 - 5$ ______ **21.** $9 + (2^2 + 3)^2 \times 2$ ______ **22.** $6 + 5 - 4 \times 3 \div 2$ ______

Reading Start-Up

Visualize Vocabulary

Use the ✔ words to complete the chart. You may put more than one word in each box.

÷, or put into equal groups	×, or repeated addition
Multiplying and Dividing Whole Numbers	
$4 \times 1 = 4$	$32 \div 4 = 8$

Understand Vocabulary

Complete the sentences using the review words.

1. A ____________________ is a number that is less than 0. A ____________________ is a number that is greater than 0.
2. Division problems have three parts. The part you want to divide into groups is called the ____________. The number that is divided into another number is called the ____________. The answer to a division problem is called the ____________.
3. ____________ are all whole numbers and their opposites.

Vocabulary

Review Words

- ✔ divide *(dividir)*
- ✔ dividend *(dividendo)*
- ✔ divisor *(divisor)*
- integers *(enteros)*
- ✔ multiply *(multiplicar)*
- negative number *(número negativo)*
- operation *(operación)*
- opposites *(opuestos)*
- positive number *(número positivo)*
- ✔ product *(producto)*
- ✔ quotient *(cociente)*

Active Reading

Double-Door Fold Create a double-door fold to help you understand the concepts in this module. Label one flap "Multiplying Integers" and the other flap "Dividing Integers." As you study each lesson, write important ideas under the appropriate flap. Include information that will help you remember the concepts later when you look back at your notes.

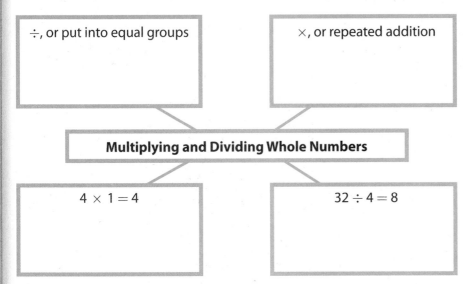

GETTING READY FOR

Multiplying and Dividing Integers

Understanding the standards and the vocabulary terms in the standards will help you know exactly what you are expected to learn in this module.

 CA CC **7.NS.2a**

Understand that multiplication is extended from fractions to rational numbers by requiring that operations continue to satisfy the properties of operations, particularly the distributive property, leading to products such as $(-1)(-1) = 1$ and the rules for multiplying signed numbers. Interpret products of rational numbers by describing real-world contexts.

Key Vocabulary

integer *(entero)*
A member of the set of whole numbers and their opposites.

What It Means to You

You will use your knowledge of multiplication of whole numbers and addition of negative numbers to multiply integers.

EXAMPLE 7.NS.2a

Show that $(-1)(-1) = 1$.

$0 = -1(0)$ Multiplication property of 0

$0 = -1(-1 + 1)$ Addition property of opposites

$0 = (-1)(-1) + (-1)(1)$ Distributive Property

$0 = (-1)(-1) + (-1)$ Multiplication property of 1

So, $(-1)(-1) = 1$. Definition of opposites

In general, a negative number times a negative number is always a positive number.

 CA CC **7.NS.2b**

Understand that integers can be divided, provided that the divisor is not zero, and every quotient of integers (with non-zero divisor) is a rational number. If p and q are integers, then $-\left(\frac{p}{q}\right) = \frac{(-p)}{q} = \frac{p}{(-q)}$. Interpret quotients of rational numbers by describing real-world contexts.

What It Means to You

You will use your knowledge of division of whole numbers and multiplication of integers to divide integers.

EXAMPLE 7.NS.2b

The temperature in Fairbanks, Alaska, dropped over four consecutive hours from 0° F to −44°F. If the temperature dropped the same amount each hour, how much did the temperature change each hour?

$\frac{-44}{4} = -11$

The quotient of −44 and 4 is the same as the negative quotient of 44 and 4.

A negative number divided by a positive number is negative.

Visit **my.hrw.com** to see all **CA Common Core Standards** explained.

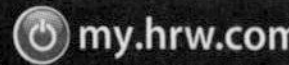 my.hrw.com

LESSON

2.1 Multiplying Integers

Apply and extend previous understandings of multiplication and division and of fractions to multiply and divide rational numbers. *Also 7.NS.2a*

ESSENTIAL QUESTION

How do you multiply integers?

EXPLORE ACTIVITY 1

CA CC 7.NS.2, 7.NS.2a

Multiplying Integers Using a Number Line

You can use a number line to see what happens when you multiply a positive number by a negative number.

A Henry made three withdrawals of $2 each from his savings account. What was the change in his balance?

Find 3(−2).

To graph −2, you would start at 0 and move ______ units to the left.

3(−2) means (______) + (______) + (______).

To graph 3(−2), start at 0 and move

2 units to the left ______ times.

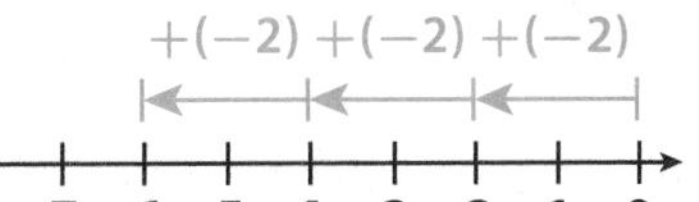

The result is ______.

The change in Henry's balance was ______

B Lisa plays a video game in which she loses points. She loses 3 points 2 times. What is her score?

Find 2(−3).

2(−3) means (______) + (______).
Show this on the number line.

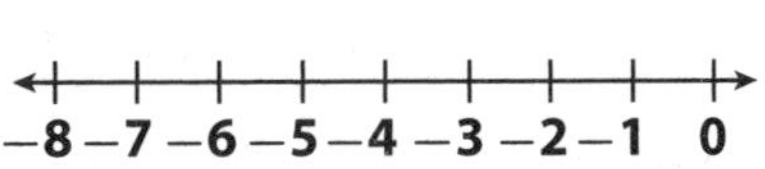

Lisa has a score of ______.

Reflect

1. What do you notice about the product of two integers with different signs?

______

______

EXPLORE ACTIVITY 2 CA CC 7.NS.2, 7.NS.2a

Modeling Integer Multiplication

Counters representing positive and negative numbers can help you understand how to find the product of two negative integers.

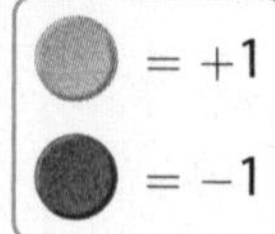

Find the product of −3 and −4.

Write (−3)(−4) as −3(−4), which means the *opposite* of 3(−4).

STEP 1 Use negative counters to model 3(−4).

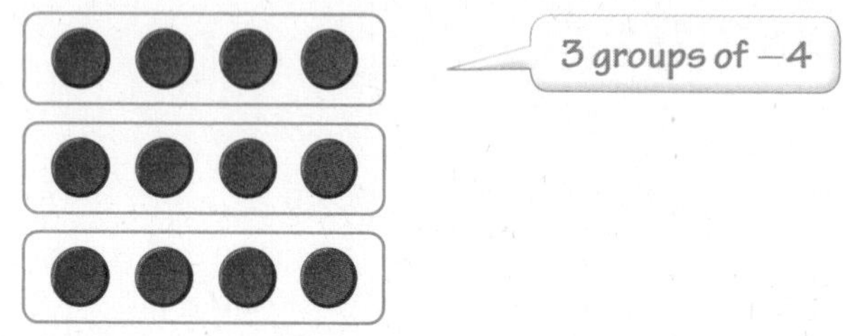

STEP 2 Make the same model using positive counters to find the *opposite* of 3(−4).

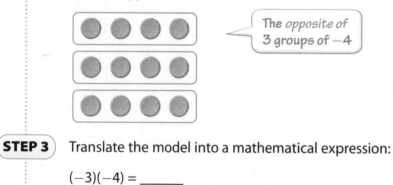

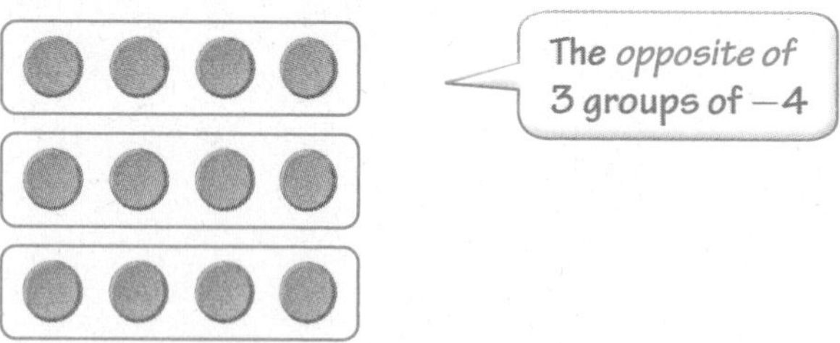

STEP 3 Translate the model into a mathematical expression:

(−3)(−4) = ______

The product of −3 and −4 is ______.

Reflect

2. What do you notice about the sign of the product of two negative integers?

____

3. **Make a Conjecture** What can you conclude about the sign of the product of two integers with the same sign?

____

____

____

____

Multiplying Integers

The product of two integers with opposite signs is negative. The product of two integers with the same sign is positive. The product of 0 and any other integer is 0.

You can use the Multiplication property of 0 and the Distributive Property to show that a negative number times a negative number is always a positive number.

Show that $(-1)(-1) = 1$.

$0 = -1(0)$	*Multiplication property of 0*
$0 = -1(-1 + 1)$	*Addition property of opposites*
$0 = (-1)(-1) + (-1)(1)$	*Distributive Property*
$0 = (-1)(-1) + (-1)$	*Multiplication property of 1*
So, $(-1)(-1) = 1$.	*Definition of opposites*

EXAMPLE 1

A Multiply: $(13)(-3)$.

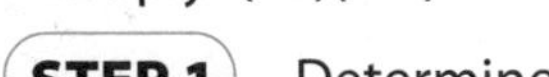

STEP 1 Determine the sign of the product.

13 is positive and -3 is negative. Since the numbers have opposite signs, the product will be negative.

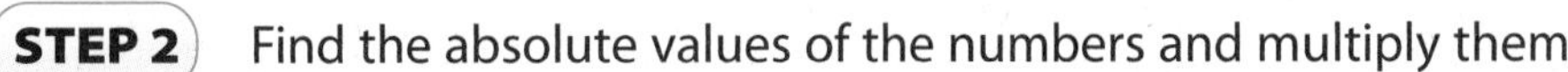

STEP 2 Find the absolute values of the numbers and multiply them.

$|13| = 13$ $|-3| = 3$

$13 \times 3 = 39$

STEP 3 Assign the correct sign to the product.

$13(-3) = -39$ *The product is -39.*

B Multiply: $(-5)(-8)$.

STEP 1 Determine the sign of the product.

-5 is negative and -8 is negative. Since the numbers have the same sign, the product will be positive.

STEP 2 Find the absolute values of the numbers and multiply them.

$|-5| = 5$ $|-8| = 8$

$5 \times 8 = 40$

STEP 3 Assign the correct sign to the product.

$(-5)(-8) = 40$ *The product is 40.*

C Multiply: $(-10)(0)$.

$(-10)(0) = 0$ *One of the factors is 0, so the product is 0.*

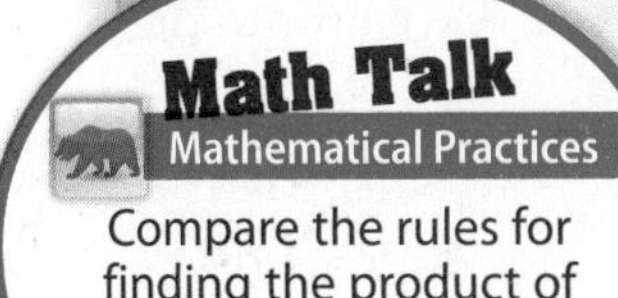

Compare the rules for finding the product of a number and zero and finding the sum of a number and 0.

YOUR TURN

Find each product.

4. $-3(5)$ ______
5. $(-10)(-2)$ ______
6. $0(-22)$ ______
7. $8(4)$ ______

Guided Practice

Find each product. (Explore Activity 2 and Example 1)

1. $-1(9)$ ______
2. $14(-2)$ ______
3. $(-9)(-6)$ ______
4. $(-2)(50)$ ______
5. $(-4)(15)$ ______
6. $-18(0)$ ______
7. $(-7)(-7)$ ______
8. $-15(9)$ ______
9. $(8)(-12)$ ______
10. $-3(-100)$ ______
11. $0(-153)$ ______
12. $-6(32)$ ______

13. Flora made 7 withdrawals of $75 each from her bank account. What was the overall change in her account? (Example 1)

______

14. A football team lost 5 yards on each of 3 plays. Explain how you could use a number line to find the team's change in field position after the 3 plays. (Explore Activity 1)

______

______

15. The temperature dropped 2 °F every hour for 6 hours. What was the total number of degrees the temperature changed in the 6 hours? (Explore Activity 1)

______

ESSENTIAL QUESTION CHECK-IN

16. Explain the process for finding the product of two integers.

______

______

______

Name ______ Class ______ Date ______

2.1 Independent Practice

7.NS.2

Personal Math Trainer

Online Practice and Help

17. **Critique Reasoning** Lisa used a number line to model −2(3). Does her number line make sense? Explain why or why not.

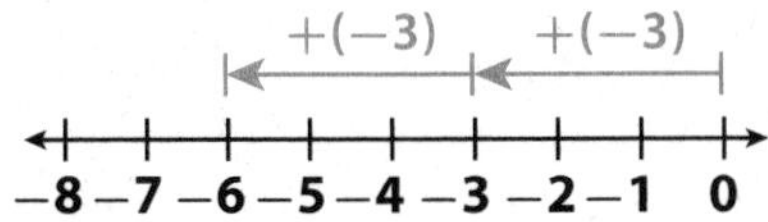

18. **Represent Real-World Problems** Mike got on an elevator and went down 3 floors. He meant to go to a lower level, so he stayed on the elevator and went down 3 more floors. How many floors did Mike go down altogether?

Solve. Show your work.

19. When Brooke buys lunch at the cafeteria, money is withdrawn from a lunch account. The table shows amounts withdrawn in one week. By how much did the amount in Brooke's lunch account change by the end of that week?

Lunch Account			
Week 1	**Lunch**	**Cost**	**Balance**
			$28
Monday	Pizza	$4	
Tuesday	Fish Tacos	$4	
Wednesday	Spaghetti	$4	
Thursday	Sandwich	$4	
Friday	Chicken	$4	

20. Adam is scuba diving. He descends 5 feet below sea level. He descends the same distance 4 more times. What is Adam's final elevation?

21. The price of jeans was reduced $6 per week for 7 weeks. By how much did the price of the jeans change over the 7 weeks?

22. Casey uses some of his savings on batting practice. The cost of renting a batting cage for 1 hour is $6. He rents a cage for 9 hours in each of two months. What is the change in Casey's savings after two months?

23. Volunteers at Sam's school use some of the student council's savings for a special project. They buy 7 backpacks for $8 each and fill each backpack with paper and pens that cost $5. By how much did the student council's savings change because of this project?

24. Communicate Mathematical Ideas Describe a real-world situation that can be represented by the product 8(−20). Then find the product and explain what the product means in terms of the real-world situation.

____

____

____

25. What If? The rules for multiplying two integers can be extended to a product of 3 or more integers. Find the following products by using the Associative Property to multiply 2 numbers at a time.

a. 3(3)(−3) ________ **b.** 3(−3)(−3) ________ **c.** −3(−3)(−3) ________

d. 3(3)(3)(−3) ________ **e.** 3(3)(−3)(−3) ________ **f.** 3(−3)(−3)(−3) ________

g. Make a Conjecture Based on your results, complete the following statements:

When a product of integers has an odd number of negative factors,

then the sign of the product is ____________.

When a product of integers has an even number of negative factors,

then the sign of the product is ____________.

H.O.T. FOCUS ON HIGHER ORDER THINKING

Work Area

26. Multiple Representations The product of three integers is −3. Determine all of the possible values for the three factors.

____

27. Analyze Relationships When is the product of two integers less than or equal to both of the two factors?

____

____

28. Justify Reasoning The sign of the product of two integers with the same sign is positive. What is the sign of the product of three integers with the same sign? Explain your thinking.

____

____

____

____

____

LESSON

2.2 Dividing Integers

CA CC 7.NS.2

Apply and extend previous understandings of multiplication and division and of fractions to multiply and divide rational numbers. *Also 7.NS.2b, 7.NS.3*

ESSENTIAL QUESTION

How do you divide integers?

EXPLORE ACTIVITY

A diver needs to descend to a depth of 100 feet. She wants to do it in 5 equal descents. How far should she travel in each descent?

A Use the number line at the right to find how far the diver should travel in each of the 5 descents.

____

B To solve this problem, you can set up a division problem: $\frac{-100}{\square} = ?$

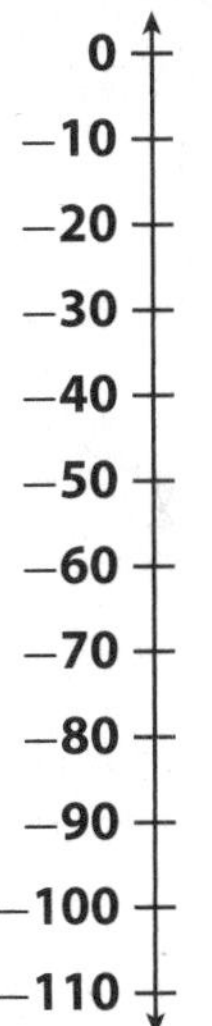

C Rewrite the division problem as a multiplication problem. Think: Some number multiplied by 5 equals −100.

________ $\times ? = -100$

D Remember the rules for integer multiplication. If the product is negative, one of the factors must be negative. Since ________ is positive, the unknown factor must be **positive / negative.**

E You know that $5 \times$ ________ $= 100$. So, using the rules for integer multiplication you can say that $5 \times$ ________ $= -100$.

The diver should descend ________ feet in each descent.

F Use the process you just learned to find each of the quotients below.

$\frac{14}{-7} =$ ________ $\frac{-36}{-9} =$ ________ $\frac{-55}{11} =$ ________ $\frac{-45}{-5} =$ ________

Reflect

1. **Make a Conjecture** Make a conjecture about the quotient of two integers with different signs. Make a conjecture about the quotient of two integers with the same sign.

____

____

Dividing Integers

You used the relationship between multiplication and division to make conjectures about the signs of quotients of integers. You can use multiplication to understand why division by zero is not possible.

Think about the division problem below and its related multiplication problem.

$$5 \div 0 = ? \qquad 0 \times ? = 5$$

The multiplication sentence says that there is some number times 0 that equals 5. You already know that 0 times any number equals 0. This means division by 0 is not possible, so we say that division by 0 is undefined.

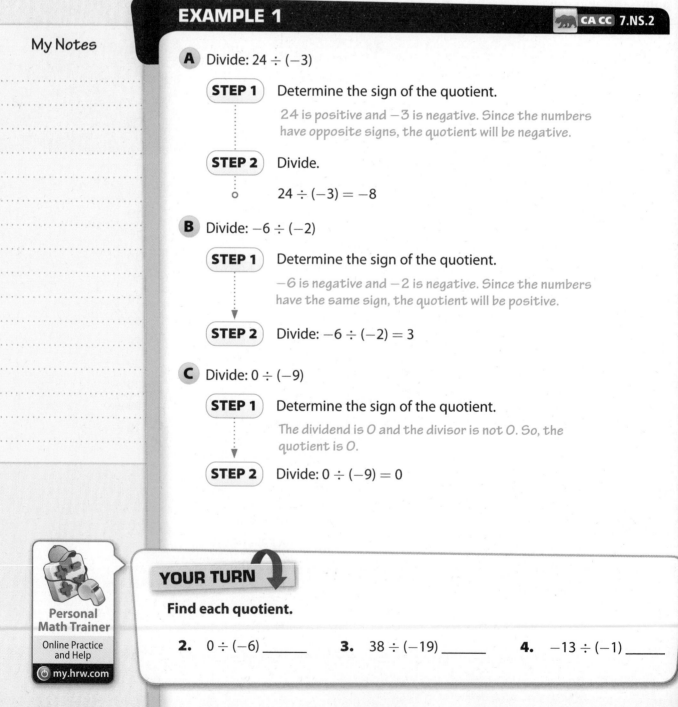

My Notes

EXAMPLE 1

CA CC 7.NS.2

A Divide: $24 \div (-3)$

STEP 1 Determine the sign of the quotient.

24 is positive and −3 is negative. Since the numbers have opposite signs, the quotient will be negative.

STEP 2 Divide.

$24 \div (-3) = -8$

B Divide: $-6 \div (-2)$

STEP 1 Determine the sign of the quotient.

−6 is negative and −2 is negative. Since the numbers have the same sign, the quotient will be positive.

STEP 2 Divide: $-6 \div (-2) = 3$

C Divide: $0 \div (-9)$

STEP 1 Determine the sign of the quotient.

The dividend is 0 and the divisor is not 0. So, the quotient is 0.

STEP 2 Divide: $0 \div (-9) = 0$

Find each quotient.

2. $0 \div (-6)$ ______ **3.** $38 \div (-19)$ ______ **4.** $-13 \div (-1)$ ______

Using Integer Division to Solve Problems

You can use integer division to solve real-world problems. For some problems, you may need to perform more than one step. Be sure to check that the sign of the quotient makes sense for the situation.

EXAMPLE 2 

Jake answers questions in two different online Olympic trivia quizzes. In each quiz, he loses points when he gives an incorrect answer. The table shows the points lost for each wrong answer in each quiz and Jake's total points lost in each quiz. In which quiz did he have more wrong answers?

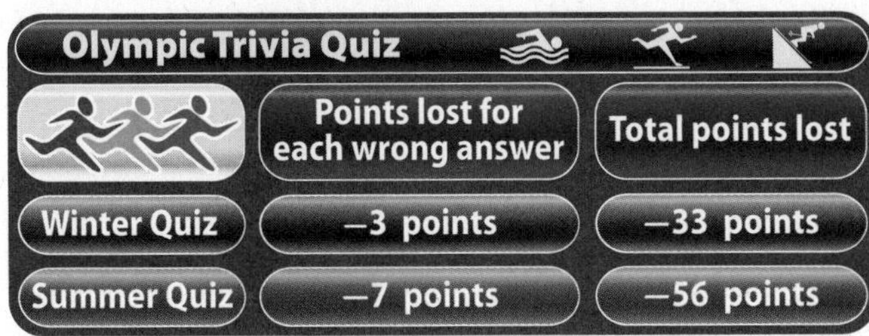

Olympic Trivia Quiz	Points lost for each wrong answer	Total points lost
Winter Quiz	−3 points	−33 points
Summer Quiz	−7 points	−56 points

STEP 1 Find the number of incorrect answers in the winter quiz.

$-33 \div (-3) = 11$ *Divide the total points lost by the number of points lost per wrong answer.*

STEP 2 Find the number of incorrect answers Jake gave in the summer quiz.

$-56 \div (-7) = 8$ *Divide the total points lost by the number of points lost per wrong answer.*

STEP 3 Compare the numbers of wrong answers.

$11 > 8$, so Jake had more wrong answers in the winter quiz.

What is the sign of each quotient in Steps 1 and 2? Why does this make sense for the situation?

5. A penalty in Meteor-Mania is −5 seconds. A penalty in Cosmic Calamity is −7 seconds. Yolanda had penalties totaling −25 seconds in a game of Meteor-Mania and −35 seconds in a game of Cosmic Calamity. In which game did Yolanda receive more penalties? Justify your answer.

____

____

____

Personal Math Trainer
Online Practice and Help
my.hrw.com

Guided Practice

Find each quotient. (Example 1)

1. $\frac{-14}{2}$ ____________

2. $21 \div (-3)$ ____________

3. $\frac{26}{-13}$ ____________

4. $0 \div (-4)$ ____________

5. $\frac{-45}{-5}$ ____________

6. $-30 \div (10)$ ____________

7. $\frac{-11}{-1}$ ____________

8. $-31 \div (-31)$ ____________

9. $\frac{0}{-7}$ ____________

10. $\frac{-121}{-11}$ ____________

11. $84 \div (-7)$ ____________

12. $\frac{500}{-25}$ ____________

13. $-6 \div (0)$ ____________

14. $\frac{-63}{-21}$ ____________

Write a division expression for each problem. Then find the value of the expression. (Example 2)

15. Clark made four of his truck payments late and was fined four late fees. The total change to his savings from late fees was −$40. How much was one late fee?

____

16. Jan received −22 points on her exam. She got 11 questions wrong out of 50 questions. How much was Jan penalized for each wrong answer?

____

17. Allen's score in a video game was changed by −75 points because he missed some targets. He got −15 points for each missed target. How many targets did he miss?

____

18. Louisa's savings change by −$9 each time she goes bowling. In all, it changed by −$99 during the summer. How many times did she go bowling in the summer?

____

? ESSENTIAL QUESTION CHECK-IN

19. How is the process of dividing integers similar to the process of multiplying integers?

____

____

____

Name ______________________ Class ______________ Date ______________

2.2 Independent Practice

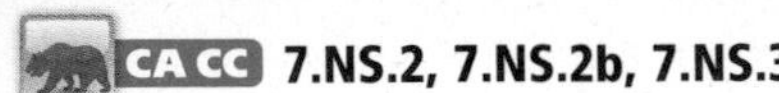
CA CC 7.NS.2, 7.NS.2b, 7.NS.3

20. Walter buys a bus pass for \$30. Every time he rides the bus, money is deducted from the value of the pass. He rode 12 times and \$24 was deducted from the value of the pass. How much does each bus ride cost?

____

21. **Analyze Relationships** Elisa withdrew \$20 at a time from her bank account and withdrew a total of \$140. Francis withdrew \$45 at a time from his bank account and withdrew a total of \$270. Who made the greater number of withdrawals? Justify your answer.

____

____

____

22. **Multistep** At 7 p.m. last night, the temperature was 10 °F. At 7 a.m. the next morning, the temperature was −2 °F.

a. By how much did the temperature change from 7 p.m. to 7 a.m.?

____

b. The temperature changed by a steady amount overnight. By how much did it change each hour?

____

____

23. **Analyze Relationships** Nola hiked down a trail at a steady rate for 10 minutes. Her change in elevation was −200 feet. Then she continued to hike down for another 20 minutes at a different rate. Her change in elevation for this part of the hike was −300 feet. During which portion of the hike did she walk down at a faster rate? Explain your reasoning.

____

____

____

24. Write a real world description to fit the expression $-50 \div 5$.

____

____

____

25. **Communicate Mathematical Ideas** Two integers, *a* and *b*, have different signs. The absolute value of integer *a* is divisible by the absolute value of integer *b*. Find two integers that fit this description. Then decide if the product of the integers is greater than or less than the quotient of the integers. Show your work.

____

____

____

Determine if each statement is true or false. Justify your answer.

26. For any two nonzero integers, the product and quotient have the same sign.

____

____

____

27. Any nonzero integer divided by 0 equals 0.

____

____

H.O.T. FOCUS ON HIGHER ORDER THINKING

Work Area

28. **Multi-step** A perfect score on a test with 25 questions is 100. Each question is worth the same number of points.

a. How many points is each question on the test worth? ______________

b. Fred got a score of 84 on the test. Write a division sentence using negative numbers where the quotient represents the number of questions Fred answered incorrectly. ______________

29. **Persevere in Problem Solving** Colleen divided integer *a* by −3 and got 8. Then she divided 8 by integer *b* and got −4.

Find the quotient of integer *a* and integer *b*. ______________

30. **Justify Reasoning** The quotient of two negative integers results in an integer. How does the value of the quotient compare to the value of the original two integers? Explain.

____

____

____

LESSON 2.3

Applying Integer Operations

CA CC 7.NS.3

Solve real-world and mathematical problems involving the four operations with rational numbers. *Also 7.NS.2a, 7.NS.2c, 7.EE.3*

ESSENTIAL QUESTION

How can you use integer operations to solve real-world problems?

Using the Order of Operations with Integers

The order of operations applies to integer operations as well as positive number operations. Perform multiplication and division first, and then addition and subtraction. Work from left to right in the expression.

EXAMPLE 1

CA CC 7.NS.2c, 7.NS.2a

Hannah made four withdrawals of $20 from her checking account. She also wrote a check for $215. By how much did the amount in her checking account change?

Analyze Information

You need to find the total *change* in Hannah's account. Since withdrawals and writing a check represent a decrease in her account, use negative numbers to represent these amounts.

Formulate a Plan

Write a product to represent the four withdrawals.

$-20 + (-20) + (-20) + (-20) = 4(-20)$

Add -215 to represent the check that Hannah wrote.

$4(-20) + (-215)$

Solve

Evaluate the expression to find by how much the amount in the account changed.

$4(-20) - 215 = -80 - 215$ Multiply first.

$= -295$ Then subtract.

The amount in the account decreased by $295.

Justify and Evaluate

The value -295 represents a decrease of 295 dollars. This makes sense, since withdrawals and writing checks remove money from the checking account.

YOUR TURN

1. Reggie lost 3 spaceships in level 3 of a video game. He lost 30 points for each spaceship. When he completed level 3, he earned a bonus of 200 points. By how much did his score change?

____

____

2. Simplify: $-6(13) - 21$ ______________________

Using Negative Integers to Represent Quantities

You can use positive and negative integers to solve problems involving amounts that increase or decrease. Sometimes you may need to use more than one operation.

EXAMPLE 2  

CA CC 7.NS.3, 7.EE.3

Three brothers each have their own savings. They borrow \$72 from their parents for concert tickets. Each brother must pay back an equal share of this amount. Also, the youngest brother owes his parents \$15. By how much will the youngest brother's savings change after he pays his parents?

STEP 1 Determine the signs of the values and the operations you will use. Write an expression.

Since the money is being paid back, it will *decrease* the amount in each brother's savings. Use -72 and -15.

Since an *equal share* of the \$72 will be paid back, use division to determine 3 equal parts of -72. Then add -15 to one of these equal parts.

Change to youngest brother's savings $= (-72) \div 3 + (-15)$

Math Talk
Mathematical Practices

Suppose the youngest brother has \$60 in savings. How much will he have left after he pays his parents what he owes?

STEP 2 Evaluate the expression.

$(-72) \div 3 + (-15) = -24 + (-15)$ Divide.

$= -39$ Add.

The youngest brother's savings will decrease by \$39.

Reflect

3. **What If?** Suppose there were four brothers in Example 2. How much would the youngest brother need to pay?

____

Simplify each expression.

4. $(-12) \div 6 + 2$ ________

5. $-87 \div (-3) - 9$ ________

6. $40 \div (-5) + 30$ ________

7. $-39 \div 3 - 15$ ________

Comparing Values of Expressions

Often, problem situations require making comparisons between two values. Use integer operations to calculate values. Then compare the values.

EXAMPLE 3 

CA CC 7.NS.3, 7.EE.3

Jill and Tony play a board game in which they move counters along a board. Jill moves her counter back 3 spaces four times, and then moves her counter forward 6 spaces. Tony moves his counter back 2 spaces three times, and then moves his player forward 3 spaces one time. Find each player's overall change in position. Who moved farther?

Find each player's overall change in position.

Jill: $4(-3) + 6 = -12 + 6 = -6$ — *Jill moves back 6 spaces.*

Tony: $3(-2) + 3 = -6 + 3 = -3$ — *Tony moves back 3 spaces.*

STEP 2 Compare the numbers of spaces moved by the players.

$|-6| > |-3|$ — *Compare absolute values.*

Jill moves farther back than Tony.

Math Talk
Mathematical Practices

Why do you compare absolute values in Step 2?

YOUR TURN

8. Amber and Will are in line together to buy tickets. Amber moves back by 3 places three times to talk to friends. She then is invited to move 5 places up in line. Will moved back by 4 places twice, and then moved up in line by 3 places. Overall, who moved farther back in line?

____

Evaluate each expression. Circle the expression with the greater value.

9. $(-10) \div 2 - 2 =$ ________

$(-28) \div 4 + 1 =$ ________

10. $42 \div (-3) + 9 =$ ________

$(-36) \div 9 - 2 =$ ________

Guided Practice

Evaluate each expression. (Example 1)

1. $-6(-5) + 12$ ______
2. $3(-6) - 3$ ______
3. $-2(8) + 7$ ______
4. $4(-13) + 20$ ______
5. $(-4)(0) - 4$ ______
6. $-3(-5) - 16$ ______

Write an expression to represent the situation. Evaluate the expression and answer the question. (Example 2)

7. Bella pays 7 payments of $5 each to a game store. She returns one game and receives $20 back. What is the change to the amount of money she has?

______

8. Ron lost 10 points seven times playing a video game. He then lost an additional 100 points for going over the time limit. What was the total change in his score?

______

9. Ned took a test with 25 questions. He lost 4 points for each of the 6 questions he got wrong and earned an additional 10 points for answering a bonus question correctly. How many points did Ned receive or lose overall?

______

10. Mr. Harris has some money in his wallet. He pays the babysitter $12 an hour for 4 hours of babysitting. His wife gives him $10, and he puts the money in his wallet. By how much does the amount in his wallet change?

______

Compare the values of the two expressions using $<$, $=$, or $>$. (Example 3)

11. $-3(-2) + 3$ ______ $3(-4) + 9$
12. $-8(-2) - 20$ ______ $3(-2) + 2$
13. $-7(5) - 9$ ______ $-3(20) + 10$
14. $-16(0) - 3$ ______ $-8(-2) - 3$

ESSENTIAL QUESTION CHECK-IN

15. When you solve a problem involving money, what can a negative answer represent?

______

______

______

Name ____________________ Class ____________ Date ____________

2.3 Independent Practice

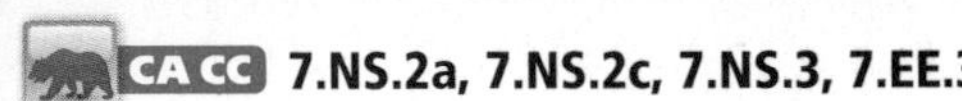
CA CC 7.NS.2a, 7.NS.2c, 7.NS.3, 7.EE.3

Evaluate each expression.

16. $-12(-3) + 7$ ____________

17. $-42 \div (-6) + 5 - 8$ ____________

18. $10(-60) - 18$ ____________

19. $(-11)(-7) + 5 - 82$ ____________

20. $35 \div (-7) + 6$ ____________

21. $-13(-2) - 16 - 8$ ____________

22. **Multistep** Lily and Rose are playing a game. In the game, each player starts with 0 points and the player with the most points at the end wins. Lily gains 5 points two times, loses 12 points, and then gains 3 points. Rose loses 3 points two times, loses 1 point, gains 6 points, and then gains 7 points.

a. Write and evaluate an expression to find Lily's score.

____

b. Write and evaluate an expression to find Rose's score.

____

c. Who won the game?

____

Write an expression from the description. Then evaluate the expression.

23. 8 less than the product of 5 and -4

____

24. 9 more than the quotient of -36 and -4.

____

25. **Multistep** Arleen has a gift card for a local lawn and garden store. She uses the gift card to rent a tiller for 4 days. It costs \$35 per day to rent the tiller. She also buys a rake for \$9.

a. Find the change to the value on her gift card.

____

b. The original amount on the gift card was \$200. Does Arleen have enough left on the card to buy a wheelbarrow for \$50? Explain.

____

____

26. Carlos made up a game where, in a deck of cards, the red cards (hearts and diamonds) are negative and the black cards (spades and clubs) are positive. All face cards are worth 10 points, and number cards are worth their value.

a. Samantha has a king of hearts, a jack of diamonds, and a 3 of spades. Write an expression to find the value of her cards.

____

b. Warren has a 7 of clubs, a 2 of spades, and a 7 of hearts. Write an expression to find the value of his cards.

____

c. If the greater score wins, who won?

____

d. If a player always gets three cards, describe two different ways to receive a score of 7.

____

____

FOCUS ON HIGHER ORDER THINKING

Work Area

27. Represent Real-World Problems Write a problem that the expression $3(-7) - 10 + 25 = -6$ could represent.

____

____

____

28. Critique Reasoning Jim found the quotient of two integers and got a positive integer. He added another integer to the quotient and got a positive integer. His sister Kim says that all the integers Jim used to get this result must be positive. Do you agree? Explain.

____

____

____

29. Persevere in Problem Solving Lisa is standing on a dock beside a lake. She drops a rock from her hand into the lake. After the rock hits the surface of the lake, the rock's distance from the lake's surface changes at a rate of -5 inches per second. If Lisa holds her hand 5 feet above the lake's surface, how far from Lisa's hand is the rock 4 seconds after it hits the surface?

____

MODULE QUIZ

Ready to Go On?

2.1 Multiplying Integers

Find each product.

1. $(-2)(3)$ ____________

2. $(-5)(-7)$ ____________

3. $(8)(-11)$ ____________

4. $(-3)(2)(-2)$ ____________

5. The temperature dropped 3 °C every hour for 5 hours. Write an integer that represents the change in temperature. ____________

2.2 Dividing Integers

Find each quotient.

6. $\frac{-63}{7}$ ____________

7. $\frac{-15}{-3}$ ____________

8. $0 \div (-15)$ ____________

9. $96 \div (-12)$ ____________

10. An elephant at the zoo lost 24 pounds over 6 months. The elephant lost the same amount of weight each month. Write an integer that represents the change in the elephant's weight each month. ____________

2.3 Applying Integer Operations

Evaluate each expression.

11. $(-4)(5) + 8$ ____________

12. $(-3)(-6) - 7$ ____________

13. $-27 \div 9 - 11$ ____________

14. $\frac{-24}{-3} - (-2)$ ____________

ESSENTIAL QUESTION

15. Write and solve a real-world problem that can be represented by the expression $(-3)(5) + 10$.

____

____

____

____

MODULE 2
MIXED REVIEW

Assessment Readiness

1. Look at each expression. Does it have a value of 0?

Select Yes or No for expressions A–C.

A. $\frac{28}{-4} + 7$ ◯ Yes ◯ No
B. $(-4)(-7) + 28$ ◯ Yes ◯ No
C. $-4 - \left(\frac{-28}{7}\right)$ ◯ Yes ◯ No

2. An addition problem is shown below.

$$2 + (-3)$$

Choose True or False for the accurate representations of the solution.

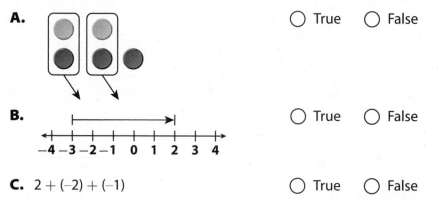

A. ◯ True ◯ False

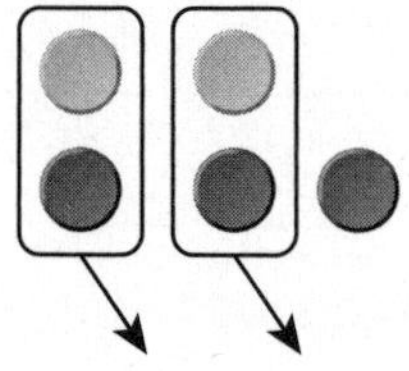

B. ◯ True ◯ False

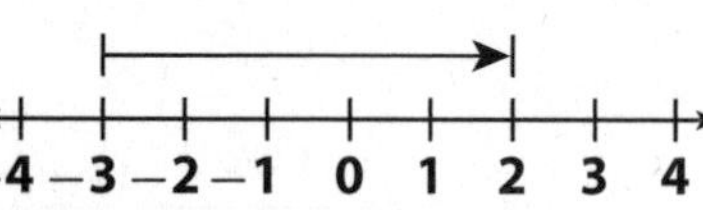

C. $2 + (-2) + (-1)$ ◯ True ◯ False

3. A diver descends from an elevation of 6 feet below sea level to an elevation of 98 feet below sea level in 4 equal intervals. What was the diver's change in elevation in each interval? Explain how you solved this problem.

4. An elevator starts at the 6th floor. It goes up 7 floors twice, and then it goes down 10 floors. A second elevator starts on the 20th floor. It goes down 5 floors 3 times, and then it goes up 12 floors. Which elevator ends on a higher floor? Explain how you know.

Rational Numbers

ESSENTIAL QUESTION

How can you use rational numbers to solve real-world problems?

my.hrw.com

Real-World Video

In many competitive sports, scores are given as decimals. For some events, the judges' scores are averaged to give the athlete's final score.

LESSON 3.1

Rational Numbers and Decimals

CA CC 7.NS.2b, 7.NS.2d

LESSON 3.2

Adding Rational Numbers

CA CC 7.NS.1a, 7.NS.1b, 7.NS.1d, 7.NS.3

LESSON 3.3

Subtracting Rational Numbers

CA CC 7.NS.1, 7.NS.1c

LESSON 3.4

Multiplying Rational Numbers

CA CC 7.NS.2, 7.NS.2a, 7.NS.2c

LESSON 3.5

Dividing Rational Numbers

CA CC 7.NS.2, 7.NS.2b, 7.NS.2c

LESSON 3.6

Applying Rational Number Operations

CA CC 7.NS.3, 7.EE.3

GO DIGITAL
my.hrw.com

my.hrw.com

Go digital with your write-in student edition, accessible on any device.

Math On the Spot

Scan with your smart phone to jump directly to the online edition, video tutor, and more.

Animated Math

Interactively explore key concepts to see how math works.

Personal Math Trainer

Get immediate feedback and help as you work through practice sets.

Are YOU Ready?

Complete these exercises to review skills you will need for this module.

Multiply Fractions

EXAMPLE $\frac{3}{8} \times \frac{4}{9}$ $\quad \frac{3}{8} \times \frac{4}{9} = \frac{\overset{1}{\cancel{3}}}{\underset{2}{\cancel{8}}} \times \frac{\overset{1}{\cancel{4}}}{\underset{3}{\cancel{9}}}$ Divide by the common factors.

$= \frac{1}{6}$ Simplify.

Multiply. Write the product in simplest form.

1. $\frac{9}{14} \times \frac{7}{6}$ ______ **2.** $\frac{3}{5} \times \frac{4}{7}$ ______ **3.** $\frac{11}{8} \times \frac{10}{33}$ ______ **4.** $\frac{4}{9} \times 3$ ______

Operations with Fractions

EXAMPLE $\frac{2}{5} \div \frac{7}{10} = \frac{2}{5} \times \frac{10}{7}$ Multiply by the reciprocal of the divisor.

$= \frac{2}{\underset{1}{\cancel{5}}} \times \frac{\overset{2}{\cancel{10}}}{7}$ Divide by the common factors.

$= \frac{4}{7}$ Simplify.

Divide.

5. $\frac{1}{2} \div \frac{1}{4}$ ______ **6.** $\frac{3}{8} \div \frac{13}{16}$ ______ **7.** $\frac{2}{5} \div \frac{14}{15}$ ______ **8.** $\frac{4}{9} \div \frac{16}{27}$ ______

9. $\frac{3}{5} \div \frac{5}{6}$ ______ **10.** $\frac{1}{4} \div \frac{23}{24}$ ______ **11.** $6 \div \frac{3}{5}$ ______ **12.** $\frac{4}{5} \div 10$ ______

Order of Operations

EXAMPLE

$50 - 3(3 + 1)^2$	To evaluate, first operate within parentheses.
$50 - 3(4)^2$	Next simplify exponents.
$50 - 3(16)$	Then multiply and divide from left to right.
$50 - 48$	Finally add and subtract from left to right.
2	

Evaluate each expression.

13. $21 - 6 \div 3$ ____ **14.** $18 + (7 - 4) \times 3$ ____ **15.** $5 + (8 - 3)^2$ ____

16. $9 + 18 \div 3 + 10$ ____ **17.** $60 - (3 - 1)^4 \times 3$ ____ **18.** $10 - 16 \div 4 \times 2 + 6$ ____

Reading Start-Up

Vocabulary

Review Words

integers (*enteros*)
✔ negative numbers (*números negativos*)
pattern (*patrón*)
✔ positive numbers (*números positivos*)
✔ whole numbers (*números enteros*)

Preview Words

additive inverse (*inverso aditivo*)
opposite (*opuesto*)
rational number (*número racional*)
repeating decimal (*decimal periódico*)
terminating decimal (*decimal finito*)

Visualize Vocabulary

Use the ✔ words to complete the graphic. You can put more than one word in each section of the triangle.

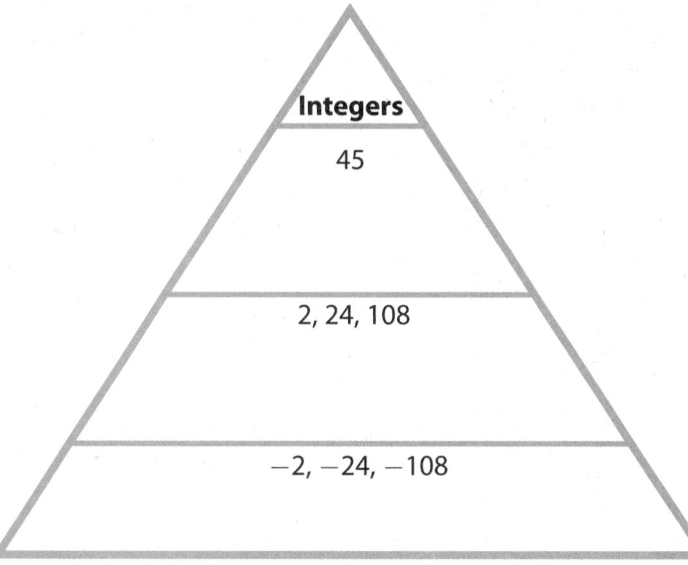

Understand Vocabulary

Complete the sentences using the preview words.

1. A decimal number for which the decimals come to an end is a ____________________ decimal.
2. The ____________________ , or ______________, of a number is the same distance from 0 on a number line as the original number, but on the other side of 0.

Active Reading

Layered Book Before beginning the module, create a layered book to help you learn the concepts in this module. At the top of the first flap, write the title of the module, "Rational Numbers." Label the other flaps "Adding," "Subtracting," "Multiplying," and "Dividing." As you study each lesson, write important ideas, such as vocabulary and processes, on the appropriate flap.

GETTING READY FOR

Rational Numbers

Understanding the Standards and the vocabulary terms in the Standards will help you know exactly what you are expected to learn in this module.

 CA CC 7.NS.3

Solve real-world and mathematical problems involving the four operations with rational numbers.

Key Vocabulary

rational number *(número racional)*
Any number that can be expressed as a ratio of two integers.

What It Means to You

You will add, subtract, multiply, and divide rational numbers.

EXAMPLE 7.NS.3

$-15 \cdot \frac{2}{3} - 12 \div 1\frac{1}{3}$

$-\frac{15}{1} \cdot \frac{2}{3} - \frac{12}{1} \div \frac{4}{3}$ — Write as fractions.

$-\frac{15}{1} \cdot \frac{2}{3} - \frac{12}{1} \cdot \frac{3}{4}$ — To divide, multiply by the reciprocal.

$-\frac{\overset{5}{\cancel{15}} \cdot 2}{1 \cdot \underset{1}{\cancel{3}}} - \frac{\overset{3}{\cancel{12}} \cdot 3}{1 \cdot \underset{1}{\cancel{4}}}$ — Simplify.

$-\frac{10}{1} - \frac{9}{1} = -10 - 9 = -19$ — Multiply.

 CA CC 7.NS.3

Solve real-world and mathematical problems involving the four operations with rational numbers.

What It Means to You

You will solve real-world and mathematical problems involving the four operations with rational numbers.

EXAMPLE 7.NS.3

In 1954, the Sunshine Skyway Bridge toll for a car was \$1.75. In 2012, the toll was $\frac{5}{7}$ of the toll in 1954. What was the toll in 2012?

$1.75 \cdot \frac{5}{7} = 1\frac{3}{4} \cdot \frac{5}{7}$ — Write the decimal as a fraction.

$= \frac{7}{4} \cdot \frac{5}{7}$ — Write the mixed number as an improper fraction.

$= \frac{\overset{1}{\cancel{7}} \cdot 5}{4 \cdot \underset{1}{\cancel{7}}}$ — Simplify.

$= \frac{5}{4} = 1.25$ — Multiply, then write as a decimal.

The Sunshine Skyway Bridge toll for a car was \$1.25 in 2012.

Visit **my.hrw.com** to see all **CA Common Core Standards** explained.

my.hrw.com

LESSON 3.1

Rational Numbers and Decimals

CA CC 7.NS.2d

Convert a rational number to a decimal using long division; know that the decimal form of a rational number terminates in 0s or eventually repeats. Also *7.NS.2b*

ESSENTIAL QUESTION

How can you convert a rational number to a decimal?

EXPLORE ACTIVITY

CA CC 7.NS.2b, 7.NS.2d

Describing Decimal Forms of Rational Numbers

A **rational number** is a number that can be written as a ratio of two integers *a* and *b*, where *b* is not zero. For example, $\frac{4}{7}$ is a rational number, as is 0.37 because it can be written as the fraction $\frac{37}{100}$.

A Use a calculator to find the equivalent decimal form of each fraction. Remember that numbers that repeat can be written as 0.333… or $0.\overline{3}$.

Fraction	$\frac{1}{4}$	$\frac{5}{8}$	$\frac{2}{3}$	$\frac{2}{9}$	$\frac{12}{5}$		
Decimal Equivalent						0.2	0.875

B Now find the corresponding fraction of the decimal equivalents given in the last two columns in the table. Write the fractions in simplest form.

C **Conjecture** What do you notice about the digits after the decimal point in the decimal forms of the fractions? Compare notes with your neighbor and refine your conjecture if necessary.

____

Reflect

1. Consider the decimal 0.101001000100001000001…. Do you think this decimal represents a rational number? Why or why not?

____

____

2. Do you think a negative sign affects whether or not a number is a rational number? Use $-\frac{8}{5}$ as an example.

____

____

EXPLORE ACTIVITY *(cont'd)*

3. Do you think a mixed number is a rational number? Explain.

____

____

____

Writing Rational Numbers as Decimals

You can convert a rational number to a decimal using long division. Some decimals are **terminating decimals** because the decimals come to an end. Other decimals are **repeating decimals** because one or more digits repeat infinitely.

EXAMPLE 1

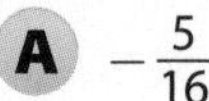

Write each rational number as a decimal.

A $-\frac{5}{16}$

Divide 5 by 16.
Add a zero after the decimal point.
Subtract 48 from 50.
Use the grid to help you complete the long division.

		0.	3	1	2	5	
1	6)	5.	0	0	0	0	
	−	4	8				
			2	0			
		−	1	6			
				4	0		
			−	3	2		
					8	0	
				−	8	0	
						0	

Add zeros in the dividend and continue dividing until the remainder is 0.

The decimal equivalent of $-\frac{5}{16}$ is -0.3125.

B $\frac{13}{33}$

Divide 13 by 33.
Add a zero after the decimal point.
Subtract 99 from 130.
Use the grid to help you complete the long division.

			0.	3	9	3	9	
3	3)	1	3.	0	0	0	0	
		−9	9					
		3	1	0				
		−2	9	7				
			1	3	0			
				−9	9			
				3	1	0		
				−2	9	7		
					1	3		

You can stop dividing once you discover a repeating pattern in the quotient.

Write the quotient with its repeating pattern and indicate that the repeating numbers continue.

The decimal equivalent of $\frac{13}{33}$ is 0.3939…, or $0.\overline{39}$.

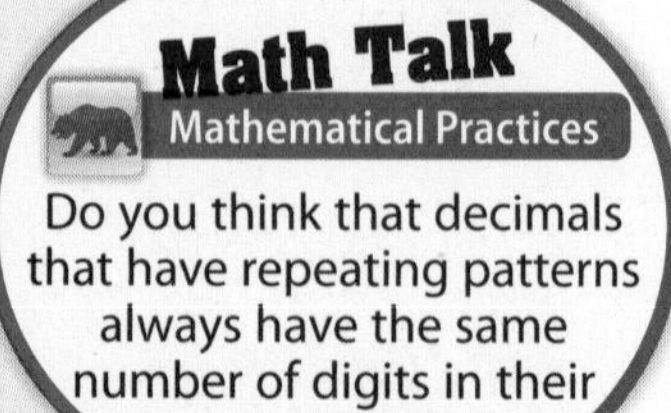

Do you think that decimals that have repeating patterns always have the same number of digits in their pattern? Explain.

YOUR TURN

Write each rational number as a decimal.

4. $-\frac{4}{7}$ ________ **5.** $\frac{1}{3}$ ________ **6.** $-\frac{9}{20}$ ________

Personal Math Trainer

Online Practice and Help

my.hrw.com

Writing Mixed Numbers as Decimals

You can convert a mixed number to a decimal by rewriting the fractional part of the number as a decimal.

Math On the Spot

my.hrw.com

EXAMPLE 2 

CA CC 7.NS.2d

Shawn rode his bike $6\frac{3}{4}$ miles to the science museum. Write $6\frac{3}{4}$ as a decimal.

STEP 1 Rewrite the fractional part of the number as a decimal.

$$\begin{array}{r} 0.75 \\ 4\overline{)3.00} \\ -28 \\ \hline 20 \\ -20 \\ \hline 0 \end{array}$$

Divide the numerator by the denominator.

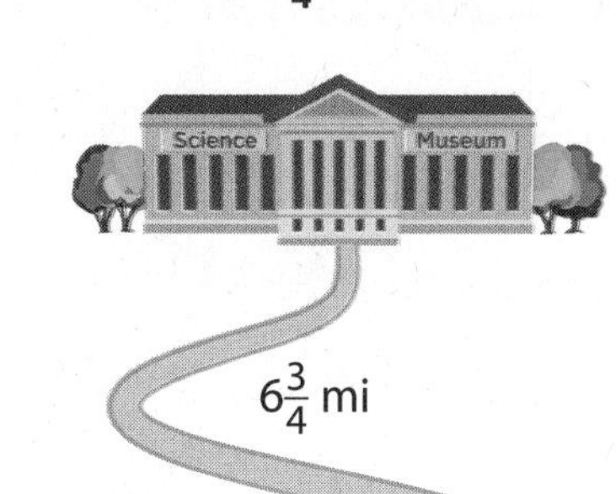

STEP 2 Rewrite the mixed number as the sum of the whole part and the decimal part.

$6\frac{3}{4} = 6 + \frac{3}{4}$

$= 6 + 0.75 \quad = 6.75$

My Notes

YOUR TURN

7. The change (\$) in a stock value was $-2\frac{3}{4}$ per share. Write $-2\frac{3}{4}$ as a decimal. $-2\frac{3}{4} =$ ________

Is the decimal equivalent a terminating or repeating decimal?

____

8. Yvonne bought a watermelon that weighed $7\frac{1}{3}$ pounds. Write $7\frac{1}{3}$ as a decimal. $7\frac{1}{3} =$ ________

Is the decimal equivalent a terminating or repeating decimal?

____

Personal Math Trainer

Online Practice and Help

my.hrw.com

Guided Practice

Write each rational number as a decimal. Then tell whether each decimal is a terminating or a repeating decimal. (Explore Activity and Example 1)

1. $\frac{3}{5} =$ ________ ________

2. $-\frac{89}{100} =$ ________ ________

3. $\frac{4}{12} =$ ________ ________

4. $\frac{25}{99} =$ ________ ________

5. $-\frac{7}{9} =$ ________ ________

6. $-\frac{9}{25} =$ ________ ________

7. $\frac{1}{25} =$ ________ ________

8. $-\frac{25}{176} =$ ________ ________

9. $\frac{12}{1,000} =$ ________ ________

Write each mixed number as a decimal. (Example 2)

10. $-11\frac{1}{6} =$ ________

11. $2\frac{9}{10} =$ ________

12. $-8\frac{23}{100} =$ ________

13. $7\frac{3}{15} =$ ________

14. $54\frac{3}{11} =$ ________

15. $-3\frac{1}{18} =$ ________

16. Maggie bought $3\frac{2}{3}$ lb of apples to make some apple pies. What is the weight of the apples written as a decimal? (Example 2)

$3\frac{2}{3} =$ ________

17. Harry's dog lost $2\frac{7}{8}$ pounds. What is the change in the dog's weight written as a decimal? (Example 2)

$-2\frac{7}{8} =$ ________

ESSENTIAL QUESTION CHECK-IN

18. Tom is trying to write $\frac{3}{47}$ as a decimal. He used long division and divided until he got the quotient 0.0638297872, at which point he stopped. Since the decimal doesn't seem to terminate or repeat, he concluded that $\frac{3}{47}$ is not rational. Do you agree or disagree? Why?

____

____

____

____

____

Name ____________________ Class ____________ Date ____________

3.1 Independent Practice

CA CC 7.NS.2b, 7.NS.2d

Personal Math Trainer

Online Practice and Help

Use the table for 19–23. Write each ratio in the form $\frac{a}{b}$ and then as a decimal. Tell whether each decimal is a terminating or a repeating decimal.

Team Sports	
Sport	**Number of Players**
Baseball	9
Basketball	5
Football	11
Hockey	6
Lacrosse	10
Polo	4
Rugby	15
Soccer	11

19. basketball players to football players

____

20. hockey players to lacrosse players

____

21. polo players to football players

____

22. lacrosse players to rugby players

____

23. football players to soccer players

____

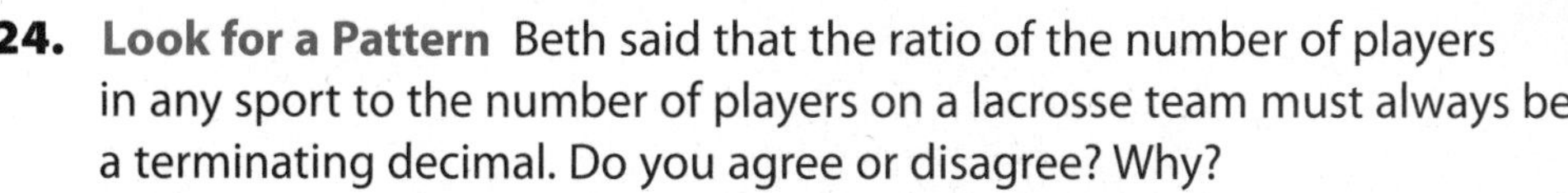

24. **Look for a Pattern** Beth said that the ratio of the number of players in any sport to the number of players on a lacrosse team must always be a terminating decimal. Do you agree or disagree? Why?

____

____

____

____

25. The change in the water level at the lake was $-4\frac{7}{8}$ inches for the month.

a. What is $-4\frac{7}{8}$ written as an improper fraction? ____________

b. What is $-4\frac{7}{8}$ written as a decimal? ____________

c. **Communicate Mathematical Ideas** If the water level at the lake continued to change at the same rate for 3 months in a row, explain how you could estimate the total change in the water level at the end of the 3 month period.

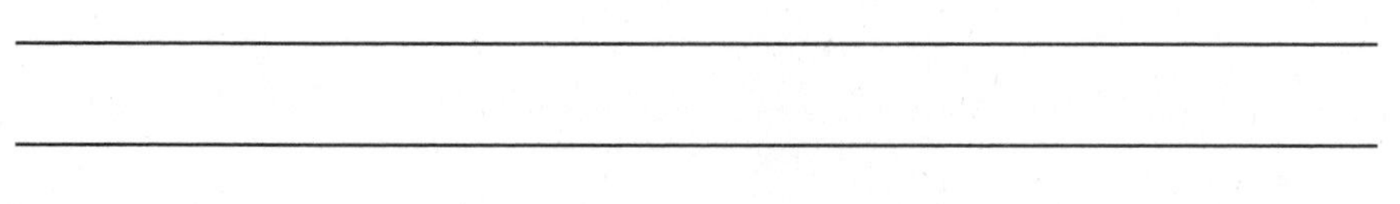

____

____

____

26. Vocabulary A rational number can be written as the ratio of one

__________________ to another and can be represented by a repeating

or __________________ decimal.

27. Problem Solving Marcus is $5\frac{7}{24}$ feet tall. Ben is $5\frac{5}{16}$ feet tall. Which of the two boys is taller? Justify your answer.

____

28. Represent Real-World Problems If one store is selling $\frac{3}{4}$ of a bushel of apples for $9, and another store is selling $\frac{2}{3}$ of a bushel of apples for $9, which store has the better deal? Explain your answer.

____

____

____

____

H.O.T. FOCUS ON HIGHER ORDER THINKING

Work Area

29. Analyze Relationships You are given a fraction in simplest form. The numerator is not zero. When you write the fraction as a decimal, it is a repeating decimal. Which numbers from 1 to 10 could be the denominator?

____

____

30. Communicate Mathematical Ideas Julie got 21 of the 23 questions on her math test correct. She got 29 of the 32 questions on her science test correct. On which test did she get a higher score? Can you compare the fractions $\frac{21}{23}$ and $\frac{29}{32}$ by comparing 29 and 21? Explain. How can Julie compare her scores?

____

____

____

____

31. Look for a Pattern Look at the decimal 0.121122111222.... If the pattern continues, is this a repeating decimal? Explain.

____

____

____

LESSON 3.2

Adding Rational Numbers

CA CC 7.NS.1d

Apply properties of operations as strategies to add and subtract rational numbers. *Also 7.NS.1a, 7.NS.1b, 7.NS.3*

ESSENTIAL QUESTION

How can you add rational numbers?

Adding Rational Numbers with the Same Sign

To add rational numbers with the same sign, apply the rules for adding integers. The sum has the same sign as the sign of the rational numbers.

EXAMPLE 1

CA CC 7.NS.1b

A **Malachi hikes for 2.5 miles and stops for lunch. Then he hikes for 1.5 more miles. How many miles did he hike altogether?**

STEP 1 Use positive numbers to represent the distance Malachi hiked.

STEP 2 Find $2.5 + 1.5$.

STEP 3 Start at 2.5.

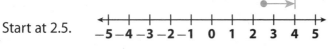

−5 −4 −3 −2 −1 0 1 2 3 4 5

STEP 4 Move 1.5 units to the *right* because the second addend is *positive*.

The result is 4.

Malachi hiked 4 miles.

B **Kyle pours out $\frac{3}{4}$ liter of liquid from a beaker. Then he pours out another $\frac{1}{2}$ liter of liquid. What is the overall change in the amount of liquid in the beaker?**

STEP 1 Use negative numbers to represent amounts the change each time Kyle pours liquid from the beaker.

STEP 2 Find $-\frac{3}{4} + \left(-\frac{1}{2}\right)$.

STEP 3 Start at $-\frac{3}{4}$.

−2 −1 0

STEP 4 Move $\left|-\frac{1}{2}\right| = \frac{1}{2}$ unit to the *left* because the second addend is *negative*.

The result is $-1\frac{1}{4}$.

The amount of liquid in the beaker has decreased by $1\frac{1}{4}$ liters.

Reflect

1. Explain how to determine whether to move right or left on the number line when adding rational numbers.

____

____

Use a number line to find each sum.

2. $3 + 1\frac{1}{2} =$ ________

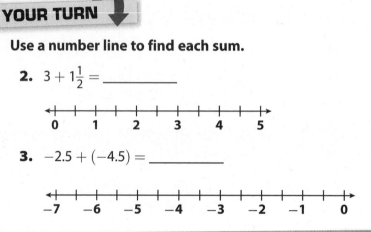

0 1 2 3 4 5

3. $-2.5 + (-4.5) =$ ________

−7 −6 −5 −4 −3 −2 −1 0

Adding Rational Numbers with Different Signs

To add rational numbers with different signs, find the difference of their absolute values. Then use the sign of the rational number with the greater absolute value.

EXAMPLE 2

CA CC 7.NS.1b

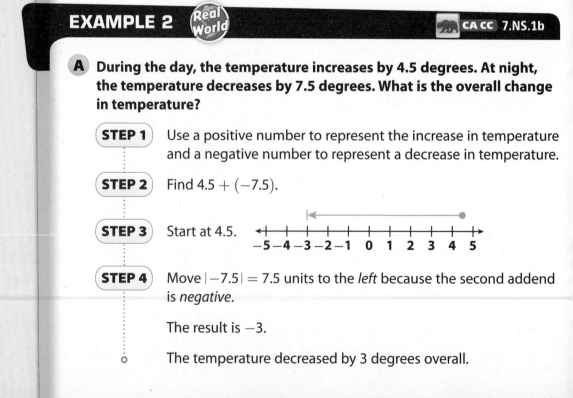

A **During the day, the temperature increases by 4.5 degrees. At night, the temperature decreases by 7.5 degrees. What is the overall change in temperature?**

STEP 1 Use a positive number to represent the increase in temperature and a negative number to represent a decrease in temperature.

STEP 2 Find $4.5 + (-7.5)$.

STEP 3 Start at 4.5.

−5 −4 −3 −2 −1 0 1 2 3 4 5

STEP 4 Move $|-7.5| = 7.5$ units to the *left* because the second addend is *negative*.

The result is −3.

The temperature decreased by 3 degrees overall.

B **Ernesto writes a check for \$2.50. Then he deposits \$6 in his checking account. What is the overall increase or decrease in the account balance?**

STEP 1 Use a positive number to represent a deposit and a negative number to represent a withdrawal or a check.

STEP 2 Find $-2.5 + 6$.

STEP 3 Start at -2.5.

−5 −4 −3 −2 −1 0 1 2 3 4 5

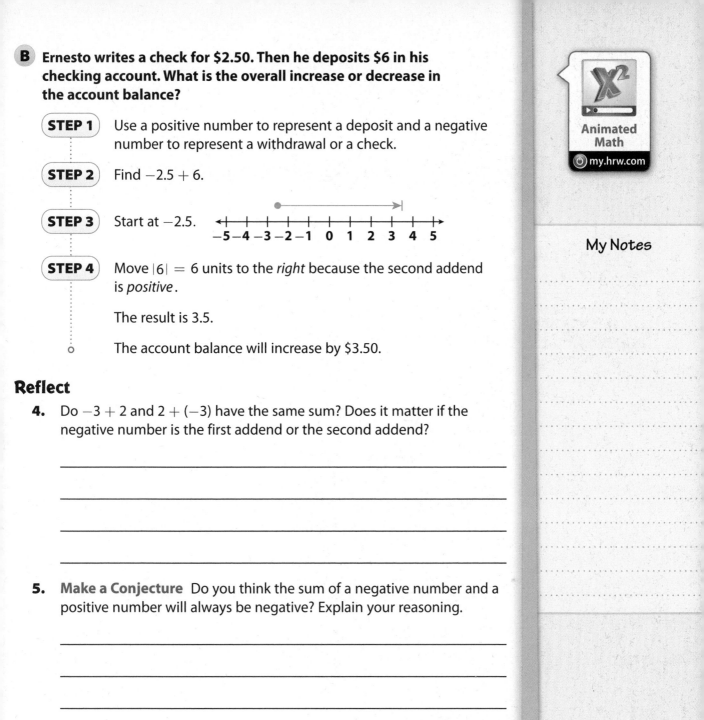

STEP 4 Move $|6| = 6$ units to the *right* because the second addend is *positive*.

The result is 3.5.

The account balance will increase by \$3.50.

My Notes

Reflect

4. Do $-3 + 2$ and $2 + (-3)$ have the same sum? Does it matter if the negative number is the first addend or the second addend?

____

____

____

____

5. **Make a Conjecture** Do you think the sum of a negative number and a positive number will always be negative? Explain your reasoning.

____

____

____

YOUR TURN

Use a number line to find each sum.

6. $-8 + 5 =$ ________

−8 −7 −6 −5 −4 −3 −2 −1 0 1 2

7. $\frac{1}{2} + \left(-\frac{3}{4}\right) =$ ________

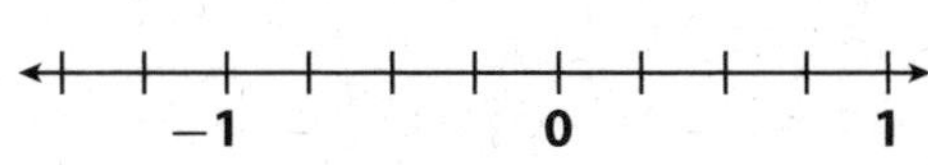

8. $-1 + 7 =$ ________

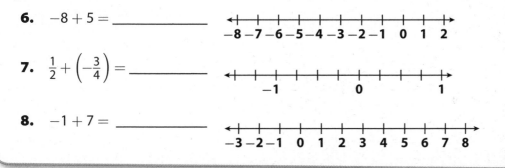

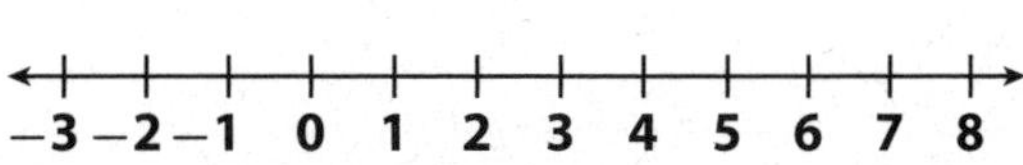

Finding the Additive Inverse

The **opposite**, or **additive inverse**, of a number is the same distance from 0 on a number line as the original number, but on the other side of 0. Zero is its own additive inverse.

EXAMPLE 3

CA CC 7.NS.1a, 7.NS.1b, 7.NS.1d

A **A football team loses 3.5 yards on their first play. On the next play, they gain 3.5 yards. What is the overall increase or decrease in yards?**

STEP 1 Use a positive number to represent the gain in yards and a negative number to represent the loss in yards.

STEP 2 Find $-3.5 + 3.5$.

STEP 3 Start at -3.5.

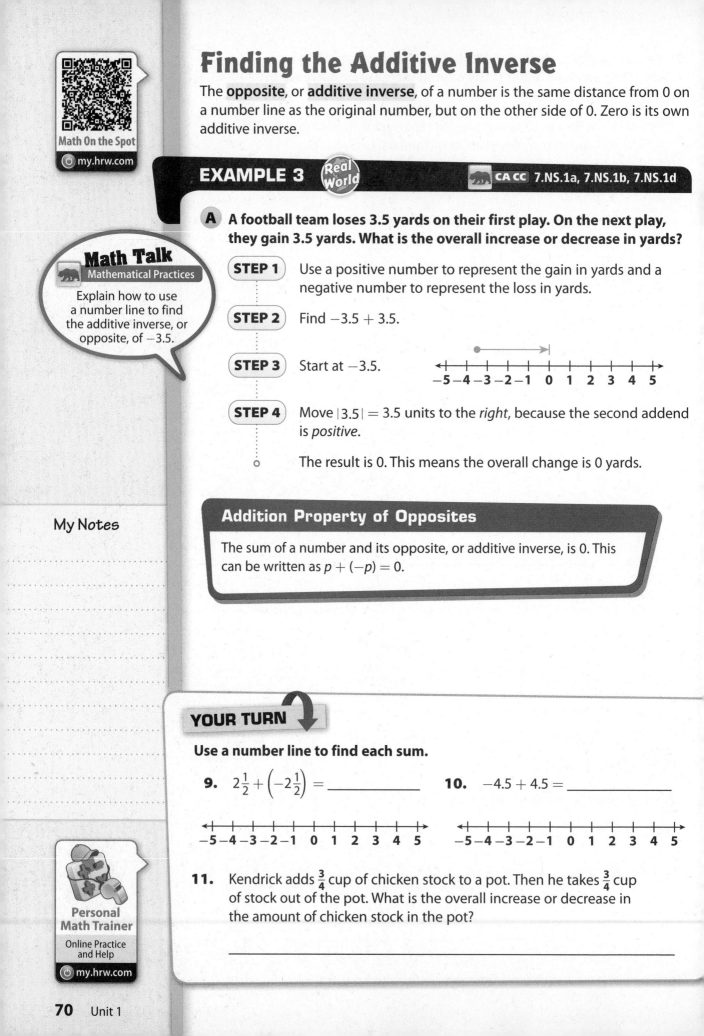

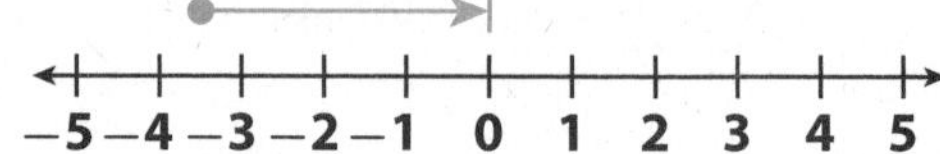

STEP 4 Move $|3.5| = 3.5$ units to the *right*, because the second addend is *positive*.

The result is 0. This means the overall change is 0 yards.

Math Talk
Mathematical Practices

Explain how to use a number line to find the additive inverse, or opposite, of -3.5.

My Notes

Addition Property of Opposites

The sum of a number and its opposite, or additive inverse, is 0. This can be written as $p + (-p) = 0$.

YOUR TURN

Use a number line to find each sum.

9. $2\frac{1}{2} + \left(-2\frac{1}{2}\right) =$ ______

10. $-4.5 + 4.5 =$ ______

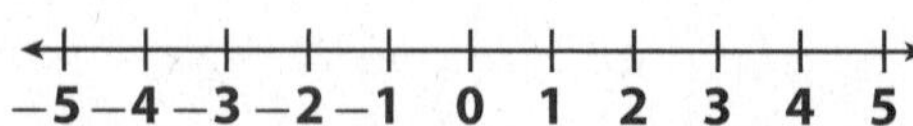

11. Kendrick adds $\frac{3}{4}$ cup of chicken stock to a pot. Then he takes $\frac{3}{4}$ cup of stock out of the pot. What is the overall increase or decrease in the amount of chicken stock in the pot?

______

Adding Three or More Rational Numbers

Recall that the Associative Property of Addition states that if you are adding more than two numbers, you can group any of the numbers together. This property can help you add numbers with different signs.

EXAMPLE 4  

7.NS.1d, 7.NS.3

Tina spent \$5.25 on craft supplies to make friendship bracelets. She made \$6.75 and spent an additional \$3.25 for supplies on Monday. On Tuesday, she sold an additional \$4.50 worth of bracelets. What was Tina's overall profit or loss?

Profit means the difference between income and costs is positive.

Use *negative* numbers to represent the amount Tina *spent* and *positive* numbers to represent the money Tina *earned*.

Find $-5.25 + 6.75 + (-3.25) + 4.50$.

Group numbers with the same sign.

$-5.25 + (-3.25) + 6.75 + 4.50$ Commutative Property

$(-5.25 + (-3.25)) + (6.75 + 4.50)$ Associative Property

STEP 4 $-8.50 + 11.25$ Add the numbers inside the parentheses.

Find the difference of the absolute values: $11.25 - 8.50$

2.75 Use the sign of the number with the greater absolute value. The sum is positive.

Tina earned a profit of \$2.75.

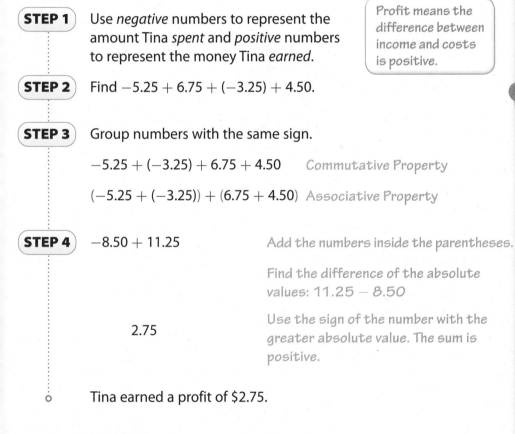

Find each sum.

12. $-1.5 + 3.5 + 2 =$ ______________

13. $3\frac{1}{4} + (-2) + \left(-2\frac{1}{4}\right) =$ ______________

14. $-2.75 + (-3.25) + 5 =$ ______________

15. $15 + 8 + (-3) =$ ______________

Guided Practice

Use a number line to find each sum. (Example 1 and Example 2)

1. $-3 + (-1.5) =$ ____________

−5 −4 −3 −2 −1 0 1 2 3 4 5

2. $1.5 + 3.5 =$ ____________

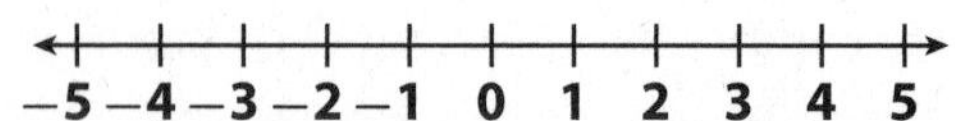

3. $\frac{1}{4} + \frac{1}{2} =$ ____________

−1 −0.5 0 0.5 1

4. $-1\frac{1}{2} + \left(-1\frac{1}{2}\right) =$ ____________

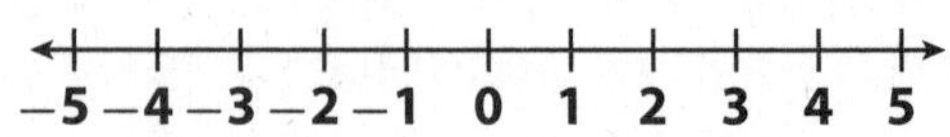

5. $3 + (-5) =$ ____________

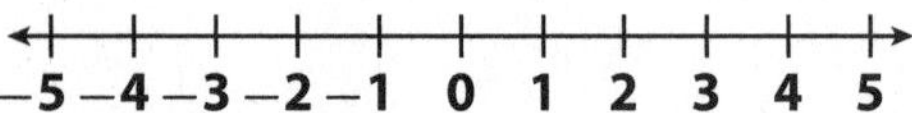

6. $-1.5 + 4 =$ ____________

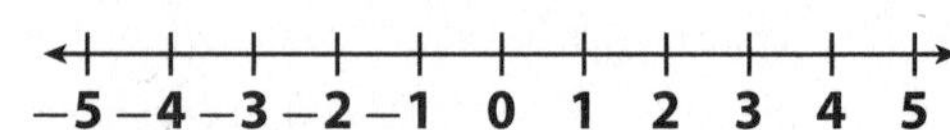

7. Victor borrowed $21.50 from his mother to go to the theater. A week later, he paid her $21.50 back. How much does he still owe her? (Example 3)

____

8. Sandra used her debit card to buy lunch for $8.74 on Monday. On Tuesday, she deposited $8.74 back into her account. What is the overall increase or decrease in her bank account? (Example 3)

____

Find each sum without using a number line. (Example 4)

9. $2.75 + (-2) + (-5.25) =$ ____________

10. $-3 + \left(1\frac{1}{2}\right) + \left(2\frac{1}{2}\right) =$ ____________

11. $-12.4 + 9.2 + 1 =$ ____________

12. $-12 + 8 + 13 =$ ____________

13. $4.5 + (-12) + (-4.5) =$ ____________

14. $\frac{1}{4} + \left(-\frac{3}{4}\right) =$ ____________

15. $-4\frac{1}{2} + 2 =$ ____________

16. $-8 + \left(-1\frac{1}{8}\right) =$ ____________

ESSENTIAL QUESTION CHECK-IN

17. How can you use a number line to find the sum of −4 and 6?

____

____

Name ______ Class ______ Date ______

3.2 Independent Practice

CA CC 7.NS.1a, 7.NS.1b, 7.NS.1d, 7.NS.3

18. Samuel walks forward 19 steps. He represents this movement with a positive 19. How would he represent the opposite of this number? ______

19. Julia spends \$2.25 on gas for her lawn mower. She earns \$15.00 mowing her neighbor's yard. What is Julia's profit? ______

20. A submarine submerged at a depth of -35.25 meters dives an additional 8.5 meters. What is the new depth of the submarine? ______

21. Renee hiked for $4\frac{3}{4}$ miles. After resting, Renee hiked back along the same route for $3\frac{1}{4}$ miles. How many more miles does Renee need to hike to return to the place where she started? ______

22. **Geography** The average elevation of the city of New Orleans, Louisiana, is 0.5 m below sea level. The highest point in Louisiana is Driskill Mountain at about 163.5 m higher than New Orleans. How high is Driskill Mountain? ______

23. **Problem Solving** A contestant on a game show has 30 points. She answers a question correctly to win 15 points. Then she answers a question incorrectly and loses 25 points. What is the contestant's final score?

______

Financial Literacy **Use the table for 24–26. Kameh owns a bakery. He recorded the bakery income and expenses in a table.**

Month	Income (\$)	Expenses (\$)
January	1,205	1,290.60
February	1,183	1,345.44
March	1,664	1,664.00
June	2,413	2,106.23
July	2,260	1,958.50
August	2,183	1,845.12

24. In which months were the expenses greater than the income? Name the month and find how much money was lost. ______

25. In which months was the income greater than the expenses? Name the months and find how much money was gained.

______

26. **Communicate Mathematical Ideas** If the bakery started with an extra \$250 from the profits in December, describe how to use the information in the table to figure out the profit or loss of money at the bakery by the end of August. Then calculate the profit or loss.

______

______

______

______

27. **Vocabulary** -2 is the ______________________________ of 2.

28. The basketball coach made up a game to play where each player takes 10 shots at the basket. For every basket made, the player gains 10 points. For every basket missed, the player loses 15 points.

 a. The player with the highest score sank 7 baskets and missed 3. What was the highest score?

 ____

 b. The player with the lowest score sank 2 baskets and missed 8. What was the lowest score?

 ____

 c. Write an expression using addition to find out what the score would be if a player sank 5 baskets and missed 5 baskets.

 ____

 ____

FOCUS ON HIGHER ORDER THINKING

Work Area

29. **Communicate Mathematical Ideas** Explain the different ways it is possible to add two rational numbers and get a negative number.

____

____

____

____

30. **Explain the Error** A student evaluated $-4 + x$ for $x = -9\frac{1}{2}$ and got an answer of $5\frac{1}{2}$. What might the student have done wrong?

____

____

31. **Draw Conclusions** Can you find the sum $[5.5 + (-2.3)] + (-5.5 + 2.3)$ without performing any additions? Explain.

____

____

____

LESSON 3.3

Subtracting Rational Numbers

CA CC 7.NS.1c

Understand subtraction of rational numbers as adding the additive inverse, $p - q = p + (-q)$. Show that the distance between two rational numbers on the number line is the absolute value of their difference, and apply this principle in real-world contexts. *Also 7.NS.1*

ESSENTIAL QUESTION

How do you subtract rational numbers?

Subtracting Positive Rational Numbers

To subtract rational numbers, you can apply the same rules you use to subtract integers.

EXAMPLE 1

CA CC 7.NS.1

The temperature on an outdoor thermometer on Monday was 5.5 °C. The temperature on Thursday was 7.25 degrees less than the temperature on Monday. What was the temperature on Thursday?

Subtract to find the temperature on Thursday.

STEP 1 Find $5.5 - 7.25$.

STEP 2 Start at 5.5.

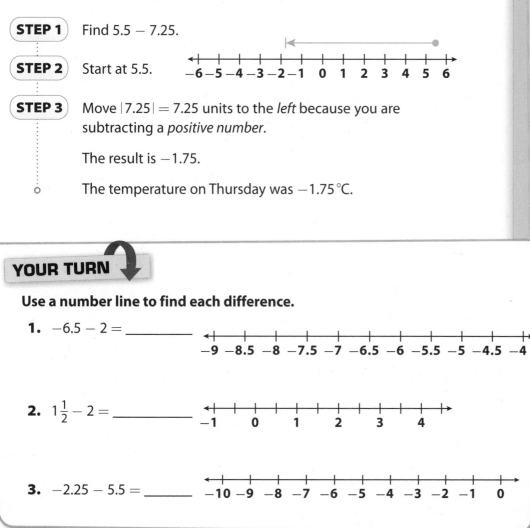

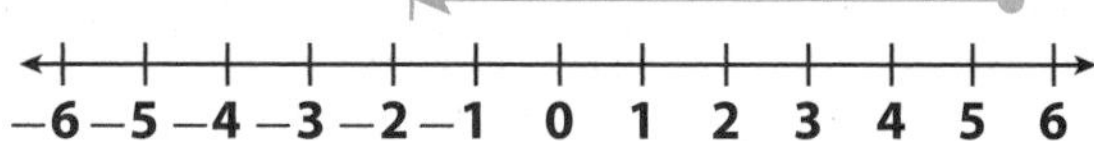

STEP 3 Move $|7.25| = 7.25$ units to the *left* because you are subtracting a *positive number.*

The result is -1.75.

The temperature on Thursday was -1.75 °C.

Use a number line to find each difference.

1. $-6.5 - 2 =$ ________

−9 −8.5 −8 −7.5 −7 −6.5 −6 −5.5 −5 −4.5 −4

2. $1\frac{1}{2} - 2 =$ ________

−1 0 1 2 3 4

3. $-2.25 - 5.5 =$ ________

−10 −9 −8 −7 −6 −5 −4 −3 −2 −1 0

Subtracting Negative Rational Numbers

To subtract negative rational numbers, move in the opposite direction on the number line.

EXAMPLE 2 

During the hottest week of the summer, the water level of the Muskrat River was $\frac{5}{6}$ foot below normal. The following week, the level was $\frac{1}{3}$ foot below normal. What is the overall change in the water level?

Subtract to find the difference in water levels.

STEP 1 Find $-\frac{1}{3} - \left(-\frac{5}{6}\right)$.

STEP 2 Start at $-\frac{1}{3}$.

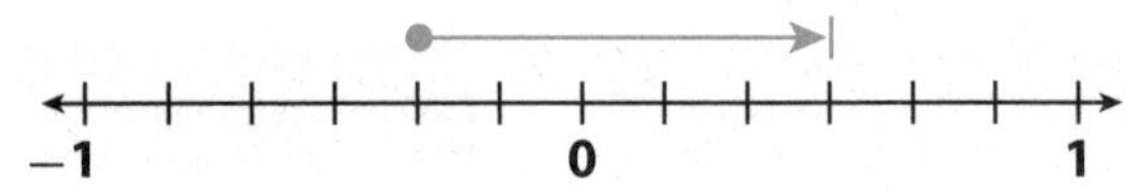

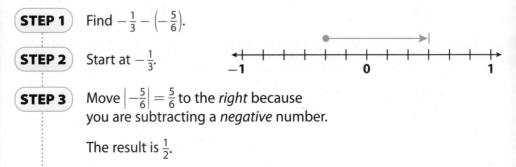

STEP 3 Move $\left|-\frac{5}{6}\right| = \frac{5}{6}$ to the *right* because you are subtracting a *negative* number.

The result is $\frac{1}{2}$.

So, the water level changed $\frac{1}{2}$ foot.

Reflect

4. Work with other students to compare addition of negative numbers on a number line to subtraction of negative numbers on a number line.

____

____

5. Compare the methods used to solve Example 1 and Example 2.

____

____

____

____

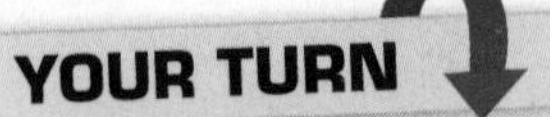

Use a number line to find each difference.

6. $0.25 - (-1.50) =$ ______________________________

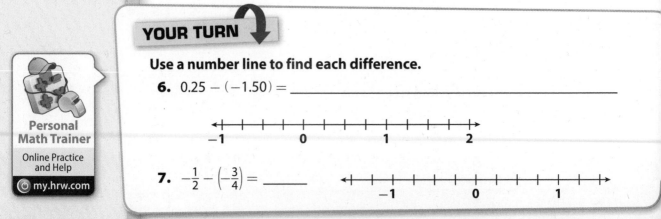

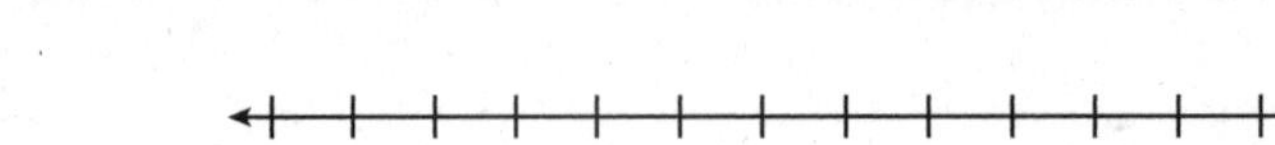

7. $-\frac{1}{2} - \left(-\frac{3}{4}\right) =$ ______

−1 0 1

EXPLORE ACTIVITY 1 Real World

CA CC 7.NS.1c

Adding the Opposite

Joe is diving $2\frac{1}{2}$ feet below sea level. He decides to descend $7\frac{1}{2}$ more feet. How many feet below sea level is he?

STEP 1 Use negative numbers to represent the number of feet below sea level.

STEP 2 Find $-2\frac{1}{2} - 7\frac{1}{2}$.

STEP 3 Start at $-2\frac{1}{2}$.

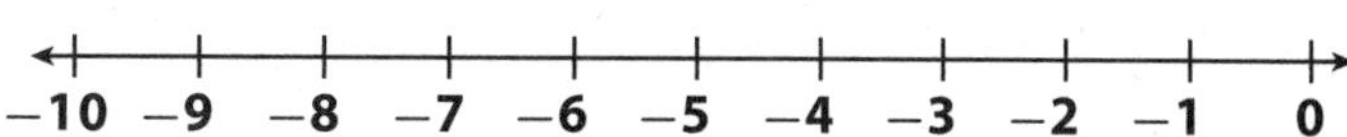

STEP 4 Move $\left|7\frac{1}{2}\right| = 7\frac{1}{2}$ units to the ________________

because you are subtracting a ________________ number.

The result is -10.

Joe is ________________ sea level.

You move left on a number line to add a negative number. You move the same direction to subtract a positive number.

Reflect

8. Compare the difference $-3.5 - 5.8$ to the sum $-3.5 + (-5.8)$.

____

____

9. **Analyze Relationships** Work with other students to explain how to change a subtraction problem into an addition problem.

____

____

____

Adding the Opposite

To subtract a number, add its opposite. This can also be written as $p - q = p + (-q)$.

EXPLORE ACTIVITY 2 

Finding the Distance between Two Numbers

A cave explorer climbed from an elevation of −11 meters to an elevation of −5 meters. What vertical distance did the explorer climb?

There are two ways to find the vertical distance.

A Start at ________.

Count the number of units on the vertical number line up to −5.

The explorer climbed ________ meters.

This means that the vertical distance between

−11 meters and −5 meters is ________ meters.

0, −1, −2, −3, −4, −5, −6, −7, −8, −9, −10, −11

B Find the difference between the two elevations and use absolute value to find the distance.

$-11 - (-5) =$ ________

Take the absolute value of the difference because distance traveled is always a nonnegative number.

$|-11 - (-5)| =$ ________

The vertical distance is ________ meters.

Reflect

10. Does it matter which way you subtract the values when finding distance? Explain.

____

____

11. Would the same methods work if both the numbers were positive? What if one of the numbers were positive and the other negative?

____

Distance Between Two Numbers

The distance between two values a and b on a number line is represented by the absolute value of the difference of a and b.

Distance between a and $b = |a - b|$ or $|b - a|$.

Guided Practice

Use a number line to find each difference. (Example 1, Example 2 and Explore Activity 1)

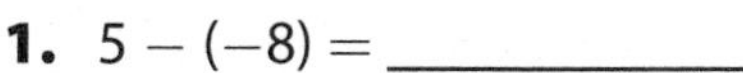

1. $5 - (-8) =$ ________

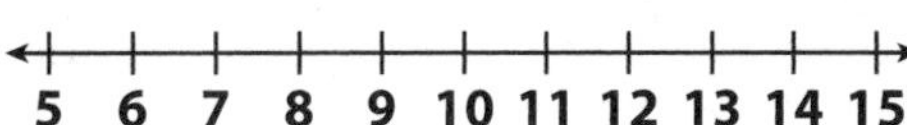

2. $-3\frac{1}{2} - 4\frac{1}{2} =$ ________

−9 −8 −7 −6 −5 −4 −3

3. $-7 - 4 =$ ________

−15 −14 −13 −12 −11 −10 −9 −8 −7 −6 −5

4. $-0.5 - 3.5 =$ ________

−6 −5 −4 −3 −2 −1 0 1

Find each difference. (Explore Activity 1)

5. $-14 - 22 =$ ________ **6.** $-12.5 - (-4.8) =$ ________ **7.** $\frac{1}{3} - \left(-\frac{2}{3}\right) =$ ________

8. $65 - (-14) =$ ________ **9.** $-\frac{2}{9} - (-3) =$ ________ **10.** $24\frac{3}{8} - \left(-54\frac{1}{8}\right) =$ ________

11. A girl is snorkeling 1 meter below sea level and then dives down another 0.5 meter. How far below sea level is the girl? (Explore Activity 1) ________

12. The first play of a football game resulted in a loss of $12\frac{1}{2}$ yards. Then a penalty resulted in another loss of 5 yards. What is the total loss or gain? (Explore Activity 1) ________

13. A climber starts descending from 533 feet above sea level and keeps going until she reaches 10 feet below sea level. How many feet did she descend? (Explore Activity 2) ________

14. Eleni withdrew $45.00 from her savings account. She then used her debit card to buy groceries for $30.15. What was the total amount Eleni took out of her account? (Explore Activity 1) ________

? ESSENTIAL QUESTION CHECK-IN

15. Mandy is trying to subtract $4 - 12$, and she has asked you for help. How would you explain the process of solving the problem to Mandy, using a number line?

____

____

____

Name ____________________ Class ____________________ Date ____________________

3.3 Independent Practice

CA CC 7.NS.1, 7.NS.1c

16. **Science** At the beginning of a laboratory experiment, the temperature of a substance is $-12.6\,°C$. During the experiment, the temperature of the substance decreases $7.5\,°C$. What is the final temperature of the substance?

____

17. A diver went 25.65 feet below the surface of the ocean, and then 16.5 feet further down, he then rose 12.45 feet. Write and solve an expression to find the diver's new depth.

____

____

____

Astronomy **Use the table for problems 18–19.**

Elevations on Planets		
	Lowest (ft)	Highest (ft)
Earth	$-36{,}198$	29,035
Mars	$-26{,}000$	70,000
Venus	$-9{,}500$	35,000

18. How much deeper is the deepest canyon on Mars than the deepest canyon on Venus?

____

19. **Persevere in Problem Solving** What is the difference between Earth's highest mountain and its deepest ocean canyon? What is the difference between Mars' highest mountain and its deepest canyon? Which difference is greater? How much greater is it?

____

____

20. A city known for its temperature extremes started the day at -5 degrees Fahrenheit. The temperature increased by 78 degrees Fahrenheit by midday, and then dropped 32 degrees by nightfall.

a. What expression can you write to find the temperature at nightfall? _______________

b. What expression can you write to describe the overall change in temperature? *Hint*: Do not include the temperature at the beginning of the day since you only want to know about how much the temperature changed. _______________

c. What is the final temperature at nightfall? What is the overall change in temperature? _______________

21. Financial Literacy On Monday, your bank account balance was −\$12.58. Because you didn't realize this, you wrote a check for \$30.72 for groceries.

a. What is the new balance in your checking account? ____________

b. The bank charges a \$25 fee for paying a check on a negative balance. What is the balance in your checking account after this fee? ____________

c. How much money do you need to deposit to bring your account balance back up to \$0 after the fee? ____________

22. Pamela wants to make some friendship bracelets for her friends. Each friendship bracelet needs 5.2 inches of string.

a. If Pamela has 20 inches of string, does she have enough to make bracelets for 4 of her friends?

b. If so, how much string would she had left over? If not, how much more string would she need?

23. Jeremy is practicing some tricks on his skateboard. One trick takes him forward 5 feet, then he flips around and moves backwards 7.2 feet, then he moves forward again for 2.2 feet.

a. What expression could be used to find how far Jeremy is from his starting position when he finishes the trick?

b. How far from his starting point is he when he finishes the trick? Explain.

24. Esteban has \$20 from his allowance. There is a comic book he wishes to buy that costs \$4.25, a cereal bar that costs \$0.89, and a small remote control car that costs \$10.99.

a. Does Esteban have enough to buy everything?

b. If so, how much will he have left over? If not, how much does he still need?

H.O.T. FOCUS ON HIGHER ORDER THINKING

Work Area

25. **Look for a Pattern** Show how you could use the Commutative Property to simplify the evaluation of the expression $-\frac{7}{16} - \frac{1}{4} - \frac{5}{16}$.

26. **Problem Solving** The temperatures for five days in Kaktovik, Alaska, are given below.

−19.6 °F, −22.5 °F, −20.9 °F, −19.5 °F, −22.4 °F

Temperatures for the following week are expected to be approximately twelve degrees lower each day than the given temperatures. What are the highest and lowest temperatures expected for the corresponding 5 days next week?

27. **Make a Conjecture** Must the difference between two rational numbers be a rational number? Explain.

28. **Look for a Pattern** Evan said that the difference between two negative numbers must be negative. Was he right? Use examples to illustrate your answer.

LESSON 3.4

Multiplying Rational Numbers

CA CC 7.NS.2

Apply and extend previous understandings of multiplication and division and of fractions to multiply and divide rational numbers. *Also 7.NS.2a, 7.NS.2c*

ESSENTIAL QUESTION

How do you multiply rational numbers?

Multiplying Rational Numbers with Different Signs

The rules for the signs of products of rational numbers with different signs are summarized below. Let p and q be rational numbers.

Products of Rational Numbers

Sign of Factor p	Sign of Factor q	Sign of Product pq
+	−	−
−	+	−

You can also use the fact that multiplication is repeated addition.

EXAMPLE 1  CA CC 7.NS.2, 7.NS.2a

Gina hiked down a canyon and stopped each time she descended $\frac{1}{2}$ mile to rest. She hiked a total of 4 sections. What is her overall change in elevation?

 Use a negative number to represent the change in elevation.

STEP 2 Find $4\left(-\frac{1}{2}\right)$.

STEP 3 Start at 0. Move $\frac{1}{2}$ unit to the left 4 times.

The result is −2.

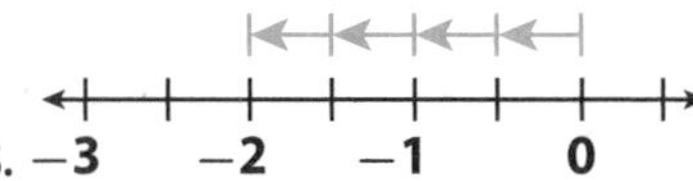

The overall change is −2 miles.

Check: Use the rules for multiplying rational numbers.

$4\left(-\frac{1}{2}\right) = \left(-\frac{4}{2}\right)$ A negative times a positive equals a negative.

$= -2$ ✓ Simplify.

YOUR TURN

1. Use a number line to find 2(−3.5). __________

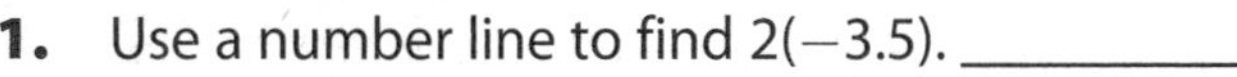

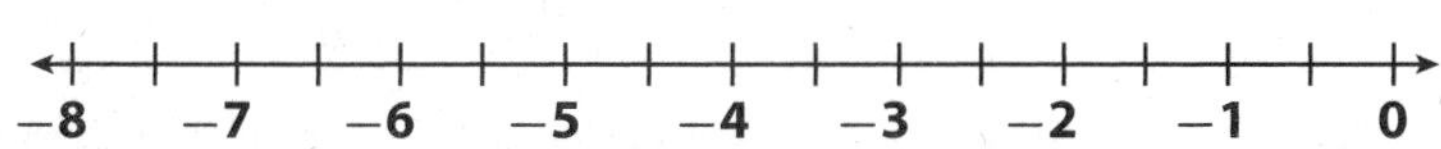

Multiplying Rational Numbers with the Same Sign

The rules for the signs of products with the same signs are summarized below.

Products of Rational Numbers

Sign of Factor p	Sign of Factor q	Sign of Product pq
+	+	+
−	−	+

You can also use a number line to find the product of rational numbers with the same signs.

My Notes

EXAMPLE 2

Multiply −2(−3.5).

STEP 1 First, find the product 2(−3.5).

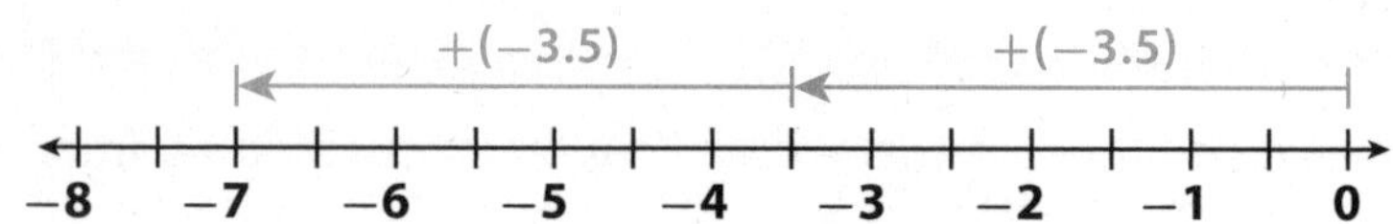

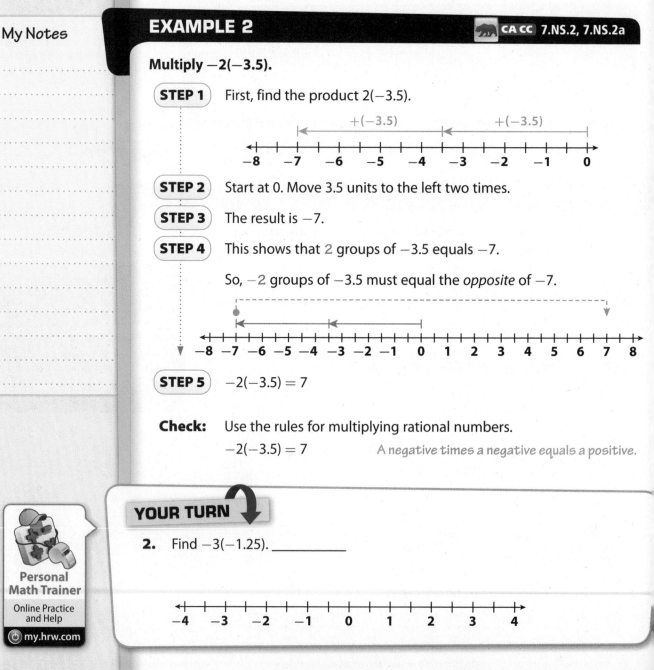

STEP 2 Start at 0. Move 3.5 units to the left two times.

STEP 3 The result is −7.

STEP 4 This shows that 2 groups of −3.5 equals −7.

So, −2 groups of −3.5 must equal the *opposite* of −7.

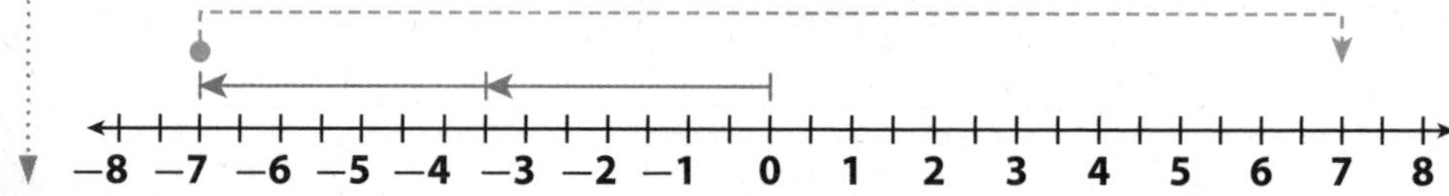

STEP 5 −2(−3.5) = 7

Check: Use the rules for multiplying rational numbers.

−2(−3.5) = 7 A negative times a negative equals a positive.

YOUR TURN

2. Find −3(−1.25). ___________

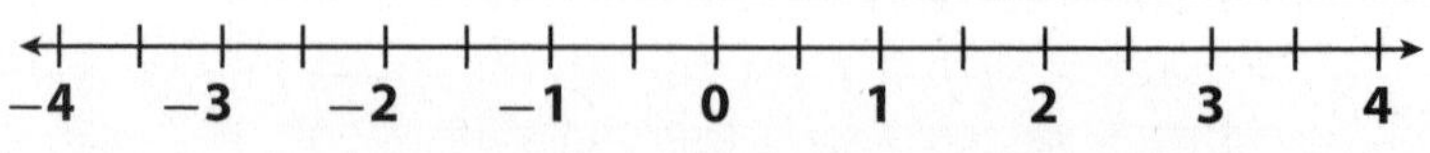

Personal Math Trainer
Online Practice and Help
my.hrw.com

Multiplying More Than Two Rational Numbers

If you multiply three or more rational numbers, you can use a pattern to find the sign of the product.

EXAMPLE 3

CA CC 7.NS.2, 7.NS.2c

Multiply $\left(-\frac{2}{3}\right)\left(-\frac{1}{2}\right)\left(-\frac{3}{5}\right)$.

STEP 1 First, find the product of the first two factors. Both factors are negative, so their product will be positive.

STEP 2 $\left(-\frac{2}{3}\right)\left(-\frac{1}{2}\right) = +\left(\frac{2}{3} \cdot \frac{1}{2}\right)$

$= \frac{1}{3}$

STEP 3 Now, multiply the result, which is positive, by the third factor, which is negative. The product will be negative.

STEP 4 $\frac{1}{3}\left(-\frac{3}{5}\right) = \frac{1}{3}\left(-\frac{3}{5}\right)$

STEP 5 $\left(-\frac{2}{3}\right)\left(-\frac{1}{2}\right)\left(-\frac{3}{5}\right) = -\frac{1}{5}$

Suppose you find the product of several rational numbers, one of which is zero. What can you say about the product?

Reflect

3. **Look for a Pattern** You know that the product of two negative numbers is positive, and the product of three negative numbers is negative. Write a rule for finding the sign of the product of n negative numbers.

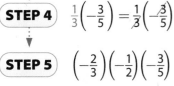

______

______

______

YOUR TURN

Find each product.

4. $\left(-\frac{3}{4}\right)\left(-\frac{4}{7}\right)\left(-\frac{2}{3}\right)$ ______

5. $\left(-\frac{2}{3}\right)\left(-\frac{3}{4}\right)\left(\frac{4}{5}\right)$ ______

6. $\left(\frac{2}{3}\right)\left(-\frac{9}{10}\right)\left(\frac{5}{6}\right)$ ______

Guided Practice

Use a number line to find each product. (Example 1 and Example 2)

1. $5\left(-\frac{2}{3}\right) =$ ______

−5 −4 −3 −2 −1 0

2. $3\left(-\frac{1}{4}\right) =$ ______

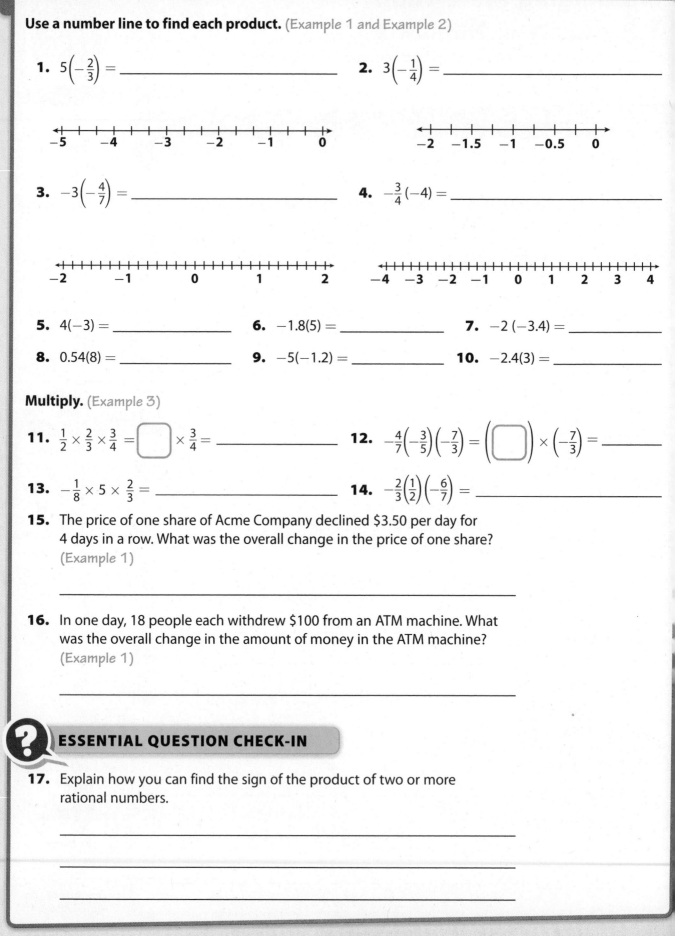

−2 −1.5 −1 −0.5 0

3. $-3\left(-\frac{4}{7}\right) =$ ______

−2 −1 0 1 2

4. $-\frac{3}{4}(-4) =$ ______

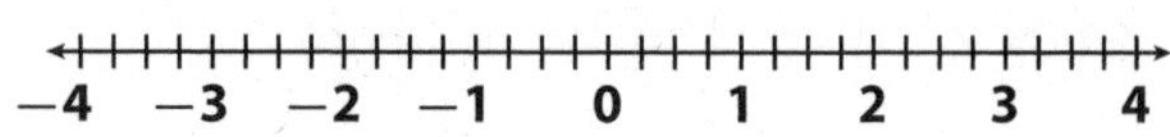

5. $4(-3) =$ ______

6. $-1.8(5) =$ ______

7. $-2\ (-3.4) =$ ______

8. $0.54(8) =$ ______

9. $-5(-1.2) =$ ______

10. $-2.4(3) =$ ______

Multiply. (Example 3)

11. $\frac{1}{2} \times \frac{2}{3} \times \frac{3}{4} = \square \times \frac{3}{4} =$ ______

12. $-\frac{4}{7}\left(-\frac{3}{5}\right)\left(-\frac{7}{3}\right) = (\square) \times \left(-\frac{7}{3}\right) =$ ______

13. $-\frac{1}{8} \times 5 \times \frac{2}{3} =$ ______

14. $-\frac{2}{3}\left(\frac{1}{2}\right)\left(-\frac{6}{7}\right) =$ ______

15. The price of one share of Acme Company declined $3.50 per day for 4 days in a row. What was the overall change in the price of one share? (Example 1)

______

16. In one day, 18 people each withdrew $100 from an ATM machine. What was the overall change in the amount of money in the ATM machine? (Example 1)

______

ESSENTIAL QUESTION CHECK-IN

17. Explain how you can find the sign of the product of two or more rational numbers.

______

______

______

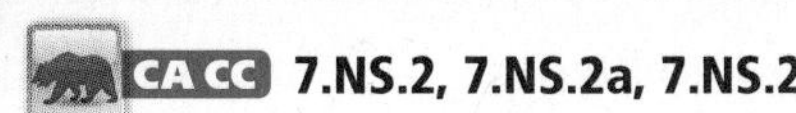

CA CC 7.NS.2, 7.NS.2a, 7.NS.2c

18. Financial Literacy Sandy has \$200 in her bank account.

a. If she writes 6 checks for exactly \$19.98, what expression describes the change in her bank account?

____

b. What is her account balance after the checks are cashed?

____

19. Communicating Mathematical Ideas Explain, in words, how to find the product of $-4(-1.5)$ using a number line. Where do you end up?

____

20. Greg sets his watch for the correct time on Wednesday. Exactly one week later, he finds that his watch has lost $3\frac{1}{4}$ minutes. If his watch continues to lose time at the same rate, what will be the overall change in time after 8 weeks?

____

21. A submarine dives below the surface, heading downward in three moves. If each move downward was 325 feet, where is the submarine after it is finished diving?

____

22. Multistep For Home Economics class, Sandra has 5 cups of flour. She made 3 batches of cookies that each used 1.5 cups of flour. Write and solve an expression to find the amount of flour Sandra has left after making the 3 batches of cookies.

____

23. Critique Reasoning In class, Matthew stated, "I think that a negative is like an opposite. That is why multiplying a negative times a negative equals a positive. The opposite of negative is positive, so it is just like multiplying the opposite of a negative twice, which is two positives." Do you agree or disagree with this statement? What would you say in response to him?

____

24. Kaitlin is on a long car trip. Every time she stops to buy gas, she loses 15 minutes of travel time. If she has to stop 5 times, how late will she be getting to her destination?

____

25. The table shows the scoring system for quarterbacks in Jeremy's fantasy football league. In one game, Jeremy's quarterback had 2 touchdown passes, 16 complete passes, 7 incomplete passes, and 2 interceptions. How many total points did Jeremy's quarterback score?

____

Quarterback Scoring	
Action	**Points**
Touchdown pass	6
Complete pass	0.5
Incomplete pass	−0.5
Interception	−1.5

FOCUS ON HIGHER ORDER THINKING

Work Area

26. **Represent Real-World Problems** The ground temperature at Brigham Airport is 12 °C. The temperature decreases by 6.8 °C for every increase of 1 kilometer above the ground. What is the temperature outside a plane flying at an altitude of 5 kilometers above Brigham Airport?

____

27. **Identify Patterns** The product of four numbers, *a*, *b*, *c*, and *d*, is a negative number. The table shows one combination of positive and negative signs of the four numbers that could produce a negative product. Complete the table to show the seven other possible combinations.

a	*b*	*c*	*d*
+	+	+	−

28. **Reason Abstractly** Find two integers whose sum is −7 and whose product is 12. Explain how you found the numbers.

____

____

____

____

LESSON 3.5

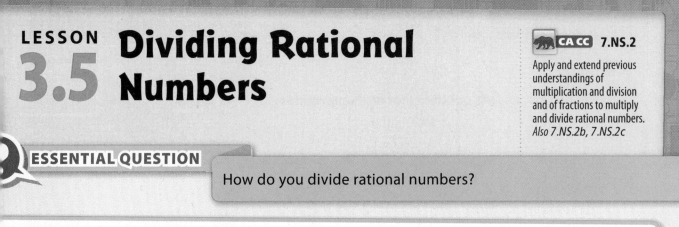

Dividing Rational Numbers

CA CC 7.NS.2

Apply and extend previous understandings of multiplication and division and of fractions to multiply and divide rational numbers. *Also 7.NS.2b, 7.NS.2c*

ESSENTIAL QUESTION

How do you divide rational numbers?

EXPLORE ACTIVITY CA CC 7.NS.2b

Placement of Negative Signs in Quotients

Quotients can have negative signs in different places.

Let p and q be rational numbers.

Quotients of Rational Numbers

Sign of Dividend p	Sign of Divisor q	Sign of Quotient $\frac{p}{q}$
+	−	−
−	+	−
+	+	+
−	−	+

Are the rational numbers $\frac{12}{-4}$, $\frac{-12}{4}$, and $-\left(\frac{12}{4}\right)$ equivalent?

A Find each quotient. Then use the rules in the table to make sure the sign of the quotient is correct.

$\frac{12}{-4} =$ ______ $\frac{-12}{4} =$ ______ $-\left(\frac{12}{4}\right) =$ ______

B What do you notice about each quotient?

______

C The rational numbers **are / are not** equivalent.

D **Conjecture** Explain how the placement of the negative sign in the rational number affects the sign of the quotients.

______

______

E If p and q are rational numbers and q is not zero, what do you know about $-\left(\frac{p}{q}\right)$, $\frac{-p}{q}$, and $\frac{p}{-q}$?

______

EXPLORE ACTIVITY *(cont'd)*

Reflect

Write two equivalent quotients for each expression.

1. $\frac{14}{-7}$ ________, ________

2. $\frac{-32}{-8}$ ________, ________

Quotients of Rational Numbers

The rules for dividing rational numbers are the same as dividing integers.

EXAMPLE 1

Over 5 months, Carlos wrote 5 checks for a total of $323.75 to pay for his cable TV service. His cable bill is the same amount each month. What was the change in Carlos's bank account each month to pay for cable?

Find the quotient: $\frac{-323.75}{5}$

STEP 1 Use a negative number to represent the withdrawal from his account each month.

STEP 2 Find $\frac{-323.75}{5}$.

STEP 3 Determine the sign of the quotient.

The quotient will be negative because the signs are different.

STEP 4 Divide.

$$\frac{-323.75}{5} = -64.75$$

Carlos withdrew $64.75 each month to pay for cable TV.

YOUR TURN

Find each quotient.

3. $\frac{2.8}{-4} =$ ________ **4.** $\frac{-6.64}{-0.4} =$ ________ **5.** $-\frac{5.5}{0.5} =$ ________

6. A diver descended 42.56 feet in 11.2 minutes. What was the diver's average change in elevation per minute?

____

Complex Fractions

A **complex fraction** is a fraction that has a fraction in its numerator, denominator, or both.

$$\frac{\frac{a}{b}}{\frac{c}{d}} = \frac{a}{b} \div \frac{c}{d}$$

My Notes

EXAMPLE 2 

CA CC 7.NS.2c, 7.NS.3

A Find $\frac{\frac{7}{10}}{-\frac{1}{5}}$.

STEP 1 Determine the sign of the quotient.
The quotient will be negative because the signs are different.

STEP 2 Write the complex fraction as division: $\frac{\frac{7}{10}}{-\frac{1}{5}} = \frac{7}{10} \div -\frac{1}{5}$

STEP 3 Rewrite using multiplication: $\frac{7}{10} \times \left(-\frac{5}{1}\right)$ Multiply by the reciprocal.

STEP 4 $\frac{7}{10} \times \left(-\frac{5}{1}\right) = -\frac{35}{10}$ Multiply.

$= -\frac{7}{2}$ Simplify.

$\frac{\frac{7}{10}}{-\frac{1}{5}} = -\frac{7}{2}$

B Maya wants to divide a $\frac{3}{4}$-pound box of trail mix into small bags. Each bag will hold $\frac{1}{12}$ pound of trail mix. How many bags of trail mix can Maya fill?

STEP 1 Find $\frac{\frac{3}{4}}{\frac{1}{12}}$.

STEP 2 Determine the sign of the quotient.
The quotient will be positive because the signs are the same.

STEP 3 Write the complex fraction as division: $\frac{\frac{3}{4}}{\frac{1}{12}} = \frac{3}{4} \div \frac{1}{12}$.

STEP 4 Rewrite using multiplication: $\frac{3}{4} \times \frac{12}{1}$. Multiply by the reciprocal.

STEP 5 $\frac{3}{4} \times \frac{12}{1} = \frac{36}{4} = 9$ Multiply. Simplify.

$\frac{\frac{3}{4}}{\frac{1}{12}} = 9$

Maya can fill 9 bags of trail mix.

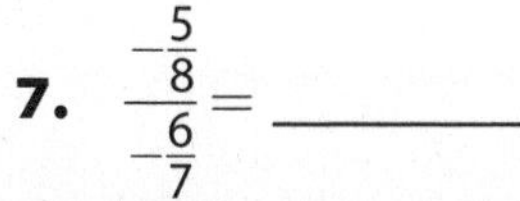
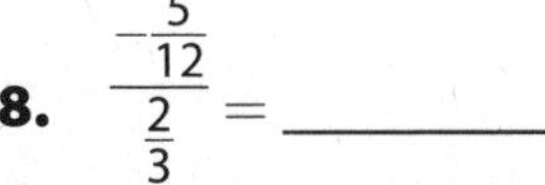
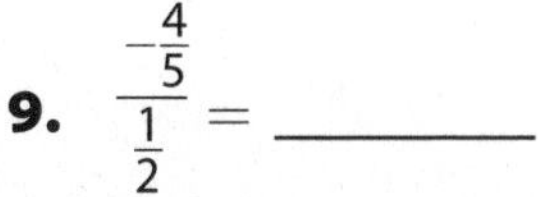

7. $\frac{-\frac{5}{8}}{-\frac{6}{7}} =$ ______ **8.** $\frac{-\frac{5}{12}}{\frac{2}{3}} =$ ______ **9.** $\frac{-\frac{4}{5}}{\frac{1}{2}} =$ ______

Guided Practice

Find each quotient. (Explore Activity 1 and 2, Example 1)

1. $\frac{0.72}{-0.9} =$ __________

2. $\left(-\frac{\frac{1}{5}}{\frac{7}{5}}\right) =$ __________

3. $\frac{56}{-7} =$ __________

4. $\frac{251}{4} \div \left(-\frac{3}{8}\right) =$ __________

5. $\frac{75}{-\frac{1}{5}} =$ __________

6. $\frac{-91}{-13} =$ __________

7. $\frac{-\frac{3}{7}}{\frac{9}{4}} =$ __________

8. $-\frac{12}{0.03} =$ __________

9. A water pail in your backyard has a small hole in it. You notice that it has drained a total of 3.5 liters in 4 days. What is the average change in water volume each day? (Example 1)

____

10. The price of one share of ABC Company decreased a total of $45.75 in 5 days. What was the average change of the price of one share per day? (Example 1)

____

11. To avoid a storm, a passenger-jet pilot descended 0.44 mile in 0.8 minute. What was the plane's average change of altitude per minute? (Example 1)

____

ESSENTIAL QUESTION CHECK-IN

12. Explain how you would find the sign of the quotient $\frac{32 \div (-2)}{-16 \div 4}$.

____

____

____

____

____

____

Name ________________ Class ________________ Date ________________

3.5 Independent Practice

CA CC 7.NS.2, 7.NS.2b, 7.NS.2c

13. $\frac{5}{-\frac{2}{8}} =$ ________________

14. $5\frac{1}{3} \div \left(-1\frac{1}{2}\right) =$ ________________

15. $\frac{-120}{-6} =$ ________________

16. $\frac{-\frac{4}{5}}{-\frac{2}{3}} =$ ________________

17. $1.03 \div (-10.3) =$ ________________

18. $\frac{-0.4}{80} =$ ________________

19. $1 \div \frac{9}{5} =$ ________________

20. $\frac{\frac{-1}{4}}{\frac{23}{24}} =$ ________________

21. $\frac{-10.35}{-2.3} =$ ________________

22. Alex usually runs for 21 hours a week, training for a marathon. If he is unable to run for 3 days, describe how to find out how many hours of training time he loses, and write the appropriate integer to describe how it affects his time.

____

23. The running back for the Bulldogs football team carried the ball 9 times for a total loss of $15\frac{3}{4}$ yards. Find the average change in field position on each run.

____

24. The 6:00 a.m. temperatures for four consecutive days in the town of Lincoln were −12.1 °C, −7.8 °C, −14.3 °C, and −7.2 °C. What was the average 6:00 a.m. temperature for the four days?

____

25. **Multistep** A seafood restaurant claims an increase of $1,750.00 over its average profit during a week where it introduced a special of baked clams.

   a. If this is true, how much extra profit did it receive per day?

   ____

   b. If it had, instead, lost $150 per day, how much money would it have lost for the week?

   ____

   c. If its total loss was $490 for the week, what was its average daily change?

   ____

26. A hot air balloon descended 99.6 meters in 12 seconds. What was the balloon's average rate of descent in meters per second?

____

27. Sanderson is having trouble with his assignment. His shown work is as follows:

$$\frac{-\frac{3}{4}}{\frac{4}{3}} = -\frac{3}{4} \times \frac{4}{3} = -\frac{12}{12} = -1$$

However, his answer does not match the answer that his teacher gives him. What is Sanderson's mistake? Find the correct answer.

____

____

____

____

28. Science Beginning in 1996, a glacier lost an average of 3.7 meters of thickness each year. Find the total change in its thickness by the end of 2012.

____

FOCUS ON HIGHER ORDER THINKING

Work Area

29. Represent Real-World Problems Describe a real-world situation that can be represented by the quotient $-85 \div 15$. Then find the quotient and explain what the quotient means in terms of the real-world situation.

____

____

____

____

30. Construct an Argument Divide 5 by 4. Is your answer a rational number? Explain.

____

____

____

31. Critical Thinking Should the quotient of an integer divided by a nonzero integer always be a rational number? Why or why not?

____

____

____

LESSON 3.6

Applying Rational Number Operations

CA CC 7.EE.3

Solve ... problems ... with positive and negative rational numbers in any form ... using tools strategically. (For the full text of the standard, see the table at the front of the book beginning on page CA2.) *Also 7.NS.3*

ESSENTIAL QUESTION

How do you use different forms of rational numbers and strategically choose tools to solve problems?

Assessing Reasonableness of Answers

Even when you understand how to solve a problem, you might make a careless solving error. You should always check your answer to make sure that it is reasonable.

EXAMPLE 1

CA CC 7.EE.3, 7.NS.3

Jon is hanging a picture. He wants to center it horizontally on the wall. The picture is $32\frac{1}{2}$ inches long, and the wall is $120\frac{3}{4}$ inches long. How far from each edge of the wall should he place the picture?

STEP 1 Find the total length of the wall not covered by the picture.

$120\frac{3}{4} - 32\frac{1}{2} = 88\frac{1}{4}$ in.

Subtract the whole number parts and then the fractional parts.

STEP 2 Find the length of the wall on each side of the picture.

$\frac{1}{2}\left(88\frac{1}{4}\right) = 44\frac{1}{8}$ in.

Jon should place the picture $44\frac{1}{8}$ inches from each edge of the wall.

STEP 3 Check the answer for reasonableness.

The wall is about 120 inches long. The picture is about 30 inches long. The length of wall space left for *both* sides of the picture is about $120 - 30 = 90$ inches. The length left for *each* side is about $\frac{1}{2}(90) = 45$ inches.

The answer is reasonable because it is close to the estimate.

1. A 30-minute TV program consists of three commercials, each $2\frac{1}{2}$ minutes long, and four equal-length entertainment segments. How long is each entertainment segment? ________________

Using Rational Numbers in Any Form

You have solved problems using integers, positive and negative fractions, and positive and negative decimals. A single problem may involve rational numbers in two or more of those forms.

EXAMPLE 2 

My Notes

Alana uses $1\frac{1}{4}$ cups of flour for each batch of blueberry muffins she makes. She has a 5-pound bag of flour that cost \$4.49 and contains seventy-six $\frac{1}{4}$-cup servings. How many batches can Alana make if she uses all the flour? How much does the flour for one batch cost?

Muffins
1¼ cups all purpose flour
3/4 cup white sugar
1/2 teaspoon salt
2 teaspoons baking powder
1/3 cup vegetable oil
1 egg
1/3 cup milk
1 cup fresh blue berries

 Analyze Information

Identify the important information.

- Each batch uses $1\frac{1}{4}$ cups of flour.
- Seventy-six $\frac{1}{4}$-cup servings of flour cost \$4.49.

Formulate a Plan

Use logical reasoning to solve the problem. Find the number of cups of flour that Alana has. Use that information to find the number of batches she can make. Use that information to find the cost of flour for each batch.

 Solve

Number of cups of flour in bag:

$76 \times \frac{1}{4}$ cup per serving $= 19$ cups

Number of batches Alana can make:

Write $1\frac{1}{4}$ as a decimal.

$$\text{total cups of flour} \div \frac{\text{cups of flour}}{\text{batch}} = 19 \text{ cups} \div \frac{1.25 \text{ cups}}{1 \text{ batch}}$$
$$= 19 \div 1.25$$
$$= 15.2$$

Alana cannot make 0.2 batch. The recipe calls for one egg, and she cannot divide one egg into tenths. So, she can make 15 batches.

Cost of flour for each batch: $\$4.49 \div 15 = \$0.299$, or about \$0.30.

 Justify and Evaluate

A bag contains about 80 quarter cups, or about 20 cups. Each batch uses about 1 cup of flour, so there is enough flour for about 20 batches. A bag costs about \$5.00, so the flour for each batch costs about $\$5.00 \div 20 = \$0.25$. The answers are close to the estimates, so the answers are reasonable.

YOUR TURN

2. A 4-pound bag of sugar contains 454 one-teaspoon servings and costs \$3.49. A batch of muffins uses $\frac{3}{4}$ cup of sugar. How many batches can you make if you use all the sugar? What is the cost of sugar for each batch? (1 cup = 48 teaspoons) ______________

Using Tools Strategically

A wide variety of tools are available to help you solve problems. Rulers, models, calculators, protractors, and software are some of the tools you can use in addition to paper and pencil. Choosing tools wisely can help you solve problems and increase your understanding of mathematical concepts.

EXAMPLE 3 

CA CC 7.EE.3, 7.NS.3

The depth of Golden Trout Lake has been decreasing in recent years. Two years ago, the depth of the lake was 186.73 meters. Since then the depth has been changing at an average rate of $-1\frac{3}{4}\%$ per year. What is the depth of the lake today?

STEP 1 Convert the percent to a decimal.

$-1\frac{3}{4}\% = -1.75\%$ *Write the fraction as a decimal.*

$= -0.0175$ *Move the decimal point two places left.*

STEP 2 Find the depth of the lake after one year. Use a calculator to simplify the computations.

$186.73 \times (-0.0175) \approx -3.27$ meters *Find the change in depth.*

$186.73 - 3.27 = 183.46$ meters *Find the new depth.*

STEP 3 Find the depth of the lake after two years.

$183.46 \times (-0.0175) \approx -3.21$ meters *Find the change in depth.*

$183.46 - 3.21 = 180.25$ meters *Find the new depth.*

STEP 4 Check the answer for reasonableness.

The original depth was about 190 meters. The depth changed by about -2% per year. Because $(-0.02)(190) = -3.8$, the depth changed by about -4 meters per year or about -8 meters over two years. So, the new depth was about 182 meters. The answer is close to the estimate, so it is reasonable.

How could you write a single expression for calculating the depth after 1 year? after 2 years?

YOUR TURN

3. Three years ago, Jolene bought $750 worth of stock in a software company. Since then the value of her purchase has been increasing at an average rate of $12\frac{3}{5}$% per year. How much is the stock worth now? ________

Guided Practice

1. Mike hiked to Big Bear Lake in 4.5 hours at an average rate of $3\frac{1}{5}$ miles per hour. Pedro hiked the same distance at a rate of $3\frac{3}{5}$ miles per hour. How long did it take Pedro to reach the lake? (Example 1 and Example 2)

STEP 1 Find the distance Mike hiked.

4.5 h × ☐ miles per hour = ☐ miles

STEP 2 Find Pedro's time to hike the same distance.

☐ miles ÷ ☐ miles per hour = ☐ hours

2. Until this year, Greenville had averaged 25.68 inches of rainfall per year for more than a century. This year's total rainfall showed a change of $-2\frac{3}{8}$% with respect to the previous average. How much rain fell this year? (Example 3)

STEP 1 Use a calculator to find this year's decrease to the nearest hundredth.

☐ inches × ☐ ≈ ☐ inches

STEP 2 Find this year's total rainfall.

☐ inches − ☐ inches ≈ ☐ inches

ESSENTIAL QUESTION CHECK-IN

3. Why is it important to consider using tools when you are solving a problem?

____

____

____

Name ____________________ Class ____________________ Date ____________________

3.6 Independent Practice

CA CC 7.NS.3, 7.EE.3

Solve, using appropriate tools.

4. Three rock climbers started a climb with each person carrying 7.8 kilograms of climbing equipment. A fourth climber with no equipment joined the group. The group divided the total weight of climbing equipment equally among the four climbers. How much did each climber carry? ____________________

5. Foster is centering a photo that is $3\frac{1}{2}$ inches wide on a scrapbook page that is 12 inches wide. How far from each side of the page should he put the picture? ____________________

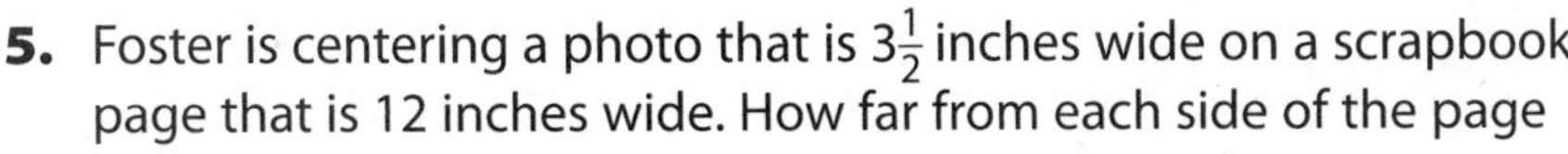

6. Diane serves breakfast to two groups of children at a daycare center. One box of Oaties contains 12 cups of cereal. She needs $\frac{1}{3}$ cup for each younger child and $\frac{3}{4}$ cup for each older child. Today's group includes 11 younger children and 10 older children. Is one box of Oaties enough for everyone? Explain. ____________________

7. The figure shows how the yard lines on a football field are numbered. The goal lines are labeled G. A referee was standing on a certain yard line as the first quarter ended. He walked $41\frac{3}{4}$ yards to a yard line with the same number as the one he had just left. How far was the referee from the nearest goal line? ____________________

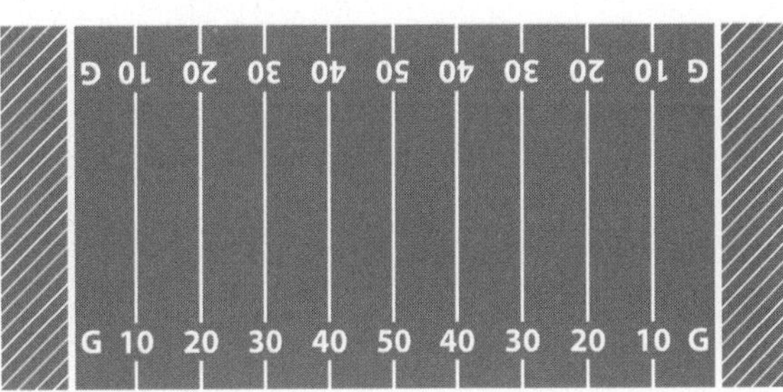

In 8–10, a teacher gave a test with 50 questions, each worth the same number of points. Donovan got 39 out of 50 questions right. Marci's score was 10 percentage points higher than Donovan's.

8. What was Marci's score? Explain.

____

9. How many more questions did Marci answer correctly? Explain.

____

10. Explain how you can check your answers for reasonableness.

____

____

____

For 11–13, use the expression 1.43 × $\left(-\frac{19}{37}\right)$.

11. **Critique Reasoning** Jamie says the value of the expression is close to −0.75. Does Jamie's estimate seem reasonable? Explain.

____

12. Find the product. Explain your method.

____

____

13. Does your answer to Exercise 12 justify your answer to Exercise 11?

____

H.O.T. FOCUS ON HIGHER ORDER THINKING

Work Area

14. **Persevere in Problem Solving** A scuba diver dove from the surface of the ocean to an elevation of $-79\frac{9}{10}$ feet at a rate of −18.8 feet per minute. After spending 12.75 minutes at that elevation, the diver ascended to an elevation of $-28\frac{9}{10}$ feet. The total time for the dive so far was $19\frac{1}{8}$ minutes. What was the rate of change in the diver's elevation during the ascent? _______

15. **Analyze Relationships** Describe two ways you could evaluate 37% of the sum of $27\frac{3}{5}$ and 15.9. Tell which method you would use and why.

____

____

____

____

____

____

16. **Represent Real-World Problems** Describe a real-world problem you could solve with the help of a yardstick and a calculator.

____

____

____

____

____

____

MODULE QUIZ

Ready to Go On?

3.1 Rational Numbers and Decimals

Write each mixed number as a decimal.

1. $4\frac{1}{5}$ ______

2. $12\frac{14}{15}$ ______

3. $5\frac{5}{32}$ ______

3.2 Adding Rational Numbers

Find each sum.

4. $4.5 + 7.1 =$ ______

5. $5\frac{1}{6} + \left(-3\frac{5}{6}\right) =$ ______

3.3 Subtracting Rational Numbers

Find each difference.

6. $-\frac{1}{8} - \left(6\frac{7}{8}\right) =$ ______

7. $14.2 - (-4.9) =$ ______

3.4 Multiplying Rational Numbers

Multiply.

8. $-4\left(\frac{7}{10}\right) =$ ______

9. $-3.2(-5.6)(4) =$ ______

3.5 Dividing Rational Numbers

Find each quotient.

10. $-\frac{19}{2} \div \frac{38}{7} =$ ______

11. $\frac{-32.01}{-3.3} =$ ______

3.6 Applying Rational Number Operations

12. Luis bought stock at \$83.60. The next day, the price increased \$15.35. This new price changed by $-4\frac{3}{4}\%$ the following day. What was the final stock price? Is your answer reasonable? Explain.

______

______

ESSENTIAL QUESTION

13. How can you use negative numbers to represent real-world problems?

______

______

MODULE 3
MIXED REVIEW

Assessment Readiness

1. Consider each expression. Is the value of the expression negative?

Select Yes or No for expressions A–C.

A. $-\frac{1}{2} \div (-8)$ ○ Yes ○ No

B. $-\frac{3}{4} \times \frac{5}{8}$ ○ Yes ○ No

C. $-0.7 - (-0.62)$ ○ Yes ○ No

2. Randall had \$75 in his bank account. He made 3 withdrawals of \$18 each.

Choose True or False for each statement.

A. The change in Randall's balance is −\$54. ○ True ○ False

B. The account balance is equal to \$75 − 3(−\$18). ○ True ○ False

C. Randall now has a negative balance. ○ True ○ False

3. The water level in a lake was 12 inches below normal at the beginning of March. The water level decreased by $2\frac{1}{4}$ inches in March and increased by $1\frac{5}{8}$ inches in April. What was the water level compared to normal at the end of April? Explain how you solved this problem.

4. A butcher has $10\frac{3}{4}$ pounds of ground beef that will be priced at \$3.40 per pound. He divides the meat into 8 equal packages. To the nearest cent, what will be the price of each package? Explain how you know that your answer is reasonable.

Study Guide Review

MODULE 1 Adding and Subtracting Integers

Key Vocabulary
additive inverse *(inverso aditivo)*

ESSENTIAL QUESTION

How can you use addition and subtraction of integers to solve real-world problems?

EXAMPLE 1

Add.

A. $-8 + (-7)$ — The signs of both integers are the same.

$8 + 7 = 15$ — Find the sum of the absolute values.

$-8 + (-7) = -15$ — Use the sign of integers to write the sum.

B. $-5 + 11$ — The signs of the integers are different.

$|11| - |-5| = 6$ — Greater absolute value – lesser absolute value.

$-5 + 11 = 6$ — 11 has the greater absolute value, so the sum is positive.

EXAMPLE 2

The temperature Tuesday afternoon was 3 °C. Tuesday night, the temperature was −6 °C. Find the change in temperature.

Find the difference $-6 - 3$.

Rewrite as $-6 + (-3)$. — -3 is the opposite of 3.

$-6 + (-3) = -9$

The temperature decreased 9 °C.

EXERCISES

Add. (Lessons 1.1, 1.2)

1. $-10 + (-5)$ ________ **2.** $9 + (-20)$ ________ **3.** $-13 + 32$ ________

Subtract. (Lesson 1.3)

4. $-12 - 5$ ________ **5.** $25 - (-4)$ ________ **6.** $-3 - (-40)$ ________

7. Antoine has $13 in his checking account. He buys some school supplies and ends up with $5 in his account. What was the overall change in Antoine's account? (Lesson 1.4) ________

MODULE 2

Multiplying and Dividing Integers

ESSENTIAL QUESTION

How can you use multiplication and division of integers to solve real-world problems?

EXAMPLE 1

Multiply.

A. $(13)(-3)$

Find the sign of the product. The numbers have different signs, so the product will be negative. Multiply the absolute values. Assign the correct sign to the product.

$13(-3) = -39$

B. $(-5)(-8)$

Find the sign of the product. The numbers have the same sign, so the product will be positive. Multiply the absolute values. Assign the correct sign to the product.

$(-5)(-8) = 40$

EXAMPLE 2

Christine received -25 points on her exam for 5 wrong answers. How many points did Christine receive for each wrong answer?

Divide -25 by 5.

$-25 \div 5 = -5$ The signs are different. The quotient is negative.

Christine received -5 points for each wrong answer.

EXAMPLE 3

Simplify: $15 + (-3) \times 8$

$15 + (-24)$ Multiply first.

-9 Add.

EXERCISES

Multiply or divide. (Lessons 2.1, 2.2)

1. $-9 \times (-5)$ ______ **2.** $0 \times (-10)$ ______ **3.** $12 \times (-4)$ ______

4. $-32 \div 8$ ______ **5.** $-9 \div (-1)$ ______ **6.** $-56 \div 8$ ______

Simplify. (Lesson 2.3)

7. $-14 \div 2 - 3$ ______ **8.** $8 + (-20) \times 3$ ______ **9.** $36 \div (-6) \times -15$ ______

10. Tony bought 3 packs of pencils for \$4 each and a pencil box for \$7. Mario bought 4 binders for \$6 each and used a coupon for \$6 off. Write and evaluate expressions to find who spent more money. (Lesson 2.3)

______

11. Sumaya is reading a book with 288 pages. She has already read 90 pages. She plans to read 20 more pages each day until she finishes the book. Determine how many days Sumaya will need to finish the book. In your answer, count part of a day as a full day. Show that your answer is reasonable.

____

____

MODULE 3 Rational Numbers

Key Vocabulary

rational number *(número racional)*

repeating decimal *(decimal periódico)*

terminating decimal *(decimal finito)*

ESSENTIAL QUESTION

How can you use rational numbers to solve real-world problems?

EXAMPLE 1

Eddie walked $1\frac{2}{3}$ miles on a hiking trail. Write $1\frac{2}{3}$ as a decimal. Use the decimal to classify $1\frac{2}{3}$ according to the number group(s) to which it belongs.

$1\frac{2}{3} = \frac{5}{3}$ Write $1\frac{2}{3}$ as an improper fraction.

$$\begin{array}{r} 1.66 \\ 3\overline{)5.00} \\ -3 \\ \hline 2\,0 \\ -1\,8 \\ \hline 20 \\ -18 \\ \hline 2 \end{array}$$

Divide the numerator by the denominator.

The decimal equivalent of $1\frac{2}{3}$ is 1.66..., or $1.\overline{6}$. It is a repeating decimal, and therefore can be classified as a rational number.

EXAMPLE 2

Find each sum or difference.

A. $-2 + 4.5$

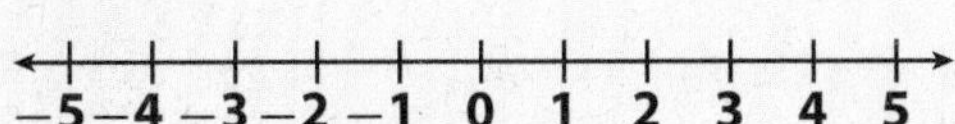

Start at -2 and move 4.5 units to the right: $-2 + 4.5 = 2.5$.

B. $-\frac{2}{5} - \left(-\frac{4}{5}\right)$

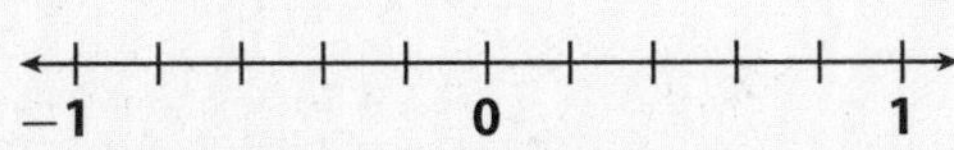

Start at $-\frac{2}{5}$. Move $\left|-\frac{4}{5}\right| = \frac{4}{5}$ unit to the right because you are subtracting a negative number: $-\frac{2}{5} - \left(-\frac{4}{5}\right) = \frac{2}{5}$.

EXAMPLE 3

Find the product: $3\left(-\frac{1}{6}\right)\left(-\frac{2}{5}\right)$.

$3\left(-\frac{1}{6}\right) = -\frac{1}{2}$ — Find the product of the first two factors. One is positive and one is negative, so the product is negative.

$-\frac{1}{2}\left(-\frac{2}{5}\right) = \frac{1}{5}$ — Multiply the result by the third factor. Both are negative, so the product is positive.

$3\left(-\frac{1}{6}\right)\left(-\frac{2}{5}\right) = \frac{1}{5}$

EXAMPLE 4

Find the quotient: $\frac{15.2}{-2}$.

$\frac{15.2}{-2} = -7.6$ — The quotient is negative because the signs are different.

EXAMPLE 5

A lake's level dropped an average of $3\frac{4}{5}$ inches per day for 21 days. A heavy rain then raised the level 8.25 feet, after which it dropped $9\frac{1}{2}$ inches per day for 4 days. Jayden says that overall, the lake level changed about $-1\frac{1}{2}$ feet. Is this answer reasonable?

Yes; the lake drops about 4 inches, or $\frac{1}{3}$ foot, per day for 21 days, rises about 8 feet, then falls about $\frac{3}{4}$ foot for 4 days:
$-\frac{1}{3}(21) + 8 - \frac{3}{4}(4) = -7 + 8 - 3 = -2$ feet.

EXERCISES

Write each mixed number as a whole number or decimal. Classify each number according to the group(s) to which it belongs: rational numbers, integers, or whole numbers. (Lesson 3.1)

1. $\frac{3}{4}$ ________

2. $\frac{8}{2}$ ________

3. $\frac{11}{3}$ ________

4. $\frac{5}{2}$ ________

Find each sum or difference. (Lessons 3.2, 3.3)

5. $-5 + 9.5$ ________

6. $\frac{1}{6} + \left(-\frac{5}{6}\right)$ ________

7. $-0.5 + (-8.5)$ ________

8. $-3 - (-8)$ ________

9. $5.6 - (-3.1)$ ________

10. $3\frac{1}{2} - 2\frac{1}{4}$ ________

11. Jorge records his hours each day on a time sheet. Last week when he was ill, his time sheet was incomplete. If Jorge worked a total of 30.5 hours last week, how many hours are missing? Show your work. Then show that your answer is reasonable.

Mon	Tues	Wed	Thurs	Fri
8	$7\frac{1}{4}$	$8\frac{1}{2}$		

____

____

____

Find each product or quotient. (Lessons 3.4, 3.5)

12. $-9 \times (-5)$ ______ **13.** $0 \times (-7)$ ______ **14.** -8×8 ______

15. $\frac{-56}{8}$ ______ **16.** $\frac{-130}{-5}$ ______ **17.** $\frac{34.5}{1.5}$ ______

18. $-\frac{2}{5}\left(-\frac{1}{2}\right)\left(-\frac{5}{6}\right)$ ______ **19.** $\left(\frac{1}{5}\right)\left(-\frac{5}{7}\right)\left(\frac{3}{4}\right)$ ______

20. Lei withdrew \$50 from her bank account every day for a week. What was the change in her account in that week?

____

21. Dan is cutting 4.75-foot lengths of twine from a 240-foot spool of twine. He needs to cut 42 lengths and says that 40.5 feet of twine will remain. Show that this is reasonable.

____

22. Jackson works as a veterinary technician and earns \$12.20 per hour.

a. Jackson normally works 40 hours a week. In a normal week, what is his total pay before taxes and other deductions?

____

b. Last week, Jackson was ill and missed some work. His total pay before deductions was \$372.10. Write and solve an equation to find the number of hours Jackson worked.

____

23. When Jackson works more than 40 hours in a week, he earns 1.5 times his normal hourly rate for each of the extra hours. Jackson worked 43 hours one week. What was his total pay before deductions? Justify your answer.

____

Unit Project

CA CC 7.NS.1, 7.NS.2

It's Okay to Be Negative!

In 2012, film director James Cameron piloted a craft called the *Deepsea Challenger* to the deepest point in the Pacific Ocean, 6.8 miles below sea level. The descent took 2.6 hours.

You can use this information and operations with negative rational numbers to find the average rate of descent.

$$\text{rate} = \frac{\text{distance}}{\text{time}} = \frac{-6.8 \text{ mi}}{2.6 \text{ h}} \approx -2.62 \text{ mi/h}$$

For this project, you can use any source in which you can find real-world data involving negative rational numbers. Create a presentation of four original real-world math problems involving negative rational numbers, including their solutions.

You should have one problem for each operation: addition, subtraction, multiplication, and division. Your presentation should include the sources for the information that you used. Use the space below to write down any questions you have or important information from your teacher.

MATH IN CAREERS | ACTIVITY

Urban Planner Armand is an urban planner, and he has proposed a site for a new town library. The site is between city hall and the post office on Main Street.

City hall — **Library site** — **Post office**

The distance between city hall and the post office is 6.5 miles. City hall is 1.25 miles closer to the library site than it is to the post office. Determine the distance from city hall to the library site and the distance from the post office to the library site.

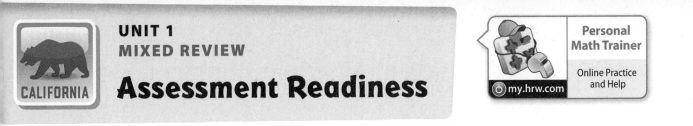

UNIT 1
MIXED REVIEW

Assessment Readiness

1. Look at each number or expression. Is its value equal to the rational number $\frac{-7}{12}$?

Select Yes or No.

A. $\frac{7}{-12}$ ○ Yes ○ No

B. $-7 \div 12$ ○ Yes ○ No

C. 0.583 ○ Yes ○ No

2. Choose True or False for A–D to indicate whether the model can represent $4 - (-3)$.

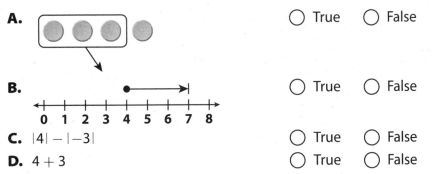

A. 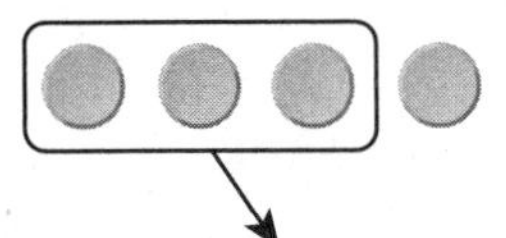 ○ True ○ False

B. ○ True ○ False

0 1 2 3 4 5 6 7 8

C. $|4| - |-3|$ ○ True ○ False

D. $4 + 3$ ○ True ○ False

3. A submarine starts at an elevation of –35 meters compared to sea level. It then makes 3 equal descents of 145 meters each. Is the final depth of the submarine greater than 500 meters? Explain how you solved this problem.

4. A website sells used comic books. The table shows how the price of *Painted Tiger,* Volume 1, has changed over the last 4 months. If the price started at $7.37, what is the current price? Explain how you know that your answer is reasonable.

Month	Change in Price ($)
1	+0.50
2	−0.38
3	+0.32
4	−0.12

Performance Tasks

★**5.** A trail has markers every $\frac{1}{8}$ mile. Jody starts at the $2\frac{1}{4}$-mile marker, hikes to the $4\frac{3}{8}$-mile marker, and then hikes back to the $1\frac{1}{2}$-mile marker. Did Jody hike more than 4 miles? Explain.

★★**6.** The table shows the bills that Rosemary has this month. She begins the month with $54.30 in her bank account.

Bill	Amount ($)
Phone	27.56
Dance uniform	65.95
Dance shoes	55.00

a. Without any deposits, what would be her bank account balance after paying her bills? What does the sign of your answer indicate?

b. Rosemary will babysit for a total of 14.5 hours this month. She earns $8 per hour. What would be the account balance after depositing all that she earns and paying all her bills?

c. Rosemary wants to buy a gift for her little brother this month. Should she buy a baseball glove for $22.95 or a T-shirt for $13.95? Use mathematics to justify your choice.

★★★**7.** The table shows the weekly change in the water level in a swimming pool. After 4 weeks, the pool owner adds water to return the water level back to the original level. Raising the water level by 1 inch requires 320 gallons. The water hose has a flow rate of 5.75 gallons of water per minute. Will it take less than an hour to fill the pool back to return the water level to the original level? Explain your reasoning.

Week	1	2	3	4
Change (in.)	$-\frac{1}{2}$	$+\frac{3}{4}$	$-1\frac{1}{8}$	$-1\frac{3}{8}$

UNIT 2

Ratios and Proportional Relationships

MODULE 4

Ratios and Proportionality

CA CC 7.RP.1, 7.RP.2, 7.RP.2a, 7.RP.2b, 7.RP.2c, 7.RP.2d

MODULE 5

Proportions and Percent

CA CC 7.RP.3, 7.EE.2, 7.EE.3

MATH IN CAREERS

Architect Architects create detailed construction plans for all types of buildings and structures. These detailed plans called blueprints show the building's appearance as well as details for its construction including plumbing and electrical systems. Architects use ratios and proportions to create blueprints. Other types of mathematics are used to analyze structural issues and ensure that the building remains standing and stable.

If you are interested in a career as an architect, you should study these mathematical subjects:

- Algebra
- Trigonometry
- Calculus
- Probability and Statistics

Research other careers that require the understanding of trigonometry.

ACTIVITY At the end of the unit, check out how **architects** use math.

Unit Project Preview

To Infinity (Almost)...and Beyond!

In the Unit Project at the end of this unit you will calculate the sizes of the Sun and planets in a scale model of the solar system. To successfully complete the Unit Project you'll need to master these skills:

- Write proportions.
- Solve proportions.
- Convert units.

Sun
Venus
Jupiter
Mercury
Uranus
Earth
Pluto
Mars
Saturn
Neptune

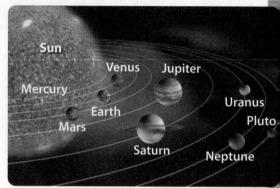

1. What is a scale model of an object?

____

____

____

2. Tony said that the school playground was 3,600 inches long. Explain how you could write 3,600 inches in a way that might be easier to understand.

____

____

____

____

Tracking Your Learning Progression

This unit addresses important California Common Core Standards in the Critical Area of developing understanding of and applying proportional relationships.

Domain 7.RP Ratios and Proportionality

Cluster Analyze proportional relationships and use them to solve real-world and mathematical problems.

The unit also supports additional standards.

Domain 7.EE Expressions and Equations

Cluster Solve real-life and mathematical problems using numerical and algebraic expressions and equations.

Ratios and Proportionality

ESSENTIAL QUESTION

How can you use rates and proportionality to solve real-world problems?

LESSON 4.1

Unit Rates

CA CC 7.RP.1

LESSON 4.2

Constant Rates of Change

CA CC 7.RP.2, 7.RP.2a, 7.RP.2b, 7.RP.2c

LESSON 4.3

Proportional Relationships and Graphs

CA CC 7.RP.2a, 7.RP.2b, 7.RP.2c, 7.RP.2d

Real-World Video

You can use rates to describe lots of real-world situations. A cyclist can compute rates such as miles per hour or rotations per minute.

my.hrw.com

GO DIGITAL
my.hrw.com

my.hrw.com

Go digital with your write-in student edition, accessible on any device.

Math On the Spot

Scan with your smart phone to jump directly to the online edition, video tutor, and more.

Animated Math

Interactively explore key concepts to see how math works.

Personal Math Trainer

Get immediate feedback and help as you work through practice sets.

Are YOU Ready?

Complete these exercises to review skills you will need for this module.

Personal Math Trainer
Online Practice and Help
my.hrw.com

Operations with Fractions

EXAMPLE $\frac{3}{10} \div \frac{5}{8} = \frac{3}{10} \times \frac{8}{5}$ Multiply by the reciprocal of the divisor.

$= \frac{3}{\cancel{10}_5} \times \frac{\cancel{8}^4}{5}$ Divide by the common factors.

$= \frac{12}{25}$ Simplify.

Divide.

1. $\frac{3}{4} \div \frac{4}{5}$ ______ **2.** $\frac{5}{9} \div \frac{10}{11}$ ______ **3.** $\frac{3}{8} \div \frac{1}{2}$ ______ **4.** $\frac{16}{21} \div \frac{8}{9}$ ______

Ordered Pairs

EXAMPLE

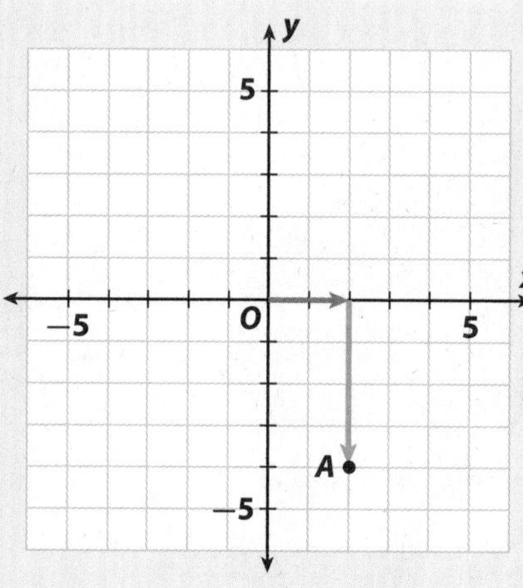

To write the ordered pair for *A*, start at the origin.
Move 2 units right.
Then move 4 units down.
The ordered pair for point *A* is (2, −4).

Write the ordered pair for each point.

5. *B* ______ **6.** *C* ______

7. *D* ______ **8.** *E* ______

9. *F* ______ **10.** *G* ______

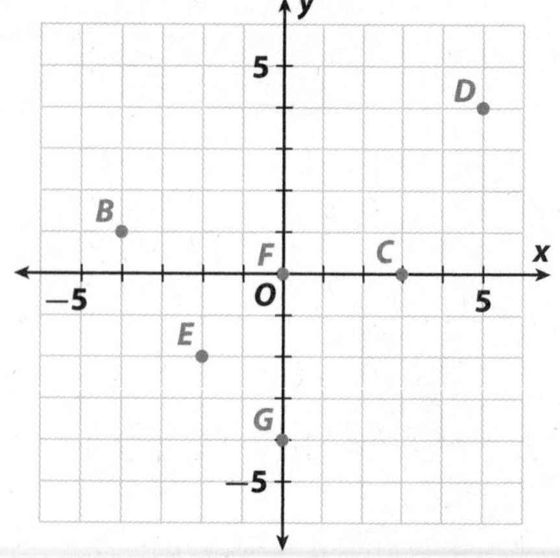

Reading Start-Up

Visualize Vocabulary

Use the ✔ words to complete the graphic. You can put more than one word in each bubble.

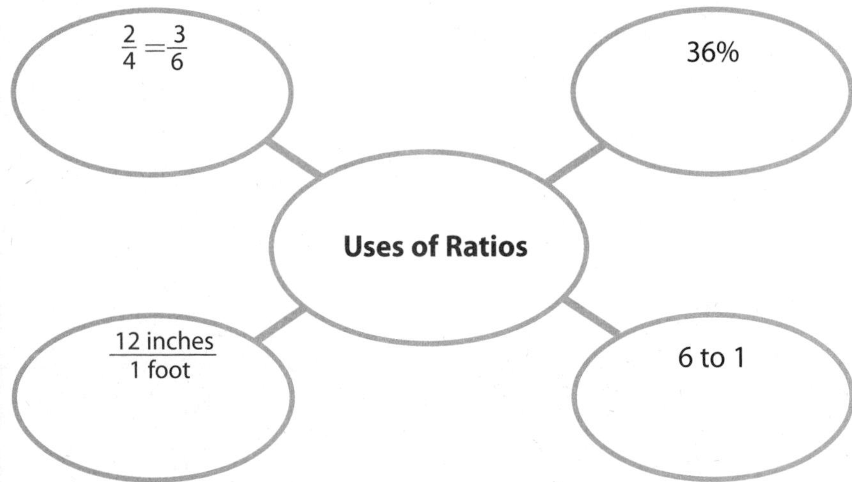

Vocabulary

Review Words

constant *(constante)*
✔ conversion factor *(factor de conversión)*
✔ equivalent ratios *(razones equivalentes)*
✔ percent *(porcentaje)*
rate *(tasa)*
✔ ratio *(razón)*

Preview Words

complex fraction *(fracción compleja)*
constant of proportionality *(constante de proporcionalidad)*
proportion *(proporción)*
proportional relationship *(relación proporcional)*
rate of change *(tasa de cambio)*
unit rates *(tasas unitarias)*

Understand Vocabulary

Match the term on the left to the definition on the right.

1. rate of change — **A.** Statement that two rates or ratios are equivalent.

2. proportion — **B.** A rate that describes how one quantity changes in relation to another quantity.

3. unit rate — **C.** Rate in which the second quantity is one unit.

Active Reading

Three-Panel Flip Chart Before beginning the module, create a three-panel flip chart to help you organize what you learn. Label each flap with one of the lesson titles from this module. As you study each lesson, write important ideas like vocabulary, properties, and formulas under the appropriate flap.

GETTING READY FOR

Ratios and Proportionality

Understanding the standards and the vocabulary terms in the standards will help you know exactly what you are expected to learn in this module.

 **CA CC 7.RP.1**

Compute unit rates associated with ratios of fractions, including ratios of lengths, areas and other quantities measured in like or different units.

Key Vocabulary

rate *(tasa)*
A ratio that compares two quantities measured in different units.

unit rate *(tasa unitaria)*
A rate in which the second quantity in the comparison is one unit.

What It Means to You

Given a rate, you can find the equivalent unit rate by dividing the numerator by the denominator.

EXAMPLE 7.RP.1

Lisa hikes $\frac{1}{3}$ mile every $\frac{1}{6}$ hour. How far does she hike in 1 hour?

$$\frac{\frac{1}{3}}{\frac{1}{6}} = \frac{1}{3} \div \frac{1}{6}$$

$$= \frac{1}{\cancel{3}_1} \cdot \frac{\cancel{6}^2}{1}$$

$$= 2 \text{ miles}$$

 **CA CC 7.RP.2b**

Identify the constant of proportionality (unit rate) in tables, graphs, equations, diagrams, and verbal descriptions of proportional relationships.

Key Vocabulary

constant *(constante)*
A value that does not change.

constant of proportionality *(constante de proporcionalidad)*
A constant ratio of two variables related proportionally.

What It Means to You

You will determine the constant of proportionality for proportional relationships.

EXAMPLE 7.RP.2b

The graph shows the distance a bicyclist travels over time. How fast does the bicyclist travel?

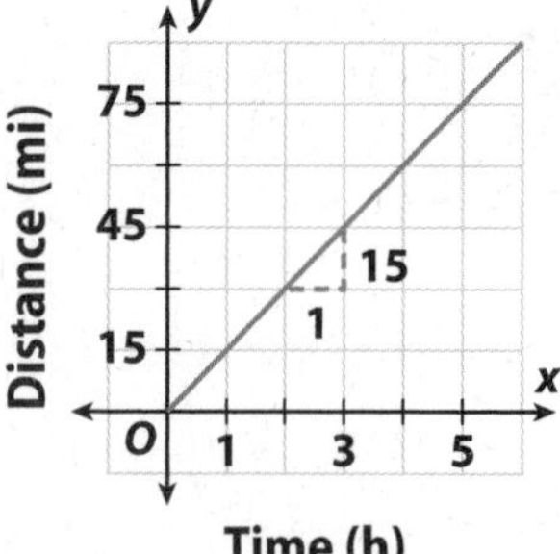

$$\text{slope (speed)} = \frac{\text{rise (distance)}}{\text{run (time)}}$$

$$= \frac{15}{1}$$

The bicyclist travels at 15 miles per hour.

The bicyclist's speed is a unit rate. It is indicated on the graphed line by the point (1, 15).

Visit **my.hrw.com** to see all **CA Common Core Standards** explained.

my.hrw.com

LESSON

4.1 Unit Rates

CA CC 7.RP.1

Compute unit rates associated with ratios of fractions, including ratios of lengths, areas and other quantities measured in like or different units.

ESSENTIAL QUESTION

How do you find and use unit rates?

EXPLORE ACTIVITY 

Exploring Rates

Commonly used rates like miles per hour make it easy to understand and compare rates.

Jeff hikes $\frac{1}{2}$ mile every 15 minutes, or $\frac{1}{4}$ hour. Lisa hikes $\frac{1}{3}$ mile every 10 minutes, or $\frac{1}{6}$ hour. How far do they each hike in 1 hour? 2 hours?

A Use the bar diagram to help you determine how many miles Jeff hikes. How many $\frac{1}{4}$-hours are in 1 hour? How far does Jeff hike in 1 hour?

? miles

$\frac{1}{4}$ hour	$\frac{1}{4}$ hour	$\frac{1}{4}$ hour	$\frac{1}{4}$ hour

$\frac{1}{2}$ mile

____

B Complete the table for Jeff's hike.

Distance (mi)	$\frac{1}{2}$				
Time (h)	$\frac{1}{4}$	$\frac{1}{2}$	$\frac{3}{4}$	1	2

C Complete the bar diagram to help you determine how far Lisa hikes. How many miles does she hike in 1 hour?

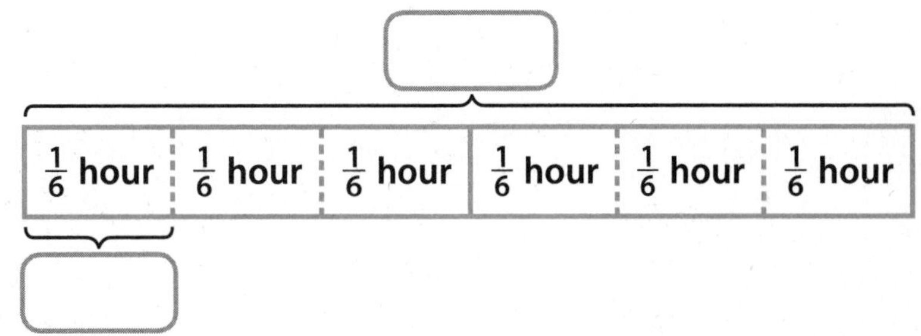

____

D Complete the table for Lisa's hike.

Distance (mi)	$\frac{1}{3}$				
Time (h)	$\frac{1}{6}$	$\frac{1}{3}$	$\frac{1}{2}$	1	2

EXPLORE ACTIVITY *(cont'd)*

Reflect

1. How did you find Jeff's distance for $\frac{3}{4}$ hour?

____

2. Which hiker walks farther in one hour? Which is faster?

____

Finding Unit Rates

A rate is a comparison of two quantities that have different units, such as miles and hours. Ratios and rates can be expressed as fractions. A rate or ratio with a denominator of 1 unit is called a **unit rate**.

$$\frac{60 \text{ miles} \div 2}{2 \text{ hours} \div 2} = \frac{30 \text{ miles}}{1 \text{ hour}}$$ This means 30 miles per hour.

When one or both of the quantities being compared in the rate is a fraction, the rate is expressed as a *complex fraction*.

$$\frac{15 \text{ miles}}{\frac{1}{2} \text{ hour}}$$ This means 15 miles per $\frac{1}{2}$ hour.

While remodeling her kitchen, Angela is repainting. She estimates that she paints 55 square feet every half-hour. How many square feet does Angela paint per hour?

Determine the units of the rate.

The rate is **area in square feet** per **time in hours**.

Find Angela's rate of painting in area painted per time.

area painted: 55 sq ft **time:** $\frac{1}{2}$ hour

$$\frac{\text{area painted}}{\text{time}} = \frac{55 \text{ square feet}}{\frac{1}{2} \text{ hour}}$$

The fraction represents area in square feet per time in hours.

STEP 3 Find Angela's unit rate of painting in square feet per hour.

$$\frac{55 \text{ square feet}}{\frac{1}{2} \text{ hour}} = 55 \div \frac{1}{2}$$ Rewrite the fraction as division.

$$= \frac{55}{1} \times \frac{2}{1}$$ Multiply by the reciprocal.

$$= \frac{110 \text{ square feet}}{1 \text{ hour}}$$ The unit rate has a denominator of 1.

Angela paints 110 square feet per hour.

YOUR TURN

3. Paige mows $\frac{1}{6}$ acre in $\frac{1}{4}$ hour. How many acres does Paige mow per hour?

____

4. Greta uses 3 cups of pasta for every $\frac{3}{4}$ cup of sauce. How much pasta does she use per cup of sauce? _______________

Using Unit Rates

You can use unit rates to simplify rates and ratios that appear complicated, such as those containing fractions in both the numerator and denominator.

Math On the Spot
my.hrw.com

EXAMPLE 2

Two pools are leaking. After 15 minutes, pool A has leaked $\frac{2}{3}$ gallon. After 20 minutes, pool B has leaked $\frac{3}{4}$ gallon. Which pool is leaking faster?

STEP 1 Find the rate in volume (gallons) per time (hours) at which each pool is leaking. First convert minutes to hours.

Pool A

$$\frac{\frac{2}{3}\text{ gal}}{15\text{ min}} = \frac{\frac{2}{3}\text{ gal}}{\frac{1}{4}\text{ h}}$$

15 min $= \frac{1}{4}$ h

Pool B

$$\frac{\frac{3}{4}\text{ gal}}{20\text{ min}} = \frac{\frac{3}{4}\text{ gal}}{\frac{1}{3}\text{ h}}$$

20 min $= \frac{1}{3}$ h

STEP 2 To find the unit rates, first rewrite the fractions.

Pool A

$$\frac{\frac{2}{3}\text{ gal}}{\frac{1}{4}\text{ h}} = \frac{2}{3} \div \frac{1}{4}$$

Pool B

$$\frac{\frac{3}{4}\text{ gal}}{\frac{1}{3}\text{ h}} = \frac{3}{4} \div \frac{1}{3}$$

STEP 3 To divide, multiply by the reciprocal.

Pool A

$$\frac{2}{3} \div \frac{1}{4} = \frac{2}{3} \times \frac{4}{1}$$
$$= \frac{8}{3}\text{, or } 2\frac{2}{3}\text{ gal per h}$$

Pool B

$$\frac{3}{4} \div \frac{1}{3} = \frac{3}{4} \times \frac{3}{1}$$
$$= \frac{9}{4}\text{, or } 2\frac{1}{4}\text{ gal per h}$$

STEP 4 Compare the unit rates.

Pool A **Pool B**

$$2\frac{2}{3} > 2\frac{1}{4}$$

So, Pool A is leaking faster.

My Notes

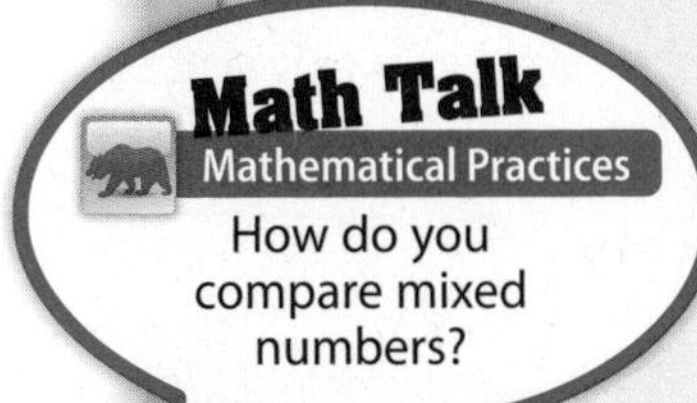

Math Talk
Mathematical Practices
How do you compare mixed numbers?

YOUR TURN

5. Jaylan makes limeade using $\frac{3}{4}$ cup water per $\frac{1}{5}$ cup lime juice. Wanchen makes limeade using $\frac{2}{3}$ cup water per $\frac{1}{6}$ cup lime juice. Find the unit rates of water (cups) per lime juice (cups). Whose limeade has a weaker lime flavor? Explain.

Guided Practice

1. Brandon enters bike races. He bikes $8\frac{1}{2}$ miles every $\frac{1}{2}$ hour. Complete the table to find how far Brandon bikes for each time interval. (Explore Activity)

Distance (mi)	$8\frac{1}{2}$				
Time (h)	$\frac{1}{2}$	1	$1\frac{1}{2}$	2	$2\frac{1}{2}$

Find each unit rate. (Example 1)

2. Julio walks $3\frac{1}{2}$ miles in $1\frac{1}{4}$ hours.

3. Kenny reads $\frac{5}{8}$ page in $\frac{2}{3}$ minute.

4. A garden snail moves $\frac{1}{6}$ foot in $\frac{1}{3}$ hour.

5. A machine covers $\frac{5}{8}$ square foot in $\frac{1}{4}$ hour.

Find each unit rate. Determine which is lower. (Example 2)

6. Brand A: 240 mg sodium for $\frac{1}{3}$ pickle
or Brand B: 325 mg sodium for $\frac{1}{2}$ pickle

7. Ingredient C: $\frac{1}{4}$ cup for $\frac{2}{3}$ serving
or Ingredient D: $\frac{1}{3}$ cup for $\frac{3}{4}$ serving

ESSENTIAL QUESTION CHECK-IN

8. How can you find a unit rate when given a rate?

Name ______________________ Class ______________ Date ______________

4.1 Independent Practice

CA CC 7.RP.1

9. The information for two pay-as-you-go cell phone companies is given.

On Call	Talk Time
3.5 hours: $10	$\frac{1}{2}$ hour: $1.25

a. What is the unit rate in dollars per hour for each company?

____

____

b. **Analyze Relationships** Which company offers the best deal? Explain your answer.

____

____

c. **What If?** Another company offers a rate of $0.05 per minute. How would you find the unit rate per hour?

____

____

d. **Draw Conclusions** Is the rate in part **c** a better deal than On Call or Talk Time? Explain.

____

____

10. **Represent Real-World Problems** Your teacher asks you to find a recipe that includes two ingredients with a ratio of $\frac{\frac{1}{2}\text{ cup}}{\frac{1}{8}\text{ cup}}$.

a. Give an example of two ingredients in a recipe that would meet this requirement.

____

____

____

b. If you needed to triple the recipe, would the ratio change? Explain.

____

____

____

c. What is the unit rate of the ingredients in your recipe?

____

____

11. A radio station requires DJs to play 2 commercials for every 10 songs they play. What is the unit rate of songs to commercials?

____

12. **Multistep** Terrance and Jesse are training for a long-distance race. Terrance trains at a rate of 6 miles every half hour, and Jesse trains at a rate of 2 miles every 15 minutes.

a. What is the unit rate in miles per hour for each runner?

____

____

b. How long will each person take to run a total of 50 miles at the given rates?

____

____

c. Sandra runs at a rate of 8 miles in 45 minutes. How does her unit rate compare to Terrance's and to Jesse's?

____

____

13. **Analyze Relationships** Eli takes a typing test and types all 300 words in $\frac{1}{10}$ hour. He takes the test a second time and types the words in $\frac{1}{12}$ hour. Was he faster or slower on the second attempt? Explain.

____

____

H.O.T. FOCUS ON HIGHER ORDER THINKING

Work Area

14. **Justify Reasoning** An online retailer sells two packages of protein bars.

Package	10-pack of 2.1 ounce bars	12-pack of 1.4 ounce bars
Cost ($)	15.37	15.35

a. Which package has the better price per bar?

____

____

____

b. Which package has the better price per ounce?

____

____

____

c. Which package do you think is a better buy? Justify your reasoning.

____

____

15. **Check for Reasonableness** A painter painted about half a room in half a day. Coley estimated the painter would paint 7 rooms in 7 days. Is Coley's estimate reasonable? Explain.

____

____

16. **Communicate Mathematical Ideas** If you know the rate of a water leak in gallons per hour, how can you find the number of hours it takes for 1 gallon to leak out? Justify your answer.

____

____

____

LESSON 4.2

Constant Rates of Change

Recognize and represent proportional relationships between quantities. Also *7.RP.2a, 7.RP.2b, 7.RP.2c*

ESSENTIAL QUESTION

How can you identify and represent proportional relationships?

EXPLORE ACTIVITY 

Discovering Proportional Relationships

It takes a giant tortoise 3 seconds to travel 10.5 inches.

A The diagram shows the rate at which one tortoise moves. Use the diagram to determine if the tortoise is moving at a steady pace. Explain.

____

____

B What unit rate is represented in the diagram?

____

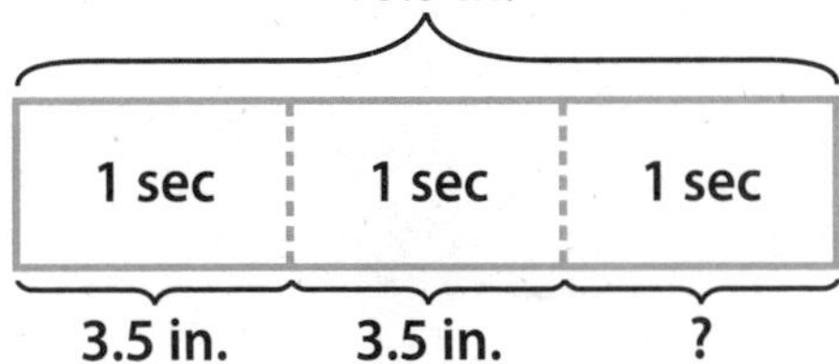

C Complete the table.

Time (sec)	1	2	3	4	5
Distance (in.)			10.5		

D For each column of the table, write a rate that compares the distance and the time. Put distance in the numerator and time in the denominator. Divide to write the rate as a decimal.

E What do you notice about the decimal forms of the rates?

____

F **Conjecture** How do you think the distance the tortoise travels is related to the time?

____

EXPLORE ACTIVITY *(cont'd)*

Reflect

1. Suppose the tortoise travels for 12 seconds. Explain how you could find the distance the tortoise travels.

____

2. How would you describe the rate of speed at which a tortoise travels?

____

Proportional Relationships

A **proportion** is a statement that two rates or ratios are equivalent. For example, $\frac{6\text{ mi}}{2\text{ h}} = \frac{3\text{ mi}}{1\text{ h}}$, or $\frac{2}{4} = \frac{1}{2}$.

A **rate of change** is a rate that describes how one quantity changes in relation to another quantity. A **proportional relationship** between two quantities is one in which the rate of change is constant or one in which the ratio of one quantity to the other is constant.

Proportional relationships are often described using words such as *per* or *for each*. For example, the rate $\frac{\$1.25}{1\text{ pound}}$ could be described as \$1.25 per pound or \$1.25 for each pound.

My Notes

EXAMPLE 1

7.RP.2a, 7.RP.2b

Callie earns money by dog sitting. Based on the table, is the relationship between the amount Callie earns and the number of days a proportional relationship?

Number of Days	1	2	3	4	5
Amount Earned ($)	16	32	48	64	80

STEP 1 Write the rates.

$\frac{\text{Amount earned}}{\text{Number of days}} = \frac{\$16}{1\text{ day}}$ — *Put the amount earned in the numerator and the number of days in the denominator.*

$\frac{\$32}{2\text{ days}} = \frac{\$16}{1\text{ day}}$

$\frac{\$48}{3\text{ days}} = \frac{\$16}{1\text{ day}}$ — *Each rate is equal to $\frac{\$16}{1\text{ day}}$, or \$16 per day.*

$\frac{\$64}{4\text{ days}} = \frac{\$16}{1\text{ day}}$

$\frac{\$80}{5\text{ days}} = \frac{\$16}{1\text{ day}}$

STEP 2 Compare the rates. The rates are all equal. This means the rate is constant, so the relationship is proportional.

The constant rate of change is \$16 per day.

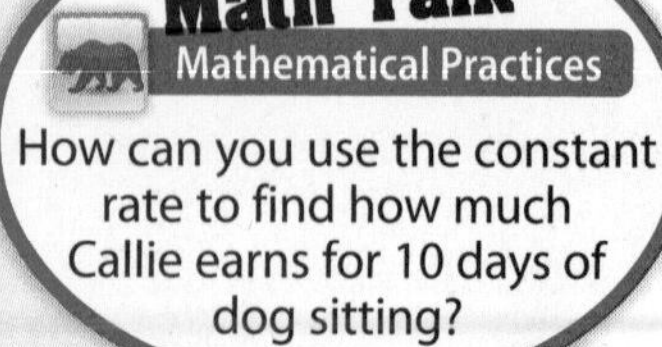

How can you use the constant rate to find how much Callie earns for 10 days of dog sitting?

3. The table shows the distance Allison drove on one day of her vacation. Is the relationship between the distance and the time a proportional relationship? Did she drive at a constant speed? Explain.

Time (h)	1	2	3	4	5
Distance (mi)	65	120	195	220	300

____

Writing an Equation for a Proportional Relationship

If there is a proportional relationship between x and y, you can describe that relationship using the equation $y = kx$. The variable k is called the **constant of proportionality**, and it represents the constant rate of change or constant ratio between x and y. The value of k is represented by the equation $k = \frac{y}{x}$.

EXAMPLE 2 

Two pounds of the cashews shown cost $19, and 8 pounds cost $76. Show that the relationship between the number of pounds of cashews and the cost is a proportional relationship. Then write an equation for the relationship. Describe the proportional relationship in words.

Make a table relating cost in dollars to pounds.

Number of Pounds	2	3	8
Cost ($)	19	28.50	76

Write the rates. Put cost in the numerator and pounds in the denominator. Write each rate as a decimal.

$$\frac{\text{Cost}}{\text{Number of Pounds}} \longrightarrow \frac{19}{2} = 9.50 \qquad \frac{28.50}{3} = 9.50 \qquad \frac{76}{8} = 9.50$$

The rates are all equal to $9.50 per pound. They are constant, so the relationship is proportional. The constant rate of change is $9.50 per pound.

To write an equation, first tell what the variables represent.

- Let x represent the number of pounds of cashews.
- Let y represent the cost in dollars.
- Use the decimal form of the constant rate of change as the constant of proportionality.

The equation for the relationship is $y = 9.5x$.

The cost is $9.50 per pound.

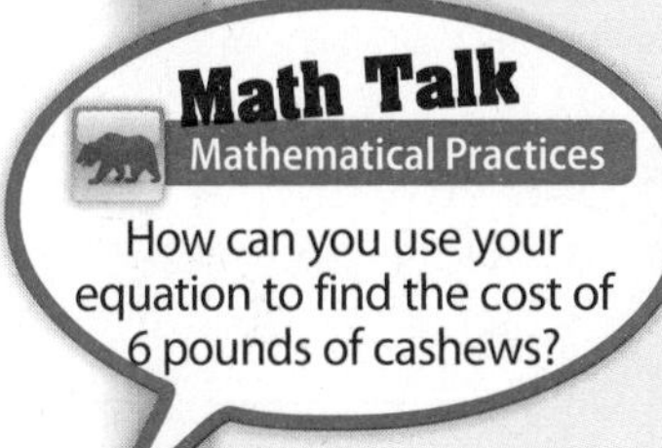

Math Talk
Mathematical Practices
How can you use your equation to find the cost of 6 pounds of cashews?

YOUR TURN

4. For a school field trip, there must be 1 adult to accompany 12 students, 3 adults to accompany 36 students, and 5 adults to accompany 60 students. Show that the relationship between the number of adults and the number of students is a proportional relationship. Then write an equation for the relationship.

Number of students	12	36	60
Number of adults	1	3	5

____

____

Guided Practice

1. Based on the information in the table, is the relationship between time and the number of words typed a proportional relationship? (Explore Activity and Example 1)

Time (min)	1	2	3	4
Number of words	45	90	135	180

$\frac{\text{Number of words}}{\text{Minutes}}$: $\frac{45}{1} = \square$ $\frac{\square}{\square} = \square$ $\frac{\square}{\square} = \square$ $\frac{\square}{\square} = \square$

The relationship **is / is not** proportional.

Find the constant of proportionality *k*. Then write an equation for the relationship between *x* and *y*. (Example 2)

2.

x	2	4	6	8
y	10	20	30	40

____

3.

x	8	16	24	32
y	2	4	6	8

____

ESSENTIAL QUESTION CHECK-IN

4. How can you represent a proportional relationship using an equation?

____

____

Name ______________________ Class ______________________ Date ______________________

4.2 Independent Practice

 CA CC 7.RP.2, 7.RP.2a, 7.RP.2b, 7.RP.2c

Information on three car-rental companies is given.

Rent-All				
Days	3	4	5	6
Total Cost ($)	55.50	74.00	92.50	111.00

A-1 Rentals
The cost y of renting a car for x days is $10.99 for each half day.

Car Town
The cost of renting a car from us is just $19.25 per day!

5. Write an equation that gives the cost y of renting a car for x days from Rent-All. ______________

6. What is the cost per day of renting a car from A-1? ______________

7. **Analyze Relationships** Which company offers the best deal? Why?

____

____

8. **Critique Reasoning** A skydiver jumps out of an airplane. After 0.8 second, she has fallen 100 feet. After 3.1 seconds, she has fallen 500 feet. Emtiaz says that the skydiver should fall about 187.5 feet in 1.5 seconds. Is his answer reasonable? Explain.

____

____

____

Steven earns extra money babysitting. He charges $31.25 for 5 hours and $50 for 8 hours.

9. Explain why the relationship between how much Steven charges and time is a proportional relationship.

____

10. **Interpret the Answer** Explain what the constant rate of change means in this context.

____

11. Write an equation to represent the relationship. Tell what the variables represent.

____

____

12. How much would Steven charge for 3 hours? ______________

A submarine dives 300 feet every 2 minutes, and 6,750 feet every 45 minutes.

13. Find the constant rate at which the submarine dives. Give your answer in feet per minute and in feet per hour.

____

14. Let x represent the time of the dive. Let y represent the depth of the submarine. Write an equation for the proportional relationship using the rate in feet per minute.

____

15. **Draw Conclusions** If you wanted to find the depth of a submarine during a dive, would it be more reasonable to use an equation with the rate in feet per minute or feet per hour? Explain your reasoning.

____

____

FOCUS ON HIGHER ORDER THINKING

Work Area

16. **Make a Conjecture** There is a proportional relationship between your distance from a thunderstorm and the amount of time that elapses between the time you see lightning and the time you hear thunder. If there are 9 seconds between lightning and thunder, the storm is about 3 kilometers away. If you double the amount of time between lightning and thunder, do you think the distance in kilometers also doubles? Justify your reasoning.

____

____

____

____

17. **Communicate Mathematical Ideas** A store sells 3 ears of corn for \$1. They round prices to the nearest cent as shown in the table. Tell whether you would describe the relationship between cost and number of ears of corn as a proportional relationship. Justify your answer.

Ears of corn	1	2	3	4
Amount charged (\$)	0.33	0.67	1.00	1.34

____

____

____

LESSON 4.3

Proportional Relationships and Graphs

7.RP.2a

Decide whether two quantities are in a proportional relationship. *Also 7.RP.2, 7.RP.2b, 7.RP.2c, 7.RP.2d, 7.RP.3*

ESSENTIAL QUESTION

How can you use graphs to represent and analyze proportional relationships?

EXPLORE ACTIVITY Real World

7.RP.2a, 7.RP.2b, 7.RP.2d

Graphing Proportional Relationships

The equation $y = 5x$ represents the relationship between the number of gallons of water used (y) and the number of minutes (x) for most showerheads manufactured before 1994.

A Explain why the relationship is proportional. How does the equation represent the constant of proportionality?

____

____

B Complete the table.

Time (min)	1	2	3		10
Water used (gal)	5			35	

Each minute, 5 gallons of water are used. So for 2 minutes, $2 \cdot 5$ gallons are used.

C Write the data in the table as ordered pairs (time, water used).

(1, 5), (2, ___), (3, ___), (__ , 35), (10, ___)

D Plot the ordered pairs.

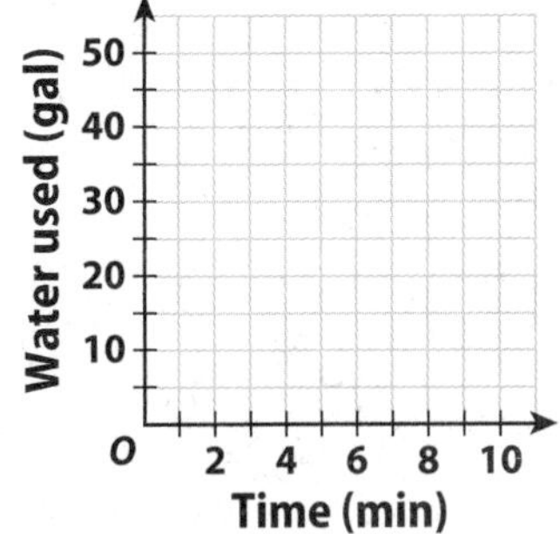

E If the showerhead is used for 0 minutes, how many gallons of water will be used? What ordered pair represents this situation? What is this location called? ______________________

F If the showerhead is used for 1 minute, how many gallons of water will be used? What ordered pair represents this situation? What does this point represent?

____

G **Draw Conclusions** If you continued the table to include 23 minutes, would the point (23, 125) be on this graph? Why or why not?

____

Identifying Proportional Relationships

In addition to using a table to determine if a relationship is proportional, you also can use a graph. A relationship is a proportional relationship if its graph is a straight line through the origin.

EXAMPLE 1

The table shows the relationship between the amount charged by a housecleaning company ($) and the amount of time worked (hours). Is the relationship a proportional relationship? Explain.

Time (h)	1	2	3	5	8
Total cost ($)	45	90	135	225	360

STEP 1 Write the data in the table as ordered pairs (time, cost).

(1, 45), (2, 90), (3, 135), (5, 225), (8, 360)

STEP 2 Graph the ordered pairs.

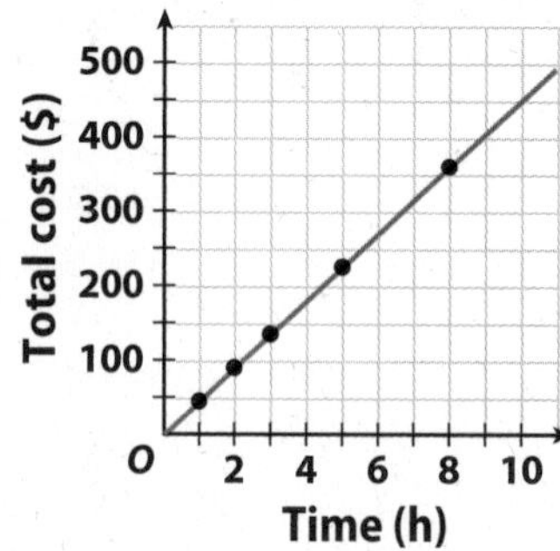

Place time on the x-axis and total cost on the y-axis.

Plot each point.

Notice that the points are on a line.

The graph is a line that goes through the origin.

The relationship is proportional. The point (1, 45) on the graph shows that the constant of proportionality, or unit rate, is $45 for 1 hour.

The housecleaning company charges $45 per hour.

YOUR TURN

1. Jared rents bowling shoes for $6 and pays $5 per bowling game. Is the relationship a proportional relationship? Explain.

Games	1	2	3	4
Total cost ($)	11	16	21	26

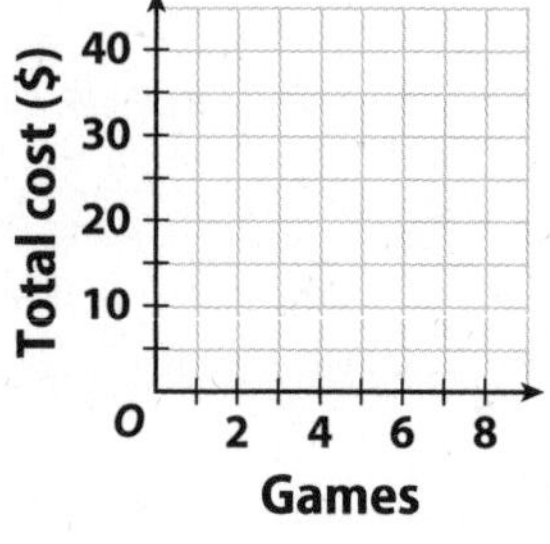

____

____

Analyzing Graphs

Recall that you can describe a proportional relationship with the equation $y = kx$. The constant of proportionality k tells you how steep the graph of the relationship is. The greater the absolute value of k, the steeper the line.

Math On the Spot
my.hrw.com

EXAMPLE 2 

CA CC 7.RP.2, 7.RP.3

The graph shows the relationship between time in minutes and the number of miles Damon runs. Write an equation for this relationship.

STEP 1 Choose a point on the graph and tell what the point represents.

The point (25, 2.5) represents the distance (2.5 miles) that Damon runs in 25 minutes.

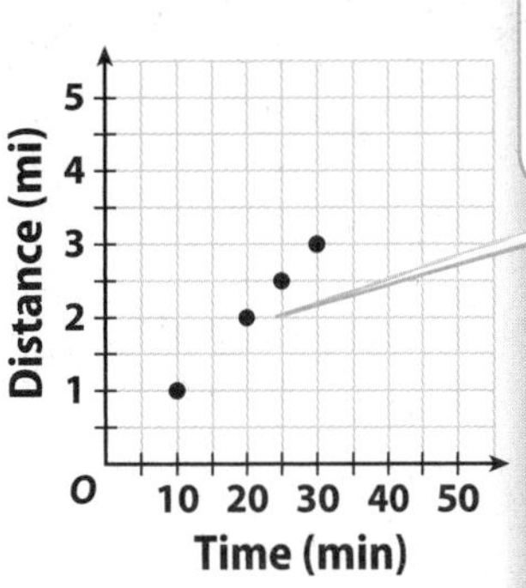

The points appear to form a line through the origin, so the relationship is proportional.

STEP 2 What is the constant of proportionality?

Because $\frac{\text{distance}}{\text{time}} = \frac{2.5 \text{ mi}}{25 \text{ min}} = \frac{1}{10}$, the constant of proportionality is $\frac{1}{10}$.

STEP 3 Write an equation in the form $y = kx$. $y = \frac{1}{10}x$

Reflect

2. What does the point (0, 0) on the graph represent? $(1, \frac{1}{10})$?

____

3. **What If?** Suppose you drew a graph representing the relationship $y = \frac{1}{8}x$ between time in minutes and the number of miles Esther runs. How would the graph compare to the one for Damon? Explain.

____

4. Use your equation to find how far Damon runs in 40 minutes. How long would it take him to run 7.5 miles?

____

What is the meaning of the point on the graph in Exercise 5 with x-coordinate 1?

YOUR TURN

5. The graph shows the relationship between the distance a bicyclist travels and the time in hours.

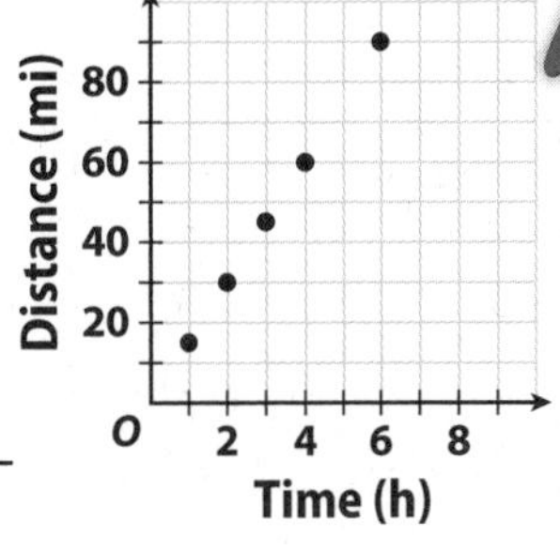

a. What does the point (4, 60) represent?

____

b. What is the constant of proportionality? __________

c. Write an equation in the form $y = kx$ for this relationship. __________

Personal Math Trainer
Online Practice and Help
my.hrw.com

Guided Practice

For each situation, tell whether the relationship is a proportional relationship. Explain why or why not. (Explore Activity)

1. The table shows the number of pages a student reads in various amounts of time.

Time (h)	3	5	9	10
Pages	195	325	585	650

2. The amount a babysitter earns is given by the equation $y = 7.5x$ where x is the number of hours and y is the amount earned in dollars.

Tell whether the relationship is a proportional relationship. Explain why or why not. (Explore Activity and Example 1)

3.

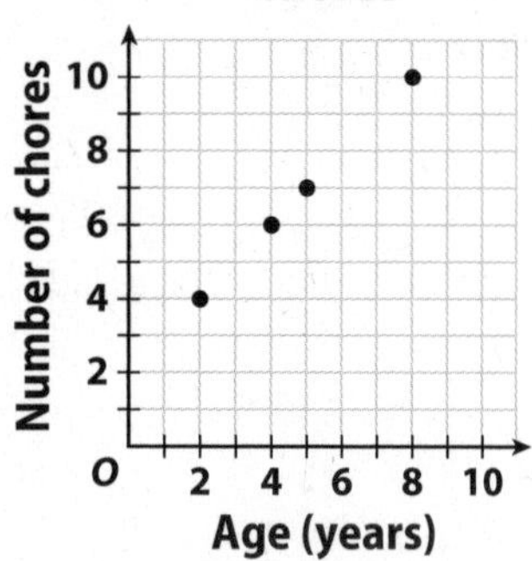

4.

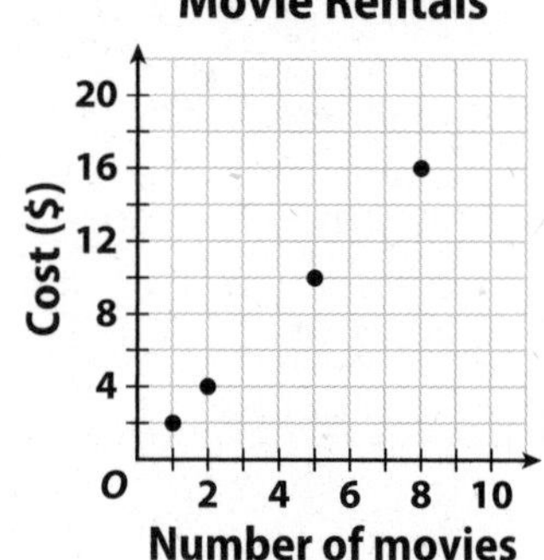

Write an equation of the form $y = kx$ for the relationship shown in each graph. (Example 2)

5.

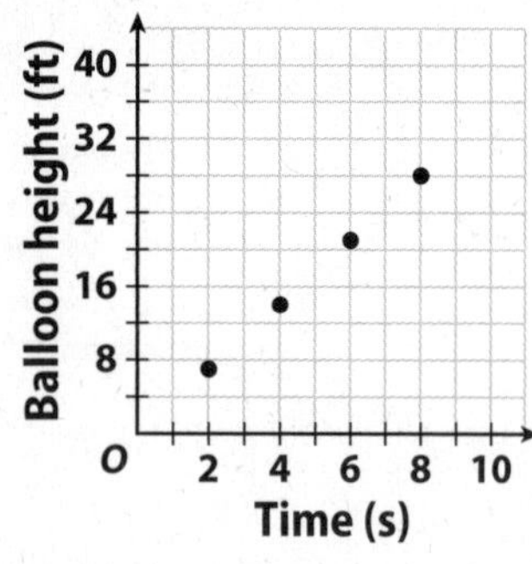

6.

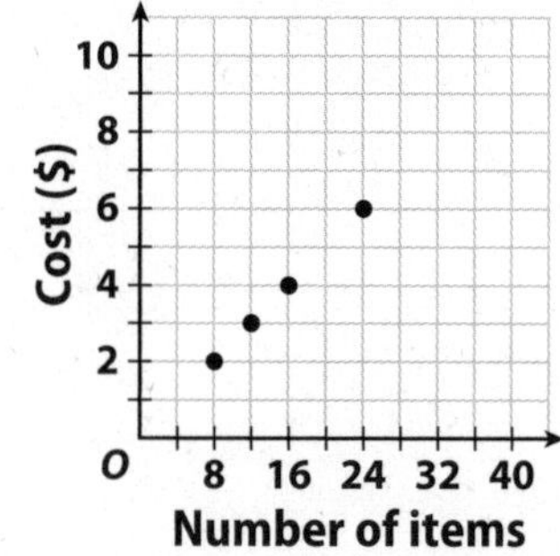

ESSENTIAL QUESTION CHECK-IN

7. How does a graph show a proportional relationship?

Name ______________________ Class ______________ Date ______________

4.3 Independent Practice

CA CC 7.RP.2, 7.RP.2a, 7.RP.2b, 7.RP.2c, 7.RP.2d, 7.RP.3

For Exercises 8–12, the graph shows the relationship between time and distance run by two horses.

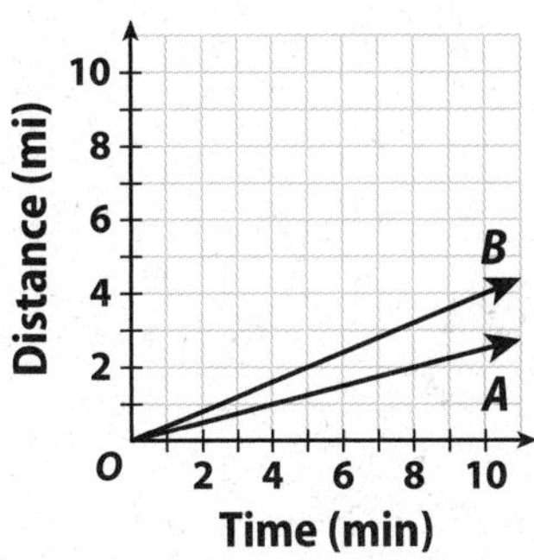

8. Explain the meaning of the point (0, 0).

____

____

9. How long does it take each horse to run a mile?

____

____

10. **Multiple Representations** Write an equation for the relationship between time and distance for each horse.

____

11. **Draw Conclusions** At the given rates, how far would each horse run in 12 minutes?

____

____

12. **Analyze Relationships** Draw a line on the graph representing a horse than runs faster than horses A and B.

____

____

13. A bullet train can travel at 170 miles per hour. Will a graph representing distance in miles compared to time in hours show a proportional relationship? Explain.

____

____

____

____

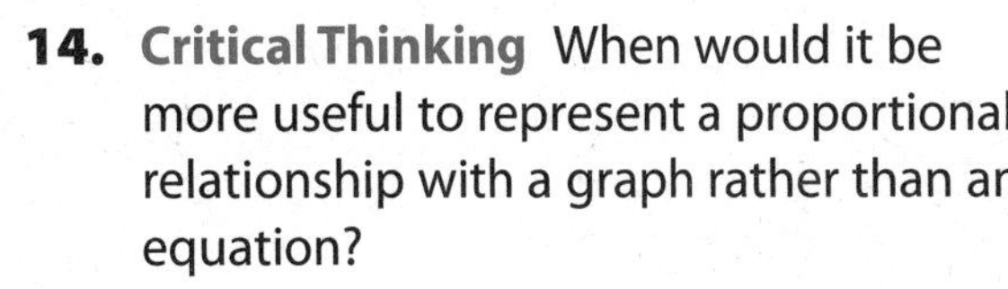

14. **Critical Thinking** When would it be more useful to represent a proportional relationship with a graph rather than an equation?

____

____

____

15. **Multiple Representations** Bargain DVDs cost $5 each at Mega Movie.

a. Graph the proportional relationship that gives the cost y in dollars of buying x bargain DVDs.

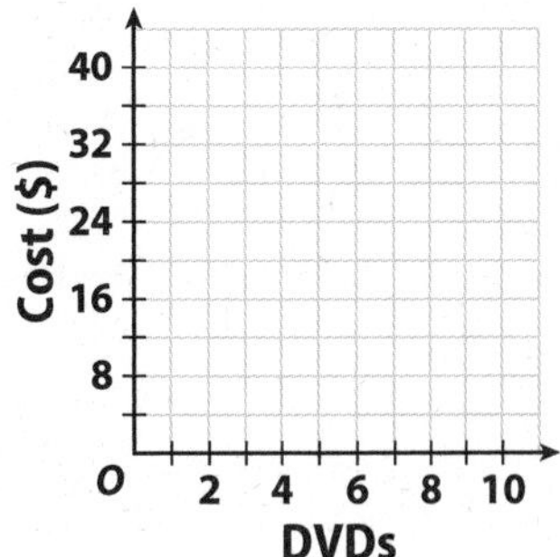

b. Give an ordered pair on the graph and explain its meaning in the real world context.

____

____

The graph shows the relationship between distance and time as Glenda swims.

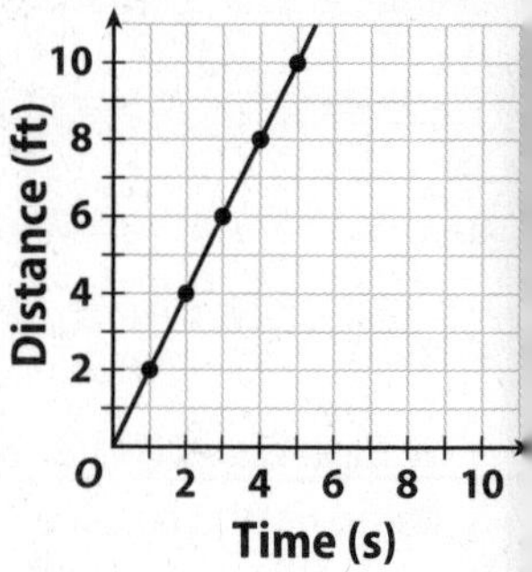

16. How far did Glenda swim in 4 seconds? ______

17. Communicate Mathematical Ideas Is this a proportional relationship? Explain your reasoning.

______

18. Multiple Representations Write an equation that shows the relationship between time and distance. Use your equation to find how long it would take in minutes for Glenda to swim $\frac{1}{2}$ mile at this rate. ______

H.O.T. FOCUS ON HIGHER ORDER THINKING

Work Area

19. Make a Conjecture If you know that a relationship is proportional and are given one ordered pair that is not (0, 0), how can you find another pair?

______

______

______

______

The tables show the distance traveled by three cars.

Car 1	
Time (h)	Distance (mi)
0	0
2	120
3	180
5	300
6	360

Car 2	
Time (h)	Distance (mi)
0	0
5	200
10	400
15	600
20	800

Car 3	
Time (h)	Distance (mi)
0	0
1	65
2	85
3	105
4	125

20. Communicate Mathematical Ideas Which car is not traveling at a constant speed? Explain your reasoning.

______

______

21. Make a Conjecture Car 4 is traveling at twice the rate of speed of car 2. How will the table values for car 4 compare to the table values for car 2?

______

______

______

MODULE QUIZ

Ready to Go On?

4.1 Unit Rates

Find each unit rate. Round to the nearest hundredth, if necessary.

1. \$140 for 18 ft^2 ________________

2. 14 lb for \$2.99 ________________

Circle the better deal in each pair. Then give the unit rate for the better deal.

3. $\frac{\$56}{25\text{ gal}}$ or $\frac{\$32.05}{15\text{ gal}}$ ________________

4. $\frac{\$160}{5\text{ g}}$ or $\frac{\$315}{9\text{ g}}$ ________________

4.2 Constant Rates of Change

5. The table shows the amount of money Tyler earns for mowing lawns. Is the relationship a proportional relationship? Why or why not?

Number of Lawns	1	2	3	4
Amount Earned ($)	15	30	48	64

____

6. On a recent day, 8 euros were worth \$9 and 24 euros were worth \$27. Write an equation of the form $y = kx$ to show the relationship between the number of euros and the value in dollars.

____________, where y is dollars and x is euros

4.3 Proportional Relationships and Graphs

7. The graph shows the number of servings in different amounts of frozen yogurt listed on a carton. Write an equation that gives the number of servings y in x pints.

____

8. A refreshment stand makes 2 large servings of frozen yogurt from 3 pints. Add the line to the graph and write its equation.

____

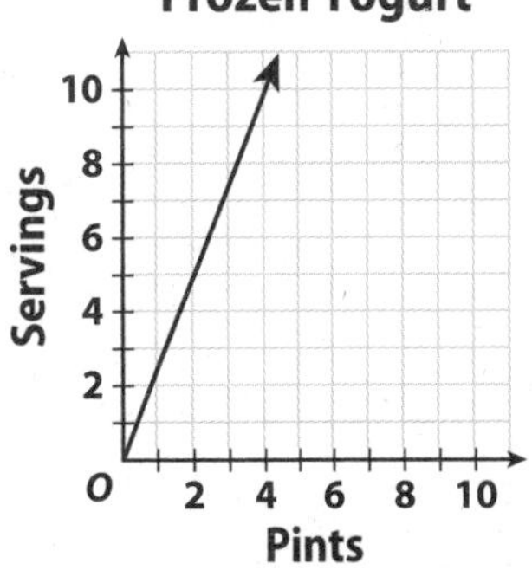

ESSENTIAL QUESTION

9. How can you use rates to determine whether a situation is a proportional relationship?

____

____

MODULE 4
MIXED REVIEW

Assessment Readiness

1. Consider each ratio. Is the ratio equivalent to a unit rate of $\frac{1}{4}$ cup of milk per cup of flour?

Select Yes or No for expressions A–C.

A. $\frac{1}{2}$ cup of milk per 2 cups of flour ◯ Yes ◯ No

B. $1\frac{1}{2}$ cups of milk per 4 cups of flour ◯ Yes ◯ No

C. $1\frac{3}{4}$ cups of milk per 7 cups of flour ◯ Yes ◯ No

2. Consider the number $-\frac{9}{20}$.

Choose True or False for each statement.

A. The number is rational. ◯ True ◯ False

B. The number can be written as a repeating decimal. ◯ True ◯ False

C. The number is less than −0.4. ◯ True ◯ False

3. The graph shows the relationship between the gallons of water a sprinkler system uses and the number of minutes the system is used. Write an equation for this relationship. Explain how you determined your answer.

Amount of water (gal)
y
48
36
24
12
O
2 4 6
x
Time (min)

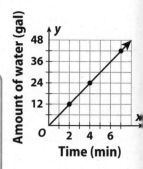

4. A blimp travels 765 feet in $\frac{1}{4}$ minute, 1,530 feet in $\frac{1}{2}$ minute, and 3,060 feet in 1 minute. Is there a proportional relationship between the distance the blimp travels and the time it travels? Justify your answer.

Proportions and Percent

ESSENTIAL QUESTION

How can you use proportions and percent to solve real-world problems?

my.hrw.com

Real-World Video

A store may have a sale with deep discounts on some items. They can still make a profit because they first markup the wholesale price by as much as 400%, then markdown the retail price.

GO DIGITAL
my.hrw.com

my.hrw.com

Go digital with your write-in student edition, accessible on any device.

Math On the Spot

Scan with your smart phone to jump directly to the online edition, video tutor, and more.

Animated Math

Interactively explore key concepts to see how math works.

Personal Math Trainer

Get immediate feedback and help as you work through practice sets.

Are YOU Ready?

Complete these exercises to review skills you will need for this module.

Percents and Decimals

EXAMPLE $147\% = 100\% + 47\%$ — *Write the percent as the sum of 1 whole and a percent remainder.*

$= \frac{100}{100} + \frac{47}{100}$ — *Write the percents as fractions.*

$= 1 + 0.47$ — *Write the fractions as decimals.*

$= 1.47$ — *Simplify.*

Write each percent as a decimal.

1. 22% _______ **2.** 75% _______ **3.** 6% _______ **4.** 189% _______

Write each decimal as a percent.

5. 0.59 _______ **6.** 0.98 _______ **7.** 0.02 _______ **8.** 1.33 _______

Find the Percent of a Number

EXAMPLE $30\% \text{ of } 45 = ?$

$30\% = 0.30$ — *Write the percent as a decimal.*

$$\begin{array}{r} 45 \\ \times 0.3 \\ \hline 13.5 \end{array}$$

Multiply.

Find the percent of each number.

9. 50% of 64 _______ **10.** 7% of 30 _______ **11.** 15% of 160 _______

12. 32% of 62 _______ **13.** 120% of 4 _______ **14.** 6% of 1,000 _______

Reading Start-Up

Visualize Vocabulary

Use the ✔ words to complete the triangle. Write the review word that fits the description in each section of the triangle.

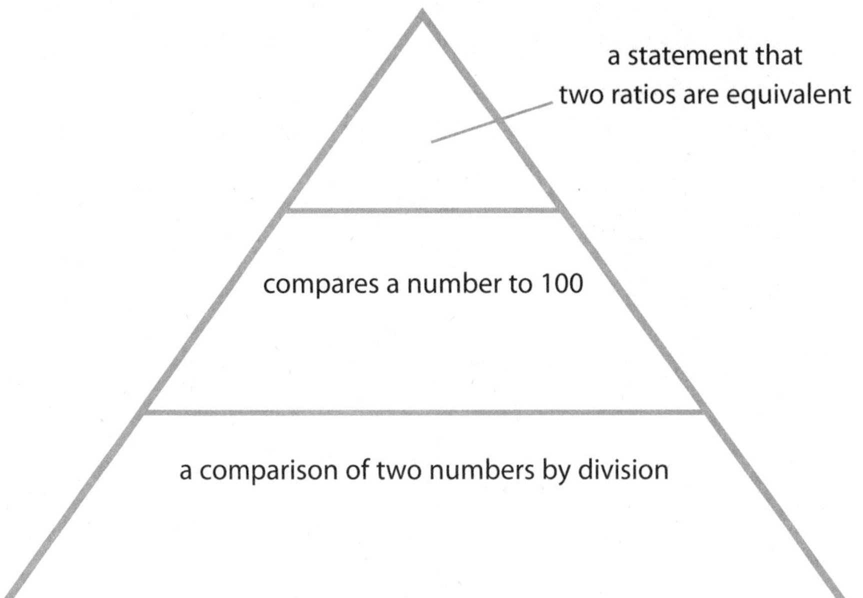

Vocabulary

Review Words

✔ proportion *(proporción)*
✔ percent *(porcentaje)*
rate *(tasa)*
✔ ratio *(razón)*
unit rate *(tasa unitaria)*

Preview Words

percent decrease *(porcentaje de disminución)*
percent increase *(porcentaje de aumento)*
principal *(capital)*
simple interest *(interés simple)*

Understand Vocabulary

Complete the sentences using the preview words.

1. A fixed percent of the principal is ____________________.
2. The original amount of money deposited or borrowed is the ____________________.
3. A ____________________ is the amount of increase divided by the original amount.

Active Reading

Tri-Fold Before beginning the module, create a tri-fold to help you learn the concepts and vocabulary in this module. Fold the paper into three sections. Label the columns "What I Know," "What I Need to Know," and "What I Learned." Complete the first two columns before you read. After studying the module, complete the third.

CALIFORNIA

GETTING READY FOR

Proportions and Percent

Understanding the Standards and the vocabulary terms in the Standards will help you know exactly what you are expected to learn in this module.

CA CC 7.RP.3

Use proportional relationships to solve multistep ratio and percent problems.

Key Vocabulary

proportion *(proporción)*
An equation that states that two ratios are equivalent.

ratio *(razón)*
A comparison of two quantities by division.

percent *(porcentaje)*
A ratio that compares a part to the whole using 100.

What It Means to You

You will use proportions to solve problems involving ratio and percent.

EXAMPLE 7.RP.3

Find the amount of sales tax if the sales tax rate is 5% and the cost of the item is $40.

$$5\% = \frac{5}{100} = \frac{1}{20}$$

Multiply $\frac{1}{20}$ times the cost to find the sales tax.

$$\frac{1}{20} \times 40 = 2$$

The sales tax is $2.

CA CC 7.EE.2

Understand that rewriting an expression in different forms in a problem context can shed light on the problem and how the quantities in it are related.

Key Vocabulary

expression *(expresión)*
A mathematical phrase containing variables, constants and operation symbols.

What It Means to You

You will find helpful ways to rewrite an expression in an equivalent form.

EXAMPLE 7.EE.2

A store advertises that all bicycle helmets will be sold at 10% off the regular price. Find two expressions that represent the value of the sale price p for the helmets that are on sale.

Sale price = original price minus 10% of the price

$$= p - 0.10p$$

Equivalently,

$$p - 0.10p = p(1 - 0.10) = 0.90p$$

Visit **my.hrw.com** to see all **CA Common Core Standards** explained.

my.hrw.com

LESSON 5.1

Percent Increase and Decrease

7.RP.3

Use proportional relationships to solve multistep ratio and percent problems.

ESSENTIAL QUESTION

How do you use percents to describe change?

Finding Percent Increase

Percents can be used to describe how an amount changes.

$$\text{Percent Change} = \frac{\text{Amount of Change}}{\text{Original Amount}}$$

The change may be an increase or a decrease. **Percent increase** describes how much a quantity increases in comparison to the original amount.

EXAMPLE 1

7.RP.3

Amber got a raise, and her hourly wage increased from \$8 to \$9.50. What is the percent increase?

STEP 1 Find the amount of change.

Amount of Change = Greater Value − Lesser Value

$= 9.50 - 8.00$ Substitute values.

$= 1.50$ Subtract.

STEP 2 Find the percent increase. Round to the nearest percent.

$\text{Percent Change} = \frac{\text{Amount of Change}}{\text{Original Amount}}$

$= \frac{1.50}{8.00}$ Substitute values.

$= 0.1875$ Divide.

$\approx 19\%$ Write as a percent and round.

Reflect

1. What does a 100% increase mean?

____

____

2. The price of a pair of shoes increases from \$52 to \$64. What is the percent increase to the nearest percent? ____________

My Notes

Finding Percent Decrease

When the change in the amount decreases, you can use a similar approach to find percent decrease. **Percent decrease** describes how much a quantity decreases in comparison to the original amount.

EXAMPLE 2 

David moved from a house that is 89 miles away from his workplace to a house that is 51 miles away from his workplace. What is the percent decrease in the distance from his home to his workplace?

STEP 1 Find the amount of change.

Amount of Change = Greater Value − Lesser Value

$= 89 - 51$ *Substitute values.*

$= 38$ *Subtract.*

STEP 2 Find the percent decrease. Round to the nearest percent.

$$\text{Percent Change} = \frac{\text{Amount of Change}}{\text{Original Amount}}$$

$= \frac{38}{89}$ *Substitute values.*

≈ 0.427 *Divide.*

$= 43\%$ *Write as a percent and round.*

Reflect

3. **Critique Reasoning** David considered moving even closer to his workplace. He claims that if he had done so, the percent of decrease would have been more than 100%. Is David correct? Explain your reasoning.

____

____

____

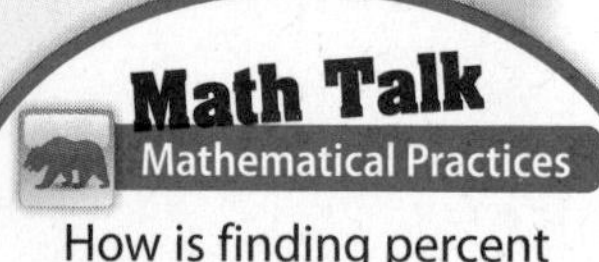

How is finding percent decrease the same as finding percent increase? How is it different?

YOUR TURN

4. The number of students in a chess club decreased from 18 to 12. What is the percent decrease? Round to the nearest percent. _______

5. Officer Brimberry wrote 16 tickets for traffic violations last week, but only 10 tickets this week. What is the percent decrease? _______

Using Percent of Change

Given an original amount and a percent increase or decrease, you can use the percent of change to find the new amount.

EXAMPLE 3  CA CC 7.RP.3

The grizzly bear population in Yellowstone National Park in 1970 was about 270. Over the next 35 years, it increased by about 115%. What was the population in 2005?

STEP 1 Find the amount of change.

$1.15 \times 270 = 310.5$ Find 115% of 270. Write 115% as a decimal.

≈ 311 Round to the nearest whole number.

STEP 2 Find the new amount.

New Amount = Original Amount + Amount of Change

$= 270 + 311$ Substitute values.

$= 581$ Add.

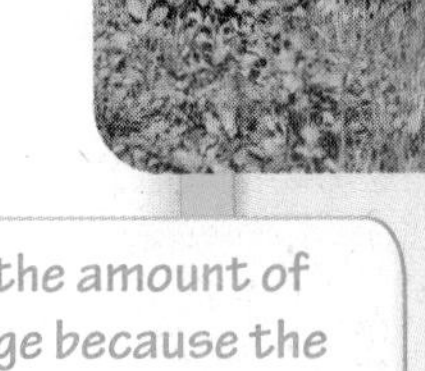

Add the amount of change because the population increased.

The population in 2005 was about 581 grizzly bears.

Reflect

6. Why will the percent of change always be represented by a positive number?

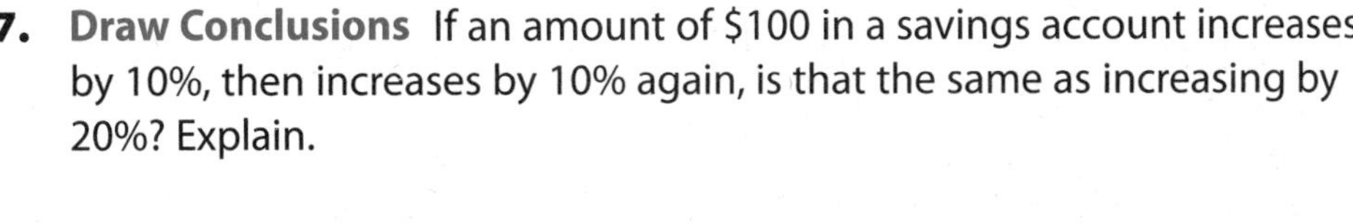

7. **Draw Conclusions** If an amount of $100 in a savings account increases by 10%, then increases by 10% again, is that the same as increasing by 20%? Explain.

____

____

____

YOUR TURN

A TV has an original price of $499. Find the new price after the given percent of change.

8. 10% increase ____________ **9.** 30% decrease ____________

Guided Practice

Find each percent increase. Round to the nearest percent. (Example 1)

1. From \$5 to \$8 ____________
2. From 20 students to 30 students ____________
3. From 86 books to 150 books ____________
4. From \$3.49 to \$3.89 ____________
5. From 13 friends to 14 friends ____________
6. From 5 miles to 16 miles ____________
7. Nathan usually drinks 36 ounces of water per day. He read that he should drink 64 ounces of water per day. If he starts drinking 64 ounces, what is the percent increase? Round to the nearest percent. (Example 1) ____________

Find each percent decrease. Round to the nearest percent. (Example 2)

8. From \$80 to \$64 ____________
9. From 95 °F to 68 °F ____________
10. From 90 points to 45 points ____________
11. From 145 pounds to 132 pounds ____________
12. From 64 photos to 21 photos ____________
13. From 16 bagels to 0 bagels ____________
14. Over the summer, Jackie played video games 3 hours per day. When school began in the fall, she was only allowed to play video games for half an hour per day. What is the percent decrease? Round to the nearest percent. (Example 2) ____________

Find the new amount given the original amount and the percent of change. (Example 3)

15. \$9; 10% increase ____________
16. 48 cookies; 25% decrease ____________
17. 340 pages; 20% decrease ____________
18. 28 members; 50% increase ____________
19. \$29,000; 4% decrease ____________
20. 810 songs; 130% increase ____________
21. Adam currently runs about 20 miles per week, and he wants to increase his weekly mileage by 30%. How many miles will Adam run per week? (Example 3) ____________

ESSENTIAL QUESTION CHECK-IN

22. What process do you use to find the percent change of a quantity?

____

____

Name ______________________ Class ______________________ Date ______________________

5.1 Independent Practice

7.RP.3

23. Complete the table.

Item	Original Price	New Price	Percent Change	Increase or Decrease
Bike	$110	$96		
Scooter	$45	$56		
Tennis Racket	$79		5%	Increase
Skis	$580		25%	Decrease

24. Multiple Representations The bar graph shows the number of hurricanes in the Atlantic Basin from 2006–2011.

a. Find the amount of change and the percent of decrease in the number of hurricanes from 2008 to 2009 and from 2010 to 2011. Compare the amounts of change and percents of decrease.

____

____

____

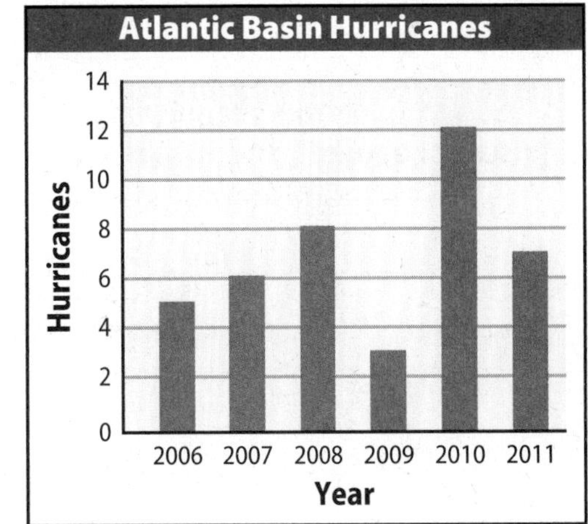

b. Between which two years was the percent of change the greatest? What was the percent of change during that period?

____

25. Represent Real-World Problems Cheese sticks that were previously priced at "5 for $1" are now "4 for $1". Find each percent of change and show your work.

a. Find the percent decrease in the number of cheese sticks you can buy for $1.

____

b. Find the percent increase in the price per cheese stick.

____

____

26. Percent error calculations are used to determine how close to the true values, or how accurate, experimental values really are. The formula is similar to finding percent of change.

$$\text{Percent Error} = \frac{|\text{Experimental Value} - \text{Actual Value}|}{\text{Actual Value}} \times 100$$

In chemistry class, Charlie records the volume of a liquid as 13.3 milliliters. The actual volume is 13.6 milliliters. What is his percent error? Round to the nearest percent. ________________

Work Area

FOCUS ON HIGHER ORDER THINKING

27. **Look for a Pattern** Leroi and Sylvia both put \$100 in a savings account. Leroi decides he will put in an additional \$10 each week. Sylvia decides to put in an additional 10% of the amount in the account each week.

a. Who has more money after the first additional deposit? Explain.

____

____

b. Who has more money after the second additional deposit? Explain.

____

____

c. How do you think the amounts in the two accounts will compare after a month? A year?

____

____

____

28. **Critical Thinking** Suppose an amount increases by 100%, then decreases by 100%. Find the final amount. Would the situation change if the original increase was 150%? Explain your reasoning.

____

____

29. **Look for a Pattern** Ariel deposited \$100 into a bank account. Each Friday she will withdraw 10% of the money in the account to spend. Ariel thinks her account will be empty after 10 withdrawals. Do you agree? Explain.

____

____

____

LESSON 5.2

Rewriting Percent Expressions

CA CC 7.EE.2

Understand that rewriting an expression in different forms in a problem context can shed light on the problem and how the quantities in it are related. *Also 7.RP.3, 7.EE.3*

ESSENTIAL QUESTION

How can you rewrite expressions to help you solve markup and markdown problems?

Calculating Markups

A *markup* is one kind of percent increase. You can use a bar model to represent the *retail price* of an item, that is, the total price including the markup.

Math On the Spot

my.hrw.com

EXAMPLE 1

CA CC 7.EE.2, 7.RP.3, 7.EE.3

To make a profit, stores mark up the prices on the items they sell. A sports store buys skateboards from a supplier for s dollars. What is the retail price for skateboards that the manager buys for \$35 and \$56 after a 42% markup?

STEP 1 Use a bar model.

Draw a bar for the cost of the skateboard s.

Then draw a bar that shows the markup: 42% of s, or $0.42s$.

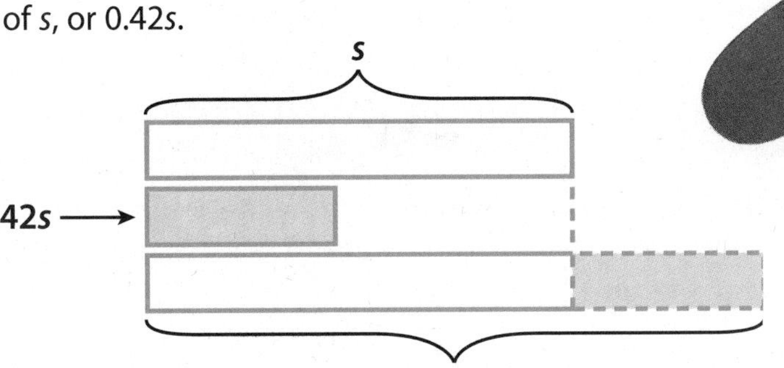

These bars together represent the cost plus the markup, $s + 0.42s$.

STEP 2 Retail price = Original cost + Markup

$$= s + 0.42s$$
$$= 1s + 0.42s$$
$$= 1.42s$$

STEP 3 Use the expression to find the retail price of each skateboard.

$s = \$35 \longrightarrow$ Retail price $= 1.42(\$35) = \$49.70$

$s = \$56 \longrightarrow$ Retail price $= 1.42(\$56) = \$79.52$

Math Talk
Mathematical Practices

Why write the retail price as the sum of two terms? as one term?

Reflect

1. **What If?** The markup is changed to 34%; how does the expression for the retail price change?

____

YOUR TURN

2. Rick buys remote control cars to resell. He applies a markup of 10%.

   a. Write two expressions that represent the retail price of the cars.

   ____

   b. If Rick buys a remote control car for $28.00, what is his selling price?

   ____

3. An exclusive clothing boutique triples the price of the items it purchases for resale.

   a. What is the boutique's markup percent? ______________________

   b. Write two expressions that represent the retail price of the clothes.

   ____

Calculating Markdowns

An example of a percent decrease is a *discount*, or *markdown*. A price after a markdown may be called a sale price. You can also use a bar model to represent the price of an item including the markdown.

EXAMPLE 2

CA CC 7.EE.2, 7.RP.3, 7.EE.3

A discount store marks down all of its holiday merchandise by 20% off the regular selling price. Find the discounted price of decorations that regularly sell for $16 and $23.

STEP 1 Use a bar model.

Draw a bar for the regular price p.

Then draw a bar that shows the discount: 20% of p, or $0.2p$.

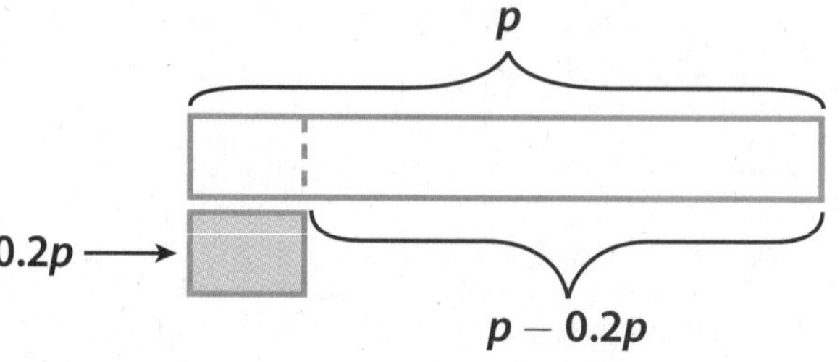

The difference between these two bars represents the price minus the discount, $p - 0.2p$.

STEP 2 Sale price = Original price − Markdown

$= p - 0.2p$

$= 1p - 0.2p$

$= 0.8p$

STEP 3 Use the expression to find the sale price of each decoration.

$p = \$16 \longrightarrow$ Sale price $= 0.8(\$16) = \$12.80$

$p = \$23 \longrightarrow$ Sale price $= 0.8(\$23) = \$18.40$

Reflect

4. **Conjecture** Compare the single term expression for retail price after a markup from Example 1 and the single term expression for sale price after a markdown from Example 2. What do you notice about the coefficients in the two expressions?

____

____

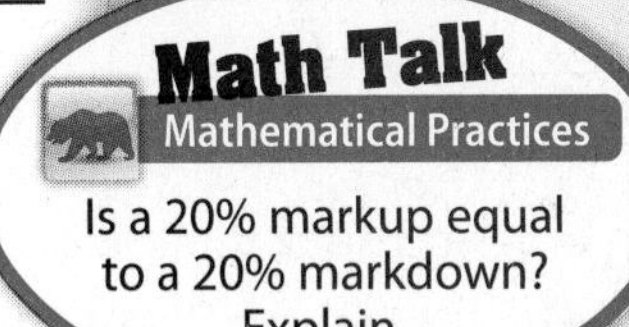

Is a 20% markup equal to a 20% markdown? Explain.

5. A bicycle shop marks down each bicycle's selling price *b* by 24% for a holiday sale.

a. Draw a bar model to represent the problem.

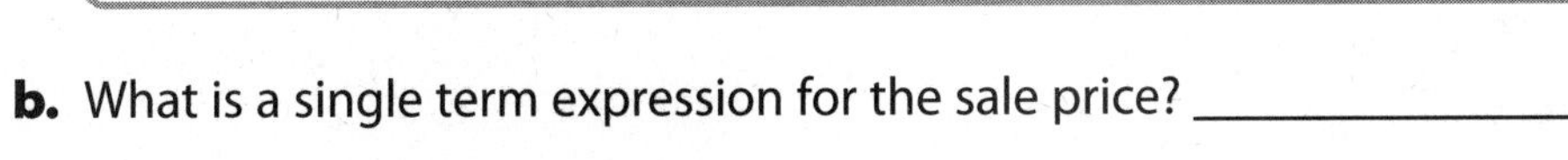

b. What is a single term expression for the sale price? ____________

6. Jane sells pillows. For a sale, she marks them down 5%.

a. Write two expressions that represent the sale price of the pillows.

____

b. If the original price of a pillow is $15.00, what is the sale price?

____

Guided Practice

1. Dana buys dress shirts from a clothing manufacturer for *s* dollars each, and then sells the dress shirts in her retail clothing store at a 35% markup. (Example 1)

   a. Write the markup as a decimal. ____________

   b. Write two expressions for the retail price of the dress shirt. ____________

   c. What is the retail price of a dress shirt that Dana purchased for $32.00? ____________

   d. How much was added to the original price of the dress shirt? ____________

List the markup and retail price of each item. Round to two decimal places when necessary. (Example 1)

	Item	Price	Markup %	Markup	Retail Price
2.	Hat	$18	15%		
3.	Book	$22.50	42%		
4.	Shirt	$33.75	75%		
5.	Shoes	$74.99	33%		
6.	Clock	$48.60	100%		
7.	Painting	$185.00	125%		

Find the sale price of each item. Round to two decimal places when necessary. (Example 2)

8. Original price: $45.00; Markdown: 22%

   ____

9. Original price: $89.00; Markdown: 33%

   ____

10. Original price: $23.99; Markdown: 44%

    ____

11. Original price: $279.99, Markdown: 75%

    ____

ESSENTIAL QUESTION CHECK-IN

12. How can you determine the sale price if you are given the regular price and the percent of markdown?

    ____

    ____

Name ______________________ Class ______________ Date ______________

5.2 Independent Practice

7.RP.3, 7.EE.2, 7.EE.3

13. A bookstore manager marks down the price of older hardcover books, which originally sell for b dollars, by 46%.

a. Write the markdown as a decimal. ______________

b. Write two expressions for the sale price of the hardcover book.

____

c. What is the sale price of a hardcover book for which the original retail price was \$29.00? ______________

d. If you buy the book in part **c**, how much do you save by paying the sale price? ______________

14. Raquela's coworker made price tags for several items that are to be marked down by 35%. Match each Regular Price to the correct Sale Price, if possible. Not all sales tags match an item.

Regular Price \$3.29	Regular Price \$4.19	Regular Price \$2.79	Regular Price \$3.09	Regular Price \$3.77

Sale Price \$2.01	Sale Price \$2.45	Sale Price \$1.15	Sale Price \$2.72	Sale Price \$2.24

15. **Communicate Mathematical Ideas** For each situation, give an example that includes the original price and final price after markup or markdown.

a. A markdown that is greater than 99% but less than 100%

____

b. A markdown that is less than 1%

____

c. A markup that is more than 200%

____

16. Represent Real-World Problems Harold works at a men's clothing store, which marks up its retail clothing by 27%. The store purchases pants for \$74.00, suit jackets for \$325.00, and dress shirts for \$48.00. How much will Harold charge a customer for two pairs of pants, three dress shirts, and a suit jacket?

____

17. Analyze Relationships Your family needs a set of 4 tires. Which of the following deals would you prefer? Explain.

(I) Buy 3, get one free **(II)** 20% off **(III)** $\frac{1}{4}$ off

____

____

H.O.T. FOCUS ON HIGHER ORDER THINKING

Work Area

18. Critique Reasoning Margo purchases bulk teas from a warehouse and marks up those prices by 20% for retail sale. When teas go unsold for more than two months, Margo marks down the retail price by 20%. She says that she is *breaking even*, that is, she is getting the same price for the tea that she paid for it. Is she correct? Explain.

____

____

____

19. Problem Solving Grady marks down some \$2.49 pens to \$1.99 for a week and then marks them back up to \$2.49. Find the percent of increase and the percent of decrease to the nearest tenth. Are the percents of change the same for both price changes? If not, which is a greater change?

____

____

20. Persevere in Problem Solving At Danielle's clothing boutique, if an item does not sell for eight weeks, she marks it down by 15%. If it remains unsold after that, she marks it down an additional 5% each week until she can no longer make a profit. Then she donates it to charity.

Rafael wants to buy a coat originally priced \$150, but he can't afford more than \$110. If Danielle paid \$100 for the coat, during which week(s) could Rafael buy the coat within his budget? Justify your answer.

____

____

____

LESSON 5.3

Applications of Percent

Use proportional relationships to solve multistep ratio and percent problems. *Also 7.EE.3*

ESSENTIAL QUESTION

How do you use percents to solve problems?

Finding Total Cost

Sales tax, which is the tax on the sale of an item or service, is a percent of the purchase price that is collected by the seller.

EXAMPLE 1 

Marcus buys a varsity jacket from a clothing store in Anaheim. The price of the jacket is \$80 and the sales tax is 8%. What is the total cost of the jacket?

STEP 1 Use a bar model to find the amount of the tax.

Draw a bar for the price of the jacket, \$80. Divide it into 10 equal parts. Each part represents 10% of \$80, or \$8.

Then draw a bar that shows the sales tax: 8% of \$80.

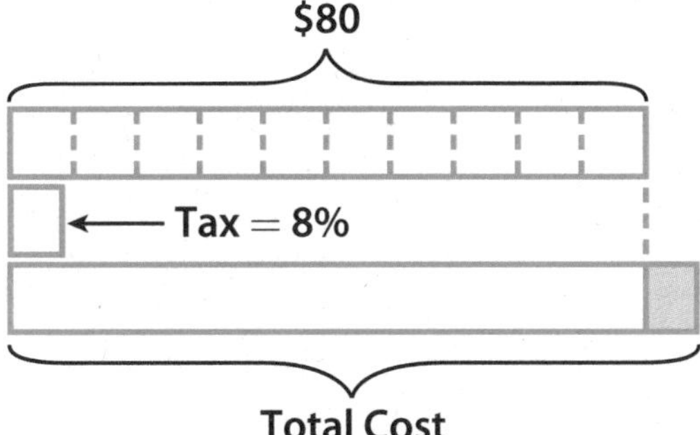

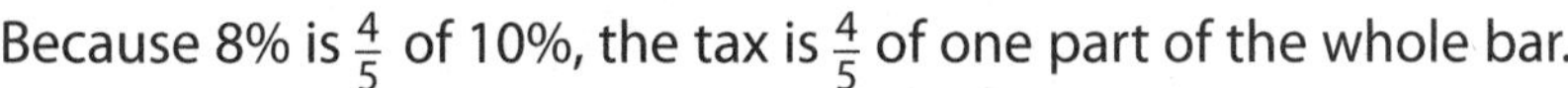
Because 8% is $\frac{4}{5}$ of 10%, the tax is $\frac{4}{5}$ of one part of the whole bar.

Each part of the whole bar is \$8.

So, the sales tax is $\frac{4}{5}$ of \$8.

$\frac{4}{5} \times \$8 = \$6.40$

The sales tax is \$6.40.

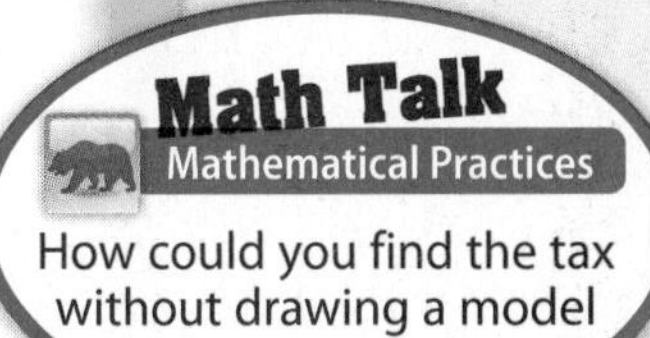

Math Talk
Mathematical Practices
How could you find the tax without drawing a model of the situation?

STEP 2 To find the total cost of the jacket, add the price of the jacket and the sales tax.

Jacket price + Sales tax = Total cost

\$80 + \$6.40 = \$86.40

YOUR TURN

1. Sharon wants to buy a shirt that costs $20. The sales tax is 5%. How much is the sales tax? What is her total cost for the shirt? ______________

Finding Simple Interest

When you deposit money in a savings account, your money usually earns interest. When you borrow money, you must pay back the original amount of the loan plus interest. **Simple interest** is a fixed percent of the *principal*. The **principal** is the original amount of money deposited or borrowed.

EXAMPLE 2 

My Notes

Terry deposits $200 into a bank account that earns 3% simple interest per year. What is the total amount in the account after 2 years?

STEP 1 Find the amount of interest earned in one year. Then calculate the amount of interest for 2 years.

Write 3% as a decimal: *0.03*

Interest Rate $\times$ Initial Deposit $=$ Interest for 1 year

$0.03 \times \$200 = \$6$

Interest for 1 year $\times$ 2 years $=$ Interest for 2 years

$\$6 \times 2 = \$12$

STEP 2 Add the interest for 2 years to the initial deposit to find the total amount in his account after 2 years.

Initial deposit $+$ Interest for 2 years $=$ Total

$\$200 + \$12 = \$212$

The total amount in the account after 2 years is $212.

Reflect

2. Write an expression you can use to find the total amount in Terry's account.

____

YOUR TURN

3. Ariane borrows $400 on a 4-year loan. She is charged 5% simple interest per year. How much interest is she charged for 4 years? What is the total amount she has to pay back? ______________

Using Multiple Percents

Some situations require applying more than one percent to a problem. For example, when you dine at a restaurant, you might pay a tax on the meal, and pay a tip to the wait staff. The tip is usually paid on the amount before tax. When you pay tax on a sale item, you pay tax only on the discounted price.

EXAMPLE 3 

The Sanchez family goes out for dinner, and the price of the meal is $60. The sales tax on the meal is 7%, and they also want to leave a 15% tip. What is the total cost of the meal?

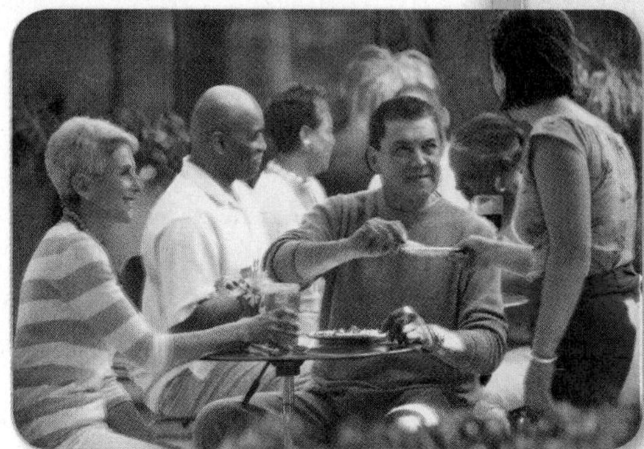

Analyze Information

Identify the important information.

- The bill for the meal is *$60*.
- The sales tax is 7%, or *0.07*.
- The tip is 15%, or *0.15*.

The total cost will be the sum of the bill for the meal, the sales tax, and the tip.

Formulate a Plan

Calculate the sales tax separately, then calculate the tip, and then add the products to the bill for the meal to find the total.

Solve

Sales tax: $0.07 \times \$60 = \$4.20$ Tip: $0.15 \times \$60 = \$9.00$

Meal + Sales tax + Tip = Total cost

$\$60 + \$4.20 + \$9 = \$73.20$

The total cost is $73.20.

Justify and Evaluate

Estimate the sales tax and tip. Sales tax is about 10% plus 15% for tip gives 25%. Find 25% of the bill: $0.25 \times \$60 = \$15$. Add this to the bill: $\$60 + \$15 = \$75$. The total cost should be about $75.

4. Kedar earns a monthly salary of $2,200 plus a 3.75% commission on the amount of his sales at a men's clothing store. One month he sold $4,500 in clothing. What was his commission that month? How much did he earn in all? Show your work.

____

____

Guided Practice

1. 5% of \$30 = ______________________

2. 15% of \$70 = ______________________

3. 0.4% of \$100 = ______________________

4. 150% of \$22 = ______________________

5. 1% of \$80 = ______________________

6. 200% of \$5 = ______________________

7. Brandon buys a radio for \$43.99 in a state where the sales tax is 7%. (Example 1)

   a. How much does he pay in taxes? ______________________

   b. What is the total Brandon pays for the radio? ______________________

8. Luisa's restaurant bill comes to \$75.50, and she leaves a 15% tip. What is Luisa's total restaurant bill? (Example 1)

   ____

9. Joe borrowed \$2,000 from the bank at a rate of 7% simple interest per year. How much interest did he pay in 5 years? (Example 2)

   ____

10. You have \$550 in a savings account that earns 3% simple interest each year. How much will be in your account in 10 years? (Example 2)

    ____

11. Martin finds a shirt on sale for 10% off at a department store. The original price was \$20. Martin must also pay 8.5% sales tax. (Example 3)

    a. How much is the shirt before taxes are applied? ______________________

    b. How much is the shirt after taxes are applied? ______________________

12. Teresa's restaurant bill comes to \$29.99 before tax. If the sales tax is 6.25% and she tips the waiter 20%, what is the total cost of the meal? (Example 3)

    ____

ESSENTIAL QUESTION CHECK-IN

13. How can you determine the total cost of an item including tax if you know the price of the item and the tax rate?

    ____

    ____

Name ________________ Class ________________ Date ________________

5.3 Independent Practice

14. Emily's meal costs $32.75 and Darren's meal costs $39.88. Emily treats Darren by paying for both meals, and leaves a 14% tip. Find the total cost.

____

15. The Jayden family eats at a restaurant that is having a 15% discount promotion. Their meal costs $78.65, and they leave a 20% tip. If the tip applies to the cost of the meal before the discount, what is the total cost of the meal?

____

16. A jeweler buys a ring from a jewelry maker for $125. He marks up the price by 135% for sale in his store. What is the selling price of the ring with 7.5% sales tax?

____

17. Luis wants to buy a skateboard that usually sells for $79.99. All merchandise is discounted by 12%. What is the total cost of the skateboard if Luis has to pay a state sales tax of 6.75%?

____

18. Samuel orders four DVDs from an online music store. Each DVD costs $9.99. He has a 20% discount code, and sales tax is 6.75%. What is the total cost of his order?

____

19. Danielle earns a 7.25% commission on everything she sells at the electronics store where she works. She also earns a base salary of $750 per week. How much did she earn last week if she sold $4,500 in electronics merchandise? Round to the nearest cent.

____

20. Francois earns a weekly salary of $475 plus a 5.5% commission on sales at a gift shop. How much would he earn in a week if he sold $700 in goods? Round to the nearest cent.

____

21. Sandra is 4 feet tall. Pablo is 10% taller than Sandra, and Michaela is 8% taller than Pablo.

a. Explain how to find Michaela's height with the given information.

____

____

____

____

____

____

____

b. What is Michaela's approximate height in feet and inches?

____

22. Eugene wants to buy jeans at a store that is giving $10 off everything. The tag on the jeans is marked 50% off. The original price is $49.98.

a. Find the total cost if the 50% discount is applied before the $10 discount.

____

b. Find the total cost if the $10 discount is applied before the 50% discount.

____

23. **Multistep** Eric downloads the coupon shown and goes shopping at Gadgets Galore, where he buys a digital camera for $95 and an extra battery for $15.99.

a. What is the total cost if the coupon is applied to the digital camera?

____

b. What is the total cost if the coupon is applied to the extra battery?

____

c. To which item should Eric apply the discount? Explain.

____

d. Eric has to pay 8% sales tax after the coupon is applied. How much is his total bill?

____

24. Two stores are having sales on the same shirts. The sale at Store 1 is "2 shirts for $22" and the sale at Store 2 is "Each $12.99 shirt is 10% off".

a. Explain how much will you save by buying at Store 1.

____

____

b. If Store 3 has shirts originally priced at $20.98 on sale for 55% off, does it have a better deal than the other stores? Justify your answer.

____

H.O.T. FOCUS ON HIGHER ORDER THINKING

Work Area

25. **Analyze Relationships** Marcus can choose between a monthly salary of $1,500 plus 5.5% of sales or $2,400 plus 3% of sales. He expects sales between $5,000 and $10,000 a month. Which salary option should he choose? Explain.

____

____

____

26. **Multistep** In chemistry class, Bob recorded the volume of a liquid as 13.2 mL. The actual volume was 13.7 mL. Use the formula to find percent error of Bob's measurement to the nearest tenth of a percent.

$$\text{Percent Error} = \frac{|\text{Experimental Value} - \text{Actual Value}|}{\text{Actual Value}} \times 100$$

____

MODULE QUIZ

Ready to Go On?

5.1 Percent Increase and Decrease

Find the percent change from the first value to the second.

1. 36; 63 ____________

2. 50; 35 ____________

3. 40; 72 ____________

4. 92; 69 ____________

5.2 Rewriting Percent Expressions

Use the original price and the markdown or markup to find the retail price.

5. Original price: \$60; Markup: 15%; Retail price: ____________

6. Original price: \$32; Markup: 12.5%; Retail price: ____________

7. Original price: \$50; Markdown: 22%; Retail price: ____________

8. Original price: \$125; Markdown: 30%; Retail price: ____________

5.3 Applications of Percent

9. Mae Ling earns a weekly salary of \$325 plus a 6.5% commission on sales at a gift shop. How much would she make in a work week if she sold \$4,800 worth of merchandise? ____________

10. Ramon earns \$1,735 each month and pays \$53.10 for electricity. To the nearest tenth of a percent, what percent of Ramon's earnings are spent on electricity each month? ____________

11. James, Priya, and Siobhan work in a grocery store. James makes \$7.00 per hour. Priya makes 20% more than James, and Siobhan makes 5% less than Priya. How much does Siobhan make per hour? ____________

12. The Hu family goes out for lunch, and the price of the meal is \$45. The sales tax on the meal is 6%, and the family also leaves a 20% tip on the pre-tax amount. What is the total cost of the meal? ____________

ESSENTIAL QUESTION

13. Give three examples of how percents are used in the real-world. Tell whether each situation represents a percent increase or a percent decrease.

____

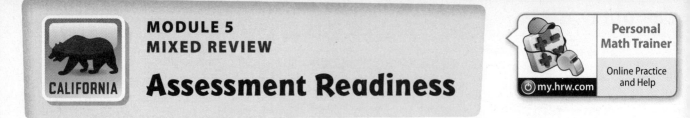

MODULE 5 MIXED REVIEW

Assessment Readiness

1. All winter coats in a store are marked down 15% off the regular selling price.

Which model(s) below could represent the sale price in dollars of a winter coat with a regular selling price of r dollars? Select Yes or No for models A–D.

A. ◯ Yes ◯ No

r

$0.15r$ ⟶

sale price

B. ◯ Yes ◯ No

r

$0.15r$

sale price

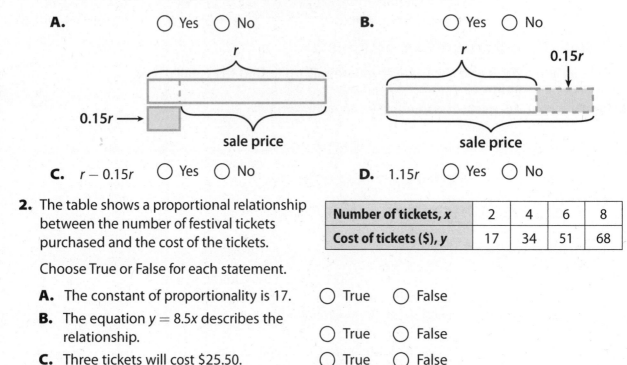

C. $r - 0.15r$ ◯ Yes ◯ No

D. $1.15r$ ◯ Yes ◯ No

2. The table shows a proportional relationship between the number of festival tickets purchased and the cost of the tickets.

Number of tickets, x	2	4	6	8
Cost of tickets (\$), y	17	34	51	68

Choose True or False for each statement.

A. The constant of proportionality is 17. ◯ True ◯ False

B. The equation $y = 8.5x$ describes the relationship. ◯ True ◯ False

C. Three tickets will cost \$25.50. ◯ True ◯ False

3. Marla has \$20 to spend on a bed for her dog. The bed she likes is priced at \$18.50, and the sales tax is 6%. Does Marla have enough money for the total cost of the bed? Explain your reasoning.

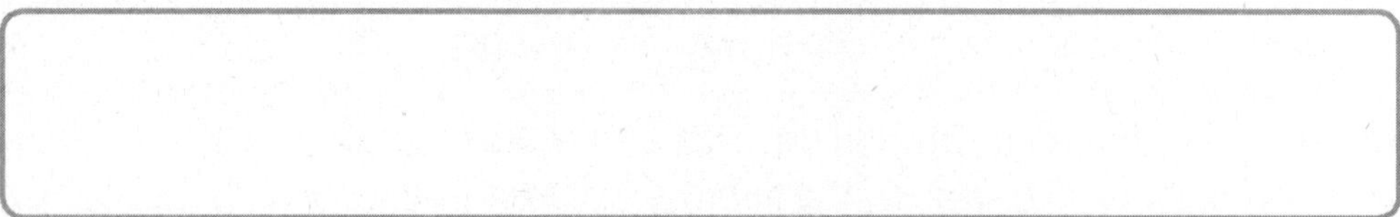

4. A store buys frozen burritos from a supplier for \$1.40 each. The store adds a markup of 80% to determine the retail price. This month the store is putting the burritos on sale for 25% off the retail price. What is the sale price of the burritos? Explain how you solved this problem.

UNIT 2

Study Guide Review

Ratios and Proportionality

ESSENTIAL QUESTION

How can you use ratios and proportionality to solve real-world problems?

Key Vocabulary

constant of proportionality *(constante de proporcionalidad)*

proportion *(proporción)*

proportional relationship *(relación proporcional)*

rate of change *(tasa de cambio)*

unit rate *(tasa unitaria)*

EXAMPLE

A store sells onions by the pound. Is the relationship between the cost of an amount of onions and the number of pounds proportional? If so, write an equation for the relationship, and represent the relationship on a graph.

Number of pounds	2	5	6
Cost ($)	3.00	7.50	9.00

Write the rates.

$$\frac{\text{cost}}{\text{number of pounds}} : \frac{\$3.00}{2 \text{ pounds}} = \frac{\$1.50}{1 \text{ pound}}$$

$$\frac{\$7.50}{5 \text{ pounds}} = \frac{\$1.50}{1 \text{ pound}}$$

$$\frac{\$9.00}{6 \text{ pounds}} = \frac{\$1.50}{1 \text{ pound}}$$

The rates are constant, so the relationship is proportional.

The constant rate of change is $1.50 per pound, so the constant of proportionality is 1.5. Let x represent the number of pounds and y represent the cost.

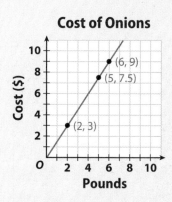

Cost of Onions

Cost ($)

10
8
6
4
2
O
2 4 6 8 10

Pounds

(6, 9)
(5, 7.5)
(2, 3)

The equation for the relationship is $y = 1.5x$.

Plot the ordered pairs (pounds, cost): (2, 3), (5, 7.5), and (6, 9).

Connect the points with a line.

EXERCISES

1. Steve uses $\frac{8}{9}$ gallon of paint to paint 4 identical birdhouses. How many gallons of paint does he use for each birdhouse? (Lesson 4.1) ______________

2. Ron walks 0.5 mile on the track in 10 minutes. Stevie walks 0.25 mile on the track in 6 minutes. Find the unit rate for each walker in miles per hour. Who is the faster walker? (Lesson 4.1)

____

____

3. The table below shows how far several animals can travel at their maximum speeds in a given time. Write each animal's speed as a unit rate in feet per second. Which animal has the fastest speed? (Lesson 4.1)

Animal Distances		
Animal	**Distance traveled (ft)**	**Time (s)**
elk	33	$\frac{1}{2}$
giraffe	115	$2\frac{1}{2}$
zebra	117	2

____

____

4. How many miles could the fastest animal travel in 2 hours if it maintained the speed you calculated in exercise **3**? Use the formula $d = rt$ and round your answer to the nearest tenth of a mile. Show your work. (Lesson 4.1)

____

____

5. The data in the table represents how fast each animal can travel at its maximum speed. Is it reasonable to expect the animal from exercise **3** to travel that distance in 2 hours? Explain why or why not. (Lesson 4.1)

____

____

6. The table below shows the proportional relationship between Juan's pay and the hours he works. Complete the table. Plot the data and connect the points with a line. (Lessons 4.2, 4.3)

Hours worked	2		5	6
Pay ($)	40	80		

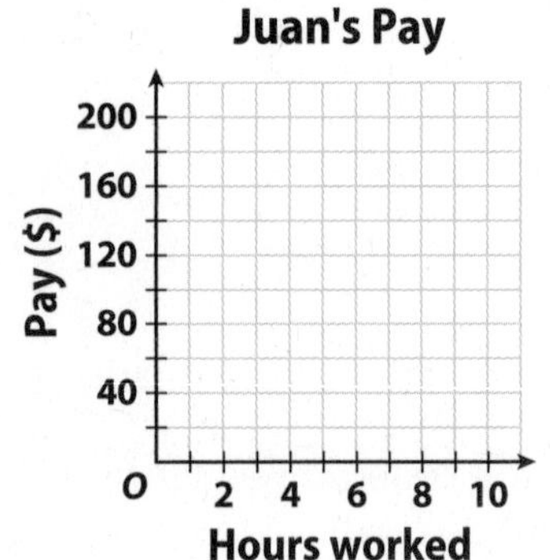

MODULE 5

Proportions and Percent

ESSENTIAL QUESTION

How can you use proportions and percent to solve real-world problems?

Key Vocabulary

percent decrease *(porcentaje de disminución)*
percent increase *(porcentaje de aumento)*
principal *(capital)*
simple interest *(interés simple)*

EXAMPLE 1

Donata had a 25-minute commute from home to work. Her company moved, and now her commute to work is 33 minutes long. Does this situation represent an increase or a decrease? Find the percent increase or decrease in her commute to work.

This situation represents an increase. Find the percent increase.

amount of change = greater value – lesser value

$33 - 25 = 8$

$$\text{percent increase} = \frac{\text{amount of change}}{\text{original amount}}$$

$$\frac{8}{25} = 0.32 = 32\%$$

Donata's commute increased by 32%.

EXERCISES

1. Michelle purchased 25 audio files in January. In February she purchased 40 audio files. Find the percent increase in the number of audio files purchased per month. (Lesson 5.1) __________

2. Sam's dog weighs 72 pounds. The vet suggests that for the dog's health, its weight should decrease by 12.5 percent. According to the vet, what is a healthy weight for the dog? (Lesson 5.1) __________

3. The original price of a barbecue grill is $79.50. The grill is marked down 15%. What is the sale price of the grill? (Lesson 5.2) __________

4. A sporting goods store marks up the cost *s* of soccer balls by 250%. Write an expression that represents the retail cost of the soccer balls. The store buys soccer balls for $5.00 each. What is the retail price of the soccer balls? (Lesson 5.2) __________

Unit Project

CA CC 7.RP.1, 7.RP.2, 7.RP.2a, 7.RP.2b, 7.RP.2c

To Infinity (Almost)...and Beyond!

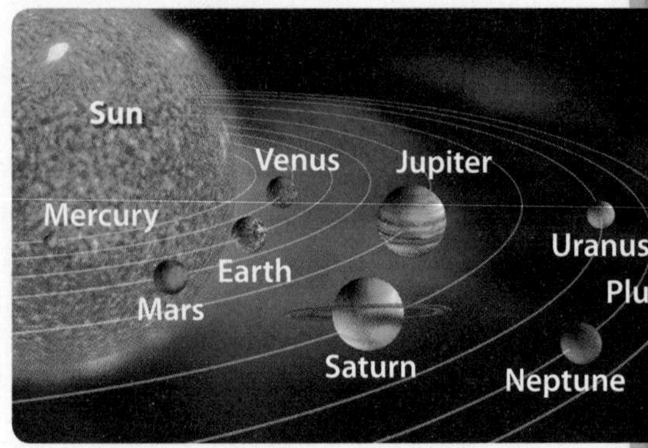

For a science project, Orlando decided to make a scale model of the solar system using a scale of 1 inch = 10,000 miles. That would make Earth a sphere about the size of a golf ball.

He quickly discovered that he would need a lot more space than the school could possibly give him. Create a presentation showing the scaled-down sizes and distances that Orlando would need to use for his model solar system. Your presentation should include each of the following:

- The scaled-down diameters, in inches, of the Sun and the planets Mercury, Venus, Mars, Jupiter, Saturn, Uranus, and Neptune, based on a scale of 1 inch = 10,000 miles
- The scaled-down distances from the Sun, in inches, of Mercury, Venus, Earth, Mars, Jupiter, Saturn, Uranus, and Neptune, based on a scale of 1 inch = 10,000 miles. Base your calculations on the average distances of the planets from the Sun.

To make the scaled-down distances from the Sun easier to visualize, you should convert those of Mercury, Venus, Earth, and Mars to feet and the rest to miles. Use the space below to write down any questions you have or important information from your teacher.

MATH IN CAREERS ACTIVITY

Architect Edith is an architect. She is currently creating a plan to renovate an old warehouse to house a new fitness center. One wall of the warehouse is 36 feet long. Edith plans to increase the length of that wall by 25%. She wants to ensure that there is a minimum of 1 electrical outlet for every 12 feet of length along the wall. What is the length of the new wall? What is the least number of outlets she should include in her plan for that wall? Explain your answer.

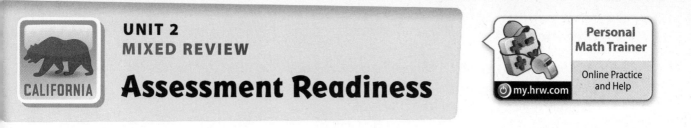

UNIT 2
MIXED REVIEW

Assessment Readiness

1. The regular prices of sandals at a shoe store are marked down by 15%. Look at each sale price and determine whether it is a 15% markdown to the nearest cent.

Select Yes or No.

A. regular price: \$24.30; sale price: \$20.66 ○ Yes ○ No

B. regular price: \$55.80; sale price: \$40.80 ○ Yes ○ No

C. regular price: \$66.50; sale price: \$56.53 ○ Yes ○ No

2. The graph shows the relationship between the number of gold beads and the number of black beads on the bracelets that Kassie makes.

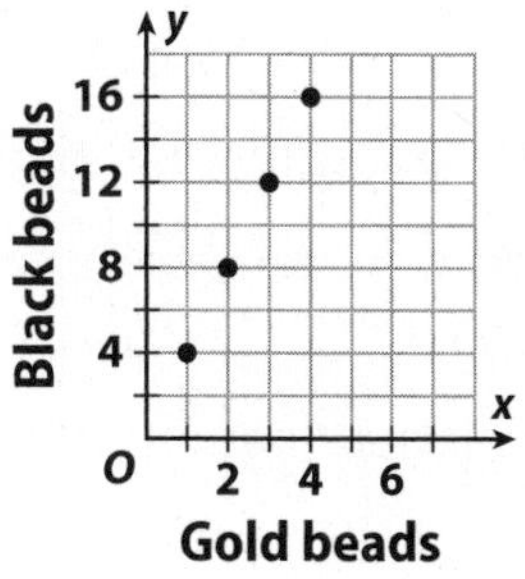

Choose True or False for each statement.

A. The relationship has a constant rate of change.

○ True ○ False

B. The relationship can be represented by $y = 4x$.

○ True ○ False

C. The point (1, 4) indicates a unit rate of 4 gold beads per black bead.

○ True ○ False

3. Last year, 20,820 people attended a kite festival. This year, 19,779 people attended it. If attendance continues to decrease by the same percent each year, how many people can be expected to attend the kite festival next year? Explain your reasoning.

4. David and Brad are competing in a 20-mile bicycle race. David rides 6.2 miles in $\frac{1}{4}$ hour. Brad rides 11.9 miles in $\frac{1}{2}$ hour. If both riders continue at the same average speed, who will finish first? Explain how you know.

Performance Tasks

★**5.** On Monday, Anya read 11 pages of a book in $\frac{1}{2}$ hour. On Tuesday, she read 18 pages in $\frac{3}{4}$ hour. Did Anya's reading speed increase by more than 10% from Monday to Tuesday? Justify your answer.

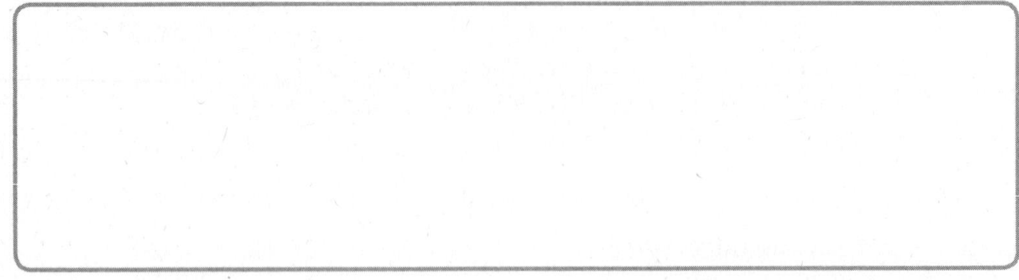

★★**6.** The table shows the relationship between the cost of a T-shirt to a store and the retail price that the store charges for T-shirts after a markup.

Cost ($), *x*	Retail Price ($), *y*
6.00	7.50
7.00	8.75
8.00	10.00
9.00	11.25

a. Graph the relationship in the table.

b. Is the relationship proportional? Explain how you know.

c. Write an equation that represents the relationship.

d. Predict the retail price that the store will charge for a T-shirt that costs the store $9.50. Justify your reasoning.

★★★**7.** The table shows how much simple interest a $1,000 deposit in a savings account at Joyner Bank will earn over time. The graph shows how much simple interest a $750 deposit will earn at Ross Bank over time. Evan has $600 that he plans to deposit in a savings account for 6 years. Which bank should he choose? Use mathematics to justify your reasoning.

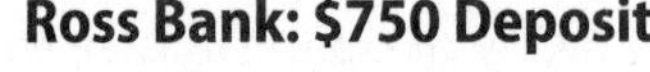

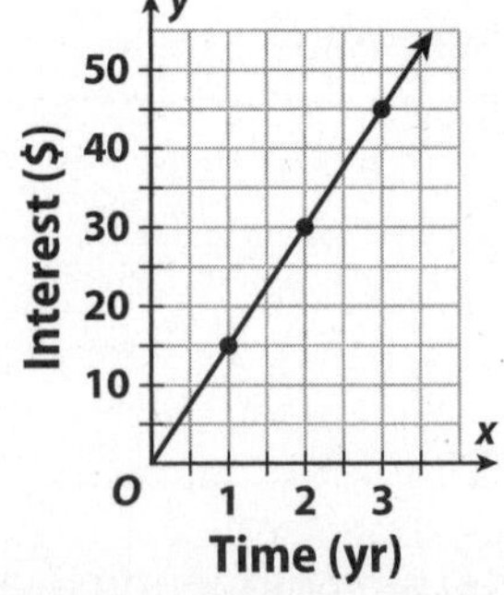

Joyner Bank: $1000 Deposit	
Time (yr)	**Interest ($)**
1	23
2	46
3	69
4	92

Expressions, Equations, and Inequalities

MODULE 6

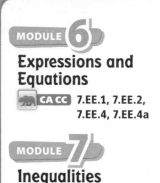

Expressions and Equations

CA CC 7.EE.1, 7.EE.2, 7.EE.4, 7.EE.4a

MODULE 7

Inequalities

CA CC 7.EE.4, 7.EE.4b

MATH IN CAREERS

Mechanical Engineer A mechanical engineer designs, develops, and manufactures mechanical devices and technological systems. Mechanical engineers use math to solve diverse problems, from calculating the strength of materials to determining energy consumption of a device.

If you are interested in a career in mechanical engineering, you should study these mathematical subjects:

- Algebra
- Geometry
- Trigonometry
- Statistics
- Calculus

Research other careers that require the daily use of mathematics to solve problems.

ACTIVITY At the end of the unit, check out how **mechanical engineers** use math.

Unit Project Preview

The Rhind Papyrus

In the Unit Project at the end of this unit, you will solve some equations that were written more than 3,600 years ago. The problems are stated in an unusual way, but you will be able to solve them using familiar algebraic methods. To successfully complete the Unit Project you'll need to master these skills:

- Apply the Distributive Property.
- Write and solve one-step equations.
- Write and solve two-step equations.

1. Here is one of the problems: "A quantity with $\frac{1}{7}$ of it added to it becomes 19." Show how you could use a variable to write the problem as an equation:

____

2. Except for the fractions $\frac{2}{3}$ and $\frac{3}{4}$, the ancient Egyptians used only "unit fractions," fractions with a numerator of 1. All other fractions they wrote as a sum of unit fractions. Show two ways you can write $\frac{5}{6}$ as a sum of unit fractions.

____

Tracking Your Learning Progression

This unit addresses important California Common Core Standards in the Critical Areas of understanding properties of operations and applying them to expressions and equations.

Domain 7.EE Expressions and Equations

Cluster Use properties of operations to generate equivalent expressions.

The unit also supports additional standards.

Domain 7.EE Expressions and Equations

Cluster Solve real-life and mathematical problems using numerical and algebraic expressions and equations.

Expressions and Equations

ESSENTIAL QUESTION

How can you use algebraic expressions and equations to solve real-world problems?

Real-World Video

When you take a taxi, you will be charged an initial fee plus a charge per mile. To describe situations like this, you can write a two-step equation.

my.hrw.com

GO DIGITAL
my.hrw.com

my.hrw.com

Go digital with your write-in student edition, accessible on any device.

Math On the Spot

Scan with your smart phone to jump directly to the online edition, video tutor, and more.

Animated Math

Interactively explore key concepts to see how math works.

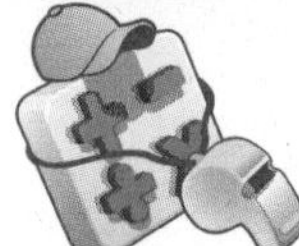

Personal Math Trainer

Get immediate feedback and help as you work through practice sets.

Are YOU Ready?

Complete these exercises to review skills you will need for this chapter.

Words for Operations

EXAMPLE the difference of 2 and b — *Difference means subtraction.*

$2 - b$

the product of -8 and a number — *Product means multiplication.*

$(-8)x$ or $-8x$ — *Let x represent the unknown number.*

Write an algebraic expression for each word expression.

1. the sum of 5 and a number x ______
2. 11 decreased by n ______
3. the quotient of -9 and y ______
4. twice a number, minus 13 ______

Evaluate Expressions

EXAMPLE Evaluate $3x - 5$ for $x = -2$.

$3x - 5 = 3(-2) - 5$ — *Substitute the given value of x for x.*

$= -6 - 5$ — *Multiply.*

$= -11$ — *Subtract.*

Evaluate each expression for the given value of x.

5. $2x + 3$ for $x = 3$ ______
6. $-4x + 7$ for $x = -1$ ______
7. $1.5x - 2.5$ for $x = 3$ ______
8. $0.4x + 6.1$ for $x = -5$ ______
9. $\frac{2}{3}x - 12$ for $x = 18$ ______
10. $-\frac{5}{8}x + 10$ for $x = -8$ ______

Operations with Fractions

EXAMPLE $\frac{2}{5} \div \frac{7}{10}$

$\frac{2}{5} \div \frac{7}{10} = \frac{2}{5} \times \frac{10}{7}$ — *Multiply by the reciprocal of the divisor.*

$= \frac{2}{\cancel{5}_1} \times \frac{\cancel{10}^2}{7}$ — *Divide by the common factors.*

$= \frac{4}{7}$ — *Simplify.*

Divide.

11. $\frac{1}{2} \div \frac{1}{4}$ ______
12. $\frac{3}{8} \div \frac{13}{16}$ ______
13. $\frac{2}{5} \div \frac{14}{15}$ ______
14. $\frac{4}{9} \div \frac{16}{27}$ ______

Reading Start-Up

Vocabulary

Review Words

algebraic expression *(expresión algebraica)*
Distributive Property *(Propiedad distributiva)*
✔ equation *(ecuación)*
factor *(factor)*
✔ operation *(operación)*
✔ solution *(solución)*
✔ variable *(variable)*

Visualize Vocabulary

Use the ✔ words to complete the graphic. You may put more than one word in each box.

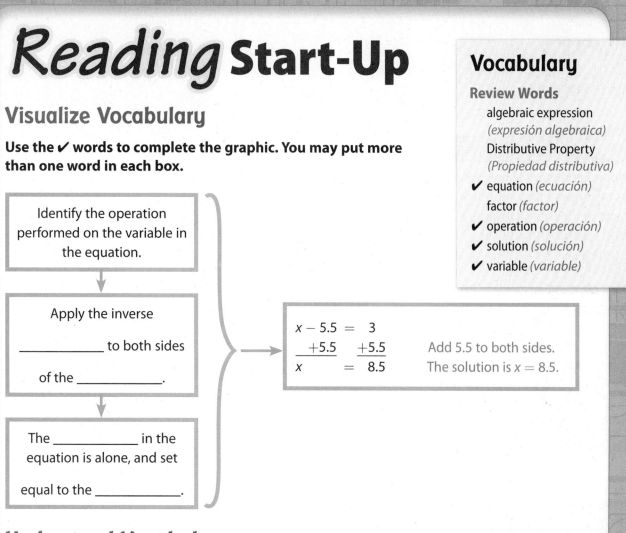

Identify the operation performed on the variable in the equation.

↓

Apply the inverse ____________ to both sides of the ____________.

↓

The ____________ in the equation is alone, and set equal to the ____________.

→

$x - 5.5$	$=$	3	
$+5.5$		$+5.5$	Add 5.5 to both sides.
x	$=$	8.5	The solution is $x = 8.5$.

Understand Vocabulary

Complete the sentences using the review words.

1. A(n) ____________________________ contains at least one variable.

2. A mathematical sentence that shows that two expressions are equivalent is called a(n) ________________________.

Active Reading

Tri-Fold Before beginning the module, create a tri-fold to help you learn the concepts and vocabulary in this module. Fold the paper into three sections. Label the columns "What I Know," "What I Need to Know," and "What I Learned." Complete the first two columns before you read. After studying the module, complete the third column.

GETTING READY FOR

Expressions and Equations

Understanding the standards and the vocabulary terms in the standards will help you know exactly what you are expected to learn in this module.

CA CC 7.EE.1

Apply properties of operations as strategies to add, subtract, factor, and expand linear expressions with rational coefficients.

Key Vocabulary

coefficient *(coeficiente)*
The number that is multiplied by the variable in an algebraic expression.

rational number *(número racional)* Any number that can be expressed as a ratio of two integers.

What It Means to You

You will use your knowledge of properties of operations to write equivalent expressions.

EXAMPLE 7.EE.1

Expand the expression $2(a + 7)$ using the distributive property.

$2(a + 7) = 2 \cdot a + 2 \cdot 7$ — Multiply each term in parentheses by 2.

$= 2a + 14$

CA CC 7.EE.4a

Solve word problems leading to equations of the form $px + q = r$ and $p(x + q) = r$, where p, q, and r are specific rational numbers. Solve equations of these forms fluently.

Key Vocabulary

equation *(ecuación)*
A mathematical sentence that shows that two expressions are equivalent.

solution *(solución)*
The value for the variable that makes the equation true.

What It Means to You

You will write and solve real-world equations that require two steps.

EXAMPLE 7.EE.4a

Jai and Lúpe plan to rent a kayak. The rental is \$12 for the first hour and \$9 for each hour after that. If they have \$50, for how long can they rent the kayak?

Rental Charge $= 12 + 9x$, where x is the number of hours after the first hour.

$50 = 12 + 9x$

$50 - 12 = 12 - 12 + 9x$ — Subtract 12 from both sides.

$38 = 9x$

$\frac{38}{9} = x$, or $x \approx 4.2$ — Divide both sides by 9.

They can rent the kayak for 4 hours.

Visit my.hrw.com to see all CA Common Core Standards explained.

my.hrw.com

LESSON

6.1 Algebraic Expressions

CA CC 7.EE.1

Apply properties of operations as strategies to add, subtract, factor, and expand linear expressions with rational coefficients. *Also 7.EE.2*

ESSENTIAL QUESTION

How do you add, subtract, factor, and multiply algebraic expressions?

Adding and Subtracting Expressions

You can use the properties of addition along with the Distributive Property to add and subtract algebraic expressions.

Math On the Spot
my.hrw.com

EXAMPLE 1 Real World — CA CC 7.EE.1, 7.EE.2

Jill and Kyle get paid per project. Jill is paid a project fee of \$25 plus \$10 per hour. Kyle is paid a project fee of \$18 plus \$14 per hour. Write an expression to represent how much a company will pay to hire both to work the same number of hours on a project.

STEP 1 Write expressions for how much the company will pay each person. Let h represent the number of hours they will work on the project.

Jill: $\$25 + \$10h$ — Fee + Hourly rate × Hours

Kyle: $\$18 + \$14h$ — Fee + Hourly rate × Hours

STEP 2 Add the expressions to represent the amount the company will pay to hire both.

$25 + 10h + 18 + 14h$ — *Combine their pay.*

$= 25 + 18 + 10h + 14h$ — *Use the Commutative Property.*

$= 43 + 24h$ — *Combine like terms.*

The company will pay $43 + 24h$ dollars to hire both Jill and Kyle.

Reflect

1. **Critical Thinking** What can you read directly from the expression $43 + 24h$ that you cannot read directly from the equivalent expression $25 + 10h + 18 + 14h$?

____

YOUR TURN

Simplify each expression.

2. $\left(3x + \frac{1}{2}\right) + \left(7x - 4\frac{1}{2}\right)$ _______________

3. $(-0.25x - 3) - (1.5x + 1.4)$ _______________

Personal Math Trainer
Online Practice and Help
my.hrw.com

Using the Distributive Property

You can use the Distributive Property to remove the parentheses from an algebraic expression like $3(x + 5)$. Sometimes this is called "simplifying" or "expanding" the expression. Multiply the quantity in front of parentheses by each term within parentheses: $3(x + 5) = 3 \cdot x + 3 \cdot 5 = 3x + 15$.

EXAMPLE 2

CA CC 7.EE.1, 7.EE.2

Simplify each expression.

A $5 - 3(7x + 8)$

$5 - 3(7x + 8)$	
$5 - 21x - 24$	Use the Distributive Property.
$5 + (-21x) + (-24)$	Rewrite subtraction as adding the opposite.
$5 + (-24) + (-21x)$	Use the Commutative Property.
$-19 + (-21x)$	Combine like terms.

B $-9a - \frac{1}{3}\left(-\frac{3}{4} - \frac{2}{3}a + 12\right)$

$-9a - \frac{1}{3}\left(-\frac{3}{4} - \frac{2}{3}a + 12\right)$	
$-9a + \frac{1}{4} + \frac{2}{9}a - 4$	Use the Distributive Property.
$-9a + \frac{1}{4} + \frac{2}{9}a + (-4)$	Rewrite subtraction as adding the opposite.
$-9a + \frac{2}{9}a + \frac{1}{4} + (-4)$	Use the Commutative Property.
$-8\frac{7}{9}a - 3\frac{3}{4}$	Combine like terms.

YOUR TURN

Simplify each expression.

4. $0.2(3b - 15c) + 6c$

____

5. $\frac{2}{3}(6e + 9f - 21g) - 7f$

____

6. $5x - 3(x - 2) - x$

____

7. $8.3 + 3.4y - 0.5(12y - 7)$

____

EXPLORE ACTIVITY CA CC 7.EE.1

Factoring Expressions

A factor is a number that is multiplied by another number to get a product. To **factor** is to write a number or an algebraic expression as a product.

Factor $4x + 8$.

A Model the expression with algebra tiles.

Use ______ positive x tiles and ______ $+1$-tiles.

B Arrange the tiles to form a rectangle. The total area represents $4x + 8$.

C Since the length multiplied by the width equals the area, the length and the width of the rectangle are the factors of $4x + 8$. Find the length and width.

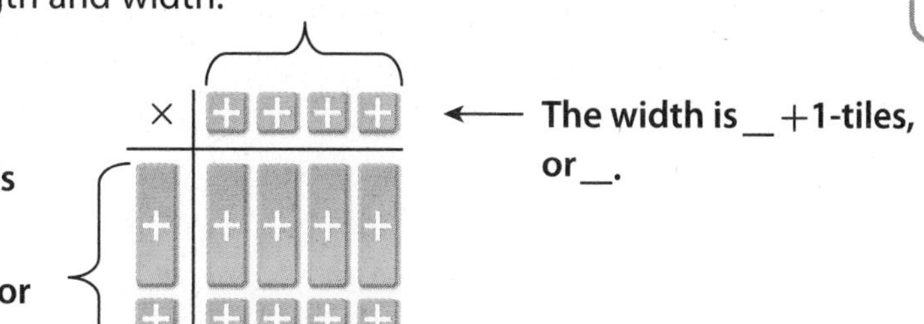
×
The width is __ +1-tiles, or __.
The length is __ x tile and __ +1-tiles, or ______.

D Use the expressions for the length and width of the rectangle to write the area of the rectangle, $4x + 8$, in factored form. __________

Reflect

8. **Communicate Mathematical Ideas** How could you use the Distributive Property to check your factoring?

____

____

Factor each expression.

9. $2x + 2$ __________

10. $3x + 9$ __________

11. $5x + 15$ __________

12. $4x + 16$ __________

Guided Practice

1. The manager of a summer camp has 14 baseballs and 23 tennis balls. The manager buys some boxes of baseballs with 12 baseballs to a box and an equal number of boxes of tennis balls with 16 tennis balls to a box. Write an expression to represent the total number of balls. (Example 1)

STEP 1 Write expressions for the total number of baseballs and tennis balls. Let n represent the number of boxes of each type.

baseballs: ______ + (______)n tennis balls: ______ + (______)n

STEP 2 Find an expression for the total number of balls.

______ + ______ + ______ + ______ *Combine the two expressions.*

______ + ______ + ______ + ______ *Use the Commutative Property.*

______ + ______ *Combine like terms.*

So the total number of baseballs and tennis balls is ______ + ______.

2. Use the expression you found above to find the total number of baseballs and tennis balls if the manager bought 9 boxes of each type. (Example 1) ______

Simplify each expression. (Example 3)

3. $14 + 5(x + 3) - 7x$

______

4. $3(t - 4) - 8(2 - 3t)$

______

5. $6.3c - 2(1.5c + 4.1)$

______

6. $9 + \frac{1}{2}(7n - 26) - 8n$

______

Factor each expression. (Explore Activity)

7. $2x + 12$

______

8. $12x + 24$

______

9. $7x + 35$

______

ESSENTIAL QUESTION CHECK-IN

10. What is the relationship between multiplying and factoring?

______

______

______

Name ____________ Class ____________ Date ____________

6.1 Independent Practice

7.EE.1, 7.EE.2

Write and simplify an expression for each situation.

11. A company rents out 15 food booths and 20 game booths at the county fair. The fee for a food booth is \$100 plus \$5 per day. The fee for a game booth is \$50 plus \$7 per day. The fair lasts for d days, and all the booths are rented for the entire time. Write and simplify an expression for the amount in dollars that the company is paid.

____

12. A rug maker is using a pattern that is a rectangle with a length of 96 inches and a width of 60 inches. The rug maker wants to increase each dimension by a different amount. Let ℓ and w be the increases in inches of the length and width. Write and simplify an expression for the perimeter of the new pattern.

____

In 13–14, identify the two factors that were multiplied together to form the array of tiles. Then identify the product of the two factors.

13. 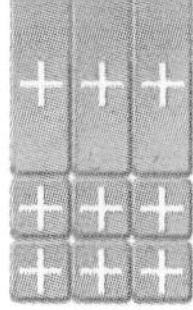 ______________________

14.  ______________________

15. Explain how the figure illustrates that $6(9) = 6(5) + 6(4)$.

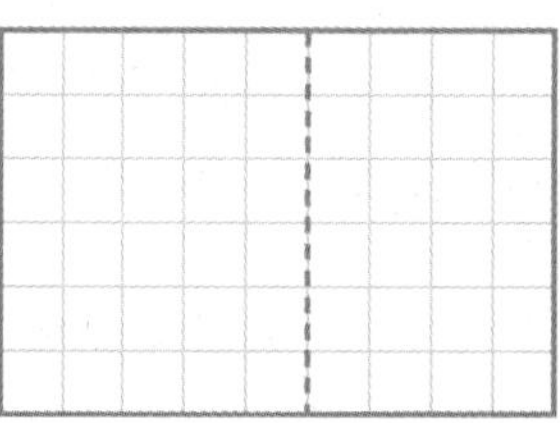

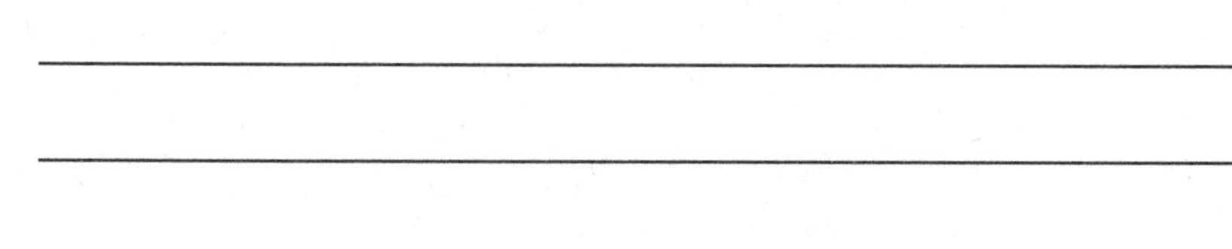

In 16–17, the perimeter of the figure is given. Find the length of the indicated side.

16.

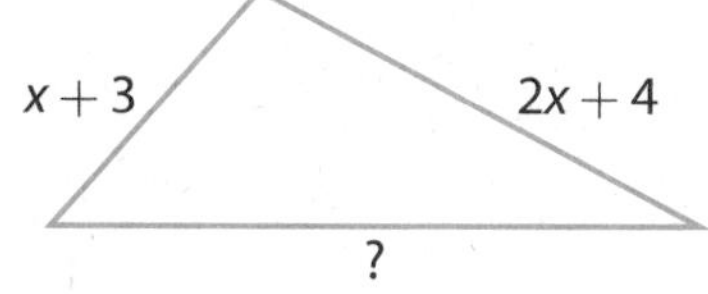

Perimeter $= 6x$ ____________

17.

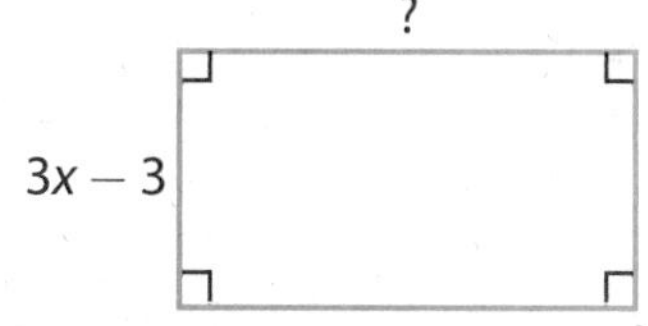

Perimeter $= 10x + 6$ ____________

18. **Persevere in Problem Solving** The figures show the dimensions of a tennis court and a basketball court given in terms of the width x in feet of the tennis court.

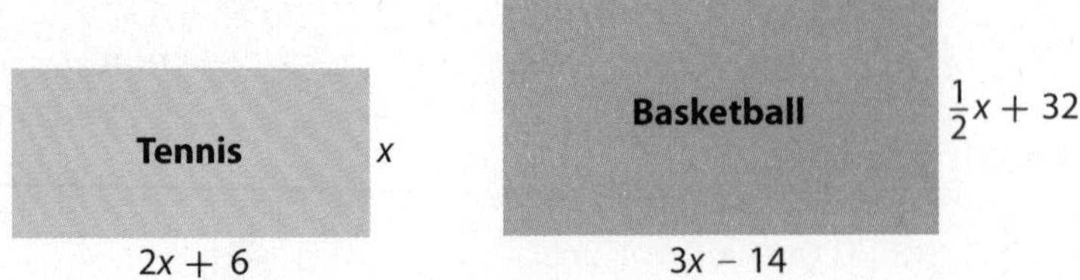

a. Write an expression for the perimeter of each court. ________________

b. Write an expression that describes how much greater the perimeter of the basketball court is than the perimeter of the tennis court. ________________

c. Suppose the tennis court is 36 feet wide. Find all dimensions of the two courts. ________________

FOCUS ON HIGHER ORDER THINKING

Work Area

19. **Draw Conclusions** Use the figure to find the product $(x + 3)(x + 2)$. (*Hint*: Find the area of each small square or rectangle, then add.)

x 1 1 1

x

1

1

$(x + 3)(x + 2) =$ ________________

20. **Communicate Mathematical Ideas** Desmond claims that the product shown at the right illustrates the Distributive Property. Do you agree? Explain why or why not.

$$\begin{array}{r} 58 \\ \times\ 23 \\ \hline 174 \\ 1160 \\ \hline 1{,}334 \end{array}$$

____

21. **Justify Reasoning** Describe two different ways that you could find the product 8×997 using mental math. Find the product and explain why your methods work.

____

LESSON 6.2

One-Step Equations with Rational Coefficients

CA CC 7.EE.4

Use variables to represent quantities in a real-world or mathematical problem, and construct simple equations and inequalities to solve problems by reasoning about the quantities.

ESSENTIAL QUESTION

How do you use one-step equations with rational coefficients to solve problems?

One-Step Equations

You have written and solved one-step equations involving whole numbers. Now you will learn to work with equations containing negative numbers.

EXAMPLE 1

CA CC 7.EE.4

Use inverse operations to solve each equation.

A $x + 3.2 = -8.5$

$$\begin{array}{rcl} x + 3.2 & = & -8.5 \\ \underline{-3.2} & & \underline{-3.2} \\ x & = & -11.7 \end{array}$$

Subtract 3.2 from both sides.

B $-\frac{2}{3} + y = 8$

$$\begin{array}{rcl} -\frac{2}{3} + y & = & 8 \\ \underline{+\frac{2}{3}} & & \underline{+\frac{2}{3}} \\ y & = & 8\frac{2}{3} \end{array}$$

Add $\frac{2}{3}$ to both sides.

C $30 = -0.5a$

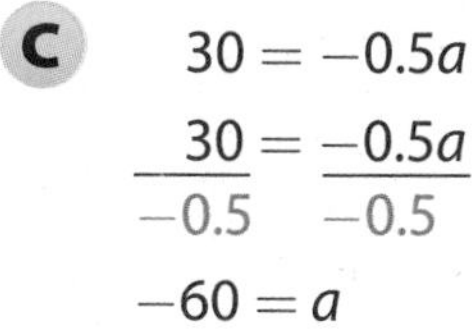

$$\frac{30}{-0.5} = \frac{-0.5a}{-0.5}$$

Divide both sides by -0.5.

$$-60 = a$$

D $-\frac{q}{3.5} = 9.2$

$$-\frac{q}{3.5}(-3.5) = 9.2\,(-3.5)$$

Multiply both sides by -3.5.

$$q = -32.2$$

YOUR TURN

Use inverse operations to solve each equation.

1. $4.9 + z = -9$ ______

2. $r - 17.1 = -4.8$ ______

3. $-3c = 36$ ______

Writing and Solving One-Step Addition and Subtraction Equations

Negative numbers often appear in real-world situations. For example, elevations below sea level are represented by negative numbers. When you increase your elevation, you are moving in a positive direction. When you decrease your elevation, you are moving in a negative direction.

EXAMPLE 2  

A scuba diver is exploring at an elevation of −12.2 meters. As the diver rises to the surface, she plans to stop and rest briefly at a reef that has an elevation of −4.55 meters. Find the vertical distance that the diver will travel.

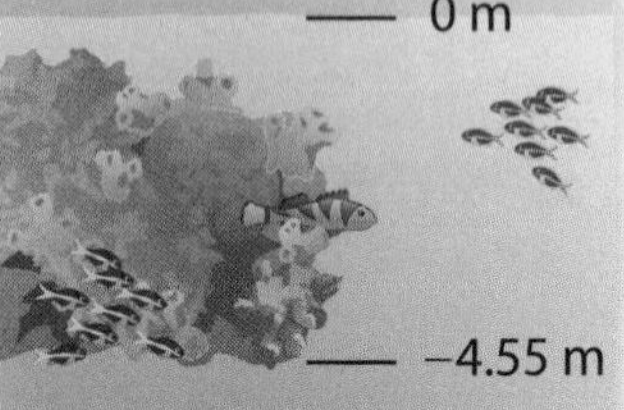

STEP 1 Write an equation. Let x represent the vertical distance between her initial elevation and the elevation of the reef.

$$-12.2 + x = -4.55$$

STEP 2 Solve the equation using an inverse operation.

$$\begin{aligned} -12.2 + x &= -4.55 \\ \underline{+12.2} \quad & \quad \underline{+12.2} \\ x &= 7.65 \end{aligned}$$

Add 12.2 to both sides.

The diver will travel a vertical distance of 7.65 meters.

Reflect

4. **Make a Prediction** Explain how you know whether the diver is moving in a positive or a negative direction before you solve the equation.

____

____

____

YOUR TURN

5. An airplane descends 1.5 miles to an elevation of 5.25 miles. Find the elevation of the plane before its descent.

____

____

Writing and Solving One-Step Multiplication and Division Problems

Temperatures can be both positive and negative, and they can increase or decrease during a given period of time. A decrease in temperature is represented by a negative number. An increase in temperature is represented by a positive number.

EXAMPLE 3 

Between the hours of 10 P.M. and 6 A.M., the temperature decreases an average of $\frac{3}{4}$ of a degree per hour. How long, in hours and minutes, will it take for the temperature to decrease by 5 °F?

STEP 1 Write an equation. Let x represent the number of hours it takes for the temperature to decrease by 5 °F.

$-\frac{3}{4}x = -5$

STEP 2 Solve the equation using an inverse operation.

$-\frac{3}{4}x = -5$

$-\frac{4}{3}\left(-\frac{3}{4}x\right) = -\frac{4}{3}(-5)$ Multiply both sides by $-\frac{4}{3}$.

$x = \frac{20}{3}$

It takes $6\frac{2}{3}$ hours.

STEP 3 Convert the fraction of an hour to minutes.

$\frac{2}{3}$ hours $\times \frac{60 \text{ minutes}}{1 \text{ hour}} = 40$ minutes

It takes 6 hours and 40 minutes for the temperature to decrease by 5 °F.

Math Talk
Mathematical Practices

Why is multiplying by $-\frac{4}{3}$ the inverse of multiplying by $-\frac{3}{4}$?

YOUR TURN

6. The value of a share of stock decreases in value at a rate of \$1.20 per hour during the first 3.5 hours of trading. Write and solve an equation to find the decrease in the value of the share of stock during that time.

____

7. After a power failure, the temperature in a freezer increased at an average rate of 2.5 °F per hour. The total increase was 7.5 °F. Write and solve an equation to find the number of hours until the power was restored.

____

Guided Practice

The table shows the average temperature in Barrow, Alaska, for three months during one year.

Month	Average Temperature (°F)
January	−13.4
June	34.0
November	−1.7

1. How many degrees warmer is the average temperature in November than in January? (Examples 1 and 2)

STEP 1 Write an equation. Let x represent ______________

____.

$x +$ ________ $=$ ________, or $x -$ ________ $=$ ________

STEP 2 Solve the equation. Show your work.

The average temperature in November is ________ warmer.

2. Suppose that during one period of extreme cold, the average daily temperature decreased $1\frac{1}{2}$ °F each day. How many days did it take for the temperature to decrease by 9 °F? (Examples 1 and 3)

STEP 1 Write an equation. Let x represent ______________

____.

________ $x =$ ________

STEP 2 Solve the equation. Show your work.

It took ________ days for the temperature to decrease by 9 °F.

Use inverse operations to solve each equation. (Example 1)

3. $-2x = 34$

____

4. $y - 3.5 = -2.1$

____

5. $\frac{2}{3}z = -6$

____

ESSENTIAL QUESTION CHECK-IN

6. How does writing an equation help you solve a problem?

____

____

Name ______________________ Class ______________ Date ______________

6.2 Independent Practice

7.EE.4

The table shows the elevation in feet at the peaks of several mountains. Use the table to write and solve an equation for 7–9.

Mountain	Elevation (feet)
Mt. McKinley	20,321.5
K2	28,251.31
Tupungato	22,309.71
Dom	14,911.42

7. Mt. Everest is 8,707.37 feet higher than Mt. McKinley. What is the elevation of Mt. Everest?

____

____

8. Liam descended from the summit of K2 to an elevation of 23,201.06 feet. What was his change in elevation?

____

____

9. K2 is 11,194.21 feet higher than Mt. Kenya. What is the elevation of Mt. Kenya?

____

____

10. A hot air balloon begins its descent at a rate of $22\frac{1}{2}$ feet per minute. How long will it take for the balloon's elevation to change by -315 feet?

____

11. During another part of its flight, the balloon in Exercise 10 had a change in elevation of -901 feet in 34 minutes. What was its rate of descent?

____

The table shows the average temperatures in several states from January through March. Use the table to write and solve an equation for 12–14.

State	Average temperature (°C)
Florida	18.1
Minnesota	−2.5
Montana	−0.7
Texas	12.5

12. How much warmer is Montana's average 3-month temperature than Minnesota's?

____

13. How much warmer is Florida's average 3-month temperature than Montana's?

____

14. How would the average temperature in Texas have had to change to match the average temperature in Florida?

____

15. A football team has a net yardage of $-26\frac{1}{3}$ yards on a series of plays. The team needs a net yardage of 10 yards to get a first down. How many yards does the team have to get on the next play to get a first down?

____

16. A diver begins at sea level and descends vertically at a rate of $2\frac{1}{2}$ feet per second. How long does the diver take to reach -15.6 feet?

17. **Analyze Relationships** In Exercise 16, what is the relationship between the rate at which the diver descends, the elevation he reaches, and the time it takes to reach that elevation?

18. **Check for Reasonableness** Jane withdrew money from her savings account in each of 5 months. The average amount she withdrew per month was $45.50. How much did she withdraw in all during the 5 months? Show that your answer is reasonable.

H.O.T. FOCUS ON HIGHER ORDER THINKING

Work Area

19. **Justify Reasoning** Consider the two problems below. Which values in the problems are represented by negative numbers? Explain why.

    (1) A diver below sea level ascends 25 feet to a reef at -35.5 feet. What was the elevation of the diver before she ascended to the reef?

    (2) A plane descends 1.5 miles to an elevation of 3.75 miles. What was the elevation of the plane before its descent?

20. **Analyze Relationships** How is solving $-4x = -4.8$ different from solving $-\frac{1}{4}x = -4.8$? How are the solutions related?

21. **Communicate Mathematical Ideas** Flynn opens a savings account. In one 3-month period, he makes deposits of $75.50 and $55.25. He makes withdrawals of $25.15 and $18.65. His balance at the end of the 3-month period is $210.85. Explain how you can find his initial deposit amount.

LESSON 6.3

Writing Two-Step Equations

7.EE.4

Use variables to represent quantities in a real-world or mathematical problem, and construct simple equations and inequalities to solve problems by reasoning about the quantities.

ESSENTIAL QUESTION

How do you write a two-step equation?

EXPLORE ACTIVITY

Modeling Two-Step Equations

You can use algebra tiles to model two-step equations.

KEY

[+] = positive variable

[−] = negative variable

[+] = 1 [−] = −1

Use algebra tiles to model $3x - 4 = 5$.

A How can you model the left side of the equation?

____

B How can you model the right side of the equation?

____

C Use algebra tiles or draw them to model the equation on the mat.

Math Talk
Mathematical Practices

Why is the mat divided into two equal halves with a line?

Reflect

1. **What If?** How would you change the algebra tile model in the Explore Activity to model $-3x + 4 = 5$?

____

____

____

Writing Two-Step Equations

You can write two-step equations to represent real-world problems by translating the words of the problems into numbers, variables, and operations.

EXAMPLE 1

CA CC 7.EE.4

A one-year membership to Metro Gym costs $460. There is a fee of $40 when you join, and the rest is paid monthly. Write an equation to represent the situation that can help members find how much they pay per month.

STEP 1 Identify what you are trying to find. This will be the variable in the equation.

Let m represent the amount of money members pay per month.

STEP 2 Identify important information in the problem that can be used to help write an equation.

one-time joining fee: **$40**
fee charged for 1 year: **$12 \cdot m$**
total cost for the year: **$460**

Convert 1 year into 12 months to find how much members pay per month.

STEP 3 Use words in the problem to tie the information together and write an equation.

One-time joining fee	plus	12	times	monthly cost	equals	$460
↓	↓	↓	↓	↓	↓	↓
$40	+	12	·	m	=	$460

The equation $40 + 12m = 460$ can help members find out their monthly fee.

Reflect

2. **Multiple Representations** Why would this equation for finding the monthly fee be difficult to model with algebra tiles?

3. Can you rewrite the equation in the form $52m = 460$? Explain.

4. Billy has a gift card with a \$150 balance. He buys several video games that cost \$35 each. After the purchases, his gift card balance is \$45. Write an equation to help find out how many video games Billy bought.

____

Writing a Verbal Description of a Two-Step Equation

You can also write a verbal description to fit a two-step equation.

EXAMPLE 2   CA CC 7.EE.4

Write a corresponding real-world problem to represent $5x + 50 = 120$.

STEP 1 Analyze what each part of the equation means mathematically.

x is the solution of the problem, the quantity you are looking for.

$5x$ means that, for a reason given in the problem, the quantity you are looking for is multiplied by 5.

$+ 50$ means that, for a reason given in the problem, 50 is added to $5x$.

$= 120$ means that after multiplying the solution x by 5 and adding 50 to it, the result is 120.

STEP 2 Think of some different situations in which a quantity x might be multiplied by 5.

You have x number of books, each weighing 5 pounds, and you want to know their total weight.	You save \$5 each week for x weeks and want to know the total amount you have saved.

STEP 3 Build on the situation and adjust it to create a verbal description that takes all of the information of the equation into account.

- A publisher ships a package of x number of books each weighing 5 pounds, plus a second package weighing 50 pounds. The total weight of both packages is 120 pounds. How many books are being shipped?
- Leon receives a birthday gift of \$50 from his parents and decides to save it. Each week he adds \$5 to his savings. How many weeks will it take for him to save \$120?

My Notes

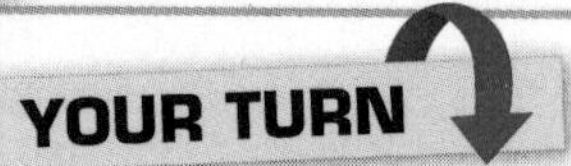

5. Write a real-world problem that can be represented by $10x + 40 = 100$.

____

____

Guided Practice

Draw algebra tiles to model the given two-step equation. (Explore Activity)

1. $2x + 5 = 7$

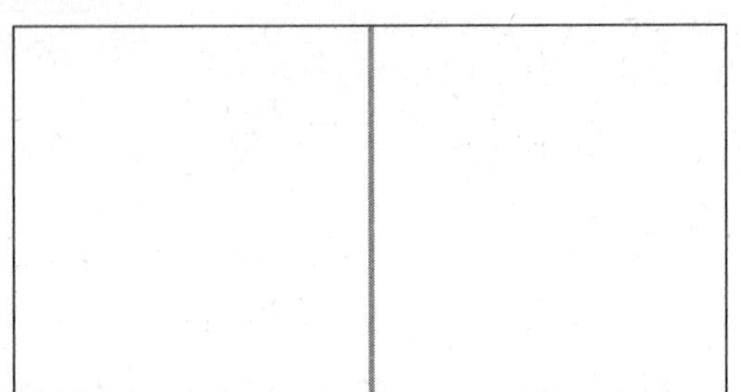

2. $-3 = 5 - 4x$

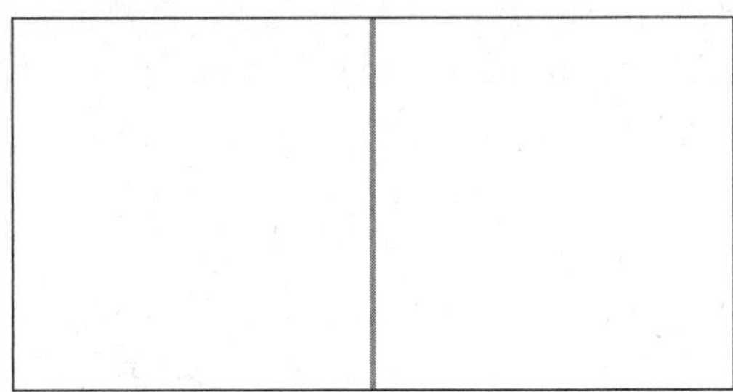

3. A group of adults plus one child attend a movie at Cineplex 15. Tickets cost \$9 for adults and \$6 for children. The total cost for the movie is \$78. Write an equation to find the number of adults in the group. (Example 1) ______________

4. Break down the equation $2x + 10 = 16$ to analyze each part. (Example 2)

x is ______________ of the problem.

$2x$ is the quantity you are looking for ______________.

$+ 10$ means 10 is ______________. $= 16$ means the ______________ is 16.

5. Write a corresponding real-world problem to represent $2x - 125 = 400$.

(Example 2) ____

____

ESSENTIAL QUESTION CHECK-IN

6. Describe the steps you would follow to write a two-step equation you can use to solve a real-world problem.

____

____

____

Name ______________________ Class ______________ Date ____________

6.3 Independent Practice

CA CC 7.EE.4

7. Describe how to model $-3x + 7 = 28$ with algebra tiles.

____

____

____

8. Val rented a bicycle while she was on vacation. She paid a flat rental fee of $55.00, plus $8.50 each day. The total cost was $123. Write an equation you can use to find the number of days she rented the bicycle.

____

9. A restaurant sells a coffee refill mug for $6.75. Each refill costs $1.25. Last month Keith spent $31.75 on a mug and refills. Write an equation you can use to find the number of refills that Keith bought.

____

10. A gym holds one 60-minute exercise class on Saturdays and several 45-minute classes during the week. Last week all of the classes lasted a total of 285 minutes. Write an equation you can use to find the number of weekday classes.

____

11. **Multiple Representations** There are 172 South American animals in the Springdale Zoo. That is 45 more than half the number of African animals in the zoo. Write an equation you could use to find n, the number of African animals in the zoo.

____

12. A school bought $548 in basketball equipment and uniforms costing $29.50 each. The total cost was $2,023. Write an equation you can use to find the number of uniforms the school purchased.

____

13. **Financial Literacy** Heather has $500 in her savings account. She withdraws $20 per week for gas. Write an equation Heather can use to see how many weeks it will take her to have a balance of $220.

____

14. **Critique Reasoning** For $9x + 25 = 88$, Deena wrote the situation "I bought some shirts at the store for $9 each and received a $25 discount. My total bill was $88. How many shirts did I buy?"

a. What mistake did Deena make?

____

____

____

b. Rewrite the equation to match Deena's situation.

____

c. How could you rewrite the situation to make it fit the equation?

____

____

____

____

____

15. Multistep Sandy charges each family that she babysits a flat fee of \$10 for the night and an extra \$5 per child. Kimmi charges \$25 per night, no matter how many children a family has.

a. Write a two-step equation that would compare what the two girls charge and find when their fees are the same. ____________

b. How many children must a family have for Sandy and Kimmi to charge the same amount? ____________

c. The Sanderson family has five children. Which babysitter should they choose if they wish to save some money on babysitting, and why?

____

____

H.O.T. FOCUS ON HIGHER ORDER THINKING

Work Area

16. Analyze Relationships Each student wrote a two-step equation. Peter wrote the equation $4x - 2 = 10$, and Andres wrote the equation $16x - 8 = 40$. The teacher looked at their equations and asked them to compare them. Describe one way in which the equations are similar.

____

____

____

____

17. What's the Error? Damon has 5 dimes and some nickels in his pocket, worth a total of \$1.20. To find the number of nickels Damon has, a student wrote the equation $5n + 50 = 1.20$. Find the error in the student's equation.

____

____

____

18. Represent Real-World Problems Write a real-world problem you could answer by solving the equation $-8x + 60 = 28$.

____

____

____

____

LESSON 6.4

Solving Two-Step Equations

CA CC 7.EE.4a

Solve word problems leading to equations of the form $px + q = r$ and $p(x + q) = r$, where p, q, and r are specific rational numbers. Solve equations of these forms fluently. Compare an algebraic solution to an arithmetic solution, identifying the sequence of the operations used in each approach. *Also 7.EE.4*

ESSENTIAL QUESTION

How do you solve a two-step equation?

Modeling and Solving Two-Step Equations

You can solve two-step equations using algebra tiles.

EXAMPLE 1

CA CC 7.EE.4

Use algebra tiles to model and solve $3n + 2 = 11$.

STEP 1 Model the equation.

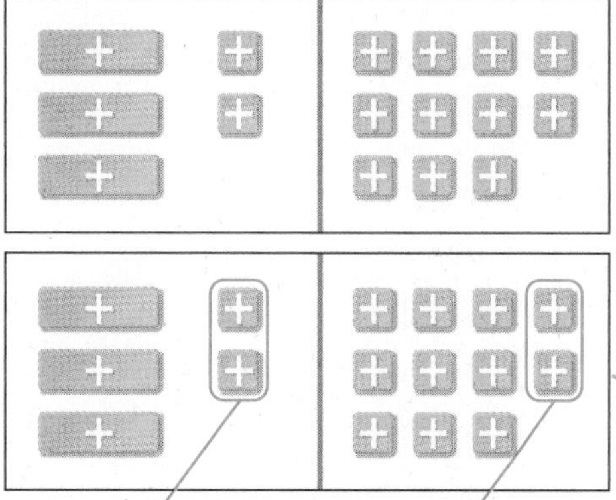

STEP 2 Remove 2 +1-tiles from each side of the mat.

Since there are +1-tiles on both sides of the equation, you can remove, or subtract, 2 +1-tiles from each side to help isolate the variable.

STEP 3 Divide each side into 3 equal groups.

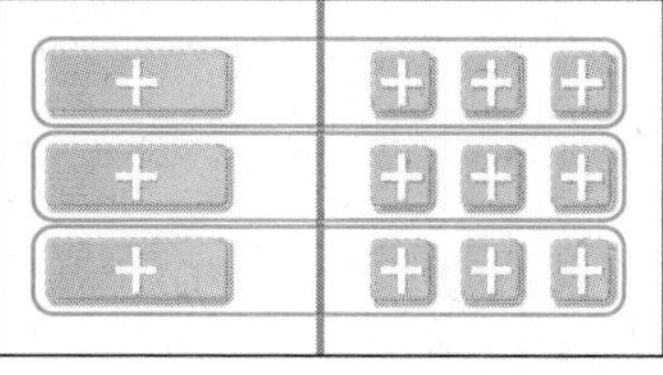

STEP 4 The solution is $n = 3$.

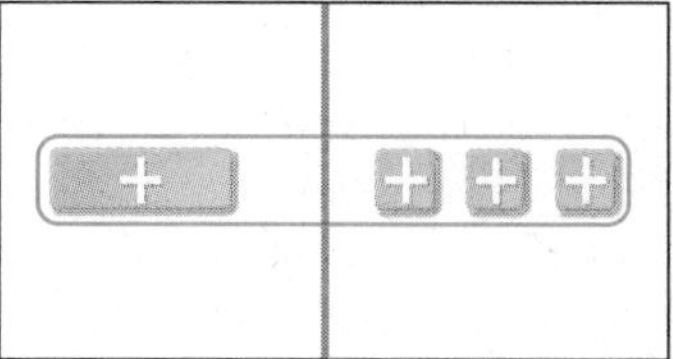

Use algebra tiles to model and solve each equation.

1. $2x + 5 = 11$ ______________
2. $3n - 1 = 8$ ______________
3. $2a - 3 = -5$ ______________
4. $-4y + 2 = -2$ ______________

Solving Two-Step Equations

You can use inverse operations to solve equations with more than one operation.

EXAMPLE 2

A dog sled driver added more gear to the sled, doubling its weight. This felt too heavy, so the driver removed 20 pounds to reach the final weight of 180 pounds. Write and solve an equation to find the sled's original weight.

STEP 1 Write an equation. Let w represent the original weight of the sled.

$2w - 20 = 180.$

STEP 2 Solve the equation.

$$2w - 20 = 180$$

$$\underline{+20} \quad \underline{+20} \qquad \text{Add 20 to both sides.}$$

$$2w = 200$$

$$\frac{2w}{2} = \frac{200}{2} \qquad \text{Divide both sides by 2.}$$

$$w = 100$$

The sled's original weight was 100 pounds.

Reflect

5. **Analyze Relationships** Describe how you could find the original weight of the sled using only arithmetic. Compare this method with the method shown in Example 2.

____

____

____

____

YOUR TURN

Solve each problem by writing and solving an equation.

6. The Wilsons have triplets and another child who is ten years old. The sum of the ages of their children is 37. How old are the triplets?

____

7. Five less than the quotient of a number and 4 is 15. What is the number?

____

Two-Step Equations with Negative Numbers

Many real-world quantities such as altitude or temperature involve negative numbers. You solve equations with negative numbers just as you did equations with positive numbers.

EXAMPLE 3 

CA CC 7.EE.4a

A **To convert a temperature from degrees Fahrenheit to degrees Celsius, first subtract 32. Then multiply the result by $\frac{5}{9}$. An outdoor thermometer showed a temperature of −10 °C. What was the temperature in degrees Fahrenheit?**

STEP 1 Write an equation. Let x represent the temperature in degrees Fahrenheit.

$$-10 = \frac{5}{9}(x - 32)$$

STEP 2 Solve the equation.

$$\frac{9}{5}(-10) = \frac{9}{5}\left(\frac{5}{9}(x - 32)\right) \quad \text{Multiply both sides by } \frac{9}{5}.$$

$$-18 = x - 32$$

$$\underline{+32} \qquad \underline{+32} \quad \text{Add 32 to both sides.}$$

$$14 = x$$

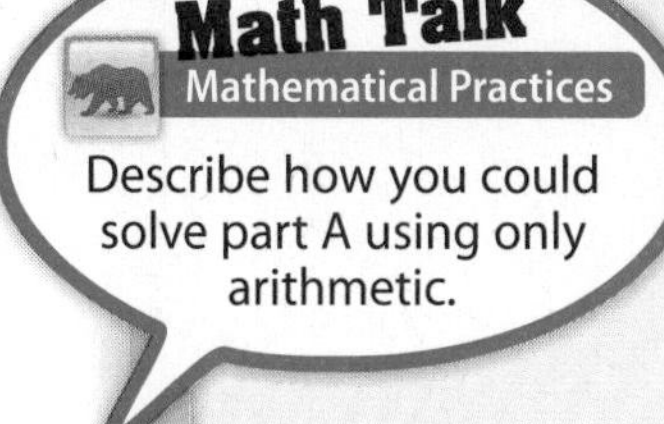

Math Talk
Mathematical Practices
Describe how you could solve part A using only arithmetic.

The temperature was 14 degrees Fahrenheit.

Check: $(14 - 32) \cdot \frac{5}{9} = -18 \cdot \frac{5}{9} = -10$ ✓

B **An airplane flies at an altitude of 38,000 feet. As it nears the airport, the plane begins to descend at a rate of 600 feet per minute. At this rate, how many minutes will the plane take to descend to 18,800 feet?**

STEP 1 Write an equation. Let m represent the number of minutes.

$$38{,}000 - 600m = 18{,}800$$

STEP 2 Solve the equation. Start by isolating the term that contains the variable.

$$38{,}000 - 600m = 18{,}800$$

$$\underline{-38{,}000} \qquad \underline{-38{,}000} \quad \text{Subtract 38,000 from both sides.}$$

$$-600m = -19{,}200$$

$$\frac{-600m}{-600} = \frac{-19{,}200}{-600} \quad \text{Divide both sides by } -600.$$

$$m = 32$$

The plane will take 32 minutes to descend to 18,800 feet.

Check: $38{,}000 - 32(600) = 38{,}000 - 19{,}200 = 18{,}800$ ✓

YOUR TURN

Solve each problem by writing and solving an equation.

8. What is the temperature in degrees Fahrenheit of a freezer kept at -20 °C?

____

9. Jenny earned 92 of a possible 120 points on a test. She lost 4 points for each incorrect answer. How many incorrect answers did she have?

____

Guided Practice

The equation $2x + 1 = 9$ is modeled below. (Example 1)

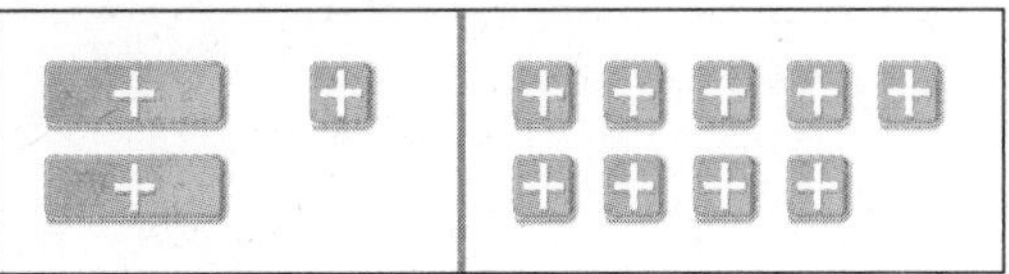

1. To solve the equation with algebra tiles, first remove _______________ .

Then divide each side into _______________ .

2. The solution is $x =$ _______________ .

Solve each problem by writing and solving an equation.

3. A rectangular picture frame has a perimeter of 58 inches. The height of the frame is 18 inches. What is the width of the frame? (Example 2)

____

4. A school store has 1200 pencils in stock, and sells an average of 25 pencils per day. The manager reorders when the number of pencils in stock is 500. In how many days will the manager have to reorder? (Example 3)

____

ESSENTIAL QUESTION CHECK-IN

5. How can you decide which operations to use to solve a two-step equation?

____

____

____

Name ____________ Class ____________ Date ____________

6.4 Independent Practice

CA CC 7.EE.4, 7.EE.4a

Solve.

6. $9s + 3 = 57$ ____________

7. $4d + 6 = 42$ ____________

8. $11.5 - 3y = -48.5$ ____________

9. $\frac{k}{2} + 9 = 30$ ____________

10. $\frac{g}{3} - 7 = 15$ ____________

11. $\frac{z}{5} + 3 = -35$ ____________

12. $-9h - 15 = 93$ ____________

13. $-\frac{1}{3}(n + 15) = -2$ ____________

14. $-17 + \frac{b}{8} = 13$ ____________

15. $7(c - 12) = -21$ ____________

16. $-3.5 + \frac{p}{7} = -5.2$ ____________

17. $46 = -6t - 8$ ____________

Solve each problem by writing and solving an equation.

18. After making a deposit, Puja had \$264 in her savings account. She noticed that if she added \$26 to the amount originally in the account and doubled the sum, she would get the new amount. How much did she originally have in the account? ____________

19. The current temperature in Smalltown is 20 °F. This is 6 degrees less than twice the temperature that it was six hours ago. What was the temperature in Smalltown six hours ago? ____________

20. One reading at an Arctic research station showed that the temperature was −35 °C. What is this temperature in degrees Fahrenheit? ____________

21. Artaud noticed that if he takes the opposite of his age and adds 40, he gets the number 28. How old is Artaud? ____________

22. Sven has 11 more than twice as many customers as when he started selling newspapers. He now has 73 customers. How many did he have when he started? ____________

23. Paula bought a ski jacket on sale for \$6 less than half its original price. She paid \$88 for the jacket. What was the original price? ____________

24. The McIntosh family went apple picking. They picked a total of 115 apples. The family ate a total of 8 apples each day. After how many days did they have 19 apples left? ____________

Use a calculator to solve each equation.

25. $-5.5x + 0.56 = -1.64$ ____________

26. $-4.2x + 31.5 = -65.1$ ____________

27. $\frac{k}{5.2} + 81.9 = 47.2$ ____________

28. Write a two-step equation that involves multiplication and subtraction, includes a negative coefficient, and has a solution of $x = 7$.

____

29. Explain the Error A student's solution to the equation $3x + 2 = 15$ is shown. Describe and correct the error that the student made.

$3x + 2 = 15$ Divide both sides by 3.

$x + 2 = 5$ Subtract 2 from both sides.

$x = 3$

____

____

30. Multiple Representations Trey has money saved for a school trip. He earns an additional $40 mowing lawns to add to his savings. Trey's parents give him enough money to double the amount he has so far for the trip. Now Trey has a total of $234 for the trip.

a. Write and solve an equation to find the amount Trey had saved before mowing lawns.

____

b. How would this compare with an arithmetic approach to this problem?

____

____

____

FOCUS ON HIGHER ORDER THINKING

Work Area

31. Reason Abstractly The formula $F = 1.8C + 32$ allows you to find the Fahrenheit (F) temperature for a given Celsius (C) temperature. Solve the equation for C to produce a formula for finding the Celsius temperature for a given Fahrenheit temperature.

____

32. Reason Abstractly The equation $P = 2(\ell + w)$ can be used to find the perimeter P of a rectangle with length ℓ and width w. Solve the equation for w to produce a formula for finding the width of a rectangle given its perimeter and length.

____

33. Reason Abstractly Solve the equation $ax + b = c$ for x.

____

MODULE QUIZ

Ready to Go On?

6.1 Algebraic Expressions

1. The Science Club went on a two-day field trip. The first day the members paid \$60 for transportation plus \$15 per ticket to the planetarium. The second day they paid \$95 for transportation plus \$12 per ticket to the geology museum. Write an expression to represent the total cost for two days for the n members of the club. ________

6.2 One-Step Equations with Rational Coefficients

Solve.

2. $h + 9.7 = -9.7$ ________

3. $-\frac{3}{4} + p = \frac{1}{2}$ ________

4. $-15 = -0.2k$ ________

5. $\frac{y}{-3} = \frac{1}{6}$ ________

6. $-\frac{2}{3}m = -12$ ________

7. $2.4 = -\frac{t}{4.5}$ ________

6.3 Writing Two-Step Equations

8. Jerry started doing sit-ups every day. The first day he did 15 sit-ups. Every day after that he did 2 more sit-ups than he had done the previous day. Today Jerry did 33 sit-ups. Write an equation that could be solved to find the number of days Jerry has been doing sit-ups, not counting the first day.

____

6.4 Solving Two-Step Equations

Solve.

9. $5n + 8 = 43$ ________

10. $\frac{y}{6} - 7 = 4$ ________

11. $8w - 15 = 57$ ________

12. $\frac{g}{3} + 11 = 25$ ________

13. $\frac{f}{5} - 2.2 = -2.5$ ________

14. $-\frac{1}{4}(p + 16) = 2$ ________

ESSENTIAL QUESTION

15. How can you use two-step equations to represent and solve real-world problems?

____

____

MODULE 6
MIXED REVIEW

Assessment Readiness

1. Consider each change in price. Is the change equivalent to a 33% increase?

Select Yes or No for expressions A–C.

A. A price increases from \$24.00 to \$35.82. ◯ Yes ◯ No

B. A price increases from \$52.00 to \$69.16. ◯ Yes ◯ No

C. A price increases from \$66.00 to \$87.78. ◯ Yes ◯ No

2. Renting a small moving truck for a day costs \$29.95 plus \$0.79 per mile that the truck is driven. Ms. Knowles rented a truck for one day and paid \$91.57. The equation $29.95 + 0.79d = 91.57$ can be used to model this situation.

Choose True or False for each statement.

A. The variable d represents the number of miles Ms. Knowles drove. ◯ True ◯ False

B. The term $0.79d$ represents the charge in dollars for the distance driven. ◯ True ◯ False

C. You can isolate the term $0.79d$ by adding 29.95 to both sides of the equation. ◯ True ◯ False

3. Two-thirds of the students who voted for student council president voted for Aisha. Aisha received 216 votes. Write and solve an equation to find the total number of students who voted in the election for student council president. Explain the steps you used.

4. An episode of a television show is 60 minutes long when it originally airs with commercials. On a DVD without commercials, the episode is only $41\frac{1}{2}$ minutes long. How many $\frac{1}{2}$-minute commercials did the episode include when it originally aired? Write and solve an equation to justify your answer.

Inequalities

ESSENTIAL QUESTION

How can you use inequalities to solve real-world problems?

my.hrw.com

Real-World Video

Many school groups and other organizations hold events to raise money. Members can write and solve inequalities to represent the financial goals they are trying to achieve.

my.hrw.com

my.hrw.com

Go digital with your write-in student edition, accessible on any device.

Math On the Spot

Scan with your smart phone to jump directly to the online edition, video tutor, and more.

Animated Math

Interactively explore key concepts to see how math works.

Personal Math Trainer

Get immediate feedback and help as you work through practice sets.

Are YOU Ready?

Complete these exercises to review skills you will need for this module.

Inverse Operations

EXAMPLE

$3x = 24$ — *x is multiplied by 3.*

$\frac{3x}{3} = \frac{24}{3}$ — *Use the inverse operation, division. Divide both sides by 3.*

$x = 8$

$z + 6 = 4$ — *6 is added to z.*

$\underline{-6} = \underline{-6}$ — *Use the inverse operation, subtraction.*

$z = -2$ — *Subtract 6 from both sides.*

Solve each equation, using inverse operations.

1. $9w = -54$ ________ **2.** $b - 12 = 3$ ________ **3.** $\frac{n}{4} = -11$ ________

Locate Points on a Number Line

EXAMPLE

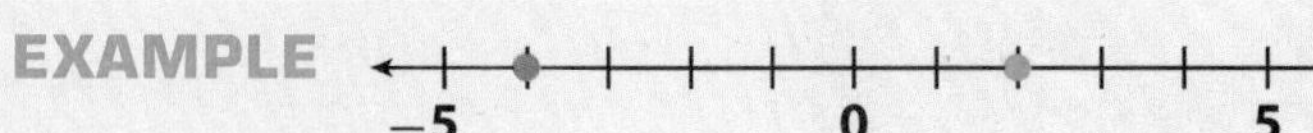

Graph +2 by starting at 0 and counting 2 units to the right.

Graph −4 by starting at 0 and counting 4 units to the left.

Graph each number on the number line.

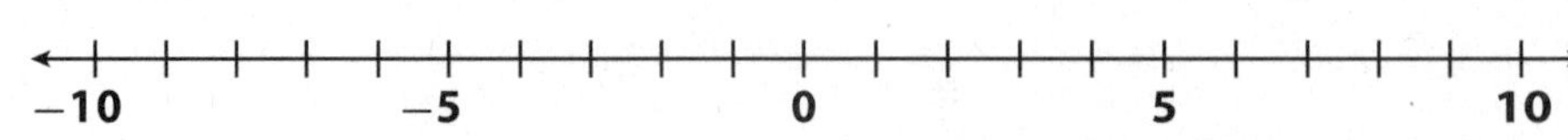

4. 3 **5.** −9 **6.** 7 **7.** −3

Integer Operations

EXAMPLE

$-7 - (-4) = -7 + 4$ — *To subtract an integer, add its opposite.*

$= |-7| - |4|$ — *The signs are different, so find the difference of the absolute values.*

$= 7 - 4$, or 3

$= -3$ — *Use the sign of the number with the greater absolute value.*

8. $3 - (-5)$ ______ **9.** $-4 - 5$ ______ **10.** $6 - 10$ ______ **11.** $-5 - (-3)$ ______

12. $8 - (-8)$ ______ **13.** $9 - 5$ ______ **14.** $-3 - 9$ ______ **15.** $0 - (-6)$ ______

Reading Start-Up

Visualize Vocabulary

Use the ✔ words to complete the graphic. You may put more than one word in each box.

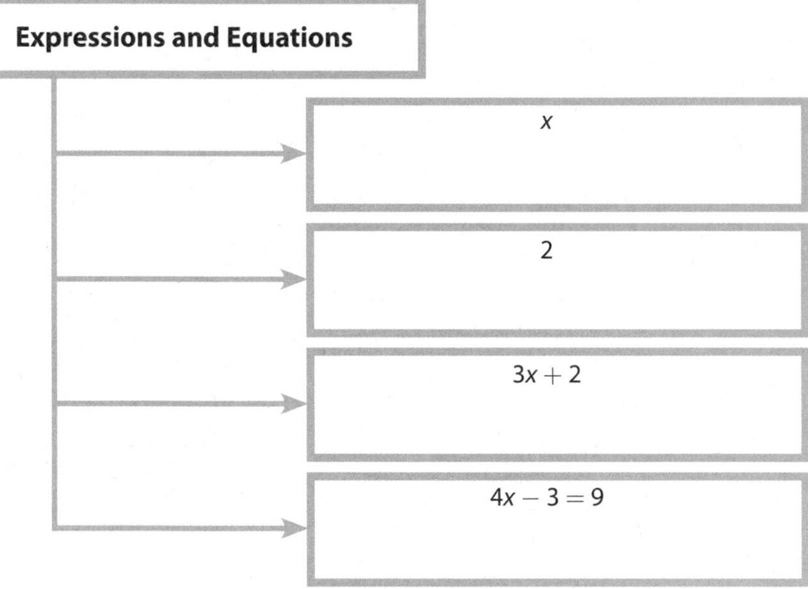

Vocabulary

Review Words

- ✔ algebraic expression *(expresión algebraica)*
- coefficient *(coeficiente)*
- ✔ constant *(constante)*
- ✔ equation *(ecuación)*
- greater than *(mayor que)*
- ✔ inequality *(desigualdad)*
- integers *(enteros)*
- less than *(menor que)*
- operations *(operaciones)*
- solution *(solución)*
- ✔ variable *(variable)*

Understand Vocabulary

Complete each sentence, using the review words.

1. A value of the variable that makes the equation true is a __________.
2. The set of all whole numbers and their opposites are ____________.
3. An ________________________ is an expression that contains at least one variable.

Active Reading

Layered Book Before beginning the module, create a layered book to help you learn the concepts in this module. At the top of the first flap, write the title of the module, "Inequalities." Then label each flap with one of the lesson titles in this module. As you study each lesson, write important ideas, such as vocabulary and processes, under the appropriate flap.

GETTING READY FOR

Inequalities

Understanding the standards and the vocabulary terms in the standards will help you know exactly what you are expected to learn in this module.

CA CC 7.EE.4

Use variables to represent quantities in a real-world or mathematical problem, and construct simple equations and inequalities to solve problems by reasoning about the quantities.

Key Vocabulary

inequality *(desigualdad)*
A mathematical sentence that shows that two quantities are not equal.

What It Means to You

You will write an inequality to solve a real-world problem.

EXAMPLE 7.EE.4

To rent a certain car for a day costs \$39 plus \$0.29 for every mile the car is driven. Write an inequality to show the maximum number of miles you can drive and keep the rental cost under \$100.

The expression for the cost of the rental is $39 + 0.29m$. The total cost of the rental must be under \$100. So the inequality is as shown.

$$39 + 0.29m < 100$$

CA CC 7.EE.4b

Solve word problems leading to inequalities of the form $px + q > r$ or $px + q < r$, where p, q, and r are specific rational numbers. Graph the solution set of the inequality and interpret it in the context of the problem.

Key Vocabulary

solution *(solución)*
The value(s) for the variable that makes the inequality true.

What It Means to You

You will solve inequalities that involve two steps and interpret the solutions.

EXAMPLE 7.EE.4b

Solve and graph the solution of $-3x + 7 > -8$.

$-3x + 7 > -8$

$-3x > -7 - 8$ Subtract 7 from both sides.

$-3x > -15$ Simplify.

$x < 5$ Divide both sided by -5, and reverse the inequality.

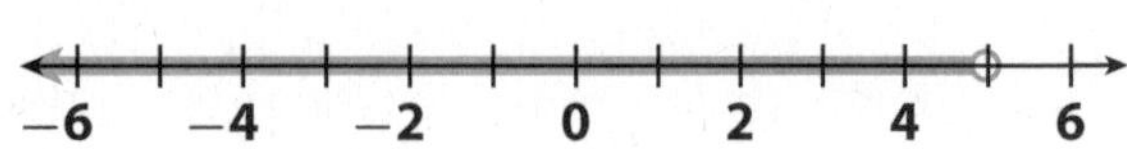

All numbers less than 5 are solutions for this inequality.

Visit **my.hrw.com** to see all **CA Common Core Standards** explained.

my.hrw.com

LESSON 7.1

Writing and Solving One-Step Inequalities

CA CC 7.EE.4

Use variables to represent quantities in a real-world or mathematical problem, and construct simple equations and inequalities to solve problems by reasoning about the quantities. *Also 7.EE.4b*

ESSENTIAL QUESTION

How do you write and solve one-step inequalities?

EXPLORE ACTIVITY  Prep. for 7.EE.4

Investigating Inequalities

You know that when you perform any of the four basic operations on both sides of an equation, the resulting equation is still true. What effect does performing these operations on both sides of an *inequality* have?

A Complete the table.

Inequality	Add to both sides:	New Inequality	Is new inequality true or false?
$2 \geq -3$	**3**		
$-1 \leq 6$	**−1**		
$-8 > -10$	**−8**		

Reflect

1. **Make a Conjecture** When you add the same number to both sides of an inequality, is the inequality still true? Explain how you know that your conjecture holds for *subtracting* the same number.

____

B Complete the table.

Inequality	Divide both sides by:	New Inequality	Is new inequality true or false?
$4 < 8$	**4**		
$12 \geq -15$	**3**		
$-16 \leq 12$	**−4**		
$15 > 5$	**−5**		

What do you notice when you divide both sides of an inequality by the same negative number?

____

EXPLORE ACTIVITY (cont'd)

Reflect

2. **Make a Conjecture** What could you do to make the inequalities that are not true into true statements?

____

3. **Communicate Mathematical Ideas** Explain how you know that your conjecture holds for multiplying both sides of an inequality by a negative number.

____

Solving Inequalities Involving Addition and Subtraction

You can use properties of inequality to solve inequalities involving addition and subtraction with rational numbers.

Addition and Subtraction Properties of Inequality

Addition Property of Inequality	Subtraction Property of Inequality
You can add the same number to both sides of an inequality and the inequality will remain true.	You can subtract the same number from both sides of an inequality and the inequality will remain true.

EXAMPLE 1

Solve each inequality. Graph and check the solution.

A $x + 5 < -12$

STEP 1 Solve the inequality.

$x + 5 < -12$ — Use the Subtraction Property of Inequality.

$\frac{-5}{x} < \frac{-5}{-17}$ — Subtract 5 from both sides.

STEP 2 Graph the solution.

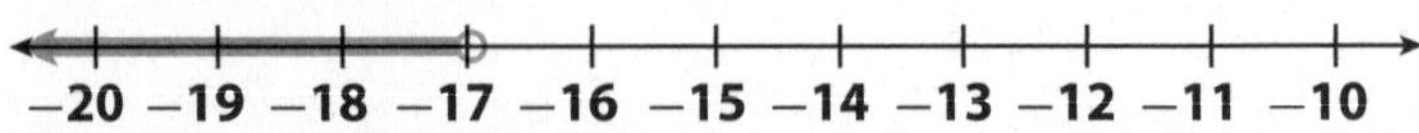

STEP 3 Check the solution. Substitute a solution from the shaded part of your number line into the original inequality.

$-18 + 5 \overset{?}{<} -12$ — Substitute −18 for x into $x + 5 < -12$.

$-13 < -12$ — The inequality is true.

B $8 \leq y - 3$

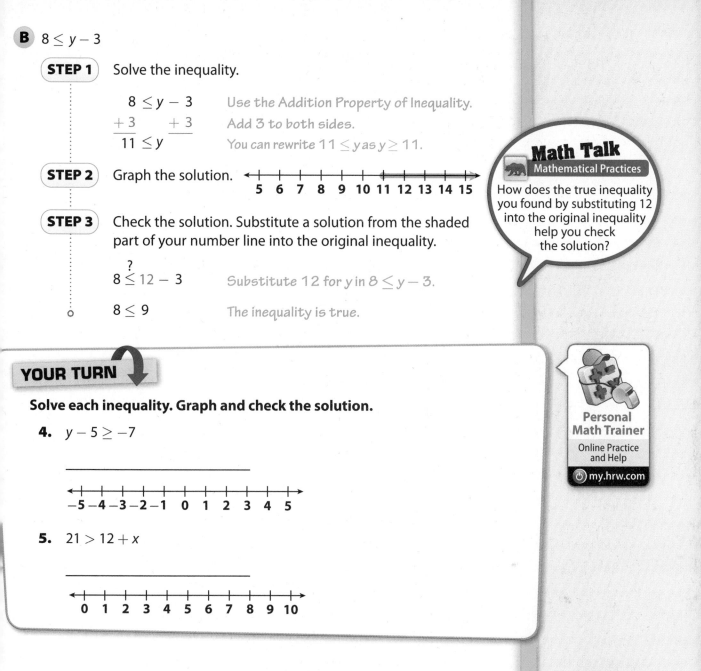

STEP 1 Solve the inequality.

$$\begin{aligned} 8 &\leq y - 3 \\ +3 & \quad\ \ +3 \\ \hline 11 &\leq y \end{aligned}$$

Use the Addition Property of Inequality.

Add 3 to both sides.

You can rewrite $11 \leq y$ as $y \geq 11$.

STEP 2 Graph the solution.

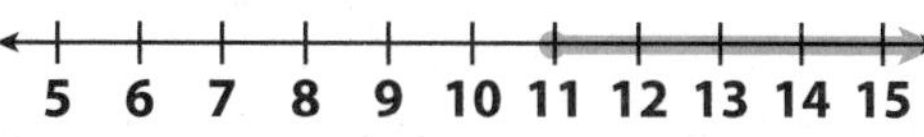

How does the true inequality you found by substituting 12 into the original inequality help you check the solution?

STEP 3 Check the solution. Substitute a solution from the shaded part of your number line into the original inequality.

$8 \overset{?}{\leq} 12 - 3$ Substitute 12 for y in $8 \leq y - 3$.

$8 \leq 9$ The inequality is true.

YOUR TURN

Solve each inequality. Graph and check the solution.

4. $y - 5 \geq -7$

____

5. $21 > 12 + x$

____

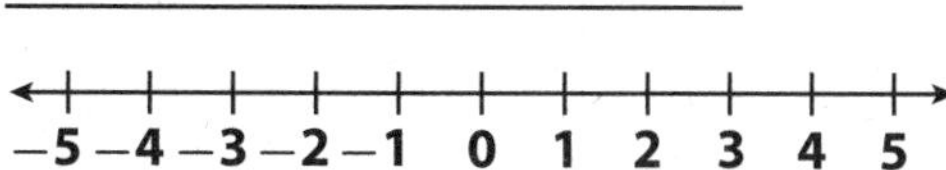

Solving Inequalities Involving Multiplication and Division

You can use properties of inequality to solve inequalities involving multiplication and division with rational numbers.

Multiplication and Division Properties of Inequality

- You can multiply or divide both sides of an inequality by the same positive number and the inequality will remain true.
- If you multiply or divide both sides of an inequality by the same negative number, you must reverse the inequality symbol for the statement to still be true.

EXAMPLE 2

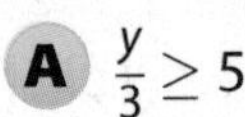

7.EE.4

Solve each inequality. Graph and check the solution.

A $\frac{y}{3} \geq 5$

STEP 1 Solve the inequality.

$3\left(\frac{y}{3}\right) \geq 3(5)$ Multiply both sides by 3.

$y \geq 15$

Use a closed circle to show that 15 is a solution.

STEP 2 Graph the solution.

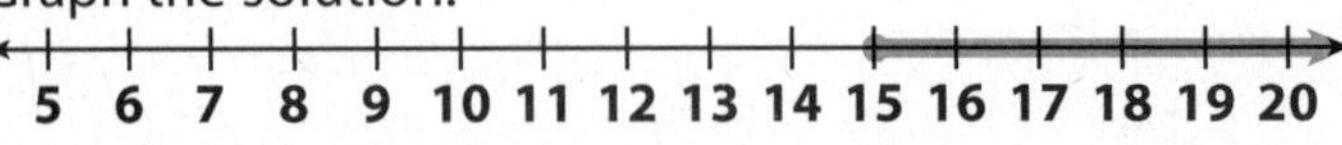

STEP 3 Check the solution by substituting a solution from the shaded part of the graph into the original inequality. For convenience, choose a multiple of 3.

$\frac{18}{3} \stackrel{?}{\geq} 5$ Substitute 18 for x in the original inequality.

$6 \geq 5$ The inequality is true.

B $-4x > 52$

STEP 1 Solve the inequality.

$-4x > 52$

$\frac{-4x}{-4} < \frac{52}{-4}$ Divide both sides by −4. Reverse the inequality symbol.

$x < -13$

STEP 2 Graph the solution.

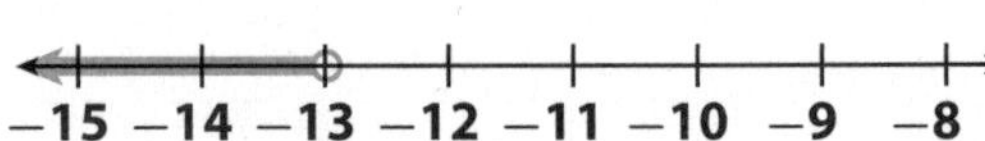

STEP 3 Check your answer using substitution.

$-4(-15) \stackrel{?}{>} 52$ Substitute −15 for x in $-4x > 52$.

$60 > 52$ The statement is true.

My Notes

YOUR TURN

Solve each inequality. Graph and check the solution.

6. $-10y < 60$ ____________

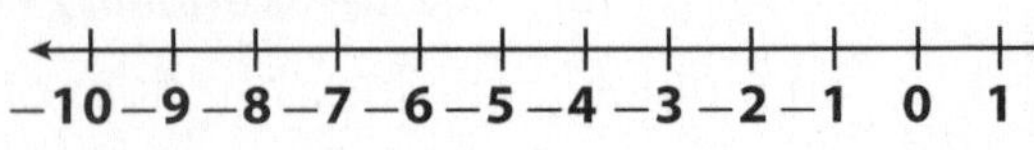

7. $7 \geq -\frac{t}{6}$ ____________

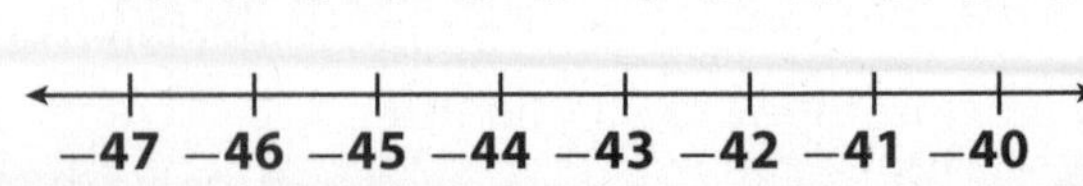

Solving a Real-World Problem

Although elevations below sea level are represented by negative numbers, we often use absolute values to describe these elevations. For example, −50 feet relative to sea level might be described as 50 feet below sea level.

EXAMPLE 3 Problem Solving

CA CC 7.EE.4b

A marine submersible descends more than 40 feet below sea level. As it descends from sea level, the change in elevation is −5 feet per second. For how many seconds does it descend?

Analyze Information

Rewrite the question as a statement.

- Find the number of seconds that the submersible descends below sea level.

List the important information:

- Final elevation > 40 feet below sea level or final elevation < −40 feet
- Rate of descent = −5 feet per second

Formulate a Plan

Write and solve an inequality. Use this fact:

Rate of change in elevation × Time in seconds = Final elevation

Solve

$-5t < -40$ *Rate of change × Time < Final elevation*

$\frac{-5t}{-5} > \frac{-40}{-5}$ *Divide both sides by −5. Reverse the inequality symbol.*

$t > 8$

The submersible descends for more than 8 seconds.

Justify and Evaluate

Check your answer by substituting a value greater than 8 seconds in the original inequality.

$-5(9) \stackrel{?}{<} -40$ *Substitute 9 for t in the inequality −5t < −40.*

$-45 < -40$ *The statement is true.*

YOUR TURN

8. Every month, \$35 is withdrawn from Tony's savings account to pay for his gym membership. He has enough savings to withdraw no more than \$315. For how many months can Tony pay for his gym membership?

____

____

Guided Practice

Write the resulting inequality. (Explore Activity)

1. $-5 \leq -2$; Add 7 to both sides ________________

2. $-6 < -3$; Divide both sides by -3 ________________

3. $7 > -4$; Subtract 7 from both sides ________________

4. $-1 \geq -8$; Multiply both sides by -2 ________________

Solve each inequality. Graph and check the solution. (Examples 1 and 2)

5. $n - 5 \geq -2$ ________________

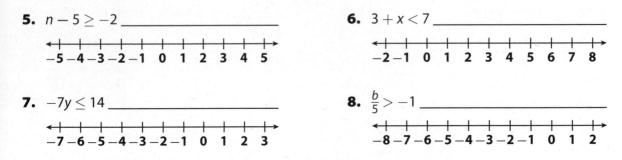

−5 −4 −3 −2 −1 0 1 2 3 4 5

6. $3 + x < 7$ ________________

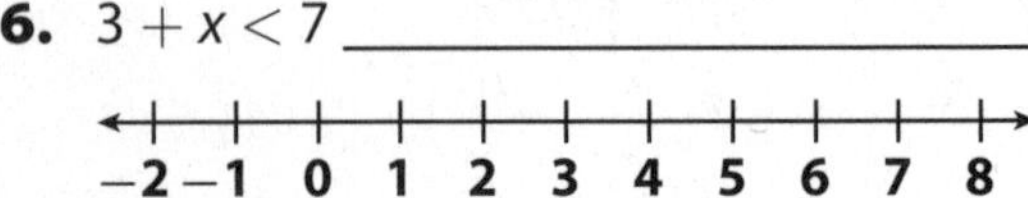

7. $-7y \leq 14$ ________________

−7 −6 −5 −4 −3 −2 −1 0 1 2 3

8. $\frac{b}{5} > -1$ ________________

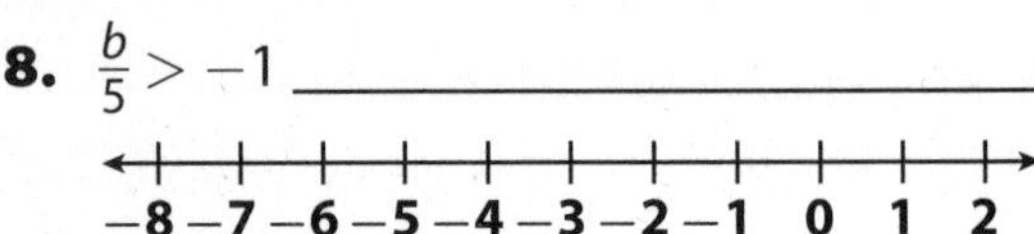

9. For a scientific experiment, a physicist must make sure that the temperature of a metal at 0 °C gets no colder than −80 °C. The physicist changes the metal's temperature at a steady rate of −4 °C per hour. For how long can the physicist change the temperature? (Example 3)

a. Let *t* represent temperature in degrees Celsius. Write an inequality. Use the fact that the rate of change in temperature times the number of hours equals the final temperature.

____

b. Solve the inequality in part **a**. How long can the physicist change the temperature of the metal?

____

c. The physicist has to repeat the experiment if the metal gets cooler than −80 °C. How many hours would the physicist have to cool the metal for this to happen?

____

ESSENTIAL QUESTION CHECK-IN

10. Suppose you are solving an inequality. Under what circumstances do you reverse the inequality symbol?

____

Name ______________________ Class ______________ Date ____________

7.1 Independent Practice

CA CC 7.EE.4, 7.EE.4b

In 11–16, solve each inequality. Graph and check the solution.

11. $x - 35 > 15$ ______________

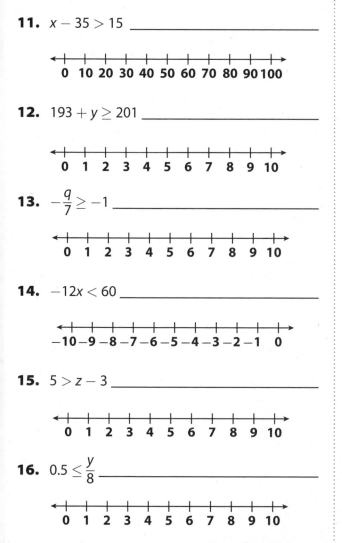

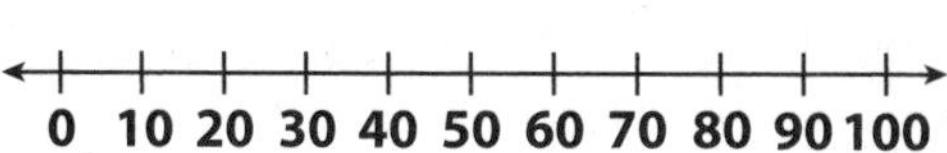

12. $193 + y \geq 201$ ______________

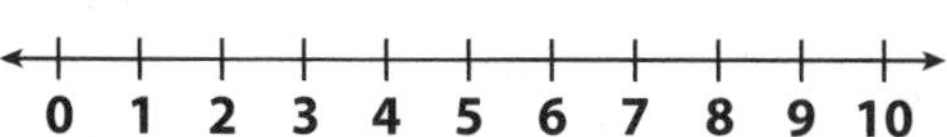

13. $-\frac{q}{7} \geq -1$ ______________

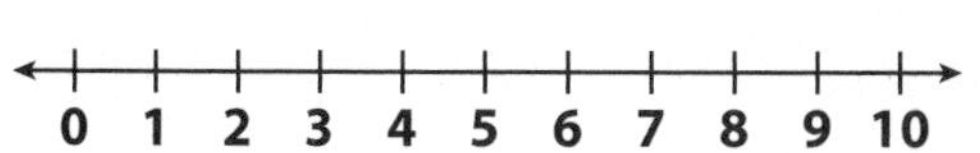

14. $-12x < 60$ ______________

−10 −9 −8 −7 −6 −5 −4 −3 −2 −1 0

15. $5 > z - 3$ ______________

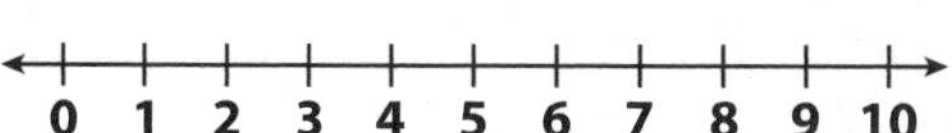

16. $0.5 \leq \frac{y}{8}$ ______________

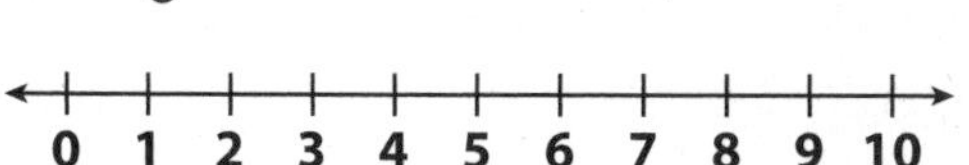

To solve 17–21, write and solve an inequality.

17. The vet says that Lena's puppy will grow to be at most 28 inches tall. Lena's puppy is currently 1 foot tall. How many more inches will the puppy grow?

____

18. Each of 7 kittens, weighs less than 3.5 ounces. Find all the possible values of the combined weights of the kittens.

____

19. **Geometry** The sides of the hexagon shown are equal in length. The perimeter of the hexagon is at most 42 inches. Find the possible side lengths of the hexagon.

____

20. To get a free meal at his favorite restaurant, Tom needs to spend \$50 or more at the restaurant. He has already spent \$30.25. How much more does Tom need to spend to get his free meal?

____

21. To cover a rectangular region of her yard, Penny needs at least 170.5 square feet of sod. The length of the region is 15.5 feet. What are the possible widths of the region?

____

22. **Draw Conclusions** A submarine descends from sea level to the entrance of an underwater cave. The elevation of the entrance is −120 feet. The rate of change in the submarine's elevation is less than −12 feet per second. Can the submarine reach the entrance to the cave in less than 10 seconds? Explain.

____

____

____

____

The sign shows some prices at a produce stand.

Produce	Price per Pound
Onions	\$1.25
Yellow Squash	\$0.99
Spinach	\$3.00
Potatoes	\$0.50

23. Selena has \$10. What is the greatest amount of spinach she can buy?

24. Gary has enough money to buy at most 5.5 pounds of potatoes. How much money does Gary have?

25. Florence wants to spend no more than \$3 on onions. Will she be able to buy 2.5 pounds of onions? Explain.

FOCUS ON HIGHER ORDER THINKING

Work Area

26. **Counterexamples** John says that if one side of an inequality is 0, you don't have to reverse the inequality symbol when you multiply or divide both sides by a negative number. Find an inequality that you can use to disprove John's statement. Explain your thinking.

27. **Look for a Pattern** Solve $x + 1 > 10$, $x + 11 > 20$, and $x + 21 > 30$. Describe a pattern. Then use the pattern to predict the solution of $x + 9{,}991 > 10{,}000$.

28. **Persevere in Problem Solving** The base of a rectangular prism has a length of 13 inches and a width of $\frac{1}{2}$ inch. The volume of the prism is less than 65 cubic inches. Find all possible heights of the prism. Show your work.

LESSON 7.2

Writing Two-Step Inequalities

7.EE.4

Use variables to represent quantities in a real-world or mathematical problem, and construct simple equations and inequalities to solve problems by reasoning about the quantities.

ESSENTIAL QUESTION

How do you write a two-step inequality?

EXPLORE ACTIVITY CA CC Prep for 7.EE.4

Modeling Two-Step Inequalities

You can use algebra tiles to model two-step inequalities.

Use algebra tiles to model $2k + 5 \geq -3$.

A Using the line on the mat, draw in the inequality symbol shown in the inequality.

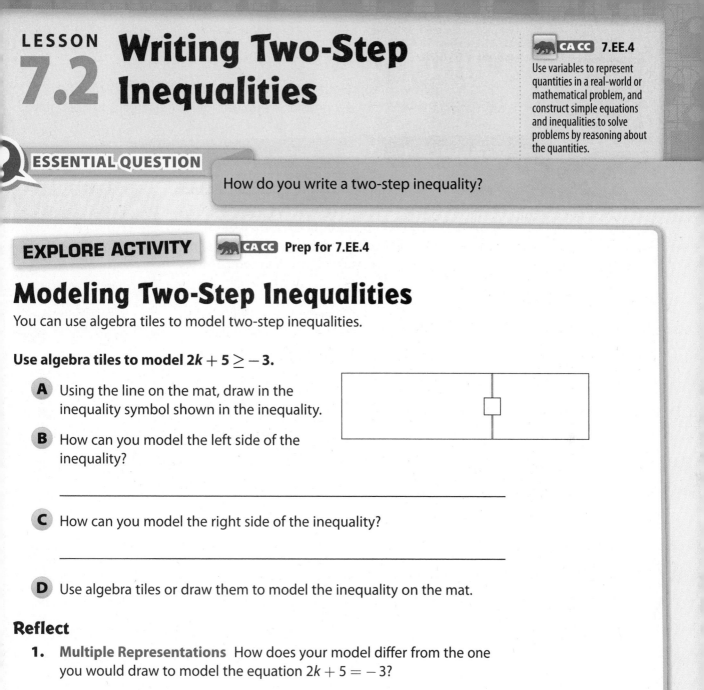

B How can you model the left side of the inequality?

____

C How can you model the right side of the inequality?

____

D Use algebra tiles or draw them to model the inequality on the mat.

Reflect

1. **Multiple Representations** How does your model differ from the one you would draw to model the equation $2k + 5 = -3$?

____

____

____

2. Why might you need to change the inequality sign when you solve an inequality using algebra tiles?

____

____

____

Writing Two-Step Inequalities

You can write two-step inequalities to represent real-world problems by translating the words of the problems into numbers, variables, and operations.

EXAMPLE 1 

CA CC 7.EE.4

A mountain climbing team is camped at an altitude of 18,460 feet on Mount Everest. The team wants to reach the 29,029-foot summit within 6 days. Write an inequality to find the average number of feet per day the team must climb to accomplish its objective.

STEP 1 Identify what you are trying to find. This will be the variable in the inequality.

Let d represent the average altitude the team must gain each day.

STEP 2 Identify important information in the problem that you can use to write an inequality.

starting altitude: **18,460 ft** target altitude: **29,029 ft**
number of days times altitude gained to reach target altitude: $6 \cdot d$

STEP 3 Use words in the problem to tie the information together and write an inequality.

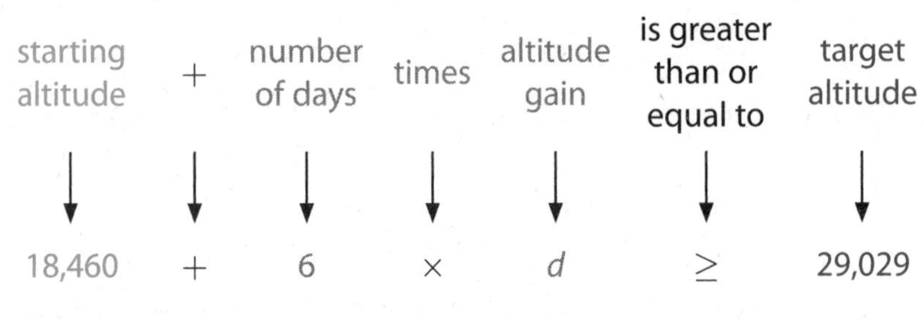

starting altitude	+	number of days	times	altitude gain	is greater than or equal to	target altitude
↓	↓	↓	↓	↓	↓	↓
18,460	+	6	×	d	≥	29,029

$18{,}460 + 6d \geq 29{,}029$

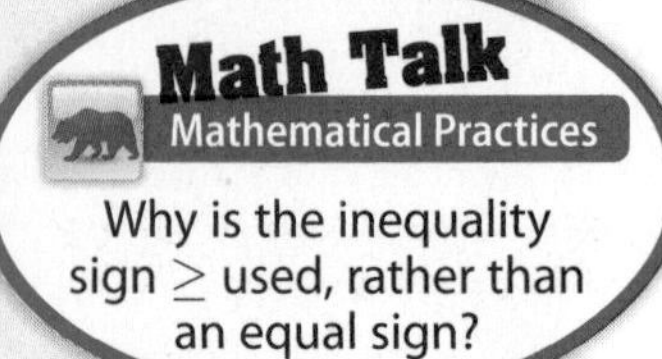

YOUR TURN

3. The 45 members of the glee club are trying to raise $6,000 so they can compete in the state championship. They already have $1,240. What inequality can you write to find the amount each member must raise, on average, to meet the goal? ______________________

4. Ella has $40 to spend at the State Fair. Admission is $6 and each ride costs $3. Write an inequality to find the greatest number of rides she can go on.

____

Writing a Verbal Description of a Two-Step Inequality

You can also write a verbal description to fit a two-step inequality.

EXAMPLE 2 

CA CC 7.EE.4

Write a corresponding real-world problem to represent $2x + 20 \leq 50$.

My Notes

STEP 1 Analyze what each part of the inequality means mathematically.

x is the solution of the problem, the quantity you are looking for.

$2x$ means that, for a reason given in the problem, the quantity you are looking for is multiplied by 2.

$+ 20$ means that, for a reason given in the problem, 20 is added to $2x$.

≤ 50 means that after multiplying the solution x by 2 and adding 20 to it, the result can be no greater than 50.

STEP 2 Think of some different situations in which a quantity x is multiplied by 2.

You run x miles per day for 2 days. So, $2x$ is the total distance run.	You buy 2 items each costing x dollars. So, $2x$ is the total cost.

STEP 3 Build on the situation and adjust it to create a verbal description that takes all of the information into account.

- Tomas has run 20 miles so far this week. If he intends to run 50 miles or less, how many miles on average should he run on each of the 2 days remaining in the week?
- Manny buys 2 work shirts that are each the same price. After using a $20 gift card, he can spend no more than $50. What is the maximum amount he can spend on each shirt?

YOUR TURN

Write a real-world problem for each inequality.

5. $3x + 10 > 30$

6. $5x - 50 \leq 100$

Guided Practice

Draw algebra tiles to model each two-step inequality. (Explore Activity)

1. $4x - 5 < 7$

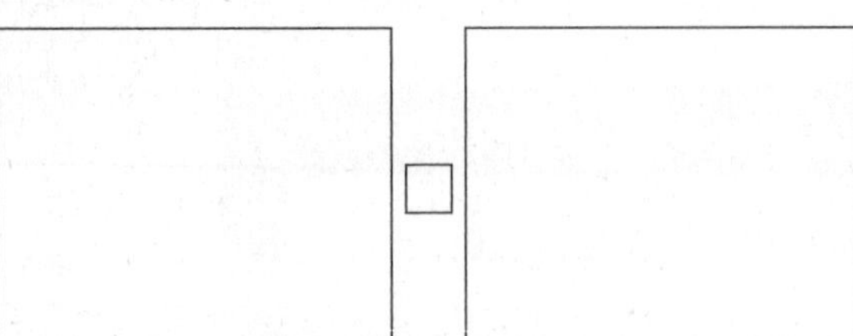

2. $-3x + 6 > 9$

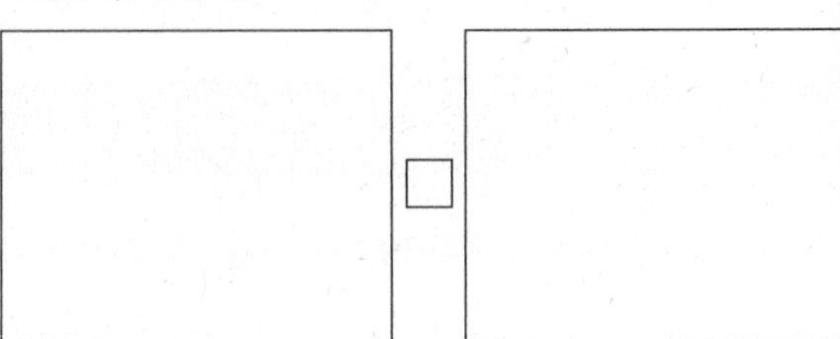

3. The booster club needs to raise at least $7,000 for new football uniforms. So far, they have raised $1,250. Write an inequality to find the average amounts each of the 92 members can raise to meet the club's objective. (Example 1)

Let *a* represent the amount each member must raise.

amount to be raised: ________ amount already raised: ________ number of members: ________

Use clues in the problem to write an equation.

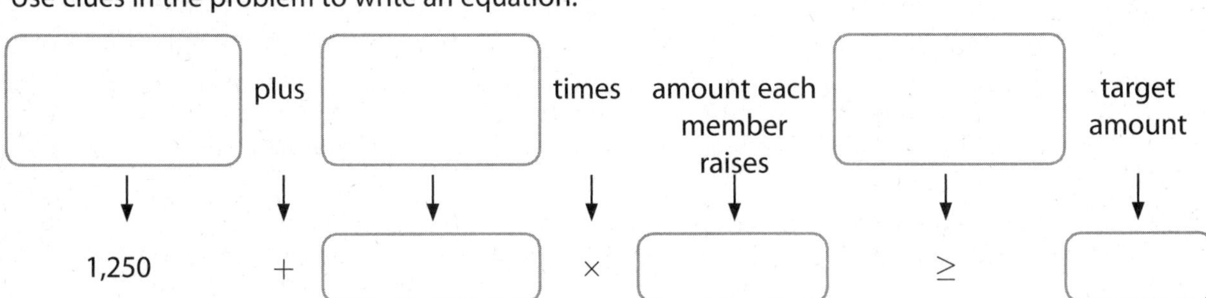

The inequality that represents the situation is ________________.

4. Analyze what each part of $7x - 18 \leq 32$ means mathematically. (Example 2)

x is ________________. $7x$ is ________________.

-18 means that ________________.

≤ 32 means that ________________

5. Write a real-world problem to represent $7x - 18 \leq 32$.

____

? ESSENTIAL QUESTION CHECK-IN

6. Describe the steps you would follow to write a two-step inequality you can use to solve a real-world problem.

____

____

Name ____________ Class ____________ Date ____________

7.2 Independent Practice

CA CC 7.EE.4

7. Three friends earned more than \$200 washing cars. They paid their parents \$28 for supplies and divided the rest of money equally. Write an inequality to find possible amounts each friend earned. Identify what your variable represents.

____

____

8. Nick has \$7.00. Bagels cost \$0.75 each, and a small container of cream cheese costs \$1.29. Write an inequality to find the numbers of bagels Nick can buy. Identify what your variable represents.

____

____

9. Chet needs to buy 4 work shirts, all costing the same amount. After he uses a \$25 gift certificate, he can spend no more than \$75. Write an inequality to find the possible costs for a shirt. Identify what your variable represents.

____

____

10. Due to fire laws, no more than 720 people may attend a performance at Metro Auditorium. The balcony holds 120 people. There are 32 rows on the ground floor, each with the same number of seats. Write an inequality to find the numbers of people that can sit in a ground-floor row if the balcony is full. Identify what your variable represents.

____

____

11. Liz earns a salary of \$2,100 per month, plus a commission of 5% of her sales. She wants to earn at least \$2,400 this month. Write an inequality to find amounts of sales that will meet her goal. Identify what your variable represents.

____

____

12. Lincoln Middle School plans to collect more than 2,000 cans of food in a food drive. So far, 668 cans have been collected. Write an inequality to find numbers of cans the school can collect on each of the final 7 days of the drive to meet this goal. Identify what your variable represents.

____

____

13. Joanna joins a CD club. She pays \$7 per month plus \$10 for each CD that she orders. Write an inequality to find how many CDs she can purchase in a month if she spends no more than \$100. Identify what your variable represents.

____

____

14. Lionel wants to buy a belt that costs \$22. He also wants to buy some shirts that are on sale for \$17 each. He has \$80. What inequality can you write to find the number of shirts he can buy? Identify what your variable represents.

____

____

____

15. Write a situation for $15x - 20 \leq 130$ and solve.

____

____

____

Analyze Relationships Write $>$, $<$, $\geq$, or $\leq$ in the blank to express the given relationship.

16. m is at least 25 m ______ 25

17. k is no greater than 9 k ______ 9

18. p is less than 48 p ______ 48

19. b is no more than -5 b ______ -5

20. h is at most 56 h ______ 56

21. w is no less than 0 w ______ 0

22. Critical Thinking Marie scored 95, 86, and 89 on three science tests. She wants her average score for 6 tests to be at least 90. What inequality can you write to find the average scores that she can get on her next three tests to meet this goal? Use s to represent the lowest average score.

____

____

H.O.T. FOCUS ON HIGHER ORDER THINKING

Work Area

23. Communicate Mathematical Ideas Write an inequality that expresses the reason the lengths 5 feet, 10 feet, and 20 feet could not be used to make a triangle. Explain how the inequality demonstrates that fact.

____

____

____

____

____

24. Analyze Relationships The number m satisfies the relationship $m < 0$. Write an inequality expressing the relationship between $-m$ and 0. Explain your reasoning.

____

____

____

25. Analyze Relationships The number n satisfies the relationship $n > 0$. Write three inequalities to express the relationship between n and $\frac{1}{n}$.

____

LESSON 7.3 Solving Two-Step Inequalities

CA CC 7.EE.4b

Solve word problems leading to inequalities of the form $px + q > r$ or $px + q < r$, where p, q, and r are specific rational numbers. Graph the solution set of the inequality and interpret it in the context of the problem.

ESSENTIAL QUESTION

How do you solve a two-step inequality?

Modeling and Solving Two-Step Inequalities

You can solve two-step inequalities using algebra tiles. The method is similar to the one you used to solve two-step equations.

EXAMPLE 1

CA CC Prep for 7.EE.4b

Use algebra tiles to model and solve $4d - 3 \geq 9$.

STEP 1 Model the inequality. Use a "$\geq$" symbol between the mats.

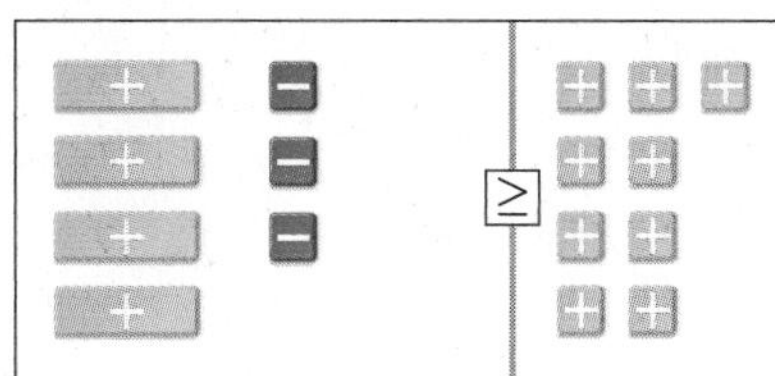

STEP 2 Add three +1 tiles to both sides of the mat.

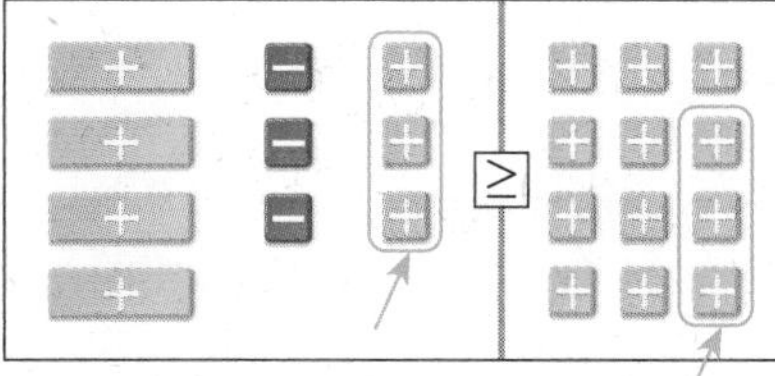

STEP 3 Remove zero pairs from the left side of the mat.

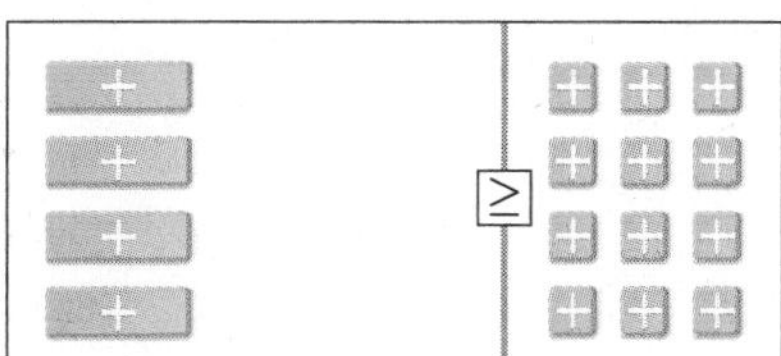

STEP 4 Divide each side into 4 equal groups.

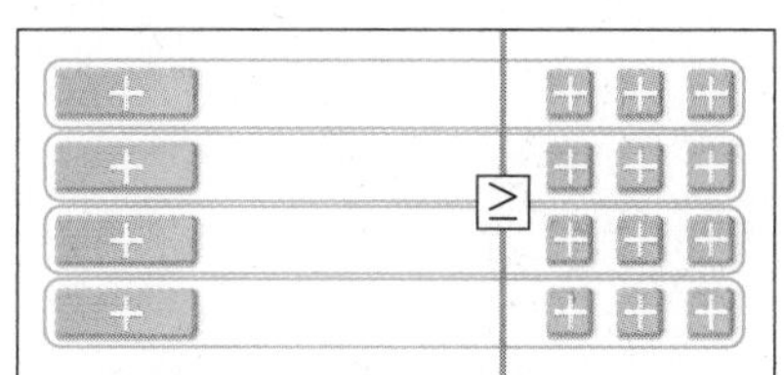

STEP 5 The solution is $d \geq 3$.

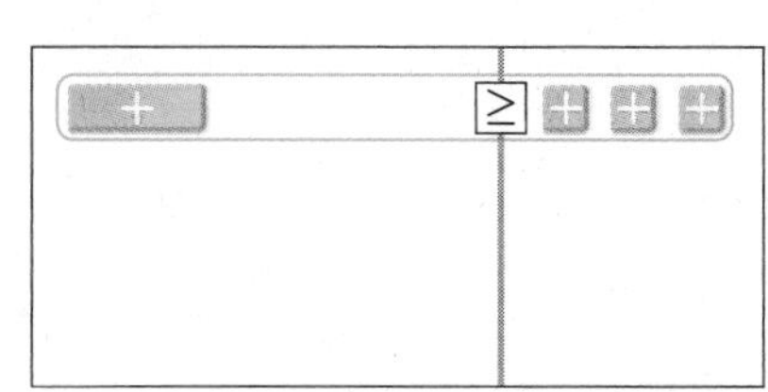

Math Talk
Mathematical Practices

Why are three +1-tiles added to both sides of the mat in Step 2?

Use algebra tiles to model and solve each inequality.

1. $2x + 7 > 11$ ________________

2. $5h - 4 \geq 11$ ________________

Solving and Interpreting Solutions

You can apply what you know about solving two-step equations and one-step inequalities to solving two-step inequalities.

EXAMPLE 2

CA CC 7.EE.4b

Serena wants to complete the first 3 miles of a 10-mile run in 45 minutes or less running at a steady pace. The inequality $10 - 0.75p \leq 7$ can be used to find p, the pace, in miles per hour, she can run to reach her goal. Solve the inequality. Then graph and interpret the solution.

STEP 1 Use inverse operations to solve the inequality.

$$10 - 0.75p \leq 7$$ Subtract 10 from both sides.

$$\underline{-10} \qquad \underline{-10}$$

$$-0.75p \leq -3$$

$$\frac{-0.75p}{-0.75} \geq \frac{-3}{-0.75}$$ Divide both sides by −0.75. Reverse the inequality symbol.

$$p \geq 4$$

STEP 2 Graph the inequality and interpret the circle and the arrow.

Serena can meet her goal by running at a pace of 4 miles per hour.

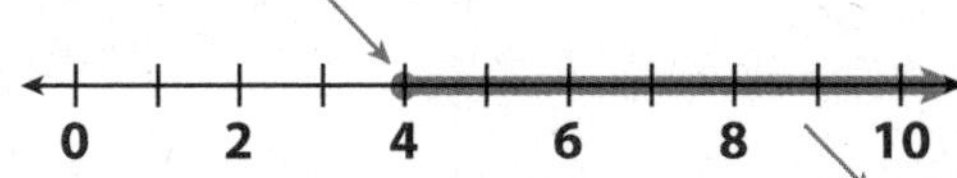

Serena can run at paces faster than 4 miles per hour and reach her goal.

Serena has to run at a steady pace of at least 4 miles per hour.

Math Talk
Mathematical Practices

In Example 2, how will the graph change if Serena's maximum pace is 12 miles per hour?

YOUR TURN

3. Joshua wants to complete the first mile of a 5-mile run in 10 minutes or less running at a steady pace. The inequality $5 - \frac{p}{6} \leq 4$ can be used to find p, the pace, in miles per hour, he can run to reach his goal. Solve the inequality. Then graph and interpret the solution.

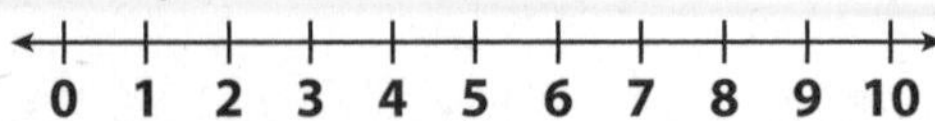

____

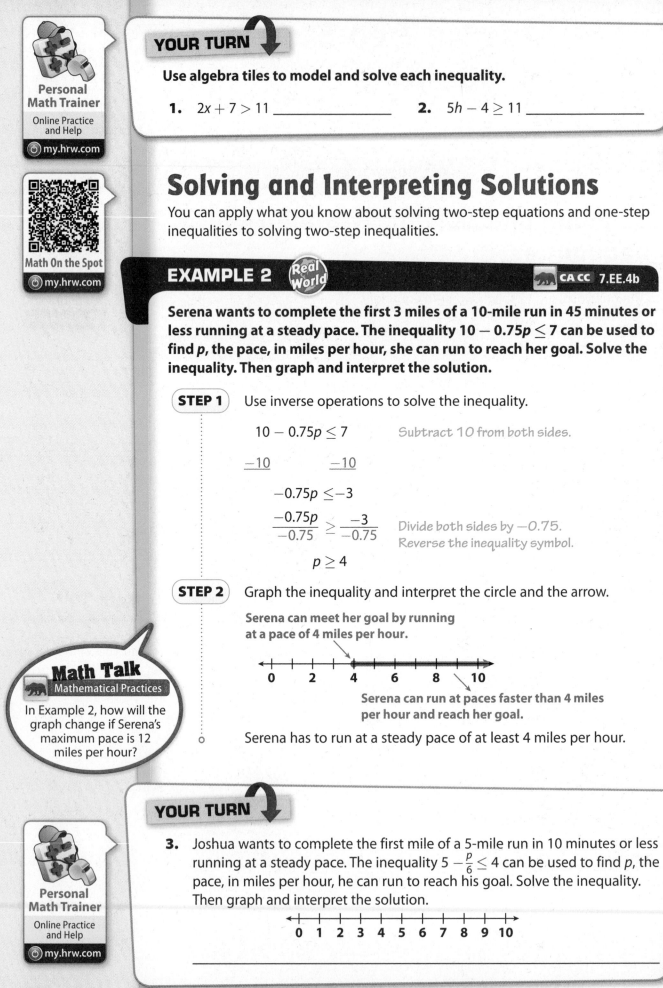

Determining if a Given Value Makes the Inequality True

You can use substitution to decide whether a given value is the solution of an inequality.

EXAMPLE 3 

CA CC 7.EE.4b

My Notes

At Gas 'n' Wash, gasoline sells for \$4.00 a gallon and a car wash costs \$12. Harika wants to have her car washed and keep her total purchase under \$60. The inequality $4g + 12 < 60$ can be used to find g, the number of gallons of gas she can buy. Determine which, if any, of these values is a solution: $g = 10$; $g = 11$; $g = 12$.

STEP 1 Substitute each value for g in the inequality $4g + 12 < 60$.

$g = 10$	$g = 11$	$g = 12$
$4(10) + 12 < 60$	$4(11) + 12 < 60$	$4(12) + 12 < 60$

STEP 2 Evaluate each expression to see if a true inequality results.

$4(10) + 12 \overset{?}{<} 60$	$4(11) + 12 \overset{?}{<} 60$	$4(12) + 12 \overset{?}{<} 60$
$40 + 12 \overset{?}{<} 60$	$44 + 12 \overset{?}{<} 60$	$48 + 12 \overset{?}{<} 60$
$52 \overset{?}{<} 60$	$56 \overset{?}{<} 60$	$60 \overset{?}{<} 60$
true ✓	true ✓	*not* true ✗

So, Harika can buy 10 or 11 gallons of gas but not 12 gallons.

Check: Solve and graph the inequality.

$4g + 12 < 60$

$4g < 48$

$g < 12$

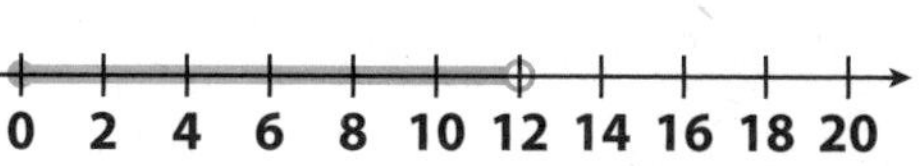

The closed circle at zero represents the minimum amount she can buy, zero gallons. She cannot buy a negative number of gallons. The open circle at 12 means that she can buy any amount up to but not including 12 gallons.

YOUR TURN

Circle any given values that make the inequality true.

4. $3v - 8 > 22$

$v = 9$; $v = 10$; $v = 11$

5. $5h + 12 \leq -3$

$h = -3$; $h = -4$; $h = -5$

Guided Practice

1. Describe how to solve the inequality $3x + 4 < 13$ using algebra tiles. (Example 1)

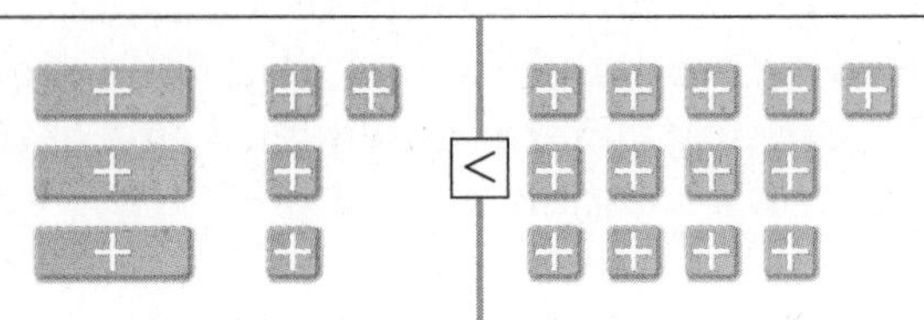

____

____

Solve each inequality. Graph and check the solution. (Example 2)

2. $5d - 13 < 32$ ____________________

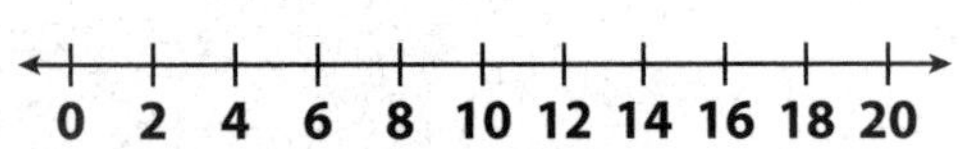

3. $-4b + 9 \leq -7$ ____________________

0 2 4 6 8 10 12 14 16 18 20

Circle any given values that make the inequality true. (Example 3)

4. $2m + 18 > -4$

$m = -12$; $m = -11$; $m = -10$

5. $-6y + 3 \geq 0$

$y = 1$; $y = \frac{1}{2}$; $y = 0$

6. Lizzy has 6.5 hours to tutor 4 students and spend 1.5 hours in a lab. She plans to tutor each student the same amount of time. The inequality $6.5 - 4t \geq 1.5$ can be used to find t, the amount of time in hours Lizzy could spend with each student. Solve the inequality. Graph and interpret the solution. Can Lizzy tutor each student for 1.5 hours? Explain. (Examples 2 and 3)

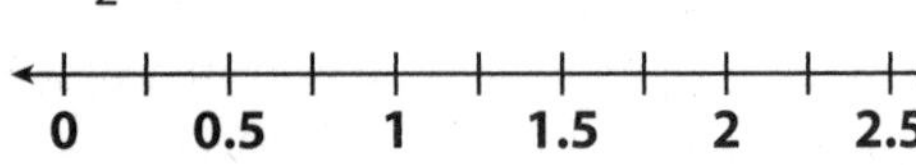

____

____

ESSENTIAL QUESTION CHECK-IN

7. How do you solve a two-step inequality?

____

____

____

Name ________________ Class ________________ Date ________________

7.3 Independent Practice

7.EE.4b

Solve each inequality. Graph and check the solution.

8. $2s + 5 \geq 49$ ________________

10 12 14 16 18 20 22 24 26 28 30

9. $-3t + 9 \geq -21$ ________________

–10 –8 –6 –4 –2 0 2 4 6 8 10

10. $55 > -7v + 6$ ________________

–10 –9 –8 –7 –6 –5 –4 –3 –2 –1 0

11. $21\frac{1}{3} > 3m - 2\frac{2}{3}$ ________________

0 1 2 3 4 5 6 7 8 9 10

12. $\frac{a}{-8} + 15 > 23$ ________________

–70 –69 –68 –67 –66 –65 –64 –63 –62 –61 –60

13. $\frac{f}{2} - 22 < 48$ ________________

100 105 110 115 120 125 130 135 140 145 150

14. $-25 + \frac{t}{2} \geq 50$ ________________

15. $10 + \frac{g}{-9} > 12$ ________________

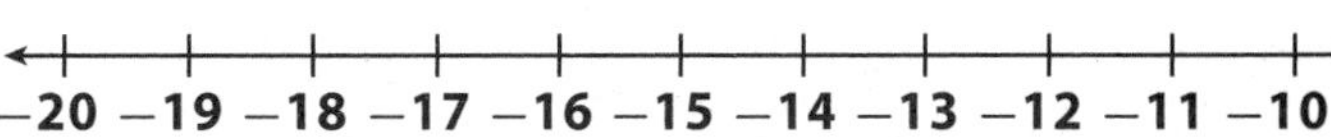

16. $25.2 \leq -1.5y + 1.2$ ________________

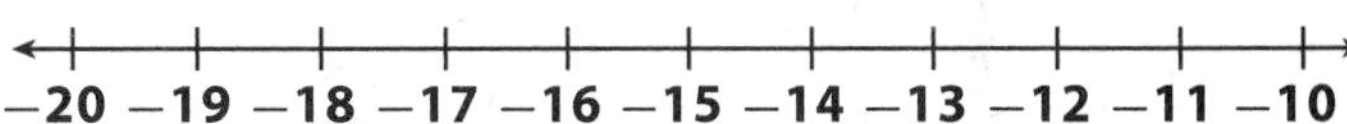

17. $-3.6 \geq -0.3a + 1.2$ ________________

10 11 12 13 14 15 16 17 18 19 20

18. **What If?** The perimeter of a rectangle is at most 80 inches. The length of the rectangle is 25 inches. The inequality $80 - 2w \geq 50$ can be used to find w, the width of the rectangle in inches. Solve the inequality and interpret the solution. How will the solution change if the width must be at least 10 inches and a whole number?

____

____

____

19. **Interpret the Answer** Grace earns \$7 for each car she washes. She always saves \$25 of her weekly earnings. This week, she wants to have at least \$65 in spending money. How many cars must she wash? Write and solve an inequality to represent this situation. Interpret the solution in context.

____

____

Work Area

H.O.T. FOCUS ON HIGHER ORDER THINKING

20. **Critical Thinking** Is there any value of x with the property that $x < x - 1$? Explain your reasoning.

____

____

____

21. **Analyze Relationships** A *compound inequality* consists of two simple equalities joined by the word "*and*" or "*or*." Graph the solution sets of each of these compound inequalities.

a. $x > 2$ and $x < 7$

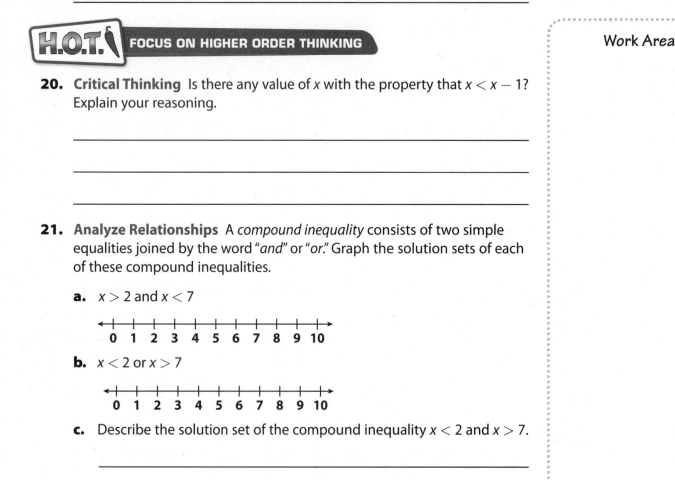

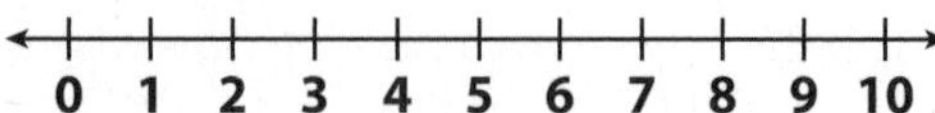

b. $x < 2$ or $x > 7$

0 1 2 3 4 5 6 7 8 9 10

c. Describe the solution set of the compound inequality $x < 2$ and $x > 7$.

____

d. Describe the solution set of the compound inequality $x > 2$ or $x < 7$.

____

22. **Communicate Mathematical Ideas** Joseph used the problem-solving strategy Work Backward to solve the inequality $2n + 5 < 13$. Shawnee solved the inequality using the algebraic method you used in this lesson. Compare the two methods.

____

____

____

____

____

____

MODULE QUIZ

Ready to Go On?

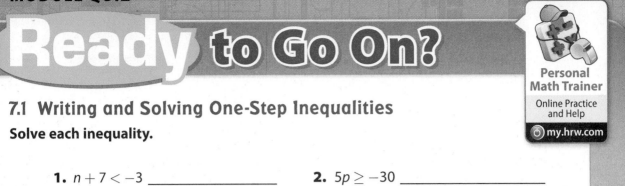

7.1 Writing and Solving One-Step Inequalities

Solve each inequality.

1. $n + 7 < -3$ ________________

2. $5p \geq -30$ ________________

3. $14 < k + 11$ ________________

4. $\frac{d}{-3} \leq -6$ ________________

5. $c - 2.5 \leq 2.5$ ________________

6. $12 \geq -3b$ ________________

7. Jose has scored 562 points on his math tests so far this semester. To get an A for the semester, he must score at least 650 points. Write and solve an inequality to find the minimum number of points he must score on the remaining tests in order to get an A.

____

7.2 Writing Two-Step Inequalities

8. During a scuba dive, Lainey descended to a point 20 feet below the ocean surface. She continued her descent at a rate of 20 feet per minute. Write an inequality you could solve to find the number of minutes she can continue to descend if she does not want to reach a point more than 100 feet below the ocean surface.

____

7.3 Solving Two-Step Inequalities

Solve.

9. $2s + 3 > 15$ ________________

10. $-\frac{d}{12} - 6 < 1$ ________________

11. $-6w - 18 \geq 36$ ________________

12. $\frac{z}{4} + 22 \leq 38$ ________________

13. $\frac{b}{9} - 34 < -36$ ________________

14. $-2p + 12 > 8$ ________________

ESSENTIAL QUESTION

15. How can you recognize whether a real-world situation should be represented by an equation or an inequality?

____

____

MODULE 7
MIXED REVIEW

Assessment Readiness

1. Which expression(s) below are equivalent to $-3x + 6$? Select all that apply.

- ○ $(4x + 2) + (-7x + 4)$
- ○ $(-4x + 4) - (x - 2)$
- ○ $-3(x - 2)$
- ○ $\frac{1}{2}(-6x + 12)$

2. Consider the inequality $\frac{1}{2}n - 6 \geq -5\frac{2}{3}$.

Choose True or False for each statement.

A. $n = -4$ is a solution. ○ True ○ False

B. $n = \frac{2}{3}$ is a solution. ○ True ○ False

C. $n = 2\frac{1}{2}$ is a solution. ○ True ○ False

3. Darian wants to run more than 5 miles this week. So far, he has run $2\frac{3}{4}$ miles. Write and solve an inequality to determine how many more miles Darian must run to meet his goal. Explain how you can check your solution.

4. The owner of a miniature golf course plans to spend no more than \$300 on supplies. Golf balls cost \$6.30 per dozen, and putters cost \$10.95 each. The owner decides to buy 10 dozen golf balls. Can the owner also afford to buy 20 putters? Write and solve an inequality to justify your answer.

UNIT 3

Study Guide Review

MODULE 6 Expressions and Equations

Key Vocabulary
algebraic expression *(expresión algebraica)*
equation *(ecuación)*

ESSENTIAL QUESTION

How can you use equations to solve real-world problems?

EXAMPLE 1

Huang and Belita both repair computers. Huang makes \$50 a day plus \$25 per repair. Belita makes \$20 a day plus \$35 per repair. Write an expression for Huang and Belita's total daily earnings if they make the same number of repairs *r*.

Huang: $\$50 + \$25r$ Belita: $\$20 + \$35r$

Together: $(50 + 25r) + (20 + 35r) = 50 + 20 + 25r + 35r = 70 + 60r$

Huang and Belita earn $\$70 + \$60r$ together.

EXAMPLE 2

Simplify the expression.

$1.2(3m - 5) - 7m$

$1.2(3m - 5) - 7m$

$3.6m - 6 - 7m$ Use the Distributive Property.

$3.6m + (-6) + (-7m)$ Rewrite subtraction as adding the opposite.

$3.6m + (-7m) + (-6)$ Use the Commutative Property.

$-3.4m - 6$ Combine like terms.

EXAMPLE 3

A skydiver's parachute opens at a height of 2,790 feet. He then falls at a rate of $-15\frac{1}{2}$ feet per second. How long will it take the skydiver to reach the ground?

Let *x* represent the number of seconds it takes to reach the ground.

$-15\frac{1}{2}x = -2{,}790$

$-\frac{31}{2}x = -2{,}790$ Write as a fraction.

$\left(-\frac{2}{31}\right)\left(-\frac{31}{2}x\right) = \left(-\frac{2}{31}\right)(-2{,}790)$ Multiply both sides by the reciprocal.

$x = 180$

It takes 180 seconds for the skydiver to reach the ground.

EXAMPLE 4

A clothing store sells clothing for 2 times the wholesale cost plus $10. The store sells a pair of pants for $48. How much did the store pay for the pants? Represent the solution on a number line.

Let w represent the wholesale cost of the pants, or the price paid by the store.

$2w + 10 = 48$

10 11 12 13 14 15 16 17 18 19 20

$2w = 38$ Subtract 10 from both sides.

$w = 19$ Divide both sides by 2.

The store paid $19 for the pants.

EXERCISES

Simplify each expression. (Lesson 6.1)

1. $(2x + 3\frac{2}{5}) + (5x - \frac{4}{5})$ ________

2. $(-0.5x - 4) - (1.5x + 2.3)$ ________

3. $9(3t + 4b)$ ________

4. $0.7(5a - 13p)$ ________

Factor each expression. (Lesson 6.1)

5. $8x + 56$ ________

6. $3x + 57$ ________

Use inverse operations to solve each equation. (Lesson 6.2)

7. $1.6 + y = -7.3$ ________

8. $-\frac{2}{3}n = 12$ ________

9. The cost of a ticket to an amusement park is $42 per person. For groups of up to 8 people, the cost per ticket decreases by $3 for each person in the group. Marcos's ticket cost $30. Write and solve an equation to find the number of people in Marcos's group. (Lessons 6.3, 6.4)

____

Solve each equation. Graph the solution on a number line. (Lesson 6.4)

10. $8x - 28 = 44$

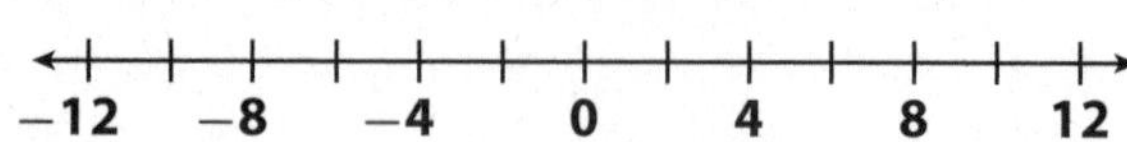

____

11. $-5z + 4 = 34$

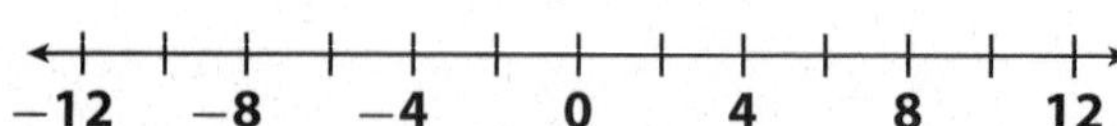

____

MODULE 7

Inequalities

Key Vocabulary
Inequalities
(desigualdad)

ESSENTIAL QUESTION

How can you use inequalities to solve real-world problems?

EXAMPLE 1

Amy is having her birthday party at a roller skating rink. The rink charges a fee of $50 plus $8 per person. If Amy wants to spend at most $170 for the party at the rink, how many people can she invite to her party?

Let p represent the number of people skating at the party.

$50 + 8p \leq 170$

$8p \leq 120$ Subtract 50 from both sides.

$\frac{8p}{8} \leq \frac{120}{8}$ Divide both sides by 8.

$p \leq 15$

Up to 15 people can skate, so Amy can invite up to 14 people to her party.

EXAMPLE 2

Determine which, if any, of these values makes the inequality $-7x + 42 \leq 28$ true: $x = -1, x = 2, x = 5$.

Substitute each value for x in the inequality and evaluate the expression to see if a true inequality results.

$-7(-1) + 42 \leq 28$ $-7(2) + 42 \leq 28$ $-7(5) + 42 \leq 28$

$x = 2$ and $x = 5$

EXERCISES

1. Prudie needs $90 or more to be able to take her family out to dinner. She has already saved $30 and wants to take her family out to eat in 4 days. (Lesson 7.2)

a. Suppose that Prudie earns the same each day. Write an inequality to find how much she needs to earn each day.

____

b. Suppose that Prudie earns $18 each day. Will she have enough money to take her family to dinner in 4 days? Explain.

____

Solve each inequality. Graph and check the solution. (Lesson 7.3)

2. $11 - 5y < -19$

3. $7x - 2 \leq 61$

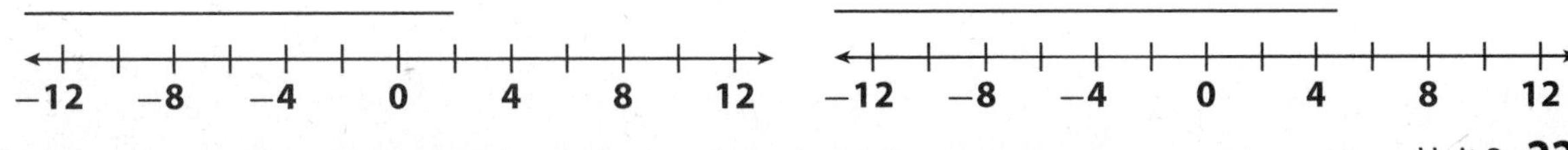

Unit Project

CA CC 7.EE.1, 7.EE.2, 7.EE.4, 7.EE.4a

The Rhind Papyrus

More than 3,600 years ago, an Egyptian scribe named Ahmose wrote this problem on a type of paper called papyrus: "A quantity with $\frac{1}{7}$ of it added to it becomes 19. What is the quantity?" The problem is Number 24 of 84 problems that are preserved in an ancient manuscript called the Rhind Papyrus. Today we would solve it by writing and solving this equation: $x + \frac{1}{7}x = 19$.

For this project, use the Internet to create a presentation in which you write and solve Problems 24–30, 32, and 34 of the Rhind Papyrus. Express your answers as fractions or mixed numbers.

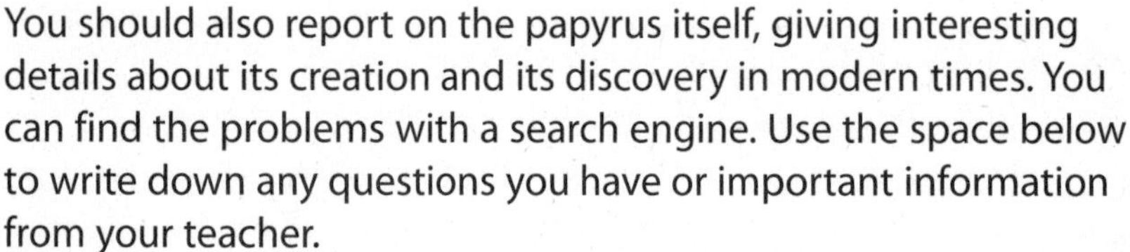

You should also report on the papyrus itself, giving interesting details about its creation and its discovery in modern times. You can find the problems with a search engine. Use the space below to write down any questions you have or important information from your teacher.

MATH IN CAREERS | **ACTIVITY**

Mechanical Engineer A mechanical engineer is testing the amount of force needed to make a spring stretch by a given amount. The force y is measured in units called *Newtons*, abbreviated N. The stretch x is measured in centimeters. Her results are shown in the graph. Write an equation for the line. Next, explain how you know the graph is proportional. Then, identify the rate of change and the constant of proportionality. Finally, what is the meaning of the constant of proportionality in the context of the problem?

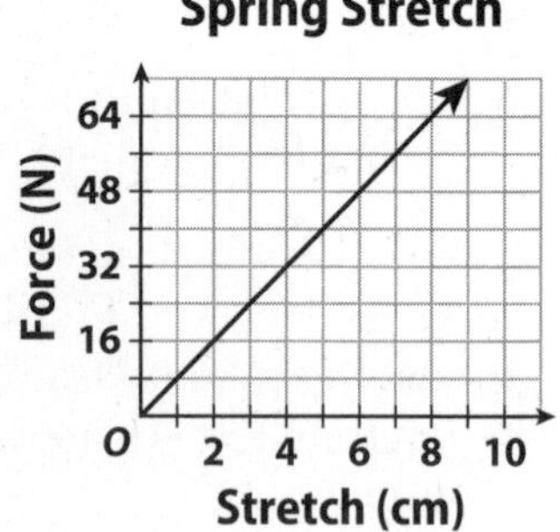

UNIT 3
MIXED REVIEW

Assessment Readiness

1. Look at each expression. Is the expression equivalent to $12x - 18$?

Select Yes or No for each expression.

A. $-2(-6x + 9)$ ○ Yes ○ No

B. $6(2x - 3)$ ○ Yes ○ No

C. $12(x - 6)$ ○ Yes ○ No

2. Consider the inequality $-3c + 8 \leq -1$.

Choose True or False for each statement.

A. The graph of the inequality has a closed circle at 3. ○ True ○ False

B. The graph of the inequality is shaded to the right of an endpoint. ○ True ○ False

C. The number 0 is included in the shaded region of the graph of the inequality. ○ True ○ False

3. A worker at a pet store tells Jillian that the total length of the fish in her aquarium should be no more than 10 inches. Black phantom tetras are 2 inches long, and neon tetras are 1.25 inches long. Jillian buys 3 black phantom tetras. Write an inequality that Jillian can use to decide how many neon tetras to buy for her aquarium. Tell what each part of your inequality represents.

4. The orange-and-purple-striped sweaters at a store were not selling, so the store put them on sale for half of the original price. The sweaters still did not sell, so the store reduced the price by an additional \$10. The sweaters are now priced at \$7.50. Write and solve an equation to find the original price of the sweaters. Explain each step of your solution.

Performance Tasks

★**5.** Mr. Arnold needs to repaint the outside of his house. He estimates that the area he needs to paint is about 1,600 square feet. Each gallon of paint will cover about 250 square feet. Mr. Arnold has 1 gallon of paint left over from the last time he painted that he can use this time. Will Mr. Arnold need to buy more than 5 gallons of paint? Use an equation to explain your reasoning.

★★**6.** A restaurant owner is ordering new chef uniforms. Each uniform has a jacket and pants. The jackets cost \$37.99 each, plus a one-time fee of \$70.00 to add the restaurant's logo. The pants cost \$27.99 each.

a. Write and simplify an expression for the total cost of *n* uniforms.

b. The restaurant owner can spend \$550 for uniforms. Write an inequality to find the number of uniforms she can afford to buy.

c. Can the owner buy 8 uniforms? Explain your reasoning.

d. Suppose the restaurant owner decides not to have the logo put on the chef jackets. Does this decision change your answer to part **c**? Explain.

★★★**7.** Kaylee has a \$20 gift card to spend at an online entertainment store. The table shows the categories of items she can buy. Kaylee wants to buy only songs and TV episodes with her card. If Kaylee buys at least 4 TV episodes, what combinations of songs and TV episodes can she afford? Use inequalities to justify your reasoning.

Category	Price
App	\$0.99
Song*	\$1.29
TV episode	\$2.99
Movie	\$9.99

*This week's special: Buy 6 songs and get 1 free!

UNIT 4

Geometry

MODULE 8

Modeling Geometric Figures

CA CC 7.G.1, 7.G.2, 7.G.3, 7.G.5

MODULE 9

Circumference, Area, and Volume

CA CC 7.G.4, 7.G.6

MATH IN CAREERS

Product Design Engineer A product design engineer works to design and develop manufactured products and equipment. A product design engineer uses math to design and modify models, and to calculate costs in producing their designs.

If you are interested in a career in product design engineering, you should study these mathematical subjects:

- Algebra
- Geometry
- Trigonometry
- Statistics
- Calculus

Research other careers that require the use of mathematics to design and modify products.

ACTIVITY At the end of the unit, check out how **product design engineers** use math.

Unit Project Preview

Buffon's Needle

In the Unit Project at the end of this unit you will conduct an experiment to approximate the value of π. The image shows the "needle" and "target" you will use in the experiment. To successfully complete the Unit Project you'll need to master these skills:

- Calculate circumference of circles.
- Calculate area of circles.
- Multiply and divide rational numbers.

Understand the meaning of π.

1. Describe a real-world situation in which you might need to calculate the circumference of a circle.

____

____

2. Describe a real-world situation in which you might need to calculate the area of a circle.

____

____

Tracking Your Learning Progression

This unit addresses important California Common Core Standards in the Critical Areas of understanding geometrical figures and solving problems involving plane and solid figures.

Domain 7.G Geometry

Cluster Draw, construct, and describe geometrical figures and describe the relationships between them.

The unit also supports additional standards.

Domain 7.G Geometry

Cluster Solve real-life and mathematical problems involving angle measure, area, surface area, and volume.

Modeling Geometric Figures

ESSENTIAL QUESTION

How can you use proportions to solve real-world geometry problems?

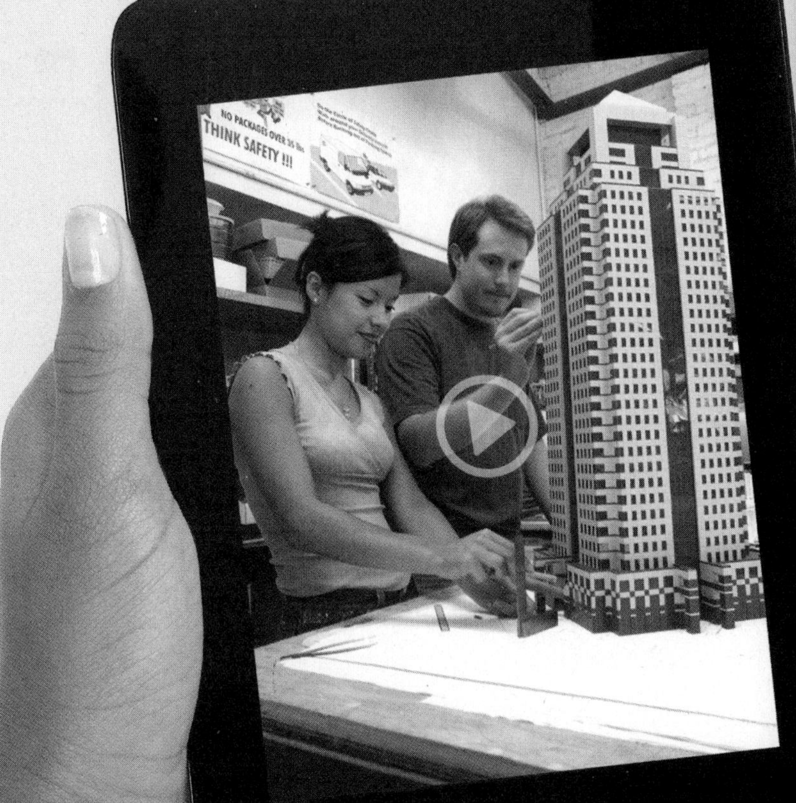

my.hrw.com

Real-World Video

Architects make blueprints and models of their designs to show clients and contractors. These scale drawings and scale models have measurements in proportion to those of the project when built.

GO DIGITAL
my.hrw.com

my.hrw.com

Go digital with your write-in student edition, accessible on any device.

Math On the Spot

Scan with your smart phone to jump directly to the online edition, video tutor, and more.

Animated Math

Interactively explore key concepts to see how math works.

Personal Math Trainer

Get immediate feedback and help as you work through practice sets.

Are YOU Ready?

Complete these exercises to review skills you will need for this module.

Personal Math Trainer

Online Practice and Help

Solve Two-Step Equations

EXAMPLE

$5x + 3 = -7$

$5x + 3 - 3 = -7 - 3$ Subtract 3 from both sides.

$5x = -10$ Simplify.

$\frac{5x}{5} = \frac{-10}{5}$ Divide both sides by 5.

$x = -2$

Solve.

1. $3x + 4 = 10$ __________
2. $5x - 11 = 34$ __________
3. $-2x + 5 = -9$ __________
4. $-11 = 8x + 13$ __________
5. $4x - 7 = -27$ __________
6. $\frac{1}{2}x + 16 = 39$ __________
7. $12 = 2x - 16$ __________
8. $5x - 15 = -65$ __________

Solve Proportions

EXAMPLE

$\frac{a}{4} = \frac{27}{18}$

What do you multiply 27 by to get a? $18 \times \frac{2}{9} = 4$.

So multiply 27 by $\frac{2}{9}$.

$a = 27 \times \frac{2}{9} = 6$

Solve for *x*.

9. $\frac{x}{5} = \frac{18}{30}$ __________
10. $\frac{x}{12} = \frac{24}{36}$ __________
11. $\frac{3}{9} = \frac{x}{3}$ __________
12. $\frac{14}{15} = \frac{x}{75}$ __________
13. $\frac{8}{x} = \frac{14}{7}$ __________
14. $\frac{14}{x} = \frac{2}{5}$ __________
15. $\frac{5}{6} = \frac{x}{15}$ __________
16. $\frac{81}{33} = \frac{x}{5.5}$ __________

Reading Start-Up

Visualize Vocabulary

Use the ✔ words to complete the graphic. You may put more than one word on each line.

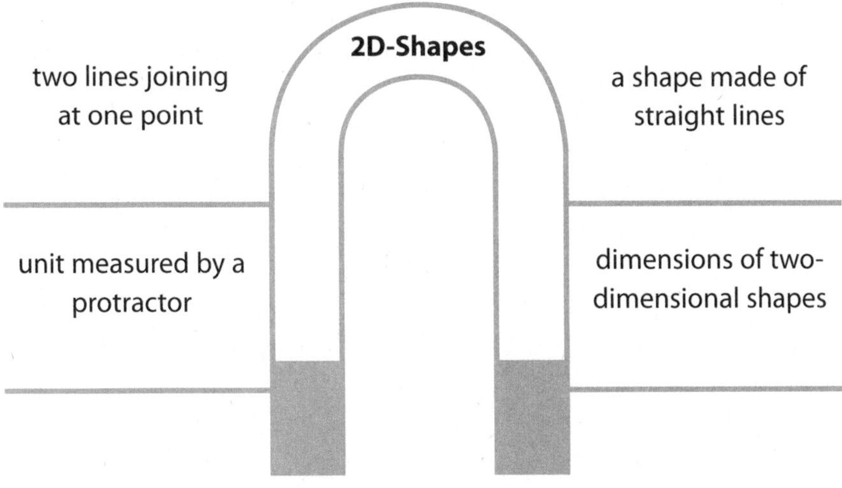

Understand Vocabulary

Complete each sentence using a preview word.

1. What is a proportional two-dimensional drawing of an object?

   ____

2. ____________________ are angles that have the same measure.

3. ____________________ are angles whose measures have a sum of 90°.

Vocabulary

Review Words

✔ angle *(ángulo)*
✔ degree *(grado)*
dimension *(dimensión)*
✔ length *(longitud)*
proportion *(proporción)*
✔ polygon *(polígono)*
ratio *(razón)*
✔ width *(ancho)*

Preview Words

adjacent angles *(ángulos adyacentes)*
complementary angles *(ángulos complementarios)*
congruent angles *(ángulos congruentes)*
cross section *(sección transversal)*
intersection *(intersección)*
scale *(escala)*
scale drawing *(dibujo a escala)*
supplementary angles *(ángulos suplementarios)*
vertical angles *(ángulos verticales)*

Active Reading

Key-Term Fold Before beginning the module, create a key-term fold to help you learn the vocabulary in this module. Write each highlighted vocabulary word on one side of a flap. Write the definition for each word on the other side of the flap. Use the key-term fold to quiz yourself on the definitions in this module.

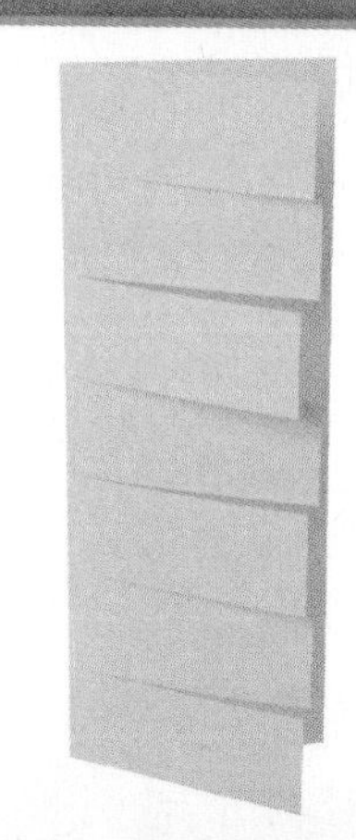

GETTING READY FOR

Modeling Geometric Figures

Understanding the standards and the vocabulary terms in the standards will help you know exactly what you are expected to learn in this module.

 CA CC **7.G.1**

Solve problems involving scale drawings of geometric figures, including computing actual lengths and areas from a scale drawing and reproducing a scale drawing at a different scale.

Key Vocabulary

scale *(escala)*
The ratio between two sets of measurements.

What It Means to You

You will learn how to calculate actual measurements from a scale drawing.

EXAMPLE 7.G.1

A photograph of a painting has dimensions 5.4 cm and 4 cm. The scale factor is $\frac{1}{15}$. Find the length and width of the actual painting.

$$\frac{1}{15} = \frac{5.4}{\ell} \qquad \frac{1}{15} = \frac{4}{w}$$

$$\frac{1 \times 5.4}{15 \times 5.4} = \frac{5.4}{\ell} \qquad \frac{1 \times 4}{15 \times 4} = \frac{4}{w}$$

$$15 \times 5.4 = \ell \qquad 15 \times 4 = w$$

$$81 = \ell \qquad 60 = w$$

The painting is 81 cm long and 60 cm wide.

CA CC **7.G.5**

Use facts about supplementary, complementary, vertical, and adjacent angles in a multi-step problem to write and solve simple equations for an unknown angle in a figure.

Key Vocabulary

supplementary angles
(ángulos suplementarios)
Two angles whose measures have a sum of 180°.

What It Means to You

You will learn about supplementary, complementary, vertical, and adjacent angles. You will solve simple equations to find the measure of an unknown angle in a figure.

EXAMPLE 7.G.5

Suppose $m\angle 1 = 55°$.

Adjacent angles formed by two intersecting lines are supplementary.

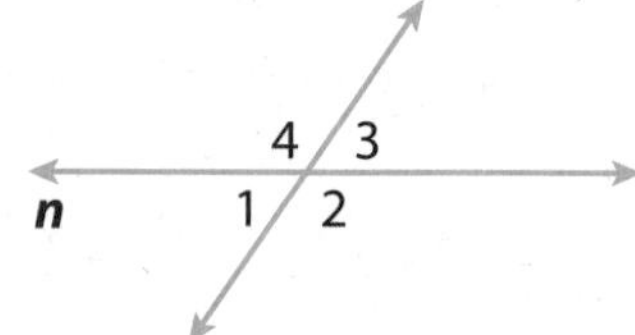

$m\angle 1 + m\angle 2 = 180°$

$55° + m\angle 2 = 180°$ Substitute.

$m\angle 2 = 180° - 55°$

$= 125°$

Visit **my.hrw.com** to see all **CA Common Core Standards** explained.

my.hrw.com

LESSON 8.1

Similar Shapes and Scale Drawings

CA CC 7.G.1

Solve problems involving scale drawings of geometric figures, including computing actual lengths and areas from a scale drawing and reproducing a scale drawing at a different scale. *Also 7.RP.1, 7.RP.2b*

ESSENTIAL QUESTION

How can you use scale drawings to solve problems?

EXPLORE ACTIVITY 1

Finding Dimensions

Scale drawings and scale models are used in mapmaking, construction, and other trades.

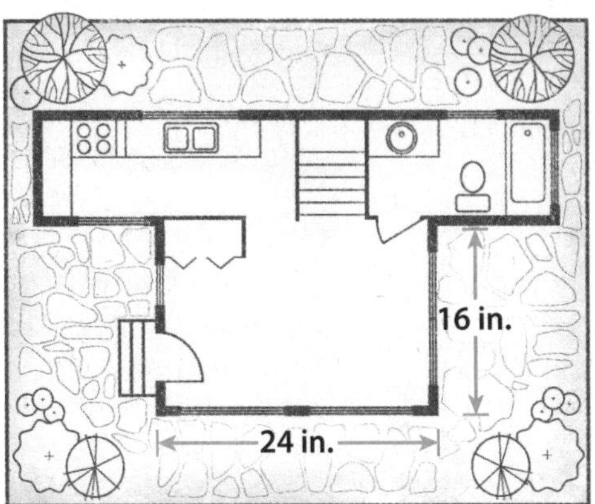

A blueprint is a technical drawing that usually displays architectural plans. Pete's blueprint shows a layout of a house. Every 4 inches in the blueprint represents 3 feet of the actual house. One of the walls in the blueprint is 24 inches long. What is the actual length of the wall?

A Complete the table to find the actual length of the wall.

Blueprint length (in.)	4	8	12	16	20	24
Actual length (ft)	3	6				

Reflect

1. In Pete's blueprint the length of a side wall is 16 inches. Find the actual length of the wall.

____

2. The back wall of the house is 33 feet long. What is the length of the back wall in the blueprint?

____

3. **Check for Reasonableness** How do you know your answer to **2** is reasonable?

____

____

____

____

Using a Scale Drawing to Find Area

Similar shapes are proportional figures that have the same shape but not necessarily the same size.

A **scale drawing** is a proportional two-dimensional drawing that is *similar* to an actual object. Scale drawings can represent objects that are smaller or larger than the actual object.

A **scale** is a ratio between 2 sets of measurements. It shows how a dimension in a scale drawing is related to the actual object. Scales are usually shown as two numbers separated by a colon such as 1:20 or 1 cm:1 m. Scales can be shown in the same unit or in different units.

My Notes

EXAMPLE 1

CA CC 7.G.1, 7.RP.1

The art class is planning to paint a mural on an outside wall. This figure is a scale drawing of the wall. What is the area of the actual wall?

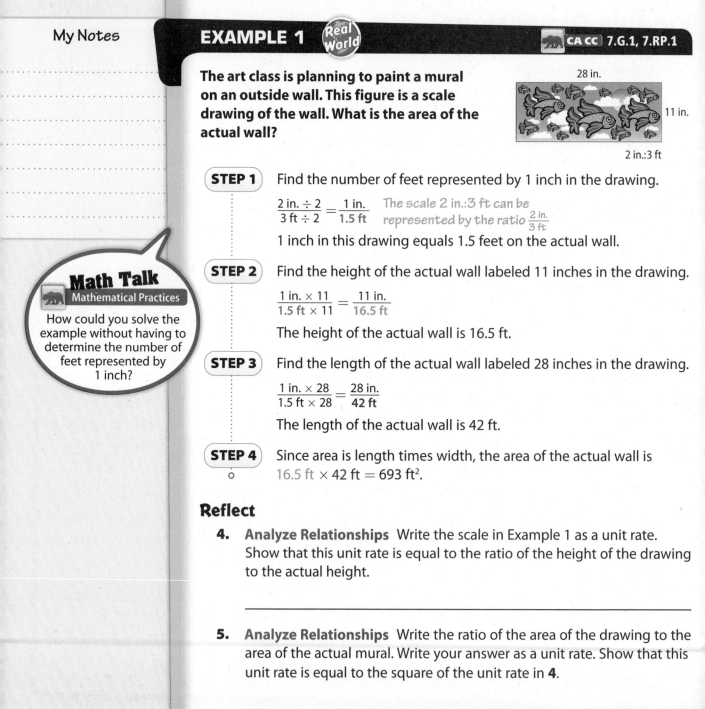

STEP 1 Find the number of feet represented by 1 inch in the drawing.

$\frac{2 \text{ in.} \div 2}{3 \text{ ft} \div 2} = \frac{1 \text{ in.}}{1.5 \text{ ft}}$ The scale 2 in.:3 ft can be represented by the ratio $\frac{2 \text{ in.}}{3 \text{ ft}}$

1 inch in this drawing equals 1.5 feet on the actual wall.

STEP 2 Find the height of the actual wall labeled 11 inches in the drawing.

$\frac{1 \text{ in.} \times 11}{1.5 \text{ ft} \times 11} = \frac{11 \text{ in.}}{16.5 \text{ ft}}$

The height of the actual wall is 16.5 ft.

STEP 3 Find the length of the actual wall labeled 28 inches in the drawing.

$\frac{1 \text{ in.} \times 28}{1.5 \text{ ft} \times 28} = \frac{28 \text{ in.}}{42 \text{ ft}}$

The length of the actual wall is 42 ft.

STEP 4 Since area is length times width, the area of the actual wall is $16.5 \text{ ft} \times 42 \text{ ft} = 693 \text{ ft}^2$.

Math Talk
Mathematical Practices
How could you solve the example without having to determine the number of feet represented by 1 inch?

Reflect

4. **Analyze Relationships** Write the scale in Example 1 as a unit rate. Show that this unit rate is equal to the ratio of the height of the drawing to the actual height.

5. **Analyze Relationships** Write the ratio of the area of the drawing to the area of the actual mural. Write your answer as a unit rate. Show that this unit rate is equal to the square of the unit rate in **4**.

6. The drawing plan for an art studio shows a rectangle that is 13.2 inches by 6 inches. The scale in the plan is 3 in.:5 ft. Find the length and width of the actual studio. Then find the area of the actual studio.

____

EXPLORE ACTIVITY 2 

Drawing in Different Scales

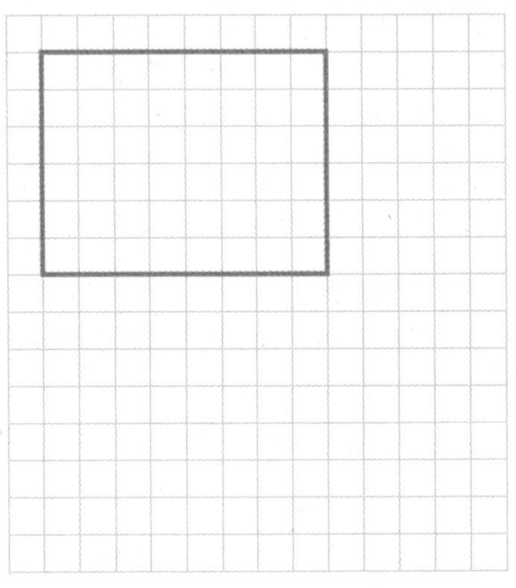

A A scale drawing of a meeting hall is drawn on centimeter grid paper as shown. The scale is 1 cm:3 m.

Suppose you redraw the rectangle on centimeter grid paper using a scale of 1 cm:6 m. In the new scale, 1 cm represents **more than/less than** 1 cm in the old scale.

The measurement of each side of the new drawing will be **twice/half** as long as the measurement of the original drawing.

B Draw the rectangle for the new scale 1 cm:6 m.

Reflect

7. Find the actual length and width of the hall using the original scale. Then find the actual length and width of the hall using the new scale. How do you know your answers are correct?

____

____

____

____

8. Explain how you know that there is a proportional relationship between the first and second drawings.

____

____

____

Guided Practice

1. The scale of a room in a blueprint is 3 in.:5 ft. A wall in the same blueprint is 18 in. Complete the table. (Explore Activity 1)

Blueprint length (in.)	3					
Actual length (ft)						

a. How long is the actual wall? ______________________

b. A window in the room has an actual width of 2.5 feet. Find the width of the window in the blueprint. __________

2. The scale in the drawing is 2 in.:4 ft. What are the length and width of the actual room? Find the area of the actual room. (Example 1)

14 in.

7 in.

____

____

3. The scale in the drawing is 2 cm:5 m. What are the length and width of the actual room? Find the area of the actual room. (Example 1)

10 cm

6 cm

____

4. A scale drawing of a cafeteria is drawn on centimeter grid paper as shown. The scale is 1 cm:4 m. (Explore Activity 2)

a. Redraw the rectangle on centimeter grid paper using a scale of 1 cm:6 m.

b. What is the actual length and width of the cafeteria using the original scale? What are the actual dimensions of the cafeteria using the new scale?

____

ESSENTIAL QUESTION CHECK-IN

5. If you have an accurate, complete scale drawing and the scale, which measurements of the object of the drawing can you find?

____

____

Name ______________________ Class ______________ Date ______________

8.1 Independent Practice

CA CC 7.G.1, 7.RP.1, 7.RP.2b

6. Art Marie has a small copy of Rene Magritte's famous painting, *The Schoolmaster*. Her copy has dimensions 2 inches by 1.5 inches. The scale of the copy is 1 in.:40 cm.

a. Find the dimensions of the original painting.

____

b. Find the area of the original painting.

____

c. Since 1 inch is 2.54 centimeters, find the dimensions of the original painting in inches.

____

d. Find the area of the original painting in square inches.

____

7. A game room has a floor that is 120 feet by 75 feet. A scale drawing of the floor on grid paper uses a scale of 1 unit:5 feet. What are the dimensions of the scale drawing?

____

8. Multiple Representations The length of a table is 6 feet. On a scale drawing, the length is 2 inches. Write three possible scales for the drawing.

____

9. Analyze Relationships A scale for a scale drawing is 10 cm:1 mm. Which is larger, the actual object or the scale drawing? Explain.

____

____

10. Architecture The scale model of a building is 5.4 feet tall.

a. If the original building is 810 meters tall, what was the scale used to make the model?

____

b. If the model is made out of tiny bricks each measuring 0.4 inch in height, how many bricks tall is the model?

____

11. You have been asked to build a scale model of your school out of toothpicks. Imagine your school is 30 feet tall. Your scale is 1 ft:1.26 cm.

   a. If a toothpick is 6.3 cm tall, how many toothpicks tall will your model be?

   ____

   b. Your mother is out of toothpicks, and suggests you use cotton swabs instead. You measure them, and they are 7.6 cm tall. How many cotton swabs tall will your model be?

   ____

H.O.T. FOCUS ON HIGHER ORDER THINKING

Work Area

12. **Draw Conclusions** The area of a square floor on a scale drawing is 100 square centimeters, and the scale of the drawing is 1 cm:2 ft. What is the area of the actual floor? What is the ratio of the area in the drawing to the actual area?

____

13. **Multiple Representations** Describe how to redraw a scale drawing with a new scale.

____

____

____

____

____

____

14. The scale drawing of a room is drawn on a grid that represents quarter-inch grid paper. The scale is $\frac{1}{4}$ in.:4 ft. Redraw the scale drawing of the same room using a different scale. What scale did you use? What is the length and width of the actual room? What is the area of the actual room?

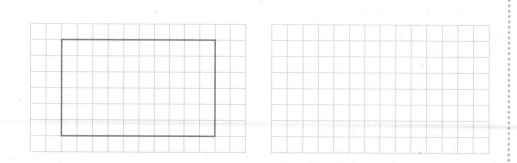

____

LESSON

8.2 Geometric Drawings

CA CC 7.G.2

Draw (freehand, with ruler and protractor, and with technology) geometric shapes with given conditions. Focus on constructing triangles from three measures of angles or sides, noticing when the conditions determine a unique triangle, more than one triangle, or no triangle.

ESSENTIAL QUESTION

How can you draw shapes that satisfy given conditions?

EXPLORE ACTIVITY 1 CA CC 7.G.2

Drawing Three Sides

Use geometry software to draw a triangle whose sides have the following lengths: 2 units, 3 units, and 4 units.

A Draw the segments.

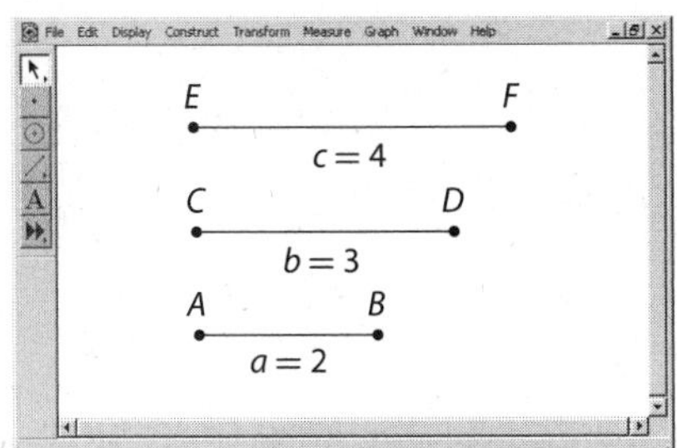

B Let $\overline{AB}$ be the base of the triangle. Place point C on top of point B and point E on top of point A.

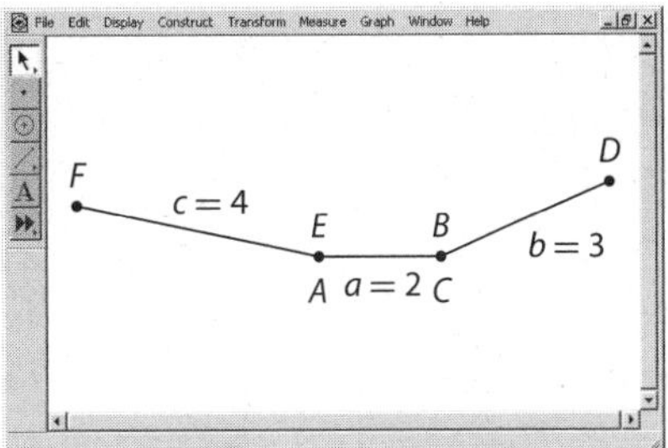

C Using the points C and E as fixed vertices, rotate points F and D to see if they will meet in a single point.

Note that the line segments form a triangle.

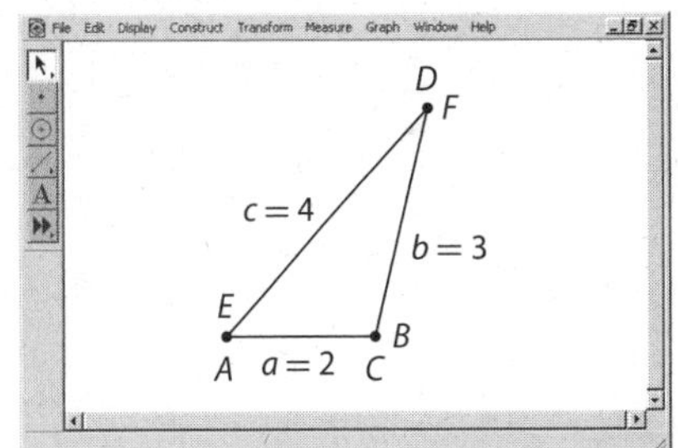

D Repeat **A** and **B**, but use a different segment as the base. Do the segments form a triangle? If so, is it the same as the original triangle?

____

E Use geometry software to draw a triangle with sides of length 2, 3, and 6 units, and one with sides of length 2, 3, and 5 units. Do the line segments form triangles? How does the sum of the lengths of the two shorter sides of each triangle compare to the length of the third side?

____

Reflect

1. **Conjecture** Do two segments of lengths a and b units and a longer segment of length c units form one triangle, more than one, or none?

____

EXPLORE ACTIVITY 2 CA CC 7.G.2

Two Angles and Their Included Side

Use a ruler and a protractor to draw each triangle.

Triangle 1	Triangle 2
Angles: 30° and 80°	Angles: 55° and 50°
Length of included side: 2 inches	Length of included side: 1 inch

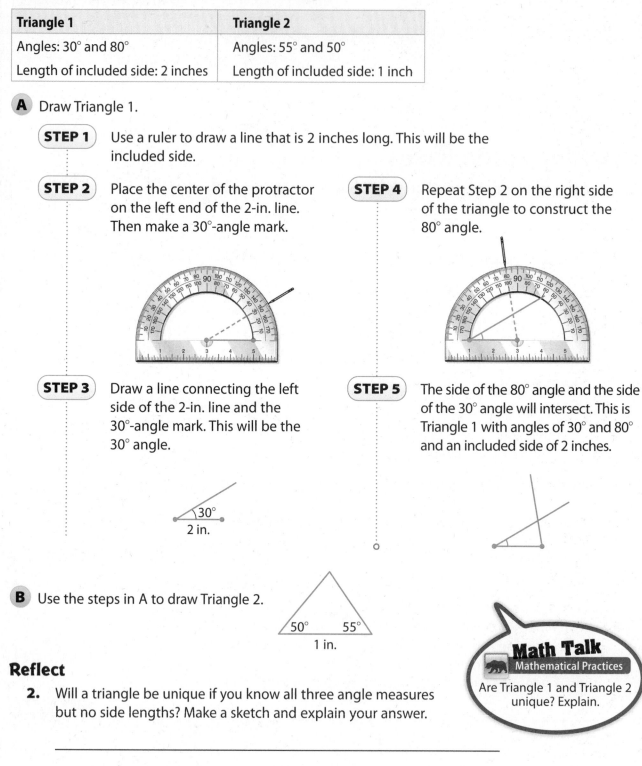

A Draw Triangle 1.

STEP 1 Use a ruler to draw a line that is 2 inches long. This will be the included side.

STEP 2 Place the center of the protractor on the left end of the 2-in. line. Then make a 30°-angle mark.

STEP 3 Draw a line connecting the left side of the 2-in. line and the 30°-angle mark. This will be the 30° angle.

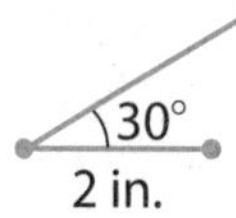

STEP 4 Repeat Step 2 on the right side of the triangle to construct the 80° angle.

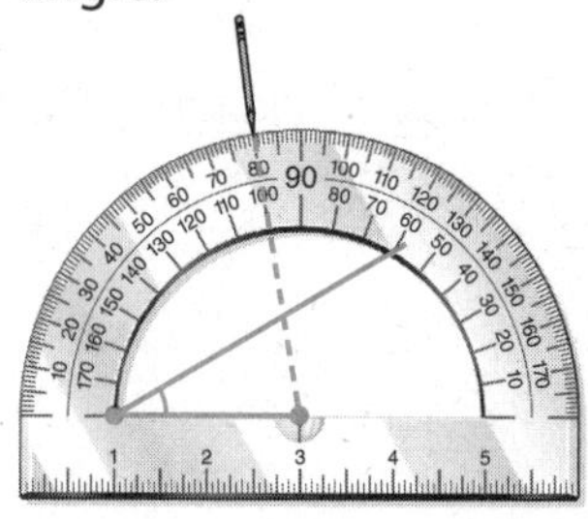

STEP 5 The side of the 80° angle and the side of the 30° angle will intersect. This is Triangle 1 with angles of 30° and 80° and an included side of 2 inches.

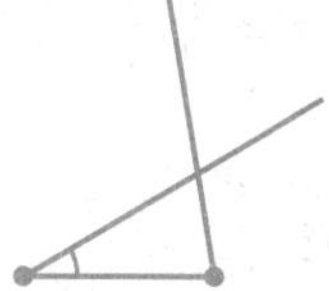

B Use the steps in A to draw Triangle 2.

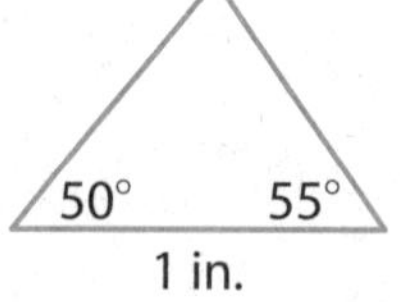

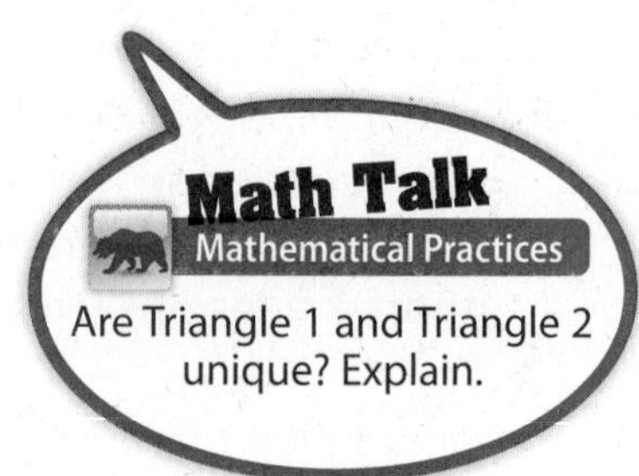

Math Talk
Mathematical Practices
Are Triangle 1 and Triangle 2 unique? Explain.

Reflect

2. Will a triangle be unique if you know all three angle measures but no side lengths? Make a sketch and explain your answer.

Name____________________ Class____________ Date____________

Guided Practice

Tell whether each figure creates the conditions to form a unique triangle, more than one triangle, or no triangle. (Explore Activities 1 and 2)

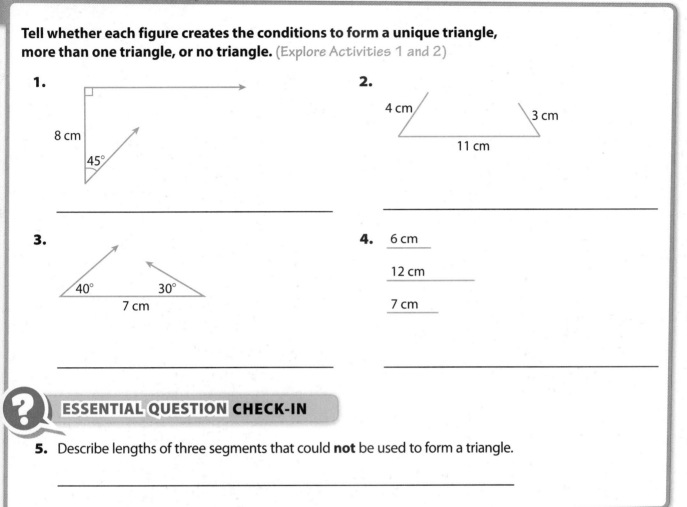

1.

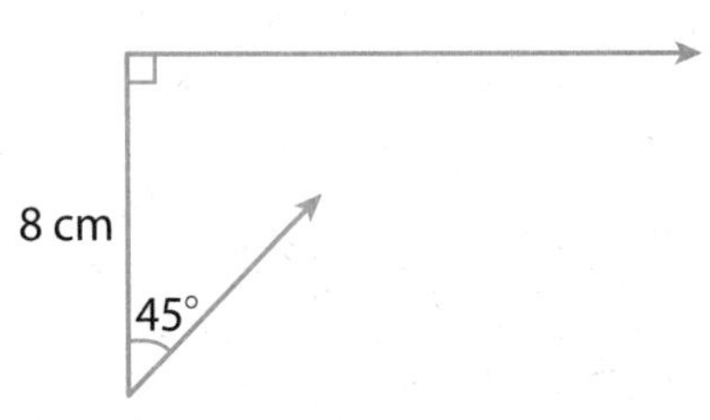

____

2.

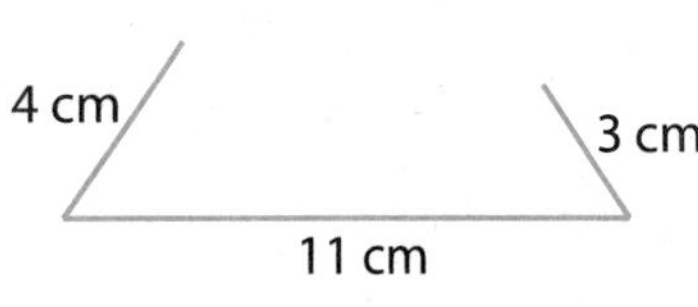

____

3.

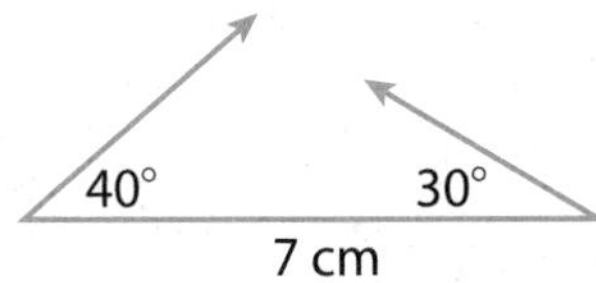

____

4. 6 cm

12 cm

7 cm

____

ESSENTIAL QUESTION CHECK-IN

5. Describe lengths of three segments that could **not** be used to form a triangle.

____

8.2 Independent Practice

7.G.2

6. On a separate piece of paper, try to draw a triangle with side lengths of 3 centimeters and 6 centimeters, and an included angle of 120°. Determine whether the given segments and angle produce a unique triangle, more than one triangle, or no triangle.

____

7. A landscape architect submitted a design for a triangle-shaped flower garden with side lengths of 21 feet, 37 feet, and 15 feet to a customer. Explain why the architect was not hired to create the flower garden.

____

____

8. Make a Conjecture The angles in an actual triangle-shaped traffic sign all have measures of 60°. The angles in a scale drawing of the sign all have measures of 60°. Explain how you can use this information to decide whether three given angle measures can be used to form a unique triangle or more than one triangle.

____

____

Work Area

H.O.T. FOCUS ON HIGHER ORDER THINKING

9. Communicate Mathematical Ideas The figure on the left shows a line segment 2 inches long forming a 45° angle with a dashed line whose length is not given. The figure on the right shows a compass set at a width of $1\frac{1}{2}$ inches with its point on the top end of the 2-inch segment. An arc is drawn intersecting the dashed line twice.

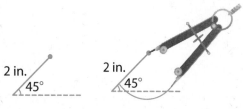

2 in. 45°   2 in. 45°

Explain how you can use this figure to decide whether two sides and an angle **not** included between them can be used to form a unique triangle, more than one triangle, or no triangle.

____

____

____

____

____

____

10. Critical Thinking Two sides of an isosceles triangle have lengths of 6 inches and 15 inches, respectively. Find the length of the third side. Explain your reasoning.

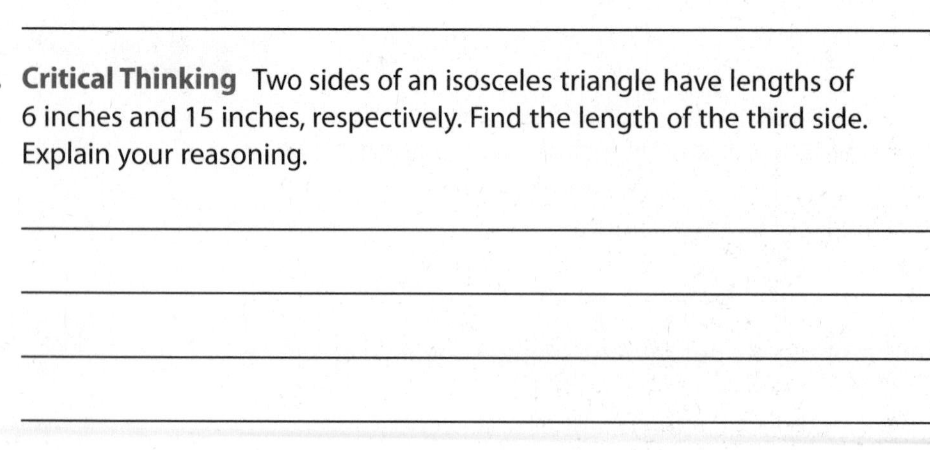

____

____

____

____

LESSON

8.3 Cross Sections

CA CC 7.G.3

Describe the two-dimensional figures that result from slicing three-dimensional figures, as in plane sections of right rectangular prisms and right rectangular pyramids.

ESSENTIAL QUESTION

How can you describe cross sections of three-dimensional figures?

EXPLORE ACTIVITY 1

Cross Sections of a Right Rectangular Prism

An **intersection** is a point or set of points common to two or more geometric figures. A **plane** is a flat surface that extends forever in all directions. A **cross section** is the intersection of a three-dimensional figure and a plane. Imagine a plane slicing through the pyramid shown, or through a cone or a prism.

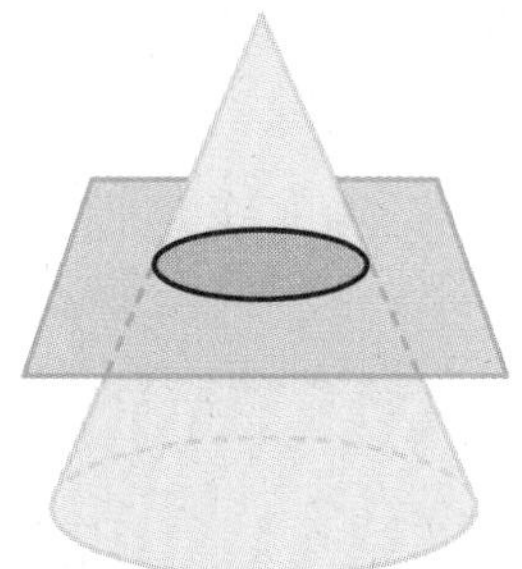

This figure shows the intersection of a cone and a plane. The cross section is a circle.

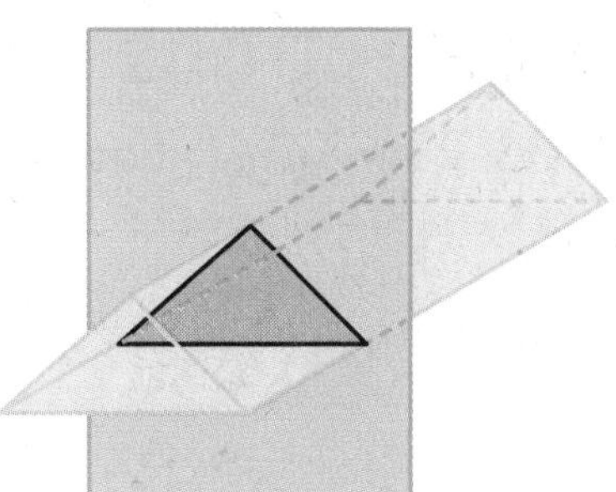

This figure shows the intersection of a triangular prism and a plane. The cross section is a triangle.

A three-dimensional figure can have several different cross sections depending on the position and the direction of the slice. For example, if the intersection of the plane and cone were vertical, the cross section would form a triangle.

Describe each cross section of the right rectangular prism with the name of its shape.

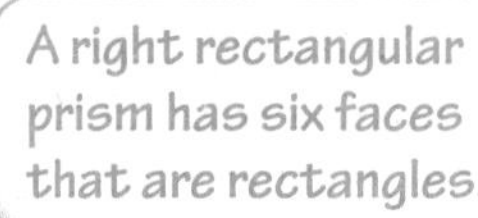

A right rectangular prism has six faces that are rectangles.

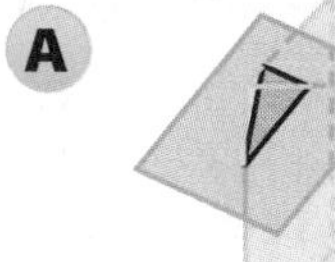

A

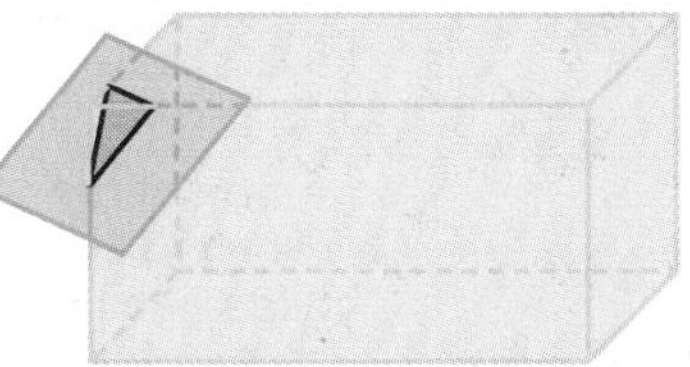

____

B

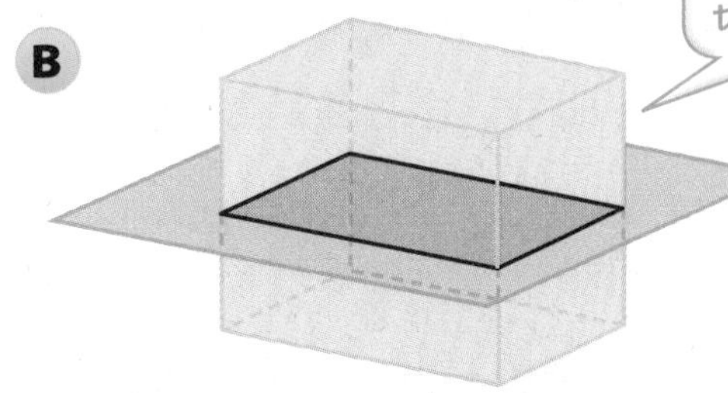

____

EXPLORE ACTIVITY 1 *(cont'd)*

C

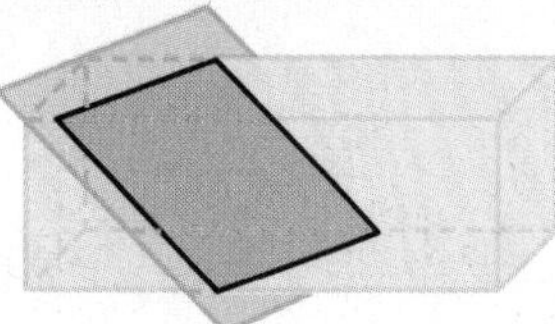

D

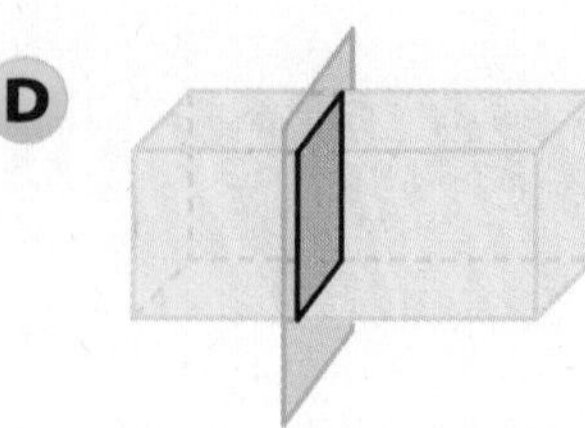

______________________________ ______________________________

Reflect

1. **Conjecture** Is it possible to have a circular cross section in a right rectangular prism?

____

EXPLORE ACTIVITY 2

Describing Cross Sections

A right rectangular pyramid with a non-square base is shown. (In a *right* pyramid, the point where the triangular sides meet is centered over the base.)

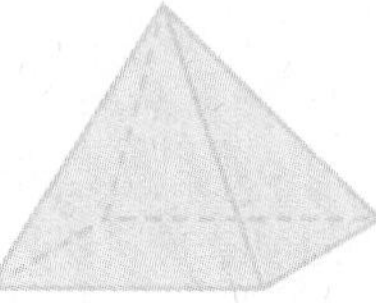

A The shape of the base is a ______________________________.

The shape of each side is a ______________________________.

B Is it possible for a cross section of the pyramid to have each shape?

square	rectangle	triangle	circle	trapezoid
______	______	______	______	______

C Sketch the cross sections of the right rectangular pyramid below.

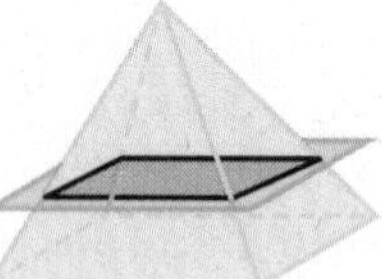

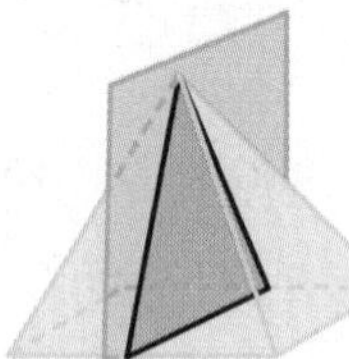

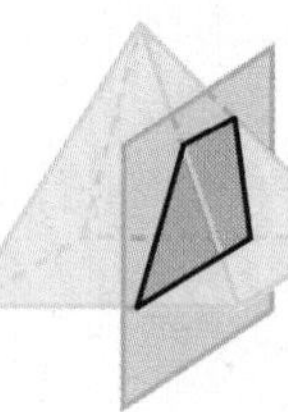

Reflect

2. **What If?** Suppose the figure in **B** had a square base. Would your answers in **B** be the same? Explain.

____

____

Math Talk

Describe and compare the cross sections created when two horizontal planes intersect a right rectangular pyramid.

Name ______________________ Class ______________ Date ____________

Guided Practice

Describe the cross section of each given figure with the name of its shape.

1. cube (Explore Activity 1)

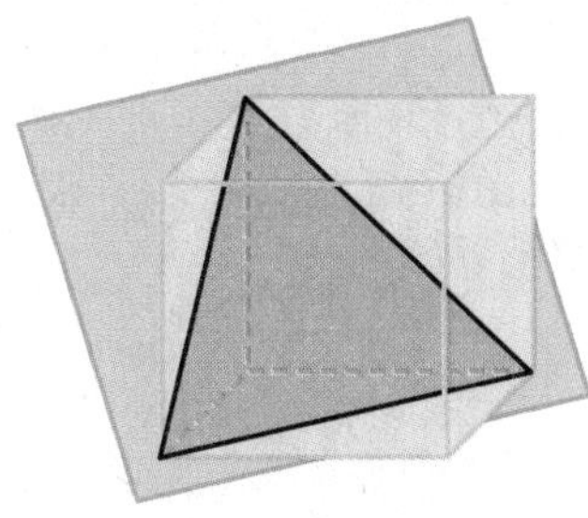

____

2. cylinder (Explore Activity 2)

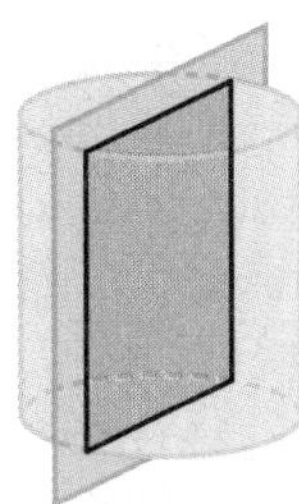

____

3. triangular prism (Explore Activity 2)

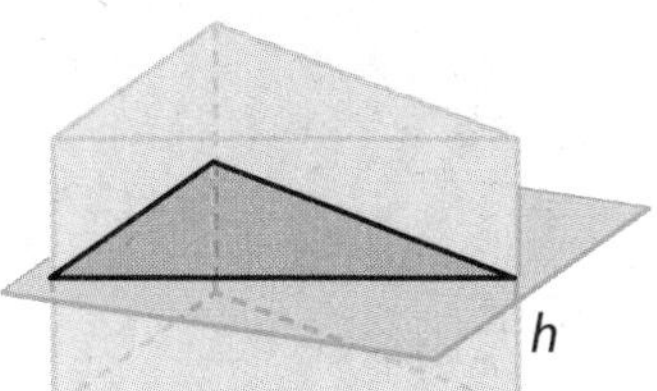

____

4. cone (Explore Activity 2)

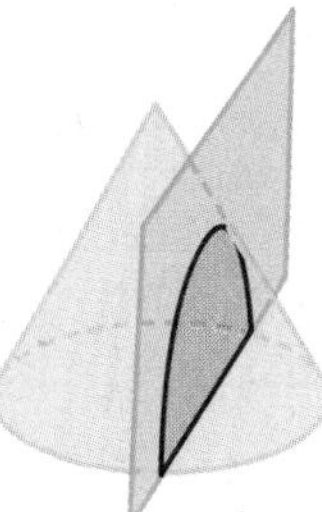

____

ESSENTIAL QUESTION CHECK-IN

5. What is the first step in describing what figure results when a given plane intersects a given three-dimensional figure?

____

8.3 Independent Practice

7.G.3

Personal Math Trainer
Online Practice and Help

6. Describe different ways in which a plane might intersect the cylinder and the cross section that results.

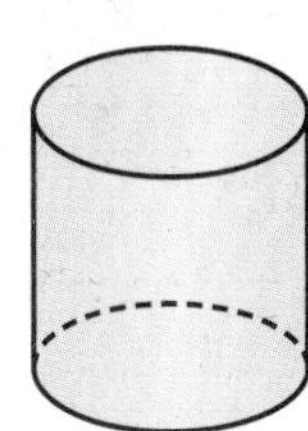

____

____

____

7. **Make a Conjecture** What cross sections might you see when a plane intersects a cone that you would **not** see when a plane intersects a pyramid or a prism? ______________________

H.O.T. FOCUS ON HIGHER ORDER THINKING

Work Area

8. **Critical Thinking** The two figures on the left below show that you can form a cross section of a cube that is a pentagon. Think of a plane cutting the cube at an angle in such a way as to slice through five of the cube's six faces. Draw dotted lines on the third cube to show how to form a cross section that is a hexagon.

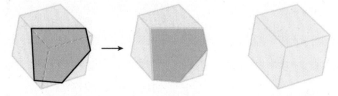

9. **Analyze Relationships** A sphere has a radius of 12 inches. A horizontal plane passes through the center of the sphere.

a. Describe the cross section formed by the plane and the sphere.

____

b. Describe the cross sections formed as the plane intersects the interior of the sphere but moves away from the center.

____

____

____

10. **Communicate Mathematical Ideas** A right rectangular prism is intersected by a horizontal plane and a vertical plane. The cross section formed by the horizontal plane and the prism is a rectangle with dimensions 8 in. and 12 in. The cross section formed by the vertical plane and the prism is a rectangle with dimensions 5 in. and 8 in. Describe the faces of the prism, including their dimensions. Then find its volume.

____

____

11. **Represent Real-World Problems** Describe a real-world situation that could be represented by planes slicing a three-dimensional figure to form cross sections.

____

____

____

LESSON

8.4 Angle Relationships

Use facts about supplementary, complementary, vertical, and adjacent angles in a multi-step problem to write and solve simple equations for an unknown angle in a figure.

ESSENTIAL QUESTION

How can you use angle relationships to solve problems?

EXPLORE ACTIVITY 

Measuring Angles

It is useful to work with pairs of angles and to understand how pairs of angles relate to each other. **Congruent angles** are angles that have the same measure.

STEP 1 Using a ruler, draw a pair of intersecting lines. Label each angle from 1 to 4.

STEP 2 Use a protractor to help you complete the chart.

Angle	Measure of Angle
$m\angle 1$	
$m\angle 2$	
$m\angle 3$	
$m\angle 4$	
$m\angle 1 + m\angle 2$	
$m\angle 2 + m\angle 3$	
$m\angle 3 + m\angle 4$	
$m\angle 4 + m\angle 1$	

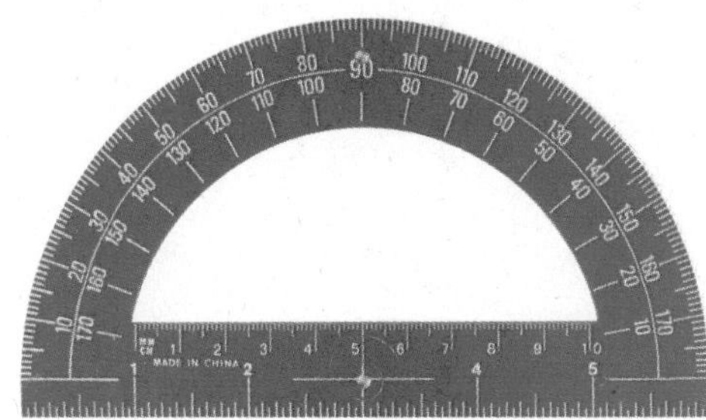

Reflect

1. **Make a Conjecture** Share your results with other students. Make a conjecture about pairs of angles that are opposite each other.

____

____

2. **Make a Conjecture** When two lines intersect to form four angles, what conjecture can you make about the pairs of angles that are next to each other?

____

Angle Pairs and One-Step Equations

Vertical angles are the opposite angles formed by two intersecting lines. Vertical angles are congruent because the angles have the same measure.

Adjacent angles are pairs of angles that share a vertex and one side but do not overlap.

Complementary angles are two angles whose measures have a sum of 90°.

Supplementary angles are two angles whose measures have a sum of 180°. You discovered in the Explore Activity that adjacent angles formed by two intersecting lines are supplementary.

EXAMPLE 1

Use the diagram.

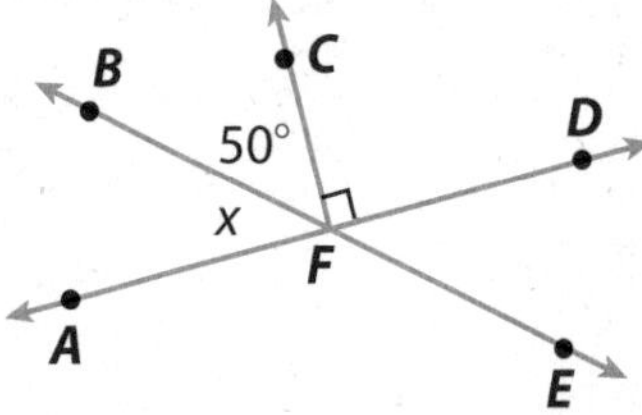

A Name a pair of vertical angles.

Vertical angles are opposite angles formed by intersecting lines.

$\angle AFB$ and $\angle DFE$ are vertical angles.

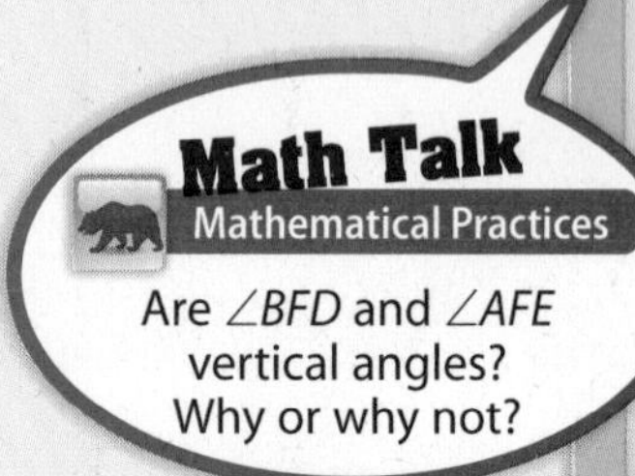

Math Talk
Mathematical Practices
Are ∠BFD and ∠AFE vertical angles? Why or why not?

B Name a pair of adjacent angles.

Adjacent angles share a vertex and a side but do not overlap.

$\angle AFB$ and $\angle BFD$ are adjacent angles.

C Name a pair of supplementary angles.

Adjacent angles formed by intersecting lines are supplementary.

$\angle AFB$ and $\angle BFD$ are supplementary angles.

D Name two pairs of supplementary angles that include $\angle DFE$.

Any angle that forms a line with $\angle DFE$ is a supplementary angle to $\angle DFE$.

$\angle DFE$ and $\angle EFA$ are supplementary angles, as are $\angle DFE$ and $\angle DFB$.

E Find the measure of $\angle AFB$.

Use the fact that $\angle AFB$ and $\angle BFD$ in the diagram are supplementary angles to find $m\angle AFB$.

$m\angle AFB + m\angle BFD = 180°$ — They are supplementary angles.

$x + 140° = 180°$ — $m\angle BFD = 50° + 90° = 140°$

$\underline{-140°} \quad \underline{-140°}$ — Subtract 140° from both sides.

$x = 40°$

The measure of $\angle AFB$ is 40°.

Reflect

3. Analyze Relationships What is the relationship between $\angle AFB$ and $\angle BFC$? Explain.

____

____

____

4. Draw Conclusions Are $\angle AFC$ and $\angle BFC$ adjacent angles? Why or why not?

____

____

____

My Notes

YOUR TURN

Use the diagram.

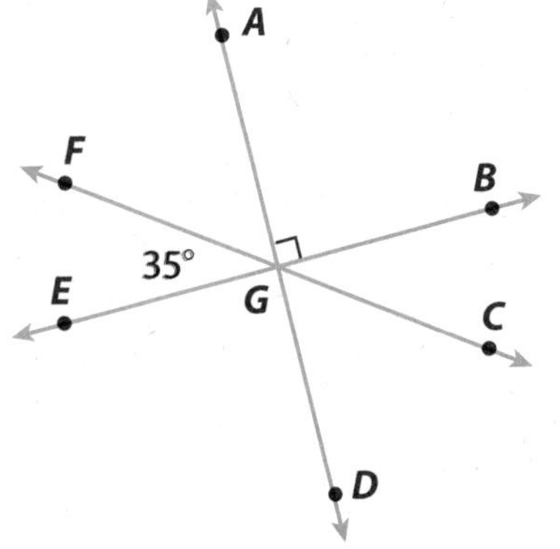

5. Name a pair of supplementary angles.

____

6. Name a pair of vertical angles.

____

7. Name a pair of adjacent angles.

____

8. Name a pair of complementary angles.

____

9. Find the measure of $\angle CGD$. ______________________________

My Notes

Angle Pairs and Two-Step Equations

Sometimes solving an equation is only the first step in using an angle relationship to solve a problem.

EXAMPLE 2

A **Find the measure of ∠*EHF*.**

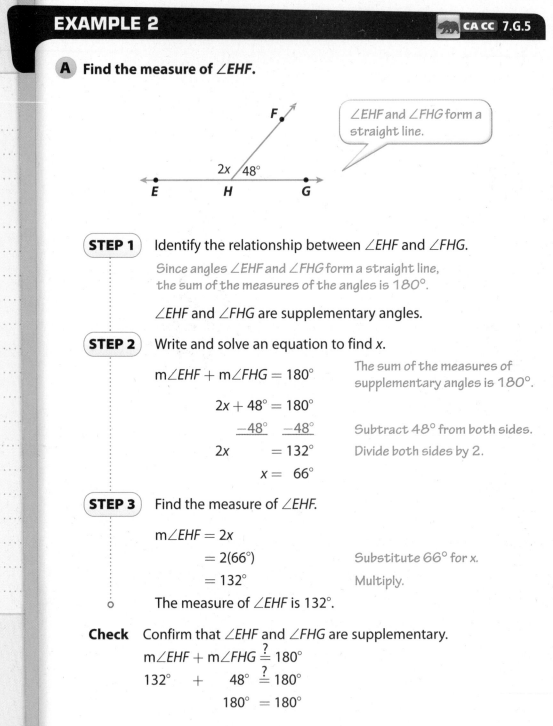

F, 2x, 48°, E, H, G

∠*EHF* and ∠*FHG* form a straight line.

STEP 1 Identify the relationship between ∠*EHF* and ∠*FHG*.

Since angles ∠*EHF* and ∠*FHG* form a straight line, the sum of the measures of the angles is 180°.

∠*EHF* and ∠*FHG* are supplementary angles.

STEP 2 Write and solve an equation to find *x*.

$m\angle EHF + m\angle FHG = 180°$ — The sum of the measures of supplementary angles is 180°.

$2x + 48° = 180°$

$\underline{-48°} \quad \underline{-48°}$ — Subtract 48° from both sides.

$2x = 132°$ — Divide both sides by 2.

$x = 66°$

STEP 3 Find the measure of ∠*EHF*.

$m\angle EHF = 2x$

$= 2(66°)$ — Substitute 66° for *x*.

$= 132°$ — Multiply.

The measure of ∠*EHF* is 132°.

Check Confirm that ∠*EHF* and ∠*FHG* are supplementary.

$m\angle EHF + m\angle FHG \stackrel{?}{=} 180°$

$132° + 48° \stackrel{?}{=} 180°$

$180° = 180°$

B **Find the measure of $\angle ZXY$.**

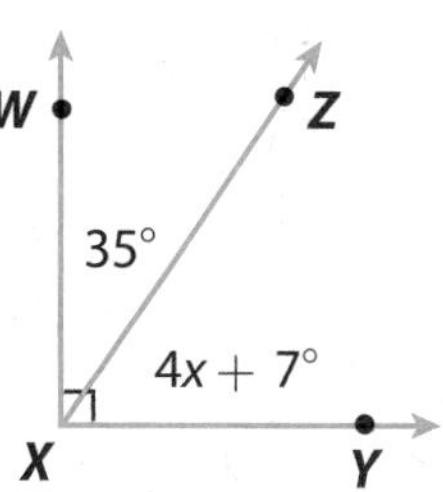

STEP 1 Identify the relationship between $\angle WXZ$ and $\angle ZXY$.

$\angle WXZ$ and $\angle ZXY$ are complementary angles.

STEP 2 Write and solve an equation to find x.

$m\angle WXZ + m\angle ZXY = 90°$	The sum of the measures of complementary angles is 90°.
$4x + 7° + 35° = 90°$	Substitute the values.
$4x + 42° = 90°$	Combine like terms.
$\underline{-42°}\ \ \underline{-42°}$	Subtract 42° from both sides.
$4x = 48°$	Divide both sides by 4.
$x = 12°$	

STEP 3 Find the measure of $\angle ZXY$.

$m\angle ZXY = 4x + 7°$	
$= 4(12°) + 7°$	Substitute 12° for x.
$= 55°$	Use the Order of Operations.

The measure of $\angle ZXY$ is 55°.

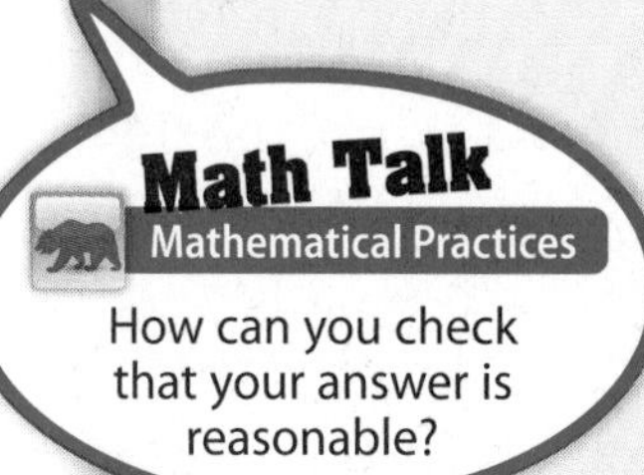

Math Talk
Mathematical Practices
How can you check that your answer is reasonable?

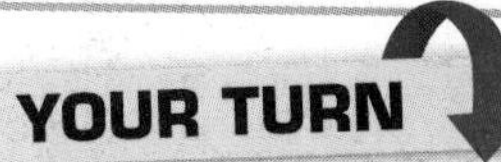

10. Write and solve an equation to find the measure of $\angle JML$.

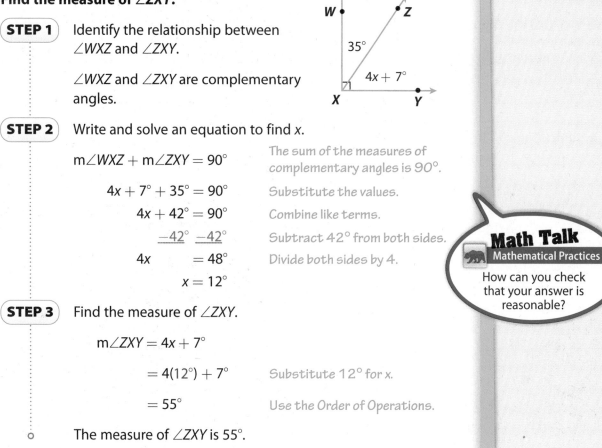

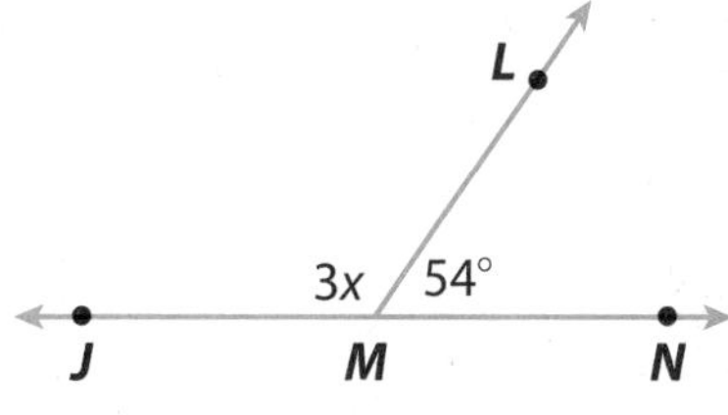

11. **Critique Reasoning** Cory says that to find $m\angle JML$ above, you can stop when you get to the solution step $3x = 126°$. Explain why this works.

____

____

____

Guided Practice

For 1–2, use the figure. (Example 1)

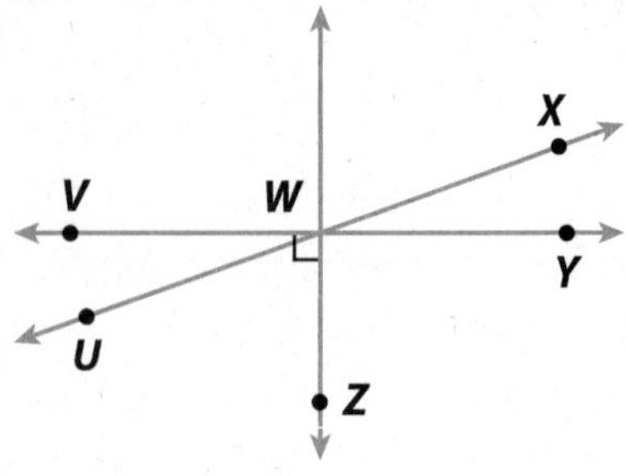

1. **Vocabulary** The sum of the measures of $\angle UWV$ and $\angle UWZ$ is 90°, so $\angle UWV$ and $\angle UWZ$ are

   __________________ angles.

2. **Vocabulary** $\angle UWV$ and $\angle VWX$ share a vertex and one side. They do not overlap, so $\angle UWV$ and $\angle VWX$ are

   __________________ angles.

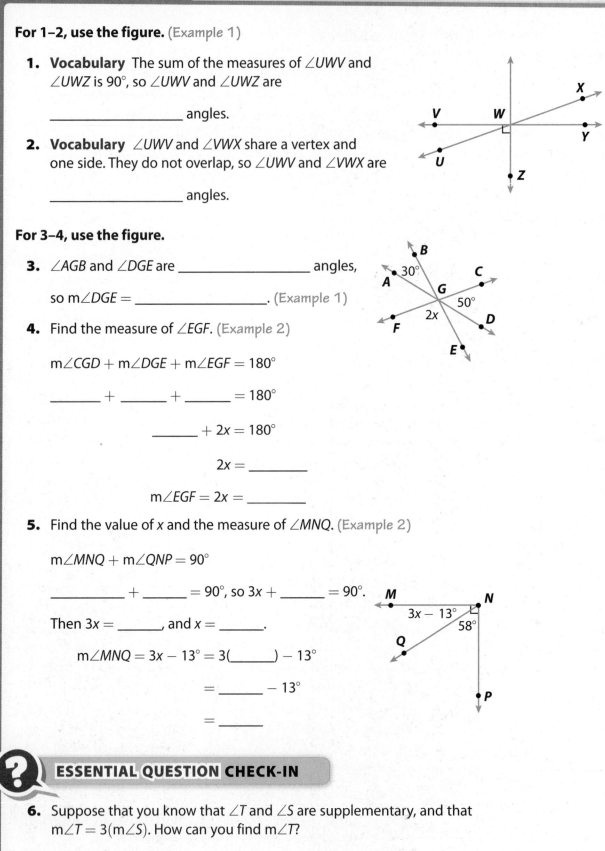

For 3–4, use the figure.

3. $\angle AGB$ and $\angle DGE$ are __________________ angles,

   so $m\angle DGE =$ __________________. (Example 1)

4. Find the measure of $\angle EGF$. (Example 2)

   $m\angle CGD + m\angle DGE + m\angle EGF = 180°$

   ______ + ______ + ______ $= 180°$

   ______ $+ 2x = 180°$

   $2x =$ ______

   $m\angle EGF = 2x =$ ______

5. Find the value of x and the measure of $\angle MNQ$. (Example 2)

   $m\angle MNQ + m\angle QNP = 90°$

   ______ + ______ $= 90°$, so $3x +$ ______ $= 90°$.

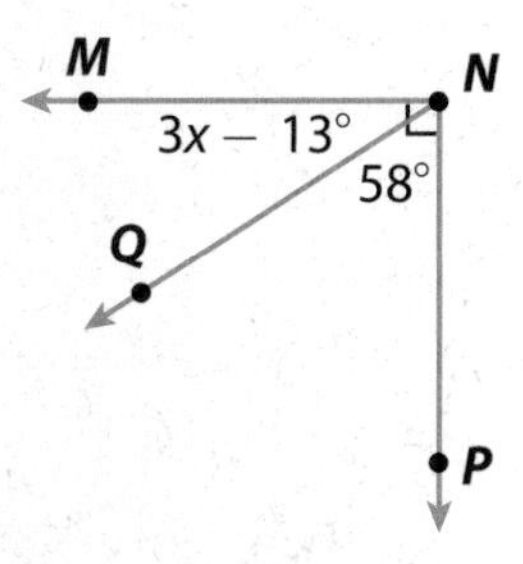

   Then $3x =$ ______, and $x =$ ______.

   $m\angle MNQ = 3x - 13° = 3($______$) - 13°$

   $=$ ______ $- 13°$

   $=$ ______

ESSENTIAL QUESTION CHECK-IN

6. Suppose that you know that $\angle T$ and $\angle S$ are supplementary, and that $m\angle T = 3(m\angle S)$. How can you find $m\angle T$?

   ____

   ____

Name ______________________ Class ______________ Date ______________

8.4 Independent Practice

7.G.5

For 7–11, use the figure.

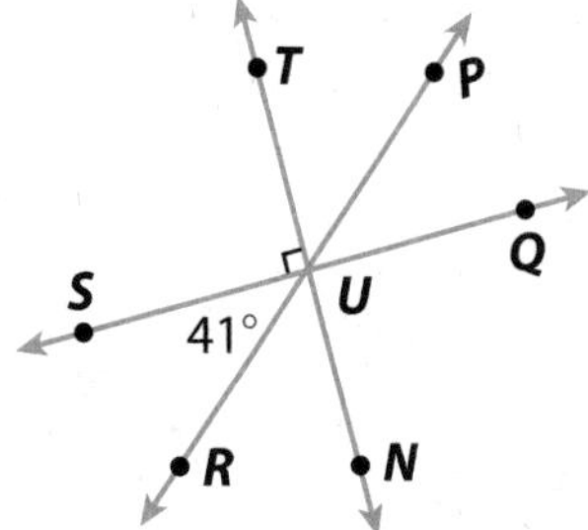

7. Name a pair of adjacent angles. Explain why they are adjacent.

8. Name a pair of acute vertical angles.

9. Name a pair of supplementary angles.

10. **Justify Reasoning** Find m∠*QUR*. Justify your answer.

11. **Draw Conclusions** Which is greater, m∠*TUR* or m∠*RUQ*? Explain.

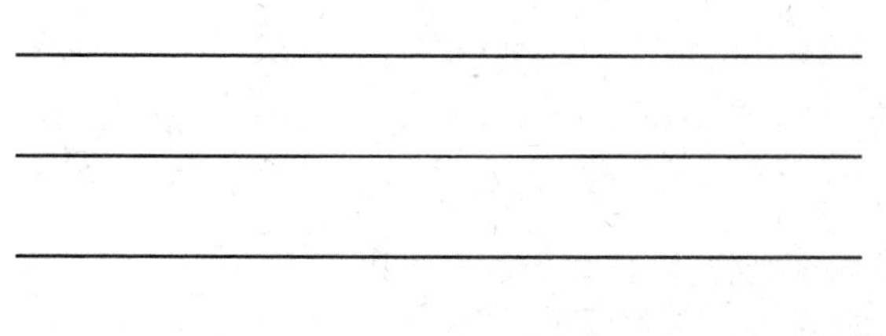

For 12–13, use the figure. A bike path crosses a road as shown. Solve for each indicated angle measure or variable.

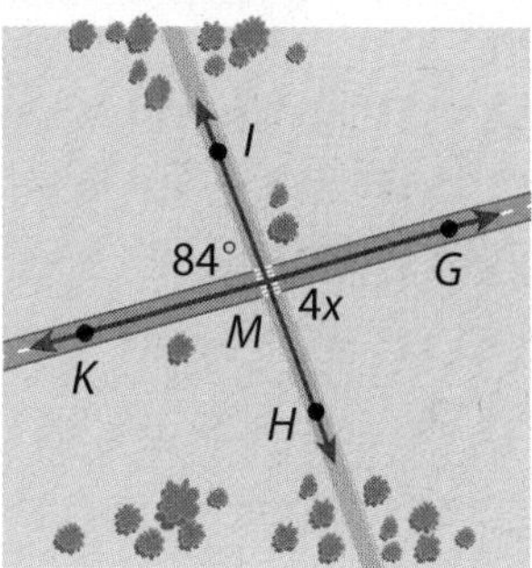

12. x ______________

13. m∠*KMH* ______________

For 14–16, use the figure. Solve for each indicated angle measure.

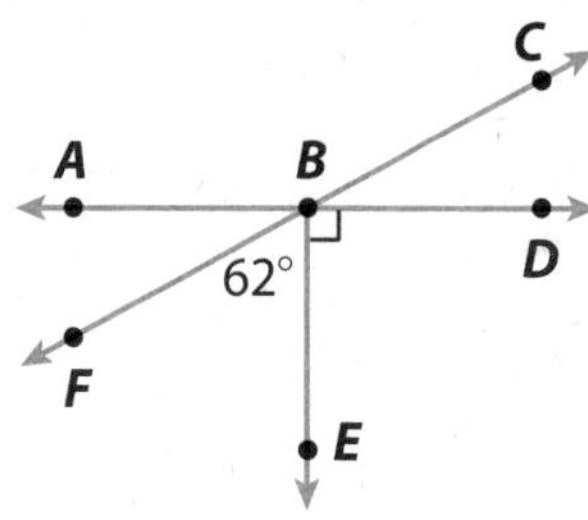

14. m∠*CBE* ______________

15. m∠*ABF* ______________

16. m∠*CBA* ______________

17. The measure of ∠*A* is 4° greater than the measure of ∠*B*. The two angles are complementary. Find the measure of each angle.

18. The measure of ∠*D* is 5 times the measure of ∠*E*. The two angles are supplementary. Find the measure of each angle.

19. **Astronomy** Astronomers sometimes use angle measures divided into degrees, minutes, and seconds. One degree is equal to 60 minutes, and one minute is equal to 60 seconds. Suppose that $\angle J$ and $\angle K$ are complementary, and that the measure of $\angle J$ is 48 degrees, 26 minutes, 8 seconds. What is the measure of $\angle K$?

____

FOCUS ON HIGHER ORDER THINKING

20. **Represent Real-World Problems** The railroad tracks meet the road as shown. The town will allow a parking lot at angle K if the measure of angle K is greater than 38°. Can a parking lot be built at angle K? Why or why not?

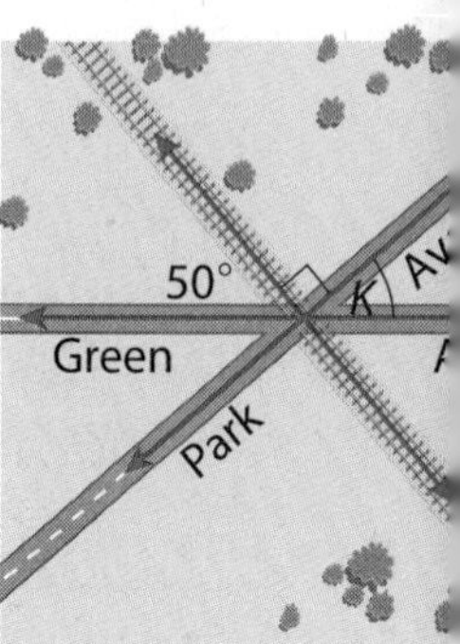

____

____

21. **Justify Reasoning** Kendra says that she can draw $\angle A$ and $\angle B$ so that $m\angle A$ is 119° and $\angle A$ and $\angle B$ are complementary angles. Do you agree or disagree? Explain your reasoning.

____

____

____

____

Work Area

22. **Draw Conclusions** If two angles are complementary, each angle is called a *complement* of the other. If two angles are supplementary, each angle is called a *supplement* of the other.

 a. Suppose $m\angle A = 77°$. What is the measure of a complement of a complement of $\angle A$? Explain.

 ____

 ____

 ____

 b. What conclusion can you draw about a complement of a complement of an angle? Explain.

 ____

 ____

 ____

 ____

 ____

MODULE QUIZ

Ready to Go On?

8.1 Similar Shapes and Scale Drawings

1. A house blueprint has a scale of 1 in.:4 ft. The length and width of each room in the actual house are shown in the table. Complete the table by finding the length and width of each room on the blueprint.

	Living room	Kitchen	Office	Bedroom	Bedroom	Bathroom
Actual $\ell \times w$ (ft)	16×20	12×12	8×12	20×12	12×12	6×8
Blueprint $\ell \times w$ (in.)						

8.2 Geometric Drawings

2. Can a triangle be formed with the side lengths of 8 cm, 4 cm, and 12 cm? ______

3. A triangle has side lengths of 11 cm and 9 cm. Which could be the value of the third side, 20 cm or 15 cm? ________________

8.3 Cross Sections

4. Name one possible cross section of a sphere. ________________

5. Name at least two shapes that are cross sections of a cylinder.

____

8.4 Angle Relationships

6. $\angle BGC$ and $\angle FGE$ are _________ angles, so $m\angle FGE =$ _________.

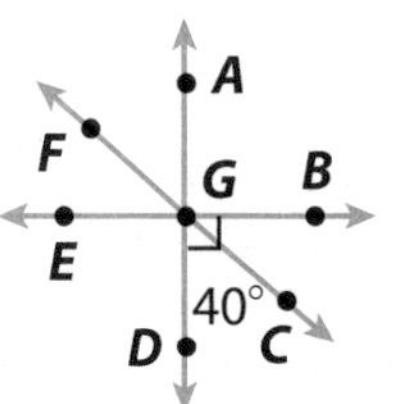

7. Suppose you know that $\angle S$ and $\angle Y$ are complementary, and that $m\angle S = 2(m\angle Y) - 30°$. Find $m\angle Y$. ____________

ESSENTIAL QUESTION

8. How can you model geometry figures to solve real-world problems?

____

____

MODULE 8
MIXED REVIEW

Assessment Readiness

Personal Math Trainer
my.hrw.com
Online Practice and Help

1. Consider each figure named below. Could the figure be a cross section of the cone as seen at right?

Select Yes or No for A–C.

A. triangle ○ Yes ○ No
B. circle ○ Yes ○ No
C. rectangle ○ Yes ○ No

2. The temperature at 7 p.m. at a weather station in Minnesota was −5 °F. The temperature began changing at a rate of −2.5 °F per hour.

Choose True or False for each statement.

A. At 10 p.m. the temperature was −7.5 °F. ○ True ○ False
B. At midnight the temperature was −12.5 °F. ○ True ○ False
C. At 9 p.m. the temperature was −10 °F. ○ True ○ False

3. The floor of the entryway to an office building will be triangular. Two angles of the triangle will measure 40°, and the side between them will have a length of 8 meters. Make a scale drawing of the entryway using a scale of 1 cm : 2 m. Explain how you made your drawing.

4. The diagram shows a portion of a wooden support for the roof of a house. A construction worker says that ∠*BDA* measures 30° more than ∠*DAC*. Is the worker correct? Use angle relationships and equations to justify your answer.

B
D
48°
108°
A
C

Circumference, Area, and Volume

ESSENTIAL QUESTION

How can you apply geometry concepts to solve real-world problems?

my.hrw.com

Real-World Video

A 16-inch pizza has a diameter of 16 inches. You can use the diameter to find circumference and area of the pizza. You can also determine how much pizza in one slice of different sizes of pizzas.

my.hrw.com

my.hrw.com

Go digital with your write-in student edition, accessible on any device.

Math On the Spot

Scan with your smart phone to jump directly to the online edition, video tutor, and more.

Animated Math

Interactively explore key concepts to see how math works.

Personal Math Trainer

Get immediate feedback and help as you work through practice sets.

Are YOU Ready?

Complete these exercises to review skills you will need for this module.

Multiply with Fractions and Decimals

EXAMPLE

$$\begin{array}{r} 7.3 \\ \times\ 2.4 \\ \hline 292 \\ +146\ \ \\ \hline 17.52 \end{array}$$

Multiply as you would with whole numbers.
Count the total number of decimal places in the two factors.

Place the decimal point in the product so that there are the same number of digits after the decimal point.

Multiply.

1. $\begin{array}{r} 4.16 \\ \times\ 13 \\ \hline \end{array}$

2. $\begin{array}{r} 6.47 \\ \times\ 0.4 \\ \hline \end{array}$

3. $\begin{array}{r} 7.05 \\ \times\ 9.4 \\ \hline \end{array}$

4. $\begin{array}{r} 25.6 \\ \times\ 0.49 \\ \hline \end{array}$

Area of Squares, Rectangles, and Triangles

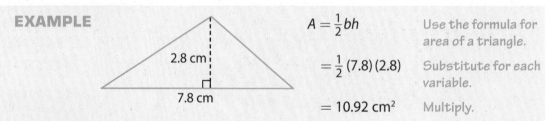

EXAMPLE

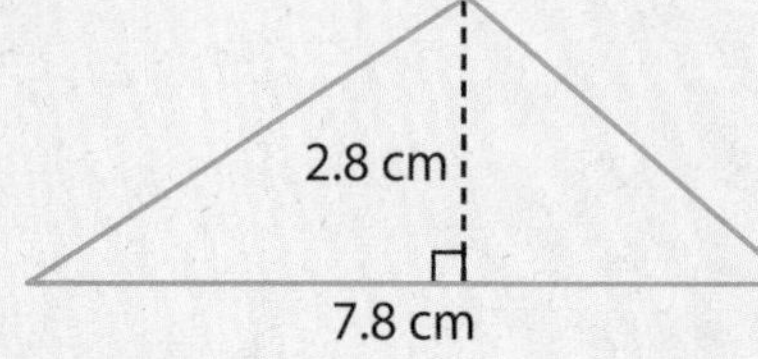

$A = \frac{1}{2}bh$ — *Use the formula for area of a triangle.*

$= \frac{1}{2}(7.8)(2.8)$ — *Substitute for each variable.*

$= 10.92 \text{ cm}^2$ — *Multiply.*

Find the area of each figure.

5. triangle with base 14 in. and height 10 in. ______________________

6. square with sides of 3.5 ft ______________________

7. rectangle with length $8\frac{1}{2}$ in. and width 6 in. ______________________

8. triangle with base 12.5 m and height 2.4 m ______________________

Reading Start-Up

Visualize Vocabulary

Use the ✔ words to complete the graphic. You will put one word in each oval. Then write examples of formulas in each rectangle.

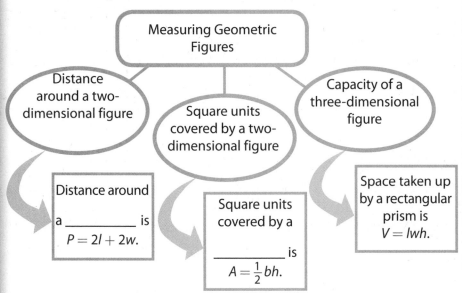

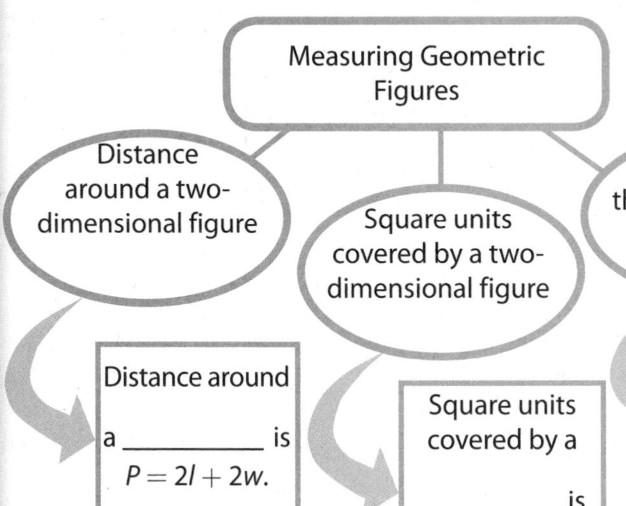

Square units covered by a __________ is $A = \frac{1}{2}bh$.

Vocabulary

Review Words

✔ area *(área)*
parallelogram *(paralelogramo)*
✔ perimeter *(perímetro)*
prism *(prisma)*
rectangle *(rectángulo)*
square *(cuadrado)*
trapezoid *(trapecio)*
triangle *(triángulo)*
✔ volume *(volumen)*

Preview Words

circumference *(circunferencia)*
composite figure *(figura compuesta)*
diameter *(diámetro)*
radius *(radio)*

Understand Vocabulary

Match the term on the left to the correct expression on the right.

1. ____ circumference
2. ____ diameter
3. ____ radius

A. A line segment that passes through the center of a circle and has endpoints on the circle, or the length of that segment.

B. A line segment with one endpoint at the center of the circle and the other on the circle, or the length of that segment.

C. The distance around a circle.

Active Reading

Four-Corner Fold Before beginning the module, create a four-corner fold to help you organize what you learn. As you study this module, note important ideas, such as vocabulary, properties, and formulas, on the flaps. Use one flap each for circumference, area, surface area, and volume. You can use your FoldNote later to study for tests and complete assignments.

GETTING READY FOR

Circumference, Area, and Volume

Understanding the standards and the vocabulary terms in the standards will help you know exactly what you are expected to learn in this module.

CA CC 7.G.6

Know the formulas for the area and circumference of a circle and use them to solve problems; give an informal derivation of the relationship between the circumference and area of a circle.

Key Vocabulary

circumference *(circunferencia)*
The distance around a circle.

What It Means to You

You will use formulas to solve problems involving the area and circumference of circles.

EXAMPLE 7.G.6

Lily is drawing plans for a circular fountain. The diameter of the fountain is 20 feet. What is the approximate circumference?

$C = \pi d$

$C \approx 3.14 \cdot 20$ Substitute.

$C \approx 62.8$

The circumference of the fountain is about 62.8 feet.

CA CC 7.G.4

Solve real-world and mathematical problems involving area, volume and surface area of two- and three-dimensional objects composed of triangles, quadrilaterals, polygons, cubes, and right prisms.

Key Vocabulary

volume *(volumen)*
The number of cubic units inside a three-dimensional solid.

surface area *(área total)*
The sum of the areas of all the surfaces of a three-dimensional solid.

What It Means to You

You will find area, volume and surface area of real-world objects.

EXAMPLE 7.G.4

Find the volume and the surface area of a tissue box before the hole is cut in the top.

The tissue box is a right rectangular prism. The base is $4\frac{3}{8}$ in. by $4\frac{3}{8}$ in. and the height is 5 in.

Use the volume and surface area formulas:

B is the area of the base, h is the height of the box, and P is the perimeter of the base.

$V = Bh$

$= \left(4\frac{3}{8} \cdot 4\frac{3}{8}\right)5$

$= 95\frac{45}{64}\text{ in}^3$

$S = 2B + Ph$

$= 2\left(4\frac{3}{8} \cdot 4\frac{3}{8}\right) + \left(4 \cdot 4\frac{3}{8}\right)5$

$= 125\frac{25}{32}\text{ in}^2$

The volume is $95\frac{45}{64}\text{ in}^3$ and the surface area is $125\frac{25}{32}\text{ in}^2$.

Visit **my.hrw.com** to see all **CA Common Core Standards** explained.

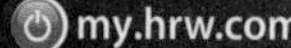

my.hrw.com

LESSON

9.1 Circumference

Know the formulas for the area and circumference of a circle and use them to solve problems; give an informal derivation of the relationship between the circumference and area of a circle.

ESSENTIAL QUESTION

How do you find and use the circumference of a circle?

EXPLORE ACTIVITY 

Exploring Circumference

A circle is a set of points in a plane that are a fixed distance from the center.

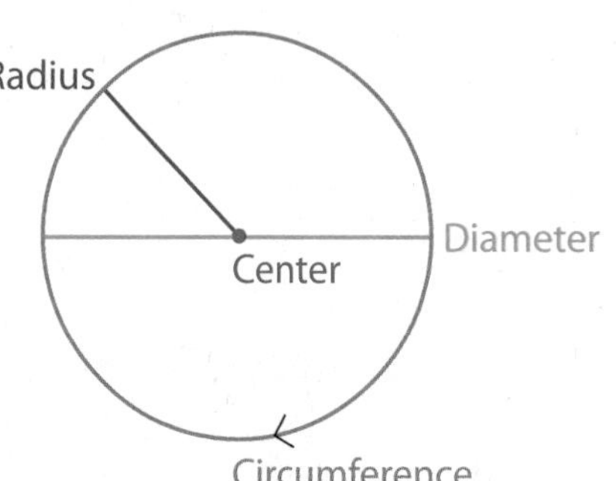

A **radius** is a line segment with one endpoint at the center of the circle and the other endpoint on the circle. The length of a radius is called the radius of the circle.

A **diameter** of a circle is a line segment that passes through the center of the circle and whose endpoints lie on the circle. The length of the diameter is twice the length of the radius. The length of a diameter is called the diameter of the circle.

The **circumference** of a circle is the distance around the circle.

A **Use a measuring tape to find the circumference of five circular objects. Then measure the distance across each item to find its diameter. Record the measurements of each object in the table below.**

Object	Circumference C	Diameter d	$\frac{C}{d}$

B **Divide the circumference of each object by its diameter. Record your answer, rounded to the nearest hundredth, in the table above.**

Reflect

1. **Make a Conjecture** Describe what you notice about the ratio $\frac{C}{d}$ in your table.

____

Finding Circumference

The ratio of the circumference to the diameter $\frac{C}{d}$ is the same for all circles. This ratio is called π or *pi*, and you can approximate it as 3.14 or as $\frac{22}{7}$. You can use π to find a formula for circumference.

For any circle, $\frac{C}{d} = \pi$. Solve the equation for C to give an equation for the circumference of a circle in terms of the diameter.

$\frac{C}{d} = \pi$	The ratio of the circumference to the diameter is π.
$\frac{C}{d} \times d = \pi \times d$	Multiply both sides by d.
$C = \pi d$	Simplify.

The diameter of a circle is twice the radius. You can use the equation $C = \pi d$ to find a formula for the circumference C in terms of the radius r.

$C = \pi d = \pi(2r) = 2\pi r$

The two equivalent formulas for circumference are $C = \pi d$ and $C = 2\pi r$.

EXAMPLE 1

An irrigation sprinkler waters a circular region with a radius of 14 feet. Find the circumference of the region watered by the sprinkler. Use $\frac{22}{7}$ for π.

14 ft

Use the formula.

$C = 2\pi r$ — The radius is 14 feet.

$C = 2\pi(14)$	Substitute 14 for r.
$C \approx 2\left(\frac{22}{7}\right)(14)$	Substitute $\frac{22}{7}$ for π.
$C \approx 88$	Multiply.

The circumference of the region watered by the sprinkler is about 88 feet.

Reflect

2. **Analyze Relationships** When is it logical to use $\frac{22}{7}$ instead of 3.14 for π?

____

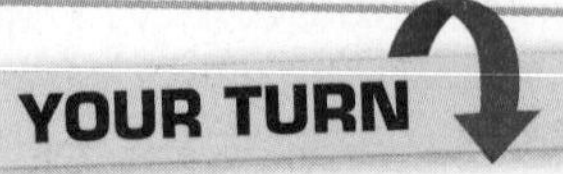

3. Find the circumference of the circle to the nearest hundredth.

11 cm

____

Using Circumference

Given the circumference of a circle, you can use the appropriate circumference formula to find the radius or the diameter of the circle. You can use that information to solve problems.

EXAMPLE 2 

A circular pond has a circumference of 628 feet. A model boat is moving directly across the pond, along a radius, at a rate of 5 feet per second. How long does it take the boat to get from the edge of the pond to the center?

STEP 1 Find the radius of the pond.

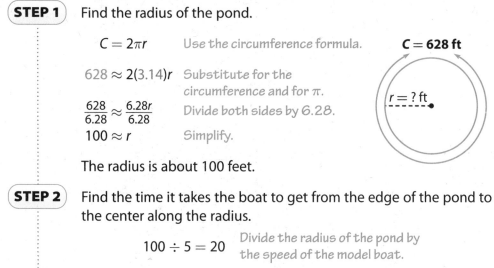

$C = 2\pi r$ Use the circumference formula.

$628 \approx 2(3.14)r$ Substitute for the circumference and for π.

$\frac{628}{6.28} \approx \frac{6.28r}{6.28}$ Divide both sides by 6.28.

$100 \approx r$ Simplify.

$C = 628$ **ft**

$r = ?$ ft

The radius is about 100 feet.

STEP 2 Find the time it takes the boat to get from the edge of the pond to the center along the radius.

$100 \div 5 = 20$ Divide the radius of the pond by the speed of the model boat.

It takes the boat about 20 seconds to get to the center of the pond.

My Notes

Reflect

4. Analyze Relationships Dante checks the answer to Step 1 by multiplying it by 6 and comparing it with the given circumference. Explain why Dante's estimation method works. Use it to check Step 1.

____

5. What If? Suppose the model boat were traveling at a rate of 4 feet per second. How long would it take the model boat to get from the edge of the pond to the center? _______________

What value will you substitute for π to find the diameter of the garden? Explain.

6. A circular garden has a circumference of 44 yards. Lars is digging a straight line along a diameter of the garden at a rate of 7 yards per hour. How many hours will it take him to dig across the garden?

____

Guided Practice

Find the circumference of each circle. (Example 1)

1. $C = \pi d$

$C \approx$ ____________

$C \approx$ ____________ inches

9 in.

2. $C = 2\pi r$

$C \approx 2\left(\frac{22}{7}\right)$ (____________)

$C \approx$ ____________ cm

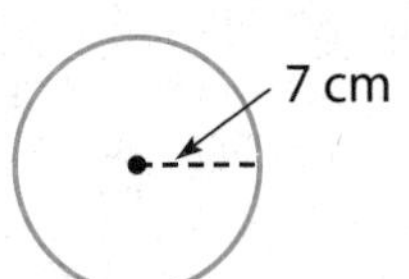

Find the circumference of each circle. Use 3.14 or $\frac{22}{7}$ for π. Round to the nearest hundredth, if necessary. (Example 1)

3.

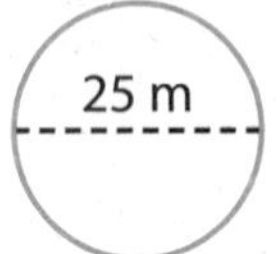

____

4.

____

5.

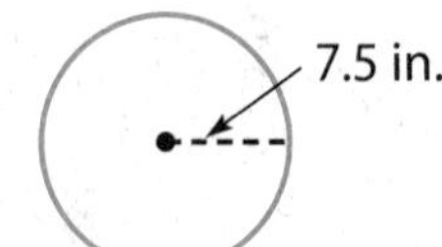

____

6. A round swimming pool has a circumference of 66 feet. Carlos wants to buy a rope to put across the diameter of the pool. The rope costs \$0.45 per foot, and Carlos needs 4 feet more than the diameter of the pool. How much will Carlos pay for the rope? (Example 2)

Find the diameter.

$C = \pi d$

_______ $\approx 3.14d$

$\frac{\square}{3.14} \approx \frac{3.14d}{3.14}$

_______ $\approx d$

Find the cost.

Carlos needs ____________ feet of rope.

_______ $\times$ \$0.45 = _______

Carlos will pay _______ for the rope.

Find each missing measurement to the nearest hundredth. Use 3.14 for π. (Examples 1 and 2)

7. $r =$ ____________

$d =$ ____________

$C = \pi$ yd

8. $r \approx$ ____________

$d \approx$ ____________

$C = 78.8$ ft

9. $r \approx$ ____________

$d \approx 3.4$ in.

$C =$ ____________

ESSENTIAL QUESTION CHECK-IN

10. Norah knows that the diameter of a circle is 13 meters. How would you tell her to find the circumference?

____

____

Name ______________________ Class ______________ Date ______________

9.1 Independent Practice

7.G.4

Personal Math Trainer

Online Practice and Help

For 11–13, find the circumference of each circle. Use 3.14 or $\frac{22}{7}$ for π. Round to the nearest hundredth, if necessary.

11.

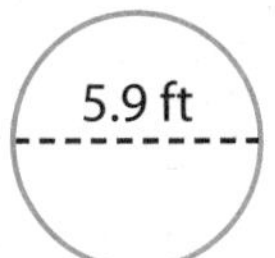

____

12.

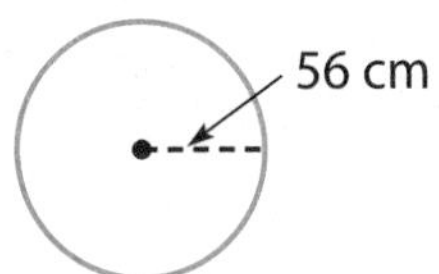

____

13.

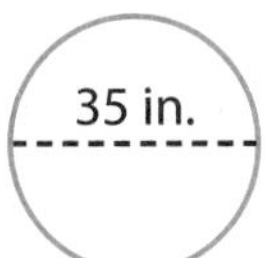

____

14. In Exercises 11–13, for which problems did you use $\frac{22}{7}$ for π? Explain your choice.

____

____

____

15. A circular fountain has a radius of 9.4 feet. Find its diameter and circumference to the nearest tenth.

____

16. Find the radius and circumference of a CD with a diameter of 4.75 inches.

____

17. A dartboard has a diameter of 18 inches. What are its radius and circumference?

____

18. **Multistep** Randy's circular garden has a radius of 1.5 feet. He wants to enclose the garden with edging that costs \$0.75 per foot. About how much will the edging cost? Explain.

____

____

19. **Represent Real-World Problems** The Ferris wheel shown makes 12 revolutions per ride. How far would someone travel during one ride?

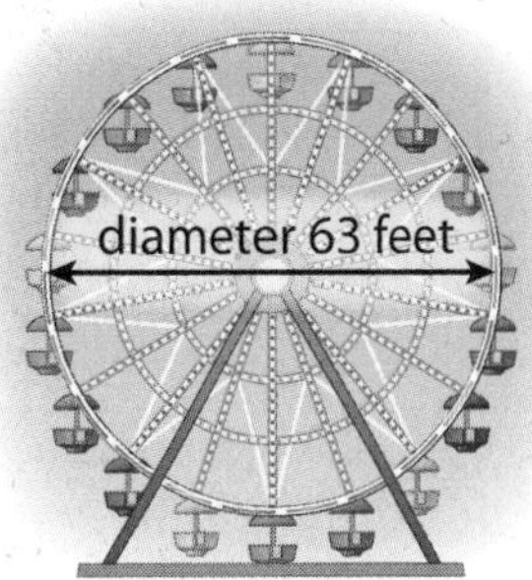

____

20. The diameter of a bicycle wheel is 2 feet. About how many revolutions does the wheel make to travel 2 kilometers? Explain. Hint: 1 km $\approx$ 3,280 ft

____

____

____

21. **Multistep** A map of a public park shows a circular pond. There is a bridge along a diameter of the pond that is 0.25 mi long. You walk across the bridge, while your friend walks halfway around the pond to meet you at the other side of the bridge. How much farther does your friend walk?

____

22. Architecture The Capitol Rotunda connects the House and the Senate sides of the U.S. Capitol. Complete the table. Round your answers to the nearest foot.

Capitol Rotunda Dimensions	
Height	180 ft
Circumference	301.5 ft
Radius	
Diameter	

FOCUS ON HIGHER ORDER THINKING

Work Area

23. Multistep A museum groundskeeper is creating a semicircular statuary garden with a diameter of 30 feet. There will be a fence around the garden. The fencing costs $9.25 per linear foot. About how much will the fencing cost altogether?

____

24. Critical Thinking Sam is placing rope lights around the edge of a circular patio with a diameter of 18 feet. The lights come in lengths of 54 inches. How many strands of lights does he need to surround the patio edge?

____

25. Represent Real-World Problems A circular path 2 feet wide has an inner diameter of 150 feet. How much farther is it around the outer edge of the path than around the inner edge?

____

26. Critique Reasoning A gear on a bicycle has the shape of a circle. One gear has a diameter of 4 inches, and a smaller one has a diameter of 2 inches. Justin says that the circumference of the larger gear is 2 inches more than the circumference of the smaller gear. Do you agree? Explain your answer.

____

____

____

____

27. Persevere in Problem Solving Consider two circular swimming pools. Pool A has a radius of 12 feet, and Pool B has a diameter of 7.5 meters. Which pool has a greater circumference? How much greater? Justify your answers.

____

____

____

____

LESSON

9.2 Area of Circles

CA CC 7.G.4

Know the formulas for the area and circumference of a circle and use them to solve problems; give an informal derivation of the relationship between the circumference and area of a circle.

ESSENTIAL QUESTION

How do you find the area of a circle?

EXPLORE ACTIVITY 1  7.G.4

Exploring Area of Circles

You can use what you know about circles and π to help find the formula for the area of a circle.

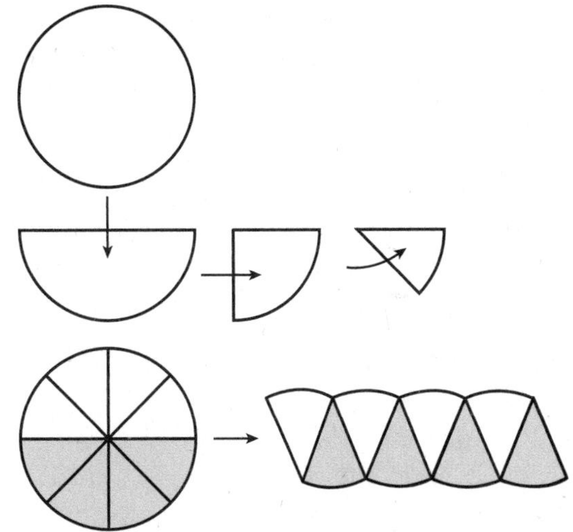

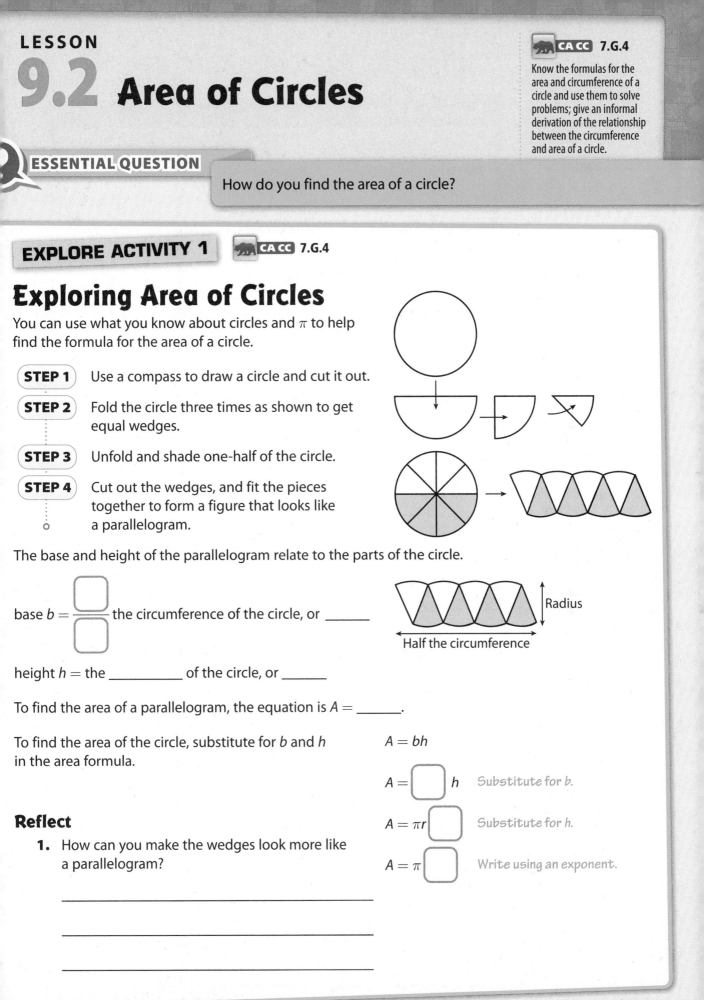

STEP 1 Use a compass to draw a circle and cut it out.

STEP 2 Fold the circle three times as shown to get equal wedges.

STEP 3 Unfold and shade one-half of the circle.

STEP 4 Cut out the wedges, and fit the pieces together to form a figure that looks like a parallelogram.

The base and height of the parallelogram relate to the parts of the circle.

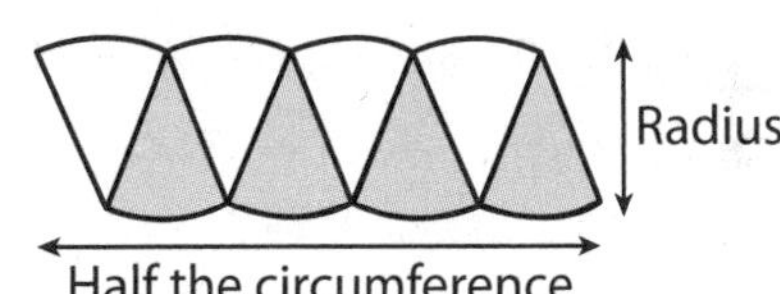

base $b = \frac{\square}{\square}$ the circumference of the circle, or ______

height $h =$ the __________ of the circle, or ______

To find the area of a parallelogram, the equation is $A =$ ______.

To find the area of the circle, substitute for b and h in the area formula.

$A = bh$

$A = \square\, h$ Substitute for b.

$A = \pi r \square$ Substitute for h.

$A = \pi \square$ Write using an exponent.

Reflect

1. How can you make the wedges look more like a parallelogram?

____

____

____

Finding the Area of a Circle

Area of a Circle

The area of a circle is equal to π times the radius squared.

$$A = \pi r^2$$

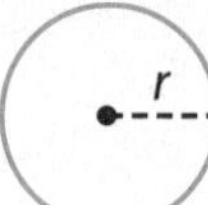

Remember that area is given in square units.

EXAMPLE 1 

A biscuit recipe calls for the dough to be rolled out and circles to be cut from the dough. The biscuit cutter has a radius of 4 cm. Find the area of the top of the biscuit once it is cut. Use 3.14 for π.

$A = \pi r^2$ — Use the formula.

$A = \pi(4)^2$ — Substitute. Use 4 for r.

$A \approx 3.14 \times 4^2$ — Substitute. Use 3.14 for π.

$A \approx 3.14 \times 16$ — Evaluate the power.

$A \approx 50.24$ — Multiply.

The area of the biscuit is about 50.24 cm^2.

Math Talk

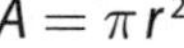
Mathematical Practices

If the radius increases by 1 centimeter, how does the area of the top of the biscuit change?

Reflect

2. Compare finding the area of a circle when given the radius with finding the area when given the diameter.

____

____

____

3. Why do you evaluate the power in the equation before multiplying by pi?

____

____

YOUR TURN

4. A circular pool has a radius of 10 feet. What is the area of the *surface* of the water in the pool? Use 3.14 for π. _______________

EXPLORE ACTIVITY 2

7.G.4

Finding the Relationship between Circumference and Area

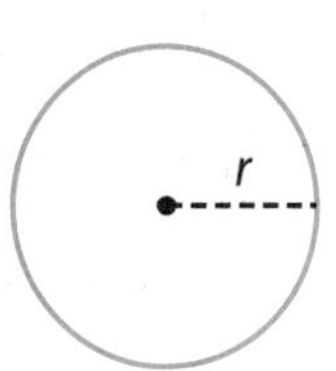

You can use what you know about circumference and area of circles to find a relationship between them.

Find the relationship between the circumference and area of a circle.

Start with a circle that has radius r.

Solve the equation $C = 2\pi r$ for r. $\quad r = \frac{\square}{\square}$

Substitute your expression for r in the formula for area of a circle. $\quad A = \pi\left(\frac{\square}{\square}\right)^2$

Remember: Because the exponent is outside the parentheses, you must apply it to the numerator and to each factor of the denominator.

Square the term in the parentheses. $\quad A = \pi\left(\frac{\square^2}{\square^2 \cdot \square^2}\right)$

Evaluate the power. $\quad A = \frac{\square \cdot \square^2}{\square \cdot \square^2}$

Simplify. $\quad A = \frac{\square^2}{\square \cdot \square}$

Solve for C^2. $\quad C^2 = 4\square\square$

The circumference of the circle squared is equal to

________________________________.

EXPLORE ACTIVITY 2 *(cont'd)*

Reflect

5. Does this formula work for a circle with a radius of 3 inches? Show your work.

Guided Practice

Find the area of each circle. Round to the nearest tenth if necessary. Use 3.14 for π. (Explore Activity 1)

1.

____

2.

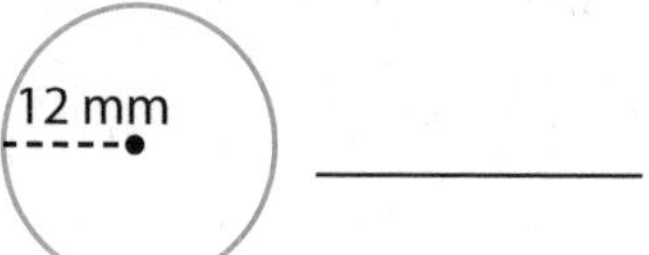

____

3.

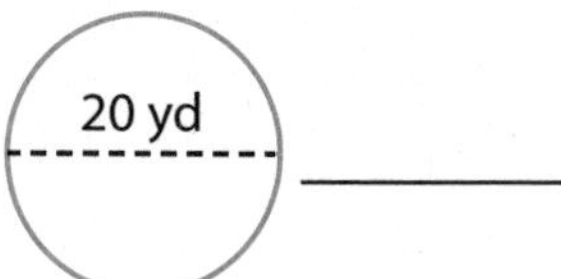

____

Solve. Use 3.14 for π. (Example 1)

4. A clock face has a radius of 8 inches. What is the area of the clock face? Round your answer to the nearest hundredth. ________

5. A DVD has a diameter of 12 centimeters. What is the area of the DVD? Round your answer to the nearest hundredth. ________

6. A company makes steel lids that have a diameter of 13 inches. What is the area of each lid? Round your answer to the nearest hundredth. ________

Find the area of each circle. Give your answers in terms of π. (Explore Activity 2)

7. $C = 4\pi$

$A =$ ________

8. $C = 12\pi$

$A =$ ________

9. $C = \frac{\pi}{2}$

$A =$ ________

10. A circular pen has an area of 64π square yards. What is the circumference of the pen? Give your answer in terms of π. (Explore Activity 2) ________

ESSENTIAL QUESTION CHECK-IN

11. What is the formula for the area A of a circle in terms of the radius r? ________

Name ________________ Class ________________ Date ________________

9.2 Independent Practice

7.G.4

12. The most popular pizza at Pavone's Pizza is the 10-inch personal pizza with one topping. What is the area of a pizza with a diameter of 10 inches? Round your answer to the nearest hundredth.

____

13. A hubcap has a radius of 16 centimeters. What is the area of the hubcap? Round your answer to the nearest hundredth.

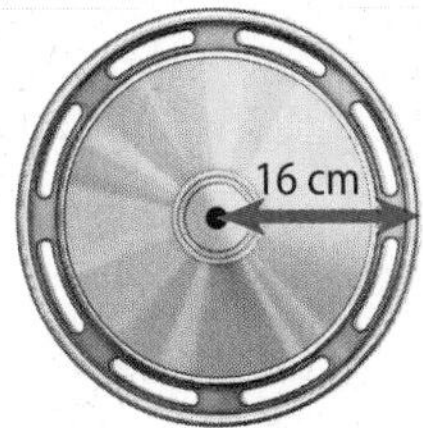

____

14. A stained glass window is shaped like a semicircle. The bottom edge of the window is 36 inches long. What is the area of the stained glass window? Round your answer to the nearest hundredth.

____

15. Analyze Relationships The point (3, 0) lies on a circle with the center at the origin. What is the area of the circle to the nearest hundredth?

____

16. Multistep A radio station broadcasts a signal over an area with a radius of 50 miles. The station can relay the signal and broadcast over an area with a radius of 75 miles. How much greater is the area of the broadcast region when the signal is relayed? Round your answer to the nearest square mile.

____

17. Multistep The sides of a square field are 12 meters. A sprinkler in the center of the field sprays a circular area with a diameter that corresponds to a side of the field. How much of the field is **not** reached by the sprinkler? Round your answer to the nearest hundredth.

____

18. Justify Reasoning A small silver dollar pancake served at a restaurant has a circumference of 2π inches. A regular pancake has a circumference of 4π inches. Is the area of the regular pancake twice the area of the silver dollar pancake? Explain.

____

____

____

____

____

____

19. Analyze Relationships A bakery offers a small circular cake with a diameter of 8 inches. It also offers a large circular cake with a diameter of 24 inches. Does the top of the large cake have three times the area of that of the small cake? If not, how much greater is its area? Explain.

____

____

____

____

____

20. Communicate Mathematical Ideas You can use the formula $A = \frac{C^2}{4\pi}$ to find the area of a circle given the circumference. Describe another way to find the area of a circle when given the circumference.

____

____

____

21. Draw Conclusions Mark wants to order a pizza. Which is the better deal? Explain.

Donnie's Pizza Palace		
Diameter (in.)	12	18
Cost ($)	10	20

____

____

____

22. Multistep A bear was seen near a campground. Searchers were dispatched to the region to find the bear.

a. Assume the bear can walk in any direction at a rate of 2 miles per hour. Suppose the bear was last seen 4 hours ago. How large an area must the searchers cover? Use 3.14 for π. Round your answer to the nearest square mile. ______________

b. What If? How much additional area would the searchers have to cover if the bear were last seen 5 hours ago? ______________

H.O.T. FOCUS ON HIGHER ORDER THINKING

Work Area

23. Analyze Relationships Two circles have the same radius. Is the combined area of the two circles the same as the area of a circle with twice the radius? Explain.

____

____

24. Look for a Pattern How does the area of a circle change if the radius is multiplied by a factor of n, where n is a whole number?

____

25. Represent Real World Problems The bull's-eye on a target has a diameter of 3 inches. The whole target has a diameter of 15 inches. What part of the whole target is the bull's-eye? Explain.

____

LESSON 9.3

Area of Composite Figures

Solve real-world and mathematical problems involving area, volume and surface area of two- and three-dimensional objects composed of triangles, quadrilaterals, polygons, cubes, and right prisms.

ESSENTIAL QUESTION

How do you find the area of composite figures?

EXPLORE ACTIVITY  

Exploring Areas of Composite Figures

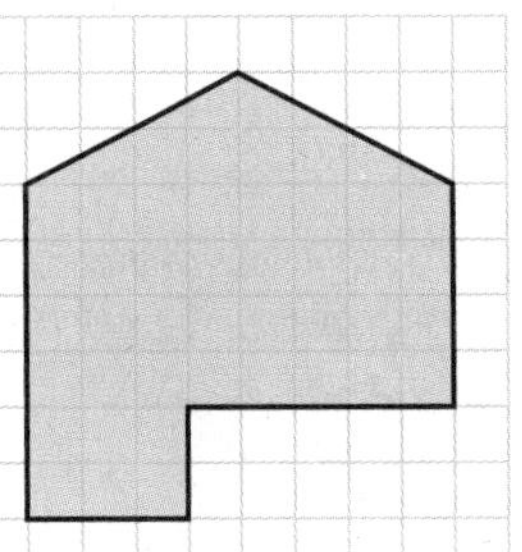

Aaron was plotting the shape of his garden on grid paper. While it was an irregular shape, it was perfect for his yard. Each square on the grid represents 1 square meter.

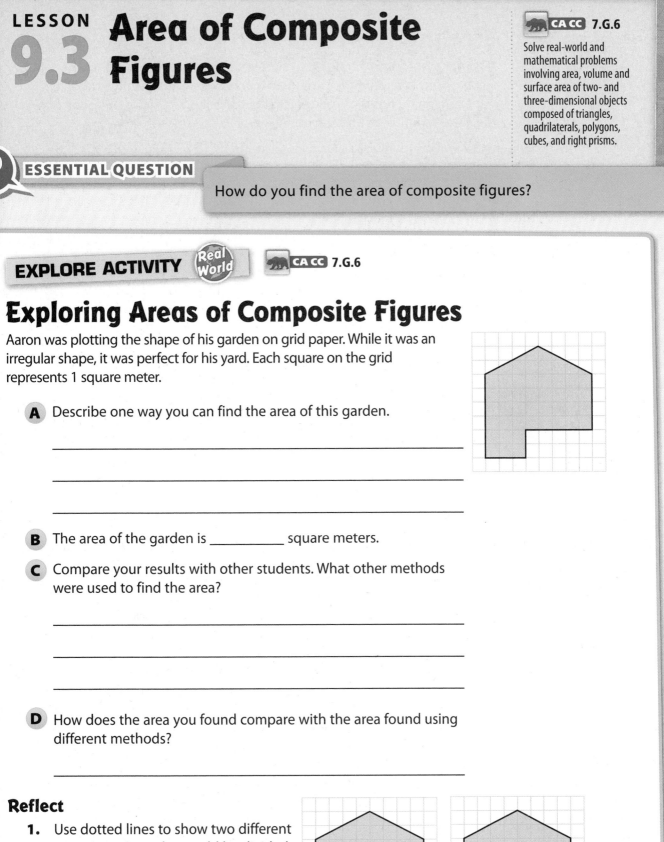

A Describe one way you can find the area of this garden.

____

____

____

B The area of the garden is ________ square meters.

C Compare your results with other students. What other methods were used to find the area?

____

____

____

D How does the area you found compare with the area found using different methods?

____

Reflect

1. Use dotted lines to show two different ways Aaron's garden could be divided up into simple geometric figures.

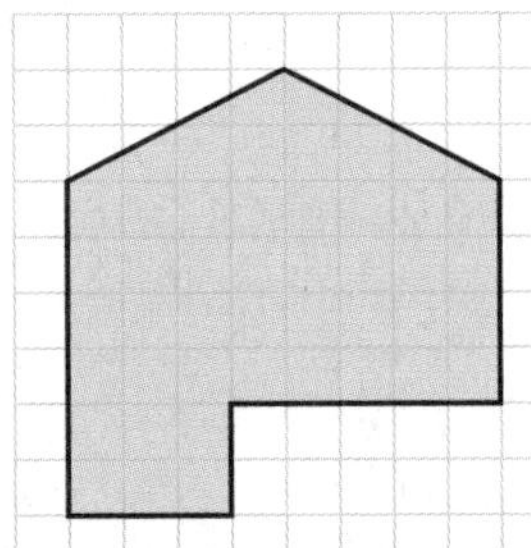

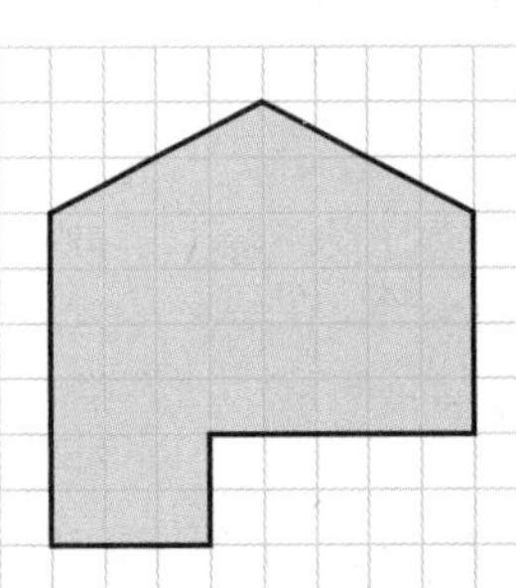

Finding the Area of a Composite Figure

A composite figure is made up of simple geometric shapes. To find the area of a composite figure or other irregular-shaped figure, divide it into simple, nonoverlapping figures. Find the area of each simpler figure, and then add the areas together to find the total area of the composite figure.

Use the chart below to review some common area formulas.

Shape	Area Formula
triangle	$A = \frac{1}{2}bh$
square	$A = s^2$
rectangle	$A = \ell w$
parallelogram	$A = bh$
trapezoid	$A = \frac{1}{2}h(b_1 + b_2)$

EXAMPLE 1

CA CC 7.G.6

Find the area of the figure.

STEP 1 Separate the figure into smaller, familiar figures: a parallelogram and a trapezoid.

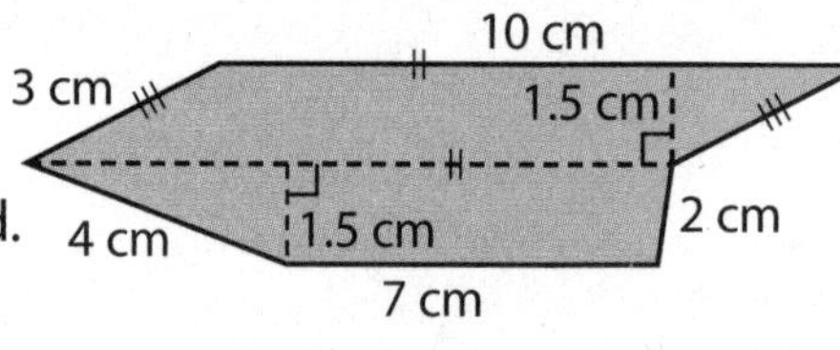

STEP 2 Find the area of each shape.

Area of the Parallelogram

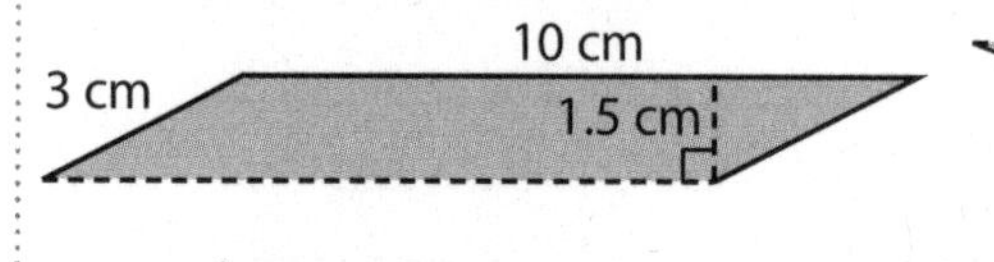

base = 10 cm

height = 1.5 cm

Use the formula.

$A = bh$

$A = 10 \cdot 1.5$

$A = 15$

The area of the parallelogram is 15 cm².

Area of the Trapezoid

$\text{base}_1 = 7$ cm $\text{base}_2 = 10$ cm

height 1.5 cm

Use the formula.

$A = \frac{1}{2}h(b_1 + b_2)$

$A = \frac{1}{2}(1.5)(7 + 10)$

$A = \frac{1}{2}(1.5)(17) = 12.75$

The area of the trapezoid is 12.75 cm².

The top base of the trapezoid is 10 cm since it is the same length as the base of the parallelogram.

STEP 3 Add the areas to find the total area.

$A = 15 + 12.75 = 27.75 \text{ cm}^2$

The area of the figure is 27.75 cm².

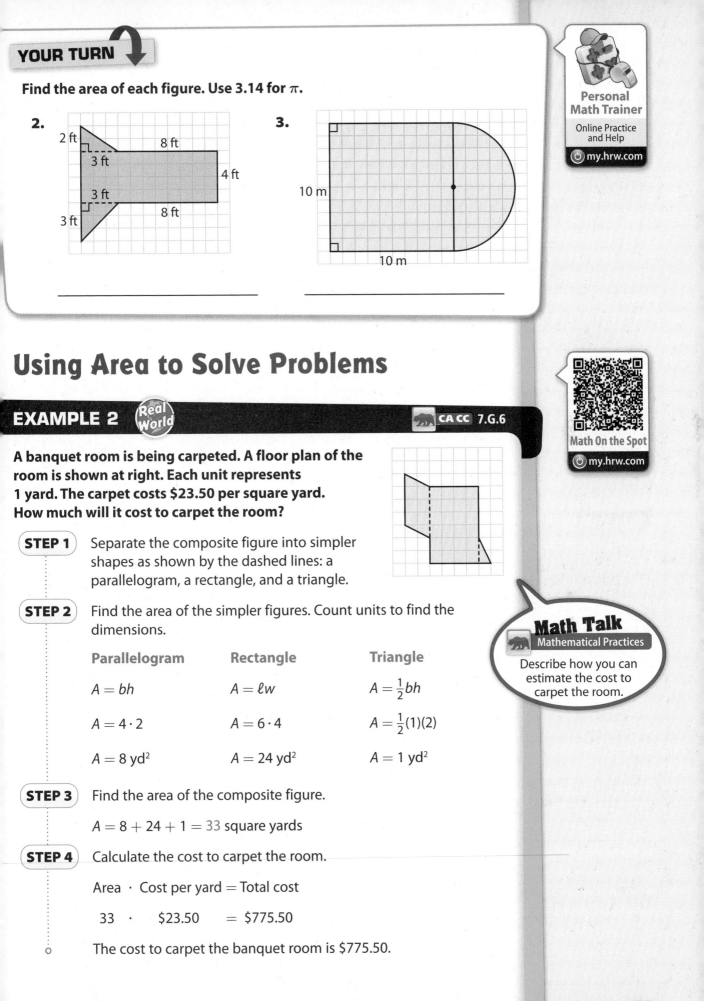

YOUR TURN

Find the area of each figure. Use 3.14 for π.

2.

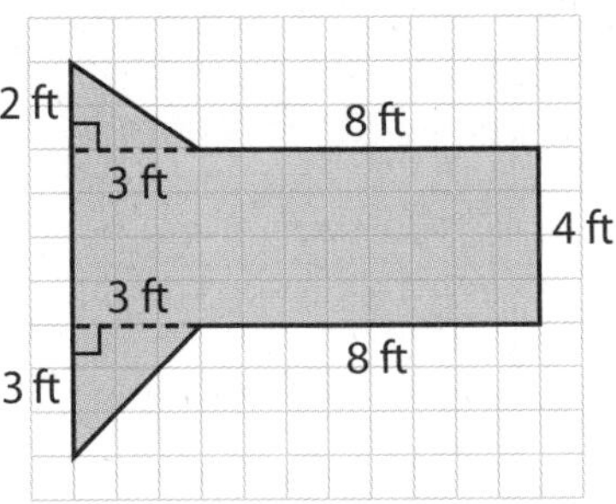

3.

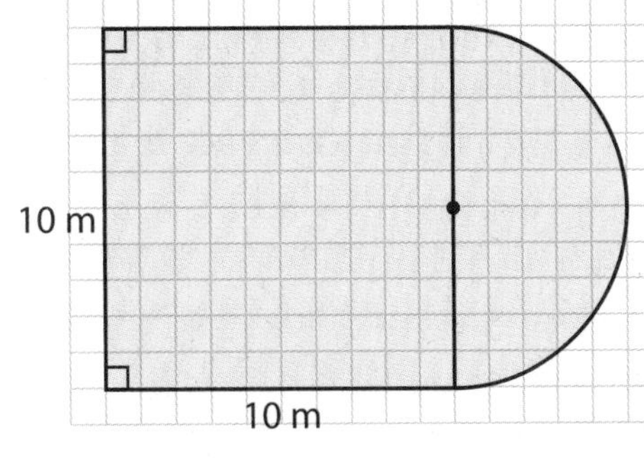

Using Area to Solve Problems

EXAMPLE 2 Real World

CA CC 7.G.6

A banquet room is being carpeted. A floor plan of the room is shown at right. Each unit represents 1 yard. The carpet costs \$23.50 per square yard. How much will it cost to carpet the room?

STEP 1 Separate the composite figure into simpler shapes as shown by the dashed lines: a parallelogram, a rectangle, and a triangle.

STEP 2 Find the area of the simpler figures. Count units to find the dimensions.

Parallelogram	Rectangle	Triangle
$A = bh$	$A = \ell w$	$A = \frac{1}{2}bh$
$A = 4 \cdot 2$	$A = 6 \cdot 4$	$A = \frac{1}{2}(1)(2)$
$A = 8 \text{ yd}^2$	$A = 24 \text{ yd}^2$	$A = 1 \text{ yd}^2$

STEP 3 Find the area of the composite figure.

$A = 8 + 24 + 1 = 33$ square yards

STEP 4 Calculate the cost to carpet the room.

Area · Cost per yard = Total cost

33 · \$23.50 = \$775.50

The cost to carpet the banquet room is \$775.50.

YOUR TURN

4. A window is being replaced with tinted glass. The plan at the right shows the design of the window. Each unit length represents 1 foot. The glass costs $28 per square foot. How much will it cost to replace the glass? Use 3.14 for π.

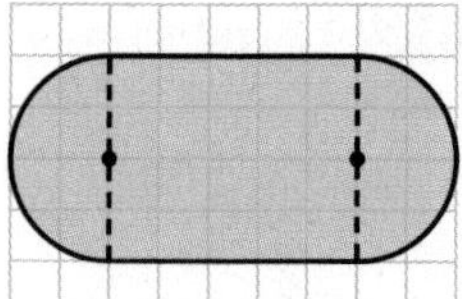

____

Guided Practice

1. A tile installer plots an irregular shape on grid paper. Each square on the grid represents 1 square centimeter. What is the area of the irregular shape? (Explore Activity, Example 2)

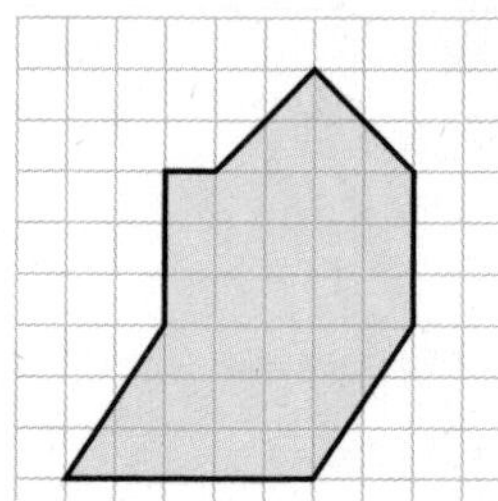

STEP 1 Separate the figure into a triangle, a _______________, and a parallelogram.

STEP 2 Find the area of each figure.

triangle: ____ cm^2; rectangle: ____ cm^2; parallelogram: ____ cm^2

STEP 3 Find the area of the composite figure: ____ + ____ + ____ = ____ cm^2

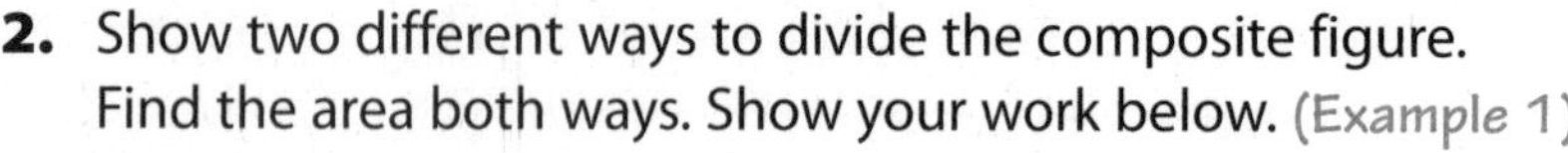

The area of the irregular shape is ____ cm^2.

2. Show two different ways to divide the composite figure. Find the area both ways. Show your work below. (Example 1)

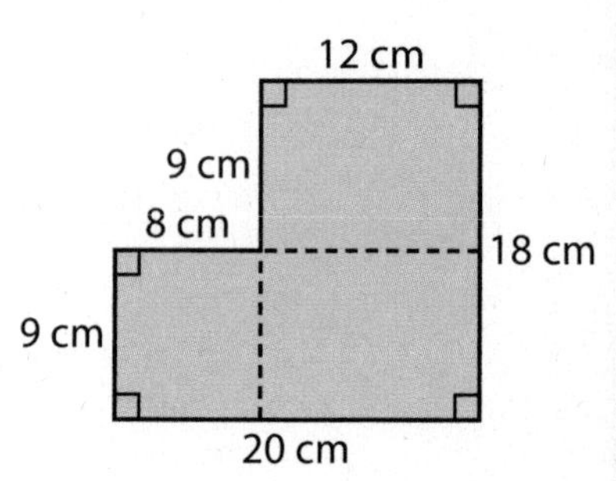

3. Sal is tiling his entryway. The floor plan is drawn on a unit grid. Each unit length represents 1 foot. Tile costs $2.25 per square foot. How much will Sal pay to tile his entryway? (Example 2)

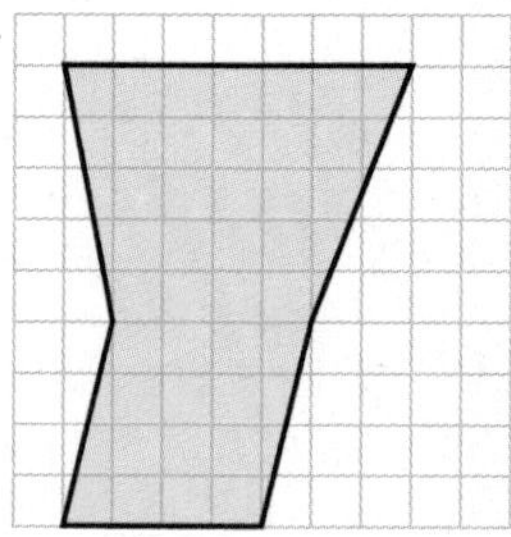

____

ESSENTIAL QUESTION CHECK-IN

4. What is the first step in finding the area of a composite figure?

____

Name ______________________ Class ______________ Date ____________

9.3 Independent Practice

5. A banner is made of a square and a semicircle. The square has side lengths of 26 inches. One side of the square is also the diameter of the semicircle. What is the total area of the banner? Use 3.14 for π.

____

6. **Multistep** Erin wants to carpet the floor of her closet. A floor plan of the closet is shown.

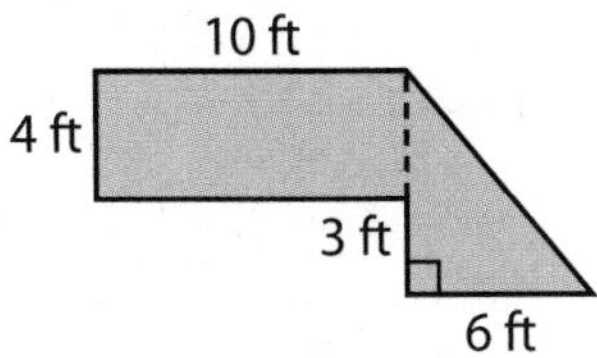

a. How much carpet does Erin need?

____

b. The carpet Erin has chosen costs \$2.50 per square foot. How much will it cost her to carpet the floor?

____

7. **Multiple Representations** Hexagon *ABCDEF* has vertices *A*(−2, 4), *B*(0, 4), *C*(2, 1), *D*(5, 1), *E*(5, −2), and *F*(−2, −2). Sketch the figure on a coordinate plane. What is the area of the hexagon?

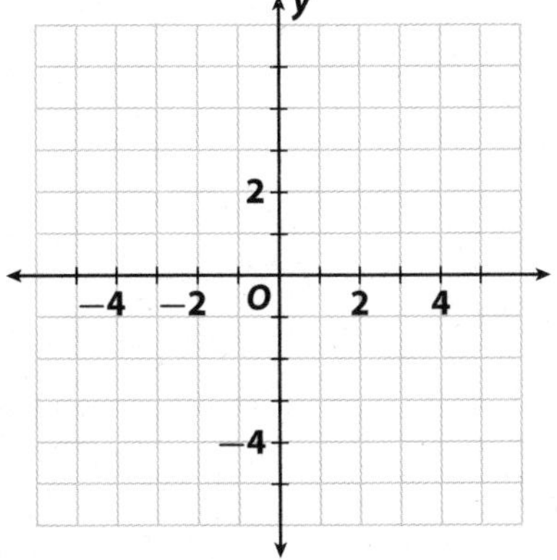

____

8. A field is shaped like the figure shown. What is the area of the field? Use 3.14 for π.

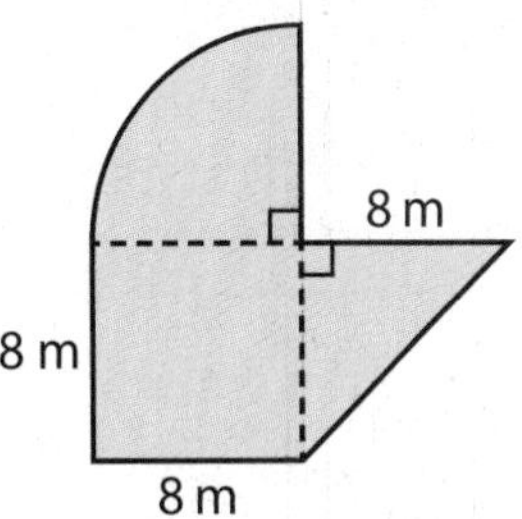

____

9. A bookmark is shaped like a rectangle with a semicircle attached at both ends. The rectangle is 12 cm long and 4 cm wide. The diameter of each semicircle is the width of the rectangle. What is the area of the bookmark? Use 3.14 for π.

____

10. **Multistep** Alex is making 12 pennants for the school fair. The pattern he is using to make the pennants is shown in the figure. The fabric for the pennants costs \$1.25 per square foot. How much will it cost Alex to make 12 pennants?

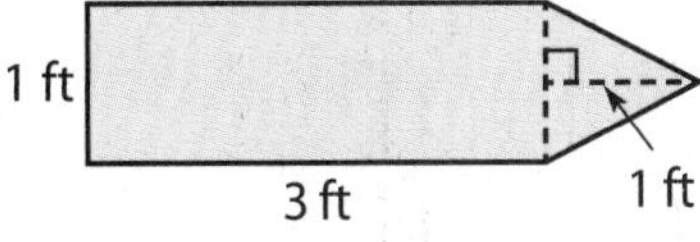

____

11. **Reasoning** A composite figure is formed by combining a square and a triangle. Its total area is 32.5 ft^2. The area of the triangle is 7.5 ft^2. What is the length of each side of the square? Explain.

____

____

____

____

FOCUS ON HIGHER ORDER THINKING

Work Area

12. Represent Real-World Problems Christina plotted the shape of her garden on graph paper. She estimates that she will get about 15 carrots from each square unit. She plans to use the entire garden for carrots. About how many carrots can she expect to grow? Explain.

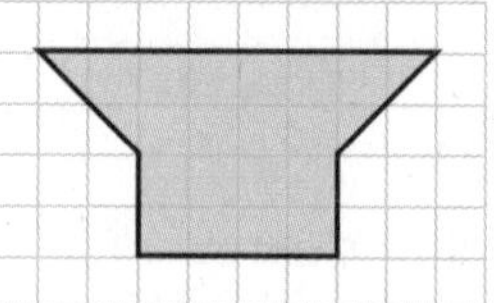

13. Analyze Relationships The figure shown is made up of a triangle and a square. The perimeter of the figure is 56 inches. What is the area of the figure? Explain.

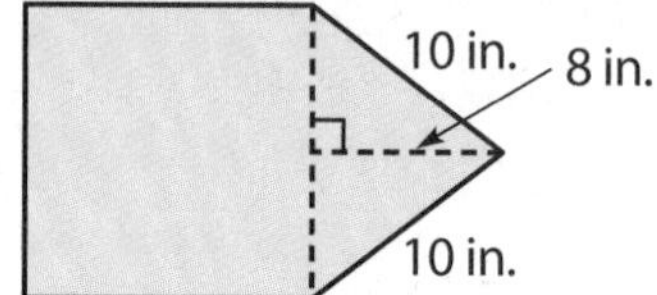

14. Critical Thinking The pattern for a scarf is shown at right. What is the area of the scarf? Use 3.14 for π.

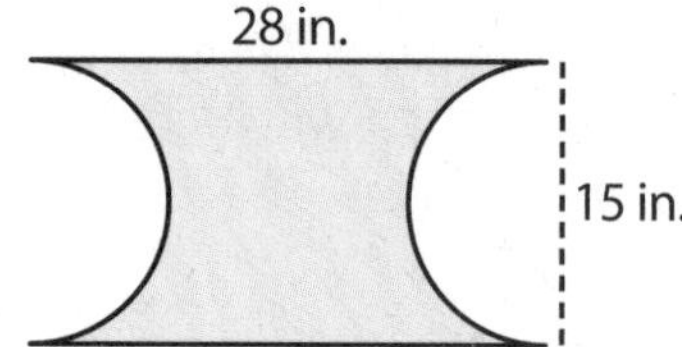

15. Persevere in Problem Solving The design for the palladium window shown includes a semicircular shape at the top. The bottom is formed by squares of equal size. A shade for the window will extend 4 inches beyond the perimeter of the window, shown by the dashed line around the window. Each square in the window has an area of 100 in^2.

a. What is the area of the window? Use 3.14 for π.

b. What is the area of the shade? Round your answer to the nearest whole number.

LESSON 9.4

Solving Surface Area Problems

CA CC 7.G.6

Solve real-world and mathematical problems involving area, volume and surface area of two- and three-dimensional objects composed of triangles, quadrilaterals, polygons, cubes, and right prisms.

ESSENTIAL QUESTION

How can you find the surface area of a figure made up of cubes and prisms?

EXPLORE ACTIVITY 

Modeling Surface Area of a Prism

The surface area of a three-dimensional figure is the sum of the areas of all its surfaces. You know how to use the net of a figure to find its surface area. Now you will discover a formula that you can use.

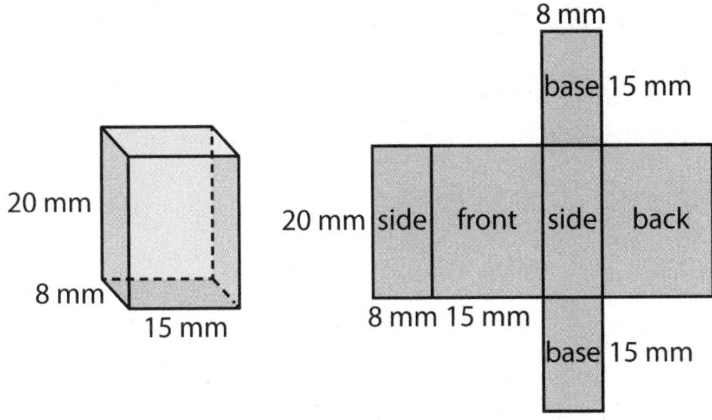

A The lateral area L of a prism is the area of all faces except the bases.

$L = 2($___________$) + 2($___________$) =$ ___________.

B The area B of each base is ___________.

C The surface area S of the prism is the sum of the lateral area L and the total area of the bases, or ___________.

Reflect

1. **Analyze Relationships** Use the net above to answer this question: How does the product of the perimeter P of the base of the prism and the height h of the prism compare to the lateral area L? ___________

2. **Critical Thinking** How can you express the surface area S of the prism in terms of P, h, and B? Use your answer to Question 1. ___________

Finding the Surface Area of a Prism

Given a prism's dimensions, you can use a formula to find the surface area.

Surface Area of a Prism

The surface area S of a prism with base perimeter P, height h, and base area B is $S = Ph + 2B$.

EXAMPLE 1

CA CC 7.G.6

My Notes

Erin is making a jewelry box of wood in the shape of a rectangular prism. The jewelry box will have the dimensions shown. She plans to spray paint the exterior of the box. How many square inches will she have to paint?

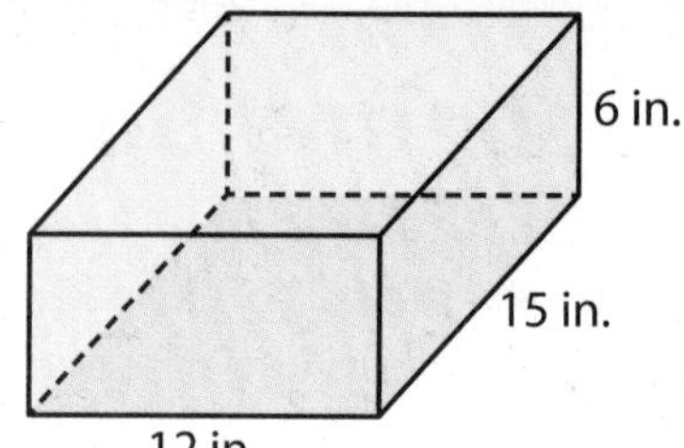

STEP 1 Identify a base, and find its area and perimeter.

Any pair of opposite faces can be the bases. For example, you can choose the bottom and top of the box as the bases.

$B = \ell \times w$

$= 12 \times 15$

$= 180$ square inches

$P = 2(12) + 2(15)$

$= 24 + 30$

$= 54$ inches

STEP 2 Identify the height, and find the surface area.

The height h of the prism is 6 inches. Use the formula to find the surface area.

$S = Ph + 2B$

$S = 54(6) + 2(180) = 684$ square inches

Erin will have to spray paint 684 square inches of wood.

Math Talk

How can you express the formula for the surface area S of a rectangular prism in terms of its dimensions ℓ, w, and h?

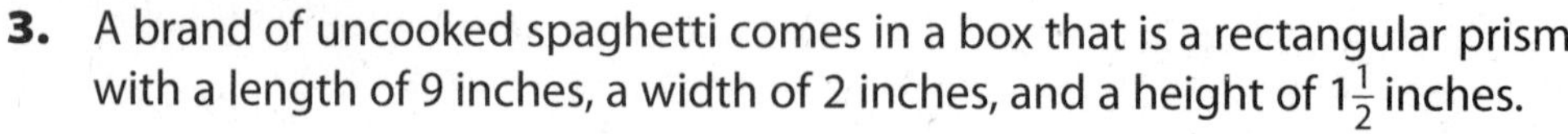

3. A brand of uncooked spaghetti comes in a box that is a rectangular prism with a length of 9 inches, a width of 2 inches, and a height of $1\frac{1}{2}$ inches.

What is the surface area of the box? Explain. ____________________

____

____

____

Finding the Surface Area of a Composite Solid

A composite solid is made up of two or more solid figures. To find the surface area of a composite solid, find the surface area of each figure. Subtract any area not on the surface.

EXAMPLE 2

CA CC 7.G.6

Daniel built the birdhouse shown. What was the surface area of the birdhouse before the hole was drilled?

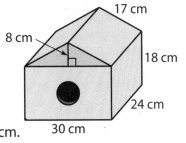

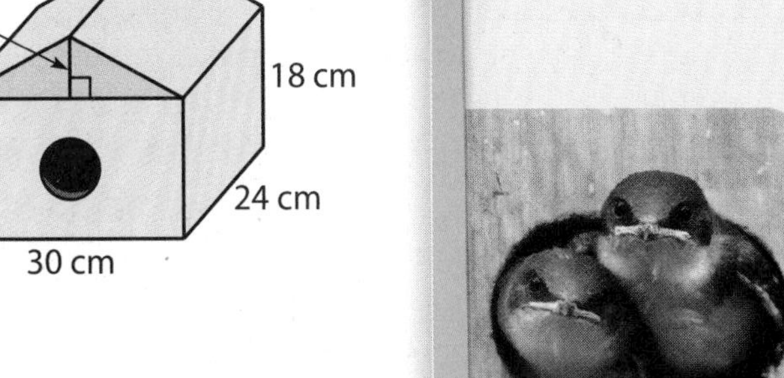

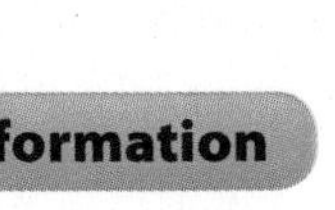

Analyze Information

Identify the important information.

- The top is a triangular prism with $h = 24$ cm. The base is a triangle with height 8 cm and base 30 cm.
- The bottom is a rectangular prism with $h = 18$ cm. The base is a 30 cm by 24 cm rectangle.
- One face of each prism is not on the surface of the figure.

Formulate a Plan

Find the surface area of each prism.

Add the surface areas. Subtract the areas of the parts not on the surface.

Solve

Find the surface area of the triangular prism.

Perimeter $= 17 + 17 + 30 = 64$ cm; Base area $= \frac{1}{2}(30)(8) = 120$ cm^2

Surface area $= Ph + 2B$

$= 64(24) + 2(120) = 1{,}776$ cm^2

Find the surface area of the rectangular prism.

Perimeter $= 2(30) + 2(24) = 108$ cm; Base area $= 30(24) = 720$ cm^2

Surface area $= Ph + 2B$

$= 108(18) + 2(720) = 3{,}384$ cm^2

Add. Then subtract the areas of the parts not on the surface.

Surface area $= 1{,}776 + 3{,}384 - 2(720) = 3{,}720$ cm^2

The surface area before the hole was drilled was 3,720 cm^2.

Justify and Evaluate

You can check your work by using a net to find the surface areas.

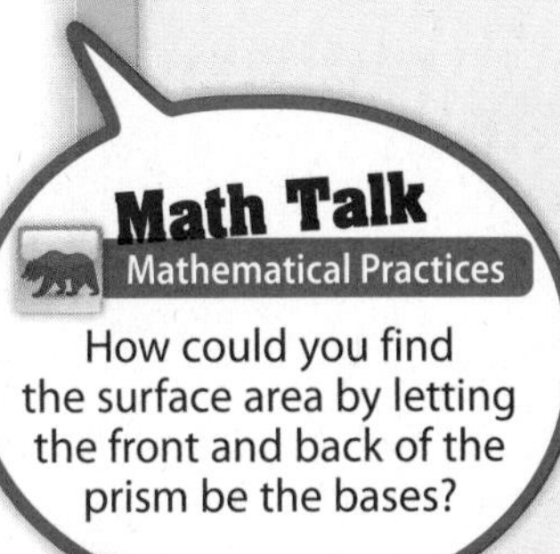

Math Talk
Mathematical Practices
How could you find the surface area by letting the front and back of the prism be the bases?

YOUR TURN

4. Dara is building a plant stand. She wants to stain the plant stand, except for the bottom of the larger prism. Find the surface area of the part of the plant stand she will stain.

____

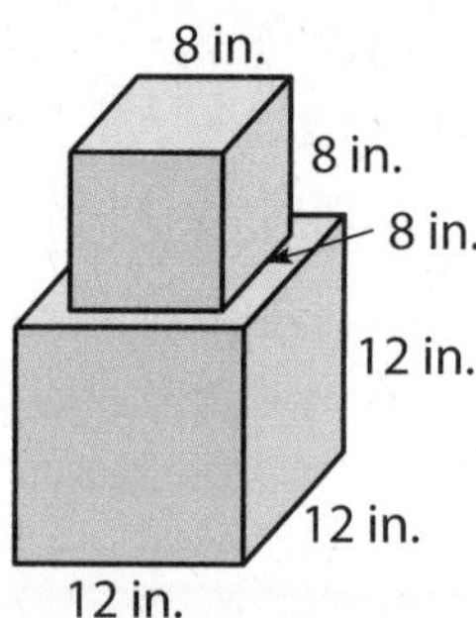

Guided Practice

Find the surface area of each solid figure. (Examples 1 and 2)

1.

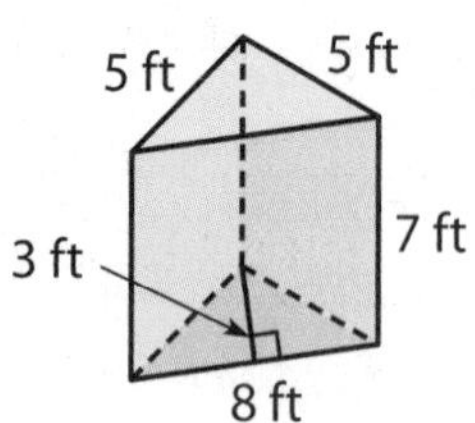

Perimeter of base = ________

Height = ________

Base area = ________

Surface area:

S = (________)(________) + 2(________)

= ________

2.

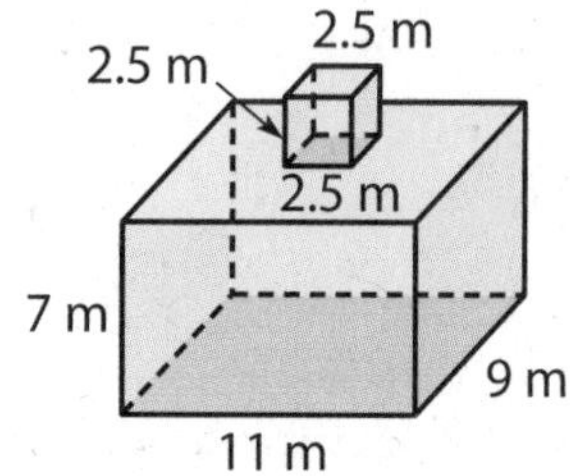

Surface area of cube:

S = __________

Surface area of rectangular prism:

S = __________

Overlapping area: A = __________

Surface area of composite figure:

= ________ + ________ − 2(________) =

________ m^2

ESSENTIAL QUESTION CHECK-IN

3. How can you find the surface area of a composite solid made up of prisms?

____

____

____

Name ______________________ Class ______________ Date ______________

9.4 Independent Practice

CA CC 7.G.6

4. Carla is wrapping a present in the box shown. How much wrapping paper does she need, not including overlap?

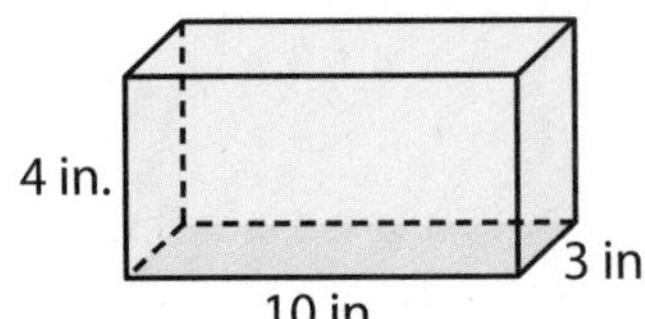

____

5. Dmitri wants to cover the top and sides of the box shown with glass tiles that are 5 mm square. How many tiles does he need?

____

6. Shera is building a cabinet. She is making wooden braces for the corners of the cabinet. Find the surface area of each brace.

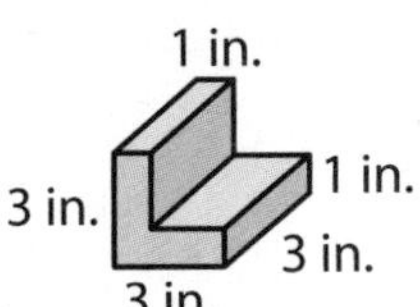

____

7. The doghouse shown has a floor, but no windows. Find the total surface area of the doghouse, including the door.

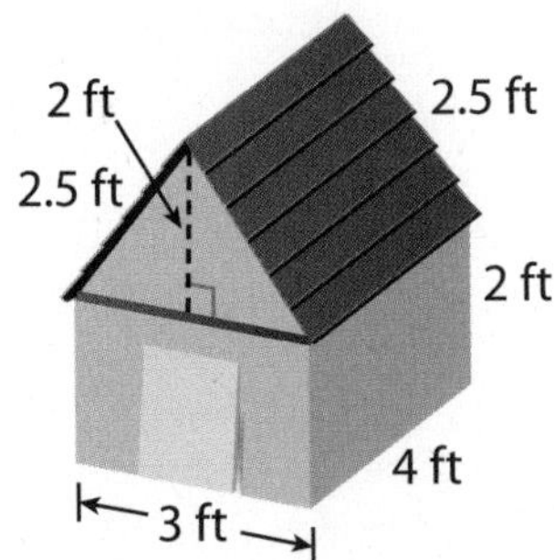

____

Eddie built the ramp shown to train his puppy to do tricks. Use the figure for 8–9.

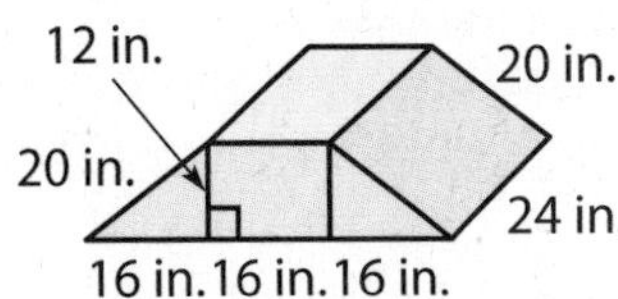

8. **Analyze Relationships** Describe two ways to find the surface area of the ramp.

____

____

____

____

9. What is the surface area of the ramp?

____

Marco and Elaine are building a stand like the one shown to display trophies. Use the figure for 10–11.

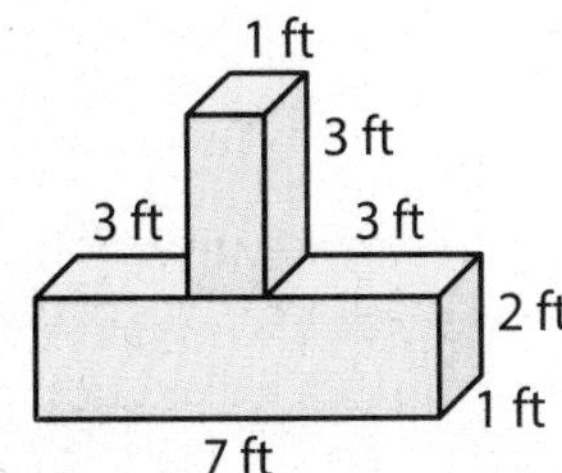

10. What is the surface area of the stand?

____

11. **Critique Reasoning** Marco and Elaine want to paint the entire stand silver. A can of paint covers 25 square feet and costs \$6.79. They set aside \$15 for paint. Is that enough? Explain.

____

____

12. Henry wants to cover the box shown with paper without any overlap. How many square centimeters will be covered with paper?

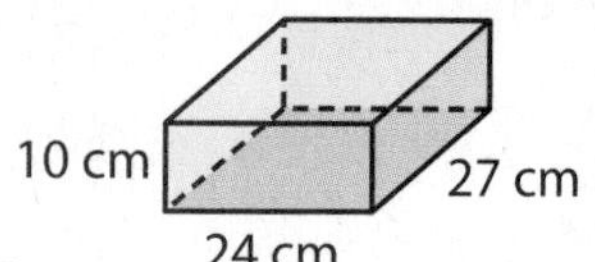

____

13. **What If?** Suppose the length and width of the box in Exercise 12 double. Does the surface area S double? Explain.

____

FOCUS ON HIGHER ORDER THINKING

Work Area

14. **Persevere in Problem Solving** Enya is building a storage cupboard in the shape of a rectangular prism. The rectangular prism has a square base with side lengths of 2.5 feet and a height of 3.5 feet. Compare the amount of paint she would use to paint all but the bottom surface of the prism to the amount she would use to paint the entire prism.

____

____

____

15. **Interpret the Answer** The oatmeal box shown is shaped like a cylinder. Use a net to find the surface area S of the oatmeal box to the nearest tenth. Then find the number of square feet of cardboard needed for 1,500 oatmeal boxes. Round your answer to the nearest whole number.

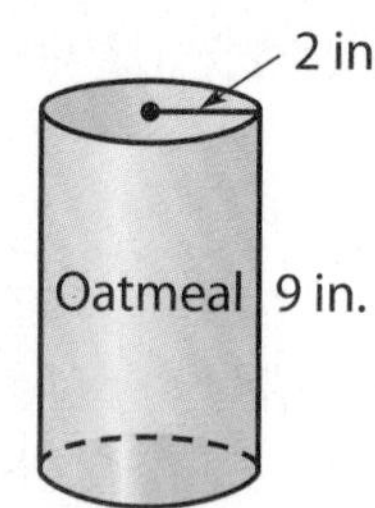

____

____

16. **Analyze Relationships** A prism is made of centimeter cubes. How can you find the surface area of the prism in Figure 1 without using a net or a formula? How does the surface area change in Figures 2, 3, and 4? Explain.

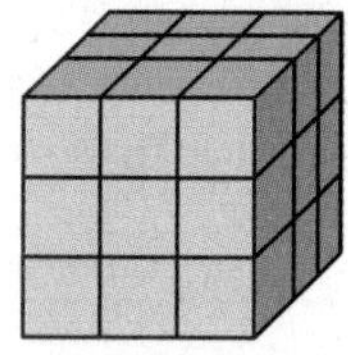
Figure 1

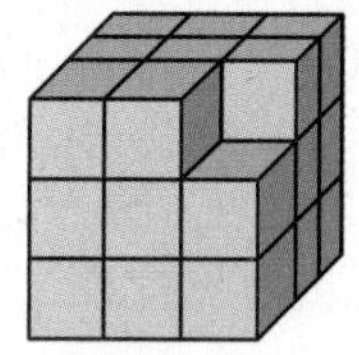
Figure 2

Figure 3

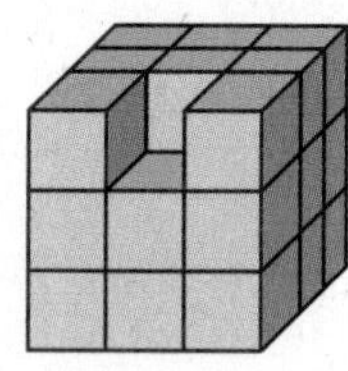
Figure 4

____

____

____

____

____

LESSON 9.5
Solving Volume Problems

7.G.6

Solve real-world and mathematical problems involving area, volume and surface area of two- and three-dimensional objects composed of triangles, quadrilaterals, polygons, cubes, and right prisms.

ESSENTIAL QUESTION

How do you find the volume of a figure made of cubes and prisms?

Volume of a Triangular Prism

The formula for the volume of a rectangular prism can be used for *any* prism.

Volume of a Prism

The volume V of a prism is the area of its base B times its height h.

$$V = Bh$$

EXAMPLE 1

CA CC 7.G.6

Bradley's tent is in the shape of a triangular prism. How many cubic feet of space are in his tent?

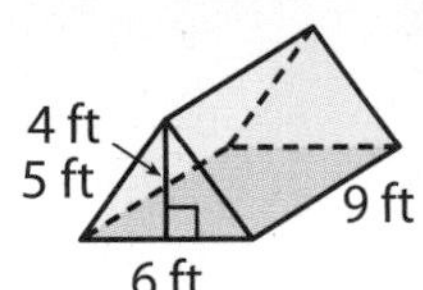

STEP 1 Find the base area B of the triangular prism.

$B = \frac{1}{2}bh$ — Area of a triangle with base length b and height h

$= \frac{1}{2}(6)(4)$ — Substitute 6 for b and 4 for h.

$= 12\text{ ft}^2$

STEP 2 Find the volume of the prism.

$V = Bh$ — Volume of a prism with base area B and height h

$= (12)(9)$ — Substitute 12 for B and 9 for h.

$= 108\text{ ft}^3$

The volume of Bradley's tent is 108 ft^3.

Reflect

1. **Analyze Relationships** For a prism that is **not** a rectangular prism, how do you determine which sides are the bases?

____

2. Find the volume of the prism.

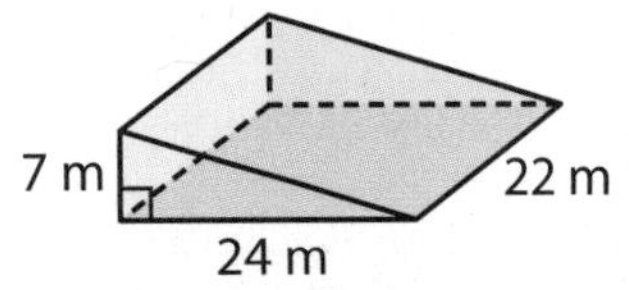

____

Volume of a Trapezoidal Prism

Prisms are named for the polygons that form their bases. In this lesson, you will focus on prisms whose bases are either triangles or quadrilaterals other than squares and rectangles.

EXAMPLE 2

Cherise is setting up her tent. Her tent is in the shape of a trapezoidal prism. How many cubic feet of space are in her tent?

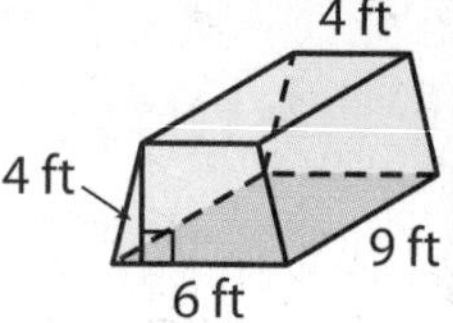

STEP 1 Find the base area B of the trapezoidal prism.

$B = \frac{1}{2}(b_1 + b_2)\,h$ — *Area of a trapezoid with bases of lengths b_1 and b_2 and height h*

$= \frac{1}{2}(6 + 4)4$ — *Substitute 6 for b_1, 4 for b_2, and 4 for h.*

$= \frac{1}{2}(10)4 = 20 \text{ ft}^2$

STEP 2 Find the volume of the prism.

$V = Bh$ — *Volume of a prism with base area B and height h*

$= (20)(9)$ — *Substitute 20 for B and 9 for h.*

$= 180 \text{ ft}^3$

The volume of Cherise's tent is 180 ft^3.

Math Talk
Mathematical Practices

Without calculating the volumes, how can you know whether Bradley's or Cherise's tent has a greater volume?

Reflect

3. **Look for a Pattern** How could you double the volume of the tent by doubling just one of its dimensions?

____

____

4. **What If?** How would doubling *all* the dimensions of the prism affect the volume of the tent?

____

YOUR TURN

5. Find the volume of the prism.

____

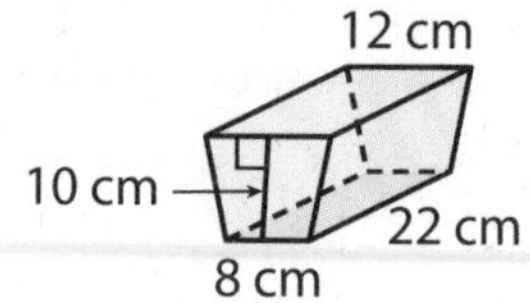

Volume of a Composite Solid

You can use the formula for the volume of a prism to find the volume of a composite figure that is made up of prisms.

Math On the Spot
my.hrw.com

EXAMPLE 3 

CA CC 7.G.6

Allie has two aquariums connected by a small square prism. Find the volume of the double aquarium.

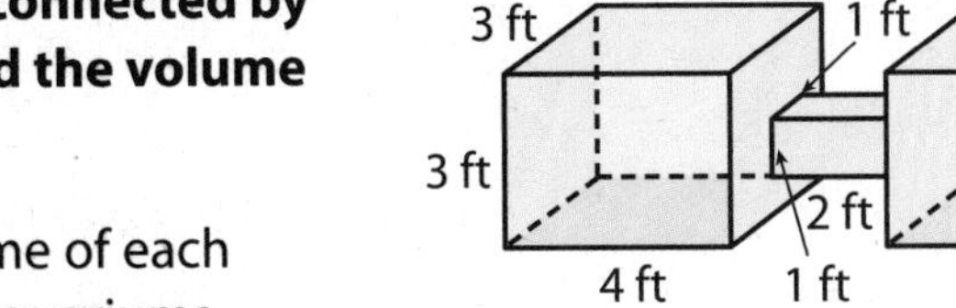

STEP 1 Find the volume of each of the larger aquariums.

$V = Bh$ *Volume of a prism*

$= (12)(3)$ Substitute $3 \times 4 = 12$ for B and 3 for h.

$= 36 \text{ ft}^3$

STEP 2 Find the volume of the connecting prism.

$V = Bh$ *Volume of a prism*

$= (1)(2)$ Substitute $1 \times 1 = 1$ for B and 2 for h.

$= 2 \text{ ft}^3$

STEP 3 Add the volumes of the three parts of the aquarium.

$V = 36 + 36 + 2 = 74 \text{ ft}^3$

The volume of the aquarium is 74 ft^3.

My Notes

Reflect

6. **What If?** Find the volume of one of the large aquariums on either end using another pair of opposite sides as the bases. Do you still get the same volume? Explain.

____

____

7. The figure is composed of a rectangular prism and a triangular prism. Find the volume of the figure.

____

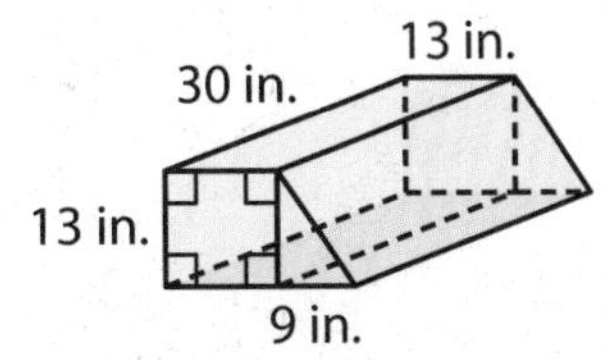

Guided Practice

1. Find the volume of the triangular prism. (Example 1)

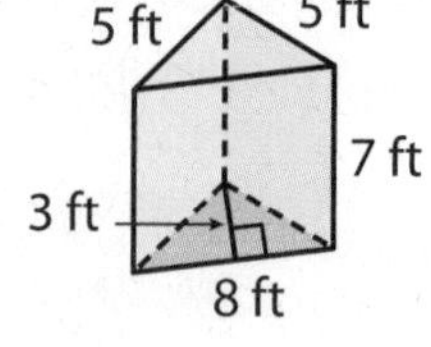

$B = \frac{1}{2}bh = \frac{1}{2}(8)(3) = 12 \text{ ft}^{\square}$

$V = Bh = (\square \times \square) \text{ ft}^{\square} = \square \text{ ft}^3$

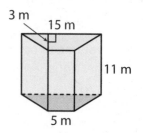

2. Find the volume of the trapezoidal prism. (Example 2)

$B = \frac{1}{2}(b_1 + b_2)h = \frac{1}{2}(15 + 5)(3) = 30 \text{ m}^{\square}$

$V = Bh = (\square \times \square) \text{ m}^{\square} = \square \text{ m}^3$

3. Find the volume of the composite figure. (Example 3)

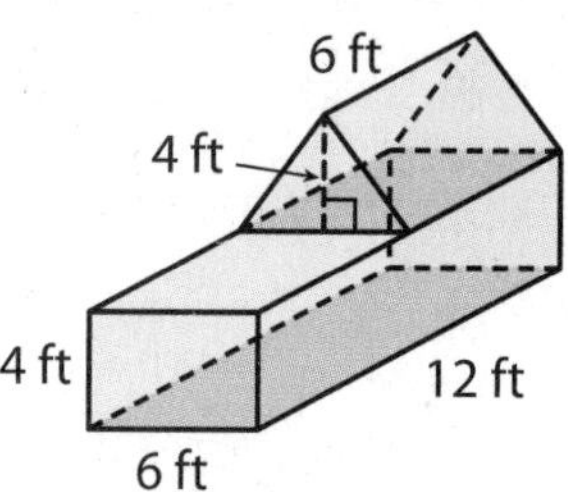

Volume of rectangular prism = ____________

Volume of triangular prism = ____________

Volume of composite figure = ____________

Find the volume of each figure. (Examples 2 and 3)

4. The figure shows a barn that Mr. Fowler is building for his farm.

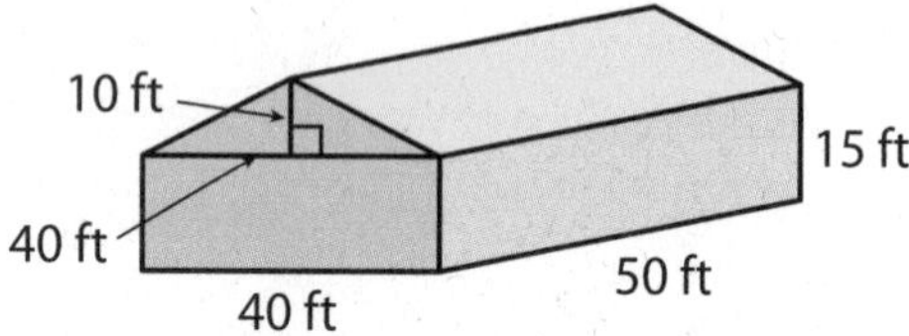

____

5. The figure shows a container, in the shape of a trapezoidal prism, that Pete filled with sand.

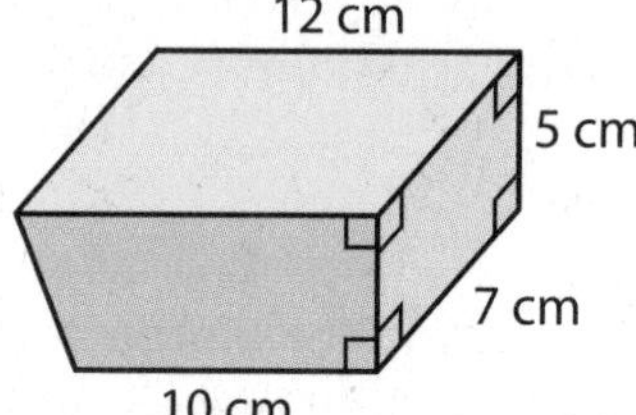

____

ESSENTIAL QUESTION CHECK-IN

6. How do you find the volume of a composite solid formed by two or more prisms?

____

____

Name________________________ Class________________ Date________________

9.5 Independent Practice

7.G.6

7. A trap for insects is in the shape of a triangular prism. The area of the base is 3.5 in^2 and the height of the prism is 5 in. What is the volume of this trap?

____

8. Arletta built a cardboard ramp for her little brothers' toy cars. Identify the shape of the ramp. Then find its volume.

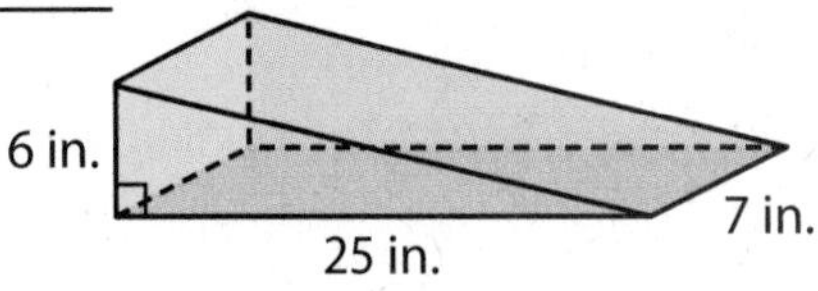

____

9. Alex made a sketch for a homemade soccer goal he plans to build. The goal will be in the shape of a triangular prism. The legs of the right triangles at the sides of his goal measure 4 ft and 8 ft, and the opening along the front is 24 ft. How much space is contained within this goal?

____

10. A gift box is in the shape of a trapezoidal prism with base lengths of 7 inches and 5 inches and a height of 4 inches. The height of the gift box is 8 inches. What is the volume of the gift box?

____

11. **Explain the Error** A student wrote this statement: "A triangular prism has a height of 15 inches and a base area of 20 square inches. The volume of the prism is 300 square inches." Identify and correct the error.

____

Find the volume of each figure. Round to the nearest hundredth if necessary.

12. $B \approx 23.4$ in^2

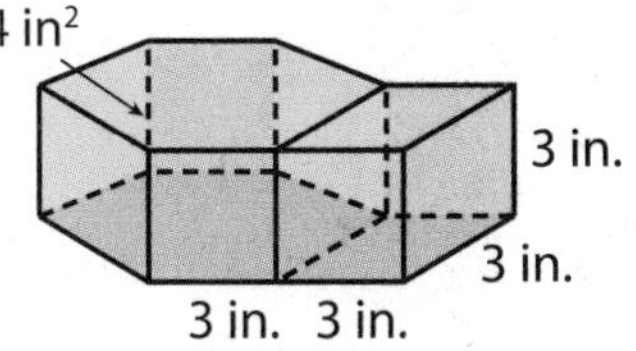

____

13.

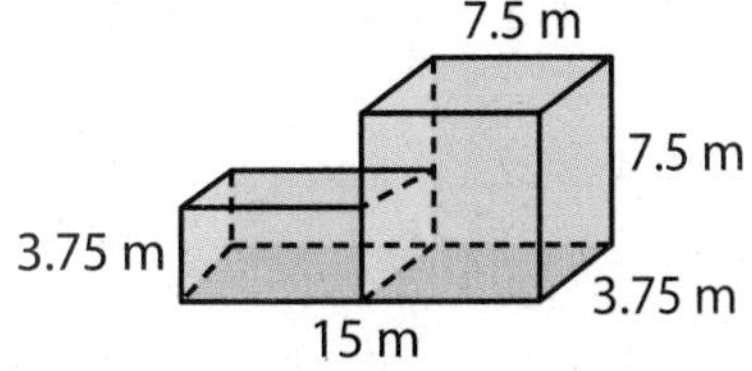

____

14. **Multi-Step** Josie has 260 cubic centimeters of candle wax. She wants to make a hexagonal prism candle with a base area of 21 square centimeters and a height of 8 centimeters. She also wants to make a triangular prism candle with a height of 14 centimeters. Can the base area of the triangular prism candle be 7 square centimeters? Explain.

____

15. A movie theater offers popcorn in two different containers for the same price. One container is a trapezoidal prism with a base area of 36 square inches and a height of 5 inches. The other container is a triangular prism with a base area of 32 square inches and a height of 6 inches. Which container is the better deal? Explain.

____

____

FOCUS ON HIGHER ORDER THINKING

Work Area

16. Critical Thinking The wading pool shown is a trapezoidal prism with a total volume of 286 cubic feet. What is the missing dimension?

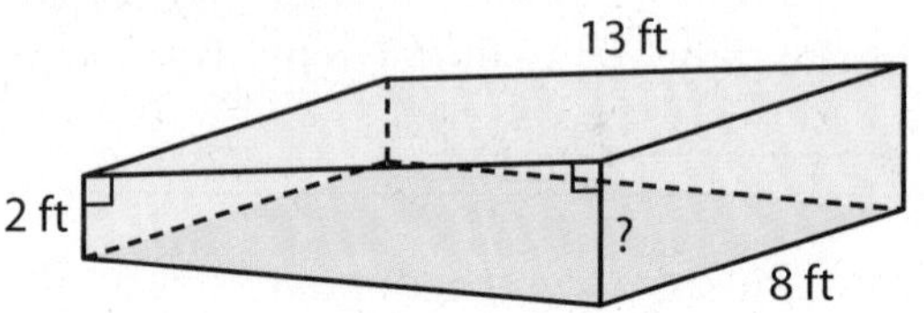

____

17. Persevere in Problem Solving Lynette has a metal doorstop with the dimensions shown. Each cubic centimeter of the metal in the doorstop has a mass of about 8.6 grams. Find the volume of the metal in the doorstop. Then find the mass of the doorstop.

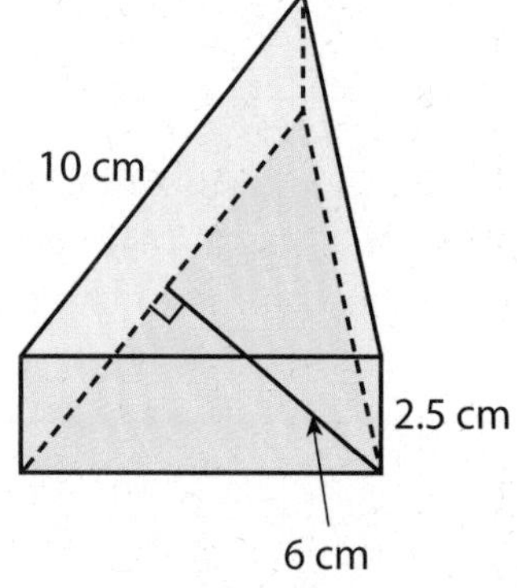

____

____

18. Analyze Relationships What effect would tripling all the dimensions of a triangular prism have on the volume of the prism? Explain your reasoning.

____

____

____

____

19. Persevere in Problem Solving Each of two trapezoidal prisms has a volume of 120 cubic centimeters. The prisms have no dimensions in common. Give possible dimensions for each prism.

____

____

____

____

MODULE QUIZ

Ready to Go On?

9.1, 9.2 Circumference and Area of Circles

Find the circumference and area of each circle. Use 3.14 for π. Round to the nearest hundredth if necessary.

1. 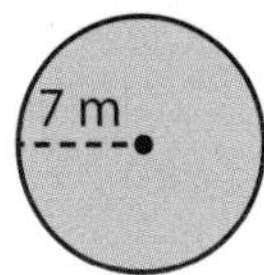

____

2. 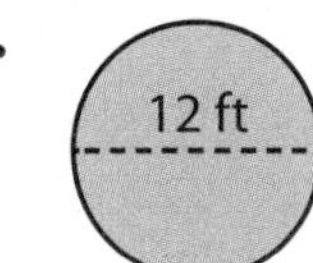

____

9.3 Area of Composite Figures

Find the area of each figure. Use 3.14 for π.

3. 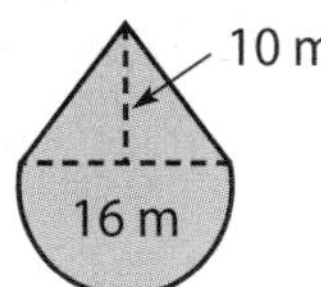

____

4. 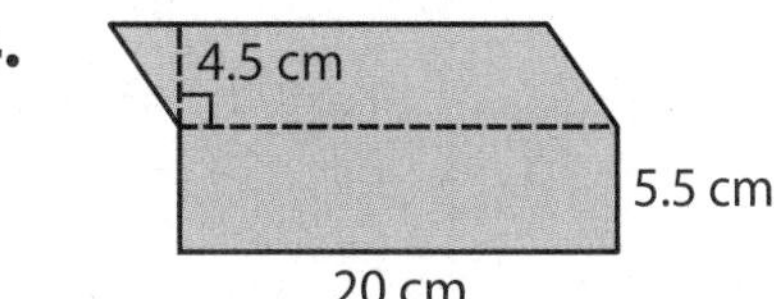

____

9.4, 9.5 Solving Surface Area and Volume Problems

Find the surface area and volume of each figure.

5. 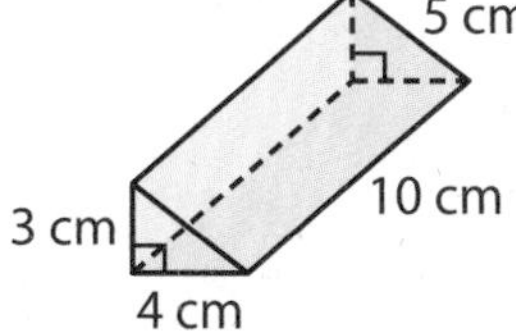

____

6. 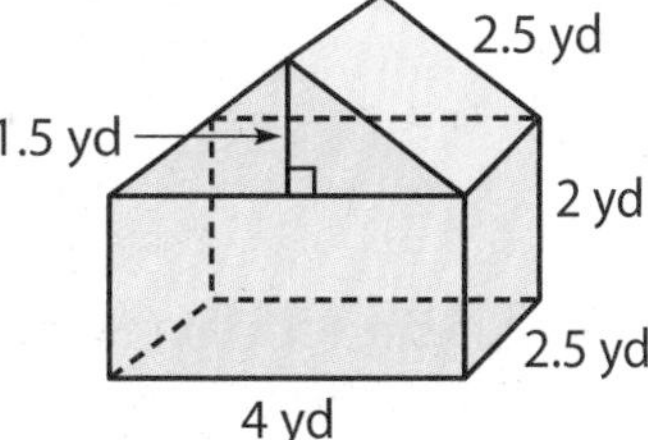

____

ESSENTIAL QUESTION

7. How can you use geometry figures to solve real-world problems?

____

____

MODULE 9
MIXED REVIEW

Assessment Readiness

Personal Math Trainer
my.hrw.com
Online Practice and Help

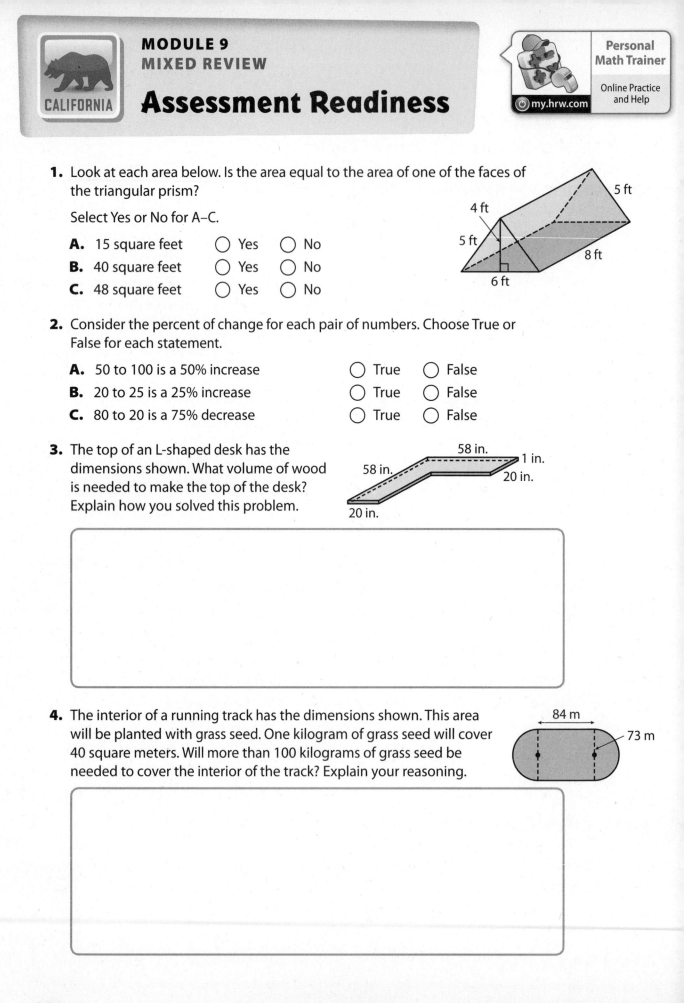

1. Look at each area below. Is the area equal to the area of one of the faces of the triangular prism?

4 ft, 5 ft, 5 ft, 6 ft, 8 ft

Select Yes or No for A–C.

A. 15 square feet ○ Yes ○ No
B. 40 square feet ○ Yes ○ No
C. 48 square feet ○ Yes ○ No

2. Consider the percent of change for each pair of numbers. Choose True or False for each statement.

A. 50 to 100 is a 50% increase ○ True ○ False
B. 20 to 25 is a 25% increase ○ True ○ False
C. 80 to 20 is a 75% decrease ○ True ○ False

3. The top of an L-shaped desk has the dimensions shown. What volume of wood is needed to make the top of the desk? Explain how you solved this problem.

58 in., 58 in., 1 in., 20 in., 20 in.

4. The interior of a running track has the dimensions shown. This area will be planted with grass seed. One kilogram of grass seed will cover 40 square meters. Will more than 100 kilograms of grass seed be needed to cover the interior of the track? Explain your reasoning.

84 m, 73 m

UNIT 4

Study Guide Review

MODULE 8

Modeling Geometric Figures

Key Vocabulary

adjacent angles *(ángulos adyacentes)*

complementary angles *(ángulos complementarios)*

congruent angles *(ángulos congruentes)*

cross section *(sección transversal)*

intersection *(intersección)*

plane *(plano)*

scale *(escala)*

scale drawing *(dibujo a escala)*

supplementary angles *(ángulos suplementarios)*

vertical angles *(ángulos opuestos por el vértice)*

ESSENTIAL QUESTION

How can you apply geometry concepts to solve real-world problems?

EXAMPLE 1

Use the scale drawing to find the perimeter of Tim's yard.

15 cm

4 cm

2 cm : 14 ft

$\frac{2 \text{ cm}}{14 \text{ ft}} = \frac{1 \text{ cm}}{7 \text{ ft}}$ 1 cm in the drawing equals 7 feet in the actual yard.

$\frac{1 \text{ cm} \times 15}{7 \text{ ft} \times 15} = \frac{15 \text{ cm}}{105 \text{ ft}}$ 15 cm in the drawing equals 105 feet in the actual yard. Tim's yard is 105 feet long.

$\frac{1 \text{ cm} \times 4}{7 \text{ ft} \times 4} = \frac{4 \text{ cm}}{28 \text{ ft}}$ 4 cm in the drawing equals 7 feet in the actual yard. Tim's yard is 28 feet wide.

Perimeter is twice the sum of the length and the width. So the perimeter of Tim's yard is $2(105 + 28) = 2(133)$, or 266 feet.

EXAMPLE 2

Find (a) the value of *x* and (b) the measure of $\angle APY$.

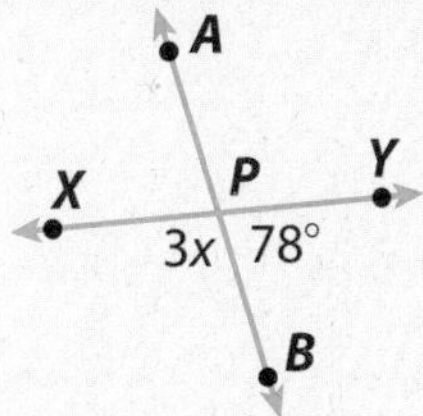

a. $\angle XPB$ and $\angle YPB$ are supplementary.

$3x + 78° = 180°$

$3x = 102°$

$x = 34°$

b. $\angle APY$ and $\angle XPB$ are vertical angles.

$m\angle APY = m\angle XPB = 3x = 102°$

EXERCISES

1. In the scale drawing of a park, the scale is 1 cm: 10 m. Find the area of the actual park.

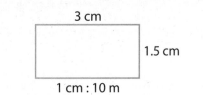

3 cm

1.5 cm

1 cm : 10 m

(Lesson 8.1) ______________________

2. Find the value of y and the measure of $\angle YPS$ (Lesson 8.4)

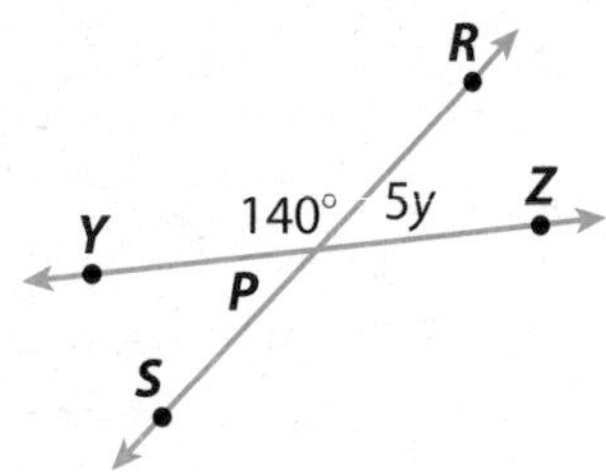

$y =$ ______________

$m\angle YPS =$ ______________

3. Kanye wants to make a triangular flower bed using logs with the lengths shown below to form the border. Can Kanye form a triangle with the logs without cutting any of them? Explain. (Lesson 8.2)

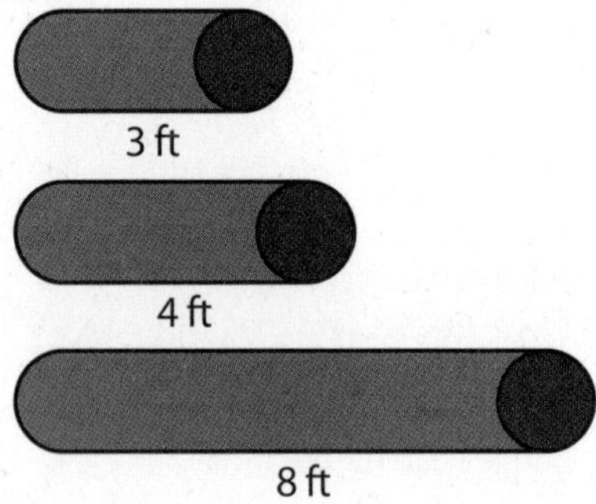

____

____

____

4. In shop class, Adriana makes a pyramid with a 4-inch square base and a height of 6 inches. She then cuts the pyramid vertically in half as shown. What is the area of each cut surface? (Lesson 8.3)

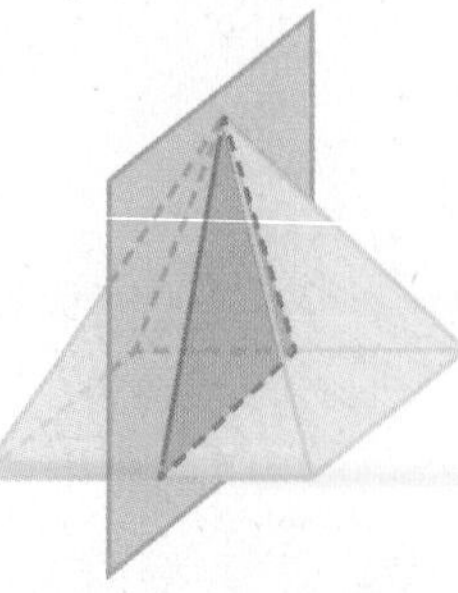

____

Circumference, Area, and Volume

ESSENTIAL QUESTION

How can you use geometry concepts to solve real-world problems?

Key Vocabulary

circumference *(circunferencia)*

composite figure *(figura compuesta)*

diameter *(diámetro)*

radius *(radio)*

EXAMPLE 1

Find the area of the composite figure. It consists of a semicircle and a rectangle.

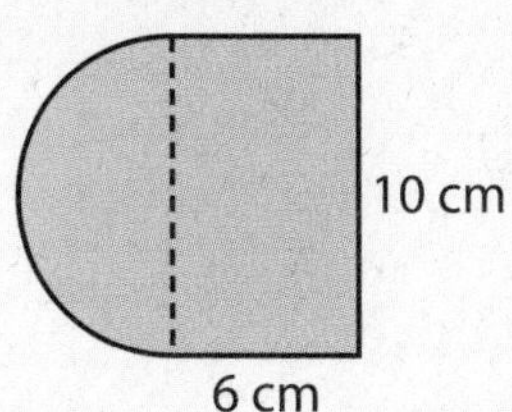

Area of semicircle $= 0.5(\pi r^2)$

$\approx 0.5(3.14)25$

$\approx 39.25 \text{ cm}^2$

Area of rectangle $= \ell w$

$= 10(6)$

$= 60 \text{ cm}^2$

The area of the composite figure is approximately 99.25 square centimeters.

EXAMPLE 2

Find the volume and surface area of the regular hexagonal prism hat box shown. Each side of the hexagonal base is 20 inches.

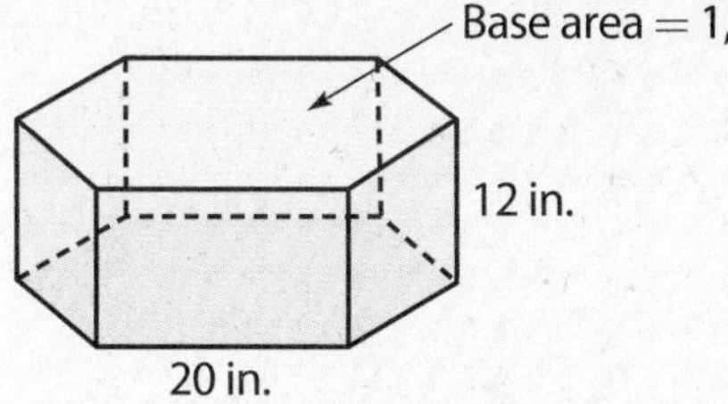

Use the formulas for volume and surface area of a prism.

$V = Bh$

$= 1{,}039(12)$

$= 12{,}468 \text{ in}^3$

$S = Ph + 2B$ Perimeter $= 6(20) = 120$ in.

$= 120(12) + 2(1{,}039)$

$= 1{,}440 + 2{,}078$

$= 3{,}518 \text{ in}^2$

EXERCISES

Find the circumference and area of each circle. Round to the nearest hundredth. (Lessons 9.1, 9.2)

1.

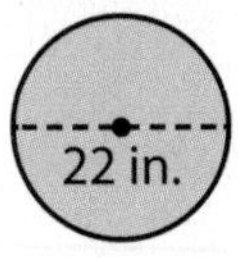

____

2.

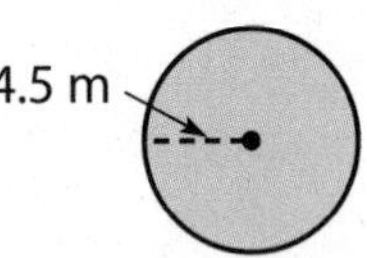

____

Find the area of each composite figure. Round to the nearest hundredth if necessary. (Lesson 9.3)

3.

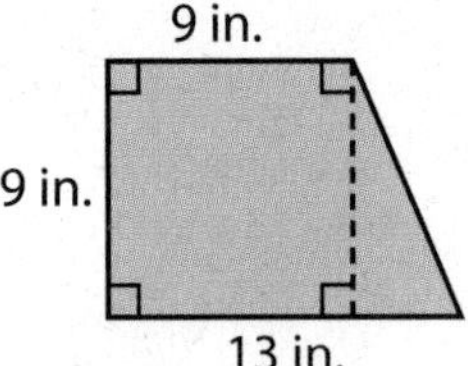

Area ______________________

4.

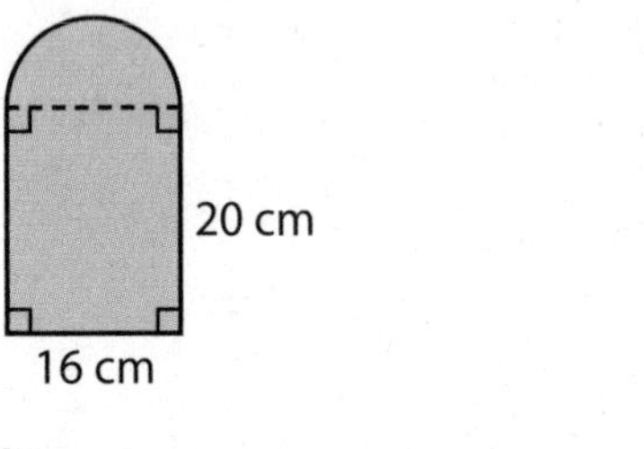

Area ______________________

Find the volume of each figure. (Lesson 9.5)

5.

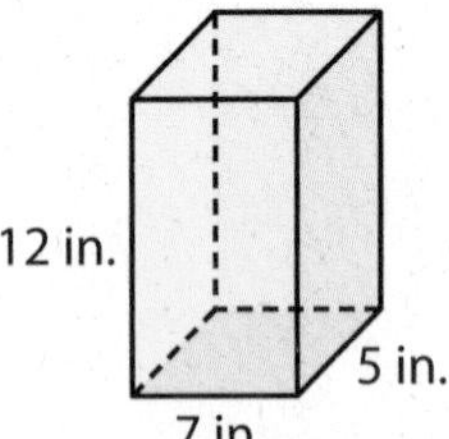

____

6. The volume of a triangular prism is 264 cubic feet. The area of a base of the prism is 48 square feet. Find the height of the prism.

(Lesson 9.5) ______________________

EXERCISES

A glass paperweight has a composite shape: a square pyramid fitting exactly on top of an 8-centimeter cube. The pyramid has a height of 3 cm. Each triangular face has a height of 5 centimeters. (Lessons 9.4, 9.5)

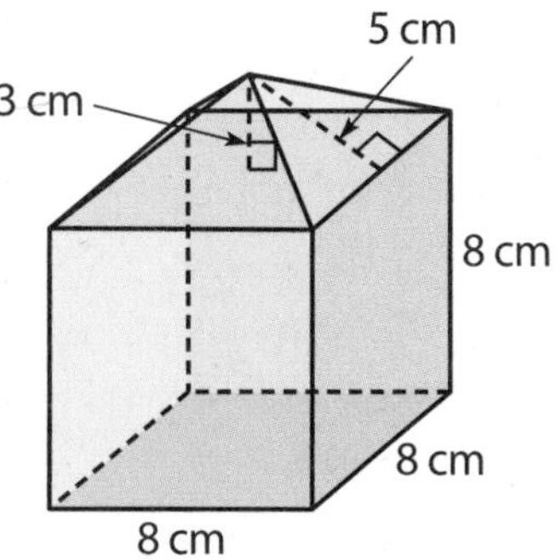

7. What is the volume of the paperweight? ___________

8. What is the total surface area of the paperweight? ___________

Li is making a stand to display a sculpture made in art class. The stand is a rectangular prism and will be 45 centimeters wide, 25 centimeters long, and 1.2 meters high.

9. What is the volume of the stand? Write your answer in cubic centimeters. (Lesson 9.5)

____

10. Li needs to fill the stand with sand so that it is heavy and stable. Each piece of wood is 1 centimeter thick. The boards are put together as shown in the figure, which is not drawn to scale. How many cubic centimeters of sand does she need to fill the stand? Explain how you found your answer. (Lesson 9.5)

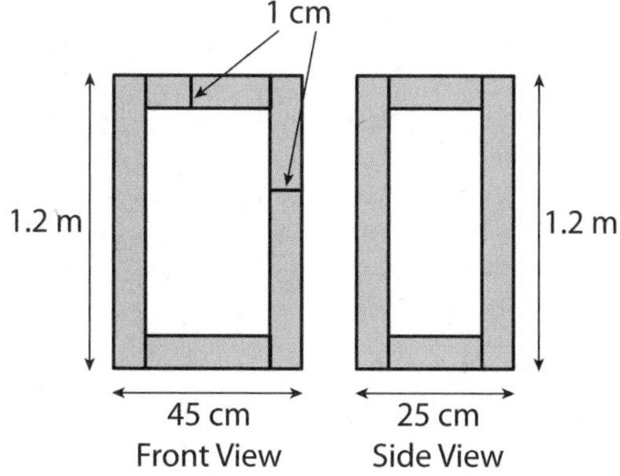

____

____

____

____

Unit Project CA CC 7.G.2.4

Buffon's Needle

In this project you will perform a famous probability experiment called "Buffon's Needle." It will enable you to calculate π to a high degree of accuracy.

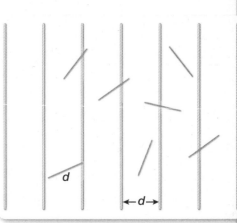

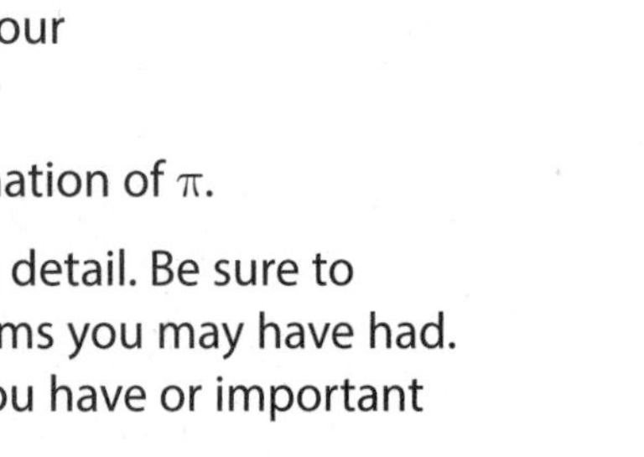

- Choose a long, thin, straight, rigid item for the "needle" such as a toothpick, a piece of uncooked spaghetti, or an unsharpened pencil. Since you will be throwing your "needle" many times, you can use many of them, but they must be identical.
- Draw or make a set of long, narrow, parallel lines. This is your "target." The lines must be the same distance apart as the length of your "needle."
- Toss or drop your needle so that it lands on the target. If the needle is intersecting one of the parallel lines when it comes to rest, record the toss as an "intersection."
- Repeat *at least* 200 times. The more times you toss your needle, the closer to π your results will be.
- Evaluate $\frac{\text{number of tosses}}{\text{number of intersections}} \times 2$ for your approximation of π.
- Create a presentation describing your experiment in detail. Be sure to explain how you created your target and any problems you may have had. Use the space below to write down any questions you have or important information from your teacher.

MATH IN CAREERS ACTIVITY

Product Design Engineer Miranda is a product design engineer working for a sporting goods company. She designs a tent in the shape of a triangular prism. The approximate dimensions of the tent are shown in the diagram. How many square feet of material does Miranda need to make the tent (including the floor)? What Is the volume of the tent? Show your work.

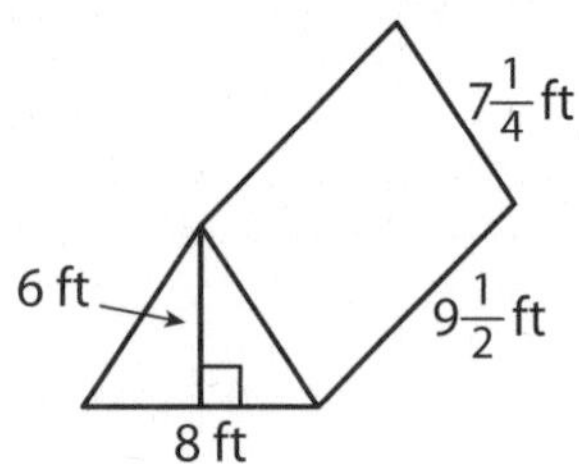

UNIT 4
MIXED REVIEW

Assessment Readiness

1. Can you draw a triangle that has these side lengths?

Select Yes or No.

A. 3 cm, 5 cm, and 7 cm ○ Yes ○ No

B. 4 cm, 6 cm, and 12 cm ○ Yes ○ No

C. 5 cm, 8 cm, and 11 cm ○ Yes ○ No

2. In the diagram, $\overleftrightarrow{AE}$ and $\overleftrightarrow{CF}$ intersect at point *G*.

Choose True or False for each statement.

A. $m\angle AGB = 76°$ ○ True ○ False

B. $m\angle AGF = 104°$ ○ True ○ False

C. $m\angle BGC = 22°$ ○ True ○ False

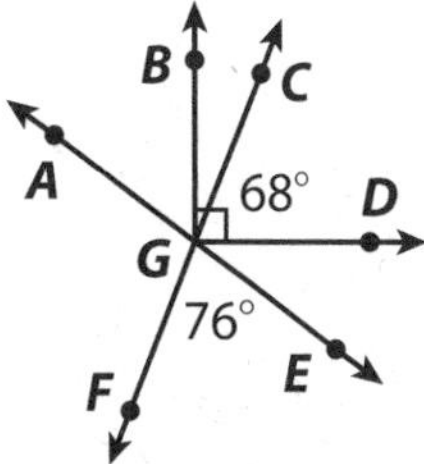

3. A bank offers a home improvement loan with simple interest at an annual rate of 12%. J.T. borrows an amount of $14,000 to pay back over 3 years. How much will he pay back altogether? Explain how you found the total amount.

4. The diagram shows the dimensions of a cat carrier before air holes are placed. The cat carrier is composed of a rectangular prism and a triangular prism. To the nearest square inch, how much cardboard, not including overlap, is needed to make the carrier? Explain how you solved this problem.

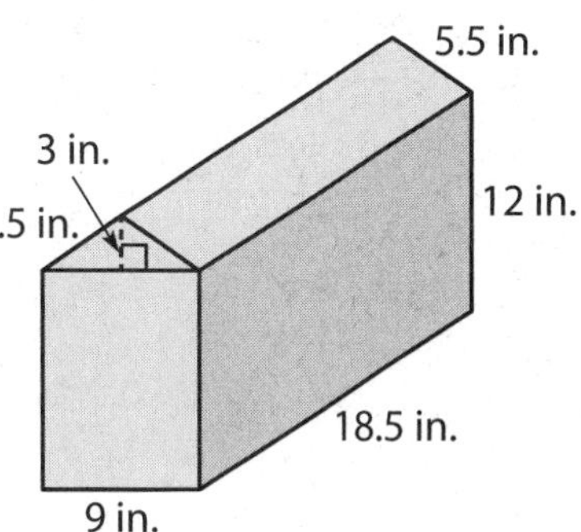

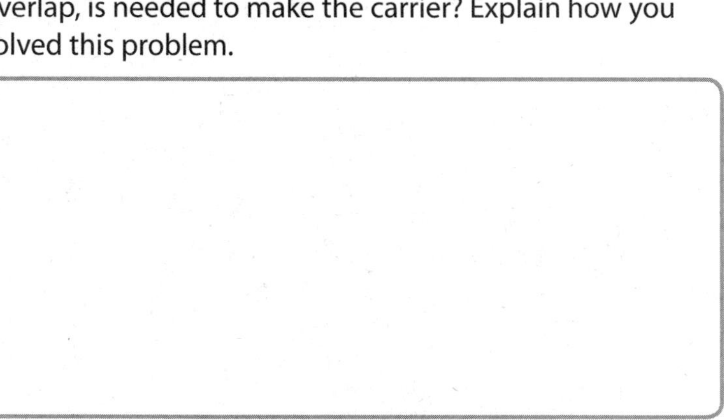

Performance Tasks

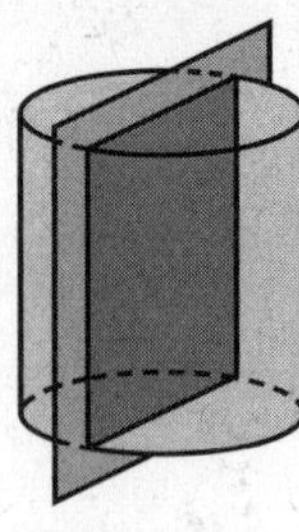

★**5.** A cylindrical piece of wood has a height of 12 inches and a base radius of 4 inches. A woodworker cuts the piece in half vertically through the center of its bases, as shown. Describe the shape of the cross section, and find its area. Justify your reasoning.

★★**6.** The scale drawing shows the patio for a house. The scale is 1 in. : 4 ft.

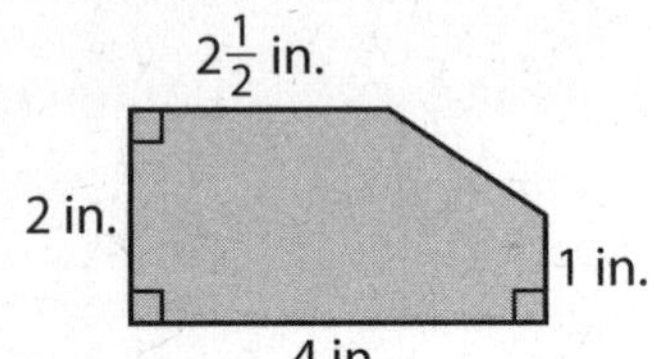

a. Label the sides with the actual side lengths.

b. Determine the area of the patio in square feet. Explain how you separated the patio into simpler shapes to find the area.

c. The patio will be made of concrete that is 4 inches thick. Determine how many cubic feet of concrete are needed to make the patio. Justify your answer.

★★★**7.** Petra fills a small cardboard box with tiny beads and fills a larger box with the same type of beads. She also plans to cover the sides of both boxes with decorative paper.

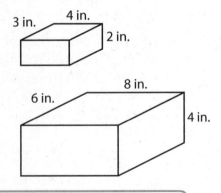

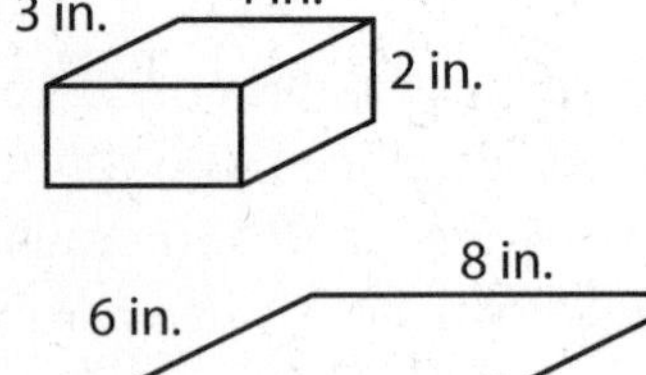

How many times the volume of beads can the larger box hold than the first? How many times as much decorative paper will it take to cover the larger box? Justify your answers.

UNIT 5

Statistics

MODULE 10

Analyzing and Comparing Data

CA CC 7.SP.3, 7.SP.4

MODULE 11

Random Samples and Populations

CA CC 7.RP.2c, 7.SP.1, 7.SP.2

MATH IN CAREERS

Entomologist An entomologist is a biologist who studies insects. These scientists analyze data and use mathematical models to understand and predict the behavior of insect populations.

If you are interested in a career in entomology, you should study these mathematical subjects:

- Algebra
- Trigonometry
- Probability and Statistics
- Calculus

Research other careers that require the analysis of data and use of mathematical models.

ACTIVITY At the end of the unit, check out how **entomologists** use math.

Unit Project Preview

A Sample? Simple!

In the Unit Project at the end of this unit, you will choose a random group of people, conduct a survey, display and interpret the results of the survey, and calculate how many people in a much larger group would respond to your survey as your group did. To successfully complete the Unit Project you'll need to master these skills:

- Choose a random sample.
- Conduct a survey.
- Draw and interpret a box plot.
- Make inferences from a random sample.

1. Kerry asked this question to 25 girls in her co-ed school: "Isn't it about time that the school had a girls' soccer team?" Do you think the school principal should use the results of Kerry's survey to decide whether or not to have a girls' soccer team? Explain.

____

____

____

2. What would have been a better question for Kerry to ask?

____

Tracking Your Learning Progression

This unit addresses important California Common Core Standards in the Critical Area of applying proportional relationships to random samples to solve problems.

Domain 7.SP Statistics and Probability

Cluster Use random sampling to draw inferences about a population.

The unit also supports additional standards.

Domain 7.RP Ratios and Proportionality

Cluster Analyze proportional relationships and use them to solve real-world and mathematical problems.

Analyzing and Comparing Data

ESSENTIAL QUESTION

How can you solve real-world problems by analyzing and comparing data?

LESSON 10.1

Comparing Data Displayed in Dot Plots

LESSON 10.2

Comparing Data Displayed in Box Plots

LESSON 10.3

Using Statistical Measures to Compare Populations

CA CC 7.SP.3, 7.SP.4

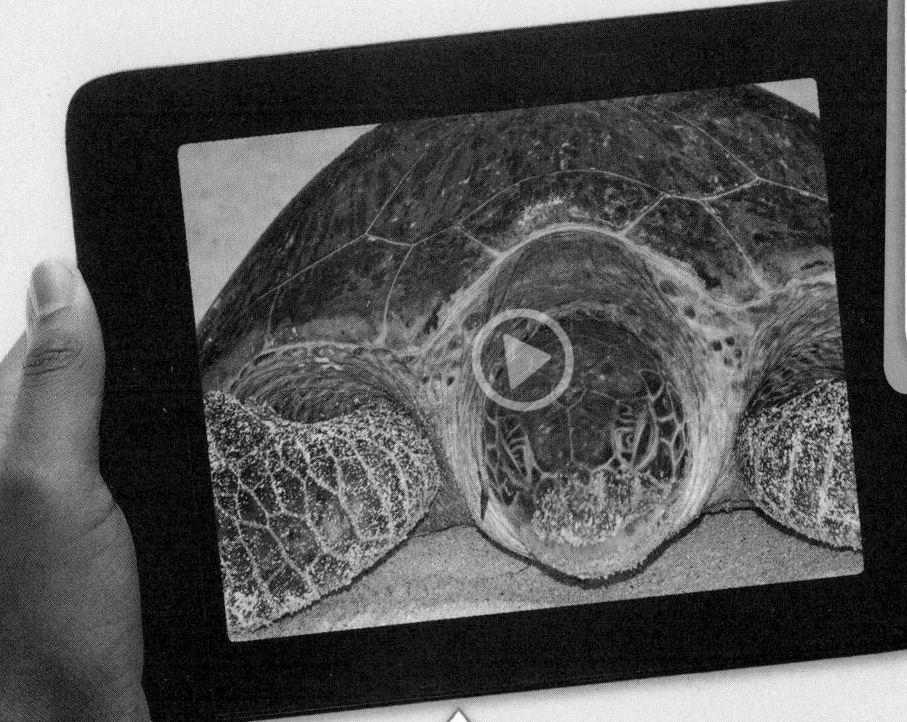

my.hrw.com

Real-World Video

Scientists place radio frequency tags on some animals within a population of that species. Then they track data, such as migration patterns, about the animals.

GO DIGITAL
my.hrw.com

my.hrw.com

Go digital with your write-in student edition, accessible on any device.

Math On the Spot

Scan with your smart phone to jump directly to the online edition, video tutor, and more.

Animated Math

Interactively explore key concepts to see how math works.

Personal Math Trainer

Get immediate feedback and help as you work through practice sets.

Are YOU Ready?

Complete these exercises to review skills you will need for this module.

Personal Math Trainer

Online Practice and Help

Fractions, Decimals, and Percents

EXAMPLE Write $\frac{13}{20}$ as a decimal and a percent.

$$\begin{array}{r} 0.65 \\ 20\overline{)13.00} \\ -12\,0 \\ \hline 1\,00 \\ -1\,00 \\ \hline 0 \end{array}$$

Write the fraction as a division problem.
Write a decimal point and zeros in the dividend.
Place a decimal point in the quotient.

$0.65 = 65\%$ *Write the decimal as a percent.*

Write each fraction as a decimal and a percent.

1. $\frac{7}{8}$ ________ **2.** $\frac{4}{5}$ ________ **3.** $\frac{1}{4}$ ________ **4.** $\frac{3}{10}$ ________

Find the Median and Mode

EXAMPLE 17, 14, 13, 16, 13, 11

11, 13, 13, 14, 16, 17 *Order the data from least to greatest.*

$\text{median} = \frac{13 + 14}{2}$

$= 13.5$ *The median is the middle item or the average of the two middle items.*

$\text{mode} = 13$ *The mode is the item that appears most frequently in the data*

Find the median and the mode of the data.

5. 11, 17, 7, 6, 7, 4, 15, 9 ________ **6.** 43, 37, 49, 51, 56, 40, 44, 50, 36 ________

Find the Mean

EXAMPLE 17, 14, 13, 16, 13, 11

$\text{mean} = \frac{17 + 14 + 13 + 16 + 13 + 11}{6}$

$= \frac{84}{6}$

$= 14$

The mean is the sum of the data items divided by the number of items.

Find the mean of the data.

7. 9, 16, 13, 14, 10, 16, 17, 9 ________ **8.** 108, 95, 104, 96, 97,106, 94 ________

Reading Start-Up

Vocabulary

Review Words

✔ data *(datos)*
interquartile range *(rango entre cuartiles)*
✔ mean *(media)*
measure of center *(medida central)*
measure of spread *(medida de dispersión)*
✔ median *(mediana)*
survey *(encuesta)*

Preview Words

box plot *(diagrama de caja)*
dot plot *(diagrama de puntos)*
mean absolute deviation (MAD) *(desviación absoluta media, (DAM))*

Visualize Vocabulary

Use the ✔ words to complete the right column of the chart.

Statistical Data		
Definition	**Example**	**Review Word**
A group of facts.	Grades on history exams: 85, 85, 90, 92, 94	
The middle value of a data set.	85, 85, 90, 92, 94	
A value that summarizes a set of values, found through addition and division.	Results of the survey show that students typically spend 5 hours a week studying.	

Understand Vocabulary

Complete each sentence using the preview words.

1. A display that uses values from a data set to show how the values are spread out is a ___________________.

2. A ___________________ uses a number line to display data.

Active Reading

Layered Book Before beginning the module, create a layered book to help you learn the concepts in this module. Label the first flap with the module title. Label the remaining flaps with the lesson titles. As you study each lesson, write important ideas, such as vocabulary and formulas, under the appropriate flap. Refer to your finished layered book as you work on exercises from this module.

GETTING READY FOR

Analyzing and Comparing Data

Understanding the standards and the vocabulary terms in the standards will help you know exactly what you are expected to learn in this module.

CA CC 7.SP.3

Informally assess the degree of visual overlap of two numerical data distributions with similar variabilities, measuring the difference between the centers by expressing it as a multiple of a measure of variability.

Key Vocabulary

measure of center *(medida de centro)*
A measure used to describe the middle of a data set; the mean and median are measures of center.

What It Means to You

You will compare two populations based on random samples.

EXAMPLE 7.SP.3

Melinda surveys a random sample of 16 students from two college dorms to find the average number of hours of sleep they get. Use the results shown in the dot plots to compare the two populations.

Average Daily Hours of Sleep

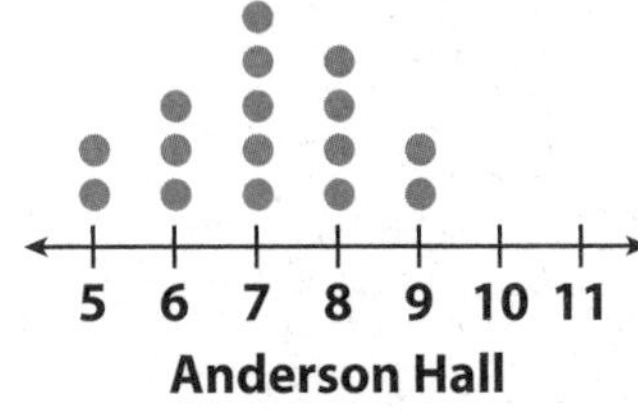

Anderson Hall

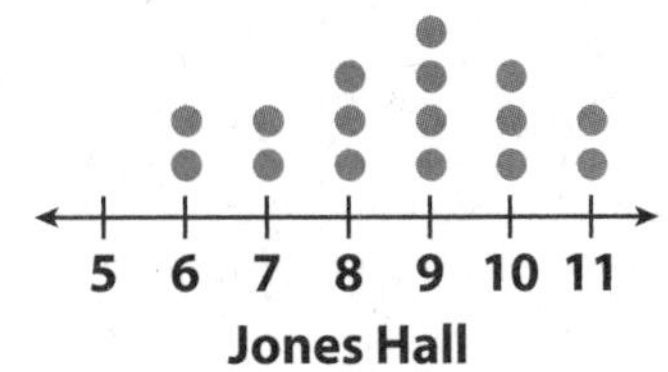

Jones Hall

Students in Jones Hall tend to sleep more than students in Anderson Hall, but the variation in the data sets is similar.

CA CC 7.SP.3

Informally assess… distributions with similar variabilities, measuring the difference between the centers by expressing it as a multiple of a measure of variability.

Key Vocabulary

measure of spread *(medida de la dispersión)*
A measure used to describe how much a data set varies; the range, IQR, and mean absolute deviation are measures of spread.

What It Means to You

You will compare two groups of data by comparing the difference in the means to the variability.

EXAMPLE 7.SP.3

The tables show the number of items that students in a class answered correctly on two different math tests. How does the difference in the means of the data sets compare to the variability?

Items Correct on Test 1
20, 13, 18, 19, 15, 18, 20, 20, 15, 15, 19, 18

Mean: 17.5; Mean absolute deviation: 2

Items Correct on Test 2
8, 12, 12, 8, 15, 16, 14, 12, 13, 9, 14, 11

Mean: 12; Mean absolute deviation: 2

The means of the two data sets differ by $\frac{17.5-12}{2} = 2.75$ times the variability of the data sets.

Visit **my.hrw.com** to see all **CA Common Core Standards** explained.

LESSON 10.1

Comparing Data Displayed in Dot Plots

7.SP.4

Use measures of center and measures of variability for numerical data from random samples to draw informal comparative inferences about two populations. *Also 7.SP.3*

ESSENTIAL QUESTION

How do you compare two sets of data displayed in dot plots?

EXPLORE ACTIVITY   7.SP.4

Analyzing Dot Plots

You can use dot plots to analyze a data set, especially with respect to its center and spread.

People once used body parts for measurements. For example, an inch was the width of a man's thumb. In the 12th century, King Henry I of England stated that a yard was the distance from his nose to his outstretched arm's thumb. The dot plot shows the different lengths, in inches, of the "yards" for students in a 7th grade class.

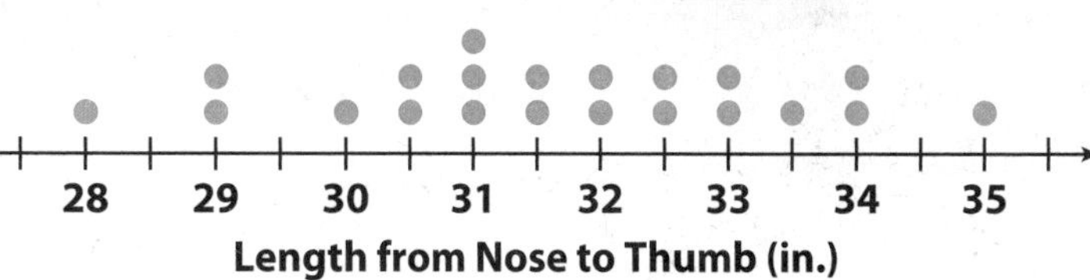

A Describe the shape of the dot plot. Are the dots evenly distributed or grouped on one side?

____

B Describe the center of the dot plot. What single dot would best represent the data?

____

____

C Describe the spread of the dot plot. Are there any outliers?

____

____

Reflect

1. Calculate the mean, median, and range of the data in the dot plot.

____

Comparing Dot Plots Visually

You can compare dot plots visually using various characteristics, such as center, spread, and shape.

EXAMPLE 1  

The dot plots show the heights of 15 high school basketball players and the heights of 15 high school softball players.

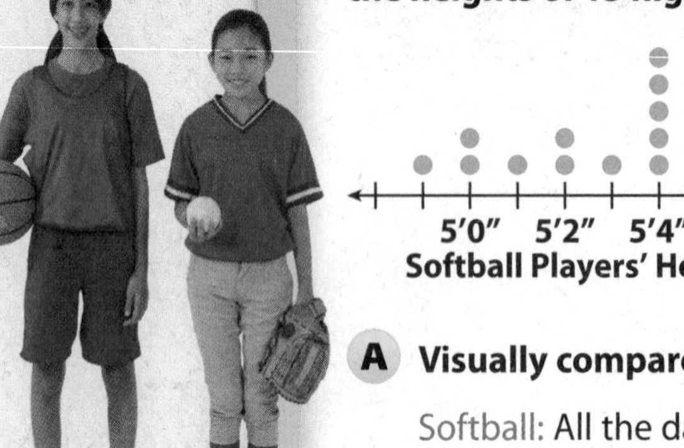

5′0″ 5′2″ 5′4″ 5′6″
Softball Players' Heights

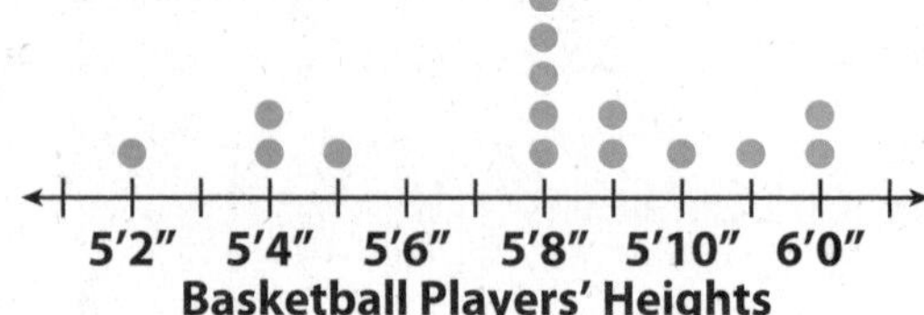

A **Visually compare the shapes of the dot plots.**

Softball: All the data is 5′6″ or less.
Basketball: Most of the data is 5′8″ or greater.
As a group, the softball players are shorter than the basketball players.

B **Visually compare the centers of the dot plots.**

Softball: The data is centered around 5′4″.
Basketball: The data is centered around 5′8″.
This means that the most common height for the softball players is 5 feet 4 inches, and for the basketball players 5 feet 8 inches.

C **Visually compare the spreads of the dot plots.**

Softball: The spread is from 4′11″ to 5′6″.
Basketball: The spread is from 5′2″ to 6′0″.
There is a greater spread in heights for the basketball players.

Math Talk
Mathematical Practices
How do the heights of field hockey players compare with the heights of softball and basketball players?

YOUR TURN

2. Visually compare the dot plot of heights of field hockey players to the dot plots for softball and basketball players.

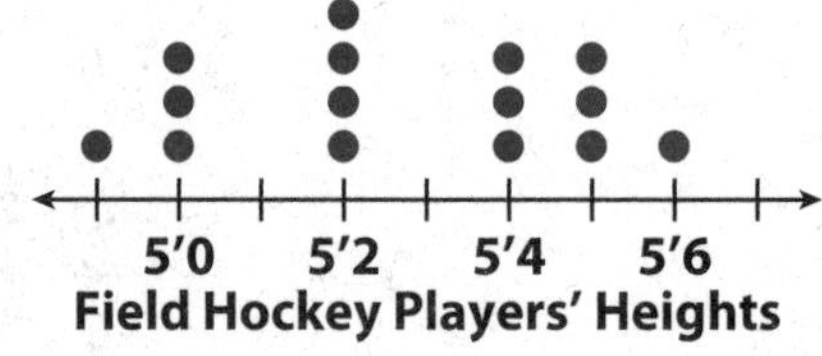

Shape: ______________________________

____

Center: ______________________________

____

Spread: ______________________________

____

Comparing Dot Plots Numerically

You can also compare the shape, center, and spread of two dot plots numerically by calculating values related to the center and spread. Remember that outliers can affect your calculations.

Numerically compare the dot plots of the number of hours a class of students exercises each week to the number of hours the students play video games each week.

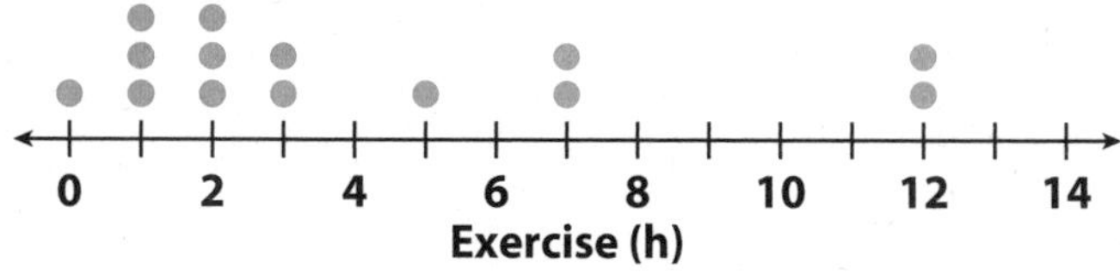

A **Compare the shapes of the dot plots.**

The dot plots appear almost opposite. The dot plots show that most students exercise less than 4 hours but most play video games more than 6 hours each week.

How do outliers affect the results of this data?

B **Compare the centers of the dot plots by finding the medians.**

The median number of hours that students exercise is 2.5 hours, which is 6.5 hours less than the median of 9 hours that students play video games.

C **Compare the spreads of the dot plots by calculating the ranges.**

The dot plots show the ranges to be similar to one another. The range for the amount of time that students exercise is 12 hours, and the range for the amount of time that students play video games is 14 hours.

3. Calculate the median and range of the data in the dot plot. Then compare the results to the dot plot for exercise in Example 2.

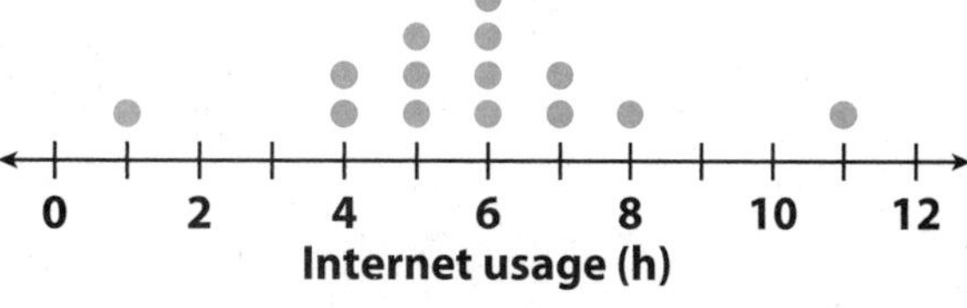

Guided Practice

The dot plots show the number of miles run per week for two different classes. For 1–5, use the dot plots shown. (Explore Activity, Example 1 and 2)

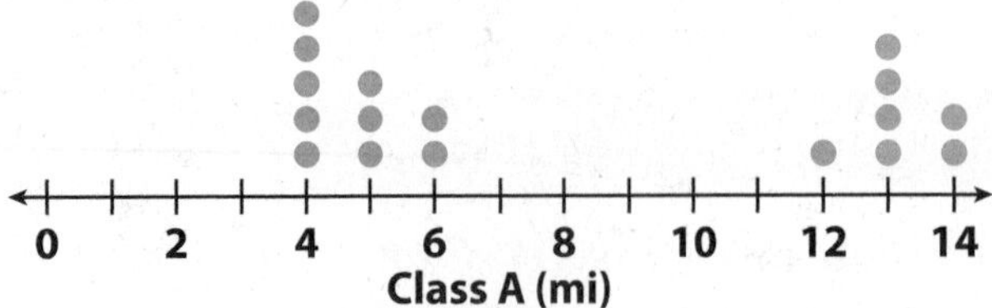

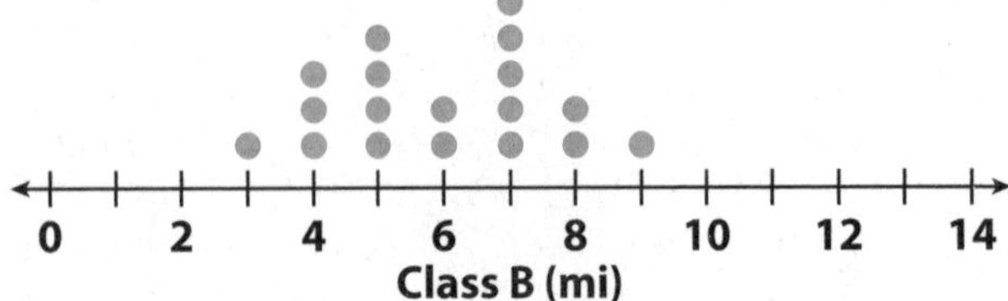

1. Compare the shapes of the dot plots.

____

____

____

2. Compare the centers of the dot plots.

____

____

3. Compare the spreads of the dot plots.

____

____

4. Calculate the medians of the dot plots.

____

5. Calculate the ranges of the dot plots.

____

ESSENTIAL QUESTION CHECK-IN

6. What do the medians and ranges of two dot plots tell you about the data?

____

____

Name______________________ Class______________________ Date______________________

10.1 Independent Practice

7.SP.3, 7.SP.4

The dot plot shows the number of letters in the spellings of the 12 months. Use the dot plot for 7–10.

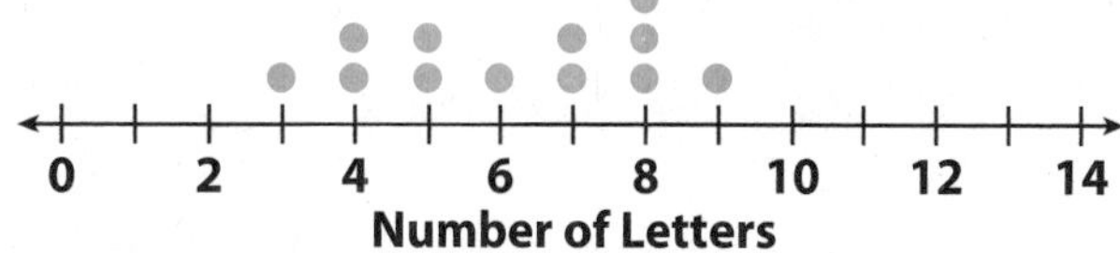

7. Describe the shape of the dot plot.

____

8. Describe the center of the dot plot.

____

9. Describe the spread of the dot plot.

____

10. Calculate the mean, median, and range of the data in the dot plot.

____

The dot plots show the mean number of days with rain per month for two cities.

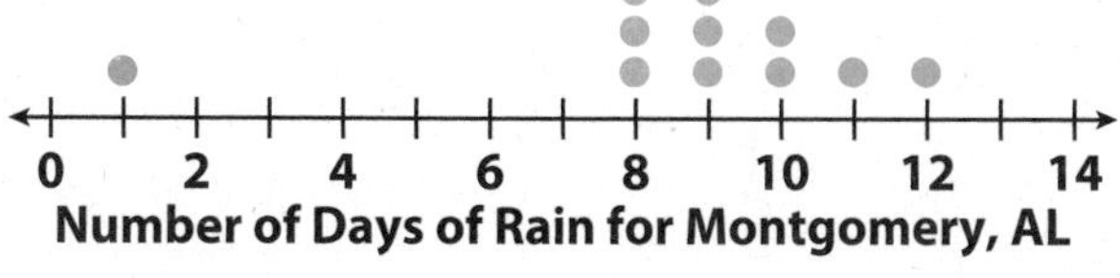

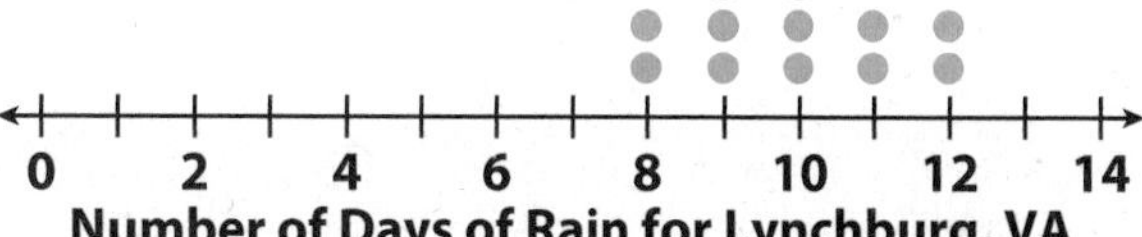

11. Compare the shapes of the dot plots.

____

____

12. Compare the centers of the dot plots.

____

____

13. Compare the spreads of the dot plots.

____

____

14. What do the dot plots tell you about the two cities with respect to their average monthly rainfall?

____

____

The dot plots show the shoe sizes of two different groups of people.

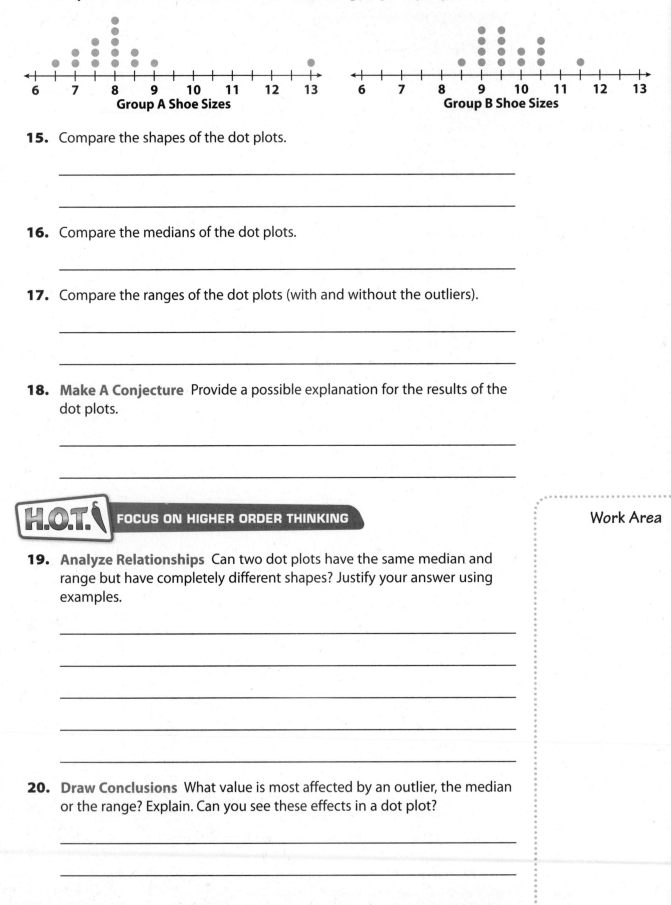

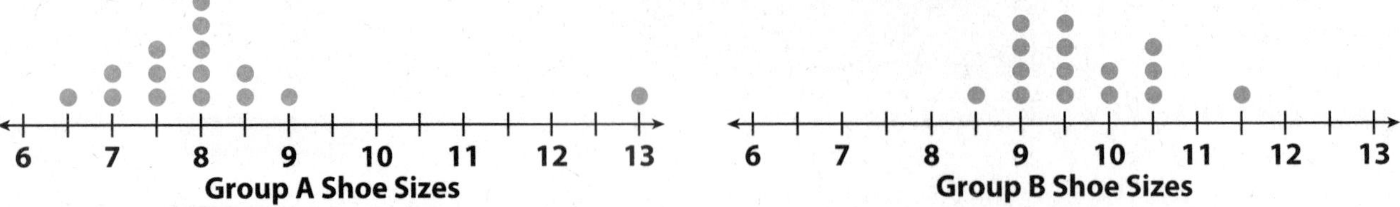

15. Compare the shapes of the dot plots.

____

____

16. Compare the medians of the dot plots.

____

17. Compare the ranges of the dot plots (with and without the outliers).

____

____

18. **Make A Conjecture** Provide a possible explanation for the results of the dot plots.

____

____

FOCUS ON HIGHER ORDER THINKING

Work Area

19. **Analyze Relationships** Can two dot plots have the same median and range but have completely different shapes? Justify your answer using examples.

____

____

____

____

____

20. **Draw Conclusions** What value is most affected by an outlier, the median or the range? Explain. Can you see these effects in a dot plot?

____

____

____

LESSON 10.2

Comparing Data Displayed in Box Plots

Informally assess the degree of visual overlap of two numerical data distributions with similar variabilities, measuring the difference between the centers by expressing it as a multiple of a measure of variability. *Also 7.SP.4*

ESSENTIAL QUESTION

How do you compare two sets of data displayed in box plots?

EXPLORE ACTIVITY

Analyzing Box Plots

Box plots show five key values to represent a set of data, the least and greatest values, the lower and upper quartile, and the median. To create a box plot, arrange the data in order, and divide them into four equal-size parts or quarters. Then draw the box and the whiskers as shown.

The number of points a high school basketball player scored during the games he played this season are organized in the box plot shown.

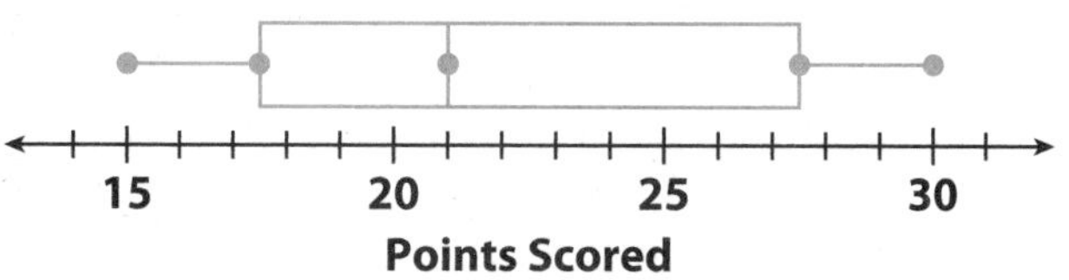

A Find the least and greatest values.

Least value: ________ Greatest value: ________

B Find the median and describe what it means for the data.

____

____

____

C Find and describe the lower and upper quartiles.

____

____

____

D The interquartile range is the difference between the upper and lower quartiles, which is represented by the length of the box. Find the interquartile range.

$Q_3 - Q_1 =$ ________ $-$ ________ $=$ ________

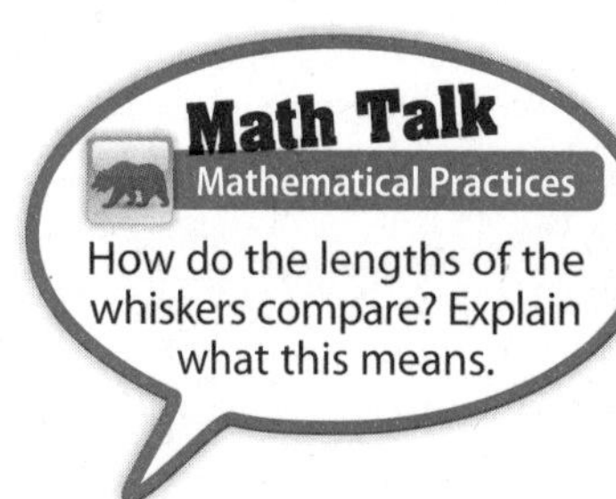

Math Talk
Mathematical Practices
How do the lengths of the whiskers compare? Explain what this means.

EXPLORE ACTIVITY (cont'd)

Reflect

1. Why is one-half of the box wider than the other half of the box?

____

____

Box Plots with Similar Variability

You can compare two box plots numerically according to their centers, or medians, and their spreads, or variability. Range and interquartile range (IQR) are both measures of spread. Box plots with similar variability should have similar boxes and whiskers.

EXAMPLE 1  

My Notes

The box plots show the distribution of times spent shopping by two different groups.

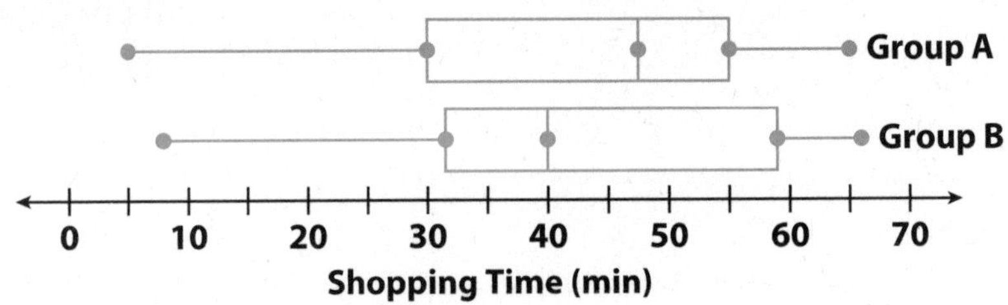

A Compare the shapes of the box plots.

The positions and lengths of the boxes and whiskers appear to be very similar. In both plots, the right whisker is shorter than the left whisker.

B Compare the centers of the box plots.

Group A's median, 47.5, is greater than Group B's, 40. This means that the median shopping time for Group A is 7.5 minutes more.

C Compare the spreads of the box plots.

The box shows the interquartile range. The boxes are similar.

Group A: $55 - 30 = 25$ min   Group B: About $59 - 32 = 27$ min

The whiskers have similar lengths, with Group A's slightly shorter than Group B's.

Math Talk
Mathematical Practices
Which store has the shopper who shops longest? Explain how you know.

Reflect

2. Which group has the greater variability in the bottom 50% of shopping times? The top 50% of shopping times? Explain how you know.

____

____

YOUR TURN

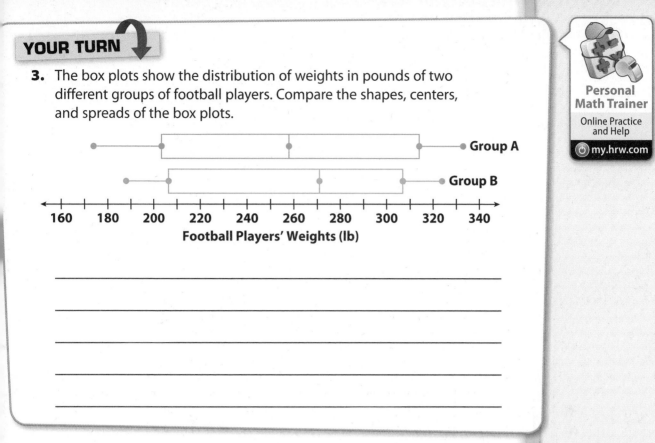

3. The box plots show the distribution of weights in pounds of two different groups of football players. Compare the shapes, centers, and spreads of the box plots.

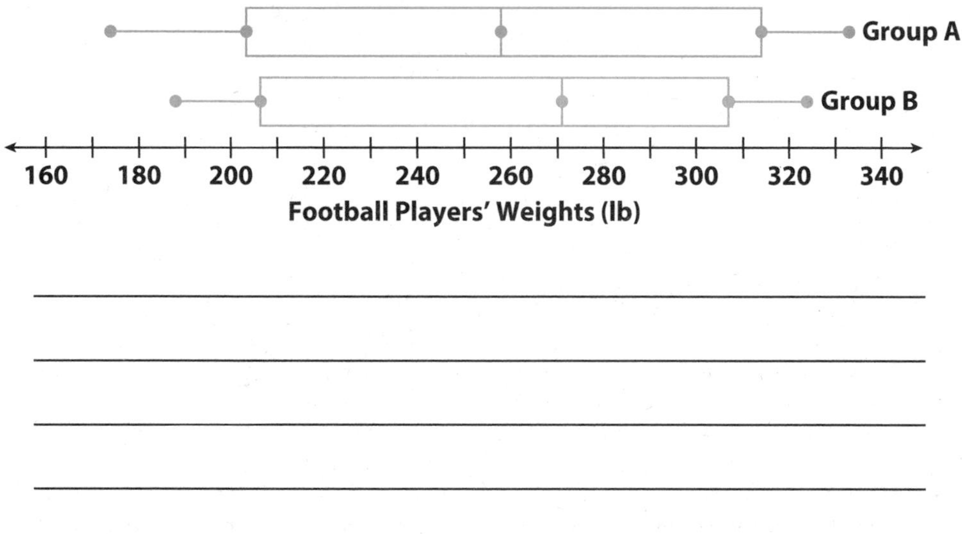

____

____

____

____

____

Box Plots with Different Variability

You can compare box plots with greater variability, where there is less overlap of the median and interquartile range.

EXAMPLE 2 

The box plots show the distribution of the number of team wristbands sold daily by two different stores over the same time period.

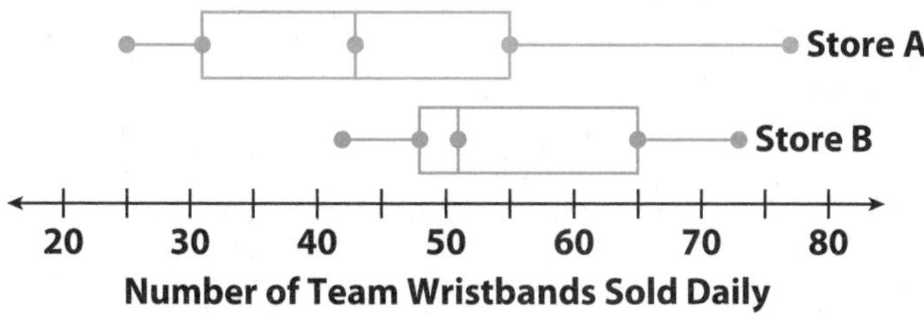

A Compare the shapes of the box plots.

Store A's box and right whisker are longer than Store B's.

B Compare the centers of the box plots.

Store A's median is about 43, and Store B's is about 51. Store A's median is close to Store B's minimum value, so about 50% of Store A's daily sales were less than sales on Store B's worst day.

C Compare the spreads of the box plots.

Store A has a greater spread. Its range and interquartile range are both greater. Four of Store B's key values are greater than Store A's corresponding value. Store B had a greater number of sales overall.

YOUR TURN

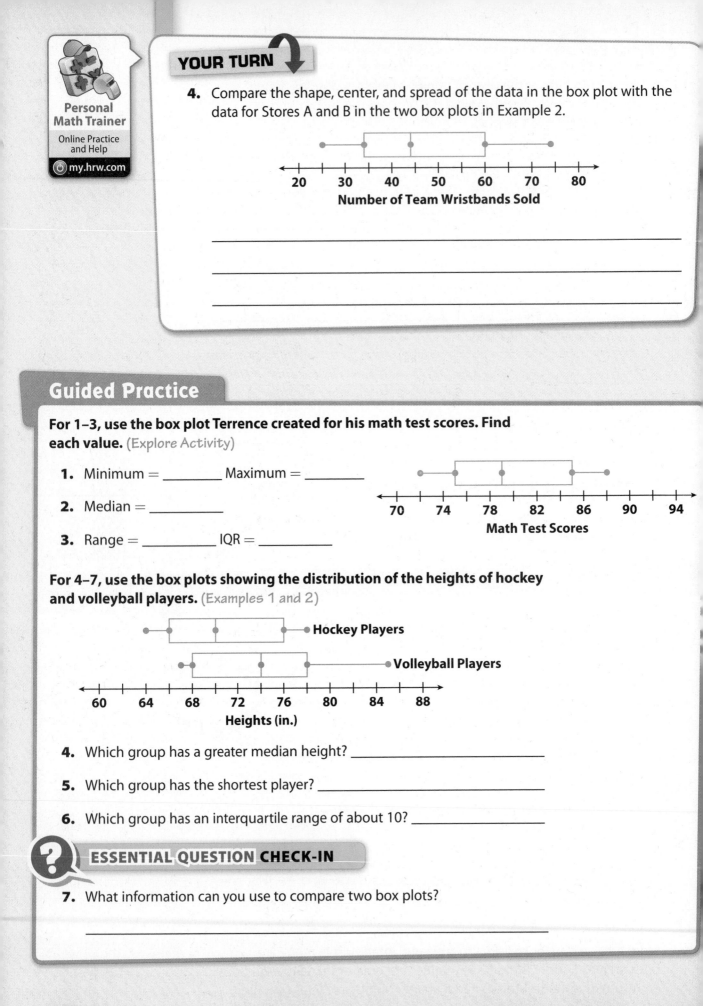

4. Compare the shape, center, and spread of the data in the box plot with the data for Stores A and B in the two box plots in Example 2.

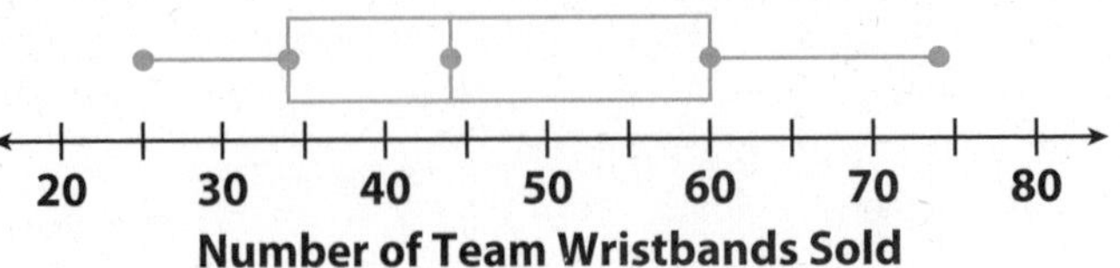

____

____

____

Guided Practice

For 1–3, use the box plot Terrence created for his math test scores. Find each value. (Explore Activity)

1. Minimum = ________ Maximum = ________

2. Median = ________

3. Range = ________ IQR = ________

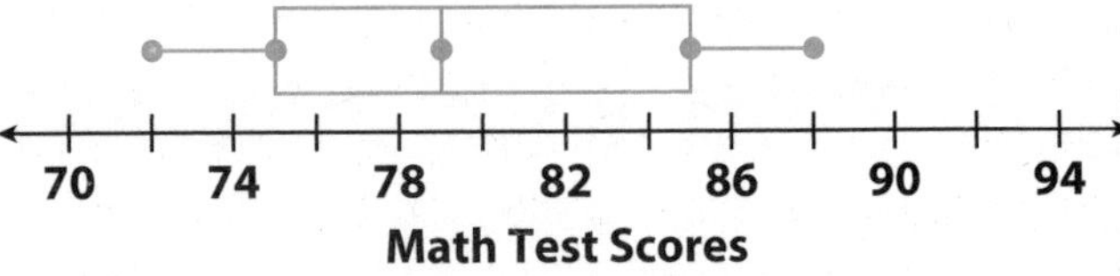

For 4–7, use the box plots showing the distribution of the heights of hockey and volleyball players. (Examples 1 and 2)

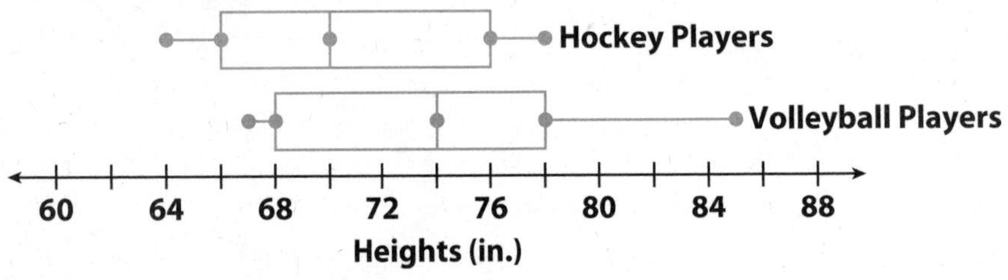

4. Which group has a greater median height? ________________

5. Which group has the shortest player? ________________

6. Which group has an interquartile range of about 10? ________________

ESSENTIAL QUESTION CHECK-IN

7. What information can you use to compare two box plots?

____

Name ________________________ Class ________________ Date ____________

10.2 Independent Practice

7.SP.3, 7.SP.4

For 8–11, use the box plots of the distances traveled by two toy cars that were jumped from a ramp.

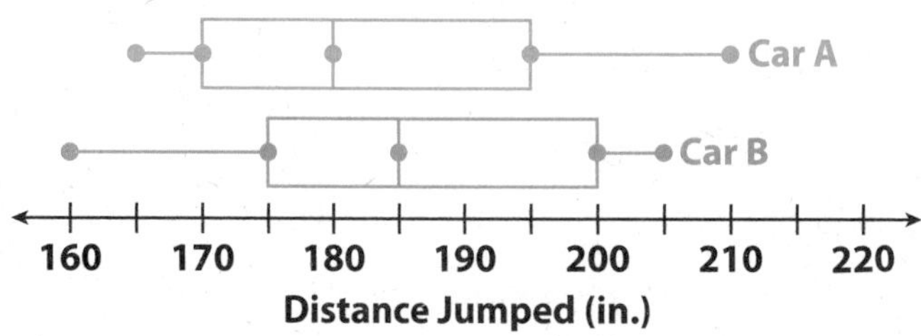

8. Compare the minimum, maximum, and median of the box plots.

____

____

____

____

____

____

9. Compare the ranges and interquartile ranges of the data in box plots.

____

____

____

10. What do the box plots tell you about the jump distances of two cars?

____

____

____

____

____

____

11. **Critical Thinking** What do the whiskers tell you about the two data sets?

____

____

____

____

____

For 12–14, use the box plots to compare the costs of leasing cars in two different cities.

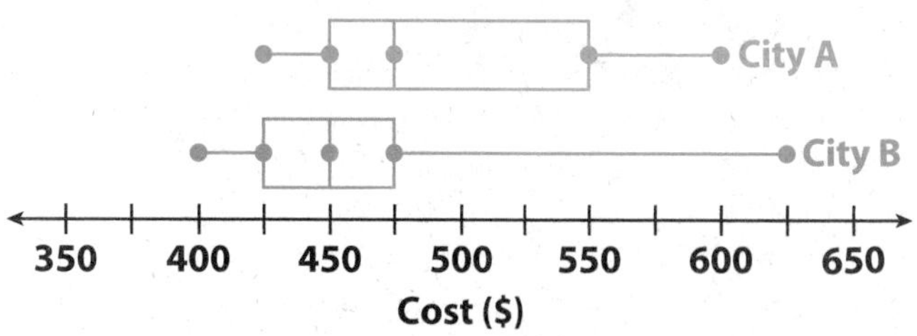

12. In which city could you spend the least amount of money to lease a car? The greatest?

____

____

____

13. Which city has a higher median price? How much higher is it?

____

14. **Make a Conjecture** In which city is it more likely to choose a car at random that leases for less than $450? Why?

____

____

____

____

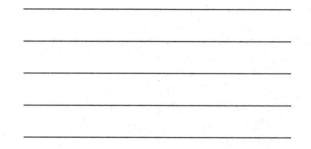

15. Summarize Look back at the box plots for 12–14 on the previous page. What do the box plots tell you about the costs of leasing cars in those two cities?

____

____

____

____

Work Area

H.O.T. FOCUS ON HIGHER ORDER THINKING

16. Draw Conclusions Two box plots have the same median and equally long whiskers. If one box plot has a longer box than the other box plot, what does this tell you about the difference between the data sets?

____

____

17. Communicate Mathematical Ideas What can you learn about a data set from a box plot? How is this information different from a dot plot?

____

____

____

____

____

____

____

____

____

____

18. Analyze Relationships In mathematics, *central tendency* is the tendency of data values to cluster around some central value. What does a measure of variability tell you about the central tendency of a set of data? Explain.

____

____

____

LESSON 10.3

Using Statistical Measures to Compare Populations

CA CC 7.SP.3

Informally assess the degree of visual overlap of two numerical data distributions with similar variabilities, measuring the difference between the centers by expressing it as a multiple of a measure of variability. *Also 7.SP.4*

ESSENTIAL QUESTION

How can you use statistical measures to compare populations?

Comparing Differences in Centers to Variability

Recall that to find the mean absolute deviation (MAD) of a data set, first find the mean of the data. Next, take the absolute value of the difference between the mean and each data point. Finally, find the mean of those absolute values.

EXAMPLE 1

CA CC 7.SP.3

The tables show the number of minutes per day students in a class spend exercising and playing video games. What is the difference of the means as a multiple of the mean absolute deviations?

Minutes Per Day Exercising
0, 7, 7, 18, 20, 38, 33, 24, 22, 18, 11, 6

Minutes Per Day Playing Video Games
13, 18, 19, 30, 32, 46, 50, 34, 36, 30, 23, 19

STEP 1 Calculate the mean number of minutes per day exercising.

$0 + 7 + 7 + 18 + 20 + 38 + 33 + 24 + 22 + 18 + 11 + 6 = 204$

$204 \div 12 = 17$ Divide the sum by the number of students.

STEP 2 Calculate the mean absolute deviation for the number of minutes exercising.

$|0-17| = 17$ $|7-17| = 10$ $|7-17| = 10$ $|18-17| = 1$

$|20-17| = 3$ $|38-17| = 21$ $|33-17| = 16$ $|24-17| = 7$

$|22-17| = 5$ $|18-17| = 1$ $|11-17| = 6$ $|6-17| = 11$

Find the mean of the absolute values.

$17 + 10 + 10 + 1 + 3 + 21 + 16 + 7 + 5 + 1 + 6 + 11 = 108$

$108 \div 12 = 9$ Divide the sum by the number of students.

My Notes

STEP 3 Calculate the mean number of minutes per day playing video games. Round to the nearest tenth.

$13 + 18 + 19 + 30 + 32 + 46 + 50 + 34 + 36 + 30 + 23 + 19 = 350$

$350 \div 12 \approx 29.2$ Divide the sum by the number of students.

STEP 4 Calculate the mean absolute deviation for the numbers of minutes playing video games.

$\lvert 13-29.2 \rvert = 16.2$	$\lvert 18-29.2 \rvert = 11.2$	$\lvert 19-29.2 \rvert = 10.2$
$\lvert 30-29.2 \rvert = 0.8$	$\lvert 32-29.2 \rvert = 2.8$	$\lvert 46-29.2 \rvert = 16.8$
$\lvert 50-29.2 \rvert = 20.8$	$\lvert 34-29.2 \rvert = 4.8$	$\lvert 36-29.2 \rvert = 6.8$
$\lvert 30-29.2 \rvert = 0.8$	$\lvert 23-29.2 \rvert = 6.2$	$\lvert 19-29.2 \rvert = 10.2$

Find the mean of the absolute values. Round to the nearest tenth.

$16.2 + 11.2 + 10.2 + 0.8 + 2.8 + 16.8 + 20.8 + 4.8 + 6.8 + 0.8 + 6.2 + 10.2 = 107.6$

$107.6 \div 12 \approx 9$ Divide the sum by the number of students.

STEP 5 Find the difference in the means.

$29.2 - 17 = 12.2$ Subtract the lesser mean from the greater mean.

STEP 6 Write the difference of the means as a multiple of the mean absolute deviations, which are similar but not identical.

$12.2 \div 9 \approx 1.36$ Divide the difference of the means by the MAD.

The means of the two data sets differ by about 1.4 times the variability of the two data sets.

YOUR TURN

1. The high jumps in inches of the students on two intramural track and field teams are shown below. What is the difference of the means as a multiple of the mean absolute deviations?

High Jumps for Students on Team 1 (in.)
44, 47, 67, 89, 55, 76, 85, 80, 87, 69, 47, 58

High Jumps for Students on Team 2 (in.)
40, 32, 52, 75, 65, 70, 72, 61, 54, 43, 29, 32

____

Personal Math Trainer

Online Practice and Help

my.hrw.com

Using Multiple Samples to Compare Populations

Many different random samples are possible for any given population, and their measures of center can vary. Using multiple samples can give us an idea of how reliable any inferences or predictions we make are.

EXAMPLE 2 

A group of about 250 students in grade 7 and about 250 students in grade 11 were asked, "How many hours per month do you volunteer?" Responses from one random sample of 10 students in grade 7 and one random sample of 10 students in grade 11 are summarized in the box plots.

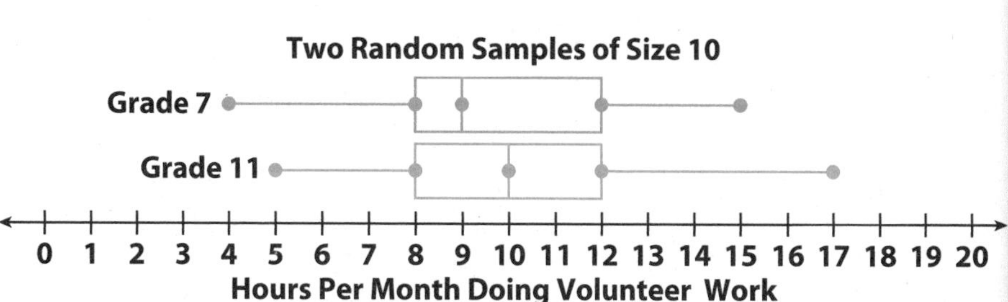

How can we tell if the grade 11 students do more volunteer work than the grade 7 students?

Math Talk
Mathematical Practices

Why doesn't the first box plot establish that students in grade 11 volunteer more than students in grade 7?

STEP 1 The median is higher for the students in grade 11. But there is a great deal of variation. To make an inference for the entire population, it is helpful to consider how the medians vary among multiple samples.

STEP 2 The box plots below show how the medians from 10 different random samples for each group vary.

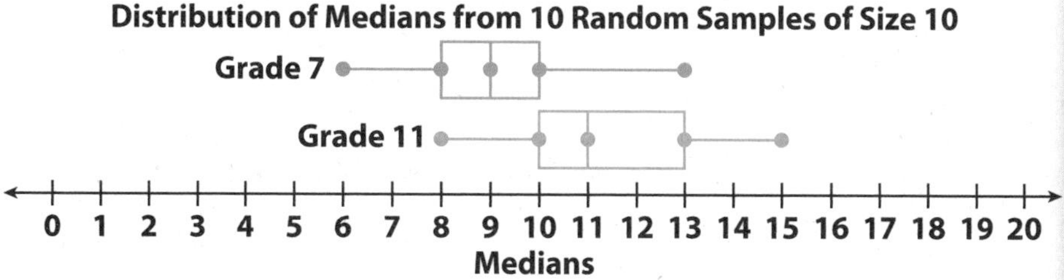

The medians vary less than the actual data. Half of the grade 7 medians are within 1 hour of 9. Half of the grade 11 medians are within 1 or 2 hours of 11. Although the distributions overlap, the middle halves of the data barely overlap. This is fairly convincing evidence that the grade 11 students volunteer more than the grade 7 students.

YOUR TURN

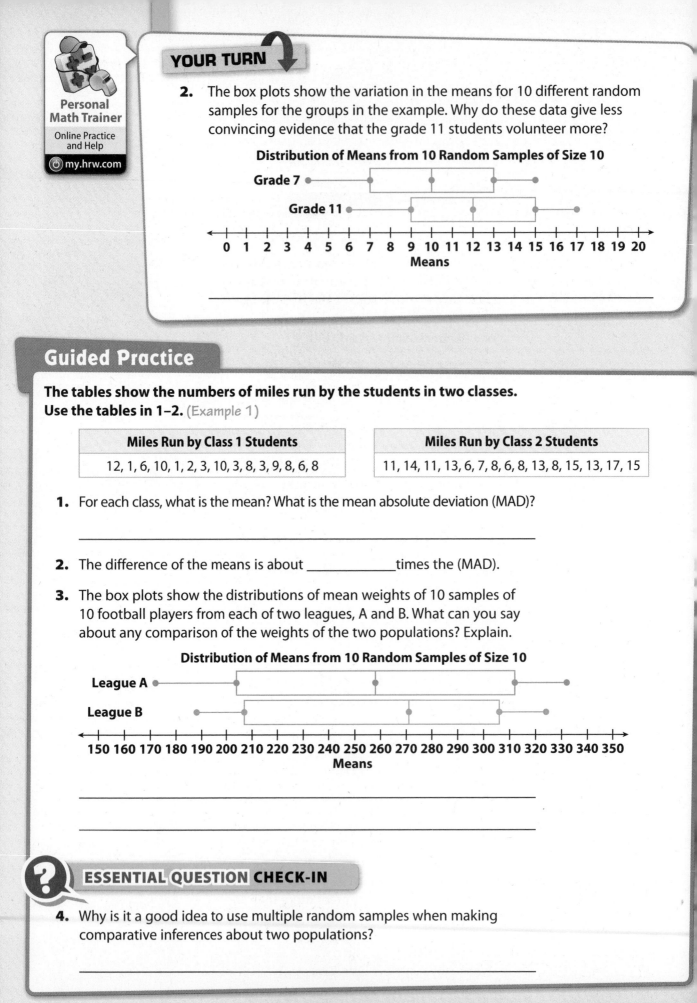

2. The box plots show the variation in the means for 10 different random samples for the groups in the example. Why do these data give less convincing evidence that the grade 11 students volunteer more?

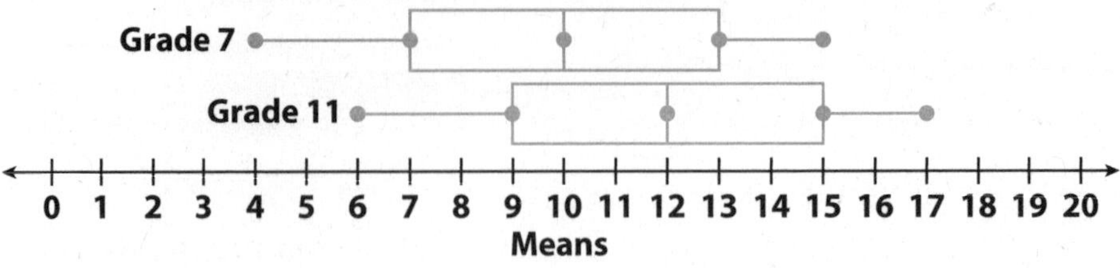

____

Guided Practice

The tables show the numbers of miles run by the students in two classes. Use the tables in 1–2. (Example 1)

Miles Run by Class 1 Students
12, 1, 6, 10, 1, 2, 3, 10, 3, 8, 3, 9, 8, 6, 8

Miles Run by Class 2 Students
11, 14, 11, 13, 6, 7, 8, 6, 8, 13, 8, 15, 13, 17, 15

1. For each class, what is the mean? What is the mean absolute deviation (MAD)?

____

2. The difference of the means is about ____________ times the (MAD).

3. The box plots show the distributions of mean weights of 10 samples of 10 football players from each of two leagues, A and B. What can you say about any comparison of the weights of the two populations? Explain.

Distribution of Means from 10 Random Samples of Size 10

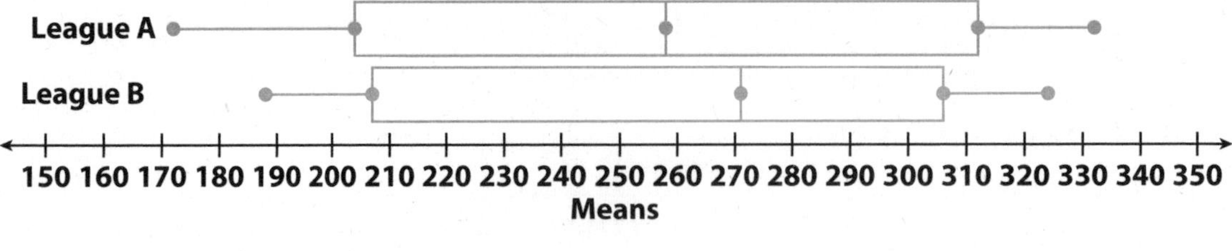

____

____

ESSENTIAL QUESTION CHECK-IN

4. Why is it a good idea to use multiple random samples when making comparative inferences about two populations?

____

Name ______________________ Class ______________________ Date ______________________

10.3 Independent Practice

7.SP.3, 7.SP.4

Josie recorded the average monthly temperatures for two cities in the state where she lives. Use the data for 5–7.

Average Monthly Temperatures for City 1 (°F)
23, 38, 39, 48, 55, 56, 71, 86, 57, 53, 43, 31

Average Monthly Temperatures for City 2 (°F)
8, 23, 24, 33, 40, 41, 56, 71, 42, 38, 28, 16

5. For City 1, what is the mean of the average monthly temperatures? What is the mean absolute deviation of the average monthly temperatures?

____

6. What is the difference between each average monthly temperature for City 1 and the corresponding temperature for City 2? ______________________

7. **Draw Conclusions** Based on your answers to Exercises 5 and 6, what do you think the mean of the average monthly temperatures for City 2 is? What do you think the mean absolute deviation of the average monthly temperatures for City 2 is? Give your answers without actually calculating the mean and the mean absolute deviation. Explain your reasoning.

____

____

8. What is the difference in the means as a multiple of the mean absolute deviations? ______________________

9. **Make a Conjecture** Mark took 10 random samples of 10 students from two schools. He asked how many minutes they spend per day going to and from school. The tables show the medians and the means of the samples. Compare the travel times using distributions of the medians and means.

School A
Medians: 28, 22, 25, 10, 40, 36, 30, 14, 20, 25
Means: 27, 24, 27, 15, 42, 36, 32, 18, 22, 29

School B
Medians: 22, 25, 20, 14, 20, 18, 21, 18, 26, 19
Means: 24, 30, 22, 15, 20, 17, 22, 15, 36, 27

____

____

____

10. Justify Reasoning Statistical measures are shown for the ages of middle school and high school teachers in two states.

State A: Mean age of middle school teachers = 38, mean age of high school teachers = 48, mean absolute deviation for both = 6

State B: Mean age of middle school teachers = 42, mean age of high school teachers = 50, mean absolute deviation for both = 4

In which state is the difference in ages between members of the two groups more significant? Support your answer.

____

____

11. Analyze Relationships The tables show the heights in inches of all the adult grandchildren of two sets of grandparents, the Smiths and the Thompsons. What is the difference in the medians as a multiple of the ranges?

Heights of the Smiths' Adult Grandchildren (in.)
64, 65, 68, 66, 65, 68, 69, 66, 70, 67

Heights of the Thompsons' Adult Grandchildren (in.)
75, 80, 78, 77, 79, 76, 75, 79, 77, 74

____

FOCUS ON HIGHER ORDER THINKING

Work Area

12. Critical Thinking Jill took many samples of 10 tosses of a standard number cube. What might she reasonably expect the median of the medians of the samples to be? Why?

____

____

13. Analyze Relationships Elly and Ramon are both conducting surveys to compare the average numbers of hours per month that men and women spend shopping. Elly plans to take many samples of size 10 from both populations and compare the distributions of both the medians and the means. Ramon will do the same, but will use a sample size of 100. Whose results will probably produce more reliable inferences? Explain.

____

____

14. Counterexamples Seth believes that it is always possible to compare two populations of numerical values by finding the difference in the means of the populations as a multiple of the mean absolute deviations. Describe a situation that explains why Seth is incorrect.

____

____

MODULE QUIZ

Ready to Go On?

10.1 Comparing Data Displayed in Dot Plots

The two dot plots show the number of miles run by 14 students at the start and at the end of the school year. Compare each measure for the two dot plots. Use the data for 1–3.

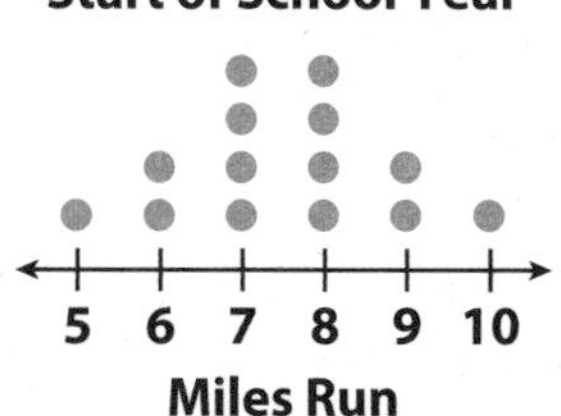

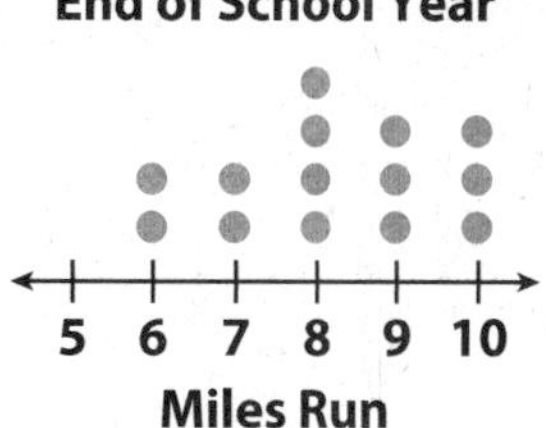

1. means ______________________

2. medians ______________________

3. ranges ______________________

10.2 Comparing Data Displayed in Box Plots

The box plots show lengths of flights in inches flown by two model airplanes. Use the data for 4–5.

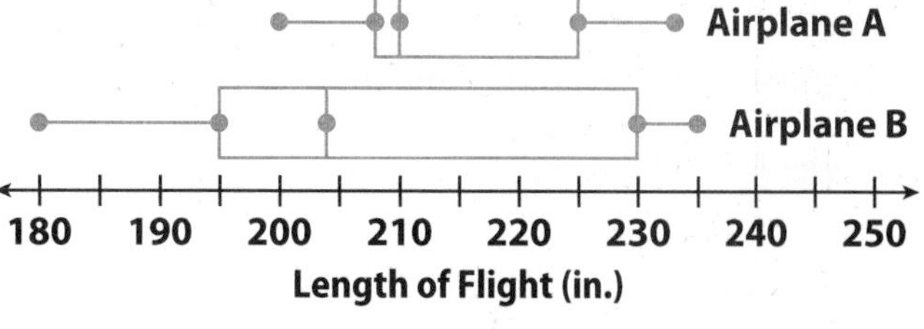

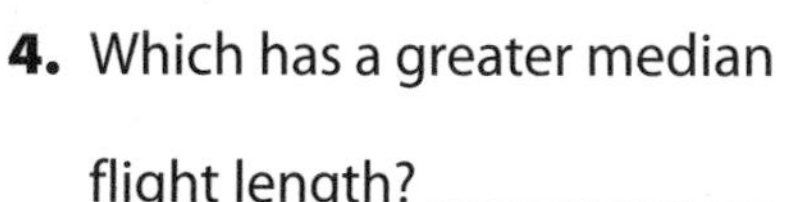

4. Which has a greater median flight length? ____________

5. Which has a greater interquartile range? ____________

10.3 Using Statistical Measures to Compare Populations

6. Roberta grows pea plants, some in shade and some in sun. She picks 8 plants of each type at random and records the heights.

Shade plant heights (in.)	7	11	11	12	9	12	8	10
Sun plant heights (in.)	21	24	19	19	22	23	24	24

Express the difference in the means as a multiple of their ranges.

____

ESSENTIAL QUESTION

7. How can you use and compare data to solve real-world problems?

____

MODULE 10
MIXED REVIEW

Assessment Readiness

Personal Math Trainer

Online Practice and Help

1. The box plots show the price of a gallon of gasoline in two cities. Look at each measure. Is the measure greater for city B?

Select Yes or No for A–C.

A. median ○ Yes ○ No

B. range ○ Yes ○ No

C. interquartile range ○ Yes ○ No

City A: 3.26 3.37 3.54 3.60 3.69

City B: 3.35 3.53 3.65 3.74 3.99

3.20 3.40 3.60 3.80 4.00

Cost of gasoline ($/gal)

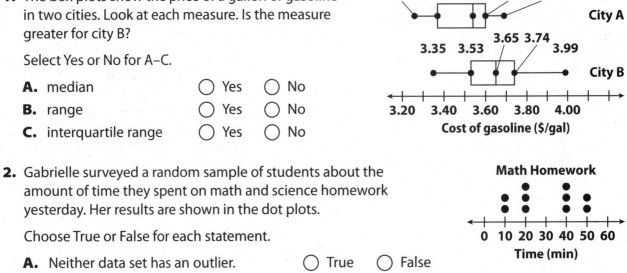

2. Gabrielle surveyed a random sample of students about the amount of time they spent on math and science homework yesterday. Her results are shown in the dot plots.

Choose True or False for each statement.

A. Neither data set has an outlier. ○ True ○ False

B. The science data is more symmetric. ○ True ○ False

C. The science data has a greater mean. ○ True ○ False

Math Homework

0 10 20 30 40 50 60

Time (min)

Science Homework

0 10 20 30 40 50 60

Time (min)

3. Use the data from Item 2. What is the difference of the means as a multiple of the mean absolute deviations? Explain how you solved this problem.

4. Tyrone buys a pair of shoes on sale for 20% off. The regular price of the shoes is $59.95, and the sales tax rate is 7.5%. How much will Tyrone pay for the shoes, including sales tax? Explain how you solved this problem.

Random Samples and Populations

ESSENTIAL QUESTION

How can you use random samples and populations to solve real-world problems?

Real-World Video

Scientists study animals like dart frogs to learn more about characteristics such as behavior, diet, and communication.

my.hrw.com

GO DIGITAL
my.hrw.com

my.hrw.com

Go digital with your write-in student edition, accessible on any device.

Math On the Spot

Scan with your smart phone to jump directly to the online edition, video tutor, and more.

Animated Math

Interactively explore key concepts to see how math works.

Personal Math Trainer

Get immediate feedback and help as you work through practice sets.

Are YOU Ready?

Complete these exercises to review skills you will need for this module.

Personal Math Trainer

Online Practice and Help

Solve Proportions

EXAMPLE $\frac{a}{1} = \frac{30}{1.5}$

$a \times 1.5 = 1 \times 30$ Write the cross products.

$1.5a = 30$ Simplify.

$\frac{1.5a}{1.5} = \frac{30}{1.5}$ Divide both sides by 1.5.

$a = 20$

Solve for *x*.

1. $\frac{x}{16} = \frac{45}{40}$ ______ **2.** $\frac{x}{5} = \frac{1}{4}$ ______ **3.** $\frac{2.5}{10} = \frac{x}{50}$ ______ **4.** $\frac{x}{6} = \frac{2}{9}$ ______

Find the Range

EXAMPLE 29, 26, 21, 30, 32, 19 Order the data from least to greatest.

19, 21, 26, 29, 30, 32

range = 32 − 19 The range is the difference between the greatest and the least data items.

= 13

Find the range of the data.

5. 52, 48, 57, 47, 49, 60, 59, 51 ______

6. 5, 9, 13, 6, 4, 5, 8, 12, 12, 6 ______

7. 97, 106, 99, 97, 115, 95, 108, 100 ______

8. 27, 13, 35, 19, 71, 12, 66, 47, 39 ______

Find the Mean

EXAMPLE 21, 15, 26, 19, 25, 14

$\text{mean} = \frac{21 + 15 + 26 + 19 + 25 + 14}{6}$ The mean is the sum of the data items divided by the number of items.

$= \frac{120}{6}$

$= 20$

Find the mean of each set of data.

9. 3, 5, 7, 3, 6, 4, 8, 6, 9, 5 ______

10. 8.1, 9.4, 11.3, 6.7, 6.2, 7.5 ______

Reading Start-Up

Visualize Vocabulary

Use the ✔ words to complete the right column of the chart.

Box Plots to Display Data	
Definition	**Review Word**
A display that uses values from a data set to show how the values are spread out.	
The middle value of a data set.	
The median of the lower half of the data.	
The median of the upper half of the data.	

Understand Vocabulary

Complete each sentence, using the preview words.

1. An entire group of objects, individuals, or events is a

____________________.

2. A ____________________ is part of the population chosen to represent the entire group.

3. A sample that does not accurately represent the population is a

____________________.

Vocabulary

Review Words

✔ box plot *(diagrama de caja)*
data *(datos)*
dot plot *(diagrama de puntos)*
interquartile range *(rango entre cuartiles)*
✔ lower quartile *(cuartil inferior)*
✔ median *(mediana)*
spread *(dispersión)*
survey *(estudio)*
✔ upper quartile *(cuartil superior)*

Preview Words

biased sample *(muestra sesgada)*
population *(población)*
random sample *(muestra aleatoria)*
sample *(muestra)*

Active Reading

Tri-Fold Before beginning the module, create a tri-fold to help you learn the concepts and vocabulary in this module. Fold the paper into three sections. Label the columns "What I Know," "What I Need to Know," and "What I Learned." Complete the first two columns before you read. After studying the module, complete the third column.

CALIFORNIA

GETTING READY FOR

Random Samples and Populations

Understanding the standards and the vocabulary terms in the standards will help you know exactly what you are expected to learn in this module.

CA CC 7.SP.1

Understand that statistics can be used to gain information about a population by examining a sample of the population; generalizations about a population from a sample are valid only if the sample is representative of that population. Understand that random sampling tends to produce representative samples and support valid inferences.

What It Means to You

You will learn how a random sample can be representative of a population.

EXAMPLE 7.SP.1

Avery wants to survey residents who live in an apartment building. She writes down all of the apartment numbers on slips of paper, and draws slips from a box without looking to decide who to survey. Will this produce a random sample?

The population is all of the residents or people who live in the apartment building. The sample is a valid random sample because every apartment number has the same chance of being selected.

CA CC 7.SP.2

Use data from a random sample to draw inferences about a population with an unknown characteristic of interest. Generate multiple samples (or simulated samples) of the same size to gauge the variation in estimates or predictions.

Key Vocabulary

population *(población)*
The entire group of objects or individuals considered for a survey.

sample *(muestra)*
A part of the population.

What It Means to You

You will use data collected from a random sample to make inferences about a population.

EXAMPLE 7.SP.2

Alexi surveys a random sample of 80 students at his school and finds that 22 of them usually walk to school. There are 1,760 students at the school. Predict the number of students who usually walk to school.

$$\frac{\text{number in sample who walk}}{\text{size of sample}} = \frac{\text{number in population who walk}}{\text{size of population}}$$

$$\frac{22}{80} = \frac{x}{1{,}760}$$

$$x = \frac{22}{80} \cdot 1{,}760$$

$$x = \frac{38{,}720}{80} = 484$$

Approximately 484 students usually walk to school.

Visit **my.hrw.com** to see all **CA Common Core Standards** explained.

my.hrw.com

LESSON **11.1**

Populations and Samples

CA CC 7.SP.1

Understand that statistics can be used to gain information about a population by examining a sample of the population; generalizations about a population from a sample are valid only if the sample is representative of that population. Understand that random sampling tends to produce representative samples and support valid inferences.

ESSENTIAL QUESTION

How can you use a sample to gain information about a population?

EXPLORE ACTIVITY  

Random and Non-Random Sampling

When information is being gathered about a group, the entire group of objects, individuals, or events is called the **population**. Because gathering information about each member of a large group can be difficult or impossible, researchers often study a part of the population, called a **sample**.

The size of a sample and the way the sample is chosen can have an effect on whether the sample is representative of the population or not.

A vegetable garden has 36 tomato plants arranged in a 6-by-6 array. The gardener wants to know the average number of tomatoes on the plants. Each white cell in the table represents a plant. The number in the cell tells how many tomatoes are on that particular plant.

						First Number Cube
	8	9	13	18	24	15	**1**
	34	42	46	20	13	41	**2**
	29	21	14	45	27	43	**3**
	22	45	46	41	22	33	**4**
	12	42	44	17	42	11	**5**
	18	26	43	32	33	26	**6**
Second Number Cube	**1**	**2**	**3**	**4**	**5**	**6**	

Because counting the number of tomatoes on all of the plants is too time-consuming, the gardener decides to choose plants at random to find the average number of tomatoes on them.

To simulate the random selection, roll two number cubes 10 times. Find the cell in the table identified by the first and second number cubes. Record the number in each randomly selected cell.

A What is the average number of tomatoes on the 10 plants that were randomly selected?

____

B Alternately, the gardener decides to choose the plants in the first row. What is the average number of tomatoes on these plants?

____

Math Talk
Mathematical Practices

How do the averages you got with each sampling method compare?

EXPLORE ACTIVITY (cont'd)

Reflect

1. How do the averages you got with each sampling method compare to the average for the entire population, which is 28.25?

____

____

2. Why might the first method give a closer average than the second method?

____

____

Random Samples and Biased Samples

A sample in which every person, object, or event has an equal chance of being selected is called a **random sample**. A random sample is more likely to be representative of the entire population than other types of samples. When a sample does not accurately represent the population, it is called a **biased sample**.

EXAMPLE 1

Identify the population. Determine whether each sample is a random sample or a biased sample. Explain your reasoning.

A Roberto wants to know the favorite sport of adults in his hometown. He surveys 50 adults at a baseball game.

The population is adults in Roberto's hometown.

The sample is biased.

Think: People who don't like baseball will not be represented in this sample.

B Paula wants to know the favorite type of music for students in her class. She puts the names of all students in a hat, draws 8 names, and surveys those students.

The population is students in Paula's class.

The sample is random.

Think: Each student has an equal chance of being selected.

Math Talk
Mathematical Practices
Why do you think samples are used? Why not survey each member of the population?

Reflect

3. How might you choose a sample of size 20 to determine the preferred practice day of all the players in a soccer league?

____

____

YOUR TURN

4. For a survey, a company manager assigned a number to each of the company's 500 employees, and put the numbers in a bag. The manager chose 20 numbers and surveyed the employees with those numbers. Did the manager choose a random sample?

____

____

Bias in Survey Questions

Once you have selected a representative sample of the population, be sure that the data is gathered without bias. Make sure that the survey questions themselves do not sway people to respond a certain way.

EXAMPLE 2 

In Madison County, residents were surveyed about a new skateboard park. Determine whether each survey question may be biased. Explain.

A Would you like to waste the taxpayers' money to build a frivolous skateboard park?

This question is biased. It discourages residents from saying yes to a new skateboard park by implying it is a waste of money.

B Do you favor a new skateboard park?

This question is not biased. It does not include an opinion on the skateboard park.

C Studies have shown that having a safe place to go keeps kids out of trouble. Would you like to invest taxpayers' money to build a skateboard park?

This question is biased. It leads people to say yes because it mentions having a safe place for kids to go and to stay out of trouble.

YOUR TURN

Determine whether each question may be biased. Explain.

5. When it comes to pets, do you prefer cats?

____

6. What is your favorite season?

____

____

Guided Practice

1. Follow each method described below to collect data to estimate the average shoe size of seventh grade boys. (Explore Activity)

Method 1

A Randomly select 6 seventh grade boys and ask each his shoe size. Record your results in a table like the one shown.

Random Sample of Seventh Grade Male Students	
Student	Shoe Size

____

B Find the mean of this data. Mean:

____

Method 2

A Find the 6 boys in your math class with the largest shoes and ask their shoe size. Record your results in a table like the one shown in Method 1.

____

B Find the mean of this data. Mean: ______________________________

2. Method 1 produces results that are **more / less** representative of the entire student population because it is a **random / biased** sample. (Example 1)

3. Method 2 produces results that are **more / less** representative of the entire student population because it is a **random / biased** sample. (Example 1)

4. Heidi decides to use a random sample to determine her classmates' favorite color. She asks, "Is green your favorite color?" Is Heidi's question biased? If so, give an example of an unbiased question that would serve Heidi better. (Example 2)

____

ESSENTIAL QUESTION CHECK-IN

5. How can you select a sample so that the information gained represents the entire population?

____

____

Name ______________________ Class ______________ Date ______________

11.1 Independent Practice

CA CC 7.SP.1

6. Paul and his friends average their test grades and find that the average is 95. The teacher announces that the average grade of all of her classes is 83. Why are the averages so different?

____

____

____

7. Nancy hears a report that the average price of gasoline is \$2.82. She averages the prices of stations near her home. She finds the average price of gas to be \$3.03. Why are the averages different?

____

____

____

____

For 8–10, determine whether each sample is a random sample or a biased sample. Explain.

8. Carol wants to find out the favorite foods of students at her middle school. She asks the boys' basketball team about their favorite foods.

____

____

9. Dallas wants to know what elective subjects the students at his school like best. He surveys students who are leaving band class.

____

____

____

10. To choose a sample for a survey of seventh graders, the student council puts pieces of paper with the names of all the seventh graders in a bag, and selects 20 names.

____

____

____

11. Members of a polling organization survey 700 of the 7,453 registered voters in a town by randomly choosing names from a list of all registered voters. Is their sample likely to be representative?

____

____

For 12–13, determine whether each question may be biased. Explain.

12. Joey wants to find out what sport seventh grade girls like most. He asks girls, "Is basketball your favorite sport?"

____

____

____

13. Jae wants to find out what type of art her fellow students enjoy most. She asks her classmates, "What is your favorite type of art?"

____

____

____

FOCUS ON HIGHER ORDER THINKING

Work Area

14. Draw Conclusions Determine which sampling method will better represent the entire population. Justify your answer.

Student Attendance at Football Games	
Sampling Method	**Results of Survey**
Collin surveys 78 students by randomly choosing names from the school directory.	63% attend football games.
Karl surveys 25 students that were sitting near him during lunch.	82% attend football games.

____

____

____

____

____

____

15. Multistep Barbara surveyed students in her school by looking at an alphabetical list of the 600 student names, dividing them into groups of 10, and randomly choosing one from each group.

a. How many students did she survey? What type of sample is this?

____

b. Barbara found that 35 of the survey participants had pets. About what percent of the students she surveyed had pets? Is it safe to believe that about the same percent of students in the school have pets? Explain your thinking.

____

____

____

16. Communicating Mathematical Ideas Carlo said a population can have more than one sample associated with it. Do you agree or disagree with his statement? Justify your answer.

____

____

____

LESSON 11.2

Making Inferences from a Random Sample

CA CC 7.SP.2

Use data from a random sample to draw inferences about a population with an unknown characteristic of interest. Generate multiple samples (or simulated samples) of the same size to gauge the variation in estimates or predictions. *Also 7.RP.2c, 7.SP.1*

ESSENTIAL QUESTION

How can you use a sample to make inferences about a population?

EXPLORE ACTIVITY 1 

Using Dot Plots to Make Inferences

After obtaining a random sample of a population, you can make inferences about the population. Random samples are usually representative and support valid inferences.

Rosee asked a random sample of students how many books they had in their backpacks. She recorded the data as a list: 2, 6, 1, 0, 4, 1, 4, 2, 2. Make a dot plot for the books carried by this sample of students.

STEP 1 Order the data from least to greatest. Find the least and greatest values in the data set.

STEP 2 Draw a number line from 0 to 6. Place a dot above each number on the number line for each time it appears in the data set.

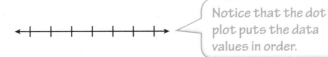

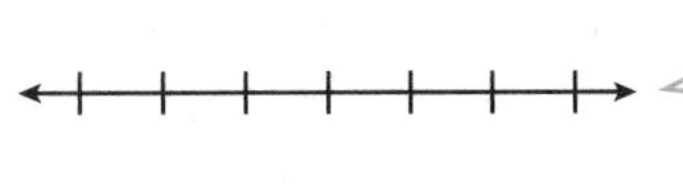

Notice that the dot plot puts the data values in order.

Math Talk
Mathematical Practices

No students in Rosee's sample carry 3 books. Do you think this is true of all the students at the school? Explain.

Reflect

1. **Critical Thinking** How are the number of dots you plotted related to the number of data values?

____

2. **Draw Conclusions** Complete each qualitative inference about the population.

   Most students have ___________ 1 book in their backpacks.

   Most students have fewer than ___________ books in their backpacks.

   Most students have between ___________ books in their backpacks.

3. **Analyze Relationships** What could Rosee do to improve the quality of her data?

____

EXPLORE ACTIVITY 2   7.SP.2

Using Box Plots to Make Inferences

You can also analyze box plots to make inferences about a population.

The number of pets owned by a random sample of students at Park Middle school is shown below. Use the data to make a box plot.

9, 2, 0, 4, 6, 3, 3, 2, 5

STEP 1 Order the data from least to greatest. Then find the least and greatest values, the median, and the lower and upper quartiles.

STEP 2 The lower and upper quartiles can be calculated by finding the medians of each "half" of the number line that includes all the data.

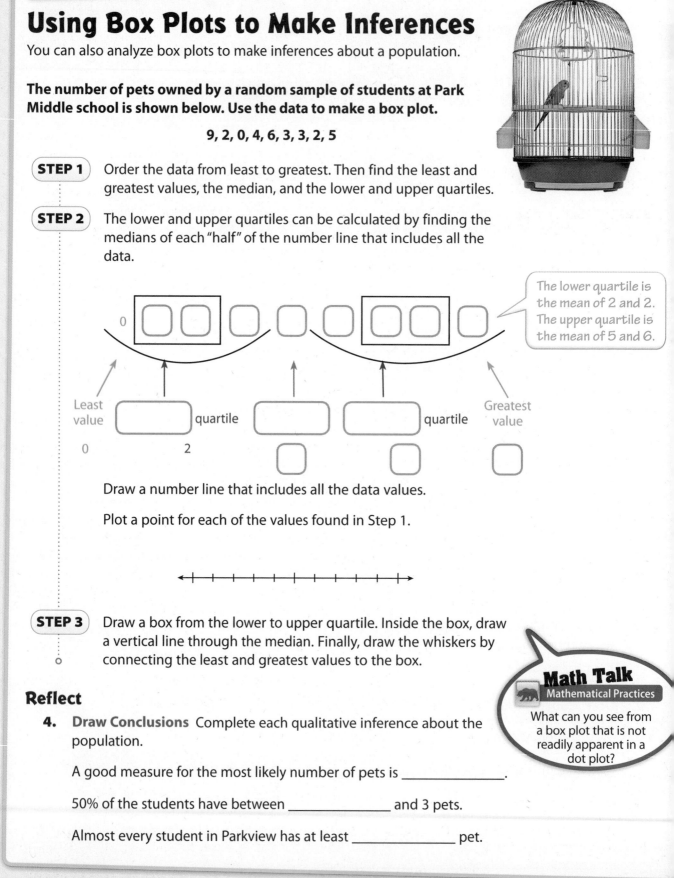

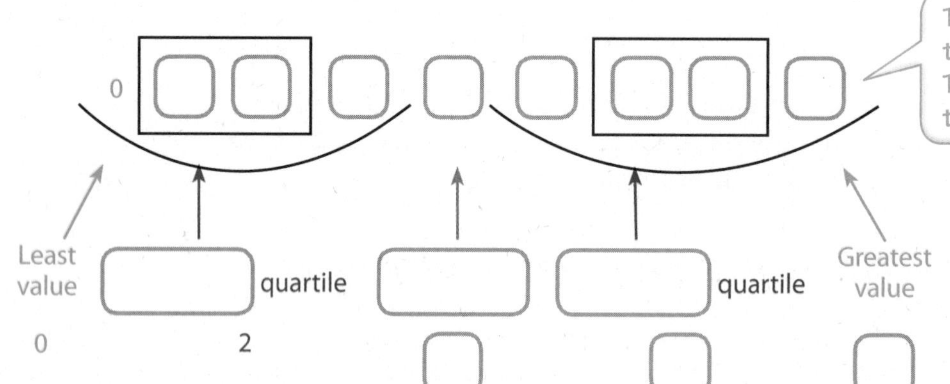

Draw a number line that includes all the data values.

Plot a point for each of the values found in Step 1.

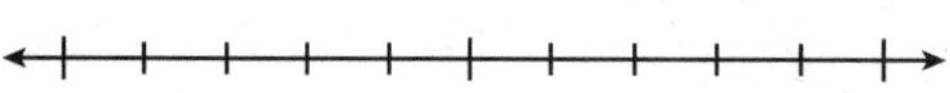

STEP 3 Draw a box from the lower to upper quartile. Inside the box, draw a vertical line through the median. Finally, draw the whiskers by connecting the least and greatest values to the box.

Reflect

4. **Draw Conclusions** Complete each qualitative inference about the population.

A good measure for the most likely number of pets is ______________.

50% of the students have between ______________ and 3 pets.

Almost every student in Parkview has at least ______________ pet.

Math Talk
Mathematical Practices
What can you see from a box plot that is not readily apparent in a dot plot?

Using Proportions to Make Inferences

You can use data based on a random sample, along with proportional reasoning, to make inferences or predictions about the population.

EXAMPLE 1 Real World CA CC 7.SP.2, 7.RP.2c

A shipment to a warehouse consists of 3,500 MP3 players. The manager chooses a random sample of 50 MP3 players and finds that 3 are defective. How many MP3 players in the shipment are likely to be defective?

It is reasonable to make a prediction about the population because this sample is random.

STEP 1 Set up a proportion.

$$\frac{\text{defective MP3s in sample}}{\text{size of sample}} = \frac{\text{defective MP3s in population}}{\text{size of population}}$$

STEP 2 Substitute values into the proportion.

$$\frac{3}{50} = \frac{x}{3{,}500}$$ Substitute known values. Let x be the number of defective MP3 players in the population.

$$\frac{3 \cdot 70}{50 \cdot 70} = \frac{x}{3{,}500}$$ $50 \cdot 70 = 3{,}500$, so multiply the numerator and denominator by 70.

$$\frac{210}{3{,}500} = \frac{x}{3{,}500}$$

$$210 = x$$

Based on the sample, you can predict that 210 MP3 players in the shipment would be defective.

YOUR TURN

5. **What If?** How many MP3 players in the shipment would you predict to be damaged if 6 MP3s in the sample had been damaged?

____

Reflect

6. **Check for Reasonableness** How could you use estimation to check if your answer is reasonable?

____

____

Guided Practice

Patrons in the children's section of a local branch library were randomly selected and asked their ages. The librarian wants to use the data to infer the ages of all patrons of the children's section so he can select age appropriate activities. In 3–6, complete each inference. (Explore Activity 1 and 2)

7, 4, 7, 5, 4, 10, 11, 6, 7, 4

1. Make a dot plot of the sample population data.

2. Make a box plot of the sample population data.

3. The most common ages of children that use the library are ______ and ______.

4. The range of ages of children that use the library is from ______ to ______.

5. The median age of children that use the library is ______.

6. A manufacturer fills an order for 4,200 smart phones. The quality inspector selects a random sample of 60 phones and finds that 4 are defective. How many smart phones in the order are likely to be defective? (Example 1)

About ________ smart phones in the order are likely to be defective.

7. Part of the population of 4,500 elk at a wildlife preserve is infected with a parasite. A random sample of 50 elk shows that 8 of them are infected. How many elk are likely to be infected? (Example 1)

____

ESSENTIAL QUESTION CHECK-IN

8. How can you use a random sample of a population to make predictions?

____

____

____

____

____

Name ______________________ Class ______________ Date ______________

11.2 Independent Practice

CA CC 7.RP.2c, 7.SP.1, 7.SP.2

9. A manager samples the receipts of every fifth person who goes through the line. Out of 50 people, 4 had a mispriced item. If 600 people go to this store each day, how many people would you expect to have a mispriced item?

____

10. Jerry randomly selects 20 boxes of crayons from the shelf and finds 2 boxes with at least one broken crayon. If the shelf holds 130 boxes, how many would you expect to have at least one broken crayon?

____

11. A random sample of dogs at different animal shelters in a city shows that 12 of the 60 dogs are puppies. The city's animal shelters collectively house 1,200 dogs each year. About how many dogs in all of the city's animal shelters are puppies?

____

12. Part of the population of 10,800 hawks at a national park are building a nest. A random sample of 72 hawks shows that 12 of them are building a nest. Estimate the number of hawks building a nest in the population.

____

13. In a wildlife preserve, a random sample of the population of 150 raccoons was caught and weighed. The results, given in pounds, were 17, 19, 20, 21, 23, 27, 28, 28, 28 and 32. Jean made the qualitative statement, "The average weight of the raccoon population is 25 pounds." Is her statement reasonable? Explain.

____

____

____

14. Greta collects the number of miles run each week from a random sample of female marathon runners. Her data are shown below. She made the qualitative statement, "25% of female marathoners run 13 or more miles a week." Is her statement reasonable? Explain. Data: 13, 14, 18, 13, 12, 17, 15, 12, 13, 19, 11, 14, 14, 18, 22, 12

____

____

____

15. A random sample of 20 of the 200 students at Garland Elementary is asked how many siblings each has. The data are ordered as shown. Make a dot plot of the data. Then make a qualitative statement about the population. Data: 0, 1, 1, 1, 1, 1, 1, 2, 2, 2, 2, 2, 3, 3, 3, 3, 4, 4, 4, 6

____

____

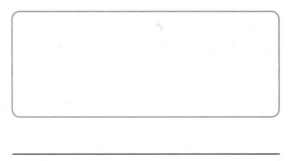

16. Linda collects a random sample of 12 of the 98 Wilderness Club members' ages. She makes an inference that most wilderness club members are between 20 and 40 years old. Describe what a box plot that would confirm Linda's inference should look like.

____

____

____

17. **What's the Error?** Kudrey was making a box plot. He first plotted the least and greatest data values. He then divided the distance into half, and then did this again for each half. What did Kudrey do wrong and what did his box plot look like?

____

____

____

____

H.O.T. FOCUS ON HIGHER ORDER THINKING

Work Area

18. **Communicating Mathematical Ideas** A dot plot includes all of the actual data values. Does a box plot include any of the actual data values?

____

____

____

____

19. **Make a Conjecture** Sammy counted the peanuts in several packages of roasted peanuts. He found that the bags had 102, 114, 97, 85, 106, 120, 107, and 111 peanuts. Should he make a box plot or dot plot to represent the data? Explain your reasoning.

____

____

____

____

____

____

20. **Represent Real-World Problems** The salaries for the eight employees at a small company are \$20,000, \$20,000, \$22,000, \$24,000, \$24,000, \$29,000, \$34,000 and \$79,000. Make a qualitative inference about a typical salary at this company. Would an advertisement that stated that the average salary earned at the company is \$31,500 be misleading? Explain.

____

____

____

LESSON 11.3

Generating Random Samples

CA CC 7.SP.2

Use data from a random sample to draw inferences about a population with an unknown characteristic of interest. Generate multiple samples (or simulated samples) of the same size to gauge the variation in estimates or predictions.

ESSENTIAL QUESTION

How can you generate and use random samples to represent a population?

EXPLORE ACTIVITY 1 

Generating a Random Sample Using Technology

In an earlier lesson, you generated random samples by rolling number cubes. You can also generate random samples by using technology. In Explore Activity 1, you will generate samples using a graphing calculator.

Each of the 200 students in a school will have a chance to vote on one of two names, Tigers or Bears, for the school's athletic teams. A group of students decides to select a random sample of 20 students and ask them for which name they intend to vote. How can the group choose a random sample to represent the entire population of 200 students?

A One way to identify a random sample is to use a graphing calculator to generate random integers.

To simulate choosing 20 students at random from among 200 students:

- Press MATH, scroll right and select **PRB**, then select **5: randInt(**.
- Enter the least value, comma, greatest possible value.

randInt (1, 200)
43
93
75
178

In this specific case, the students will enter **randInt** (☐ , ☐)

because there are ________________ students in school.

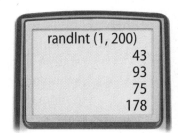

- Hit ENTER ______ times to generate ______ random numbers.

The group gets a list of all the students in the school and assigns a number to each one. The group surveys the students with the given numbers.

Of the 20 students surveyed, 9 chose Tigers. The percent choosing

Tigers was ________. What might the group infer?

____

____

B You can simulate multiple random samples to see how much statistical measures vary for different samples of size 20.

Assume that the 200 students are evenly divided among those voting for Tigers and those voting for Bears. You can generate random numbers and let each number represent a vote. Let numbers from 1 to 100 represent votes for Tigers, and numbers from 101 to 200 represent votes for Bears. For each simulated sample, use randInt(1, 200) and generate 20 numbers.

Perform the simulation 10 times and record how many numbers from 1 to 100 are generated. How many of the samples indicated that there were 9 or fewer votes for Tigers?

____

Combine your results with those of your classmates. Make a dot plot showing the number of numbers from 1 to 100 generated in each simulation.

____

Reflect

1. **Communicate Mathematical Reasoning** Assume that it was accurate to say that the 200 students are evenly divided among those voting for Tigers and those voting for Bears. Based on your results, does it seem likely that in a sample of size 20, there would be 9 or fewer votes for Tigers?

____

2. **Make a Prediction** Based on your answers, do you think it is likely that Tigers will win? Explain.

____

3. **Multiple Representations** Suppose you wanted to simulate a random sample for the situation in Explore Activity 1 without using technology. One way would be to use marbles of two different colors to represent students choosing the different names. Describe how you could perform a simulation.

____

____

____

____

____

EXPLORE ACTIVITY 2   7.SP.2

Generating a Random Sample without Technology

A tree farm has a 100 acre square field arranged in a 10-by-10 array. The farmer wants to know the average number of trees per acre. Each cell in the table represents an acre. The number in each cell represents the number of trees on that acre.

22	24	27	29	31	24	27	29	30	25
37	22	60	53	62	42	64	53	41	62
61	54	57	34	44	66	39	60	65	40
45	33	64	36	33	51	62	66	42	42
37	34	57	33	47	43	66	33	61	66
66	45	46	67	60	59	51	46	67	48
53	46	35	35	55	56	61	46	38	64
55	51	54	62	55	58	51	45	41	53
61	38	48	48	43	59	64	48	49	47
41	53	53	59	58	48	62	53	45	59

The farmer decides to choose a random sample of 10 of the acres.

A To simulate the random selection, number the table columns 1–10 from left to right, and the rows 1–10 from top to bottom. Write the numbers 1–10 on identical pieces of paper. Place the pieces into a bag. Draw one at random, replace it, and draw another. Let the first number represent a table column, and the second represent a row. For instance, a draw of 2 and then 3 represents the cell in the second column and third row of the table, an acre containing 54 trees. Repeat this process 9 more times.

B Based on your sample, predict the average number of trees per acre. How does your answer compare with the actual mean number, 48.4?

____

____

C Compare your answer to **B** with several of your classmates' answers. Do they vary a lot? Is it likely that you can make a valid prediction about the average number of trees per acre? Explain.

____

EXPLORE ACTIVITY 2 *(cont'd)*

Reflect

4. **Communicate Mathematical Ideas** Suppose that you use the method in **A** to collect a random sample of 25 acres. Do you think any resulting prediction would be more or less reliable than your original one? Explain.

____

____

5. **Multiple Representations** How could you use technology to select the acres for your sample?

____

____

Guided Practice

A manufacturer gets a shipment of 600 batteries of which 50 are defective. The store manager wants to be able to test random samples in future shipments. She tests a random sample of 20 batteries in this shipment to see whether a sample of that size produces a reasonable inference about the entire shipment. (Explore Activities 1 and 2)

1. The manager selects a random sample using the formula randInt(☐, ☐) to generate ______ random numbers.

2. She lets numbers from 1 to ______ represent defective batteries, and ______ to ______ represent working batteries. She generates this list: 120, 413, 472, 564, 38, 266, 344, 476, 486, 177, 26, 331, 358, 131, 352, 227, 31, 253, 31, 277.

3. Does the sample produce a reasonable inference?

____

____

ESSENTIAL QUESTION CHECK-IN

4. What can happen if a sample is too small or is not random?

____

____

Name ______________________ Class ______________ Date ______________

11.3 Independent Practice

7.SP.2

Maureen owns three bagel shops. Each shop sells 500 bagels per day. Maureen asks her store managers to use a random sample to see how many whole-wheat bagels are sold at each store each day. The results are shown in the table. Use the table for 5–7.

	Total bagels in sample	Whole-wheat bagels
Shop A	50	10
Shop B	100	23
Shop C	25	7

5. If you assume the samples are representative, how many whole-wheat bagels might you infer are sold at each store?

____

6. Rank the samples for the shops in terms of how representative they are likely to be. Explain your rankings.

____

____

7. Which sample or samples should Maureen use to tell her managers how many whole-wheat bagels to make each day? Explain.

____

____

____

8. In a shipment of 1,000 T-shirts, 75 do not meet quality standards. The table below simulates a manager's random sample of 20 T-shirts to inspect. For the simulation, the integers 1 to 75 represent the below-standard shirts.

124	876	76	79	12	878	86	912	435	91
340	213	45	678	544	271	714	777	812	80

In the sample, how many of the shirts are below quality standards? ______

If someone used the sample to predict the number of below standard shirts in the shipment, how far off would the prediction be?

____

____

9. Multistep A 64-acre coconut farm is arranged in an 8-by-8 array. Mika wants to know the average number of coconut palms on each acre. Each cell in the table represents an acre of land. The number in each cell tells how many coconut palms grow on that particular acre.

56	54	40	34	44	66	43	65
66	33	42	36	33	51	62	63
33	34	66	33	47	43	66	61
46	35	48	67	60	59	52	67
46	32	64	35	55	47	61	38
45	51	53	62	55	58	51	41
48	38	47	48	43	59	64	54
53	67	59	59	58	48	62	45

a. The numbers in green represent Mika's random sample of 10 acres. What is the average number of coconut palms on the randomly selected acres?

____

b. Project the number of palms on the entire farm.

____

FOCUS ON HIGHER ORDER THINKING

Work Area

10. Draw Conclusions A random sample of 15 of the 78 competitors at a middle school gymnastics competition are asked their height. The data set lists the heights in inches: 55, 57, 57, 58, 59, 59, 59, 59, 59, 61, 62, 62, 63, 64, 66. What is the mean height of the sample? Do you think this is a reasonable prediction of the mean height of all competitors? Explain.

____

____

____

____

11. Critical Thinking The six-by-six grid contains the ages of actors in a youth Shakespeare festival. Randomly select 8 cells by rolling two six-sided number cubes, with one cube representing the row and the other representing the column. Then calculate the average of the 8 values you found.

12	15	16	9	21	11
9	10	14	10	13	12
16	21	14	12	8	14
16	20	9	16	19	18
17	14	12	15	10	15
12	20	14	10	12	9

____

____

12. Communicating Mathematical Ideas Describe how the size of a random sample affects how well it represents a population as a whole.

____

____

____

MODULE QUIZ

Ready to Go On?

Personal Math Trainer

Online Practice and Help

my.hrw.com

11.1 Populations and Samples

1. A company uses a computer to identify their 600 most loyal customers from its database and then surveys those customers to find out how they like their service. Identify the population and determine whether the sample is random or biased.

____

____

11.2 Making Inferences from a Random Sample

2. A university has 30,330 students. In a random sample of 270 students, 18 speak three or more languages. Predict the number of students at the university who speak three or more languages.

____

11.3 Generating Random Samples

A store receives a shipment of 5,000 MP3 players. In a previous shipment of 5,000 MP3 players, 300 were defective. A store clerk generates random numbers to simulate a random sample of this shipment. The clerk lets the numbers 1 through 300 represent defective MP3 players, and the numbers 301 through 5,000 represent working MP3 players. The results are given.

13 2,195 3,873 525 900 167 1,094 1,472 709 5,000

3. Based on the sample, how many of the MP3 players might the clerk predict would be defective?

____

4. Can the manufacturer assume the prediction is valid? Explain.

____

ESSENTIAL QUESTION

5. How can you use random samples to solve real-world problems?

____

____

MODULE 11
MIXED REVIEW

Assessment Readiness

1. Tony is taking a survey to determine how many miles the runners in a race typically run each week. Consider each survey method. Is the survey a random sample? Select Yes or No for A–B.

A. He surveys the first 20 people to finish the race. ○ Yes ○ No

B. He puts the names of the runners in a bag, draws 20 names, and surveys those runners. ○ Yes ○ No

2. Marcella has $20 to buy 4 notebooks and a package of copy paper. The copy paper costs $5.79. The inequality $4n + 5.79 \leq 20$ can be used to find n, the amount in dollars Marcella can spend on each notebook.

Choose True or False for each statement.

A. $n = 1.89$ is a solution of the inequality. ○ True ○ False

B. $n = 2.59$ is a solution of the inequality. ○ True ○ False

C. $n = 3.79$ is a solution of the inequality. ○ True ○ False

3. A factory ships an order of 650 laptops. A worker tests a random sample of 40 laptops and finds that 1 of the laptops takes more than 30 seconds to start up. Predict the number of laptops in the shipment that will take more than 30 seconds to start up. Explain how you made your prediction.

4. The 412 students at a high school are voting on whether to change the school mascot. Tonya and Julio each asked a random sample of 10 students about their votes. The results are shown below. Can the samples be used to predict the outcome of the vote? Explain your reasoning.

Tonya's sample	yes, no, yes, no, yes, no, no, yes, yes, yes
Julio's sample	no, no, yes, no, yes, no, no, no, yes, yes

UNIT 5

Study Guide Review

MODULE 10 Analyzing and Comparing Data

Key Vocabulary

mean absolute deviation (MAD) *(desviación absoluta media, (DAM))*

ESSENTIAL QUESTION

How can you solve problems by analyzing and comparing data?

EXAMPLE

The box plots show amounts donated to two charities at a fundraising drive. Compare the shapes, centers and spreads of the box plots.

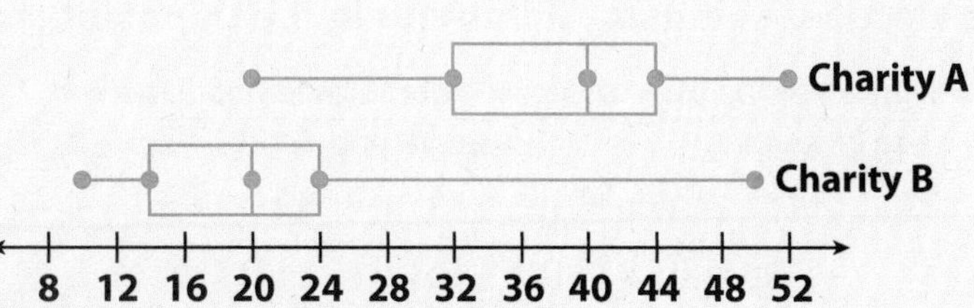

Shapes: The lengths of the boxes and overall plot lengths are fairly similar, but while the whiskers for Charity A are similar in length, Charity B has a very short whisker and a very long whisker.

Centers: The median for Charity A is \$40, and for Charity B is \$20.

Spreads: The interquartile range for Charity A is $44 - 32 = 12$. The interquartile range for Charity B is slightly less, $24 - 14 = 10$.

The donations varied more for Charity B and were lower overall.

EXERCISES

The dot plots show the number of hours a group of students spends online each week, and how many hours they spend reading. (Lesson 10.1)

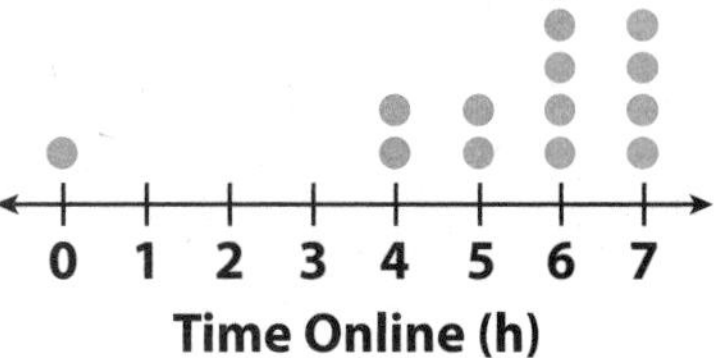

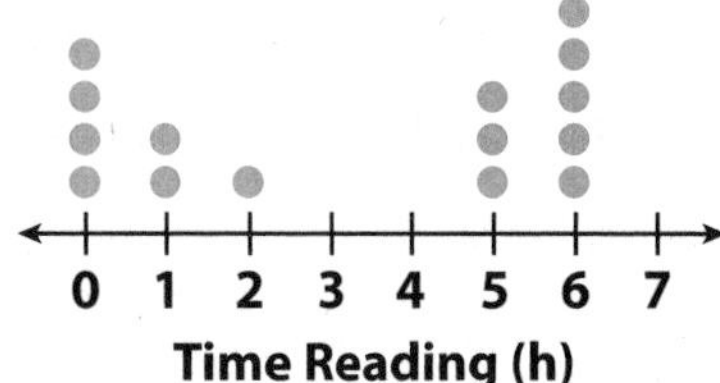

1. Calculate the medians of the dot plots. ____________________

2. The average times (in minutes) a group of students spends studying and watching TV per school day are given. (Lesson 10.3)

Studying:	25, 30, 35, 45, 60, 60, 70, 75
Watching TV:	0, 35, 35, 45, 50, 50, 70, 75

a. Find the mean times for studying and for watching TV.

____

b. Find the mean absolute deviations (MADs) for each data set.

____

c. Find the difference of the means as a multiple of the MAD. ____________

Random Samples and Populations

ESSENTIAL QUESTION

How can you use random samples and populations to solve real-world problems?

Key Vocabulary

biased sample *(muestra sesgada)*

population *(población)*

random sample *(muestra aleatoria)*

sample *(muestra)*

EXAMPLE 1

An engineer at a lightbulb factory chooses a random sample of 100 lightbulbs from a shipment of 2,500 and finds that 2 of them are defective. How many lightbulbs in the shipment are likely to be defective?

$$\frac{\text{defective lightbulbs}}{\text{size of sample}} = \frac{\text{defective lightbulbs in population}}{\text{size of population}}$$

$$\frac{2}{100} = \frac{x}{2{,}500}$$

$$\frac{2 \cdot 25}{100 \cdot 25} = \frac{x}{2{,}500}$$

$$x = 50$$

In a shipment of 2,500 lightbulbs, 50 are likely to be defective.

EXAMPLE 2

The 300 students in a school are about to vote for student body president. There are two candidates, Jay and Serena, and each candidate has about the same amount of support. Use a simulation to generate a random sample. Interpret the results.

Step 1: Write the digits 0 through 9 on 10 index cards, one digit per card. Draw and replace a card three times to form a 3-digit number. For example, if you draw 0-4-9, the number is 49. If you draw 1-0-8, the number is 108. Repeat this process until you have a sample of 30 3-digit numbers.

Step 2: Let the numbers from 1 to 150 represent votes for Jay and the numbers from 151 to 300 represent votes for Serena. For example:

Jay: 83, 37, 16, 4, 127, 93, 9, 62, 91, 75, 13, 35, 94, 26, 60, 120, 36, 73

Serena: 217, 292, 252, 186, 296, 218, 284, 278, 209, 296, 190, 300

Step 3: Notice that 18 of the 30 numbers represent votes for Jay. The results suggest that Jay will receive $\frac{18}{30} = 60\%$ of the 300 votes, or 180 votes.

Step 4: Based on this one sample, Jay will win the election. The results of samples can vary. Repeating the simulation many times and looking at the pattern across the different samples will produce more reliable results.

EXERCISES

1. Molly uses the school directory to select, at random, 25 students from her school for a survey on which sports people like to watch on television. She calls the students and asks them, "Do you think basketball is the best sport to watch on television?" (Lesson 11.1)

   a. Did Molly survey a random sample or a biased sample of the students at her school?

   ____

   b. Was the question she asked an unbiased question? Explain your answer.

   ____

   ____

2. There are 2,300 licensed dogs in Clarkson. A random sample of 50 of the dogs in Clarkson shows that 8 have ID microchips implanted. How many dogs in Clarkson are likely to have ID microchips implanted? (Lesson 11.2)

   ____

3. A store gets a shipment of 500 MP3 players. Twenty-five of the players are defective, and the rest are working. A graphing calculator is used to generate 20 random numbers to simulate a random sample of the players. (Lesson 11.3)

   A list of 20 randomly generated numbers representing MP3 players is:

474	77	101	156	378	188	116	458	230	333
78	19	67	5	191	124	226	496	481	161

   a. Let numbers 1 to 25 represent players that are ______________.

   b. Let numbers 21 to 500 represent players that are ______________.

   c. How many players in this sample are expected to be defective? ______________

   d. If 300 players are chosen at random from the shipment, how many are expected to be defective based on the sample? Does the sample provide a reasonable inference? Explain.

   ____

   ____

   ____

Unit Project

CA CC 7.RP.2c, 7.SP.1, 7.SP.2, 7.SP.3, 7.SP.4

A Sample? Simple!

For this project, choose one of the following topics. Randomly sample at least 25 people and record their answers to the question you write about the topic.

- Number of pets in a home
- Number of books read optionally in the past 6 months
- Number of cell phone lines a family uses
- Number of full-time or part-time students in a family
- Number of hours of sleep obtained *last night*

Use your data to create a presentation that includes the following:

- An explanation of how you chose your random sample
- The question you asked and the answers you received
- A box plot of your data
- Your interpretations of the data, including the median, the range, and the most common items of data
- Your inference, based on your data, of the number of 5,000 randomly chosen people who would give the answer to your question that your median group gave

Use the space below to write down any questions you have or important information from your teacher.

MATH IN CAREERS | ACTIVITY

Entomologist An entomologist is studying how two different types of flowers appeal to butterflies. The box-and-whisker plots show the number of butterflies that visited one of two different types of flowers in a field. The data were collected over a two-week period, for one hour each day. Find the median, range, and interquartile range for each data set. If you had to choose one flower as having the more consistent visits, which would you choose? Explain your reasoning.

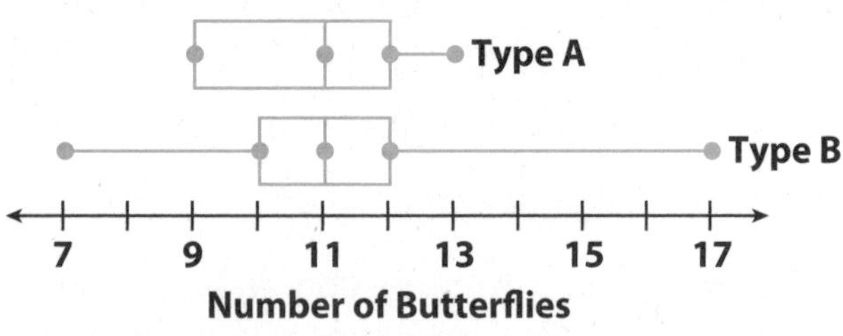

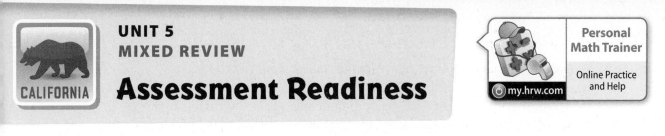

UNIT 5
MIXED REVIEW

CALIFORNIA

Assessment Readiness

Personal Math Trainer
Online Practice and Help
my.hrw.com

1. Zack wants to take a survey about the Internet use of students at his school. Consider each survey question. Is the question biased?

Select Yes or No for each question.

A. Which Internet service provider do you use? ○ Yes ○ No

B. How many hours do you waste surfing the Internet each week? ○ Yes ○ No

C. Do you agree that download times from the Internet are too slow? ○ Yes ○ No

2. Melanie randomly surveyed students about the distance they live from school. Use the box plot of the results to make an inference about most of these students. Explain your reasoning.

Distance from School

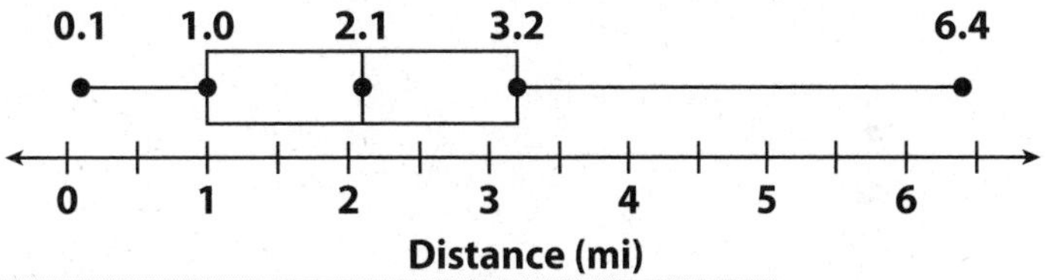

3. Melanie also made a box plot showing the distance the students in the sample live from the nearest park.

Choose True or False for each statement.

Distance from Nearest Park

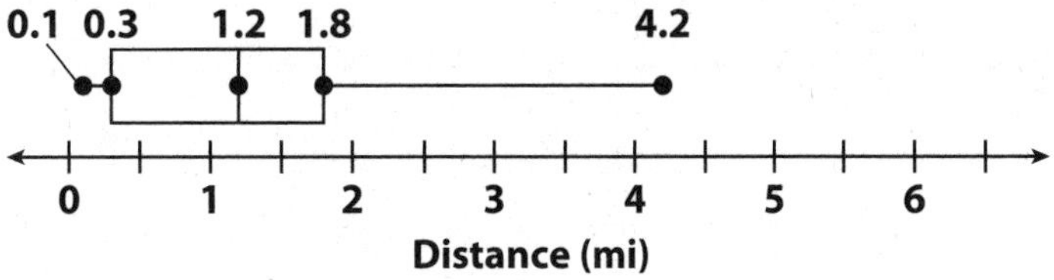

A. In general, the students live closer to a park than to school. ○ True ○ False

B. The park distances have a greater variability than the school distances. ○ True ○ False

C. The upper half of both data sets is more variable than the lower half. ○ True ○ False

4. One serving of a cereal is $\frac{3}{4}$ cup. Each box of cereal has about 9 cups of cereal and costs \$3.80. Is the price per serving greater than \$0.50? Explain.

Performance Tasks

★**5.** A random sample of 50 dogs at an animal shelter were tested for heartworms, and 4 tested positive. It costs the shelter $300 to treat a dog for heartworms. Estimate the yearly cost to treat all dogs at the shelter that test positive for heartworms, given that the shelter houses about 5,750 dogs per year. Explain your reasoning.

★★**6.** Corbin surveyed a random sample of 4th grade students and 7th grade students from his neighborhood about the number of days they exercise per week during the summer. The results are shown in the tables.

a. Make a box plot for each data set.

b. Compare the medians and the interquartile ranges of the data sets.

c. Based on the samples, do the 4th graders or the 7th graders exercise more often during the summer? Justify your answer.

Days of Exercise per Week, 4th Grade
4, 5, 2, 0, 6, 5, 7, 6, 4, 5, 5, 7

Days of Exercise per Week, 7th Grade
1, 5, 3, 2, 4, 0, 3, 0, 6, 4, 2, 2

★★★**7.** The grid contains the heights in feet of the 64 pine trees in a park.

a. Describe a method for randomly selecting 5 of the 64 pine trees. Use your method to select 2 random samples of 5 trees each.

b. Estimate the mean height of the pine trees in the park based on each sample. Are the samples large enough to give an accurate estimate of the mean height of the entire population? Justify your answer.

18	46	36	59	37	61	8	29
45	46	6	57	13	51	60	25
50	41	40	60	10	31	51	59
54	60	54	45	34	47	25	11
49	51	6	58	19	60	25	57
48	46	30	48	15	60	48	56
35	48	45	45	49	39	12	54
12	48	31	31	50	58	61	59

UNIT 6

Probability

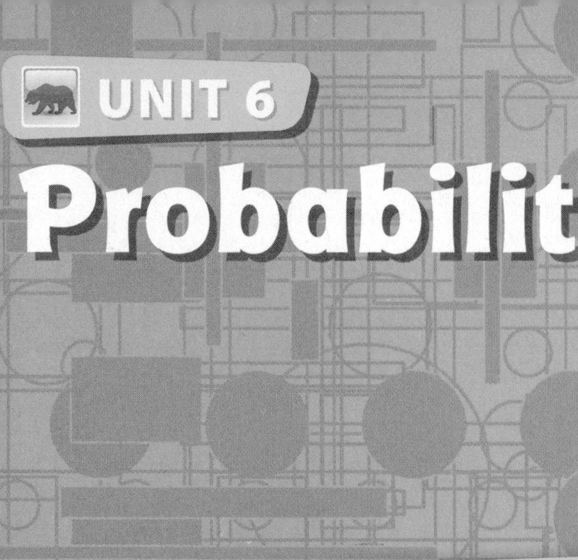

MODULE 12

Experimental Probability

CA CC 7.SP.5, 7.SP.6, 7.SP.7a, 7.SP.7b, 7.SP.8, 7.SP.8a, 7.SP.8b, 7.SP.8c

MODULE 13

Theoretical Probability and Simulations

CA CC 7.SP.6, 7.SP.7, 7.SP.7a, 7.SP.8, 7.SP.8a, 7.SP.8b, 7.SP.8c

MATH IN CAREERS

Meteorologist Meteorologists use scientific principles to explain, understand, observe, and forecast atmospheric phenomena and how the atmosphere affects us. They use math in many ways, such as calculating wind velocities, computing the probabilities of weather conditions, and creating and using mathematical models to predict weather patterns. If you are interested in a career as a meteorologist, you should study these mathematical subjects:

- Algebra
- Geometry
- Trigonometry
- Calculus
- Probability and Statistics

Research other careers that require computing probabilities and using mathematical models.

ACTIVITY At the end of the unit, check out how **meteorologists** use math.

Unit Project Preview

A Birthday Puzzle

In the Unit Project at the end of this unit, you will investigate an amazing fact about birthdays. You will explore the probability that two people in a group share the same birthday. To successfully complete the Unit Project you'll need to master these skills:

- Collect, organize, and analyze a set of data.
- Understand how to choose a random sample.
- Make predictions with experimental probability.

1. Explain how you could randomly select a sample of 25 students.

____

____

2. Describe an experiment you could perform to find the likelihood that if you tossed a paper cup, it would land on its bottom.

____

____

3. If others performed your paper cup experiment, would they get the same results? Explain.

____

Tracking Your Learning Progression

This unit addresses important California Common Core Standards in the Critical Area of developing probability models to solve real-world and mathematical problems.

Domain 7.SP Statistics and Probability

Cluster Investigate chance processes and develop, use, and evaluate probability models.

Experimental Probability

MODULE 12
CALIFORNIA

ESSENTIAL QUESTION

How can you use experimental probability to solve real-world problems?

my.hrw.com

Real-World Video

Meteorologists use sophisticated equipment to gather data about the weather. Then they use experimental probability to forecast, or predict, what the weather conditions will be.

GO DIGITAL
my.hrw.com

my.hrw.com

Go digital with your write-in student edition, accessible on any device.

Math On the Spot

Scan with your smart phone to jump directly to the online edition, video tutor, and more.

Animated Math

Interactively explore key concepts to see how math works.

Personal Math Trainer

Get immediate feedback and help as you work through practice sets.

Are YOU Ready?

Complete these exercises to review skills you will need for this module.

Personal Math Trainer

Online Practice and Help

Simplify Fractions

EXAMPLE Simplify $\frac{12}{21}$.

12: 1, 2, (3), 4, 6, 12 — List all the factors of the numerator and denominator.
21: 1, (3), 7, 21 — Circle the greatest common factor (GCF).

$\frac{12 \div 3}{21 \div 3} = \frac{4}{7}$ — Divide the numerator and denominator by the GCF.

Write each fraction in simplest form.

1. $\frac{6}{10}$ ______ **2.** $\frac{9}{15}$ ______ **3.** $\frac{16}{24}$ ______ **4.** $\frac{9}{36}$ ______

5. $\frac{45}{54}$ ______ **6.** $\frac{30}{42}$ ______ **7.** $\frac{36}{60}$ ______ **8.** $\frac{14}{42}$ ______

Write Fractions as Decimals

EXAMPLE $\frac{13}{25} \rightarrow$

$$\begin{array}{r} 0.52 \\ 25\overline{)13.00} \\ -12.5 \\ \hline 50 \\ -50 \\ \hline 0 \end{array}$$

Write the fraction as a division problem.
Write a decimal point and a zero in the dividend.
Place a decimal point in the quotient.
Write more zeros in the dividend if necessary.

Write each fraction as a decimal.

9. $\frac{3}{4}$ ______ **10.** $\frac{7}{8}$ ______ **11.** $\frac{3}{20}$ ______ **12.** $\frac{19}{50}$ ______

Percents and Decimals

EXAMPLE

$$\begin{aligned} 109\% &= 100\% + 9\% \\ &= \frac{100}{100} + \frac{9}{100} \\ &= 1 + 0.09 \\ &= 1.09 \end{aligned}$$

Write the percent as the sum of 1 whole and a percent remainder.
Write the percents as fractions.
Write the fractions as decimals.
Simplify.

Write each percent as a decimal.

13. 67% ______ **14.** 31% ______ **15.** 7% ______ **16.** 146% ______

Write each decimal as a percent.

17. 0.13 ______ **18.** 0.55 ______ **19.** 0.08 ______ **20.** 1.16 ______

Reading Start-Up

Visualize Vocabulary

Use the ✔ words to complete the graphic. You can put more than one word in each box.

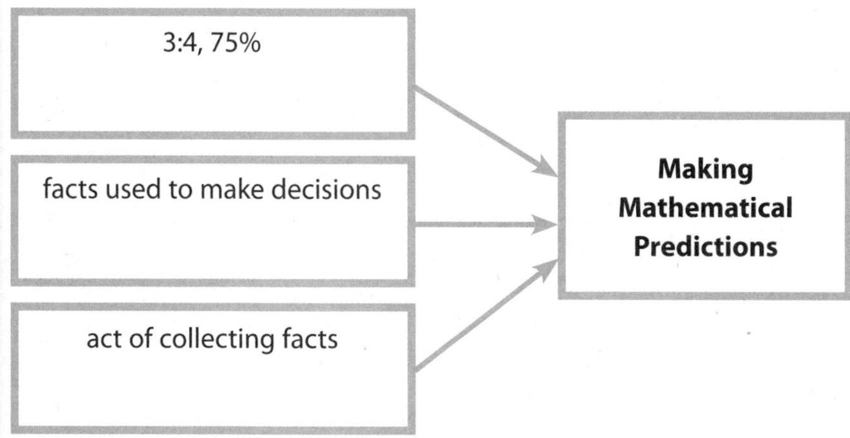

Understand Vocabulary

Match the term on the left to the definition on the right.

1. probability — **A.** Measures the likelihood that the event will occur.

2. trial — **B.** A set of one or more outcomes.

3. event — **C.** Each observation of an experiment.

Vocabulary

Review Words

✔ data *(datos)*
✔ observation *(observación)*
✔ percent *(porcentaje)*
✔ ratio *(razón)*

Preview Words

complement *(complemento)*
compound event *(suceso compuesto)*
event *(suceso)*
experiment *(experimento)*
experimental probability *(probabilidad experimental)*
outcome *(resultado)*
probability *(probabilidad)*
simple event *(suceso simple)*
simulation *(simulación)*
trial *(prueba)*

Active Reading

Pyramid Before beginning the module, create a rectangular pyramid to help you organize what you learn. Label each side with one of the lesson titles from this module. As you study each lesson, write important ideas, such as vocabulary, properties, and formulas, on the appropriate side.

GETTING READY FOR

Experimental Probability

Understanding the standards and the vocabulary terms in the standards will help you know exactly what you are expected to learn in this module.

CA CC 7.SP.6

Approximate the probability of a chance event by collecting data on the chance process that produces it and observing its long-run relative frequency, and predict the approximate relative frequency given the probability.

Key Vocabulary

simple event *(suceso simple)*
An event consisting of only one outcome.

experimental probability *(probabilidad experimental)*
The ratio of the number of times an event occurs to the total number of trials, or times that the activity is performed.

What It Means to You

You will use experimental probabilities to make predictions and solve problems.

EXAMPLE 7.SP.6

Caitlyn finds that the experimental probability of her making a goal in hockey is 30%. Out of 500 attempts to make a goal, about how many could she predict she would make?

$$\frac{3}{10} \cdot 500 = x$$

$$150 = x$$

Caitlyn can predict that she will make about 150 of the 500 goals that she attempts.

CA CC 7.SP.7b

Develop a probability model (which may not be uniform) by observing frequencies in data generated from a chance process.

Key Vocabulary

sample space *(espacio muestral)*
All possible outcomes of an experiment.

What It Means to You

You will use data to determine experimental probabilities.

EXAMPLE 7.SP.7b

Anders buys a novelty coin that is weighted more heavily on one side. He flips the coin 60 times and a head comes up 36 times. Based on his results, what is the experimental probability of flipping a head?

$$\text{experimental probability} = \frac{\text{number of times event occurs}}{\text{total number of trials}}$$

$$= \frac{36}{60} = \frac{3}{5}$$

The experimental probability of flipping a head is $\frac{3}{5}$.

Visit **my.hrw.com** to see all **CA Common Core Standards** explained.

my.hrw.com

LESSON

12.1 Probability

Understand that the probability of a chance event is a number between 0 and 1 that expresses the likelihood of the event occurring. Larger numbers indicate greater likelihood. A probability near 0 indicates an unlikely event, a probability around $\frac{1}{2}$ indicates an event that is neither unlikely nor likely, and a probability near 1 indicates a likely event. *Also 7.SP.7a*

How can you describe the likelihood of an event?

EXPLORE ACTIVITY 

Finding the Likelihood of an Event

Each time you roll a number cube, a number from 1 to 6 lands face up. This is called an *event*.

Work with a partner to decide how many of the six possible results of rolling a number cube match the described event.

Then order the events from least likely (1) to most likely (9) by writing a number in each box to the right.

Rolling a number less than 7 ______ ☐

Rolling an 8 ______ ☐

Rolling a number greater than 4 ______ ☐

Rolling a 5 ______ ☐

Rolling a number other than 6 ______ ☐

Rolling an even number ______ ☐

Rolling a number less than 5 ______ ☐

Rolling an odd number ______ ☐

Rolling a number divisible by 3 ______ ☐

Reflect

1. Are any of the events impossible? ______

______

Describing Events

An **experiment** is an activity involving chance in which results are observed. Each observation of an experiment is a **trial**, and each result is an **outcome**. A set of one or more outcomes is an **event**.

The **probability** of an event, written *P*(event), measures the likelihood that the event will occur. Probability is a measure between 0 and 1 as shown on the number line, and can be written as a fraction, a decimal, or a percent.

If the event is not likely to occur, the probability of the event is close to 0. If an event is likely to occur, the event's probability is closer to 1.

Impossible	Unlikely	As likely as not	Likely	Certain
0		$\frac{1}{2}$		1
0		0.5		1.0
0%		50%		100%

EXAMPLE 1

Tell whether each event is impossible, unlikely, as likely as not, likely, or certain. Then, tell whether the probability is 0, close to 0, $\frac{1}{2}$, close to 1, or 1.

A You roll a six-sided number cube and the number is 1 or greater.

This event is certain to happen. Its probability is 1.

> Because you can roll the numbers 1, 2, 3, 4, 5, and 6 on a number cube, there are 6 possible outcomes.

B You roll two number cubes and the sum of the numbers is 3.

This event is unlikely to happen. Its probability is close to 0.

C A bowl contains disks marked with the numbers 1 through 10. You close your eyes and select a disk at random. You pick an odd number.

This event is as likely as not. The probability is $\frac{1}{2}$.

D A spinner has 8 equal sections marked 0 through 7. You spin and land on a prime number.

This event is as likely as not. The probability is $\frac{1}{2}$.

> Remember that a prime number is a whole number greater than 1 and has exactly 2 divisors, 1 and itself.

Math Talk
Mathematical Practices

Is an event that is *not* certain an impossible event? Explain.

Reflect

2. The probability of event *A* is $\frac{1}{3}$. The probability of event *B* is $\frac{1}{4}$. What can you conclude about the two events?

YOUR TURN

3. A hat contains pieces of paper marked with the numbers 1 through 16. Tell whether picking an even number is impossible, unlikely, as likely as not, likely, or certain. Tell whether the probability is 0, close to 0, $\frac{1}{2}$, close to 1, or 1.

____

Personal Math Trainer

Online Practice and Help

my.hrw.com

Finding Probability

A **sample space** is the set of all possible outcomes for an experiment. A sample space can be small, such as the 2 outcomes when a coin is flipped. Or a sample space can be large, such as the possible number of Texas Classic automobile license plates. Identifying the sample space can help you calculate the probability of an event.

Math On the Spot

my.hrw.com

Probability of An Event

$$P(\text{event}) = \frac{\text{number of outcomes in the event}}{\text{number of outcomes in the sample space}}$$

EXAMPLE 2

What is the probability of rolling an even number on a standard number cube?

STEP 1 Find the sample space for a standard number cube.

{1, 2, 3, 4, 5, 6}   *There are 6 possible outcomes.*

STEP 2 Find the number of ways to roll an even number.

2, 4, 6   *The event can occur 3 ways.*

STEP 3 Find the probability of rolling an even number.

$$P(\text{even}) = \frac{\text{number of ways to roll an even number}}{\text{number of faces on a number cube}}$$

$$= \frac{3}{6} = \frac{1}{2}$$ *Substitute values and simplify.*

The probability of rolling an even number is $\frac{1}{2}$.

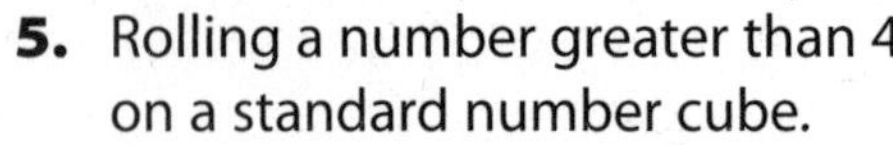

YOUR TURN

Find each probability. Write your answer in simplest form.

4. Picking a purple marble from a jar with 10 green and 10 purple marbles. ______

5. Rolling a number greater than 4 on a standard number cube. ______

Using the Complement of an Event

The **complement** of an event is the set of all outcomes in the sample space that are *not* included in the event. For example, in the event of rolling a 3 on a number cube, the complement is rolling any number other than 3, which means the complement is rolling a 1, 2, 4, 5, or 6.

An Event and Its Complement

The sum of the probabilities of an event and its complement equals 1.

$$P(\text{event}) + P(\text{complement}) = 1$$

You can apply probabilities to situations involving random selection, such as drawing a card out of a shuffled deck or pulling a marble out of a closed bag.

EXAMPLE 3

There are 2 red jacks in a standard deck of 52 cards. What is the probability of not getting a red jack if you select one card at random?

$$P(\text{event}) + P(\text{complement}) = 1$$

$P(\text{red jack}) + P(\text{not a red jack}) = 1$ — The probability of getting a red jack is $\frac{2}{52}$.

$\frac{2}{52} + P(\text{not a red jack}) = 1$ — Substitute $\frac{2}{52}$ for $P(\text{red jack})$.

$\frac{2}{52} + P(\text{not a red jack}) = \frac{52}{52}$ — Subtract $\frac{2}{52}$ from both sides.

$-\frac{2}{52} \qquad\qquad -\frac{2}{52}$

$P(\text{not a red jack}) = \frac{50}{52}$

$P(\text{not a red jack}) = \frac{25}{26}$ — Simplify.

The probability that you will not draw a red jack is $\frac{25}{26}$. It is likely that you will not select a red jack.

Reflect

6. Why do the probability of an event and the probability of its complement add up to 1?

____

____

____

____

____

YOUR TURN

7. A jar contains 8 marbles marked with the numbers 1 through 8. You pick a marble at random. What is the probability of not picking the marble marked with the number 5? __________

8. You roll a standard number cube. Use the probability of rolling an even number to find the probability of rolling an odd number. __________

Personal Math Trainer

Online Practice and Help

my.hrw.com

Guided Practice

1. In a hat, you have index cards with the numbers 1 through 10 written on them. Order the events from least likely to happen (1) to most likely to happen (8) when you pick one card at random. In the boxes, write a number from 1 to 8 to order the eight different events. (Explore Activity)

You pick a number greater than 0.	☐
You pick an even number.	☐
You pick a number that is at least 2.	☐
You pick a number that is at most 0.	☐
You pick a number divisible by 3.	☐
You pick a number divisible by 5.	☐
You pick a prime number.	☐
You pick a number less than the greatest prime number.	☐

Guided Practice

Determine whether each event is impossible, unlikely, as likely as not, likely, or certain. Then, tell whether the probability is 0, close to 0, $\frac{1}{2}$, close to 1, or 1. (Example 1)

2. randomly picking a green card from a standard deck of playing cards

____

3. randomly picking a red card from a standard deck of playing cards

____

4. picking a number less than 15 from a jar with papers labeled from 1 to 12

____

5. picking a number that is divisible by 5 from a jar with papers labeled from 1 to 12

____

Find each probability. Write your answer in simplest form. (Example 2)

6. spinning a spinner that has 5 equal sections marked 1 through 5 and landing on an even number

____

7. picking a diamond from a standard deck of playing cards which has 13 cards in each of four suits: spades, hearts, diamonds and clubs

____

Use the complement to find each probability. (Example 3)

8. What is the probability of not rolling a 5 on a standard number cube?

____

9. A spinner has 3 equal sections that are red, white, and blue. What is the probability of not landing on blue?

____

10. A spinner has 5 equal sections marked 1 through 5. What is the probability of not landing on 4?

____

11. There are 4 queens in a standard deck of 52 cards. You pick one card at random. What is the probability of not picking a queen?

____

ESSENTIAL QUESTION CHECK-IN

12. Describe an event that has a probability of 0% and an event that has a probability of 100%.

____

____

____

Name ________________ Class ________________ Date ________________

12.1 Independent Practice

7.SP.5, 7.SP.7a

13. There are 4 aces and 4 kings in a standard deck of 52 cards. You pick one card at random. What is the probability of selecting an ace or a king? Explain your reasoning.

____

____

14. There are 12 pieces of fruit in a bowl. Seven of the pieces are apples and two are peaches. What is the probability that a randomly selected piece of fruit will not be an apple or a peach? Justify your answer.

____

____

15. **Critique Reasoning** For breakfast, Clarissa can choose from oatmeal, cereal, French toast, or scrambled eggs. She thinks that if she selects a breakfast at random, it is likely that it will be oatmeal. Is she correct? Explain your reasoning.

____

____

____

16. **Draw Conclusions** A researcher's garden contains 90 sweet pea plants, which have either white or purple flowers. About 70 of the plants have purple flowers, and about 20 have white flowers. Would you expect that one plant randomly selected from the garden will have purple or white flowers? Explain.

____

____

____

____

17. The power goes out as Sandra is trying to get dressed. If she has 4 white T-shirts and 10 colored T-shirts in her drawer, is it likely that she will pick a colored T-shirt in the dark? What is the probability she will pick a colored T-shirt? Explain your answers.

____

____

18. James counts the hair colors of the 22 people in his class, including himself. He finds that there are 4 people with blonde hair, 8 people with brown hair, and 10 people with black hair. What is the probability that a randomly chosen student in the class does not have red hair? Explain.

____

____

19. **Persevere in Problem Solving** A bag contains 8 blue coins and 6 red coins. A coin is removed at random and replaced by three of the other color.

a. What is the probability that the removed coin is blue?

____

b. If the coin removed is blue, what is the probability of drawing a red coin after three red coins are put in the bag to replace the blue one?

____

c. If the coin removed is red, what is the probability of drawing a red coin after three blue coins are put in the bag to replace the red one?

____

H.O.T. FOCUS ON HIGHER ORDER THINKING

Work Area

20. **Draw Conclusions** Give an example of an event in which all of the outcomes are not equally likely. Explain.

____

____

____

21. **Critique Reasoning** A box contains 150 black pens and 50 red pens. Jose said the sum of the probability that a randomly selected pen will not be black and the probability that the pen will not be red is 1. Explain whether you agree.

____

____

____

22. **Communicate Mathematical Ideas** A spinner has 7 identical sections. Two sections are blue, 1 is red, and 4 of the sections are green. Suppose the probability of an event happening is $\frac{2}{7}$. What does each number in the ratio represent? What outcome matches this probability?

____

____

LESSON 12.2

Experimental Probability of Simple Events

CA CC 7.SP.6

Approximate the probability of a chance event by collecting data on the chance process that produces it and observing its long-run relative frequency, and predict the approximate relative frequency given the probability. *Also 7.SP.7b*

ESSENTIAL QUESTION

How do you find the experimental probability of a simple event?

EXPLORE ACTIVITY

CA CC 7.SP.6, 7.SP.7b

Finding Experimental Probability

You can toss a paper cup to demonstrate *experimental probability*.

A Consider tossing a paper cup. Fill in the Outcome column of the table with the three different ways the cup could land.

B Toss a paper cup twenty times. Record your observations in the table.

Outcome	Number of Times

Reflect

1. Do the outcomes appear to be equally likely? ____________________

2. Describe the three outcomes using the words *likely* and *unlikely*.

____

____

3. Use the number of times each event occurred to approximate the probability of each event.

4. **Make a Prediction** What do you think would happen if you performed more trials?

____

____

____

5. What is the sum of the probabilities in 3?

____

Outcome	Experimental Probability
Open-end up	$\frac{\text{open-end up}}{20} = \frac{\square}{20}$
Open-end down	$\frac{\text{open-end down}}{20} = \frac{\square}{20}$
On its side	$\frac{\text{on its side}}{20} = \frac{\square}{20}$

Calculating Experimental Probability

You can use *experimental probability* to approximate the probability of an event. An **experimental probability** of an event is found by comparing the number of times the event occurs to the total number of trials. When there is only one outcome for an event, it is called a **simple event**.

Experimental Probability

For a given experiment:

$$\text{Experimental probability} = \frac{\text{number of times the event occurs}}{\text{total number of trials}}$$

EXAMPLE 1

CA CC 7.SP.7b

Martin has a bag of marbles. He removed one marble at random, recorded the color and then placed it back in the bag. He repeated this process several times and recorded his results in the table. Find the experimental probability of drawing each color.

Color	Frequency
Red	12
Blue	10
Green	15
Yellow	13

STEP 1 Identify the number of trials: $12 + 10 + 15 + 13 = 50$

STEP 2 Complete the table of experimental probabilities. Write each answer as a fraction in simplest form.

Color	Experimental Probability
Red	$\frac{\text{frequency of the event}}{\text{total number of trials}} = \frac{12}{50} = \frac{6}{25}$
Blue	$\frac{\text{frequency of the event}}{\text{total number of trials}} = \frac{10}{50} = \frac{1}{5}$
Green	$\frac{\text{frequency of the event}}{\text{total number of trials}} = \frac{15}{50} = \frac{3}{10}$
Yellow	$\frac{\text{frequency of the event}}{\text{total number of trials}} = \frac{13}{50}$

Substitute the results recorded in the table. You can also write each probability as a decimal or as a percent.

Reflect

6. **Communicate Mathematical Ideas** What are two different ways you could find the experimental probability of the event that Martin does **not** draw a red marble?

7. A spinner has three unequal sections: red, yellow, and blue. The table shows the results of Nolan's spins. Find the experimental probability of landing on each color. Write your answers in simplest form.

Color	Frequency
Red	10
Yellow	14
Blue	6

____

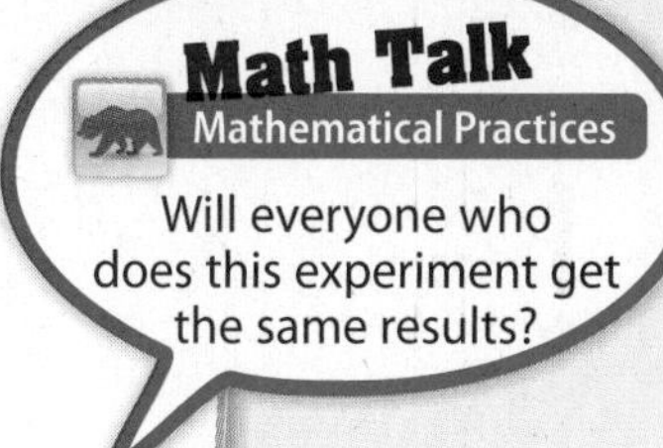

Math Talk
Mathematical Practices
Will everyone who does this experiment get the same results?

Making Predictions with Experimental Probability

A **simulation** is a model of an experiment that would be difficult or inconvenient to actually perform. You can use a simulation to find an experimental probability and make a prediction.

EXAMPLE 2

My Notes

A baseball team has a batting average of 0.250 so far this season. This means that the team's players get hits in 25% of their chances at bat. Use a simulation to predict the number of hits the team's players will have in their next 34 chances at bat.

STEP 1 Choose a model.

Batting average $= 0.250 = \frac{250}{1,000} = \frac{1}{4}$

A standard deck of cards has four suits, hearts, diamonds, spades, and clubs. Since $\frac{1}{4}$ of the cards are hearts, you can let hearts represent a "hit." Diamonds, clubs, and spades then represent "no hit."

STEP 2 Perform the simulation.

Draw a card at random from the deck, record the result, and put the card back into the deck. Continue until you have drawn and replaced 34 cards in all.

Since the team has 34 chances at bat, you must draw a card 34 times.

(H = heart, D = diamond, C = club, S = spade)

H D D S H C H S D H C D C C D H H
S D D H C C H C H H D S S S C H D

STEP 3 Make a prediction.

Count the number of hearts in the simulation.

Since there are 11 hearts, you can predict that the team will have 11 hits in its next 34 chances at bat.

YOUR TURN

8. A toy machine has equal numbers of red, white, and blue foam balls which it releases at random. Ross wonders which color ball will be released next. Describe how you could use a standard number cube to predict the answer.

____

____

____

____

____

Guided Practice

1. A spinner has four sections lettered A, B, C, and D. The table shows the results of several spins. Find the experimental probability of spinning each letter as a fraction in simplest form, a decimal, and a percent. (Explore Activity and Example 1)

Letter	A	B	C	D
Frequency	14	7	11	8

A: _______________ B: _______________

C: _______________ D: _______________

2. Rachel's free-throw average for basketball is 60%. She wants to predict how many times in the next 50 tries she will make a free throw. Describe how she could use 10 index cards to predict the answer. (Example 2)

____

____

____

ESSENTIAL QUESTION CHECK-IN

3. **Essential Question Follow Up** How do you find an experimental probability of a simple event?

____

____

Name__________ Class__________ Date__________

12.2 Independent Practice

7.SP.6, 7.SP.7b

4. Dree rolls a strike in 6 out of the 10 frames of bowling. What is the experimental probability that Dree will roll a strike in the first frame of the next game? Explain why a number cube would not be a good way to simulate this situation.

____

____

____

5. To play a game, you spin a spinner like the one shown. You win if the arrow lands in one of the areas marked "WIN". Lee played this game many times and recorded her results. She won 8 times and lost 40 times. Use Lee's data to explain how to find the experimental probability of winning this game.

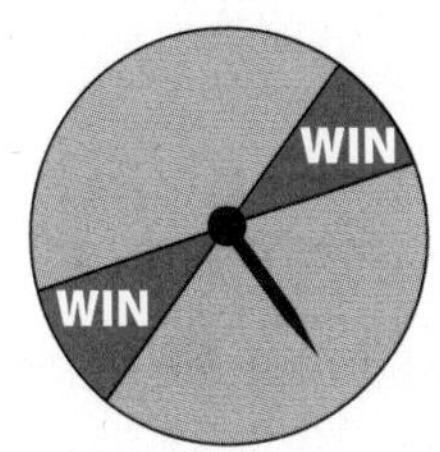

____

____

6. The names of the students in Mr. Hayes' math class are written on the board. Mr. Hayes writes each name on an index card and shuffles the cards. Each day he randomly draws a card, and the chosen student explains a math problem at the board. What is the probability that Ryan is chosen today? What is the probability that Ryan is **not** chosen today?

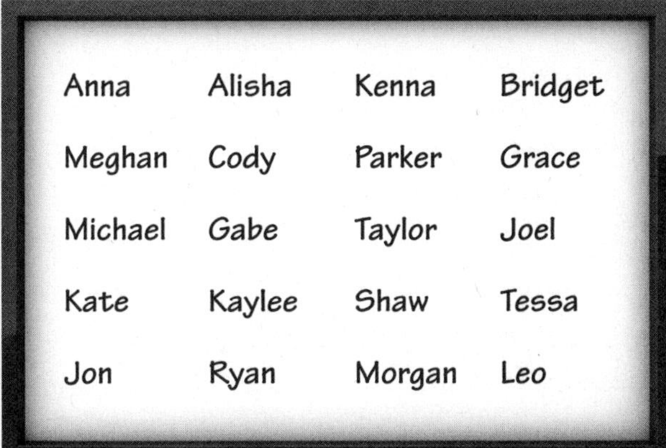

Anna
Alisha
Kenna
Bridget
Meghan
Cody
Parker
Grace
Michael
Gabe
Taylor
Joel
Kate
Kaylee
Shaw
Tessa
Jon
Ryan
Morgan
Leo

____

7. **Critique Reasoning** A meteorologist reports an 80% chance of precipitation. Is this an example of experimental probability, written as a percent? Explain your reasoning.

____

8. Mica and Joan are on the same softball team. Mica got 8 hits out of 48 times at bat, while Joan got 12 hits out of 40 times at bat. Who do you think is more likely to get a hit her next time at bat? Explain.

9. **Make a Prediction** In tennis, Gabby serves an ace, a ball that can't be returned, 4 out of the 10 times she serves. What is the experimental probability that Gabby will serve an ace in the first match of the next game? Make a prediction about how many aces Gabby will have for the next 40 serves. Justify your reasoning.

10. **Represent Real-World Problems** Patricia finds that the experimental probability that her dog will want to go outside between 4 P.M. and 5 P.M. is $\frac{7}{12}$. About what percent of the time does her dog **not** want to go out between 4 P.M. and 5 P.M.?

H.O.T. FOCUS ON HIGHER ORDER THINKING

Work Area

11. **Explain the Error** Talia tossed a penny many times. She got 40 heads and 60 tails. She said the experimental probability of getting heads was $\frac{40}{60}$. Explain and correct her error.

12. **Communicate Mathematical Ideas** A high school has 438 students, with about the same number of males as females. Describe a simulation to predict how many of the first 50 students who leave school at the end of the day are female.

13. **Critical Thinking** For a scavenger hunt, Chessa put one coin in each of 10 small boxes. Four coins are quarters, 4 are dimes, and 2 are nickels. How could you simulate choosing one box at random? Would you use the same simulation if you planned to put these coins in your pocket and choose one? Explain your reasoning.

LESSON 12.3

Experimental Probability of Compound Events

CA CC 7.SP.8

Find probabilities of compound events using organized lists, tables, tree diagrams, and simulation. *Also 7.SP.8a, 7.SP.8b, 7.SP.8c*

ESSENTIAL QUESTION

How do you find the experimental probability of a compound event?

EXPLORE ACTIVITY CA CC 7.SP.8a, 7.SP.8b

Exploring Compound Probability

A **compound event** is an event that includes two or more simple events, such as flipping a coin *and* rolling a number cube. A compound event can include events that depend on each other or are independent. Events are independent if the occurrence of one event does not affect the probability of the other event, such as flipping a coin and rolling a number cube.

A What are the possible outcomes of flipping a coin once? ______

B What are the possible outcomes of rolling a standard number cube once? ______

C Complete the list for all possible outcomes for flipping a coin *and* rolling a number cube.

H1, H2, ____, ____, ____, ____, T1, ____, ____, ____, ____, ____

There are ______ possible outcomes for this compound event.

H1 would mean the coin landed on heads, and the number cube showed a 1.

D Flip a coin and roll a number cube 50 times. Use tally marks to record your results in the table.

	1	2	3	4	5	6
H						
T						

E Based on your data, which compound event had the greatest experimental probability and what was it? The least experimental probability? ______

F **Draw Conclusions** Did you expect to have the same probability for each possible combination of flips and rolls? Why or why not?

______

______

Calculating Experimental Probability of Compound Events

The experimental probability of a compound event can be found using recorded data.

EXAMPLE 1

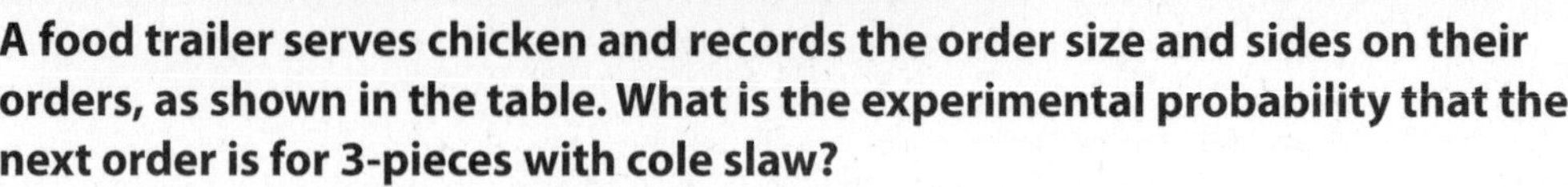

A food trailer serves chicken and records the order size and sides on their orders, as shown in the table. What is the experimental probability that the next order is for 3-pieces with cole slaw?

	Green Salad	Macaroni & Cheese	French Fries	Cole Slaw
2 pieces	33	22	52	35
3 pieces	13	55	65	55

STEP 1 Find the total number of trials, or orders.

$33 + 22 + 52 + 35 + 13 + 55 + 65 + 55 = 330$

STEP 2 Find the number of orders that are for 3 pieces with cole slaw: 55.

STEP 3 Find the experimental probability.

$$P(3 \text{ piece} + \text{slaw}) = \frac{\text{number of 3 piece} + \text{slaw}}{\text{total number of orders}}$$

$$= \frac{55}{330} \quad \textit{Substitute the values.}$$

$$= \frac{1}{6} \quad \textit{Simplify.}$$

The experimental probability that the next order is for 3 pieces of chicken with cole slaw is $\frac{1}{6}$.

Javier said the total number of orders is 8 and not 330. Is he correct? Explain.

YOUR TURN

1. Drink sales for an afternoon at the school carnival were recorded in the table. What is the experimental probability that the next drink is a small cocoa?

	Soda	Water	Cocoa
Small	77	98	60
Large	68	45	52

____

Using a Simulation to Make a Prediction

You can use a simulation or model of an experiment to find the experimental probability of compound events.

EXAMPLE 2 Real World  CA CC 7.SP.8c

At a street intersection, a vehicle is classified either as a *car* or a *truck*, and it can turn *left*, *right*, or go *straight*. About an equal number of cars and trucks go through the intersection and turn in each direction. Use a simulation to find the experimental probability that the next vehicle will be a car that turns right.

STEP 1 Choose a model.

Use a coin toss to model the two vehicle types.
Let Heads = Car and Tails = Truck

Use a spinner divided into 3 equal sectors to represent the *three* directions as shown.

STEP 2 Find the sample space for the compound event.

There are 6 possible outcomes: CL, CR, CS, TL, TR, TS

STEP 3 Perform the simulation.

A coin was tossed and a spinner spun 50 times. The results are shown in the table.

	Car	Truck
Left	8	9
Right	6	11
Straight	9	7

STEP 4 Find the experimental probability that a car turns right.

$$P(\text{Car turns right}) = \frac{\text{frequency of compound event}}{\text{total number of trials}}$$

$$= \frac{6}{50} \quad \text{Substitute the values.}$$

$$= \frac{3}{25} \quad \text{Simplify.}$$

Based on the simulation, the experimental probability is $\frac{3}{25}$ that the next vehicle will be a car that turns right.

My Notes

Reflect

2. **Make a Prediction** Predict the number of cars that turn right out of 100 vehicles that enter the intersection. Explain your reasoning.

____

____

YOUR TURN

3. A jeweler sells necklaces made in three sizes and two different metals. Use the data from a simulation to find the experimental probability that the next necklace sold is a 20-inch gold necklace.

	Silver	Gold
12 in.	12	22
16 in.	16	8
20 in.	5	12

____

Guided Practice

1. A dentist has 400 male and female patients that range in ages from 10 years old to 50 years old and up as shown in the table. What is the experimental probability that the next patient will be female and in the age range 22–39? (Explore Activity and Example 1)

	Range: 10–21	Range: 22–39	Range: 40–50	Range: 50+
Male	44	66	32	53
Female	36	50	45	74

____

2. At a car wash, customers can choose the type of wash and whether to use the interior vacuum. Customers are equally likely to choose each type of wash and whether to use the vacuum. Use a simulation to find the experimental probability that the next customer purchases a deluxe wash and no interior vacuum. Describe your simulation. (Example 2)

____

____

____

ESSENTIAL QUESTION CHECK-IN

3. How do you find the experimental probability of a compound event?

____

____

Name ____________ Class ____________ Date ____________

12.3 Independent Practice

 CA CC 7.SP.8, 7.SP.8a, 7.SP.8b, 7.SP.8c

Personal Math Trainer

Online Practice and Help

4. **Represent Real-World Problems** For the same food trailer mentioned in Example 1, explain how to find the experimental probability that the next order is two pieces of chicken with a green salad.

____

____

The school store sells spiral notebooks in four colors and three different sizes. The table shows the sales by size and color for 400 notebooks.

	Red	Green	Blue	Yellow
100 Pages	55	37	26	12
150 Pages	60	44	57	27
200 Pages	23	19	21	19

5. What is the experimental probability that the next customer buys a red notebook with 150 pages?

____

6. What is the experimental probability that the next customer buys any red notebooks?

____

7. **Analyze Relationships** How many possible combined page count and color choices are possible? How does this number relate to the number of page size choices and to the number of color choices?

____

____

A middle school English teacher polled random students about how many pages of a book they read per week.

	6th	7th	8th
75 Pages	24	18	22
100 Pages	22	32	24
150 Pages	30	53	25

8. **Critique Reasoning** Jennie says the experimental probability that a 7th grade student reads at least 100 pages per week is $\frac{16}{125}$. What is her error and the correct experimental probability?

____

9. **Analyze Relationships** Based on the data, which group(s) of students should be encouraged to read more? Explain your reasoning.

____

____

Work Area

10. Make a Conjecture Would you expect the probability for the simple event "rolling a 6" to be greater than or less than the probability of the compound event "rolling a 6 and getting heads on a coin"? Explain.

____

____

11. Critique Reasoning Donald says he uses a standard number cube for simulations that involve 2, 3, or 6 equal outcomes. Explain how Donald can do this.

____

____

____

12. Draw Conclusions Data collected in a mall recorded the shoe styles worn by 150 male and for 150 female customers. What is the probability that the next customer is male and has an open-toe shoe (such as a sandal)? What is the probability that the next male customer has an open-toe shoe? Are the two probabilities the same? Explain.

	Male	Female
Open toe	11	92
Closed toe	139	58

____

____

____

13. What If? Suppose you wanted to perform a simulation to model the shoe style data shown in the table. Could you use two coins? Explain.

____

____

14. Represent Real-World Problems A middle school is made up of grades 6, 7, and 8, and has about the same number of male and female students in each grade. Explain how to use a simulation to find the experimental probability that the first 50 students who arrive at school are male and 7th graders.

____

____

____

____

LESSON 12.4

Making Predictions with Experimental Probability

CA CC 7.SP.6

Approximate the probability of a chance event by collecting data on the chance process that produces it and observing its long-run relative frequency, and predict the approximate relative frequency given the probability.

ESSENTIAL QUESTION

How do you make predictions using experimental probability?

Using Experimental Probability to Make a Prediction

Scientists study data to make predictions. You can use probabilities to make predictions in your daily life.

EXAMPLE 1

CA CC 7.SP.6

Danae found that the experimental probability of her making a bull's-eye when throwing darts is $\frac{2}{10}$, or 20%. Out of 75 throws, about how many bull's-eyes could she predict she would make?

Method 1: Use a proportion.

$\frac{2}{10} = \frac{x}{75}$ Write a proportion. 2 out of 10 is how many out of 75?

$\frac{2}{10} = \frac{x}{75}$ ($\times 7.5$)

$\frac{2}{10} = \frac{15}{75}$ ($\times 7.5$) Since 10 times 7.5 is 75, multiply 2 times 7.5 to find the value of x.

$x = 15$

Method 2: Use a percent equation.

$0.20 \cdot 75 = x$ Find 20% of 75.

$15 = x$

You can write probabilities as ratios, decimals, or percents.

Danae can predict that she will make about 15 bull's-eye throws out of 75.

YOUR TURN

1. A car rental company sells accident insurance to 24% of its customers. Out of 550 customers, about how many customers are predicted to purchase insurance? ________________

Using Experimental Probability to Make a Qualitative Prediction

A prediction is something you reasonably expect to happen in the future. A qualitative prediction helps you decide which situation is more likely in general.

EXAMPLE 2 

A doctor's office records data and concludes that, on average, 11% of patients call to reschedule their appointments per week. The office manager predicts that 23 appointments will be rescheduled out of the 240 total appointments during next week. Explain whether the prediction is reasonable.

Method 1: Use a proportion.

$\frac{11}{100} = \frac{x}{240}$ Write a proportion. 11 out of 100 is how many out of 240?

$\frac{11}{100} = \frac{x}{240}$ (× 2.4)

$\frac{11}{100} = \frac{26.4}{240}$ (× 2.4) Since 100 times 2.4 is 240, multiply 11 times 2.4 to find the value of x.

$x = 26.4$

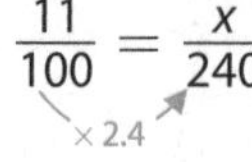

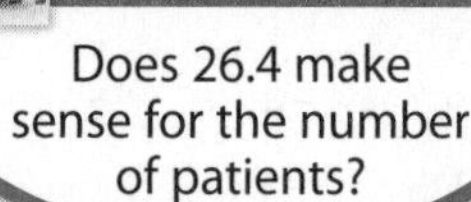

Does 26.4 make sense for the number of patients?

26.4 is the average number of patients that would call to reschedule.

Method 2: Use a percent equation.

$0.11 \cdot 240 = x$ Find 11% of 240.

$26.4 = x$ Solve for x.

The prediction of 23 is reasonable but a little low, because 23 is a little less than 26.4.

YOUR TURN

2. In emails to monthly readers of a newsletter 3% of the emails come back undelivered. The editor predicts that if he sends out 12,372 emails, he will receive 437 notices for undelivered email. Do you agree with his prediction?

Explain. ____

____

____

Making a Quantitative Prediction

You can use proportional reasoning to make quantitative predictions and compare options in real-world situations.

EXAMPLE 3

CA CC 7.SP.6

An online poll for a movie site shows its polling results for a new movie. If a newspaper surveys 150 people leaving the movie, how many people can it predict will like the movie based on the online poll? Is the movie site's claim accurate if the newspaper has 104 people say they like the movie?

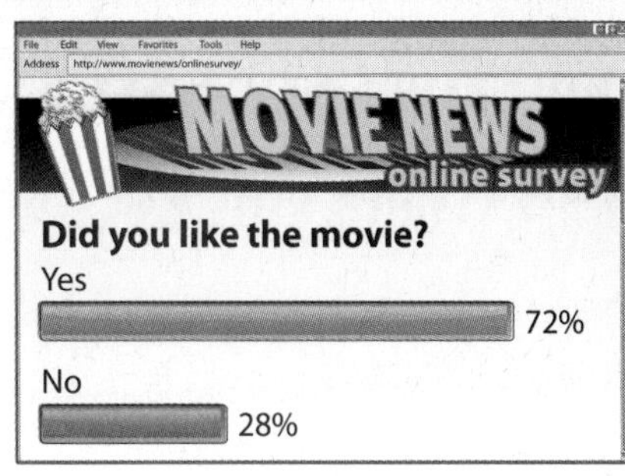

Analyze Information

The **answer** is a prediction for how many people out of 150 will like the movie based on the online poll. Also tell whether the 104 people that say they like the movie is enough to support the movie site's claim.

List the important information:

- The online poll says 72% of movie goers like the new movie.
- A newspaper surveys 150 people.

Formulate a Plan

Use a proportion to calculate 72% of the 150 people surveyed.

Solve

$\frac{72}{100} = \frac{x}{150}$ *Set up a proportion. 72 out of 100 is how many out of 150?*

$\frac{72}{100} = \frac{x}{150}$ (×1.5)

$\frac{72}{100} = \frac{108}{150}$ (×1.5) *Since 100 times 1.5 is 150, multiply 72 times 1.5 to find the value of x.*

$x = 108$

The newspaper can predict that 108 out of 150 people will say they like the movie, based on the online poll.

Justify and Evaluate

Since 108 is close to 104, the newspaper survey and the online poll show that about the same percent of people like the movie.

My Notes

YOUR TURN

3. On average, 24% of customers who buy shoes in a particular store buy two or more pairs. One weekend, 350 customers purchased shoes. How many can be predicted to buy two or more pairs? If 107 customers buy more than two pairs, did more customers than normal buy two or more pairs?

Guided Practice

1. A baseball player reaches first base 30% of the times he is at bat. Out of 50 times at bat, about how many times will the player reach first base? (Example 1)

2. The experimental probability that it will rain on any given day in Houston, Texas, is about 15%. Out of 365 days, about how many days can residents predict rain? (Example 1)

3. A catalog store has 6% of its orders returned for a refund. The owner predicts that a new candle will have 812 returns out of the 16,824 sold. Do you agree with this prediction? Explain. (Example 2)

4. On a toy assembly line, 3% of the toys are found to be defective. The quality control officer predicts that 872 toys will be found defective out of 24,850 toys made. Do you agree with this prediction? Explain. (Example 2)

5. A light-rail service claims to be on time 98% of the time. Jeanette takes the light-rail 40 times one month, how many times can she predict she will be on time? Is the light-rail's claim accurate if she is late 6 times? (Example 3)

6. On average, a college claims to accept 18% of its applicants. If the college has 5,000 applicants, predict how many will be accepted. If 885 applicants are accepted, is the college's claim accurate? (Example 3)

ESSENTIAL QUESTION CHECK-IN

7. How do you make predictions using experimental probability?

Name ______________________ Class ______________________ Date ______________________

12.4 Independent Practice

CA CC 7.SP.6

The table shows the number of students in a middle school at the beginning of the year and the percentage that can be expected to move out of the area by the end of the year.

	6th	7th	8th
Number of Students	250	200	150
% Moves	2%	4%	8%

8. How many 7th grade students are expected to move by the end of the year? If 12 students actually moved, did more or fewer 7th grade students move than expected? Justify your answer.

____

____

9. Critique Reasoning The middle school will lose some of its funding if 50 or more students move away in any year. The principal claims he only loses about 30 students a year. Do the values in the table support his claim? Explain.

____

____

____

10. Represent Real-World Problems An airline knows that, on average, the probability that a passenger will not show up for a flight is 6%. If an airplane is fully booked and holds 300 passengers, how many seats are expected to be empty? If the airline overbooked the flight by 10 passengers, about how many passengers are expected to show up for the flight? Justify your answer.

____

____

____

____

11. Draw Conclusions In a doctor's office, an average of 94% of the clients pay on the day of the appointment. If the office has 600 clients per month, how many are expected not to pay on the day of the appointment? If 40 clients do not pay on the day of their appointment in a month, did more or fewer than the average not pay?

____

12. **Counterexamples** The soccer coach claimed that, on average, only 80% of the team come to practice each day. The table shows the number of students that came to practice for 8 days. If the team has 20 members, how many team members should come to practice to uphold the coach's claim? Was the coach's claim accurate? Explain your reasoning.

	1	2	3	4	5	6	7	8
Number of Students	18	15	18	17	17	19	20	20

____

____

13. **What's the Error?** Ronnie misses the school bus 1 out of every 30 school days. He sets up the proportion $\frac{1}{30} = \frac{180}{x}$ to predict how many days he will miss the bus in the 180-day school year. What is Ronnie's error?

____

FOCUS ON HIGHER ORDER THINKING

Work Area

14. **Persevere in Problem Solving** A gas pump machine rejects 12% of credit card transactions. If this is twice the normal rejection rate for a normal gas pump, how many out of 500 credit cards transactions would a normal gas pump machine reject? ______________

15. **Make Predictions** An airline's weekly flight data showed a 98% probability of being on time. If this airline has 15,000 flights in a year, how many flights would you predict to arrive on time? Explain whether you can use the data to predict whether a specific flight with this airline will be on time.

____

____

____

____

16. **Draw Conclusions** An average response rate for a marketing letter is 4%, meaning that 4% of the people who receive the letter respond to it. A company writes a new type of marketing letter, sends out 2,400 of them, and gets 65 responses. Explain whether the new type of letter would be considered to be a success.

____

____

____

MODULE QUIZ

Ready to Go On?

Personal Math Trainer

Online Practice and Help

my.hrw.com

12.1 Probability

1. Josue tosses a coin and spins the spinner at the right. What are all the possible outcomes?

____

12.2 Experimental Probability of Simple Events

2. While bowling with friends, Brandy rolls a strike in 6 out of 10 frames. What is the experimental probability that Brandy will roll a strike in the first frame of the next game? __________

3. Ben is greeting customers at a music store. Of the first 20 people he sees enter the store, 13 are wearing jackets and 7 are not. What is the experimental probability that the next person to enter the store will be wearing a jacket? __________

12.3 Experimental Probability of Compound Events

4. Auden rolled two number cubes and recorded the results.

Roll #1	Roll #2	Roll #3	Roll #4	Roll #5	Roll #6	Roll #7
2, 1	4, 5	3, 2	2, 2	1, 3	6, 2	5, 3

What is the experimental probability that the sum of the next two numbers rolled is greater than 5? __________

12.4 Making Predictions with Experimental Probability

5. A player on a school baseball team reaches first base $\frac{3}{10}$ of the time he is at bat. Out of 80 times at bat, about how many times would you predict he will reach first base? __________

ESSENTIAL QUESTION

6. How is experimental probability used to make predictions?

____

____

____

MODULE 12
MIXED REVIEW

Assessment Readiness

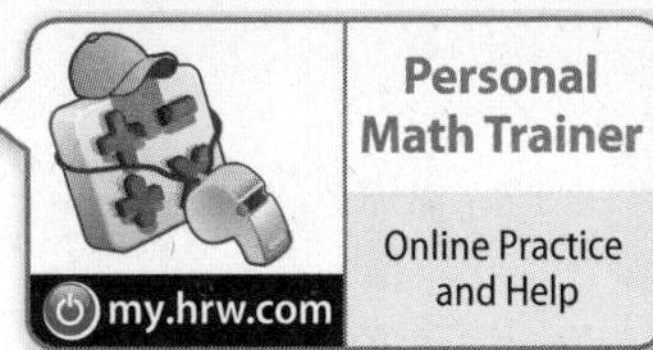

1. Consider each addition problem. Is the sum positive?

Select Yes or No for A–C.

A. $-18 + 27 + (-6)$ ◯ Yes ◯ No

B. $12 + (-19) + 5$ ◯ Yes ◯ No

C. $32 + (-24) + (-6)$ ◯ Yes ◯ No

2. The spinner at right has 8 equal sections, as shown.

Choose True or False for each statement.

A. The probability of landing on an odd number is $\frac{1}{2}$. ◯ True ◯ False

B. The probability of not landing on 6 is $\frac{7}{8}$. ◯ True ◯ False

C. The probability of landing on a number less than 3 is $\frac{3}{8}$. ◯ True ◯ False

3. The table shows the sizes and colors of T-shirts sold at a store in the past week. To the nearest percent, what is the experimental probability that the next customer who buys a T-shirt at the store will buy a large blue T-shirt? Explain how you solved this problem.

	Small	Medium	Large
White	32	49	28
Blue	12	36	20
Black	20	42	23

4. The experimental probability that a delivery service will deliver a package late is 3%. An employee at the delivery service predicts that 45 out of 15,000 packages will be delivered late. Is this prediction reasonable? Justify your answer.

Theoretical Probability and Simulations

ESSENTIAL QUESTION

How can you use theoretical probability to solve real-world problems?

my.hrw.com

Real-World Video

Many carnival games rely on theoretical probability to set the chance of winning fairly low. Understanding how the game is set up might help you be more likely to win.

GO DIGITAL
my.hrw.com

my.hrw.com

Go digital with your write-in student edition, accessible on any device.

Math On the Spot

Scan with your smart phone to jump directly to the online edition, video tutor, and more.

Animated Math

Interactively explore key concepts to see how math works.

Personal Math Trainer

Get immediate feedback and help as you work through practice sets.

Are YOU Ready?

Complete these exercises to review skills you will need for this module.

Fractions, Decimals, and Percents

EXAMPLE Write $\frac{3}{8}$ as a decimal and a percent.

$$\begin{array}{r} 0.375 \\ 8\overline{)3.000} \\ \underline{-2\,4} \\ 60 \\ \underline{-56} \\ 40 \\ \underline{-40} \\ 0 \end{array}$$

Write the fraction as a division problem. Write a decimal point and zeros in the dividend. Place a decimal point in the quotient. Divide as with whole numbers.

$0.375 = 37.5\%$. *Write the decimal as a percent.*

Write each fraction as a decimal and a percent.

1. $\frac{3}{4}$ ________ 2. $\frac{2}{5}$ ________ 3. $\frac{9}{10}$ ________ 4. $\frac{7}{20}$ ________

5. $\frac{7}{8}$ ________ 6. $\frac{1}{20}$ ________ 7. $\frac{19}{25}$ ________ 8. $\frac{23}{50}$ ________

Operations with Fractions

EXAMPLE

$1 - \frac{7}{12} = \frac{12}{12} - \frac{7}{12}$ *Use the denominator of the fraction to write 1 as a fraction.*

$= \frac{12 - 7}{12}$ *Subtract the numerators.*

$= \frac{5}{12}$ *Simplify.*

Find each difference.

9. $1 - \frac{1}{5}$ ______ 10. $1 - \frac{2}{9}$ ______ 11. $1 - \frac{8}{13}$ ______ 12. $1 - \frac{3}{20}$ ______

Multiply Fractions

EXAMPLE

$\frac{4}{15} \times \frac{5}{6} = \frac{\overset{2}{\cancel{4}}}{\underset{3}{\cancel{15}}} \times \frac{\overset{1}{\cancel{5}}}{\underset{3}{\cancel{6}}}$ *Divide by the common factors.*

$= \frac{2}{9}$ *Simplify.*

Multiply. Write each product in simplest form.

13. $\frac{8}{15} \times \frac{5}{8}$ ______ 14. $\frac{2}{9} \times \frac{3}{4}$ ______ 15. $\frac{9}{16} \times \frac{12}{13}$ ______ 16. $\frac{7}{10} \times \frac{5}{28}$ ______

Reading Start-Up

Visualize Vocabulary

Use the ✔ words to complete the graphic.

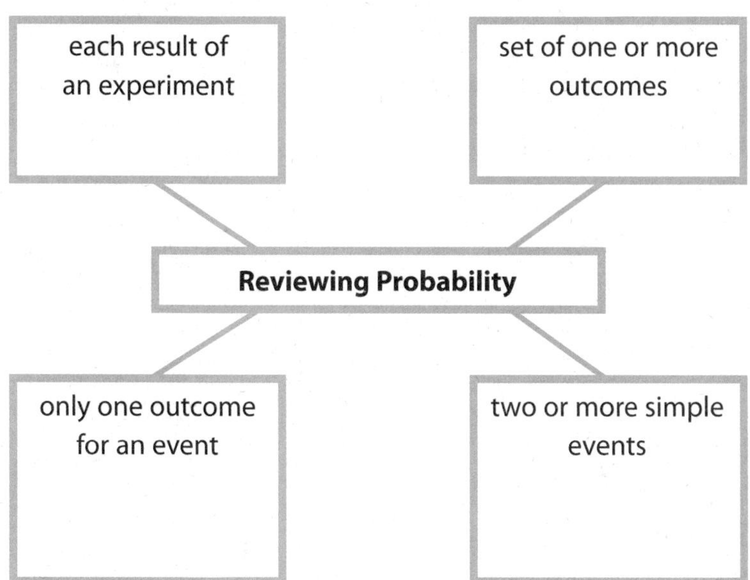

Vocabulary

Review Words

complement *(complemento)*
✔ compound event *(suceso compuesto)*
✔ event *(suceso)*
experiment *(experimento)*
✔ outcome *(resultado)*
✔ simple event *(suceso simple)*
probability *(probabilidad)*

Preview Words

theoretical probability *(probabilidad teórica)*

Understand Vocabulary

Match the term on the left to the correct expression on the right.

1. compound event
2. theoretical probability
3. complement

A. The set of all outcomes that are not the desired event.
B. An event made of two or more simple events.
C. The ratio of the number of equally likely outcomes in an event to the total number of possible outcomes.

Active Reading

Two-Panel Flip Chart Create a two-panel flip chart, to help you understand the concepts in this module. Label one flap "Simple Events" and the other flap "Compound Events." As you study each lesson, write important ideas under the appropriate flap. Include information that will help you remember the concepts later when you look back at your notes.

GETTING READY FOR

Theoretical Probability and Simulations

Understanding the standards and the vocabulary terms in the standards will help you know exactly what you are expected to learn in this module.

CA CC 7.SP.7a

Develop a uniform probability model by assigning equal probability to all outcomes, and use the model to determine probabilities of events.

What It Means to You

You will find the probabilities of a simple event and its complement.

EXAMPLE 7.SP.7A

Tara has a bag that contains 8 white marbles, 10 green marbles, and 7 red marbles. She selects a marble at random. Find the probability that the marble is red, and the probability that it is **not** red.

$$P(\text{red}) = \frac{\text{number of red marbles}}{\text{total number of marbles}}$$

$$= \frac{7}{25}$$

$$P\,(\text{not red}) = 1 - P\,(\text{red}) = 1 - \frac{7}{25} = \frac{25}{25} - \frac{7}{25} = \frac{18}{25}$$

The probability that the marble is red is $\frac{7}{25}$, and the probability that it is not red is $\frac{18}{25}$.

CA CC 7.SP.8b

Represent sample spaces for compound events using methods such as organized lists, tables and tree diagrams. For an event described in everyday language (e.g., "rolling double sixes"), identify the outcomes in the sample space which compose the event.

Key Vocabulary

compound event *(suceso compuesto)*
An event made of two or more simple events.

What It Means to You

You will identify the outcomes in the sample space of a compound event.

EXAMPLE 7.SP.8B

Identify the sample space for flipping a coin and rolling a number cube.

Make a table to organize the information.

		Number Cube Outcomes					
		1	2	3	4	5	6
COIN	H	H1	H2	H3	H4	H5	H6
	T	T1	T2	T3	T4	T5	T6

The sample space includes 12 possible outcomes: H1, H2, H3, H4, H5, H6, T1, T2, T3, T4, T5, and T6.

Visit **my.hrw.com** to see all **CA Common Core Standards** explained.

my.hrw.com

LESSON 13.1

Theoretical Probability of Simple Events

CA CC 7.SP.7a

Develop a uniform probability model by assigning equal probability to all outcomes, and use the model to determine probabilities of events. *Also 7.SP.6, 7.SP.7*

ESSENTIAL QUESTION

How can you find the theoretical probability of a simple event?

EXPLORE ACTIVITY 1 

Finding Theoretical Probability

In previous lessons, you found probabilities based on observing data, or experimental probabilities. In this lesson, you will find *theoretical probabilities.*

Spinner A

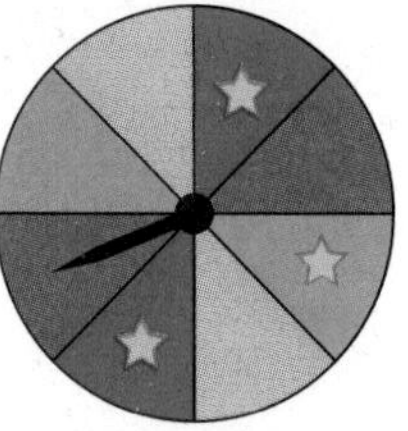

At a school fair, you have a choice of spinning Spinner A or Spinner B. You win an MP3 player if the spinner lands on a section with a star in it. Which spinner should you choose if you want a better chance of winning?

A Complete the table.

	Spinner A	Spinner B
Total number of outcomes		
Number of sections with stars		
***P*(winning MP3)** $= \frac{\text{number of sections with stars}}{\text{total number of outcomes}}$		

Spinner B

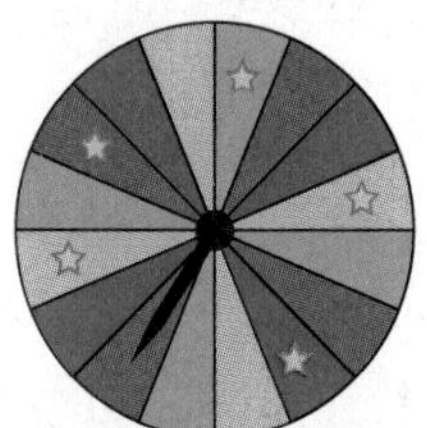

B Compare the ratios for Spinner A and Spinner B.

The ratio for Spinner ________ is greater than the ratio for Spinner _______.

I should choose ________________ for a better chance of winning.

Math Talk
Mathematical Practices

Describe a way to change Spinner B to make your chances of winning equal to your chances of not winning. Explain.

Reflect

1. *Theoretical probability* is a way to describe how you found the chance of winning an MP3 player in the scenario above. Using the spinner example to help you, explain in your own words how to find the theoretical probability of an event.

____

____

____

Calculating Theoretical Probability of Simple Events

Theoretical probability is the probability that an event occurs when all of the outcomes of the experiment are equally likely.

Theoretical Probability

$$P(\text{event}) = \frac{\text{number of ways the event can occur}}{\text{total number of equally likely outcomes}}$$

Probability can be written as a fraction, a decimal, or a percent. For example, the probability you win with Spinner B is $\frac{5}{16}$. You can also write that as 0.3125 or as 31.25%.

EXAMPLE 1

A bag contains 6 red marbles and 12 blue ones. You select one marble at random from the bag. What is the probability that you select a red marble? Write your answer in simplest form.

STEP 1 Find the number of ways the event can occur, that is, the number of red marbles: 6

STEP 2 Add to find the total number of equally likely outcomes.

number of red marbles	+	number of blue marbles	=	total number of marbles
6	+	12	=	**18**

There are 18 possible outcomes in the sample space.

STEP 3 Find the probability of selecting a red marble.

$$P(\text{red marble}) = \frac{\text{number of red marbles}}{\text{total number of marbles}} = \frac{6}{\mathbf{18}}$$

The probability that you select a red marble is $\frac{6}{18}$, or $\frac{1}{3}$.

Math Talk
Mathematical Practices
Describe a situation that has a theoretical probability of $\frac{1}{4}$.

YOUR TURN

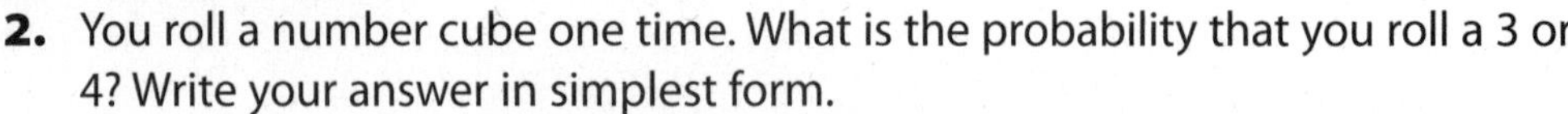

2. You roll a number cube one time. What is the probability that you roll a 3 or 4? Write your answer in simplest form.

$P(\text{rolling a 3 or 4}) = \frac{\square}{\square} = \frac{\square}{\square} = \frac{\square}{\square}$

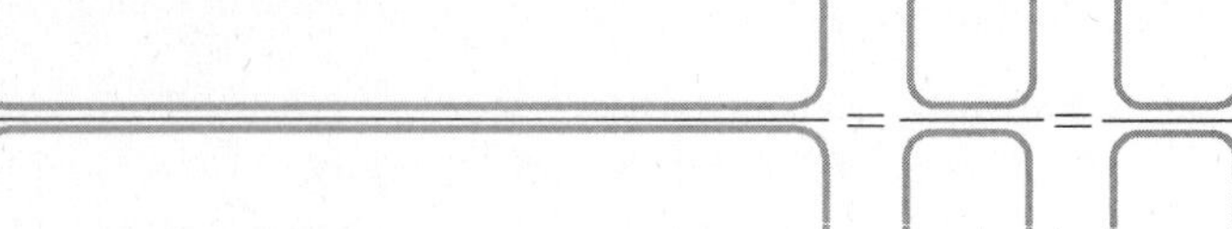

3. How is the sample space for an event related to the formula for theoretical probability? ______________________

____

EXPLORE ACTIVITY 2 

7.SP.7, 7.SP.6

Comparing Theoretical and Experimental Probability

Now that you have calculated theoretical probabilities, you may wonder how theoretical and experimental probabilities compare.

Six students are performing in a talent contest. You roll a number cube to determine the order of the performances.

STEP 1 You roll the number cube once. Complete the table of theoretical probabilities for the different outcomes.

Number	1	2	3	4	5	6
Theoretical probability						

STEP 2 Predict the number of times each number will be rolled out of 30 total rolls.

1: ☐ times 3: ☐ times 5: ☐ times

2: ☐ times 4: ☐ times 6: ☐ times

STEP 3 Roll a number cube 30 times. Complete the table for the frequency of each number and then find its experimental probability.

Number	1	2	3	4	5	6
Frequency						
Experimental probability						

STEP 4 Look at the tables you completed. How do the experimental probabilities compare with the theoretical probabilities?

____

____

STEP 5 **Conjecture** By performing more trials, you tend to get experimental results that are closer to the theoretical probabilities. Combine your table from **Step 3** with those of your classmates to make one table for the class. How do the class experimental probabilities compare with the theoretical probabilities?

____

____

EXPLORE ACTIVITY 2 *(cont'd)*

Reflect

4. Could the experimental probabilities ever be exactly equal to the theoretical probability? If so, how likely is it? If not, why not?

____

____

Guided Practice

At a school fair, you have a choice of randomly picking a ball from Basket A or Basket B. Basket A has 5 green balls, 3 red balls, and 8 yellow balls. Basket B has 7 green balls, 4 red balls, and 9 yellow balls. You can win a digital book reader if you pick a red ball. (Explore Activity 1)

	Basket A	Basket B
Total number of outcomes		
Number of red balls		
***P*(win) =** $\frac{\text{number of red balls}}{\text{total number of outcomes}}$		

1. Complete the chart. Write each answer in simplest form.

2. Which basket should you choose if you want the better chance of winning? ____________

A spinner has 11 equal-sized sections marked 1 through 11. Find each probability. (Example 1)

3. You spin once and land on an odd number.

$P(\text{odd}) = \frac{\text{number of \_\_\_\_ sections}}{\text{total number of \_\_\_\_}} = \frac{\square}{\square}$

4. You spin once and land on an even number.

$P(\text{even}) = \frac{\text{number of \_\_\_\_ sections}}{\text{total number of \_\_\_\_}} = \frac{\square}{\square}$

You roll a number cube once.

5. What is the theoretical probability that you roll a 3 or 4? (Example 1) ____________

6. Suppose you rolled the number cube 199 more times. Would you expect the experimental probability of rolling a 3 or 4 to be the same as your answer to Exercise 5? (Explore Activity 2)

____

ESSENTIAL QUESTION CHECK-IN

7. How can you find the probability of a simple event if the total number of equally likely outcomes is 20?

____

Name________________________ Class________________ Date__________

13.1 Independent Practice

CA CC 7.SP.7, 7.SP.7a

Find the probability of each event. Write each answer as a fraction in simplest form, as a decimal to the nearest hundredth, and as a percent to the nearest whole number.

8. You spin the spinner shown. The spinner lands on yellow.

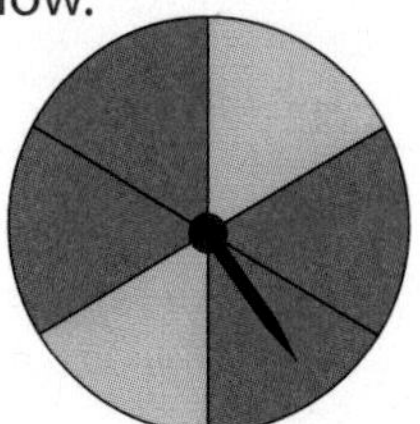

____

9. You spin the spinner shown. The spinner lands on blue or green.

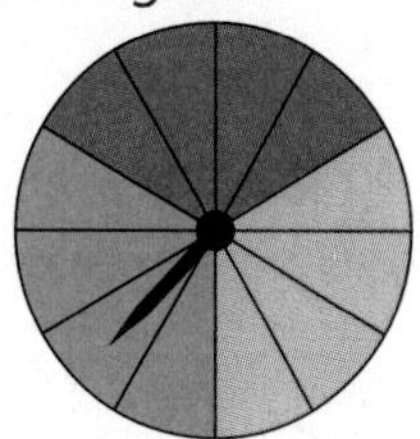

____

10. A jar contains 4 cherry cough drops and 10 honey cough drops. You choose one cough drop without looking. The cough drop is cherry. _______________

11. You pick one card at random from a standard deck of 52 playing cards. You pick a black card. _______________

12. There are 12 pieces of fruit in a bowl. Five are lemons and the rest are limes. You choose a piece of fruit without looking. The piece of fruit is a lime. _______________

13. You choose a movie CD at random from a case containing 8 comedy CDs, 5 science fiction CDs, and 7 adventure CDs. The CD is **not** a comedy. _______________

14. You roll a number cube. You roll a number that is greater than 2 and less than 5. _______________

15. **Communicate Mathematical Ideas** The theoretical probability of a given event is $\frac{9}{13}$. Explain what each number represents.

____

____

____

16. Leona has 4 nickels, 6 pennies, 4 dimes, and 2 quarters in a change purse. Leona lets her little sister Daisy pick a coin at random. If Daisy is equally likely to pick each type of coin, what is the probability that her coin is worth more than five cents? Explain.

____

____

____

Work Area

17. **Critique Reasoning** A bowl of flower seeds contains 5 petunia seeds and 15 begonia seeds. Riley calculated the probability that a randomly selected seed is a petunia seed as $\frac{1}{3}$. Describe and correct Riley's error.

18. There are 20 seventh graders and 15 eighth graders in a club. A club president will be chosen at random.

a. **Analyze Relationships** Compare the probabilities of choosing a seventh grader or an eighth grader.

b. **Critical Thinking** If a student from one grade is more likely to be chosen than a student from the other, is the method unfair? Explain.

A jar contains 8 red marbles, 10 blue ones, and 2 yellow ones. One marble is chosen at random. The color is recorded in the table, and then it is returned to the jar. This is repeated 40 times.

Red	Blue	Yellow
14	16	10

19. **Communicate Mathematical Ideas** Use proportional reasoning to explain how you know that for each color, the theoretical and experimental probabilities are not the same.

20. **Persevere in Problem Solving** For which color marble is the experimental probability closest to the theoretical probability? Explain.

LESSON

13.2 Theoretical Probability of Compound Events

CA CC 7.SP.8

Find probabilities of compound events using organized lists, tables, tree diagrams, and simulation. *7.SP.8a, 7.SP.8b*

ESSENTIAL QUESTION

How do you find the probability of a compound event?

EXPLORE ACTIVITY

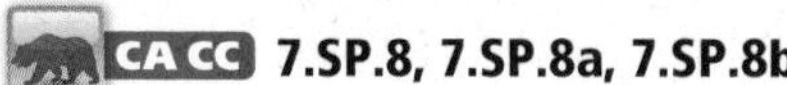

CA CC 7.SP.8, 7.SP.8a, 7.SP.8b

Finding Probability Using a Table

Recall that a compound event consists of two or more simple events. To find the probability of a compound event, you write a ratio of the number of ways the compound event can happen to the total number of equally likely possible outcomes.

Jacob rolls two fair number cubes. Find the probability that the sum of the numbers he rolls is 8.

STEP 1 Use the table to find the sample space for rolling a particular sum on two number cubes. Each cell is the sum of the first number in that row and column.

	1	2	3	4	5	6
1						
2						
3						
4						
5						
6						

STEP 2 How many possible outcomes are in the sample space? ________

STEP 3 Circle the outcomes that give the sum of 8.

STEP 4 How many ways are there to roll a sum of 8? ________

STEP 5 What is the probability of rolling a sum of 8? ________

Reflect

1. Give an example of an event that is more likely than rolling a sum of 8.

____

2. Give an example of an event that is less likely than rolling a sum of 8.

____

Finding Probability Using a Tree Diagram

You can also use a tree diagram to calculate theoretical probabilities of compound events.

EXAMPLE 1

A deli prepares sandwiches with one type of bread (white or wheat), one type of meat (ham, turkey, or chicken), and one type of cheese (cheddar or Swiss). Each combination is equally likely. Find the probability of choosing a sandwich at random and getting turkey and Swiss on wheat bread.

STEP 1 Make a tree diagram to find the sample space for the compound event.

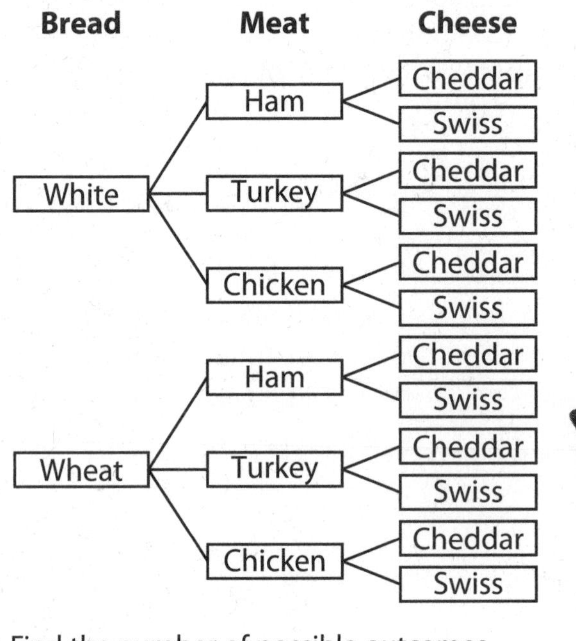

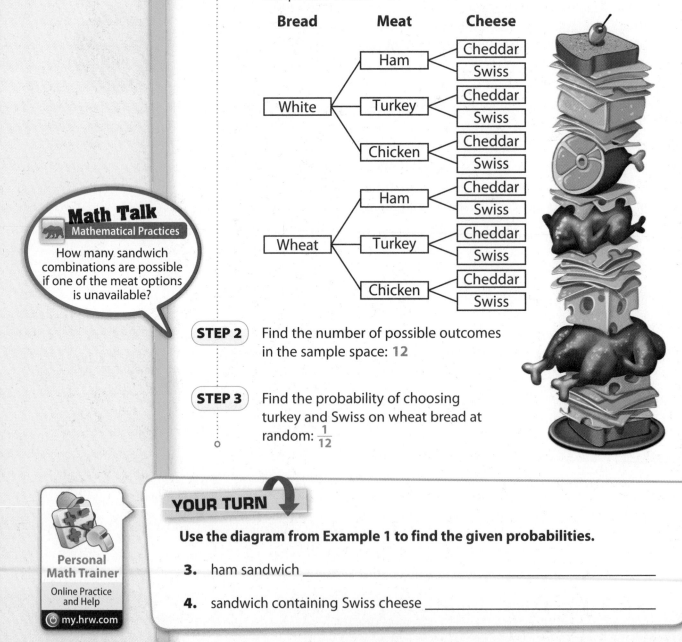

Math Talk
Mathematical Practices
How many sandwich combinations are possible if one of the meat options is unavailable?

STEP 2 Find the number of possible outcomes in the sample space: **12**

STEP 3 Find the probability of choosing turkey and Swiss on wheat bread at random: $\frac{1}{12}$

Use the diagram from Example 1 to find the given probabilities.

3. ham sandwich ____________________

4. sandwich containing Swiss cheese ____________________

Finding Probability Using a List

One way to provide security for a locker or personal account is to assign it an access code number known only to the owner.

Math On the Spot
my.hrw.com

EXAMPLE 2 

 CA CC 7.SP.8, 7.SP.8b

The combination for Khiem's locker is a 3-digit code that uses the numbers 1, 2, and 3. Any of these numbers may be repeated. Find the probability that Khiem's randomly-assigned number is 222.

Make an organized list to find the sample space.

STEP 1 List all the codes that start with 1 and have 1 as a second digit.

1	1	1
1	1	2
1	1	3

STEP 2 List all the codes that start with 1 and have 2 as a second digit.

1	2	1
1	2	2
1	2	3

STEP 3 List all the codes that start with 1 and have 3 as a second digit.

1	3	1
1	3	2
1	3	3

STEP 4 You have now listed all the codes that start with 1. Repeat Steps 1–3 for codes that start with 2, and then for codes that start with 3.

2	1	1
2	1	2
2	1	3

2	2	1
2	2	2
2	2	3

2	3	1
2	3	2
2	3	3

3	1	1
3	1	2
3	1	3

3	2	1
3	2	2
3	2	3

3	3	1
3	3	2
3	3	3

STEP 5 Find the number of outcomes in the sample space by counting all the possible codes. There are **27** such codes.

STEP 6 Find the probability that Khiem's locker code is 222.

$$P(\text{Code } 222) = \frac{\text{number of favorable outcomes}}{\text{total number of possible outcomes}} = \frac{1}{27}$$

My Notes

Notice that there are 3 possible first numbers, 3 possible second numbers, and 3 possible third numbers, or $3 \times 3 \times 3 = 27$ numbers in all.

Math Talk
Mathematical Practices

How could you find the probability that Khiem's locker code includes exactly two 1s?

YOUR TURN

5. Martha types a 4-digit code into a keypad to unlock her car doors. The code uses the numbers 1 and 0. If the digits are selected at random, what is the probability of getting a code with exactly two 0s? ________

Personal Math Trainer
Online Practice and Help
my.hrw.com

Guided Practice

Drake rolls two fair number cubes. (Explore Activity)

1. Complete the table to find the sample space for rolling a particular product on two number cubes.

	1	2	3	4	5	6
1						
2						
3						
4						
5						
6						

2. What is the probability that the product of the two numbers Drake rolls is a multiple of 4? ______________

3. What is the probability that the product of the two numbers Drake rolls is less than 13? ______________

You flip three coins and want to explore probabilities of certain events. (Examples 1 and 2)

4. Complete the tree diagram and make a list to find the sample space.

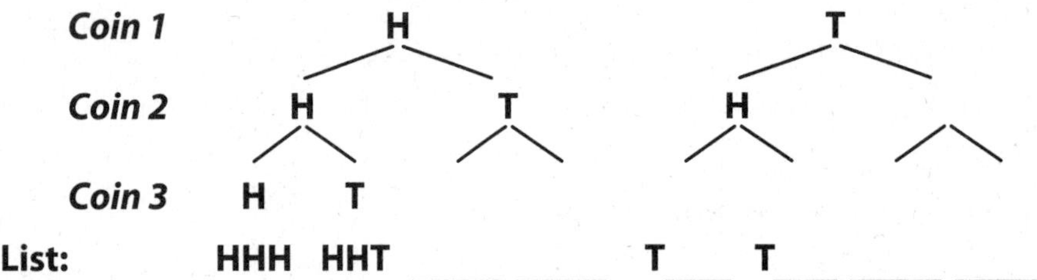

List: HHH HHT _____ _____ T____ T____ _____ _____

5. How many outcomes are in the sample space? _______

6. List all the ways to get three tails. _______

7. Complete the expression to find the probability of getting three tails.

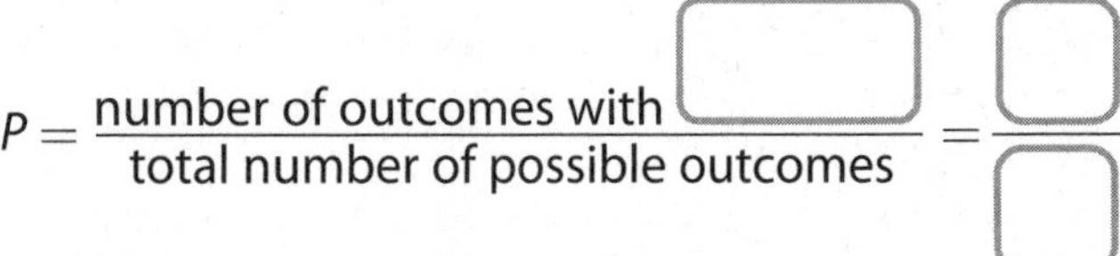

$$P = \frac{\text{number of outcomes with } \square}{\text{total number of possible outcomes}} = \frac{\square}{\square}$$

The probability of getting three tails when three coins are flipped is _______.

8. What is the probability of getting exactly two heads?

There are _______ way(s) to obtain exactly two heads: HHT, ______________

$$P = \frac{\text{number of outcomes with } \square}{\text{total number of possible outcomes}} = \frac{\square}{\square}$$

ESSENTIAL QUESTION CHECK-IN

9. There are 6 ways a given compound event can occur. What else do you need to know to find the theoretical probability of the event?

____

Name ______________________ Class ______________ Date ______________

13.2 Independent Practice

CA CC 7.SP.8, 7.SP.8a, 7.SP.8b

In Exercises 10–12, use the following information. Mattias gets dressed in the dark one morning and chooses his clothes at random. He chooses a shirt (green, red, or yellow), a pair of pants (black or blue), and a pair of shoes (checkered or red).

10. Use the space below to make a tree diagram to find the sample space.

11. What is the probability that Mattias picks an outfit at random that includes red shoes? ______________

12. What is the probability that no part of Mattias's outfit is red? ______________

13. Rhee and Pamela are two of the five members of a band. Every week, the band picks two members at random to play on their own for five minutes. What is the probability that Rhee and Pamela are chosen this week? ______________

14. Ben rolls two number cubes. What is the probability that the sum of the numbers he rolls is less than 6? ______________

15. Nhan is getting dressed. He considers two different shirts, three pairs of pants, and three pairs of shoes. He chooses one of each of the articles at random. What is the probability that he will wear his jeans but not his sneakers?

Shirt	Pants	Shoes
collared	khakis	sneakers
T-shirt	jeans	flip-flops
	shorts	sandals

____

16. Communicate Mathematical Ideas A ski resort has 3 chair lifts, each with access to 6 ski trails. Explain how you can find the number of possible outcomes when choosing a chair lift and a ski trail without making a list, a tree diagram, or table.

____

17. Explain the Error For breakfast, Sarah can choose eggs, granola or oatmeal as a main course, and orange juice or milk for a drink. Sarah says that the sample space for choosing one of each contains $3^2 = 9$ outcomes. What is her error? Explain.

____

18. Represent Real-World Problems A new shoe comes in two colors, black or red, and in sizes from 5 to 12, including half sizes. If a pair of the shoes is chosen at random for a store display, what is the probability it will be red and size 9 or larger? ___________

Work Area

H.O.T. FOCUS ON HIGHER ORDER THINKING

19. Analyze Relationships At a diner, Sondra tells the server, "Give me one item from each column." Gretchen says, "Give me one main dish and a vegetable." Who has a greater probability of getting a meal that includes salmon? Explain.

Main Dish	Vegetable	Side
Pasta	Carrots	Tomato soup
Salmon	Peas	Tossed salad
Beef	Asparagus	
Pork	Sweet potato	

____

____

20. The digits 1 through 5 are used for a set of locker codes.

a. Look for a Pattern Suppose the digits cannot repeat. Find the number of possible two-digit codes and three-digit codes. Describe any pattern and use it to predict the number of possible five-digit codes.

____

____

____

b. Look for a Pattern Repeat part **a**, but allow digits to repeat.

____

____

____

c. Justify Reasoning Suppose that a gym plans to issue numbered locker codes by choosing the digits at random. Should the gym use codes in which the digits can repeat or not? Justify your reasoning.

____

____

____

LESSON 13.3

Making Predictions with Theoretical Probability

CA CC 7.SP.6

Approximate the probability of a chance event by collecting data on the chance process that produces it and observing its long-run relative frequency, and predict the approximate relative frequency given the probability. *Also 7.SP.7a*

ESSENTIAL QUESTION

How do you make predictions using theoretical probability?

Using Theoretical Probability to Make a Quantitative Prediction

You can make quantitative predictions based on theoretical probability just as you did with experimental probability earlier.

My Notes

EXAMPLE 1 

A **You roll a standard number cube 150 times. Predict how many times you will roll a 3 or a 4.**

The probability of rolling a 3 or a 4 is $\frac{2}{6} = \frac{1}{3}$.

Method 1: Set up a proportion.

$\frac{1}{3} = \frac{x}{150}$ Write a proportion. 1 out of 3 is how many out of 150?

$\frac{1}{3} = \frac{x}{150}$ (× 50)

$\frac{1}{3} = \frac{50}{150}$ (× 50) Since 3 times 50 is 150, multiply 1 times 50 to find the value of x.

$x = 50$

Method 2: Set up an equation and solve.

p(rolling a 3 or 4) · Number of events = Prediction

$\frac{1}{3} \cdot 150 = x$ Multiply the probability by the total number of rolls.

$50 = x$ Solve for x.

You can expect to roll a 3 or a 4 about 50 times out of 150.

B **Celia volunteers at her local animal shelter. She has an equally likely chance to be assigned to the dog, cat, bird, or reptile section. If she volunteers 24 times, about how many times should she expect to be assigned to the dog section?**

Set up a proportion. The probability of being assigned to the dog section is $\frac{1}{4}$.

$\frac{1}{4} = \frac{x}{24}$ — Write a proportion. 1 out of 4 is how many out of 24?

$\frac{1}{4} = \frac{x}{24}$ ($\times 6$ from 4 to 24)

$\frac{1}{4} = \frac{x}{24}$ ($\times 6$ from 1 to x; $\times 6$ from 4 to 24) — Since 4 times 6 is 24, multiply 1 times 6 to find the value of x.

$x = 6$

Celia can expect to be assigned to the dog section about 6 times out of 24.

YOUR TURN

1. Predict how many times you will roll a number less than 5 if you roll a standard number cube 250 times.

____

2. You flip a fair coin 18 times. About how many times would you expect heads to appear?

____

Using Theoretical Probability to Make a Qualitative Prediction

Earlier, you learned how to make predictions using experimental probability. You can use theoretical probabilities in the same way to help you predict or compare how likely events are.

EXAMPLE 2 Real World

CA CC 7.SP.6, 7.SP.7a

A **Herschel pulls a sock out of his drawer without looking and puts it on. The sock is black. There are 7 black socks, 8 white socks, and 5 striped socks left in the drawer. He pulls out a second sock without looking. Is it likely that he will be wearing matching socks to school?**

Find the theoretical probability that Herschel picks a matching sock and the probability that he picks one that does not match.

$P(\text{matching}) = \frac{7}{20}$ $\quad$ $P(\text{not matching}) = 1 - \frac{7}{20} = \frac{13}{20}$

$P(\text{not matching}) = 1 - P(\text{matching})$

The probability that Herschel picks a matching sock is about half the probability that he picks one that does not match. It is likely that he will **not** be wearing matching socks to school.

B **All 2,000 customers at a gym are randomly assigned a 3-digit security code that they use to access their online accounts. The codes are made up of the digits 0 through 4, and the digits can be repeated. Is it likely that fewer than 10 of the customers are issued the code 103?**

Set up a proportion. The probability of the code 103 is $\frac{1}{125}$.

There are 5 possible first numbers, 5 possible second numbers, and 5 possible third numbers. So, the probability of any one code is $\frac{1}{5} \cdot \frac{1}{5} \cdot \frac{1}{5} = \frac{1}{125}$.

$\frac{1}{125} = \frac{x}{2{,}000}$ $\quad$ *Write a proportion. 1 out of 125 is how many out of 2,000?*

$\frac{1}{125} = \frac{16}{2{,}000}$ ($\times 16$) $\quad$ *Since 125 times 16 is 2,000, multiply 1 times 16 to find the value of x.*

It is **not** likely that fewer than 10 of the customers get the same code. It is more likely that 16 members get the code 103.

YOUR TURN

3. A bag of marbles contains 8 red marbles, 4 blue marbles, and 5 white marbles. Tom picks a marble at random. Is it more likely that he picks a red marble or a marble of another color?

____

4. At a fundraiser, a school group charges $6 for tickets for a "grab bag." You choose one bill at random from a bag that contains 40 $1 bills, 20 $5 bills, 5 $10 bills, 5 $20 bills, and 1 $100 bill. Is it likely that you will win enough to pay for your ticket? Justify your answer.

____

____

____

Guided Practice

1. Bob works at a construction company. He has an equally likely chance to be assigned to work different crews every day. He can be assigned to work on crews building apartments, condominiums, or houses. If he works 18 days a month, about how many times should he expect to be assigned to the house crew? (Example 1)

STEP 1 Find the probabilities of being assigned to each crew.

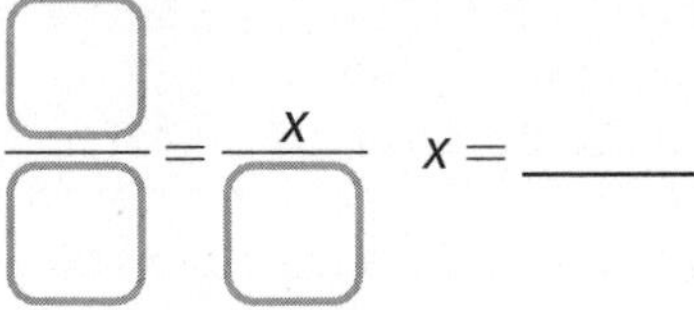

Apartment ☐ Condo ☐ House ☐

The probability of being assigned to the house crew is ________

STEP 2 Set up and solve a proportion.

$\frac{\square}{\square} = \frac{x}{\square}$ $x =$ ______

Bob can expect to be assigned to the house crew about

______ times out of 18.

2. During a raffle drawing, half of the ticket holders will receive a prize. The winners are equally likely to win one of three prizes: a book, a gift certificate to a restaurant, or a movie ticket. If there are 300 ticket holders, predict the number of people who will win a movie ticket. (Example 1) ______________

3. In Mr. Jawarani's first period math class, there are 9 students with hazel eyes, 10 students with brown eyes, 7 students with blue eyes, and 2 students with green eyes. Mr. Jawarani picks a student at random. Which color eyes is the student most likely to have? Explain. (Example 2)

____

____

____

ESSENTIAL QUESTION CHECK-IN

4. How do you make predictions using theoretical probability?

____

____

____

Name ____________ Class ____________ Date ____________

13.3 Independent Practice

CA CC 7.SP.6, 7.SP.7a

5. A bag contains 6 red marbles, 2 white marbles, and 1 gray marble. You randomly pick out a marble, record its color, and put it back in the bag. You repeat this process 45 times. How many white or gray marbles do you expect to get?

____

6. Using the blank circle below, draw a spinner with 8 equal sections and 3 colors—red, green, and yellow. The spinner should be such that you are equally likely to land on green or yellow, but more likely to land on red than either on green or yellow.

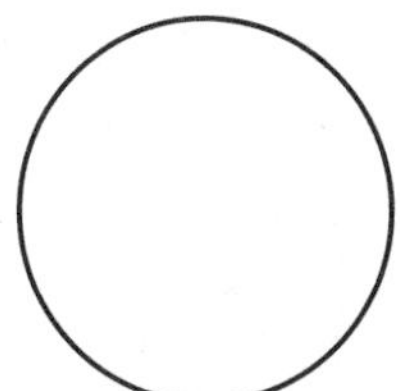

Use the following for Exercises 7–9. In a standard 52-card deck, half of the cards are red and half are black. The 52 cards are divided evenly into 4 suits: spades, hearts, diamonds, and clubs. Each suit has three face cards (jack, queen, king), and an ace. Each suit also has 9 cards numbered from 2 to 10.

7. Dawn draws 1 card, replaces it, and draws another card. Is it more likely that she draws 2 red cards or 2 face cards?

____

____

8. Luis draws 1 card from a deck, 39 times. Predict how many times he draws an ace.

____

9. Suppose a solitaire player has played 1,000 games. Predict how many times the player turned over a red card as the first card.

____

10. John and O'Neal are playing a board game in which they roll two number cubes. John needs to get a sum of 8 on the number cubes to win. O'Neal needs a sum of 11. If they take turns rolling the number cube, who is more likely to win? Explain.

____

____

____

11. Every day, Navya's teacher randomly picks a number from 1 to 20 to be the number of the day. The number of the day can be repeated. There are 180 days in the school year. Predict how many days the number of the day will be greater than 15. ____________

12. Eben rolls two standard number cubes 36 times. Predict how many times he will roll a sum of 4. ____________

13. **Communicate Mathematical Ideas** Can you always show that a prediction based on theoretical probability is true by performing the event often enough? If so, explain why. If not, describe a situation that justifies your response.

____

____

____

____

____

14. Represent Real-World Problems Give a real-world example of an experiment in which all of the outcomes are not equally likely. Can you make a prediction for this experiment, using theoretical probability?

H.O.T. FOCUS ON HIGHER ORDER THINKING

Work Area

15. Critical Thinking Pierre asks Sherry a question involving the theoretical probability of a compound event in which you flip a coin and draw a marble from a bag of marbles. The bag of marbles contains 3 white marbles, 8 green marbles, and 9 black marbles. Sherry's answer, which is correct, is $\frac{12}{40}$. What was Pierre's question?

16. Make a Prediction Horace is going to roll a standard number cube and flip a coin. He wonders if it is more likely that he rolls a 5 **and** the coin lands on heads, or that he rolls a 5 **or** the coin lands on heads. Which event do you think is more likely to happen? Find the probability of both events to justify or reject your initial prediction.

17. Communicate Mathematical Ideas Cecil solved a theoretical prediction problem and got this answer: "The spinner will land on the red section 4.5 times." Is it possible to have a prediction that is not a whole number? If so, give an example.

LESSON 13.4

Using Technology to Conduct a Simulation

CA CC 7.SP.8c

Design and use a simulation to generate frequencies for compound events. *Also 7.SP.8*

ESSENTIAL QUESTION

How can you use technology simulations to estimate probabilities?

Designing and Conducting a Simulation for a Simple Event

You can use a graphing calculator or computer to generate random numbers and conduct a simulation.

EXAMPLE 1

A cereal company is having a contest. There are codes for winning prizes in 30% of its cereal boxes. Find an experimental probability that you have to buy *exactly* 3 boxes of cereal before you find a winning code.

STEP 1 Choose a model.

The probability of finding a winning code is $30\% = \frac{3}{10}$.

Use whole numbers from 1 to 10.
Let three numbers represent buying a box with a winning code.

Winning code: 1, 2, 3 Nonwinning code: 4, 5, 6, 7, 8, 9, 10

STEP 2 Generate random numbers from 1 to 10 until you get one that represents a box with a winning code. Record how many boxes you bought before finding a winning code.

5 numbers generated: 9, 6, 7, 8, 1

1 represents a box with a winning code.

STEP 3 Perform multiple trials by repeating Step 2.

Trial	Numbers generated	Boxes bought
1	9, 6, 7, 8, 1	5
2	2	1
3	10, 4, 8, 1	4
4	4, 10, 7, 1	4
5	2	1
6	4, 3	2
7	3	1
8	7, 5, 2	3
9	8, 5, 4, 8, 10, 3	6
10	9, 1	2

Trial 8 represents a winning code after buying 3 boxes.

STEP 4 Find the experimental probability.

In 1 of 10 trials, you bought exactly 3 boxes of cereal before finding a winning code. The experimental probability is $\frac{1}{10}$, or 10%.

YOUR TURN

1. An elephant has a 50% chance of giving birth to a male or a female calf. Use a simulation to find an experimental probability that the elephant gives birth to 3 male calves before having a female calf. (*Hint:* Use 0s and 1s. Let 0 represent a male calf, and 1 represent a female calf. Generate random numbers until you get a 1.)

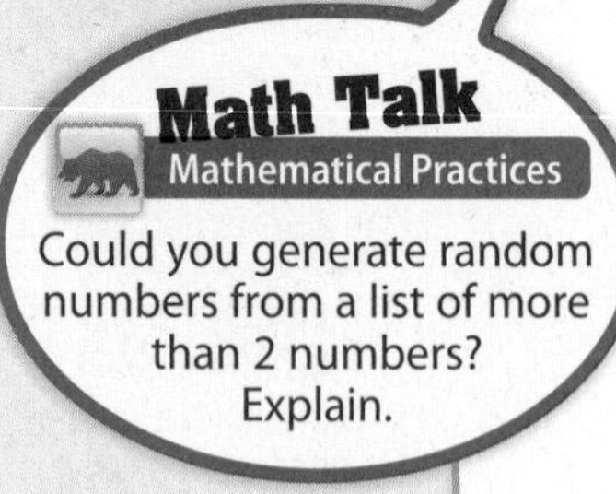

Trial	Numbers generated	3 Males first
1		
2		
3		
4		
5		

Trial	Numbers generated	3 Males first
6		
7		
8		
9		
10		

____

Designing and Conducting a Simulation for a Compound Event

You can use random numbers to simulate compound events as well as simple events.

EXAMPLE 2 

Suppose that there is a 20% chance that a particular volcano will erupt in any given decade. Find an experimental probability that the volcano will erupt in at least 1 of the next 5 decades.

STEP 1 Choose a model.

The probability of an eruption is $20\% = \frac{1}{5}$.

Use whole numbers from 1 to 5.

Let 1 represent a decade with an eruption.

Let 2, 3, 4, and 5 represent a decade without an eruption.

STEP 2 Generate 5 random numbers from 1 to 5. Record the number of decades with an eruption.

5 numbers generated: 3, 1, 3, 4, 2 Eruption decades: 1

STEP 3 Perform multiple trials by repeating Step 2. Calculate the percent of trials in which there was an eruption in at least 1 of the 5 decades.

Trial	Numbers generated	Eruption decades
1	3, 1, 3, 4, 2	1
2	3, 2, 2, 4, 5	0
3	1, 3, 3, 2, 5	1
4	5, 3, 4, 5, 4	0
5	5, 5, 3, 2, 4	0

Trial	Numbers generated	Eruption decades
6	2, 3, 3, 4, 2	0
7	1, 2, 4, 1, 4	2
8	1, 3, 2, 1, 5	2
9	1, 2, 4, 2, 5	1
10	5, 5, 3, 2, 4	0

In 5 out of the 10 trials, there was an eruption in at least 1 of the 5 decades. The experimental probability of an eruption in at least 1 of the next 5 decades is $\frac{5}{10} = 50\%$.

YOUR TURN

2. Matt guesses the answers on a quiz with 5 true-false questions. The probability of guessing a correct answer on each question is 50%. Use a simulation to find an experimental probability that he gets at least 2 questions right. (*Hint:* Use 0s and 1s. Let 0s represent incorrect answers, and 1s represent correct answers. Perform 10 trials, generating 5 random numbers in each, and count the number of 1s.)

Trial	Numbers generated	Correct answers
1		
2		
3		
4		
5		

Trial	Numbers generated	Correct answers
6		
7		
8		
9		
10		

____

Guided Practice

There is a 30% chance that T'Shana's county will have a drought during any given year. She performs a simulation to find the experimental probability of a drought in at least 1 of the next 4 years. (Examples 1 and 2)

1. T'Shana's model involves the whole numbers from 1 to 10. Complete the description of her model.

Let the numbers 1 to 3 represent [ ]

and the numbers 4 to 10 represent [ ]

Perform multiple trials, generating [ ] random numbers each time.

2. Suppose T'Shana used the model described in Exercise 1 and got the results shown in the table. Complete the table.

Trial	Numbers generated	Drought years
1	10, 3, 5, 1	
2	10, 4, 6, 5	
3	3, 2, 10, 3	
4	2, 10, 4, 4	
5	7, 3, 6, 3	

Trial	Numbers generated	Drought years
6	8, 4, 8, 5	
7	6, 2, 2, 8	
8	6, 5, 2, 4	
9	2, 2, 3, 2	
10	6, 3, 1, 5	

3. According to the simulation, what is the experimental probability that there will be a drought in the county in at least 1 of the next 4 years? ________

ESSENTIAL QUESTION CHECK-IN

4. You want to generate random numbers to simulate an event with a 75% chance of occurring. Describe a model you could use.

____

____

____

____

Name ____________________ Class ____________________ Date ____________________

13.4 Independent Practice

CA CC 7.SP.8, 7.SP.8c

Every contestant on a game show has a 40% chance of winning. In the simulation below, the numbers 1–4 represent a winner, and the numbers 5–10 represent a nonwinner. Numbers were generated until one that represented a winner was produced.

Trial	Numbers generated
1	7, 4
2	6, 5, 2
3	1
4	9, 1
5	3

Trial	Numbers generated
6	8, 8, 6, 2
7	2
8	5, 9, 4
9	10, 3
10	1

5. In how many of the trials did it take exactly 4 contestants to get a winner? __________

6. Based on the simulation, what is the experimental probability that it will take exactly 4 contestants to get a winner? __________

Over a 100-year period, the probability that a hurricane struck Rob's city in any given year was 20%. Rob performed a simulation to find an experimental probability that a hurricane would strike the city in at least 4 of the next 10 years. In Rob's simulation, 1 represents a year with a hurricane.

Trial	Numbers generated
1	2, 5, 3, 2, 5, 5, 1, 4, 5, 2
2	1, 1, 5, 2, 2, 1, 3, 1, 1, 5
3	4, 5, 4, 5, 5, 4, 3, 5, 1, 1
4	1, 5, 5, 5, 1, 2, 2, 3, 5, 3
5	5, 1, 5, 3, 5, 3, 4, 5, 3, 2

Trial	Numbers generated
6	1, 1, 5, 5, 1, 4, 2, 2, 3, 4
7	2, 1, 5, 3, 1, 5, 1, 2, 1, 4
8	2, 4, 3, 2, 4, 4, 2, 1, 3, 1
9	3, 2, 1, 4, 5, 3, 5, 5, 1, 2
10	3, 4, 2, 4, 3, 5, 2, 3, 5, 1

7. According to Rob's simulation, what was the experimental probability that a hurricane would strike the city in at least 4 of the next 10 years? __________

8. **Analyze Relationships** Suppose that over the 10 years following Rob's simulation, there was actually 1 year in which a hurricane struck. How did this compare to the results of Rob's simulation?

____

____

9. Communicate Mathematical Ideas You generate three random whole numbers from 1 to 10. Do you think that it is unlikely or even impossible that all of the numbers could be 10? Explain?

10. Erika collects baseball cards, and 60% of the packs contain a player from her favorite team. Use a simulation to find an experimental probability that she has to buy exactly 2 packs before she gets a player from her favorite team.

H.O.T. FOCUS ON HIGHER ORDER THINKING

Work Area

11. Represent Real-World Problems When Kate plays basketball, she usually makes 37.5% of her shots. Design and conduct a simulation to find the experimental probability that she makes at least 3 of her next 10 shots. Justify the model for your simulation.

12. Justify Reasoning George and Susannah used a simulation to simulate the flipping of 8 coins 50 times. In all of the trials, at least 5 heads came up. What can you say about their simulation? Explain.

MODULE QUIZ

Ready to Go On?

13.1, 13.2 Theoretical Probability of Simple and Compound Events

Find the probability of each event. Write your answer as a fraction, as a decimal, and as a percent.

1. You choose a marble at random from a bag containing 12 red, 12 blue, 15 green, 9 yellow, and 12 black marbles. The marble is red. ________

2. You draw a card at random from a shuffled deck of 52 cards. The deck has four 13-card suits (diamonds, hearts, clubs, spades). The card is a diamond or a spade. ________

13.3 Making Predictions with Theoretical Probability

3. A bag contains 23 red marbles, 25 green marbles, and 18 blue marbles. You choose a marble at random from the bag. What color marble will you most likely choose? ________

13.4 Using Technology to Conduct a Simulation

4. Bay City has a 25% chance of having a flood in any given decade. The table shows the results of a simulation using random numbers to find the experimental probability that there will be a flood in Bay City in at least 1 of the next 5 decades. In the table, the number 1 represents a decade with a flood. The numbers 2 through 5 represent a decade without a flood.

Trial	Numbers generated	Trial	Numbers generated
1	2, 2, 5, 5, 5	6	4, 2, 2, 5, 4
2	3, 2, 3, 5, 4	7	1, 3, 2, 4, 4
3	5, 5, 5, 4, 3	8	3, 5, 5, 2, 1
4	5, 1, 3, 3, 5	9	4, 3, 3, 2, 5
5	4, 5, 5, 3, 2	10	5, 4, 1, 2, 1

According to the simulation, what is the experimental probability of a flood in Bay City in at least 1 of the next 5 decades? ________

ESSENTIAL QUESTION

5. How can you use theoretical probability to make predictions in real-world situations?

____

____

MODULE 13
MIXED REVIEW

Assessment Readiness

1. Is it possible for a cross section of a cylinder to have these shapes?

Select Yes or No for A–C.

A. oval ○ Yes ○ No

B. rectangle ○ Yes ○ No

C. triangle ○ Yes ○ No

2. A bag contains 12 red marbles, 6 blue marbles, and 2 green marbles.

Choose True or False for each statement.

A. The probability of randomly selecting a blue marble from the bag is $\frac{1}{6}$. ○ True ○ False

B. The probability of randomly selecting a red marble or a green marble from the bag is 70%. ○ True ○ False

C. If you choose and replace a marble 30 times, you can expect about 3 of the marbles to be green. ○ True ○ False

3. The table shows the taco options at a restaurant. Each month, the manager randomly chooses a meat, a tortilla, and a salsa for the taco special. What is the probability that the taco special in June will be chicken on a corn tortilla with mango salsa? Explain your answer.

Meat	Tortilla	Salsa
beef	corn	chipotle
chicken	flour	mango
pork		verde

4. A weather forecast states that there is a 20% probability of rain on each of the next 3 days. Describe a simulation you could perform using random numbers to find the experimental probability that it will not rain on any of the next 3 days.

UNIT 6

Study Guide Review

MODULE 12 Experimental Probability

Key Vocabulary

complement *(complemento)*
compound event *(suceso compuesto)*
event *(suceso)*
experiment *(experimento)*
experimental probability *(probabilidad experimental)*
outcome *(resultado)*
probability *(probabilidad)*
sample space *(espacio muestral)*
simple event *(suceso simple)*
simulation *(simulación)*
trial *(prueba)*

ESSENTIAL QUESTION

How can you use experimental probability to solve real-world problems?

EXAMPLE 1

What is the probability of picking a red marble from a jar with 5 green marbles and 2 red marbles?

$P(\text{picking a red marble}) = \frac{\text{number of red marbles}}{\text{number of total marbles}}$

$= \frac{2}{7}$ There are 2 red marbles. The total number of marbles is $2 + 5 = 7$.

EXAMPLE 2

For one month, a doctor recorded information about new patients as shown in the table.

	Senior	Adult	Young adult	Child
Female	5	8	2	14
Male	3	10	1	17

What is the experimental probability that his next new patient is a female adult?

$P\left(\begin{array}{l}\text{new patient is a}\\ \text{female adult}\end{array}\right) = \frac{\text{number of female adults}}{\text{total number of patients}}$

$P = \frac{8}{60} = \frac{2}{15}$

What is the experimental probability that his next new patient is a child?

$P\left(\begin{array}{l}\text{new patient is}\\ \text{a child}\end{array}\right) = \frac{\text{number of children}}{\text{total number of patients}}$

$P = \frac{31}{60}$

EXERCISES

Find the probability of each event. (Lesson 12.1)

1. Rolling a 5 on a fair number cube.

____

2. Picking a 7 from a standard deck of 52 cards. A standard deck includes 4 cards of each number from 2 to 10.

____

3. Picking a blue marble from a bag of 4 red marbles, 6 blue marbles, and 1 white marble.

____

4. Rolling a number greater than 7 on a 12-sided number cube.

____

5. Christopher picked coins randomly from his piggy bank and got the numbers of coins shown in the table. Find each experimental probability. (Lessons 12.2, 12.3)

Penny	Nickel	Dime	Quarter
7	2	8	6

a. The next coin that Christopher picks is a quarter. ________________

b. The next coin that Christopher picks is not a quarter. ____________

c. The next coin that Christopher picks is a penny or a nickel. _______

6. A grocery store manager found that 54% of customers usually bring their own bags. In one afternoon, 82 out of 124 customers brought their own grocery bags. Did a greater or lesser number of people than usual bring their own bags? (Lesson 12.4)

____

MODULE 13 Theoretical Probability

Key Vocabulary
theoretical probability
(probabilidad teórica)

ESSENTIAL QUESTION

How can you use theoretical probability to solve real-world problems?

EXAMPLE 1

A. Lola rolls two fair number cubes. What is the probability that the two numbers Lola rolls include at least one 4 and have a product of at least 16?

There are 5 pairs of numbers that include a 4 and have a product of at least 16:

(4, 4), (4, 5), (4, 6), (5, 4), (6, 4)

Find the probability.

$$P = \frac{\text{number of possible ways}}{\text{total number of possible outcomes}} = \frac{5}{36}$$

	1	2	3	4	5	6
1	1	2	3	4	5	6
2	2	4	6	8	10	12
3	3	6	9	12	15	18
4	4	8	12	16	20	24
5	5	10	15	20	25	30
6	6	12	18	24	30	36

B. Suppose Lola rolls the two number cubes 180 times. Predict how many times she will roll two numbers that include a pair of numbers like the ones described above.

One way to answer is to write and solve an equation.

$\frac{5}{36} \times 180 = x$ Multiply the probability by the total number of rolls.

$25 = x$ Solve for x.

Lola can expect to roll two numbers that include at least one 4 and have a product of 16 or more about 25 times.

EXAMPLE 2

A store has a sale bin of soup cans. There are 6 cans of chicken noodle soup, 8 cans of split pea soup, 8 cans of minestrone, and 13 cans of vegetable soup. Find the probability of picking each type of soup at random. Then predict what kind of soup a customer is most likely to pick.

$P(\text{chicken noodle}) = \frac{6}{35}$

$P(\text{split pea}) = \frac{8}{35}$

$P(\text{minestrone}) = \frac{8}{35}$

$P(\text{vegetable}) = \frac{13}{35}$

The customer is most likely to pick vegetable soup. That is the event that has the greatest probability.

EXERCISES

Find the probability of each event. (Lessons 13.1, 13.2)

1. Graciela picks a white mouse at random from a bin of 8 white mice, 2 gray mice, and 2 brown mice.

____

2. Theo spins a spinner that has 12 equal sections marked 1 through 12. It does **not** land on 1.

____

3. Patty tosses a coin and rolls a number cube. (Lesson 13.3)

a. Find the probability that the coin lands on heads and the cube lands on an even number.

____

b. Patty tosses the coin and rolls the number cube 60 times. Predict how many times the coin will land on heads and the cube will land on an even number.

____

4. Rajan's school is having a raffle. The school sold raffle tickets with 3-digit numbers. Each digit is either 1, 2, or 3. The school also sold 2 tickets with the number 000. Which number is more likely to be picked, 123 or 000? (Lesson 13.3)

____

5. Suppose you know that over the last 10 years, the probability that your town would have at least one major storm was 40%. Describe a simulation that you could use to find the experimental probability that your town will have at least one major storm in at least 3 of the next 5 years. (Lesson 13.4)

____

____

____

____

Unit Project

CA CC 7.SP.5, 7.SP.6, 7.SP.7a, 7.SP.7b

A Birthday Puzzle

Here's a fact that you may find hard to believe: In any group of 23 randomly chosen people, it is more likely than unlikely that two of them share the same birthday!

To test the rule, collect information for a list of 23 people and their birthdays. The people on your list should be randomly chosen from a well-defined group, such as 23 members of a major league baseball team, the first 23 governors of your state, 23 Olympic swimming champions, or 23 Nobel Prize winners in chemistry. Create a presentation showing the names and birthdays. Tell whether any two of your people share the same birthday and explain how you determined that fact. Then share your results with the other students in your class. Determine how many of them had results that supported the "23" rule and how many did not.

Use the space below to write down any questions you have or important information from your teacher.

MATH IN CAREERS | ACTIVITY

Meteorologist A meteorologist predicts a 20% chance of rain for the next two nights and a 75% chance of rain on the third night.

Tara would like to go camping for the next 3 nights but will not go if it is likely to rain on all 3 nights. Should she go? Use probability to justify your answer.

UNIT 6
MIXED REVIEW

Assessment Readiness

1. Look at each expression. Is the expression equivalent to $6x + 8$?

Select Yes or No for each expression.

A. $(4x - 5) + (2x + 13)$ ○ Yes ○ No
B. $(8x - 1) - (2x + 9)$ ○ Yes ○ No
C. $2(3x + 4)$ ○ Yes ○ No

2. Sofia spins the pointer of a spinner that has 5 equal sections numbered 1 to 5.

Choose True or False for each statement.

A. It is likely that the pointer will land on a factor of 4. ○ True ○ False
B. It is as likely as not that the pointer will land on an odd number. ○ True ○ False
C. It is unlikely that the pointer will land on a number greater than 3. ○ True ○ False

3. The experimental probability that a person in the United States has the A+ blood type is 35.7%. The experimental probability that a person in the United States has the AB– blood type is 0.6%. Last week, a blood bank received 224 donations. Predict how many more A+ donations the bank received than AB– donations. Explain your reasoning.

4. Bag A contains 24 white marbles, 18 blue marbles, and 5 green marbles. Bag B contains 36 white marbles, 28 blue marbles, and 8 green marbles. Felix will win a prize if he randomly chooses a green marble from a bag. Should he choose from Bag A or Bag B to have a better chance of winning? Justify your answer.

Performance Tasks

★**5.** Darrin tosses a quarter and a penny 20 times. He gets heads on both coins twice. Compare the theoretical probability of getting heads on both coins with Darrin's experimental probability of getting heads on both coins. Why might the probabilities differ?

★★**6.** A board game has the spinner shown at the right. On each turn, a player spins the pointer twice and adds the numbers that the pointer lands on.

4 1
3 2

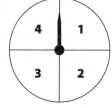

a. Make a table that shows the sample space of the sums a player could get on each turn.

b. A player who spins a sum of 7 gets to pick a Lucky card. What is the probability that Evelyn will get to pick a Lucky card on her next turn? Explain your reasoning.

c. A player who spins a sum of 2 has to pick an Unlucky card. If Evelyn has 30 turns during a game, how many more Lucky cards than Unlucky cards can she expect to get? Justify your answer.

★★★**7.** A restaurant gives out a scratch-off card to every customer. The probability that a customer will win a prize from a scratch-off card is 25%. Design and conduct a simulation using random numbers to find the experimental probability that a customer will need more than 3 cards in order to win a prize. Justify the model for your simulation, and conduct at least 10 trials.

UNIT 7

Real Numbers, Exponents, and Scientific Notation

MODULE 14
Real Numbers
CA CC 8.NS.1, 8.NS.2, 8.EE.2

MODULE 15
Exponents and Scientific Notation
CA CC 8.EE.1, 8.EE.3, 8.EE.4

MATH IN CAREERS

Astronomer An astronomer is a scientist who studies and tries to interpret the universe beyond Earth. Astronomers use math to calculate distances to celestial objects and to create mathematical models to help them understand the dynamics of systems from stars and planets to black holes. If you are interested in a career as an astronomer, you should study the following mathematical subjects:

- Algebra
- Geometry
- Trigonometry
- Calculus

Research other careers that require creating mathematical models to understand physical phenomena.

ACTIVITY At the end of the unit, check out how **astronomers** use math.

Unit Project Preview

The Large and the Small of It

The Unit Project at the end of this unit will ask you to research amazing facts involving extremely large and extremely small numbers. You will illustrate the facts and write each of them in both standard and scientific notation. To successfully complete the Unit Project you'll need to master these skills:

- Understand integer exponents.
- Write numbers in scientific notation with positive powers of 10.
- Write numbers in scientific notation with negative powers of 10.

1. How is a number like 73,000,000,000,000,000 more challenging to write and comprehend than a number like 73?

____

____

2. What does 10^4 mean?

____

3. How can you use exponents to write 10,000,000?

____

Tracking Your Learning Progression

This unit addresses important California Common Core Standards in the Critical Area of working with non-rational numbers, radicals, and integer exponents.

Domain 8.NS The Number System

Cluster Know that there are numbers that are not rational, and approximate them by rational numbers.

The unit also supports additional standards.

Domain 8.EE Expressions and Equations

Cluster Work with radicals and integer exponents.

Real Numbers

ESSENTIAL QUESTION

How can you use real numbers to solve real-world problems?

LESSON 14.1

Rational and Irrational Numbers

 CA CC 8.NS.1, 8.NS.2, 8.EE.2

LESSON 14.2

Sets of Real Numbers

 CA CC 8.NS.1

LESSON 14.3

Ordering Real Numbers

 CA CC 8.NS.2

my.hrw.com

Real-World Video

Living creatures can be classified into groups. The sea otter belongs to the kingdom Animalia and class Mammalia. Numbers can also be classified into groups such as rational numbers and integers.

GO DIGITAL
my.hrw.com

my.hrw.com

Go digital with your write-in student edition, accessible on any device.

Math On the Spot

Scan with your smart phone to jump directly to the online edition, video tutor, and more.

Animated Math

Interactively explore key concepts to see how math works.

Personal Math Trainer

Get immediate feedback and help as you work through practice sets.

Are YOU Ready?

Complete these exercises to review skills you will need for this module.

Find the Square of a Number

EXAMPLE Find the square of $\frac{2}{3}$.

$\frac{2}{3} \times \frac{2}{3} = \frac{2 \times 2}{3 \times 3}$ Multiply the number by itself.

$= \frac{4}{9}$ Simplify.

Find the square of each number.

1. 7 ________ **2.** 21 ________ **3.** -3 ________ **4.** $\frac{4}{5}$ ________

5. 2.7 ________ **6.** $-\frac{1}{4}$ ________ **7.** -5.7 ________ **8.** $1\frac{2}{5}$ ________

Exponents

EXAMPLE $5^3 = 5 \times 5 \times 5$ Use the base, 5, as a factor 3 times.

$= 25 \times 5$ Multiply from left to right.

$= 125$

Simplify each exponential expression.

9. 9^2 ________ **10.** 2^4 ________ **11.** $\left(\frac{1}{3}\right)^2$ ________ **12.** $(-7)^2$ ________

13. 4^3 ________ **14.** $(-1)^5$ ________ **15.** 4.5^2 ________ **16.** 10^5 ________

Write a Mixed Number as an Improper Fraction

EXAMPLE $2\frac{2}{5} = 2 + \frac{2}{5}$ Write the mixed number as a sum of a whole number and a fraction.

$= \frac{10}{5} + \frac{2}{5}$ Write the whole number as an equivalent fraction with the same denominator as the fraction in the mixed number.

$= \frac{12}{5}$ Add the numerators.

Write each mixed number as an improper fraction.

17. $3\frac{1}{3}$ ________ **18.** $1\frac{5}{8}$ ________ **19.** $2\frac{3}{7}$ ________ **20.** $5\frac{5}{6}$ ________

Reading Start-Up

Visualize Vocabulary

Use the ✔ words to complete the graphic. You can put more than one word in each section of the triangle.

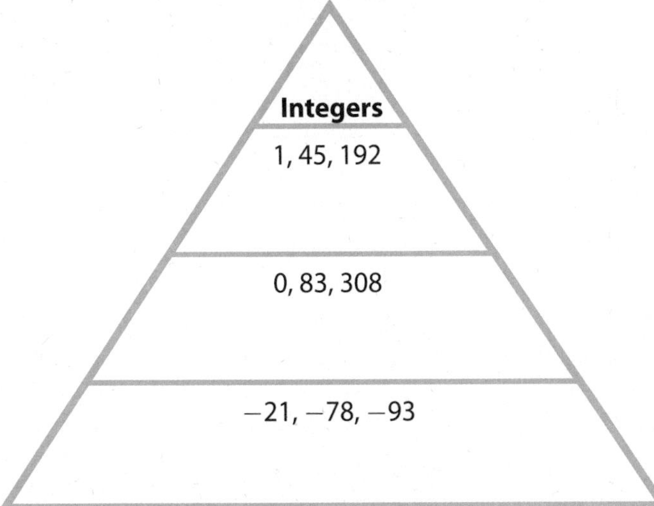

Understand Vocabulary

Complete the sentences using the preview words.

1. One of the two equal factors of a number is a ______________.
2. A ________________________ has integers as its square roots.
3. The ________________________ is the nonnegative square root of a number.

Vocabulary

Review Words

integers *(enteros)*
✔ negative numbers *(números negativos)*
✔ positive numbers *(números positivos)*
✔ whole number *(número entero)*

Preview Words

cube root *(raiz cúbica)*
irrational numbers *(número irracional)*
perfect cube *(cubo perfecto)*
perfect square *(cuadrado perfecto)*
principal square root *(raíz cuadrada principal)*
rational number *(número racional)*
real numbers *(número real)*
repeating decimal *(decimal periódico)*
square root *(raíz cuadrada)*
terminating decimal *(decimal finito)*

Active Reading

Layered Book Before beginning the lessons in this module, create a layered book to help you learn the concepts in this module. Label the flaps "Rational Numbers," "Irrational Numbers," "Square Roots," and "Real Numbers." As you study each lesson, write important ideas such as vocabulary, models, and sample problems under the appropriate flap.

GETTING READY FOR

Real Numbers

Understanding the standards and the vocabulary terms in the standards will help you know exactly what you are expected to learn in this module.

 CA CC **8.NS.1**

Know that numbers that are not rational are called irrational. Understand informally that every number has a decimal expansion; for rational numbers show that the decimal expansion repeats eventually, and convert a decimal expansion which repeats eventually into a rational number.

Key Vocabulary

rational number *(número racional)*
A number that can be expressed as a ratio of two integers.

irrational number *(número irracional)*
A number that cannot be expressed as a ratio of two integers or as a repeating or terminating decimal.

What It Means to You

You will recognize a number as rational or irrational by looking at its fraction or decimal form.

EXAMPLE 8.NS.1

Classify each number as rational or irrational.

$0.\overline{3} = \frac{1}{3}$ $\qquad$ $0.25 = \frac{1}{4}$

These numbers are rational because they can be written as ratios of integers or as repeating or terminating decimals.

$\pi \approx 3.141592654\ldots$ $\qquad$ $\sqrt{5} \approx 2.236067977\ldots$

These numbers are irrational because they cannot be written as ratios of integers or as repeating or terminating decimals.

 CA CC **8.NS.2**

Use rational approximations of irrational numbers to compare the size of irrational numbers, locate them approximately on a number line diagram, and estimate the value of expressions (e.g., π^2).

What It Means to You

You will learn to estimate the values of irrational numbers.

EXAMPLE 8.NS.2

Estimate the value of $\sqrt{8}$.

8 is not a perfect square. Find the two perfect squares closest to 8.

8 is between the perfect squares 4 and 9.
So $\sqrt{8}$ is between $\sqrt{4}$ and $\sqrt{9}$.
$\sqrt{8}$ is between 2 and 3.

8 is closer to 9, so $\sqrt{8}$ is closer to 3.
$2.8^2 = 7.84$ $\qquad$ $2.9^2 = 8.41$
$\sqrt{8}$ is between 2.8 and 2.9
A good estimate for $\sqrt{8}$ is 2.85.

Visit **my.hrw.com** to see all **CA Common Core Standards** explained.

my.hrw.com

LESSON 14.1

Rational and Irrational Numbers

CA CC 8.NS.1

Know that numbers that are not rational are called irrational. Understand informally that every number has a decimal expansion; for rational numbers show that the decimal expansion repeats eventually, and convert a decimal expansion which repeats eventually into a relation number. *Also 8.NS.2, 8.EE.2*

ESSENTIAL QUESTION

How do you rewrite rational numbers and decimals, take square roots and cube roots, and approximate irrational numbers?

Expressing Rational Numbers as Decimals

A **rational number** is any number that can be written as a ratio in the form $\frac{a}{b}$, where a and b are integers and b is not 0. Examples of rational numbers are 6 and 0.5.

6 can be written as $\frac{6}{1}$.   0.5 can be written as $\frac{1}{2}$.

Every rational number can be written as a terminating decimal or a repeating decimal. A **terminating decimal**, such as 0.5, has a finite number of digits. A **repeating decimal** has a block of one or more digits that repeat indefinitely.

EXAMPLE 1

Write each fraction as a decimal.

A $\frac{1}{4}$

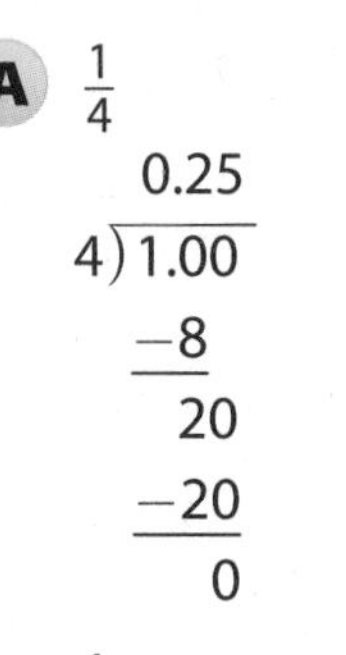

$$\begin{array}{r} 0.25 \\ 4\overline{)1.00} \\ \underline{-8} \\ 20 \\ \underline{-20} \\ 0 \end{array}$$

$\frac{1}{4} = 0.25$

Remember that the fraction bar means "divided by." Divide the numerator by the denominator.

Divide until the remainder is zero, adding zeros after the decimal point in the dividend as needed.

B $\frac{1}{3}$

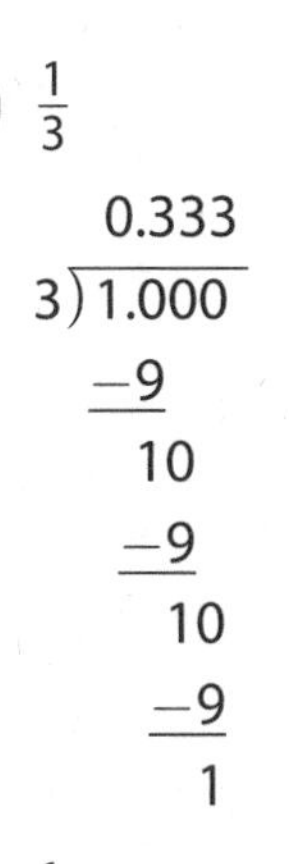

$$\begin{array}{r} 0.333 \\ 3\overline{)1.000} \\ \underline{-9} \\ 10 \\ \underline{-9} \\ 10 \\ \underline{-9} \\ 1 \end{array}$$

$\frac{1}{3} = 0.\overline{3}$

Divide until the remainder is zero or until the digits in the quotient begin to repeat.

Add zeros after the decimal point in the dividend as needed.

When a decimal has one or more digits that repeat indefinitely, write the decimal with a bar over the repeating digit(s).

My Notes

YOUR TURN

Write each fraction as a decimal.

1. $\frac{5}{11}$ ________ **2.** $\frac{1}{8}$ ________ **3.** $2\frac{1}{3}$ ________

Expressing Decimals as Rational Numbers

You can express terminating and repeating decimals as rational numbers.

EXAMPLE 2

My Notes

Write each decimal as a fraction in simplest form.

A 0.825

The decimal 0.825 means "825 thousandths." Write this as a fraction.

$\frac{825}{1000}$ *To write "825 thousandths", put 825 over 1000.*

Then simplify the fraction.

$\frac{825 \div 25}{1000 \div 25} = \frac{33}{40}$ *Divide both the numerator and the denominator by 25.*

$0.825 = \frac{33}{40}$

B $0.\overline{37}$

Let $x = 0.\overline{37}$. The number $0.\overline{37}$ has 2 repeating digits, so multiply each side of the equation $x = 0.\overline{37}$ by 10^2, or 100.

$x = 0.\overline{37}$

$(100)x = 100(0.\overline{37})$

$100x = 37.\overline{37}$ *100 times $0.\overline{37}$ is $37.\overline{37}$.*

Because $x = 0.\overline{37}$, you can subtract x from one side and $0.\overline{37}$ from the other.

$100x = 37.\overline{37}$

$-x \quad -0.\overline{37}$

$99x = 37$ *$37.\overline{37}$ minus $0.\overline{37}$ is 37.*

Now solve the equation for x. Simplify if necessary.

$\frac{99x}{99} = \frac{37}{99}$ *Divide both sides of the equation by 99.*

$x = \frac{37}{99}$

YOUR TURN

Write each decimal as a fraction in simplest form.

4. 0.12 ________ **5.** $0.\overline{57}$ ________ **6.** 1.4 ________

Math On the Spot
my.hrw.com

Finding Square Roots and Cube Roots

The **square root** of a positive number p is x if $x^2 = p$. There are two square roots for every positive number. For example, the square roots of 36 are 6 and -6 because $6^2 = 36$ and $(-6)^2 = 36$. The square roots of $\frac{1}{25}$ are $\frac{1}{5}$ and $-\frac{1}{5}$. You can write the square roots of $\frac{1}{25}$ as $\pm\frac{1}{5}$. The symbol $\sqrt{\ }$ indicates the positive, or **principal square root**.

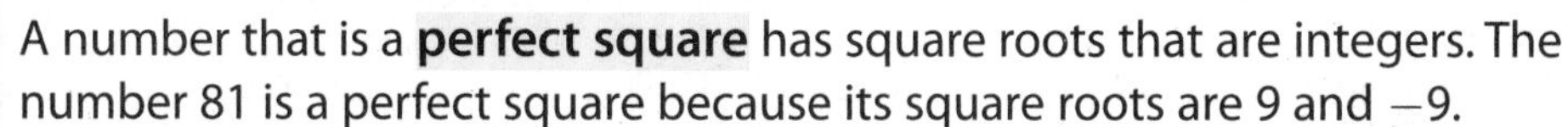

A number that is a **perfect square** has square roots that are integers. The number 81 is a perfect square because its square roots are 9 and -9.

The **cube root** of a positive number p is x if $x^3 = p$. There is one cube root for every positive number. For example, the cube root of 8 is 2 because $2^3 = 8$. The cube root of $\frac{1}{27}$ is $\frac{1}{3}$ because $\left(\frac{1}{3}\right)^3 = \frac{1}{27}$. The symbol $\sqrt[3]{\ }$ indicates the cube root.

A number that is a **perfect cube** has a cube root that is an integer. The number 125 is a perfect cube because its cube root is 5.

EXAMPLE 3

CA CC 8.EE.2

Solve each equation for x.

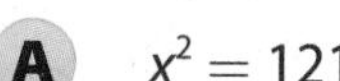

A $x^2 = 121$

$x^2 = 121$ Solve for x by taking the square root of both sides.

$x = \pm\sqrt{121}$ Apply the definition of square root.

$x = \pm 11$ Think: What numbers squared equal 121?

The solutions are 11 and -11.

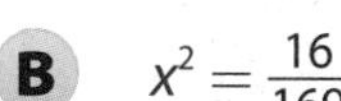

B $x^2 = \frac{16}{169}$

$x^2 = \frac{16}{169}$ Solve for x by taking the square root of both sides.

$x = \pm\sqrt{\frac{16}{169}}$ Apply the definition of square root.

$x = \pm\frac{4}{13}$ Think: What numbers squared equal $\frac{16}{169}$?

The solutions are $\frac{4}{13}$ and $-\frac{4}{13}$.

Can you square an integer and get a negative number? What does this indicate about whether negative numbers have square roots?

C $729 = x^3$

$\sqrt[3]{729} = \sqrt[3]{x^3}$ — Solve for x by taking the cube root of both sides.

$\sqrt[3]{729} = x$ — Apply the definition of cube root.

$9 = x$ — Think: What number cubed equals 729?

The solution is 9.

D $x^3 = \frac{8}{125}$

$\sqrt[3]{x^3} = \sqrt[3]{\frac{8}{125}}$ — Solve for x by taking the cube root of both sides.

$x = \sqrt[3]{\frac{8}{125}}$ — Apply the definition of cube root.

$x = \frac{2}{5}$ — Think: What number cubed equals $\frac{8}{125}$?

The solution is $\frac{2}{5}$.

Personal Math Trainer

Online Practice and Help

my.hrw.com

YOUR TURN

Solve each equation for *x*.

7. $x^2 = 196$ ________________

8. $x^2 = \frac{9}{256}$ ________________

9. $x^3 = 512$ ________________

10. $x^3 = \frac{64}{343}$ ________________

EXPLORE ACTIVITY CA CC 8.NS.2, 8.EE.2

Estimating Irrational Numbers

Irrational numbers are numbers that are not rational. In other words, they cannot be written in the form $\frac{a}{b}$, where a and b are integers and b is not 0. Square roots of perfect squares are rational numbers. Square roots of numbers that are not perfect squares are irrational. Some equations like those in Example 3 involve square roots of numbers that are not perfect squares.

$x^2 = 2$ $\qquad$ $x = \pm\sqrt{2}$ $\qquad$ $\sqrt{2}$ is irrational.

Estimate the value of $\sqrt{2}$.

A Find two consecutive perfect squares that 2 is between. Complete the inequality by writing these perfect squares in the boxes.

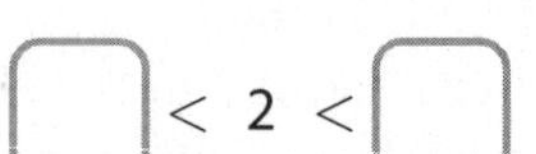

$\square < 2 < \square$

B Now take the square root of each number.

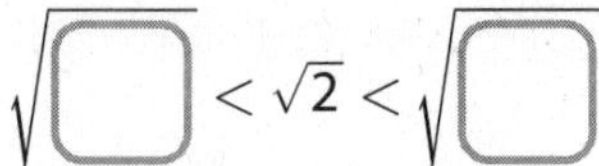

$\sqrt{\square} < \sqrt{2} < \sqrt{\square}$

C Simplify the square roots of perfect squares.

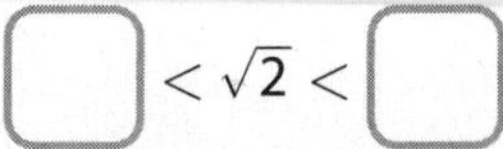

$\square < \sqrt{2} < \square$

$\sqrt{2}$ is between ________ and ________.

D Estimate that $\sqrt{2} \approx 1.5$.

$\sqrt{2} \approx 1.5$

0 1 2 3 4

E To find a better estimate, first choose some numbers between 1 and 2 and square them. For example, choose 1.3, 1.4, and 1.5.

$1.3^2 =$ ________ $1.4^2 =$ ________ $1.5^2 =$ ________

Is $\sqrt{2}$ between 1.3 and 1.4? How do you know?

____

____

Is $\sqrt{2}$ between 1.4 and 1.5? How do you know?

____

____

2 is closer to ________ than to ________, so $\sqrt{2} \approx$ ________.

F Locate and label this value on the number line.

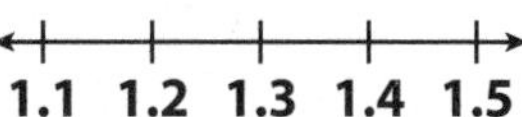

Reflect

11. How could you find an even better estimate of $\sqrt{2}$?

____

____

12. Find a better estimate of $\sqrt{2}$.

$1.41^2 =$ ________ $1.42^2 =$ ________ $1.43^2 =$ ________

2 is closer to ________ than to ________, so $\sqrt{2} \approx$ ________.

Draw a number line and locate and label your estimate.

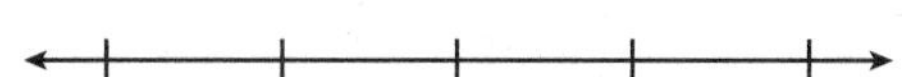

13. Solve $x^2 = 7$. Write your answer as a radical expression. Then estimate to one decimal place.

____

Guided Practice

Write each fraction or mixed number as a decimal. (Example 1)

1. $\frac{2}{5}$ ________
2. $\frac{8}{9}$ ________
3. $3\frac{3}{4}$ ________
4. $\frac{7}{10}$ ________
5. $2\frac{3}{8}$ ________
6. $\frac{5}{6}$ ________

Write each decimal as a fraction or mixed number in simplest form. (Example 2)

7. 0.675 ________
8. 5.6 ________
9. 0.44 ________
10. $0.\overline{4}$

$10x = \square$

$-x \quad -\square$

$\square x = \square$

$x =$ ________

11. $0.\overline{26}$

$100x = \square$

$-x \quad -\square$

$\square x = \square$

$x =$ ________

12. $0.\overline{325}$

$1000x = \square$

$-x \quad -\square$

$\square x = \square$

$x =$ ________

Solve each equation for *x*. (Example 3 and Explore Activity)

13. $x^2 = 17$

$x = \pm\sqrt{\square} \approx \pm\square$

14. $x^2 = \frac{25}{289}$

$x = \pm\sqrt{\frac{\square}{\square}} = \pm\frac{\square}{\square}$

15. $x^3 = 216$

$x = \sqrt[3]{\square} = \square$

Approximate each irrational number to one decimal place without a calculator. (Explore Activity)

16. $\sqrt{5} \approx \square$
17. $\sqrt{3} \approx \square$
18. $\sqrt{10} \approx \square$

ESSENTIAL QUESTION CHECK-IN

19. What is the difference between rational and irrational numbers?

____

____

____

Name ____________________ Class ____________________ Date ____________________

14.1 Independent Practice

CA CC 8.NS.1, 8.NS.2, 8.EE.2

20. A $\frac{7}{16}$-inch-long bolt is used in a machine. What is this length written as a decimal?

____

21. The weight of an object on the moon is $\frac{1}{6}$ its weight on Earth. Write $\frac{1}{6}$ as a decimal.

____

22. The distance to the nearest gas station is $2\frac{4}{5}$ kilometers. What is this distance written as a decimal?

____

23. A baseball pitcher has pitched $98\frac{2}{3}$ innings. What is the number of innings written as a decimal?

____

24. A heartbeat takes 0.8 second. How many seconds is this written as a fraction?

____

25. There are 26.2 miles in a marathon. Write the number of miles using a fraction.

____

26. The average score on a biology test was $72.\overline{1}$. Write the average score using a fraction.

____

27. The metal in a penny is worth about 0.505 cent. How many cents is this written as a fraction?

____

28. **Multistep** An artist wants to frame a square painting with an area of 400 square inches. She wants to know the length of the wood trim that is needed to go around the painting.

a. If x is the length of one side of the painting, what equation can you set up to find the length of a side? How many solutions does the equation have?

____

b. Do all of the solutions that you found make sense in the context of the problem? Explain.

____

____

c. What is the length of the wood trim needed to go around the painting?

____

Solve each equation for x. Write your answers as radical expressions. Then estimate to one decimal place, if necessary.

29. $x^2 = 14$ ______________________

30. $x^3 = 1331$ ______________________

31. $x^2 = 144$ ______________________

32. $x^2 = 29$ ______________________

33. **Analyze Relationships** To find $\sqrt{15}$, Beau found $3^2 = 9$ and $4^2 = 16$. He said that since 15 is between 9 and 16, $\sqrt{15}$ must be between 3 and 4. He thinks a good estimate for $\sqrt{15}$ is $\frac{3+4}{2} = 3.5$. Is Beau's estimate high, low, or correct? Explain.

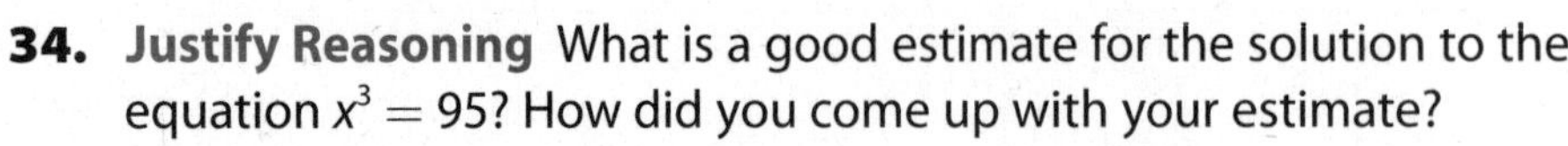

34. **Justify Reasoning** What is a good estimate for the solution to the equation $x^3 = 95$? How did you come up with your estimate?

35. The volume of a sphere is 36π ft^3. What is the radius of the sphere? Use the formula $V = \frac{4}{3}\pi r^3$ to find your answer.

FOCUS ON HIGHER ORDER THINKING

Work Area

36. **Draw Conclusions** Can you find the cube root of a negative number? If so, is it positive or negative? Explain your reasoning.

37. **Make a Conjecture** Evaluate and compare the following expressions.

$$\sqrt{\frac{4}{25}} \text{ and } \frac{\sqrt{4}}{\sqrt{25}} \qquad \sqrt{\frac{16}{81}} \text{ and } \frac{\sqrt{16}}{\sqrt{81}} \qquad \sqrt{\frac{36}{49}} \text{ and } \frac{\sqrt{36}}{\sqrt{49}}$$

Use your results to make a conjecture about a division rule for square roots. Since division is multiplication by the reciprocal, make a conjecture about a multiplication rule for square roots.

38. **Persevere in Problem Solving** The difference between the solutions to the equation $x^2 = a$ is 30. What is a? Show that your answer is correct.

LESSON 14.2
Sets of Real Numbers

CA CC 8.NS.1

Know that numbers that are not rational are called irrational. Understand informally that every number has a decimal expansion; for rational numbers show that the decimal expansion repeats eventually, and convert a decimal expansion which repeats eventually into a relation number.

ESSENTIAL QUESTION

How can you describe relationships between sets of real numbers?

Classifying Real Numbers

Biologists classify animals based on shared characteristics. A cardinal is an animal, a vertebrate, a bird, and a passerine.

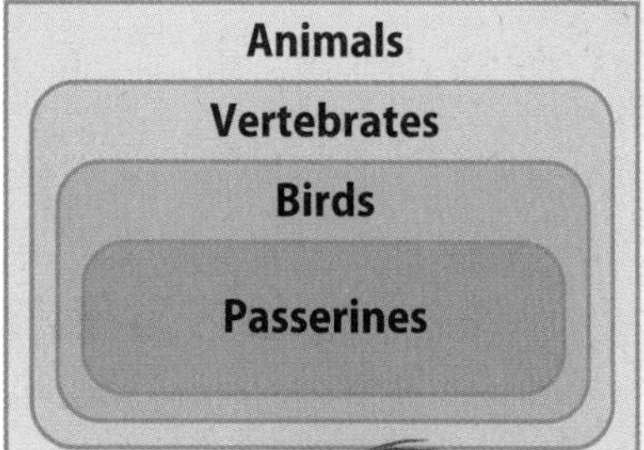

You already know that the set of rational numbers consists of whole numbers, integers, and fractions. The set of **real numbers** consists of the set of rational numbers and the set of irrational numbers.

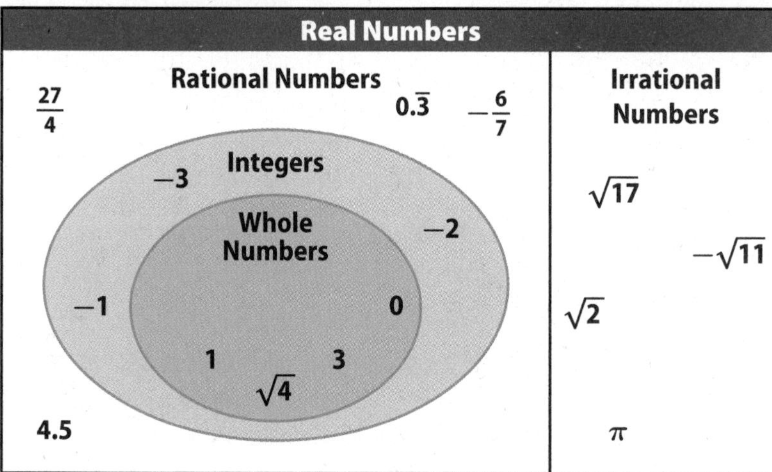

Passerines, such as the cardinal, are also called "perching birds."

EXAMPLE 1

CA CC 8.NS.1

Animated Math my.hrw.com

Write all names that apply to each number.

A $\sqrt{5}$ — 5 is a whole number that is not a perfect square.

irrational, real

B -17.84 — -17.84 is a terminating decimal.

rational, real

C $\frac{\sqrt{81}}{9}$ — $\frac{\sqrt{81}}{9} = \frac{9}{9} = 1$

whole, integer, rational, real

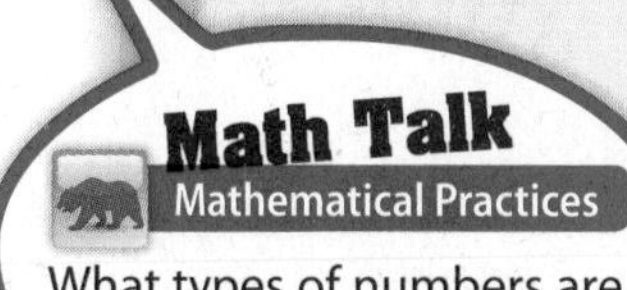

Math Talk
Mathematical Practices
What types of numbers are between 3.1 and 3.9 on a number line?

YOUR TURN

Write all names that apply to each number.

1. A baseball pitcher has pitched $12\frac{2}{3}$ innings.

____

2. The length of the side of a square that has an area of 10 square yards. _______________

Understanding Sets and Subsets of Real Numbers

By understanding which sets are subsets of types of numbers, you can verify whether statements about the relationships between sets are true or false.

EXAMPLE 2

Tell whether the given statement is true or false. Explain your choice.

A All irrational numbers are real numbers.

True. Every irrational number is included in the set of real numbers. The irrational numbers are a subset of the real numbers.

B No rational numbers are whole numbers.

False. A whole number can be written as a fraction with a denominator of 1, so every whole number is included in the set of rational numbers. The whole numbers are a subset of the rational numbers.

Math Talk
Mathematical Practices

Give an example of a rational number that is a whole number. Show that the number is both whole and rational.

YOUR TURN

Tell whether the given statement is true or false. Explain your choice.

3. All rational numbers are integers.

____

____

____

4. Some irrational numbers are integers.

____

____

Personal Math Trainer
Online Practice and Help
my.hrw.com

Identifying Sets for Real-World Situations

Real numbers can be used to represent real-world quantities. Highways have posted speed limit signs that are represented by natural numbers such as 55 mph. Integers appear on thermometers. Rational numbers are used in many daily activities, including cooking. For example, ingredients in a recipe are often given in fractional amounts such as $\frac{2}{3}$ cup flour.

EXAMPLE 3  

CA CC 8.NS.1

Identify the set of numbers that best describes each situation. Explain your choice.

A the number of people wearing glasses in a room

The set of whole numbers best describes the situation. The number of people wearing glasses may be 0 or a counting number.

B the circumference of a flying disk has a diameter of 8, 9, 10, 11, or 14 inches

The set of irrational numbers best describes the situation. Each circumference would be a product of π and the diameter, and any multiple of π is irrational.

My Notes

Identify the set of numbers that best describes the situation. Explain your choice.

5. the amount of water in a glass as it evaporates

____

____

____

6. the weight of a person in pounds

____

____

____

Guided Practice

Write all names that apply to each number. (Example 1)

1. $\frac{7}{8}$

2. $\sqrt{36}$

3. $\sqrt{24}$

4. 0.75

5. 0

6. $-\sqrt{100}$

7. $5.\overline{45}$

8. $-\frac{18}{6}$

Tell whether the given statement is true or false. Explain your choice. (Example 2)

9. All whole numbers are rational numbers.

10. No irrational numbers are whole numbers.

Identify the set of numbers that best describes each situation. Explain your choice. (Example 3)

11. the change in the value of an account when given to the nearest dollar

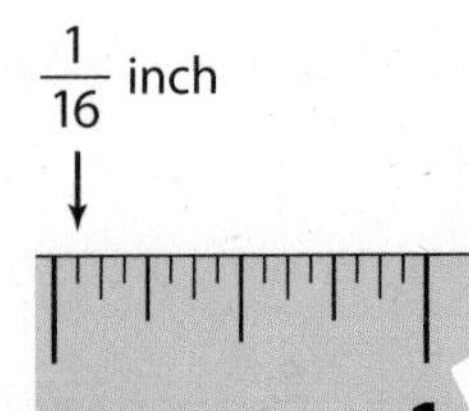

12. the markings on a standard ruler

ESSENTIAL QUESTION CHECK-IN

13. What are some ways to describe the relationships between sets of numbers?

Name ______________________ Class ______________ Date ______________

14.2 Independent Practice

8.NS.1

Write all names that apply to each number. Then place the numbers in the correct location on the Venn diagram.

14. $-\sqrt{9}$ ______________

15. 257 ______________

16. $\sqrt{50}$ ______________

17. $8\frac{1}{2}$ ______________

18. 16.6 ______________

19. $\sqrt{16}$ ______________

Real Numbers	
Rational Numbers (Integers (Whole Numbers))	Irrational Numbers

Identify the set of numbers that best describes each situation. Explain your choice.

20. the height of an airplane as it descends to an airport runway

____

21. the score with respect to par of several golfers: 2, −3, 5, 0, −1

____

____

22. **Critique Reasoning** Ronald states that the number $\frac{1}{11}$ is not rational because, when converted into a decimal, it does not terminate. Nathaniel says it is rational because it is a fraction. Which boy is correct? Explain.

____

____

23. Critique Reasoning The circumference of a circular region is shown. What type of number best describes the diameter of the circle? Explain your answer. ____________

π mi

24. Critical Thinking A number is not an integer. What type of number can it be?

____

25. A grocery store has a shelf with half-gallon containers of milk. What type of number best represents the total number of gallons?

____

H.O.T. FOCUS ON HIGHER ORDER THINKING

Work Area

26. Explain the Error Katie said, "Negative numbers are integers." What was her error?

____

____

27. Justify Reasoning Can you ever use a calculator to determine if a number is rational or irrational? Explain.

____

____

____

____

____

____

____

28. Draw Conclusions The decimal $0.\overline{3}$ represents $\frac{1}{3}$. What type of number best describes $0.\overline{9}$, which is $3 \cdot 0.\overline{3}$? Explain.

____

29. Communicate Mathematical Ideas Irrational numbers can never be precisely represented in decimal form. Why is this?

____

____

____

____

LESSON 14.3

Ordering Real Numbers

CA CC 8.NS.2

Use rational approximations of irrational numbers to compare the size of irrational numbers, locate them approximately on a number line diagram, and estimate the value of expressions (e.g., π^2).

ESSENTIAL QUESTION

How do you order a set of real numbers?

Comparing Irrational Numbers

Between any two real numbers is another real number. To compare and order real numbers, you can approximate irrational numbers as decimals.

EXAMPLE 1

CA CC 8.NS.2

Compare $\sqrt{3} + 5$ ○ $3 + \sqrt{5}$. Write <, >, or =.

STEP 1 First approximate $\sqrt{3}$.

$\sqrt{3}$ is between 1 and 2.

Next approximate $\sqrt{5}$.

$\sqrt{5}$ is between 2 and 3.

Use perfect squares to estimate square roots. $1^2 = 1 \quad 2^2 = 4 \quad 3^2 = 9$

STEP 2 Then use your approximations to simplify the expressions.

$\sqrt{3} + 5$ is between 6 and 7.

$3 + \sqrt{5}$ is between 5 and 6.

So, $\sqrt{3} + 5 > 3 + \sqrt{5}$.

My Notes

Reflect

1. If $7 + \sqrt{5}$ is equal to $\sqrt{5}$ plus a number, what do you know about the number? Why?

____

2. What are the closest two integers that $\sqrt{300}$ is between?

____

Compare. Write <, >, or =.

3. $\sqrt{2} + 4$ ○ $2 + \sqrt{4}$

4. $\sqrt{12} + 6$ ○ $12 + \sqrt{6}$

Personal Math Trainer

Online Practice and Help

my.hrw.com

Ordering Real Numbers

You can compare and order real numbers and list them from least to greatest.

EXAMPLE 2

Order $\sqrt{22}$, $\pi + 1$, and $4\frac{1}{2}$ from least to greatest.

STEP 1 First approximate $\sqrt{22}$.

$\sqrt{22}$ is between 4 and 5. Since you don't know where it falls between 4 and 5, you need to find a better estimate for $\sqrt{22}$ so you can compare it to $4\frac{1}{2}$.

Since 22 is closer to 25 than 16, use squares of numbers between 4.5 and 5 to find a better estimate of $\sqrt{22}$.

$4.5^2 = 20.25$ $4.6^2 = 21.16$ $4.7^2 = 22.09$ $4.8^2 = 23.04$

Since $4.7^2 = 22.09$, an approximate value for $\sqrt{22}$ is 4.7.

An approximate value of π is 3.14. So an approximate value of $\pi + 1$ is 4.14.

STEP 2 Plot $\sqrt{22}$, $\pi + 1$, and $4\frac{1}{2}$ on a number line.

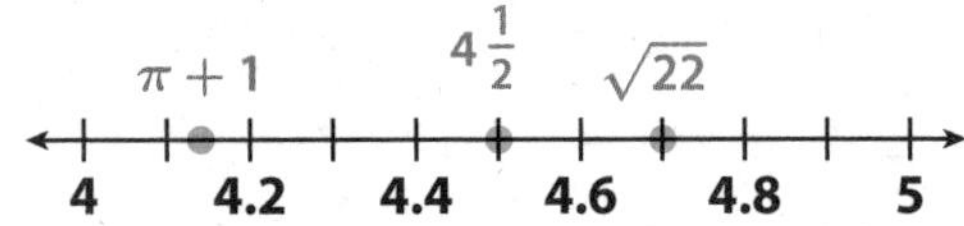

Read the numbers from left to right to place them in order from least to greatest.

From least to greatest, the numbers are $\pi + 1$, $4\frac{1}{2}$, and $\sqrt{22}$.

YOUR TURN

Order the numbers from least to greatest. Then graph them on the number line.

5. $\sqrt{5}$, 2.5, $\sqrt{3}$ ______________________

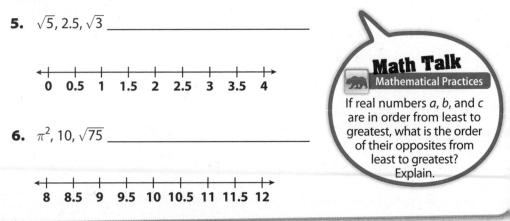

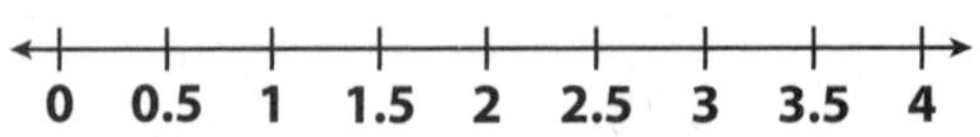

6. π^2, 10, $\sqrt{75}$ ______________________

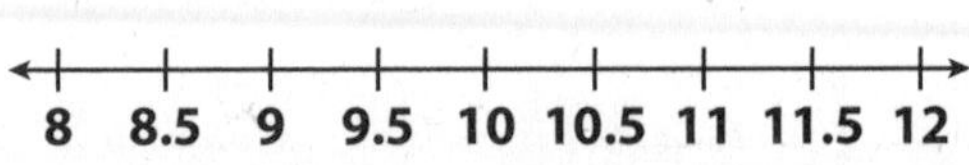

If real numbers *a*, *b*, and *c* are in order from least to greatest, what is the order of their opposites from least to greatest? Explain.

Ordering Real Numbers in a Real-World Context

Calculations and estimations in the real world may differ. It can be important to know not only which are the most accurate but which give the greatest or least values, depending upon the context.

EXAMPLE 3 

Four people have found the distance in kilometers across a canyon using different methods. Their results are given in the table. Order the distances from greatest to least.

Distance Across Quarry Canyon (km)			
Juana	**Lee Ann**	**Ryne**	**Jackson**
$\sqrt{28}$	$\frac{23}{4}$	$5.\overline{5}$	$5\frac{1}{2}$

STEP 1 Write each value as a decimal.

$\sqrt{28}$ is between 5.2 and 5.3. Since $5.3^2 = 28.09$, an approximate value for $\sqrt{28}$ is 5.3.

$\frac{23}{4} = 5.75$

$5.\overline{5}$ is 5.555..., so $5.\overline{5}$ to the nearest hundredth is 5.56.

$5\frac{1}{2} = 5.5$

STEP 2 Plot $\sqrt{28}$, $\frac{23}{4}$, $5.\overline{5}$, and $5\frac{1}{2}$ on a number line.

From greatest to least, the distances are:

$\frac{23}{4}$ km, $5.\overline{5}$ km, $5\frac{1}{2}$ km, $\sqrt{28}$ km.

My Notes

YOUR TURN

7. Four people have found the distance in miles across a crater using different methods. Their results are given below.

Jonathan: $\frac{10}{3}$, Elaine: $3.\overline{45}$, José: $3\frac{1}{2}$, Lashonda: $\sqrt{10}$

Order the distances from greatest to least.

____

Guided Practice

Compare. Write <, >, or =. (Example 1)

1. $\sqrt{3} + 2$ ◯ $\sqrt{3} + 3$

2. $\sqrt{8} + 17$ ◯ $\sqrt{11} + 15$

3. $\sqrt{6} + 5$ ◯ $6 + \sqrt{5}$

4. $\sqrt{9} + 3$ ◯ $9 + \sqrt{3}$

5. $\sqrt{17} - 3$ ◯ $-2 + \sqrt{5}$

6. $12 - \sqrt{2}$ ◯ $14 - \sqrt{8}$

7. $\sqrt{7} + 2$ ◯ $\sqrt{10} - 1$

8. $\sqrt{17} + 3$ ◯ $3 + \sqrt{11}$

9. Order $\sqrt{3}$, 2π, and 1.5 from least to greatest. Then graph them on the number line. (Example 2)

$\sqrt{3}$ is between ____________ and ____________, so $\sqrt{3} \approx$ ____________.

$\pi \approx 3.14$, so $2\pi \approx$ ____________.

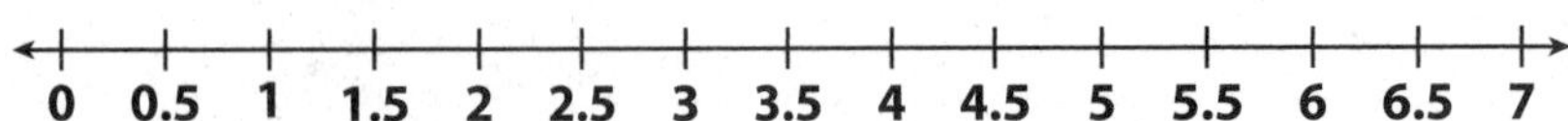

From least to greatest, the numbers are ____________, ____________,

____________.

10. Four people have found the perimeter of a forest using different methods. Their results are given in the table. Order their calculations from greatest to least. (Example 3)

____

____

Forest Perimeter (km)			
Leon	Mika	Jason	Ashley
$\sqrt{17} - 2$	$1 + \frac{\pi}{2}$	$\frac{12}{5}$	2.5

ESSENTIAL QUESTION CHECK-IN

11. Explain how to order a set of real numbers.

____

____

____

____

____

Name________________________ Class________________ Date____________

14.3 Independent Practice

CA CC 8.NS.2

Order the numbers from least to greatest.

12. $\sqrt{7}, 2, \frac{\sqrt{8}}{2}$

____

13. $\sqrt{10}, \pi, 3.5$

____

14. $\sqrt{220}, -10, \sqrt{100}, 11.5$

____

15. $\sqrt{8}, -3.75, 3, \frac{9}{4}$

____

16. Your sister is considering two different shapes for her garden. One is a square with side lengths of 3.5 meters, and the other is a circle with a diameter of 4 meters.

a. Find the area of the square. _______________

b. Find the area of the circle. _______________

c. Compare your answers from parts **a** and **b**. Which garden would give your sister the most space to plant?

____

____

17. Winnie measured the length of her father's ranch four times and got four different distances. Her measurements are shown in the table.

Distance Across Father's Ranch (km)			
1	2	3	4
$\sqrt{60}$	$\frac{58}{8}$	$7.\overline{3}$	$7\frac{3}{5}$

a. To estimate the actual length, Winnie first approximated each distance to the nearest hundredth. Then she averaged the four numbers. Using a calculator, find Winnie's estimate.

____

____

b. Winnie's father estimated the distance across his ranch to be $\sqrt{56}$ km. How does this distance compare to Winnie's estimate?

____

Give an example of each type of number.

18. a real number between $\sqrt{13}$ and $\sqrt{14}$ _______________

19. an irrational number between 5 and 7 _______________

20. A teacher asks his students to write the numbers shown in order from least to greatest. Paul thinks the numbers are already in order. Sandra thinks the order should be reversed. Who is right?

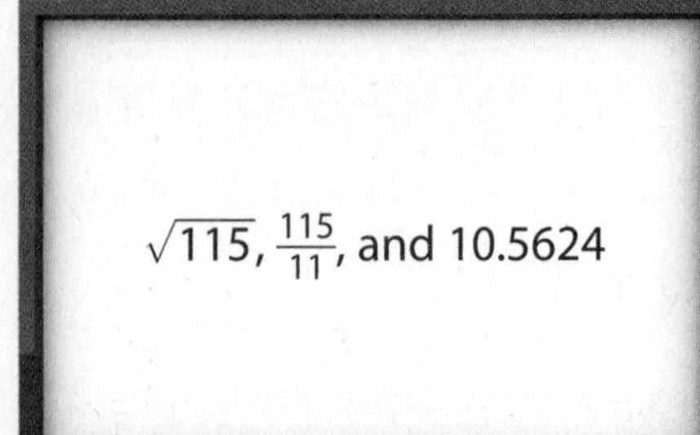

____

____

____

21. **Math History** There is a famous irrational number called Euler's number, symbolized with an e. Like π, its decimal form never ends or repeats. The first few digits of e are 2.7182818284.

a. Between which two square roots of integers could you find this number?

____

b. Between which two square roots of integers can you find π?

____

FOCUS ON HIGHER ORDER THINKING

Work Area

22. **Analyze Relationships** There are several approximations used for π, including 3.14 and $\frac{22}{7}$. π is approximately 3.14159265358979…

a. Label π and the two approximations on the number line.

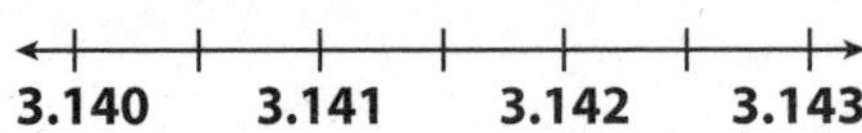

b. Which of the two approximations is a better estimate for π? Explain.

____

c. Find a whole number x so that the ratio $\frac{x}{113}$ is a better estimate for π than the two given approximations. _______________

23. **Communicate Mathematical Ideas** If a set of six numbers that include both rational and irrational numbers is graphed on a number line, what is the fewest number of distinct points that need to be graphed? Explain.

____

____

____

24. **Critique Reasoning** Jill says that $12.\overline{6}$ is less than 12.63. Explain her error.

____

MODULE QUIZ

Ready to Go On?

14.1 Rational and Irrational Numbers

Write each fraction as a decimal or each decimal as a fraction.

1. $\frac{7}{20}$ ________

2. $1.\overline{27}$ ________

3. $1\frac{7}{8}$ ________

Solve each equation for *x*.

4. $x^2 = 81$ ________

5. $x^3 = 343$ ________

6. $x^2 = \frac{1}{100}$ ________

7. A square patio has an area of 200 square feet. How long is each side of the patio to the nearest tenth? ________

14.2 Sets of Real Numbers

Write all names that apply to each number.

8. $\frac{121}{\sqrt{121}}$ ________

9. $\frac{\pi}{2}$ ________

10. Tell whether the statement "All integers are rational numbers" is true or false. Explain your choice.

____

____

14.3 Ordering Real Numbers

Compare. Write <, >, or =.

11. $\sqrt{8} + 3$ ◯ $8 + \sqrt{3}$

12. $\sqrt{5} + 11$ ◯ $5 + \sqrt{11}$

Order the numbers from least to greatest.

13. $\sqrt{99}, \pi^2, 9.\overline{8}$ ________

14. $\sqrt{\frac{1}{25}}, \frac{1}{4}, 0.\overline{2}$ ________

ESSENTIAL QUESTION

15. How are real numbers used to describe real-world situations?

____

____

MODULE 14
MIXED REVIEW

Assessment Readiness

1. Look at each number. Is the number between 2π and $\sqrt{52}$?

Select Yes or No for expressions A–C.

A. $6\frac{2}{3}$ ○ Yes ○ No

B. $\frac{5\pi}{2}$ ○ Yes ○ No

C. $3\sqrt{5}$ ○ Yes ○ No

2. Consider the number $-\frac{11}{15}$.

Choose True or False for each statement.

A. The number is rational. ○ True ○ False

B. The number can be written as a repeating decimal. ○ True ○ False

C. The number is less than −0.8. ○ True ○ False

3. The volume of a cube is given by $V = x^3$, where x is the length of an edge of the cube. A cube-shaped end table has a volume of $3\frac{3}{8}$ cubic feet. What is the length of an edge of the end table? Explain how you solved this problem.

4. A student says that $\sqrt{83}$ is greater than $\frac{29}{3}$. Is the student correct? Justify your reasoning.

Exponents and Scientific Notation

ESSENTIAL QUESTION

How can you use scientific notation to solve real-world problems?

LESSON 15.1

Integer Exponents

8.EE.1

LESSON 15.2

Scientific Notation with Positive Powers of 10

8.EE.3

LESSON 15.3

Scientific Notation with Negative Powers of 10

8.EE.3

LESSON 15.4

Operations with Scientific Notation

CA CC 8.EE.4, 8.EE.3

Real-World Video

my.hrw.com

The distance from Earth to other planets, moons, and stars is a very great number of kilometers. To make it easier to write very large and very small numbers, we use scientific notation.

GO DIGITAL
my.hrw.com

my.hrw.com

Go digital with your write-in student edition, accessible on any device.

Math On the Spot

Scan with your smart phone to jump directly to the online edition, video tutor, and more.

Animated Math

Interactively explore key concepts to see how math works.

Personal Math Trainer

Get immediate feedback and help as you work through practice sets.

Are YOU Ready?

Complete these exercises to review skills you will need for this module.

Personal Math Trainer

Online Practice and Help

Exponents

EXAMPLE $10^4 = 10 \times 10 \times 10 \times 10$ — *Write the exponential expression as a product.*

$= 10{,}000$ — *Simplify.*

Write each exponential expression as a decimal.

1. 10^2 ________ **2.** 10^3 ________ **3.** 10^5 ________ **4.** 10^7 ________

Multiply and Divide by Powers of 10

EXAMPLE $0.0478 \times 10^5 = 0.0478 \times 100{,}000$

$= 4{,}780$

Identify the number of zeros in the power of 10. When multiplying, move the decimal point to the right the same number of places as the number of zeros.

$37.9 \div 10^4 = 37.9 \div 10{,}000$

$= 0.00379$

Identify the number of zeros in the power of 10. When dividing, move the decimal point to the left the same number of places as the number of zeros.

Find each product or quotient.

5. 45.3×10^3 ________

6. $7.08 \div 10^2$ ________

7. 0.00235×10^6 ________

8. $3{,}600 \div 10^4$ ________

9. 0.5×10^2 ________

10. $67.7 \div 10^5$ ________

11. 0.0057×10^4 ________

12. $195 \div 10^6$ ________

Reading Start-Up

Visualize Vocabulary

Use the ✔ words to complete the Venn diagram. You can put more than one word in each section of the diagram.

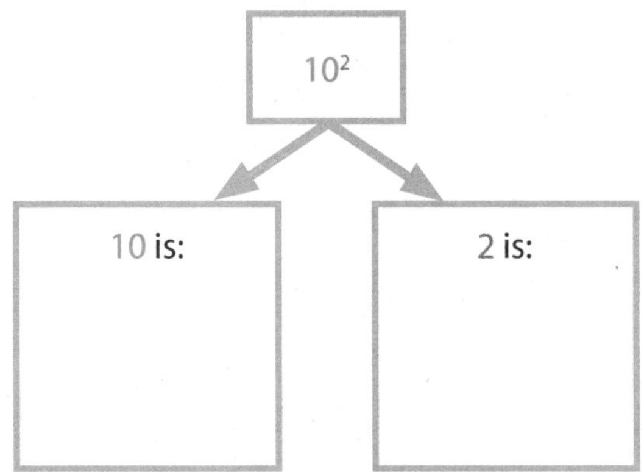

Understand Vocabulary

Complete the sentences using the preview words.

1. A number produced by raising a base to an exponent is a ______________________.

2. ______________________ is a method of writing very large or very small numbers by using powers of 10.

3. A ______________________ is any number that can be expressed as a ratio of two integers.

Vocabulary

Review Words

✔ base *(base)*
✔ exponent *(exponente)*
integers *(enteros)*
✔ positive number *(número positivo)*
standard notation *(notación estándar)*

Preview Words

power *(potencia)*
rational number *(número racional)*
real numbers *(número real)*
scientific notation *(notación científica)*
whole number *(número entero)*

Active Reading

Two-Panel Flip Chart Create a two-panel flip chart to help you understand the concepts in this module. Label one flap "Positive Powers of 10" and the other flap "Negative Powers of 10." As you study each lesson, write important ideas under the appropriate flap. Include sample problems that will help you remember the concepts later when you look back at your notes.

GETTING READY FOR

Exponents and Scientific Notation

Understanding the standards and the vocabulary terms in the standards will help you know exactly what you are expected to learn in this module.

CA CC 8.EE.1

Know and apply the properties of integer exponents to generate equivalent numerical expressions.

Key Vocabulary

integer *(entero)*
The set of whole numbers and their opposites

exponent *(exponente)*
The number that indicates how many times the base is used as a factor.

What It Means to You

You will use the properties of integer exponents to find equivalent expressions.

EXAMPLE 8.EE.1

Evaluate two different ways.

$\frac{8^3}{8^5}$ $\quad \frac{8^3}{8^5} = \frac{8 \cdot 8 \cdot 8}{8 \cdot 8 \cdot 8 \cdot 8 \cdot 8} = \frac{1}{8 \cdot 8} = \frac{1}{64}$

$\frac{8^3}{8^5} = 8^{(3-5)} = 8^{-2} = \frac{1}{8^2} = \frac{1}{8 \cdot 8} = \frac{1}{64}$

$(3^2)^4$ $\quad (3^2)^4 = (3^2)(3^2)(3^2)(3^2) = 3^{2+2+2+2} = 3^8 = 6{,}561$

$(3^2)^4 = 3^{(2 \cdot 4)} = 3^8 = 6{,}561$

CA CC 8.EE.3

Use numbers expressed in the form of a single digit times an integer power of 10 to estimate very large or very small quantities, and to express how many times as much one is than the other.

Key Vocabulary

scientific notation *(notación científica)*
A method of writing very large or very small numbers by using powers of 10.

What It Means to You

You will convert very large numbers to scientific notation.

EXAMPLE 8.EE.3

There are about 55,000,000,000 cells in an average-sized adult. Write this number in scientific notation.

Move the decimal point to the left until you have a number that is greater than or equal to 1 and less than 10.

5.5 0 0 0 0 0 0 0 0 0 — *Move the decimal point 10 places to the left.*

5.5 — *Remove the extra zeros.*

You would have to multiply 5.5 by 10^{10} to get 55,000,000,000.

$55{,}000{,}000{,}000 = 5.5 \times 10^{10}$

Visit **my.hrw.com** to see all **CA Common Core Standards** explained.

my.hrw.com

LESSON

15.1 Integer Exponents

CA CC 8.EE.1

Know and apply the properties of integer exponents to generate equivalent numerical expressions.

ESSENTIAL QUESTION

How can you develop and use the properties of integer exponents?

EXPLORE ACTIVITY 1 

Using Patterns of Integer Exponents

The table below shows powers of 5, 4, and 3.

$5^4 = 625$	$5^3 = 125$	$5^2 = 25$	$5^1 = 5$	$5^0 =$ ☐	$5^{-1} =$ ☐	$5^{-2} =$ ☐
$4^4 = 256$	$4^3 = 64$	$4^2 = 16$	$4^1 = 4$	$4^0 =$ ☐	$4^{-1} =$ ☐	$4^{-2} =$ ☐
$3^4 = 81$	$3^3 = 27$	$3^2 = 9$	$3^1 = 3$	$3^0 =$ ☐	$3^{-1} =$ ☐	$3^{-2} =$ ☐

A What pattern do you see in the powers of 5?

____

____

B What pattern do you see in the powers of 4?

____

____

C What pattern do you see in the powers of 3?

____

____

D Complete the table for the values of $5^0, 5^{-1}, 5^{-2}$.

E Complete the table for the values of $4^0, 4^{-1}, 4^{-2}$.

F Complete the table for the values of $3^0, 3^{-1}, 3^{-2}$.

Reflect

1. **Make a Conjecture** Write a general rule for the value of a^0, $a \neq 0$. ______________

2. **Make a Conjecture** Write a general rule for the value of a^{-n}, where $a \neq 0$ and n is an integer. ______________

EXPLORE ACTIVITY 2  CA CC 8.EE.1

Exploring Properties of Integer Exponents

A Complete the following equations:

$3 \cdot 3 \cdot 3 \cdot 3 \cdot 3 = 3^{\square}$

$(3 \cdot 3 \cdot 3 \cdot 3) \cdot 3 = 3^{\square} \cdot 3^{\square} = 3^{\square}$

$(3 \cdot 3 \cdot 3) \cdot (3 \cdot 3) = 3^{\square} \cdot 3^{\square} = 3^{\square}$

What pattern do you see when multiplying two powers with the same base?

____

____

Use your pattern to complete this equation: $5^2 \cdot 5^5 = 5^{\square}$.

B Complete the following equation:

$\frac{4^5}{4^3} = \frac{4 \cdot 4 \cdot 4 \cdot 4 \cdot 4}{4 \cdot 4 \cdot 4} = \frac{\cancel{4}^1 \cdot \cancel{4}^1 \cdot \cancel{4}^1 \cdot 4 \cdot 4}{\cancel{4}_1 \cdot \cancel{4}_1 \cdot \cancel{4}_1} = 4 \cdot 4 = 4^{\square}$

What pattern do you see when dividing two powers with the same base?

____

____

____

Use your pattern to complete this equation: $\frac{6^8}{6^3} = 6^{\square}$.

C Complete the following equations:

$(5^3)^2 = (5 \cdot 5 \cdot 5)^{\square} = (5 \cdot 5 \cdot 5) \cdot (5 \cdot 5 \cdot 5) = 5^{\square}$

What pattern do you see when raising a power to a power?

____

____

Use your pattern to complete this equation: $(7^2)^4 = 7^{\square}$.

Math Talk
Mathematical Practices

Do the patterns you found in parts A–D apply if the exponents are negative? If so, give an example of each.

D Complete the following equation:

$(3 \cdot 4)^2 = (3 \cdot 4) \cdot (3 \cdot 4) = (3 \cdot 3) \cdot (4 \cdot 4) = 3^{\square} \cdot 4^{\square}$

What pattern do you see when raising a product to a power?

___

Use your pattern to complete this equation: $(5 \cdot 6)^3 = 5^{\square} 6^{\square}$.

Reflect

Let *m* and *n* be integers.

3. **Make a Conjecture** Write a general rule for the value of $a^m \cdot a^n$. ___

4. **Make a Conjecture** Write a general rule for the value of $\frac{a^m}{a^n}$, $a \neq 0$. ___

5. **Make a Conjecture** Write a general rule for the value of $(a^m)^n$. ___

6. **Make a Conjecture** Write a general rule for the value of $(a \cdot b)^n$. ___

Simplifying Expressions with Powers

You can use the general rules you found in the Explore Activities to simplify expressions involving powers.

EXAMPLE 1

CA CC 8.EE.1

Simplify each expression.

A $(10^3)^2 = 10^{3 \cdot 2}$
$= 10^6$
$= 1{,}000{,}000$

B $4^3 \cdot 5^3 = (4 \cdot 5)^3$
$= 20^3$
$= 8000$

C $8^0 \cdot 8^{-3} \cdot 8^5 = 1 \cdot 8^{-3+5}$
$= 1 \cdot 8^2$
$= 8^2$
$= 64$

D $\frac{7^9}{7^{11}} = 7^{9-11}$
$= 7^{-2}$
$= \frac{1}{7^2}$
$= \frac{1}{49}$

Simplify each expression.

7. $(2 \cdot 11)^2$ ___ **8.** $(2^2)^3$ ___ **9.** $5^3 \cdot 5^{-4} \cdot 5^{-1}$ ___

Applying Properties of Integer Exponents

The general rules you found in the Explore Activities are summarized below. You can use them to simplify more complicated expressions.

Properties of Integer Exponents

Let *m* and *n* be integers.

Property	Rule	Example
Zero Exponent Property	$a^0 = 1, a \neq 0$	$2^0 = 1$
Negative Exponent Property	$a^{-n} = \frac{1}{a^n}, a \neq 0$	$3^{-2} = \frac{1}{3^2} = \frac{1}{9}$
Product of Powers Property	$a^m \cdot a^n = a^{m+n}$	$2^3 \cdot 2^4 = 2^7 = 128$
Quotient of Powers Property	$\frac{a^m}{a^n} = a^{m-n}, a \neq 0$	$\frac{2^7}{2^4} = 2^3 = 8$
Power of a Product Property	$(a \cdot b)^n = a^n \cdot b^n$	$(2 \cdot 3)^2 = 2^2 \cdot 3^2 = 36$
Power of a Power Property	$(a^m)^n = a^{mn}$	$(3^2)^3 = 3^6 = 729$

My Notes

EXAMPLE 2

Simplify each expression.

A $(5 - 2)^5 \cdot 3^{-8} + (5 + 2)^0$

$(3)^5 \cdot 3^{-8} + (7)^0$ — Simplify within parentheses.

$3^{5+(-8)} + 1$ — Use properties of exponents.

$3^{-3} + 1$ — Simplify.

$\frac{1}{27} + 1 = 1\frac{1}{27}$ — Apply the rule for negative exponents and add.

B $\frac{[(3 + 1)^2]^3}{(7 - 3)^2}$

$\frac{(4^2)^3}{4^2}$ — Simplify within parentheses.

$\frac{4^6}{4^2}$ — Use properties of exponents.

4^{6-2} — Use properties of exponents.

$4^4 = 256$ — Simplify.

YOUR TURN

Simplify each expression.

10. $\frac{[(6 - 1)^2]^2}{(3 + 2)^3}$ ________

11. $(2^2)^3 - (10 - 6)^3 \cdot 4^{-5}$ ________

Guided Practice

Find the value of each power. (Explore Activity 1)

1. $8^{-1} =$ ______ **2.** $6^{-2} =$ ______ **3.** $256^{0} =$ ______

4. $10^{2} =$ ______ **5.** $5^{4} =$ ______ **6.** $2^{-5} =$ ______

7. $4^{-5} =$ ______ **8.** $89^{0} =$ ______ **9.** $11^{-3} =$ ______

Use properties of exponents to write an equivalent expression. (Explore Activity 2)

10. $4 \cdot 4 \cdot 4 = 4^{\square}$

11. $(2 \cdot 2) \cdot (2 \cdot 2 \cdot 2) = 2^{\square} \cdot 2^{\square} = 2^{\square}$

12. $\frac{6^7}{6^5} = \frac{6 \cdot 6 \cdot 6 \cdot 6 \cdot 6 \cdot 6 \cdot 6}{6 \cdot 6 \cdot 6 \cdot 6 \cdot 6} = \square^{\square}$

13. $\frac{8^{12}}{8^9} = 8^{\square - \square} = \square^{\square}$

14. $5^{10} \cdot 5 \cdot 5 = 5^{\square}$

15. $7^8 \cdot 7^5 = \square^{\square}$

16. $(6^2)^4 = 6^{\square \cdot \square} = 6^{\square}$

17. $(8 \cdot 12)^3 = 8^{\square} \cdot 12^{\square}$

Simplify each expression. (Examples 1 and 2)

18. $6^9 \cdot 6^0 \cdot 6^{-10}$ ______

19. $\frac{10^2 \cdot 10^7}{10^5}$ ______

20. $(10 - 6)^3 \cdot 4^2 + (10 + 2)^2$ ______

21. $\frac{(12 - 5)^7}{\left[(3 + 4)^2\right]^2}$ ______

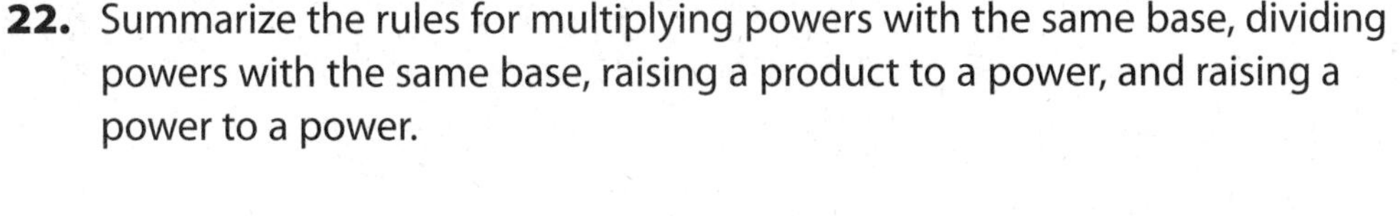

ESSENTIAL QUESTION CHECK-IN

22. Summarize the rules for multiplying powers with the same base, dividing powers with the same base, raising a product to a power, and raising a power to a power.

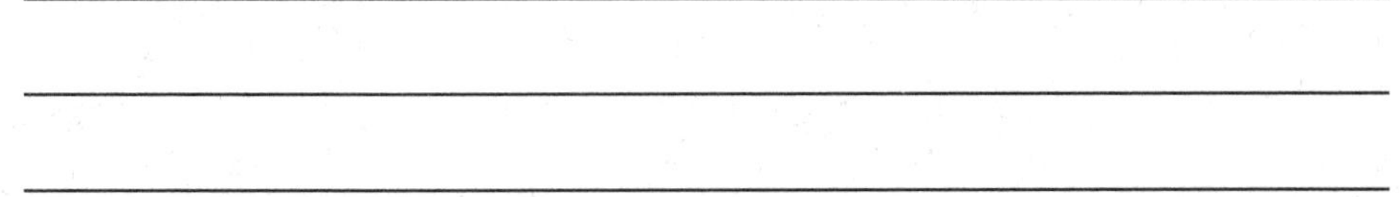

Name ______________________ Class ______________ Date ____________

15.1 Independent Practice

8.EE.1

Simplify each expression.

23. $5^{-7} \cdot 5^{12} \cdot 5^{-2}$ ____________

24. $8^{12} \cdot (8^7)^{-2}$ ____________

25. $5 \cdot (3 \cdot 5)^2$ ____________

26. $\frac{9^2}{9^5}$ ____________

27. $\frac{(6^2)^5}{6^8}$ ____________

28. $\frac{11^{10}}{11^3 \cdot 11^5}$ ____________

29. $(2^2)^3 + 2^0 + 2^7 \cdot 2^{-5}$ ____________

30. $3^{-2} \cdot (7-4)^2 + (7+4)^2$ ____________

31. $10^4 \cdot [(8+2)^2]^{-3}$ ____________

32. $\frac{7^5(2+5)^4}{(8-1)^7}$ ____________

33. $\frac{[(4+2)^3]^5}{(9-3)^{12}}$ ____________

34. $\frac{(4 \cdot 6)^3}{(5+1)^3}$ ____________

35. **Vocabulary** Identify the property that is being applied at each step to simplify the expression.

$$4^{-5} \cdot (4 \cdot 9)^5 \cdot 9^{-3} = 4^{-5} \cdot (4^5 \cdot 9^5) \cdot 9^{-3}$$ ____________

$$= (4^{-5} \cdot 4^5) \cdot (9^5 \cdot 9^{-3})$$ ____________

$$= 4^0 \cdot 9^2$$ ____________

$$= 1 \cdot 9^2$$ ____________

$$= 9^2$$ ____________

$$= 81$$ ____________

36. **Communicate Mathematical Ideas** Camille simplified an expression as shown. Discuss why this method is justified.

$$\frac{6 \cdot 10^5}{3 \cdot 10^2} = \frac{6}{3} \cdot \frac{10^5}{10^2} = 2 \cdot 10^3 = 2000$$

____

____

____

____

____

37. Explain why the exponents cannot be added in the product $12^3 \cdot 11^3$.

____

____

38. List three ways to express 3^5 as a product of powers.

____

39. **Astronomy** The distance from Earth to the moon is about 22^4 miles. The distance from Earth to Neptune is about 22^7 miles. Which distance is the greater distance, and about how many times greater is it?

____

40. **Critique Reasoning** A student claims that $8^3 \cdot 8^{-5}$ is greater than 1. Explain whether the student is correct or not.

____

____

____

Find the missing exponent.

41. $(b^2)^{\square} = b^{-6}$

42. $x^{\square} \cdot x^6 = x^9$

43. $\dfrac{y^{25}}{y^{\square}} = y^6$

44. **Communicate Mathematical Ideas** Why do you subtract exponents when dividing powers with the same base?

____

____

____

____

45. **Astronomy** The mass of the Sun is about 2×10^{27} metric tons, or 2×10^{30} kilograms. How many kilograms are in one metric ton?

____

46. **Represent Real-World Problems** In computer technology, a kilobyte is 2^{10} bytes in size. A gigabyte is 2^{30} bytes in size. The size of a terabyte is the product of the size of a kilobyte and the size of a gigabyte. What is the size of a terabyte?

____

47. Write equivalent expressions for $x^7 \cdot x^{-2}$ and $\frac{x^7}{x^2}$. What do you notice? Explain how your results relate to the properties of integer exponents.

A toy store is creating a large window display of different colored cubes stacked in a triangle shape. The table shows the number of cubes in each row of the triangle, starting with the top row.

Row	1	2	3	4
Number of cubes in each row	3	3^2	3^3	3^4

48. Look for a Pattern Describe any pattern you see in the table.

49. Using exponents, how many cubes will be in Row 6? How many times as many cubes will be in Row 6 than in Row 3?

50. Justify Reasoning If there are 6 rows in the triangle, what is the total number of cubes in the triangle? Explain how you found your answer.

FOCUS ON HIGHER ORDER THINKING

Work Area

51. Critique Reasoning A student simplified the expression $\frac{6^2}{36^2}$ as $\frac{1}{3}$. Do you agree with this student? Explain why or why not.

52. Draw Conclusions Evaluate $-a^n$ when $a = 3$ and $n = 2, 3, 4$, and 5. Now evaluate $(-a)^n$ when $a = 3$ and $n = 2, 3, 4$, and 5. Based on this sample, does it appear that $-a^n = (-a)^n$? If not, state the relationships, if any, between $-a^n$ and $(-a)^n$.

53. Persevere in Problem Solving A number to the 12th power divided by the same number to the 9th power equals 125. What is the number?

LESSON 15.2

Scientific Notation with Positive Powers of 10

8.EE.3

Use numbers expressed in the form of a single digit times an integer power of 10 to estimate very large or very small quantities, and to express how many times as much one is than the other.

ESSENTIAL QUESTION

How can you use scientific notation to express very large quantities?

EXPLORE ACTIVITY 

8.EE.3

Using Scientific Notation

Scientific notation is a method of expressing very large and very small numbers as a product of a number greater than or equal to 1 and less than 10, and a power of 10.

The weights of various sea creatures are shown in the table. Write the weight of the blue whale in scientific notation.

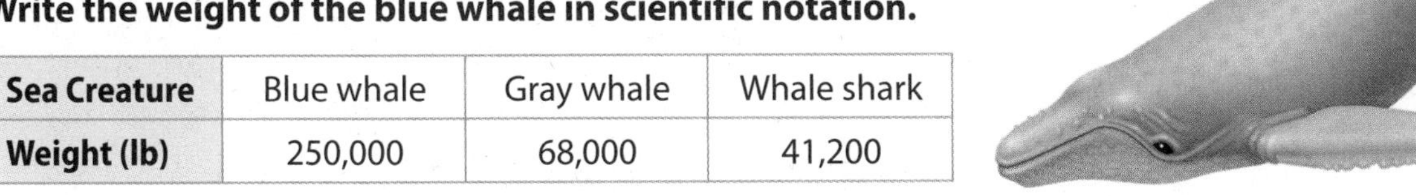

Sea Creature	Blue whale	Gray whale	Whale shark
Weight (lb)	250,000	68,000	41,200

A Move the decimal point in 250,000 to the left as many places as necessary to find a number that is greater than or equal to 1 and less than 10.

What number did you find? ______________________

B Divide 250,000 by your answer to **A**. Write your answer as a power of 10.

____

C Combine your answers to **A** and **B** to represent 250,000.

$250{,}000 = \square \times 10^{\square}$

Repeat steps **A** through **C** to write the weight of the whale shark in scientific notation.

$41{,}200 = \square \times 10^{\square}$

Reflect

1. How many places to the left did you move the decimal point to write 41,200 in scientific notation? ______________________

2. What is the exponent on 10 when you write 41,200 in scientific notation?

____

Writing a Number in Scientific Notation

To translate between standard notation and scientific notation, you can count the number of places the decimal point moves.

Writing Large Quantities in Scientific Notation

When the number is greater than or equal to 10, use a positive exponent.	$84{,}000 = 8.4 \times 10^4$	*The decimal point moves 4 places to the left.*

EXAMPLE 1 

The distance from Earth to the Sun is about 93,000,000 miles. Write this distance in scientific notation.

STEP 1 Move the decimal point in 93,000,000 to the left until you have a number that is greater than or equal to 1 and less than 10.

9.3 0 0 0 0 0 0. — Move the decimal point 7 places to the left.

9.3 — Remove extra zeros.

STEP 2 Divide the original number by the result from Step 1.

10,000,000 — Divide 93,000,000 by 9.3.

10^7 — Write your answer as a power of 10.

STEP 3 Write the product of the results from Steps 1 and 2.

$93{,}000{,}000 = 9.3 \times 10^7$ miles — Write a product to represent 93,000,000 in scientific notation.

Math Talk
Mathematical Practices

Is 12×10^7 written in scientific notation? Explain.

YOUR TURN

Write each number in scientific notation.

3. 6,400

______

4. 570,000,000,000

______

5. A light-year is the distance that light travels in a year and is equivalent to 9,461,000,000,000 km. Write this distance in scientific notation.

______

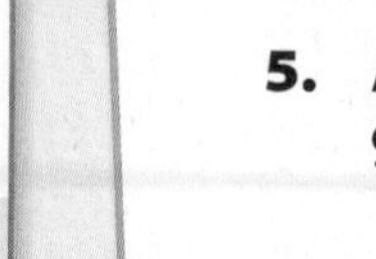

Personal Math Trainer
Online Practice and Help
my.hrw.com

Writing a Number in Standard Notation

To translate between scientific notation and standard notation, move the decimal point the number of places indicated by the exponent in the power of 10. When the exponent is positive, move the decimal point to the right and add placeholder zeros as needed.

EXAMPLE 2

CA CC 8.EE.3

Write 3.5×10^6 in standard notation.

STEP 1 Use the exponent of the power of 10 to see how many places to move the decimal point. — 6 places

STEP 2 Place the decimal point. Since you are going to write a number greater than 3.5, move the decimal point to the *right*. Add placeholder zeros if necessary. — 3 5 0 0 0 0 0.

The number 3.5×10^6 written in standard notation is 3,500,000.

My Notes

Reflect

6. Explain why the exponent in 3.5×10^6 is 6, while there are only 5 zeros in 3,500,000.

______

______

______

7. What is the exponent on 10 when you write 5.3 in scientific notation?

______

YOUR TURN

Write each number in standard notation.

8. 7.034×10^9 ______

9. 2.36×10^5 ______

10. The mass of one roosting colony of Monarch butterflies in Mexico was estimated at 5×10^6 grams. Write this mass in standard notation.

______

Guided Practice

Write each number in scientific notation. (Explore Activity and Example 1)

1. 58,927
Hint: Move the decimal left 4 places.

____

2. 1,304,000,000
Hint: Move the decimal left 9 places.

____

3. 6,730,000

____

4. 13,300

____

5. An ordinary quarter contains about 97,700,000,000,000,000,000,000 atoms.

____

6. The distance from Earth to the Moon is about 384,000 kilometers.

____

Write each number in standard notation. (Example 2)

7. 4×10^5
Hint: Move the decimal right 5 places.

____

8. 1.8499×10^9
Hint: Move the decimal right 9 places.

____

9. 6.41×10^3

____

10. 8.456×10^7

____

11. 8×10^5

____

12. 9×10^{10}

____

13. Diana calculated that she spent about 5.4×10^4 seconds doing her math homework during October. Write this time in standard notation. (Example 2)

____

14. The town recycled 7.6×10^6 cans this year. Write the number of cans in standard notation. (Example 2)

____

? ESSENTIAL QUESTION CHECK-IN

15. Describe how to write 3,482,000,000 in scientific notation.

____

____

____

____

Name ______________________ Class ______________________ Date ______________________

15.2 Independent Practice

8.EE.3

Paleontology Use the table for problems 16–21. Write the estimated weight of each dinosaur in scientific notation.

Estimated Weight of Dinosaurs	
Name	**Pounds**
Argentinosaurus	220,000
Brachiosaurus	100,000
Apatosaurus	66,000
Diplodocus	50,000
Camarasaurus	40,000
Cetiosauriscus	19,850

16. *Apatosaurus* ______________________

17. *Argentinosaurus* ______________________

18. *Brachiosaurus* ______________________

19. *Camarasaurus* ______________________

20. *Cetiosauriscus* ______________________

21. *Diplodocus* ______________________

22. A single little brown bat can eat up to 1000 mosquitoes in a single hour. Express in scientific notation how many mosquitoes a little brown bat might eat in 10.5 hours.

____

23. Multistep Samuel can type nearly 40 words per minute. Use this information to find the number of hours it would take him to type 2.6×10^5 words.

____

____

24. Entomology A tropical species of mite named *Archegozetes longisetosus* is the record holder for the strongest insect in the world. It can lift up to 1.182×10^3 times its own weight.

a. If you were as strong as this insect, explain how you could find how many pounds you could lift.

____

____

____

b. Complete the calculation to find how much you could lift, in pounds, if you were as strong as an *Archegozetes longisetosus* mite. Express your answer in both scientific notation and standard notation.

____

____

25. During a discussion in science class, Sharon learns that at birth an elephant weighs around 230 pounds. In four herds of elephants tracked by conservationists, about 20 calves were born during the summer. In scientific notation, express approximately how much the calves weighed all together.

____

26. Classifying Numbers Which of the following numbers are written in scientific notation?

0.641×10^3 $\quad$ 9.999×10^4

2×10^1 $\quad$ 4.38×5^{10}

____

27. **Explain the Error** Polly's parents' car weighs about 3500 pounds. Samantha, Esther, and Polly each wrote the weight of the car in scientific notation. Polly wrote 35.0×10^2, Samantha wrote 0.35×10^4, and Esther wrote 3.5×10^4.

a. Which of these girls, if any, is correct?

____

b. Explain the mistakes of those who got the question wrong.

____

____

____

28. **Justify Reasoning** If you were a biologist counting very large numbers of cells as part of your research, give several reasons why you might prefer to record your cell counts in scientific notation instead of standard notation.

____

____

____

H.O.T. FOCUS ON HIGHER ORDER THINKING

Work Area

29. **Draw Conclusions** Which measurement would be least likely to be written in scientific notation: number of stars in a galaxy, number of grains of sand on a beach, speed of a car, or population of a country? Explain your reasoning.

____

____

30. **Analyze Relationships** Compare the two numbers to find which is greater. Explain how you can compare them without writing them in standard notation first.

$$4.5 \times 10^6 \qquad 2.1 \times 10^8$$

____

____

31. **Communicate Mathematical Ideas** To determine whether a number is written in scientific notation, what test can you apply to the first factor, and what test can you apply to the second factor?

____

____

LESSON 15.3

Scientific Notation with Negative Powers of 10

Use numbers expressed in the form of a single digit times an integer power of 10 to estimate very large or very small quantities, and to express how many times as much one is than the other.

ESSENTIAL QUESTION

How can you use scientific notation to express very small quantities?

EXPLORE ACTIVITY 

Negative Powers of 10

You can use what you know about writing very large numbers in scientific notation to write very small numbers in scientific notation.

A typical human hair has a diameter of 0.000025 meter. Write this number in scientific notation.

A Notice how the decimal point moves in the list below. Complete the list.

1.345×10^0	= 1.3 4 5	It moves one place to the right with each increasing power of 10.	1.345×10^0	= 1.3 4 5	It moves one place to the left with each decreasing power of 10.
1.345×10^1	= 1 3.4 5		1.345×10^{-1}	= 0.1 3 4 5	
1.345×10^2	= 1 3 4.5		1.345×10^{-2}	= 0.0 1 3 4 5	
$1.345 \times 10^{\square}$	= 1 3 4 5.		$1.345 \times 10^{\square}$	= 0.0 0 1 3 4 5	

B Move the decimal point in 0.000025 to the right as many places as necessary to find a number that is greater than or equal to 1 and less than 10. What number did you find? ______________

C Divide 0.000025 by your answer to **B**. ______________

Write your answer as a power of 10. ______________

D Combine your answers to **B** and **C** to represent 0.000025 in scientific notation. ______________

Reflect

1. When you move the decimal point, how can you know whether you are increasing or decreasing the number?

____

2. Explain how the two steps of moving the decimal and multiplying by a power of 10 leave the value of the original number unchanged.

____

Writing a Number in Scientific Notation

To write a number less than 1 in scientific notation, move the decimal point right and use a negative exponent.

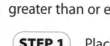

Writing Small Quantities in Scientific Notation		
When the number is between 0 and 1, use a negative exponent.	 $0.0783 = 7.83 \times 10^{-2}$	*The decimal point moves 2 places to the right.*

EXAMPLE 1 Real World

The average size of an atom is about 0.00000003 centimeter across. Write the average size of an atom in scientific notation.

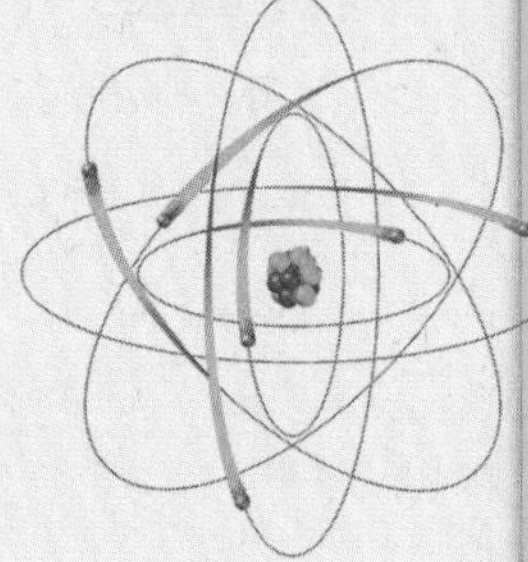

Move the decimal point as many places as necessary to find a number that is greater than or equal to 1 and less than 10.

STEP 1 Place the decimal point. 3.0

STEP 1 Count the number of places you moved the decimal point. 8

STEP 3 Multiply 3.0 times a power of 10. 3.0×10^{-8}

Since 0.00000003 is less than 1, you moved the decimal point to the right and the exponent on 10 is negative.

The average size of an atom in scientific notation is 3.0×10^{-8}.

Reflect

3. **Critical Thinking** When you write a number that is less than 1 in scientific notation, how does the power of 10 differ from when you write a number greater than 1 in scientific notation?

____

Write each number in scientific notation.

4. 0.0000829 _______________

5. 0.000000302 _______________

6. A typical red blood cell in human blood has a diameter of approximately 0.000007 meter. Write this diameter in scientific notation. _______________

Writing a Number in Standard Notation

To translate between scientific notation and standard notation with very small numbers, you can move the decimal point the number of places indicated by the exponent on the power of 10. When the exponent is negative, move the decimal point to the left.

EXAMPLE 2

Platelets are one component of human blood. A typical platelet has a diameter of approximately 2.33×10^{-6} meter. Write 2.33×10^{-6} in standard notation.

STEP 1 Use the exponent of the power of 10 to see how many places to move the decimal point.

6 places

STEP 1 Place the decimal point. Since you are going to write a number less than 2.33, move the decimal point to the *left*. Add placeholder zeros if necessary.

0.0 0 0 0 0 2 3 3

The number 2.33×10^{-6} in standard notation is 0.00000233.

Math Talk
Mathematical Practices

Describe the two factors that multiply together to form a number written in scientific notation.

Reflect

7. **Justify Reasoning** Explain whether 0.9×10^{-5} is written in scientific notation. If not, write the number correctly in scientific notation.

____

____

____

8. Which number is larger, 2×10^{-3} or 3×10^{-2}? Explain.

____

YOUR TURN

Write each number in standard notation.

9. 1.045×10^{-6} _______________

10. 9.9×10^{-5} _______________

11. Jeremy measured the length of an ant as 1×10^{-2} meter. Write this length in standard notation.

____

Guided Practice

Write each number in scientific notation. (Explore Activity and Example 1)

1. 0.000487
Hint: Move the decimal right 4 places.

____

2. 0.000028
Hint: Move the decimal right 5 places.

____

3. 0.000059

____

4. 0.0417

____

5. Picoplankton can be as small as 0.00002 centimeter.

____

6. The average mass of a grain of sand on a beach is about 0.000015 gram.

____

Write each number in standard notation. (Example 2)

7. 2×10^{-5}
Hint: Move the decimal left 5 places.

____

8. 3.582×10^{-6}
Hint: Move the decimal left 6 places.

____

9. 8.3×10^{-4}

____

10. 2.97×10^{-2}

____

11. 9.06×10^{-5}

____

12. 4×10^{-5}

____

13. The average length of a dust mite is approximately 0.0001 meter. Write this number in scientific notation. (Example 1)

____

14. The mass of a proton is about 1.7×10^{-24} gram. Write this number in standard notation. (Example 2)

____

ESSENTIAL QUESTION CHECK-IN

15. Describe how to write 0.0000672 in scientific notation.

____

____

____

Name ______________________ Class ______________ Date ____________

15.3 Independent Practice

8.EE.3

Use the table for problems 16–21. Write the diameter of the fibers in scientific notation.

Average Diameter of Natural Fibers	
Animal	**Fiber Diameter (cm)**
Vicuña	0.0008
Angora rabbit	0.0013
Alpaca	0.00277
Angora goat	0.0045
Llama	0.0035
Orb web spider	0.015

16. Alpaca

____

17. Angora rabbit

____

18. Llama

____

19. Angora goat

____

20. Orb web spider

____

21. Vicuña

____

22. **Make a Conjecture** Which measurement would be least likely to be written in scientific notation: the thickness of a dog hair, the radius of a period on this page, the ounces in a cup of milk? Explain your reasoning.

____

____

23. **Multiple Representations** Convert the length 7 centimeters to meters. Compare the numerical values when both numbers are written in scientific notation.

____

____

____

____

24. **Draw Conclusions** A graphing calculator displays 1.89×10^{12} as 1.89E12. How do you think it would display 1.89×10^{-12}? What does the E stand for?

____

____

25. **Communicate Mathematical Ideas** When a number is written in scientific notation, how can you tell right away whether or not it is greater than or equal to 1?

____

____

____

26. The volume of a drop of a certain liquid is 0.000047 liter. Write the volume of the drop of liquid in scientific notation.

____

27. **Justify Reasoning** If you were asked to express the weight in ounces of a ladybug in scientific notation, would the exponent of the 10 be positive or negative? Justify your response.

____

____

Physical Science The table shows the length of the radii of several very small or very large items. Complete the table.

	Item	Radius in Meters (Standard Notation)	Radius in Meters (Scientific Notation)
28.	The Moon	1,740,000	
29.	Atom of silver		1.25×10^{-10}
30.	Atlantic wolfish egg	0.0028	
31.	Jupiter		7.149×10^{7}
32.	Atom of aluminum	0.000000000182	
33.	Mars		3.397×10^{6}

34. List the items in the table in order from the smallest to the largest.

____

____

FOCUS ON HIGHER ORDER THINKING

Work Area

35. Analyze Relationships Write the following diameters from least to greatest.
1.5×10^{-2} m 1.2×10^{2} m 5.85×10^{-3} m 2.3×10^{-2} m 9.6×10^{-1} m

____

____

36. Critique Reasoning Jerod's friend Al had the following homework problem:

Express 5.6×10^{-7} in standard form.

Al wrote 56,000,000. How can Jerod explain Al's error and how to correct it?

____

____

____

37. Make a Conjecture Two numbers are written in scientific notation. The number with a positive exponent is divided by the number with a negative exponent. Describe the result. Explain your answer.

____

____

____

LESSON 15.4

Operations with Scientific Notation

CA CC 8.EE.4

Perform operations ... in scientific notation. ... choose units of appropriate size for measurements .... Interpret scientific notation ... generated by technology. (For the full text of the standard, see the table at the front of the book beginning on page CA2.) *Also 8.EE.3*

ESSENTIAL QUESTION

How do you add, subtract, multiply, and divide using scientific notation?

Adding and Subtracting with Scientific Notation

Numbers in scientific notation can be added and subtracted, either directly or by rewriting them in standard form.

EXAMPLE 1

The table below shows the population of the three largest countries in North America in 2011. Find the total population of these countries.

Country	United States	Canada	Mexico
Population	3.1×10^8	3.38×10^7	1.1×10^8

Method 1:

STEP 1 First, write each population with the same power of 10.

United States: 3.1×10^8

Canada: 0.338×10^8

Mexico: 1.1×10^8

STEP 2 Add the multipliers for each population.

$3.1 + 0.338 + 1.1 = 4.538$

STEP 3 Write the final answer in scientific notation: 4.538×10^8.

Method 2:

STEP 1 First, write each number in standard notation.

United States: 310,000,000

Canada: 33,800,000

Mexico: 110,000,000

STEP 2 Find the sum of the numbers in standard notation.

$310{,}000{,}000 + 33{,}800{,}000 + 110{,}000{,}000 = 453{,}800{,}000$

STEP 3 Write the answer in scientific notation: 4.538×10^8.

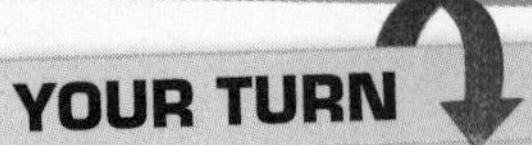

1. Using the population table in the example, how many more people live in Mexico than in Canada? Write your answer in scientific notation.

____

Multiplying and Dividing with Scientific Notation

Numbers in scientific notation can be multiplied and divided directly by using properties of exponents.

EXAMPLE 2 

When the Sun makes an orbit around the center of the Milky Way, it travels 2.025×10^{14} kilometers. The orbit takes 225 million years. At what rate does the Sun travel? Write your answer in scientific notation.

 **Analyze Information**

The answer is the number of kilometers per year that the Sun travels around the Milky Way.

 **Formulate a Plan**

Set up a division problem using Rate $= \frac{\text{Distance}}{\text{Time}}$ to represent the situation.

 **Solve**

STEP 1 Substitute the values from the problem into the Rate formula.

$$\text{Rate} = \frac{2.025 \times 10^{14} \text{ kilometers}}{225{,}000{,}000 \text{ years}}$$

STEP 2 Write the expression for rate with years in scientific notation.

$$\text{Rate} = \frac{2.025 \times 10^{14} \text{ kilometers}}{2.25 \times 10^{8} \text{ years}}$$

225 million $= 2.25 \times 10^8$

STEP 3 Find the quotient by dividing the decimals and using the laws of exponents.

$2.025 \div 2.25 = 0.9$ *Divide the multipliers.*

$\frac{10^{14}}{10^{8}} = 10^{14-8} = 10^6$ *Divide the powers of 10.*

STEP 4 Combine the answers to write the rate in scientific notation.

Rate $= 0.9 \times 10^6 = 9.0 \times 10^5$ km per year

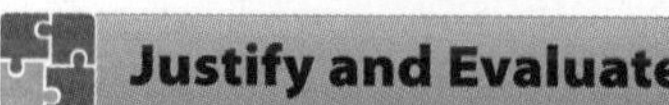

Use estimation to check the reasonableness of your answer.

$$\frac{2.025 \times 10^{14}}{225{,}000{,}000} \approx \frac{2 \times 10^{14}}{2 \times 10^{8}} = 10^6$$

9.0×10^5 is close to 10^6, so the answer is reasonable.

Could you write 2.025×10^{14} in standard notation to do the division? Would this be a good way to solve the problem?

YOUR TURN

2. Light travels at a speed of 1.86×10^5 miles per second. It takes light from the Sun about 4.8×10^3 seconds to reach Saturn. Find the approximate distance from the Sun to Saturn. Write your answer in scientific notation. ________________

3. Light travels at the speed of 1.17×10^7 miles per minute. Pluto's average distance from the Sun is 3,670,000,000 miles. On average, how long does it take sunlight to reach Pluto? Write your answer in scientific notation. ________________

Scientific Notation on a Calculator

On many scientific calculators, you can enter numbers in scientific notation by using a function labeled "ee" or "EE". Usually, the letter "E" takes the place of "$\times 10$". So, the number 4.1×10^9 would appear as 4.1E9 on the calculator.

Math On the Spot
my.hrw.com

EXAMPLE 3

8.EE.4

The table shows the approximate areas for three continents given in square meters. What is the total area of these three continents? Write the answer in scientific notation using more appropriate units.

Continent	Asia	Africa	Europe
Area (m^2)	4.4×10^{13}	3.02×10^{13}	1.04×10^{13}

Find $4.4 \times 10^{13} + 3.02 \times 10^{13} + 1.04 \times 10^{13}$.

Enter 4.4E13 + 3.02E13 + 1.04E13 on your calculator.

Write the results from your calculator: 8.46E13.

Write this number in scientific notation: 8.46×10^{13} m^2.

Square kilometers is more appropriate: 8.46×10^7 km^2.

Because 1 km = 1,000 m, 1 km^2 = $1{,}000^2$ m^2, or 10^6 m^2. Divide by 10^6.

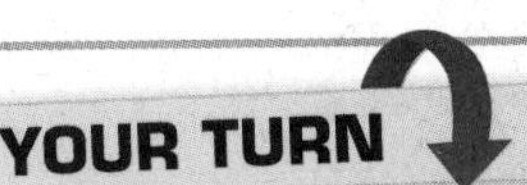

Write each number using calculator notation.

4. 7.5×10^5 ________

5. 3×10^{-7} ________

6. 2.7×10^{13} ________

Write each number using scientific notation.

7. 4.5E−1 ________

8. 5.6E12 ________

9. 6.98E−8 ________

Guided Practice

Add or subtract. Write your answer in scientific notation. (Example 1)

1. $4.2 \times 10^6 + 2.25 \times 10^5 + 2.8 \times 10^6$

$4.2 \times 10^6 + \square \times 10^{\square} + 2.8 \times 10^6$

$4.2 + \square + \square$

$\square \times 10^{\square}$

2. $8.5 \times 10^3 - 5.3 \times 10^3 - 1.0 \times 10^2$

$8.5 \times 10^3 - 5.3 \times 10^3 - \square \times 10^{\square}$

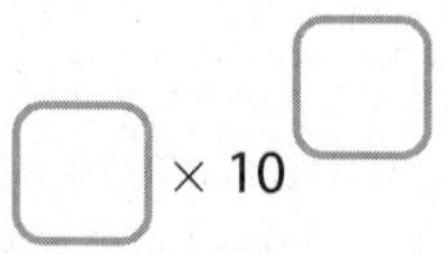

3. $1.25 \times 10^2 + 0.50 \times 10^2 + 3.25 \times 10^2$ ______

4. $6.2 \times 10^5 - 2.6 \times 10^4 - 1.9 \times 10^2$ ______

Multiply or divide. Write your answer in scientific notation. (Example 2)

5. $(1.8 \times 10^9)(6.7 \times 10^{12})$ ______

6. $\frac{3.46 \times 10^{17}}{2 \times 10^9}$ ______

7. $(5 \times 10^{12})(3.38 \times 10^6)$ ______

8. $\frac{8.4 \times 10^{21}}{4.2 \times 10^{14}}$ ______

Write each number using calculator notation. (Example 3)

9. 3.6×10^{11} ______

10. 7.25×10^{-5} ______

11. 8×10^{-1} ______

Write each number using scientific notation. (Example 3)

12. 7.6E–4 ______

13. 1.2E16 ______

14. 9E1 ______

? ESSENTIAL QUESTION CHECK-IN

15. How do you add, subtract, multiply, and divide numbers written in scientific notation?

______

______

______

______

______

Name ______________________ Class ______________________ Date ______________________

15.4 Independent Practice

16. An adult blue whale can eat 4.0×10^7 krill in a day. At that rate, how many krill can an adult blue whale eat in 3.65×10^2 days?

____

17. A newborn baby has about 26,000,000,000 cells. An adult has about 4.94×10^{13} cells. About how many times as many cells does an adult have than a newborn? Write your estimate in standard notation.

____

____

Represent Real-World Problems **The table shows the number of tons of waste generated and recovered (recycled) in 2010.**

	Paper	Glass	Plastics
Tons generated	7.131×10^7	1.153×10^7	3.104×10^7
Tons recovered	4.457×10^7	0.313×10^7	0.255×10^7

18. What is the total amount of paper, glass, and plastic waste generated?

____

____

19. What is the total amount of paper, glass, and plastic waste recovered?

____

20. What is the total amount of paper, glass, and plastic waste ***not*** recovered?

____

21. Which type of waste has the lowest recovery ratio?

____

Social Studies **The table shows the approximate populations of three countries.**

Country	China	France	Australia
Population	1.3×10^9	6.48×10^7	2.15×10^7

22. How many more people live in France than in Australia?

____

23. The area of Australia is 2.95×10^6 square miles. What is the approximate average number of people per square mile in Australia?

____

____

24. How many times greater is the population of China than the population of France? Write your answer in standard notation.

____

____

25. Mia is 7.01568×10^6 minutes old. Convert her age to more appropriate units. Assume that each year has 6 months that have 30 days and 6 months that have 31 days.

____

____

26. Courtney takes 2.4×10^4 steps during her a long-distance run. Each step covers an average of 810 mm. What total distance (in mm) did Courtney cover during her run? Write your answer in scientific notation. Then convert the distance to a more appropriate unit. Write that answer in standard form.

____

27. **Social Studies** The U.S. public debt as of October 2010 was $\$9.06 \times 10^{12}$. Estimate the average U.S. public debt per American if the population in 2010 was 3.08×10^8 people.

____

H.O.T. FOCUS ON HIGHER ORDER THINKING

Work Area

28. **Communicate Mathematical Ideas** How is multiplying and dividing numbers in scientific notation different from adding and subtracting numbers in scientific notation?

____

____

____

____

____

29. **Explain the Error** A student found the product of 8×10^6 and 5×10^9 to be 4×10^{15}. What is the error? What is the correct product?

____

____

30. **Communicate Mathematical Ideas** Describe a procedure that can be used to simplify $\frac{(4.87 \times 10^{12}) - (7 \times 10^{10})}{(3 \times 10^7) + (6.1 \times 10^8)}$. Write the expression in scientific notation in simplified form.

____

____

____

____

____

____

____

MODULE QUIZ

Ready to Go On?

15.1 Integer Exponents

Find the value of each power.

1. 3^{-4} ________ **2.** 35^0 ________ **3.** 4^4 ________

Use the properties of exponents to write an equivalent expression.

4. $8^3 \cdot 8^7$ ________ **5.** $\frac{12^6}{12^2}$ ________ **6.** $(10^3)^5$ ________

15.2 Scientific Notation with Positive Powers of 10

Convert each number to scientific notation or standard notation.

7. 2,000 ________ **8.** 91,007,500 ________

9. 1.0395×10^9 ________ **10.** 4×10^2 ________

15.3 Scientific Notation with Negative Powers of 10

Convert each number to scientific notation or standard notation.

11. 0.02 ________ **12.** 0.000701 ________

13. 8.9×10^{-5} ________ **14.** 4.41×10^{-2} ________

15.4 Operations with Scientific Notation

Perform the operation. Write your answer in scientific notation.

15. $7 \times 10^6 - 5.3 \times 10^6$ ________ **16.** $3.4 \times 10^4 + 7.1 \times 10^5$ ________

17. $(2 \times 10^4)(5.4 \times 10^6)$ ________ **18.** $\frac{7.86 \times 10^9}{3 \times 10^4}$ ________

19. Neptune's average distance from the Sun is 4.503×10^9 km. Mercury's average distance from the Sun is 5.791×10^7 km. About how many times farther from the Sun is Neptune than Mercury? Write your answer in scientific notation.

____

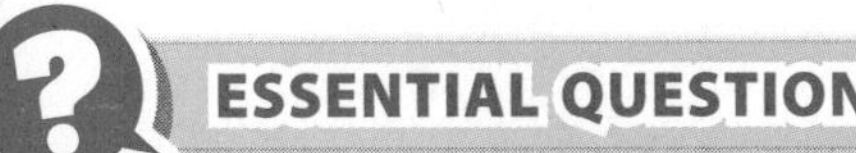

20. How is scientific notation used in the real world?

____

____

MODULE 15
MIXED REVIEW

Assessment Readiness

1. Consider each expression. Is the expression equivalent to 2^{-4}?

Select Yes or No for expressions A–C.

A. $2^2 - 2^6$ ○ Yes ○ No

B. $(2^{-2})^2$ ○ Yes ○ No

C. $\frac{2^3}{2^7}$ ○ Yes ○ No

2. The variable *r* represents a rational number.

Choose True or False for each statement.

A. *r* is a real number. ○ True ○ False

B. *r* could be a repeating decimal. ○ True ○ False

C. *r* could be $\sqrt{39}$. ○ True ○ False

3. So far this year, a company has sold 8.28×10^5 tablet computers. How many more tablets must the company sell for its tablet sales to reach 1 million this year? Explain how you solved this problem.

4. Brazil has an area of approximately 8.51×10^6 square kilometers and a population of about 1.99×10^8 people. Portugal has an area of approximately 9.21×10^4 square kilometers and a population of about 1.08×10^7 people. On average, which country has a greater number of people per square kilometer? Explain how you know.

UNIT 7

Study Guide Review

MODULE 14 Real Numbers

ESSENTIAL QUESTION

How can you use real numbers to solve real-world problems?

Key Vocabulary

cube root *(raiz cúbica)*
irrational number *(número irracional)*
perfect cube *(cubo perfecto)*
perfect square *(cuadrado perfecto)*
principal square root *(raíz cuadrada principal)*
rational number *(número racional)*
real number *(número real)*
repeating decimal *(decimal periódico)*
square root *(raíz cuadrada)*
terminating decimal *(decimal finito)*

EXAMPLE 1

Write $0.\overline{81}$ as a fraction in simplest form.

$$x = 0.\overline{81}$$

$$(100)x = (100)0.\overline{81}$$

$$100x = 81.\overline{81}$$ 100 times $0.\overline{81}$ is $81.\overline{81}$.

$$-x = -0.\overline{81}$$

$$99x = 81$$

$$x = \frac{81}{99}$$ Divide both sides by 99.

$$x = \frac{9}{11}$$ Simplify.

EXAMPLE 2

Solve each equation for *x*.

A $x^2 = 289$

$x = \pm\sqrt{289}$

$x = \pm 17$

The solutions are 17 and -17.

B $x^3 = 1000$

$x = \sqrt[3]{1000}$

$x = 10$

The solution is 10.

EXAMPLE 3

Write all names that apply to each number.

A $5.\overline{4}$
rational, real

$5.\overline{4}$ is a repeating decimal.

B $\frac{8}{4}$
whole, integer, rational, real

$\frac{8}{4} = 2$

C $\sqrt{13}$
irrational, real

13 is a whole number that is not a perfect square.

EXAMPLE 4

Order 6, 2π, and $\sqrt{38}$ from least to greatest.

2π is approximately equal to 2×3.14, or 6.28.

$\sqrt{38}$ is approximately 6.15 based on the following reasoning.

$\sqrt{36} < \sqrt{38} < \sqrt{49}$ $6 < \sqrt{38} < 7$ $6.1^2 = 37.21$ $6.2^2 = 38.44$

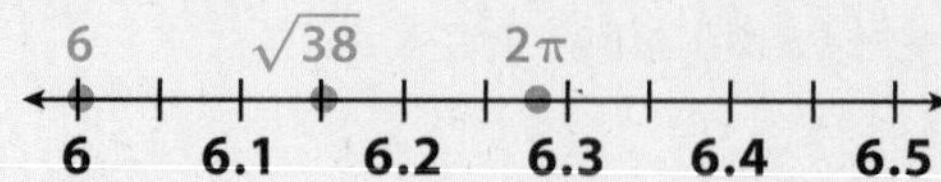

From least to greatest, the numbers are 6, $\sqrt{38}$, and 2π.

EXERCISES

Find the two square roots of each number. If the number is not a perfect square, approximate the values to one decimal place. (Lesson 14.1)

1. 16 ______ **2.** $\frac{4}{25}$ ______ **3.** 225 ______

4. $\frac{1}{49}$ ______ **5.** $\sqrt{10}$ ______ **6.** $\sqrt{18}$ ______

Write each decimal as a fraction in simplest form. (Lesson 14.1)

7. $0.\overline{5}$ ______ **8.** $0.\overline{63}$ ______ **9.** $0.\overline{214}$ ______

Solve each equation for *x*. (Lesson 14.1)

10. $x^2 = 361$ ______ **11.** $x^3 = 1728$ ______ **12.** $x^2 = \frac{49}{121}$ ______

Write all names that apply to each number. (Lesson 14.2)

13. $\frac{2}{3}$ ______ **14.** $-\sqrt{100}$ ______

15. $\frac{15}{5}$ ______ **16.** $\sqrt{21}$ ______

Compare. Write $<$, $>$, or $=$. (Lesson 14.3)

17. $\sqrt{7} + 5$ ◯ $7 + \sqrt{5}$ **18.** $6 + \sqrt{8}$ ◯ $\sqrt{6} + 8$ **19.** $\sqrt{4} - 2$ ◯ $4 - \sqrt{2}$

Order the numbers from least to greatest. (Lesson 14.3)

20. $\sqrt{81}, \frac{72}{7}, 8.9$ ______ **21.** $\sqrt{7}, 2.55, \frac{7}{3}$ ______

MODULE 15

Exponents and Scientific Notation

Key Vocabulary
scientific notation
(notación científica)

ESSENTIAL QUESTION

How can you use scientific notation to solve real-world problems?

EXAMPLE 1

Write each measurement in scientific notation.

A The diameter of Earth at the equator is approximately 12,700 kilometers.

Move the decimal point in 12,700 four places to the left: 1.2 7 0 0.

$12{,}700 = 1.27 \times 10^4$

B The diameter of a human hair is approximately 0.00254 centimeters.

Move the decimal point in 0.00254 three places to the right: 0.0 0 2.5 4

$0.00254 = 2.54 \times 10^{-3}$

EXAMPLE 2

Find the quotient: $\frac{2.4 \times 10^7}{9.6 \times 10^3}$.

Divide the multipliers: $2.4 \div 9.6 = 0.25$

Divide the powers of ten: $\frac{10^7}{10^3} = 10^{7-3} = 10^4$

Combine the answers and write the product in scientific notation.

$0.25 \times 10^4 = 0.25 \times (10 \times 10^3) = (0.25 \times 10) \times 10^3 = 2.5 \times 10^3$

EXERCISES

Write each number in scientific notation. (Lessons 15.2, 15.3)

1. 25,500,000 ____________

2. 0.00734 ____________

Write each number in standard notation. (Lessons 15.2, 15.3)

3. 5.23×10^4 ____________

4. 1.33×10^{-5} ____________

Simplify each expression. (Lessons 15.1, 15.4)

5. $(9 - 7)^3 \cdot 5^0 + (8 + 3)^2$ ____________

6. $\frac{(4 + 2)^2}{[(9 - 3)^3]^2}$ ____________

7. $3.2 \times 10^5 + 1.25 \times 10^4 + 2.9 \times 10^5$

____

8. $(2600)(3.24 \times 10^4)$

____

Unit Project

The Large and the Small of It

Did you know that, according to one estimate, there are about 300,000,000,000 birds in the world? Or that the mass of a dust particle is about 0.0000000008 kg?

For this project, find five interesting facts that involve numbers greater than one million. Find five more facts that involve positive numbers less than one-millionth. Then create a presentation that includes the following:

- Each of the ten numbers written in both standard notation and scientific notation
- A description of the fact that each number represents
- The source where you found the information
- An image for each fact

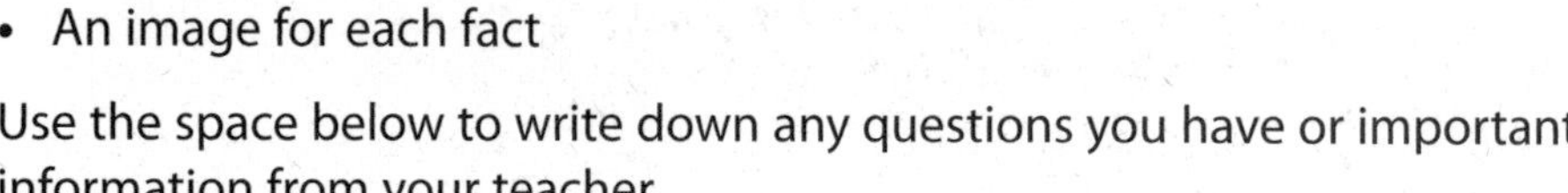

Use the space below to write down any questions you have or important information from your teacher.

MATH IN CAREERS | **ACTIVITY**

Astronomer An astronomer is studying Mercury, which is the closest planet to our Sun. Mercury is 57,910,000,000 meters away from the Sun. Earth is 149,600,000,000 meters away from the Sun. How much longer does it take for light to travel from the Sun to Earth than to Mercury? The speed of light is 3.0×10^8 miles per second.

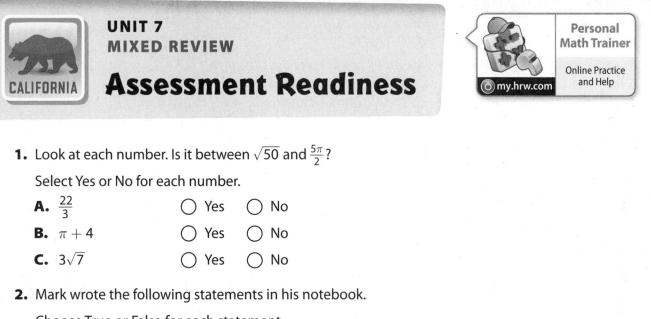

UNIT 7
MIXED REVIEW

Assessment Readiness

1. Look at each number. Is it between $\sqrt{50}$ and $\frac{5\pi}{2}$?

Select Yes or No for each number.

A. $\frac{22}{3}$ ○ Yes ○ No

B. $\pi + 4$ ○ Yes ○ No

C. $3\sqrt{7}$ ○ Yes ○ No

2. Mark wrote the following statements in his notebook.

Choose True or False for each statement.

A. Integers can be irrational numbers. ○ True ○ False

B. All integers are whole numbers. ○ True ○ False

C. All whole numbers are integers. ○ True ○ False

3. The total land area on Earth is about 6×10^7 square miles. The land area of Australia is about 3×10^6 square miles. About how many times larger is the land area on Earth than the land area of Australia? Explain your reasoning.

4. Jonathan says that the simplest form of the expression below is 49.

$$\frac{[(9-2)^2]^4}{(4+3)^5}$$

Is he correct? Explain.

Performance Tasks

★**5.** Amanda says the human fingernail has a thickness of about 4.2×10^{-4} meters. Justin says a human fingernail has a thickness of about 0.42 millimeter. Do Amanda's and Justin's estimations agree? Explain.

★★**6.** Cory is making a poster of common geometric shapes. He draws a square with a side of length 4^3 cm, an equilateral triangle with a height of $\sqrt{200}$ cm, a circle with a circumference of 8π cm, a rectangle with a length of $\frac{122}{5}$ cm, and a parallelogram with a base of 3.14 cm.

a. Write the numbers in this problem in order from least to greatest.

b. Explain how you decided on your arrangement.

★★★**7.** The closest star to our Sun, Proxima Centauri, is 39,900,000,000,000,000 meters away from Earth.

a. Write this distance in scientific notation.

b. Light travels at a speed of 3.0×10^8 meters per second. How can you calculate the time in seconds that it takes light from Proxima Centauri to reach Earth? How many seconds does it take? Write your answer in scientific notation and standard notation.

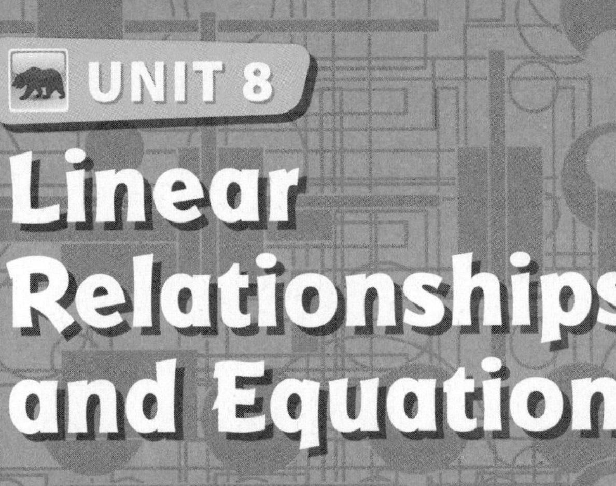

Linear Relationships and Equations

MODULE 16
Proportional Relationships
CA CC 8.EE.5, 8.EE.6, 8.F.2, 8.F.4

MODULE 17
Nonproportional Relationships
CA CC 8.EE.6, 8.F.2, 8.F.3, 8.F.4

MODULE 18
Solving Linear Equations
CA CC 8.EE.7, 8.EE.7a, 8.EE.7b

MATH IN CAREERS

Cost Estimator A cost estimator determines the cost of a product or project, which helps businesses decide whether or not to manufacture a product or build a structure. Cost estimators analyze the costs of labor, materials, and use of equipment, among other things. Cost estimators use math when they assemble and analyze data. If you are interested in a career as a cost estimator, you should study these mathematical subjects:

- Algebra
- Trigonometry
- Calculus

Research other careers that require analyzing costs.

ACTIVITY At the end of the unit, check out how **cost estimators** use math.

Unit Project Preview

Proportional or Nonproportional?

In the Unit Project at the end of this unit, you will choose two companies in your community that are in the same business and that charge by the hour for their services. You will research their charges, compile a table of values relating time and total charges, and graph the relationships. To successfully complete the Unit Project you'll need to master these skills:

- Collect real-world data.
- Make a table of values relating two variables.
- Graph and interpret a relationship between two variables.

1. Explain how you would find the total charge for n hours of a service costing \$15 per hour plus a flat \$30 service fee.

____

____

2. Terri charges \$28 for 4 hours of babysitting, including a \$4 charge for transportation. What is her hourly rate for babysitting?

____

Tracking Your Learning Progression

This unit addresses important California Common Core Standards in the Critical Areas of applying proportional relationships to lines and linear equations and understanding linear equations.

Domain 8.EE Expressions and Equations

Cluster Understand the connections between proportional relationships, lines, and linear equations.

The unit also supports additional standards.

Domain 8.EE Expressions and Equations

Cluster Analyze and solve linear equations and pairs of simultaneous linear equations.

Proportional Relationships

ESSENTIAL QUESTION

How can you use proportional relationships to solve real-world problems?

LESSON 16.1

Representing Proportional Relationships

CA CC 8.EE.6, 8.F.4

LESSON 16.2

Rate of Change and Slope

CA CC 8.F.4

LESSON 16.3

Interpreting the Unit Rate as Slope

CA CC 8.EE.5, 8.F.2, 8.F.4

my.hrw.com

Real-World Video

Speedboats can travel at fast rates while sailboats travel more slowly. If you graphed distance versus time for both types of boats, you could tell by the steepness of the graph which boat was faster.

GO DIGITAL

my.hrw.com

my.hrw.com

Go digital with your write-in student edition, accessible on any device.

Math On the Spot

Scan with your smart phone to jump directly to the online edition, video tutor, and more.

Animated Math

Interactively explore key concepts to see how math works.

Personal Math Trainer

Get immediate feedback and help as you work through practice sets.

Are YOU Ready?

Complete these exercises to review skills you will need for this module.

Personal Math Trainer

Online Practice and Help

Write Fractions as Decimals

EXAMPLE $\frac{1.7}{2.5} = ?$

Multiply the numerator and the denominator by a power of 10 so that the denominator is a whole number. $\frac{1.7 \times 10}{2.5 \times 10} = \frac{17}{25}$

Write the fraction as a division problem.
Write a decimal point and zeros in the dividend.
Place a decimal point in the quotient.
Divide as with whole numbers.

$$\begin{array}{r} 0.68 \\ 25\overline{)17.00} \\ \underline{-150} \\ 200 \\ \underline{-200} \\ 0 \end{array}$$

Write each fraction as a decimal.

1. $\frac{3}{8}$ ________
2. $\frac{0.3}{0.4}$ ________
3. $\frac{0.13}{0.2}$ ________
4. $\frac{0.39}{0.75}$ ________
5. $\frac{4}{5}$ ________
6. $\frac{0.1}{2}$ ________
7. $\frac{3.5}{14}$ ________
8. $\frac{7}{14}$ ________
9. $\frac{0.3}{10}$ ________

Solve Proportions

EXAMPLE $\frac{5}{7} = \frac{x}{14}$

$\frac{5 \times 2}{7 \times 2} = \frac{x}{14}$ $7 \times 2 = 14$, so multiply the numerator and denominator by 2.

$\frac{10}{14} = \frac{x}{14}$ $5 \times 2 = 10$

$x = 10$

Solve each proportion for *x*.

10. $\frac{20}{18} = \frac{10}{x}$ ________
11. $\frac{x}{12} = \frac{30}{72}$ ________
12. $\frac{x}{4} = \frac{4}{16}$ ________
13. $\frac{11}{x} = \frac{132}{120}$ ________
14. $\frac{36}{48} = \frac{x}{4}$ ________
15. $\frac{x}{9} = \frac{21}{27}$ ________
16. $\frac{24}{16} = \frac{x}{2}$ ________
17. $\frac{30}{15} = \frac{6}{x}$ ________
18. $\frac{3}{x} = \frac{18}{36}$ ________

Reading Start-Up

Visualize Vocabulary

Use the ✔ words to complete the diagram.

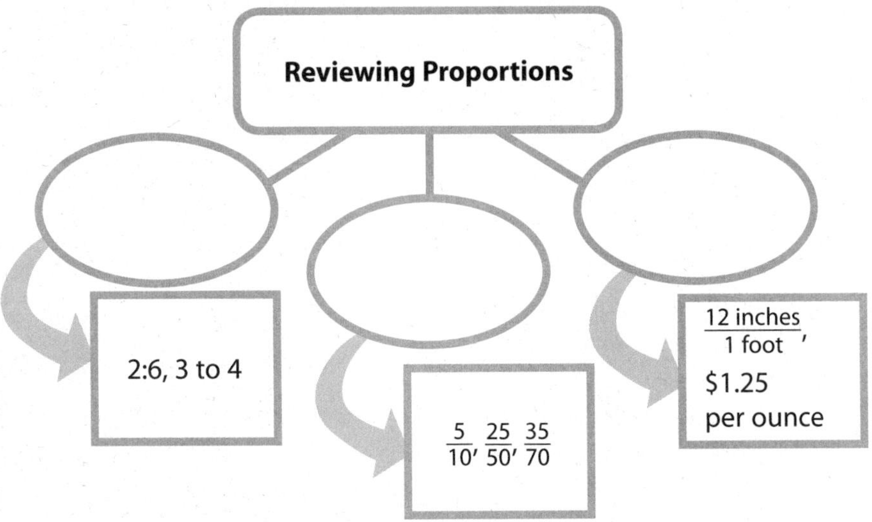

Vocabulary

Review Words

constant *(constante)*

✔ equivalent ratios *(razones equivalentes)*

proportion *(proporción)*

rate *(tasa)*

✔ ratios *(razón)*

✔ unit rates *(tasas unitarias)*

Preview Words

constant of proportionality *(constante de proporcionalidad)*

proportional relationship *(relación proporcional)*

rate of change *(tasa de cambio)*

slope *(pendiente)*

Understand Vocabulary

Match the term on the left to the definition on the right.

1. unit rate	**A.** A constant ratio of two variables related proportionally.
2. constant of proportionality	**B.** A rate in which the second quantity in the comparison is one unit.
3. proportional relationship	**C.** A relationship between two quantities in which the ratio of one quantity to the other quantity is constant.

Active Reading

Key-Term Fold Before beginning the module, create a key-term fold to help you learn the vocabulary in this module. Write the highlighted vocabulary words on one side of the flap. Write the definition for each word on the other side of the flap. Use the key-term fold to quiz yourself on the definitions used in this module.

GETTING READY FOR

Proportional Relationships

Understanding the standards and the vocabulary terms in the standards will help you know exactly what you are expected to learn in this module.

 CA CC **8.EE.5**

Graph proportional relationships, interpreting the unit rate as the slope of the graph. Compare two different proportional relationships represented in different ways.

Key Vocabulary

proportional relationship *(relación proporcional)*
A relationship between two quantities in which the ratio of one quantity to the other quantity is constant.

slope *(pendiente)*
A measure of the steepness of a line on a graph; the rise divided by the run.

unit rate *(tasa unitaria)*
A rate in which the second quantity in the comparison is one unit.

What It Means to You

You will use data from a table and a graph to apply your understanding of rates to analyzing real-world situations.

EXAMPLE 8.EE.5

The table shows the volume of water released by Hoover Dam over a certain period of time. Use the data to make a graph. Find the slope of the line and explain what it shows.

Water Released from Hoover Dam	
Time (s)	**Volume of water (m^3)**
5	75,000
10	150,000
15	225,000
20	300,000

Water Released from Hoover Dam

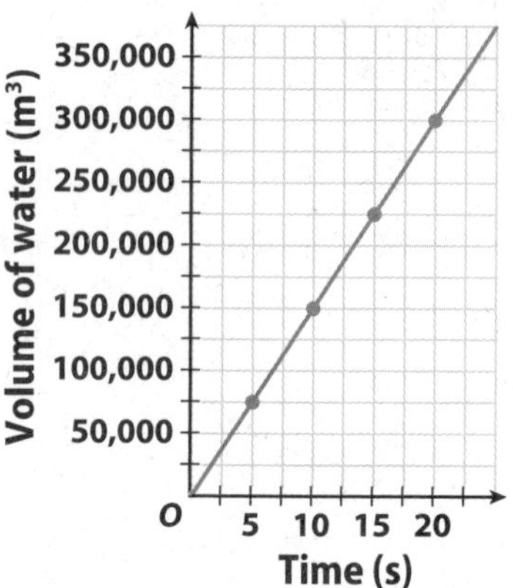

The slope of the line is 15,000. This means that for every second that passed, 15,000 m^3 of water was released from Hoover Dam.

Suppose another dam releases water over the same period of time at a rate of 180,000 m^3 per minute. How do the two rates compare?

180,000 m^3 per minute is equal to 3,000 m^3 per second. This rate is one fifth the rate released by the Hoover Dam over the same time period.

Visit **my.hrw.com** to see all **CA Common Core Standards** explained.

my.hrw.com

LESSON 16.1

Representing Proportional Relationships

8EE.6

Graph proportional relationships, interpreting the unit rate as the slope of the graph. Compare two different proportional relationships represented in different ways.

ESSENTIAL QUESTION

How can you use tables, graphs, and equations to represent proportional situations?

EXPLORE ACTIVITY 

Prep for 8.EE.6

Representing Proportional Relationships with Tables

In 1870, the French writer Jules Verne published *20,000 Leagues Under the Sea*, one of the most popular science fiction novels ever written. One definition of a *league* is a unit of measure equaling 3 miles.

A Complete the table.

Distance (leagues)	1	2	6		20,000
Distance (miles)	3			36	

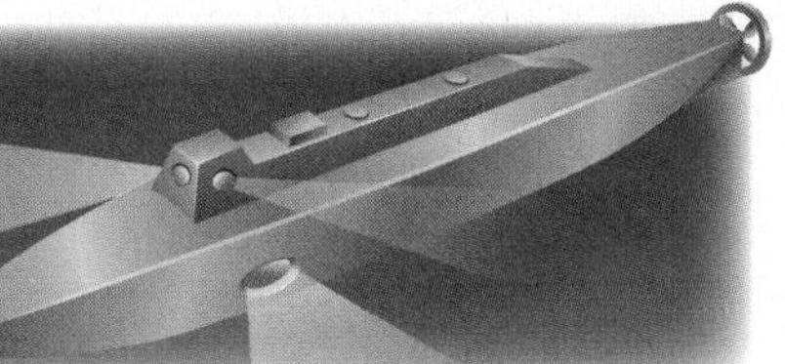

B What relationships do you see among the numbers in the table?

____

____

C For each column of the table, find the ratio of the distance in miles to the distance in leagues. Write each ratio in simplest form.

$\frac{3}{1} = \square$ $\quad \frac{\square}{2} = \square$ $\quad \frac{\square}{6} = \square$ $\quad \frac{36}{\square} = \square$ $\quad \frac{\square}{20,000} = \square$

D What do you notice about the ratios? ______________________________

Reflect

1. If you know the distance between two points in leagues, how can you find the distance in miles? ______________________________

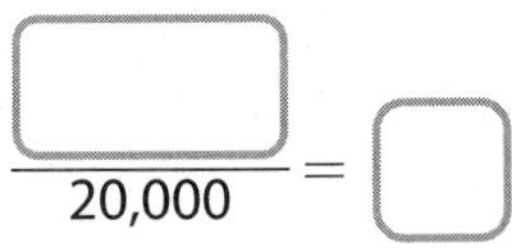

2. If you know the distance between two points in miles, how can you find the distance in leagues? ______________________________

Representing Proportional Relationships with Equations

The ratio of the distance in miles to the distance in leagues is constant. This relationship is said to be *proportional*. A **proportional relationship** is a relationship between two quantities in which the ratio of one quantity to the other quantity is constant.

A proportional relationship can be described by an equation of the form $y = kx$, where k is a number called the **constant of proportionality**.

Sometimes it is useful to use another form of the equation, $k = \frac{y}{x}$.

EXAMPLE 1

Meghan earns $12 an hour at her part-time job. Show that the relationship between the amount she earned and the number of hours she worked is a proportional relationship. Then write an equation for the relationship.

STEP 1 Make a table relating amount earned to number of hours.

For every hour Meghan works, she earns $12. So, for 8 hours of work, she earns $8 \times \$12 = \$96$.

Number of hours	1	2	4	8
Amount earned ($)	12	24	48	96

STEP 2 For each number of hours, write the relationship of the amount earned and the number of hours as a ratio in simplest form.

$$\frac{\text{amount earned}}{\text{number of hours}} \quad \frac{12}{1} = \frac{12}{1} \quad \frac{24}{2} = \frac{12}{1} \quad \frac{48}{4} = \frac{12}{1} \quad \frac{96}{8} = \frac{12}{1}$$

Since the ratios for the two quantities are all equal to $\frac{12}{1}$, the relationship is proportional.

STEP 3 Write an equation.

First tell what the variables represent.

Let x represent the number of hours.
Let y represent the amount earned.

Use the ratio as the constant of proportionality in the equation $y = kx$.

The equation is $y = \frac{12}{1}x$ or $y = 12x$.

Describe two real-world quantities with a proportional relationship that can be described by the equation $y = 25x$.

Personal Math Trainer
Online Practice and Help
my.hrw.com

YOUR TURN

3. Fifteen bicycles are produced each hour at the Speedy Bike Works. Show that the relationship between the number of bikes produced and the number of hours is a proportional relationship. Then write an equation for the relationship. ______________

Representing Proportional Relationships with Graphs

You can represent a proportional relationship with a graph. The graph will be a line that passes through the origin (0, 0). The graph shows the relationship between distance measured in miles to distance measured in leagues.

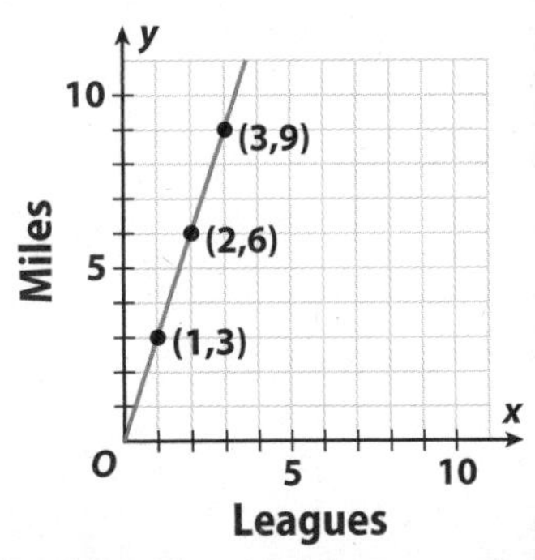

EXAMPLE 2

CA CC 8.EE.6

The graph shows the relationship between the weight of an object on the Moon and its weight on Earth. Write an equation for this relationship.

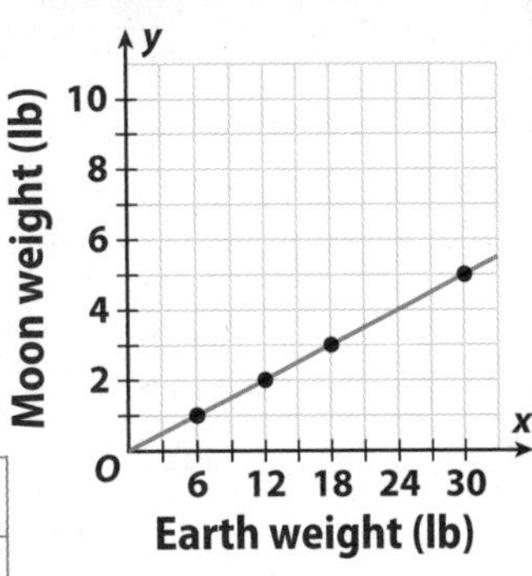

STEP 1 Use the points on the graph to make a table.

Earth weight (lb)	6	12	18	30
Moon weight (lb)	1	2	3	5

STEP 2 Find the constant of proportionality.

$\frac{\text{Moon weight}}{\text{Earth weight}}$ $\quad \frac{1}{6} = \frac{1}{6} \quad \frac{2}{12} = \frac{1}{6} \quad \frac{3}{18} = \frac{1}{6} \quad \frac{5}{30} = \frac{1}{6}$

The constant of proportionality is $\frac{1}{6}$.

STEP 3 Write an equation.

Let x represent weight on Earth.

Let y represent weight on the Moon.

The equation is $y = \frac{1}{6}x$. *Replace k with $\frac{1}{6}$ in $y = kx$.*

YOUR TURN

The graph shows the relationship between the amount of time that a backpacker hikes and the distance traveled.

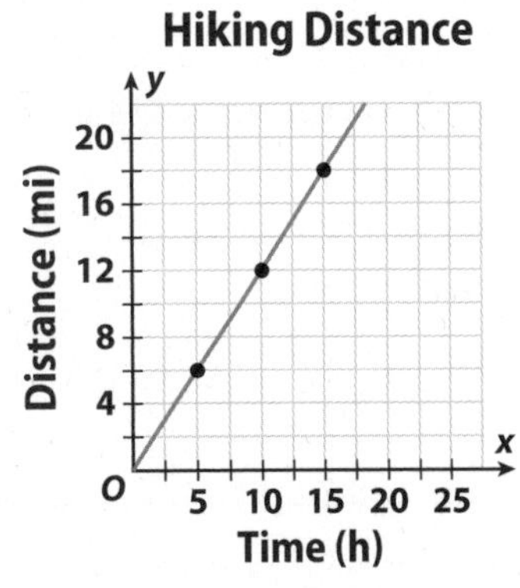

4. What does the point (5, 6) represent?

____

5. What is the equation of the relationship?

____

Guided Practice

1. **Vocabulary** A proportional relationship is a relationship between two quantities in which the ratio of one quantity to the other quantity **is / is not** constant.

2. **Vocabulary** When writing an equation of a proportional relationship in the form $y = kx$, k represents the ______________________.

3. Write an equation that describes the proportional relationship between the number of days and the number of weeks in a given length of time. (Explore Activity and Example 1)

   a. Complete the table.

Time (weeks)	1	2	4		10
Time (days)	7			56	

   b. Let x represent ______________________.

   Let y represent ______________________.

   The equation that describes the relationship is ____________.

Each table or graph represents a proportional relationship. Write an equation that describes the relationship. (Example 1 and Example 2)

4. **Physical Science** The relationship between the numbers of oxygen atoms and hydrogen atoms in water

Oxygen atoms	2	5		120
Hydrogen atoms	4		34	

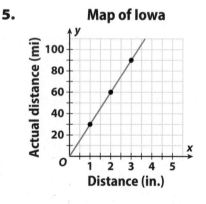

____

5. **Map of Iowa**

____

ESSENTIAL QUESTION CHECK-IN

6. If you know the equation of a proportional relationship, how can you draw the graph of the equation?

____

____

Name ______________________ Class ______________________ Date ______________________

16.1 Independent Practice

The table shows the relationship between temperatures measured on the Celsius and Fahrenheit scales.

Celsius temperature	0	10	20	30	40	50
Fahrenheit temperature	32	50	68	86	104	122

7. Is the relationship between the temperature scales proportional? Why or why not?

____

____

8. Describe the graph of the Celsius-Fahrenheit relationship.

____

____

9. **Analyze Relationships** Ralph opened a savings account with a deposit of \$100. Every month after that, he deposited \$20 more.

a. Why is the relationship described not proportional?

____

____

b. How could the situation be changed to make the situation proportional?

____

____

10. **Represent Real-World Problems** Describe a real-world situation that can be modeled by the equation $y = \frac{1}{20}x$. Be sure to describe what each variable represents.

____

____

Look for a Pattern **The variables *x* and *y* are related proportionally.**

11. When $x = 8$, $y = 20$. Find y when $x = 42$. ______________________

12. When $x = 12$, $y = 8$. Find x when $y = 12$. ______________________

13. The graph shows the relationship between the distance that a snail crawls and the time that it crawls.

Snail Crawling

a. Use the points on the graph to make a table.

Time (min)					
Distance (in.)					

b. Write the equation for the relationship and tell what each variable represents.

____

c. How long does it take the snail to crawl 85 inches? ______________

Work Area

H.O.T. FOCUS ON HIGHER ORDER THINKING

14. Communicate Mathematical Ideas Explain why all of the graphs in this lesson show the first quadrant but omit the other three quadrants.

____

____

____

____

15. Analyze Relationships Complete the table.

Length of side of square	1	2	3	4	5
Perimeter of square					
Area of square					

a. Are the length of a side of a square and the perimeter of the square related proportionally? Why or why not?

____

____

b. Are the length of a side of a square and the area of the square related proportionally? Why or why not?

____

____

16. Make a Conjecture A table shows a proportional relationship where k is the constant of proportionality. The rows are then switched. How does the new constant of proportionality relate to the original one?

____

LESSON 16.2

Rate of Change and Slope

CA CC 8. F.4

Construct a function to model a linear relationship between two quantities. Determine the rate of change and initial value of the function from a description of a relationship or from two (x, y) values, including reading these from a table or from a graph. Interpret the rate of change and initial value of a linear function in terms of the situation it models, and in terms of its graph or a table of values.

ESSENTIAL QUESTION

How do you find a rate of change or a slope?

Investigating Rates of Change

A **rate of change** is a ratio of the amount of change in the dependent variable to the amount of change in the independent variable.

EXAMPLE 1

CA CC 8.F.4

Eve keeps a record of the number of lawns she has mowed and the money she has earned. Tell whether the rates of change are constant or variable.

	Day 1	Day 2	Day 3	Day 4
Number of lawns	1	3	6	8
Amount earned ($)	15	45	90	120

STEP 1 Identify the independent and dependent variables.

independent: number of lawns   dependent: amount earned

STEP 2 Find the rates of change.

Day 1 to Day 2: $\frac{\text{change in \$}}{\text{change in lawns}} = \frac{45 - 15}{3 - 1} = \frac{30}{2} = 15$

Day 2 to Day 3: $\frac{\text{change in \$}}{\text{change in lawns}} = \frac{90 - 45}{6 - 3} = \frac{45}{3} = 15$

Day 3 to Day 4: $\frac{\text{change in \$}}{\text{change in lawns}} = \frac{120 - 90}{8 - 6} = \frac{30}{2} = 15$

The rates of change are constant: $15 per lawn.

Math Talk

Would you expect the rates of change of a car's speed during a drive through a city to be constant or variable? Explain.

YOUR TURN

1. The table shows the approximate height of a football after it is kicked. Tell whether the rates of change are constant or variable.

Time (s)	Height (ft)
0	0
0.5	18
1.5	31
2	26

Find the rates of change:

____

The rates of change are **constant / variable.**

EXPLORE ACTIVITY   CA CC 8.F.4

Using Graphs to Find Rates of Change

You can also use a graph to find rates of change.

The graph shows the distance Nathan bicycled over time. What is Nathan's rate of change?

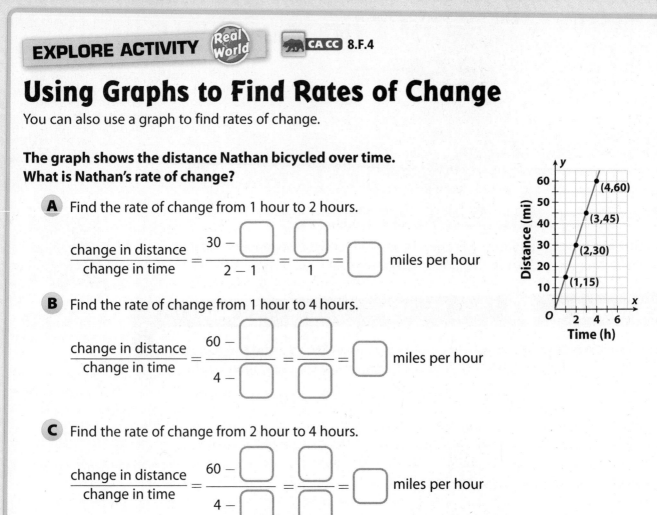

A Find the rate of change from 1 hour to 2 hours.

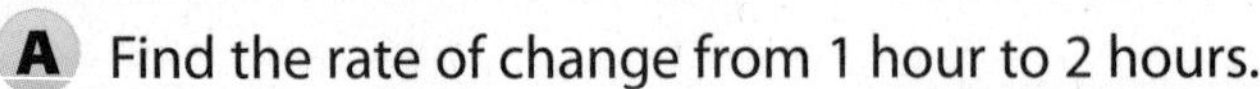

$$\frac{\text{change in distance}}{\text{change in time}} = \frac{30 - \square}{2 - 1} = \frac{\square}{1} = \square \text{ miles per hour}$$

B Find the rate of change from 1 hour to 4 hours.

$$\frac{\text{change in distance}}{\text{change in time}} = \frac{60 - \square}{4 - \square} = \frac{\square}{\square} = \square \text{ miles per hour}$$

C Find the rate of change from 2 hour to 4 hours.

$$\frac{\text{change in distance}}{\text{change in time}} = \frac{60 - \square}{4 - \square} = \frac{\square}{\square} = \square \text{ miles per hour}$$

D Recall that the graph of a proportional relationship is a line through the origin. Explain whether the relationship between Nathan's time and distance is a proportional relationship.

____

____

Reflect

2. **Make a Conjecture** Does a proportional relationship have a constant rate of change?

____

3. Does it matter what interval you use when you find the rate of change of a proportional relationship? Explain.

____

____

Calculating Slope m

When the rate of change of a relationship is constant, any segment of its graph has the same steepness. The constant rate of change is called the *slope* of the line.

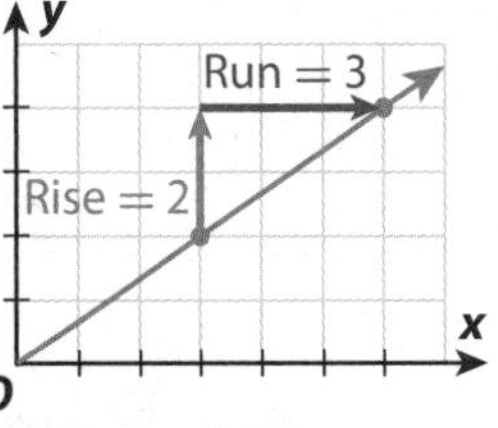

Slope Formula

The **slope** of a line is the ratio of the change in y-values (rise) for a segment of the graph to the corresponding change in x-values (run).

$$m = \frac{y_2 - y_1}{x_2 - x_1}$$

EXAMPLE 2

Find m the slope of the line.

STEP 1 Choose two points on the line.

$P_1(x_1, y_1)$ $P_2(x_2, y_2)$

STEP 2 Find the change in y-values (rise $= y_2 - y_1$) and the change in x-values (run $= x_2 - x_1$) as you move from one point to the other.

$$\textbf{rise} = y_2 - y_1 = 4 - 2 = 2$$

$$\textbf{run} = x_2 - x_1 = -6 - (-3) = -3$$

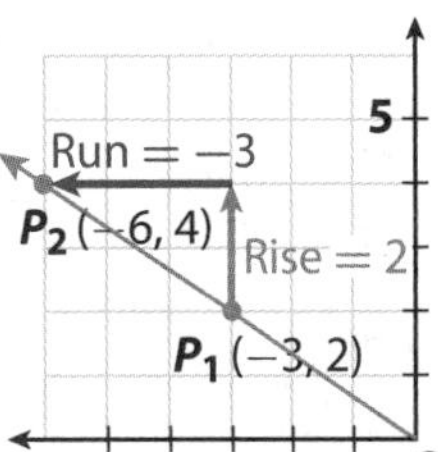

If you move up or right, the change is positive. If you move down or left, the change is negative.

STEP 3 $m = \frac{\text{rise}}{\text{run}} = \frac{y_2 - y_1}{x_2 - x_1}$

$= \frac{2}{-3}$

$= -\frac{2}{3}$

My Notes

YOUR TURN

4. The graph shows the rate at which water is leaking from a tank. The slope of the line gives the leaking rate in gallons per minute. Find the slope of the line.

Rise = ________ Run = ________

Slope = ________

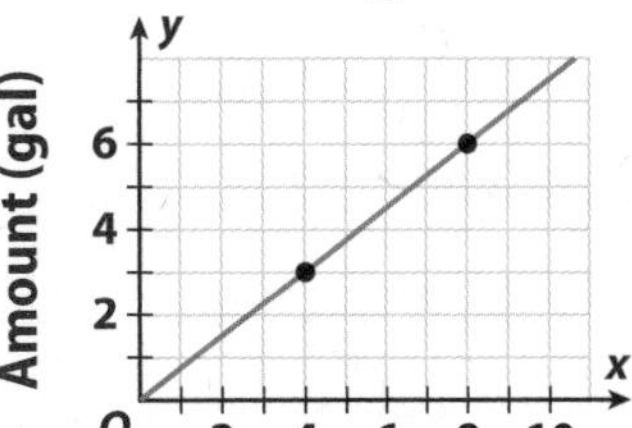

Guided Practice

Tell whether the rates of change are constant or variable. (Example 1)

1. building measurements ________________

Feet	3	12	27	75
Yards	1	4	9	25

2. computers sold ________________

Week	2	4	9	20
Number Sold	6	12	25	60

3. distance an object falls ________________

Distance (ft)	16	64	144	256
Time (s)	1	2	3	4

4. cost of sweaters ________________

Number	2	4	7	9
Cost ($)	38	76	133	171

Erica walks to her friend Philip's house. The graph shows Erica's distance from home over time. (Explore Activity)

5. Find the rate of change from 1 minute to 2 minutes.

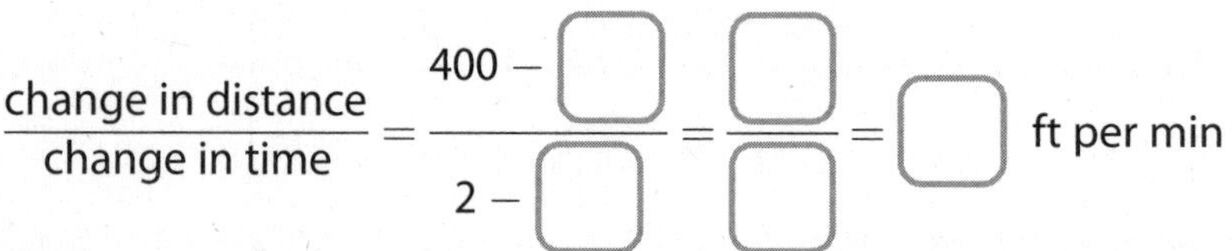

$$\frac{\text{change in distance}}{\text{change in time}} = \frac{400 - \square}{2 - \square} = \frac{\square}{\square} = \square \text{ ft per min}$$

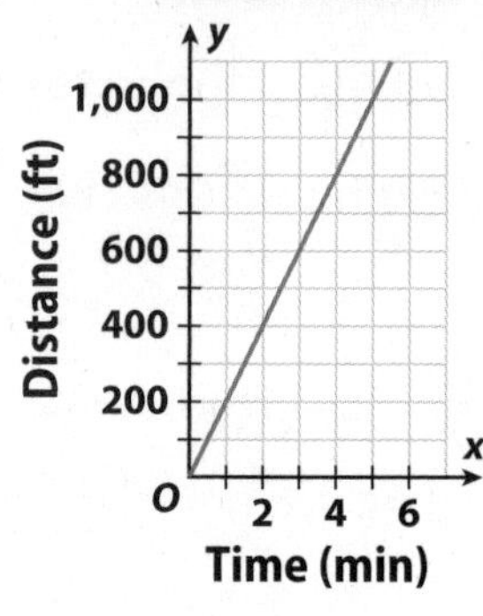

6. Find the rate of change from 1 minute to 4 minutes. ________________

Find the slope of each line. (Example 2)

7.

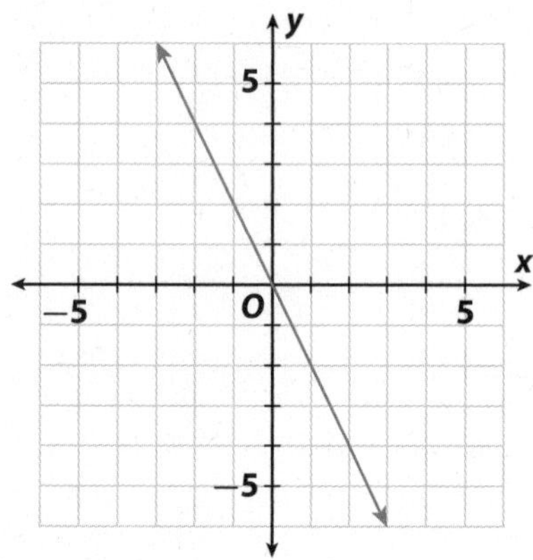

slope = ________________

8.

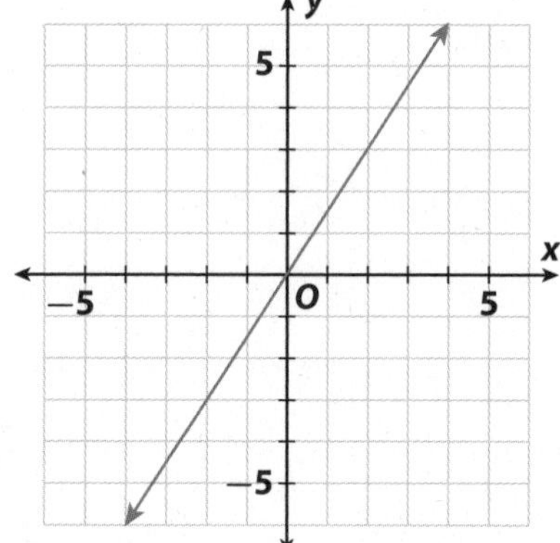

slope = ________________

ESSENTIAL QUESTION CHECK-IN

9. If you know two points on a line, how can you find the rate of change of the variables being graphed?

____

____

____

Name ______________________ Class ______________ Date ______________

16.2 Independent Practice

CA CC 8.F.4

10. Rectangle *EFGH* is graphed on a coordinate plane with vertices at $E(-3, 5)$, $F(6, 2)$, $G(4, -4)$, and $H(-5, -1)$.

a. Find the slopes of each side.

____

____

b. What do you notice about the slopes of opposite sides?

____

c. What do you notice about the slopes of adjacent sides?

____

11. A bicyclist started riding at 8:00 A.M. The diagram below shows the distance the bicyclist had traveled at different times. What was the bicyclist's average rate of speed in miles per hour?

8:00 A.M. ← 4.5 miles → 8:18 A.M. ← 7.5 miles → 8:48 A.M.

____

12. Multistep A line passes through (6, 3), (8, 4), and $(n, -2)$. Find the value of n.

____

13. A large container holds 5 gallons of water. It begins leaking at a constant rate. After 10 minutes, the container has 3 gallons of water left.

a. At what rate is the water leaking?

____

b. After how many minutes will the container be empty?

____

14. Critique Reasoning Billy found the slope of the line through the points (2, 5) and $(-2, -5)$ using the equation $\frac{2-(-2)}{5-(-5)} = \frac{2}{5}$. What mistake did he make?

____

____

15. Multiple Representations Graph parallelogram *ABCD* on a coordinate plane with vertices at *A*(3, 4), *B*(6, 1), *C*(0, −2), and *D*(−3, 1).

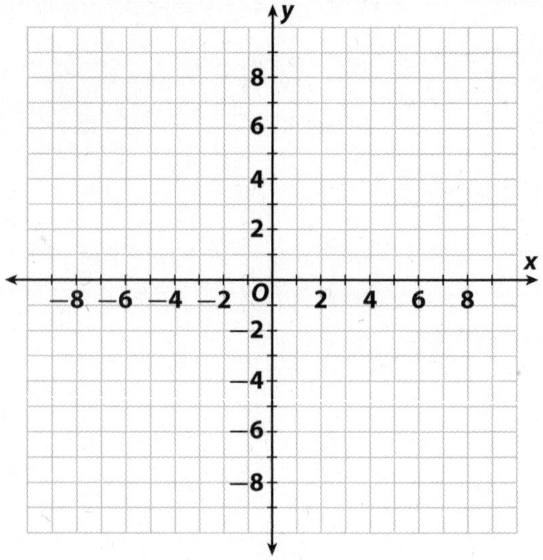

a. Find the slope of each side.

____

____

b. What do you notice about the slopes?

____

____

c. Draw another parallelogram on the coordinate plane. Do the slopes have the same characteristics?

____

H.O.T. FOCUS ON HIGHER ORDER THINKING

Work Area

16. Communicate Mathematical Ideas Ben and Phoebe are finding the slope of a line. Ben chose two points on the line and used them to find the slope. Phoebe used two different points to find the slope. Did they get the same answer? Explain.

____

____

____

17. Analyze Relationships Two lines pass through the origin. The lines have slopes that are opposites. Compare and contrast the lines.

____

____

____

____

____

18. Reason Abstractly What is the slope of the *x*-axis? Explain.

____

____

____

LESSON 16.3

Interpreting the Unit Rate as Slope

8.EE.5

Graph proportional relationships, interpreting the unit rate as the slope of the graph. Compare two different proportional relationships represented in different ways. *Also 8.F.2, 8.F.4*

ESSENTIAL QUESTION

How do you interpret the unit rate as slope?

EXPLORE ACTIVITY 

Relating the Unit Rate to Slope

A rate is a comparison of two quantities that have different units, such as miles and hours. A **unit rate** is a rate in which the second quantity in the comparison is one unit.

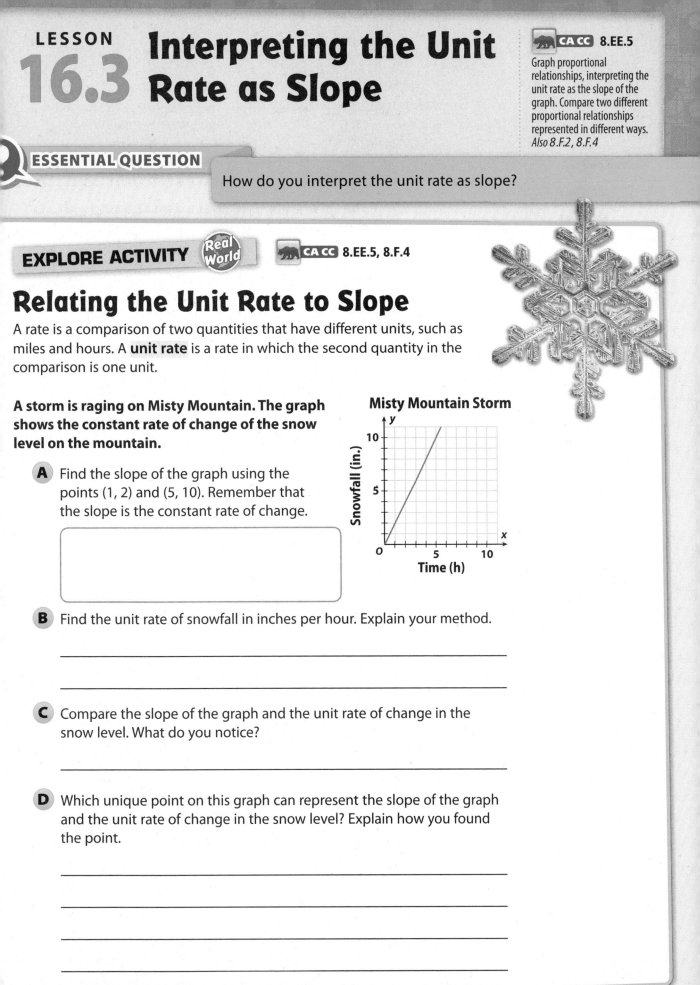

A storm is raging on Misty Mountain. The graph shows the constant rate of change of the snow level on the mountain.

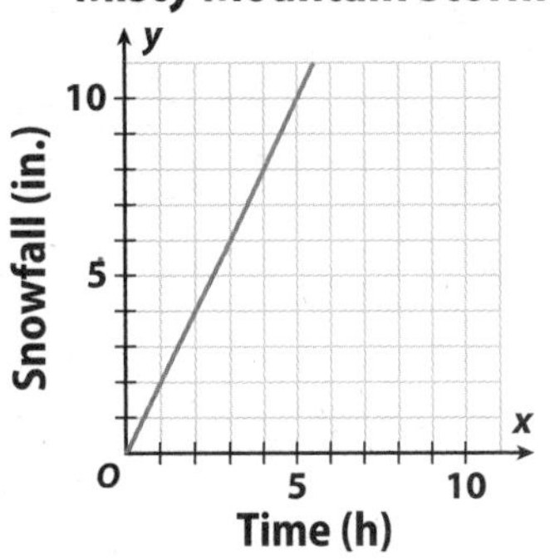

A Find the slope of the graph using the points (1, 2) and (5, 10). Remember that the slope is the constant rate of change.

B Find the unit rate of snowfall in inches per hour. Explain your method.

____

____

C Compare the slope of the graph and the unit rate of change in the snow level. What do you notice?

____

D Which unique point on this graph can represent the slope of the graph and the unit rate of change in the snow level? Explain how you found the point.

____

____

____

____

Graphing Proportional Relationships

You can use a table or a graph to find the unit rate and slope that describe a real-world proportional relationship. The constant of proportionality for a proportional relationship is the same as the slope and the unit rate.

EXAMPLE 1

Every 3 seconds, 4 cubic feet of water pass over a dam. Draw a graph of the situation. Find the unit rate of this proportional relationship.

STEP 1 Make a table.

Time (sec)	3	6	9	12	15
Volume (ft³)	4	8	12	16	20

Animated Math
my.hrw.com

STEP 2 Draw a graph.

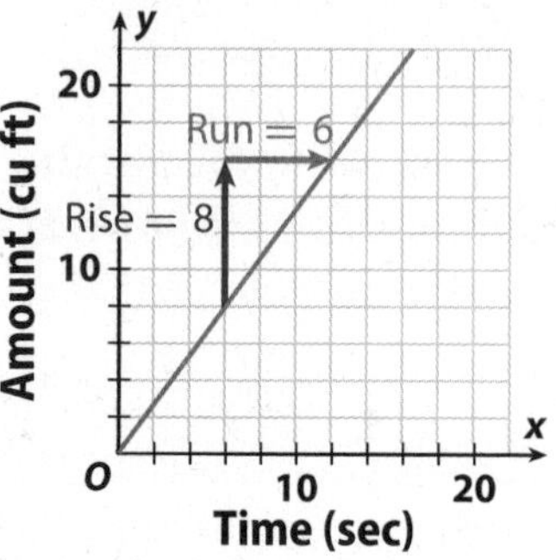

STEP 3 Find the slope.

$$\text{slope} = \frac{\text{rise}}{\text{run}} = \frac{8}{6}$$

$$= \frac{4}{3}$$

Math Talk
Mathematical Practices
In a proportional relationship, how are the constant of proportionality, the unit rate, and the slope of the graph of the relationship related?

The slope and the unit rate of the graph are equal, therefore $\frac{4}{3}$ cubic feet per second is the unit rate and the slope.

Reflect

1. **What If?** Without referring to the graph, how do you know that the point $\left(1, \frac{4}{3}\right)$ is on the graph?

____

____

YOUR TURN

2. Tomas rides his bike at a steady rate of 4 miles every 6 minutes. Graph the situation. Find the unit rate of this proportional relationship.

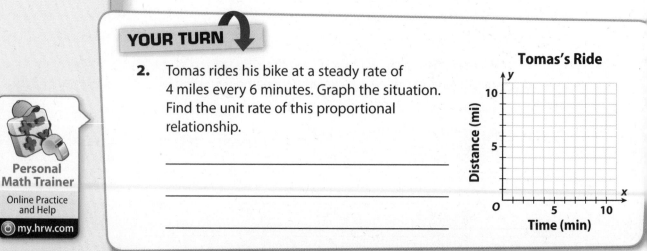

____

____

____

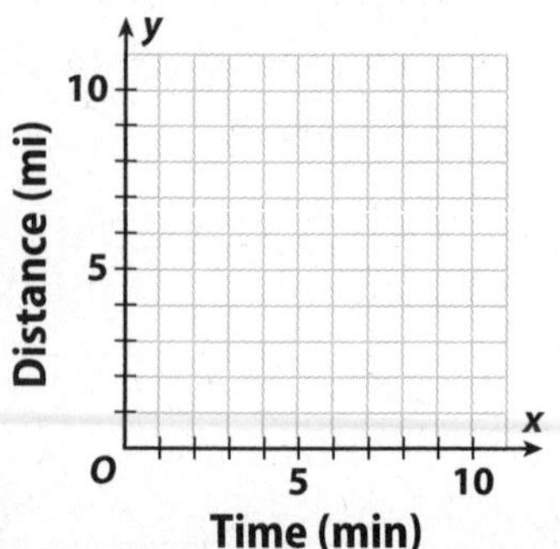

Online Practice and Help
my.hrw.com

Using Slopes to Compare Unit Rates

You can compare proportional relationships presented in different ways.

EXAMPLE 2 

CA CC 8.EE.5, 8.F.2

The equation $y = 2.75x$ represents the rate, in barrels per hour, that oil is pumped from Well A. The graph represents the rate that oil is pumped from Well B. Which well pumped oil at a faster rate?

Well B Pumping Rate

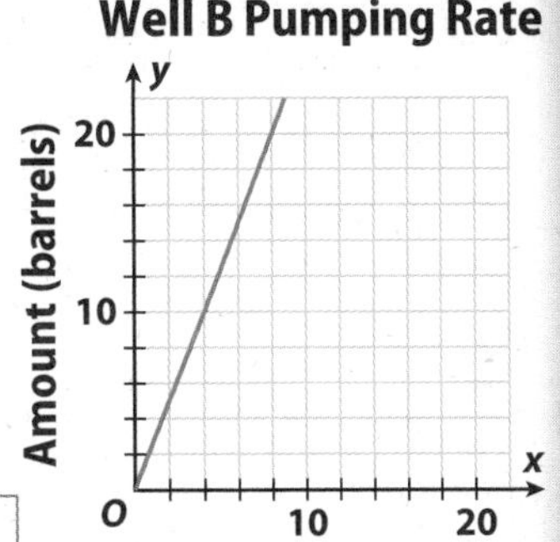

STEP 1 Use the equation $y = 2.75x$ to make a table for Well A's pumping rate, in barrels per hour.

Time (h)	1	2	3	4
Quantity (barrels)	2.75	5.5	8.25	11

STEP 2 Use the table to find the slope of the graph of Well A.

slope = unit rate = $\frac{5.5 - 2.75}{2 - 1} = \frac{2.75}{1} = \mathbf{2.75}$ barrels/hour

STEP 3 Use the graph to find the slope of the graph of Well B.

slope = unit rate = $\frac{\text{rise}}{\text{run}} = \frac{10}{4} = \mathbf{2.5}$ barrels/hour

STEP 4 Compare the unit rates.

$2.75 > 2.5$, so Well A's rate, 2.75 barrels/hour, is faster.

Reflect

3. Describe the relationships among the slope of the graph of Well A's rate, the equation representing Well A's rate, and the constant of proportionality.

___

___

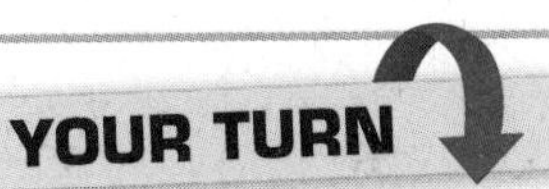

4. The equation $y = 375x$ represents the relationship between x, the time that a plane flies in hours, and y, the distance the plane flies in miles for Plane A. The table represents the relationship for Plane B. Find the slope of the graph for each plane and the plane's rate of speed. Determine which plane is flying at a faster rate of speed.

Time (h)	1	2	3	4
Distance (mi)	425	850	1275	1700

___

Guided Practice

Give the slope of the graph and the unit rate. (Explore Activity and Example 1)

1. Jorge: 5 miles every 6 hours

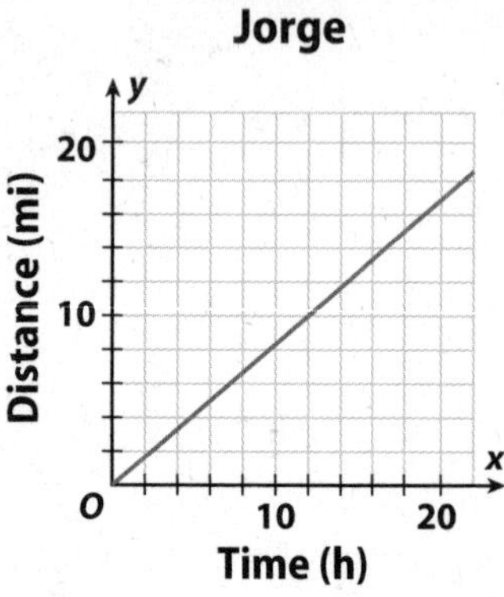

____

2. Akiko

Time (h)	Distance (mi)
4	5
8	10
12	15
16	20

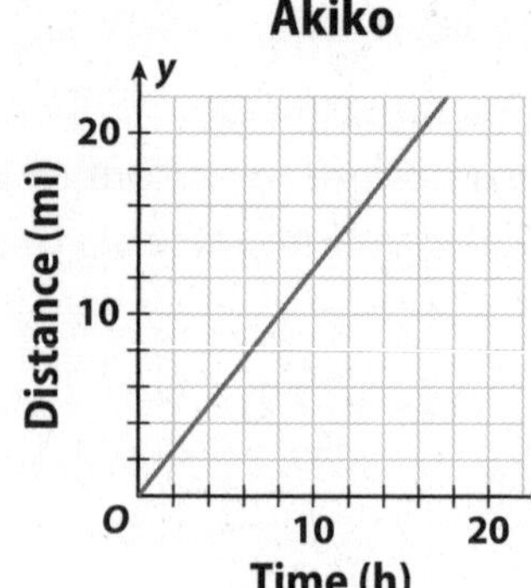

____

3. The equation $y = 0.5x$ represents the distance Henry hikes in miles per hour. The graph represents the rate that Clark hikes. Determine which hiker is faster. Explain. (Example 2)

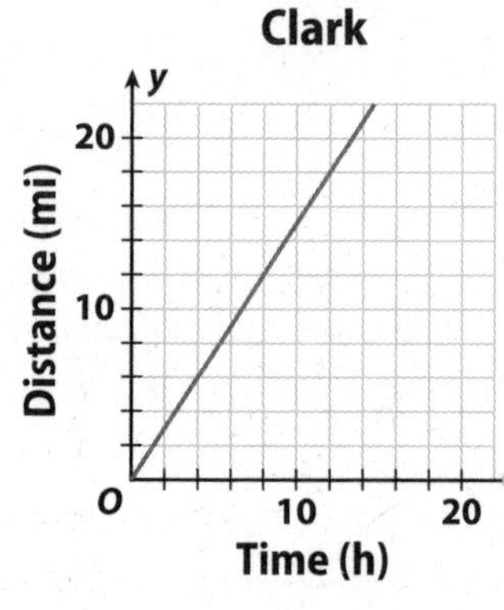

____

____

____

Write an equation relating the variables in each table. (Example 2)

4.

Time (x)	1	2	4	6
Distance (y)	15	30	60	90

____

5.

Time (x)	16	32	48	64
Distance (y)	6	12	18	24

____

? ESSENTIAL QUESTION CHECK-IN

6. Describe methods you can use to show a proportional relationship between two variables, x and y. For each method, explain how you can find the unit rate and the slope.

____

____

____

____

____

Name _______________ Class _______________ Date _______________

16.3 Independent Practice

CA CC 8.EE.5, 8.F.2, 8.F.4

7. A Canadian goose migrated at a steady rate of 3 miles every 4 minutes.

a. Fill in the table to describe the relationship.

Time (min)	4	8			20
Distance (mi)			9	12	

b. Graph the relationship.

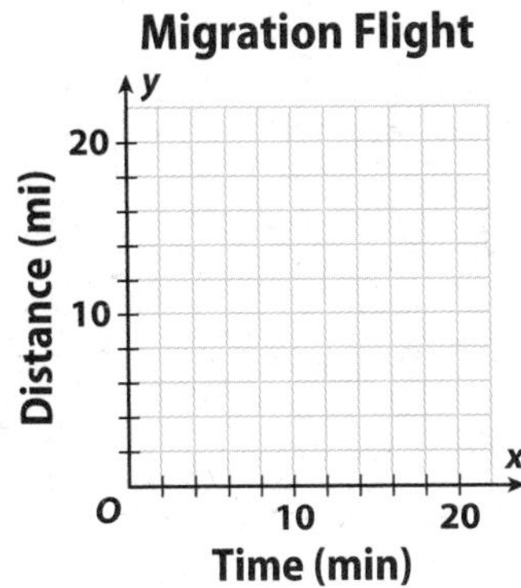

c. Find the slope of the graph and describe what it means in the context of this problem.

____

____

____

____

8. Vocabulary A unit rate is a rate in which the **first quantity / second quantity** in the comparison is one unit.

9. The table and the graph represent the rate at which two machines are bottling milk in gallons per second.

Machine 1

Time (s)	1	2	3	4
Amount (gal)	0.6	1.2	1.8	2.4

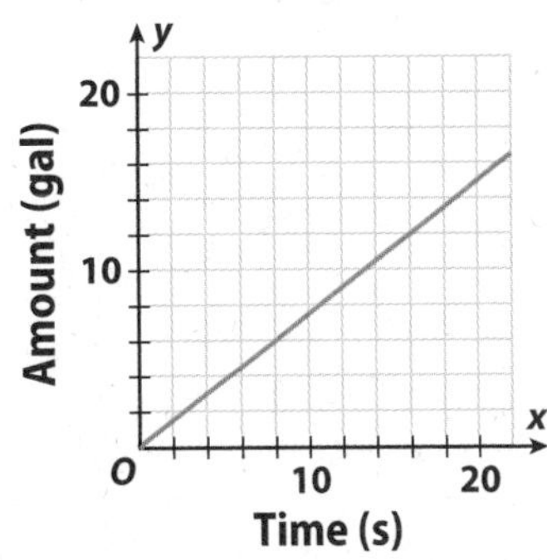

a. Determine the slope and unit rate of each machine.

____

____

b. Determine which machine is working at a faster rate.

____

10. **Cycling** The equation $y = \frac{1}{9}x$ represents the distance y, in kilometers, that Patrick traveled in x minutes while training for the cycling portion of a triathlon. The table shows the distance y Jennifer traveled in x minutes in her training. Who has the faster training rate?

Time (min)	40	64	80	96
Distance (km)	5	8	10	12

H.O.T. FOCUS ON HIGHER ORDER THINKING

Work Area

11. **Analyze Relationships** There is a proportional relationship between minutes and dollars per minute, shown on a graph of printing expenses. The graph passes through the point (1, 4.75). What is the slope of the graph? What is the unit rate? Explain.

12. **Draw Conclusions** Two cars start at the same time and travel at different constant rates. A graph for Car A passes through the point (0.5, 27.5), and a graph for Car B passes through (4, 240). Both graphs show distance in miles and time in hours. Which car is traveling faster? Explain.

13. **Critical Thinking** The table shows the rate at which water is being pumped into a swimming pool.

Time (min)	2	5	7	12
Amount (gal)	36	90	126	216

Use the unit rate and the amount of water pumped after 12 minutes to find how much water will have been pumped into the pool after $13\frac{1}{2}$ minutes. Explain your reasoning.

MODULE QUIZ

Ready to Go On?

16.1 Representing Proportional Relationships

1. Find the constant of proportionality for the table of values.

x	2	3	4	5
y	3	4.5	6	7.5

____

2. Phil is riding his bike. He rides 25 miles in 2 hours, 37.5 miles in 3 hours, and 50 miles in 4 hours. Find the constant of proportionality and write an equation to describe the situation. ______________________

16.2 Rate of Change and Slope

Find the slope of each line.

3.

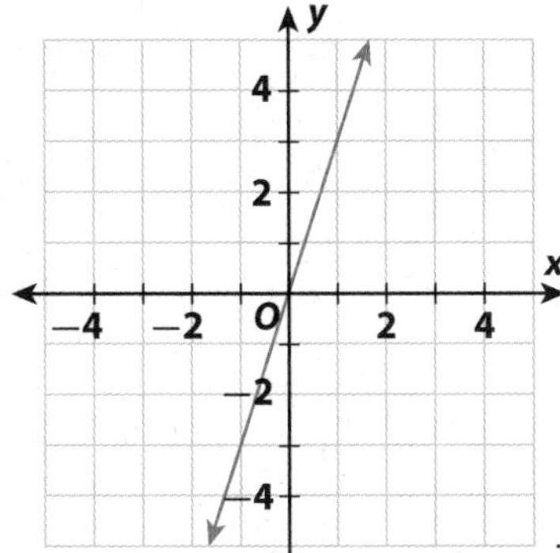

____

4.

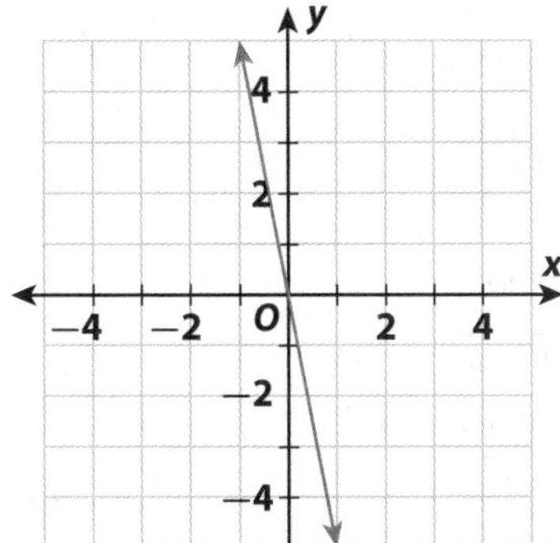

____

16.3 Interpreting the Unit Rate as Slope

5. The distance Train A travels is represented by $d = 70t$, where d is the distance in kilometers and t is the time in hours. The distance Train B travels at various times is shown in the table. What is the unit rate of each train? Which train is going faster?

Time (hours)	Distance (km)
2	150
4	300
5	375

____

ESSENTIAL QUESTION

6. What is the relationship among proportional relationships, lines, rates of change, and slope?

____

____

MODULE 16
MIXED REVIEW

Assessment Readiness

1. Consider each table. Are the rates of change within each table constant?

Select Yes or No for tables A–C.

A.

Time (s)	1	2	5	8
Height (m)	14	28	70	112

○ Yes ○ No

B.

Time (s)	1	2	3	4
Height (m)	60	30	15	7.5

○ Yes ○ No

C.

Time (s)	2	6	10	12
Height (m)	40	120	200	240

○ Yes ○ No

2. An influenza virus has a length of 1.3×10^{-7} meter.

Choose True or False if a virus is longer than the influenza virus.

A. a hepatitis virus with a length of 4.5×10^{-8} m ○ True ○ False

B. a measles virus with a length of 0.00000022 m ○ True ○ False

C. a phage virus with a length of 2×10^{-7} m ○ True ○ False

The table shows travel distance and fuel usage for a train. Use the table for items 3 and 4.

Distance (mi), *x*	20	40	60	80
Amount of fuel (gal), *y*	120	240	360	480

3. Write an equation for the relationship shown in the table and explain how you determined your answer.

4. The equation $y = 6.5x$ gives the number of gallons of fuel that a second train uses to travel a distance of x miles. Which train uses fuel at a greater rate? Explain how you know.

Nonproportional Relationships

MODULE 17

CALIFORNIA

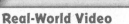

ESSENTIAL QUESTION

How can you use non-proportional relationships to solve real-world problems?

Real-World Video

The distance a car can travel on a tank of gas or a full battery charge in an electric car depends on factors such as fuel capacity and the car's efficiency. This is described by a nonproportional relationship.

my.hrw.com

GO DIGITAL
my.hrw.com

my.hrw.com

Go digital with your write-in student edition, accessible on any device.

Math On the Spot

Scan with your smart phone to jump directly to the online edition, video tutor, and more.

Animated Math

Interactively explore key concepts to see how math works.

Personal Math Trainer

Get immediate feedback and help as you work through practice sets.

Are YOU Ready?

Complete these exercises to review skills you will need for this module.

Integer Operations

EXAMPLE $-7-(-4) = -7+4$ *To subtract an integer, add its opposite.*

$|-7| - |4|$ *The signs are different, so find the difference*

$7-4$, or 3 *of the absolute values.*

$= -3$ *Use the sign of the number with the greater absolute value.*

Find each difference.

1. $3-(-5)$ ________
2. $-4-5$ ________
3. $6-10$ ________
4. $-5-(-3)$ ________
5. $8-(-8)$ ________
6. $9-5$ ________
7. $-3-9$ ________
8. $0-(-6)$ ________
9. $12-(-9)$ ________
10. $-6-(-4)$ ________
11. $-7-10$ ________
12. $5-14$ ________

Graph Ordered Pairs (First Quadrant)

EXAMPLE

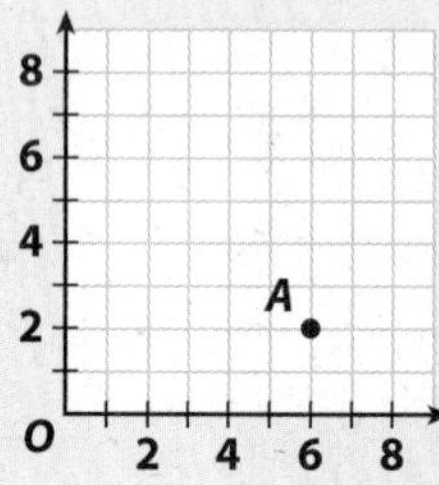

To graph a point at (6, 2), start at the origin.

Move 6 units right.

Then move 2 units up.

Graph point $A(6, 2)$.

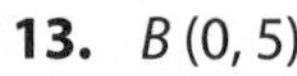

Graph each point on the coordinate grid.

13. $B(0, 5)$
14. $C(8, 0)$
15. $D(5, 7)$
16. $E(2, 3)$

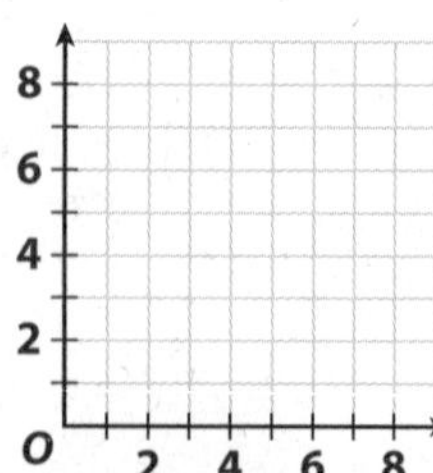

Reading Start-Up

Visualize Vocabulary

Use the ✔ words to complete the diagram. You can put more than one word in each box.

Reviewing Slope

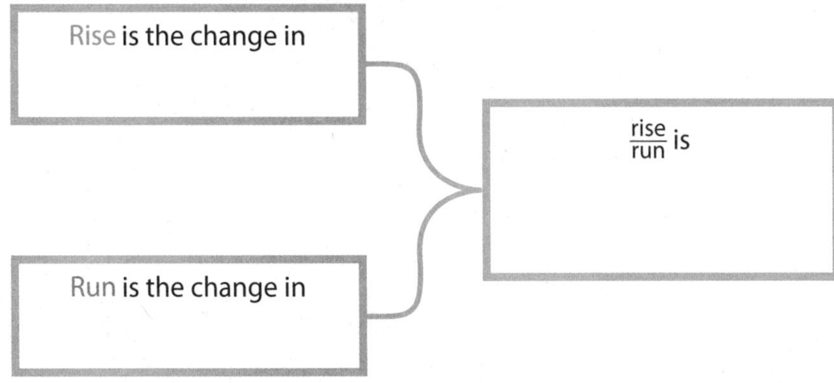

Understand Vocabulary

Complete the sentences using the preview words.

1. The *y*-coordinate of the point where a graph of a line intersects the *y*-axis is the ________________________.

2. A ________________________ is an equation whose solutions form a straight line on a coordinate plane.

3. A linear equation written in the form $y = mx + b$ is the ____.

Vocabulary

Review Words

- ordered pair *(par ordenado)*
- proportional relationship *(relación proporcional)*
- ✔ rate of change *(tasa de cambio)*
- ✔ slope *(pendiente)*
- ✔ *x*-coordinate *(coordenada x)*
- ✔ *y*-coordinate *(coordenada y)*

Preview Words

- linear equation *(ecuación lineal)*
- slope-intercept form of an equation *(forma de pendiente-intersección)*
- *y*-intercept *(intersección con el eje y)*

Active Reading

Booklet Before beginning the module, create a booklet to help you learn the concepts. Write the main idea of each lesson on each page of the booklet. As you study each lesson, write important details that support the main idea, such as vocabulary and formulas. Refer to your finished booklet as you work on assignments and study for tests.

CALIFORNIA

GETTING READY FOR

Nonproportional Relationships

Understanding the standards and the vocabulary terms in the standards will help you know exactly what you are expected to learn in this module.

CA CC 8.F.3

Interpret the equation $y = mx + b$ as defining a linear function, whose graph is a straight line; give examples of functions that are not linear.

Key Vocabulary

slope *(pendiente)*
A measure of the steepness of a line on a graph; the rise divided by the run.

***y*-intercept** *(intersección con el eje y)*
The *y*-coordinate of the point where the graph of a line crosses the *y*-axis.

What It Means to You

You will identify the slope and the *y*-intercept of a line by looking at its equation and use them to graph the line.

EXAMPLE 8.F.3

Graph $y = 3x - 2$ using the slope and the *y*-intercept.

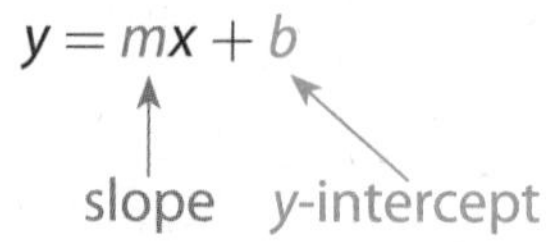

The slope m is 3, and the *y*-intercept is -2.

Plot the point $(0, -2)$. Use the slope $3 = \frac{3}{1}$ to find another point by moving *up* 3 and to the *right* 1. Connect the points.

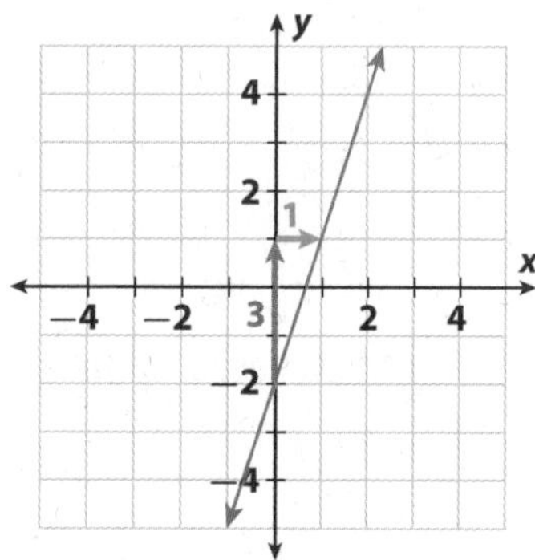

CA CC 8.F.3

Interpret the equation $y = mx + b$ as defining a linear function, whose graph is a straight line; give examples of functions that are not linear.

Key Vocabulary

function *(función)*
An input-output relationship that has exactly one output for each input.

linear function *(función lineal)*
A function whose graph is a straight line.

Visit **my.hrw.com** to see all **CA Common Core Standards** explained.

my.hrw.com

What It Means to You

You will distinguish linear relationships from nonlinear relationships by looking at graphs.

EXAMPLE 8.F.3

Which relationship is linear and which is nonlinear?

$P = 4s$

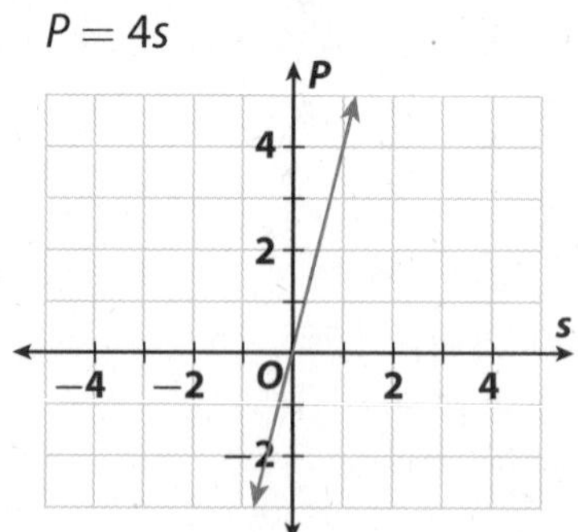

$P = 4s$ is linear because its graph is a line.

$A = s^2$

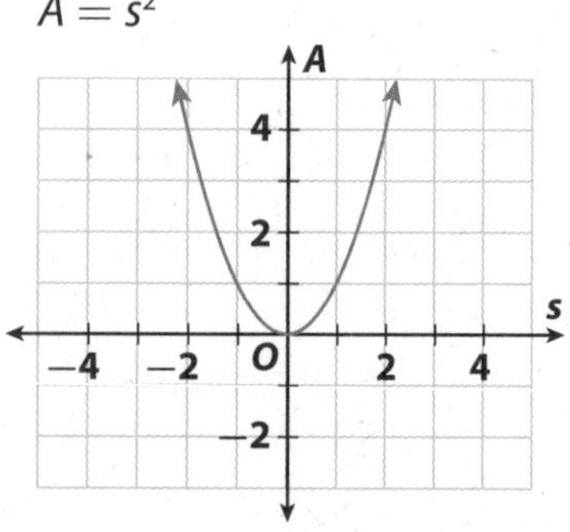

$A = s^2$ is not linear because its graph is not a line.

LESSON 17.1

Representing Linear Nonproportional Relationships

CA CC 8.F.3

Interpret the equation $y = mx + b$ as defining a linear function, whose graph is a straight line; give examples of functions that are not linear.

ESSENTIAL QUESTION

How can you use tables, graphs, and equations to represent linear nonproportional situations?

Representing Linear Relationships Using Tables

You can use an equation to describe the relationship between two quantities in a real-world situation. You can use a table to show some values that make the equation true.

EXAMPLE 1

The equation $y = 3x + 2$ gives the total charge for one person, y, renting a pair of shoes and bowling x games at Baxter Bowling Lanes based on the prices shown. Make a table of values for this situation.

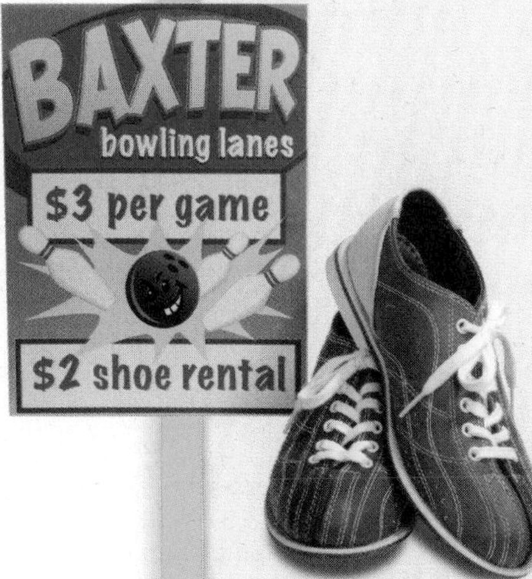

STEP 1 Choose several values for x that make sense in context.

x (number of games)	1	2	3	4
y (total cost in dollars)				

STEP 2 Use the equation $y = 3x + 2$ to find y for each value of x.

x (number of games)	1	2	3	4
y (total cost in dollars)	5	8	11	14

Substitute 1 for x: $y = 3(1) + 2 = 5$.

1. Francisco makes $12 per hour doing part-time work on Saturdays. He spends $4 on transportation to and from work. The equation $y = 12x - 4$ gives his earnings y, after transportation costs, for working x hours. Make a table of values for this situation.

x (number of hours)				
y (earnings in dollars)				

EXPLORE ACTIVITY   CA CC 8.F.3

Examining Linear Relationships

Recall that a proportional relationship is a relationship between two quantities in which the ratio of one quantity to the other quantity is constant. The graph of a proportional relationship is a line through the origin. When ratios between quantities are not constant, a relationship may be linear but not proportional and the graph does not pass through the origin.

The entrance fee for Mountain World theme park is $20. Visitors purchase additional $2 tickets for rides, games, and food. The equation $y = 2x + 20$ gives the total cost, y, to visit the park, including purchasing x tickets.

STEP 1 Complete the table.

x (number of tickets)	0	2	4	6	8
y (total cost in dollars)	20				

STEP 2 Plot ordered pairs from the information in the table. Describe the shape of the graph.

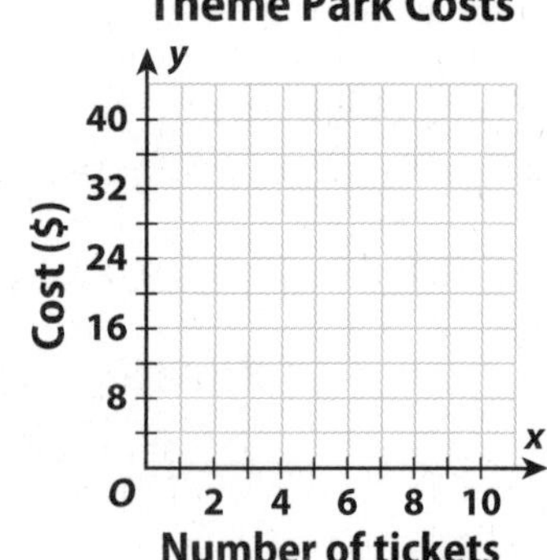

____

STEP 3 Find the rate of change between each point and the next. Is the rate constant?

____

STEP 4 Calculate rates of change for the values in the table. Explain why the relationship between number of tickets and total cost is not proportional.

____

____

____

Reflect

2. **Analyze Relationships** Would it be possible to add more points to the graph from $x = 0$ to $x = 10$? Would it make sense to connect the points with a line? Explain.

____

____

____

____

Representing Linear Relationships Using Graphs

A **linear equation** is an equation whose solutions are ordered pairs that form a line when graphed on a coordinate plane. Linear equations can be written in the form $y = mx + b$. When $b \neq 0$, the relationship between x and y is *nonproportional*.

EXAMPLE 2

The diameter of a Douglas fir tree is currently 10 inches when measured at chest height. Over the next 50 years, the diameter is expected to increase by an average growth rate of $\frac{2}{5}$ inch per year. The equation $y = \frac{2}{5}x + 10$ gives y, the diameter of the tree in inches, after x years. Draw a graph of the equation. Describe the relationship.

STEP 1 Make a table. Choose several values for x that make sense in context. To make calculations easier, choose multiples of 10.

x (years)	0	10	20	30	50
y (diameter in inches)	10	14	18	22	30

STEP 2 Plot ordered pairs from the information in the table. Then draw a line connecting the points to represent all the possible solutions.

STEP 3 The relationship is linear but nonproportional. The graph is a line but it does not go through the origin.

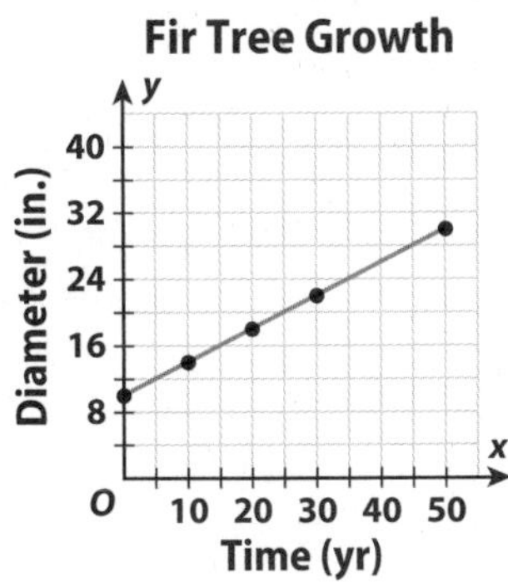

Math Talk
Mathematical Practices

Why can a line be drawn connecting the points in this example, but not in the preceding Explore Activity?

YOUR TURN

3. Make a table and graph the solutions of the equation $y = -2x + 1$.

x	−1	0	1	2
y				

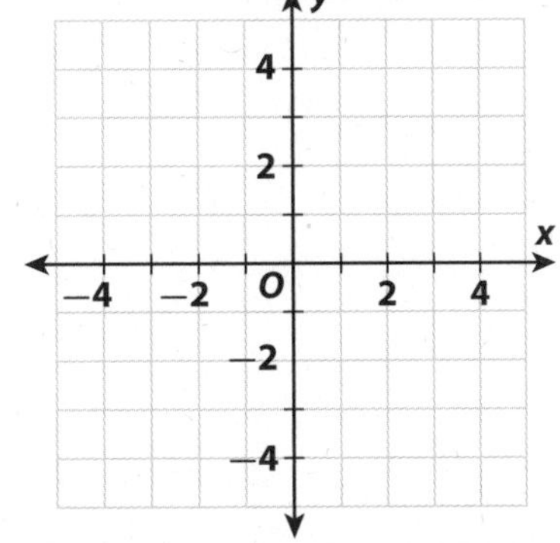

Guided Practice

Make a table of values for each equation. (Example 1)

1. $y = 2x + 5$

x	−2	−1	0	1	2
y					

2. $y = \frac{3}{8}x - 5$

x	−8	0	8		
y					

Explain why each relationship is not proportional. (Explore Activity)

3.

x	0	2	4	6	8
y	3	7	11	15	19

First calculate $\frac{y}{x}$ for the values in the table.

4.

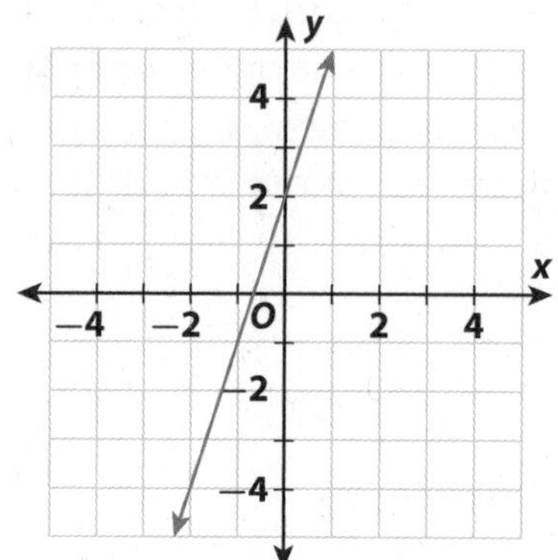

Complete the table for the equation. Then use the table to graph the equation. (Example 2)

5. $y = x - 1$

x	−2	−1	0	1	2
y					

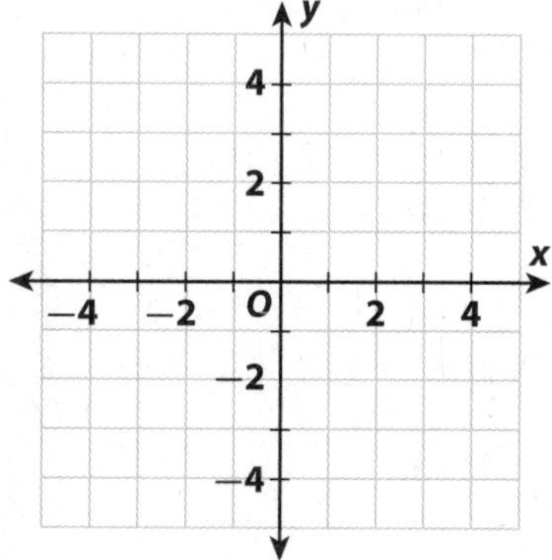

ESSENTIAL QUESTION CHECK-IN

6. How can you choose values for x when making a table of values representing a real world situation?

Name ______________________ Class ______________ Date ______________

17.1 Independent Practice

8.F.3

State whether the graph of each linear relationship is a solid line or a set of unconnected points. Explain your reasoning.

7. The relationship between the number of \$4 lunches you buy with a \$100 school lunch card and the money remaining on the card

____

____

____

____

8. The relationship between time and the distance remaining on a 3-mile walk for someone walking at a steady rate of 2 miles per hour

____

____

____

____

9. **Analyze Relationships** Simone paid \$12 for an initial year's subscription to a magazine. The renewal rate is \$8 per year. This situation can be represented by the equation $y = 8x + 12$, where x represents the number of years the subscription is renewed and y represents the total cost.

a. Make a table of values for this situation.

b. Draw a graph to represent the situation. Include a title and axis labels.

c. Explain why this relationship is not proportional.

____

____

____

____

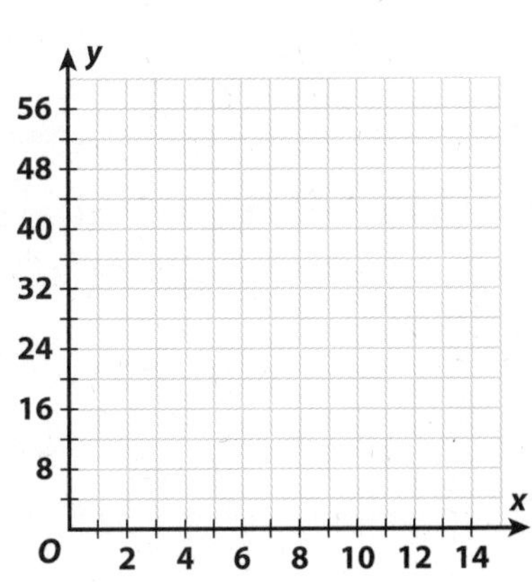

d. Does it make sense to connect the points on the graph with a solid line? Explain.

____

____

____

10. Analyze Relationships A proportional relationship is a linear relationship because the rate of change is constant (and equal to the constant of proportionality). What is required of a proportional relationship that is *not* required of a general linear relationship?

____

____

11. Communicate Mathematical Ideas Explain how you can identify a linear non-proportional relationship from a table, a graph, and an equation.

____

____

____

H.O.T. FOCUS ON HIGHER ORDER THINKING

Work Area

12. Critique Reasoning George observes that for every increase of 1 in the value of x, there is an increase of 60 in the corresponding value of y. He claims that the relationship represented by the table is proportional. Critique George's reasoning.

x	1	2	3	4	5
y	90	150	210	270	330

____

____

____

____

____

13. Make a Conjecture Two parallel lines are graphed on a coordinate plane. How many of the lines could represent proportional relationships? Explain.

____

____

____

____

____

____

LESSON 17.2

Determining Slope and y-intercept

CA CC 8.EE.6

Use similar triangles to explain why the slope m is the same between any two distinct points on a non-vertical line in the coordinate plane; derive the equation $y = mx$ for a line through the origin and the equation $y = mx + b$ for a line intercepting the vertical axis at b. *Also 8.F.4*

ESSENTIAL QUESTION

How can you determine the slope and the y-intercept of a line?

EXPLORE ACTIVITY 1 

Investigating Slope and y-intercept

The graph of every nonvertical line crosses the y-axis. The **y-intercept** is the y-coordinate of the point where the graph intersects the y-axis. The x-coordinate of this point is always 0.

The graph represents the linear equation $y = -\frac{2}{3}x + 4$.

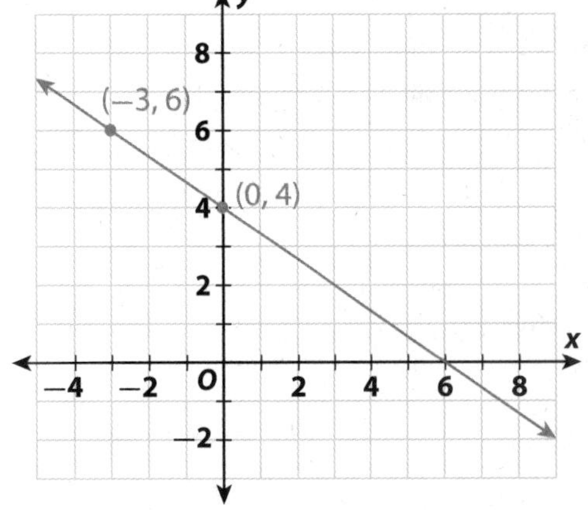

STEP 1 Find the slope of the line using the points (0, 4) and (−3, 6).

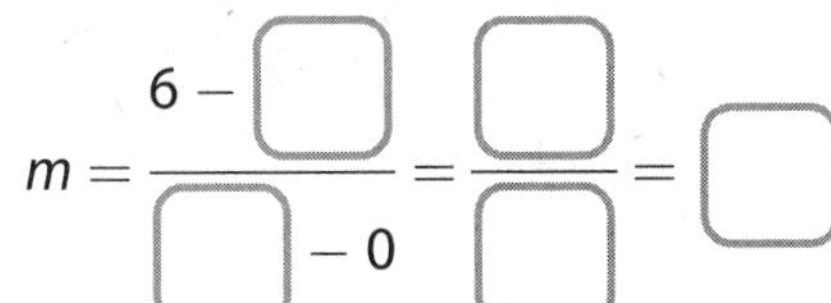

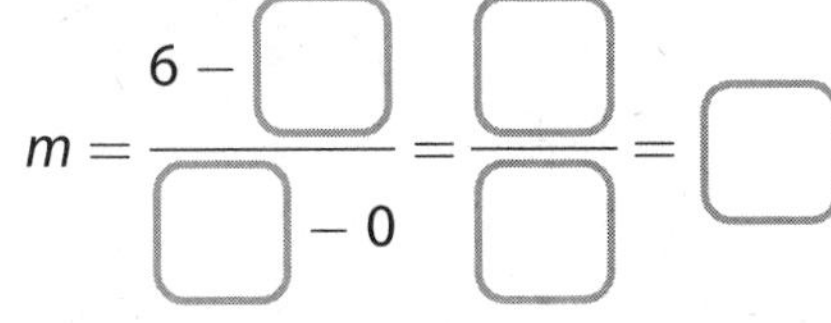

$$m = \frac{6 - \square}{\square - 0} = \frac{\square}{\square} = \square$$

STEP 2 The line also contains the point (6, 0). What is the slope using (0, 4) and (6, 0)? Using (−3, 6) and (6, 0). What do you notice?

____

STEP 3 Compare your answers in Steps 1 and 2 with the equation of the graphed line.

____

____

STEP 4 Find the value of y when $x = 0$ using the equation $y = -\frac{2}{3}x + 4$. Describe the point on the graph that corresponds to this solution.

____

STEP 5 Compare your answer in Step 4 with the equation of the line.

____

____

Determining Rate of Change and Initial Value

The linear equation shown is written in the **slope-intercept form of an equation**. Its graph is a line with **slope m** and **y-intercept b**.

$$y = mx + b$$

A linear relationship has a constant rate of change. You can find the **rate of change m** and the **initial value b** for a linear situation from a table of values.

EXAMPLE 1 Real World

CA CC 8.F.4

A phone salesperson is paid a minimum weekly salary and a commission for each phone sold, as shown in the table. Confirm that the relationship is linear and give the constant rate of change and the initial value.

STEP 1 Confirm that the rate of change is constant.

$$\frac{\text{change in income}}{\text{change in phones sold}} = \frac{630-480}{20-10} = \frac{150}{10} = \mathbf{15}$$

$$\frac{\text{change in income}}{\text{change in phones sold}} = \frac{780-630}{30-20} = \frac{150}{10} = \mathbf{15}$$

$$\frac{\text{change in income}}{\text{change in phones sold}} = \frac{930-780}{40-30} = \frac{150}{10} = \mathbf{15}$$

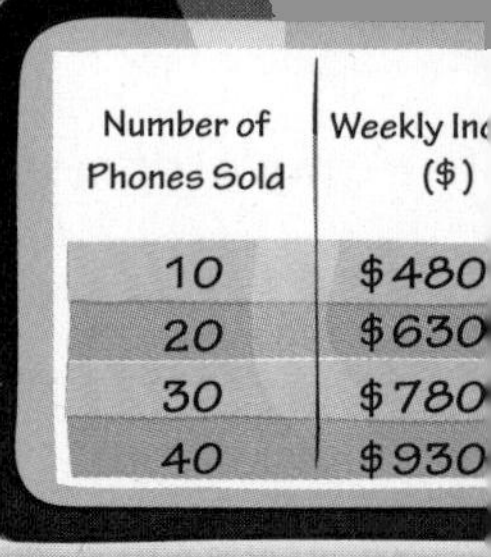

Number of Phones Sold	Weekly Inc ($)
10	$480
20	$630
30	$780
40	$930

The rate of change is a constant, **15**.

The salesperson receives a $15 commission for each phone sold.

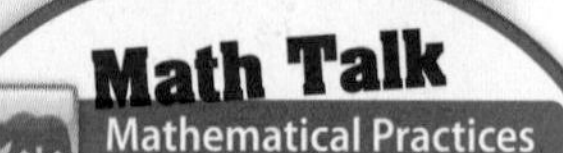

Math Talk Mathematical Practices

How do you use the rate of change to work backward to find the initial value?

STEP 2 Find the initial value when the number of phones sold is 0.

−10 −10

Number of phones sold	0	10	20
Weekly income ($)	330	480	630

−150 −150

Work backward from $x = 10$ to $x = 0$ to find the initial value.

The initial value is $330. The salesperson receives a salary of $330 each week before commissions.

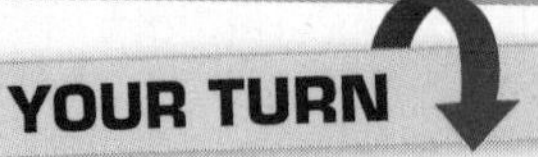

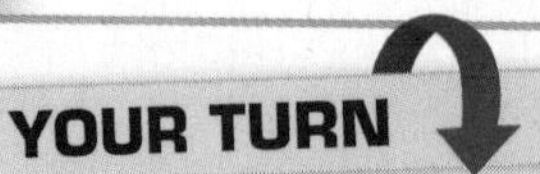

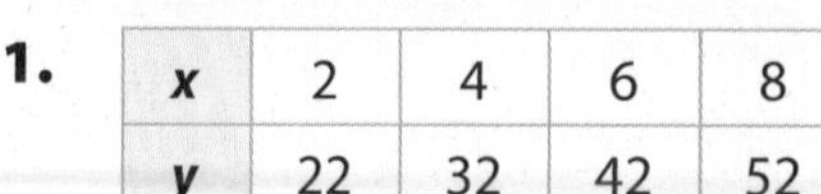

YOUR TURN

Find the slope and y-intercept of the line represented by each table.

1.

x	2	4	6	8
y	22	32	42	52

____

2.

x	1	2	3	4
y	8	15	22	29

____

EXPLORE ACTIVITY 2

 8.EE.6

Deriving the Slope-intercept Form of an Equation

In the following Explore Activity, you will derive the slope-intercept form of an equation.

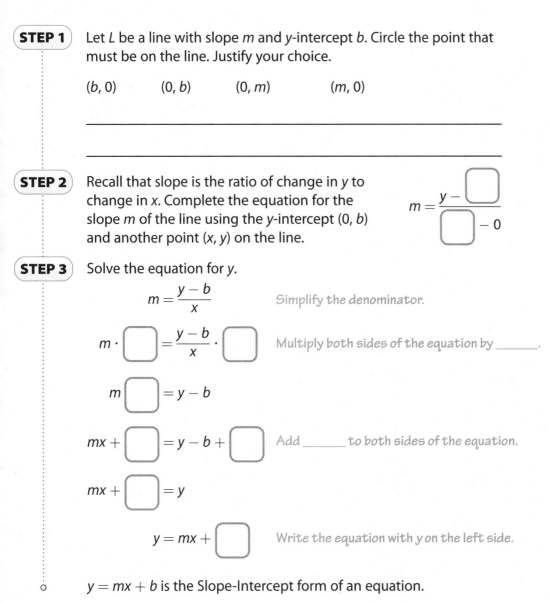

STEP 1 Let L be a line with slope m and y-intercept b. Circle the point that must be on the line. Justify your choice.

$(b, 0)$ $(0, b)$ $(0, m)$ $(m, 0)$

____

____

STEP 2 Recall that slope is the ratio of change in y to change in x. Complete the equation for the slope m of the line using the y-intercept $(0, b)$ and another point (x, y) on the line.

$$m = \frac{y - \square}{\square - 0}$$

STEP 3 Solve the equation for y.

$$m = \frac{y - b}{x}$$ Simplify the denominator.

$$m \cdot \square = \frac{y - b}{x} \cdot \square$$ Multiply both sides of the equation by ______.

$$m\square = y - b$$

$$mx + \square = y - b + \square$$ Add ______ to both sides of the equation.

$$mx + \square = y$$

$$y = mx + \square$$ Write the equation with y on the left side.

$y = mx + b$ is the Slope-Intercept form of an equation.

Reflect

3. **Critical Thinking** Write the equation of a line with slope m that passes through the origin. Explain your reasoning.

____

____

____

Guided Practice

Find the slope and y-intercept of the line in each graph. (Explore Activity 1)

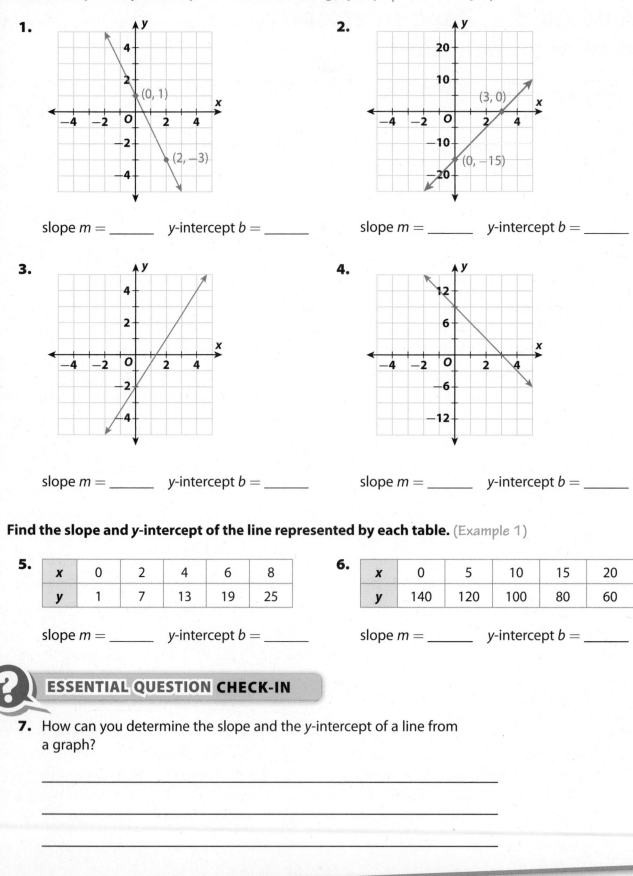

1.

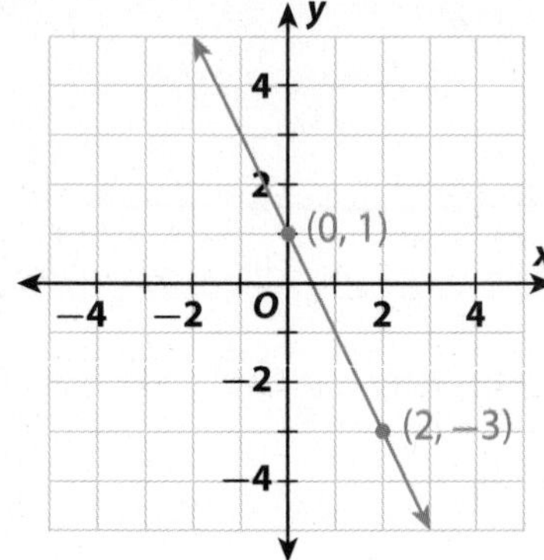

slope $m =$ ______ y-intercept $b =$ ______

2.

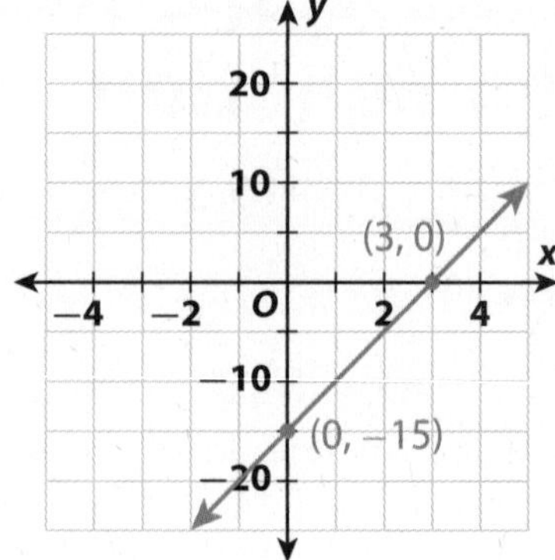

slope $m =$ ______ y-intercept $b =$ ______

3.

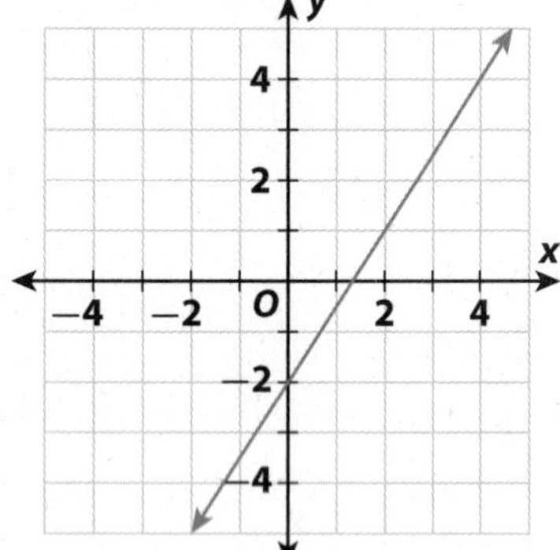

slope $m =$ ______ y-intercept $b =$ ______

4.

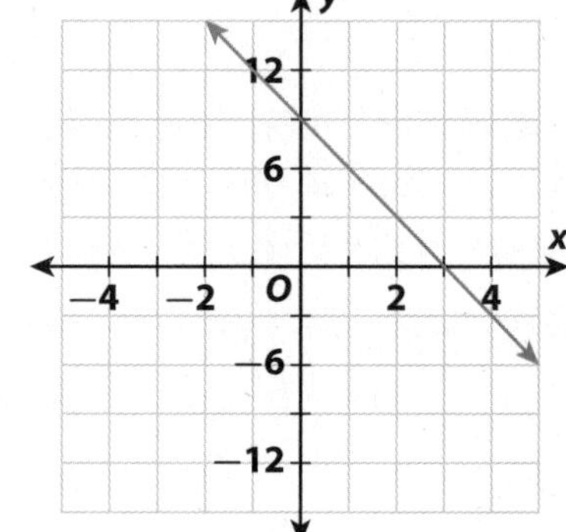

slope $m =$ ______ y-intercept $b =$ ______

Find the slope and y-intercept of the line represented by each table. (Example 1)

5.

x	0	2	4	6	8
y	1	7	13	19	25

slope $m =$ ______ y-intercept $b =$ ______

6.

x	0	5	10	15	20
y	140	120	100	80	60

slope $m =$ ______ y-intercept $b =$ ______

ESSENTIAL QUESTION CHECK-IN

7. How can you determine the slope and the y-intercept of a line from a graph?

____

____

____

Name ____________________ Class ____________________ Date ____________________

17.2 Independent Practice

8.EE.6, 8.F.4

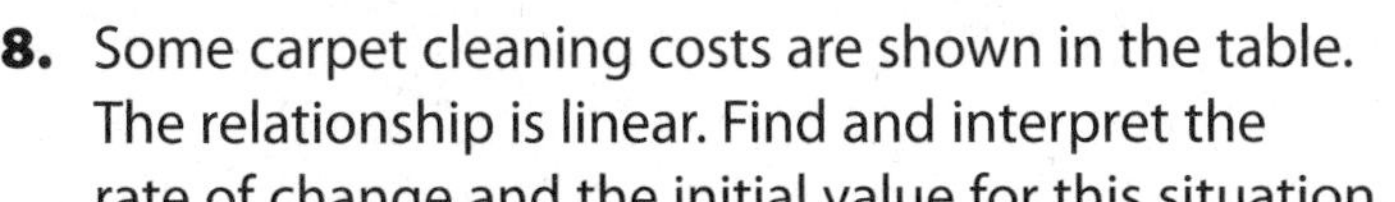

8. Some carpet cleaning costs are shown in the table. The relationship is linear. Find and interpret the rate of change and the initial value for this situation.

Rooms cleaned	1	2	3	4
Cost ($)	125	175	225	275

____

____

____

9. Make Predictions The total cost to pay for parking at a state park for the day and rent a paddleboat are shown.

Number of Hours	**Cost ($)**
1	$17
2	$29
3	$41
4	$53

a. Find the cost to park for a day and the hourly rate to rent a paddleboat.

____

b. What will Lin pay if she rents a paddleboat for 3.5 hours and splits the total cost with a friend? Explain.

____

____

10. Multi-Step Raymond's parents will pay for him to take sailboard lessons during the summer. He can take half-hour group lessons or half-hour private lessons. The relationship between cost and number of lessons is linear.

Lessons	1	2	3	4
Group ($)	55	85	115	145
Private ($)	75	125	175	225

a. Find the rate of change and the initial value for the group lessons.

____

____

b. Find the rate of change and the initial value for the private lessons.

____

____

c. Compare and contrast the rates of change and the initial values.

____

____

____

Vocabulary **Explain why each relationship is not linear.**

11.

x	1	2	3	4
y	4.5	6.5	8.5	11.5

____

____

12.

x	3	5	7	9
y	140	126	110	92

____

____

13. **Communicate Mathematical Ideas** Describe the procedure you performed to derive the slope-intercept form of a linear equation.

____

____

____

FOCUS ON HIGHER ORDER THINKING

Work Area

14. **Critique Reasoning** Your teacher asked your class to describe a real-world situation in which a y-intercept is 100 and the slope is 5. Your partner gave the following description: *My younger brother originally had 100 small building blocks, but he has lost 5 of them every month since.*

a. What mistake did your partner make?

____

____

b. Describe a real-world situation that does match the situation.

____

____

15. **Justify Reasoning** John has a job parking cars. He earns a fixed weekly salary of $300 plus a fee of $5 for each car he parks. His potential earnings for a week are shown in the graph. At what point does John begin to earn more from fees than his fixed salary? Justify your answer.

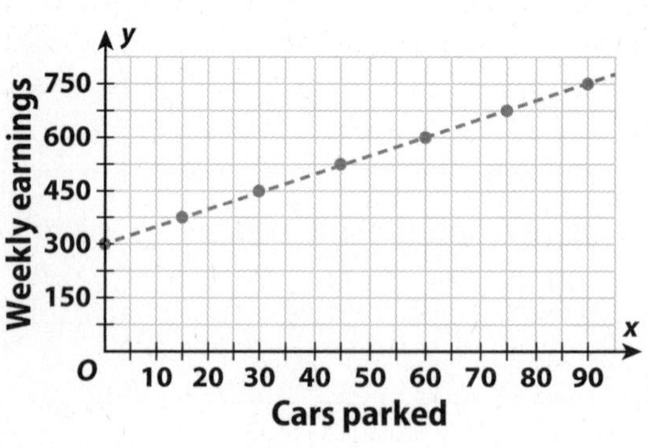

____

____

____

LESSON 17.3

Graphing Linear Nonproportional Relationships Using Slope and *y*-intercept

CA CC 8.F.4

Construct a function to model a linear relationship between two quantities. Determine the rate of change and initial value of the function from a description of a relationship or from two (*x*, *y*) values, including reading these from a table or from a graph. Interpret the rate of change and initial value of a linear function in terms of the situation it models, and in terms of its graph or a table of values. *Also 8.F.3*

ESSENTIAL QUESTION

How can you graph a line using the slope and *y*-intercept?

Using Slope-intercept Form to Graph a Line

Recall that $y = mx + b$ is the slope-intercept form of the equation of a line. In this form, it is easy to see the slope *m* and the *y*-intercept *b*. So you can use this form to quickly graph a line by plotting the point (0, *b*) and using the slope to find a second point.

EXAMPLE 1

CA CC 8.F.3

Animated Math
my.hrw.com

A Graph $y = \frac{2}{3}x - 1$.

STEP 1 The *y*-intercept is $b = -1$. Plot the point that contains the *y*-intercept: (0, −1).

STEP 2 The slope is $m = \frac{2}{3}$. Use the slope to find a second point. From (0, −1), count *up* 2 and *right* 3. The new point is (3, 1).

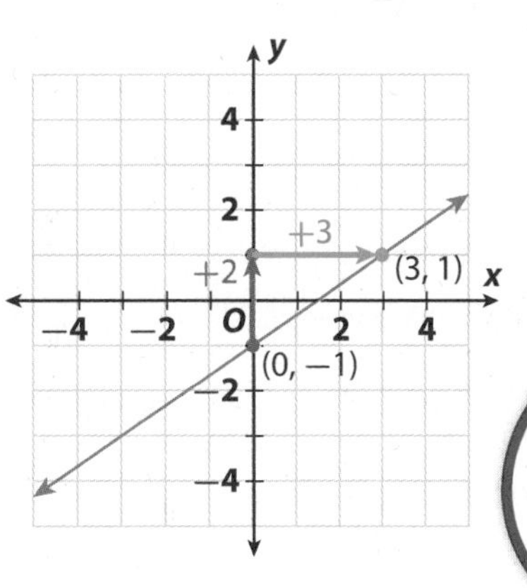

STEP 3 Draw a line through the points.

Math Talk
Mathematical Practices
Is a line with a positive slope always steeper than a line with a negative slope? Explain.

B Graph $y = -\frac{5}{2}x + 3$.

STEP 1 The *y*-intercept is $b = 3$. Plot the point that contains the *y*-intercept: (0, 3).

STEP 2 The slope is $m = -\frac{5}{2}$. Use the slope to find a second point. From (0, 3), count *down* 5 and *right* 2, or *up* 5 and *left* 2. The new point is (2, −2) or (−2, 8).

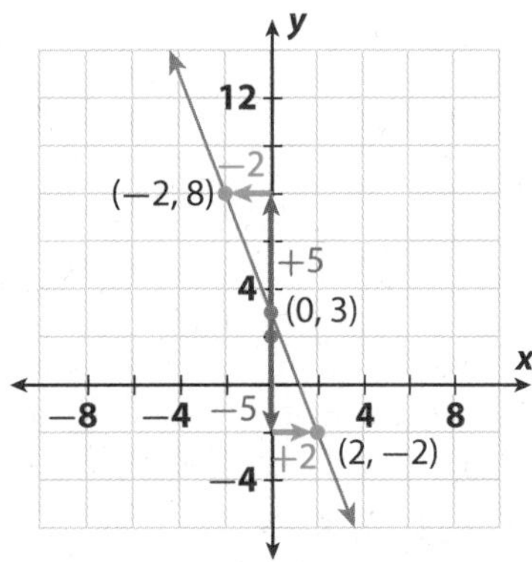

STEP 3 Draw a line through the points.

Note that the line passes through all three points: (−2, 8), (0, 3), and (2, −2).

Reflect

1. **Draw Conclusions** How can you use the slope of a line to predict the way the line will be slanted? Explain.

____

____

Graph each equation.

2. $y = \frac{1}{2}x + 1$

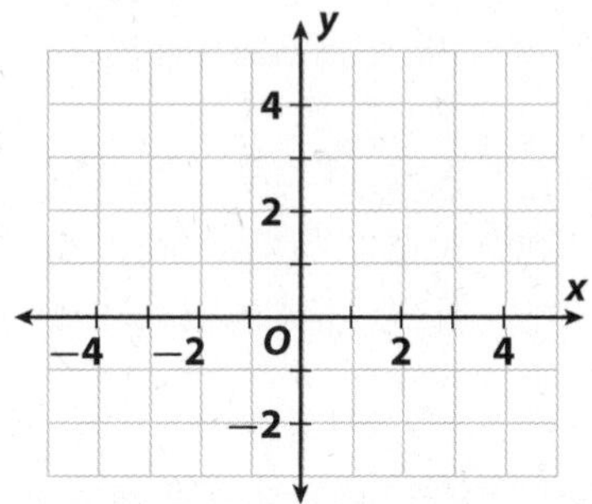

3. $y = -3x + 4$

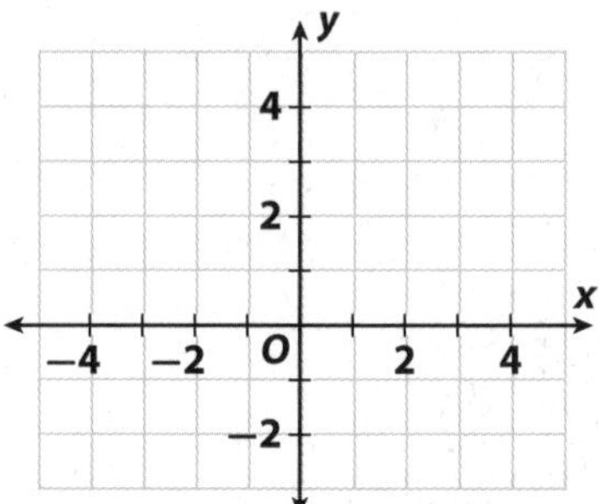

Analyzing a Graph

Many real-world situations can be represented by linear relationships. You can use graphs of linear relationships to visualize situations and solve problems.

EXAMPLE 2

Ken has a weekly goal of burning 2400 calories by taking brisk walks. The equation $y = -300x + 2400$ represents the number of calories y Ken has left to burn after x hours of walking which burns 300 calories per hour.

A Graph the equation $y = -300x + 2400$.

STEP 1 Write the slope as a fraction.

$$m = \frac{-300}{1} = \frac{-600}{2} = \frac{-900}{3}$$

Using the slope as $\frac{-900}{3}$ helps in drawing a more accurate graph.

STEP 2 Plot the point for the y-intercept: (0, 2400).

STEP 3 Use the slope to locate a second point.

From (0, 2400), count *down* 900 and *right* 3.

The new point is (3, 1500).

STEP 4 Draw a line through the two points.

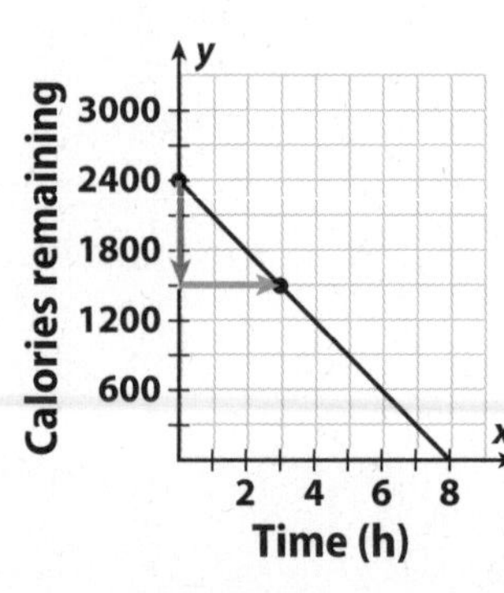

B After how many hours of walking will Ken have 600 calories left to burn? After how many hours will he reach his weekly goal?

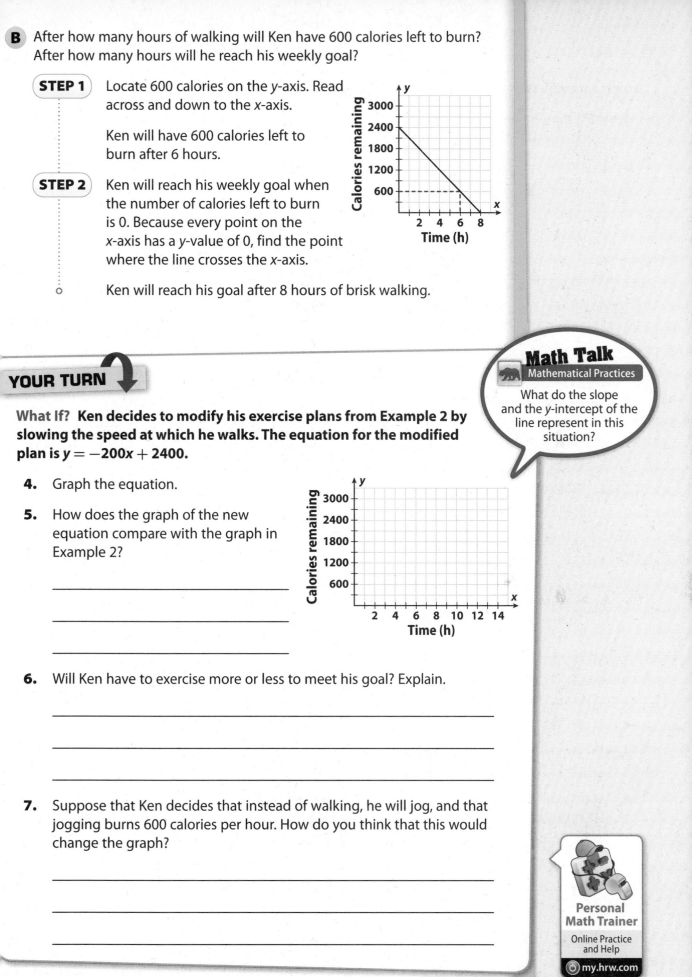

STEP 1 Locate 600 calories on the y-axis. Read across and down to the x-axis.

Ken will have 600 calories left to burn after 6 hours.

STEP 2 Ken will reach his weekly goal when the number of calories left to burn is 0. Because every point on the x-axis has a y-value of 0, find the point where the line crosses the x-axis.

Ken will reach his goal after 8 hours of brisk walking.

YOUR TURN

Math Talk
Mathematical Practices

What do the slope and the y-intercept of the line represent in this situation?

What If? Ken decides to modify his exercise plans from Example 2 by slowing the speed at which he walks. The equation for the modified plan is $y = -200x + 2400$.

4. Graph the equation.

5. How does the graph of the new equation compare with the graph in Example 2?

____

____

____

6. Will Ken have to exercise more or less to meet his goal? Explain.

____

____

____

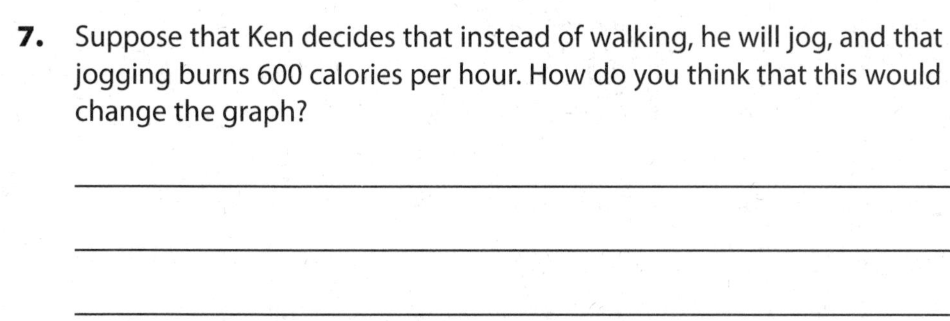

7. Suppose that Ken decides that instead of walking, he will jog, and that jogging burns 600 calories per hour. How do you think that this would change the graph?

____

____

____

Guided Practice

Graph each equation using the slope and the *y*-intercept. (Example 1)

1. $y = \frac{1}{2}x - 3$

slope = ______ *y*-intercept = ______

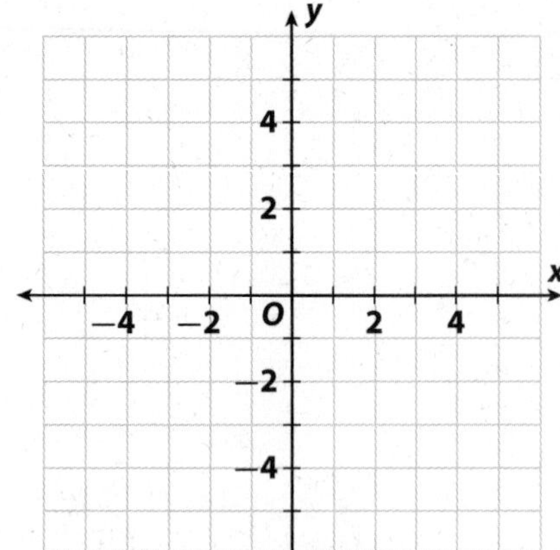

2. $y = -3x + 2$

slope = ______ *y*-intercept = ______

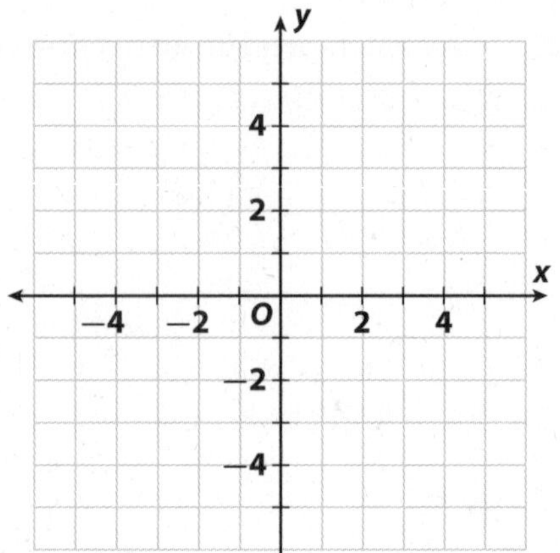

3. A friend gives you two baseball cards for your birthday. Afterward, you begin collecting them. You buy 4 cards each week. The equation $y = 4x + 2$ describes the number of cards, *y*, you have after *x* weeks. (Example 2)

a. Find and interpret the slope and the *y*-intercept of the line that represents this situation. Graph $y = 4x + 2$. Include axis labels.

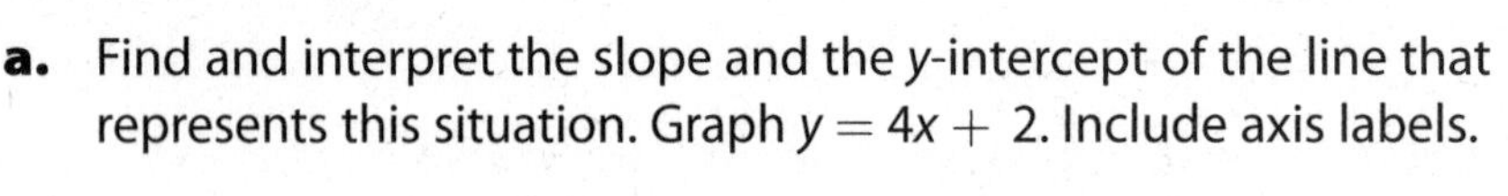

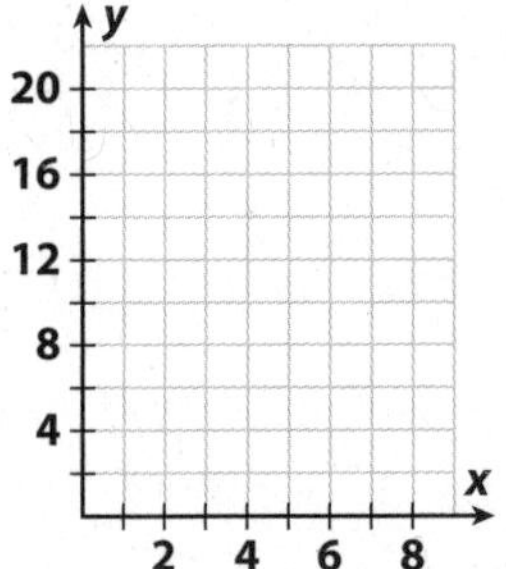

____

____

b. Discuss which points on the line do not make sense in this situation. Then plot three more points on the line that do make sense.

____

____

____

ESSENTIAL QUESTION CHECK-IN

4. Why might someone choose to use the *y*-intercept and the slope to graph a line?

____

____

____

____

Name ______________________ Class ______________ Date ______________

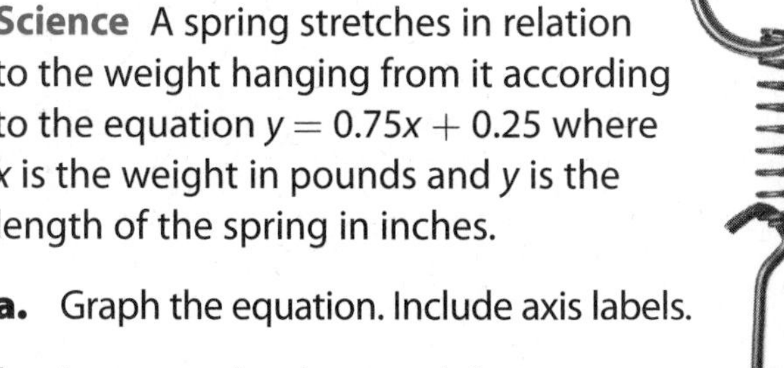

17.3 Independent Practice

CA CC 8.F.3, 8.F.4

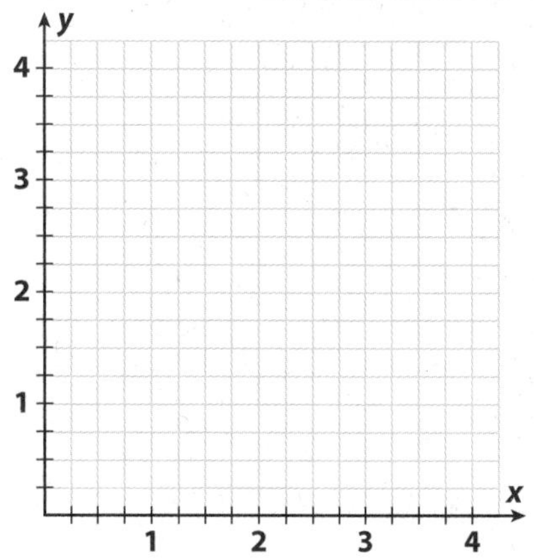

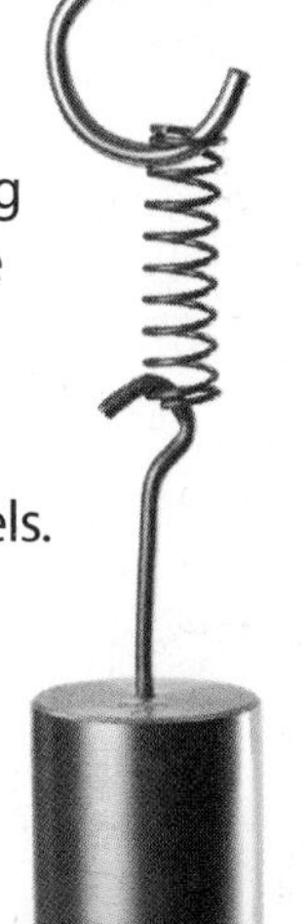

5. **Science** A spring stretches in relation to the weight hanging from it according to the equation $y = 0.75x + 0.25$ where x is the weight in pounds and y is the length of the spring in inches.

   a. Graph the equation. Include axis labels.

   b. Interpret the slope and the y-intercept of the line.

   ____

   ____

   ____

   ____

   ____

   c. How long will the spring be if a 2-pound weight is hung on it? Will the length double if you double the weight? Explain

   ____

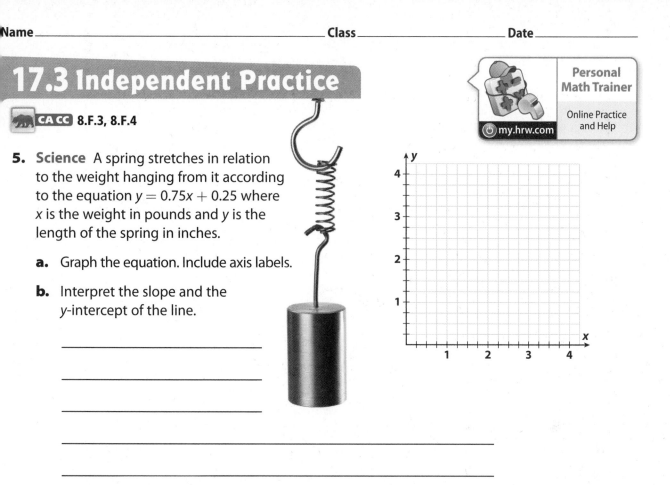

Look for a Pattern **Identify the coordinates of four points on the line with each given slope and *y*-intercept.**

6. slope $= 5$, y-intercept $= -1$

   ____

7. slope $= -1$, y-intercept $= 8$

   ____

8. slope $= 0.2$, y-intercept $= 0.3$

   ____

9. slope $= 1.5$, y-intercept $= -3$

   ____

10. slope $= -\frac{1}{2}$, y-intercept $= 4$

    ____

11. slope $= \frac{2}{3}$, y-intercept $= -5$

    ____

12. A music school charges a registration fee in addition to a fee per lesson. Music lessons last 0.5 hour. The equation $y = 40x + 30$ represents the total cost y of x lessons. Find and interpret the slope and y-intercept of the line that represents this situation. Then find four points on the line.

    ____

    ____

13. A public pool charges a membership fee and a fee for each visit. The equation $y = 3x + 50$ represents the cost y for x visits.

a. After locating the y-intercept on the coordinate plane shown, can you move up three gridlines and right one gridline to find a second point? Explain.

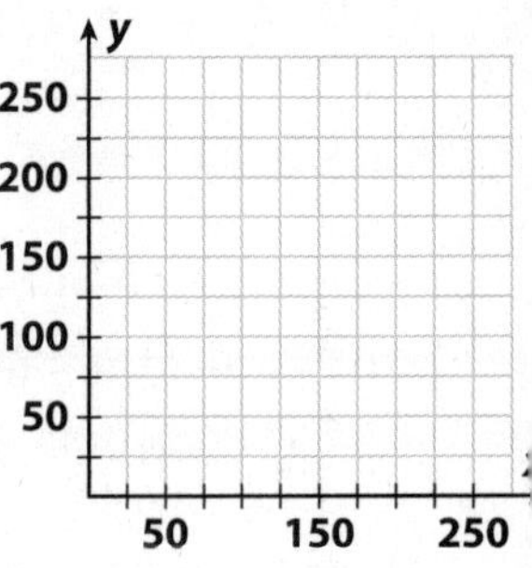

____

____

____

b. Graph the equation $y = 3x + 50$. Include axis labels. Then interpret the slope and y-intercept.

____

____

c. How many visits to the pool can a member get for \$200?

____

FOCUS ON HIGHER ORDER THINKING

Work Area

14. Explain the Error A student says that the slope of the line for the equation $y = 20 - 15x$ is 20 and the y-intercept is 15. Find and correct the error.

____

____

____

15. Critical Thinking Suppose you know the slope of a linear relationship and a point that its graph passes through. Can you graph the line even if the point provided does *not* represent the y-intercept? Explain.

____

____

____

16. Make a Conjecture Graph the lines $y = 3x$, $y = 3x - 3$, and $y = 3x + 3$. What do you notice about the lines? Make a conjecture based on your observation.

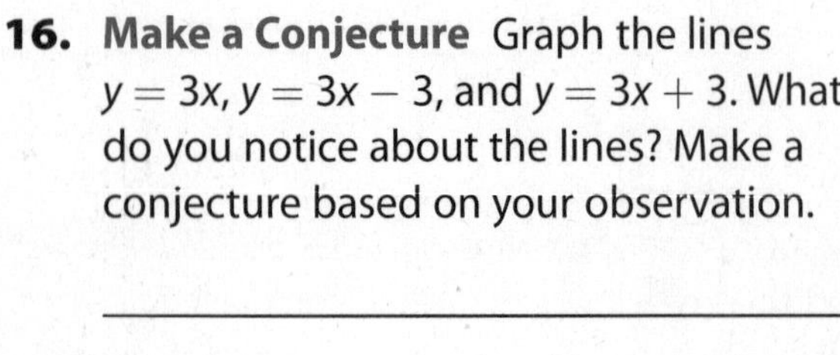

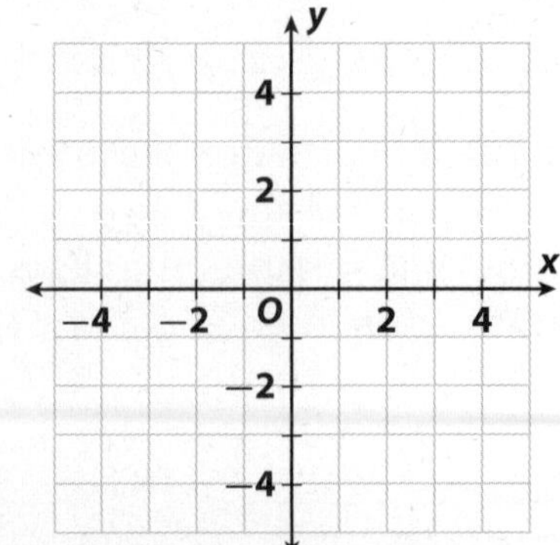

____

____

____

LESSON 17.4

Proportional and Nonproportional Situations

CA CC 8.F.2

Compare properties of two functions each represented in a different way (algebraically, graphically, numerically in tables, or by verbal descriptions). *Also 8.F.3, 8.F.4*

ESSENTIAL QUESTION

How can you distinguish between proportional and nonproportional situations?

Distinguish Between Proportional and Nonproportional Situations Using a Graph

If a relationship is nonlinear, it is nonproportional. If it is linear, it may be either proportional or nonproportional. When the graph of the linear relationship contains the origin, the relationship is proportional.

EXAMPLE 1

CA CC 8.F.3

The graph shows the sales tax charged based on the amount spent at a video game store in a particular city. Does the graph show a linear relationship? Is the relationship proportional or nonproportional?

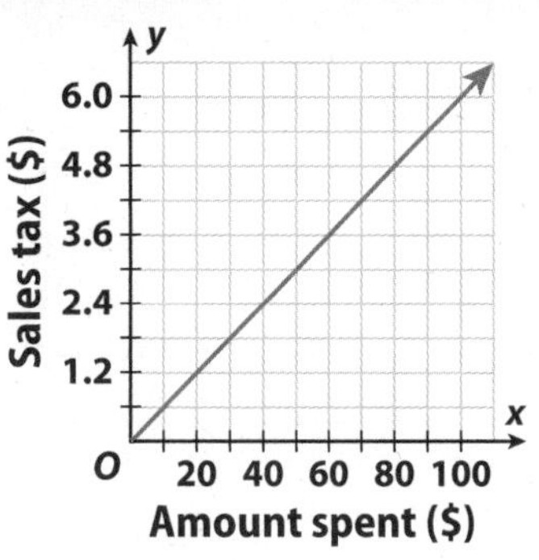

The graph shows a linear proportional relationship because it is a line that contains the origin.

Math Talk
Mathematical Practices

What do the slope and the *y*-intercept of the graph represent in this situation?

YOUR TURN

Determine if each of the following graphs represents a proportional or nonproportional relationship.

1.

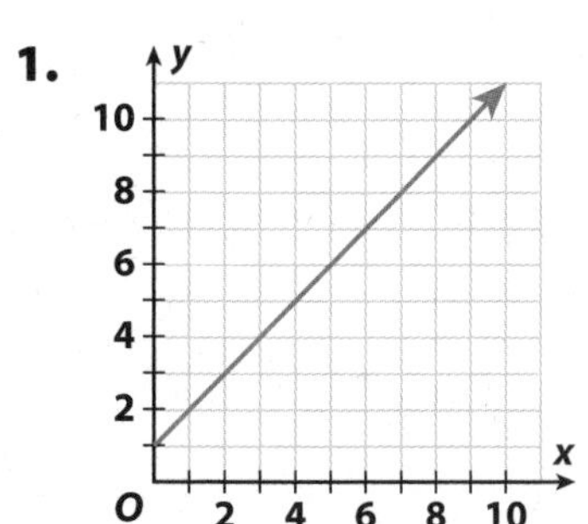

____

2.

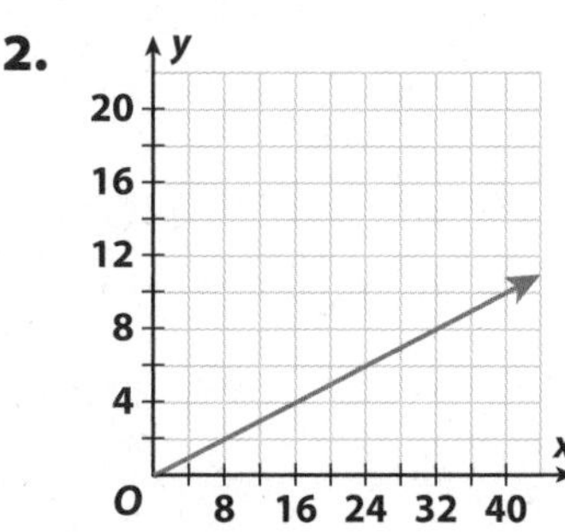

____

Distinguish Between Proportional and Nonproportional Situations Using an Equation

If an equation is not a linear equation, it represents a nonproportional relationship. A linear equation of the form $y = mx + b$ may represent either a proportional ($b = 0$) or nonproportional ($b \neq 0$) relationship.

EXAMPLE 2  

CA CC 8.F.4

The number of years since Keith graduated from middle school can be represented by the equation $y = a - 14$, where y is the number of years and a is his age. Is the relationship between the number of years since Keith graduated and his age proportional or nonproportional?

$$y = a - 14$$

The equation is in the form $y = mx + b$, with a being used as the variable instead of x. The value of m is 1, and the value of b is -14. Since b is not 0, the relationship between the number of years since Keith graduated and his age is nonproportional.

Reflect

3. Communicate Mathematical Ideas In a proportional relationship, the ratio $\frac{y}{x}$ is constant. Show that this ratio is not constant for the equation $y = a - 14$.

____

____

4. What If? Suppose another equation represents Keith's age in months y given his age in years a. Is this relationship proportional? Explain.

____

____

YOUR TURN

Determine if each of the following equations represents a proportional or nonproportional relationship.

5. $d = 65t$

____

6. $p = 0.1s + 2000$

____

7. $n = 450 - 3p$

____

8. $36 = 12d$

____

Distinguish Between Proportional and Nonproportional Situations Using a Table

If there is not a constant rate of change in the data displayed in a table, then the table represents a nonlinear nonproportional relationship.

A linear relationship represented by a table is a proportional relationship when the quotient of each pair of numbers is constant. Otherwise, the linear relationship is nonproportional.

EXAMPLE 3

The values in the table represent the numbers of U.S. dollars three tourists traded for Mexican pesos. The relationship is linear. Is the relationship proportional or nonproportional?

U.S. Dollars Traded	Mexican Pesos Received
130	1,690
255	3,315
505	6,565

$\frac{1,690}{130} = \frac{169}{13} = 13$

$\frac{3,315}{255} = \frac{221}{17} = 13$

$\frac{6,565}{505} = \frac{1,313}{101} = 13$

Simplify the ratios to compare the pesos received to the dollars traded.

The ratio of pesos received to dollars traded is constant at 13 Mexican pesos per U.S. dollar. This is a proportional relationship.

Math Talk
Mathematical Practices

How could you confirm that the values in the table have a linear relationship?

YOUR TURN

Determine if the linear relationship represented by each table is a proportional or nonproportional relationship.

9.

x	y
2	30
8	90
14	150

____

10.

x	y
5	1
40	8
65	13

____

Comparing Proportional and Nonproportional Situations

You can use what you have learned about proportional and nonproportional relationships to compare similar real-world situations that are given using different representations.

EXAMPLE 4 

A **A laser tag league has the choice of two arenas for a tournament. In both cases, x is the number of hours and y is the total charge. Compare and contrast these two situations.**

Arena A

$y = 225x$

Arena B

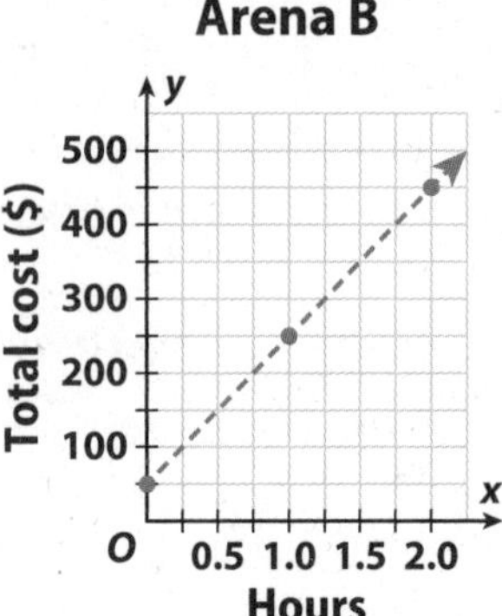

- **Arena A's** equation has the form $y = mx + b$, where $b = 0$. So, Arena A's charges are a proportional relationship. The hourly rate, $225, is greater than Arena B's, but there is no additional fee.
- **Arena B's** graph is a line that does not include the origin. So, Arena B's charges are a nonproportional relationship. Arena B has a $50 initial fee but its hourly rate, $200, is lower.

B **Jessika is remodeling and has the choice of two painters. In both cases, x is the number of hours and y is the total charge. Compare and contrast these two situations.**

Painter A

$y = \$45x$

Painter B

x	0	1	2	3
y	20	55	90	125

- **Painter A's** equation has the form $y = mx + b$, where $b = 0$. So, Painter A's charges are proportional. The hourly rate, $45, is greater than Painter B's, but there is no additional fee.
- **Painter B's** table is a nonproportional relationship because the ratio of y to x is not constant. Because the table contains the ordered pair (0, 20), Painter B charges an initial fee of $20, but the hourly rate, $35, is less than Painter A's.

Math Talk

How might graphing the equation for Arena A help you to compare the situations?

My Notes

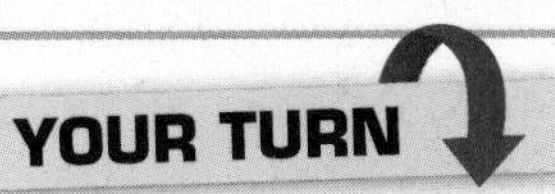

11. Compare and contrast the following two situations.

Test-Prep Center A	Test-Prep Center B
The cost for Test-Prep Center A is given by $c = 20h$, where c is the cost in dollars and h is the number of hours you attend.	Test-Prep Center B charges $25 per hour to attend, but you have a $100 coupon that you can use to reduce the cost.

Guided Practice

Determine if each relationship is a proportional or nonproportional situation. Explain your reasoning. (Example 1, Example 2, Example 4)

1.

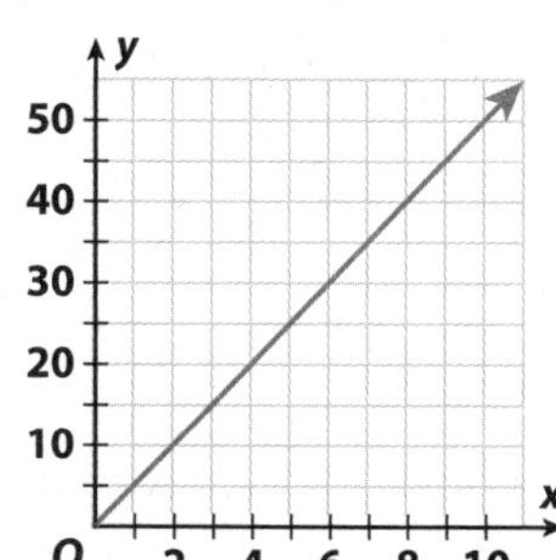

Look at the origin.

2.

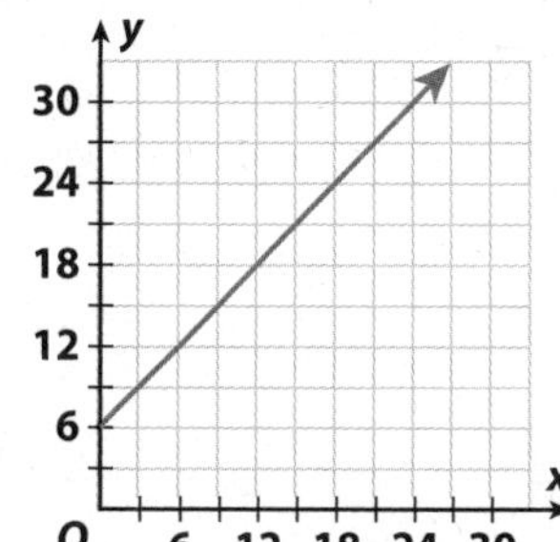

3. $q = 2p + \frac{1}{2}$

Compare the equation with $y = mx + b$.

4. $v = \frac{1}{10}u$

The tables represent linear relationships. Determine if each relationship is a proportional or nonproportional situation. (Example 3, Example 4)

5.

x	y
3	12
9	36
21	84

Find the quotient of y and x.

6.

x	y
22	4
46	8
58	10

7. The values in the table represent the numbers of households that watched three TV shows and the ratings of the shows. The relationship is linear. Describe the relationship in other ways. (Example 4)

Number of Households that Watched TV Show	TV Show Rating
15,000,000	12
20,000,000	16
25,000,000	20

ESSENTIAL QUESTION CHECK-IN

8. How are using graphs, equations, and tables similar when distinguishing between proportional and nonproportional situations?

Name________________________ Class________________ Date____________

17.4 Independent Practice

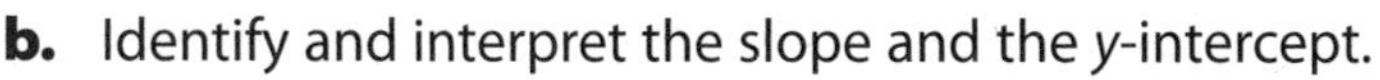

CA CC 8.F.2, 8.F.3, 8.F.4

9. The graph shows the weight of a cross-country team's beverage cooler based on how much sports drink it contains.

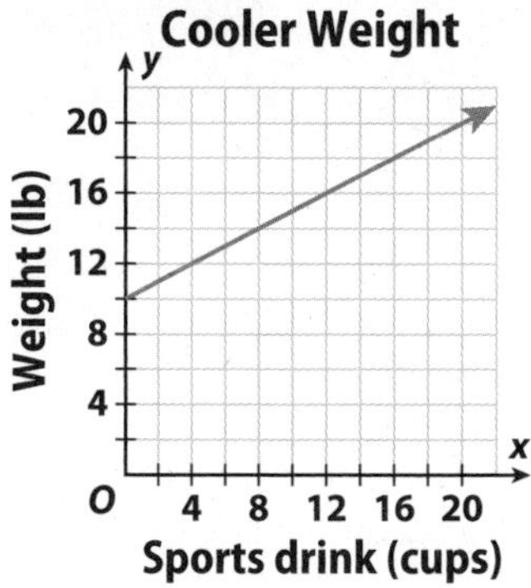

a. Is the relationship proportional or nonproportional? Explain.

____

____

b. Identify and interpret the slope and the y-intercept.

____

____

In 10–11, tell if the relationship between a rider's height above the first floor and the time since the rider stepped on the elevator or escalator is proportional or nonproportional. Explain your reasoning.

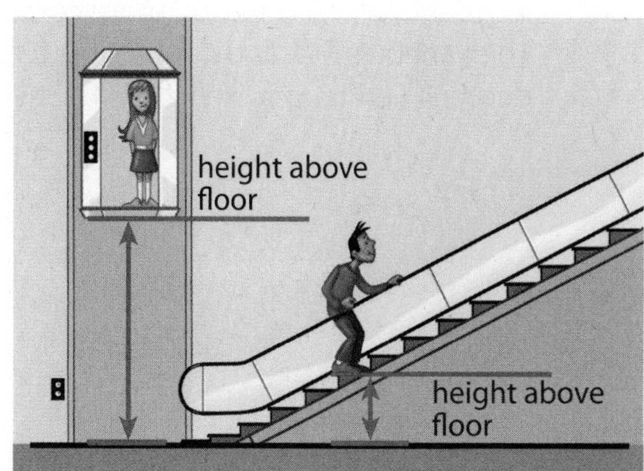

10. The elevator paused for 10 seconds after you stepped on before beginning to rise at a constant rate of 8 feet per second.

____

____

____

11. Your height in feet above the first floor on the escalator, h, is given by $h = 0.75t$, where t is the time in seconds.

____

12. Analyze Relationships Compare and contrast the two graphs.

Graph A

$y = \frac{1}{3}x$

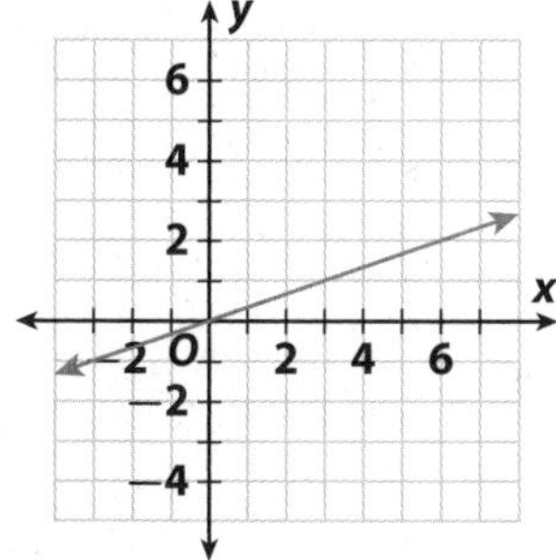

Graph B

$y = \sqrt{x}$

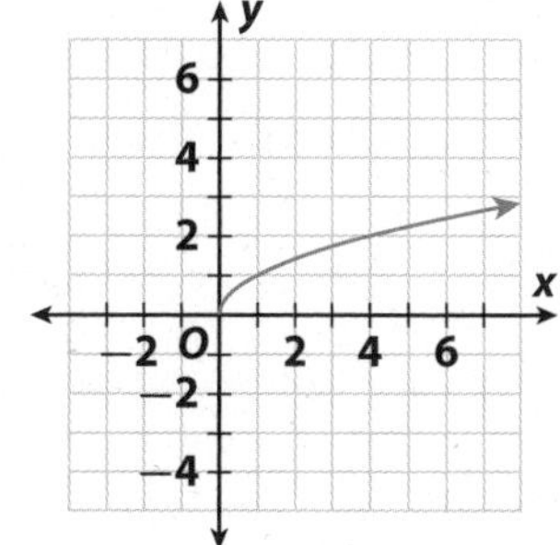

____

____

13. Represent Real-World Problems Describe a real-world situation where the relationship is linear and nonproportional.

____

____

H.O.T. FOCUS ON HIGHER ORDER THINKING

Work Area

14. Mathematical Reasoning Suppose you know the slope of a linear relationship and one of the points that its graph passes through. How can you determine if the relationship is proportional or nonproportional?

____

____

____

15. Multiple Representations An entrant at a science fair has included information about temperature conversion in various forms, as shown. The variables *F*, *C*, and *K* represent temperatures in degrees Fahrenheit, degrees Celsius, and kelvin, respectively.

Equations	Table C	
	Degrees Celsius	**kelvin**
Equation A $F = \frac{9}{5}C + 32$	8	281.15
Equation B $K = C + 273.15$	15	288.15
	36	309.15

a. Is the relationship between kelvins and degrees Celsius proportional? Justify your answer in two different ways.

____

____

____

____

b. Is the relationship between degrees Celsius and degrees Fahrenheit proportional? Why or why not?

____

____

____

____

MODULE QUIZ

Ready to Go On?

17.1 Representing Linear Nonproportional Relationships

1. Complete the table using the equation $y = 3x + 2$.

x	−1	0	1	2	3
y					

17.2 Determining Slope and y-intercept

2. Find the slope and y-intercept of the line in the graph.

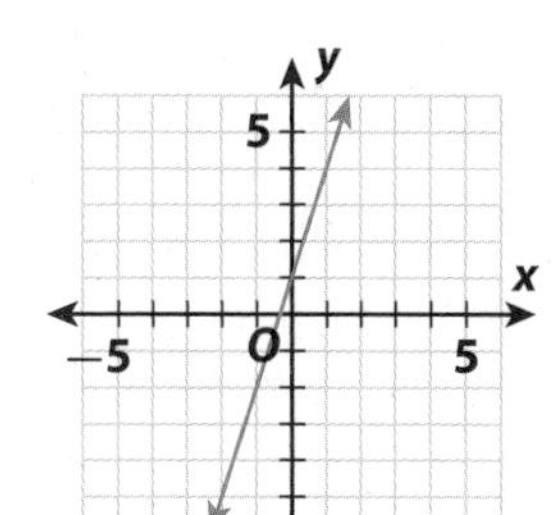

____

17.3 Graphing Linear Nonproportional Relationships

3. Graph the equation $y = 2x - 3$ using slope and y-intercept.

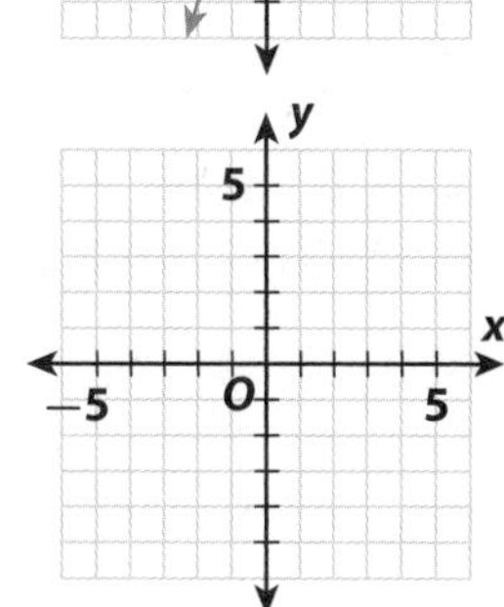

17.4 Proportional and Nonproportional Situations

4. Does the table represent a proportional or a nonproportional linear relationship?

x	1	2	3	4	5
y	4	8	12	16	20

____

5. Does the graph in Exercise 2 represent a proportional or a nonproportional linear relationship? _______________

6. Does the graph in Exercise 3 represent a proportional or a nonproportional relationship? _______________

ESSENTIAL QUESTION

7. How can you identify a linear nonproportional relationship from a table, a graph, and an equation?

____

____

MODULE 17 MIXED REVIEW

Assessment Readiness

1. Consider each table. Does the table represent a proportional relationship?

Select Yes or No for tables A–C.

A.

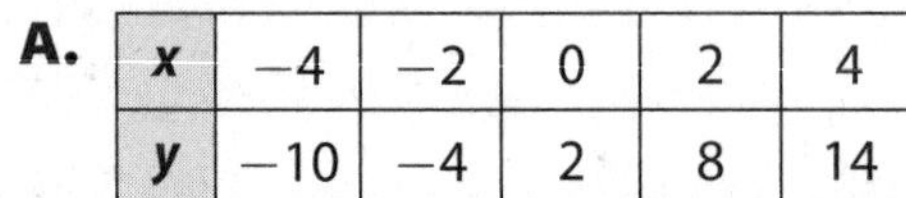

x	−4	−2	0	2	4
y	−10	−4	2	8	14

○ Yes ○ No

B.

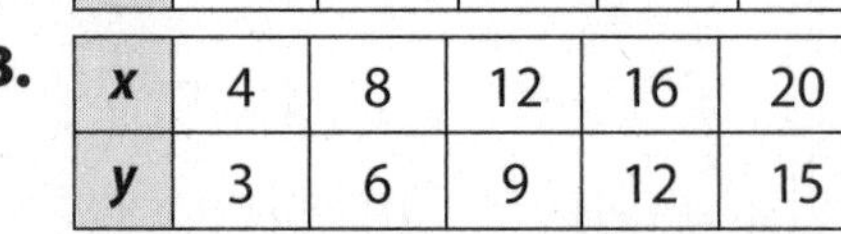

x	4	8	12	16	20
y	3	6	9	12	15

○ Yes ○ No

C.

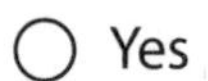

x	−3	−1	1	3	5
y	−12	−4	4	12	20

○ Yes ○ No

2. The graph shows the relationship between the hours Leann works and the money she earns.

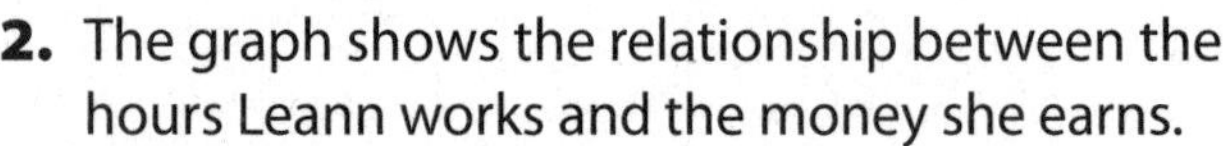

Choose True or False for each statement.

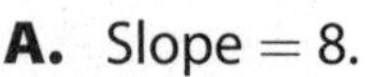

A. Slope = 8. ○ True ○ False

B. Unit rate = \$8/h. ○ True ○ False

C. Equation is $y = \frac{x}{8}$ ○ True ○ False

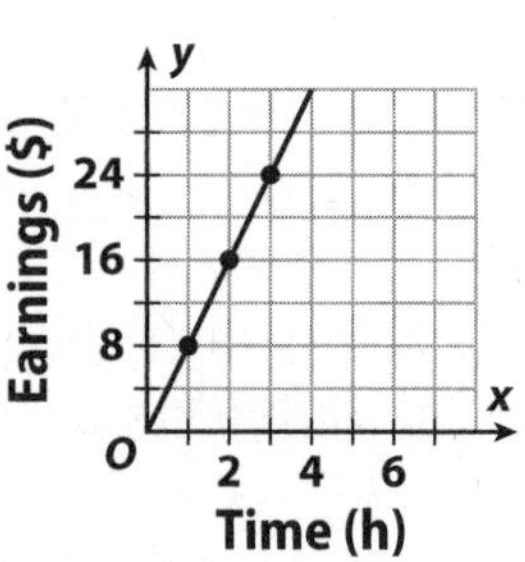

3. There is an initial fee to join a gym, plus a monthly charge. The table represents the linear relationship between the total cost of joining the gym and the number of months a person is a member. What is the y-intercept of the line, and what does it represent in this situation?

Time (months), x	Total Cost (\$), y
1	125
2	155
3	185

4. The equation $y = 35x - 5$ gives y as the cost of x tickets to a theme park with a \$5 coupon. After the park raises ticket prices by \$3, what is the new equation? How are the graphs of the two equations different?

Solving Linear Equations

ESSENTIAL QUESTION

How can you use equations with the variable on both sides to solve real-world problems?

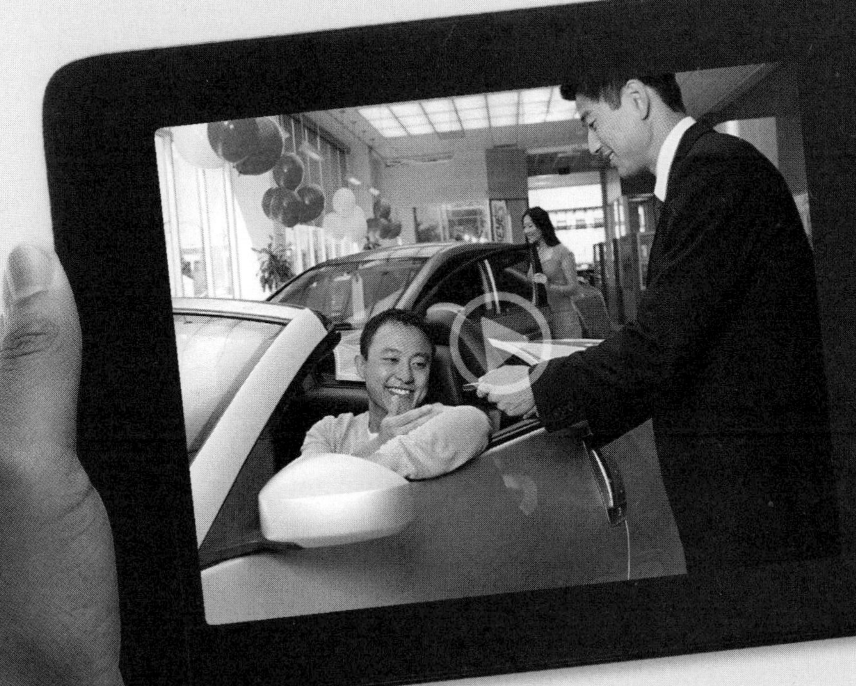

Real-World Video

my.hrw.com

Some employees earn commission plus their salary when they make a sale. There may be options about their pay structure. They can find the best option by solving an equation with the variable on both sides.

GO DIGITAL
my.hrw.com

my.hrw.com

Go digital with your write-in student edition, accessible on any device.

Math On the Spot

Scan with your smart phone to jump directly to the online edition, video tutor, and more.

Animated Math

Interactively explore key concepts to see how math works.

Personal Math Trainer

Get immediate feedback and help as you work through practice sets.

Are YOU Ready?

Complete these exercises to review skills you will need for this module.

Find Common Denominators

EXAMPLE Find the LCD of 3, 5, and 10.

3: 3, 6, 9, 12, 15, 18, 21, 24, 27, 30,...
5: 5, 10, 15, 20, 25, 30, 35,...
10: 10, 20, 30, 40, 50,...

List the multiples of each number. Choose the least multiple the lists have in common.
LCD(3, 5, 10) = 30

Find the LCD.

1. 8, 12 ________ **2.** 9, 12 ________ **3.** 15, 20 ________ **4.** 8, 10 ________

Multiply Decimals by Powers of 10

EXAMPLE 3.719×100 *Count the zeros in 100: 2 zeros*

$3.719 \times 100 = 371.9$ *Move the decimal point 2 places to the right.*

Find the product.

5. 0.683×100 **6.** $9.15 \times 1{,}000$ **7.** 0.005×100 **8.** $1{,}000 \times 1{,}000$

________ ________ ________ ________

Connect Words and Equations

EXAMPLE Two times a number decreased by 5 is −6.

Two times x decreased by 5 is −6. *Represent the unknown with a variable.*

$2x - 5$ is -6 *Times means multiplication. Decreased by means subtraction.*

$2x - 5 = -6$ *Place the equal sign.*

Write an algebraic equation for the sentence.

9. The difference between three times a number and 7 is 14. ________

10. The quotient of five times a number and 7 is no more than 10. ________

11. 14 less than 3 times a number is 5 more than half of the number. ________

Reading Start-Up

Vocabulary

Review Words

✔ algebraic expression *(expresión algebraica)*
coefficient *(coeficiente)*
common denominator *(denominador común)*
✔ constant *(constante)*
✔ equation *(ecuación)*
integers *(entero)*
least common multiple *(mínimo común múltiplo)*
operations *(operaciones)*
solution *(solución)*
✔ variable *(variable)*

Visualize Vocabulary

Use the ✔ words to complete the bubble map. You may put more than one word in each oval.

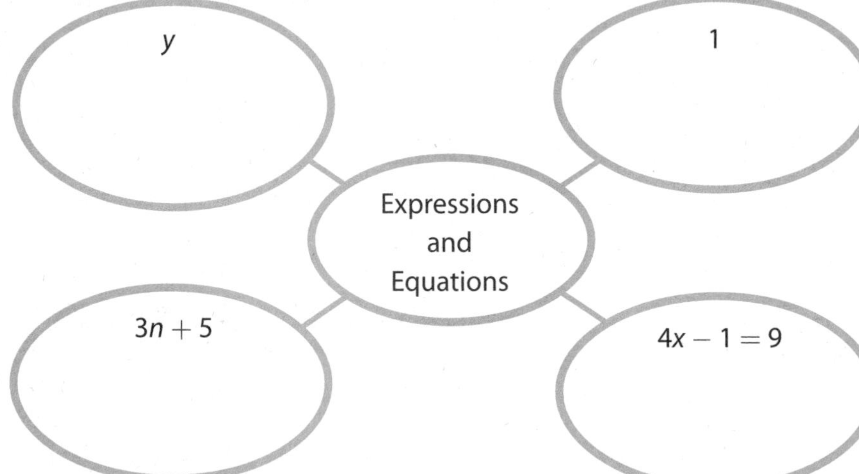

Understand Vocabulary

Complete the sentences using the review words.

1. A value of the variable that makes an equation true is a ________________.
2. The set of all whole numbers and their opposites are ________________.
3. An ______________________________ is an expression that contains at least one variable.

Active Reading

Layered Book Before beginning the module, create a layered book to help you learn the concepts in this module. At the top of the first flap, write the title of the book, "Solving Linear Equations." Then label each flap with one of the lesson titles in this module. As you study each lesson, write important ideas, such as vocabulary and formulas, under the appropriate flap.

GETTING READY FOR

Solving Linear Equations

Understanding the standards and the vocabulary terms in the standards will help you know exactly what you are expected to learn in this module.

CA CC 8.EE.7a

Give examples of linear equations in one variable with one solution, infinitely many solutions, or no solutions. Show which of these possibilities is the case by successively transforming the given equation into simpler forms, until an equivalent equation of the form $x = a$, $a = a$, or $a = b$ results (where a and b are different numbers).

Key Vocabulary

linear equation in one variable *(ecuación lineal en una variable)*
An equation that can be written in the form $ax = b$ where a and b are constants and $a \neq 0$.

What It Means to You

You will identify the number of solutions an equation has.

EXAMPLE 8.EE.7a

Your gym charges \$50 per month. Find the number of months for which your costs will equal the cost of membership at each gym shown.

A: \$40 per month plus \$100 one-time fee
$50x = 40x + 100 \rightarrow x = 10$
Equal in 10 months → one solution

B: \$50 per month plus \$25 one-time fee
$50x = 50x + 25 \rightarrow 0 = 25$
Never equal → no solution

C: \$40 per month plus \$10 monthly garage fee
$50x = 40x + 10x \rightarrow x = x$
Equal for any number of months → infinitely many solutions

CA CC 8.EE.7b

Solve linear equations with rational number coefficients, including equations whose solutions require expanding expressions using the distributive property and collecting like terms.

Key Vocabulary

solution *(solución)*
In an equation, the value for the variable that makes the equation true.

What It Means to You

You can write and solve an equation that has a variable on both sides of the equal sign.

EXAMPLE 8.EE.7b

Yellow Taxi has no pickup fee but charges \$0.25 per mile. AAA Taxi charges \$3 for pickup and \$0.15 per mile. Find the number of miles for which the cost of the two taxis is the same.

$$\begin{aligned} 0.25x &= 3 + 0.15x \\ 100(0.25x) &= 100(3) + 100(0.15x) \\ 25x &= 300 + 15x \\ 10x &= 300 \\ x &= 30 \end{aligned}$$

The cost is the same for 30 miles.

Visit **my.hrw.com** to see all **CA Common Core Standards** explained.

my.hrw.com

LESSON 18.1

Equations with the Variable on Both Sides

8.EE.7

Solve linear equations in one variable. *Also 8.EE.7b*

How can you represent and solve equations with the variable on both sides?

EXPLORE ACTIVITY

8.EE.7, 8.EE.7b

Modeling an Equation with a Variable on Both Sides

Algebra tiles can model equations with a variable on both sides.

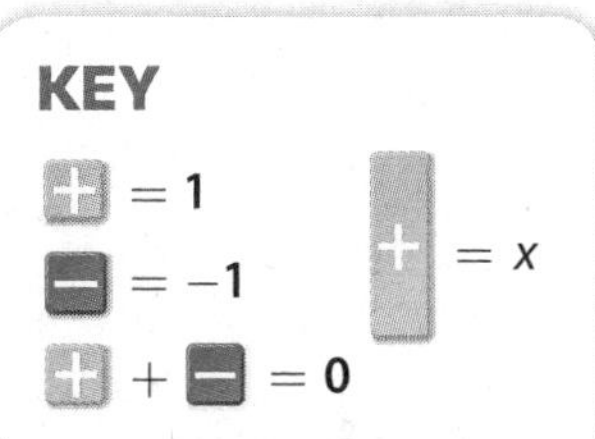

Use algebra tiles to model and solve $x + 5 = 3x - 1$.

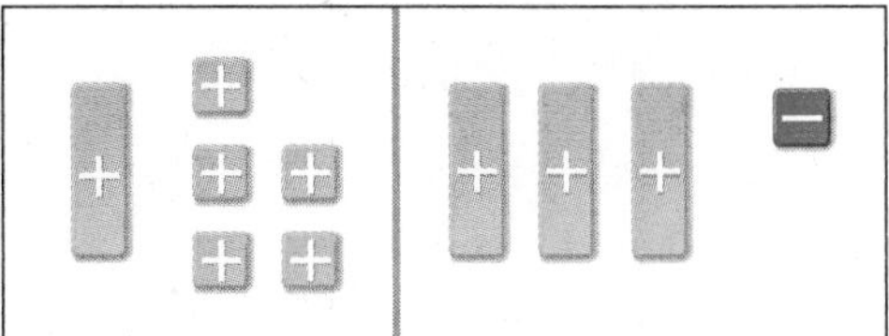

Model $x + 5$ on the left side of the mat and $3x - 1$ on the right side. Remember that $3x - 1$ is the same as

$3x +$ ________.

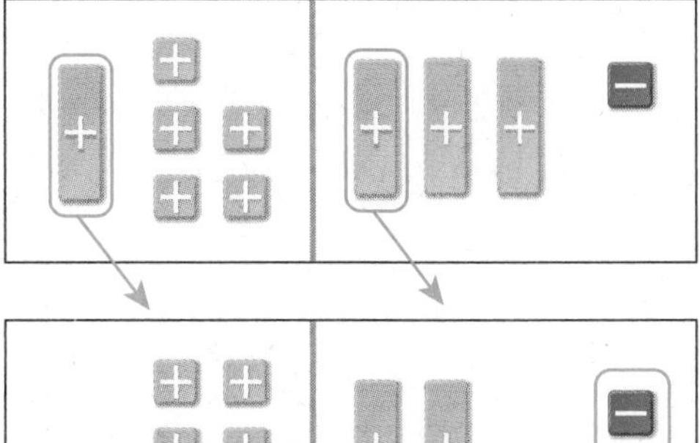

Remove one x-tile from both sides. This represents subtracting ________ from both sides of the equation.

Why is a positive unit tile added to both sides in the third step?

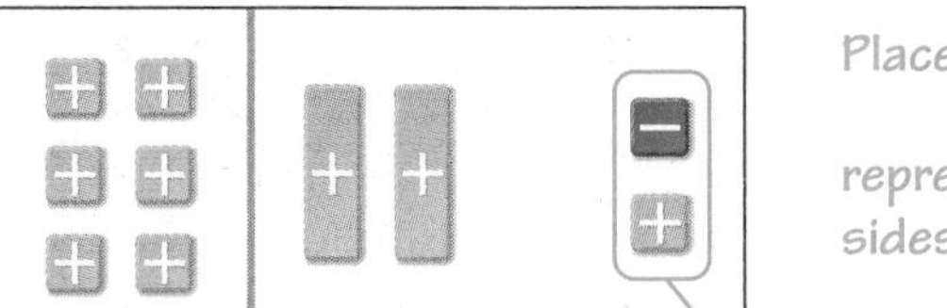

Place one +1-tile on both sides. This represents adding ________ to both sides of the equation. Remove zero pairs.

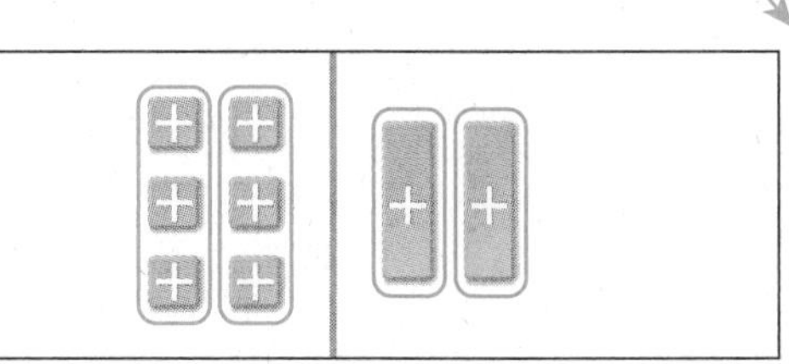

Separate each side into 2 equal groups.

One x-tile is equivalent to ________ +1-tiles.

The solution is ________ = ________.

Reflect

1. How can you check the solution to $x + 5 = 3x - 1$ using algebra tiles?

____

____

Solving an Equation with the Variable on Both Sides

Equations with the variable on both sides can be used to compare costs of real-world situations. To solve these equations, use inverse operations to get the variable terms on one side of the equation.

EXAMPLE 1

CA CC 8.EE.7, 8.EE.7b

Andy's Rental Car charges an initial fee of $20 plus an additional $30 per day to rent a car. Buddy's Rental Car charges an initial fee of $36 plus an additional $28 per day. For what number of days is the total cost charged by the companies the same?

STEP 1 Write an expression representing the total cost of renting a car from Andy's Rental Car.

Initial fee + Cost for x days

$$20 + 30x$$

STEP 2 Write an expression representing the total cost of renting a car from Buddy's Rental Car.

Initial fee + Cost for x days

$$36 + 28x$$

STEP 3 Write an equation that can be solved to find the number of days for which the total cost charged by the companies would be the same.

Total cost at Andy's = Total cost at Buddy's

$$20 + 30x = 36 + 28x$$

STEP 4 Solve the equation for x.

$$\begin{aligned} 20 + 30x &= 36 + 28x && \text{Write the equation.} \\ -28x &\quad\; -28x && \text{Subtract } 28x \text{ from both sides.} \\ 20 + 2x &= 36 \\ -20 &\quad\; -20 && \text{Subtract 20 from both sides.} \\ 2x &= 16 \\ \frac{2x}{2} &= \frac{16}{2} && \text{Divide both sides by 2.} \\ x &= 8 \end{aligned}$$

The total cost is the same if the rental is for 8 days.

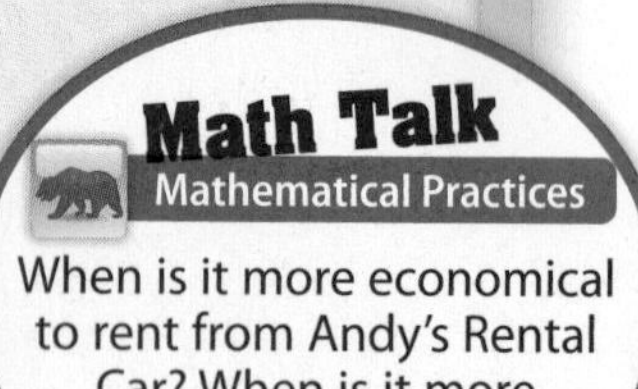

When is it more economical to rent from Andy's Rental Car? When is it more economical to rent from Buddy's?

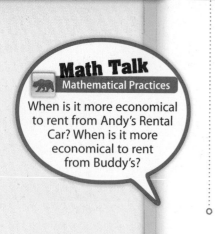

YOUR TURN

2. A water tank holds 256 gallons but is leaking at a rate of 3 gallons per week. A second water tank holds 384 gallons but is leaking at a rate of 5 gallons per week. After how many weeks will the amount of water in the two tanks be the same?

____

Writing a Real-World Situation from an Equation

As shown in Example 1, an equation with the variable on both sides can be used to represent a real-world situation. You can reverse this process by writing a real-world situation for a given equation.

EXAMPLE 2 

My Notes

Write a real-world situation that could be modeled by the equation $150 + 25x = 55x$.

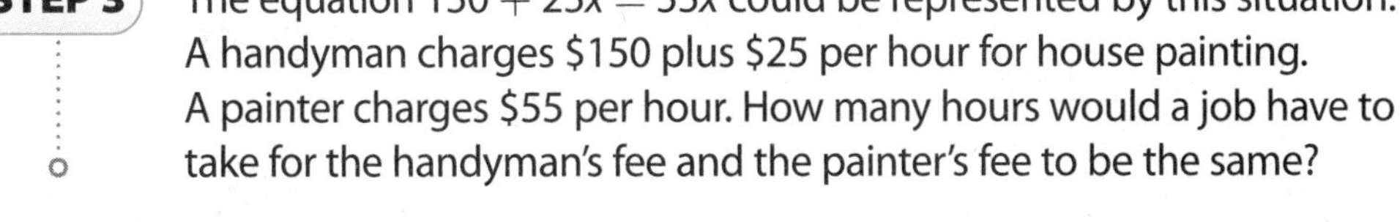

STEP 1 The left side of the equation consists of a constant plus a variable term. It could represent the total cost for doing a job where there is an initial fee plus an hourly charge.

STEP 2 The right side of the equation consists of a variable term. It could represent the cost for doing the same job based on an hourly charge only.

STEP 3 The equation $150 + 25x = 55x$ could be represented by this situation: A handyman charges $150 plus $25 per hour for house painting. A painter charges $55 per hour. How many hours would a job have to take for the handyman's fee and the painter's fee to be the same?

YOUR TURN

3. Write a real-world situation that could be modeled by the equation $30x = 48 + 22x$.

____

____

____

____

Guided Practice

Use algebra tiles to model and solve each equation. (Explore Activity)

1. $x + 4 = -x - 4$ ______

2. $2 - 3x = -x - 8$ ______

Solve each equation. (Example 1)

3. $b + 4 = 2b - 5$ ______

4. $10h + 12 = 8h + 4$ ______

5. $-6x - 29 = 5x - 7$ ______

6. $7a - 17 = 4a + 1$ ______

7. $-n + 5 = n - 11$ ______

8. $5p + 8 = 7p + 2$ ______

9. At Silver Gym, membership is \$25 per month, and personal training sessions are \$30 each. At Fit Factor, membership is \$65 per month, and personal training sessions are \$20 each. In one month, how many personal training sessions would Sarah have to buy to make the total cost at the two gyms equal? (Example 1)

______

10. A moving company charges \$840 plus \$17 per hour. Another moving company charges \$760 plus \$22 per hour. How long is a job that costs the same no matter which company is used? (Example 1)

______

11. Write a real-world situation that could be modeled by the equation $100 - 6x = 160 - 10x$. (Example 2)

______

______

______

______

ESSENTIAL QUESTION CHECK-IN

12. How can you solve an equation with the variable on both sides?

______

______

______

______

______

Name ______________________ Class ______________ Date ______________

18.1 Independent Practice

8.EE.7, 8.EE.7b

13. Derrick's Dog Sitting and Darlene's Dog Sitting are competing for new business. The companies ran the ads shown.

a. Write and solve an equation to find the number of hours for which the total cost will be the same for the two services.

____

b. **Analyze Relationships** Which dog sitting service is more economical to use if you need 5 hours of service? Explain.

____

____

14. Country Carpets charges $22 per square yard for carpeting, and an additional installation fee of $100. City Carpets charges $25 per square yard for the same carpeting, and an additional installation fee of $70.

a. Write and solve an equation to find the number of square yards of carpeting for which the total cost charged by the two companies will be the same.

____

b. **Justify Reasoning** Mr. Shu wants to hire one of the two carpet companies to install carpeting in his basement. Is he more likely to hire Country Carpets or City Carpets? Explain your reasoning.

____

____

____

____

Write an equation to represent each relationship. Then solve the equation.

15. Two less than 3 times a number is the same as the number plus 10.

____

16. A number increased by 4 is the same as 19 minus 2 times the number.

____

17. Twenty less than 8 times a number is the same as 15 more than the number.

____

18. The charges for an international call made using the calling card for two phone companies are shown in the table.

Phone Company	Charges
Company A	35¢ plus 3¢ per minute
Company B	45¢ plus 2¢ per minute

a. What is the length of a phone call that would cost the same no matter which company is used?

____

b. **Analyze Relationships** When is it better to use the card from Company B?

____

____

FOCUS ON HIGHER ORDER THINKING

Work Area

19. **Draw Conclusions** Liam is setting up folding chairs for a meeting. If he arranges the chairs in 9 rows of the same length, he has 3 chairs left over. If he arranges the chairs in 7 rows of that same length, he has 19 left over. How many chairs does Liam have?

____

20. **Explain the Error** Rent-A-Tent rents party tents for a flat fee of \$365 plus \$125 a day. Capital Rentals rents party tents for a flat fee of \$250 plus \$175 a day. Delia wrote the following equation to find the number of days for which the total cost charged by the two companies would be the same:

$$365x + 125 = 250x + 175$$

Find and explain the error in Delia's work. Then write the correct equation.

____

____

____

____

21. **Persevere in Problem Solving** Lilliana is training for a marathon. She runs the same distance every day for a week. On Monday, Wednesday, and Friday, she runs 3 laps on a running trail and then runs 6 more miles. On Tuesday and Sunday, she runs 5 laps on the trail and then runs 2 more miles. On Saturday, she just runs laps. How many laps does Lilliana run on Saturday?

____

LESSON 18.2

Equations with Rational Numbers

CA CC 8.EE.7b

Solve linear equations with rational number coefficients, including equations whose solutions require expanding expressions using the distributive property and collecting like terms. *Also 8.EE.7*

ESSENTIAL QUESTION

How can you solve equations with rational number coefficients and constants?

Solving an Equation that Involves Fractions

To solve an equation with the variable on both sides that involves fractions, start by using the least common multiple (LCM) to eliminate the fractions from the equation.

EXAMPLE 1

CA CC 8.EE.7b, 8.EE.7

Solve $\frac{7}{10}n + \frac{3}{2} = \frac{3}{5}n + 2$.

STEP 1 Determine the least common multiple of the denominators: LCM(**10**, **2**, **5**) = 10

$10 = 10 \times 1$
$= 2 \times 5$
$= 5 \times 2$

STEP 2 Multiply both sides of the equation by the LCM.

$$10\left(\frac{7}{10}n + \frac{3}{2}\right) = 10\left(\frac{3}{5}n + 2\right)$$

$$\overset{1}{\cancel{10}}\left(\frac{7}{\underset{1}{\cancel{10}}}n\right) + \overset{5}{\cancel{10}}\left(\frac{3}{\underset{1}{\cancel{2}}}\right) = \overset{2}{\cancel{10}}\left(\frac{3}{\underset{1}{\cancel{5}}}n\right) + 10(2)$$

$$7n + 15 = 6n + 20$$

STEP 3 Use inverse operations to solve the equation.

$$\begin{aligned} 7n + 15 &= 6n + 20 \\ -15 &\quad\; -15 \\ 7n &= 6n + 5 \\ -6n &\quad\; -6n \\ n &= 5 \end{aligned}$$

Subtract 15 from both sides.

Subtract $6n$ from both sides.

Math Talk Mathematical Practices

The constant on the right side, 2, is not a fraction. Why do you still need to multiply it by the LCM, 10?

Reflect

1. What is the advantage of multiplying both sides of the equation by the least common multiple of the denominators in the first step?

____

2. **What If?** What happens in the first step if you multiply both sides by a common multiple of the denominators that is not the LCM?

____

____

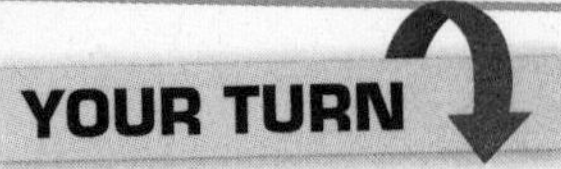

Solve.

3. $\frac{1}{7}k - 6 = \frac{3}{7}k + 4$ ______

4. $\frac{5}{6}y + 1 = -\frac{1}{2}y + \frac{1}{4}$ ______

Solving an Equation that Involves Decimals

Solving an equation with the variable on both sides that involves decimals is similar to solving an equation with fractions. But instead of first multiplying both sides by the LCM, multiply by a power of 10 to eliminate the decimals.

EXAMPLE 2

CA CC 8.EE.7, 8.EE.7b

Javier walks from his house to the zoo at a constant rate. After walking 0.75 mile, he meets his brother, Raul, and they continue walking at the same constant rate. When they arrive at the zoo, Javier has walked for 0.5 hour and Raul has walked for 0.2 hour. What is the rate in miles per hour at which the brothers walked to the zoo?

My Notes

STEP 1 Write an equation for the distance from the brothers' house to the zoo, using the fact that distance equals rate times time. Let r = the brothers' walking rate.

$$\underbrace{\text{distance to zoo}}_{0.2r + 0.75} = \underbrace{\text{distance to zoo}}_{0.5r}$$

STEP 2 Multiply both sides of the equation by $10^2 = 100$.

$$100(0.2r) + 100(0.75) = 100(0.5r)$$

$$20r + 75 = 50r$$

Multiplying by 100 clears the equation of decimals. Multiplying by 10 does not: $10 \times 0.75 = 7.5$.

STEP 3 Use inverse operations to solve the equation.

$$20r + 75 = 50r$$ Write the equation.

$$\underline{-20r} \quad \underline{-20r}$$ Subtract $20r$ from both sides.

$$75 = 30r$$

$$\frac{75}{30} = \frac{30r}{30}$$ Divide both sides by 30.

$$2.5 = r$$

So, the brothers' constant rate of speed was 2.5 miles per hour.

YOUR TURN

5. Logan has two aquariums. One aquarium contains 1.3 cubic feet of water and the other contains 1.9 cubic feet of water. The water in the larger aquarium weighs 37.44 pounds more than the water in the smaller aquarium. Write an equation with a variable on both sides to represent the situation. Then find the weight of 1 cubic foot of water.

____

Writing a Real-World Situation from an Equation

Real-world situations can often be represented by equations involving fractions and decimals. Fractions and decimals can represent quantities such as weight, volume, capacity, time, and temperature. Decimals can also be used to represent dollars and cents.

EXAMPLE 3  CA CC 8.EE.7

Write a real-world situation that can be modeled by the equation $0.95x = 0.55x + 60$.

STEP 1 The left side of the equation consists of a variable term. It could represent the total cost for x items.

STEP 2 The right side of the equation consists of a variable term plus a constant. It could represent the total cost for x items plus a flat fee.

STEP 3 The equation $0.95x = 0.55x + 60$ could be represented by this situation: Toony Tunes charges \$0.95 for each song you download. Up With Downloads charges \$0.55 for each song but also charges an annual membership fee of \$60. How many songs must a customer download in a year so that the cost will be the same at both websites?

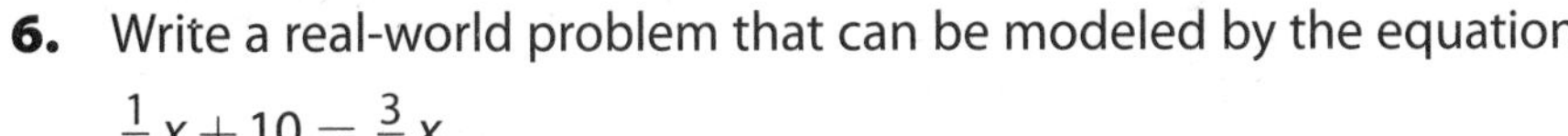

6. Write a real-world problem that can be modeled by the equation $\frac{1}{3}x + 10 = \frac{3}{5}x$.

____

____

____

Guided Practice

1. Sandy is upgrading her Internet service. Fast Internet charges \$60 for installation and \$50.45 per month. Quick Internet has free installation but charges \$57.95 per month. (Example 2)

a. Write an equation that can be used to find the number of months for which the Internet service would cost the same.

____

b. Solve the equation.

____

Solve. (Examples 1 and 2)

2. $\frac{3}{4}n - 18 = \frac{1}{4}n - 4$ ______

3. $6 + \frac{4}{5}b = \frac{9}{10}b$ ______

4. $\frac{2}{11}m + 16 = 4 + \frac{6}{11}m$ ______

5. $2.25t + 5 = 13.5t + 14$ ______

6. $3.6w = 1.6w + 24$ ______

7. $-0.75p - 2 = 0.25p$ ______

8. Write a real-world problem that can be modeled by the equation $1.25x = 0.75x + 50$. (Example 3)

____

____

____

____

____

ESSENTIAL QUESTION CHECK-IN

9. How does the method for solving equations with fractional or decimal coefficients and constants compare with the method for solving equations with integer coefficients and constants?

____

____

____

____

____

Name ____________________ Class ____________________ Date ____________________

18.2 Independent Practice

CA CC 8.EE.7, 8.EE.7b

10. Members of the Wide Waters Club pay \$105 per summer season, plus \$9.50 each time they rent a boat. Nonmembers must pay \$14.75 each time they rent a boat. How many times would a member and a non-member have to rent a boat in order to pay the same amount?

____

11. Margo can purchase tile at a store for \$0.79 per tile and rent a tile saw for \$24. At another store she can borrow the tile saw for free if she buys tiles there for \$1.19 per tile. How many tiles must she buy for the cost to be the same at both stores?

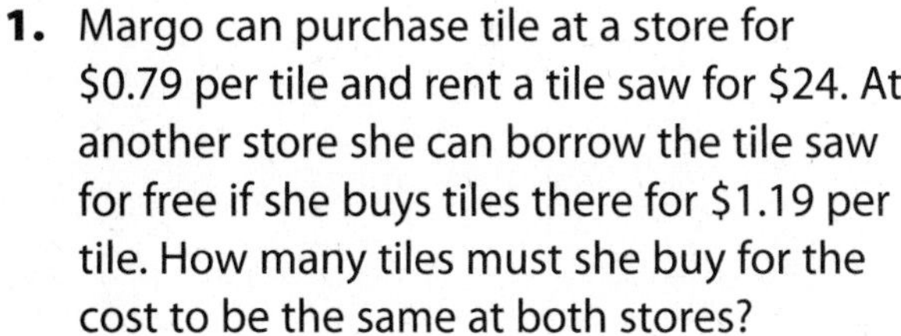

____

12. The charges for two shuttle services are shown in the table. Find the number of miles for which the cost of both shuttles is the same.

	Pickup Charge (\$)	Charge per Mile (\$)
Easy Ride	10	0.10
Best	0	0.35

____

13. **Multistep** Rapid Rental Car charges a \$40 rental fee, \$15 for gas, and \$0.25 per mile driven. For the same car, Capital Cars charges \$45 for rental and gas and \$0.35 per mile.

a. For how many miles is the rental cost at both companies the same?

____

b. What is that cost?

____

14. Write an equation with the solution $x = 20$. The equation should have the variable on both sides, a fractional coefficient on the left side, and a fraction anywhere on the right side.

____

15. Write an equation with the solution $x = 25$. The equation should have the variable on both sides, a decimal coefficient on the left side, and a decimal anywhere on the right side. One of the decimals should be written in tenths, the other in hundredths.

____

16. **Geometry** The perimeters of the rectangles shown are equal. What is the perimeter of each rectangle?

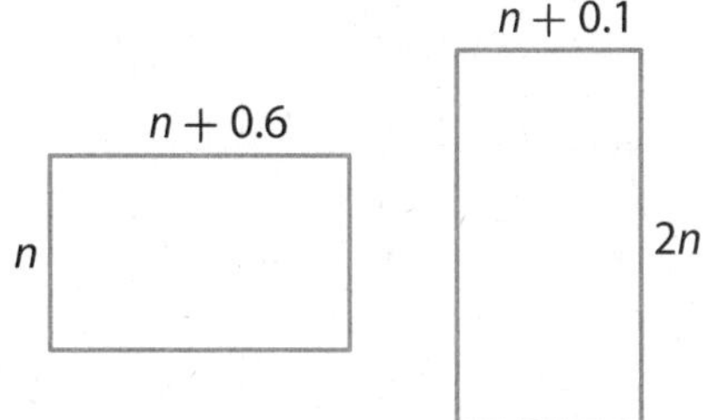

____

17. **Analyze Relationships** The formula $F = 1.8C + 32$ gives the temperature in degrees Fahrenheit (F) for a given temperature in degrees Celsius (C). There is one temperature for which the number of degrees Fahrenheit is equal to the number of degrees Celsius. Write an equation you can solve to find that temperature and then use it to find the temperature.

____

18. Explain the Error Agustin solved an equation as shown. What error did Agustin make? What is the correct answer?

$$\frac{1}{3}x - 4 = \frac{3}{4}x + 1$$
$$12\left(\frac{1}{3}x\right) - 4 = 12\left(\frac{3}{4}x\right) + 1$$
$$4x - 4 = 9x + 1$$
$$-5 = 5x$$
$$x = -1$$

FOCUS ON HIGHER ORDER THINKING

Work Area

19. Write a real-world situation that could be modeled by the equation $20 + 1.25x = 15 + 2.5x$.

20. Look for a Pattern Describe the pattern in the equation. Then solve the equation.

$$0.3x + 0.03x + 0.003x + 0.0003x + \ldots = 3$$

21. Critique Reasoning Jared wanted to find three consecutive even integers whose sum was 4 times the first of those integers. He let k represent the first integer, then wrote and solved this equation: $k + (k + 1) + (k + 2) = 4k$. Did he get the correct answer? Explain.

LESSON 18.3

Equations with the Distributive Property

CA CC 8.EE.7b

Solve linear equations with rational number coefficients, including equations whose solutions require expanding expressions using the distributive property and collecting like terms.

ESSENTIAL QUESTION

How do you use the Distributive Property to solve equations?

Using the Distributive Property

The Distributive Property can be useful in solving equations.

EXAMPLE 1

CA CC 8.EE.7b

A **Solve: $3(x - 5) + 1 = 2 + x$**

STEP 1 Use the Distributive Property.

$3x - 15 + 1 = 2 + x$ Distribute 3 to the terms within the parentheses.

$3x - 14 = 2 + x$ Simplify.

STEP 2 Use inverse operations to solve the equation.

$3x - 14 = 2 + x$

$\underline{-x \qquad\quad -x}$ Subtract x from both sides.

$2x - 14 = 2$

$\underline{+14 \quad +14}$ Add 14 to both sides.

$2x = 16$ Divide both sides by 2.

$x = 8$

B **Solve: $5 - 7k = -4(k + 1) - 3$**

STEP 1 Use the Distributive Property.

$5 - 7k = -4k - 4 - 3$ Distribute -4 to the terms within the parentheses.

$5 - 7k = -4k - 7$ Simplify.

STEP 2 Use inverse operations to solve the equation.

$5 - 7k = -4k - 7$

$\underline{+4k \quad +4k}$ Add $4k$ to both sides.

$5 - 3k = -7$

$\underline{-5 \qquad -5}$ Subtract 5 from both sides.

$-3k = -12$ Divide both sides by -3.

$k = 4$

How can you rewrite $7 - (2a + 3) = 12$ without parentheses? Explain your answer.

Personal Math Trainer

Online Practice and Help

my.hrw.com

YOUR TURN

Solve each equation.

1. $y - 5 = 3 - 9(y + 2)$ ________ **2.** $2(x - 7) - 10 = 12 - 4x$ ________

Math On the Spot

my.hrw.com

Using the Distributive Property on Both Sides

Some equations require the use of the Distributive Property on both sides.

EXAMPLE 2

CA CC 8.EE.7b

Solve: $\frac{3}{4}(x - 13) = -2(9 + x)$

Math Talk Mathematical Practices

How can you eliminate fractions if there is a fraction being distributed on both sides of an equation?

STEP 1 Eliminate the fraction.

$$\frac{3}{4}(x - 13) = -2(9 + x)$$

$$4 \times \frac{3}{4}(x - 13) = 4 \times [-2(9 + x)]$$ Multiply both sides by 4.

$$3(x - 13) = -8(9 + x)$$

STEP 2 Use the Distributive Property.

$$3x - 39 = -72 - 8x$$ Distribute 3 and −8 to the terms within the parentheses.

STEP 3 Use inverse operations to solve the equation.

$$3x - 39 = -72 - 8x$$

$$\underline{+8x} \qquad \underline{+8x}$$ Add 8x to both sides.

$$11x - 39 = -72$$

$$\underline{+39} \qquad \underline{+39}$$ Add 39 to both sides.

$$11x = -33$$

$$\frac{11x}{11} = \frac{-33}{11}$$ Divide both sides by 11.

$$x = -3$$

Personal Math Trainer

Online Practice and Help

my.hrw.com

YOUR TURN

Solve each equation.

3. $-4(-5 - b) = \frac{1}{3}(b + 16)$ ________ **4.** $\frac{3}{5}(t + 18) = -3(2 - t)$ ________

Solving a Real-World Problem Using the Distributive Property

Solving a real-world problem may involve using the Distributive Property.

EXAMPLE 3 Problem Solving — CA CC 8.EE.7b

The Coleman family had their bill at a restaurant reduced by $7.50 because of a special discount. They left a tip of $8.90, which was 20% of the reduced amount. How much was their bill before the discount?

 **Analyze Information**

The answer is the amount before the discount.

 **Formulate a Plan**

Use an equation to find the amount before the discount.

 **Solve**

STEP 1 Write the equation $0.2(x - 7.5) = 8.9$, where x is the amount of the Coleman family's bill before the discount.

STEP 2 Use the Distributive Property: $0.2x - 1.5 = 8.9$

STEP 3 Use inverse operations to solve the equation.

$$0.2x - 1.5 = 8.9$$

$$\underline{\quad + 1.5 \quad + 1.5}$$ *Add 1.5 to both sides.*

$$0.2x = 10.4$$

$$\frac{0.2x}{0.2} = \frac{10.4}{0.2}$$ *Divide both sides by 0.2.*

$$x = 52$$

The Coleman family's bill before the discount was $52.00.

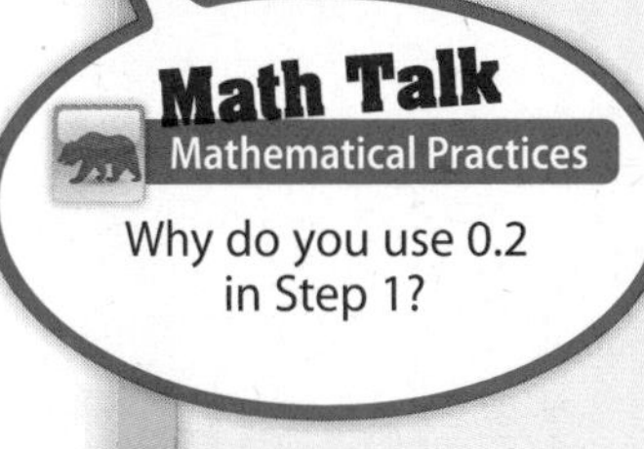

Math Talk
Mathematical Practices
Why do you use 0.2 in Step 1?

 **Justify and Evaluate**

$52.00 − $7.50 = $44.50 and 0.2($44.50) = $8.90. This is the amount of the tip the Colemans left. The answer is reasonable.

YOUR TURN

5. The Smiths spend 8% of their budget on entertainment. Their total budget this year is $2,000 more than last year, and this year they plan to spend $3,840 on entertainment. What was their total budget last year? ____________

Guided Practice

Solve each equation.

1. $4(x + 8) - 4 = 34 - 2x$ (Ex. 1)

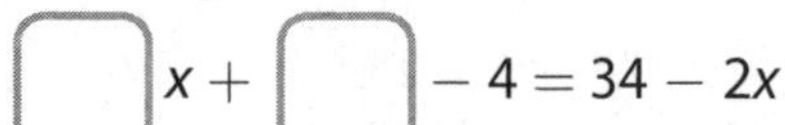

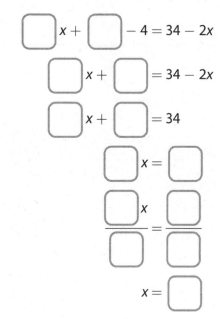

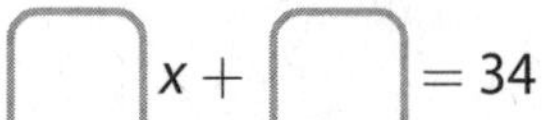

$\square x = \square$

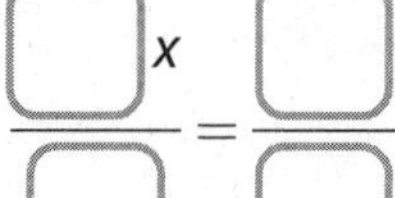

$x = \square$

2. $\frac{2}{3}(9 + x) = -5(4 - x)$ (Ex. 2)

$\square \times \frac{2}{3}(9 + x) = \square \times [-5(4 - x)]$

$\square(9 + x) = \square(4 - x)$

$\square + \square x = \square \bigcirc \square x$

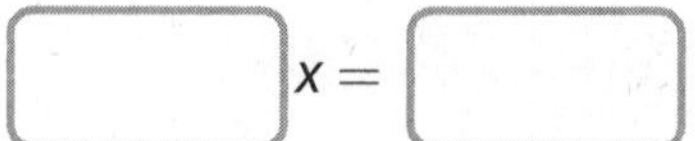

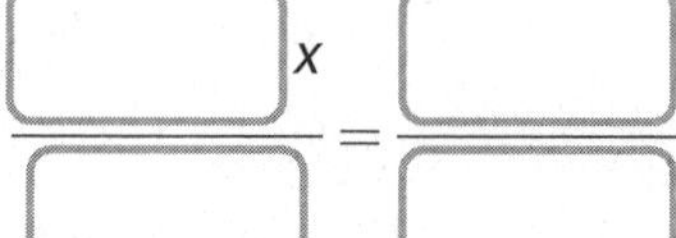

$x = \square$

3. $-3(x + 4) + 15 = 6 - 4x$ (Ex. 1)

____

4. $10 + 4x = 5(x - 6) + 33$ (Ex. 1)

____

5. $x - 9 = 8(2x + 3) - 18$ (Ex. 1)

____

6. $-6(x - 1) - 7 = -7x + 2$ (Ex. 1)

____

7. $\frac{1}{10}(x + 11) = -2(8 - x)$ (Ex. 2)

____

8. $-(4 - x) = \frac{3}{4}(x - 6)$ (Ex. 2)

____

9. $-8(8 - x) = \frac{4}{5}(x + 10)$ (Ex. 2)

____

10. $\frac{1}{2}(16 - x) = -12(x + 7)$ (Ex. 2)

____

11. Sandra saves 12% of her salary for retirement. This year her salary was $3,000 more than in the previous year, and she saved $4,200. What was her salary in the previous year? (Example 3)

Write an equation. ______________________

Sandra's salary in the previous year was ______________________.

ESSENTIAL QUESTION CHECK-IN

12. When solving an equation using the Distributive Property, if the numbers being distributed are fractions, what is your first step? Why?

____

Name ______ Class ______ Date ______

18.3 Independent Practice

8.EE.7b

13. Multistep Martina is currently 14 years older than her cousin Joey. In 5 years she will be 3 times as old as Joey. Use this information to answer the following questions.

a. If you let x represent Joey's current age, what expression can you use to represent Martina's current age?

______

b. Based on your answer to part a, what expression represents Joey's age in 5 years? What expression represents Martina's age in 5 years?

______

______

c. What equation can you write based on the information given?

______

d. What is Joey's current age? What is Martina's current age?

______

14. As part of a school contest, Sarah and Luis are playing a math game. Sarah must pick a number between 1 and 50 and give Luis clues so he can write an equation to find her number. Sarah says, "If I subtract 5 from my number, multiply that quantity by 4, and then add 7 to the result, I get 35." What equation can Luis write based on Sarah's clues and what is Sarah's number?

______

15. Critical Thinking When solving an equation using the Distributive Property that involves distributing fractions, usually the first step is to multiply by the LCD to eliminate the fractions in order to simplify computation. Is it necessary to do this to solve $\frac{1}{2}(4x + 6) = \frac{1}{3}(9x - 24)$? Why or why not?

______

______

______

16. Solve the equation given in Exercise 15 with and without using the LCD of the fractions. Are your answers the same? Explain.

______

17. Represent Real-World Problems A chemist mixed x milliliters of 25% acid solution with some 15% acid solution to produce 100 milliliters of a 19% acid solution. Use this information to complete the table.

	ml of Solution	Percent Acid as a Decimal	ml of Acid
25% Solution	x		
15% Solution			
Mixture (19% Solution)	100		

a. What is the relationship between the milliliters of acid in the 25% solution, the milliliters of acid in the 15% solution, and the milliliters of acid in the mixture?

b. What equation can you use to solve for x based on your answer to part a?

c. How many milliliters of the 25% solution and the 15% solution did the chemist use in the mixture?

FOCUS ON HIGHER ORDER THINKING

Work Area

18. Explain the Error Anne solved $5(2x) - 3 = 20x + 15$ for x by first distributing 5 on the left side of the equation. She got the answer $x = -3$. When she substituted -3 into the original equation her answer was incorrect. Explain Anne's error, and find the correct answer.

19. Communicate Mathematical Ideas Explain how to solve $5[3(x + 4) - 2(1 - x)] - x - 15 = 14x + 45$. Then solve the equation.

LESSON 18.4

Equations with Many Solutions or No Solution

8.EE.7a

Give examples of linear equations in one variable with one solution, infinitely many solutions, or no solutions. Show which of these possibilities is the case by successively transforming the given equation into simpler forms, until an equivalent equation of the form $x = a$, $a = a$, or $a = b$ results (where a and b are different numbers).

ESSENTIAL QUESTION

How can you give examples of equations with a given number of solutions?

Determining the Number of Solutions

So far, when you solved a linear equation in one variable, you found one value of x that makes the equation a true statement. When you simplify some equations, you may find that they do not have one solution.

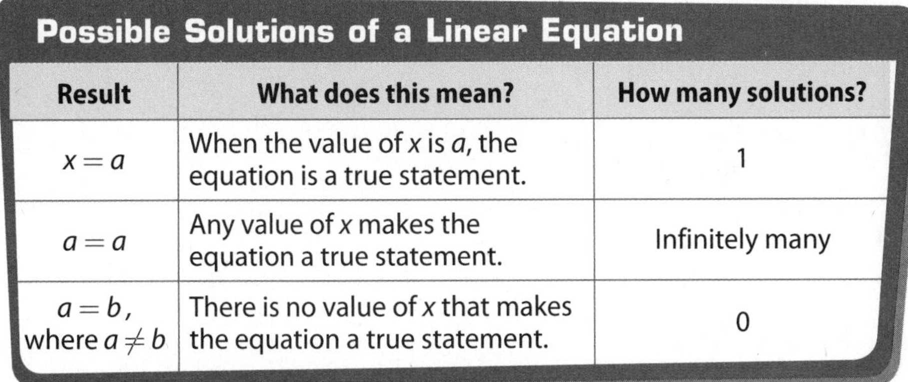

Possible Solutions of a Linear Equation

Result	What does this mean?	How many solutions?
$x = a$	When the value of x is a, the equation is a true statement.	1
$a = a$	Any value of x makes the equation a true statement.	Infinitely many
$a = b$, where $a \neq b$	There is no value of x that makes the equation a true statement.	0

EXAMPLE 1

8.EE.7a

Use the properties of equality to simplify each equation. Tell whether the equation has one, zero, or infinitely many solutions.

$4x - 3 = 2x + 13$

$$4x - 3 = 2x + 13$$

$$\underline{\quad +3} = \underline{\quad +3} \qquad \text{Add 3 to both sides.}$$

$$4x = 2x + 16$$

$$\underline{-2x} \quad \underline{-2x} \qquad \text{Subtract } 2x \text{ from both sides.}$$

$$2x = 16$$

$$\frac{2x}{2} = \frac{16}{2} \qquad \text{Divide both sides by 2.}$$

$$x = 8$$

The statement is true. There is one solution.

My Notes

B $4x - 5 = 2(2x - 1) - 3$

$4x - 5 = 2(2x - 1) - 3$

$4x - 5 = 4x - 2 - 3$ Distributive Property

$4x - 5 = 4x - 5$ Simplify.

$\underline{-4x} \quad \underline{-4x}$ Subtract $4x$ from both sides.

$-5 = -5$

The statement is true. There are infinitely many solutions.

C $4x + 2 = 4x - 5$

$4x + 2 = 4x - 5$

$\underline{-2} \quad \underline{-2}$ Subtract 2 from both sides.

$4x = 4x - 7$

$\underline{-4x} \quad \underline{-4x}$ Subtract $4x$ from both sides.

$0 = -7$

The statement is false. There is no solution.

Math Talk
Mathematical Practices

Why do you substitute values for x into the *original* equation?

Reflect

1. What happens when you substitute any value for x in the original equation in part B? In the original equation in part C?

____

____

____

YOUR TURN

Use the properties of equality to simplify each equation. Tell whether the equation has one, zero, or infinitely many solutions.

2. $2x + 1 = 5x - 8$

____

3. $3(4x + 3) - 2 = 12x + 7$

____

4. $3x - 9 = 5 + 3x$

____

Personal Math Trainer
Online Practice and Help
my.hrw.com

Writing Equations with a Given Number of Solutions

You can use the results of linear equations to write an equation that has a given number of solutions.

EXAMPLE 2

Write a linear equation in one variable that has no solution.

You can use the strategy of working backward:

STEP 1 Start with a false statement such as $3 = 5$. Add the same variable term to both sides.

$3 + x = 5 + x$ *Add x to both sides.*

STEP 2 Next, add the same constant to both sides and combine like terms on each side of the equation.

$10 + x = 12 + x$ *Add 7 to both sides.*

STEP 3 Verify that your equation has no solutions by using properties of equality to simplify your equation.

$$\begin{aligned} 10 + x &= 12 + x \\ -x &= \quad\ -x \\ \hline 10 &= 12 \end{aligned}$$

What type of statement do you start with to write an equation with infinitely many solutions? Give an example.

Reflect

5. Explain why the result of the process above is an equation with no solution.

____

____

____

____

Complete each equation so that it has the indicated number of solutions.

6. No solution: $3x + 1 = 3x +$ ______________

7. Infinitely many: $2x - 4 = 2x -$ ______________

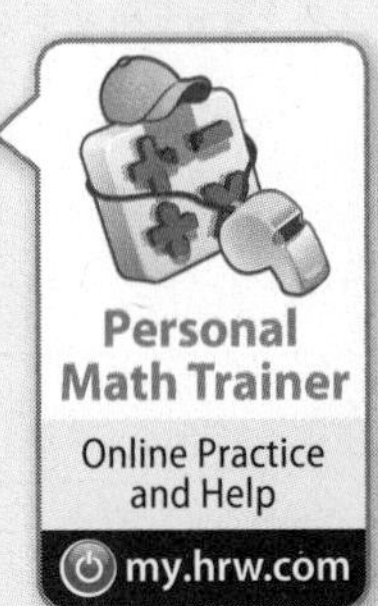

Guided Practice

Use the properties of equality to simplify each equation. Tell whether the final equation is a true statement. (Example 1)

1. $3x - 2 = 25 - 6x$ ________

   The statement is ☐.

2. $2x - 4 = 2(x - 1) + 3$ ________

   The statement is ☐.

3. How many solutions are there to the equation in Exercise 2? (Example 1)

   ____

4. After simplifying an equation, Juana gets $6 = 6$. Explain what this means. (Example 1)

   ____

   ____

Tell whether each equation has one, zero, or infinitely many solutions. (Example 1)

5. $6 + 3x = x - 8$ ________

6. $8x + 4 = 4(2x + 1)$ ________

Write a linear equation in one variable that has infinitely many solutions. (Example 2)

7. Start with a ________ statement. $10 = ☐$

   Add the ________ to both sides. $10 + x = ☐$

   Add the ________ to both sides. $10 + x + 5 = ☐$

   Combine ________ terms. $☐ = ☐$

Create an equation with the indicated number of solutions. (Example 2)

8. Infinitely many solutions:

   $2(x - 1) + 6x = 4\left(☐ - 1\right) + 2$

9. No solution:

   $3\left(x - \frac{4}{3}\right) = 3x + ☐$

ESSENTIAL QUESTION CHECK-IN

10. Give an example of an equation with an infinite number of solutions. Then make one change to the equation so that it has no solution.

    ____

    ____

Name ______________________ Class ______________________ Date ______________________

18.4 Independent Practice

8.EE.7a

Tell whether each equation has one, zero, or infinitely many solutions.

11. $-(2x + 2) - 1 = -x - (x + 3)$

____

12. $-2(z + 3) - z = -z - 4(z + 2)$

____

13. $3(2m - 1) + 5 = 6(m + 1)$

____

14. $y + 7 + 2y = -14 + 3y + 21$

____

Create an equation with the indicated number of solutions.

15. One solution of $x = -1$:

$5x - (x - 2) = 2x - (\square)$

16. Infinitely many solutions:

$-(x - 8) + 4x = 2(\square) + x$

17. **Persevere in Problem Solving** The Dig It Project is designing two gardens that have the same perimeter. One garden is a trapezoid whose nonparallel sides are equal. The other is a quadrilateral. Two possible designs are shown at the right.

$2x - 2$

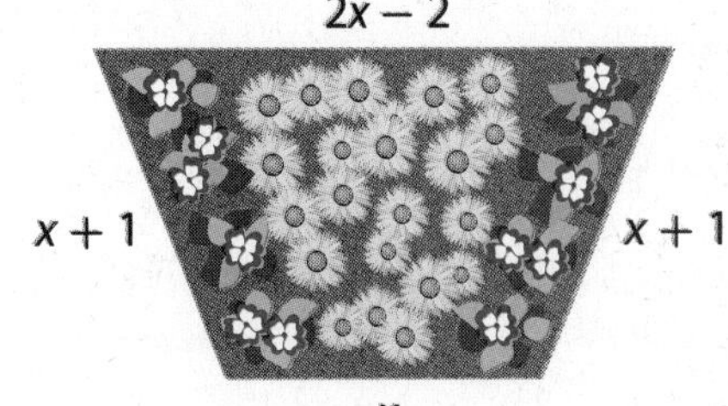

$x + 1$ $x + 1$

x

a. Based on these designs, is there more than one value for x? Explain how you know this.

____

____

____

____

____

$2x - 9$

x $x + 1$

$x + 8$

b. Why does your answer to part a make sense in this context?

____

____

____

c. Suppose the Dig It Project wants the perimeter of each garden to be 60 meters. What is the value of x in this case? How did you find this?

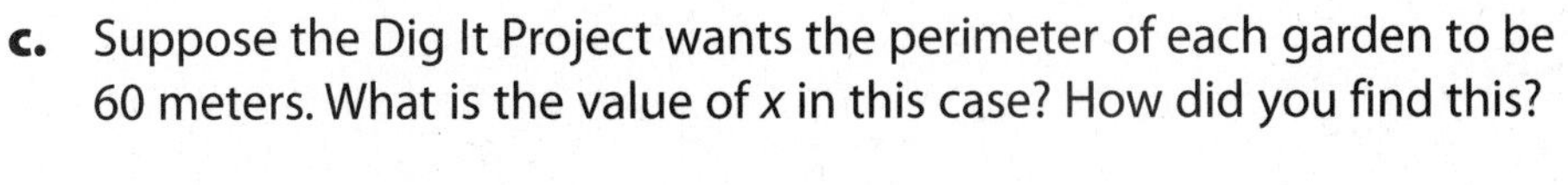

____

____

18. Critique Reasoning Lisa says that the indicated angles cannot have the same measure. Marita disagrees and says she can prove that they can have the same measure. Who do you agree with? Justify your answer.

$(9x - 25 + x)°$

$(x + 50 + 2x - 12)°$

____

____

____

____

____

19. Represent Real-World Problems Adele opens an account with \$100 and deposits \$35 a month. Kent opens an account with \$50 and also deposits \$35 a month. Will they have the same amount in their accounts at any point? If so, in how many months and how much will be in each account? Explain.

____

____

____

FOCUS ON HIGHER ORDER THINKING

Work Area

20. Communicate Mathematical Ideas Frank solved an equation and got the result $x = x$. Sarah solved the same equation and got $12 = 12$. Frank says that one of them is incorrect because you cannot get different results for the same equation. What would you say to Frank? If both results are indeed correct, explain how this happened.

____

____

____

____

21. Critique Reasoning Matt said $2x - 7 = 2(x - 7)$ has infinitely many solutions. Is he correct? Justify Matt's answer or show how he is incorrect.

____

____

____

____

MODULE QUIZ

Ready to Go On?

18.1 Equations with the Variable on Both Sides

Solve each equation.

1. $4a - 4 = 8 + a$ ______________

2. $4x + 5 = x + 8$ ______________

3. Hue is arranging chairs. She can form 6 rows of a given length with 3 chairs left over, or 8 rows of that same length if she gets 11 more chairs. Write and solve an equation to find how many chairs are in that row length.

____

18.2 Equations with Rational Numbers

Solve each equation.

4. $\frac{2}{3}n - \frac{2}{3} = \frac{n}{6} + \frac{4}{3}$ ______________

5. $1.5d + 3.25 = 1 + 2.25d$ ______________

6. Happy Paws charges $19.00 plus $1.50 per hour to keep a dog during the day. Woof Watchers charges $15.00 plus $2.75 per hour. Write and solve an equation to find for how many hours the total cost of the services is equal.

____

18.3 Equations with the Distributive Property

Solve each equation.

7. $\frac{1}{4}(x - 7) = 1 + 3x$ ______________

8. $3(x + 5) = 2(3x + 12)$ ______________

18.4 Equations with Many Solutions or No Solution

Tell whether each equation has one, zero, or infinitely many solutions.

9. $5(x - 3) + 6 = 5x - 9$ ______________

10. $5(x - 3) + 6 = 5x - 10$ ______________

ESSENTIAL QUESTION

11. How can you use equations with the variable on both sides to solve real-world problems?

____

MODULE 18
MIXED REVIEW

Assessment Readiness

Personal Math Trainer

Online Practice and Help

1. Consider each equation. Does the equation have at least one solution?

Select Yes or No for equations A–C.

A. $3(x + 2) = 2x + x + 6$ ○ Yes ○ No

B. $2x - 7 = 2(x + 4) + 3x$ ○ Yes ○ No

C. $8 + 5x = 5(x + 2) - 1$ ○ Yes ○ No

2. A ferry leaves a city and travels to an island. The distance the ferry has left to travel is modeled by the linear equation $y = 12 - 0.2x$, where y is the distance in miles and x is the time in minutes since the ferry left the city.

Choose True or False for each statement.

A. The relationship is nonproportional. ○ True ○ False

B. The slope of the line is 0.2. ○ True ○ False

C. The island is 12 miles from the city. ○ True ○ False

3. Shawn's Rental's charges \$27.50 per hour to rent a surfboard and a wetsuit. Darla's Surf Shop charges \$23.25 per hour to rent a surfboard plus \$17 extra for a wetsuit. Write and solve an equation to determine the rental period in hours for which the charges for Shawn's Rentals will be the same as the charges for Darla's Surf Shop. Explain the steps of your solution.

4. Beach towels are on sale for \$1.50 off the regular price. Ms. Ortiz buys 4 beach towels on sale for a total of \$33.96. Write and solve an equation to determine the regular price of a beach towel. Explain how you can check whether your answer is reasonable.

UNIT 8

Study Guide Review

MODULE 16 Proportional Relationships

Key Vocabulary

constant of proportionality *(constante de proporcionalidad)*

proportional relationship *(relación proporcional)*

slope *(pendiente)*

ESSENTIAL QUESTION

How can you use proportional relationships to solve real-world problems?

EXAMPLE 1

Write an equation that represents the proportional relationship shown in the graph.

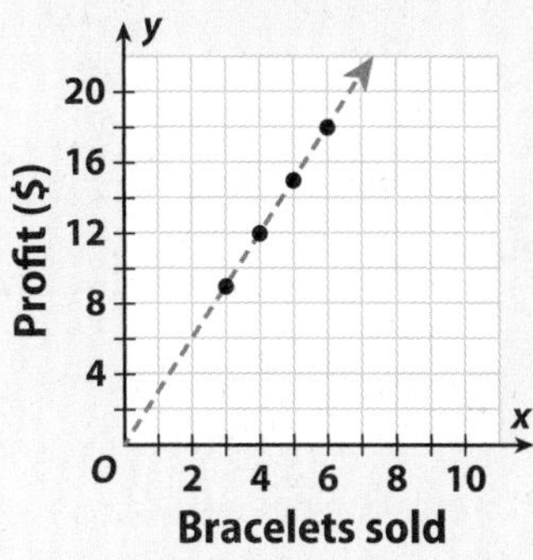

Use the points on the graph to make a table.

Bracelets sold	3	4	5	6
Profit ($)	9	12	15	18

Let x represent the number of bracelets sold.

Let y represent the profit.

The equation is $y = 3x$.

EXAMPLE 2

Find the slope of the line.

slope $= \frac{\text{rise}}{\text{run}}$

$= \frac{3}{-4}$

$= -\frac{3}{4}$

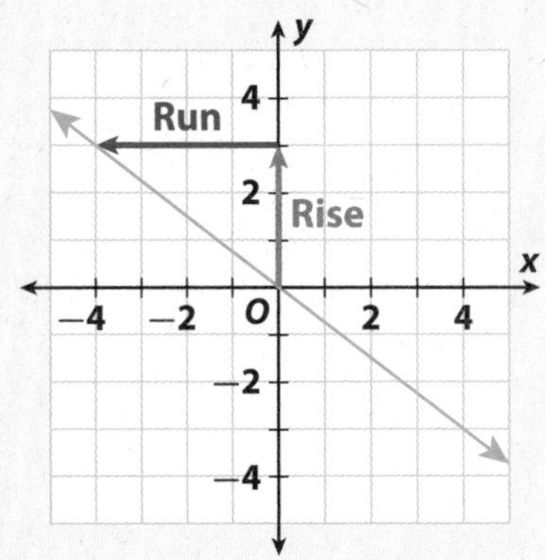

EXERCISES

1. The table represents a proportional relationship. Write an equation that describes the relationship. Then graph the relationship represented by the data. (Lessons 16.1, 16.3, 16.4)

Time (x)	6	8	10	12
Distance (y)	3	4	5	6

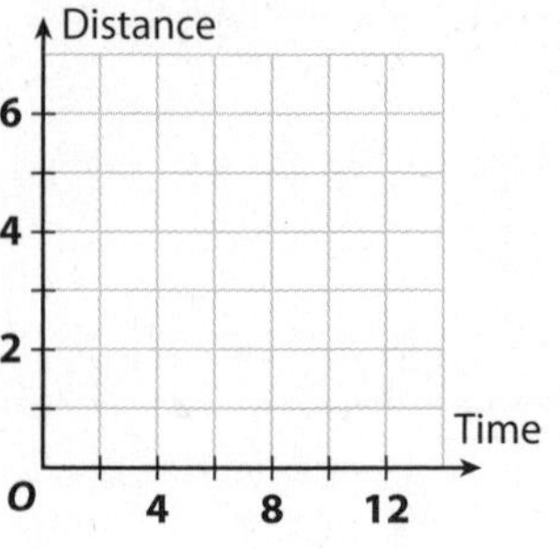

Find the slope and the unit rate represented on each graph. (Lesson 16.2)

2.

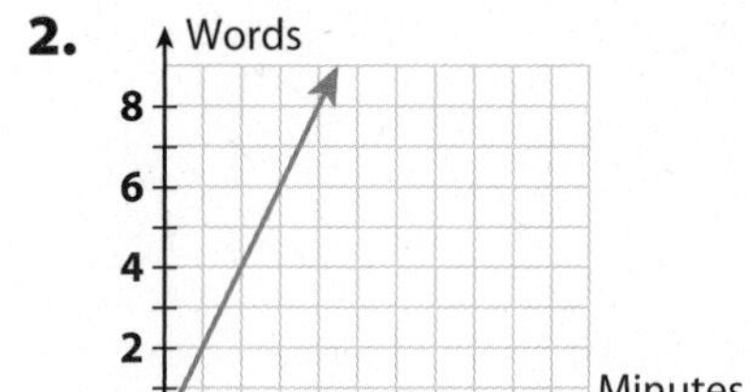

3.

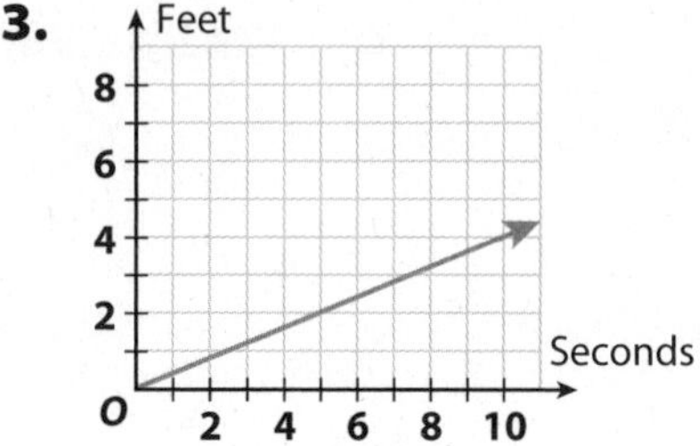

MODULE 17

Nonproportional Relationships

Key Vocabulary

linear equation (*ecuación lineal*)

slope-intercept form of an equation (*forma de pendiente-intersección*)

y-intercept (*intersección con el eje y*)

ESSENTIAL QUESTION

How can you use nonproportional relationships to solve real-world problems?

EXAMPLE 1

Jai is saving to buy his mother a birthday gift. Each week, he saves \$5. He started with \$25. The equation $y = 5x + 25$ gives the total Jai has saved, y, after x weeks. Draw a graph of the equation. Then describe the relationship.

Use the equation to make a table. Then, graph the ordered pairs from the table, and draw a line through the points.

x (weeks)	0	1	2	3	4
y (savings in dollars)	25	30	35	40	45

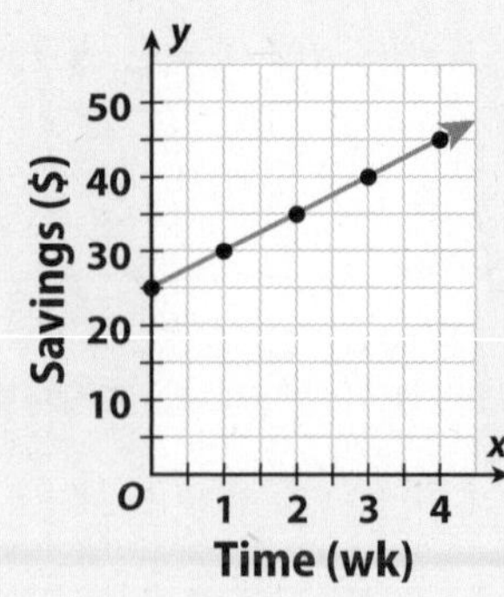

The relationship is linear but nonproportional.

EXAMPLE 2

Graph $y = -\frac{1}{2}x - 2$.

The slope is $\frac{-1}{2}$, or $-\frac{1}{2}$.

The *y*-intercept is −2.

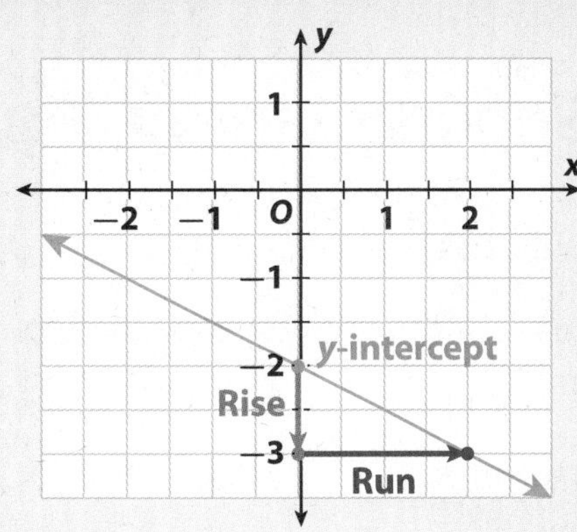

EXERCISES

Complete each table. Explain whether the relationship between *x* and *y* is proportional or nonproportional and whether it is linear. (Lesson 17.1)

1. $y = 10x - 4$

x	0	2		6
y	−4		36	

____

2. $y = -\frac{3}{2}x$

x	0		2	
y		−1.5		−4.5

____

3. Find the slope and *y*-intercept for the linear relationship shown in the table. Graph the line. Is the relationship proportional or nonproportional? (Lessons 17.2, 17.4)

x	−4	−1	0	1
y	−4	2	4	6

slope ____________

y-intercept ____________

The relationship is ______________________.

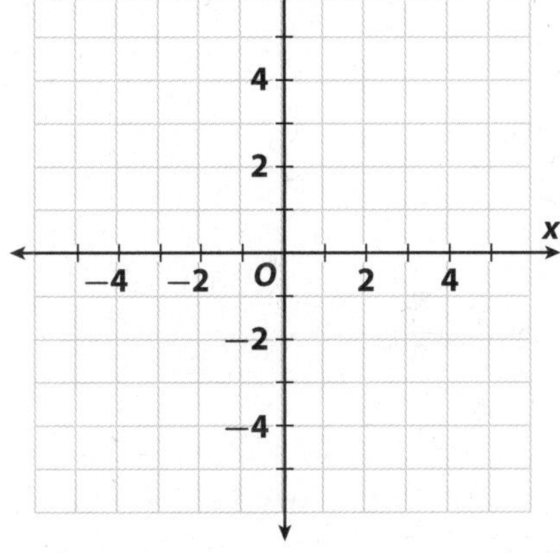

4. Tom's Taxis charges a fixed rate of \$4 per ride plus \$0.50 per mile. Carla's Cabs does not charge a fixed rate but charges \$1.00 per mile. (Lesson 17.3)

a. Write an equation that represents the cost of Tom's Taxis. ____________

b. Write an equation that represents the cost of Carla's cabs. ____________

c. Steve calculated that for the distance he needs to travel, Tom's Taxis will charge the same amount as Carla's Cabs. Graph both equations. How far is Steve going to travel and how much will he pay?

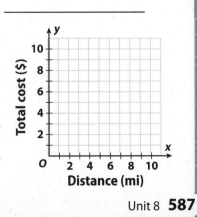

____

____

Total cost ($)
Distance (mi)

Solving Linear Equations

ESSENTIAL QUESTION

How can you use equations with the variable on both sides to solve real-world problems?

EXAMPLE 1

Solve $-2.4(3x + 5) = 0.8(x + 3.5)$.

$-2.4(3x + 5) = 0.8(x + 3.5)$

$10(-2.4)(3x + 5) = 10(0.8)(x + 3.5)$ Multiply each side by 10 to clear some decimals.

$-24(3x + 5) = 8(x + 3.5)$

$-24(3x) - 24(5) = 8(x) + 8(3.5)$ Apply the Distributive Property.

$-72x - 120 = 8x + 28$

$\underline{-8x} \quad \underline{-8x}$ Subtract 8x from both sides of the equation.

$-80x - 120 = 28$

$\underline{+120} \quad \underline{+120}$ Add 120 to both sides of the equation.

$-80x = 148$

$\frac{-80x}{-80} = \frac{148}{-80}$ Divide both sides of the equation by −80.

$x = -1.85$

EXAMPLE 2

Solve $4(3x - 6) = 2(6x - 5)$. Tell whether the equation has one, zero, or infinitely many solutions.

$4(3x - 6) = 2(6x - 5)$

$12x - 24 = 12x - 10$ Apply the Distributive Property.

$\underline{-12x} \quad \underline{-12x}$ Subtract 8x from both sides of the equation.

$-24 = -10$ The statement is false.

There is no value of x that makes a true statement. Therefore, this equation has no solution.

EXERCISES

Solve. (Lessons 18.1, 18.2, 18.3, 18.4)

1. $13.02 - 6y = 8y$

2. $\frac{1}{5}x + 5 = 19 - \frac{1}{2}x$

3. $7.3t + 22 = 2.1t - 22.2$

4. $-7(3 + t) = 4(2t + 6)$

5. $\frac{3}{4}(x + 8) = \frac{1}{3}(x + 27)$

6. $3(4x - 8) = \frac{1}{5}(35x + 30)$

7. $-1.6(2y + 15) = -1.2(2y - 10)$

8. $9(4a - 2) = 12(3a + 8)$

9. $6(x - \frac{1}{3}) = -2(x + 23)$

10. $8(p - 0.25) = 4(2p - 0.5)$

11. $4(x - 8) = 52 - 2x$

12. $0.9z + 8.25 = 1.5(2 + 2z)$

13. $\frac{1}{3}(x + 2) = \frac{1}{3}x + \frac{2}{3}$

14. $1.8(2x + 3) = 3.5(x + 2)$

15. A lawyer charges clients \$75 an hour plus a fixed cost of \$350 to write a contract. Another lawyer charges \$100 an hour plus a fixed cost of \$200.

a. For how many hours of work do the lawyers charge the same amount?

b. What amount do the lawyers charge when they charge the same amount? ____________

16. Miranda and Luci went out to dinner. They each ordered the same sandwich and drink, and they left the same amount of tip. However, Miranda got a dessert for \$2.95, and Luci did not get a dessert. Miranda tipped 15%, and Luci tipped 20%.

a. Write an equation that can be used to find the cost of the sandwich and drink. ____________

b. How much did the sandwich and drink cost? ____________

17. Stewart said that $30 - 10p$ does not equal $5(2p - 6)$ for any value of p. Do you agree with Stewart? Justify Stewart's answer, or explain why he is incorrect.

Unit Project

CA CC 8.EE.5, 8.F.2, 8.F.4

Proportional or Nonproportional?

Many businesses in your community charge a fixed hourly rate for their services. Examples may include plumbers, landscapers, babysitters, party or equipment rental services, and house cleaners. These businesses may also charge a flat service fee, which they add to the total hourly charge.

For this project, choose one such type of business. Research two companies in that business and create a presentation showing the following information:

- The names of the two companies in the business you have chosen, their hourly rates, and their service charges, if any. Explain how you found your information.
- A table of values for each company showing *y*, the total charge (hourly plus service charge, if any) for *x* hours. Each table should include at least eight coordinate pairs (*x*, *y*).
- A graph of each company's data
- For each company, a statement of whether the relationship between time and total cost is proportional or nonproportional, and an explanation of how you reached your conclusion
- An assessment of when one company is less expensive to use than the other

Use the space below to write down any questions you have or important information from your teacher.

MATH IN CAREERS **ACTIVITY**

Cost Estimator A company plans on selling MP3 players for $120. To make the MP3 players, a cost estimator determined it costs the company $1500 per week for overhead and $45 for each MP3 player made. How much profit would the company make if it sold 100 players in one week? Explain.

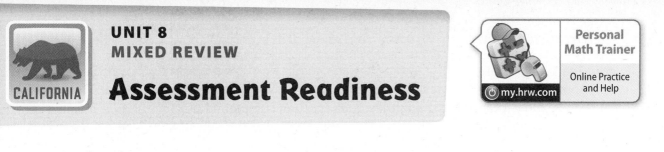

UNIT 8
MIXED REVIEW

Assessment Readiness

1. Does the equation represent a proportional relationship?

Select Yes or No for each equation.

A. $c = 0.6n$ ○ Yes ○ No

B. $s = 28 - 8t$ ○ Yes ○ No

C. $p = 6m + 9m$ ○ Yes ○ No

2. The graph shows the relationship between the number of bicycles a factory has made and the number of hours the factory has been open today.

Choose True or False for each statement.

A. The relationship is proportional. ○ True ○ False

B. The slope of the line is 400. ○ True ○ False

C. If the pattern continues, the factory will make 3200 bicycles in 6 hours. ○ True ○ False

Bicycles made: 400, 800, 1200, 1600 (y); Time since opening (h): O, 2, 4, 6 (x)

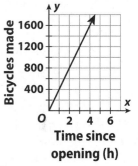

3. A baseball team is ordering caps. The table shows how the cost of a cap depends on the number of colors used in the team logo placed on a cap. Find the rate of change and the initial value of the relationship. Explain how you determined your answer.

Number of Colors, x	Cost of Cap (\$), y
1	19.95
2	22.85
3	25.75
4	28.65

4. Adrian and Rory started comic book collections at the same time. If m represents the number of months since starting the collection and c represents the number of comic books, $c = 12 + 4m$ models Adrian's collection and $c = 8 + 4m$ models Rory's collection. Will they ever have the same number of comic books? If so, after how many months? Explain how you solved this problem.

Performance Tasks

★**5.** The linear equation $y = \frac{1}{4}x + 4$ models the height y in inches of Abby's tomato plant x days after she bought it. Explain how you can use the slope and y-intercept to graph the equation. Then complete the graph.

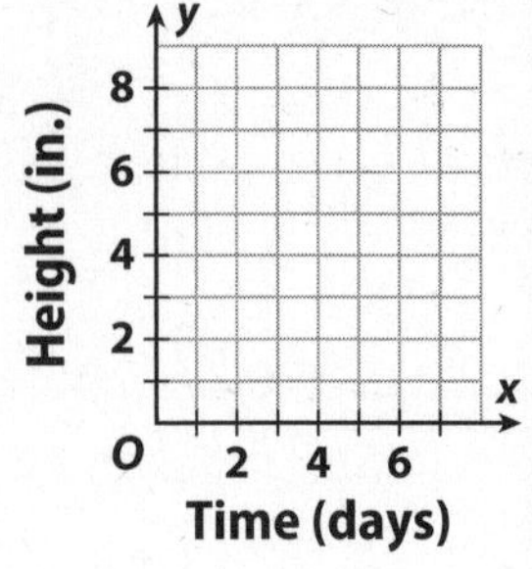

★★**6.** The table shows the amount y remaining on Barry's bus fare card after he has ridden the bus x times.

Bus Rides, x	Amount on Card (\$), y
1	13.50
2	12.00
3	10.50
4	9.00

a. Graph the relationship in the table.

b. Find the slope and y-intercept of the graph.

c. Interpret the meaning of the slope and y-intercept in this situation.

d. Predict the total number of times Barry will be able to ride the bus using his card. Justify your reasoning.

★★★**7.** Hobbs Mules charges \$80 for a 2-hour mule ride and \$144 for a 4-hour mule ride. The table shows how much McGee Mules charges for a mule ride. The relationship between the time in hours and the cost in dollars is linear for both companies.

McGee Mules	
Time (h)	Cost (\$)
0.5	25
1.0	42
1.5	59
2.0	76

a. If a group wants to take a 3-hour mule ride, which company should it choose? Justify your answer.

b. If the group decides to take a 5-hour mule ride instead, would this change your answer to part **a**? Explain your reasoning.

Transformational Geometry

MODULE 19

Transformations and Congruence

CA CC 8.G.1, 8.G.2, 8.G.3

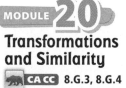

MODULE 20

Transformations and Similarity

CA CC 8.G.3, 8.G.4

MATH IN CAREERS

Contractor A contractor is engaged in the construction, repair, and dismantling of structures such as buildings, bridges, and roads. Contractors use math when researching and implementing building codes, making measurements and scaling models, and in financial management.

If you are interested in a career as a contractor, you should study the following mathematical subjects:

- Business Math
- Geometry
- Algebra
- Trigonometry

Research other careers that require the use of business math and scaling.

ACTIVITY At the end of the unit, check out how **contractors** use math.

Unit Project Preview

Transforming the World

The Unit Project at the end of this unit will ask you to extend your understanding of a mathematical concept to everyday life. In the project, you will look for real-world examples of translations, rotations, and reflections. To successfully complete the Unit Project you'll need to master these skills:

- Understand and identify translations.
- Understand and identify rotations.
- Understand and identify reflections.

1. Describe the pattern that you see in the kaleidoscope image.

____

____

____

____

____

2. What is the "reflection" of a figure?

____

____

____

____

Tracking Your Learning Progression

This unit addresses important California Common Core Standards in the Critical Area of understanding and applying congruence and similarity.

Domain **8.G** Geometry

Cluster Understand congruence and similarity using physical models, transparencies, or geometry software.

Transformations and Congruence

ESSENTIAL QUESTION

How can you use transformations and congruence to solve real-world problems?

Real-World Video

my.hrw.com

When a marching band lines up and marches across the field, they are modeling a translation. As they march, they maintain size and orientation. A translation is one type of transformation.

GO DIGITAL
my.hrw.com

my.hrw.com

Go digital with your write-in student edition, accessible on any device.

Math On the Spot

Scan with your smart phone to jump directly to the online edition, video tutor, and more.

Animated Math

Interactively explore key concepts to see how math works.

Personal Math Trainer

Get immediate feedback and help as you work through practice sets.

Are YOU Ready?

Complete these exercises to review skills you will need for this module.

Personal Math Trainer

Online Practice and Help

Integer Operations

EXAMPLE $-3 - (-6) = -3 + 6$ To subtract an integer, add its opposite.

$= |-3| - |6|$ The signs are different, so find the difference of the absolute values: $6 - 3 = 3$.

$= 3$ Use the sign of the number with the greater absolute value.

Find each difference.

1. $5 - (-9)$ ________

2. $-6 - 8$ ________

3. $2 - 9$ ________

4. $-10 - (-6)$ ________

5. $3 - (-11)$ ________

6. $12 - 7$ ________

7. $-4 - 11$ ________

8. $0 - (-12)$ ________

Measure Angles

EXAMPLE

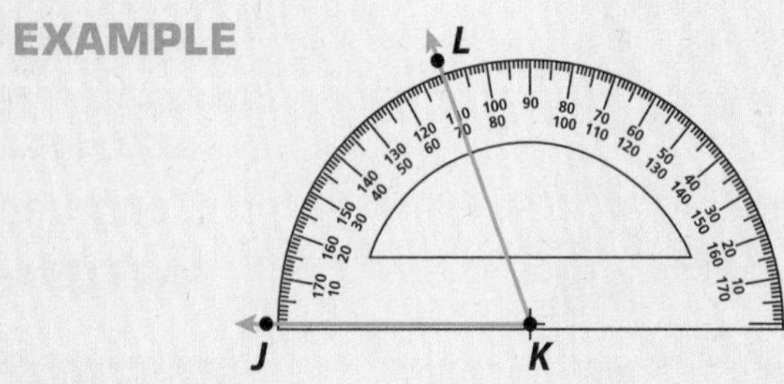

$m\angle JKL = 70°$

Place the center point of the protractor on the angle's vertex.

Align one ray with the base of the protractor.

Read the angle measure where the other ray intersects the semicircle.

Use a protractor to measure each angle.

9.

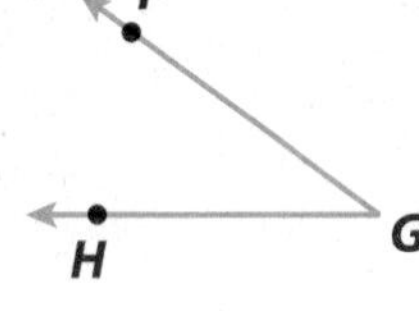

____

10.

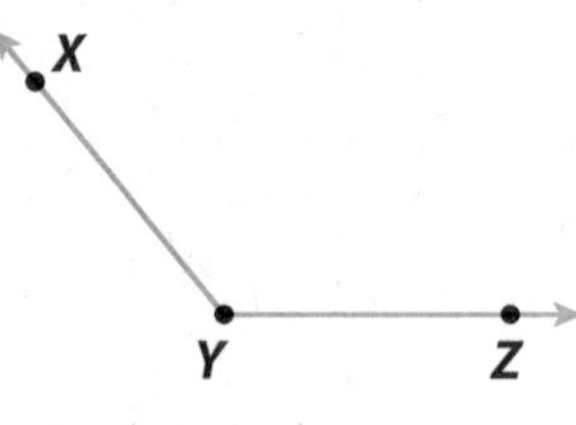

____

11.

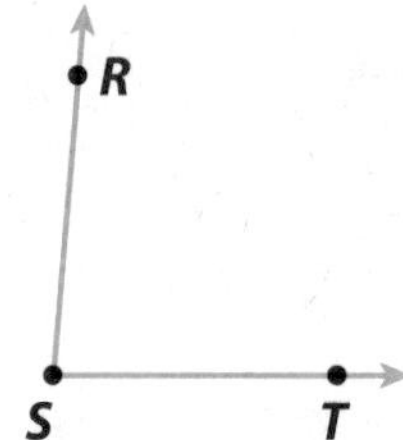

____

Reading Start-Up

Visualize Vocabulary

Use the ✔ words to complete the graphic organizer. You will put one word in each oval.

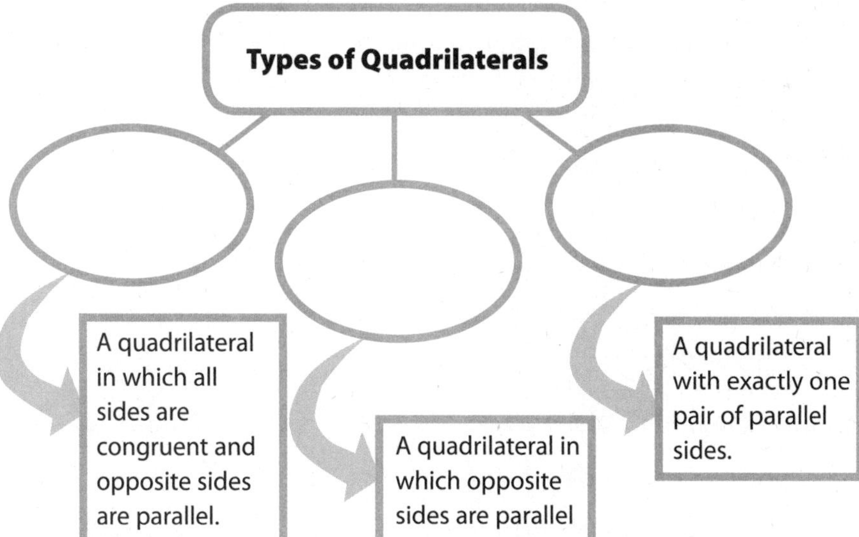

Types of Quadrilaterals
A quadrilateral in which all sides are congruent and opposite sides are parallel.
A quadrilateral in which opposite sides are parallel and congruent.
A quadrilateral with exactly one pair of parallel sides.

Understand Vocabulary

Match the term on the left to the correct expression on the right.

1. transformation **A.** A function that describes a change in the position, size, or shape of a figure.

2. reflection **B.** A function that slides a figure along a straight line.

3. translation **C.** A transformation that flips a figure across a line.

Vocabulary

Review Words

coordinate plane *(plano cartesiano)*
✔ parallelogram *(paralelogramo)*
quadrilateral *(cuadrilátero)*
✔ rhombus *(rombo)*
✔ trapezoid *(trapecio)*

Preview Words

center of rotation *(centro de rotación)*
congruent *(congruente)*
image *(imagen)*
line of reflection *(línea de reflexión)*
preimage *(imagen original)*
reflection *(reflexión)*
rotation *(rotación)*
transformation *(transformación)*
translation *(traslación)*

Active Reading

Booklet Before beginning the module, create a booklet to help you learn the concepts in this module. Write the main idea of each lesson on each page of the booklet. As you study each lesson, write important details that support the main idea, such as vocabulary and formulas. Refer to your finished booklet as you work on assignments and study for tests.

GETTING READY FOR

Transformations and Congruence

Understanding the standards and the vocabulary terms in the standards will help you know exactly what you are expected to learn in this module.

CA CC 8.G.2

Understand that a two-dimensional figure is congruent to another if the second can be obtained from the first by a sequence of rotations, reflections, and translations; given two congruent figures, describe a sequence that exhibits the congruence between them.

What It Means to You

You will identify a rotation, a reflection, a translation, and a sequence of transformations, and understand that the image has the same shape and size as the preimage.

EXAMPLE 8.G.2

The figure shows triangle *ABC* and its image after three different transformations. Identify and describe the translation, the reflection, and the rotation of triangle *ABC*.

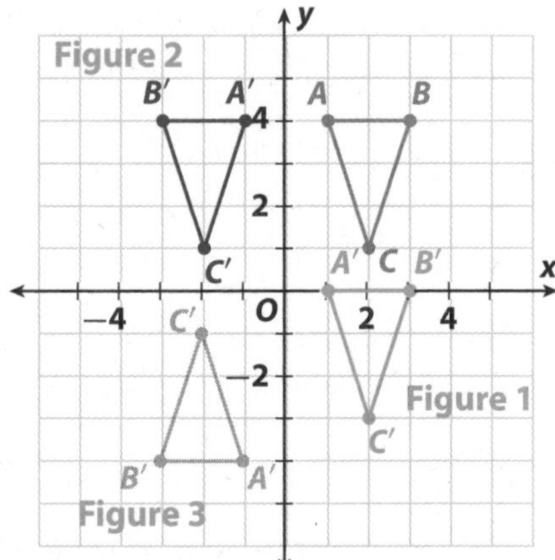

Figure 1 is a translation 4 units down. Figure 2 is a reflection across the *y*-axis. Figure 3 is a rotation of 180°.

CA CC 8.G.3

Describe the effect of dilations, translations, rotations, and reflections on two-dimensional figures using coordinates.

What It Means to You

You can use an algebraic representation to translate, reflect, or rotate a two-dimensional figure.

EXAMPLE 8.G.3

Rectangle *RSTU* with vertices (−4, 1), (−1, 1), (−1, −3), and (−4, −3) is reflected across the *y*-axis. Find the coordinates of the image.

The rule to reflect across the *y*-axis is to change the sign of the *x*-coordinate.

Coordinates	Reflect across the *y*-axis (−*x*, *y*)	Coordinates of image
(−4, 1), (−1, 1), (−1, −3), (−4, −3)	(−(−4), 1), (−(−1), 1), (− (−1), −3), (−(−4), −3)	(4, 1), (1, 1), (1, −3), (4, −3)

The coordinates of the image are (4, 1), (1, 1), (1, −3), and (4, −3).

Visit **my.hrw.com** to see all **CA Common Core Standards** explained.

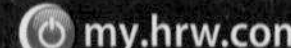

LESSON 19.1
Properties of Translations

CA CC 8.G.1a

Verify experimentally the properties of rotations, reflections, and translations: Lines are taken to lines, and line segments to line segments of the same length. *Also 8.G.1b, 8.G.1c, 8.G.3*

ESSENTIAL QUESTION

How do you describe the properties of translation and their effect on the congruence and orientation of figures?

EXPLORE ACTIVITY 1 

CA CC 8.G.1a

Exploring Translations

You learned that a function is a rule that assigns exactly one output to each input. A **transformation** is a function that describes a change in the position, size, or shape of a figure. The input of a transformation is the **preimage**, and the output of a transformation is the **image**.

A **translation** is a transformation that slides a figure along a straight line.

The triangle shown on the grid is the preimage (input). The arrow shows the motion of a translation and how point *A* is translated to point *A*′.

A Trace triangle *ABC* and line *AA*′ onto a piece of paper.

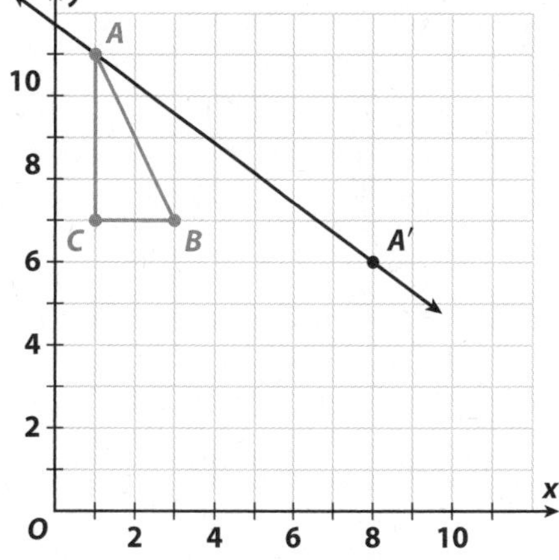

B Slide your triangle along the line to model the translation that maps point *A* to point *A*′.

C The image of the translation is the triangle produced by the translation. Sketch the image of the translation.

D The vertices of the image are labeled using prime notation. For example, the image of *A* is *A*′. Label the images of points *B* and *C*.

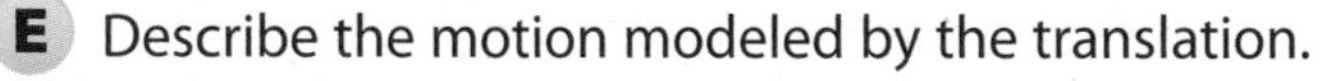

E Describe the motion modeled by the translation.

Move __________ units right and __________ units down.

F Check that the motion you described in part **E** is the same motion that maps point *A* onto *A*′, point *B* onto *B*′, and point *C* onto *C*′.

Reflect

1. How is the orientation of the triangle affected by the translation?

____

EXPLORE ACTIVITY 2 CA CC 8.G.1a

Properties of Translations

Use trapezoid *TRAP* to investigate the properties of translations.

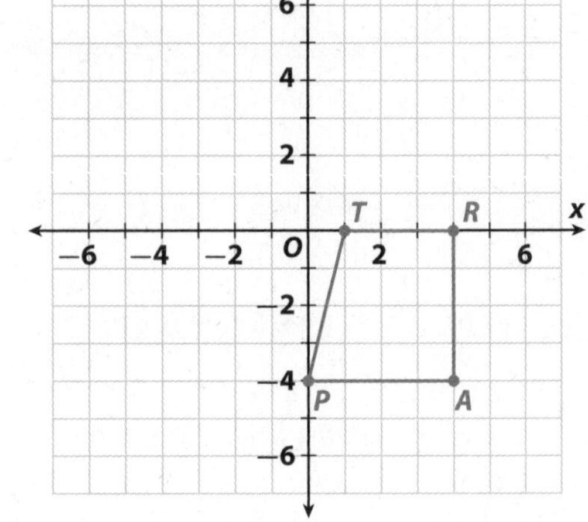

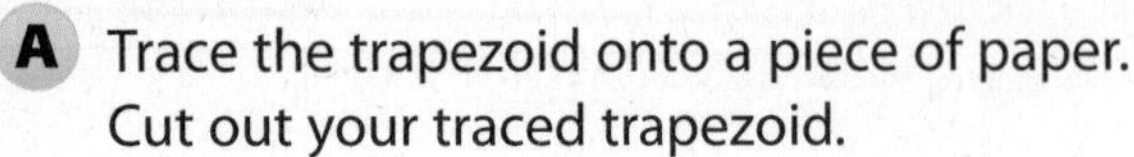

A Trace the trapezoid onto a piece of paper. Cut out your traced trapezoid.

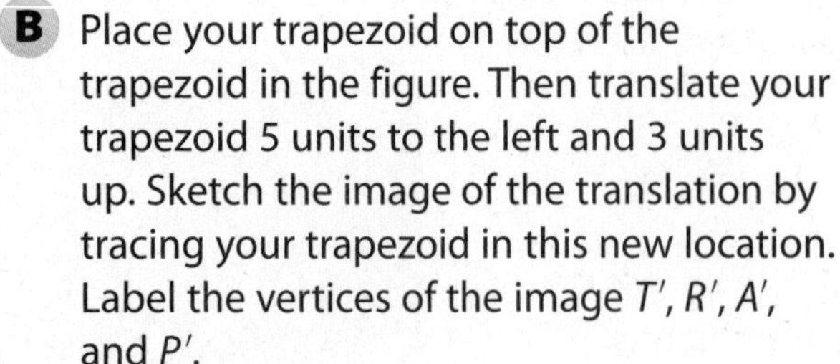

B Place your trapezoid on top of the trapezoid in the figure. Then translate your trapezoid 5 units to the left and 3 units up. Sketch the image of the translation by tracing your trapezoid in this new location. Label the vertices of the image T', R', A', and P'.

C Use a ruler to measure the sides of trapezoid *TRAP* in centimeters.

$TR =$ ________ $RA =$ ________ $AP =$ ________ $TP =$ ________

D Use a ruler to measure the sides of trapezoid $T'R'A'P'$ in centimeters.

$T'R' =$ ________ $R'A' =$ ________ $A'P' =$ ________ $T'P' =$ ________

E What do you notice about the lengths of corresponding sides of the two figures?

____

F Use a protractor to measure the angles of trapezoid *TRAP*.

$m\angle T =$ ______ $m\angle R =$ ______ $m\angle A =$ ______ $m\angle P =$ ______

G Use a protractor to measure the angles of trapezoid $T'R'A'P'$.

$m\angle T' =$ ______ $m\angle R' =$ ______ $m\angle A' =$ ______ $m\angle P' =$ ______

H What do you notice about the measures of corresponding angles of the two figures?

____

I Which sides of trapezoid *TRAP* are parallel? How do you know?

____

Which sides of trapezoid $T'R'A'P'$ are parallel? ________________

What do you notice? ________________________________

____

Reflect

2. **Make a Conjecture** Use your results from parts **E**, **H**, and **I** to make a conjecture about translations.

3. Two figures that have the same size and shape are called *congruent*. What can you say about translations and congruence?

Graphing Translations

To translate a figure in the coordinate plane, translate each of its vertices. Then connect the vertices to form the image.

Math On the Spot
my.hrw.com

EXAMPLE 1

CA CC 8.G.3

The figure shows triangle *XYZ*. Graph the image of the triangle after a translation of 4 units to the right and 1 unit up.

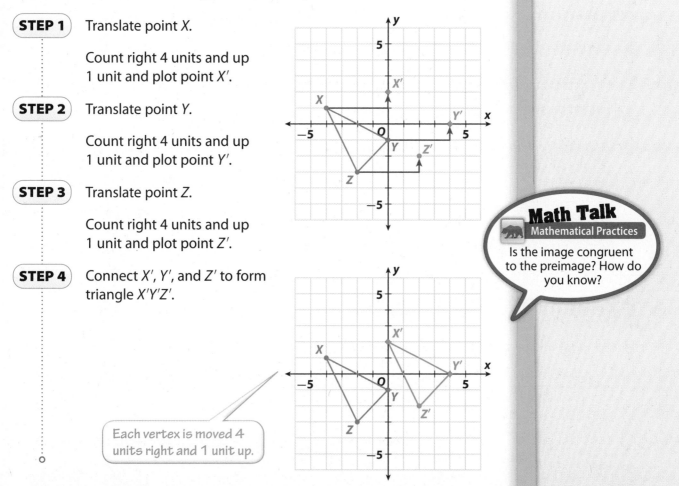

STEP 1 Translate point X.

Count right 4 units and up 1 unit and plot point X'.

STEP 2 Translate point Y.

Count right 4 units and up 1 unit and plot point Y'.

STEP 3 Translate point Z.

Count right 4 units and up 1 unit and plot point Z'.

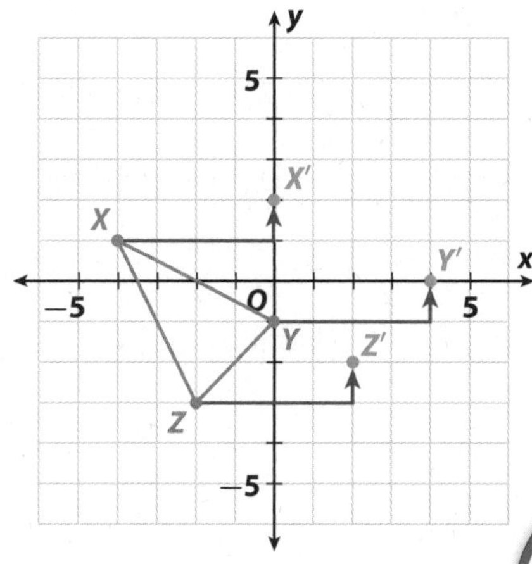

STEP 4 Connect X', Y', and Z' to form triangle $X'Y'Z'$.

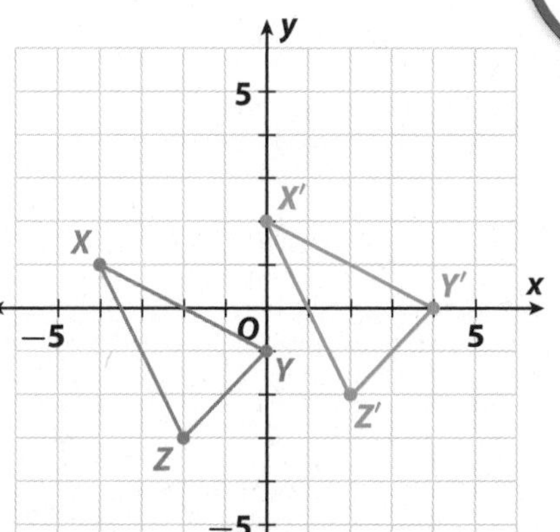

Each vertex is moved 4 units right and 1 unit up.

Math Talk
Mathematical Practices

Is the image congruent to the preimage? How do you know?

YOUR TURN

4. The figure shows parallelogram *ABCD*. Graph the image of the parallelogram after a translation of 5 units to the left and 2 units down.

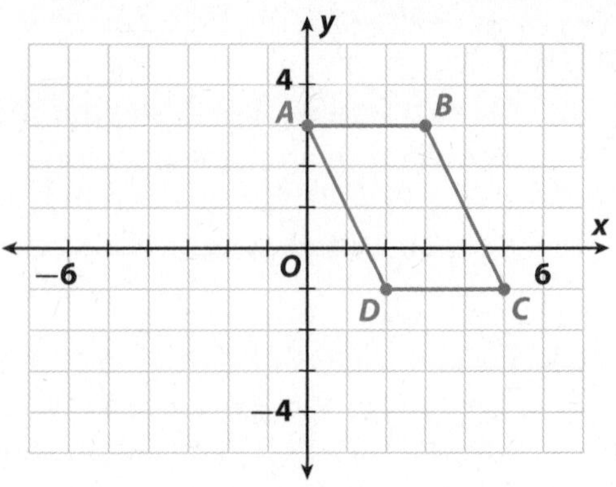

Guided Practice

1. **Vocabulary** A ____________________ is a change in the position, size, or shape of a figure.

2. **Vocabulary** When you perform a transformation of a figure on the coordinate plane, the input of the transformation is called the ____________________, and the output of the transformation is called the ____________________.

3. Joni translates a right triangle 2 units down and 4 units to the right. How does the orientation of the image of the triangle compare with the orientation of the preimage? (Explore Activity 1)

____

4. Rashid drew rectangle *PQRS* on a coordinate plane. He then translated the rectangle 3 units up and 3 units to the left and labeled the image *P'Q'R'S'*. How do rectangle *PQRS* and rectangle *P'Q'R'S'* compare? (Explore Activity 2)

____

5. The figure shows trapezoid *WXYZ*. Graph the image of the trapezoid after a translation of 4 units up and 2 units to the left. (Example 1)

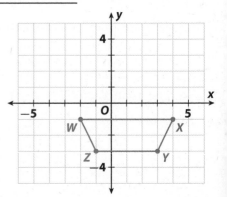

ESSENTIAL QUESTION CHECK-IN

6. What are the properties of translations?

____

____

Name ________________ Class ________________ Date ________________

19.1 Independent Practice

CA CC 8.G.1a, 8.G.1b, 8.G.1c, 8.G.3

Personal Math Trainer
my.hrw.com
Online Practice and Help

7. The figure shows triangle *DEF*.

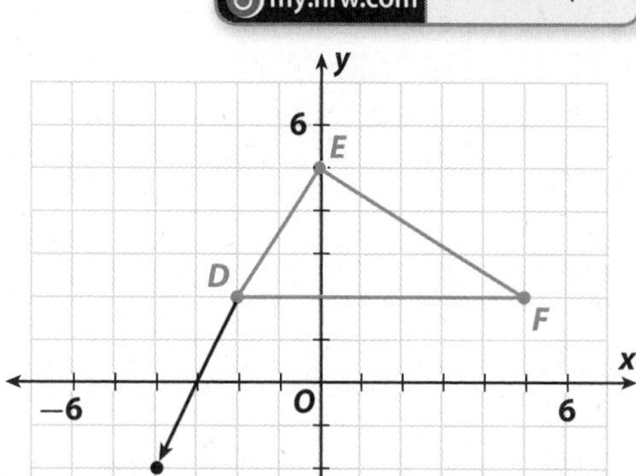

a. Graph the image of the triangle after the translation that maps point *D* to point *D′*.

b. How would you describe the translation?

____

____

c. How does the image of triangle *DEF* compare with the preimage?

____

8. a. Graph quadrilateral *KLMN* with vertices *K*(−3, 2), *L*(2, 2), *M*(0, −3), and *N*(−4, 0) on the coordinate grid.

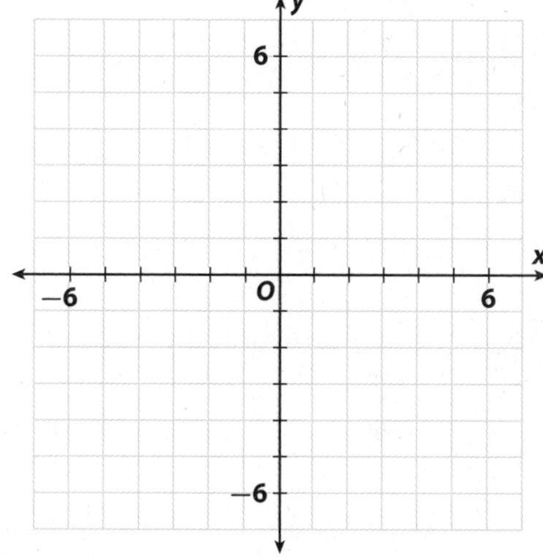

b. On the same coordinate grid, graph the image of quadrilateral *KLMN* after a translation of 3 units to the right and 4 units up.

c. Which side of the image is congruent to side $\overline{LM}$?

____

Name three other pairs of congruent sides.

____

Draw the image of the figure after each translation.

9. 4 units left and 2 units down

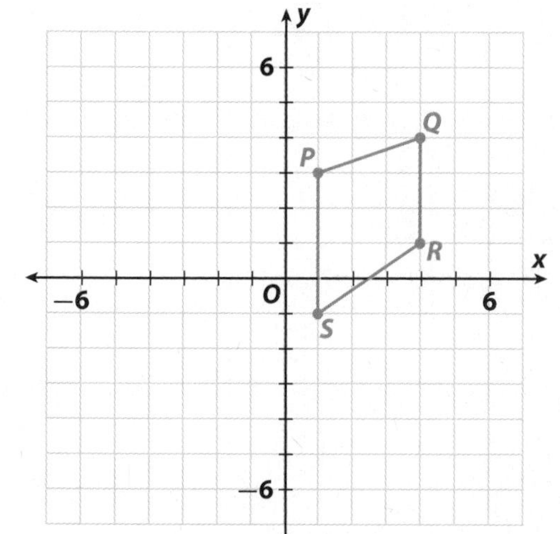

10. 5 units right and 3 units up

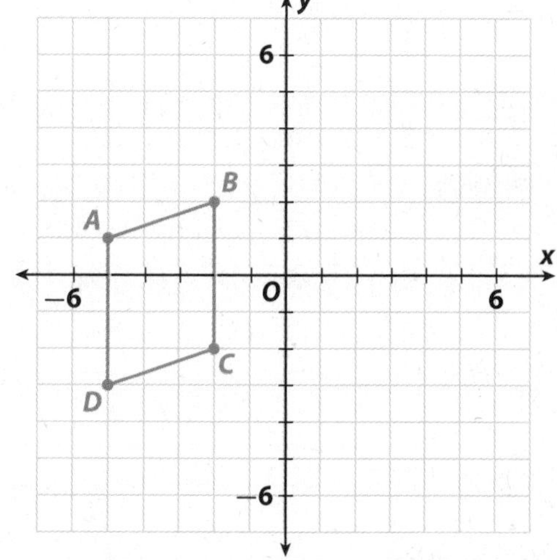

11. The figure shows the ascent of a hot air balloon. How would you describe the translation?

____

____

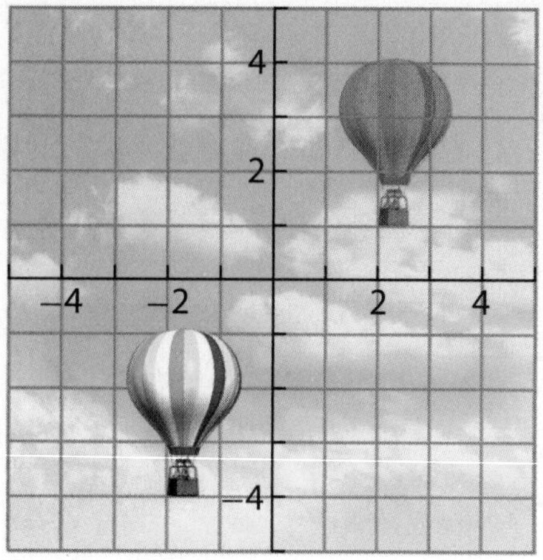

12. **Critical Thinking** Is it possible that the orientation of a figure could change after it is translated? Explain.

____

____

____

H.O.T. FOCUS ON HIGHER ORDER THINKING

13. a. **Multistep** Graph triangle XYZ with vertices $X(-2, -5)$, $Y(2, -2)$, and $Z(4, -4)$ on the coordinate grid.

b. On the same coordinate grid, graph and label triangle $X'Y'Z'$, the image of triangle XYZ after a translation of 3 units to the left and 6 units up.

c. Now graph and label triangle $X''Y''Z''$, the image of triangle $X'Y'Z'$ after a translation of 1 unit to the left and 2 units down.

d. **Analyze Relationships** How would you describe the translation that maps triangle XYZ onto triangle $X''Y''Z''$?

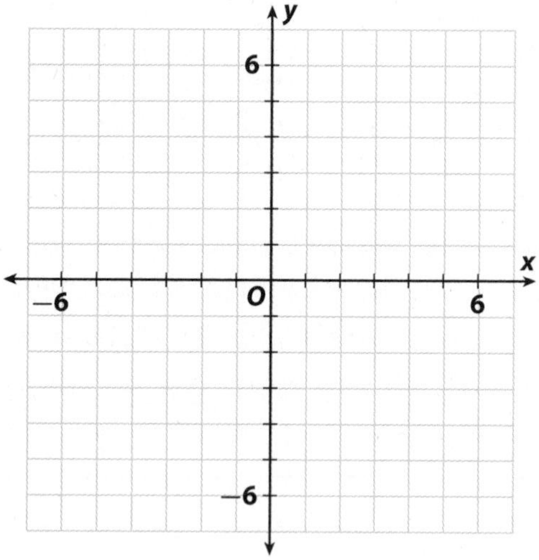

____

____

14. **Critical Thinking** The figure shows rectangle $P'Q'R'S'$, the image of rectangle $PQRS$ after a translation of 5 units to the right and 7 units up. Graph and label the preimage $PQRS$.

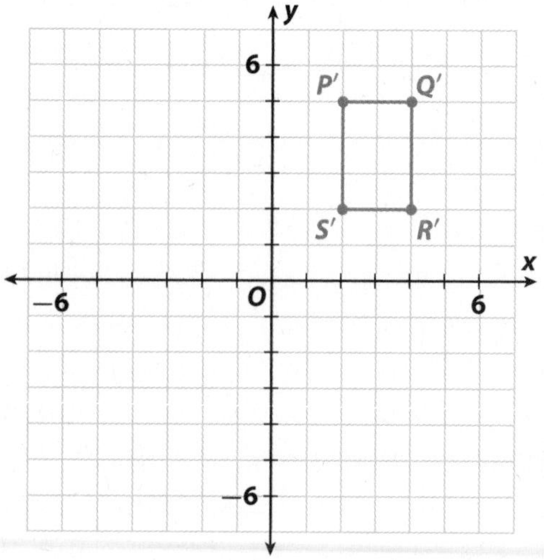

15. **Communicate Mathematical Ideas** Explain why the image of a figure after a translation is congruent to its preimage.

____

____

____

____

____

LESSON 19.2

Properties of Reflections

CA CC 8.G.1b

Verify experimentally the properties of rotations, reflections, and translations: Angles are taken to angles of the same measure. *Also 8.G.1a, 8.G.1c, 8.G.3*

ESSENTIAL QUESTION

How do you describe the properties of reflection and their effect on the congruence and orientation of figures?

EXPLORE ACTIVITY 1  CA CC 8.G.1b

Exploring Reflections

A **reflection** is a transformation that flips a figure across a line. The line is called the **line of reflection**. Each point and its image are the same distance from the line of reflection.

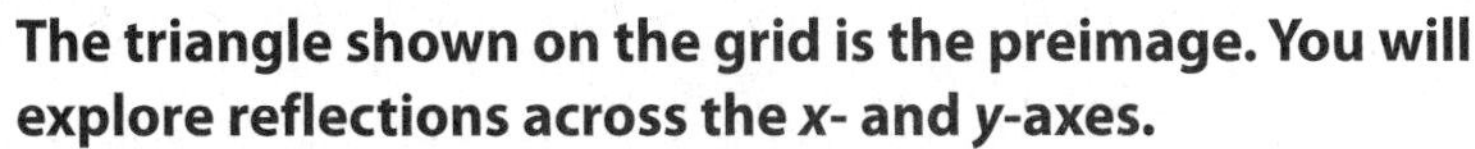

The triangle shown on the grid is the preimage. You will explore reflections across the *x*- and *y*-axes.

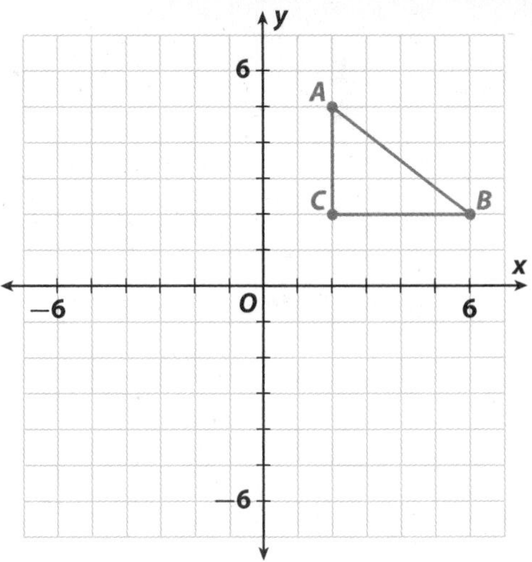

A Trace triangle *ABC* and the *x*- and *y*-axes onto a piece of paper.

B Fold your paper along the *x*-axis and trace the image of the triangle on the opposite side of the *x*-axis. Unfold your paper and label the vertices of the image *A*′, *B*′, and *C*′.

C What is the line of reflection for this transformation?

____

D Find the perpendicular distance from each point to the line of reflection.

Point *A* ________ Point *B* ________ Point *C* ________

E Find the perpendicular distance from each point to the line of reflection.

Point *A*′ ________ Point *B*′ ________ Point *C*′ ________

F What do you notice about the distances you found in **D** and **E**?

____

Reflect

1. Fold your paper from **A** along the *y*-axis and trace the image of triangle *ABC* on the opposite side. Label the vertices of the image *A*″, *B*″, and *C*″. What is the line of reflection for this transformation? ________

2. How does each image in your drawings compare with its preimage?

____

EXPLORE ACTIVITY 2 CA CC 8.G.1b

Properties of Reflections

Use trapezoid *TRAP* to investigate the properties of reflections.

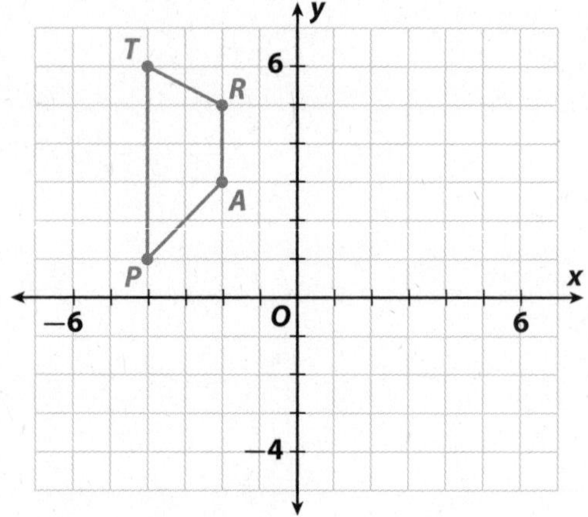

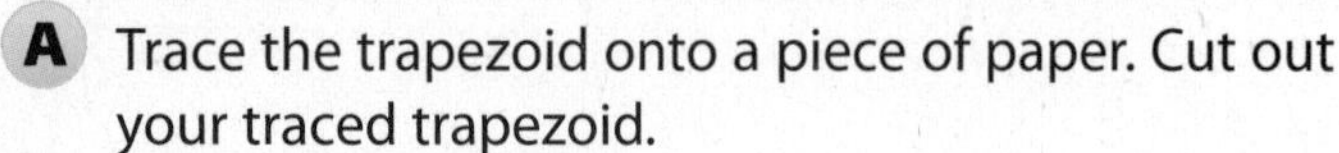

A Trace the trapezoid onto a piece of paper. Cut out your traced trapezoid.

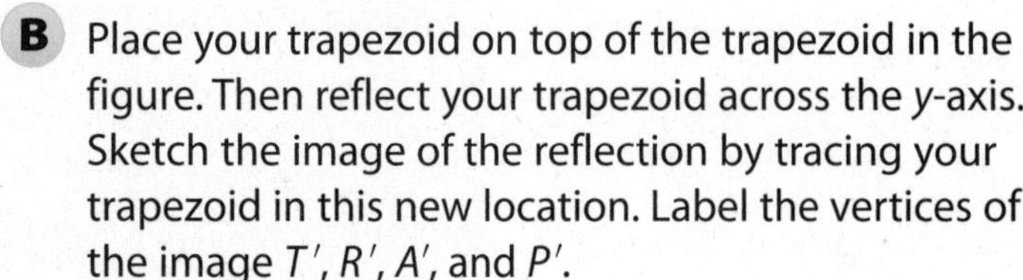

B Place your trapezoid on top of the trapezoid in the figure. Then reflect your trapezoid across the *y*-axis. Sketch the image of the reflection by tracing your trapezoid in this new location. Label the vertices of the image T', R', A', and P'.

C Use a ruler to measure the sides of trapezoid *TRAP* in centimeters.

$TR =$ ________ $RA =$ ________ $AP =$ ________ $TP =$ ________

D Use a ruler to measure the sides of trapezoid $T'R'A'P'$ in centimeters.

$T'R' =$ ________ $R'A' =$ ________ $A'P' =$ ________ $T'P' =$ ________

E What do you notice about the lengths of corresponding sides of the two figures?

____

____

F Use a protractor to measure the angles of trapezoid *TRAP*.

$m\angle T =$ ______ $m\angle R =$ ______ $m\angle A =$ ______ $m\angle P =$ ______

G Use a protractor to measure the angles of trapezoid $T'R'A'P'$.

$m\angle T' =$ ______ $m\angle R' =$ ______ $m\angle A' =$ ______ $m\angle P' =$ ______

H What do you notice about the measures of corresponding angles of the two figures?

____

____

I Which sides of trapezoid *TRAP* are parallel? ____________________

Which sides of trapezoid $T'R'A'P'$ are parallel? ____________________
What do you notice?

____

____

Reflect

3. **Make a Conjecture** Use your results from **E**, **H**, and **I** to make a conjecture about reflections.

____

____

____

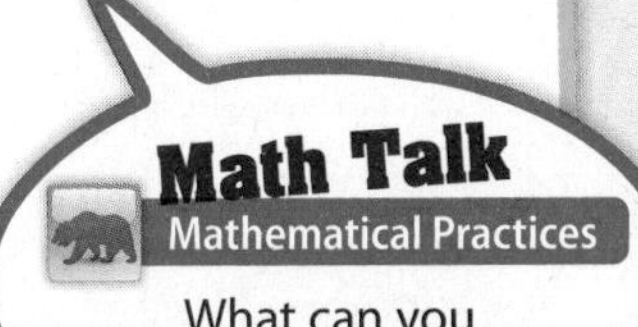

Math Talk
Mathematical Practices
What can you say about reflections and congruence?

Graphing Reflections

To reflect a figure across a line of reflection, reflect each of its vertices. Then connect the vertices to form the image. Remember that each point and its image are the same distance from the line of reflection.

EXAMPLE 1

CA CC 8.G.3

The figure shows triangle *XYZ*. Graph the image of the triangle after a reflection across the *x*-axis.

STEP 1 Reflect point *X*.

Point *X* is 3 units below the *x*-axis. Count 3 units above the *x*-axis and plot point *X′*.

STEP 2 Reflect point *Y*.

Point *Y* is 1 unit below the *x*-axis. Count 1 unit above the *x*-axis and plot point *Y′*.

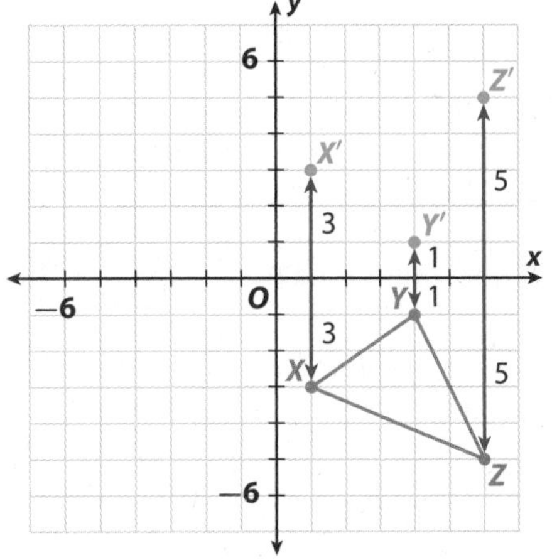

STEP 3 Reflect point *Z*.

Point *Z* is 5 units below the *x*-axis. Count 5 units above the *x*-axis and plot point *Z′*.

STEP 4 Connect *X′*, *Y′*, and *Z′* to form triangle *X′Y′Z′*.

Each vertex of the image is the same distance from the *x*-axis as the corresponding vertex in the original figure.

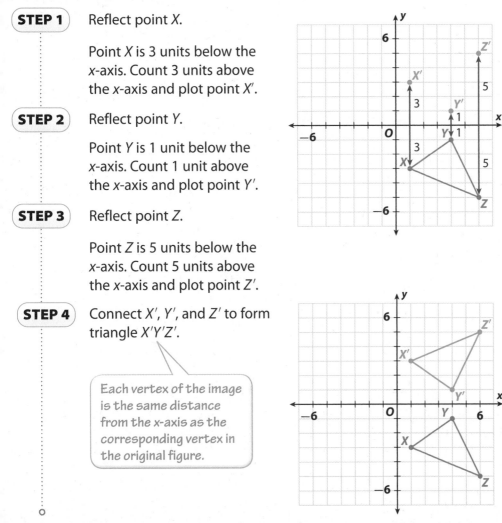

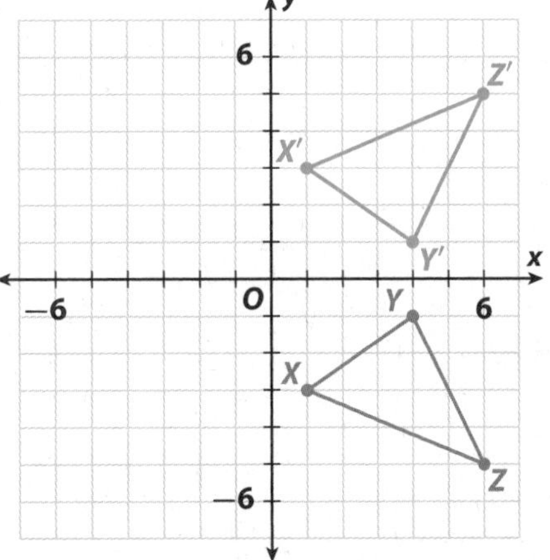

My Notes

YOUR TURN

4. The figure shows pentagon *ABCDE*. Graph the image of the pentagon after a reflection across the *y*-axis.

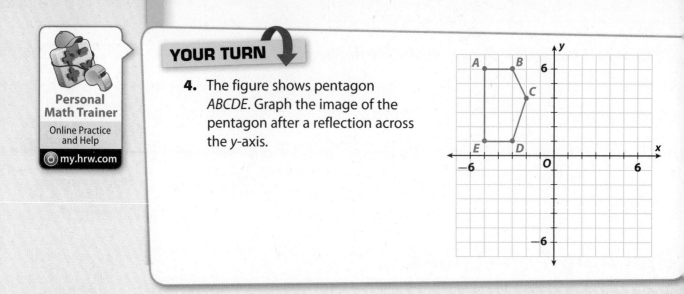

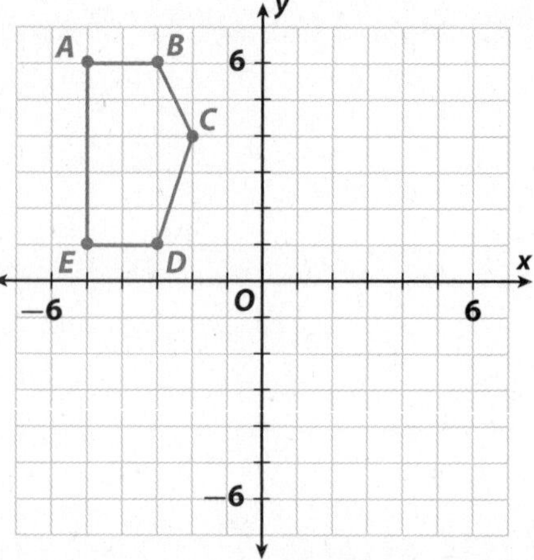

Guided Practice

1. **Vocabulary** A reflection is a transformation that flips a figure across a line called the ________________.

2. The figure shows trapezoid *ABCD*. (Explore Activities 1 and 2 and Example 1)

   a. Graph the image of the trapezoid after a reflection across the *x*-axis. Label the vertices of the image.

   b. How do trapezoid *ABCD* and trapezoid *A'B'C'D'* compare?

   ____

   c. **What If?** Suppose you reflected trapezoid *ABCD* across the *y*-axis. How would the orientation of the image of the trapezoid compare with the orientation of the preimage?

   ____

   ____

   ____

   ____

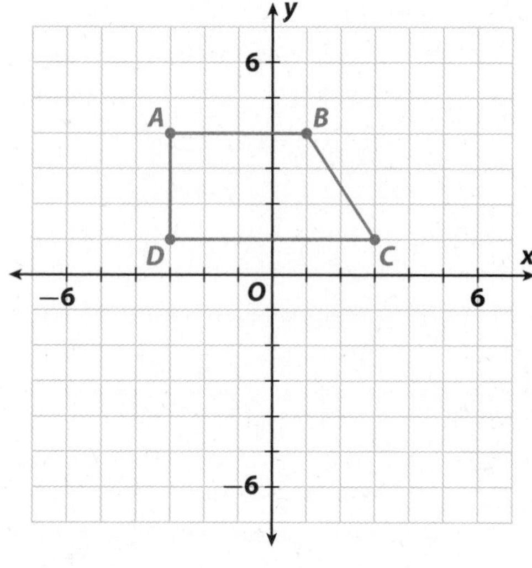

ESSENTIAL QUESTION CHECK-IN

3. What are the properties of reflections?

____

____

Name ______________________ Class ______________ Date ______________

19.2 Independent Practice

CA CC 8.G.1a, 8.G.1b, 8.G.1c, 8.G.3

The graph shows four right triangles. Use the graph for Exercises 4–7.

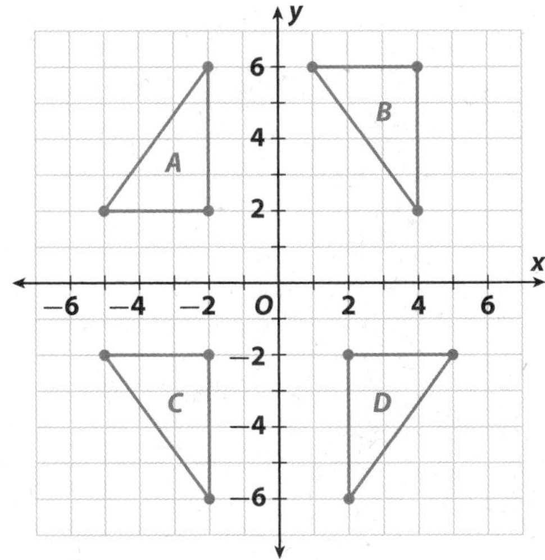

4. Which two triangles are reflections of each other across the x-axis?

____

5. For which two triangles is the line of reflection the y-axis?

____

6. Which triangle is a translation of triangle C? How would you describe the translation?

____

7. Which triangles are congruent? How do you know?

____

8. a. Graph quadrilateral $WXYZ$ with vertices $W(-2, -2)$, $X(3, 1)$, $Y(5, -1)$, and $Z(4, -6)$ on the coordinate grid.

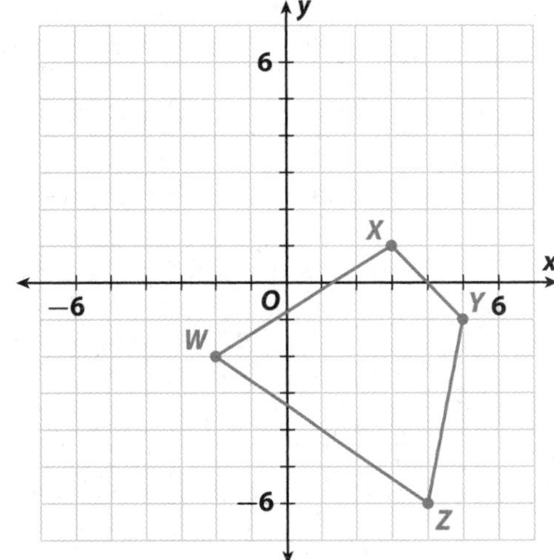

b. On the same coordinate grid, graph quadrilateral $W'X'Y'Z'$, the image of quadrilateral $WXYZ$ after a reflection across the x-axis.

c. Which side of the image is congruent to side $\overline{YZ}$?

____

Name three other pairs of congruent sides.

____

d. Which angle of the image is congruent to $\angle X$?

____

Name three other pairs of congruent angles.

____

9. **Critical Thinking** Is it possible that the image of a point after a reflection could be the same point as the preimage? Explain.

____

____

FOCUS ON HIGHER ORDER THINKING

10. **a.** Graph the image of the figure shown after a reflection across the *y*-axis.

b. On the same coordinate grid, graph the image of the figure you drew in part **a** after a reflection across the *x*-axis.

c. **Make a Conjecture** What other sequence of transformations would produce the same final image from the original preimage? Check your answer by performing the transformations. Then make a conjecture that generalizes your findings.

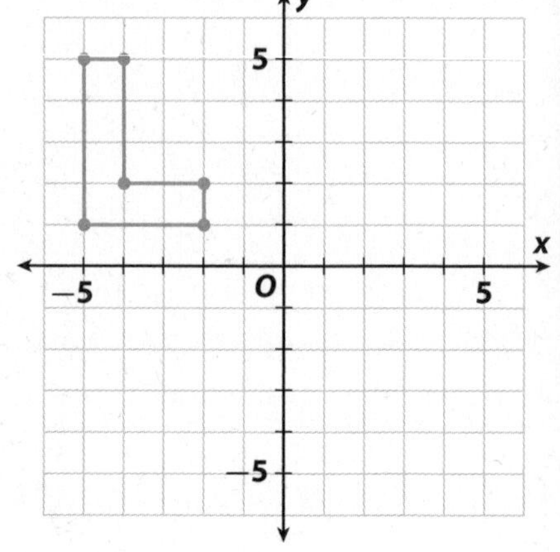

____

____

____

____

____

____

11. **a.** Graph triangle *DEF* with vertices *D*(2, 6), *E*(5, 6), and *F*(5, 1) on the coordinate grid.

b. Next graph triangle *D′E′F′*, the image of triangle *DEF* after a reflection across the *y*-axis.

c. On the same coordinate grid, graph triangle *D″E″F″*, the image of triangle *D′E′F′* after a translation of 7 units down and 2 units to the right.

d. **Analyze Relationships** Find a different sequence of transformations that will transform triangle *DEF* to triangle *D″E″F″*.

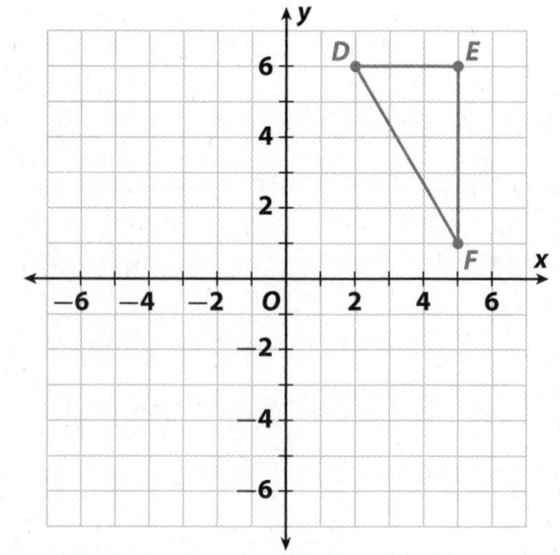

____

____

____

____

LESSON 19.3

Properties of Rotations

CA CC 8.G.1c

Verify experimentally the properties of rotations, reflections, and translations: Parallel lines are taken to parallel lines. *Also 8.G.1a, 8.G.1b, 8.G.3*

ESSENTIAL QUESTION

How do you describe the properties of rotation and their effect on the congruence and orientation of figures?

EXPLORE ACTIVITY 1 CA CC 8.G.1c

Exploring Rotations

A **rotation** is a transformation that turns a figure around a given point called the **center of rotation**. The image has the same size and shape as the preimage.

The triangle shown on the grid is the preimage. You will use the origin as the center of rotation.

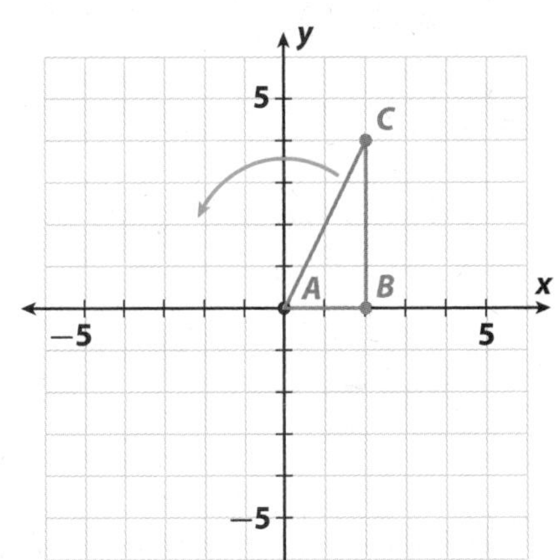

A Trace triangle *ABC* onto a piece of paper. Cut out your traced triangle.

B Rotate your triangle 90° counterclockwise about the origin. The side of the triangle that lies along the *x*-axis should now lie along the *y*-axis.

C Sketch the image of the rotation. Label the images of points *A*, *B*, and *C* as *A′*, *B′*, and *C′*.

D Describe the motion modeled by the rotation.

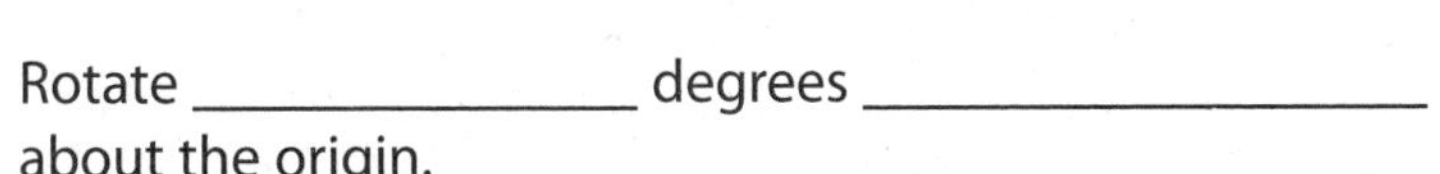

Rotate ________________ degrees ____________________ about the origin.

E Check that the motion you described in **D** is the same motion that maps point *A* onto *A′*, point *B* onto *B′*, and point *C* onto *C′*.

Reflect

1. **Communicate Mathematical Ideas** How are the size and the orientation of the triangle affected by the rotation?

____

____

____

2. Rotate triangle *ABC* 90° clockwise about the origin. Sketch the result on the coordinate grid above. Label the image vertices *A″*, *B″*, and *C″*.

EXPLORE ACTIVITY 2 CA CC 8.G.1c

Properties of Rotations

Use trapezoid *TRAP* to investigate the properties of rotations.

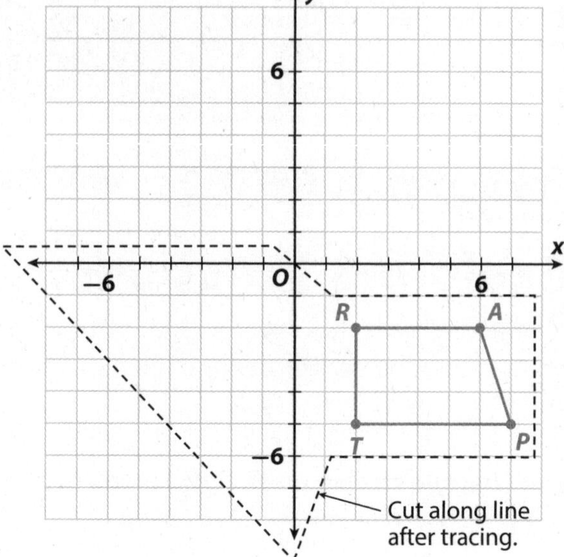

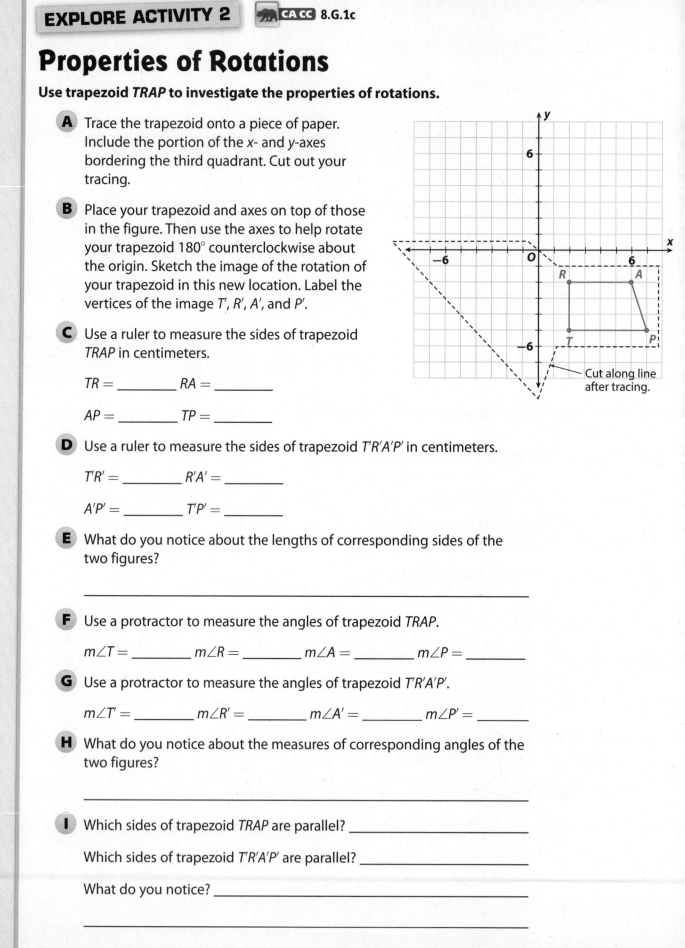

A Trace the trapezoid onto a piece of paper. Include the portion of the *x*- and *y*-axes bordering the third quadrant. Cut out your tracing.

B Place your trapezoid and axes on top of those in the figure. Then use the axes to help rotate your trapezoid 180° counterclockwise about the origin. Sketch the image of the rotation of your trapezoid in this new location. Label the vertices of the image T', R', A', and P'.

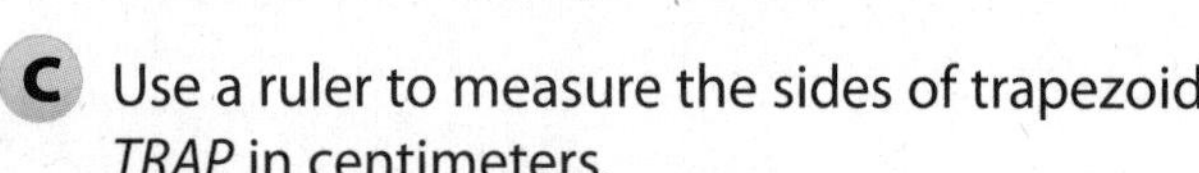

C Use a ruler to measure the sides of trapezoid *TRAP* in centimeters.

$TR =$ ________ $RA =$ ________

$AP =$ ________ $TP =$ ________

D Use a ruler to measure the sides of trapezoid $T'R'A'P'$ in centimeters.

$T'R' =$ ________ $R'A' =$ ________

$A'P' =$ ________ $T'P' =$ ________

E What do you notice about the lengths of corresponding sides of the two figures?

____

F Use a protractor to measure the angles of trapezoid *TRAP*.

$m\angle T =$ ________ $m\angle R =$ ________ $m\angle A =$ ________ $m\angle P =$ ________

G Use a protractor to measure the angles of trapezoid $T'R'A'P'$.

$m\angle T' =$ ________ $m\angle R' =$ ________ $m\angle A' =$ ________ $m\angle P' =$ ________

H What do you notice about the measures of corresponding angles of the two figures?

____

I Which sides of trapezoid *TRAP* are parallel? ________________

Which sides of trapezoid $T'R'A'P'$ are parallel? ________________

What do you notice? ________________________________

____

Reflect

3. **Make a Conjecture** Use your results from **E**, **H**, and **I** to make a conjecture about rotations.

____

____

4. Place your tracing back in its original position. Then perform a 180° *clockwise* rotation about the origin. Compare the result with the result in **B**.

____

____

Graphing Rotations

To rotate a figure in the coordinate plane, rotate each of its vertices. Then connect the vertices to form the image.

EXAMPLE 1

CA CC 8.G.3

The figure shows triangle *ABC*. Graph the image of triangle *ABC* after a rotation of 90° clockwise.

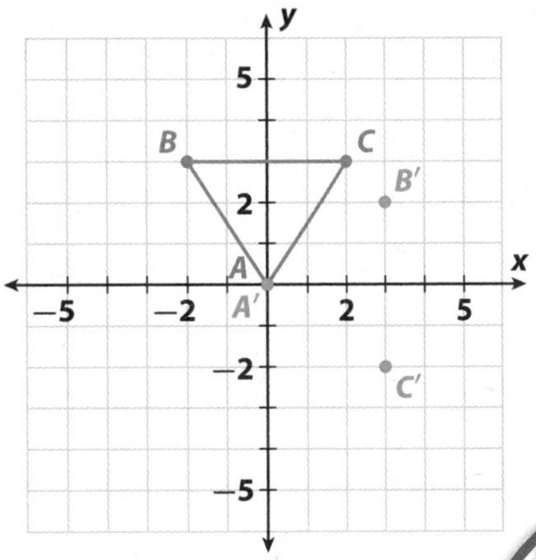

STEP 1 Rotate the figure clockwise from the *y*-axis to the *x*-axis. Point *A* will still be at (0, 0).

Point *B* is 2 units to the left of the *y*-axis, so point *B*′ is 2 units above the *x*-axis.

Point *C* is 2 units to the right of the *y*-axis, so point *C*′ is 2 units below the *x*-axis.

STEP 2 Connect *A*′, *B*′, and *C*′ to form the image triangle *A*′*B*′*C*′.

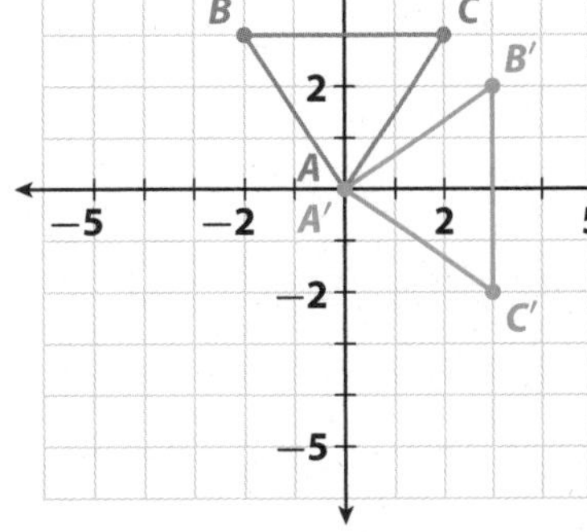

Math Talk
Mathematical Practices
How is the orientation of the triangle affected by the rotation?

Reflect

5. Is the image congruent to the preimage? How do you know?

____

____

____

____

YOUR TURN

Graph the image of quadrilateral *ABCD* after each rotation.

6. 180°
7. 270° clockwise
8. Find the coordinates of Point *C* after a 90° counterclockwise rotation followed by a 180° rotation.

____

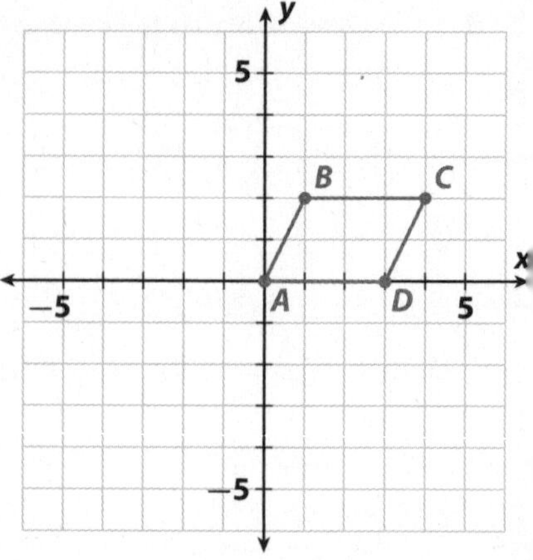

Guided Practice

1. **Vocabulary** A rotation is a transformation that turns a figure around a given _______________ called the center of rotation.

Siobhan rotates a right triangle 90° counterclockwise about the origin.

2. How does the orientation of the image of the triangle compare with the orientation of the preimage? (Explore Activity 1)

____

3. Is the image of the triangle congruent to the preimage? (Explore Activity 2)

____

Draw the image of the figure after the given rotation about the origin. (Example 1)

4. 90° counterclockwise

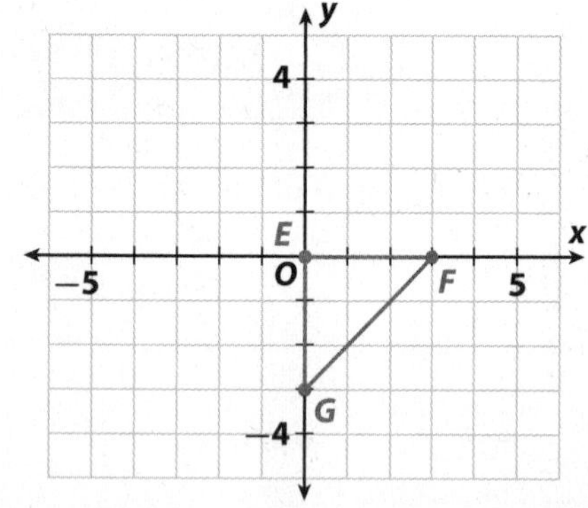

5. 180°

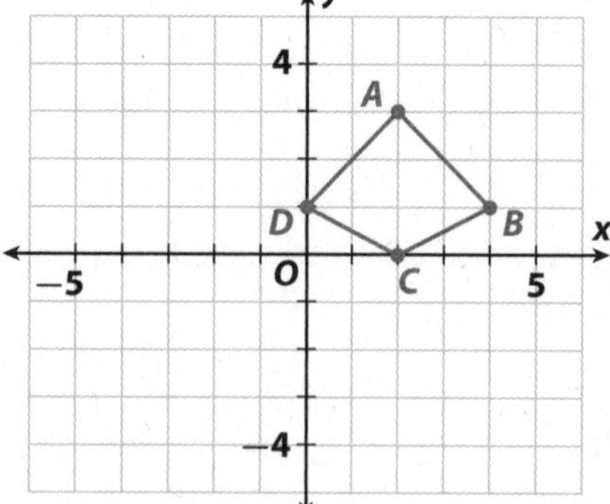

ESSENTIAL QUESTION CHECK-IN

6. What are the properties of rotations?

____

Name ______________________ Class ______________________ Date ______________________

19.3 Independent Practice

CA CC 8.G.1a, 8.G.1b, 8.G.1c, 8.G.3

7. The figure shows triangle *ABC* and a rotation of the triangle about the origin.

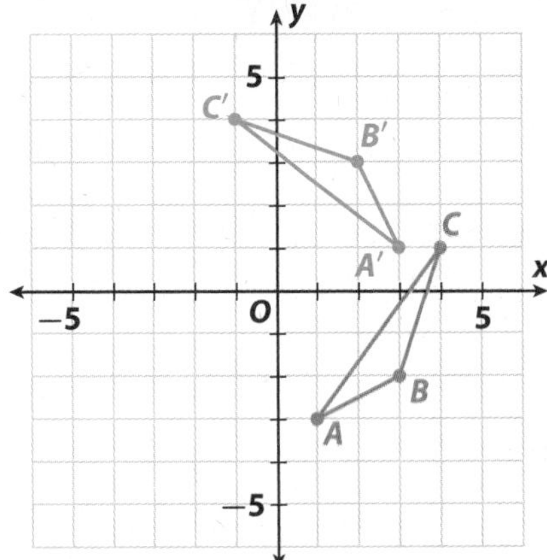

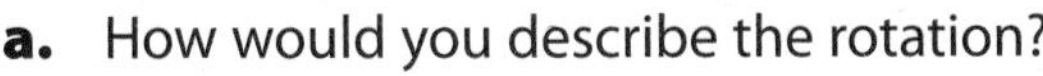

a. How would you describe the rotation?

____

____

b. What are the coordinates of the image?

____________, ____________, ____________

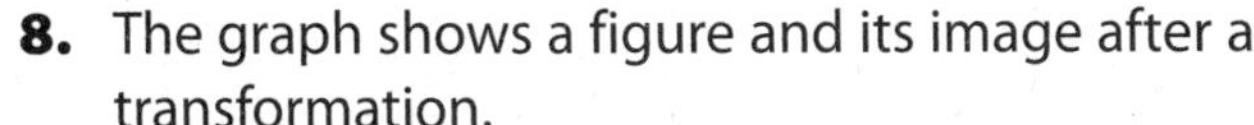

8. The graph shows a figure and its image after a transformation.

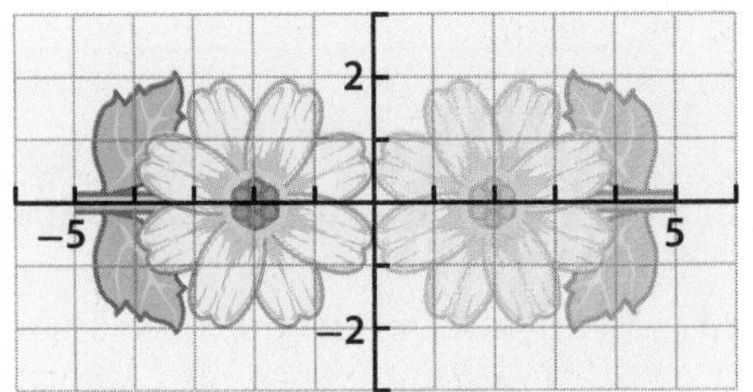

a. How would you describe this as a rotation?

____

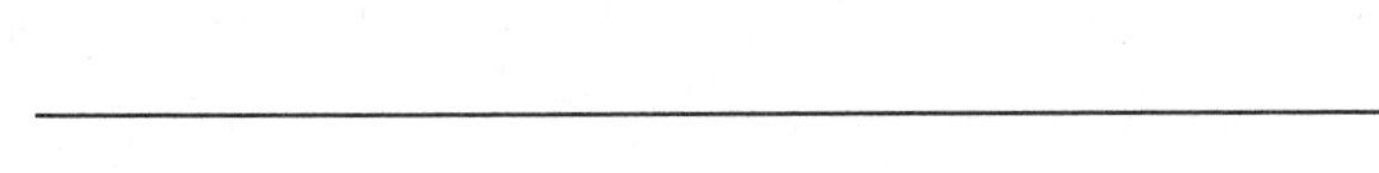

____

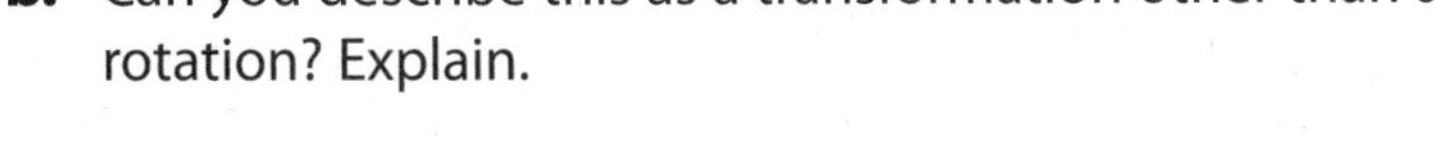

b. Can you describe this as a transformation other than a rotation? Explain.

____

____

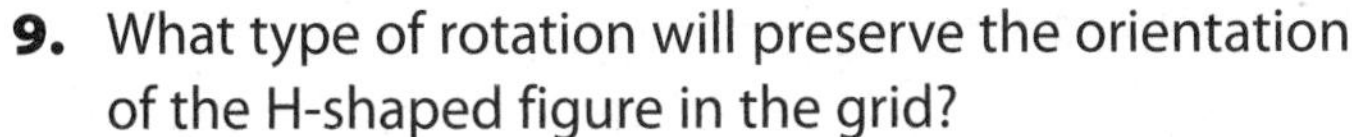

9. What type of rotation will preserve the orientation of the H-shaped figure in the grid?

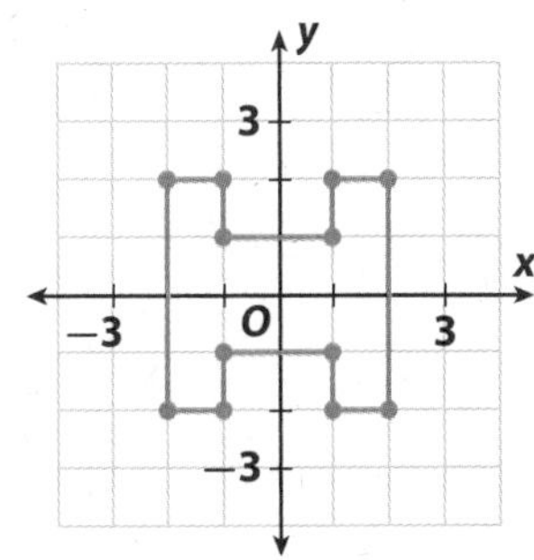

____

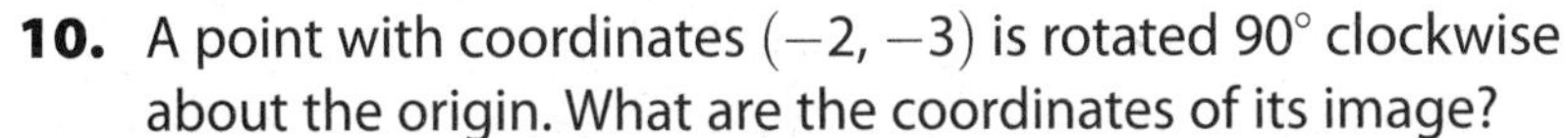

10. A point with coordinates $(-2, -3)$ is rotated 90° clockwise about the origin. What are the coordinates of its image?

____

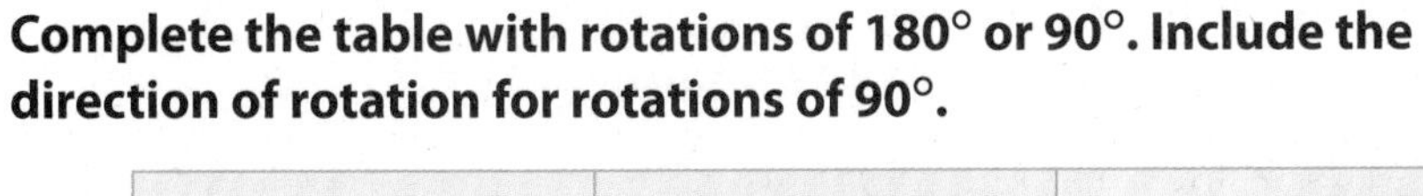

Complete the table with rotations of 180° or 90°. Include the direction of rotation for rotations of 90°.

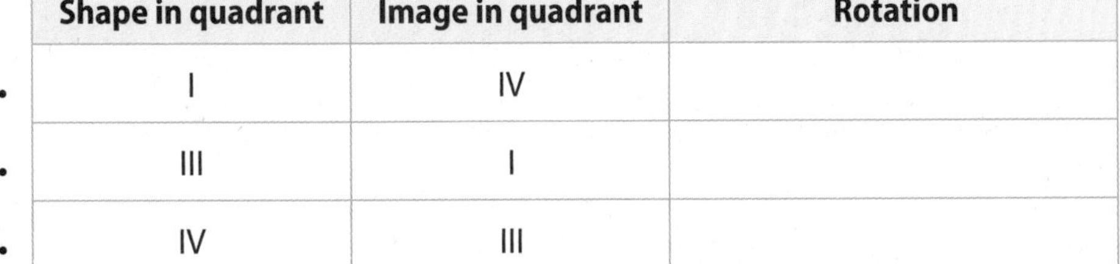

	Shape in quadrant	Image in quadrant	Rotation
11.	I	IV	
12.	III	I	
13.	IV	III	

Draw the image of the figure after the given rotation about the origin.

14. 180°

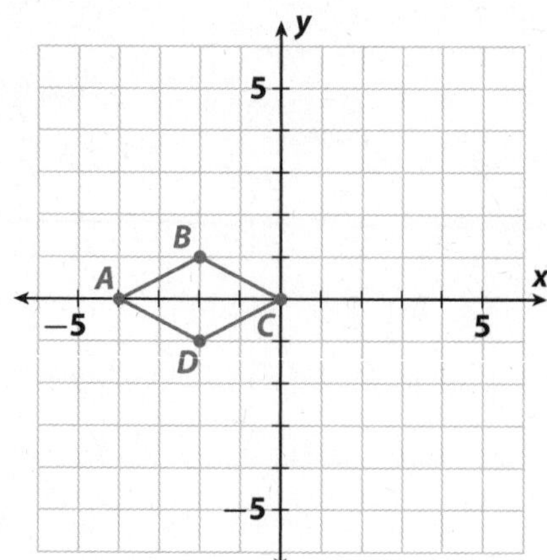

15. 270° counterclockwise

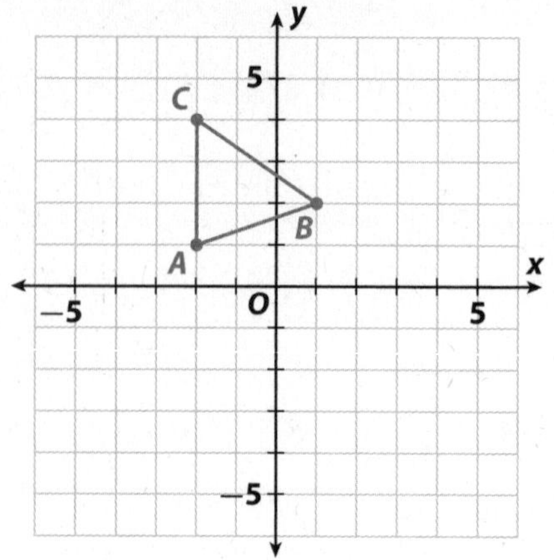

16. Is there a rotation for which the orientation of the image is always the same as that of the preimage? If so, what?

___

FOCUS ON HIGHER ORDER THINKING

Work Area

17. Problem Solving Lucas is playing a game where he has to rotate a figure for it to fit in an open space. Every time he clicks a button, the figure rotates 90 degrees clockwise. How many times does he need to click the button so that each figure returns to its original orientation?

Figure A ___

Figure B ___

Figure C ___

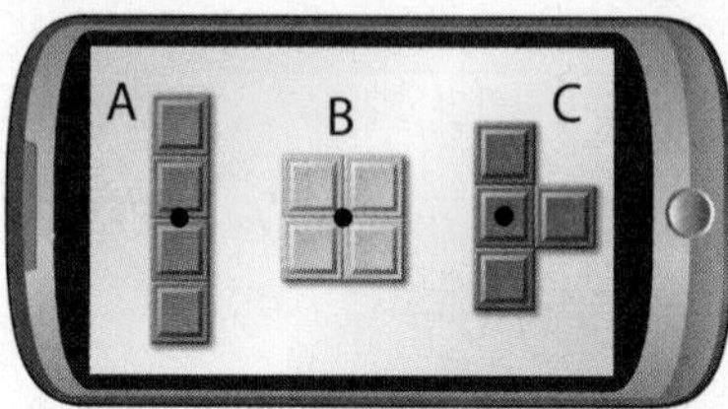

18. Make a Conjecture Triangle *ABC* is reflected across the *y*-axis to form the image *A′B′C′*. Triangle *A′B′C′* is then reflected across the *x*-axis to form the image *A″B″C″*. What type of rotation can be used to describe the relationship between triangle *A″B″C″* and triangle *ABC*?

___

19. Communicate Mathematical Ideas Point *A* is on the *y*-axis. Describe all possible locations of image *A′* for rotations of 90°, 180°, and 270°. Include the origin as a possible location for *A*.

___

___

___

___

LESSON 19.4

Algebraic Representations of Transformations

8.G.3

Describe the effect of dilations, translations, rotations, and reflections on two-dimensional figures using coordinates.

ESSENTIAL QUESTION

How can you describe the effect of a translation, rotation, or reflection on coordinates using an algebraic representation?

Algebraic Representations of Translations

The rules shown in the table describe how coordinates change when a figure is translated up, down, right, and left on the coordinate plane.

Translations

Right *a* units	Add *a* to the *x*-coordinate: $(x, y) \rightarrow (x + a, y)$
Left *a* units	Subtract *a* from the *x*-coordinate: $(x, y) \rightarrow (x - a, y)$
Up *b* units	Add *b* to the *y*-coordinate: $(x, y) \rightarrow (x, y + b)$
Down *b* units	Subtract *b* from the *y*-coordinate: $(x, y) \rightarrow (x, y - b)$

EXAMPLE 1

CA CC 8.G.3

Triangle *XYZ* has vertices *X*(0, 0), *Y*(2, 3), and *Z*(4, −1). Find the vertices of triangle *X′Y′Z′* after a translation of 3 units to the right and 1 unit down. Then graph the triangle and its image.

STEP 1 Apply the rule to find the vertices of the image.

Add 3 to the x-coordinate of each vertex and subtract 1 from the y-coordinate of each vertex.

Vertices of $\triangle XYZ$	Rule: $(x + 3, y - 1)$	Vertices of $\triangle X'Y'Z'$
$X(0, 0)$	$(0 + 3, 0 - 1)$	$X'(3, -1)$
$Y(2, 3)$	$(2 + 3, 3 - 1)$	$Y'(5, 2)$
$Z(4, -1)$	$(4 + 3, -1 - 1)$	$Z'(7, -2)$

STEP 2 Graph triangle *XYZ* and its image.

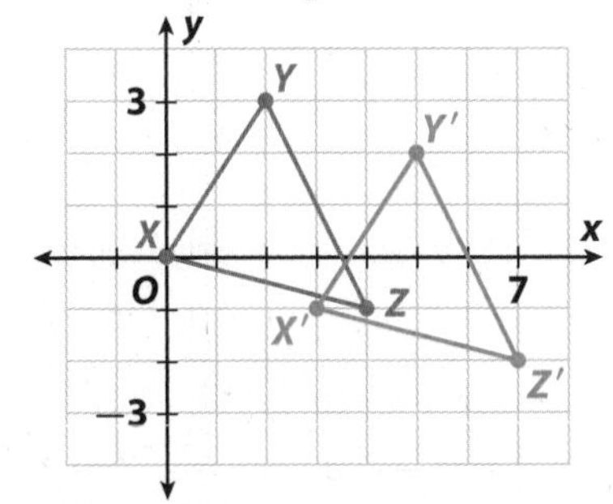

Math Talk
Mathematical Practices

When you translate a figure to the left or right, which coordinate do you change?

YOUR TURN

1. A rectangle has vertices at (0, −2), (0, 3), (3, −2), and (3, 3). What are the coordinates of the vertices of the image after the translation $(x, y) \rightarrow (x - 6, y - 3)$? Describe the translation.

____

____

Algebraic Representations of Reflections

The signs of the coordinates of a figure change when the figure is reflected across the *x*-axis and *y*-axis. The table shows the rules for changing the signs of the coordinates after a reflection.

Reflections	
Across the *x*-axis	Multiply each *y*-coordinate by −1: $(x, y) \rightarrow (x, -y)$
Across the *y*-axis	Multiply each *x*-coordinate by −1: $(x, y) \rightarrow (-x, y)$

EXAMPLE 2

CA CC 8.G.3

My Notes

Rectangle *RSTU* has vertices *R*(−4, −1), *S*(−1, −1), *T*(−1, −3), and *U*(−4, −3). Find the vertices of rectangle *R′S′T′U′* after a reflection across the *y*-axis. Then graph the rectangle and its image.

STEP 1 Apply the rule to find the vertices of the image.

Vertices of *RSTU*	Rule: $(-1 \cdot x, y)$	Vertices of *R′S′T′U′*
R(−4, −1)	(−1 · (−4), − 1)	*R′*(4, −1)
S(−1, −1)	(−1 · (−1), − 1)	*S′*(1, −1)
T(−1, −3)	(−1 · (−1), − 3)	*T′*(1, −3)
U(−4, −3)	(−1 · (−4), − 3)	*U′*(4, −3)

STEP 2 Graph rectangle *RSTU* and its image.

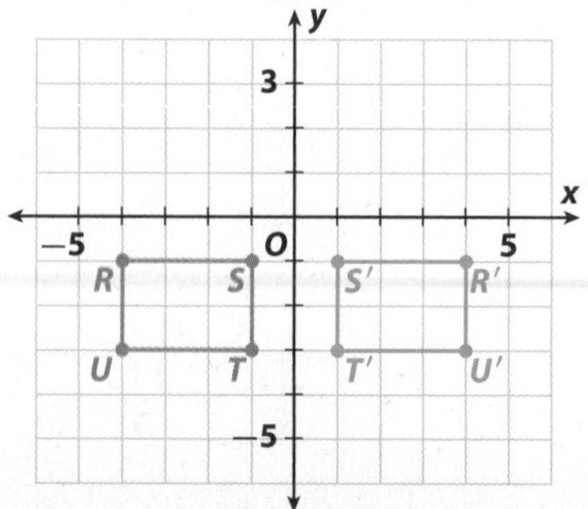

2. Triangle ABC has vertices $A(-2, 6)$, $B(0, 5)$, and $C(3, -1)$. Find the vertices of triangle $A'B'C'$ after a reflection across the x-axis.

____

Algebraic Representations of Rotations

When points are rotated about the origin, the coordinates of the image can be found using the rules shown in the table.

Rotations	
90° clockwise	Multiply each x-coordinate by -1; then switch the x- and y-coordinates: $(x, y) \rightarrow (y, -x)$
90° counterclockwise	Multiply each y-coordinate by -1; then switch the x- and y-coordinates: $(x, y) \rightarrow (-y, x)$
180°	Multiply both coordinates by -1: $(x, y) \rightarrow (-x, -y)$

EXAMPLE 3

Quadrilateral $ABCD$ has vertices at $A(-4, 2)$, $B(-3, 4)$, $C(2, 3)$, and $D(0, 0)$. Find the vertices of quadrilateral $A'B'C'D'$ after a 90° clockwise rotation. Then graph the quadrilateral and its image.

STEP 1 Apply the rule to find the vertices of the image.

Multiply the x-coordinate of each vertex by −1, and then switch the x- and y-coordinates.

Vertices of $ABCD$	Rule: $(y, -x)$	Vertices of $A'B'C'D'$
$A(-4, 2)$	$(2, -1 \cdot (-4))$	$A'(2, 4)$
$B(-3, 4)$	$(4, -1 \cdot (-3))$	$B'(4, 3)$
$C(2, 3)$	$(3, -1 \cdot 2)$	$C'(3, -2)$
$D(0, 0)$	$(0, -1 \cdot 0)$	$D'(0, 0)$

STEP 2 Graph the quadrilateral and its image.

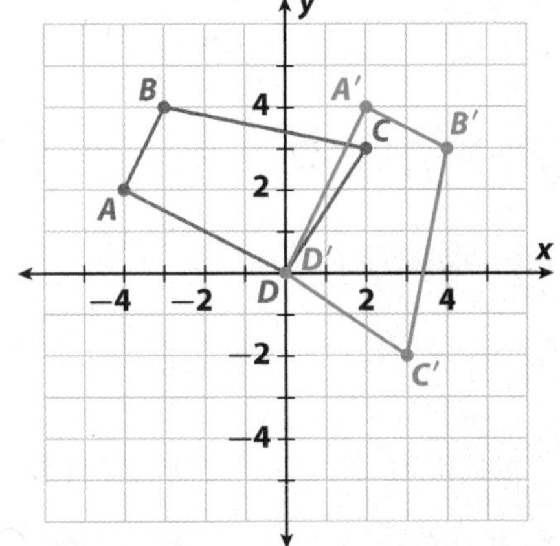

Reflect

3. **Communicate Mathematical Ideas** How would you find the vertices of an image if a figure were rotated 270° clockwise? Explain.

______

______

______

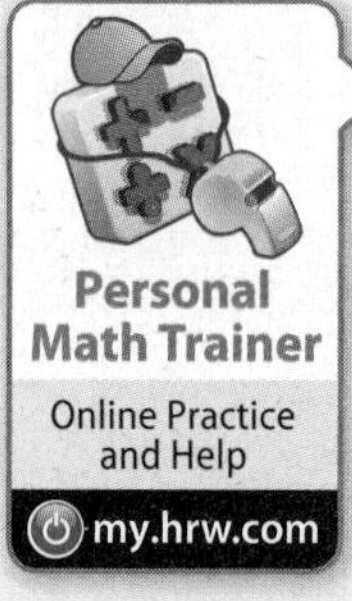

YOUR TURN

4. A triangle has vertices at $J(-2, -4)$, $K(1, 5)$, and $L(2, 2)$. What are the coordinates of the vertices of the image after the triangle is rotated 90° counterclockwise?

______

Guided Practice

1. Triangle XYZ has vertices $X(-3, -2)$, $Y(-1, 0)$, and $Z(1, -6)$. Find the vertices of triangle $X'Y'Z'$ after a translation of 6 units to the right. Then graph the triangle and its image. (Example 1)

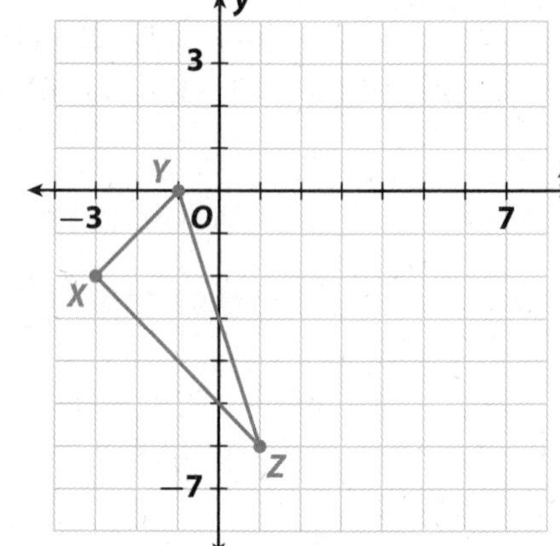

______

2. Describe what happens to the x- and y-coordinates after a point is reflected across the x-axis. (Example 2)

______

______

3. Use the rule $(x, y) \rightarrow (y, -x)$ to graph the image of the triangle at right. Then describe the transformation. (Example 3)

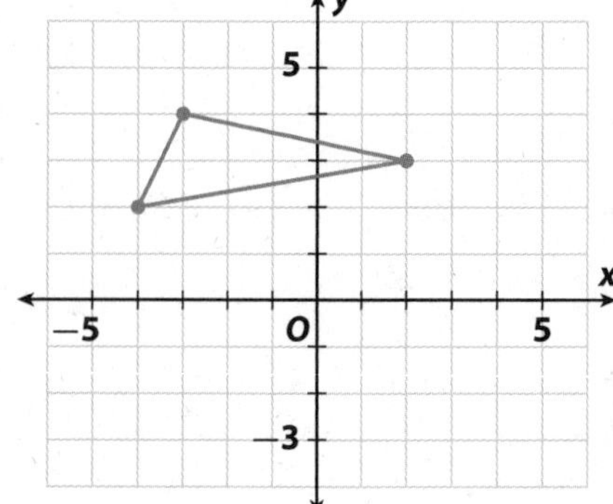

______

ESSENTIAL QUESTION CHECK-IN

4. How do the x- and y-coordinates change when a figure is translated right a units and down b units?

______

______

Name________________________ Class________________________ Date________________

19.4 Independent Practice

CA CC 8.G.3

Write an algebraic rule to describe each transformation. Then describe the transformation.

5.

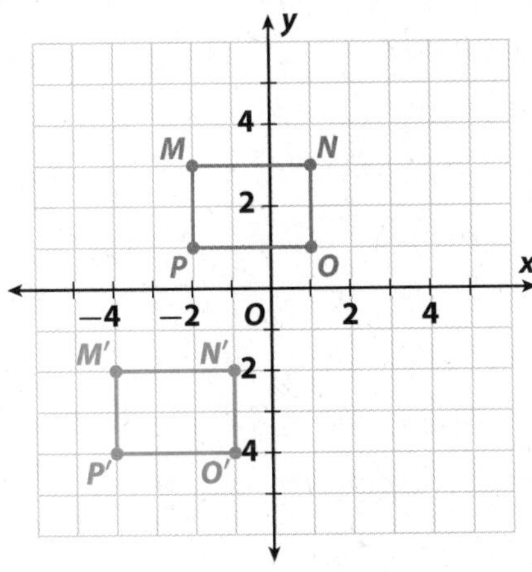

____

____

6.

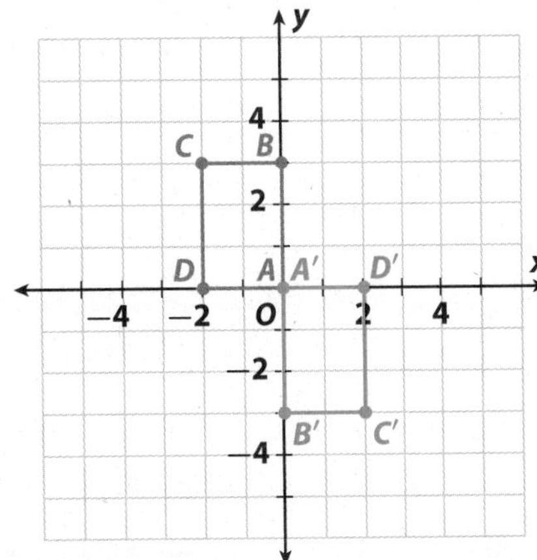

____

____

7. Triangle XYZ has vertices $X(6, -2.3)$, $Y(7.5, 5)$, and $Z(8, 4)$. When translated, X' has coordinates $(2.8, -1.3)$. Write a rule to describe this transformation. Then find the coordinates of Y' and Z'.

____

8. Point L has coordinates $(3, -5)$. The coordinates of point L' after a reflection are $(-3, -5)$. Without graphing, tell which axis point L was reflected across. Explain your answer.

____

____

____

9. Use the rule $(x, y) \rightarrow (x - 2, y - 4)$ to graph the image of the rectangle. Then describe the transformation.

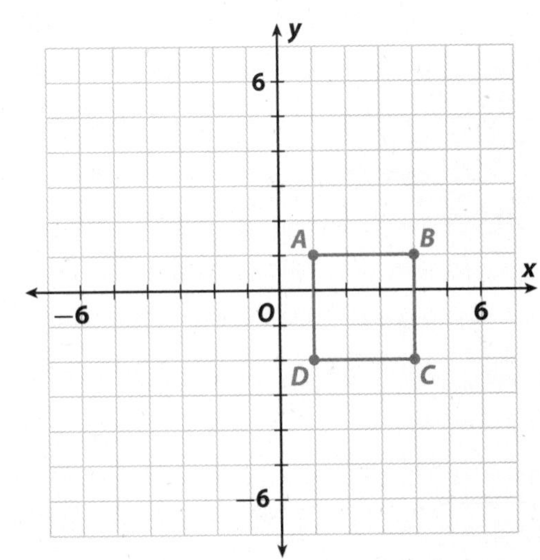

____

____

10. Parallelogram $ABCD$ has vertices $A(-2, -5\frac{1}{2})$, $B(-4, -5\frac{1}{2})$, $C(-3, -2)$, and $D(-1, -2)$. Find the vertices of parallelogram $A'B'C'D'$ after a translation of $2\frac{1}{2}$ units down.

____

____

11. Alexandra drew the logo shown on half-inch graph paper. Write a rule that describes the translation Alexandra used to create the shadow on the letter A.

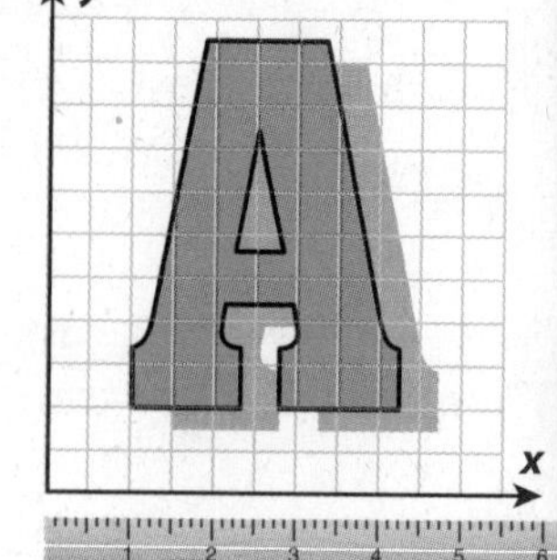

____

12. Kite *KLMN* has vertices at *K*(1, 3), *L*(2, 4), *M*(3, 3), and *N*(2, 0). After the kite is rotated, *K'* has coordinates (−3, 1). Describe the rotation, and include a rule in your description. Then find the coordinates of *L'*, *M'*, and *N'*.

____

____

FOCUS ON HIGHER ORDER THINKING

13. Make a Conjecture Graph the triangle with vertices (−3, 4), (3, 4), and (−5, −5). Use the transformation (*y*, *x*) to graph its image.

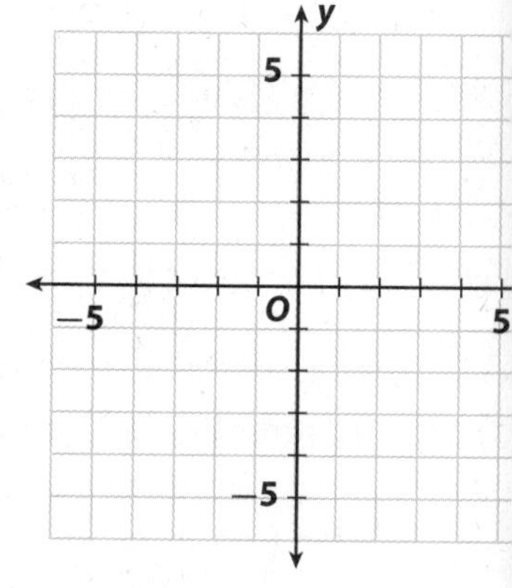

a. Which vertex of the image has the same coordinates as a vertex of the original figure? Explain why this is true.

____

____

b. What is the equation of a line through the origin and this point?

____

c. Describe the transformation of the triangle.

____

Work Area

14. Critical Thinking Mitchell says the point (0, 0) does not change when reflected across the *x*- or *y*-axis or when rotated about the origin. Do you agree with Mitchell? Explain why or why not.

____

____

____

15. Analyze Relationships Triangle *ABC* with vertices *A*(−2, −2), *B*(−3, 1), and *C*(1, 1) is translated by (*x*, *y*) → (*x* − 1, *y* + 3). Then the image, triangle *A'B'C'*, is translated by (*x*, *y*) → (*x* + 4, *y* − 1), resulting in *A''B''C''*.

a. Find the coordinates for the vertices of triangle *A''B''C''*.

____

b. Write a rule for one translation that maps triangle *ABC* to triangle *A''B''C''*.

____

LESSON

19.5 Congruent Figures

CA CC 8.G.2

Understand that a two-dimensional figure is congruent to another if the second can be obtained from the first by a sequence of rotations, reflections, and translations; given two congruent figures, describe a sequence that exhibits the congruence between them.

ESSENTIAL QUESTION

How can transformations be used to verify that two figures have the same shape and size?

EXPLORE ACTIVITY

8.G.2

Combining Transformations

Apply the indicated series of transformations to the triangle. Each transformation is applied to the image of the previous transformation, not the original figure. Label each image with the letter of the transformation applied.

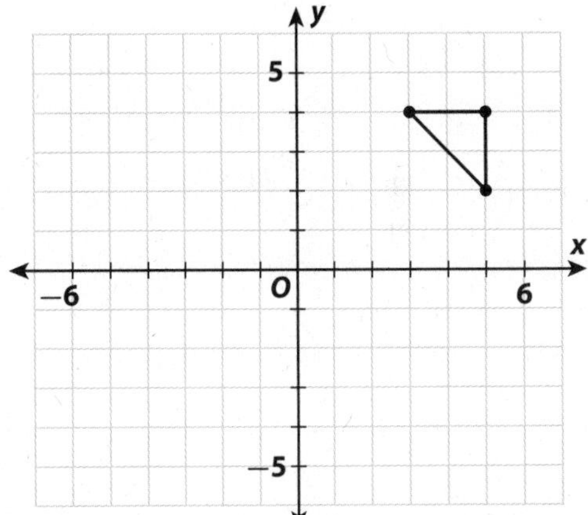

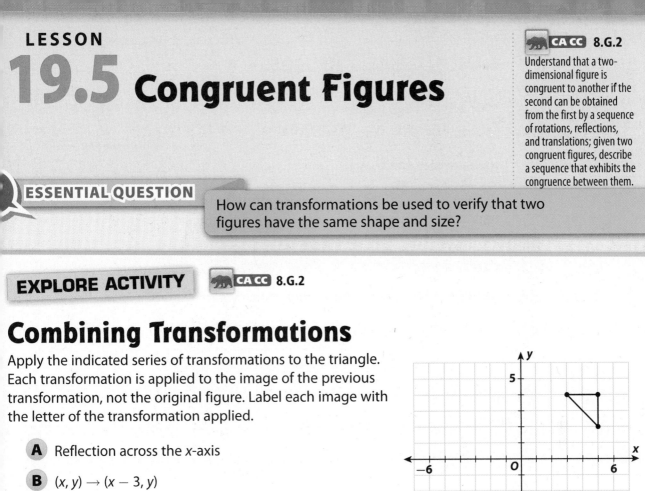

A Reflection across the x-axis

B $(x, y) \rightarrow (x - 3, y)$

C Reflection across the y-axis

D $(x, y) \rightarrow (x, y + 4)$

E Rotation 90° clockwise around the origin

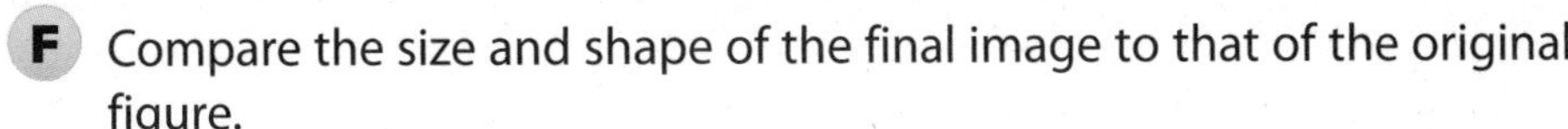

F Compare the size and shape of the final image to that of the original figure.

____

____

Reflect

1. Which transformation(s) change the orientation of figures? Which do not?

____

2. **Make a Conjecture** After a series of transformations, two figures have the same size and shape, but different orientations. What does this indicate about the transformations?

____

____

____

Congruent Figures

Recall that segments and their images have the same length and angles and their images have the same measure under a translation, reflection, or rotation. Two figures are said to be **congruent** if one can be obtained from the other by a sequence of translations, reflections, and rotations. Congruent figures have the same size and shape.

When you are told that two figures are congruent, there must be a sequence of translations, reflections, and/or rotations that transforms one into the other.

EXAMPLE 1

A Identify a sequence of transformations that will transform figure *A* into figure *B*.

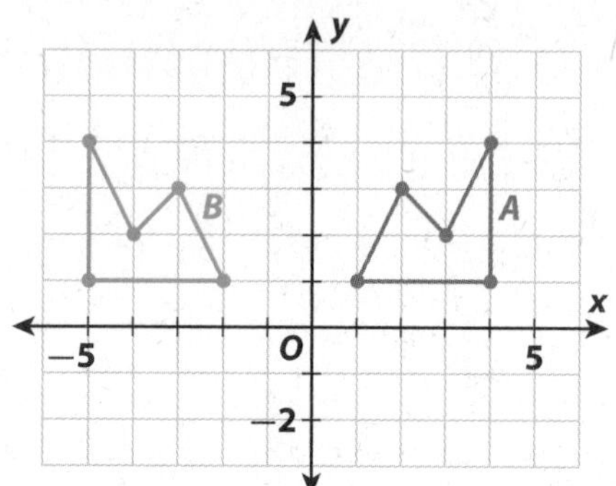

To transform figure *A* into figure *B*, you need to reflect it over the *y*-axis and translate one unit to the left. A sequence of transformations that will accomplish this is $(x, y) \rightarrow (-x, y)$ and $(x, y) \rightarrow (x - 1, y)$.

B Identify a sequence of transformations that will transform figure *B* into figure *C*.

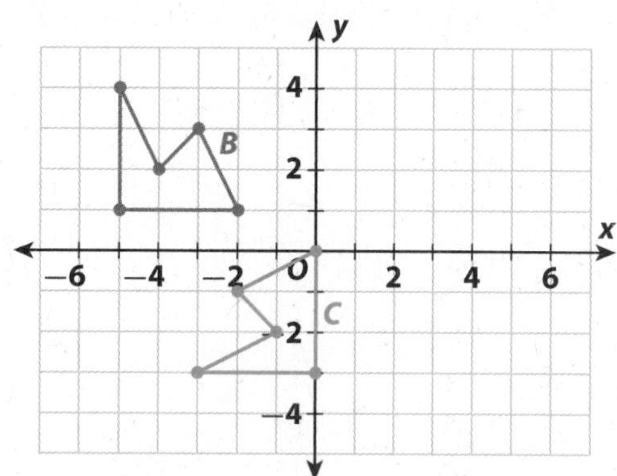

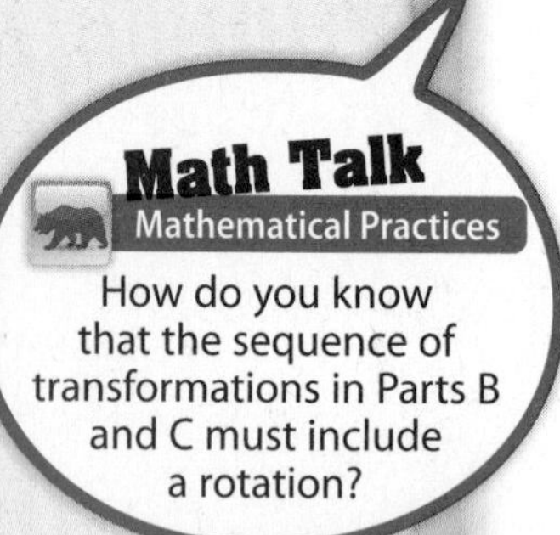

Math Talk
Mathematical Practices
How do you know that the sequence of transformations in Parts B and C must include a rotation?

Any sequence of transformations that changes figure *B* into figure *C* will need to include a rotation. A 90° counterclockwise rotation around the origin would properly orient figure *B*, but not locate it in the same position as figure *C*. The rotated figure would be 2 units below and 1 unit to the left of where figure *C* is. You would need to translate the rotated figure up 2 units and right 1 unit.

A sequence of transformations is a 90° counterclockwise rotation about the origin, $(x, y) \rightarrow (-y, x)$, followed by $(x, y) \rightarrow (x + 1, y + 2)$.

C Identify a sequence of transformations that will transform figure D into figure E.

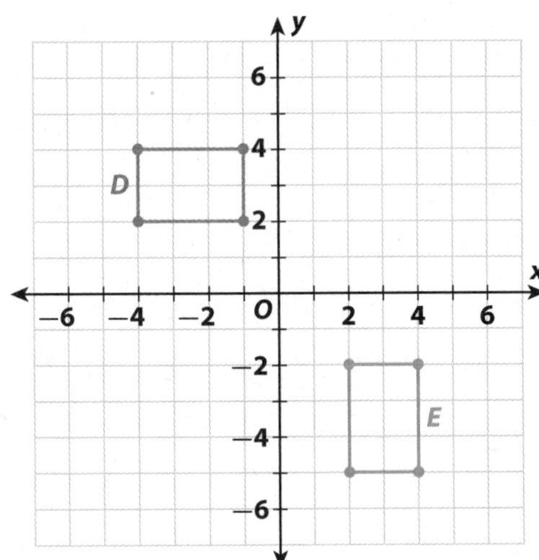

A sequence of transformations that changes figure D to figure E will need to include a rotation. A 90° clockwise rotation around the origin would result in the figure being oriented as figure E.

However, the rotated figure would be 6 units above where figure E is. You would need to translate the rotated figure down 6 units.

A sequence of transformations is a 90° clockwise rotation about the origin, $(x, y) \rightarrow (y, -x)$, followed by $(x, y) \rightarrow (x, y - 6)$.

My Notes

YOUR TURN

3. Identify a sequence of transformations that will transform figure A into figure B.

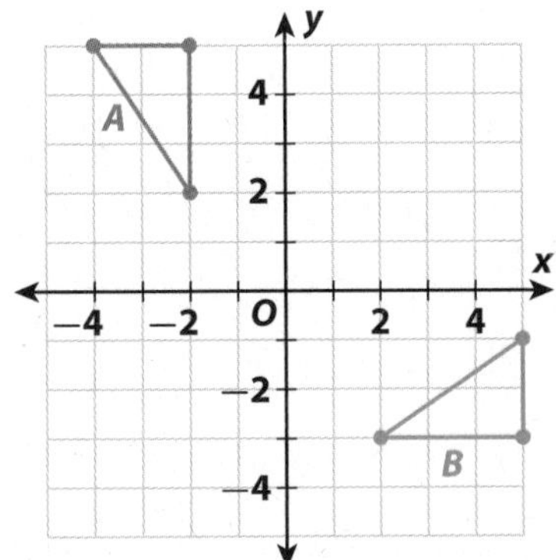

____

____

____

Guided Practice

1. Apply the indicated series of transformations to the rectangle. Each transformation is applied to the image of the previous transformation, not the original figure. Label each image with the letter of the transformation applied. (Explore Activity)

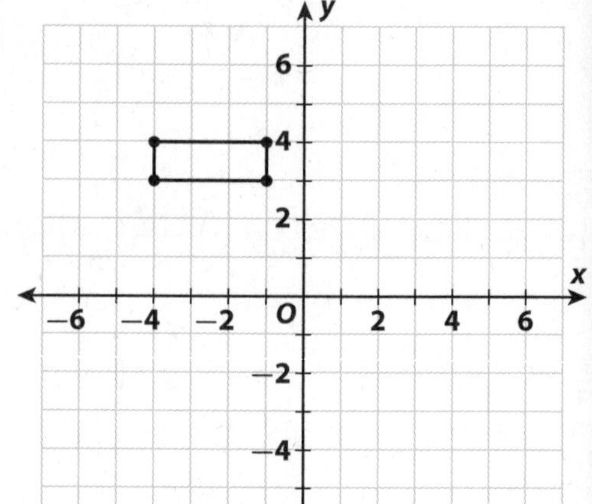

A. Reflection across the y-axis

B. Rotation 90° clockwise around the origin

C. $(x, y) \rightarrow (x - 2, y)$

D. Rotation 90° counterclockwise around the origin

E. $(x, y) \rightarrow (x - 7, y - 2)$

Identify a sequence of transformations that will transform figure *A* into figure *C*. (Example 1)

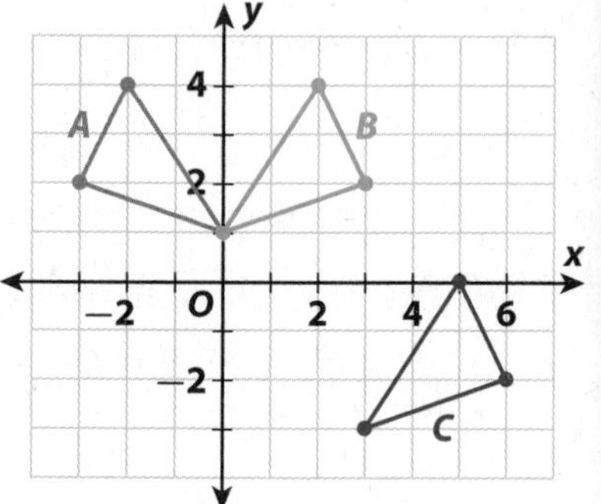

2. What transformation is used to transform figure A into figure B?

____

____

3. What transformation is used to transform figure B into figure C?

____

____

4. What sequence of transformations is used to transform figure A into figure C? Express the transformations algebraically.

____

____

5. **Vocabulary** What does it mean for two figures to be congruent?

____

____

ESSENTIAL QUESTION CHECK-IN

6. After a sequence of translations, reflections, and rotations, what is true about the first figure and the final figure?

____

____

Name ________________ Class ________________ Date ________________

19.5 Independent Practice

8.G.2

For each given figure *A*, graph figures *B* and *C* using the given sequence of transformations. State whether figures *A* and *C* have the same or different orientation.

7.

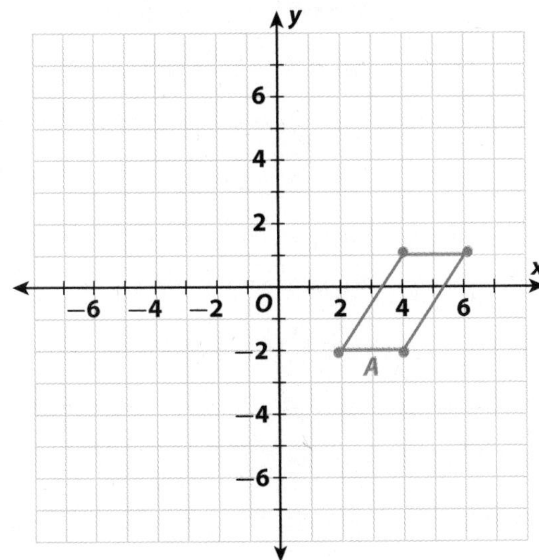

Figure *B*: a translation of 1 unit to the right and 3 units up

Figure *C*: a 90° clockwise rotation around the origin

____

8.

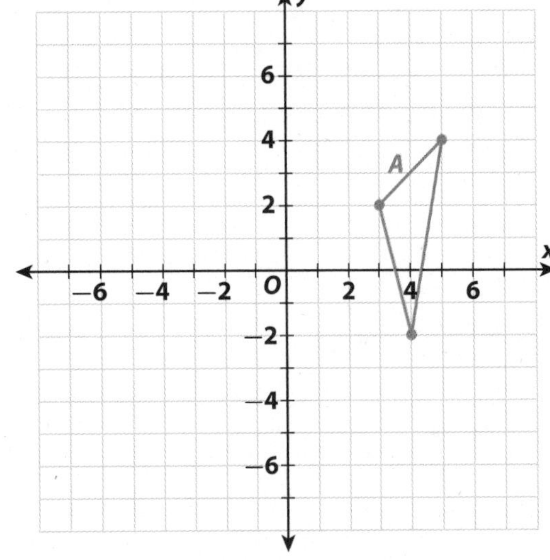

Figure *B*: a reflection across the *y*-axis

Figure *C*: a 180° rotation around the origin

____

9.

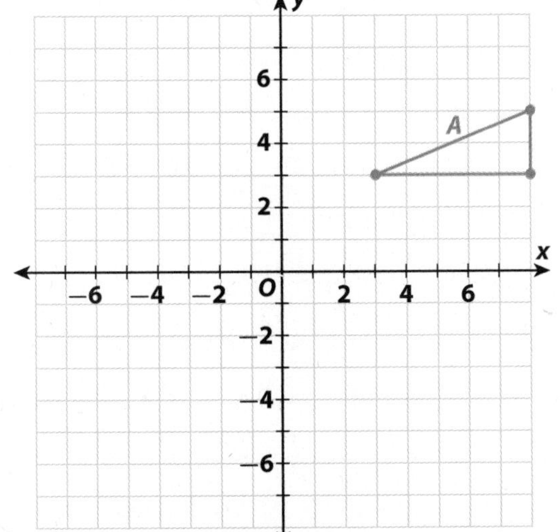

Figure *B*: a reflection across the *y*-axis

Figure *C*: a translation 2 units down

____

10.

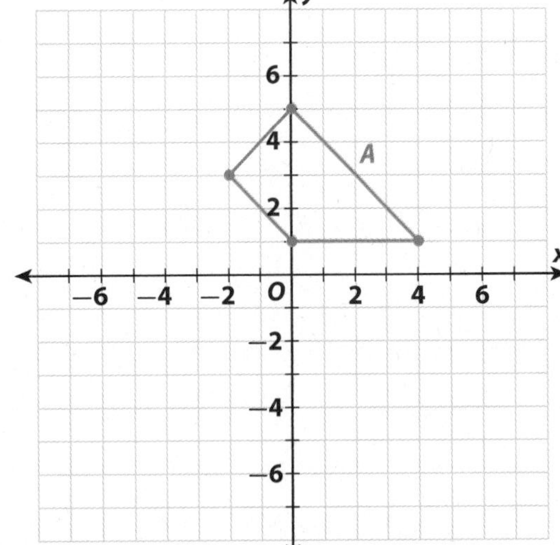

Figure *B*: a translation 2 units up

Figure *C*: a rotation of 180° around the origin

____

11. Represent Real-World Problems A city planner wanted to place the new town library at site *A*. The mayor thought that it would be better at site *B*. What transformations were applied to the building at site *A* to relocate the building to site *B*? Did the mayor change the size or orientation of the library?

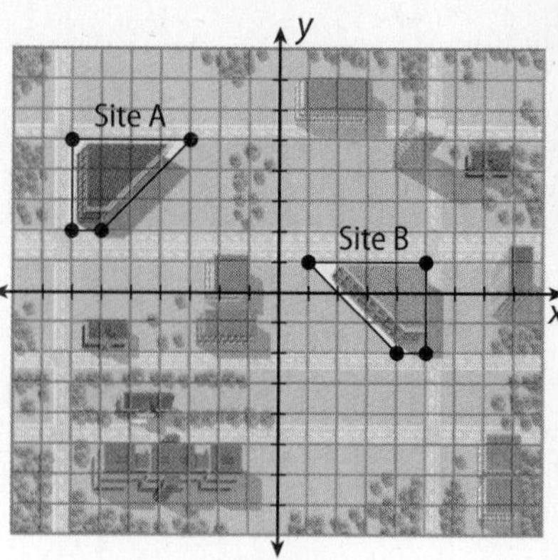

____

____

____

12. Persevere in Problem Solving Find a sequence of three transformations that can be used to obtain figure *D* from figure *A*. Graph the figures *B* and *C* that are created by the transformations.

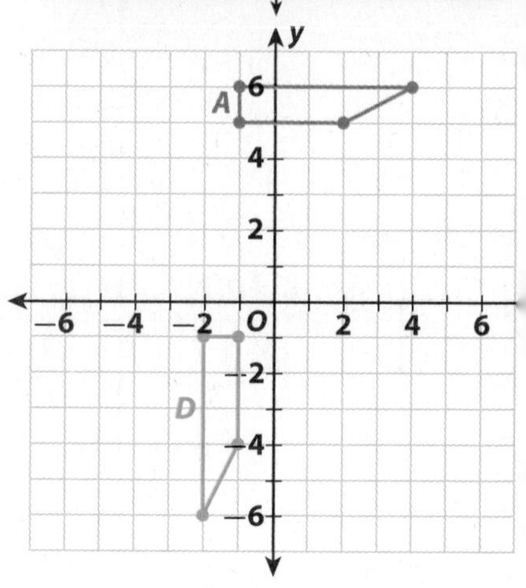

____

____

____

____

FOCUS ON HIGHER ORDER THINKING

Work Area

13. Counterexamples The Commutative Properties for Addition and Multiplication state that the order of two numbers being added or multiplied does not change the sum or product. Are translations and rotations commutative? If not, give a counterexample.

____

____

____

____

____

14. Multiple Representations For each representation, describe a possible sequence of transformations.

a. $(x, y) \rightarrow (-x - 2, y + 1)$

____

____

b. $(x, y) \rightarrow (y, -x - 3)$

____

____

MODULE QUIZ

Ready to Go On?

Personal Math Trainer
Online Practice and Help
my.hrw.com

19.1–19.3 Properties of Translations, Reflections, and Rotations

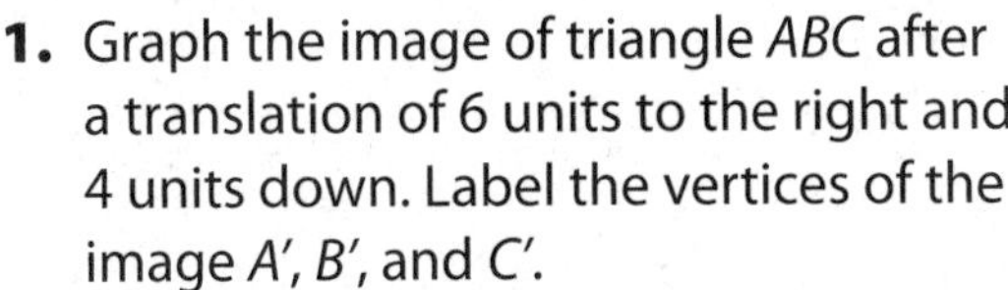

1. Graph the image of triangle *ABC* after a translation of 6 units to the right and 4 units down. Label the vertices of the image *A′*, *B′*, and *C′*.

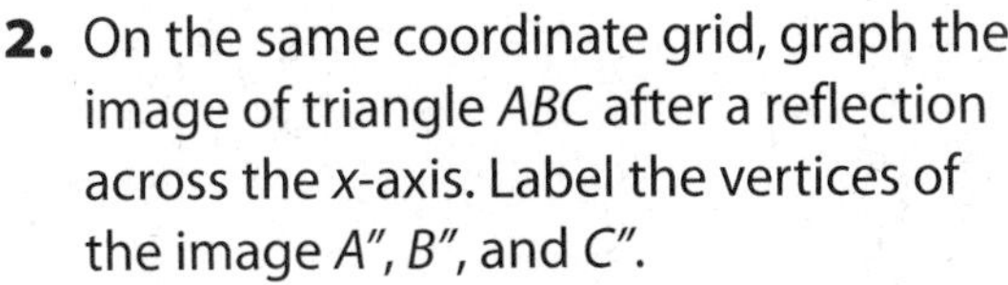

2. On the same coordinate grid, graph the image of triangle *ABC* after a reflection across the *x*-axis. Label the vertices of the image *A″*, *B″*, and *C″*.

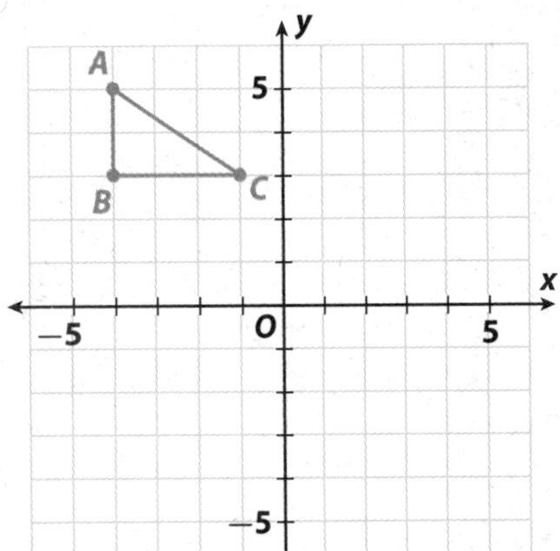

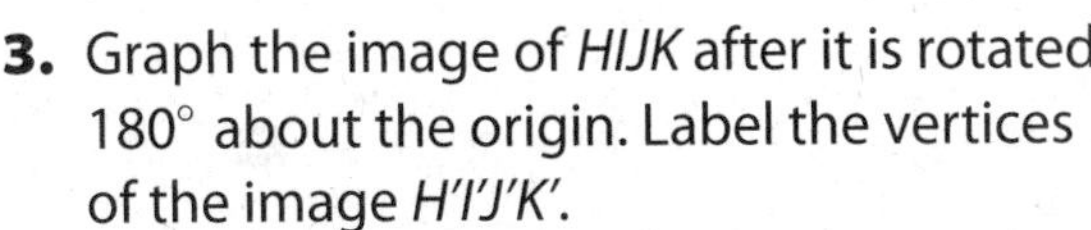

3. Graph the image of *HIJK* after it is rotated 180° about the origin. Label the vertices of the image *H′I′J′K′*.

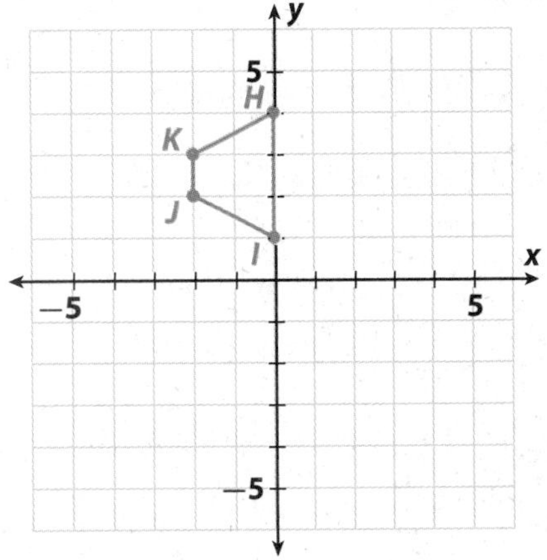

19.4 Algebraic Representations of Transformations

4. A triangle has vertices at (2, 3), (−2, 2), and (−3, 5). What are the coordinates of the vertices of the image after the translation $(x, y) \rightarrow (x + 4, y - 3)$?

____

19.5 Congruent Figures

5. **Vocabulary** Translations, reflections, and rotations produce a figure

that is ______________ to the original figure.

6. Use the coordinate grid for Exercise 3. Reflect *H′I′J′K′* over the *y*-axis, then rotate it 180° about the origin. Label the new figure *H″I″J″K″*.

ESSENTIAL QUESTION

7. What properties allow transformations to be used as problem solving tools?

____

____

MODULE 19
MIXED REVIEW

Assessment Readiness

1. Consider each rational number. Is the number greater than $-2\frac{1}{3}$ but less than $-\frac{4}{5}$?

Select Yes or No for A–C.

A. -0.4 ○ Yes ○ No
B. $-\frac{9}{7}$ ○ Yes ○ No
C. -0.9 ○ Yes ○ No

2. Triangle *DEF* is rotated 90° clockwise about the origin.

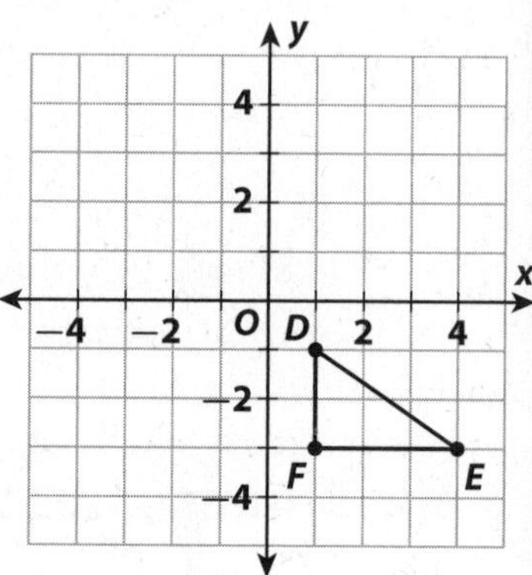

Choose True or False for each statement.

A. $E'F' = 3$ ○ True ○ False
B. $m\angle F' = 90°$ ○ True ○ False
C. $\overline{D'F'}$ is vertical. ○ True ○ False

3. A graphic artist is working on a logo for a car company. The artist draws parallelogram *LMNP* with vertices *L*(1, 0), *M*(2, 2), *N*(5, 3), and *P*(4, 1). The artist then reflects the parallelogram across the *x*-axis. Find the coordinates of the vertices of parallelogram *L′M′N′P′*, and describe the algebraic rule you used to find the coordinates.

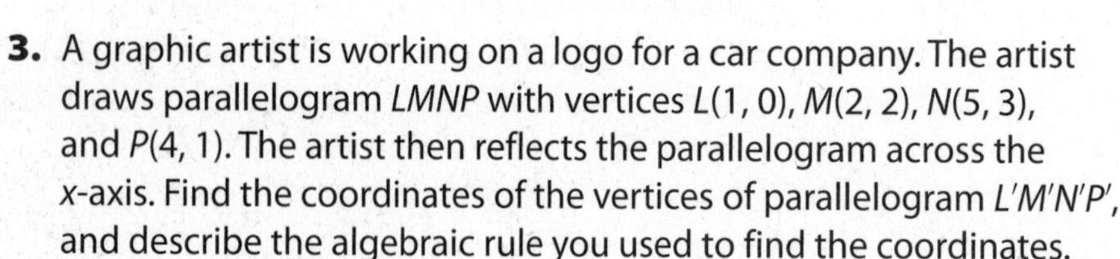

4. The map shows two of a farmer's fields. Is field *A* congruent to field *B*? Use a sequence of transformations to explain your reasoning.

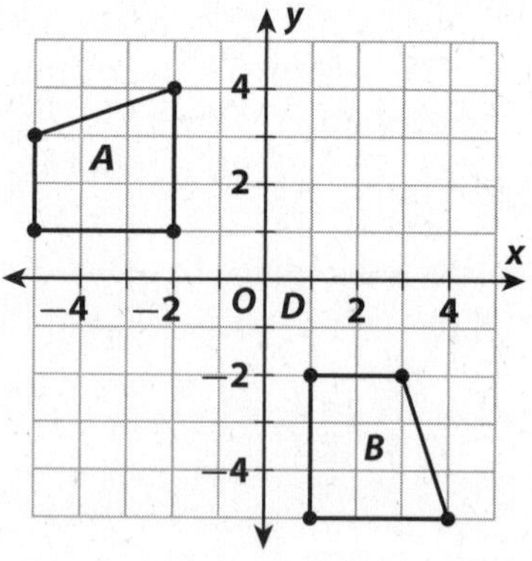

Transformations and Similarity

ESSENTIAL QUESTION

How can you use dilations and similarity to solve real-world problems?

my.hrw.com

Real-World Video

To plan a mural, the artist first makes a smaller drawing showing what the mural will look like. Then the image is enlarged by a scale factor on the mural canvas. This enlargement is called a dilation.

my.hrw.com

my.hrw.com

Go digital with your write-in student edition, accessible on any device.

Math On the Spot

Scan with your smart phone to jump directly to the online edition, video tutor, and more.

Animated Math

Interactively explore key concepts to see how math works.

Personal Math Trainer

Get immediate feedback and help as you work through practice sets.

Are YOU Ready?

Complete these exercises to review skills you will need for this module.

Simplify Ratios

EXAMPLE $\frac{35}{21} = \frac{35 \div 7}{21 \div 7}$ To write a ratio in simplest form, find the greatest common factor of the numerator and denominator.

$= \frac{5}{3}$ Divide the numerator and denominator by the GCF.

Write each ratio in simplest form.

1. $\frac{6}{15}$ ________ **2.** $\frac{8}{20}$ ________ **3.** $\frac{30}{18}$ ________ **4.** $\frac{36}{30}$ ________

Multiply with Fractions and Decimals

EXAMPLE $2\frac{3}{5} \times 20$

$= \frac{13 \times 20}{5 \times 1}$ Write numbers as fractions and multiply.

$= \frac{13 \times \overset{4}{\cancel{20}}}{{}_{1}\cancel{5} \times 1}$ Simplify.

$= 52$

$$\begin{array}{r} 68 \\ \times 4.5 \\ \hline 340 \\ +272 \\ \hline 306.0 \end{array}$$

Multiply as you would with whole numbers.

Place the decimal point in the answer based on the total number of decimal places in the two factors.

Multiply.

5. $60 \times \frac{25}{100}$ ________ **6.** 3.5×40 ________ **7.** 4.4×44 ________ **8.** $24 \times \frac{8}{9}$ ________

Graph Ordered Pairs (First Quadrant)

EXAMPLE

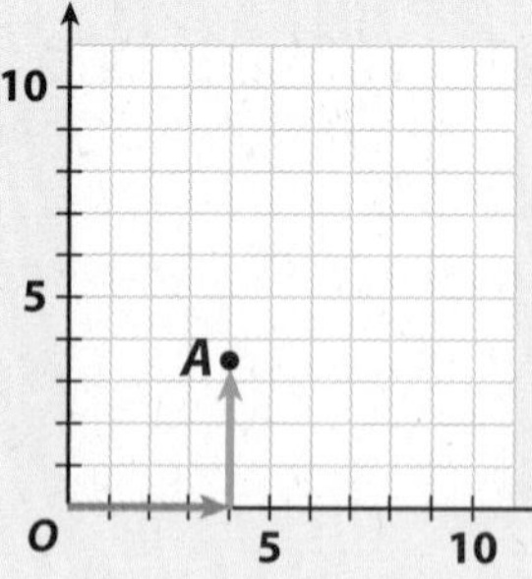

Graph the point $A(4, 3.5)$.
Start at the origin.
Move 4 units right.
Then move 3.5 units up.
Graph point $A(4, 3.5)$.

Graph each point on the coordinate grid above.

9. B (9, 0) **10.** C (2, 7) **11.** D (0, 4.5) **12.** E (6, 2.5)

Reading Start-Up

Vocabulary

Review Words

coordinate plane *(plano cartesiano)*
image *(imagen)*
✔ origin *(origen)*
preimage *(imagen original)*
✔ quadrants *(cuadrante)*
ratio *(razón)*
scale *(escala)*
✔ *x*-axis *(eje x)*
✔ *y*-axis *(eje y)*

Preview Words

center of dilation *(centro de dilatación)*
dilation *(dilatación)*
enlargement *(agrandamiento)*
reduction *(reducción)*
scale factor *(factor de escala)*
similar *(similar)*

Visualize Vocabulary

Use the ✔ words to complete the graphic organizer. You will put one word in each rectangle.

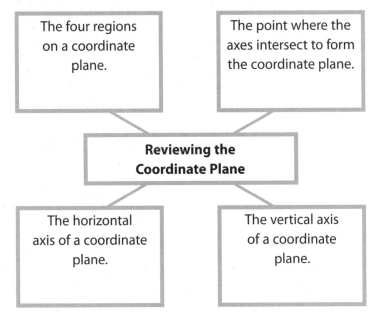

The four regions on a coordinate plane.

The point where the axes intersect to form the coordinate plane.

Reviewing the Coordinate Plane

The horizontal axis of a coordinate plane.

The vertical axis of a coordinate plane.

Understand Vocabulary

Complete the sentences using the preview words.

1. A figure larger than the original, produced through dilation, is an _________________.

2. A figure smaller than the original, produced through dilation, is a _________________.

Active Reading

Key-Term Fold Before beginning the module, create a key-term fold to help you learn the vocabulary in this module. Write the highlighted vocabulary words on one side of the flap. Write the definition for each word on the other side of the flap. Use the key-term fold to quiz yourself on the definitions used in this module.

CALIFORNIA

GETTING READY FOR

Transformations and Similarity

Understanding the standards and the vocabulary terms in the standards will help you know exactly what you are expected to learn in this module.

CA CC 8.G.3

Describe the effect of dilations, translations, rotations, and reflections on two-dimensional figures using coordinates.

What It Means to You

You will use an algebraic representation to describe a dilation.

EXAMPLE 8.G.3

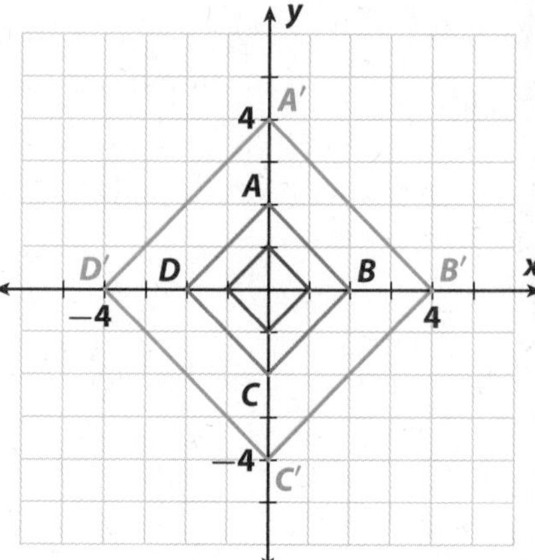

The blue square *ABCD* is the preimage. Write two algebraic representations, one for the dilation to the green square and one for the dilation to the purple square.

The coordinates of the vertices of the original image are multiplied by 2 for the green square.

Green square: $(x, y) \rightarrow (2x, 2y)$

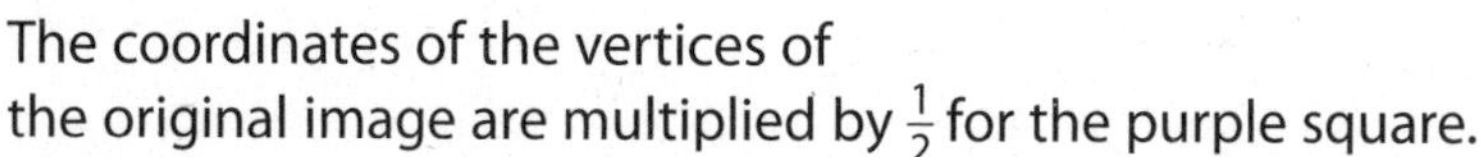

The coordinates of the vertices of the original image are multiplied by $\frac{1}{2}$ for the purple square.

Purple square: $(x, y) \rightarrow \left(\frac{1}{2}x, \frac{1}{2}y\right)$

CA CC 8.G.4

Understand that a two-dimensional figure is similar to another if the second can be obtained from the first by a sequence of rotations, reflections, translations, and dilations; given two similar two-dimensional figures, describe a sequence that exhibits the similarity between them.

What It Means to You

You will describe a sequence of transformations between two similar figures.

EXAMPLE 8.G.4

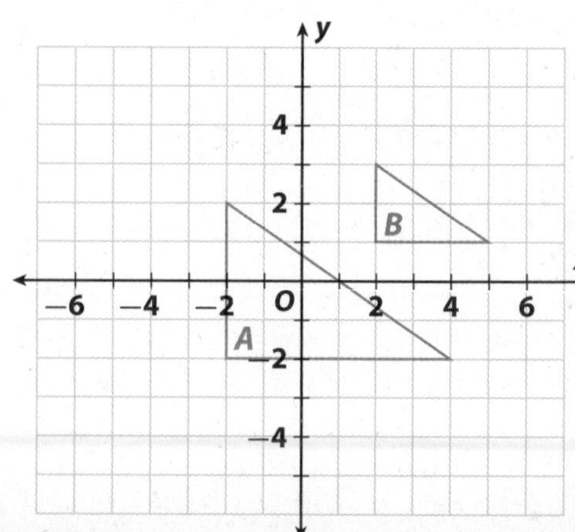

Identify a sequence of two transformations that will transform figure *A* into figure *B*.

Dilate with center at the origin by a scale factor of $\frac{1}{2}$.

Then translate right 3 units and up 2 units.

Visit **my.hrw.com** to see all **CA Common Core Standards** explained.

my.hrw.com

LESSON 20.1

Properties of Dilations

CA CC 8.G.4

Understand that a two-dimensional figure is similar to another if the second can be obtained from the first by a sequence of rotations, reflections, translations, and dilations; given two similar two-dimensional figures, describe a sequence that exhibits the similarity between them. *Also 8.G.3*

ESSENTIAL QUESTION

How do you describe the properties of dilations?

EXPLORE ACTIVITY 1 

CA CC 8.G.4

Exploring Dilations

The missions that placed 12 astronauts on the moon were controlled at the Johnson Space Center in Houston. The toy models at the right are scaled-down replicas of the Saturn V rocket that powered the moon flights. Each replica is a transformation called a **dilation**. Unlike the other transformations you have studied—translations, rotations, and reflections—dilations change the size (but not the shape) of a figure.

Every dilation has a fixed point called the **center of dilation** located where the lines connecting corresponding parts of figures intersect.

Triangle $R'S'T'$ is a dilation of triangle RST. Point C is the center of dilation.

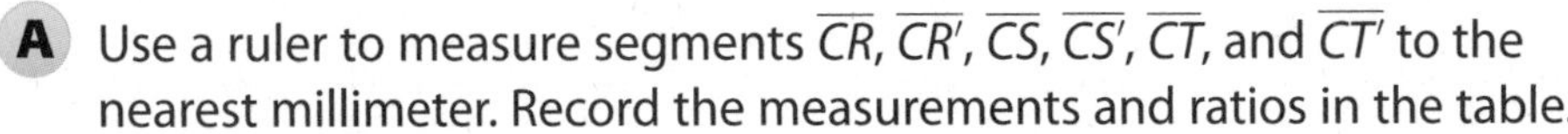

A Use a ruler to measure segments $\overline{CR}$, $\overline{CR'}$, $\overline{CS}$, $\overline{CS'}$, $\overline{CT}$, and $\overline{CT'}$ to the nearest millimeter. Record the measurements and ratios in the table.

CR'	CR	$\frac{CR'}{CR}$	CS'	CS	$\frac{CS'}{CS}$	CT'	CT	$\frac{CT'}{CT}$

B Write a conjecture based on the ratios in the table.

____

C Measure and record the corresponding side lengths of the triangles.

$R'S'$	RS	$\frac{R'S'}{RS}$	$S'T'$	ST	$\frac{S'T'}{ST}$	$R'T'$	RT	$\frac{R'T'}{RT}$

D Write a conjecture based on the ratios in the table.

____

E Measure the corresponding angles and describe your results.

____

EXPLORE ACTIVITY 1 (cont'd)

Reflect

1. Two figures that have the same shape but different sizes are called *similar*. Are triangles RST and $R'S'T'$ similar? Why or why not?

____

____

2. Compare the orientation of a figure with the orientation of its dilation.

____

EXPLORE ACTIVITY 2  8.G.3

Exploring Dilations on a Coordinate Plane

In this activity you will explore how the coordinates of a figure on a coordinate plane are affected by a dilation.

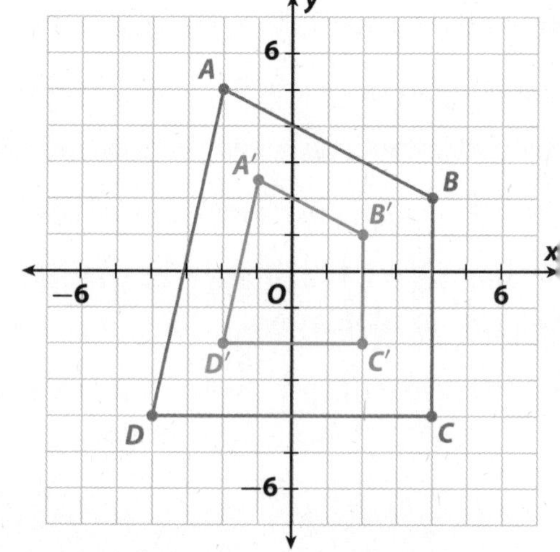

A Complete the table. Record the *x*- and *y*-coordinates of the points in the two figures and the ratios of the *x*-coordinates and the *y*-coordinates.

Vertex	*x*	*y*	Vertex	*x*	*y*	Ratio of *x*-coordinates ($A'B'C'D' \div ABCD$)	Ratio of *y*-coordinates ($A'B'C'D' \div ABCD$)
A′			*A*				
B′			*B*				
C′			*C*				
D′			*D*				

B Write a conjecture about the ratios of the coordinates of a dilation image to the coordinates of the original figure.

____

____

Reflect

3. In Explore Activity 1, triangle $R'S'T'$ was larger than triangle RST. How is the relationship between quadrilateral $A'B'C'D'$ and quadrilateral $ABCD$ different?

___

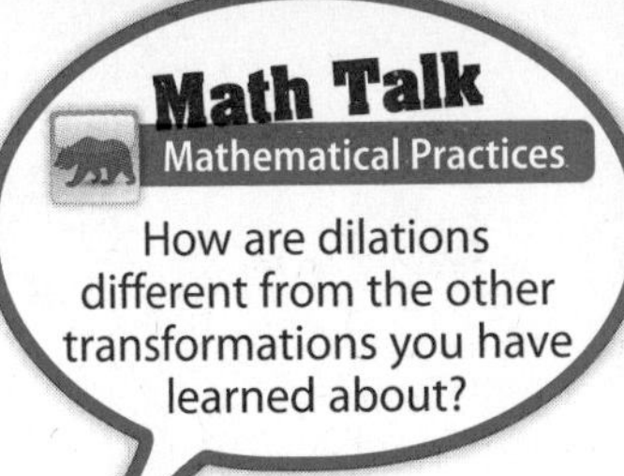

Math Talk
Mathematical Practices
How are dilations different from the other transformations you have learned about?

Finding a Scale Factor

As you have seen in the two activities, a dilation can produce a larger figure (an **enlargement**) or a smaller figure (a **reduction**). The **scale factor** describes how much the figure is enlarged or reduced. The scale factor is the ratio of a length of the image to the corresponding length on the original figure.

In Explore Activity 1, the side lengths of triangle $R'S'T'$ were twice the length of those of triangle RST, so the scale factor was 2. In Explore Activity 2, the side lengths of quadrilateral $A'B'C'D'$ were half those of quadrilateral $ABCD$, so the scale factor was 0.5.

EXAMPLE 1  CA CC 8.G.4

An art supply store sells several sizes of drawing triangles. All are dilations of a single basic triangle. The basic triangle and one of its dilations are shown on the grid. Find the scale factor of the dilation.

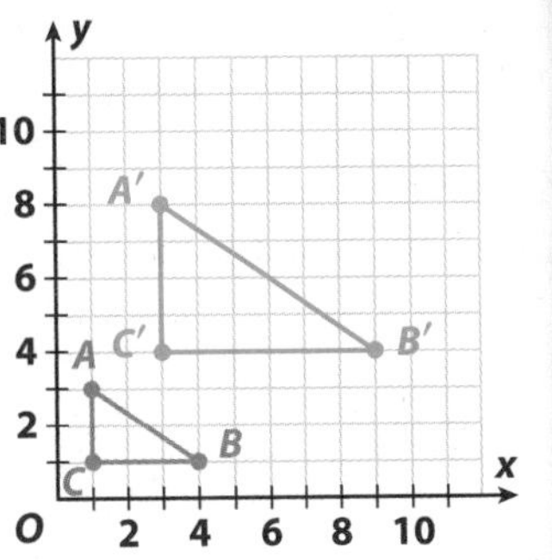

STEP 1 Use the coordinates to find the lengths of the sides of each triangle.

Triangle ABC: $AC = 2 \quad CB = 3$

Triangle $A'B'C'$: $A'C' = 4 \quad C'B' = 6$

Since the scale factor is the same for all corresponding sides, you can record just two pairs of side lengths. Use one pair as a check on the other.

STEP 2 Find the ratios of the corresponding sides.

$\frac{A'C'}{AC} = \frac{4}{2} = 2 \qquad \frac{C'B'}{CB} = \frac{6}{3} = 2$

The scale factor of the dilation is 2.

Reflect

4. Is the dilation an enlargement or a reduction? How can you tell?

___

___

Math Talk
Mathematical Practices

Which scale factors lead to enlargements? Which scale factors lead to reductions?

YOUR TURN

5. Find the scale factor of the dilation.

____

____

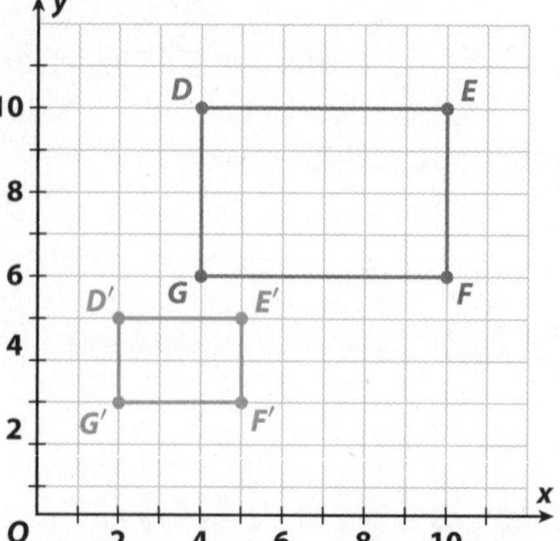

Guided Practice

Use triangles *ABC* and *A′B′C′* for 1–5. (Explore Activities 1 and 2, Example 1)

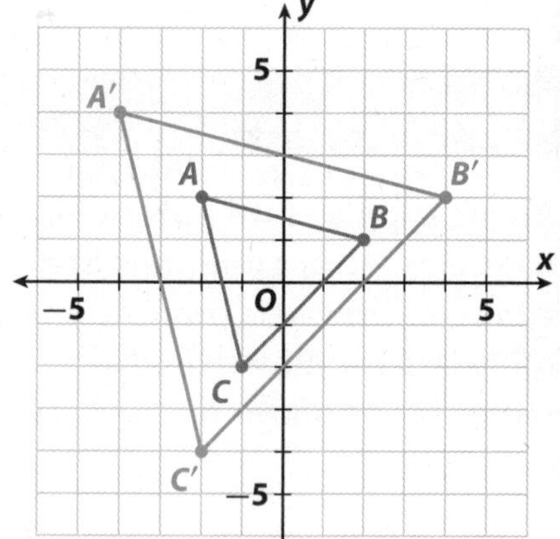

1. For each pair of corresponding vertices, find the ratio of the *x*-coordinates and the ratio of the *y*-coordinates.

   ratio of *x*-coordinates = _______________

   ratio of *y*-coordinates = _______________

2. I know that triangle *A′B′C′* is a dilation of triangle *ABC* because the ratios of the corresponding *x*-coordinates are _______________ and the ratios of the corresponding *y*-coordinates are _______________.

3. The ratio of the lengths of the corresponding sides of triangle *A′B′C′* and triangle *ABC* equals _______________.

4. The corresponding angles of triangle *ABC* and triangle *A′B′C′* are _______________.

5. The scale factor of the dilation is _______________.

ESSENTIAL QUESTION CHECK-IN

6. How can you find the scale factor of a dilation?

____

____

Name ______ Class ______ Date ______

20.1 Independent Practice

CA CC 8.G.3, 8.G.4

For 7–11, tell whether one figure is a dilation of the other or not. Explain your reasoning.

7. Quadrilateral *MNPQ* has side lengths of 15 mm, 24 mm, 21 mm, and 18 mm. Quadrilateral *M′N′P′Q′* has side lengths of 5 mm, 8 mm, 7 mm, and 4 mm.

______

8. Triangle *RST* has angles measuring 38° and 75°. Triangle *R′S′T′* has angles measuring 67° and 38°. The sides are proportional.

______

9. Two triangles, Triangle 1 and Triangle 2, are similar.

______

10. Quadrilateral *MNPQ* is the same shape but a different size than quadrilateral *M′N′P′Q*.

______

11. On a coordinate plane, triangle *UVW* has coordinates *U*(20, −12), *V*(8, 6), and *W*(−24, −4). Triangle *U′V′W′* has coordinates *U′*(15, −9), *V′*(6, 4.5), and *W′*(−18, −3).

______

Complete the table by writing "same" or "changed" to compare the image with the original figure in the given transformation.

		Image Compared to Original Figure		
		Orientation	Size	Shape
12.	**Translation**			
13.	**Reflection**			
14.	**Rotation**			
15.	**Dilation**			

16. Describe the image of a dilation with a scale factor of 1.

______

Identify the scale factor used in each dilation.

17.

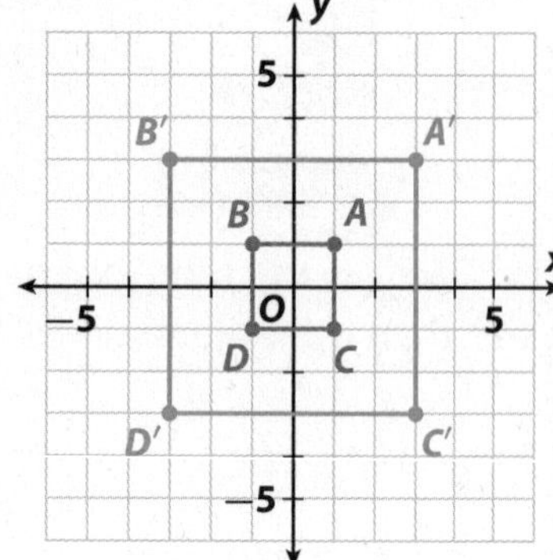

18.

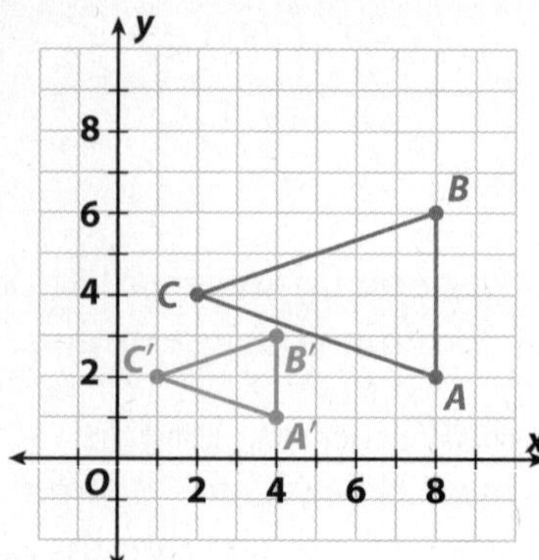

____

____

H.O.T. FOCUS ON HIGHER ORDER THINKING

Work Area

19. Critical Thinking Explain how you can find the center of dilation of a triangle and its dilation.

____

____

____

20. Make a Conjecture

a. A square on the coordinate plane has vertices at (−2, 2), (2, 2), (2, −2), and (−2, −2). A dilation of the square has vertices at (−4, 4), (4, 4), (4, −4), and (−4, −4). Find the scale factor and the perimeter of each square.

____

____

b. A square on the coordinate plane has vertices at (−3, 3), (3, 3), (3, −3), and (−3, −3). A dilation of the square has vertices at (−6, 6), (6, 6), (6, −6), and (−6, −6). Find the scale factor and the perimeter of each square.

____

____

c. Make a conjecture about the relationship of the scale factor to the perimeter of a square and its image.

____

____

LESSON 20.2

Algebraic Representations of Dilations

CA CC 8.G.3

Describe the effect of dilations, translations, rotations, and reflections on two-dimensional figures using coordinates.

ESSENTIAL QUESTION

How can you describe the effect of a dilation on coordinates using an algebraic representation?

EXPLORE ACTIVITY 1 

Graphing Enlargements

When a dilation in the coordinate plane has the origin as the center of dilation, you can find points on the dilated image by multiplying the x- and y-coordinates of the original figure by the scale factor. For scale factor k, the algebraic representation of the dilation is $(x, y) \rightarrow (kx, ky)$. For enlargements, $k > 1$.

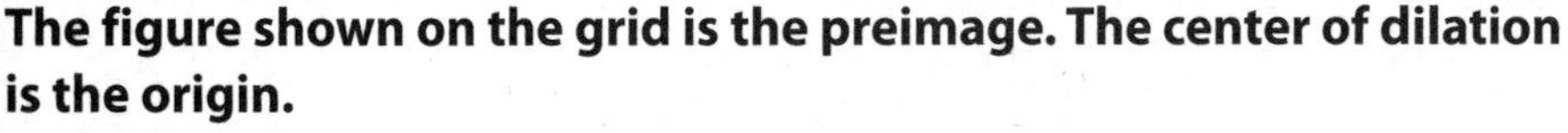

The figure shown on the grid is the preimage. The center of dilation is the origin.

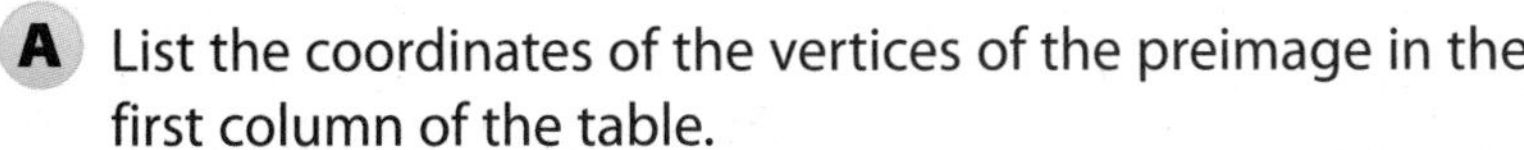

A List the coordinates of the vertices of the preimage in the first column of the table.

Preimage (x, y)	Image $(3x, 3y)$
(2, 2)	(6, 6)

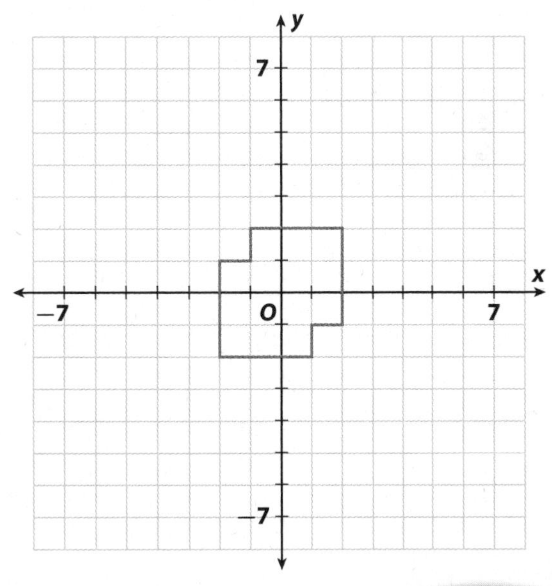

B What is the scale factor for the dilation? ________________

C Apply the dilation to the preimage and write the coordinates of the vertices of the image in the second column of the table.

D Sketch the image after the dilation on the coordinate grid.

What effect would the dilation $(x, y) \rightarrow (4x, 4y)$ have on the radius of a circle?

Reflect

1. How does the dilation affect the length of line segments?

____

____

2. How does the dilation affect angle measures?

____

EXPLORE ACTIVITY 2

8.G.3

Graphing Reductions

For scale factors between 0 and 1, the image is smaller than the preimage. This is called a reduction.

The arrow shown is the preimage. The center of dilation is the origin.

A List the coordinates of the vertices of the preimage in the first column of the table.

B What is the scale factor for the dilation? ______

C Apply the dilation to the preimage and write the coordinates of the vertices of the image in the second column of the table.

Preimage (x, y)	Image $\left(\frac{1}{2}x, \frac{1}{2}y\right)$

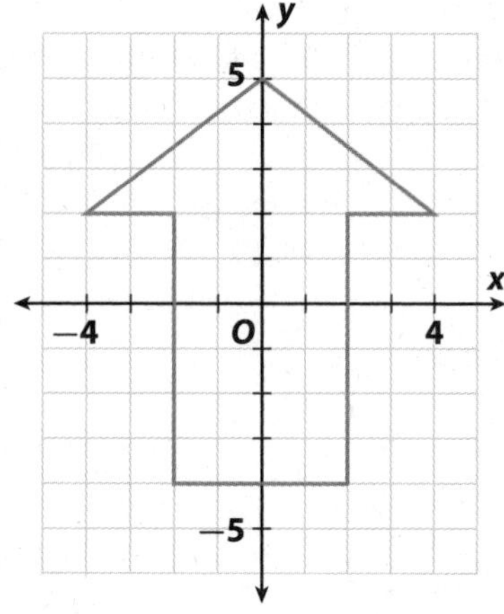

D Sketch the image after the dilation on the coordinate grid.

Reflect

3. How does the dilation affect the length of line segments?

____

4. How would a dilation with scale factor 1 affect the preimage?

____

Center of Dilation Outside the Image

The center of dilation can be inside *or* outside the original image and the dilated image. The center of dilation can be anywhere on the coordinate plane as long as the lines that connect each pair of corresponding vertices between the original and dilated image intersect at the center of dilation.

EXAMPLE 1

CA CC 8.G.3

Graph the image of $\triangle ABC$ after a dilation with the origin as its center and a scale factor of 3. What are the vertices of the image?

STEP 1 Multiply each coordinate of the vertices of $\triangle ABC$ by 3 to find the vertices of the dilated image.

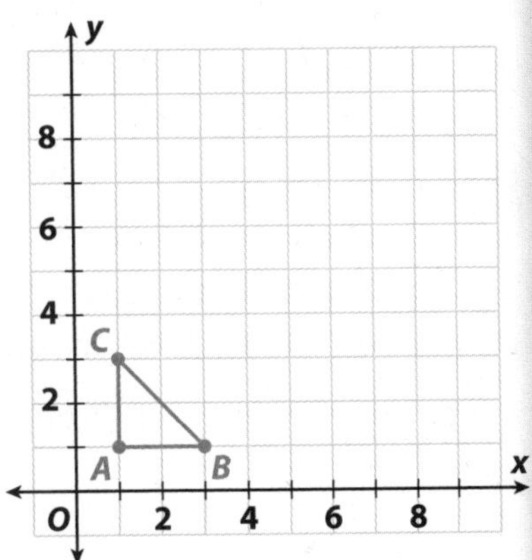

$\triangle ABC\ (x, y) \rightarrow (3x, 3y)\ \triangle A'B'C'$

$A(1, 1) \rightarrow A'(1 \cdot 3, 1 \cdot 3) \rightarrow A'(3, 3)$

$B(3, 1) \rightarrow B'(3 \cdot 3, 1 \cdot 3) \rightarrow B'(9, 3)$

$C(1, 3) \rightarrow C'(1 \cdot 3, 3 \cdot 3) \rightarrow C'(3, 9)$

The vertices of the dilated image are $A'(3, 3)$, $B'(9, 3)$, and $C'(3, 9)$.

STEP 2 Graph the dilated image.

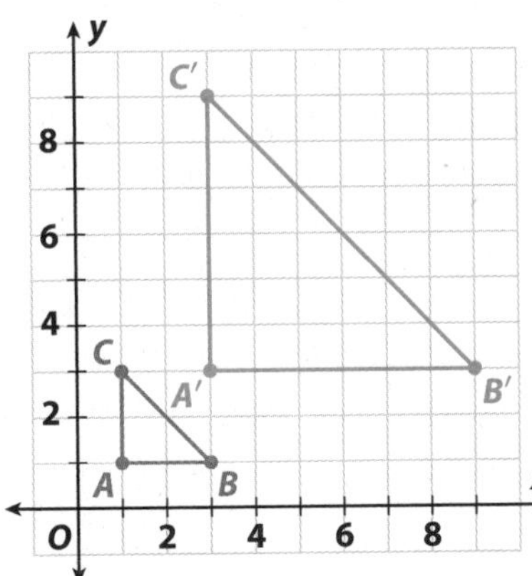

Math Talk
Mathematical Practices

Describe how you can check graphically that you have drawn the image triangle correctly.

YOUR TURN

5. Graph the image of $\triangle XYZ$ after a dilation with a scale factor of $\frac{1}{3}$ and the origin as its center. Then write an algebraic rule to describe the dilation.

____

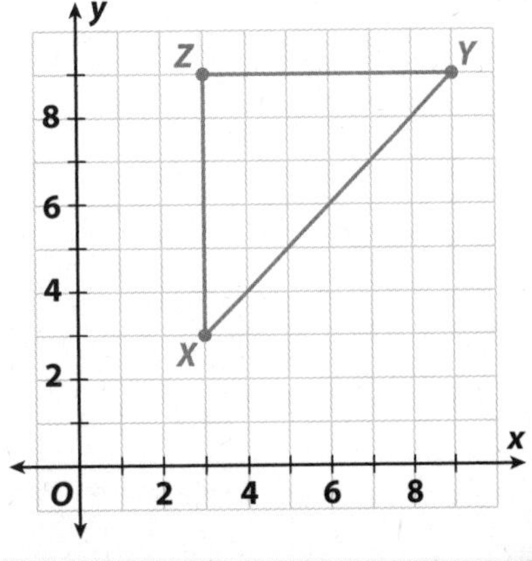

Guided Practice

1. The grid shows a diamond-shaped preimage. Write the coordinates of the vertices of the preimage in the first column of the table. Then apply the dilation $(x, y) \rightarrow \left(\frac{3}{2}x, \frac{3}{2}y\right)$ and write the coordinates of the vertices of the image in the second column. Sketch the image of the figure after the dilation. (Explore Activities 1 and 2)

Preimage	Image
(2, 0)	(3, 0)

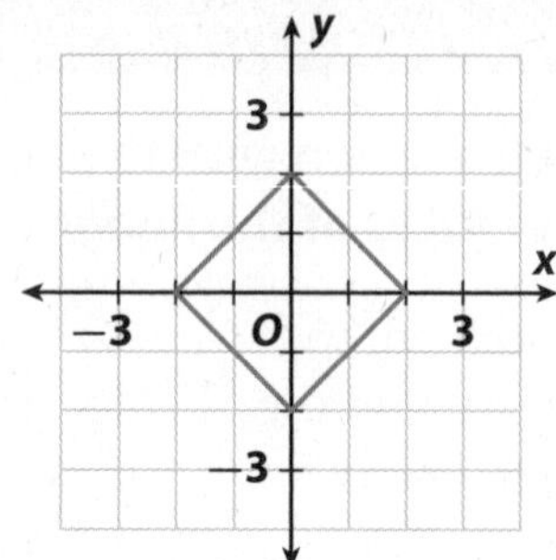

Graph the image of each figure after a dilation with the origin as its center and the given scale factor. Then write an algebraic rule to describe the dilation. (Example 1)

2. scale factor of 1.5

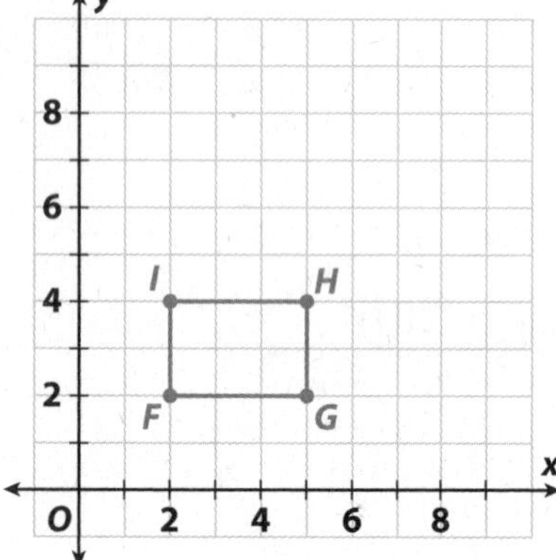

____

3. scale factor of $\frac{1}{3}$

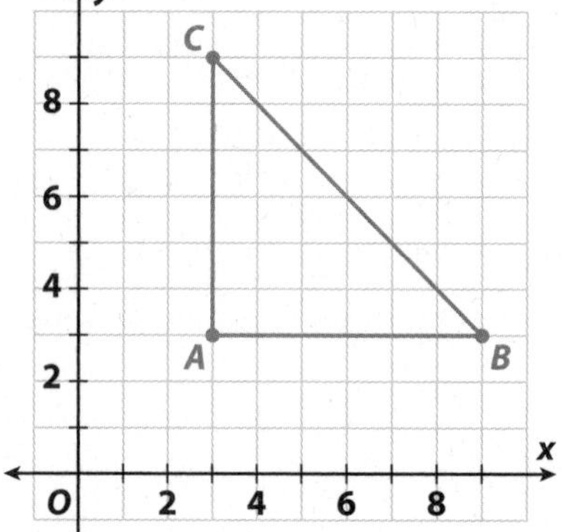

____

ESSENTIAL QUESTION CHECK-IN

4. A dilation of $(x, y) \rightarrow (kx, ky)$ when $0 < k < 1$ has what effect on the figure? What is the effect on the figure when $k > 1$?

____

____

____

____

Name ____________ Class ____________ Date ____________

20.2 Independent Practice

CA CC 8.G.3

5. The blue square is the preimage. Write two algebraic representations, one for the dilation to the green square and one for the dilation to the purple square.

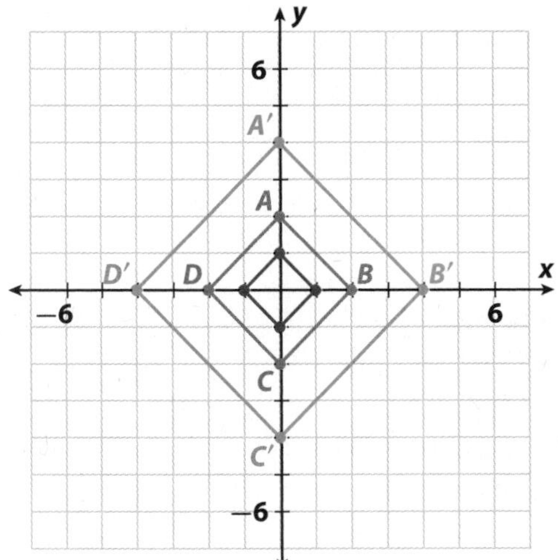

____

____

6. Critical Thinking A triangle has vertices $A(-5, -4)$, $B(2, 6)$, and $C(4, -3)$. The center of dilation is the origin and $(x, y) \rightarrow (3x, 3y)$. What are the vertices of the dilated image?

____

____

7. Critical Thinking $M'N'O'P'$ has vertices at $M'(3, 4)$, $N'(6, 4)$, $O'(6, 7)$, and $P'(3, 7)$. The center of dilation is the origin. $MNOP$ has vertices at $M(4.5, 6)$, $N(9, 6)$, $O'(9, 10.5)$, and $P'(4.5, 10.5)$. What is the algebraic representation of this dilation?

____

8. Critical Thinking A dilation with center (0,0) and scale factor k is applied to a polygon. What dilation can you apply to the image to return it to the original preimage?

____

9. Represent Real-World Problems The blueprints for a new house are scaled so that $\frac{1}{4}$ inch equals 1 foot. The blueprint is the preimage and the house is the dilated image. The blueprints are plotted on a coordinate plane.

a. What is the scale factor in terms of inches to inches?

____

b. One inch on the blueprint represents how many inches in the actual house? How many feet?

____

c. Write the algebraic representation of the dilation from the blueprint to the house.

____

d. A rectangular room has coordinates $Q(2, 2)$, $R(7, 2)$, $S(7, 5)$, and $T(2, 5)$ on the blueprint. The homeowner wants this room to be 25% larger. What are the coordinates of the new room?

____

____

____

e. What are the dimensions of the new room, in inches, on the blueprint? What will the dimensions of the new room be, in feet, in the new house?

____

____

____

____

10. Write the algebraic representation of the dilation shown.

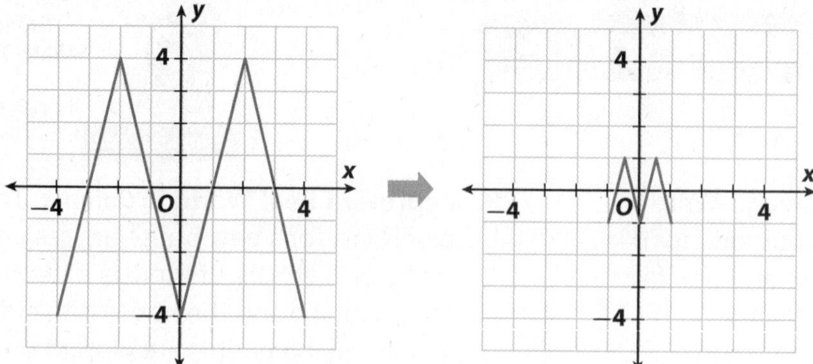

____

H.O.T. FOCUS ON HIGHER ORDER THINKING

Work Area

11. Critique Reasoning The set for a school play needs a replica of a historic building painted on a backdrop that is 20 feet long and 16 feet high. The actual building measures 400 feet long and 320 feet high. A stage crewmember writes $(x, y) \rightarrow \left(\frac{1}{12}x, \frac{1}{12}y\right)$ to represent the dilation. Is the crewmember's calculation correct if the painted replica is to cover the entire backdrop? Explain.

____

____

12. Communicate Mathematical Ideas Explain what each of these algebraic transformations does to a figure.

a. $(x, y) \rightarrow (y, -x)$ ______________________

b. $(x, y) \rightarrow (-x, -y)$ ______________________

c. $(x, y) \rightarrow (x, 2y)$ ______________________

____

d. $(x, y) \rightarrow \left(\frac{2}{3}x, y\right)$ ______________________

____

e. $(x, y) \rightarrow (0.5x, 1.5y)$ ______________________

____

13. Communicate Mathematical Ideas Triangle *ABC* has coordinates *A*(1, 5), *B*(−2, 1), and *C*(−2, 4). Sketch triangle *ABC* and *A′B′C′* for the dilation $(x, y) \rightarrow (-2x, -2y)$. What is the effect of a negative scale factor?

____

____

LESSON

20.3 Similar Figures

CA CC 8.G.4

Understand that a two-dimensional figure is similar to another if the second can be obtained from the first by a sequence of rotations, reflections, translations, and dilations; given two similar two-dimensional figures, describe a sequence that exhibits the similarity between them.

ESSENTIAL QUESTION

What is the connection between transformations and the orientations of similar figures?

EXPLORE ACTIVITY  8.G.4

Combining Transformations with Dilations

When creating an animation, figures need to be translated, reflected, rotated, and sometimes dilated. As an example of this, apply the indicated sequence of transformations to the rectangle. Each transformation is applied to the image of the previous transformation, not to the original figure. Label each image with the letter of the transformation applied.

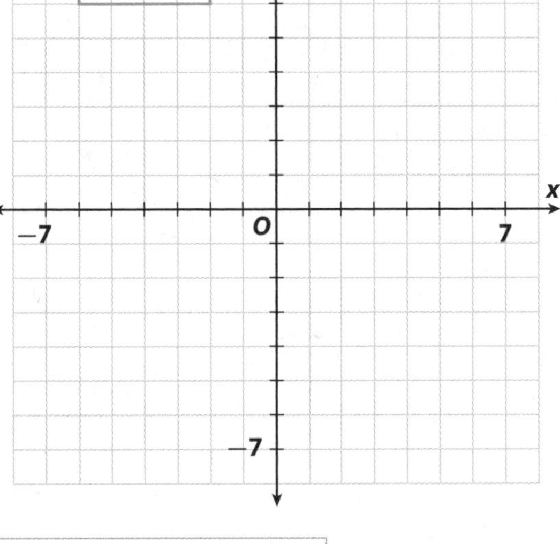

A $(x, y) \rightarrow (x + 7, y - 2)$

B $(x, y) \rightarrow (x, -y)$

C rotation 90° clockwise around the origin

D $(x, y) \rightarrow (x + 5, y + 3)$

E $(x, y) \rightarrow (3x, 3y)$

F List the coordinates of the vertices of rectangle *E*.

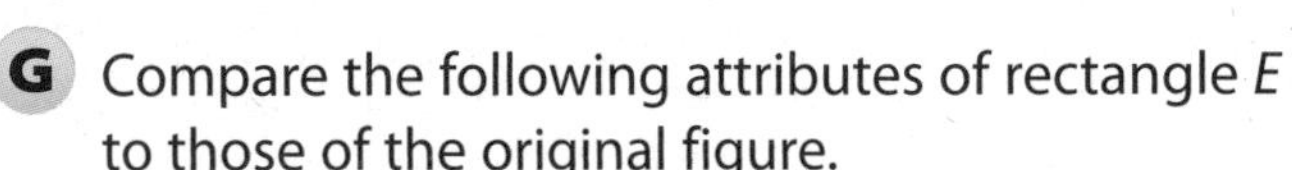

G Compare the following attributes of rectangle *E* to those of the original figure.

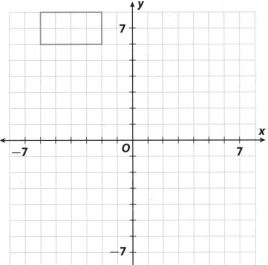

Shape	
Size	
Angle Measures	

EXPLORE ACTIVITY *(cont'd)*

Reflect

1. Which transformation represents the dilation? How can you tell?

____

____

2. A sequence of transformations containing a single dilation is applied to a figure. Are the original figure and its final image congruent? Explain.

____

____

Similar Figures

Two figures are **similar** if one can be obtained from the other by a sequence of translations, reflections, rotations, and dilations. Similar figures have the same shape but may be different sizes.

When you are told that two figures are similar, there must be a sequence of translations, reflections, rotations, and/or dilations that can transform one to the other.

EXAMPLE 1

CA CC 8.G.4

My Notes

A Identify a sequence of transformations that will transform figure *A* into figure *B*. Tell whether the figures are congruent. Tell whether they are similar.

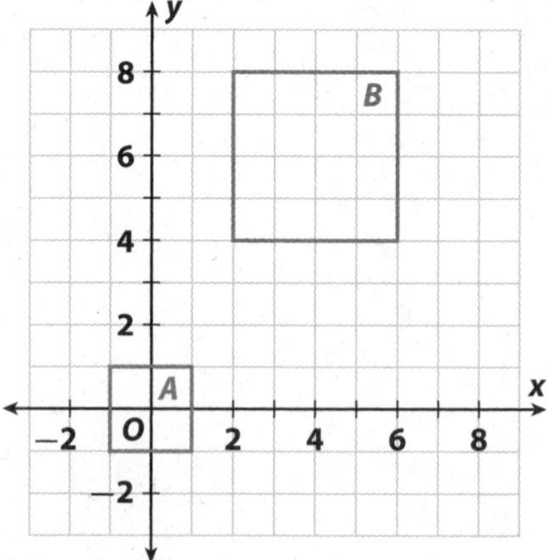

Both figures are squares whose orientations are the same, so no reflection or rotation is needed. Figure *B* has sides twice as long as figure *A*, so a dilation with a scale factor of 2 is needed. Figure *B* is moved to the right and above figure *A*, so a translation is needed. A sequence of transformations that will accomplish this is a dilation by a scale factor of 2 centered at the origin followed by the translation $(x, y) \rightarrow (x + 4, y + 6)$. The figures are not congruent, but they are similar.

B Identify a sequence of transformations that will transform figure *C* into figure *D*. Include a reflection. Tell whether the figures are congruent. Tell whether they are similar.

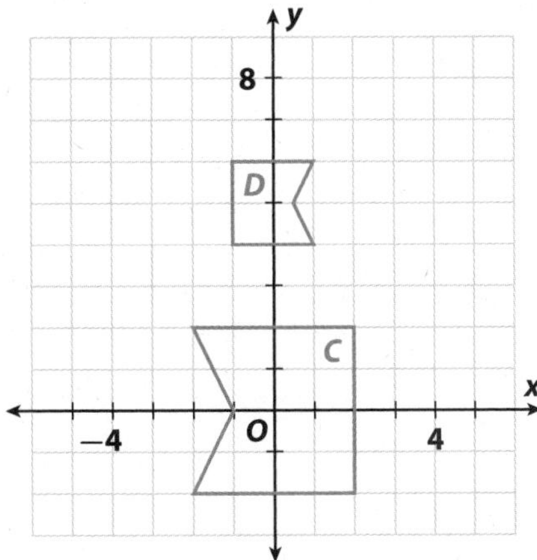

The orientation of figure *D* is reversed from that of figure *C*, so a reflection over the *y*-axis is needed. Figure *D* has sides that are half as long as figure *C*, so a dilation with a scale factor of $\frac{1}{2}$ is needed. Figure *D* is moved above figure *C*, so a translation is needed. A sequence of transformations that will accomplish this is a dilation by a scale factor of $\frac{1}{2}$ centered at the origin, followed by the reflection $(x, y) \rightarrow (-x, y)$, followed by the translation $(x, y) \rightarrow (x, y + 5)$. The figures are not congruent, but they are similar.

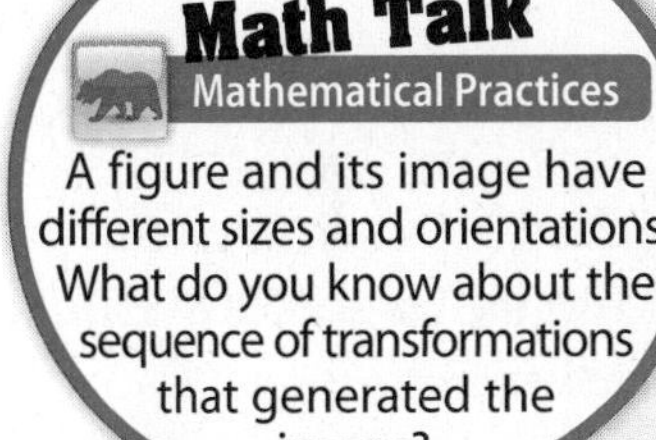

Math Talk
Mathematical Practices
A figure and its image have different sizes and orientations. What do you know about the sequence of transformations that generated the image?

C Identify a sequence of transformations that will transform figure *C* into figure *D*. Include a rotation.

The orientation of figure *D* is reversed from that of figure *C*, so a rotation of 180° is needed. Figure *D* has sides that are half as long as figure *C*, so a dilation with a scale factor of $\frac{1}{2}$ is needed. Figure *D* is moved above figure *C*, so a translation is needed. A sequence of transformations that will accomplish this is a rotation of 180° about the origin, followed by a dilation by a scale factor of $\frac{1}{2}$ centered at the origin, followed by the translation $(x, y) \rightarrow (x, y + 5)$.

YOUR TURN

3. Look again at the Explore Activity. Start with the original figure. Create a new sequence of transformations that will yield figure *E*, the final image. Your transformations do not need to produce the images in the same order in which they originally appeared.

____

____

____

Personal Math Trainer

Online Practice and Help

my.hrw.com

Guided Practice

1. Apply the indicated sequence of transformations to the square. Apply each transformation to the image of the previous transformation. Label each image with the letter of the transformation applied. (Explore Activity)

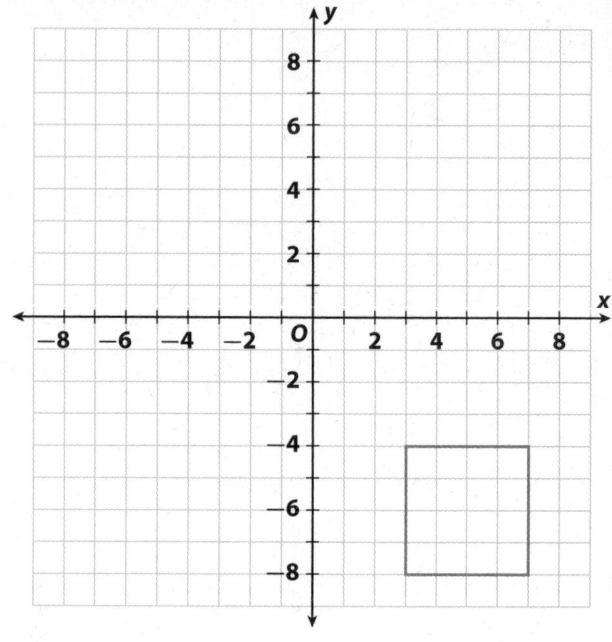

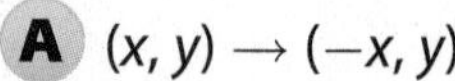

A $(x, y) \rightarrow (-x, y)$

B Rotate the square 180° around the origin.

C $(x, y) \rightarrow (x - 5, y - 6)$

D $(x, y) \rightarrow \left(\frac{1}{2}x, \frac{1}{2}y\right)$

Identify a sequence of two transformations that will transform figure A into the given figure. (Example 1)

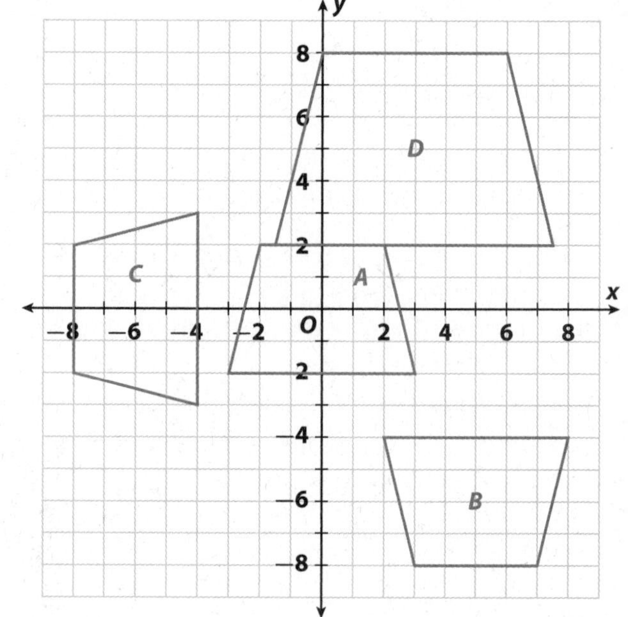

2. figure *B*

____

____

3. figure *C*

____

____

4. figure *D*

____

____

ESSENTIAL QUESTION CHECK-IN

5. If two figures are similar but not congruent, what do you know about the sequence of transformations used to create one from the other?

____

____

Name ______________________ Class ______________________ Date ______________________

20.3 Independent Practice

8.G.4

6. A designer creates a drawing of a triangular sign on centimeter grid paper for a new business. The drawing has sides measuring 6 cm, 8 cm, and 10 cm, and angles measuring 37°, 53°, and 90°. To create the actual sign shown, the drawing must be dilated using a scale factor of 40.

   a. Find the lengths of the sides of the actual sign.

   ____

   b. Find the angle measures of the actual sign.

   ____

   c. The drawing has the hypotenuse on the bottom. The business owner would like it on the top. Describe two transformations that will do this.

   ____

   ____

   d. The shorter leg of the drawing is currently on the left. The business owner wants it to remain on the left after the hypotenuse goes to the top. Which transformation in part c will accomplish this?

   ____

In Exercises 7–10, the transformation of a figure into its image is described. Describe the transformations that will transform the image back into the original figure. Then write them algebraically.

7. The figure is reflected across the *x*-axis and dilated by a scale factor of 3.

   ____

   ____

8. The figure is dilated by a scale factor of 0.5 and translated 6 units left and 3 units up.

   ____

   ____

9. The figure is dilated by a scale factor of 5 and rotated 90° clockwise.

   ____

   ____

10. The figure is reflected across the y-axis and dilated by a scale factor of 4.

Work Area

11. Draw Conclusions A figure undergoes a sequence of transformations that include dilations. The figure and its final image are congruent. Explain how this can happen.

12. Multistep A graphic artist is using transformations to sketch ideas for a logo design. Start with the image provided and label each transformation with the letter of the sequence that is applied. Apply each sequence of transformations to the previous image.

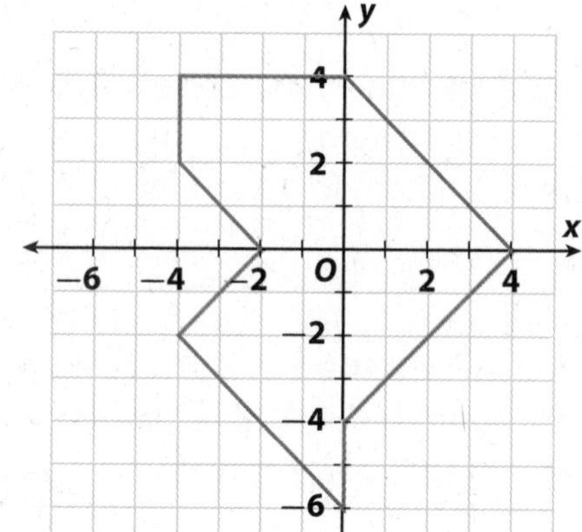

A. $(x, y) \rightarrow \left(\frac{1}{2}x, \frac{1}{2}y\right)$ with the center at the origin, $(x, y) \rightarrow (x, y - 1)$.

B. $(x, y) \rightarrow (x - 4, y + 1)$, $(x, y) \rightarrow (x, -y)$.

13. Justify Reasoning In Exercise 12A, the sketch was dilated by a scale factor of $\frac{1}{2}$ and translated down 1 unit. Is this the same as translating the sketch down 1 unit and then dilating by a scale factor of $\frac{1}{2}$? Explain how the two results are related.

MODULE QUIZ

Ready to Go On?

20.1 Properties of Dilations

Determine whether one figure is a dilation of the other. Justify your answer.

1. Triangle XYZ has angles measuring 54° and 29°. Triangle $X'Y'Z'$ has angles measuring 29° and 92°.

____

2. Quadrilateral $DEFG$ has sides measuring 16 m, 28 m, 24 m, and 20 m. Quadrilateral $D'E'F'G'$ has sides measuring 20 m, 35 m, 30 m, and 25 m.

____

____

20.2 Algebraic Representations of Dilations

Dilate each figure with the origin as the center of dilation.

3. $(x, y) \rightarrow (0.8x, 0.8y)$

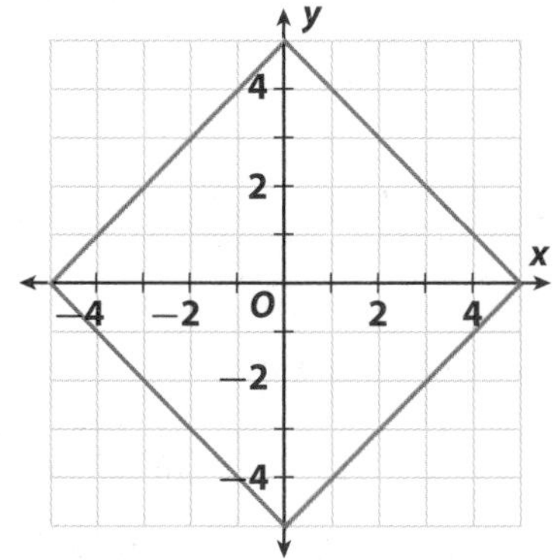

4. $(x, y) \rightarrow (2.5x, 2.5y)$

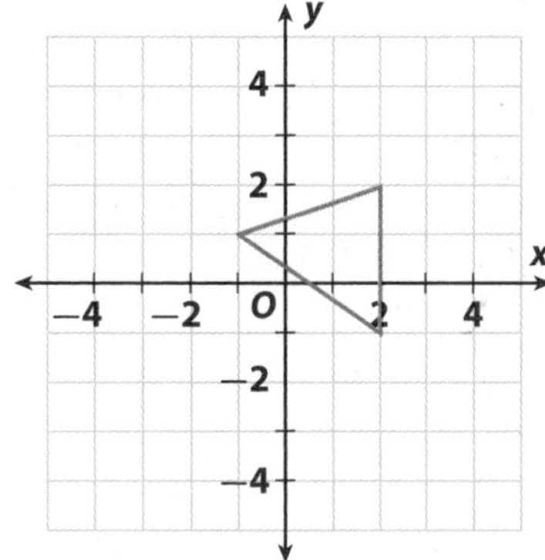

20.3 Similar Figures

5. Describe what happens to a figure when the given sequence of transformations is applied to it: $(x, y) \rightarrow (-x, y)$; $(x, y) \rightarrow (0.5x, 0.5y)$; $(x, y) \rightarrow (x - 2, y + 2)$

____

____

ESSENTIAL QUESTION

6. How can you use dilations to solve real-world problems?

____

MODULE 20
MIXED REVIEW

Assessment Readiness

1. Triangle *ABC* is dilated by a scale factor of 2 with the origin as its center and then reflected across the *y*-axis. Look at each ordered pair. Is the ordered pair a vertex of the image?

Select Yes or No for ordered pairs A–C.

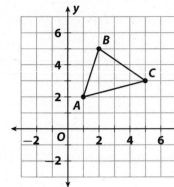

A. (−4, 10) ◯ Yes ◯ No
B. (−2, 4) ◯ Yes ◯ No
C. (10, −6) ◯ Yes ◯ No

2. Choose True or False for each statement.

A. No integers are irrational numbers. ◯ True ◯ False
B. No real numbers are rational numbers. ◯ True ◯ False
C. All integers are whole numbers. ◯ True ◯ False
D. All whole numbers are integers. ◯ True ◯ False

3. In a video game, a rectangular map has vertices *M*(10, 10), *N*(10, 20), *P*(40, 20), and *Q*(40, 10). When a player clicks the map, it is enlarged by a scale factor of 4.5 with the origin as the center of dilation. What are the coordinates of the vertices of the enlarged map? Describe the algebraic rule you used to find the coordinates.

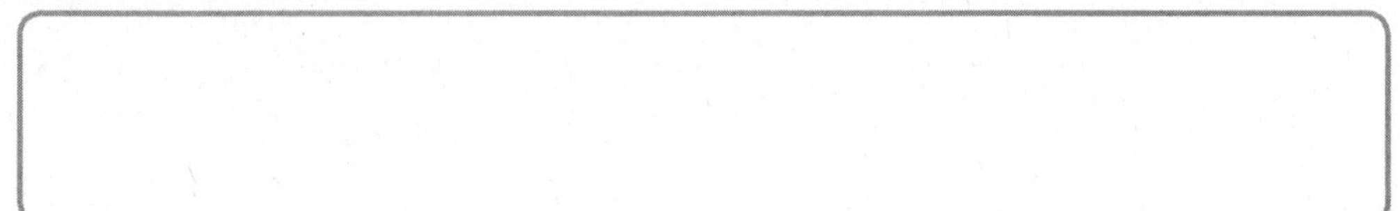

4. An engineer is working on the design of a bridge. He draws the two triangles shown. Is triangle *A* similar to triangle *B*? Use a sequence of transformations to explain how you know.

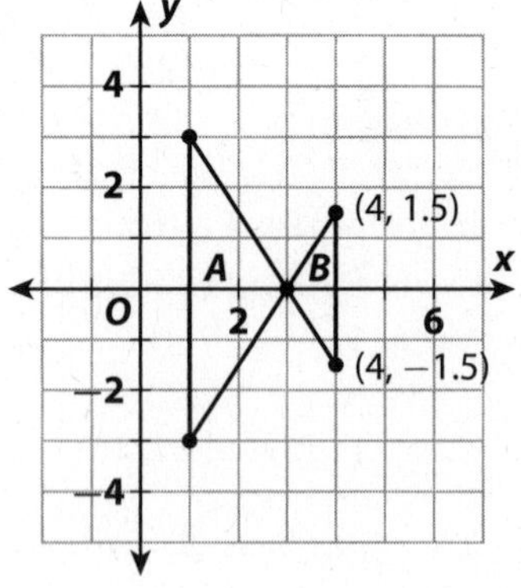

UNIT 9

Study Guide Review

MODULE 19 Transformations and Congruence

Key Vocabulary

center of rotation *(centro de rotación)*
congruent *(congruente)*
image *(imagen)*
line of reflection *(línea de reflexión)*
preimage *(imagen original)*
reflection *(reflexión)*
rotation *(rotación)*
transformation *(transformación)*
translation *(traslación)*

ESSENTIAL QUESTION

How can you use transformations and congruence to solve real-world problems?

EXAMPLE

Translate triangle *XYZ* left 4 units and down 2 units. Graph the image and label the vertices.

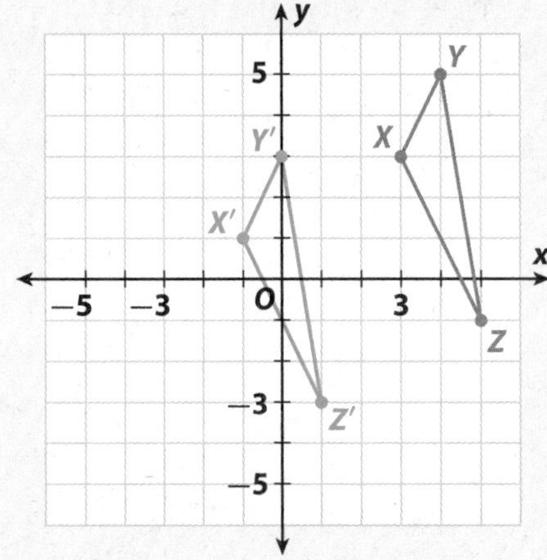

Translate the vertices by subtracting 4 from each *x*-coordinate and 2 from each *y*-coordinate. The new vertices are $X'(-1, 1)$, $Y'(0, 3)$, and $Z'(1, -3)$.

Connect the vertices to draw triangle $X'Y'Z'$.

EXERCISES

Perform the transformation shown. (Lessons 19.1, 19.2, 19.3)

1. Reflection over the *x*-axis

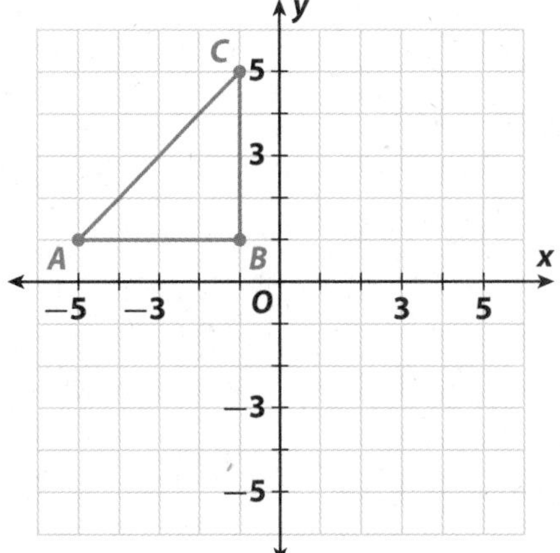

2. Translation 5 units right

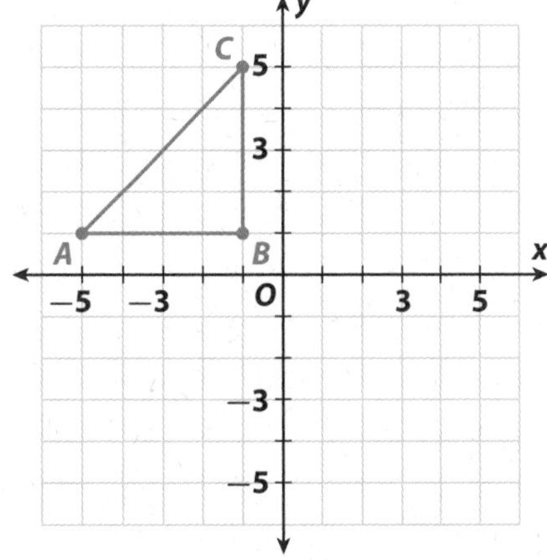

3. Rotation 90° counterclockwise about the origin

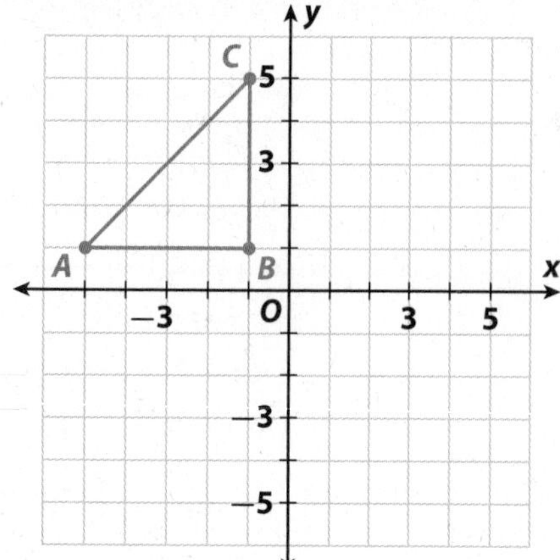

4. Translation 4 units right and 4 units down

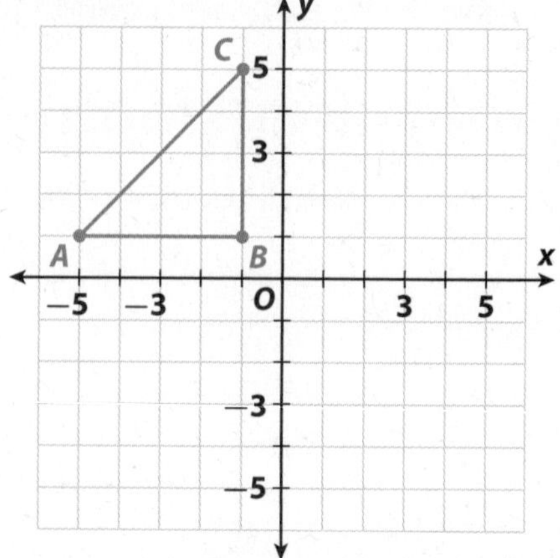

5. Quadrilateral *ABCD* with vertices *A*(4, 4), *B*(5, 1), *C*(5, −1) and *D*(4, −2) is translated left 2 units and down 3 units. Graph the preimage and the image. (Lesson 19.4)

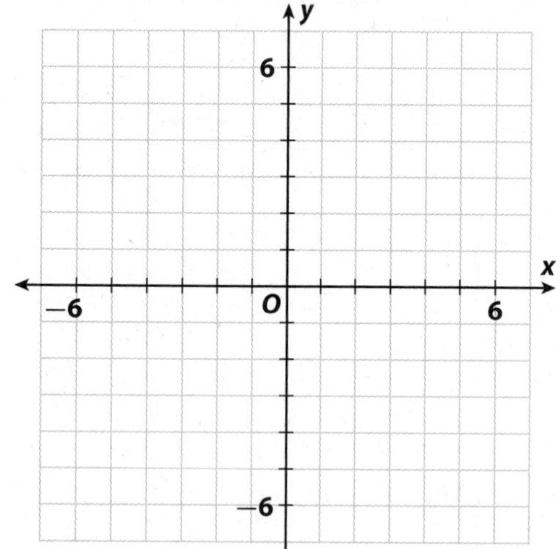

6. Triangle *ABC* with vertices *A*(1, 2), *B*(1, 4), and *C*(3, 3) is translated by $(x, y) \rightarrow (x - 4, y)$, and the result is reflected by $(x, y) \rightarrow (x, -y)$. Graph the preimage and the image. (Lesson 19.5)

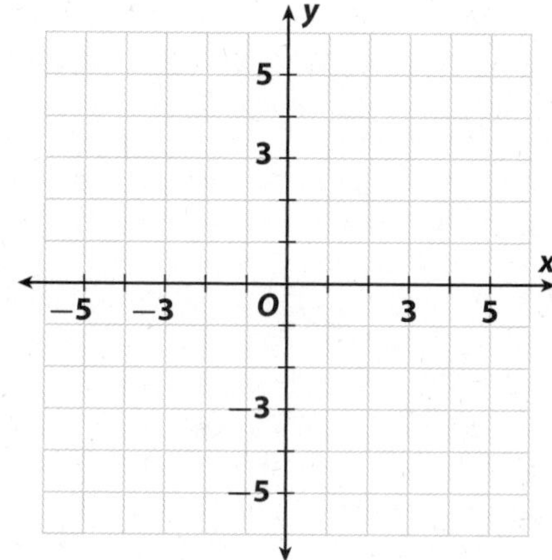

7. Triangle *RST* has vertices at (−8, 2), (−4, 0), and (−12, 8). Find the vertices after the triangle has been reflected over the *y*-axis. (Lesson 19.4)

____

8. Triangle *XYZ* has vertices at (3, 7), (9, 14), and (12, −1). Find the vertices after the triangle has been rotated 180° about the origin. (Lesson 19.4)

____

9. Triangle *MNP* has its vertices located at (−1, −4), (−2, −5), and (−3, −3). Find the vertices after the triangle has been reflected by $(x, y) \rightarrow (x, -y)$ and translated by $(x, y) \rightarrow (x + 6, y)$. (Lesson 19.5)

____

MODULE 20

Transformations and Similarity

ESSENTIAL QUESTION

How can you use dilations, similarity, and proportionality to solve real-world problems?

Key Vocabulary

center of dilation *(centro de dilatación)*
dilation *(dilatación)*
enlargement *(agrandamiento)*
reduction *(reducción)*
scale factor *(factor de escala)*
similar *(semejante/sio)*

EXAMPLE

Dilate triangle *ABC* with the origin as the center of dilation and scale factor $\frac{1}{2}$. Graph the dilated image.

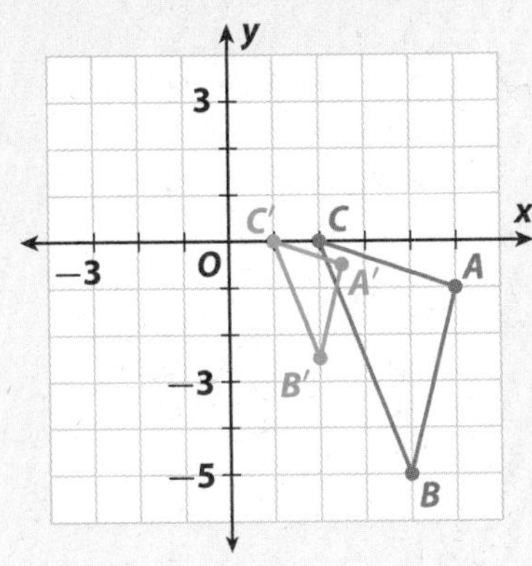

Multiply each coordinate of the vertices of *ABC* by $\frac{1}{2}$ to find the vertices of the dilated image.

$$A(5, -1) \rightarrow A'\left(5 \cdot \tfrac{1}{2}, -1 \cdot \tfrac{1}{2}\right) \rightarrow A'\left(2\tfrac{1}{2}, -\tfrac{1}{2}\right)$$
$$B(4, -5) \rightarrow B'\left(4 \cdot \tfrac{1}{2}, -5 \cdot \tfrac{1}{2}\right) \rightarrow B'\left(2, -2\tfrac{1}{2}\right)$$
$$C(2, 0) \rightarrow C'\left(2 \cdot \tfrac{1}{2}, 0 \cdot \tfrac{1}{2}\right) \rightarrow C'(1, 0)$$

EXERCISES

Dilate each figure with the origin as the center of the dilation. List the vertices of the dilated figure then graph the figure. (Lesson 20.2)

1. $(x, y) \rightarrow \left(\frac{1}{4}x, \frac{1}{4}y\right)$

____

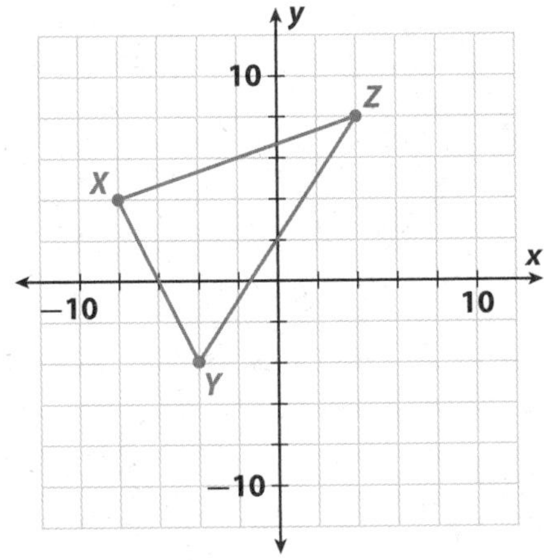

2. $(x, y) \rightarrow (2x, 2y)$

____

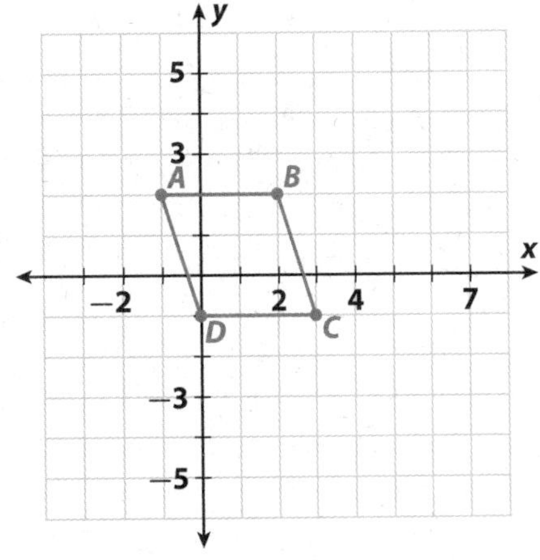

3. Rectangle *WXYZ* has vertices at (−2, −1), (−2, 1), (2, −1), and (2, 1). It is first dilated by $(x, y) \rightarrow (2x, 2y)$, and then translated by $(x, y) \rightarrow (x, y + 3)$. (Lesson 20.3)

What are the vertices of the image? ____________________

Unit Project

CA CC 8.G.1, 8.G.3

Transforming the World

For this project, create a presentation that shows real-world examples of transformations. Include three rotations, three translations, and three reflections. Your project can show photographs or drawings that you have found during your research. Your examples do not have to illustrate exact transformations. For example, you can include a photo of a flower with a shape that closely resembles, but does not precisely match, a rotational pattern.

In your project, identify the object, the transformation displayed, and the source where you found the object. Use the space below to write down any questions you have or important information from your teacher.

MATH IN CAREERS | ACTIVITY

Contractor Fernando is expanding his dog's play yard. The original yard has a fence represented by rectangle *LMNO* on the coordinate plane. Fernando hires a contractor to construct a new fence that should enclose 6 times as much area as the current fence. The shape of the yard must remain the same. The contractor constructs the fence shown by rectangle *L′M′N′O′*. Determine if the contractor met Fernando's requirements for the new fence. Explain your answer.

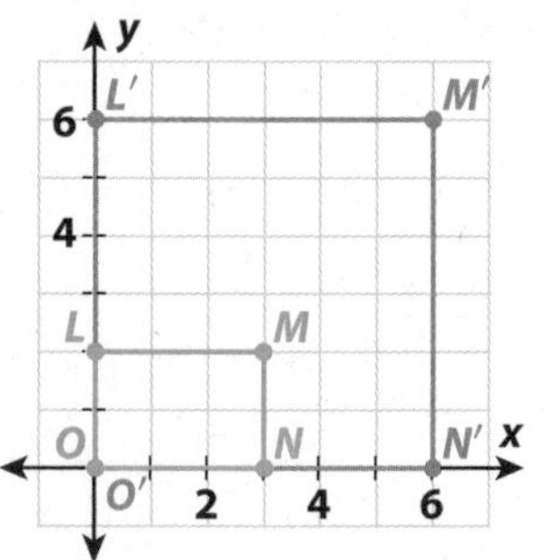

UNIT 9
MIXED REVIEW

Assessment Readiness

1. Triangle *DEF* has sides measuring 18 inches, 24 inches, and 36 inches. Look at each set of side lengths below. Could they be the side lengths of a dilation of triangle *DEF*?

Select Yes or No.

A. 9 inches, 18 inches, and 27 inches ○ Yes ○ No

B. 12 inches, 16 inches, and 24 inches ○ Yes ○ No

C. 27 inches, 36 inches, and 54 inches ○ Yes ○ No

2. Which transformation could be used to transform triangle *A* into triangle *B*?

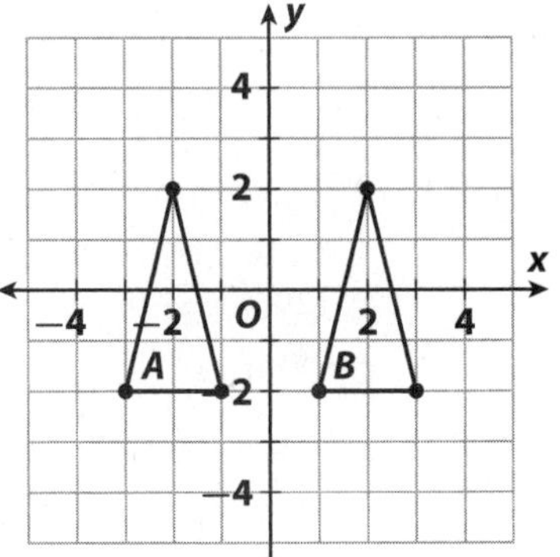

Select Yes or No.

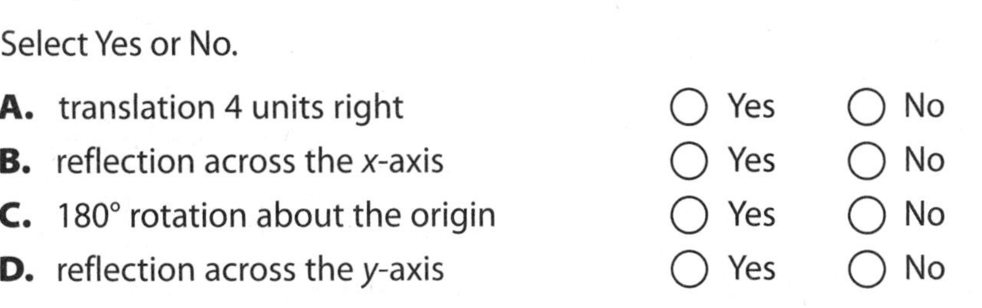

A. translation 4 units right ○ Yes ○ No

B. reflection across the *x*-axis ○ Yes ○ No

C. 180° rotation about the origin ○ Yes ○ No

D. reflection across the *y*-axis ○ Yes ○ No

3. A prop assistant needs to rent a telescope to use for a scene in a movie. One company charges $58 per day plus a flat fee of $32 to rent a telescope. Another company charges $62 per day with no flat fee. For how many days would the total cost of renting a telescope be the same at both companies? Justify your answer by writing and solving an equation.

4. An artist is working on the design for a deck. She starts by drawing quadrilateral *JKLM*. She then translates the quadrilateral 3 units right and 2 units down. What are the coordinates of the vertices of the image of the translation? Describe the algebraic rule you used to find the coordinates.

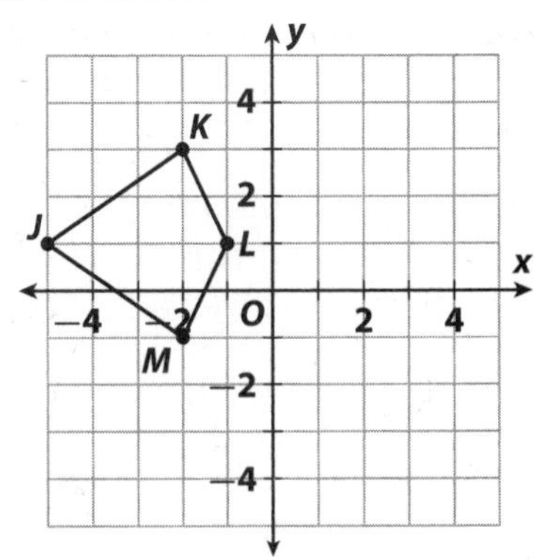

Performance Tasks

★**5.** The location of a shelter in a park is shown by trapezoid *S* on the map. Another shelter with the same size and shape as the first needs to be shown on the map as trapezoid *T* with vertices at (3, 1), (1, 1), and (0, 3). Draw trapezoid *T*, and explain how you determined the coordinates of its fourth vertex.

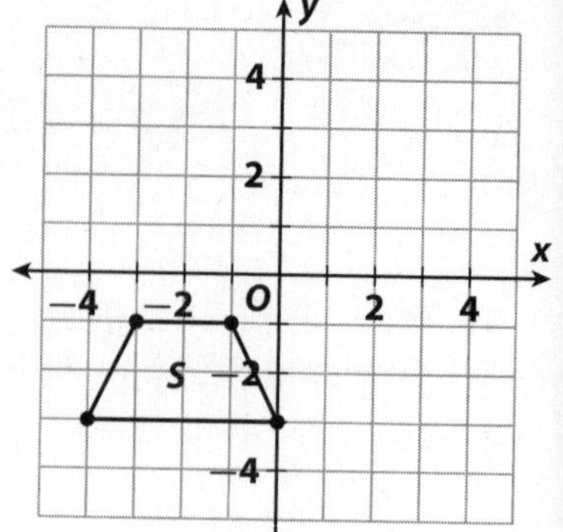

★★**6.** A rancher has a pen shown on the grid, where 1 unit represents 1 meter. The rancher needs a larger pen to be a dilation of the smaller pen by a scale factor of 3.5 with the origin as the center of dilation.

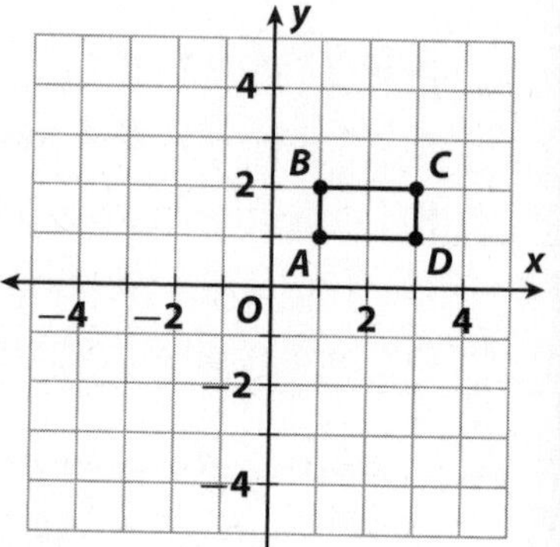

a. Graph the larger pen on a separate coordinate plane, and list the coordinates of its vertices.

b. How can you check that it is a dilation?

c. How many times the perimeter of the smaller pen is the perimeter of the larger pen? Explain how you know.

d. How many times the area of the smaller pen is the area of the larger pen? Explain how you know.

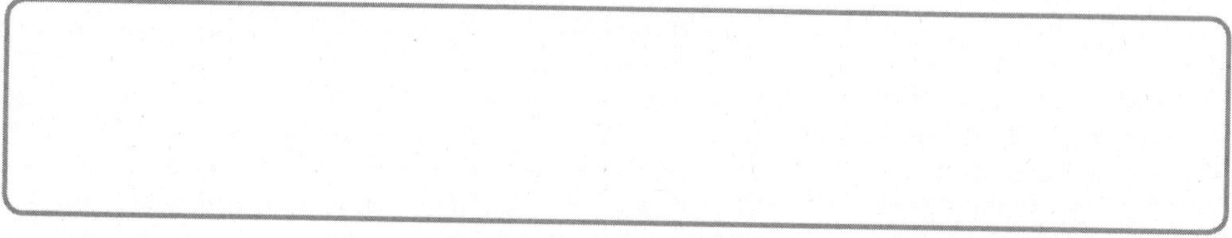

★★★**7.** A T-shirt designer is working on the design for a new shirt.

a. Describe how the designer can create the design shown by using transformations on triangle *A* to produce the other triangles.

b. Which of the triangles in the design are congruent, and which are similar? Explain how you know.

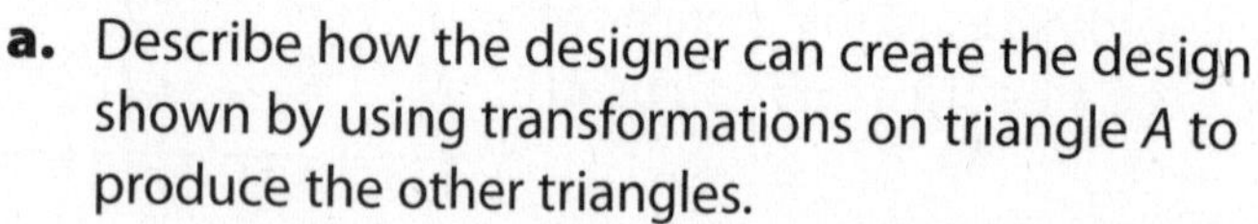

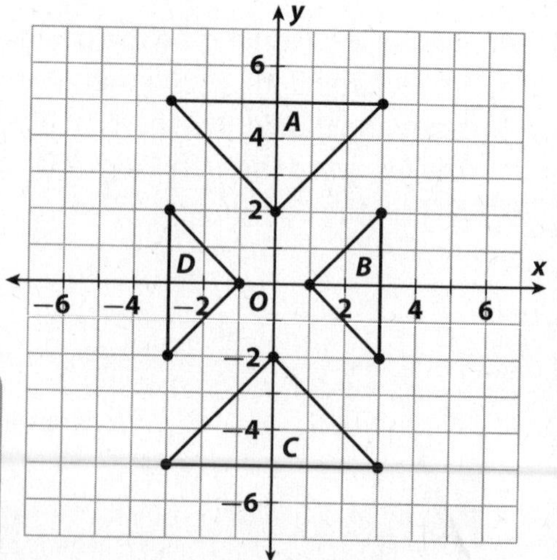

UNIT 10

Measurement Geometry

MODULE 21

Angle Relationships in Parallel Lines and Triangles

CA CC 8.G.5

MODULE 22

Volume

CA CC 8.G.9

MATH IN CAREERS

Hydrologist A hydrologist is a scientist who studies and solves water-related issues. A hydrologist might work to prevent or clean up polluted water sources, locate water supplies for urban or rural needs, or control flooding and erosion. A hydrologist uses math to assess water resources and mathematical models to understand water systems, as well as statistics to analyze phenomena such as rainfall patterns.

If you are interested in a career as a hydrologist, you should study the following mathematical subjects:

- Algebra
- Trigonometry
- Calculus
- Statistics

Research other careers that require creating and using mathematical models to understand physical phenomena.

ACTIVITY At the end of the unit, check out how **hydrologists** use math.

Unit Project Preview

The Volume of a Sphere

In the Unit Project at the end of this unit you will choose a model of a sphere and then determine a method for finding its volume and other key information. In addition, you will compare the volume of the sphere with the volumes of a cone, a cylinder, and a cube. To successfully complete the Unit Project you'll need to master these skills:

- Calculate radiuses and circumferences of circles.
- Calculate volumes of solid figures.
- Multiply and divide rational numbers.

1. Describe a real-world situation in which you might wish to calculate the volume of a sphere.

____

____

____

____

2. Explain how you can find the radius of a circle if you know the circumference.

____

____

Tracking Your Learning Progression

This unit addresses important California Common Core Standards in the Critical Area of solving problems involving solid figures.

Domain 8.G Geometry

Cluster Solve real-life and mathematical problems involving volume of cylinders, cones, and spheres.

Angle Relationships in Parallel Lines and Triangles

ESSENTIAL QUESTION

How can you use angle relationships in parallel lines and triangles to solve real-world problems?

Real-World Video

my.hrw.com

Many cities are designed on a grid with parallel streets. If another street runs across the parallel lines, it is a transversal. Special relationships exist between parallel lines and transversals.

my.hrw.com

my.hrw.com

Go digital with your write-in student edition, accessible on any device.

Math On the Spot

Scan with your smart phone to jump directly to the online edition, video tutor, and more.

Animated Math

Interactively explore key concepts to see how math works.

Personal Math Trainer

Get immediate feedback and help as you work through practice sets.

Are YOU Ready?

Complete these exercises to review skills you will need for this module.

Solve Two-Step Equations

EXAMPLE

$7x + 9 = 30$ Write the equation.

$7x + 9 - 9 = 30 - 9$ Subtract 9 from both sides.

$7x = 21$ Simplify.

$\frac{7x}{7} = \frac{21}{7}$ Divide both sides by 7.

$x = 3$ Simplify.

Solve for *x*.

1. $6x + 10 = 46$ ____

2. $7x - 6 = 36$ ____

3. $3x + 26 = 59$ ____

4. $2x + 5 = -25$ ____

5. $6x - 7 = 41$ ____

6. $\frac{1}{2}x + 9 = 30$ ____

7. $\frac{1}{3}x - 7 = 15$ ____

8. $0.5x - 0.6 = 8.4$ ____

Name Angles

EXAMPLE

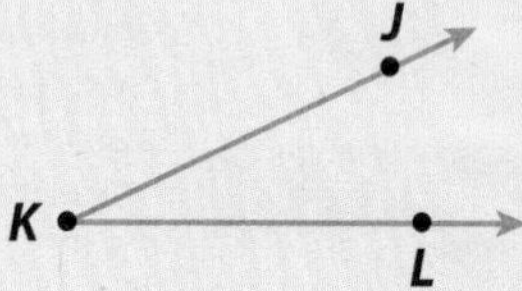

Use three points of an angle, including the vertex, to name the angle. Write the vertex between the other two points: ∠*JKL* or ∠*LKJ*. You can also use just the vertex letter to name the angle if there is no danger of confusing the angle with another. This is also ∠*K*.

Give two names for the angle formed by the dashed rays.

9. ____

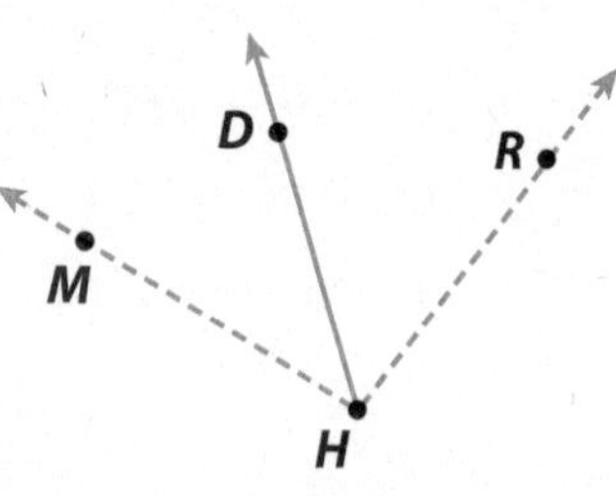

10. ____

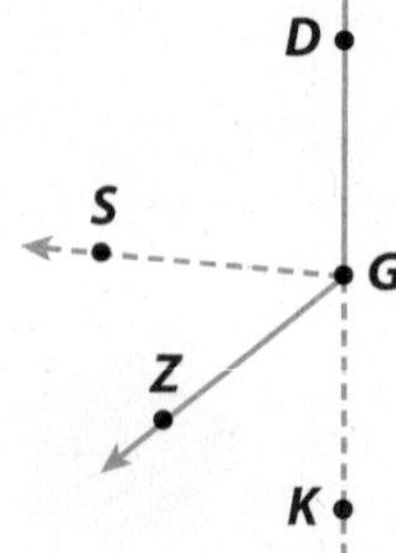

11. ____

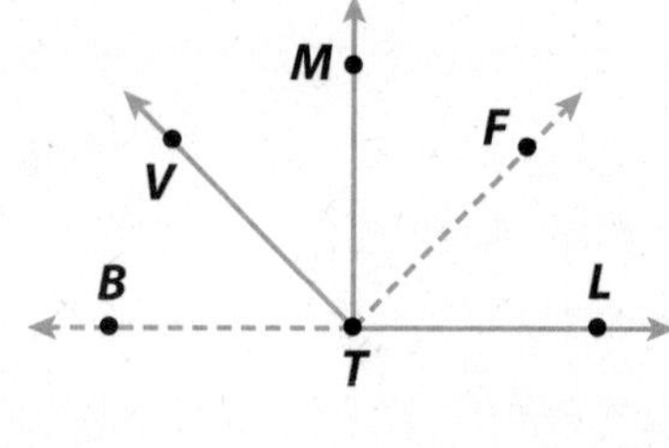

Reading Start-Up

Visualize Vocabulary

Use the ✔ words to complete the graphic. You can put more than one word in each section of the triangle.

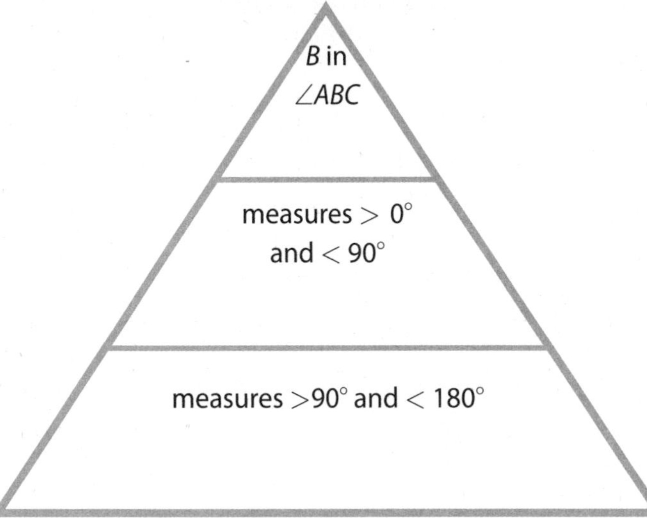

Understand Vocabulary

Complete the sentences using preview words.

1. A line that intersects two or more lines is a ___________________.

2. Figures with the same shape but not necessarily the same size are ___________________.

3. An ___________________ is an angle formed by one side of the triangle and the extension of an adjacent side.

Vocabulary

Review Words

✔ acute angle *(ángulo agudo)*
✔ angle *(ángulo)*
congruent *(congruente)*
✔ obtuse angle *(ángulo obtuso)*
parallel lines *(líneas paralelas)*
✔ vertex *(vértice)*

Preview Words

alternate exterior angles *(ángulos alternos externos)*
alternate interior angles *(ángulos alternos internos)*
corresponding angles *(ángulos correspondientes (para líneas))*
exterior angle *(ángulo externo de un polígono)*
interior angle *(ángulos internos)*
remote interior angle *(ángulo interno remoto)*
same-side interior angles *(ángulos internos del mismo lado)*
similar *(semejantes)*
transversal *(transversal)*

Active Reading

Pyramid Before beginning the module, create a pyramid to help you organize what you learn. Label each side with one of the lesson titles from this module. As you study each lesson, write important ideas like vocabulary, properties, and formulas on the appropriate side.

GETTING READY FOR

Angle Relationships in Parallel Lines and Triangles

Understanding the standards and the vocabulary terms in the standards will help you know exactly what you are expected to learn in this module.

8.G.5

Use informal arguments to establish facts about the angle sum and exterior angle of triangles, about the angles created when parallel lines are cut by a transversal, and the angle-angle criterion for similarity of triangles.

Key Vocabulary

transversal *(transversal)*
A line that intersects two or more lines.

What It Means to You

You will learn about the special angle relationships formed when parallel lines are intersected by a third line called a transversal.

EXAMPLE 8.G.5

Which angles formed by the transversal and the parallel lines seem to be congruent?

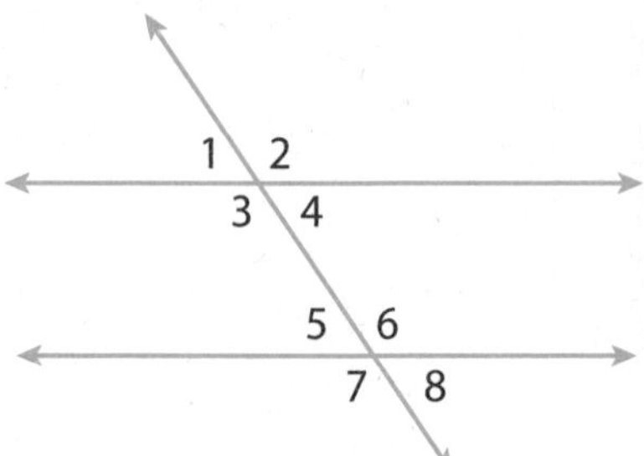

It appears that the angles below are congruent.

$\angle 1 \cong \angle 4 \cong \angle 5 \cong \angle 8$

$\angle 2 \cong \angle 3 \cong \angle 6 \cong \angle 7$

CA CC **8.G.5**

Use informal arguments to establish facts about the angle sum and exterior angle of triangles, about the angles created when parallel lines are cut by a transversal, and the angle-angle criterion for similarity of triangles.

What It Means to You

You will use the angle-angle criterion to determine similarity of two triangles.

EXAMPLE 8.G.5

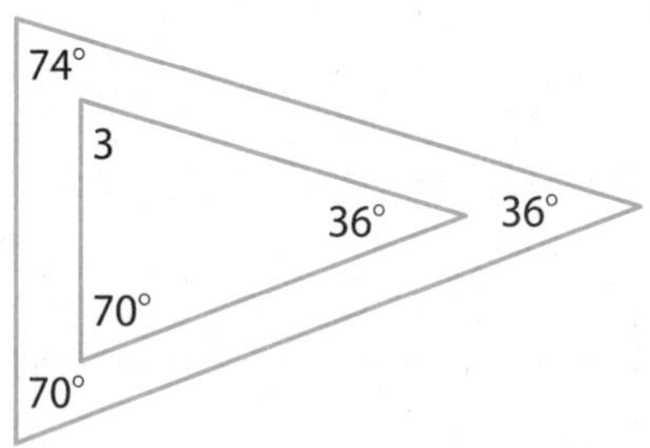

Explain whether the triangles are similar.

Two angles in the large triangle are congruent to two angles in the smaller triangle, so the third pair of angles must also be congruent, which makes the triangles similar.

$70° + 36° + m\angle 3 = 180°$

$m\angle 3 = 74°$

Visit **my.hrw.com** to see all **CA Common Core Standards** unpacked.

LESSON 21.1

Parallel Lines Cut by a Transversal

CA CC 8.G.5

Use informal arguments to establish facts about the angle sum and exterior angle of triangles, about the angles created when parallel lines are cut by a transversal, and the angle-angle criterion for similarity of triangles. *Also 8.EE.7b*

ESSENTIAL QUESTION

What can you conclude about the angles formed by parallel lines that are cut by a transversal?

EXPLORE ACTIVITY 1

Parallel Lines and Transversals

A **transversal** is a line that intersects two lines in the same plane at two different points. Transversal *t* and lines *a* and *b* form eight angles.

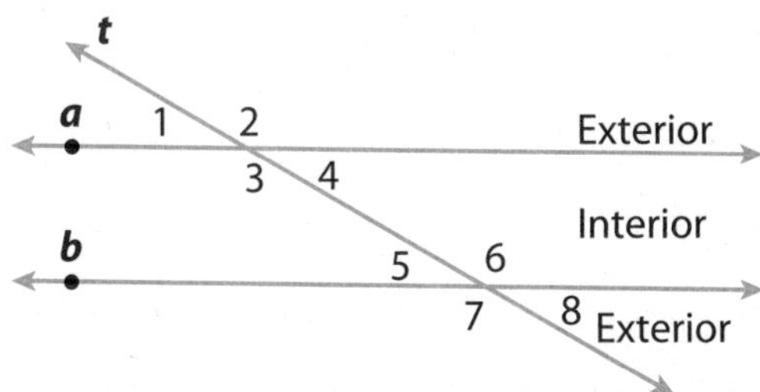

Angle Pairs Formed by a Transversal

Term	Example
Corresponding angles lie on the same side of the transversal *t*, on the same side of lines *a* and *b*.	$\angle 1$ and $\angle 5$
Alternate interior angles are nonadjacent angles that lie on opposite sides of the transversal *t*, between lines *a* and *b*.	$\angle 3$ and $\angle 6$
Alternate exterior angles lie on opposite sides of the transversal *t*, outside lines *a* and *b*.	$\angle 1$ and $\angle 8$
Same-side interior angles lie on the same side of the transversal *t*, between lines *a* and *b*.	$\angle 3$ and $\angle 5$

Use geometry software to explore the angles formed when a transversal intersects parallel lines.

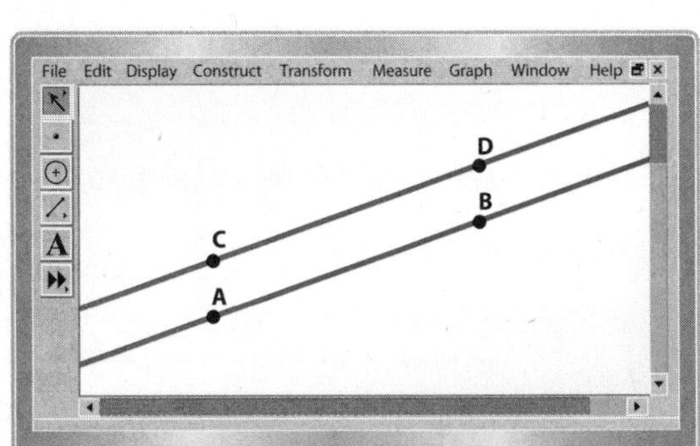

A Construct a line and label two points on the line *A* and *B*.

B Create point *C* not on $\overleftrightarrow{AB}$. Then construct a line parallel to $\overleftrightarrow{AB}$ through point *C*. Create another point on this line and label it *D*.

EXPLORE ACTIVITY 1 *(cont'd)*

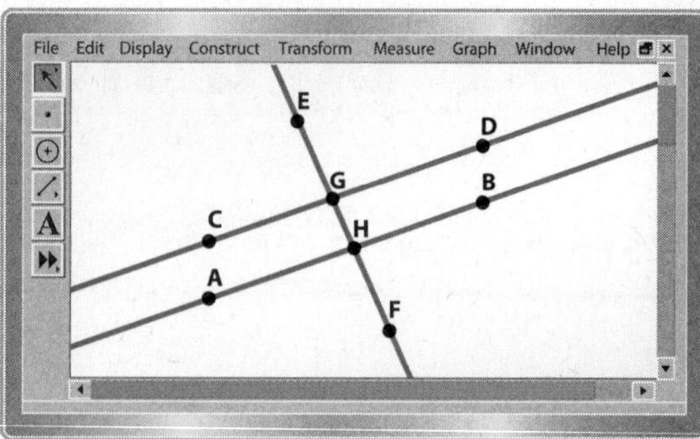

C Create two points outside the two parallel lines and label them *E* and *F*. Construct transversal $\overleftrightarrow{EF}$. Label the points of intersection *G* and *H*.

D Measure the angles formed by the parallel lines and the transversal. Write the angle measures in the table below.

E Drag point *E* or point *F* to a different position. Record the new angle measures in the table.

Angle	*∠CGE*	*∠DGE*	*∠CGH*	*∠DGH*	*∠AHG*	*∠BHG*	*∠AHF*	*∠BHF*
Measure								
Measure								

Reflect

Make a Conjecture Identify the pairs of angles in the diagram. Then make a conjecture about their angle measures. Drag a point in the diagram to confirm your conjecture.

1. corresponding angles

____

____

____

2. alternate interior angles

____

____

3. alternate exterior angles

____

____

4. same-side interior angles

____

____

____

EXPLORE ACTIVITY 2 CA CC 8.G.5

Justifying Angle Relationships

You can use tracing paper to informally justify your conclusions from the first Explore Activity.

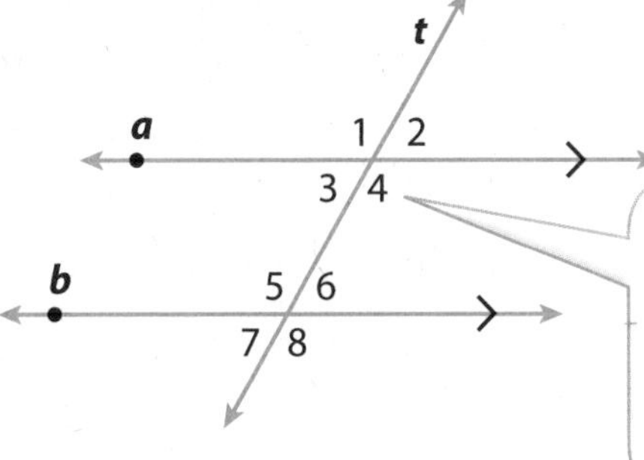

Recall that vertical angles are the opposite angles formed by two intersecting lines. ∠1 and ∠4 are vertical angles.

Lines *a* and *b* are parallel. (The black arrows on the diagram indicate parallel lines.)

A Trace the diagram onto tracing paper.

B Position the tracing paper over the original diagram so that ∠1 on the tracing is over ∠5 on the original diagram. Compare the two angles. Do they appear to be congruent?

____

____

C Use the tracing paper to compare all eight angles in the diagram to each other. List all of the congruent angle pairs.

____

____

____

Math Talk

How does a decrease in the measure of ∠1 affect the other angle measures?

Finding Unknown Angle Measures

You can find any unknown angle measure when two parallel lines are cut by a transversal if you are given at least one other angle measure.

EXAMPLE 1 CA CC 8.EE.7b

A **Find m∠2 when m∠7 = 125°.**

∠2 is congruent to ∠7 because they are alternate exterior angles.

Therefore, m∠2 = 125°.

B **Find m∠*VWZ*.**

∠*VWZ* is supplementary to ∠*YVW* because they are same-side interior angles.
m∠*VWZ* + m∠*YVW* = 180°

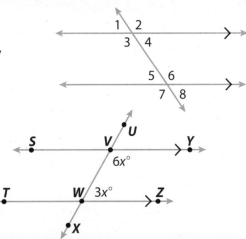

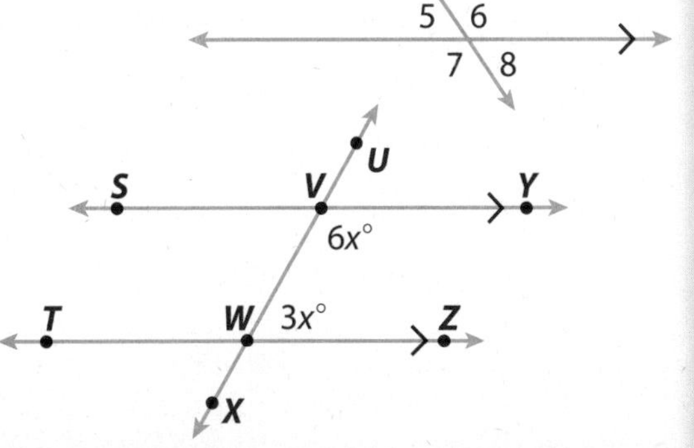

From the previous page, $m\angle VWZ + m\angle YVW = 180°$, $m\angle VWZ = 3x°$, and $m\angle YVW = 6x°$.

$$m\angle VWZ + m\angle YVW = 180°$$

$$3x° + 6x° = 180° \quad \text{Replace } m\angle VWZ \text{ with } 3x° \text{ and } m\angle YVW \text{ with } 6x°.$$

$$9x = 180 \quad \text{Combine like terms.}$$

$$\frac{9x}{9} = \frac{180}{9} \quad \text{Divide both sides by 9.}$$

$$x = 20 \quad \text{Simplify.}$$

$$m\angle VWZ = 3x° = (3 \cdot 20)° = 60°$$

YOUR TURN

Find each angle measure.

5. $m\angle GDE =$ __________

6. $m\angle BEF =$ __________

7. $m\angle CDG =$ __________

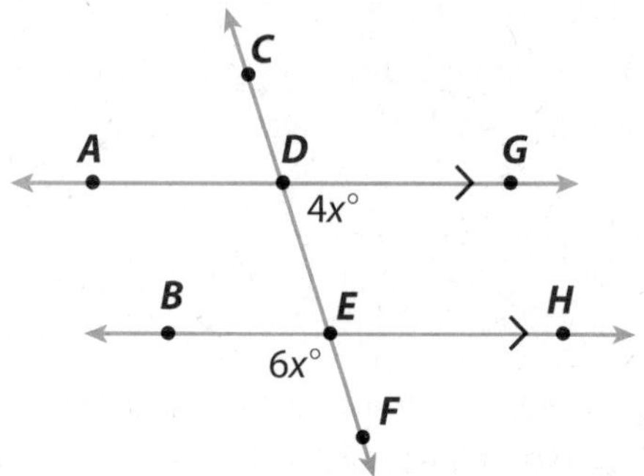

Guided Practice

Use the figure for Exercises 1–4. (Explore Activity 1 and Example 1)

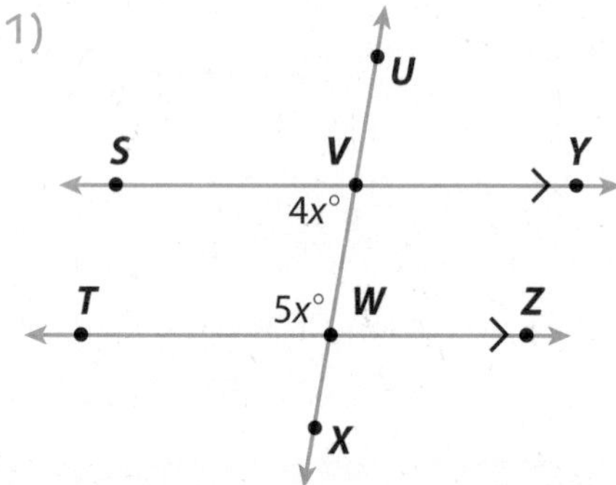

1. $\angle UVY$ and ________ are a pair of corresponding angles.

2. $\angle WVY$ and $\angle VWT$ are ________________ angles.

3. Find $m\angle SVW$. __________

4. Find $m\angle VWT$. __________

5. Vocabulary When two parallel lines are cut by a transversal, ________________ angles are supplementary. (Explore Activity 1)

ESSENTIAL QUESTION CHECK-IN

6. What can you conclude about the interior angles formed when two parallel lines are cut by a transversal?

____

____

Name ______________________ Class ______________ Date ______________

21.1 Independent Practice

CA CC 8.EE.7b, 8.G.5

Vocabulary Use the figure for Exercises 7–10.

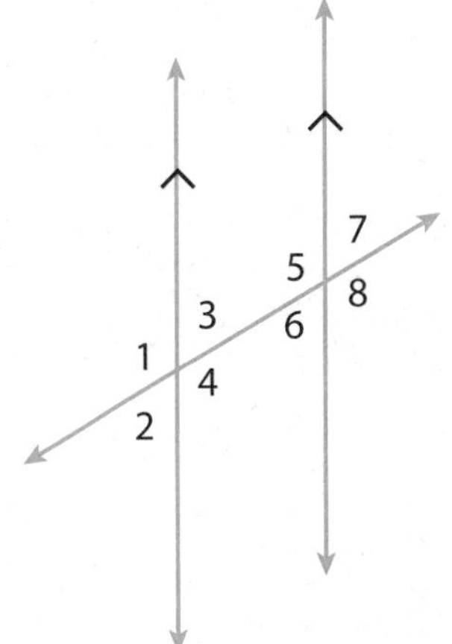

7. Name all pairs of corresponding angles.

____

8. Name both pairs of alternate exterior angles.

____

9. Name the relationship between $\angle 3$ and $\angle 6$.

____

10. Name the relationship between $\angle 4$ and $\angle 6$.

____

Find each angle measure.

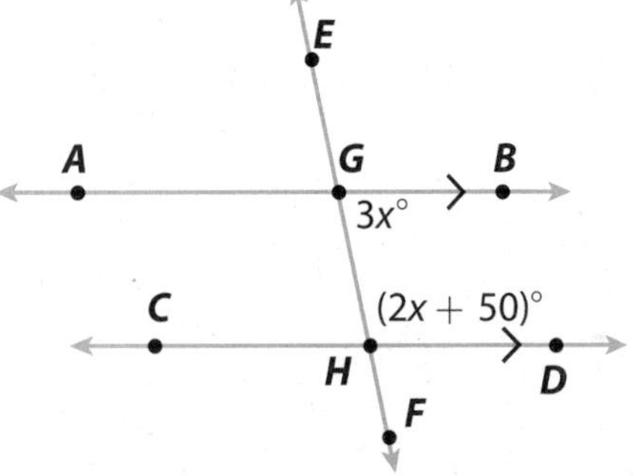

11. $m\angle AGE$ when $m\angle FHD = 30°$ ________

12. $m\angle AGH$ when $m\angle CHF = 150°$ ________

13. $m\angle CHF$ when $m\angle BGE = 110°$ ________

14. $m\angle CHG$ when $m\angle HGA = 120°$ ________

15. $m\angle BGH =$ ________

16. $m\angle GHD =$ ________

17. The Cross Country Bike Trail follows a straight line where it crosses 350th and 360th Streets. The two streets are parallel to each other. What is the measure of the larger angle formed at the intersection of the bike trail and 360th Street? Explain.

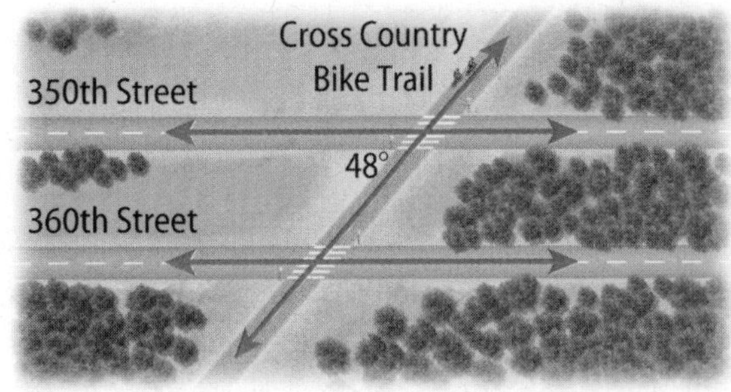

____

____

____

18. Critical Thinking How many different angles would be formed by a transversal intersecting three parallel lines? How many different angle measures would there be?

____

____

19. Communicate Mathematical Ideas In the diagram at the right, suppose $m\angle 6 = 125°$. Explain how to find the measures of each of the other seven numbered angles.

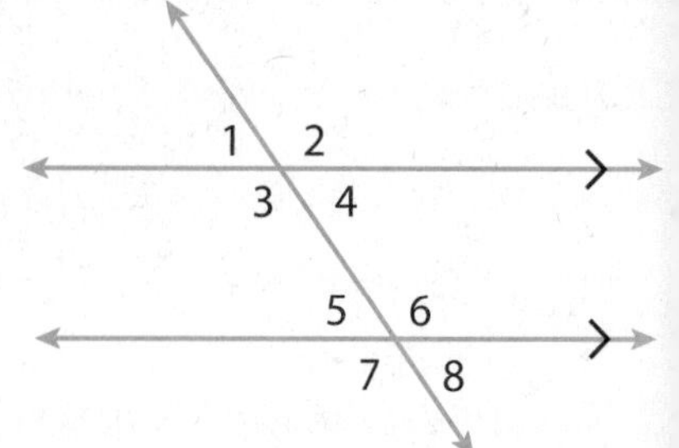

H.O.T. FOCUS ON HIGHER ORDER THINKING

Work Area

20. Draw Conclusions In a diagram showing two parallel lines cut by a transversal, the measures of two same-side interior angles are both given as $3x°$. Without writing and solving an equation, can you determine the measures of both angles? Explain. Then write and solve an equation to find the measures.

21. Make a Conjecture Draw two parallel lines and a transversal. Choose one of the eight angles that are formed. How many of the other seven angles are congruent to the angle you selected? How many of the other seven angles are supplementary to your angle? Will your answer change if you select a different angle?

22. Critique Reasoning In the diagram at the right, $\angle 2$, $\angle 3$, $\angle 5$, and $\angle 8$ are all congruent, and $\angle 1$, $\angle 4$, $\angle 6$, and $\angle 7$ are all congruent. Aiden says that this is enough information to conclude that the diagram shows two parallel lines cut by a transversal. Is he correct? Justify your answer.

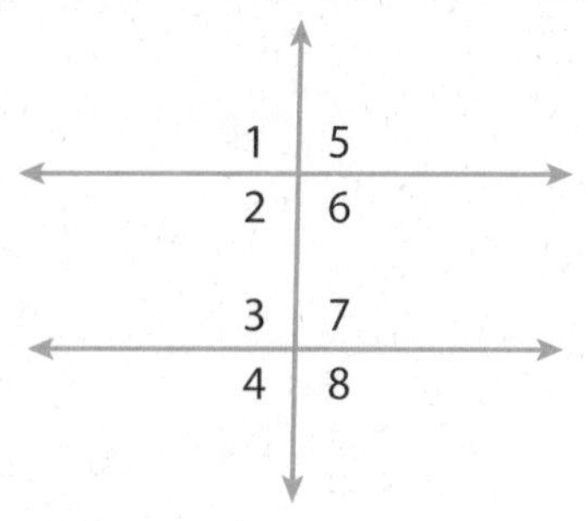

LESSON 21.2

Angle Theorems for Triangles

CA CC 8.G.5

Use informal arguments to establish facts about the angle sum and exterior angle of triangles, about the angles created when parallel lines are cut by a transversal, and the angle-angle criterion for similarity of triangles. *Also 8.EE.7, 8.EE.7b*

ESSENTIAL QUESTION

What can you conclude about the measures of the angles of a triangle?

EXPLORE ACTIVITY 1 

CA CC 8.G.5

Sum of the Angle Measures in a Triangle

There is a special relationship between the measures of the interior angles of a triangle.

A Draw a triangle and cut it out. Label the angles *A*, *B*, and *C*.

B Tear off each "corner" of the triangle. Each corner includes the vertex of one angle of the triangle.

C Arrange the vertices of the triangle around a point so that none of your corners overlap and there are no gaps between them.

D What do you notice about how the angles fit together around a point?

____

E What is the measure of a straight angle? ____________________

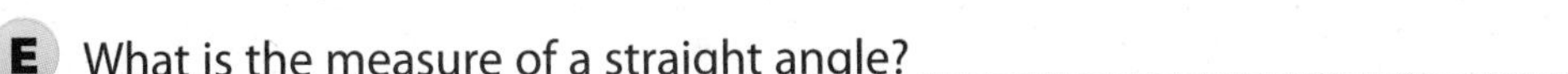

F Describe the relationship among the measures of the angles of $\triangle ABC$.

____

The Triangle Sum Theorem states that for $\triangle ABC$, $m\angle A + m\angle B + m\angle C =$ _____.

Reflect

1. **Justify Reasoning** Can a triangle have two right angles? Explain.

____

2. **Analyze Relationships** Describe the relationship between the two acute angles in a right triangle. Explain your reasoning.

____

EXPLORE ACTIVITY 2  CA CC 8.G.5

Justifying the Triangle Sum Theorem

You can use your knowledge of parallel lines intersected by a transversal to informally justify the Triangle Sum Theorem.

Follow the steps to informally prove the Triangle Sum Theorem. You should draw each step on your own paper. The figures below are provided for you to check your work.

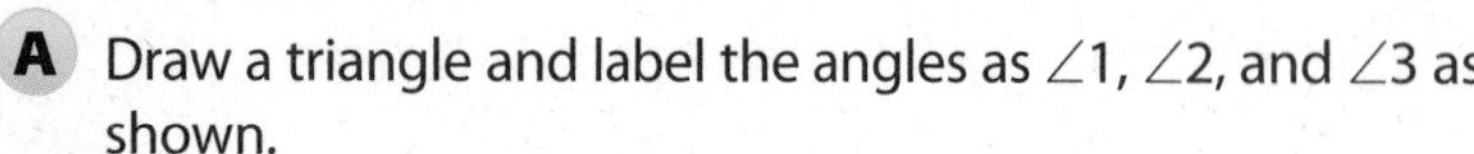

A Draw a triangle and label the angles as ∠1, ∠2, and ∠3 as shown.

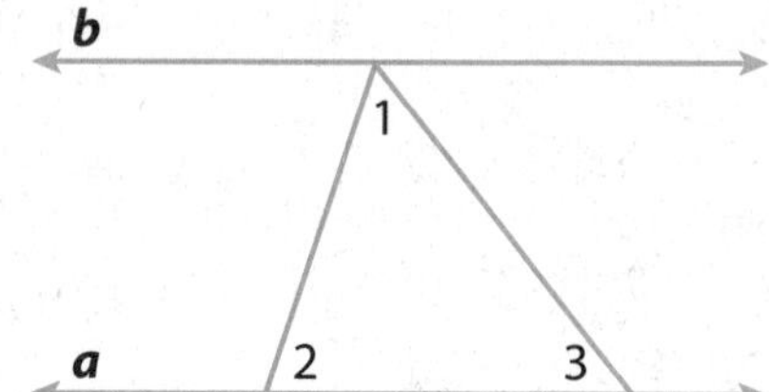

B Draw line *a* through the base of the triangle.

C The Parallel Postulate states that through a point not on a line ℓ, there is exactly one line parallel to line ℓ. Draw line *b* parallel to line *a*, through the vertex opposite the base of the triangle.

D Extend each of the non-base sides of the triangle to form transversal *s* and transversal *t*. Transversals *s* and *t* intersect parallel lines *a* and *b*.

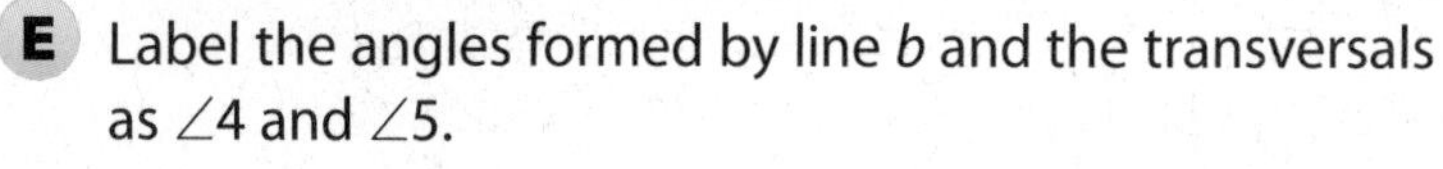

E Label the angles formed by line *b* and the transversals as ∠4 and ∠5.

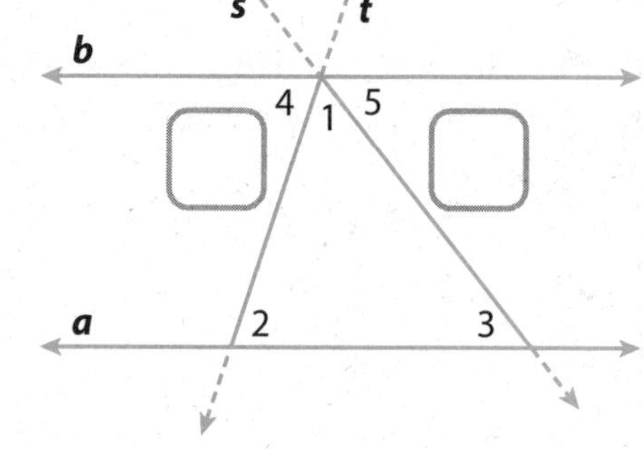

F Because ∠4 and ________________ are alternate interior angles, they are ________________.

Label ∠4 with the number of the angle to which it is congruent.

G Because ∠5 and ________________ are alternate interior angles, they are ________________.

Label ∠5 with the number of the angle to which it is congruent.

H The three angles that lie along line *b* at the vertex of the triangle are ∠1, ∠4, and ∠5. Notice that these three angles lie along a line.

So, m∠1 + m∠2 + m∠5 = ________________.

Because angles 2 and 4 are congruent and angles 3 and 5 are congruent, you can substitute m∠2 for m∠4 and m∠3 for m∠5 in the equation above.

So, m∠1 + m∠2 + m∠3 = ________________.

This shows that the sum of the angle measures in a triangle is always ________________.

Reflect

3. **Analyze Relationships** How can you use the fact that $m\angle 4 + m\angle 1 + m\angle 5 = 180°$ to show that $m\angle 2 + m\angle 1 + m\angle 3 = 180°$?

____

____

____

Finding Missing Angle Measures in Triangles

If you know the measures of two angles in a triangle, you can use the Triangle Sum Theorem to find the measure of the third angle.

EXAMPLE 1

CA CC 8.EE.7

My Notes

Find the missing angle measure.

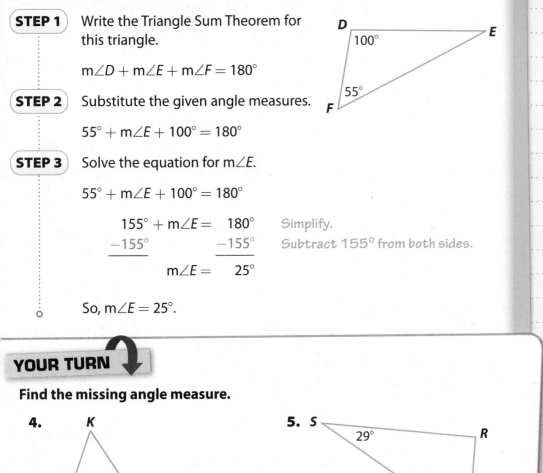

STEP 1 Write the Triangle Sum Theorem for this triangle.

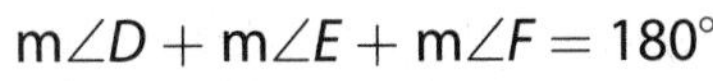

$m\angle D + m\angle E + m\angle F = 180°$

STEP 2 Substitute the given angle measures.

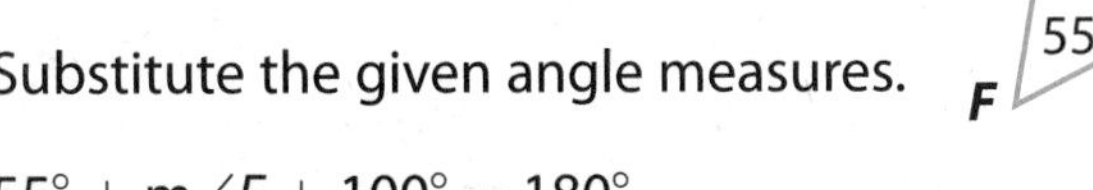

$55° + m\angle E + 100° = 180°$

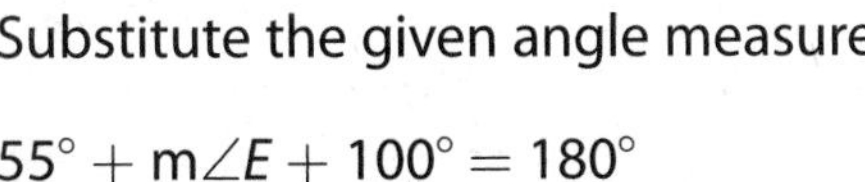

STEP 3 Solve the equation for $m\angle E$.

$55° + m\angle E + 100° = 180°$

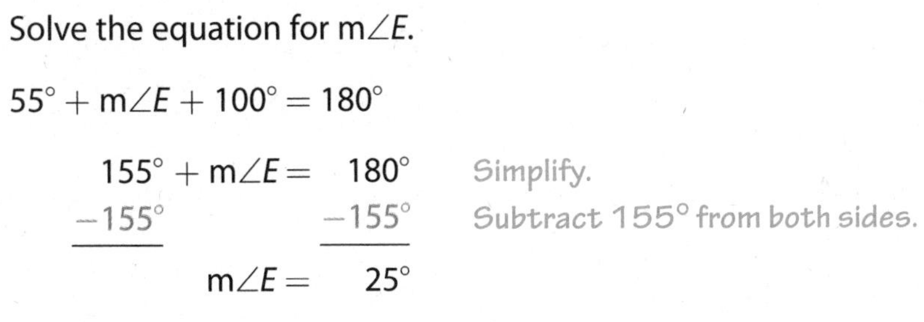

$155° + m\angle E = 180°$ Simplify.

$\underline{-155°} \qquad \underline{-155°}$ Subtract 155° from both sides.

$m\angle E = 25°$

So, $m\angle E = 25°$.

YOUR TURN

Find the missing angle measure.

4. 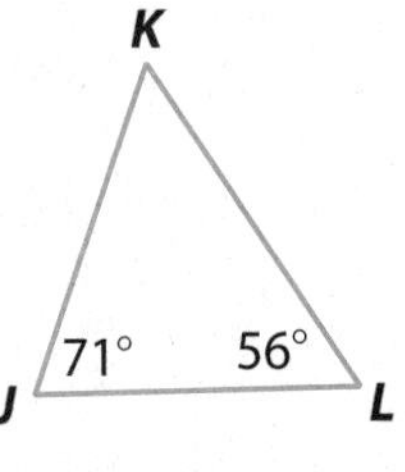

$m\angle K =$ ______________

5. 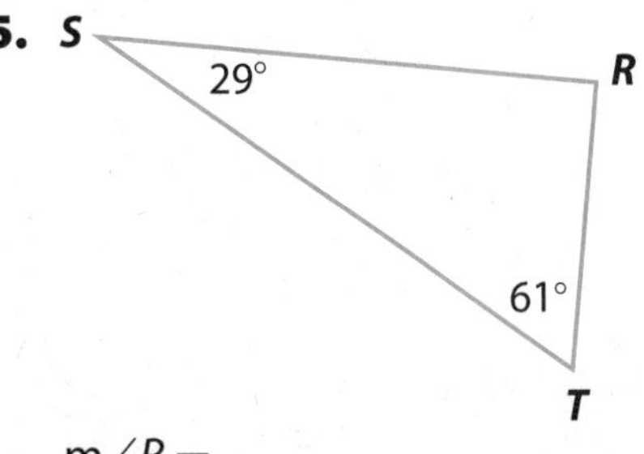

$m\angle R =$ ______________

EXPLORE ACTIVITY 3

Exterior Angles and Remote Interior Angles

An **interior angle** of a triangle is formed by two sides of the triangle. An **exterior angle** is formed by one side of the triangle and the extension of an adjacent side. Each exterior angle has two remote interior angles. A **remote interior angle** is an interior angle that is not adjacent to the exterior angle.

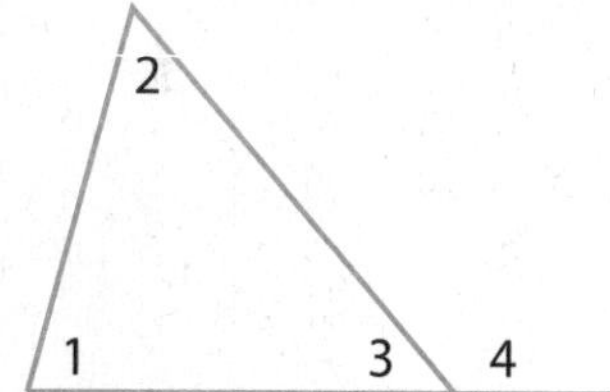

- $\angle 1$, $\angle 2$, and $\angle 3$ are interior angles.
- $\angle 4$ is an exterior angle.
- $\angle 1$ and $\angle 2$ are remote interior angles to $\angle 4$.

There is a special relationship between the measure of an exterior angle and the measures of its remote interior angles.

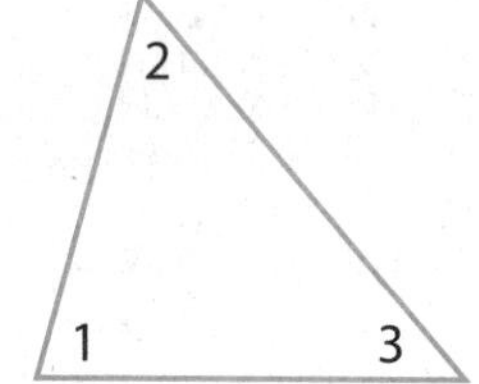

A Extend the base of the triangle and label the exterior angle as $\angle 4$.

B The Triangle Sum Theorem states:

$m\angle 1 + m\angle 2 + m\angle 3 =$ ________.

C $\angle 3$ and $\angle 4$ form a ________________________,

so $m\angle 3 + m\angle 4 =$ ________________________.

D Use the equations in **B** and **C** to complete the following equation:

$m\angle 1 + m\angle 2 +$ ____________ $=$ ____________ $+ m\angle 4$

E Use properties of equality to simplify the equation in **D**:

____

The Exterior Angle Theorem states that the measure of an ____________ angle is equal to the sum of its ____________ angles.

Reflect

6. Sketch a triangle and draw all of its exterior angles. How many exterior angles does a triangle have at each vertex?

____

7. How many total exterior angles does a triangle have?

____

Using the Exterior Angle Theorem

You can use the Exterior Angle Theorem to find the measures of the interior angles of a triangle.

EXAMPLE 2

CA CC 8.EE.7b

Find m∠*A* and m∠*B*.

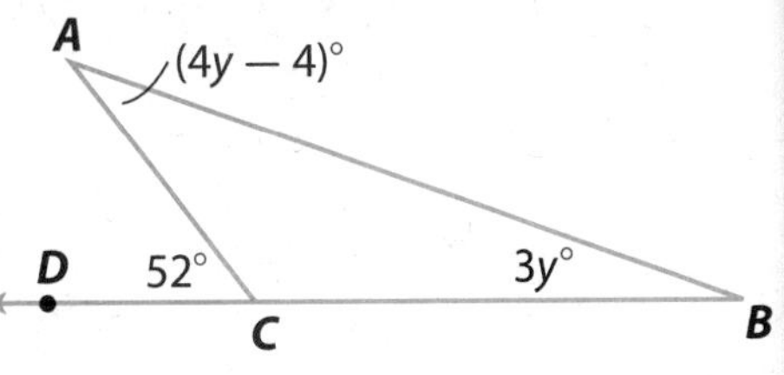

STEP 1 Write the Exterior Angle Theorem as it applies to this triangle.

$m\angle A + m\angle B = m\angle ACD$

STEP 2 Substitute the given angle measures.

$(4y - 4)^\circ + 3y^\circ = 52^\circ$

STEP 3 Solve the equation for *y*.

$(4y - 4)^\circ + 3y^\circ = 52^\circ$

$4y^\circ - 4^\circ + 3y^\circ = 52^\circ$ Remove parentheses.

$7y^\circ - 4^\circ = 52^\circ$ Simplify.

$\underline{+4^\circ} \quad \underline{+4^\circ}$ Add 4° to both sides.

$7y^\circ = 56^\circ$ Simplify.

$\frac{7y^\circ}{7} = \frac{56^\circ}{7}$ Divide both sides by 7.

$y = 8$ Simplify.

STEP 4 Use the value of *y* to find m∠*A* and m∠*B*.

$m\angle A = 4y - 4$
$= 4(8) - 4$
$= 32 - 4$
$= 28$

$m\angle B = 3y$
$= 3(8)$
$= 24$

So, $m\angle A = 28^\circ$ and $m\angle B = 24^\circ$.

Math Talk
Mathematical Practices
Describe two ways to find m∠ACB.

8. Find m∠*M* and m∠*N*.

m∠*M* = __________

m∠*N* = __________

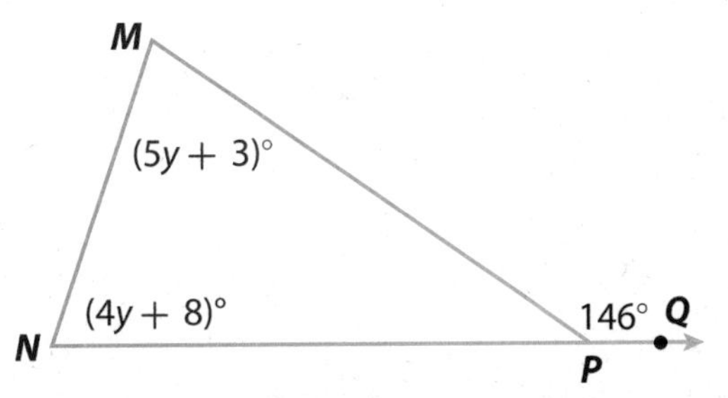

Guided Practice

Find each missing angle measure. (Explore Activity 1 and Example 1)

1.

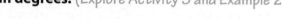

$m\angle M =$ ______

2.

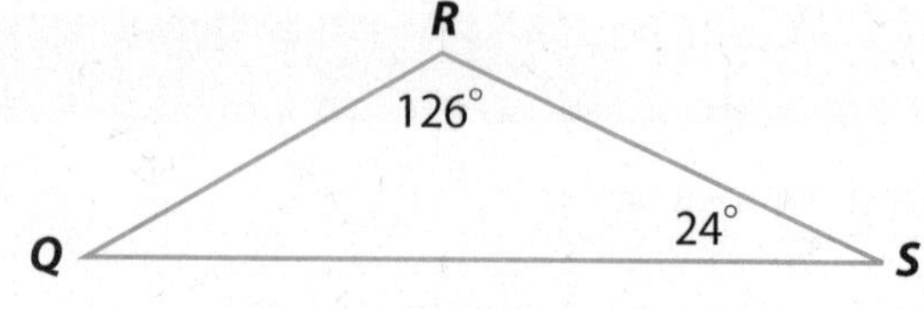

$m\angle Q =$ ______

Use the Triangle Sum Theorem to find the measure of each angle in degrees. (Explore Activity 2 and Example 1)

3.

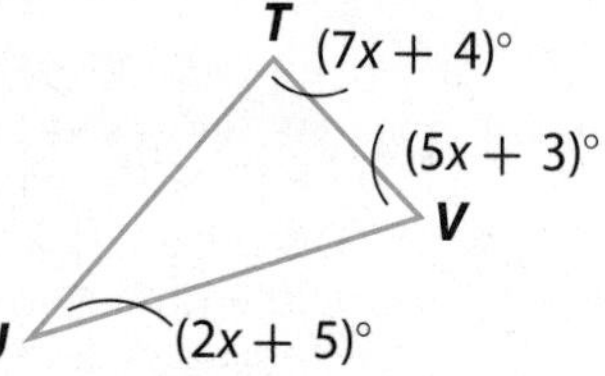

$m\angle T =$ ______, $m\angle U =$ ______,

$m\angle V =$ ______

4.

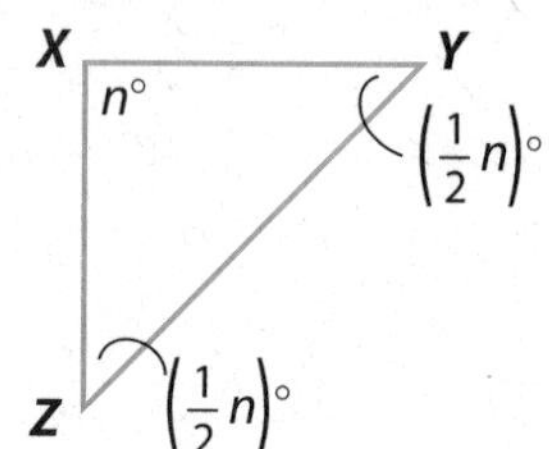

$m\angle X =$ ______, $m\angle Y =$ ______,

$m\angle Z =$ ______

Use the Exterior Angle Theorem to find the measure of each angle in degrees. (Explore Activity 3 and Example 2)

5.

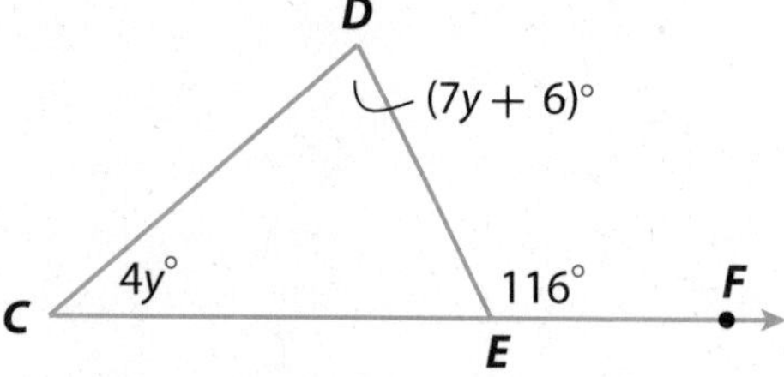

$m\angle C =$ ______, $m\angle D =$ ______,

$m\angle DEC =$ ______

6.

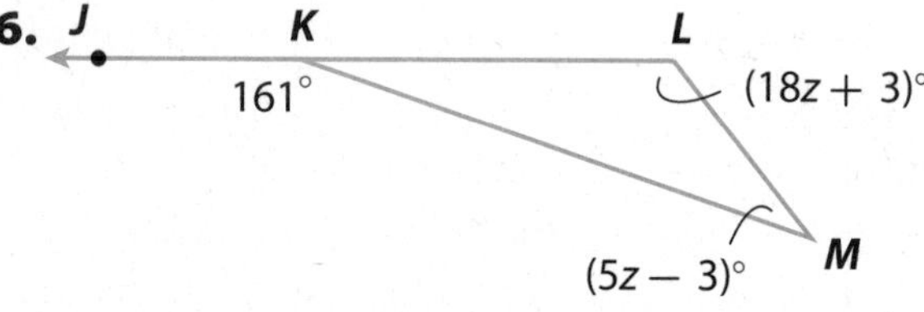

$m\angle L =$ ______, $m\angle M =$ ______,

$m\angle LKM =$ ______

ESSENTIAL QUESTION CHECK-IN

7. Describe the relationships among the measures of the angles of a triangle.

______

______

______

Name ________________ Class ________________ Date ________________

21.2 Independent Practice

CA CC 8.EE.7, 8.EE.7b, 8.G.5

Find the measure of each angle.

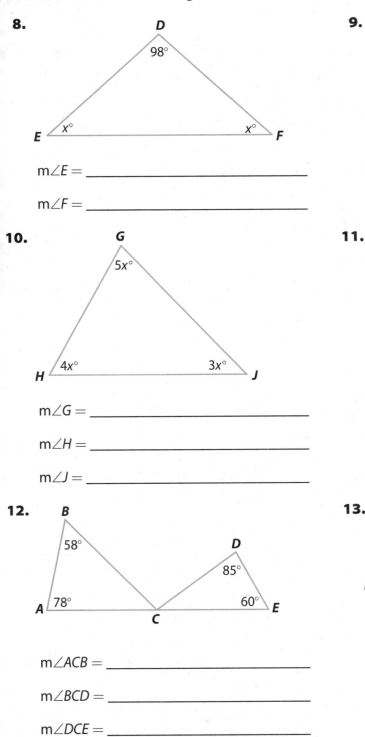

8.

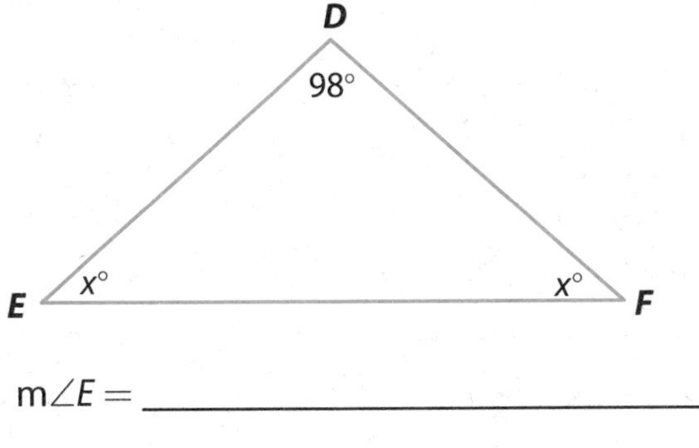

m∠E = ________________

m∠F = ________________

9.

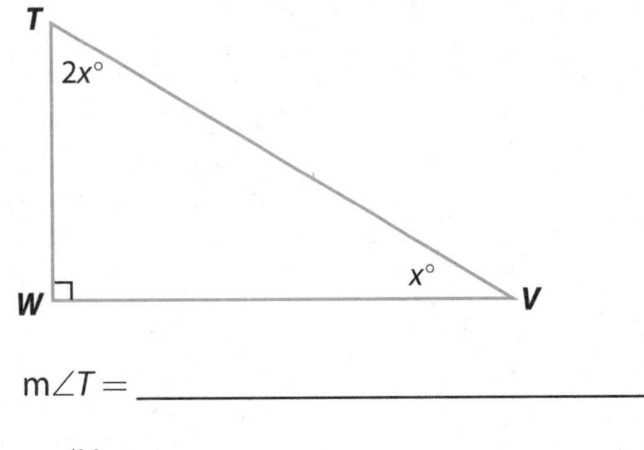

m∠T = ________________

m∠V = ________________

10.

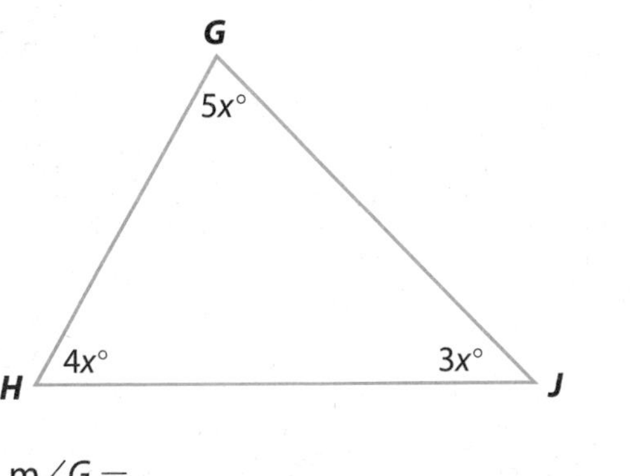

m∠G = ________________

m∠H = ________________

m∠J = ________________

11.

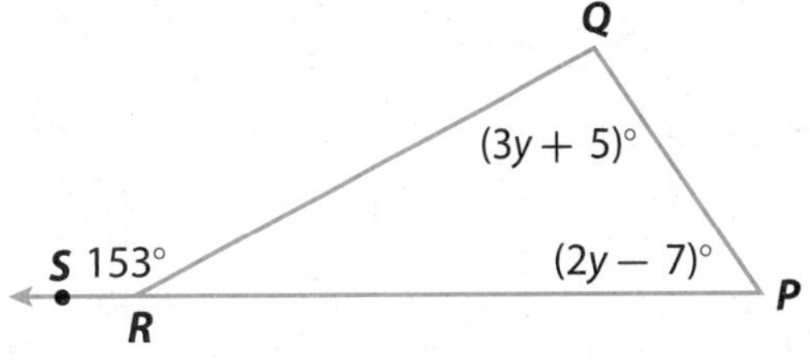

m∠Q = ________________

m∠P = ________________

m∠QRP = ________________

12.

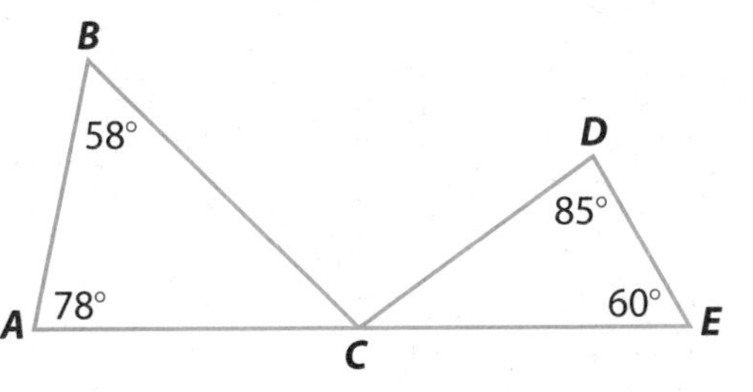

m∠ACB = ________________

m∠BCD = ________________

m∠DCE = ________________

13.

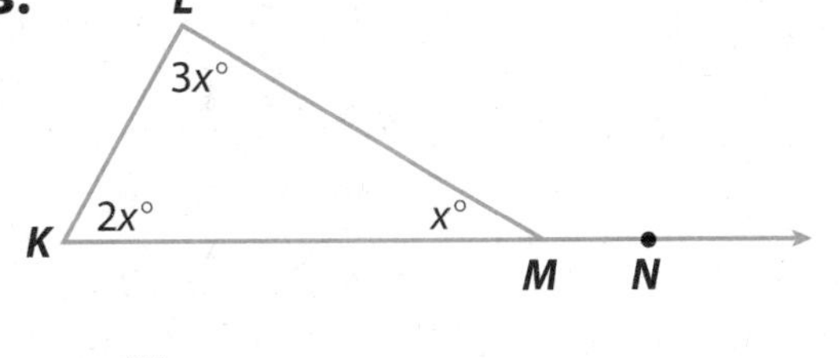

m∠K = ________________

m∠L = ________________

m∠KML = ________________

m∠LMN = ________________

14. Multistep The second angle in a triangle is five times as large as the first. The third angle is two-thirds as large as the first. Find the angle measures. ________________

15. Analyze Relationships Can a triangle have two obtuse angles? Explain.

H.O.T. FOCUS ON HIGHER ORDER THINKING

Work Area

16. Critical Thinking Explain how you can use the Triangle Sum Theorem to find the measures of the angles of an equilateral triangle.

17. a. Draw Conclusions Find the sum of the measures of the angles in quadrilateral *ABCD*. (Hint: Draw diagonal $\overline{AC}$. How can you use the figures you have formed to find the sum?)

A B C D

Sum = __________

b. Make a Conjecture Write a "Quadrilateral Sum Theorem." Explain why you think it is true.

18. Communicate Mathematical Ideas Describe two ways that an exterior angle of a triangle is related to one or more of the interior angles.

LESSON 21.3

Angle-Angle Similarity

CA CC 8.G.5

Use informal arguments to establish facts about the angle sum and exterior angle of triangles, about the angles created when parallel lines are cut by a transversal, and the angle-angle criterion for similarity of triangles. *Also 8.EE.6, 8.EE.7*

ESSENTIAL QUESTION

How can you determine when two triangles are similar?

EXPLORE ACTIVITY 1 CA CC 8.G.5

Discovering Angle-Angle Similarity

Similar figures have the same shape but may have different sizes. Two triangles are **similar** if their corresponding angles are congruent and the lengths of their corresponding sides are proportional.

A Use your protractor and a straightedge to draw a triangle. Make one angle measure 45° and another angle measure 60°.

B Compare your triangle to those drawn by your classmates. How are the triangles the same?

____

How are they different?

____

C Use the Triangle Sum Theorem to find the measure of the third angle of your triangle.

____

Reflect

1. If two angles in one triangle are congruent to two angles in another triangle, what do you know about the third pair of angles?

____

2. **Make a Conjecture** Are two pairs of congruent angles enough information to conclude that two triangles are similar? Explain.

____

____

____

____

Using the AA Similarity Postulate

Angle-Angle (AA) Similarity Postulate

If two angles of one triangle are congruent to two angles of another triangle, then the triangles are similar.

EXAMPLE 1

Explain whether the triangles are similar.

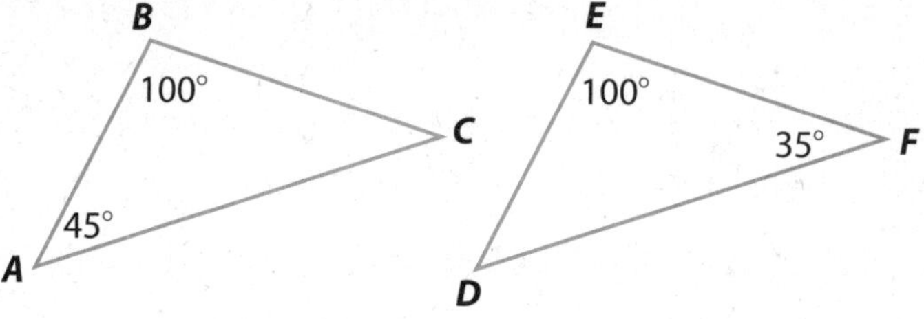

The figure shows only one pair of congruent angles. Find the measure of the third angle in each triangle.

$$45° + 100° + m\angle C = 180°$$

$$145° + m\angle C = 180°$$

$$145° + m\angle C - 145° = 180° - 145°$$

$$m\angle C = 35°$$

$$100° + 35° + m\angle D = 180°$$

$$135° + m\angle D = 180°$$

$$135° + m\angle D - 135° = 180° - 135°$$

$$m\angle D = 45°$$

Because two angles in one triangle are congruent to two angles in the other triangle, the triangles are similar.

Are all right triangles similar? Why or why not?

YOUR TURN

3. Explain whether the triangles are similar.

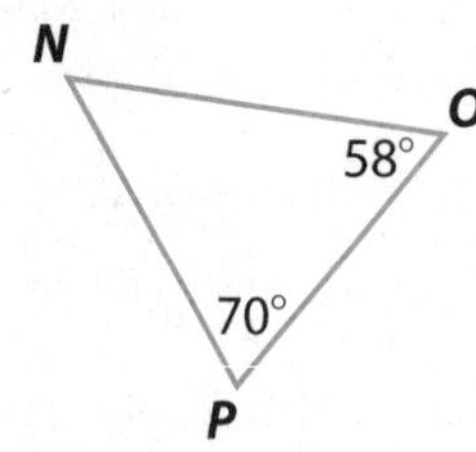

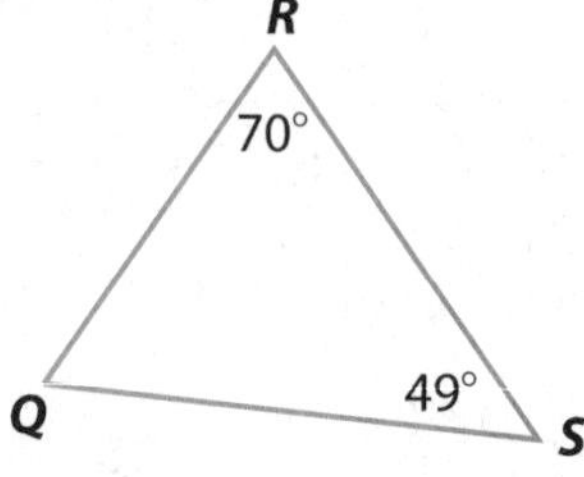

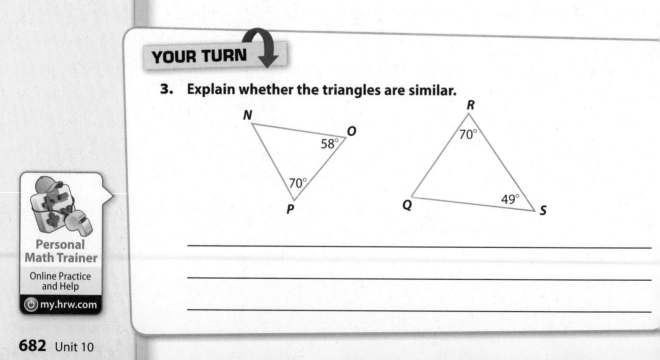

Finding Missing Measures in Similar Triangles

Because corresponding angles are congruent and corresponding sides are proportional in similar triangles, you can use similar triangles to solve real-world problems.

EXAMPLE 2  

CA CC 8.EE.7

While playing tennis, Matt is 12 meters from the net, which is 0.9 meter high. He needs to hit the ball so that it just clears the net and lands 6 meters beyond the base of the net. At what height should Matt hit the tennis ball?

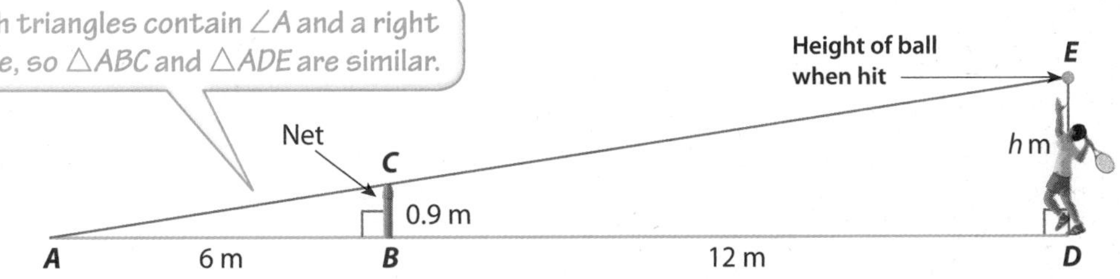

In similar triangles, corresponding side lengths are proportional.

$$\frac{AD}{AB} = \frac{DE}{BC} \longrightarrow \frac{6 + 12}{6} = \frac{h}{0.9}$$ Substitute the lengths from the figure.

$$0.9 \times \frac{18}{6} = \frac{h}{0.9} \times 0.9$$ Use properties of equality to get h by itself.

$$0.9 \times 3 = h$$ Simplify.

$$2.7 = h$$ Multiply.

Matt should hit the ball at a height of 2.7 meters.

Reflect

4. What If? Suppose you set up a proportion so that each ratio compares parts of one triangle, as shown below.

height of △ABC ⟶ $\frac{BC}{AB} = \frac{DE}{AD}$ ⟵ height of △ADE
base of △ABC ⟶ ⟵ base of △ADE

Show that this proportion leads to the same value for h as in Example 2.

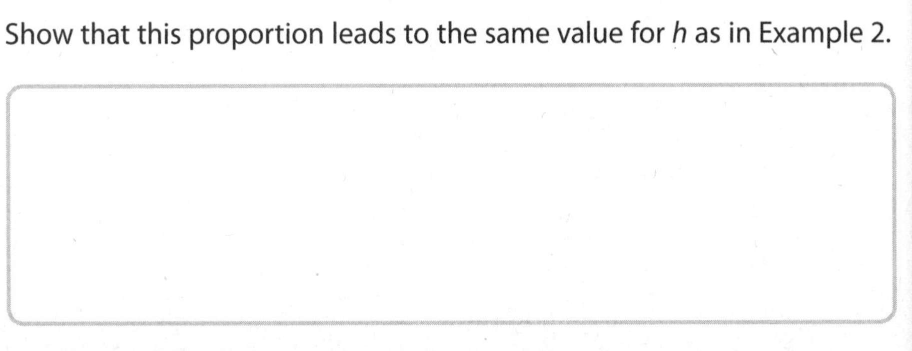

My Notes

YOUR TURN

5. Rosie is building a wheelchair ramp that is 24 feet long and 2 feet high. She needs to install a vertical support piece 8 feet from the end of the ramp. What is the length of the support piece in inches?

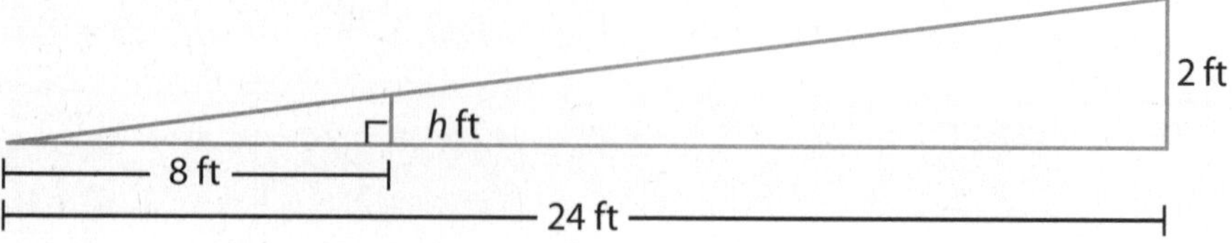

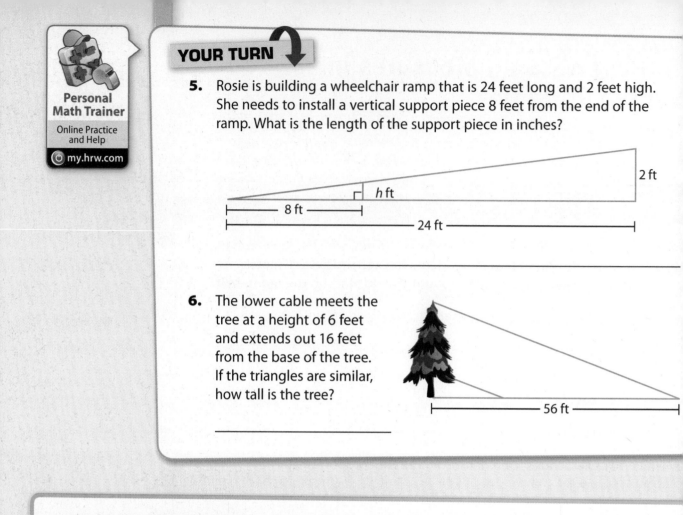

6. The lower cable meets the tree at a height of 6 feet and extends out 16 feet from the base of the tree. If the triangles are similar, how tall is the tree?

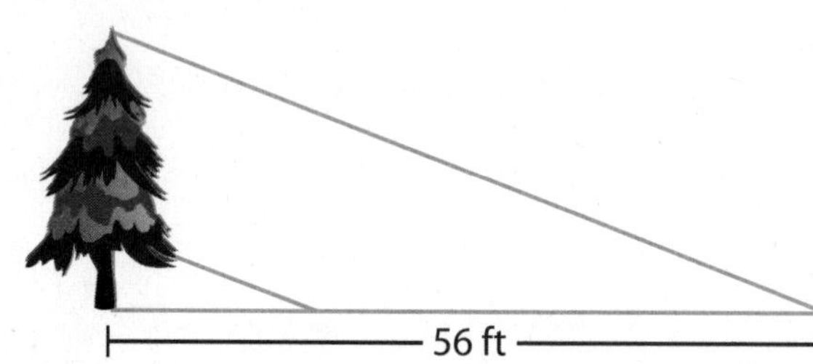

EXPLORE ACTIVITY 2

Using Similar Triangles to Explain Slope

You can use similar triangles to show that the slope of a line is constant.

A Draw a line ℓ that is not a horizontal line. Label four points on the line as *A*, *B*, *C*, and *D*.

You need to show that the slope between points *A* and *B* is the same as the slope between points *C* and *D*.

B Draw the rise and run for the slope between points *A* and *B*. Label the intersection as point *E*. Draw the rise and run for the slope between points *C* and *D*. Label the intersection as point *F*.

C Write expressions for the slope between *A* and *B* and between *C* and *D*.

Slope between *A* and *B*: $\frac{BE}{\square}$ Slope between *C* and *D*: $\frac{\square}{CF}$

D Extend $\overleftrightarrow{AE}$ and $\overleftrightarrow{CF}$ across your drawing. $\overleftrightarrow{AE}$ and $\overleftrightarrow{CF}$ are both horizontal lines, so they are parallel.

Line ℓ is a ______________ that intersects parallel lines.

E Complete the following statements:

$\angle BAE$ and ________ are corresponding angles and are ______________.

$\angle BEA$ and ________ are right angles and are ______________.

F By Angle–Angle Similarity, $\triangle ABE$ and ________ are similar triangles.

G Use the fact that the lengths of corresponding sides of similar triangles are proportional to complete the following ratios: $\frac{BE}{DF} = \frac{\square}{CF}$

H Recall that you can also write the proportion so that the ratios compare parts of the same triangle: $\frac{\square}{AE} = \frac{DF}{\square}$.

I The proportion you wrote in step **H** shows that the ratios you wrote in **C** are equal. So, the slope of line ℓ is constant.

Reflect

7. **What If?** Suppose that you label two other points on line ℓ as *G* and *H*. Would the slope between these two points be different than the slope you found in the Explore Activity? Explain.

____

____

____

Guided Practice

1. Explain whether the triangles are similar. Label the angle measures in the figure. (Explore Activity 1 and Example 1)

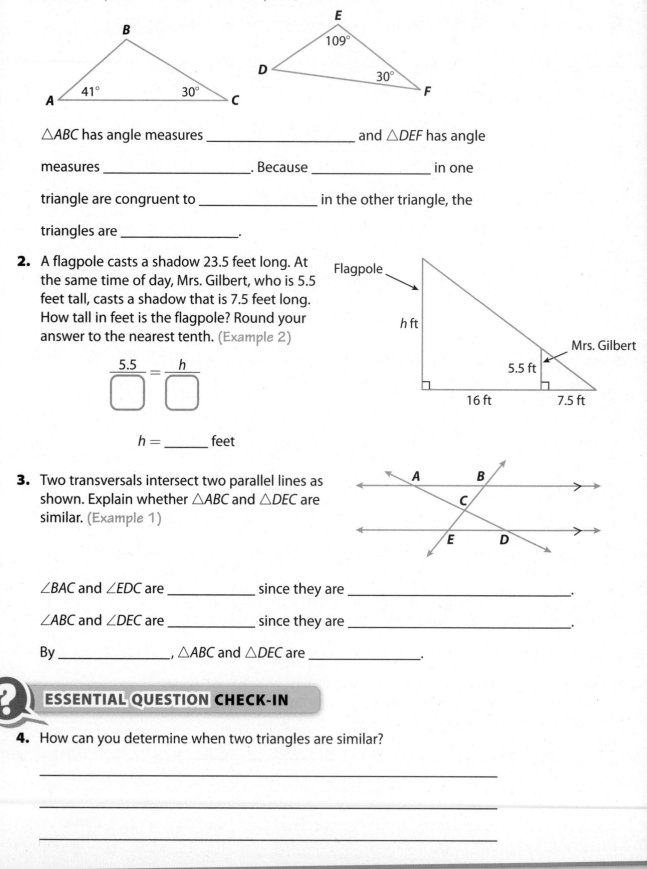

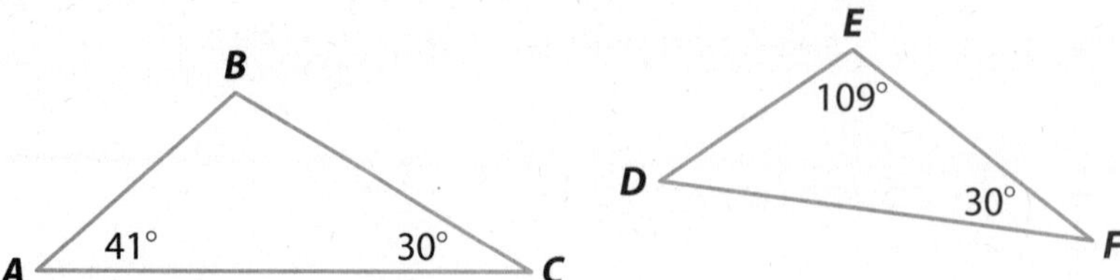

$\triangle ABC$ has angle measures ____________ and $\triangle DEF$ has angle measures ____________. Because ____________ in one triangle are congruent to ____________ in the other triangle, the triangles are ____________.

2. A flagpole casts a shadow 23.5 feet long. At the same time of day, Mrs. Gilbert, who is 5.5 feet tall, casts a shadow that is 7.5 feet long. How tall in feet is the flagpole? Round your answer to the nearest tenth. (Example 2)

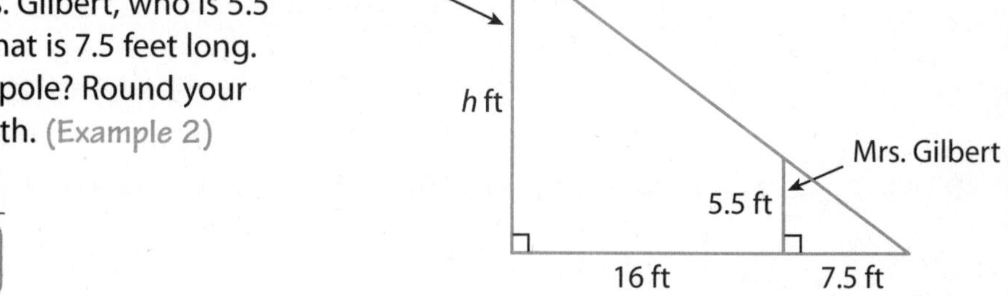

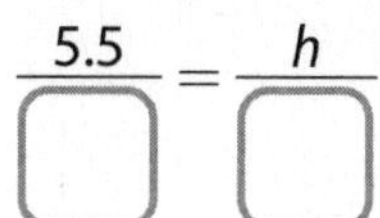

$h =$ ______ feet

3. Two transversals intersect two parallel lines as shown. Explain whether $\triangle ABC$ and $\triangle DEC$ are similar. (Example 1)

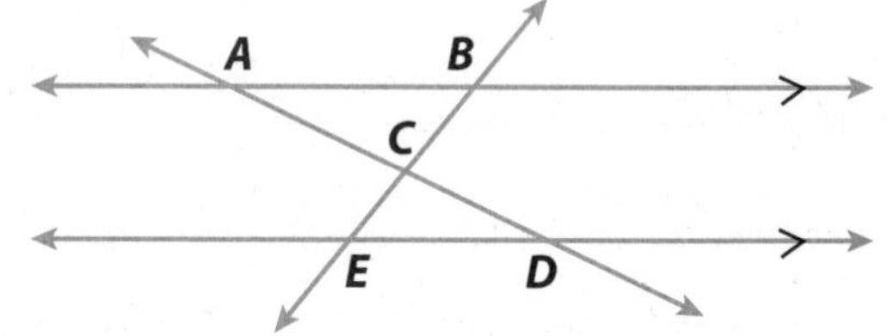

$\angle BAC$ and $\angle EDC$ are ____________ since they are ____________.

$\angle ABC$ and $\angle DEC$ are ____________ since they are ____________.

By ____________, $\triangle ABC$ and $\triangle DEC$ are ____________.

ESSENTIAL QUESTION CHECK-IN

4. How can you determine when two triangles are similar?

____

____

____

Name ______ Class ______ Date ______

21.3 Independent Practice

Use the diagrams for Exercises 5–7.

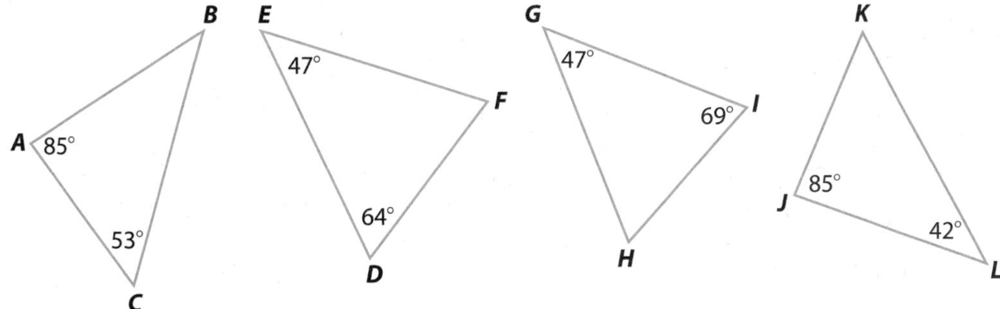

5. Find the missing angle measures in the triangles.

______

6. Which triangles are similar?

______

7. **Analyze Relationships** Determine which angles are congruent to the angles in $\triangle ABC$.

______

8. **Multistep** A tree casts a shadow that is 20 feet long. Frank is 6 feet tall, and while standing next to the tree he casts a shadow that is 4 feet long.

a. How tall is the tree? ______

b. How much taller is the tree than Frank? ______

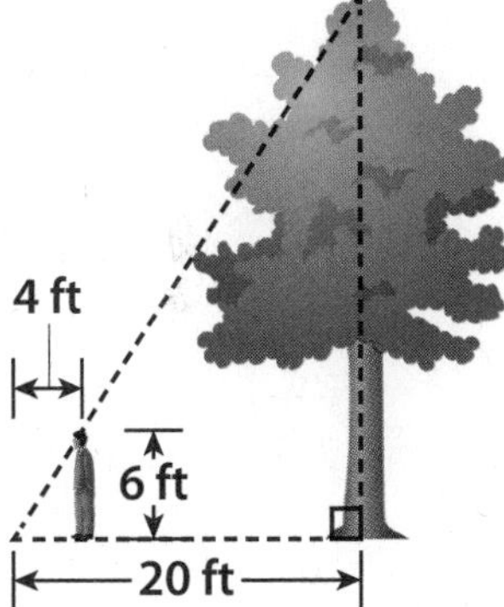

9. **Represent Real-World Problems** Sheila is climbing on a ladder that is attached against the side of a jungle gym wall. She is 5 feet off the ground and 3 feet from the base of the ladder, which is 15 feet from the wall. Draw a diagram to help you solve the problem. How high up the wall is the top of the ladder?

______

10. **Justify Reasoning** Are two equilateral triangles always similar? Explain.

______

______

______

11. **Critique Reasoning** Ryan calculated the missing measure in the diagram shown. What was his mistake?

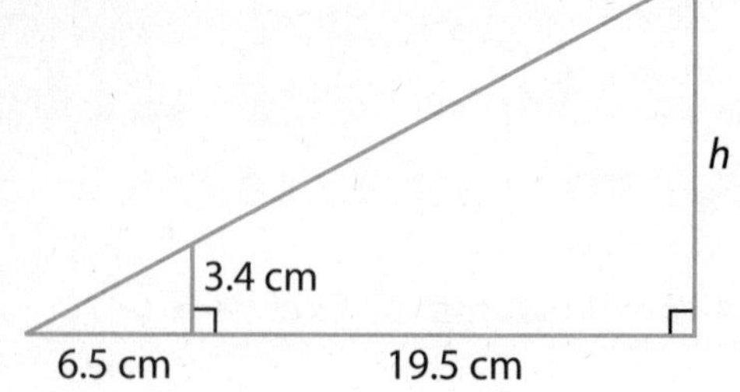

$$\frac{3.4}{6.5} = \frac{h}{19.5}$$

$$19.5 \times \frac{3.4}{6.5} = \frac{h}{19.5} \times 19.5$$

$$\frac{66.3}{6.5} = h$$

$$10.2 \text{ cm} = h$$

____

____

____

H.O.T. FOCUS ON HIGHER ORDER THINKING

Work Area

12. **Communicate Mathematical Ideas** For a pair of triangular earrings, how can you tell if they are similar? How can you tell if they are congruent?

____

____

____

____

13. **Critical Thinking** When does it make sense to use similar triangles to measure the height and length of objects in real life?

____

____

____

14. **Justify Reasoning** Two right triangles on a coordinate plane are similar but not congruent. Each of the legs of both triangles are extended by 1 unit, creating two new right triangles. Are the resulting triangles similar? Explain using an example.

____

____

____

____

____

MODULE QUIZ

Ready to Go On?

21.1 Parallel Lines Cut by a Transversal

In the figure, line $p \parallel$ line q. Find the measure of each angle if $m\angle 8 = 115°$.

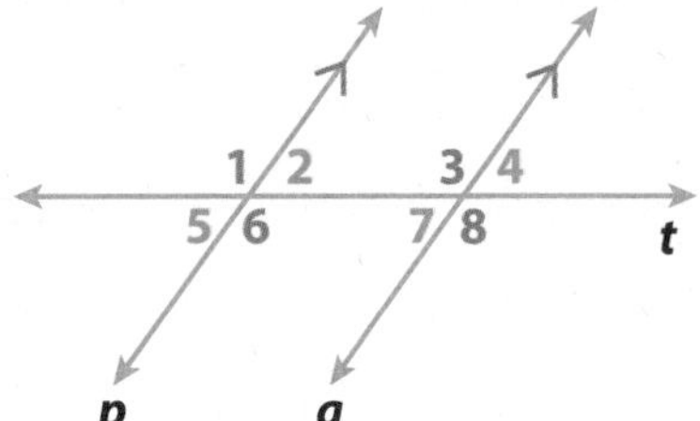

1. $m\angle 7 =$ ______________

2. $m\angle 6 =$ ______________

3. $m\angle 1 =$ ______________

21.2 Angle Theorems for Triangles

Find the measure of each angle.

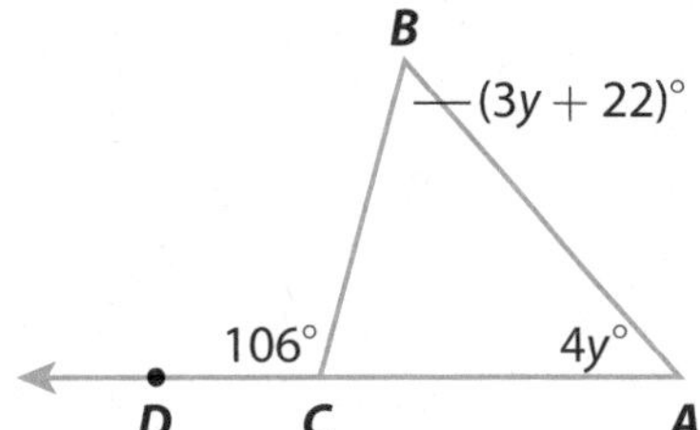

4. $m\angle A =$ ______________

5. $m\angle B =$ ______________

6. $m\angle BCA =$ ______________

21.3 Angle-Angle Similarity

Triangle *FEG* is similar to triangle *IHJ*. Find the missing values.

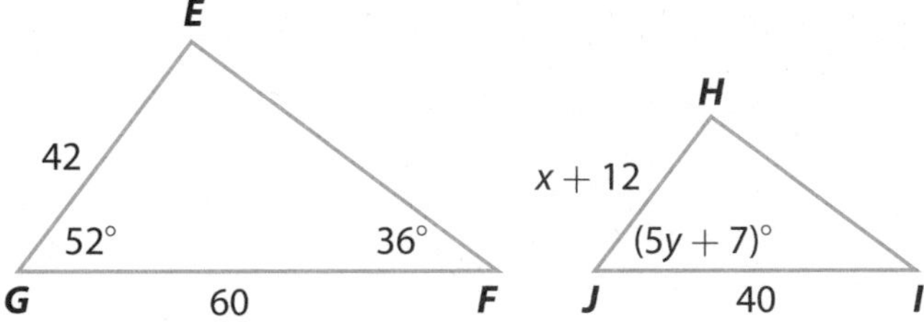

7. $x =$ __________ **8.** $y =$ __________ **9.** $m\angle H =$ __________

ESSENTIAL QUESTION

10. How can you use similar triangles to solve real-world problems?

____

____

____

MODULE 21
MIXED REVIEW

Assessment Readiness

1. In the diagram, lines *a* and *b* are parallel and lines *p* and *q* are parallel. Look at each pair of angles. Are the angles congruent?

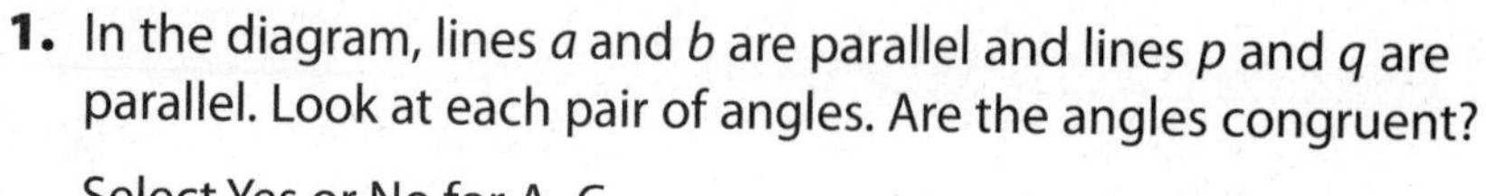

Select Yes or No for A–C.

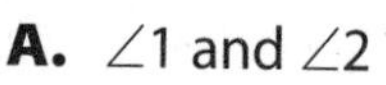

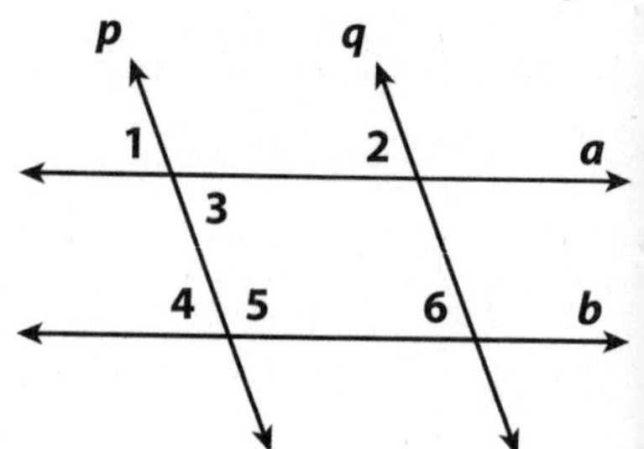

A. $\angle 1$ and $\angle 2$ ◯ Yes ◯ No

B. $\angle 3$ and $\angle 4$ ◯ Yes ◯ No

C. $\angle 5$ and $\angle 6$ ◯ Yes ◯ No

2. The variables *x* and *y* are related proportionally, and when $x = 18$, $y = 12$.

Choose True or False for each statement.

A. When $x = 3$, $y = 5$. ◯ True ◯ False

B. When $x = 27$, $y = 18$. ◯ True ◯ False

C. When $x = 63$, $y = 42$. ◯ True ◯ False

3. An artist is designing a triangular pane of glass for a stained glass window, as shown in the diagram. Given that $\angle ABC$ is an exterior angle, what is the measure of each interior angle of the triangle? Explain your reasoning.

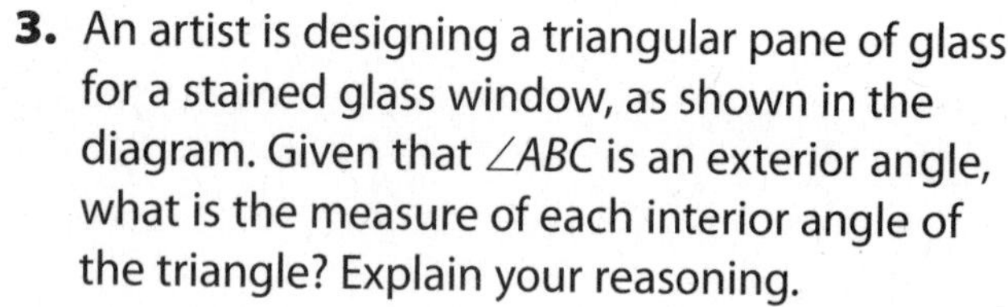

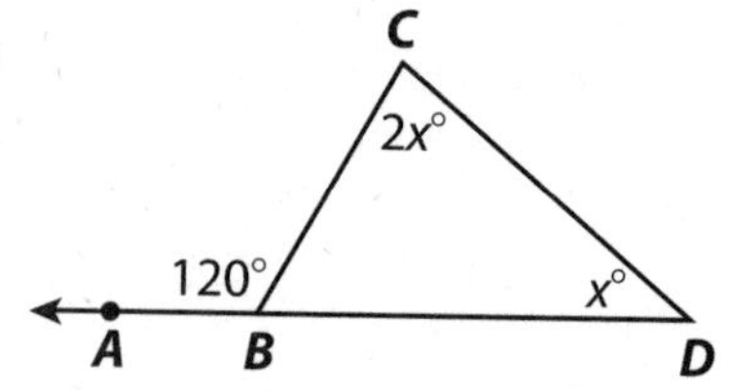

4. The diagram shows several of the boards that form part of the frame of a roof. Is $\triangle JKN$ similar to $\triangle JLM$? Explain how you know.

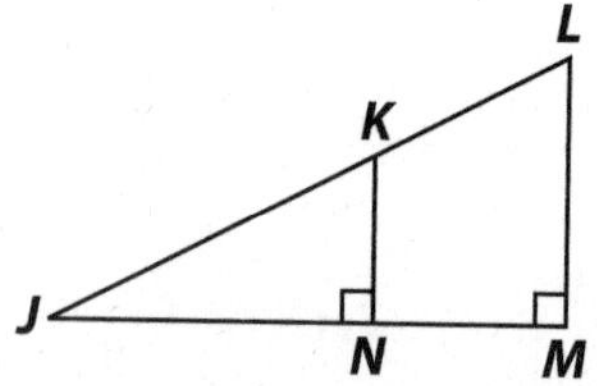

Volume

MODULE 22

CALIFORNIA

ESSENTIAL QUESTION

How can you use volume to solve real-world problems?

my.hrw.com

Real-World Video

Aquariums are in the shape of cylinders and rectangular prisms. To find out how much water an aquarium holds, you can use formulas for volume.

GO DIGITAL
my.hrw.com

my.hrw.com

Go digital with your write-in student edition, accessible on any device.

Math On the Spot

Scan with your smart phone to jump directly to the online edition, video tutor, and more.

Animated Math

Interactively explore key concepts to see how math works.

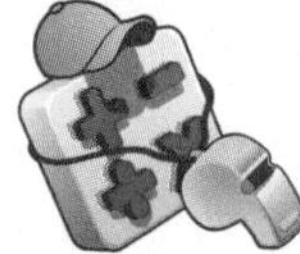

Personal Math Trainer

Get immediate feedback and help as you work through practice sets.

Are YOU Ready?

Complete these exercises to review skills you will need for this module.

Personal Math Trainer

Online Practice and Help

Exponents

EXAMPLE $6^3 = 6 \times 6 \times 6$ Multiply the base (6) by itself the number of times indicated by the exponent (3).

$= 36 \times 6$ Find the product of the first two terms.

$= 216$ Find the product of all the terms.

Evaluate each exponential expression.

1. 11^2 ________ **2.** 2^5 ________ **3.** $\left(\frac{1}{5}\right)^3$ ________ **4.** $(0.3)^2$ ________

5. 2.1^3 ________ **6.** 0.1^3 ________ **7.** $\left(\frac{9.6}{3}\right)^2$ ________ **8.** 100^3 ________

Round Decimals

EXAMPLE Round 43.2<u>6</u>85 to the underlined place.

43.2685 → 43.27

The digit to be rounded: 6
The digit to its right is 8.
8 is *5 or greater,* so round *up.*
The rounded number is 43.27.

Round to the underlined place.

9. 2.3<u>7</u>4 ______ **10.** 12<u>6</u>.399 ______ **11.** 13.<u>9</u>577 ______ **12.** 42.6<u>9</u>0 ______

13. 134.<u>9</u>5 ______ **14.** 2.<u>0</u>486 ______ **15.** 63.6<u>3</u>52 ______ **16.** 98.<u>9</u>499 ______

Simplify Numerical Expressions

EXAMPLE $\frac{1}{3}(3.14)(4)^2(3) = \frac{1}{3}(3.14)(16)(3)$ Simplify the exponent.

$= 50.24$ Multiply from left to right.

Simplify each expression.

17. $3.14(5)^2(10)$ ________ **18.** $\frac{1}{3}(3.14)(3)^2(5)$ ________ **19.** $\frac{4}{3}(3.14)(3)^3$ ________

20. $\frac{4}{3}(3.14)(6)^3$ ________ **21.** $3.14(4)^2(9)$ ________ **22.** $\frac{1}{3}(3.14)(9)^2\left(\frac{2}{3}\right)$ ________

Reading Start-Up

Visualize Vocabulary

Use the ✔ words to complete the empty columns in the chart. You may use words more than once.

Shape	Distance Around	Attributes	Associated Review Words
circle		*r*, *d*	
square		90° corner, sides	
rectangle		90° corner, sides	

Vocabulary

Review Words

area *(área)*
base *(base, en numeración)*
✔ circumference *(circunferencia)*
✔ diameter *(diámetro)*
height *(altura)*
✔ length *(longitud)*
✔ perimeter *(perímetro)*
✔ radius *(radio)*
✔ right angle *(ángulo recto)*
✔ width *(ancho)*

Preview Words

cone *(cono)*
cylinder *(cilindro)*
sphere *(esfera)*

Understand Vocabulary

Complete the sentences using the preview words.

1. A three-dimensional figure that has one vertex and one circular base is a ______________.
2. A three-dimensional figure with all points the same distance from the center is a ______________.
3. A three-dimensional figure that has two congruent circular bases is a ______________.

Active Reading

Three-Panel Flip Chart Before beginning the module, create a three-panel flip chart to help you organize what you learn. Label each flap with one of the lesson titles from this module. As you study each lesson, write important ideas like vocabulary, properties, and formulas under the appropriate flap.

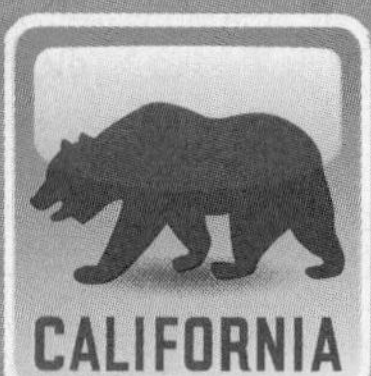

GETTING READY FOR

Volume

Understanding the standards and the vocabulary terms in the standards will help you know exactly what you are expected to learn in this module.

 CA CC **8.G.9**

Know the formulas for the volumes of cones, cylinders, and spheres and use them to solve real-world and mathematical problems.

Key Vocabulary

volume *(volumen)*
The number of cubic units needed to fill a given space.

cylinder *(cilindro)*
A three-dimensional figure with two parallel, congruent circular bases connected by a curved lateral surface.

What It Means to You

You will learn the formula for the volume of a cylinder.

EXAMPLE 8.G.9

The Asano Taiko Company of Japan built the world's largest drum in 2000. The drum's diameter is 4.8 meters, and its height is 4.95 meters. Estimate the volume of the drum.

$d = 4.8 \approx 5$

$h = 4.95 \approx 5$

$r = \frac{d}{2} \approx \frac{5}{2} = 2.5$

$V = (\pi r^2)h$ *Volume of a cylinder*

$\approx (3)\ (2.5)^2 \cdot 5$ *Use 3 for π.*

$= (3)\ (6.25)\ (5)$

$= 18.75 \cdot 5$

$= 93.75 \approx 94$

The volume of the drum is approximately 94 m^3.

 CA CC **8.G.9**

Know the formulas for the volumes of cones, cylinders, and spheres and use them to solve real-world and mathematical problems.

Key Vocabulary

cone *(cono)*
A three-dimensional figure with one vertex and one circular base.

sphere *(esfera)*
A three-dimensional figure with all points the same distance from the center.

What It Means to You

You will learn formulas for the volume of a cone and a sphere.

EXAMPLE 8.G.9

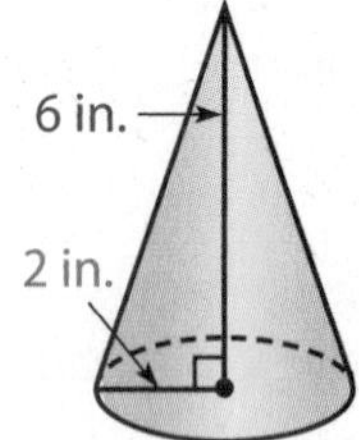

Find the volume of the cone. Use 3.14 for π.

$B = \pi(2^2) = 4\pi \text{ in}^2$

$V = \frac{1}{3} \cdot 4\pi \cdot 6$ *$V = \frac{1}{3}Bh$*

$V = 8\pi$ *Use 3.14 for π.*

$\approx 25.1 \text{ in}^3$

The volume of the cone is approximately 25.1 in^3.

The volume of a sphere with the same radius is $V = \frac{4}{3}\pi r^3 \approx \frac{4}{3}(3)(2)^3 = 32 \text{ in}^3$.

Visit **my.hrw.com** to see all **CA Common Core Standards** unpacked.

my.hrw.com

LESSON
22.1 Volume of Cylinders

8.G.9

Know the formulas for the volumes of cones, cylinders, and spheres and use them to solve real-world and mathematical problems.

ESSENTIAL QUESTION

How do you find the volume of a cylinder?

EXPLORE ACTIVITY 

8.G.9

Modeling the Volume of a Cylinder

A **cylinder** is a three-dimensional figure that has two congruent circular bases that lie in parallel planes. The volume of any three-dimensional figure is the number of cubic units needed to fill the space taken up by the solid figure.

One cube represents one cubic unit of volume. You can develop the formula for the volume of a cylinder using an empty soup can or other cylindrical container. First, remove one of the bases.

A Arrange centimeter cubes in a single layer at the bottom of the cylinder. Fit as many cubes into the layer as possible. How many cubes are in this layer?

____

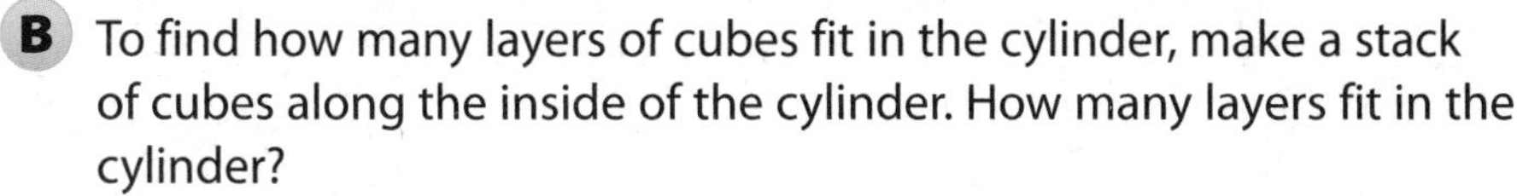

B To find how many layers of cubes fit in the cylinder, make a stack of cubes along the inside of the cylinder. How many layers fit in the cylinder?

____

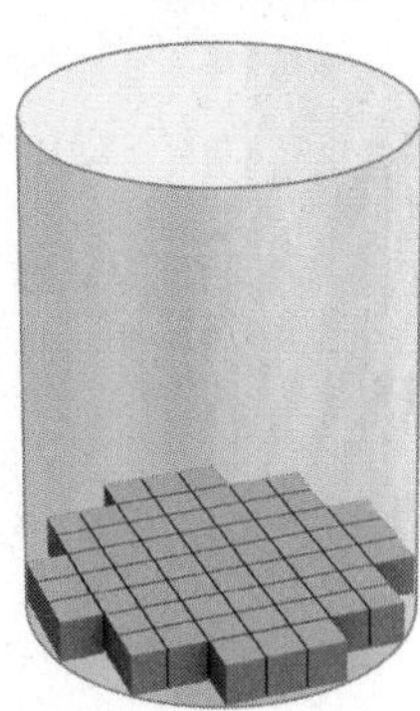

C How can you use what you know to find the approximate number of cubes that would fit in the cylinder?

____

____

Reflect

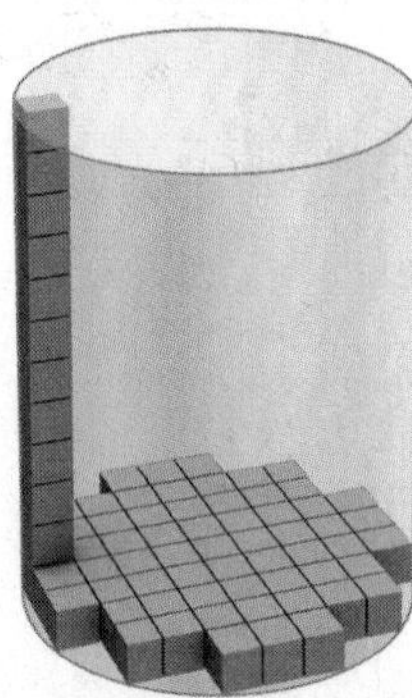

1. **Make a Conjecture** Suppose you know the area of the base of a cylinder and the height of the cylinder. How can you find the cylinder's volume?

____

2. Let the area of the base of a cylinder be *B* and the height of the cylinder be *h*. Write a formula for the cylinder's volume *V*. _________

Finding the Volume of a Cylinder Using a Formula

Finding volumes of cylinders is similar to finding volumes of prisms. You find the volume V of both a prism and a cylinder by multiplying the height h by the area of the base B, so $V = Bh$.

The base of a cylinder is a circle, so for a cylinder, $B = \pi r^2$.

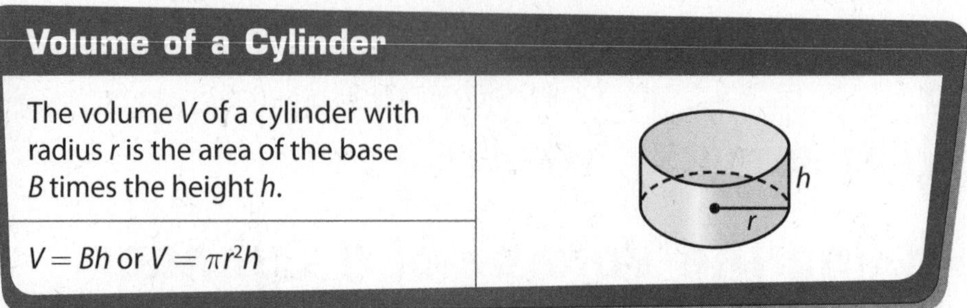

Volume of a Cylinder

The volume V of a cylinder with radius r is the area of the base B times the height h.	
$V = Bh$ or $V = \pi r^2 h$	

EXAMPLE 1

Find the volume of each cylinder. Round your answers to the nearest tenth if necessary. Use 3.14 for π.

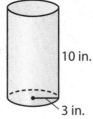

A (cylinder: 10 in., 3 in.)

$V = \pi r^2 h$

$\approx 3.14 \cdot 3^2 \cdot 10$ Substitute.

$\approx 3.14 \cdot 9 \cdot 10$ Simplify.

≈ 282.6 Multiply.

The volume is about 282.6 in^3.

B

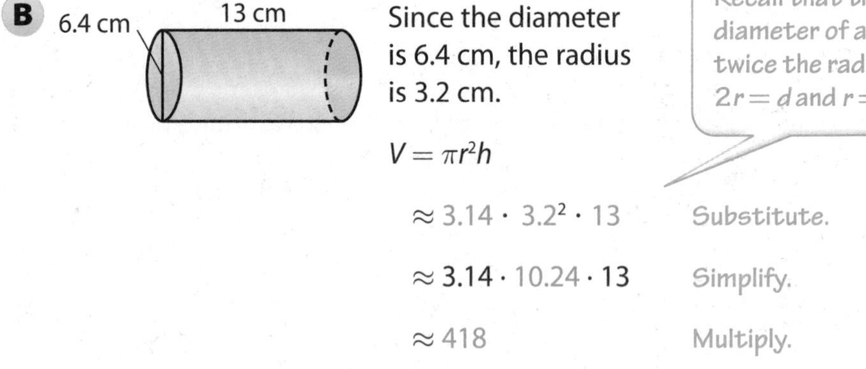

Since the diameter is 6.4 cm, the radius is 3.2 cm.

Recall that the diameter of a circle is twice the radius, so $2r = d$ and $r = \frac{d}{2}$.

$V = \pi r^2 h$

$\approx 3.14 \cdot 3.2^2 \cdot 13$ Substitute.

$\approx 3.14 \cdot 10.24 \cdot 13$ Simplify.

≈ 418 Multiply.

The volume is about 418 cm^3.

Reflect

3. **What If?** If you want a formula for the volume of a cylinder that involves the diameter d instead of the radius r, how can you rewrite it?

YOUR TURN

Find the volume of each cylinder. Round your answers to the nearest tenth if necessary. Use 3.14 for π.

4. 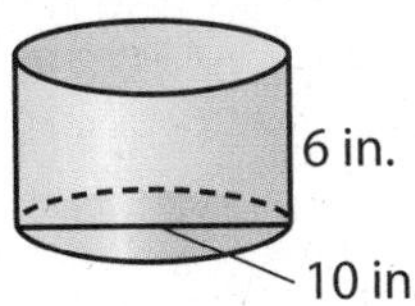

____

5. 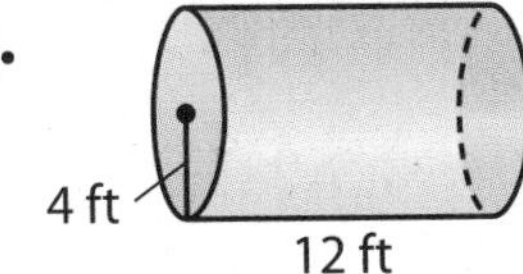

____

Finding the Volume of a Cylinder in a Real-World Context

You can find the volume of a bass drum by using the formula for the volume of a cylinder.

EXAMPLE 2

CA CC 8.G.9

One of the bass drums used in a marching band has a diameter of 18 inches and a depth of 14 inches. Find the volume of the drum to the nearest tenth. Use 3.14 for π.

STEP 1 Find the radius of the drum.

$$r = \frac{d}{2} = \frac{18}{2} = 9 \text{ in.}$$

STEP 2 Find the volume of the drum.

$V = \pi r^2 h$

$\approx 3.14 \cdot 9^2 \cdot 14$ *Substitute.*

$\approx 3.14 \cdot 81 \cdot 14$ *Simplify the exponent.*

≈ 3560.76 *Multiply.*

The volume of the drum is about 3560.8 in^3.

YOUR TURN

6. A drum company advertises a snare drum that is 4 inches high and 12 inches in diameter. Find the volume of the drum to the nearest tenth. Use 3.14 for π.

____

Guided Practice

1. Vocabulary Describe the bases of a cylinder. (Explore Activity)

____

2. Figure 1 shows a view from above of inch cubes on the bottom of a cylinder. Figure 2 shows the highest stack of cubes that will fit inside the cylinder. Estimate the volume of the cylinder. Explain your reasoning. (Explore Activity)

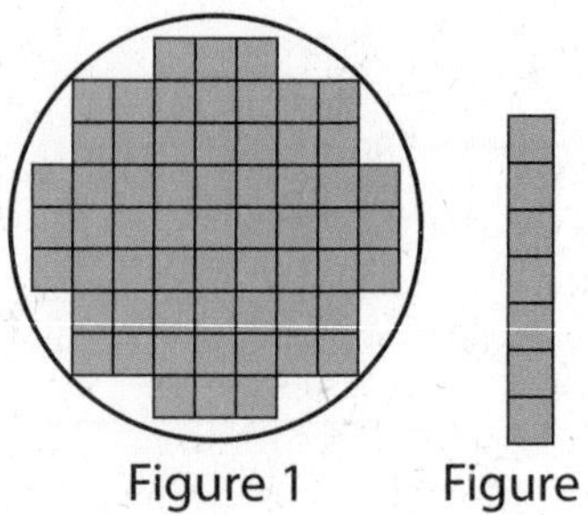

Figure 1 Figure 2

____

____

____

3. Find the volume of the cylinder to the nearest tenth. Use 3.14 for π. (Example 1)

$V = \pi r^2 h$

$V = \pi \cdot \square^2 \cdot \square$

$\approx 3.14 \cdot \square \cdot \square$

$\approx \square$

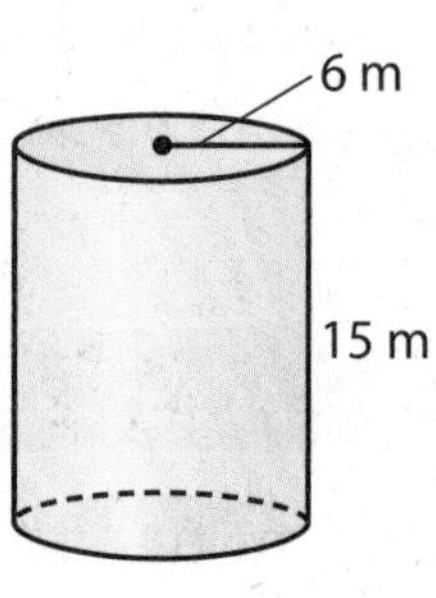

The volume of the cylinder is approximately ________ m^3.

4. A Japanese odaiko is a very large drum that is made by hollowing out a section of a tree trunk. A museum in Takayama City has three odaikos of similar size carved from a single tree trunk. The largest measures about 2.7 meters in both diameter and length, and weighs about 4.5 metric tons. Using the volume formula for a cylinder, approximate the volume of the drum to the nearest tenth. (Example 2)

The radius of the drum is about ________ m.

The volume of the drum is about ________ m^3.

ESSENTIAL QUESTION CHECK-IN

5. How do you find the volume of a cylinder? Describe which measurements of a cylinder you need to know.

____

____

____

Name________________ Class________________ Date________________

22.1 Independent Practice

8.G.9

Find the volume of each figure. Round your answers to the nearest tenth if necessary. Use 3.14 for π.

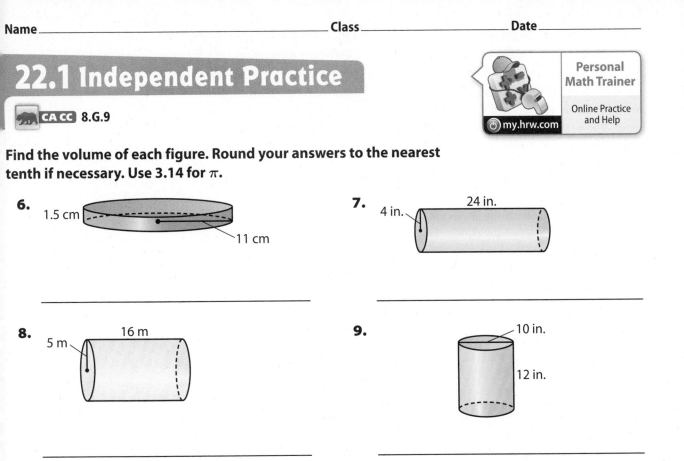

6.
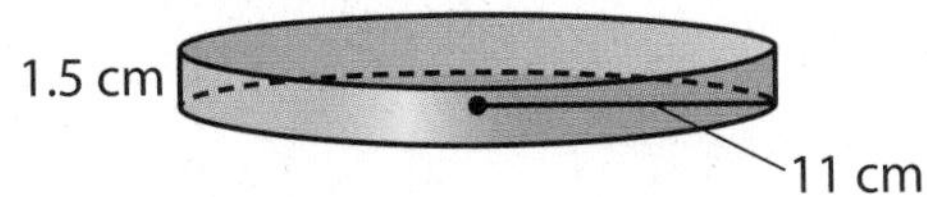

____

7.
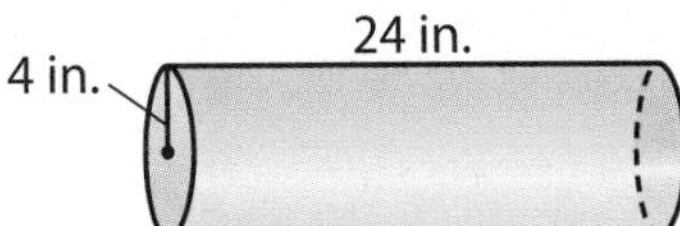

____

8.
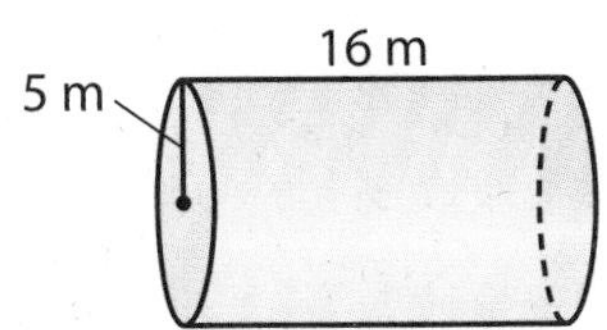

____

9.
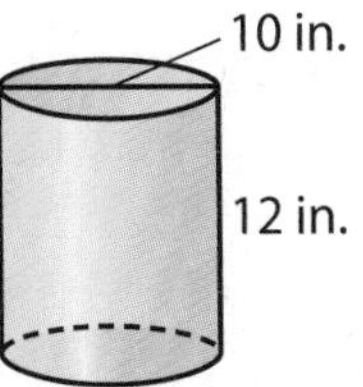

____

10. A cylinder has a radius of 4 centimeters and a height of 40 centimeters.

____

11. A cylinder has a radius of 8 meters and a height of 4 meters.

____

Round your answer to the nearest tenth, if necessary. Use 3.14 for π.

12. The cylindrical Giant Ocean Tank at the New England Aquarium in Boston is 24 feet deep and has a radius of 18.8 feet. Find the volume of the tank.

____

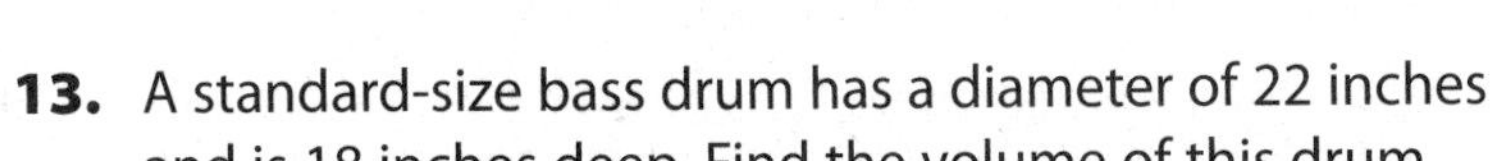

13. A standard-size bass drum has a diameter of 22 inches and is 18 inches deep. Find the volume of this drum.

____

14. Grain is stored in cylindrical structures called silos. Find the volume of a silo with a diameter of 11.1 feet and a height of 20 feet.

____

15. The Frank Erwin Center, or "The Drum," at the University of Texas in Austin can be approximated by a cylinder that is 120 meters in diameter and 30 meters in height. Find its volume.

____

16. A barrel of crude oil contains about 5.61 cubic feet of oil. How many barrels of oil are contained in 1 mile (5280 feet) of a pipeline that has an inside diameter of 6 inches and is completely filled with oil? How much is "1 mile" of oil in this pipeline worth at a price of $100 per barrel?

____

17. A pan for baking French bread is shaped like half a cylinder. It is 12 inches long and 3.5 inches in diameter. What is the volume of uncooked dough that would fill this pan?

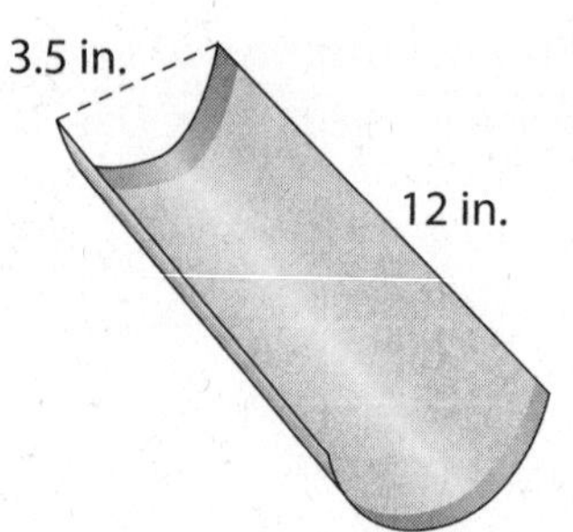

____

FOCUS ON HIGHER ORDER THINKING

Work Area

18. **Explain the Error** A student said the volume of a cylinder with a 3-inch diameter is two times the volume of a cylinder with the same height and a 1.5-inch radius. What is the error?

____

____

____

19. **Communicate Mathematical Ideas** Explain how you can find the height of a cylinder if you know the diameter and the volume. Include an example with your explanation.

____

____

____

____

____

____

20. **Analyze Relationships** Cylinder A has a radius of 6 centimeters. Cylinder B has the same height and a radius half as long as cylinder A. What fraction of the volume of cylinder A is the volume of cylinder B? Explain.

____

____

____

____

LESSON

22.2 Volume of Cones

8.G.9

Know the formulas for the volumes of cones, cylinders, and spheres and use them to solve real-world and mathematical problems.

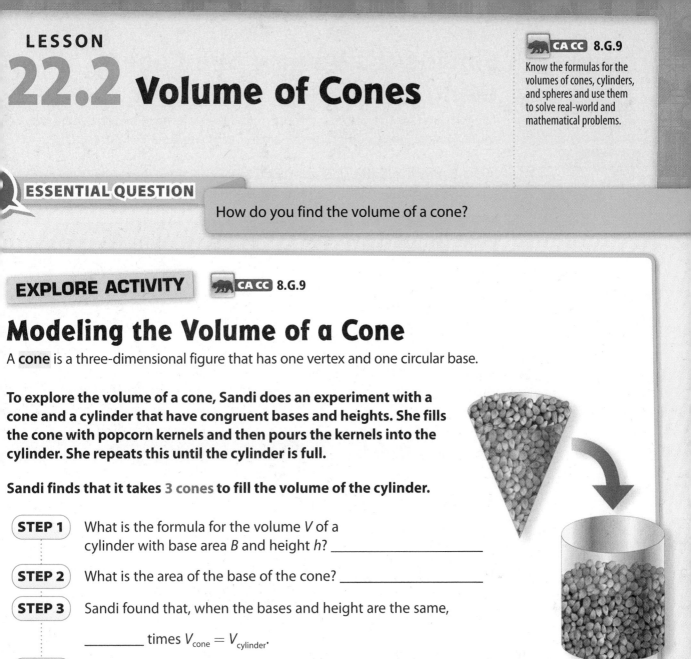

ESSENTIAL QUESTION

How do you find the volume of a cone?

EXPLORE ACTIVITY  8.G.9

Modeling the Volume of a Cone

A **cone** is a three-dimensional figure that has one vertex and one circular base.

To explore the volume of a cone, Sandi does an experiment with a cone and a cylinder that have congruent bases and heights. She fills the cone with popcorn kernels and then pours the kernels into the cylinder. She repeats this until the cylinder is full.

Sandi finds that it takes 3 cones to fill the volume of the cylinder.

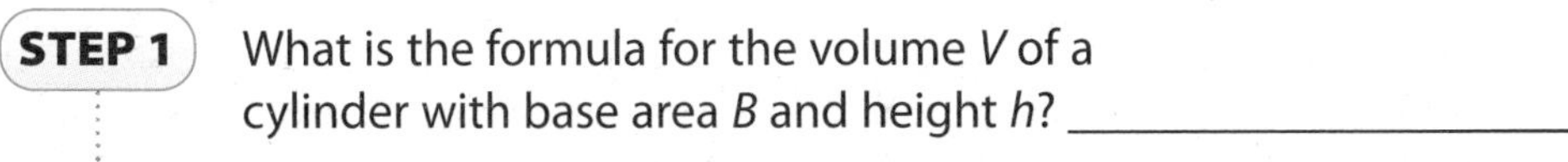

STEP 1 What is the formula for the volume V of a cylinder with base area B and height h? ____________

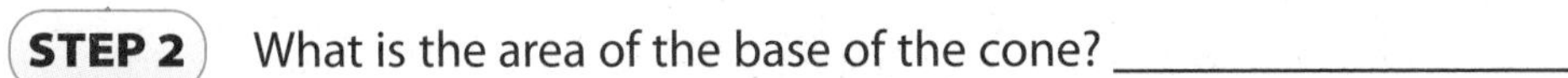

STEP 2 What is the area of the base of the cone? ____________

STEP 3 Sandi found that, when the bases and height are the same,

________ times $V_{cone} = V_{cylinder}$.

STEP 4 How does the volume of the cone compare to the volume of the cylinder?

Volume of the cone: $V_{cone} = \frac{\square}{\square} \cdot V_{cylinder}$

Reflect

1. Use the conclusion from this experiment to write a formula for the volume of a cone in terms of the height and the radius. Explain.

____

____

____

Finding the Volume of a Cone Using a Formula

The formulas for the volume of a prism and the volume of a cylinder are the same: multiply the height h by the area of the base B, so $V = Bh$.

In the **Explore Activity**, you saw that the volume of a cone is one third the volume of a cylinder with the same base and height.

Volume of a Cone

The volume V of a cone with radius r is one third the area of the base B times the height h.	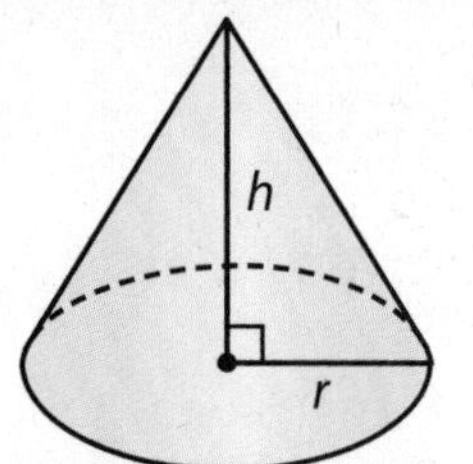
$V = \frac{1}{3}Bh$ or $V = \frac{1}{3}\pi r^2 h$	

EXAMPLE 1

CA CC 8.G.9

Find the volume of each cone. Round your answers to the nearest tenth. Use 3.14 for π.

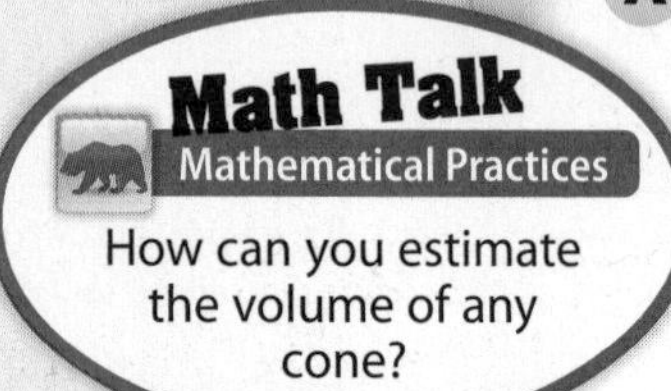

Math Talk
Mathematical Practices
How can you estimate the volume of any cone?

A

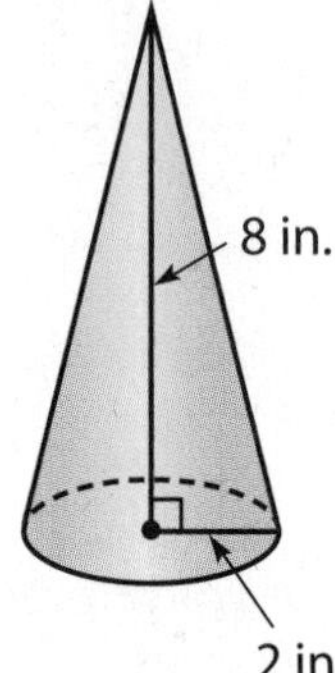

$V = \frac{1}{3}\pi r^2 h$

$\approx \frac{1}{3} \cdot 3.14 \cdot 2^2 \cdot 8$ Substitute.

$\approx \frac{1}{3} \cdot 3.14 \cdot 4 \cdot 8$ Simplify.

≈ 33.5 Multiply.

The volume is about 33.5 in^3.

B Since the diameter is 8 ft, the radius is 4 ft.

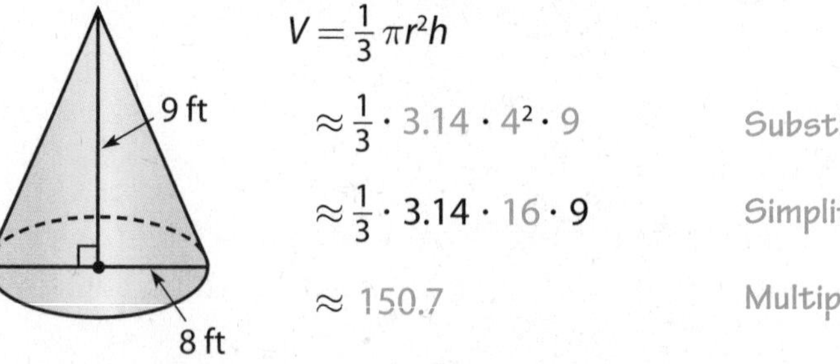

$V = \frac{1}{3}\pi r^2 h$

$\approx \frac{1}{3} \cdot 3.14 \cdot 4^2 \cdot 9$ Substitute.

$\approx \frac{1}{3} \cdot 3.14 \cdot 16 \cdot 9$ Simplify.

≈ 150.7 Multiply.

The volume is about 150.7 ft^3.

Reflect

2. How can you rewrite the formula for the volume of a cone using the diameter d instead of the radius r? ____________

YOUR TURN

Find the volume of each cone. Round your answers to the nearest tenth. Use 3.14 for π.

3.

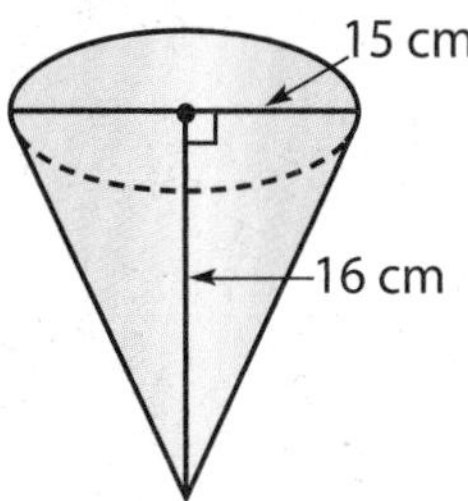

____

4.

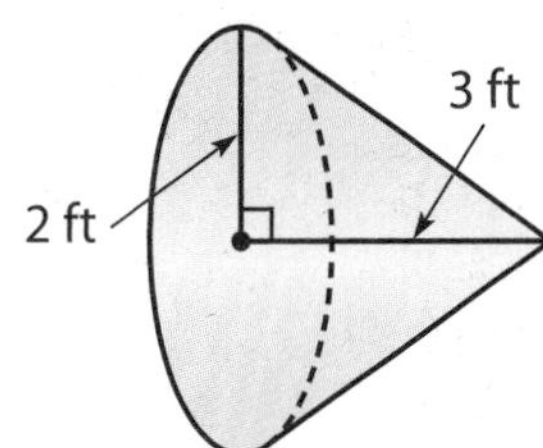

____

Finding the Volume of a Volcano

The mountain created by a volcano is often cone–shaped.

EXAMPLE 2

CA CC 8.G.9

For her geography project, Karen built a clay model of a volcano in the shape of a cone. Her model has a diameter of 12 inches and a height of 8 inches. Find the volume of clay in her model to the nearest tenth. Use 3.14 for π.

STEP 1 Find the radius.

$r = \frac{12}{2} = 6$ in.

STEP 2 Find the volume of clay.

$V = \frac{1}{3}\pi r^2 h$

$\approx \frac{1}{3} \cdot 3.14 \cdot 6^2 \cdot 8$ Substitute.

$\approx \frac{1}{3} \cdot 3.14 \cdot 36 \cdot 8$ Simplify.

≈ 301.44 Multiply.

The volume of the clay is about 301.4 in^3.

5. The cone of the volcano Parícutin in Mexico had a height of 410 meters and a diameter of 424 meters. Find the volume of the cone to the nearest tenth. Use 3.14 for π.

____

Guided Practice

1. The area of the base of a cylinder is 45 square inches and its height is 10 inches. A cone has the same area for its base and the same height. What is the volume of the cone? (Explore Activity)

$V_{cylinder} = Bh = \square \cdot \square = \square$

$V_{cone} = \frac{1}{3} V_{cylinder}$

$= \frac{1}{3} \square$

$= \square$

The volume of the cone is ________ in^3.

2. A cone and a cylinder have congruent height and bases. The volume of the cone is 18 m^3. What is the volume of the cylinder? Explain. (Explore Activity)

____

____

____

____

____

____

____

Find the volume of each cone. Round your answer to the nearest tenth if necessary. Use 3.14 for π. (Example 1)

3. 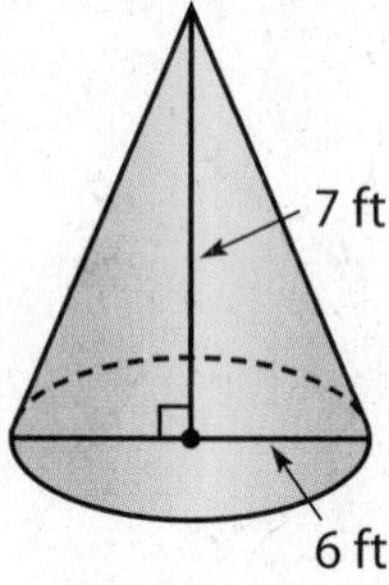

____

4. 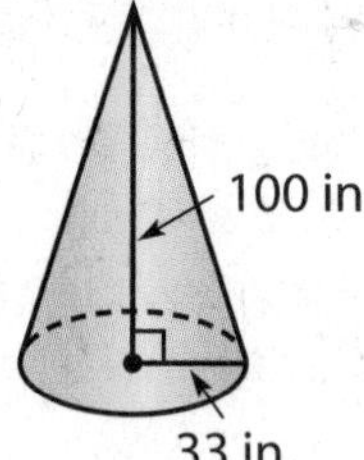

____

5. Gretchen made a paper cone to hold a gift for a friend. The paper cone was 15 inches high and had a radius of 3 inches. Find the volume of the paper cone to the nearest tenth. Use 3.14 for π. (Example 2) ________

6. A cone-shaped building is commonly used to store sand. What would be the volume of a cone-shaped building with a diameter of 50 meters and a height of 20 meters? Round your answer to the nearest tenth. Use 3.14 for π. (Example 2) ________

ESSENTIAL QUESTION CHECK-IN

7. How do you find the volume of a cone?

____

____

____

Name ______________________ Class ______________________ Date ______________________

22.2 Independent Practice

CA CC 8.G.9

Find the volume of each cone. Round your answers to the nearest tenth if necessary. Use 3.14 for π.

8.

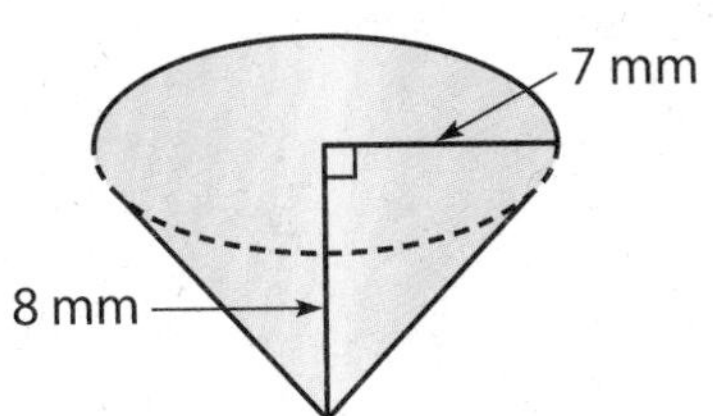

____

9.

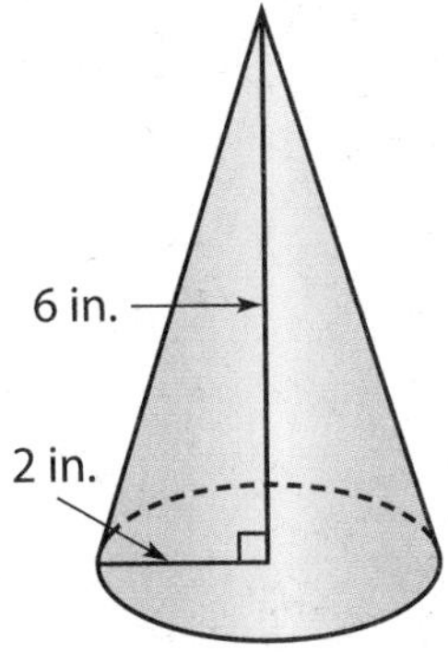

____

10. A cone has a diameter of 6 centimeters and a height of 11.5 centimeters.

____

11. A cone has a radius of 3 meters and a height of 10 meters.

____

Round your answers to the nearest tenth if necessary. Use 3.14 for π.

12. Antonio is making mini waffle cones. Each waffle cone is 3 inches high and has a radius of $\frac{3}{4}$ inch. What is the volume of a waffle cone?

____

13. A snack bar sells popcorn in cone-shaped containers. One container has a diameter of 8 inches and a height of 10 inches. How many cubic inches of popcorn does the container hold?

____

14. A volcanic cone has a diameter of 300 meters and a height of 150 meters. What is the volume of the cone?

____

15. **Multistep** Orange traffic cones come in a variety of sizes. Approximate the volume, in cubic inches, of a traffic cone that has a height of 2 feet and a diameter of 10 inches. Use 3.14 for π.

____

Find the missing measure for each cone. Round your answers to the nearest tenth if necessary. Use 3.14 for π.

16. radius = ______________

height = 6 in.

volume = 100.48 in^3

17. diameter = 6 cm

height = ______________

volume = 56.52 cm^3

18. The diameter of a cone-shaped container is 4 inches, and its height is 6 inches. How much greater is the volume of a cylinder-shaped container with the same diameter and height? Round your answer to the nearest hundredth. Use 3.14 for π.

____

FOCUS ON HIGHER ORDER THINKING

Work Area

19. Alex wants to know the volume of sand in an hourglass. When all the sand is in the bottom, he stands a ruler up beside the hourglass and estimates the height of the cone of sand.

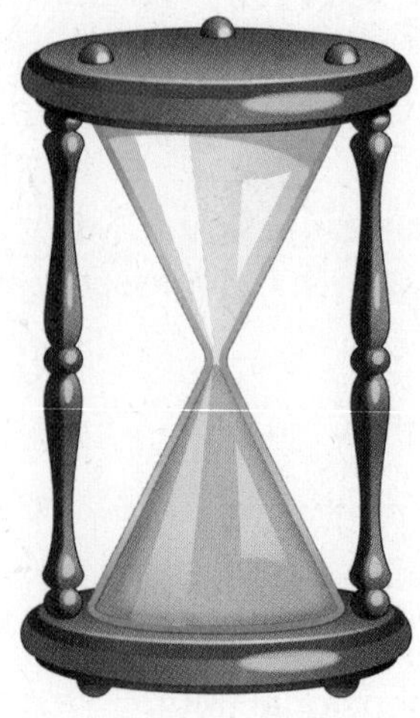

a. What else does he need to measure to find the volume of sand?

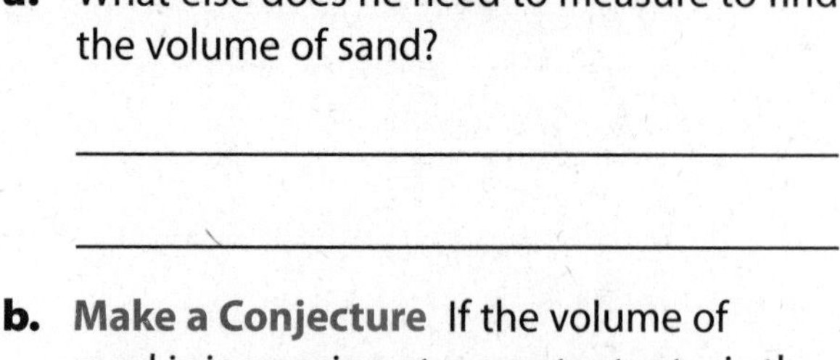

b. **Make a Conjecture** If the volume of sand is increasing at a constant rate, is the height increasing at a constant rate? Explain.

____

____

____

20. **Problem Solving** The diameter of a cone is x cm, the height is 18 cm, and the volume is 301.44 cm^3. What is x? Use 3.14 for π.

____

21. **Analyze Relationships** A cone has a radius of 1 foot and a height of 2 feet. How many cones of liquid would it take to fill a cylinder with a diameter of 2 feet and a height of 2 feet? Explain.

____

____

____

22. **Critique Reasoning** Herb knows that the volume of a cone is one third that of a cylinder with the same base and height. He reasons that a cone with the same height as a given cylinder but 3 times the radius should therefore have the same volume as the cylinder, since $\frac{1}{3} \cdot 3 = 1$. Is Herb correct? Explain.

____

____

____

____

____

LESSON

22.3 Volume of Spheres

CA CC 8.G.9

Know the formulas for the volumes of cones, cylinders, and spheres and use them to solve real-world and mathematical problems.

ESSENTIAL QUESTION

How do you find the volume of a sphere?

EXPLORE ACTIVITY 

CA CC 8.G.9

Modeling the Volume of a Sphere

A **sphere** is a three-dimensional figure with all points the same distance from the center. The **radius** of a sphere is the distance from the center to any point on the sphere.

You have seen that a cone fills $\frac{1}{3}$ of a cylinder of the same radius and height h. If you were to do a similar experiment with a sphere of the same radius, you would find that a sphere fills $\frac{2}{3}$ of the cylinder. The cylinder's height is equal to twice the radius of the sphere.

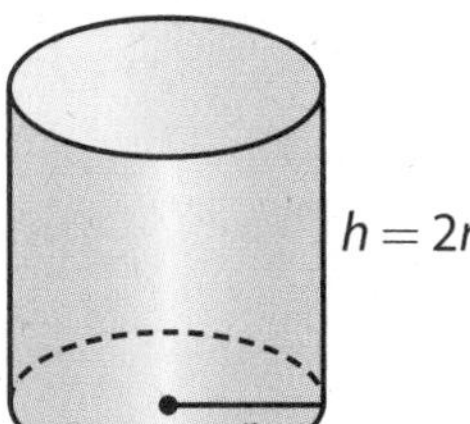
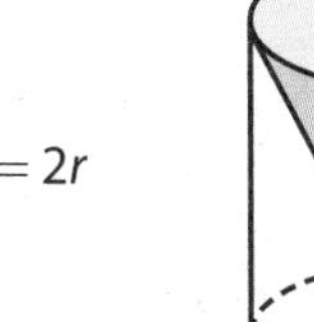
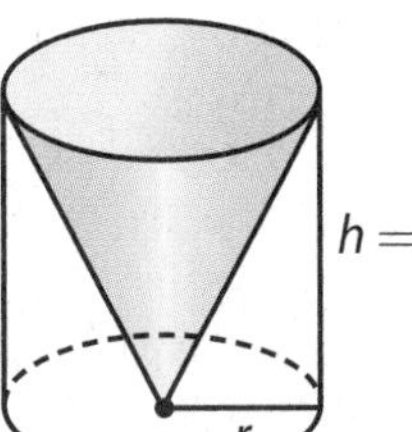
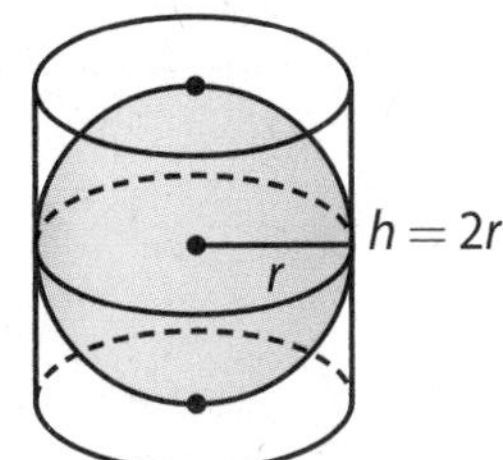

STEP 1 Write the formula $V = Bh$ for each shape. Use $B = \pi r^2$ and substitute the fractions you know for the cone and sphere.

Cylinder	Cone	Sphere
$V = \pi r^2 h$	$V = \frac{1}{3}\pi r^2 h$	$V = \frac{2}{3}\pi r^2 h$

STEP 2 Notice that a sphere always has a height equal to twice the radius. Substitute $2r$ for h. $V = \frac{2}{3}\pi r^2(2r)$

STEP 3 Simplify this formula for the volume of a sphere. $V = \square\,\pi r^3$

Reflect

1. **Analyze Relationships** A cone has a radius of r and a height of $2r$. A sphere has a radius of r. Compare the volume of the sphere and cone.

____

____

____

Finding the Volume of a Sphere Using a Formula

The Explore Activity illustrates a formula for the volume of a sphere with radius r.

Volume of a Sphere

The volume V of a sphere is $\frac{4}{3}\pi$ times the cube of the radius r.	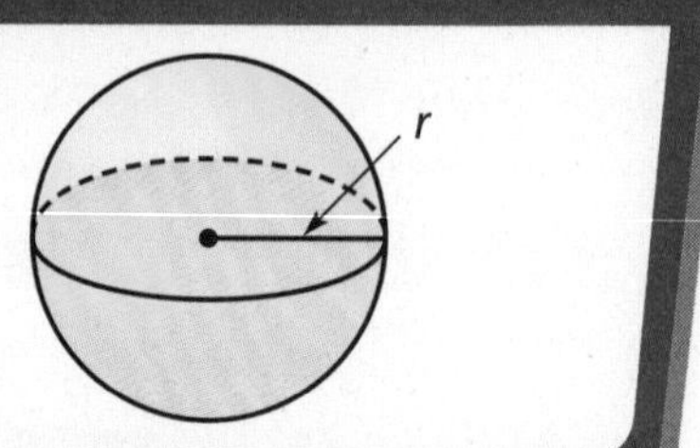
$V = \frac{4}{3}\pi r^3$	

EXAMPLE 1

CA CC 8.G.9

Find the volume of each sphere. Round your answers to the nearest tenth if necessary. Use 3.14 for π.

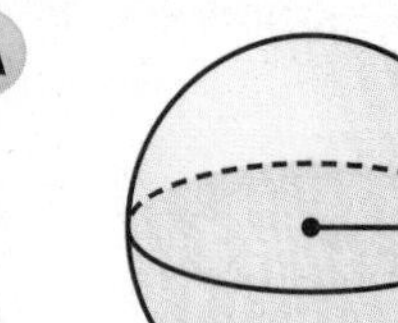

$V = \frac{4}{3}\pi r^3$

$\approx \frac{4}{3} \cdot 3.14 \cdot 2.1^3$ Substitute.

$\approx \frac{4}{3} \cdot 3.14 \cdot 9.26$ Simplify.

≈ 38.8 Multiply.

The volume is about 38.8 cm^3.

Math Talk

If you know the diameter of a sphere, how would the formula for the volume of a sphere be written in terms of d?

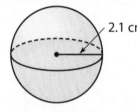

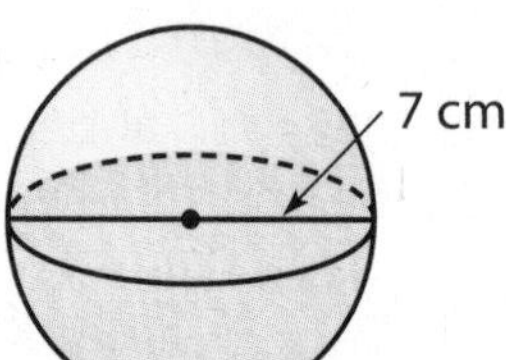

Since the diameter is 7 cm, the radius is 3.5 cm.

$V = \frac{4}{3}\pi r^3$

$\approx \frac{4}{3} \cdot 3.14 \cdot 3.5^3$ Substitute.

$\approx \frac{4}{3} \cdot 3.14 \cdot 42.9$ Simplify.

≈ 179.6 Multiply.

The volume is about 179.6 cm^3.

YOUR TURN

Find the volume of each sphere. Round your answers to the nearest tenth. Use 3.14 for π.

2. A sphere has a radius of 10 centimeters. ______________

3. A sphere has a diameter of 3.4 meters. ______________

Finding the Volume of a Sphere in a Real-World Context

Many sports, including golf and tennis, use a ball that is spherical in shape.

EXAMPLE 2 

CA CC 8.G.9

Soccer balls come in several different sizes. One soccer ball has a diameter of 22 centimeters. What is the volume of this soccer ball? Round your answer to the nearest tenth. Use 3.14 for π.

STEP 1 Find the radius.

$r = \frac{d}{2} = 11 \text{ cm}$

STEP 2 Find the volume of the soccer ball.

$V = \frac{4}{3}\pi r^3$

$\approx \frac{4}{3} \cdot 3.14 \cdot 11^3$ Substitute.

$\approx \frac{4}{3} \cdot 3.14 \cdot 1331$ Simplify.

≈ 5572.4533 Multiply.

The volume of the soccer ball is about 5572.5 cm^3.

Reflect

4. What is the volume of the soccer ball in terms of π, to the nearest whole number multiple? Explain your answer.

5. **Analyze Relationships** The diameter of a basketball is about 1.1 times that of a soccer ball. The diameter of a tennis ball is about 0.3 times that of a soccer ball. How do the volumes of these balls compare to that of a soccer ball? Explain.

YOUR TURN

6. Val measures the diameter of a ball as 12 inches. How many cubic inches of air does this ball hold, to the nearest tenth? Use 3.14 for π.

Guided Practice

1. **Vocabulary** A sphere is a three-dimensional figure with all points ________________ from the center. (Explore Activity)

2. **Vocabulary** The ________________ is the distance from the center of a sphere to a point on the sphere. (Explore Activity)

Find the volume of each sphere. Round your answers to the nearest tenth if necessary. Use 3.14 for π. (Example 1)

3.

1 in.

____

4.

20 cm

____

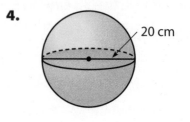

5. A sphere has a radius of 1.5 feet. ________________

6. A sphere has a diameter of 2 yards. ________________

7. A baseball has a diameter of 2.9 inches. Find the volume of the baseball. Round your answer to the nearest tenth if necessary. Use 3.14 for π. (Example 2) ________________

8. A basketball has a radius of 4.7 inches. What is its volume to the nearest cubic inch. Use 3.14 for π. (Example 2) ________________

9. A company is deciding whether to package a ball in a cubic box or a cylindrical box. In either case, the ball will touch the bottom, top, and sides. (Explore Activity)

r

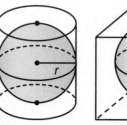

r

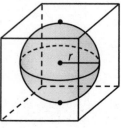

   a. What portion of the space inside the cylindrical box is empty? Explain.

   ____

   b. Find an expression for the volume of the cubic box. ________________

   c. About what portion of the space inside the cubic box is empty? Explain.

   ____

   ____

ESSENTIAL QUESTION CHECK-IN

10. Explain the steps you use to find the volume of a sphere.

____

Name ____________ Class ____________ Date ____________

22.3 Independent Practice

8.G.9

Personal Math Trainer

Online Practice and Help

Find the volume of each sphere. Round your answers to the nearest tenth if necessary. Use 3.14 for π.

11. radius of 3.1 meters ____________

12. diameter of 18 inches ____________

13. $r = 6$ in. ____________

14. $d = 36$ m ____________

15.

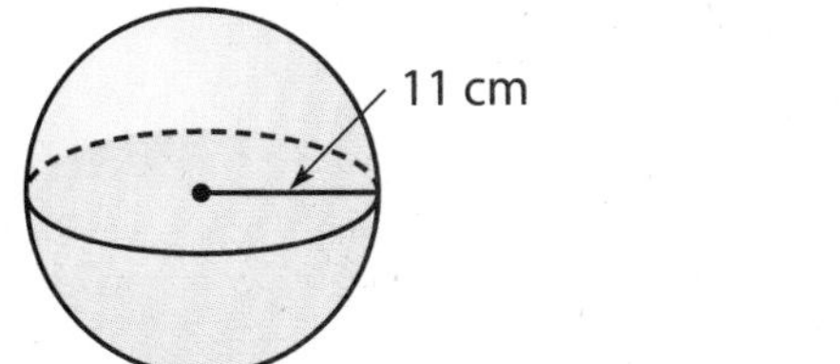

____

16.

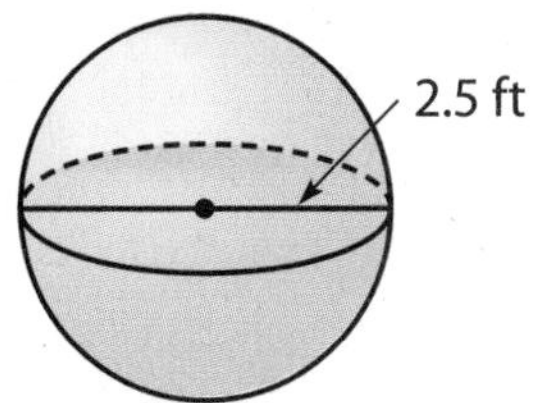

____

The eggs of birds and other animals come in many different shapes and sizes. Eggs often have a shape that is nearly spherical. When this is true, you can use the formula for a sphere to find their volume.

17. The green turtle lays eggs that are approximately spherical with an average diameter of 4.5 centimeters. Each turtle lays an average of 113 eggs at one time. Find the total volume of these eggs, to the nearest cubic centimeter.

____

18. Hummingbirds lay eggs that are nearly spherical and about 1 centimeter in diameter. Find the volume of an egg. Round your answer to the nearest tenth.

____

19. Fossilized spherical eggs of dinosaurs called titanosaurid sauropods were found in Patagonia. These eggs were 15 centimeters in diameter. Find the volume of an egg. Round your answer to the nearest tenth.

____

20. **Persevere in Problem Solving** An ostrich egg has about the same volume as a sphere with a diameter of 5 inches. If the eggshell is about $\frac{1}{12}$ inch thick, find the volume of just the shell, not including the interior of the egg. Round your answer to the nearest tenth.

____

21. **Multistep** Write the steps you would use to find a formula for the volume of the figure at right. Then write the formula.

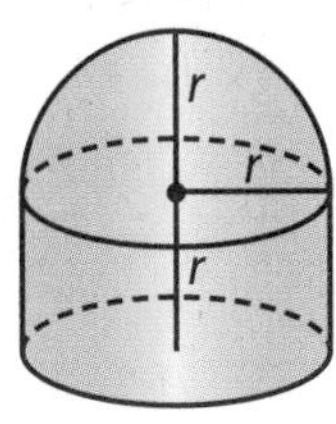

____

22. Critical Thinking Explain what happens to the volume of a sphere if you double the radius.

____

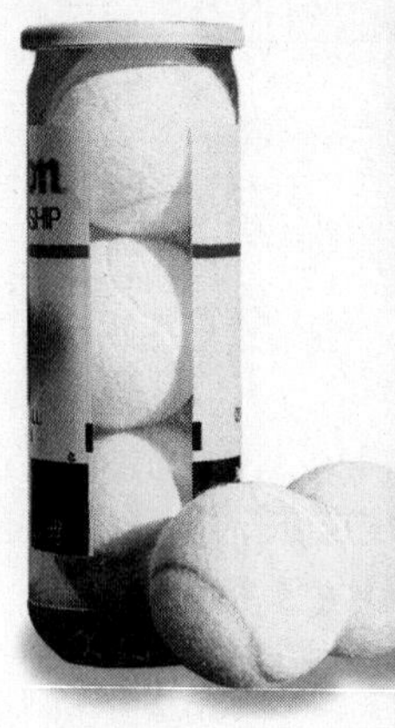

23. Multistep A cylindrical can of tennis balls holds a stack of three balls so that they touch the can at the top, bottom, and sides. The radius of each ball is 1.25 inches. Find the volume inside the can that is not taken up by the three tennis balls.

____

H.O.T. FOCUS ON HIGHER ORDER THINKING

Work Area

24. Critique Reasoning A sphere has a radius of 4 inches, and a cube-shaped box has an edge length of 7.5 inches. J.D. says the box has a greater volume, so the sphere will fit in the box. Is he correct? Explain.

____

____

____

25. Critical Thinking Which would hold the most water: a bowl in the shape of a hemisphere with radius r, a cylindrical glass with radius r and height r, or a cone-shaped drinking cup with radius r and height r? Explain.

____

____

____

26. Analyze Relationships Hari has models of a sphere, a cylinder, and a cone. The sphere's diameter and the cylinder's height are the same, $2r$. The cylinder has radius r. The cone has diameter $2r$ and height $2r$. Compare the volumes of the cone and the sphere to the volume of the cylinder.

____

____

____

27. A spherical helium balloon that is 8 feet in diameter can lift about 17 pounds. What does the diameter of a balloon need to be to lift a person who weighs 136 pounds? Explain.

____

____

____

MODULE QUIZ

Ready to Go On?

22.1 Volume of Cylinders

Find the volume of each cylinder. Round your answers to the nearest tenth if necessary. Use 3.14 for π.

1.

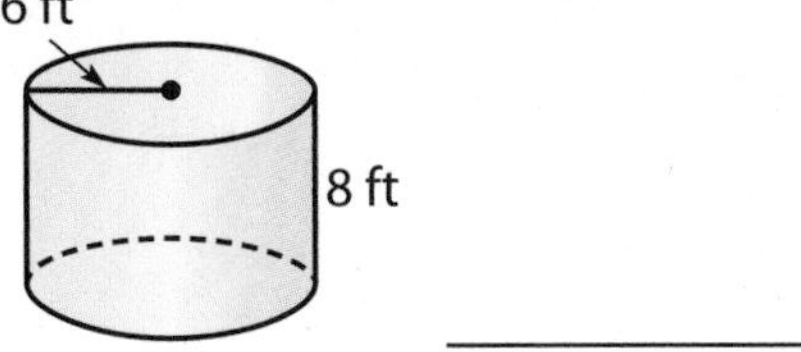

____

2. A can of juice has a radius of 4 inches and a height of 7 inches. What is the volume of the can?

____

22.2 Volume of Cones

Find the volume of each cone. Round your answers to the nearest tenth if necessary. Use 3.14 for π.

3.

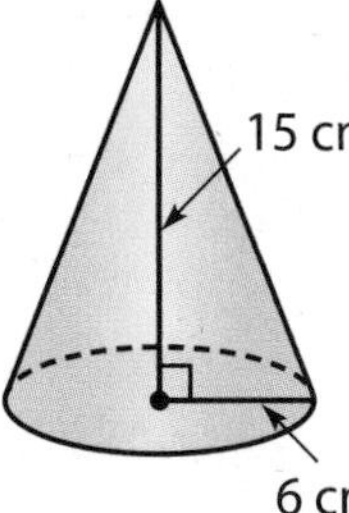

____

4.

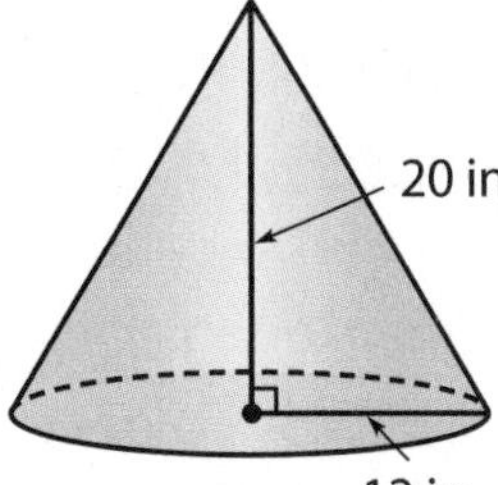

____

22.3 Volume of Spheres

Find the volume of each sphere. Round your answers to the nearest tenth if necessary. Use 3.14 for π.

5.

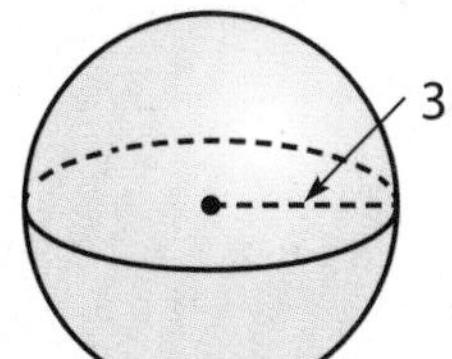

____

6.

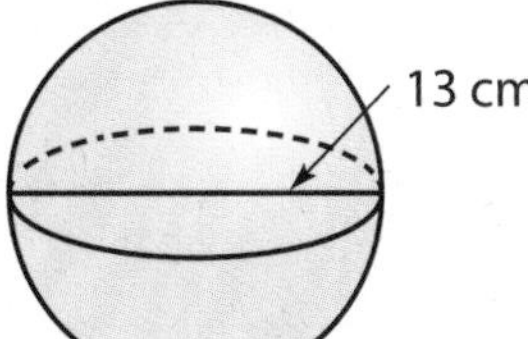

____

ESSENTIAL QUESTION

7. What measurements do you need to know to find the volume of a cylinder? a cone? a sphere?

____

____

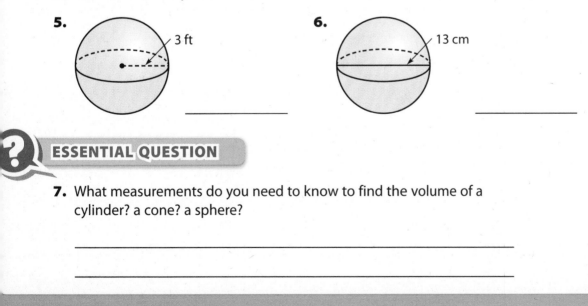

MODULE 22
MIXED REVIEW

Assessment Readiness

1. Triangle *JKL* is dilated by a scale factor of 1.5 with the origin as the center of dilation. Look at each ordered pair. Does the ordered pair represent a vertex of the image?

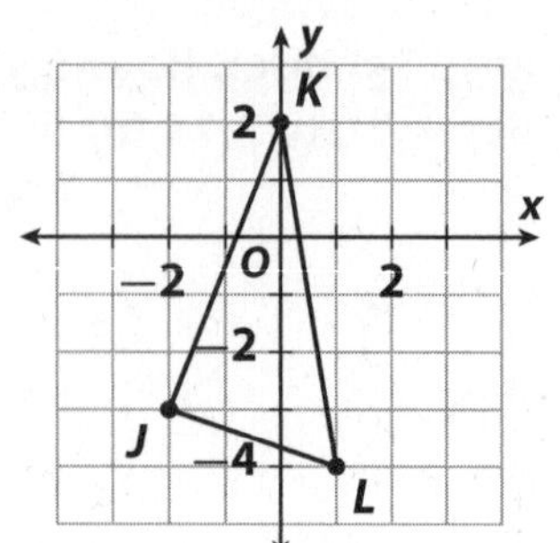

Select Yes or No for A–C.

A. (−3, −4.5) ◯ Yes ◯ No

B. (1.5, −6) ◯ Yes ◯ No

C. (3, 0) ◯ Yes ◯ No

2. A sphere has a radius of 4 inches.

Choose True or False for each statement.

A. A sphere with half the radius has $\frac{1}{8}$ of the volume. ◯ True ◯ False

B. A sphere with twice the radius has 6 times the volume. ◯ True ◯ False

C. A sphere with 3 times the radius has 27 times the volume. ◯ True ◯ False

3. A pile of sand is shaped like a cone with a height of 4 feet and a base diameter of 13 feet. Each cubic foot of sand weighs 90 pounds. Does the pile of sand weigh more than a ton (2000 pounds)? Explain how you know.

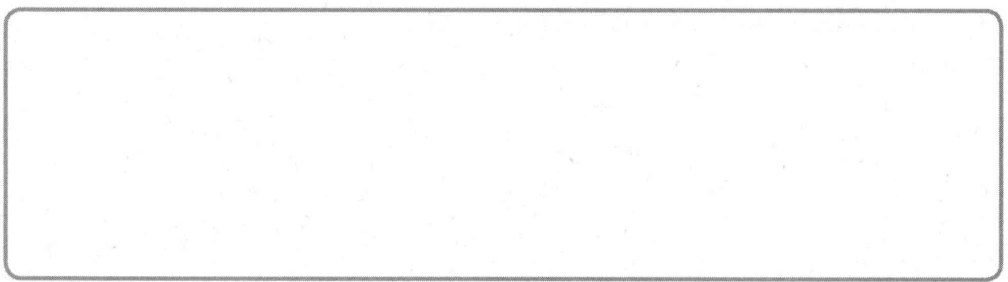

4. A cylindrical drinking glass has a base radius of 3.2 centimeters and a height of 14.0 centimeters. Given that 1 cubic centimeter is equivalent to 1 milliliter, how many milliliters of water does the glass hold when it is $\frac{3}{4}$ full? Round to the nearest milliliter.

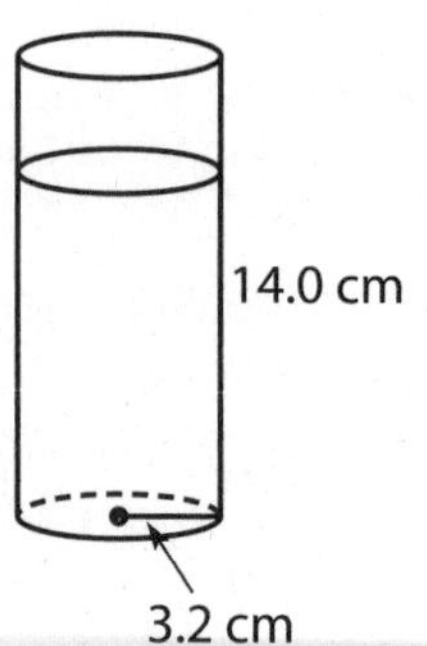

UNIT 10

Study Guide Review

MODULE 21 Angle Relationships in Parallel Lines and Triangles

Key Vocabulary

alternate exterior angles *(ángulos alternos externos)*

alternate interior angles *(ángulos alternos internos)*

corresponding angles *(ángulos correspondientes (para líneas))*

exterior angle *(ángulo externo)*

interior angle *(ángulos internos)*

remote interior angle *(ángulo interno remoto)*

same-side interior angles *(ángulos internos del mismo lado)*

similar *(semejantes)*

transversal *(transversal)*

ESSENTIAL QUESTION

How can you solve real-world problems that involve angle relationships in parallel lines and triangles?

EXAMPLE 1

Find each angle measure when $m\angle 6 = 81°$.

A $m\angle 5$

$m\angle 5 = 180° - 81° = 99°$

5 and 6 are supplementary angles.

B $m\angle 1$

$m\angle 1 = 99°$

1 and 5 are corresponding angles.

C $m\angle 3$

$m\angle 3 = 180° - 81° = 99°$

3 and 6 are same-side interior angles.

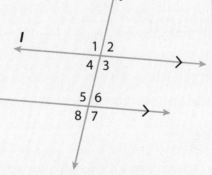

EXAMPLE 2

Are the triangles similar? Explain your answer.

$y = 180° - (67° + 35°)$

$y = 78°$

$x = 180° - (67° + 67°)$

$x = 46°$

The triangles are not similar, because they do not have 2 or more pairs of corresponding congruent angles.

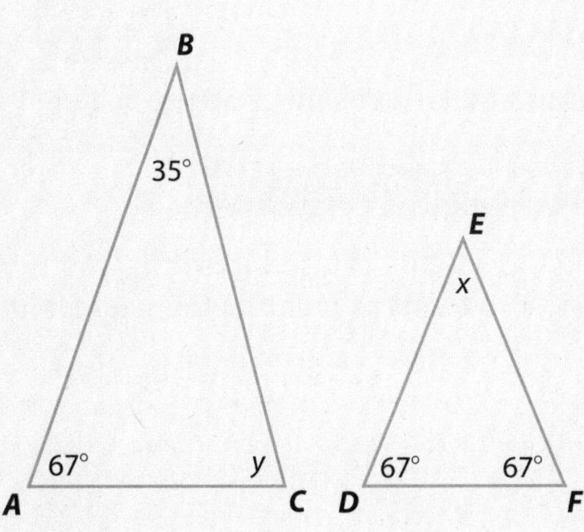

EXERCISES

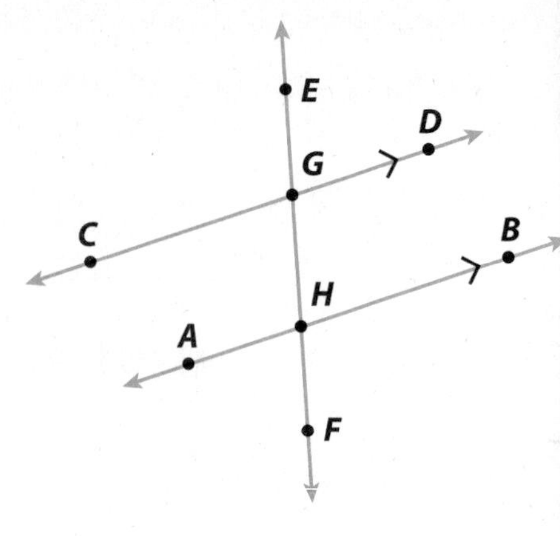

1. If m∠$GHA = 106°$, find the measures of the given angles. (Lesson 21.1)

   m∠EGC = __________

   m∠EGD = __________

   m∠BHF = __________

   m∠HGD = __________

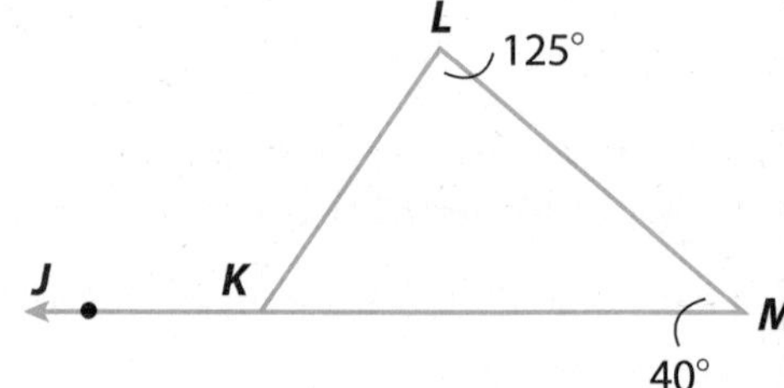

2. Find the missing angle measures. (Lesson 21.2)

   m∠JKL = __________

   m∠LKM = __________

MODULE 22 Volume

Key Vocabulary
cone *(cono)*
cylinder *(cilindro)*
sphere *(esfera)*

ESSENTIAL QUESTION

How can you solve real-world problems that involve volume?

EXAMPLE 1

Find the volume of the cistern. Round your answer to the nearest hundredth. Use 3.14 for π.

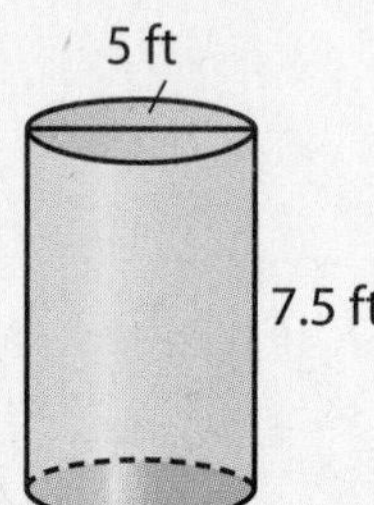

$V = \pi r^2 h$

$\approx 3.14 \cdot 2.5^2 \cdot 7.5$

$\approx 3.14 \cdot 6.25 \cdot 7.5$

≈ 147.19

The cistern has a volume of approximately 147.19 cubic feet.

EXAMPLE 2

Find the volume of a sphere with a radius of 3.7 cm. Write your answer in terms of π and to the nearest hundredth.

$V = \frac{4}{3}\pi r^3$	$V = \frac{4}{3}\pi r^3$
$\approx \frac{4}{3} \cdot \pi \cdot 3.7^3$	$\approx \frac{4}{3} \cdot 3.14 \cdot 3.7^3$
$\approx \frac{4}{3} \cdot \pi \cdot 50.653$	$\approx \frac{4}{3} \cdot 3.14 \cdot 50.653$
$\approx 67.54\pi$	≈ 212.07

The volume of the sphere is approximately 67.54π cm³, or 212.07 cm³.

EXERCISES

Find the volume of each figure. Round your answers to the nearest hundredth. Use 3.14 for π. (Lessons 22.1, 22.2, 22.3)

1. 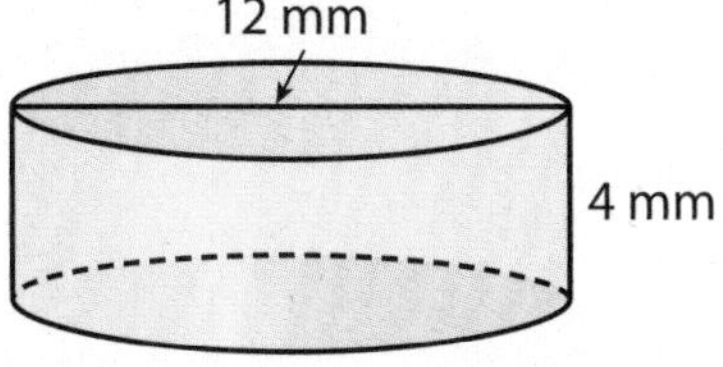

2. 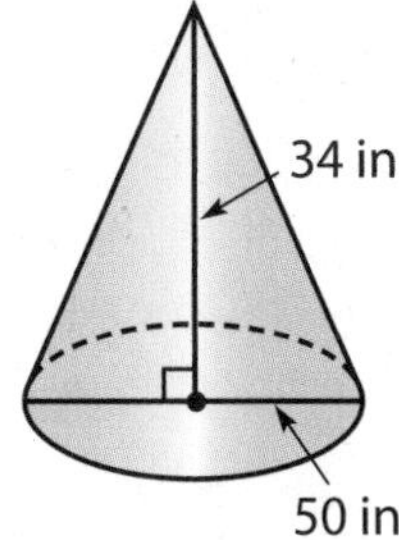

3. 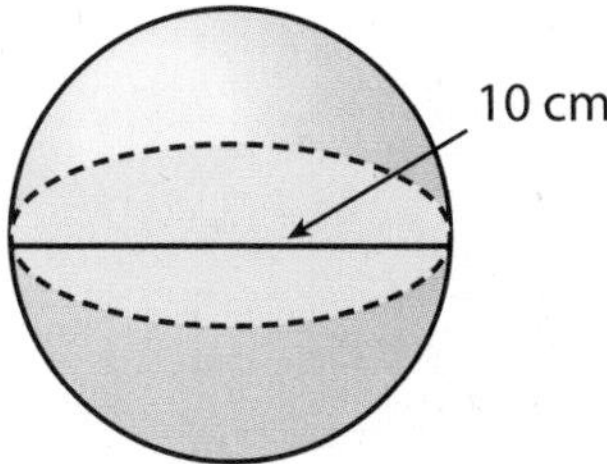

4. 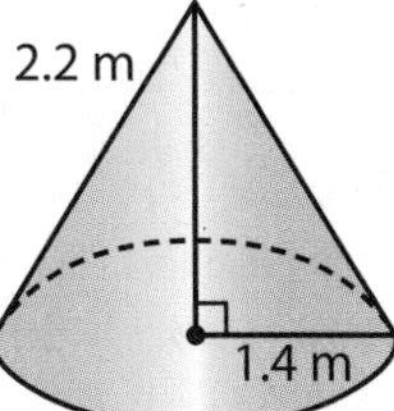

5. 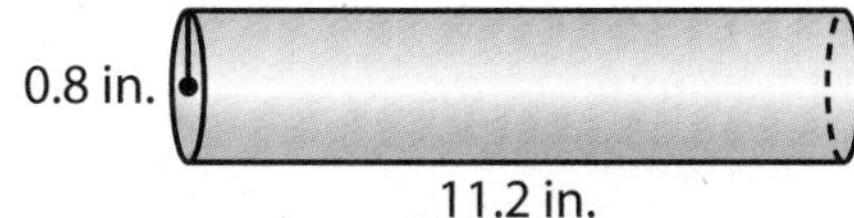

6. 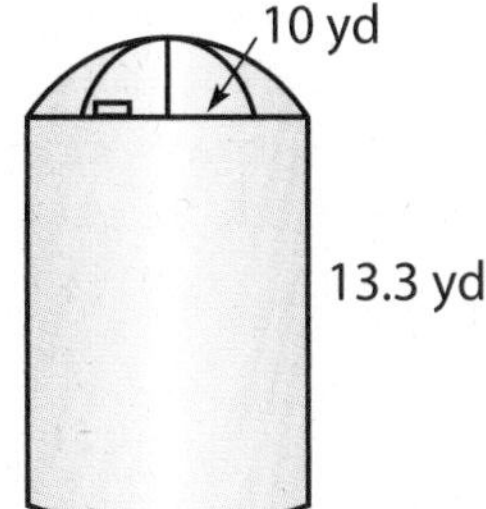

7. Find the volume of a ball with a radius of 1.68 inches. ________

8. A round above-ground swimming pool has a diameter of 15 ft and a height of 4.5 ft. What is the volume of the swimming pool? ________

9. A paper cup in the shape of a cone has a height of 4.7 inches and a diameter of 3.6 inches. What is the volume of the paper cup? ________

Unit Project CA CC 8.G.9

The Volume of a Sphere

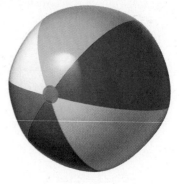

For this project you'll need a sphere. You may use a world globe, an exercise ball, a beach ball, or any sports ball such as a basketball or soccer ball. It can be hollow or solid. If you use an inflatable ball, be sure it is fully inflated.

- Measure the circumference of the sphere and explain how you did it.
- Use the formula for the circumference of a circle to calculate the radius of the sphere.
- Find the volume of the sphere.

Now answer each of the following questions. For each question, assume that you begin with your sphere filled with water.

- How much water would remain in the sphere if you poured its water into a cone with the same diameter and height as the diameterof the sphere?
- How much *more* water would you need to fill an empty cylinder with the same diameter and height as the sphere?
- How much *more* water would you need to fill an empty cube with the same length, width, and height as the diameter of the sphere?

Create a presentation with all of the above information and any other information you think should be included. Use the space below to write down any questions you have or important information from your teacher.

MATH IN CAREERS | ACTIVITY

Hydrologist A hydrologist needs to determine if an underground aquifer, which is roughly cylindrical in shape, is totally filled with water. The diameter of the aquifer is 70 meters, and its depth is 9 meters. The mass of the water in it is 2.7×10^7 kilograms. One cubic meter of water has a mass of about 1000 kilograms. Is the aquifer totally filled with water? Explain how you determined your answer.

UNIT 10
MIXED REVIEW

Assessment Readiness

1. Consider each operation. Would the operation eliminate all of the fractions from the equation $\frac{3}{4}x + \frac{1}{2} = \frac{1}{3}x + 3$?

Select Yes or No.

A. Multiply both sides by 6. ◯ Yes ◯ No
B. Multiply both sides by 12. ◯ Yes ◯ No
C. Multiply both sides by 24. ◯ Yes ◯ No

2. Angle *ABC* is an exterior angle of $\angle BCD$.

Choose True or False for each statement.

A. $m\angle D = 40°$ ◯ True ◯ False
B. $m\angle ABC = 110°$ ◯ True ◯ False
C. $m\angle CBD = 70°$ ◯ True ◯ False

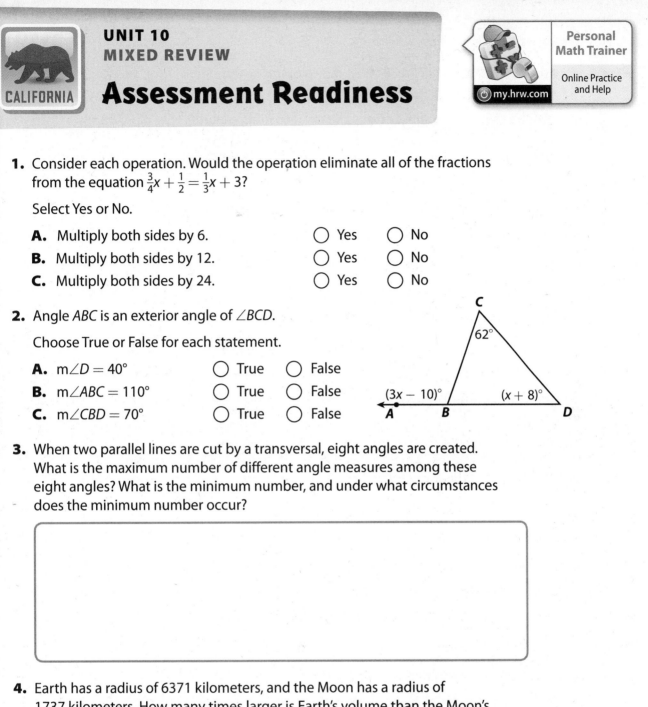

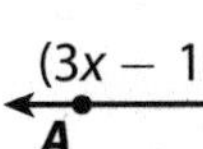

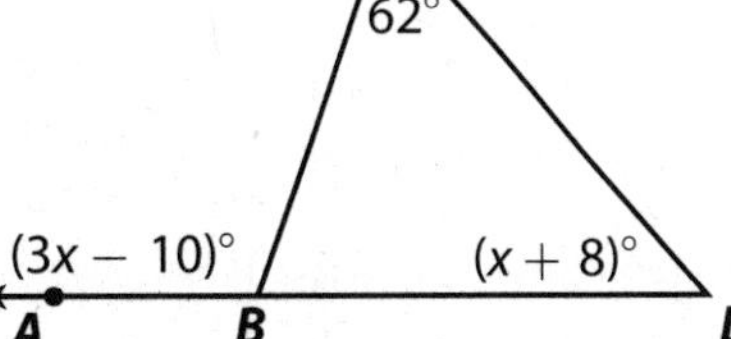

3. When two parallel lines are cut by a transversal, eight angles are created. What is the maximum number of different angle measures among these eight angles? What is the minimum number, and under what circumstances does the minimum number occur?

4. Earth has a radius of 6371 kilometers, and the Moon has a radius of 1737 kilometers. How many times larger is Earth's volume than the Moon's volume? Explain how you determined the answer.

Performance Tasks

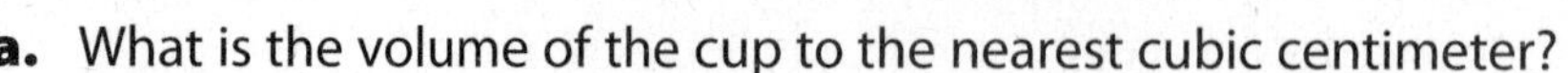

★**5.** A paper cup is shaped like a cone. The radius of the opening is 4.6 centimeters, and the height is 12.8 centimeters.

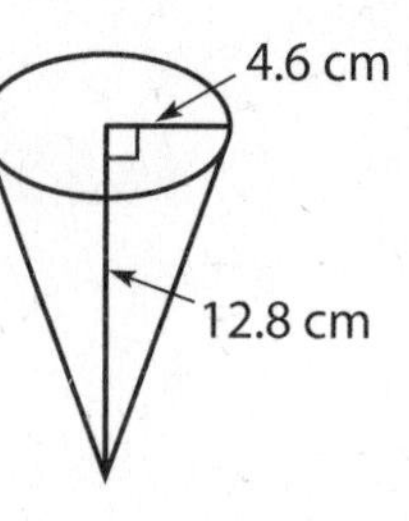

a. What is the volume of the cup to the nearest cubic centimeter?

b. If the cup is filled with water to half its height, what is the volume of water to the nearest cubic centimeter? What percent is this of the cup's total volume?

★★**6.** A potter makes a cylindrical vase that is 14 inches high and 8 inches wide. The base and sides of the vase are 0.25 inch thick.

a. How tall and wide is the hollow cylindrical interior of this vase? Explain your reasoning.

b. What is the volume of the interior? Use 3.14 for π. Round your answer to the nearest cubic inch.

c. The potter makes another vase with the same dimensions, but with a thickness of only 0.125 inch. How does its interior volume compare to the volume of the first vase?

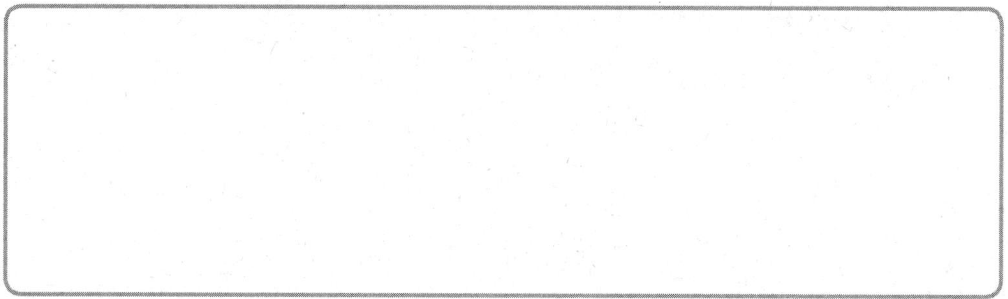

★★★**7.** The diagram shows how several steel beams intersect to form part of the structure of a building. In the diagram line p is parallel to line q. What is the length of the beam with endpoints at A and B? Justify each step of your work. (*Hint:* First show similar triangles.)

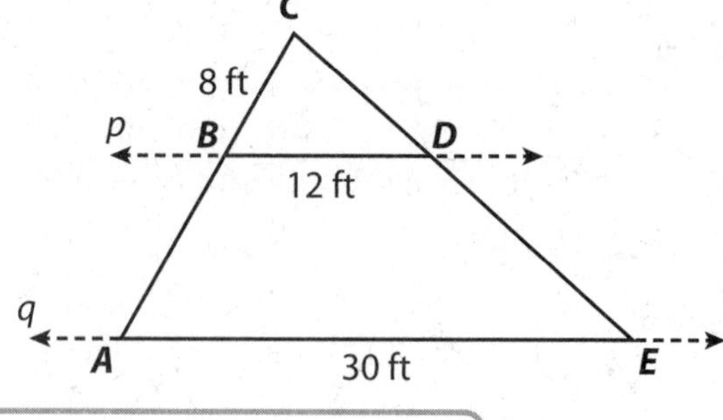

LESSON A.1

The Pythagorean Theorem

CA CC 8.G.7

Apply the Pythagorean Theorem to determine unknown side lengths in right triangles in real-world and mathematical problems in two and three dimensions. *Also 8.G.6*

ESSENTIAL QUESTION

How can you prove the Pythagorean Theorem and use it to solve problems?

EXPLORE ACTIVITY  8.G.6

Proving the Pythagorean Theorem

In a right triangle, the two sides that form the right angle are the **legs**. The side opposite the right angle is the **hypotenuse**.

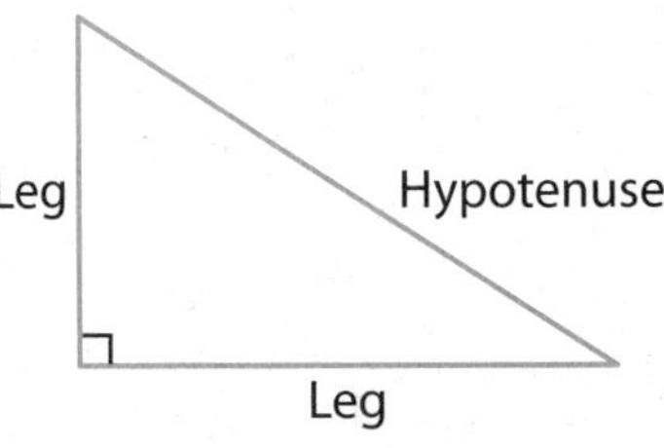

The Pythagorean Theorem

In a right triangle, the sum of the squares of the lengths of the legs is equal to the square of the length of the hypotenuse.

If a and b are legs and c is the hypotenuse, $a^2 + b^2 = c^2$.

A Draw a right triangle on a piece of paper and cut it out. Make one leg shorter than the other.

B Trace your triangle onto another piece of paper four times, arranging them as shown. For each triangle, label the shorter leg a, the longer leg b, and the hypotenuse c.

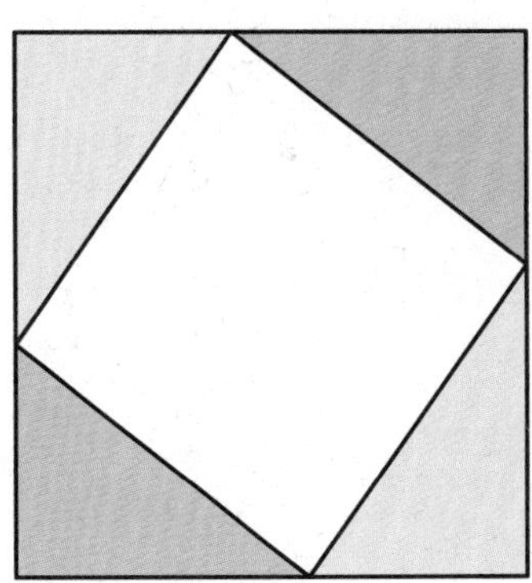

C What is the area of the unshaded square?

____

Label the unshaded square with its area.

D Trace your original triangle onto a piece of paper four times again, arranging them as shown. Draw a line outlining a larger square that is the same size as the figure you made in **B**.

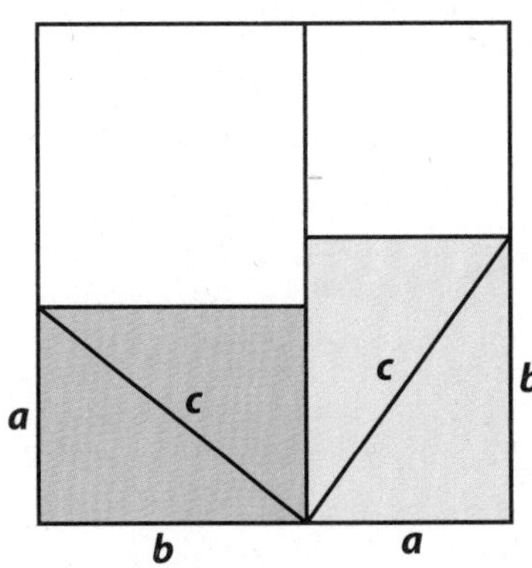

E What is the area of the unshaded square at the top right of the figure in **D**? at the top left?

____

Label the unshaded squares with their areas.

F What is the total area of the unshaded regions in **D**?

____

EXPLORE ACTIVITY *(cont'd)*

Reflect

1. Explain whether the figures in **B** and **D** have the same area.

____

2. Explain whether the unshaded regions of the figures in **B** and **D** have the same area.

____

____

____

3. **Analyze Relationships** Write an equation relating the area of the unshaded region in step **B** to the unshaded region in **D**.

____

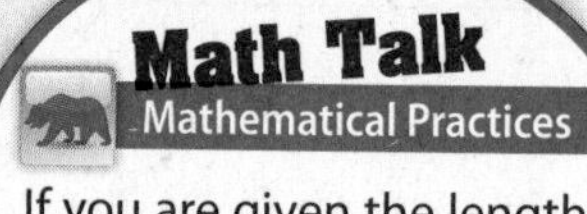

If you are given the length of the hypotenuse and one leg, does it matter whether you solve for *a* or *b*? Explain.

Using the Pythagorean Theorem

You can use the Pythagorean Theorem to find the length of a side of a right triangle when you know the lengths of the other two sides.

EXAMPLE 1

Find the length of the missing side.

A

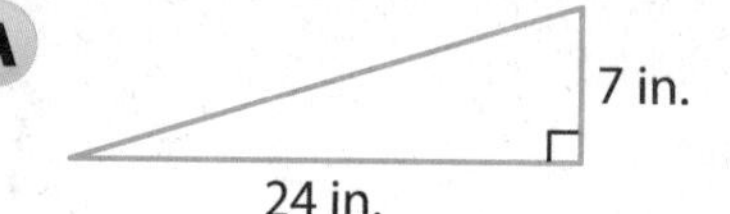

$a^2 + b^2 = c^2$

$24^2 + 7^2 = c^2$ — Substitute into the formula.

$576 + 49 = c^2$ — Simplify.

$625 = c^2$ — Add.

$25 = c$ — Take the square root of both sides.

The length of the hypotenuse is 25 inches.

B

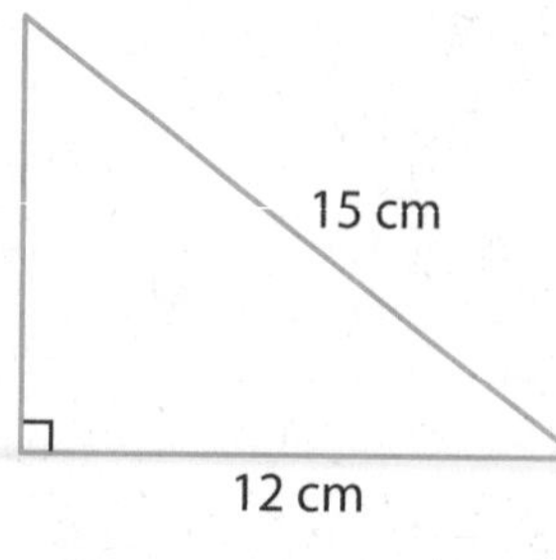

$a^2 + b^2 = c^2$

$a^2 + 12^2 = 15^2$ — Substitute into the formula.

$a^2 + 144 = 225$ — Simplify.

$a^2 = 81$ — Use properties of equality to get a^2 by itself.

$a = 9$ — Take the square root of both sides.

The length of the leg is 9 centimeters.

YOUR TURN

Find the length of the missing side.

4.

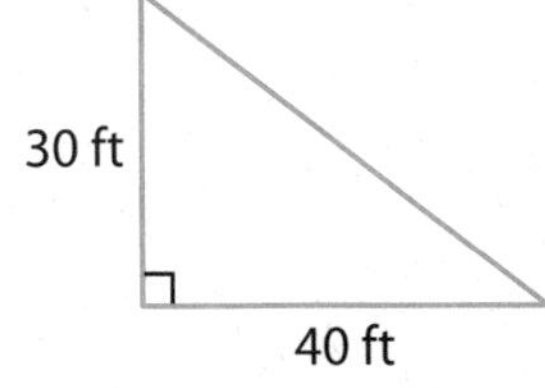

____

5.

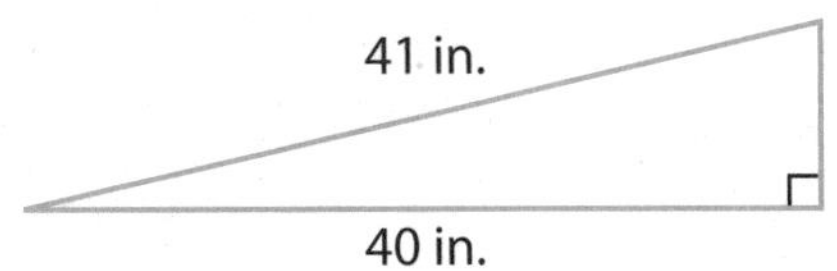

____

Pythagorean Theorem in Three Dimensions

You can use the Pythagorean Theorem to solve problems in three dimensions.

EXAMPLE 2

CA CC 8.G.7

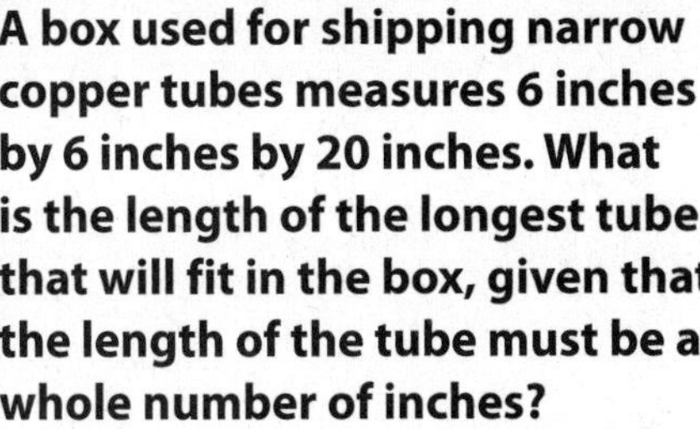

A box used for shipping narrow copper tubes measures 6 inches by 6 inches by 20 inches. What is the length of the longest tube that will fit in the box, given that the length of the tube must be a whole number of inches?

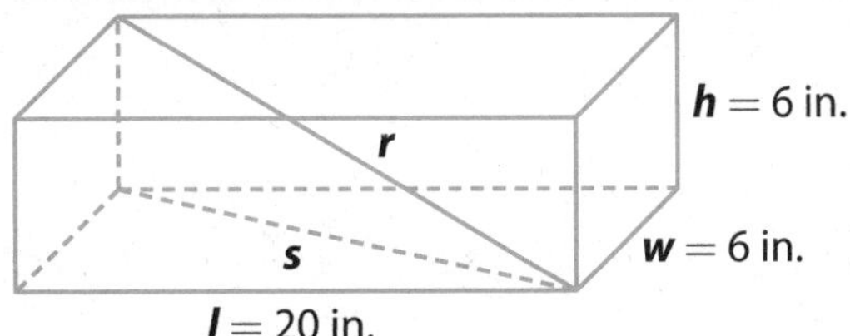

STEP 1 You want to find r, the length from a bottom corner to the opposite top corner. First, find s, the length of the diagonal across the bottom of the box.

$w^2 + l^2 = s^2$

$6^2 + 20^2 = s^2$ Substitute into the formula.

$36 + 400 = s^2$ Simplify.

$436 = s^2$ Add.

STEP 2 Use your expression for s to find r.

$h^2 + s^2 = r^2$

$6^2 + 436 = r^2$ Substitute into the formula.

$472 = r^2$ Add.

$\sqrt{472} = r$ Take the square root of both sides.

$21.7 \approx r$ Use a calculator to round to the nearest tenth.

The length of the longest tube that will fit in the box is 21 inches.

Math Talk
Mathematical Practices

Looking at Step 2, why did the calculations in Step 1 stop before taking the square root of both sides of the final equation?

YOUR TURN

6. Tina ordered a replacement part for her desk. It was shipped in a box that measures 4 in. by 4 in. by 14 in. What is the greatest length in whole inches that the part could have been?

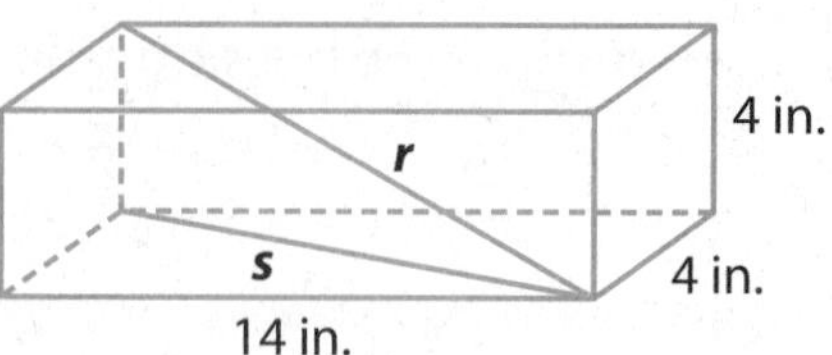

Guided Practice

1. Find the length of the missing side of the triangle. (Explore Activity 1 and Example 1)

$a^2 + b^2 = c^2 \rightarrow 24^2 + \square = c^2 \rightarrow \square = c^2$

The length of the hypotenuse is $\square$ feet.

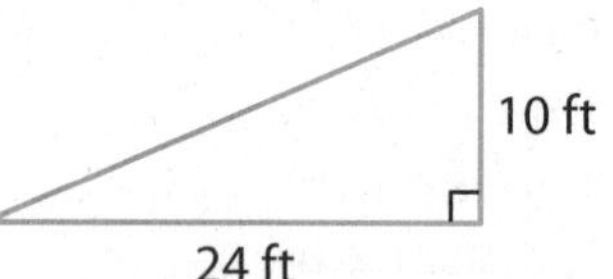

2. Mr. Woo wants to ship a fishing rod that is 42 inches long to his son. He has a box with the dimensions shown. (Example 2)

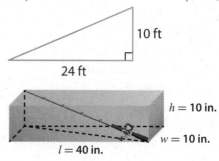

$h = 10$ in.
$w = 10$ in.
$l = 40$ in.

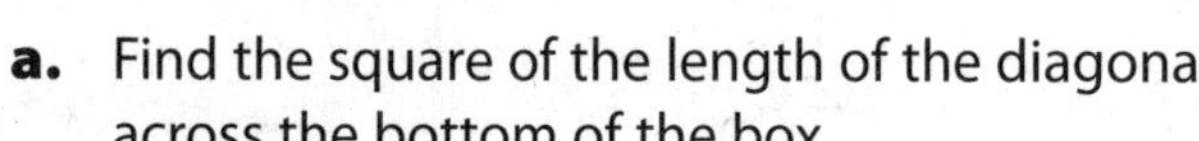

a. Find the square of the length of the diagonal across the bottom of the box. ________

b. Find the length from a bottom corner to the opposite top corner to the nearest tenth. Will the fishing rod fit? ________

ESSENTIAL QUESTION CHECK-IN

3. State the Pythagorean Theorem and tell how you can use it to solve problems.

____

____

____

____

Name ______________________ Class ______________________ Date ______________________

A.1 Independent Practice

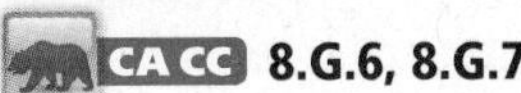

Find the length of the missing side of each triangle. Round your answers to the nearest tenth.

4.

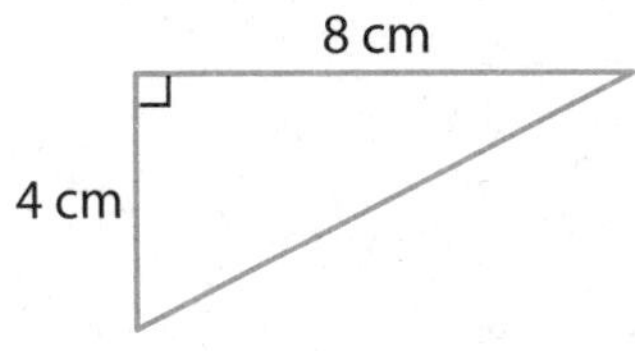

____

5.

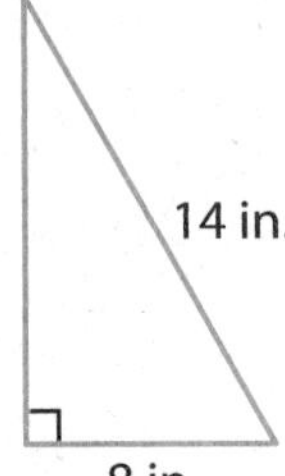

____

6. The diagonal of a rectangular big-screen TV screen measures 152 cm. The length measures 132 cm. What is the height of the screen? ______________________

7. Dylan has a square piece of metal that measures 10 inches on each side. He cuts the metal along the diagonal, forming two right triangles. What is the length of the hypotenuse of each right triangle to the nearest tenth of an inch? ______________________

8. **Represent Real-World Problems** A painter has a 24-foot ladder that he is using to paint a house. For safety reasons, the ladder must be placed at least 8 feet from the base of the side of the house. To the nearest tenth of a foot, how high can the ladder safely reach? ______________________

9. What is the longest flagpole (in whole feet) that could be shipped in a box that measures 2 ft by 2 ft by 12 ft?

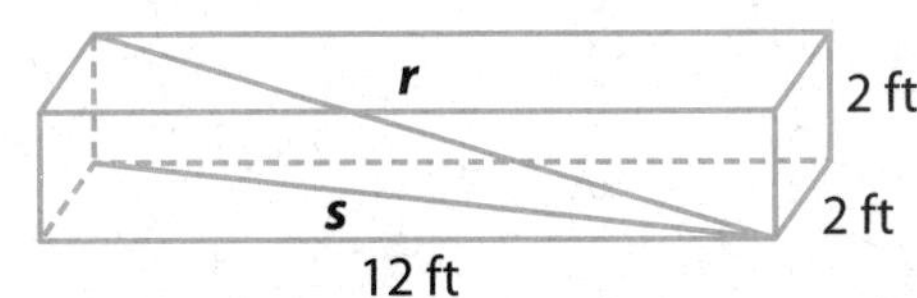

____

10. **Sports** American football fields measure 100 yards long between the end zones, and are $53\frac{1}{3}$ yards wide. Is the length of the diagonal across this field more or less than 120 yards? Explain.

____

11. **Justify Reasoning** A tree struck by lightning broke at a point 12 ft above the ground as shown. What was the height of the tree to the nearest tenth of a foot? Explain your reasoning.

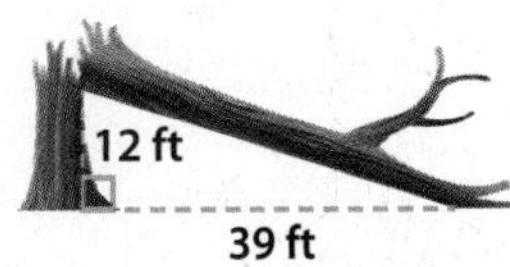

____

____

____

H.O.T. FOCUS ON HIGHER ORDER THINKING

Work Area

12. **Multistep** Main Street and Washington Avenue meet at a right angle. A large park begins at this corner. Joe's school lies at the opposite corner of the park. Usually Joe walks 1.2 miles along Main Street and then 0.9 miles up Washington Avenue to get to school. Today he walked in a straight path across the park and returned home along the same path. What is the difference in distance between the two round trips? Explain.

13. **Analyze Relationships** An isosceles right triangle is a right triangle with congruent legs. If the length of each leg is represented by *x*, what algebraic expression can be used to represent the length of the hypotenuse? Explain your reasoning.

14. **Persevere in Problem Solving** A square hamburger is centered on a circular bun. Both the bun and the burger have an area of 16 square inches.

   a. How far, to the nearest hundredth of an inch, does each corner of the burger stick out from the bun? Explain.

   b. How far does each bun stick out from the center of each side of the burger?

   c. Are the distances in part **a** and part **b** equal? If not, which sticks out more, the burger or the bun? Explain.

LESSON A.2

Converse of the Pythagorean Theorem

CA CC 8.G.6

Explain a proof of the Pythagorean Theorem and its converse.

ESSENTIAL QUESTION

How can you test the converse of the Pythagorean Theorem and use it to solve problems?

EXPLORE ACTIVITY 

Testing the Converse of the Pythagorean Theorem

The Pythagorean Theorem states that if a triangle is a right triangle, then $a^2 + b^2 = c^2$.

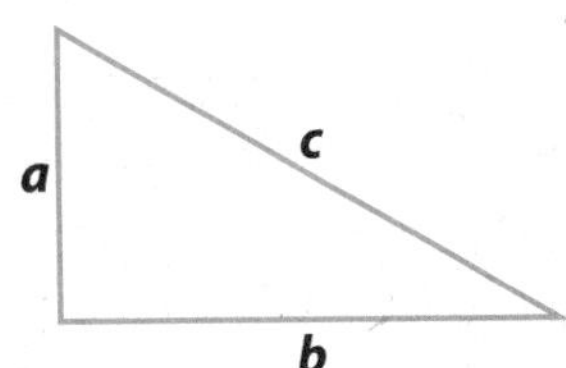

The *converse* of the Pythagorean Theorem states that if $a^2 + b^2 = c^2$, then the triangle is a right triangle.

Decide whether the converse of the Pythagorean Theorem is true.

A Verify that the following sets of lengths make the equation $a^2 + b^2 = c^2$ true. Record your results in the table.

a	*b*	*c*	Is $a^2 + b^2 = c^2$ true?	Makes a right triangle?
3	4	5		
5	12	13		
7	24	25		
8	15	17		
20	21	29		

B For each set of lengths in the table, cut strips of grid paper with a width of one square and lengths that correspond to the values of *a*, *b*, and *c*.

C For each set of lengths, use the strips of grid paper to try to form a right triangle. An example using the first set of lengths is shown. Record your findings in the table.

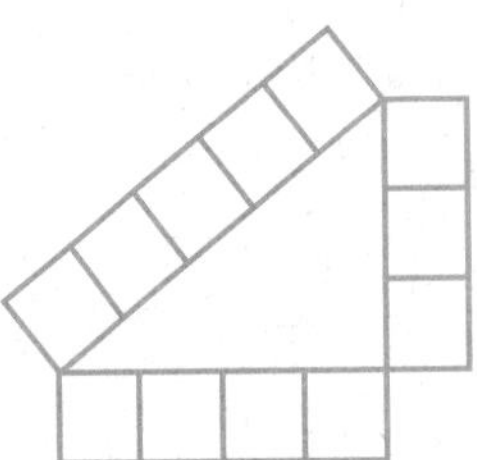

Reflect

1. **Draw Conclusions** Based on your observations, explain whether you think the converse of the Pythagorean Theorem is true.

Identifying a Right Triangle

The converse of the Pythagorean Theorem gives you a way to tell if a triangle is a right triangle when you know the side lengths.

EXAMPLE 1

My Notes

Tell whether each triangle with the given side lengths is a right triangle.

A 9 inches, 40 inches, and 41 inches

Let $a = 9$, $b = 40$, and $c = 41$.

$$a^2 + b^2 = c^2$$

$$9^2 + 40^2 \stackrel{?}{=} 41^2$$ Substitute into the formula.

$$81 + 1600 \stackrel{?}{=} 1681$$ Simpify.

$$1681 = 1681$$ Add.

Since $9^2 + 40^2 = 41^2$, the triangle is a right triangle by the converse of the Pythagorean Theorem.

B 8 meters, 10 meters, and 12 meters

Let $a = 8$, $b = 10$, and $c = 12$.

$$a^2 + b^2 = c^2$$

$$8^2 + 10^2 \stackrel{?}{=} 12^2$$ Substitute into the formula.

$$64 + 100 \stackrel{?}{=} 144$$ Simpify.

$$164 \neq 144$$ Add.

Since $8^2 + 10^2 \neq 12^2$, the triangle is not a right triangle by the converse of the Pythagorean Theorem.

YOUR TURN

Tell whether each triangle with the given side lengths is a right triangle.

2. 14 cm, 23 cm, and 25 cm ______

3. 16 in., 30 in., and 34 in. ______

4. 27 ft, 36 ft, 45 ft ______

5. 11 mm, 18 mm, 21 mm ______

Using the Converse of the Pythagorean Theorem

You can use the converse of the Pythagorean Theorem to solve real-world problems.

EXAMPLE 2  

Katya is buying edging for a triangular flower garden she plans to build in her backyard. If the lengths of the three pieces of edging that she purchases are 13 feet, 10 feet, and 7 feet, will the flower garden be in the shape of a right triangle?

Use the converse of the Pythagorean Theorem. Remember to use the longest length for *c*.

Let $a = 7$, $b = 10$, and $c = 13$.

$$a^2 + b^2 = c^2$$

$$7^2 + 10^2 \stackrel{?}{=} 13^2 \quad \text{Substitute into the formula.}$$

$$49 + 100 \stackrel{?}{=} 169 \quad \text{Simpify.}$$

$$149 \neq 169 \quad \text{Add.}$$

Since $7^2 + 10^2 \neq 13^2$, the garden will not be in the shape of a right triangle.

Math Talk
Mathematical Practices

To what length, to the nearest tenth, can Katya trim the longest piece of edging to form a right triangle?

6. A blueprint for a new triangular playground shows that the sides measure 480 ft, 140 ft, and 500 ft. Is the playground in the shape of a right triangle? Explain.

____

____

7. A triangular piece of glass has sides that measure 18 in., 19 in., and 25 in. Is the piece of glass in the shape of a right triangle? Explain.

____

8. A corner of a fenced yard forms a right angle. Can you place a 12 foot long board across the corner to form a right triangle for which the leg lengths are whole numbers? Explain.

____

____

Guided Practice

1. Lashandra used grid paper to construct the triangle shown. (Explore Activity)

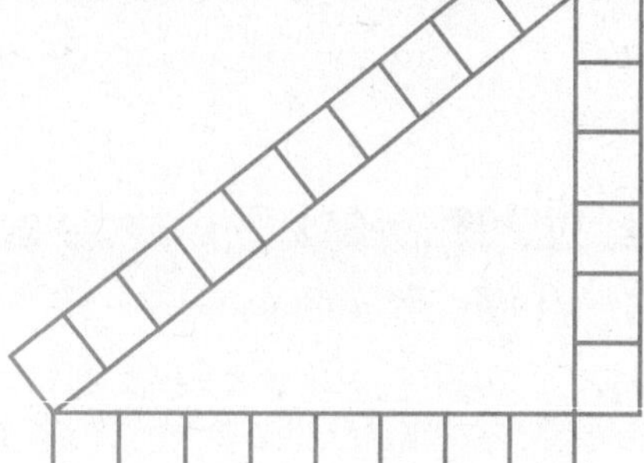

a. What are the lengths of the side of Lashandra's triangle?

________units, ________units, ________units

b. Use the converse of the Pythagorean Theorem to determine whether the triangle is a right triangle.

$$a^2 + b^2 = c^2$$

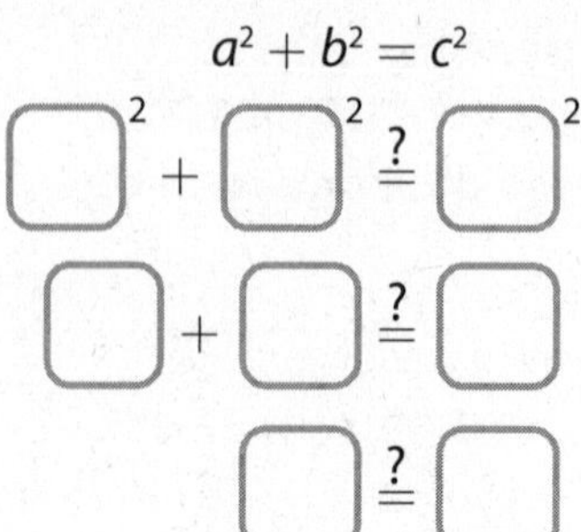

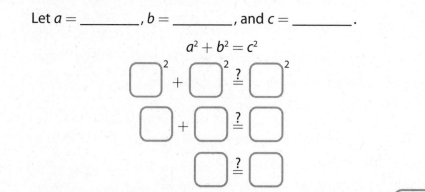

The triangle that Lashandra constructed **is / is not** a right triangle.

2. A triangle has side lengths 9 cm, 12 cm, and 16 cm. Tell whether the triangle is a right triangle. (Example 1)

Let $a =$ ________, $b =$ ________, and $c =$ ________.

$$a^2 + b^2 = c^2$$

$$\square^2 + \square^2 \overset{?}{=} \square^2$$

$$\square + \square \overset{?}{=} \square$$

$$\square \overset{?}{=} \square$$

By the converse of the Pythagorean Theorem, the triangle **is / is not** a right triangle.

3. The marketing team at a new electronics company is designing a logo that contains a circle and a triangle. On one design, the triangle's side lengths are 2.5 in., 6 in., and 6.5 in. Is the triangle a right triangle? Explain. (Example 2)

____

ESSENTIAL QUESTION CHECK-IN

4. How can you use the converse of the Pythagorean Theorem to tell if a triangle is a right triangle?

____

____

ame _______________ Class _______________ Date _______________

A.2 Independent Practice

8.G.6

ell whether each triangle with the given side lengths is a right triangle.

5. 11 cm, 60 cm, 61 cm

____

6. 5 ft, 12 ft, 15 ft

____

7. 9 in., 15 in., 17 in.

____

8. 15 m, 36 m, 39 m

____

9. 20 mm, 30 mm, 40 mm

____

10. 20 cm, 48 cm, 52 cm

____

1. 18.5 ft, 6 ft, 17.5 ft

____

12. 2 mi, 1.5 mi, 2.5 mi

____

3. 35 in., 45 in., 55 in.

____

14. 25 cm, 14 cm, 23 cm

____

15. The emblem on a college banner consists of the face of a tiger inside a triangle. The lengths of the sides of the triangle are 13 cm, 14 cm, and 15 cm. Is the triangle a right triangle? Explain.

____

16. Kerry has a large triangular piece of fabric that she wants to attach to the ceiling in her bedroom. The sides of the piece of fabric measure 4.8 ft, 6.4 ft, and 8 ft. Is the fabric in the shape of a right triangle? Explain.

____

17. A mosaic consists of triangular tiles. The smallest tiles have side lengths 6 cm, 10 cm, and 12 cm. Are these tiles in the shape of right triangles? Explain.

____

18. **History** In ancient Egypt, surveyors made right angles by stretching a rope with evenly spaced knots as shown. Explain why the rope forms a right angle.

____

____

____

19. Justify Reasoning Yoshi has two identical triangular boards as shown. Can he use these two boards to form a rectangle? Explain.

1 m
1.25 m
1.25 m
0.75 m
1

20. Critique Reasoning Shoshanna says that a triangle with side lengths 17 m, 8 m, and 15 m is not a right triangle because $17^2 + 8^2 = 353$, $15^2 = 225$, and $353 \neq 225$. Is she correct? Explain.

H.O.T. FOCUS ON HIGHER ORDER THINKING

Work Are

21. Make a Conjecture Diondre says that he can take any right triangle and make a new right triangle just by doubling the side lengths. Is Diondre's conjecture true? Test his conjecture using three different right triangles.

22. Draw Conclusions A diagonal of a parallelogram measures 37 inches. The sides measure 35 inches and 1 foot. Is the parallelogram a rectangle? Explain your reasoning.

23. Represent Real-World Problems A soccer coach is marking the lines for a soccer field on a large recreation field. The dimensions of the field are to be 90 yards by 48 yards. Describe a procedure she could use to confirm that the sides of the field meet at right angles.

LESSON **A.3**

Distance Between Two Points

CA CC 8.G.8

Apply the Pythagorean Theorem to find the distance between two points in a coordinate system.

ESSENTIAL QUESTION

How can you use the Pythagorean Theorem to find the distance between two points on a coordinate plane?

Pythagorean Theorem in the Coordinate Plane

EXAMPLE 1

CA CC 8.G.8

The figure shows a right triangle. Approximate the length of the hypotenuse to the nearest tenth using a calculator.

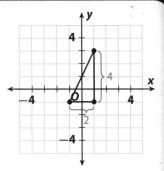

STEP 1 Find the length of each leg.

The length of the vertical leg is 4 units.

The length of the horizontal leg is 2 units.

STEP 2 Let $a = 4$ and $b = 2$. Let c represent the length of the hypotenuse. Use the Pythagorean Theorem to find c.

$a^2 + b^2 = c^2$

$4^2 + 2^2 = c^2$ Substitute into the formula.

$20 = c^2$ Add.

$\sqrt{20} = c$ Take the square root of both sides.

$\sqrt{20} \approx 4.5$ Use a calculator and round to the nearest tenth.

STEP 3 Check for reasonableness by finding perfect squares close to 20.

$\sqrt{20}$ is between $\sqrt{16}$ and $\sqrt{25}$, so $4 < \sqrt{20} < 5$.

Since 4.5 is between 4 and 5, the answer is reasonable.

The hypotenuse is about 4.5 units long.

1. Approximate the length of the hypotenuse to the nearest tenth without using a calculator.

____

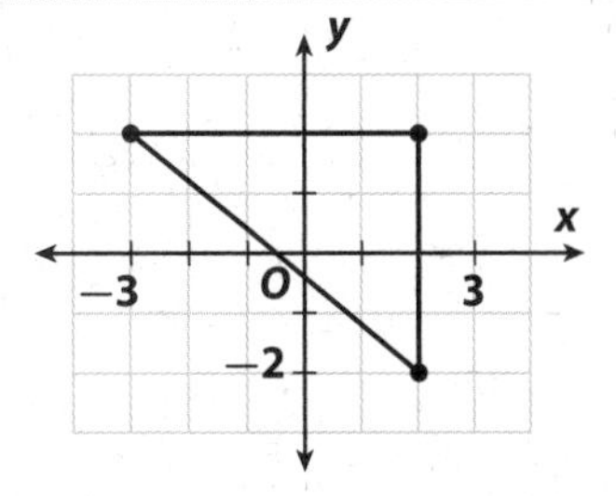

EXPLORE ACTIVITY CA CC 8.G.8

Finding the Distance Between Any Two Points

The Pythagorean Theorem can be used to find the distance between any two points (x_1, y_1) and (x_2, y_2) in the coordinate plane. The resulting expression is called the Distance Formula.

Distance Formula

In a coordinate plane, the distance d between two points (x_1, y_1) and (x_2, y_2) is

$$d = \sqrt{(x_2 - x_1)^2 + (y_2 - y_1)^2}.$$

Use the Pythagorean Theorem to derive the Distance Formula.

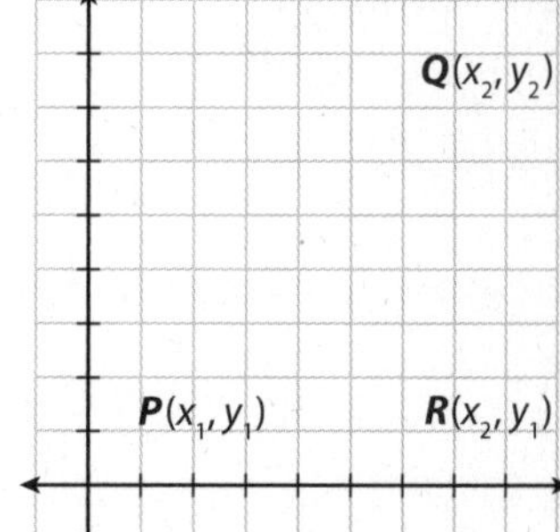

A To find the distance between points P and Q, draw segment $\overline{PQ}$ and label its length d. Then draw horizontal segment $\overline{PR}$ and vertical segment $\overline{QR}$. Label the lengths of these segments a and b. Triangle

PQR is a ______________ triangle, with hypotenuse ______________.

B Since $\overline{PR}$ is a horizontal segment, its length, a, is the difference between its x-coordinates. Therefore, $a = x_2 -$ ______________.

C Since $\overline{QR}$ is a vertical segment, its length, b, is the difference between its y-coordinates. Therefore, $b = y_2 -$ ______________.

D Use the Pythagorean Theorem to find d, the length of segment $\overline{PQ}$. Substitute the expressions from **B** and **C** for a and b.

$d^2 = a^2 + b^2$

$d = \sqrt{a^2 + b^2}$

$d = \sqrt{(\square - \square)^2 + (\square - \square)^2}$

Math Talk
Mathematical Practices

What do $x_2 - x_1$ and $y_2 - y_1$ represent in terms of the Pythagorean Theorem?

Reflect

2. Why are the coordinates of point R the ordered pair (x_2, y_1)?

____

____

____

Finding the Distance Between Two Points

The Pythagorean Theorem can be used to find the distance between two points in a real-world situation. You can do this by using a coordinate grid that overlays a diagram of the real-world situation.

EXAMPLE 2  CA CC 8.G.8

Francesca wants to find the distance between her house on one side of a lake and the beach on the other side. She marks off a third point forming a right triangle, as shown. The distances in the diagram are measured in meters.

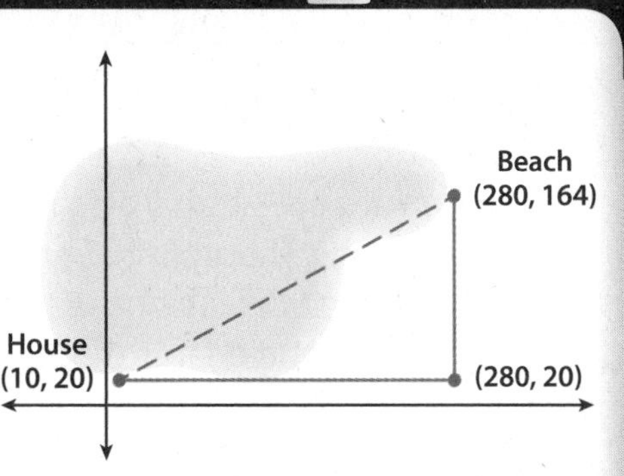

Use the Pythagorean Theorem to find the straight-line distance from Francesca's house to the beach.

STEP 1 Find the length of the horizontal leg.

The length of the horizontal leg is the absolute value of the difference between the x-coordinates of the points (280, 20) and (10, 20).

$$|280 - 10| = 270$$

The length of the horizontal leg is 270 meters.

STEP 2 Find the length of the vertical leg.

The length of the vertical leg is the absolute value of the difference between the y-coordinates of the points (280, 164) and (280, 20).

$$|164 - 20| = 144$$

The length of the vertical leg is 144 meters.

STEP 3 Let $a = 270$ and $b = 144$. Let c represent the length of the hypotenuse. Use the Pythagorean Theorem to find c.

$$a^2 + b^2 = c^2$$

$$270^2 + 144^2 = c^2 \quad \text{Substitute into the formula.}$$

$$72{,}900 + 20{,}736 = c^2 \quad \text{Simplify.}$$

$$93{,}636 = c^2 \quad \text{Add.}$$

$$\sqrt{93{,}636} = c \quad \text{Take the square root of both sides.}$$

$$306 = c \quad \text{Simplify.}$$

The distance from Francesca's house to the beach is 306 meters.

Why is it necessary to take the absolute value of the coordinates when finding the length of a segment?

Reflect

3. Show how you could use the Distance Formula to find the distance from Francesca's house to the beach.

____

____

____

YOUR TURN

4. Camp Sunshine is also on the lake. Use the Pythagorean Theorem to find the distance between Francesca's house and Camp Sunshine to the nearest tenth of a meter.

____

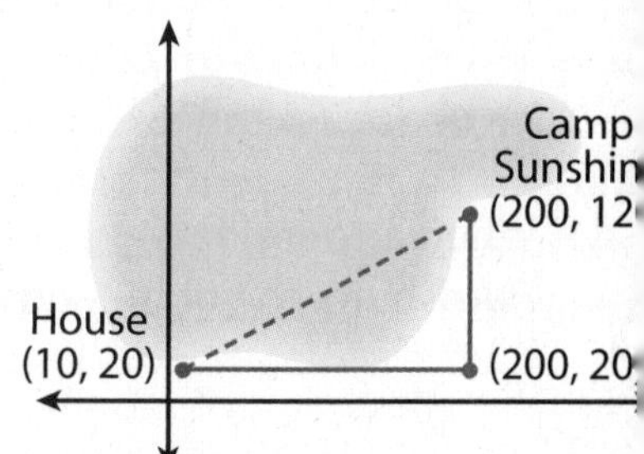

Guided Practice

1. Approximate the length of the hypotenuse of the right triangle to the nearest tenth using a calculator. (Example 1) ______________

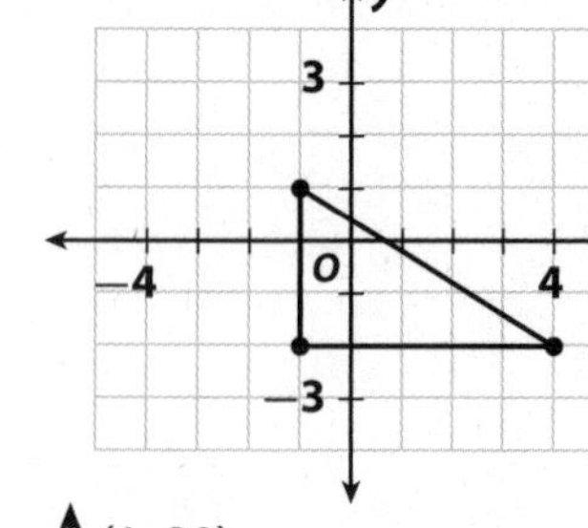

2. Find the distance between the points (3, 7) and (15, 12) on the coordinate plane. (Explore Activity) ______________

3. A plane leaves an airport and flies due north. Two minutes later, a second plane leaves the same airport flying due east. The flight plan shows the coordinates of the two planes 10 minutes later. The distances in the graph are measured in miles. Use the Pythagorean Theorem to find the distance shown between the two planes.

(Example 2) ______________

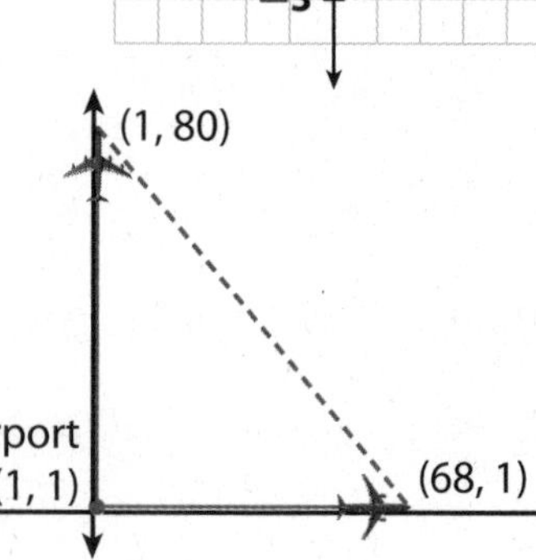

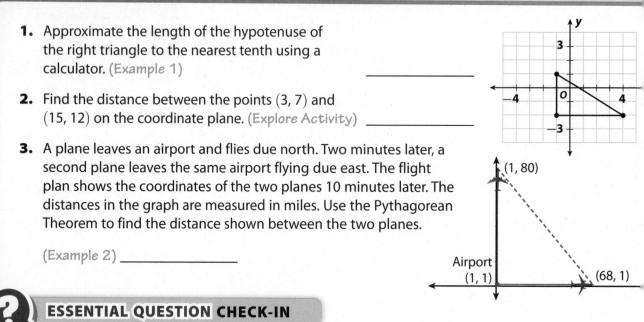

ESSENTIAL QUESTION CHECK-IN

4. Describe two ways to find the distance between two points on a coordinate plane.

____

____

____

Name ____________________ Class ____________________ Date ____________________

A.3 Independent Practice

CA CC 8.G.8

Personal Math Trainer

my.hrw.com

Online Practice and Help

5. A metal worker traced a triangular piece of sheet metal on a coordinate plane, as shown. The units represent inches. What is the length of the longest side of the metal triangle? Approximate the length to the nearest tenth of an inch using a calculator. Check that your answer is reasonable.

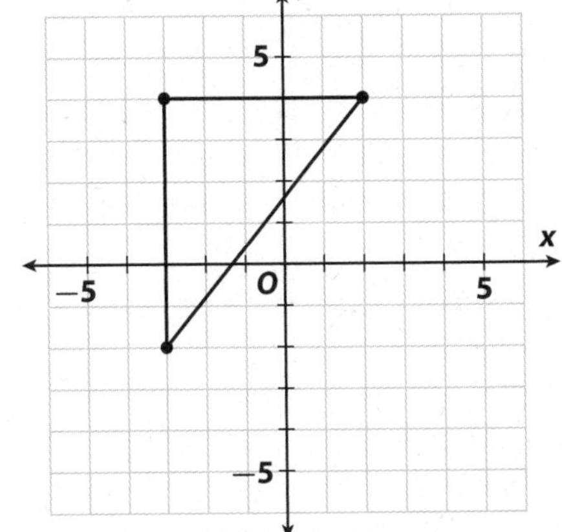

____

6. When a coordinate grid is superimposed on a map of Harrisburg, the high school is located at (17, 21) and the town park is located at (28, 13). If each unit represents 1 mile, how many miles apart are the high school and the town park? Round your answer to the nearest tenth.

____

7. The coordinates of the vertices of a rectangle are given by $R(-3, -4)$, $E(-3, 4)$, $C(4, 4)$, and $T(4, -4)$. Plot these points on the coordinate plane at the right and connect them to draw the rectangle. Then connect points E and T to form diagonal $\overline{ET}$.

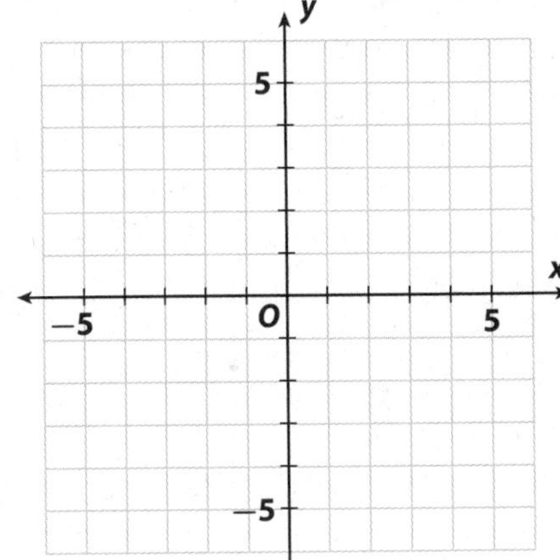

a. Use the Pythagorean Theorem to find the exact length of $\overline{ET}$.

____

b. How can you use the Distance Formula to find the length of $\overline{ET}$? Show that the Distance Formula gives the same answer.

____

____

____

____

____

____

8. **Multistep** The locations of three ships are represented on a coordinate grid by the following points: $P(-2, 5)$, $Q(-7, -5)$, and $R(2, -3)$. Which ships are farthest apart?

____

9. Make a Conjecture Find as many points as you can that are 5 units from the origin. Make a conjecture about the shape formed if all the points 5 units from the origin were connected.

10. Justify Reasoning The graph shows the location of a motion detector that has a maximum range of 34 feet. A peacock at point *P* displays its tail feathers. Will the motion detector sense this motion? Explain.

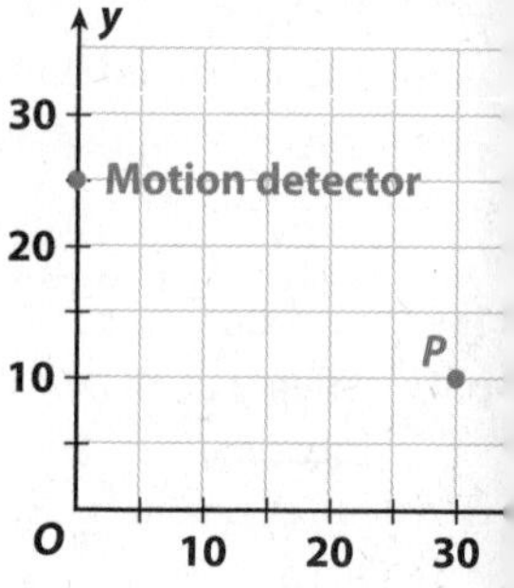

Motion detector
P

H.O.T. FOCUS ON HIGHER ORDER THINKING

Work Area

11. Persevere in Problem Solving One leg of an isosceles right triangle has endpoints (1, 1) and (6, 1). The other leg passes through the point (6, 2). Draw the triangle on the coordinate plane. Then show how you can use the Distance Formula to find the length of the hypotenuse. Round your answer to the nearest tenth.

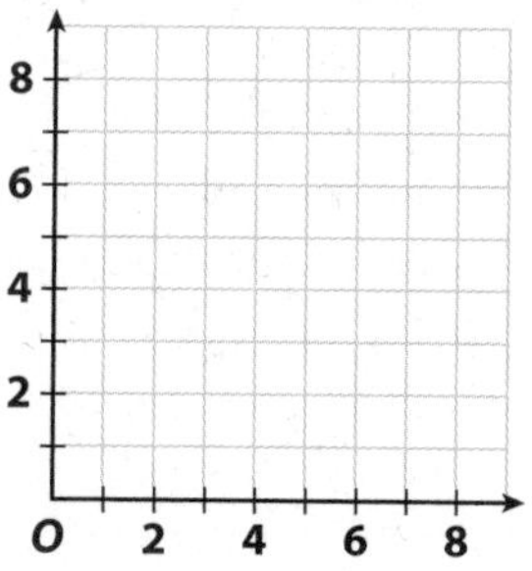

12. Represent Real-World Problems The figure shows a representation of a football field. The units represent yards. A sports analyst marks the locations of the football from where it was thrown (point *A*) and where it was caught (point *B*). Explain how you can use the Pythagorean Theorem to find the distance the ball was thrown. Then find the distance.

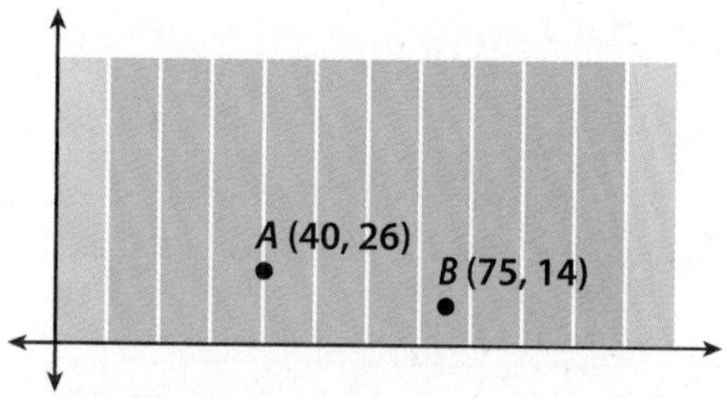

A (40, 26)
B (75, 14)

UNIT 1 Selected Answers

MODULE 1

LESSON 1.1

Your Turn

7. −9 **8.** −10 **9.** −60 **10.** −70 **11.** 300 **12.** −145 **13.** −1650 **14.** −1000

Guided Practice

1a. 6 **b.** negative **c.** −6 **2a.** 9 **b.** negative **c.** −9 **3.** −7

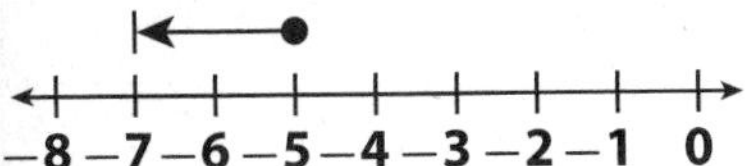

4. −4

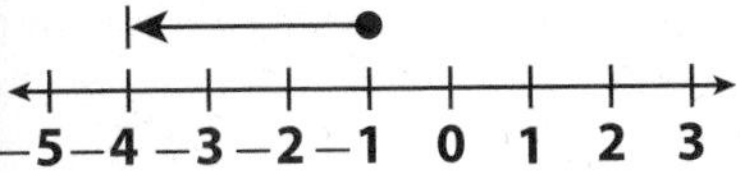

5. −10

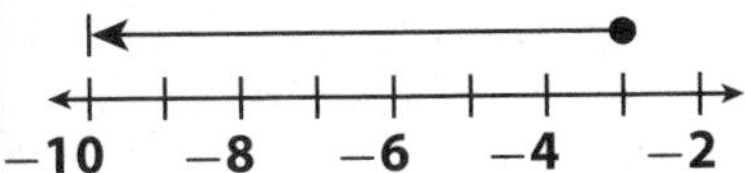

6. −5

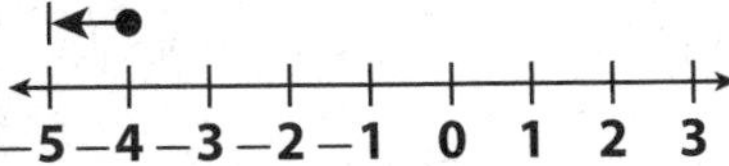

7. −4

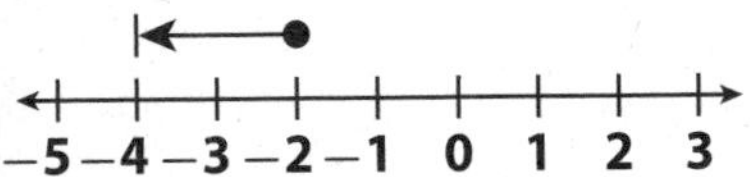

8. −14

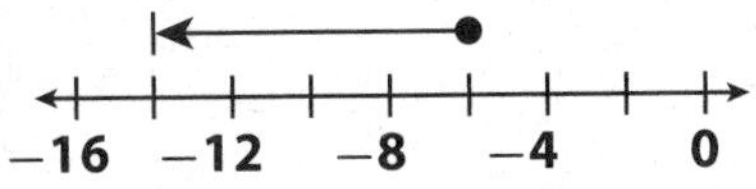

9. −9 **10.** −11 **11.** −10 **12.** −110 **13.** −100 **14.** 203 **15.** −15 **16.** −570

Independent Practice

19. −11 **21.** −54 **23.** −100 + (−75) + (−85) = −260

LESSON 1.2

Your Turn

3. 4 **4.** −2 **5.** −6 **6.** −1 **7.** −28 **8.** −8 **9.** 0 **10.** −1

Guided Practice

1. 6

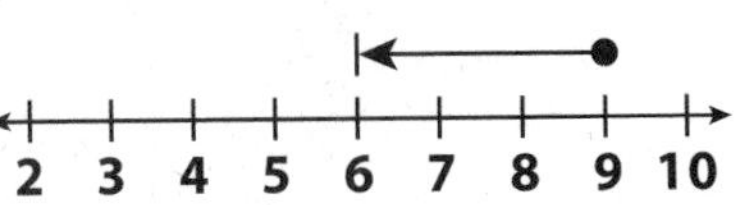

2. 5

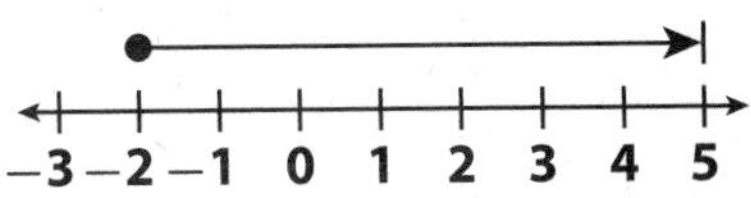

3. −11

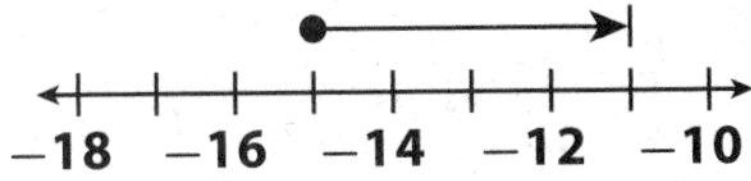

4. −3

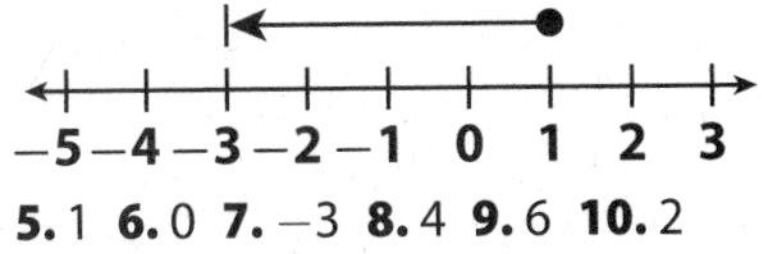

5. 1 **6.** 0 **7.** −3 **8.** 4 **9.** 6 **10.** 2 **11.** −16 **12.** 0 **13.** −5 **14.** 24

Independent Practice

17. −8 **19.** 25 **21.** −95 **23.** −7 **25.** 100 **27.** −55 + 275 = 220. The team's profit was $220.

LESSON 1.3

Your Turn

4. −9 **5.** 2 **6.** −2 **7.** −4

Guided Practice

1. −3 **2.** −2 **3.** (−5); −9 **4.** −4; −3 **5.** −3 **6.** 2 **7.** −6 **8.** −18 **9.** 5 **10.** 19 **11.** 14 **12.** 42 **13.** 38 **14.** 0

Independent Practice

17. −127 − (−225) = 98 feet **19.** −150 points **21.** Diet Chow **25.** −16, −21, −26

LESSON 1.4

Your Turn

1. −40 − 13 + 18; −35; 35 feet below the cave entrance **3.** −35 + (−45) + 180 = 100; $100 increase **4.** Jim

Guided Practice

1. −15 + 9 − 12 = −18; 18 feet below sea level **2.** −23 + 5 − 7 = −25; −25 °F **3.** 50 − 40 + 87 − 30 = 67 **4.** 24 **5.** −12 **6.** 18 **7.** 21 **8.** 97 **9.** 27 **10.** (−12 + 6 − 4) < (−34 − 3 + 39) **11.** (21 − 3 + 8) > (−14 + 31 − 6)

Independent Practice

13a. 5 − 1 + 6 − 1 = 9 **b.** over par **c.** yes **15.** Jerome did not rewrite the subtraction as adding the opposite before using the Commutative Property. 3 − 6 + 5 = 2 and 3 − 5 + 6 = 4 **17a.** 3:00 to 4:00 **b.** 87 **19.** $24 **23.** In the case in which the first number is positive, then the sum of the absolute values of the other two numbers must be greater than the value of the first number.

LESSON 2.1

Your Turn

4. −15 **5.** 20 **6.** 0 **7.** 32

Guided Practice

1. −9 **2.** −28 **3.** 54 **4.** −100 **5.** −60 **6.** 0 **7.** 49 **8.** −135 **9.** −96 **10.** 300 **11.** 0 **12.** −192 **13.** 7(−75) = −525; −$525 **14.** Start at zero and move 5 units to the left 3 times. 3(−5) = −15; −15 yards **15.** 6(−2) = −12; −12 °F

Selected Answers

Independent Practice

17. No **19.** 5(−4) = −20; $20 decrease **21.** 7(−6) = −42; the cost of the jeans decreased by $42 over the 7 weeks. **23.** 7(−8) = −56; 7(−5) = −35; −56 + (−35) = −91. The savings decreased by $91. **25a.** −27 **b.** 27 **c.** −27 **d.** −81 **e.** 81 **f.** −81 **g.** negative; positive

LESSON 2.2

Your Turn

2. 0 **3.** −2 **4.** 13 **5.** Yolanda received the same number of penalties in each game; 5. −25 ÷ (−5) = 5 and −35 ÷ (−7) = 5.

Guided Practice

1. −7 **2.** −7 **3.** −2 **4.** 0 **5.** 9 **6.** −3 **7.** 11 **8.** 1 **9.** 0 **10.** 11 **11.** −12 **12.** −20 **13.** undefined **14.** 3 **15.** −40 ÷ (4) = −10; $10 **16.** −22 ÷ (11) = −2; 2 points **17.** −75 ÷ (−15) = 5; 5 targets **18.** −99 ÷ (−9) = 11; 11 times

Independent Practice

21. Elisa; Elisa made −140 ÷ (−20) = 7 withdrawals; Francis made −270 ÷ (−45) = 6 withdrawals, and 7 > 6. **23.** the first part **27.** False; division by 0 is undefined for any dividend. **29.** 12

LESSON 2.3

Your Turn

1. Reggie earned 110 points; 3(−30) + 200 = −90 + 200 = 110. **2.** −78 − 21 = −99 **4.** 0 **5.** 20 **6.** 22 **7.** −28 **8.** Will **9.** −7; −6; (−28) ÷ 4 + 1 **10.** −5; −6; 42 ÷ (−3) + 9

Guided Practice

1. 42 **2.** −21 **3.** −9 **4.** −32 **5.** −4 **6.** −1 **7.** 7(−5) + 20 = −15; 15 dollars less **8.** 7(−10) + (−100) = −170; 170 fewer points **9.** 6(−4) + 10 = −14; lost 14 points **10.** 4(−12) + 10 = −38; $38 less **11.** > **12.** = **13.** > **14.** <

Independent Practice

17. 4 **19.** 0 **21.** 2 **23.** 5(−4) − 8 = −28 **25a.** 4(−35) − 9 = −149; $149 less **b.** Yes **29.** 80 inches

LESSON 3.1

Your Turn

4. −0.571428... **5.** 0.333... **6.** −0.45 **7.** −2.75; terminating decimal **8.** 7.333...; repeating decimal

Guided Practice

1. 0.6; terminating **2.** −0.89; terminating **3.** 0.333...; repeating **4.** 0.2525...; repeating **5.** −0.7777...; repeating **6.** −0.36; terminating **7.** 0.04; terminating **8.** −0.14204545...; repeating **9.** 0.012; terminating **10.** −11.166... **11.** 2.9 **12.** −8.23 **13.** 7.2 **14.** 54.2727... **15.** −3.0555... **16.** 3.666... **17.** −2.875

Independent Practice

19. $\frac{5}{11}$; 0.4545...; repeating **21.** $\frac{4}{11}$; 0.3636...; repeating **23.** $\frac{11}{11}$; 1; terminating **25a.** $-\frac{39}{8}$ **b.** −4.875 **27.** Ben is taller because 5.3125 > 5.2916.... **29.** When the denominator is 3, 6, 7, or 9, the result will be a repeating decimal. **31.** No; although the digits follow a pattern, the same combination of digits do not repeat.

LESSON 3.2

Your Turn

2. $4\frac{1}{2}$ **3.** −7

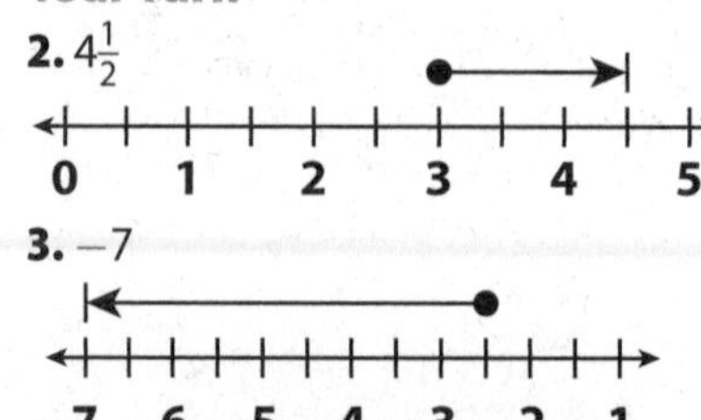

6. −3

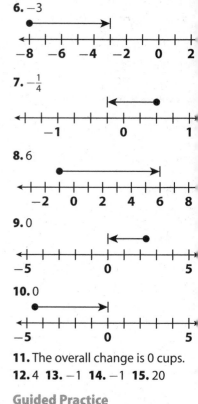

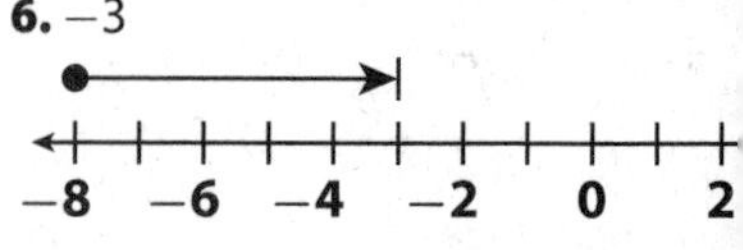

7. $-\frac{1}{4}$

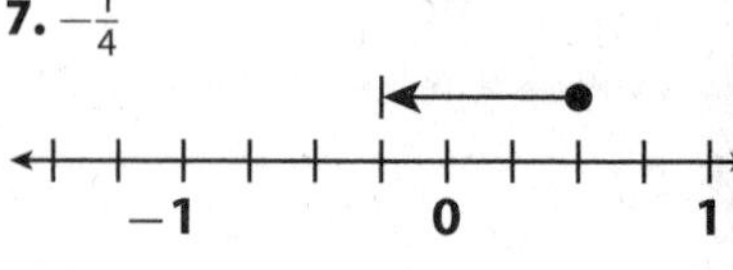

8. 6

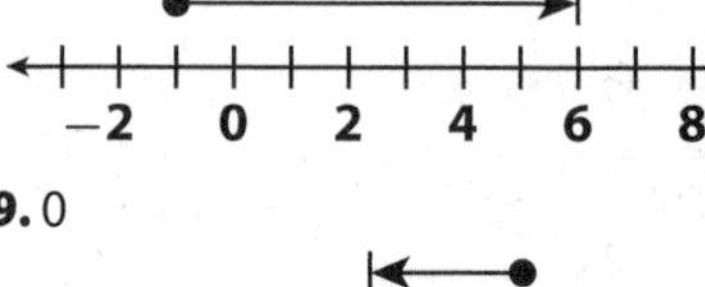

9. 0

10. 0

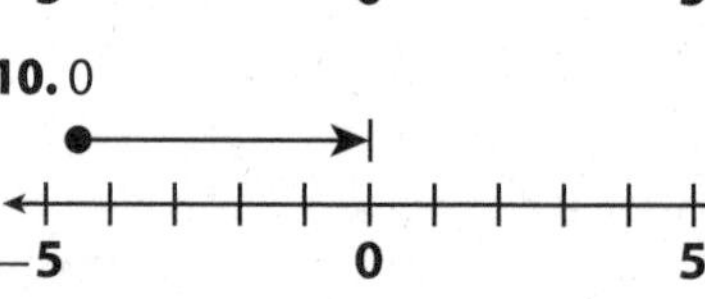

11. The overall change is 0 cups. **12.** 4 **13.** −1 **14.** −1 **15.** 20

Guided Practice

1. −4.5 **2.** 5

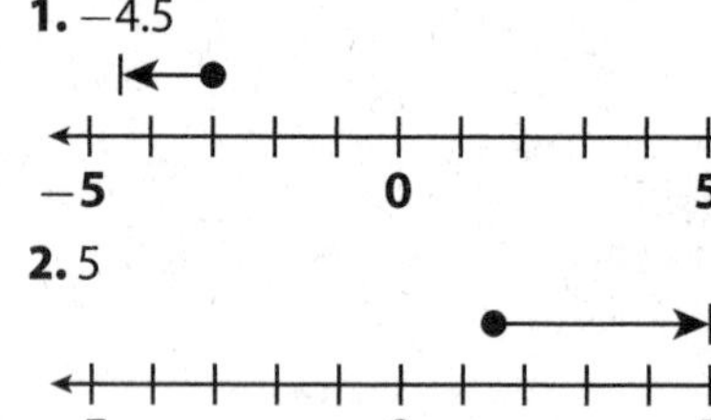

3. $\frac{3}{4}$

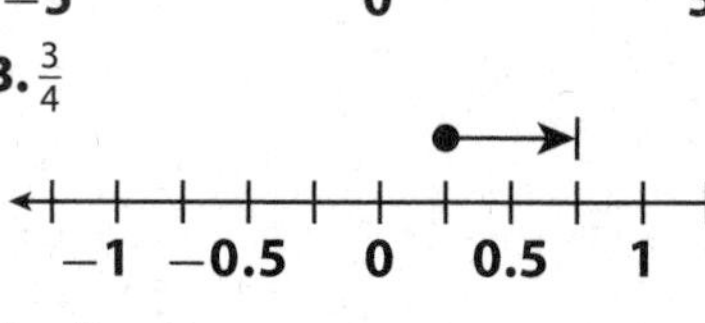

4. −3

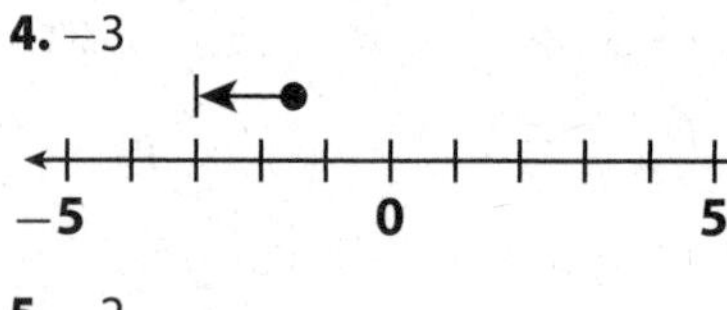

5. −2

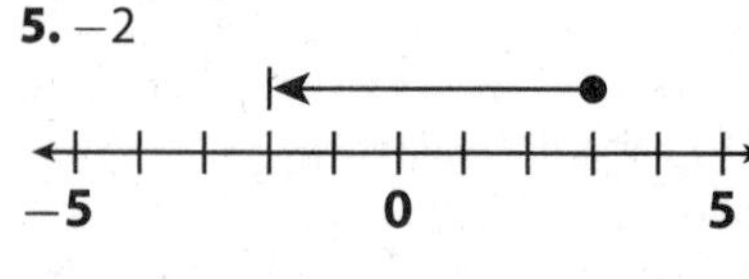

6. 2.5

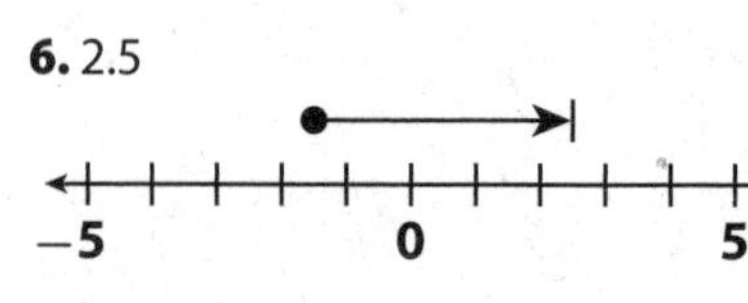

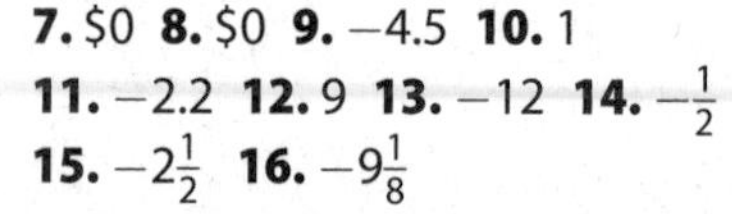

7. $0 **8.** $0 **9.** −4.5 **10.** 1 **11.** −2.2 **12.** 9 **13.** −12 **14.** $-\frac{1}{2}$ **15.** $-2\frac{1}{2}$ **16.** $-9\frac{1}{8}$

Independent Practice

19. \$12.75 **21.** $1\frac{1}{2}$ miles **23.** $30 + 15 + (-25) = 20$; the final score is 20 points **25.** June: \$306.77, July: \$301.50, Aug: \$337.88 **27.** opposite or additive inverse

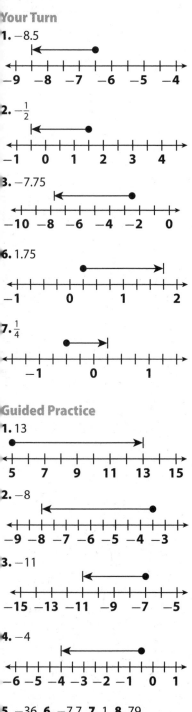

LESSON 3.3

Your Turn

1. −8.5

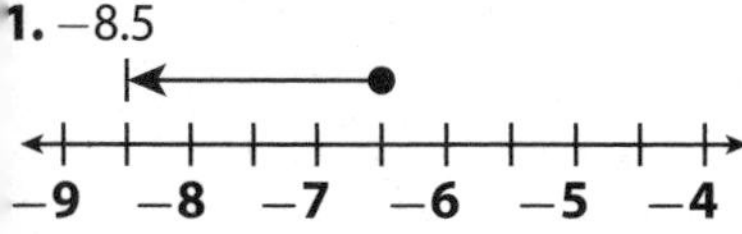

2. $-\frac{1}{2}$

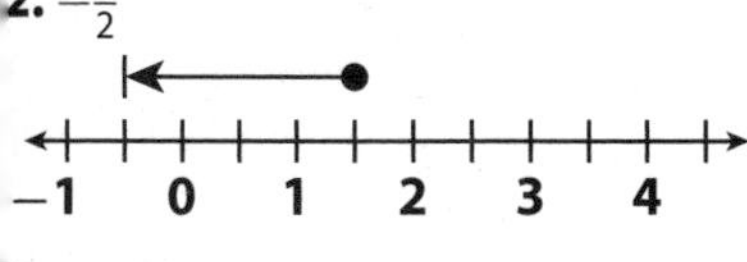

3. −7.75

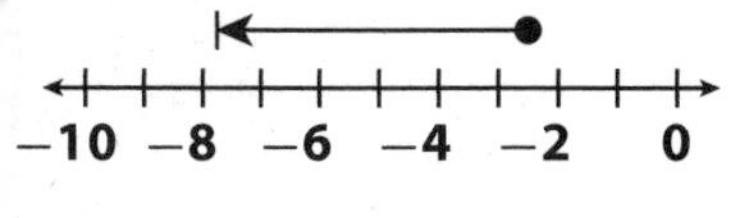

6. 1.75

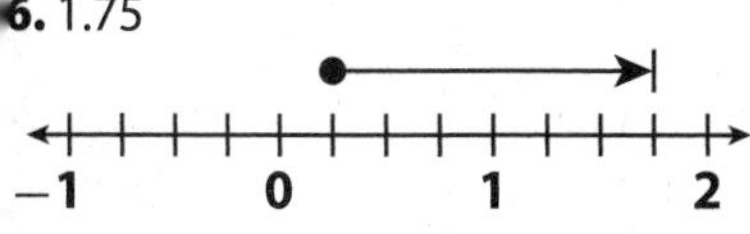

7. $\frac{1}{4}$

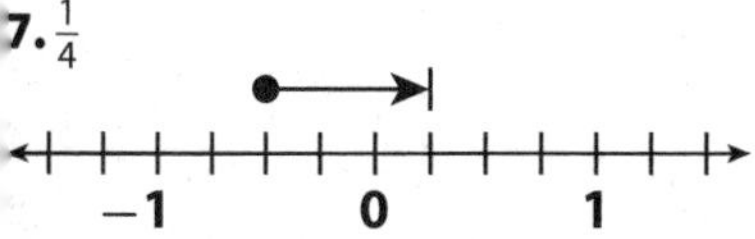

Guided Practice

1. 13

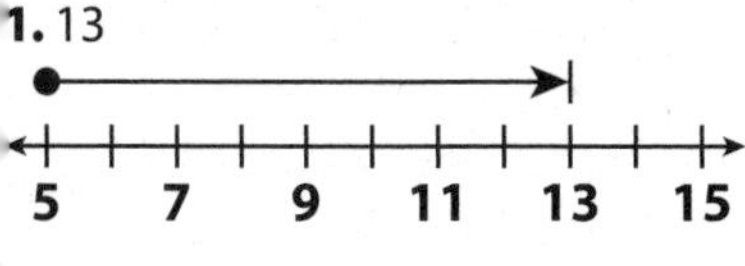

2. −8

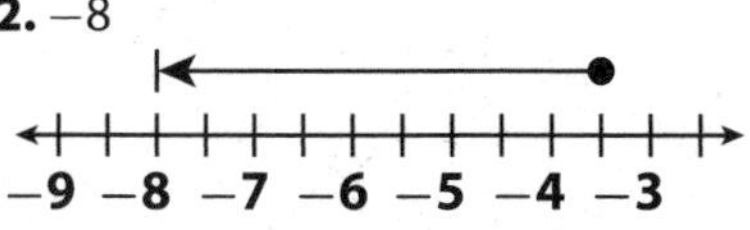

3. −11

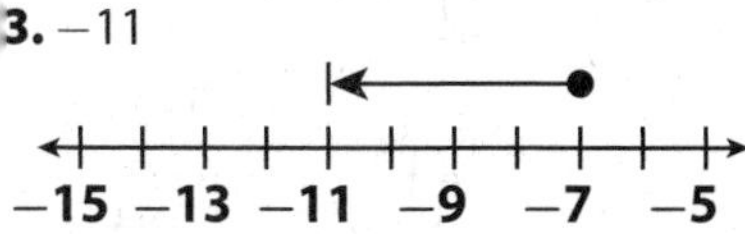

4. −4

−6 −5 −4 −3 −2 −1 0 1

5. −36 **6.** −7.7 **7.** 1 **8.** 79 **9.** $2\frac{7}{9}$ **10.** $78\frac{1}{2}$ **11.** 1.5 meters

12. $17\frac{1}{2}$ yards loss **13.** 543 feet **14.** took out \$75.15

Independent Practice

17. $-25.65 - 16.5 + 12.45$; −29.7 ft; the diver is 29.7 ft below the surface. **19.** 65,233 ft; 96,000 ft; 96,000 ft (Mars); 30,767 ft **21a.** −\$ 43.30 **b.** −\$68.30 **c.** \$68.30 **23a.** $5 - 7.2 + 2.2$ **b.** He is exactly where he started because $5 - 7.2 + 2.2 = 0$.

LESSON 3.4

Your Turn

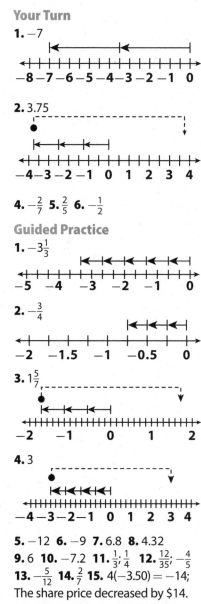

1. −7

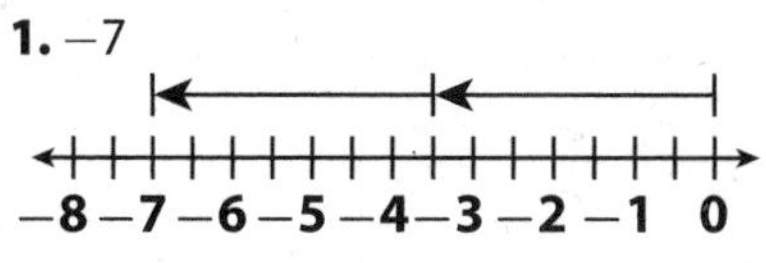

2. 3.75

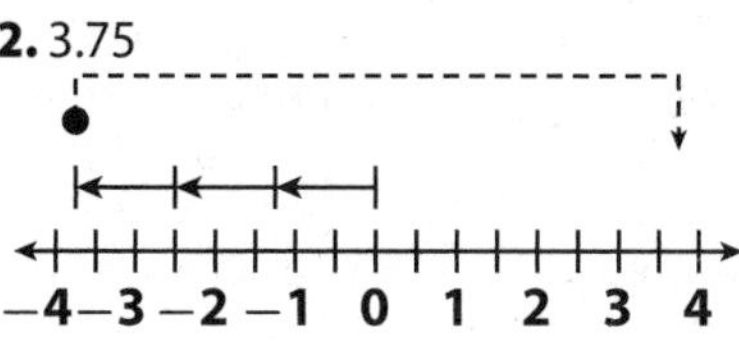

4. $-\frac{2}{7}$ **5.** $\frac{2}{5}$ **6.** $-\frac{1}{2}$

Guided Practice

1. $-3\frac{1}{3}$

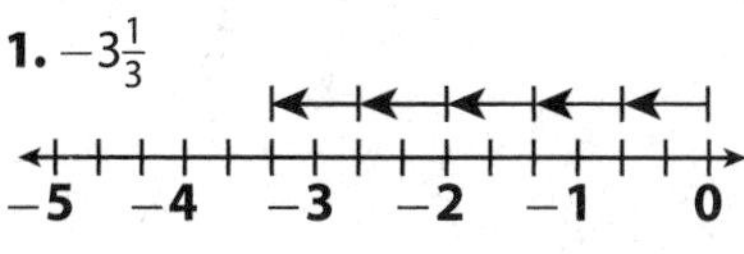

2. $-\frac{3}{4}$

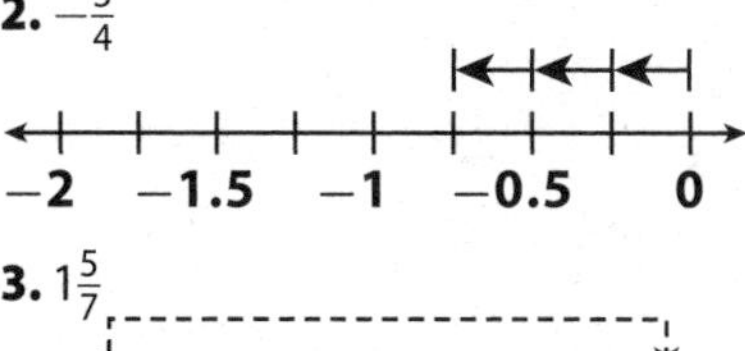

3. $1\frac{5}{7}$

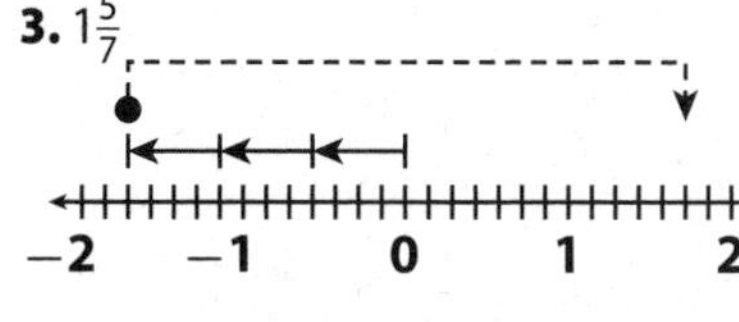

4. 3

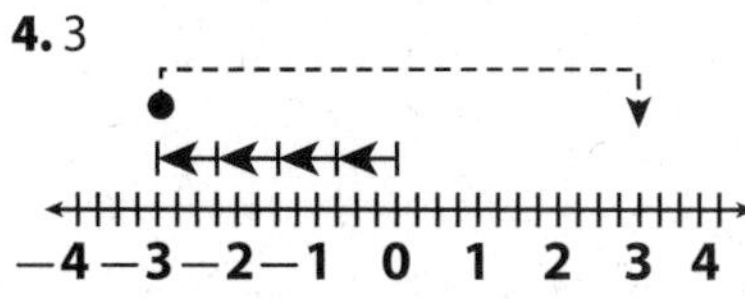

5. −12 **6.** −9 **7.** 6.8 **8.** 4.32 **9.** 6 **10.** −7.2 **11.** $\frac{1}{3}, \frac{1}{4}$ **12.** $\frac{12}{35}, -\frac{4}{5}$ **13.** $-\frac{5}{12}$ **14.** $\frac{2}{7}$ **15.** $4(-3.50) = -14$; The share price decreased by \$14. **16.** $18(-100) = -1{,}800$; The money in the ATM decreased by \$1,800.

Independent Practice

21. The submarine would be 975 feet below sea level, or −975 feet. **25.** 13.5 points

LESSON 3.5

Your Turn

3. −0.7 **4.** 16.6 **5.** −11 **6.** −3.8 feet per minute **7.** $\frac{35}{48}$ **8.** $-\frac{5}{8}$ **9.** $-1\frac{3}{5}$

Guided Practice

1. −0.8 **2.** $-\frac{1}{7}$ **3.** −8 **4.** $-\frac{502}{3}$ **5.** −375 **6.** 7 **7.** $-\frac{4}{21}$ **8.** −400 **9.** −0.875 liter per day **10.** $-45.75 \div 5 = -9.15$; −\$9.15 per day, on average **11.** −0.55 mile per minute

Independent Practice

13. −20 **15.** 20 **17.** −0.1 **19.** $\frac{5}{9}$ **21.** 4.5 **23.** $-1\frac{3}{4}$ yards **25a.** \$250 **b.** \$1,050 **c.** −\$70 **31.** Yes, since an integer divided by an integer is a ratio of two integers and the denominator is not zero, the number is rational by definition.

LESSON 3.6

Your Turn

1. $5\frac{5}{8}$ min **2.** 12 batches; \$0.29 per batch **3.** \$1,070.72

Guided Practice

1. Step 1: $3\frac{1}{5}$ or 3.2 mi/h, 14.4 mi; Step 2: 14.4 mi, $3\frac{3}{5}$ or 3.6 mi/h, 4 h **2.** Step 1: 25.68 in., −0.02375 in., −0.61 in.; Step 2: 25.68 in., 0.61 in., 25.07 in.

Independent Practice

5. $4\frac{1}{4}$ in. **7.** $29\frac{1}{8}$ yd **9.** 5 more; $88\% = \frac{88}{100} = \frac{44}{50}$ **11.** Yes, because the product is negative and about half of 1.5. **13.** Sample answer: Yes; $-0.7343 \approx -0.75$ **15.** Sample answer: (1) Convert the fraction to a decimal and find the sum of 27.6 and 15.9; then multiply the result by 0.37. (2) Convert the fraction, and then use the Distributive Property. Multiply both 27.6 and 15.9 by 0.37, and then add the products. The first method; there are fewer steps and so fewer chances to make errors.

Selected Answers

UNIT 2 Selected Answers

MODULE 4

LESSON 4.1

Your Turn

3. $\frac{1}{6} \div \frac{1}{4} = \frac{1}{6} \times \frac{4}{1} = \frac{4}{6} = \frac{2}{3}; \frac{2}{3}$ acre per hour **4.** 4 cups **5.** Jaylon's unit rate is $3\frac{3}{4}$ cups of water per cup of lime juice. Wanchen's unit rate is 4 cups of water per cup of lime juice. Wanchen's limeade has a weaker lime flavor because $4 > 3\frac{3}{4}$ and the limeade with a greater ratio of water to lime juice will have a weaker flavor.

Guided Practice

2. $2\frac{4}{5}$ miles per hour **3.** $\frac{15}{16}$ page per minute **4.** $\frac{1}{2}$ foot per hour
5. $2\frac{1}{2}$ square feet per hour
6. Brand A: 720 mg/pickle, Brand B: 650 mg/pickle; Brand B
7. Ingredient C: $\frac{3}{8}$ cup/serving, Ingredient D: $\frac{4}{9}$ cup/serving; Ingredient C

Independent Practice

9a. On Call: about $2.86 per hour; Talk Time: $2.50 per hour
b. Talk Time; its rate per hour is lower. **c.** Multiply 0.05 times 60 because there are 60 minutes in 1 hour. **d.** The unit rate is $3 per hour, so it is not a better deal. **11.** $\frac{5 \text{ songs}}{1 \text{ commercial}}$ **13.** Faster; he typed 50 words per minute before and 60 words per minute after.

LESSON 4.2

Your Turn

3. No; the rates are not equal because her speed changed.
4. Each rate is equal to $\frac{1 \text{ adult}}{12 \text{ students}}$. The relationship is proportional; $a = \frac{1}{12}s$.

Guided Practice

1. 45, $\frac{90}{2} = 45$; $\frac{135}{3} = 45$; $\frac{180}{4} = 45$; the relationship is proportional.
2. $k = 5$; $y = 5x$ **3.** $k = \frac{1}{4}$; $y = \frac{1}{4}x$

Independent Practice

5. $y = 18.50x$ **7.** Rent–All has the best deal because it has the lowest rate per day ($18.50).
9. The rates have the same unit rate, $6.25 per hour. **11.** x is the number of hours Steven babysits, and y is the amount he charges; the equation is $y = 6.25x$.
13. 150 feet per minute; 9,000 feet per hour **15.** Feet per minute

LESSON 4.3

Your Turn

1. No; a line drawn through the points does not go through the origin.

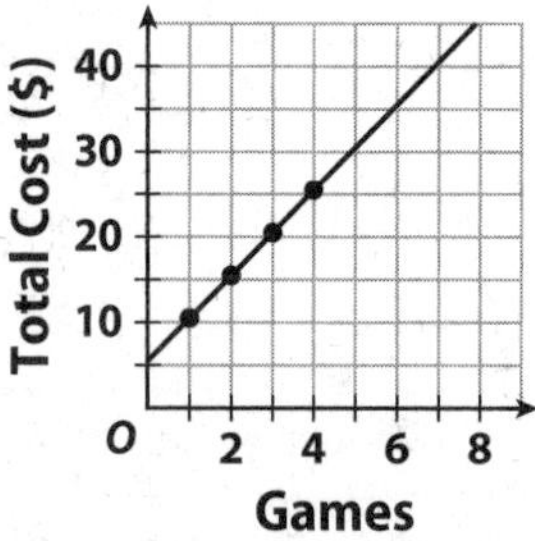

5a. The bicyclist rides 60 miles in 4 hours. **b.** 15 **c.** $y = 15x$

Guided Practice

1. proportional; pages is always 65 times the number of hours.
2. proportional; earnings are always 7.5 times the number of hours. **3.** not proportional; the line will not pass through the origin. **4.** proportional; the line will pass through the origin.
5. $y = 3.5x$ **6.** $y = \frac{1}{4}x$

Independent Practice

9. Horse A takes about 4 minutes. Horse B takes about 2.5 minutes. **11.** Horse A: $y = 3$ miles; Horse B: $y = 4\frac{4}{5}$ miles
13. Yes; A graph of miles traveled compared to number of hours will form a line that passes through the origin.

15a.

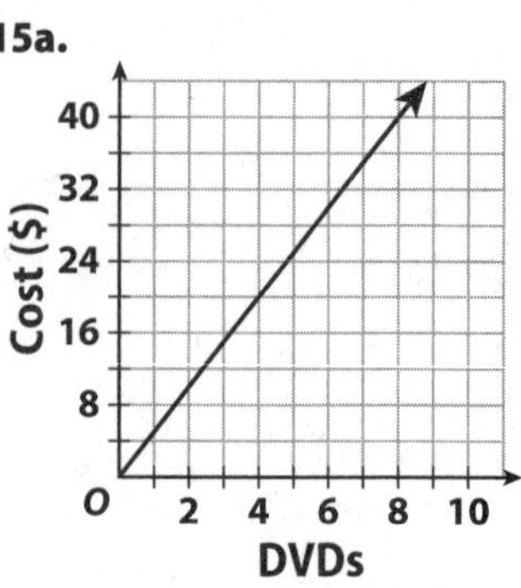

b. Sample answer: (4, 20); 4 DVDs cost $20. **17.** Yes. The graph is a line that passes through the origin. **21.** If the values in the "Time" column are the same, each value in the "Distance" column for Car 4 will be twice the corresponding value for Car 2.

LESSON 5.1

Your Turn

2. 23% **4.** 33% **5.** 37.5%
8. $548.90 **9.** $349.30

Guided Practice

1. 60% **2.** 50% **3.** 74% **4.** 11%
5. 8% **6.** 220% **7.** 78% **8.** 20%
9. 28% **10.** 50% **11.** 9% **12.** 67%
13. 100% **14.** 83% **15.** $9.90
16. 36 cookies **17.** 272 pages
18. 42 members **19.** $27,840
20. 1,863 songs **21.** 26 miles

Independent Practice

25a. Amount of change = 1; percent decrease = $\frac{1}{5}$ = 20%
27a. They have the same. $100 + $10 = $110 and $100 + 10%($100) = $110. **b.** Sylvia has more. Leroi has $110 + $10 = $120, and Sylvia has $110 + 10%($110) = $121.
29. No. Each withdrawal is less than the previous, so there will be a little money left.

LESSON 5.2

Your Turn

2a. $1c + 0.1c$; $1.1c$ **b.** $30.80
3a. 200% **b.** $1c + 2c$; $3c$
5a.

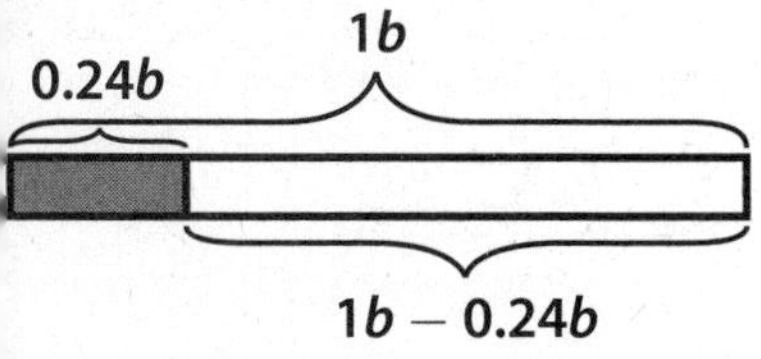

b. $0.76b$ **6a.** $1p - 0.05p$, $0.95p$
b. $14.25

Guided Practice

1a. $0.35s$ **b.** $1s + 0.35s$ or $1.35s$
c. $43.20 **d.** $11.20 **2.** $2.70; $20.70 **3.** $9.45; $31.95 **4.** $25.31; $59.06 **5.** $24.75; $99.74 **6.** $48.60; $97.20 **7.** $231.25; $416.25 **8.** $35.10 **9.** $59.63 **10.** $13.43 **11.** $70.00

Independent Practice

13a. $0.46b$ **b.** $1b - 0.46b$ or $0.54b$ **c.** $15.66 **d.** $13.34 **17.** Either buy 3, get one free or $\frac{1}{4}$ off. Either case would result in a discount of 25%, which is better than 20%.
19. No; first change: 20.1% decrease; second change: 25.1% increase. The second percent change is greater.

LESSON 5.3

Your Turn

1. $1; $21 **3.** $80; $480
4. $168.75; $2,368.75

Guided Practice

1. $1.50 **2.** $10.50 **3.** $0.40 **4.** $33 **5.** $0.80 **6.** $10 **7a.** $3.08 **b.** $47.07 **8.** $86.83 **9.** $700 **10.** $715 **11a.** $18 **b.** $19.53 **12.** $37.86

Independent Practice

15. $82.58 **17.** $75.14 **19.** $1,076.25
21a. Multiply Sandra's height by 0.10 and add the product to 4 to get Pablo's height. Then multiply Pablo's height by 0.08 and add the product to Pablo's height to get Michaela's height. **b.** about 4 feet 9 inches **23a.** $101.49 **b.** $109.39 **c.** digital camera; he can save $8. **d.** $109.61

UNIT 3 Selected Answers

LESSON 6.1

Your Turn

2. $10x - 4$ **3.** $-1.75x - 4.4$ **4.** $0.6b + 3c$ **5.** $4e - f - 14g$ **6.** $x + 6$ **7.** $11.8 - 2.6y$ **9.** $2(x + 1)$ **10.** $3(x + 3)$ **11.** $5(x + 3)$ **12.** $4(x + 4)$

Guided Practice

1. Step 1: baseballs: $14 + 12n$, tennis balls: $23 + 16n$; Step 2: $14 + 12n + 23 + 16n$, $14 + 23 + 12n + 16n$, $37 + 28n$, $37 + 28n$ **2.** 289 **3.** $29 - 2x$ **4.** $27t - 28$ **5.** $3.3c - 8.2$ **6.** $-4 - 4\frac{1}{2}n$ **7.** $2(x + 6)$ **8.** $12(x + 2)$ **9.** $7(x + 5)$

Independent Practice

11. $15(100 + 5d) + 20(50 + 7d) = 2{,}500 + 215d$ **13.** 3 and $x + 2$; $3x + 6$ **15.** The area is the product of the length and width (6×9). It is also the sum of the areas of the rectangles separated by the dashed line (6×5 and 6×4). So, $6(9) = 6(5) + 6(4)$. **17.** $2x + 6$ **19.** $x^2 + 5x + 6$ **21.** (1) Think of 997 as $1{,}000 - 3$. So, $8 \times 997 = 8(1{,}000 - 3)$. By the Distributive Property, $8(1{,}000 - 3) = 8{,}000 - 24 = 7{,}976$. (2) Think of 997 as $900 + 90 + 7$. By the Distributive Property, $8(900 + 90 + 7) = 7{,}200 + 720 + 56 = 7{,}976$.

LESSON 6.2

Your Turn

1. $z = -13.9$ **2.** $r = 12.3$ **3.** $c = -12$ **5.** $x - 1.5 = 5.25$; $x = 6.75$; the initial elevation of the plane was 6.75 miles. **6.** $\frac{x}{3.5} = -1.2$; $x = -4.2$; $4.20 **7.** $2.5x = 7.5$; $x = 3$; 3 hours

Guided Practice

1. Step 1: the number of degrees warmer the average temperature is in Nov. than in Jan., $x + (-13.4) = -1.7$ or $x - 13.4 = -1.7$; Step 2: 11.7 °F **2.** Step 1: the number of days it takes the average temperature to decrease by 9 °F, $-1\frac{1}{2}x = -9$; Step 2: 6 days **3.** $x = -17$ **4.** $y = 1.4$ **5.** $z = -9$

Independent Practice

7. 29,028.87 ft **9.** $28{,}251.31 - x = 11{,}194.21$; $x = 17{,}057.1$; 17,057.1 ft **11.** $-26\frac{1}{2}$ ft/min **13.** 18.8 °C warmer **15.** $36\frac{1}{3}$ yards **17.** Sample answer: the elevation is the product of the rate and the time. **19.** (1) The elevations of the diver and the reef; both are below sea level. (2) The change in the plane's elevation; the plane is moving from a higher to a lower elevation. **21.** Add the deposits and the withdrawals. Let x represent the amount of the initial deposit. Write and solve the equation x + deposits − withdrawals = \$210.85.

LESSON 6.3

Your Turn

4. $150 - 35x = 45$

Guided Practice

1.

2.

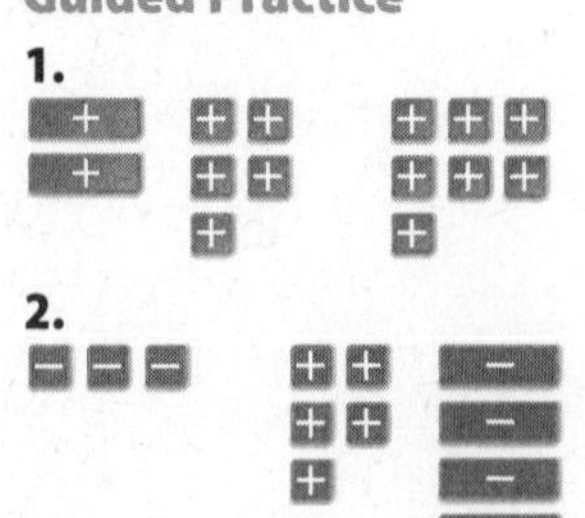

3. $6 + 9a = 78$ **4.** the solution; multiplied by 2; added to $2x$; result

Independent Practice

7. three negative variable tiles and seven +1−tiles on one side of a line and 28 +1−tiles on the other side **9.** $1.25r + 6.75 = 31.75$ **11.** $\frac{1}{2}n + 45 = 172$ **13.** $500 - 20x = 220$ **15a.** $10 + 5c = 25$ **b.** 3 children **c.** They should choose Kimmi, because she charges only \$25. If they chose Sandy, they would pay \$35. **17.** Part of the equation is written in cents and part in dollars. All of the numbers in the equation should be written either in cents or in dollars.

LESSON 6.4

Your Turn

1. $x = 3$ **2.** $n = 3$ **3.** $a = -1$ **4.** $y = 1$ **6.** $3n + 10 = 37$; the triplets are 9 years old. **7.** $\frac{n}{4} - 5 = 15$; the number is 80. **8.** $-20 = \frac{5}{9}(x - 32)$; -4 °F **9.** $120 - 4x = 92$; 7 incorrect answers

Guided Practice

1. one + 1 tile from both sides; two equal groups **2.** 4 **3.** $2(18 + w) = 58$; the width is 11 inches **4.** $1{,}200 - 25x = 500$; 28 days

Independent Practice

7. $d = 9$ **9.** $k = 42$ **11.** $z = -190$ **13.** $n = -9$ **15.** $c = 9$ **17.** $t = -9$ **19.** $2x - 6 = 20$; 13 °F **21.** $-x + 40 = 28$; 12 years old **23.** $\frac{1}{2}x - 6 = 88$; \$188 **25.** $x = 0.4$ **27.** $k = -180.44$ **29.** When dividing both sides by 3, the student did not divide 2 by 3. The solution should be $x + \frac{2}{3} = 5$, $x = 4\frac{1}{3}$.

LESSON 7.1

Your Turn

4. $y \geq -2$

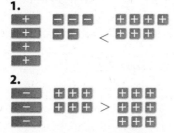

5. $x < 9$

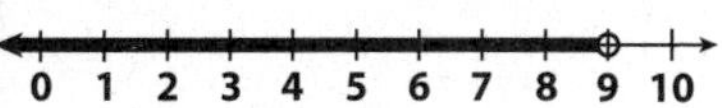

6. $y > -6$

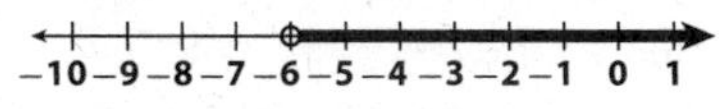

7. $t \geq -42$

−47 −46 −45 −44 −43 −42 −41 −40

8. $m \leq 9$; Tony can pay for no more than 9 months of his gym membership using this account.

Guided Practice

1. $2 \leq 5$ **2.** $2 > 1$ **3.** $0 > -11$ **4.** $2 \leq 16$ **5.** $n \geq 3$

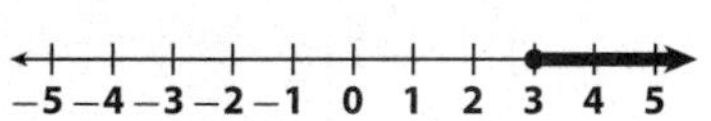

6. $x < 4$

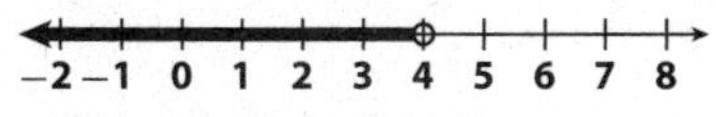

7. $y \geq -2$

−7 −6 −5 −4 −3 −2 −1 0 1 2 3

8. $b > -5$

−8 −7 −6 −5 −4 −3 −2 −1 0 1 2

9a. $-4t \geq -80$
b. 20 or fewer hours
c. more than 20 hours

Independent Practice

11. $x > 50$

0 10 20 30 40 50 60 70 80 90 100

13. $q \leq 7$

0 1 2 3 4 5 6 7 8 9 10

15. $z < 8$

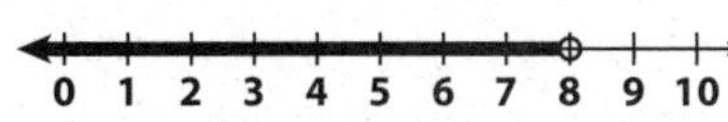

17. at most 16 in. **19.** at most 7 in. **21.** at least 11 ft **23.** $3\frac{1}{3}$ lb **25.** No; $1.25x \leq 3$; $x \leq 2.4$ so 2.4 lb of onions is the most Florence can buy. $2.4 < 2.5$, so she cannot buy 2.5 lb. **27.** $x > 9$ for each inequality; in each case the number added to x is 9 less than the number on the right side of each inequality, so $x > 9$ is the solution.

LESSON 7.2

Your Turn

3. $1{,}240 + 45a \geq 6{,}000$
4. $6 + 3n \leq 40$

Guided Practice

1.

2.

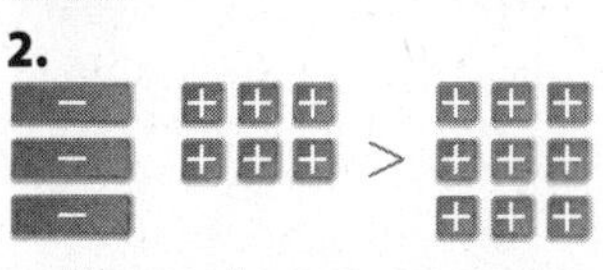

3. \$7,000; \$1,250; 92; $1{,}250 + 92a \geq 7{,}000$ **4.** the solution of the problem; the solution multiplied by 7; 18 is subtracted from $7x$; the result can be no greater than 32.

Independent Practice

7. $3a + 28 > 200$; a = possible amounts each friend earned

9. $4a - 25 \leq 75$; a = the maximum amount each shirt can cost **11.** $2{,}100 + 0.05s \geq 2{,}400$; s = the amount of her sales **13.** $7 + 10c \leq 100$; c = the number of CDs she buys **17.** $\leq$ **19.** $\leq$ **21.** $\geq$
25. $n > \frac{1}{n}$ if $n > 1$; $n < \frac{1}{n}$ if $n < 1$; $n = \frac{1}{n}$ if $n = 1$

LESSON 7.3

Your Turn

1. $x > 2$ **2.** $h \geq 3$ **3.** $p \geq 6$; Joshua has to run at a steady pace of at least 6 mi/h. **4.** $v = 11$ **5.** $h = -3$; $h = -4$; $h = -5$

Guided Practice

1. Remove 4 + 1-tiles from both sides, then divide each side into 3 equal groups; $x < 3$
2. $d < 9$

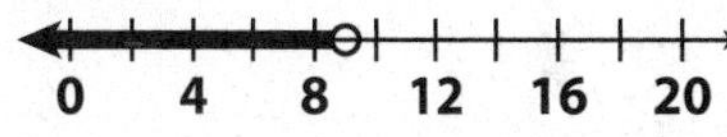

3. $b \geq 4$

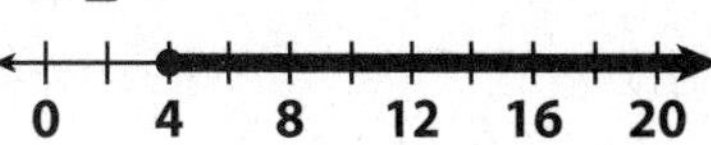

4. $m = -10$ **5.** $y = \frac{1}{2}$; $y = 0$
6. $t \leq 1.25$;

Lizzy can spend from 0 to 1.25 h with each student. No; 1.5 h per student will exceed Lizzy's available time.

Independent Practice

9. $t \leq 10$ **11.** $m < 8$
13. $f < 140$ **15.** $g < -18$
17. $a \geq 16$ **19.** $7n - 25 \geq 65$; $n \geq 12\frac{6}{7}$; Grace must wash at least 13 cars, because n must be a whole number.
21c. There is no number that satisfies both inequalities. **d.** The solution set is all numbers.

Selected Answers

UNIT 4 Selected Answers

LESSON 8.1

Your Turn

6. The length is 22 feet, and the width is 10 feet. The area is 22 feet $\times$ 10 feet, or 220 square feet.

Guided Practice

1a. The wall is 30 feet long.
b. 1.5 in. **2.** The length is 28 feet, and the width is 14 feet. The area is 28 feet $\times$ 14 feet, or 392 square feet. **3.** length: 25 meters; width: 15 meters; area: 375 square meters
4a.

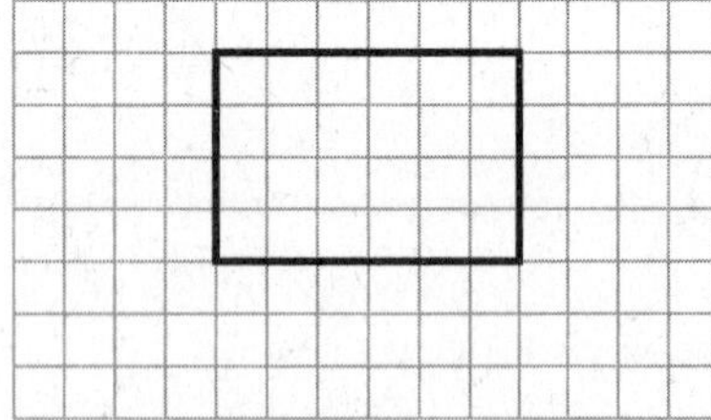

b. Length is 36 m and width is 24 m, using both scales.

Independent Practice

7. The scale drawing is 24 units by 15 units. **9.** Because the scale is 10 cm:1 mm and because 10 cm is longer than 1 mm, the drawing will be larger. **11a.** 6 toothpicks tall **b.** approximately 5 cotton swabs tall

LESSON 8.2

Guided Practice

1. a unique triangle
2. no triangle
3. a unique triangle
4. a unique triangle

Independent Practice

7. The side lengths proposed are 15, 21, and 37 ft, and $15 + 21 < 37$. No such triangle can be created.
9. More than one triangle; two triangles can be created by connecting the top of the 2-in. segment with the dashed line, once in each spot where the arc intersects the dashed line. The triangles are different, but both have sides with lengths of 2 in. and $1\frac{1}{2}$ in., and a 45° angle not included between them.

LESSON 8.3

Guided Practice

1. triangle or equilateral triangle
2. rectangle
3. triangle
4. rainbow-shaped curve

Independent Practice

7. Circles or ovals
9a. It is a circle with a radius of 12 in.
b. The cross sections will still be circles, but their radii will decrease as the plane moves away from the sphere's center.
11. Sample answer: If you think of a building shaped like a rectangular prism, you can think of horizontal planes slicing the prism to form the different floors.

LESSON 8.4

Your Turn

5. Sample answer: $\angle FGA$ and $\angle AGC$ **6.** Sample answer: $\angle FGE$ and $\angle BGC$ **7.** Sample answer: $\angle FGD$ and $\angle DGC$ **8.** Sample answer: $\angle BGC$ and $\angle CGD$
9. 55° **10.** $54° + 3x = 180°$, $3x = 126°$, $x = 42°$, $m\angle JML = 3x = 126°$
11. Sample answer: You can stop at the solution step where you find the value of $3x$ because the measure of $\angle JML$ is equal to $3x$.

Guided Practice

1. complementary **2.** adjacent
3. vertical; 30° **4.** 50°, 30°, $2x$; 80°; 100°; 100° **5.** $3x - 13$, 58°, 45°; 45°, 15°; 15°; 45°; 32°

Independent Practice

7. Sample answer: $\angle SUR$ and $\angle QUR$ **9.** Sample answer: $\angle TUS$ and $\angle QUN$ **11.** $m\angle RUQ$
13. 96° **15.** 28°
17. $m\angle A = 47°$, $m\angle B = 43°$
19. 41 degrees, 33 minutes, 52 seconds **21.** Disagree; The sum of the measures of a pair of complementary angles is 90°. So, the measure of each angle must be less than 90°. But $m\angle A = 119°$, and $119° > 90°$.

LESSON 9.1

Your Turn

3. about 34.54 cm **6.** about 2 hours

Guided Practice

1. 3.14(9); 28.26 **2.** 7; 44
3. 78.5 m **4.** 30.14 yd **5.** 47.1 in.
6. 66; 66; 21; $21 + 4 = 25$; 25; \$11.25; \$11.25 **7.** 0.5 yd; 1 yd
8. 12.55 ft; 25.10 ft **9.** 1.7 in.; 10.68 in.

Independent Practice

11. 18.53 ft **13.** 110 in.
15. $d = 18.8$ ft; $C \approx 59.0$ ft
17. $r = 9$ in.; $C \approx 56.52$ in.
19. about 2,376 ft
21. about 0.14 mi
23. about \$713.18
25. 12.56 feet **27.** Pool B; about 0.57 m or 1.84 ft

LESSON 9.2

Your Turn

1. 314 ft^2

Guided Practice

1. 153.9 m^2 **2.** 452.2 mm^2 **3.** 314 yd^2 **4.** 200.96 in^2 **5.** 113.04 cm^2 **6.** 132.67 in^2 **7.** 4π square units **8.** 36π square units **9.** $\frac{\pi}{16}$ square units **10.** 16π yd

Independent Practice

13. 803.84 cm^2 **15.** 28.26 square units **17.** 30.96 m^2 **19.** No; the top of the large cake has an area 9 times that of the small cake. The area of the top of the large cake is 144π in^2 and that of the small cake is 16π in^2. **21.** The 18-inch pizza is a better deal because it costs about 8¢ per square inch while the 12-inch pizza costs about 9¢ per square inch. **23.** No; the combined area is $2\pi r^2$ while the area of a circle with twice the radius is $4\pi r^2$. **25.** $\frac{\pi(1.5)^2}{\pi(7.5)^2} = \frac{2.25}{56.25} = \frac{1}{25}$ or 0.04 or 4%

LESSON 9.3

Your Turn

2. 51.5 ft^2 **3.** 139.25 m^2 **4.** $911.68

Guided Practice

1. rectangle; 4; 15; 15; 4; 15; 15; 34; 34 **2.** Method 1: Divide the figure into a 12 by 9 rectangle and a 20 by 9 rectangle. Method 2: Divide the figure into a 9 by 8 rectangle and a 12 by 18 rectangle. The area is 288 cm^2. **3.** $97.88

Independent Practice

5. 941.33 in^2

7. 30 square units

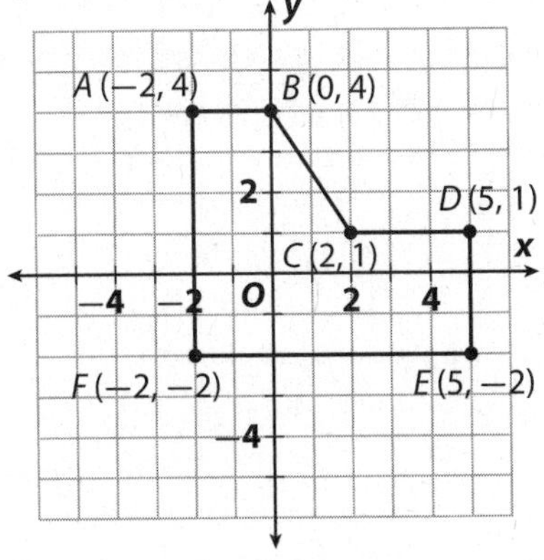

9. 60.56 cm^2 **11.** 5 ft; 32.5 ft^2 − 7.5 ft^2 = 25 ft^2; 25 ft^2 is area of the square, so each side of the square is 5 ft because $5 \times 5 = 25$ **15a.** 2,228 in^2 **b.** 3,016 in^2

LESSON 9.4

Your Turn

3. 69 in^2

4. 976 in^2

Guided Practice

1. 18 ft, 7 ft, 12 ft^2, (18 ft)(7 ft) + 2(12 ft^2), 150 ft^2 **2.** 37.5 m^2, 478 m^2, 6.25 m^2, $37.5 + 478 - 2(6.25)$, 503 m^2

Independent Practice

5. 3,720 tiles **7.** 66 ft^2

9. 3,264 in^2

11. No; they need 3 cans, which will cost 3($6.79) = $20.37.

13. No; *Ph* doubles, and 2*B* quadruples. *S* more than doubles.

15. 138.2 in^2; 1,440 ft^2 of cardboard

LESSON 9.5

Your Turn

2. 1,848 m^3

5. 2,200 cm^3

7. 6,825 in^3

Guided Practice

1. 12 ft^2; (12×7) ft^3 = 84 ft^3

2. 30 m^2; (30×11) m^3 = 330 m^3

3. 288 ft^3; 72 ft^3; 360 ft^3

4. 40,000 ft^3

5. 385 cm^3

Independent Practice

7. 17.5 in^3

9. 384 ft^3

11. The units for volume are incorrect; the volume is 300 cubic inches.

13. 316.41 m^3

15. Triangular prism; you get 192 in^3 for the same price you would pay for 180 in^3 with the trapezoidal prism.

17. $V = 30(2.5) = 75$ cm^3; mass $\approx 75(8.6) = 645$ g

19. Sample answers: (1) height of trapezoid = 4 cm, base lengths = 2 cm and 6 cm, height of prism = 7.5 cm (2) height of trapezoid = 2.5 cm, base lengths = 1 cm and 7 cm, height of prism = 12 cm

UNIT 5 Selected Answers

MODULE 10

LESSON 10.1

Your Turn

2. Dot plots for field hockey players and softball players have a similar spread. Center of the field hockey dot plot is less than the center for softball or basketball players. Dot plots for field hockey players and softball players have a similar spread.
3. median: 6 h, range: 10 h; The median is greater than the median for exercise. The range is less than the range for exercise.

Guided Practice

1. Class A: clustered around two areas; Class B: clustered in the middle **2.** Class A: two peaks at 4 and 13 mi; Class B: looks centered around 7 mi **3.** Class A: spread from 4 to 14 mi, a wide gap with no data; Class B: spread from 3 to 9 mi **4.** The median for both dot plots is 6 miles. **5.** Range for Class A: 10 mi; range for Class B: 6 mi

Independent Practice

7. The dots have a relatively even spread, with a peak at 8 letters.
9. The dots spread from 3 to 9 letters. **11.** AL: clustered in one small interval with an outlier to the left; VA: relatively uniform in height over the same interval
13. AL: spreads from 1 to 12 days of rain, an outlier at 1; VA: spreads from 8 to 12 days of rain
15. Group A: clustered to the left of size 9; Group B: clustered to the right of size 9 **17.** Group A: range with outlier = 6.5, without outlier = 2.5; Group B: range = 3 **19.** Yes; one group of five students could have the following number of pets: 1, 2, 3, 4, 5. Another group of five students could have the following number of pets: 1, 3, 3, 3, 5. For both groups of students, the median would be 3 and the range would be 4.

LESSON 10.2

Your Turn

3. Sample: The boxes have similar shapes, although Group B has a shorter box and shorter whiskers. Group B's median is greater than Group A's. Group B's shorter box means the middle 50% of the data are closer together than the middle 50% of Group A's.
4. Sample answer: The shape is similar to Store A's. The median is greater than Store A's and less than Store B's. The interquartile range is about the same as Store A's and longer than B's.

Guided Practice

1. 72; 88 **2.** 79 **3.** 16; 10
4. Volleyball players **5.** Hockey players **6.** Both groups

Independent Practice

9. Both cars have ranges of 45 in. Both cars have interquartile ranges of 25 in. **11.** Car A has less variability in the lowest quarter of its data and greater variability in the highest quarter of its data. The variability is reversed for Car B.
13. City A; $25

LESSON 10.3

Your Turn

1. About 1.1 times the MAD.
2. There is much more overlap between the two distributions.

Guided Practice

1. Class 1: 6, Class 2: 11; Class 1: 3, Class 2: 3 **2.** 1.67 **3.** The variation and overlap in the distributions make it hard to make any convincing comparison.

Independent Practice

5. Mean: 50 °F, MAD: 13 °F
7. 35 °F, 13 °F; the mean for City 2 must be 15 °F less than the mean for City 1, and the MAD must be the same.
9. Both distributions show longer travel times for school A. The distribution of the medians shows less overlap, so it is more convincing.
11. 1.75 × range **13.** Ramon's; the larger the sample size, the less variability there should be in the distributions of the medians and means.

LESSON 11.1

Your Turn

4. Yes; every employee had an equal chance of being selected.
5. The question is biased since cats are suggested. **6.** The question is not biased. It does not lead people to pick a particular season.

Guided Practice

2. more; random **3.** less; biased **4.** Yes; Sample answer: What is your favorite color?

Independent Practice

9. It is biased because students who aren't in that class won't be selected. **11.** Yes; the sample is random. **13.** Jae's question is not biased since it does not suggest a type of art to students. **15a.** 60; a random sample **b.** 58%; it appears reasonable because Barbara used a random sample and surveyed a significant percent of the students.

LESSON 11.2

Your Turn

5. 420 damaged MP3s **6.** Sample answer: 6 is a little more than 10% of 50. 10% of 3,500 is 350, and 420 is a little more than that.

Guided Practice

1.

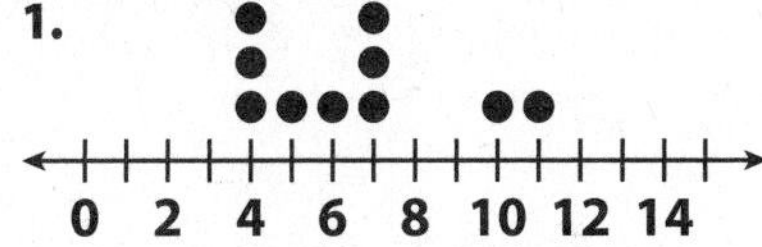

2.

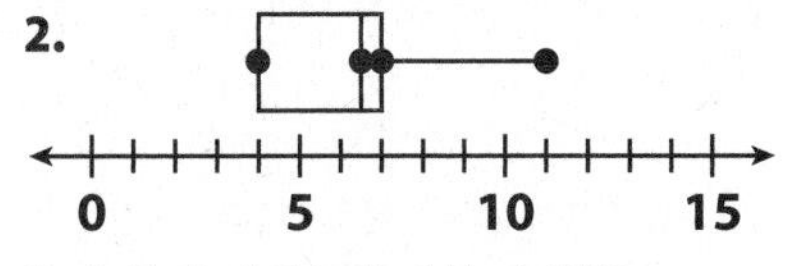

3. 4; 7 **4.** 4; 11 **5.** 6.5 **6.** 280
7. 720 elk

Independent Practice

9. 48 people **11.** 240 puppies
13. Yes, this seems reasonable because 25 is the median of the data. **17.** Kudrey needs to find the median and the lower and upper quartiles and plot those points. He assumed all quartiles would be equally long when each quartile represents an equal number of data values. **19.** a box plot

LESSON 11.3

Guided Practice

1. (1, 600); 20
2. 50; 51, 600
3. No, it has 4 defective batteries, or 20%. For the shipment, $\frac{50}{600}$, or about 8% of the batteries are defective.

Independent Practice

5. Shop A sells 100; Shop B sells 115; Shop C sells 140.
7. Shop A or Shop B; Both samples are large enough to produce a reasonably valid inference. Shop C's sample is too small.
9a. 49.8 palms **b.** about 3,187 palms

UNIT 6 Selected Answers

LESSON 12.1

Your Turn

3. as likely as not; $\frac{1}{2}$ **4.** $\frac{1}{2}$ **5.** $\frac{1}{3}$ **7.** $\frac{7}{8}$ **8.** $\frac{1}{2}$

Guided Practice

1. 8; 5; 7; 1; 3; 2; 4; 6 **2.** impossible; 0 **3.** as likely as not; $\frac{1}{2}$ **4.** certain; 1 **5.** unlikely; close to 0 **6.** $\frac{2}{5}$ **7.** $\frac{1}{4}$ **8.** $\frac{5}{6}$ **9.** $\frac{2}{3}$ **10.** $\frac{4}{5}$ **11.** $\frac{12}{13}$

Independent Practice

13. $\frac{2}{13}$; The event can occur in 8 ways. There are 52 outcomes in the sample space. $\frac{8}{52} = \frac{2}{13}$
15. No, it is unlikely that she will have oatmeal for breakfast. **19a.** $\frac{8}{14} = \frac{4}{7}$
b. $8 - 1 = 7$ blue coins and $6 + 3 = 9$ red coins; $\frac{9}{16}$
c. $8 + 3 = 11$ blue coins and $6 - 1 = 5$ red coins; $\frac{5}{16}$ **21.** Yes

LESSON 12.2

Your Turn

7. red: $\frac{1}{3}$, yellow: $\frac{7}{15}$, blue: $\frac{1}{5}$
8. Sample answer: Let 1 and 2 represent red, 3 and 4 represent white, and 5 and 6 represent blue. Toss the cube 50 times to determine the experimental probability for each color. Predict that the next ball released will be the color with the greatest experimental probability.

Guided Practice

1. A: $\frac{7}{20}$, 0.35, 35%; B: $\frac{7}{40}$, 0.175, 17.5%; C: $\frac{11}{40}$, 0.275, 27.5%; D: $\frac{1}{5}$, 0.2, 20%
2. Sample answer: Write "yes" on 6 cards and "no" on 4. Draw a card at random 50 times. Use the number of "yes" cards as her prediction.

Independent Practice

5. Sample answer: Compare the number of wins to the total number of trials; $\frac{1}{6}$.
7. Yes, because it is based on actual data of weather patterns.
9. $\frac{2}{5}$; 16 aces; $\frac{2}{5}$ of 40 is 16.
11. No; there were 40 heads in 100 trials; $P(\text{heads}) = \frac{40}{100}$.

LESSON 12.3

Your Turn

1. $\frac{60}{400} = \frac{3}{20} = 15\%$ **3.** $\frac{12}{75} = \frac{4}{25}$

Guided Practice

1. $\frac{50}{400} = \frac{1}{8}$

Independent Practice

5. $\frac{60}{400} = \frac{3}{20}$ **7.** 12; The total is the product of 3 page-count choices and 4 color choices, which is 12. **13.** No, because coins are fair and the probabilities do not appear to be equally likely.

LESSON 12.4

Your Turn

1. 132 customers **2.** No; about 371 emails out of 12,372 will come back undelivered. The prediction is high. **3.** 84 customers; Yes, 107 > 84, so more customers than normal bought two or more pairs.

Guided Practice

1. 15 times **2.** about 55 days
3. No, about 1,009 candles out of 16,824 will be returned. The prediction is low. **4.** No, about 746 toys out of 24,850 will be defective. The prediction is high. **5.** 39 times; The light-rail's claim is higher than the actual 85%. **6.** 900 students; The college's claim is close to the number actually accepted.

Independent Practice

9. Yes; 6th grade: $\frac{2}{100} = \frac{x}{250} \rightarrow x = 5$; 7th grade: $\frac{4}{100} = \frac{x}{200} \rightarrow x = 8$; 8th grade: $\frac{8}{100} = \frac{x}{150} \rightarrow x = 12$
11. 36 clients; more than would be expected on average **13.** He set up the fraction incorrectly; it should be $\frac{1}{3} = \frac{x}{180}$. **15.** 14,700 on-time flights

MODULE 13

LESSON 13.1

Your Turn

2. $\frac{1}{3}$ **3.** The total number of outcomes in the sample space is the denominator of the formula for theoretical probability.

Guided Practice

1.

	Basket A	Basket B
Total number of outcomes	16	20
Number of red balls	3	4
$P(\text{win}) = \frac{\text{number of red balls}}{\text{total number of outcomes}}$	$\frac{3}{16}$	$\frac{4}{20} = \frac{1}{5}$

2. Basket B **3.** odd, 6; sections, 11 **4.** even, 5; sections, 11
5. $\frac{2}{6} = \frac{1}{3}$ **6.** Sample answer: No, but it might be reasonably close.

Independent Practice

9. $\frac{2}{3}$, 0.67, 67% **11.** $\frac{1}{2}$, 0.50, 50% **13.** $\frac{3}{5}$, 0.60, 60% **15.** 9 represents the ways the event can occur; 13 represents the number of equally likely outcomes.

LESSON 13.2

Your Turn

3. $\frac{4}{12} = \frac{1}{3}$ **4.** $\frac{6}{12} = \frac{1}{2}$ **5.** $\frac{3}{8}$

Guided Practice

1.

	1	2	3	4	5	6
1	1	2	3	4	5	6
2	2	4	6	8	10	12
3	3	6	9	12	15	18
4	4	8	12	16	20	24
5	5	10	15	20	25	30
6	6	12	18	24	30	36

2. $\frac{15}{16}$ **3.** $\frac{23}{36}$

4.

Coin 1: H, T
Coin 2: H T, H T
Coin 3: H T H T, H T H T
List: HHH HHT HTH HTT THH THT TTH TTT

5. 8 **6.** TTT **7.** 3 tails; 1; 8; $\frac{1}{8}$ **8.** 3; HTH, THH; exactly 2 heads; $\frac{3}{8}$

Independent Practice

11. $\frac{1}{2}$ **13.** $\frac{1}{10}$ **15.** $\frac{2}{9}$ **17.** Because there are 3 choices for the first item and 2 for the second, there are $3 \cdot 2 = 6$ possible outcomes. **19.** Neither

LESSON 13.3

Your Turn

1. about 167 times **2.** about 9 times **3.** more likely that he picks a marble of another color **4.** No

Guided Practice

1. $\frac{1}{3}, \frac{1}{3}, \frac{1}{3}, \frac{1}{3}$; 1, 3, 18, 6, 6 **2.** 50 people **3.** brown; $P(\text{hazel}) = \frac{9}{28}$, $P(\text{brown}) = \frac{10}{28}$, $P(\text{blue}) = \frac{7}{28}$, and $P(\text{green}) = \frac{2}{28}$. The event with the greatest probability is choosing a person with brown eyes.

Independent Practice

5. 15 white or gray marbles **7.** It is more likely that she draws 2 red cards. **9.** 500 times **11.** 45 days **17.** Yes, but only theoretically because in reality, nothing can occur 0.5 time.

LESSON 13.4

Guided Practice

1. years with a drought; years without a drought; 4

2.

Trial	Numbers generated	Drought years
1	10, 3, 5, 1	2
2	10, 4, 6, 5	0
3	3, 2, 10, 3	3
4	2, 10, 4, 4	1
5	7, 3, 6, 3	2

Trial	Numbers generated	Drought years
6	8, 4, 8, 5	0
7	6, 2, 2, 8	2
8	6, 5, 2, 4	1
9	2, 2, 3, 2	4
10	6, 3, 1, 5	2

3. 80%

Independent Practice

5. 1 trial **7.** 20%

UNIT 7 Selected Answers

MODULE 14

LESSON 14.1

Your Turn

1. $0.\overline{45}$ **2.** 0.125 **3.** $2.\overline{3}$ **4.** $\frac{3}{25}$ **5.** $\frac{19}{33}$

6. $1\frac{2}{5}$ **7.** $x = \pm 14$ **8.** $x = \pm\frac{3}{16}$
9. $x = 8$ **10.** $x = \frac{4}{7}$

Guided Practice

1. 0.4 **2.** $0.\overline{8}$ **3.** 3.75 **4.** 0.7
5. 2.375 **6.** $0.8\overline{3}$ **7.** $\frac{27}{40}$ **8.** $5\frac{3}{5}$ **9.** $\frac{11}{25}$
10. $4.\overline{4}$; $0.\overline{4}$; 9; 4; $\frac{4}{9}$ **11.** $26.\overline{26}$; $0.\overline{26}$; 99; 26; $\frac{26}{99}$ **12.** $325.\overline{325}$; $0.\overline{325}$; 999; 325; $\frac{325}{999}$ **13.** 17; 4.1 **14.** $\frac{25}{289}$; $\pm\frac{5}{17}$
15. 216; 6 **16.** 2.2 **17.** 1.7
18. 3.2

Independent Practice

21. $0.1\overline{6}$ **23.** $98.\overline{6}$
25. $26\frac{1}{5}$ mi **27.** $\frac{101}{200}$ cent
29. $x = \pm\sqrt{14} \approx \pm 3.7$
31. $x = \pm\sqrt{144} = \pm 12$ **33.** His estimate is low because 15 is very close to 16, so $\sqrt{15}$ is very close to $\sqrt{16}$, or 4. A better estimate would be 3.8 or 3.9.
35. 3 feet
37. $\sqrt{\frac{4}{25}} = \frac{2}{5} = \frac{\sqrt{4}}{\sqrt{25}}$; $\sqrt{\frac{16}{81}} = \frac{4}{9} = \frac{\sqrt{16}}{\sqrt{81}}$; $\sqrt{\frac{36}{49}} = \frac{6}{7} = \frac{\sqrt{36}}{\sqrt{49}}$; $\frac{\sqrt{a}}{\sqrt{b}} = \sqrt{\frac{a}{b}}$; $\sqrt{a}\cdot\sqrt{b} = \sqrt{a \cdot b}$

LESSON 14.2

Your Turn

1. rational, real **2.** irrational, real **3.** False. Every integer is a rational number, but not every rational number is an integer. Rational numbers such as $\frac{3}{5}$ and $-\frac{5}{2}$ are not integers.
4. False. Real numbers are either rational or irrational numbers. Integers are rational numbers, so no integers are irrational numbers. **5.** Real numbers; the amount can be any number greater than 0. **6.** Rational numbers; a person's weight can be a decimal such as 83.5 pounds.

Guided Practice

1. rational, real **2.** whole, integer, rational, real **3.** irrational, real **4.** rational, real **5.** whole, integer, rational, real **6.** integer, rational, real **7.** rational, real **8.** integer, rational, real **9.** True. Whole numbers are a subset of the set of rational numbers and can be written as a ratio of the whole number to 1. **10.** True. Whole numbers are rational numbers. **11.** Integers; the change can be a whole dollar amount and can be positive, negative, or zero. **12.** Rational numbers; the ruler is marked every $\frac{1}{16}$th inch.

Independent Practice

15. whole, integer, rational, real **17.** rational, real **19.** whole, integer, rational, real **21.** Integers; the scores are counting numbers, their opposites, and zero.
23. Whole; the diameter is $\frac{\pi}{\pi} =$ 1 mile. **25.** rational number
27. Sample answer: If the calculator shows a terminating decimal, the number is rational. Otherwise, you cannot tell because you see only a few digits.

LESSON 14.3

Your Turn

3. $>$ **4.** $<$ **5.** $\sqrt{3}$, $\sqrt{5}$, 2.5

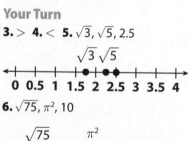

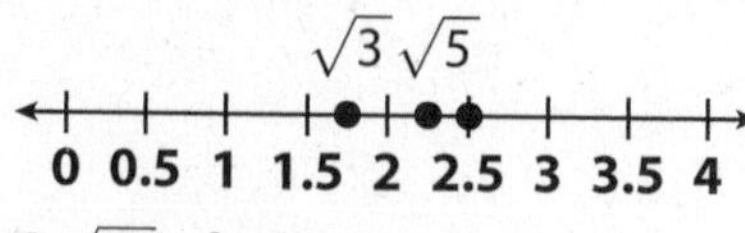

6. $\sqrt{75}$, π^2, 10

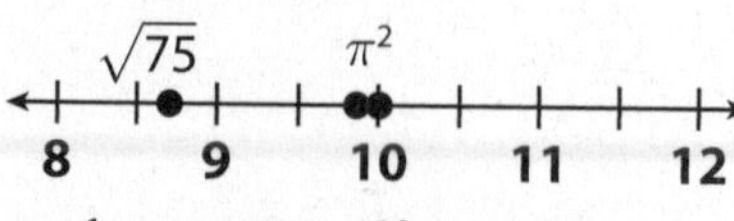

7. $3\frac{1}{2}$ mi, $3.\overline{45}$ mi, $\frac{10}{3}$ mi, $\sqrt{10}$ mi

Guided Practice

1. $<$ **2.** $>$ **3.** $<$ **4.** $<$ **5.** $>$
6. $<$ **7.** $>$ **8.** $>$ **9.** 1.7; 1.8; 1.75; 6.28; 1.5; $\sqrt{3}$; 2π **10.** $(1 + \frac{\pi}{2})$ km, 2.5 km, $\frac{12}{5}$ km, $(\sqrt{17} - 2)$ km

Independent Practice

13. π, $\sqrt{10}$, 3.5 **15.** -3.75, $\frac{9}{4}$, $\sqrt{8}$, 3
17a. $\sqrt{60} \approx 7.75$, $\frac{58}{8} = 7.25$, $7.\overline{3} \approx 7.33$, $7\frac{3}{5} = 7.60$, so the average is 7.4825 km. **b.** They are nearly identical. $\sqrt{56}$ is approximately 7.4833…
19. Sample answer: $\sqrt{31}$
21a. between $\sqrt{7} \approx 2.65$ and $\sqrt{8} \approx 2.83$ **b.** between $\sqrt{9} = 3$ and $\sqrt{10} \approx 3.16$ **23.** 2; rational numbers can have the same location, and irrational numbers can have the same location, but they cannot share a location.

MODULE 15

LESSON 15.1

Your Turn

10. 5 **11.** $63\frac{15}{16}$

Guided Practice

1. $\frac{1}{8}$ **2.** $\frac{1}{36}$ **3.** 1 **4.** 100 **5.** 625
6. $\frac{1}{32}$ **7.** $\frac{1}{1024}$ **8.** 1 **9.** $\frac{1}{1331}$ **10.** 4^3
11. $2^2 \cdot 2^3 = 2^5$ **12.** 6^2
13. $8^{12-9} = 8^3$ **14.** 5^{12} **15.** 7^{13}
16. $6^{2\cdot 4} = 6^8$ **17.** $8^3 \cdot 12^3$ **18.** $\frac{1}{6}$
19. 10,000 **20.** 1168 **21.** 343
22. When multiplying powers with the same base, you add the exponents. When dividing powers with the same base, you subtract the exponents. When raising a product to a power, you raise each factor to that power. When raising a power to a power, you multiply the exponents.

Independent Practice

23. 125 **25.** 1125 **27.** 36
29. 69 **31.** $\frac{1}{100}$ **33.** 216
37. The exponents cannot be

added because the bases are not the same. **39.** Earth to Neptune; 22^3, or 10,648, times greater. **41.** −3 **43.** 19 **45.** 10^3 kg, or 1000 kg **47.** Both expressions equal x^5, so $x^7 \cdot x^{-2} = \frac{x^7}{x^2}$. When multiplying powers with the same base, you add exponents; $7 + (-2) = 5$. When dividing powers with the same base, you subtract exponents; $7 - 2 = 5$. In cases like this, $x^n \cdot x^{-m} = \frac{x^n}{x^m}$. **49.** 3^6; 3^3

LESSON 15.2

Your Turn

3. 6.4×10^3 **4.** 5.7×10^{11} **5.** 9.461×10^{12} km **8.** 7,034,000,000 **9.** 236,000 **10.** 5,000,000 g

Guided Practice

1. 5.8927×10^4 **2.** 1.304×10^9 **3.** 6.73×10^6 **4.** 1.33×10^4 **5.** 9.77×10^{22} **6.** 3.84×10^5 **7.** 400,000 **8.** 1,849,900,000 **9.** 6410 **10.** 84,560,000 **11.** 800,000 **12.** 90,000,000,000 **13.** 54,000 s **14.** 7,600,000 cans

Independent Practice

17. 2.2×10^5 lb **19.** 4×10^4 lb **21.** 5×10^4 lb **23.** $108\frac{1}{3}$ hours or 108 hours and 20 minutes **25.** 4.6×10^3 lb **27a.** None of the girls has the correct answer. **b.** Polly and Samantha have the decimal in the wrong place; Esther miscounted the number of places the decimal moved. **29.** The speed of a car because it is likely to be less than 100. **31.** Is the first factor greater than 1 and less than 10? Is the second factor a power of 10?

LESSON 15.3

Your Turn

4. 8.29×10^{-5} **5.** 3.02×10^{-7} **6.** 7×10^{-6} m **9.** 0.000001045 **10.** 0.000099 **11.** 0.01 m

Guided Practice

1. 4.87×10^{-4} **2.** 2.8×10^{-5} **3.** 5.9×10^{-5} **4.** 4.17×10^{-2} **5.** 2×10^{-5} **6.** 1.5×10^{-5} **7.** 0.00002 **8.** 0.000003582 **9.** 0.00083 **10.** 0.0297 **11.** 0.0000906 **12.** 0.00004 **13.** 1×10^{-4} **14.** 0.0000000000000000000000017

Independent Practice

17. 1.3×10^{-3} cm **19.** 4.5×10^{-3} cm **21.** 8×10^{-4} cm **23.** 7 cm = 0.07 m, 7 cm = 7×10^0 cm; 0.07 m = 7×10^{-2} m The first factors are the same; the exponents differ by 2. **25.** If the exponent on 10 is nonnegative, the number is greater than or equal to 1. **27.** Negative, because a ladybug would weigh less than 1 ounce. **29.** 0.000000000125 **31.** 71,490,000 **33.** 3,397,000 **35.** 5.85×10^{-3} m, 1.5×10^{-2} m, 2.3×10^{-2} m, 9.6×10^{-1} m, 1.2×10^2 m **37.** The result will be greater than the number with the positive exponent because the divisor is less than 1.

LESSON 15.4

Your Turn

1. 7.62×10^7 more people **2.** 8.928×10^8 miles **3.** 3.14×10^2 minutes **4.** 7.5E5 **5.** 3E–7 **6.** 2.7E13 **7.** 4.5×10^{-1} **8.** 5.6×10^{12} **9.** 6.98×10^{-8}

Guided Practice

1. 0.225; 10^6; 0.225; 2.8; 7.225×10^6 **2.** 0.10; 10^3; 8.5; 5.3; 0.10; 3.1×10^3 **3.** 5×10^2 **4.** 5.9381×10^5 **5.** 1.206×10^{22} **6.** 1.73×10^8 **7.** 1.69×10^{19} **8.** 2×10^7 **9.** 3.6E11 **10.** 7.25E–5 **11.** 8E–1 **12.** 7.6×10^{-4} **13.** 1.2×10^{16} **14.** 9×10^1

Independent Practice

17. about 2000 as many **19.** 5.025×10^7 tons **21.** Plastics **23.** about 7 people per square mile **25.** 13 years, 3 months, 22.5 days **27.** about $\$3 \times 10^4$, or \$30,000 per person **29.** The student is off by a power of 10. The correct product is 40×10^{15}, or 4.0×10^{16}.

Selected Answers

UNIT 8 Selected Answers

LESSON 16.1

Your Turn

3. $y = 15x$ **4.** 6 miles hiked in 5 hours **5.** $y = \frac{6}{5}x$

Guided Practice

1. is **2.** constant of proportionality **3a.** The pairs (weeks, days) are (2, 14), (4, 28), (8, 56), (10, 70). **b.** the time in weeks; the time in days; $y = 7x$ **4.** The pairs (oxygen atoms, hydrogen atoms) are (5, 10), (17, 34), (120, 240); $y = 2x$ **5.** $y = 30x$

Independent Practice

7. No; the ratios of the numbers in each column are not equal.
9a. Sample answer: The account had a balance of $100 to begin with. **b.** Sample answer: Have Ralph open the account with no money to begin with and then put $20 in every month. **11.** $y = 105$
13a. The pairs (time, distance) are (1, 10), (2, 20), (3, 30), (4, 40), (5, 50).
b. $y = 10x$, where y is the distance in inches and x is the time in minutes. **c.** 8.5 minutes **15.** For $S = 1, P = 4$ and $A = 1$; For $S = 2, P = 8$ and $A = 4$; For $S = 3, P = 12$ and $A = 9$; For $S = 4, P = 16$ and $A = 16$; For $S = 5, P = 20$ and $A = 25$. **a.** Yes. The ratio of the perimeter of a square to its side length is always 4. **b.** No. The ratio of the area of a square to its side length is not constant.

LESSON 16.2

Your Turn

1. 36, 13, −10; variable **4.** +3; +4; $\frac{3}{4}$

Guided Practice

1. constant **2.** variable **3.** variable **4.** constant **5.** 200; 1; 200; 1; 200 **6.** 200 ft per min **7.** −2 **8.** $\frac{3}{2}$

Independent Practice

11. 15 miles per hour
13a. 1 gallon every 5 minutes, or 0.2 gal/min **b.** 25 minutes
15.

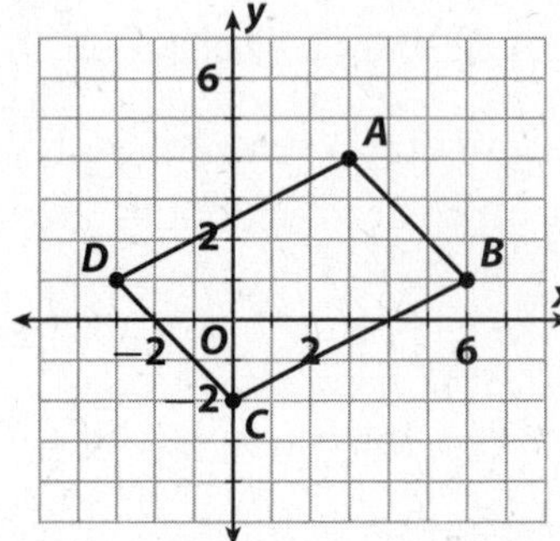

a. slope $\overline{AB} = -1$; slope $\overline{BC} = \frac{1}{2}$; slope $\overline{CD} = -1$; slope $\overline{DA} = \frac{1}{2}$
b. The slopes of the opposite sides are the same. **c.** Yes; opposite sides still have the same slope. **17.** Sample answer: One line has a positive slope and one has a negative slope. The lines are equally steep, but one slants upward left to right and the other slants downward left to right. The lines cross at the origin.

LESSON 16.3

Your Turn

2. His unit rate and the slope of a graph of the ride both equal $\frac{2}{3}$ mi/min.

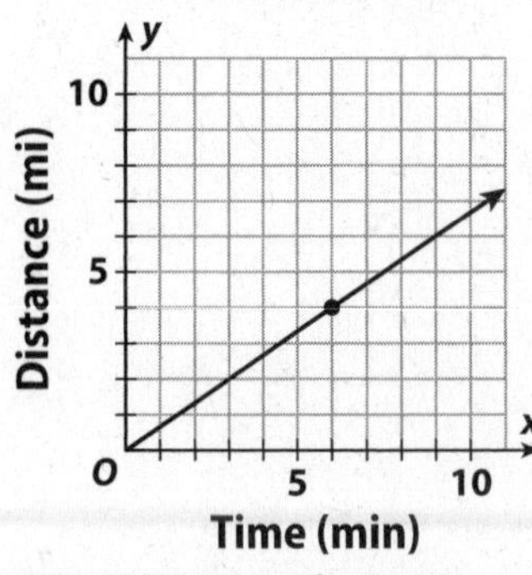

4. A: 375, 375 mi/h; B: 425, 425 mi/h; B is flying faster.

Guided Practice

1. slope = unit rate = $\frac{5}{6}$ mi/h
2. slope = unit rate = $\frac{5}{4}$ mi/h
3. Clark is faster. From the equation, Henry's rate is equal to 0.5, or $\frac{1}{2}$ mile per hour. Clark's rate is the slope of the line, which is $\frac{3}{2}$, or 1.5 miles per hour.
4. $y = 15x$ **5.** $y = \frac{3}{8}x$

Independent Practice

7a. The pairs (time, distance) are (4, 3), (8, 6), (12, 9), (16, 12), (20, 15).
b.

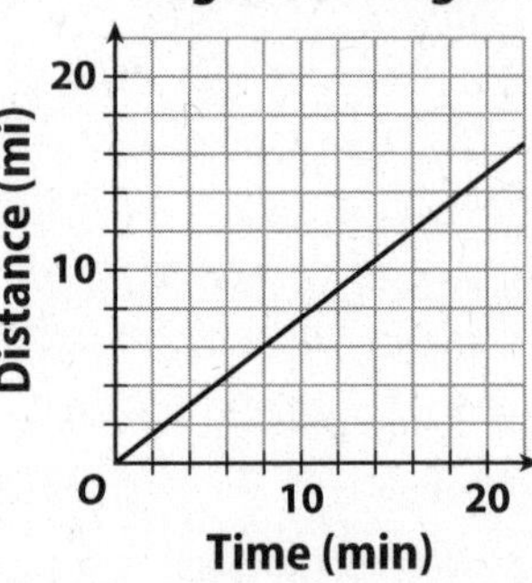

c. $\frac{3}{4}$; The unit rate of migration of the goose and the slope of the graph both equal $\frac{3}{4}$ mi/min.
9a. Machine 1: slope = unit rate = $\frac{0.6}{1} = 0.6$ gal/s; Machine 2: slope = unit rate = $\frac{3}{4} = 0.75$ gal/s
b. Machine 2 is working at a faster rate since $0.75 > 0.6$. **11.** slope = unit rate = 4.75. If the graph of a proportional relationship passes through the point $(1, r)$, then r equals the slope and the unit rate, which is $4.75/min. **13.** 243 gallons; Sample answer: The unit rate is $\frac{36}{2} = 18$ gal/min. So, $1\frac{1}{2}$ min after 12 min, an additional $18 \times 1\frac{1}{2} = 27$ gal will be pumped in. The total is $216 + 27 = 243$ gal.

LESSON 17.1

Your Turn

1. Sample answer: (2, 20), (3, 32), (4, 44), (5, 56) **3.** (−1, 3), (0, 1), (1, −1), (2, −3)

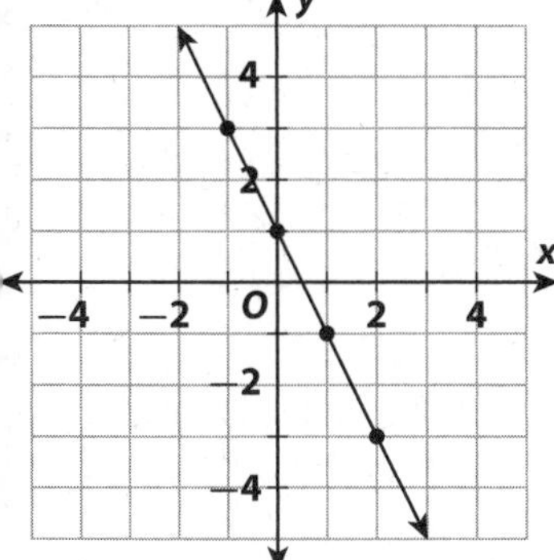

Guided Practice

1. (−2,1), (−1, 3), (0, 5), (1, 7), (2, 9) **2.** (−8, −8), (0, −5), (8, −2), (16, 1), (24, 4) **3.** Undefined, 3.5, 2.75, 2.5, 2.375; The ratio $\frac{y}{x}$ is not constant. **4.** The graph is a line, but it does not pass through the origin. **5.** (−2, −3), (−1, −2), (0, −1), (1, 0), (2, 1)

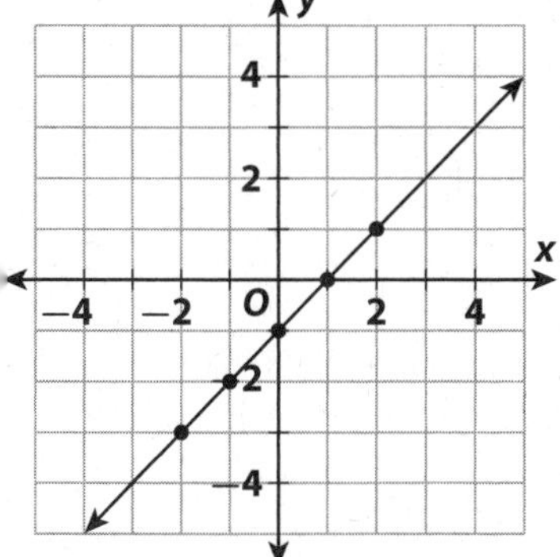

Independent Practice

7. Set of unconnected points; you cannot buy a fractional part of a lunch. **9a.** Sample answer: For (*x*, *y*) where *x* is number of years renewed and *y* is total cost in dollars: (0, 12), (1, 20), (2, 28), (3, 36), (4, 44)

b.

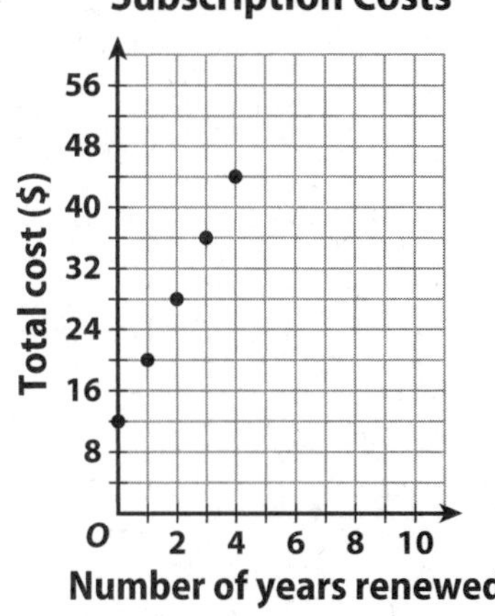

c. The graph does not include the origin. Also, the ratio of the total cost and number of years is not constant. **d.** No; the number of years must be a whole number, so total cost goes up in \$8 increments. **11.** Sample answer: In a table, the ratios $\frac{y}{x}$ will not be equal; a graph will not pass through the origin; an equation will be in the form $y = mx + b$, where $b \neq 0$. **13.** At most one. A line representing a proportional relationship must pass through the origin. A line parallel to it cannot also pass through the origin.

LESSON 17.2

Your Turn

1. $m = 5; b = 12$ **2.** $m = 7; b = 1$

Guided Practice

1. −2; 1 **2.** 5; −15 **3.** $\frac{3}{2}$; −2 **4.** −3; 9 **5.** 3; 1 **6.** −4; 140

Independent Practice

9a. \$5 to park; \$12 per hour **b.** \$23.50; (3.5 hours × \$12 per hour + \$5) ÷ 2 = \$23.50 **11.** Rate of change is constant from 1 to 2 to 3, but not from 3 to 4. **13.** Express the slope *m* between a random point (*x*, *y*) on the line and the point (0, *b*) where the line crosses the *y*-axis. Then solve the equation for *y*.

15. After parking 61 cars; John earns a fixed weekly salary of \$300 plus \$5 for each car he parks. He earns the same in fees as his fixed salary for parking 300 ÷ 5 = 60 cars.

LESSON 17.3

Your Turn

2.

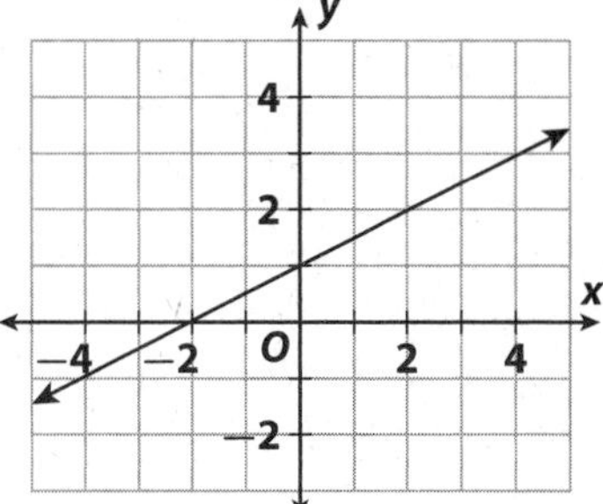

3.

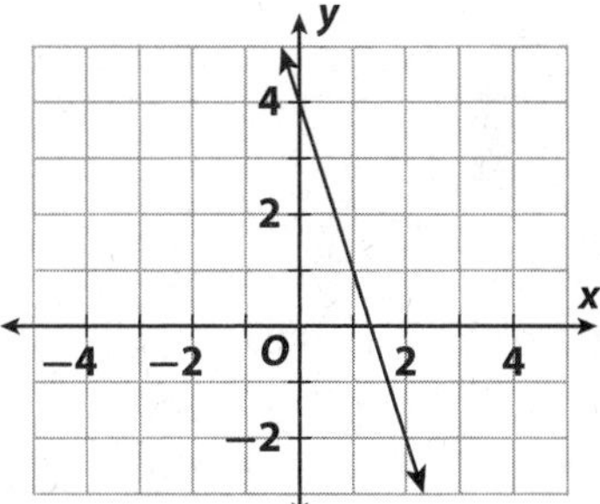

4.

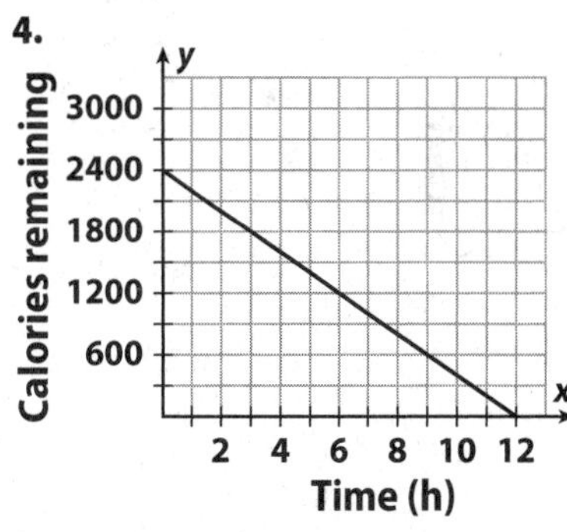

5. The new graph has the same *y*-intercept but a slope of −200 instead of −300.
6. The calories left to burn will decrease more slowly with each hour of exercise, so it will take longer for Ken to meet his goal.
7. The *y*-intercept would not change, but the slope would become −600, which is much steeper. The line would intersect the *x*-axis when $x = 4$ hours.

UNIT 8 Selected Answers *(cont'd)*

Guided Practice

1. $\frac{1}{2}$; -3

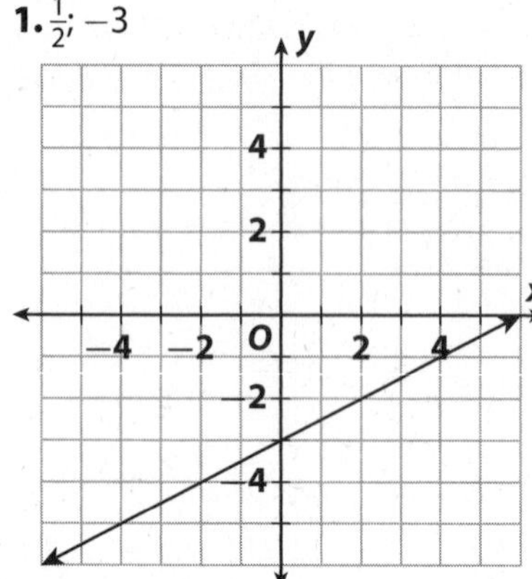

2. -3; 2

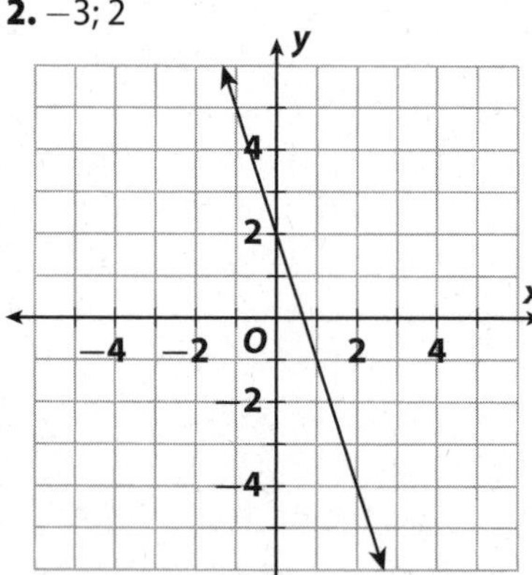

3a. Slope = 4; *y*-intercept = 2; you start with 2 cards and add 4 cards each week.

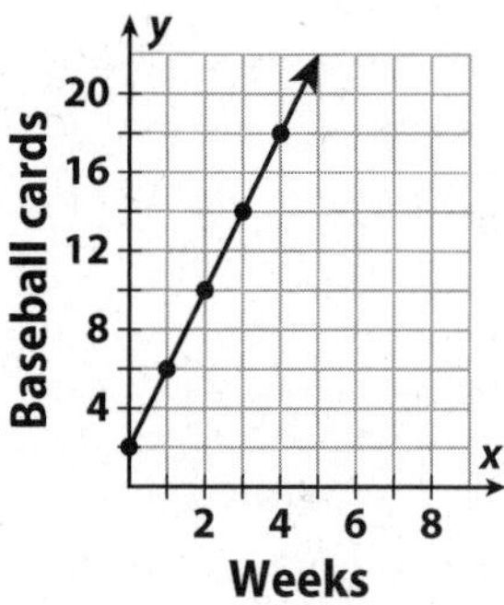

b. The points with coordinates that are not whole numbers; you will not buy part of a baseball card and you are buying only once a week.

Independent Practice

5a.

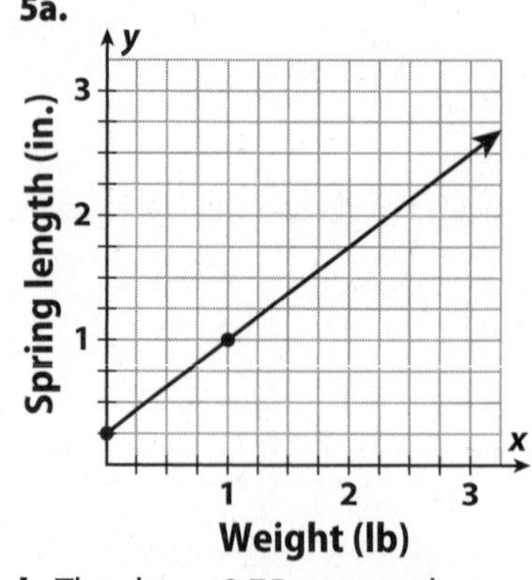

b. The slope, 0.75, means that the spring stretches by 0.75 inch with each additional pound of weight. The *y*-intercept, 0.25, is the unstretched length of the spring in inches. **c.** 1.75 inches; no; the length with a 4-pound weight is 3.25 in., not 3.5 in.
7. (0, 8), (1, 7), (2, 6), (3, 5) **9.** (0, −3), (1, −1.5), (2, 0), (3, 1.5) **11.** (0, −5), (3, −3), (6, −1), (9, 1) **13a.** Yes; since the horizontal and vertical gridlines each represent 25 units, moving up 3 gridlines and right 1 gridline represents a slope of $\frac{75}{25}$, or 3. **b.** $m = 3$ so \$3 is the charge per visit; $b = 50$ so the membership fee is \$50.

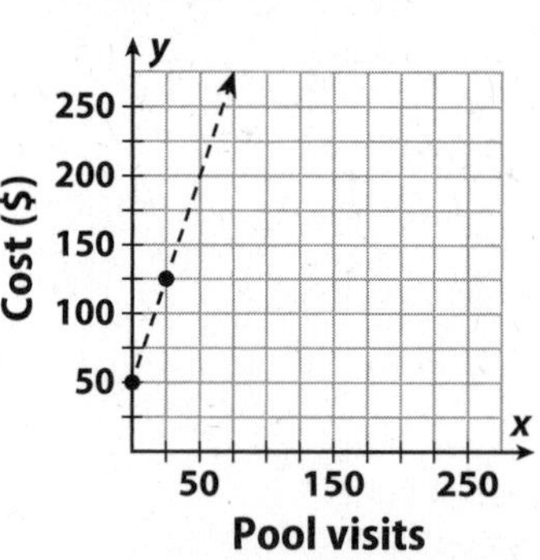

c. 50 visits **15.** Yes; plot the point and use the slope to find a second point. Then draw a line through the two points.

LESSON 17.4

Your Turn

1. nonproportional
2. proportional
5. proportional
6. nonproportional
7. nonproportional
8. nonproportional
9. nonproportional
10. proportional
11. Test-Prep Center A's charges are proportional, but B's are not. Center B offers a coupon for an initial credit, but its hourly rate, \$25, is higher than Center A's hourly rate of \$20. So, Center B will cost more in the long run.

Guided Practice

1. Proportional; the line includes the origin. **2.** Nonproportional; the line does not include the origin. **3.** Nonproportional; when the equation is written in the form $y = mx + b$, the value of b is not 0. **4.** Proportional; when the equation is written in the form $y = mx + b$, the value of b is 0. **5.** Proportional; the quotient of y and x is constant, 4, for every number pair. **6.** No; the quotient of y and x is not constant for every number pair. **7.** Sample answer: The rating is proportional to the number of households watching: the quotient of the rating and the number of households is always 0.0000008.

Independent Practice

9a. Nonproportional; the graph does not pass through the origin, so $b \neq 0$. **b.** $m = 0.5$, $b = 10$; each cup of sports drink weighs a half pound. The empty cooler weighs 10 pounds. **11.** Proportional; this equation has the form $y = mx + b$, where $b = 0$.
15a. No; from Equation B, the *y*-intercept is 273.15, not 0, so the graph does not include the origin. From Table C, the quotient of K and C is not constant.
b. No; Equation A is in the form $y = mx + b$, with F instead of y and C instead of x. The value of b is 32, not 0, so the relationship is not proportional.

LESSON 18.1

Your Turn

2. 64 weeks

Guided Practice

1. $x = -4$ **2.** $x = 5$ **3.** $b = 9$ **4.** $h = -4$ **5.** $x = -2$ **6.** $a = 6$ **7.** $n = 8$ **8.** $p = 3$ **9.** 4 personal training sessions **10.** 16 hours **11.** Sample answer: Xavier has $100 in his lunch account. He spends $6 for lunch each day. Zack has $160 in his lunch account. He spends $10 each day. After how many days will the boys have the same amount in their accounts?

Independent Practice

13a. $12 + 5x = 18 + 3x; x = 3;$ 3 hours **b.** Darlene's Dog Sitting; the cost would be $33, as opposed to $37 at Derrick's Dog Sitting. **15.** $3x - 2 = x + 10; x = 6$ **17.** $8x - 20 = x + 15; x = 5$ **19.** $9x + 3 = 7x + 19; x = 8$; 75 chairs **21.** $3x + 6 = 5x + 2; x = 2$; 6 laps

LESSON 18.2

Your Turn

3. $k = -35$ **4.** $y = -\frac{9}{16}$ **5.** $1.9x = 1.3x + 37.44$; 62.4 lb

Guided Practice

1a. $60 + 50.45x = 57.95x$ **b.** $x = 8$; 8 months **2.** $n = 28$ **3.** $b = 60$ **4.** $m = 33$ **5.** $t = -0.8$ **6.** $w = 12$ **7.** $p = -2$

Independent Practice

11. 60 tiles **13a.** 100 mi **b.** $80 **17.** $C = 1.8C + 32$; $-40°F = -40°C$

LESSON 18.3

Your Turn

1. $y = -1$ **2.** $x = 6$ **3.** $b = -4$ **4.** $t = 7$ **5.** $46,000

Guided Practice

1. 4; 32; 4; 28; 6; 28; 6; 6; 6; 6; 6; 6; $x = 1$ **2.** 3; 3; 2; −15; 18; 2; −60; +; 15; −13; −78; −13; −78; −13; −13; $x = 6$ **3.** $x = 3$ **4.** $x = 7$ **5.** $x = -1$ **6.** $x = 3$ **7.** $x = 9$ **8.** $x = -2$ **9.** $x = 10$ **10.** $x = -8$ **11.** $0.12(x + 3{,}000) = 4{,}200$; $32,000

Independent Practice

13. a. $x + 14$ **b.** Joey's age in 5 years: $x + 5$; Martina's age in 5 years: $x + 19$ **c.** $3(x + 5) = x + 19$ **d.** Joey: 2 years old; Martina: 16 years old
15. It is not necessary. In this case, distributing the fractions directly results in whole number coefficients and constants.
17. Table first row: 0.25, $0.25x$; table second row: $100 - x$, 0.15, $0.15(100 - x)$; table third row: 0.19, 19 **a.** The milliliters of acid in the 25% solution plus the milliliters of acid in the 15% solution equals the milliliters of acid in the mixture. **b.** $0.25x + 0.15(100 - x) = 19$ **c.** The chemist used 40 ml of the 25% solution and 60 ml of the 15% solution.
19. Use the Distributive Property to distribute both 3 and 2 inside the square parentheses on the left side. Combine like terms inside the square parentheses. Then use the Distributive Property again to distribute 5. Combine like terms on the left side and use inverse operations to solve the equation. $x = 1$

LESSON 18.4

Your Turn

2. $x = 3$; one solution
3. $7 = 7$; infinitely many solutions **4.** $-9 = 5$; no solution
5. You started with a false statement and performed balanced operations on both sides of the equation. This does not change the true or false nature of the original statement.
6. Sample answer: 6 **7.** 4

Guided Practice

1. $x = 3$; true
2. $-4 = 1$; false
3. none
4. Any value of x will result in a true statement; infinitely many solutions
5. One solution
6. Infinitely many solutions
7. true; same variable; same constant; like; 10; $10 + x$; $10 + x + 5$; $15 + x = 15 + x$

Independent Practice

11. $0 = 0$; infinitely many solutions
13. $2 = 6$; no solution **15.** $x + 1$
17a. Yes; because the perimeters are equal, you get the equation $(2x - 2) + (x + 1) + x + (x + 1) = (2x - 9) + (x + 1) + (x + 8) + x$, or $5x = 5x$. Since $5x = 5x$ is a true statement, there are an infinite number of values for x.
b. The condition was that the two perimeters are to be equal. However, a specific number was not given, so there are an infinite number of possible perimeters.
c. 12; Sample answer: I used the trapezoid and wrote the equation $(2x - 2) + (x + 1) + x + (x + 1) = 60$. Solving this gives $x = 12$.
19. No; setting the expressions equal to each other and solving gives $100 + 35x = 50 + 35x$, or $100 = 50$, which is false.
21. Matt is incorrect. He applied the Distributive Property to the right side incorrectly. Correctly simplified, the equation is $0 = -7$, which is false, meaning no solution.

UNIT 9 Selected Answers

MODULE 19

LESSON 19.1

Your Turn

4.

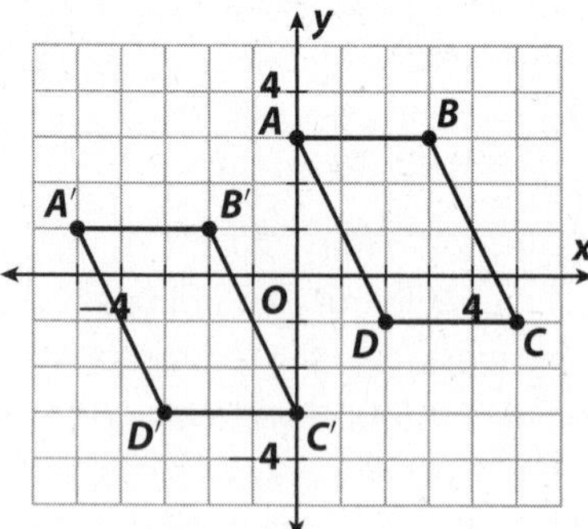

Guided Practice

1. transformation **2.** preimage; image **3.** The orientation will be the same. **4.** They are congruent.

5.

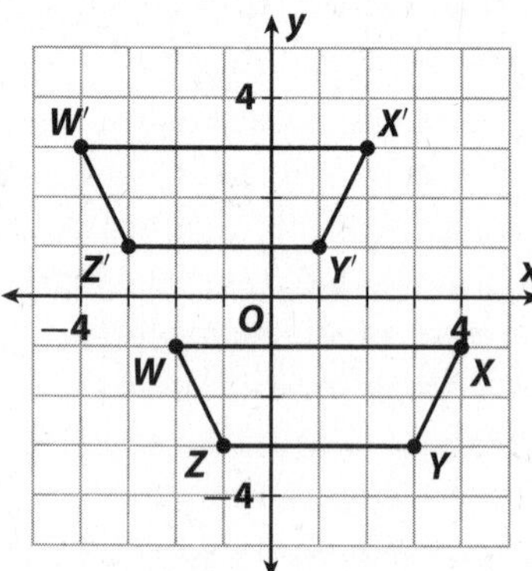

Independent Practice

7a.

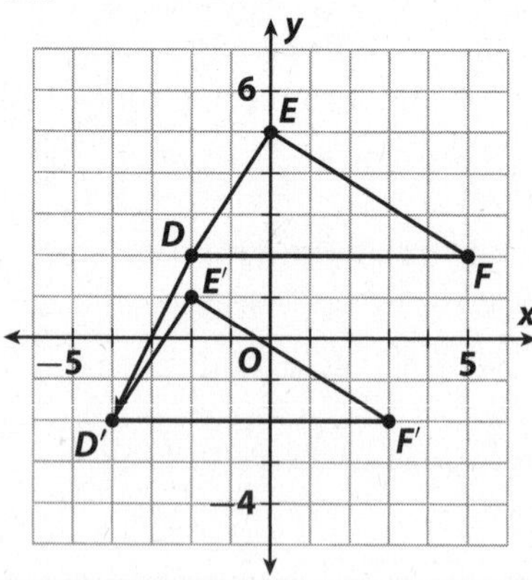

b. The translation moved the triangle 2 units to the left and 4 units down. **c.** They are congruent.

9.

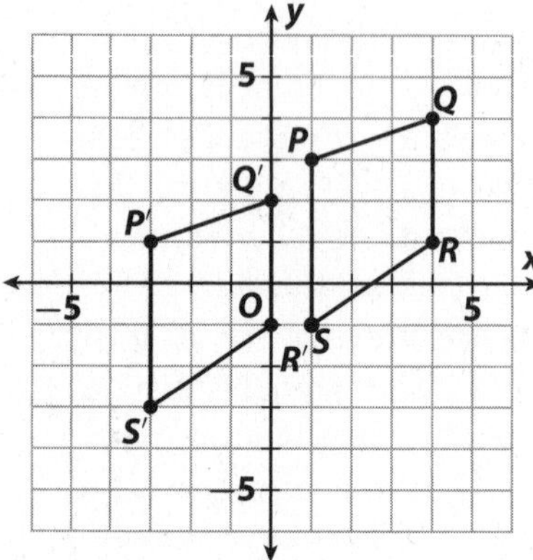

11. The hot air balloon was translated 4 units to the right and 5 units up.

13a.–c.

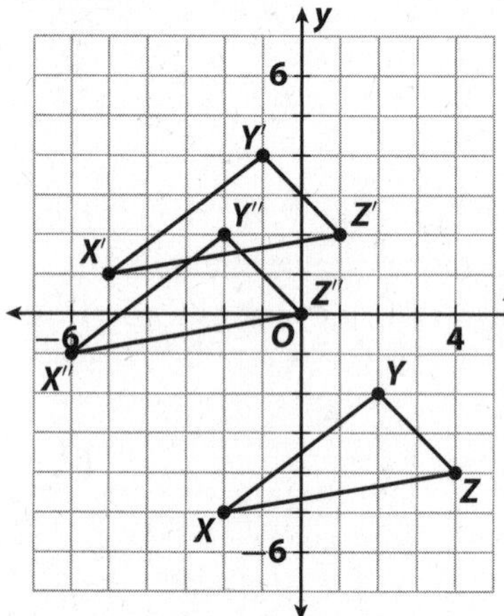

d. The original triangle was translated 4 units up and 4 units to the left.

LESSON 19.2

Your Turn

4.

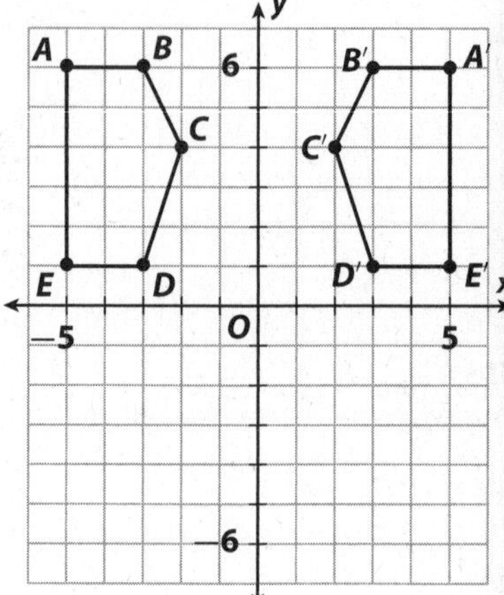

Guided Practice

1. line of reflection

2a.

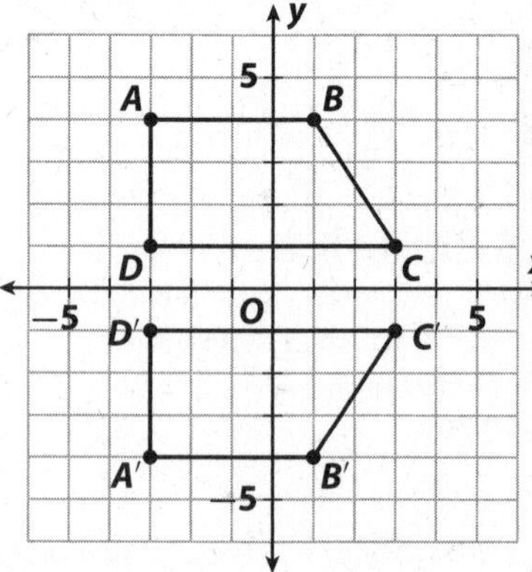

b. They are congruent. **c.** The orientation would be reversed horizontally: the figure from left to right in the preimage would match the figure from right to left in the image.

Independent Practice

5. *C* and *D* **7.** Since each triangle is either a reflection or translation of triangle *C*, they are all congruent. **9.** Yes; if the point lies on the line of reflection, then the image and the preimage will be the same point.

11a.–c.

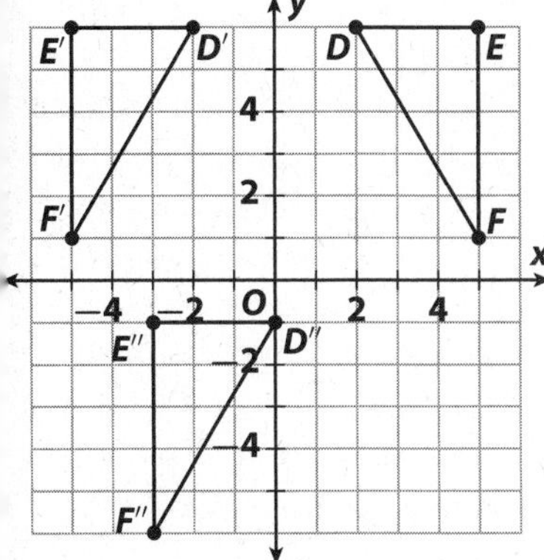

d. Sample answer: Translate triangle *DEF* 7 units down and 2 units to the left. Then reflect the image across the *y*-axis.

LESSON 19.3

Your Turn

6.–7.

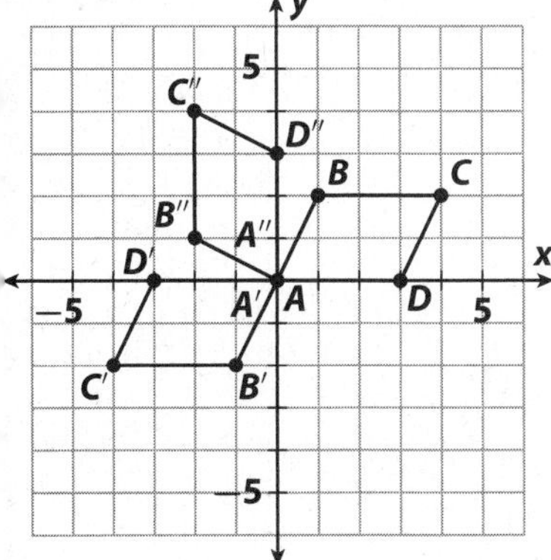

8. (2, −4)

Guided Practice

1. point **2.** Each leg in the preimage is perpendicular to its corresponding leg in the image. **3.** Yes, the figures are congruent.

4.

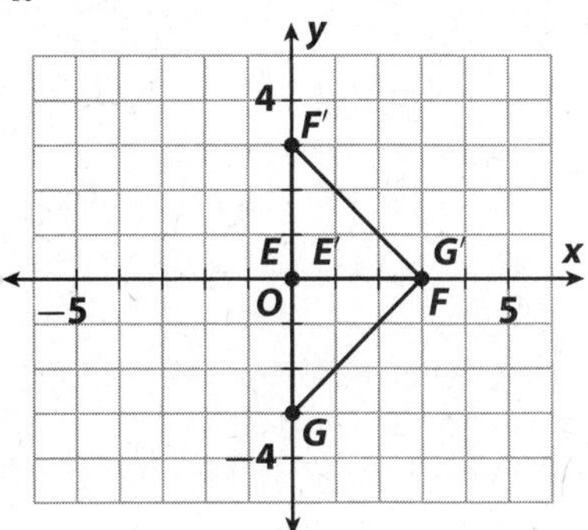

5.

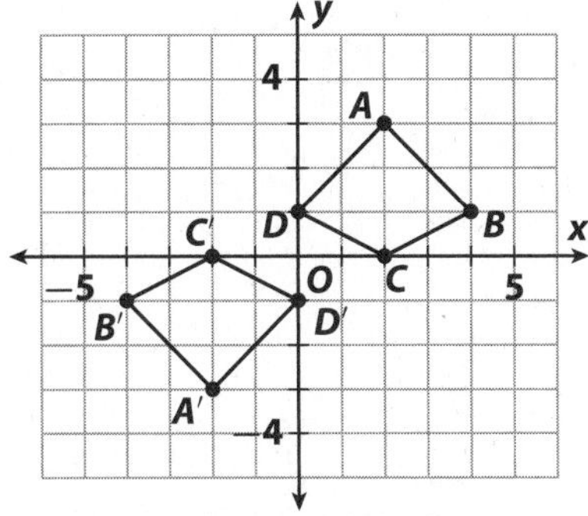

Independent Practice

7a. *ABC* was rotated 90° counterclockwise about the origin. **b.** *A*′ (3, 1); *B*′ (2, 3); *C*′ (−1, 4) **9.** 180° rotation about the origin **11.** 90° clockwise **13.** 90° clockwise **15.**

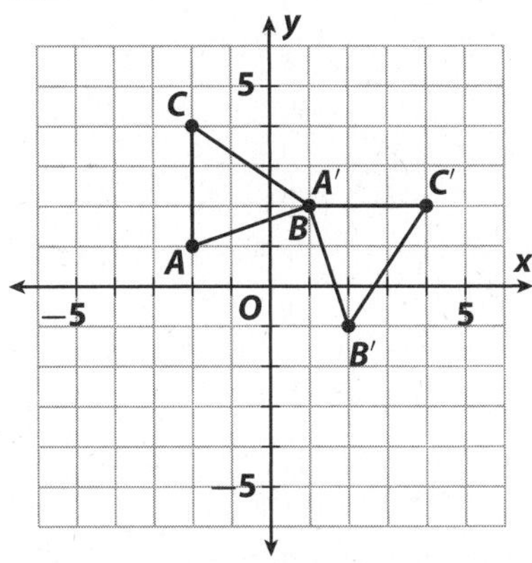

17. 2 times; 1 time; 4 times
19. If *A* is at the origin, then so is *A*′ for any rotation about the origin. Otherwise, *A*′ is on the *x*-axis for 90° and 270° rotations and on the *y*-axis for a 180° rotation.

LESSON 19.4

Your Turn

1. (−6, −5), (−6, 0), (−3, −5), and (−3, 0); the rectangle is translated 6 units to the left and 3 units down. **2.** *A*′(−2, −6), *B*′(0, −5), and *C*′(3, 1) **4.** *J*′(4, −2), *K*′(−5, 1), and *L*′(−2, 2)

Guided Practice

1. *X*′(3, −2), *Y*′(5, 0), and *Z*′(7, −6)

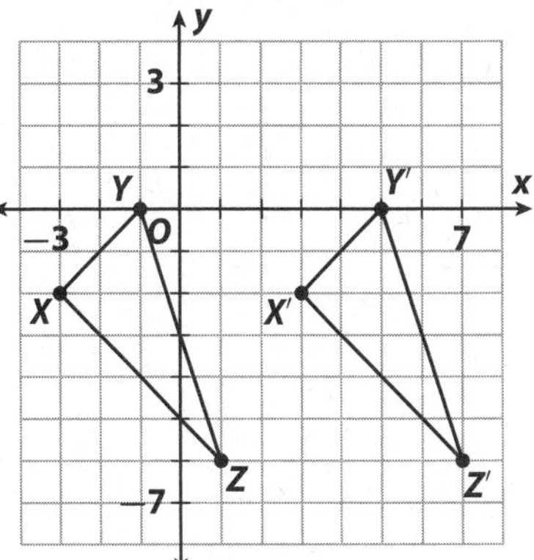

2. The *x*-coordinate remains the same, while the *y*-coordinate changes sign. **3.** The triangle is rotated 90° clockwise about the origin.

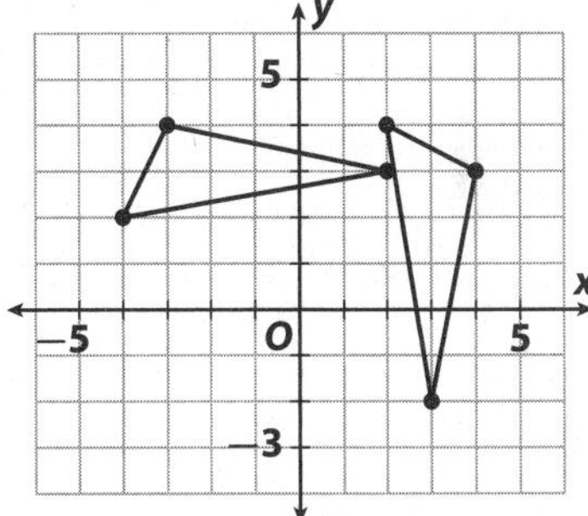

Independent Practice

5. $(x, y) \rightarrow (x - 2, y - 5)$; translation of 2 units to the left and 5 units down **7.** $(x, y) \rightarrow (x - 3.2, y + 1)$; *Y*′(4.3, 6), *Z*′(4.8, 5)
9. The rectangle is translated 2 units to the left and 4 units down.

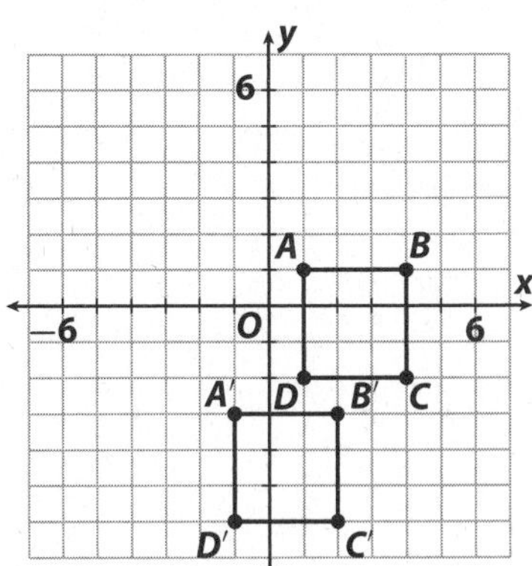

11. $(x, y) \rightarrow (x + 0.5, y - 0.25)$
13a. (−5, −5); *x* and *y* are equal, so switching *x* and *y* has no effect on the coordinates. **b.** $y = x$ **c.** The triangle is reflected across the line $y = x$.

UNIT 9 Selected Answers *(cont'd)*

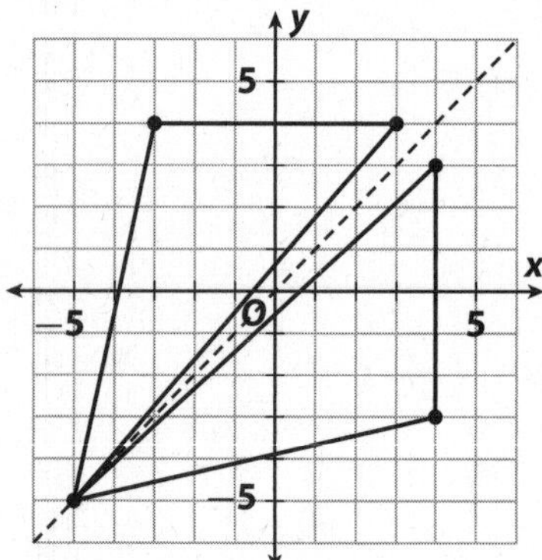

15a. $A''(1, 0)$, $B''(0, 3)$, and $C''(4, 3)$
b. $(x, y) \rightarrow (x + 3, y + 2)$

LESSON 19.5

Your Turn

3. Rotation 90° clockwise about the origin, translation 5 units down; $(x, y) \rightarrow (y, -x)$, $(x, y) \rightarrow (x, y - 5)$

Guided Practice

1.

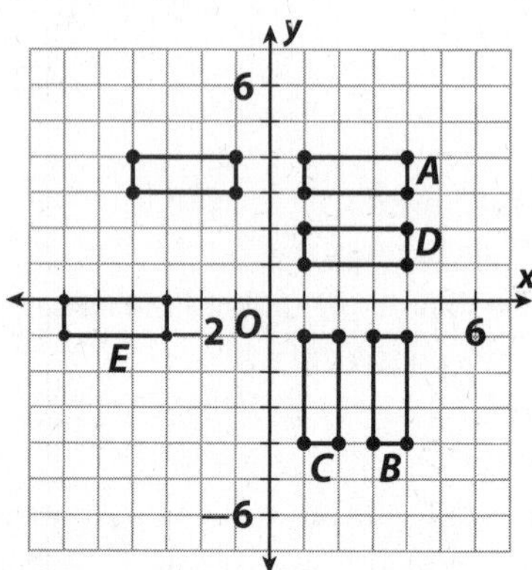

2. reflection across the *y*-axis
3. translation 3 units right and 4 units down
4. $(x, y) \rightarrow (-x, y)$, $(x, y) \rightarrow (x + 3, y - 4)$
5. The figures have the same size and the same shape.

Independent Practice

7.

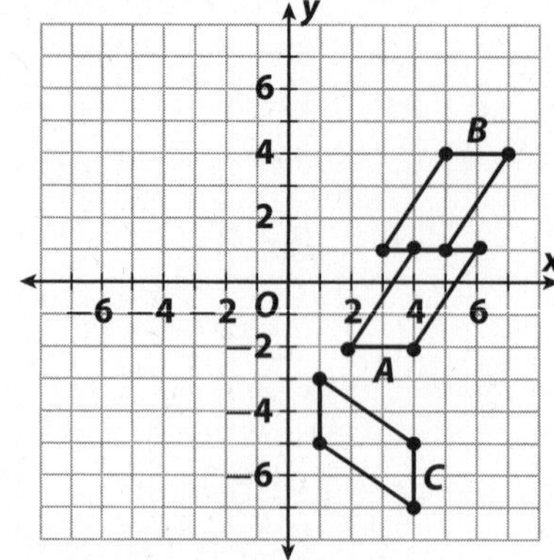

Different orientation

9.

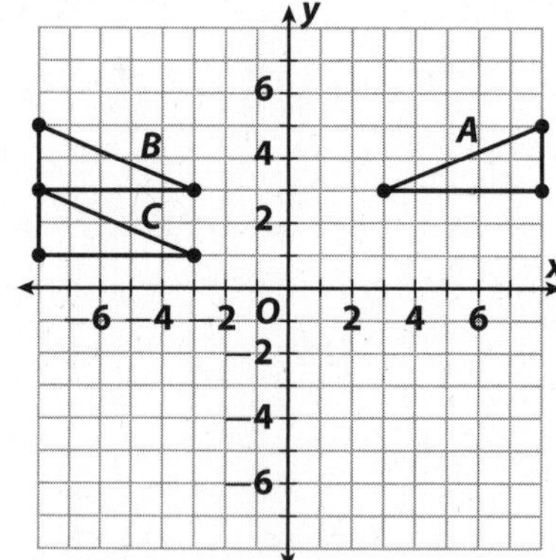

Different orientation

11. Sample answer: translation 2 units right and 4 units down, reflection across *y*-axis; size: no; orientation: yes

13. No; the point (1, 2) translated 2 units to the right becomes (3, 2), rotated 90° clockwise about the origin, it becomes (2, −3). The point (1, 2) rotated 90° clockwise around the origin becomes (2, −1), translated 2 units to the right, it becomes (4, −1), which is not the same.

MODULE 20

LESSON 20.1

Your Turn

5. The scale factor is 0.5.

Guided Practice

1. 2; 2 **2.** equal; equal **3.** 2
4. congruent **5.** 2

Independent Practice

7. No; the ratios of the lengths of the corresponding sides are not equal. **9.** Yes; a dilation produces an image similar to the original figure. **11.** Yes; each coordinate of triangle $U'V'W'$ is $\frac{3}{4}$ times the corresponding coordinate of triangle *UVW*. **13.** changed; same; same **15.** same; changed; same **17.** 3 **19.** Locate the corresponding vertices of the triangles and draw lines connecting each pair. The lines will intersect at the center of dilation.

LESSON 20.2

Your Turn

5. $(x, y) \rightarrow \left(\frac{1}{3}x, \frac{1}{3}y\right)$

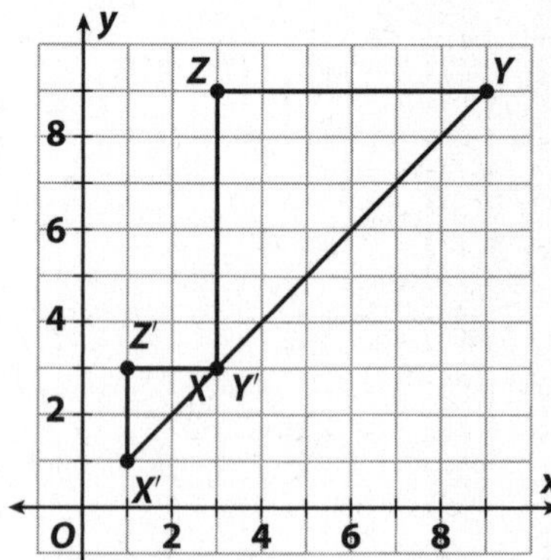

Guided Practice

1.

PreImage	Image
(2, 0)	(3, 0)
(0, 2)	(0, 3)
(−2, 0)	(−3, 0)
(0, −2)	(0, −3)

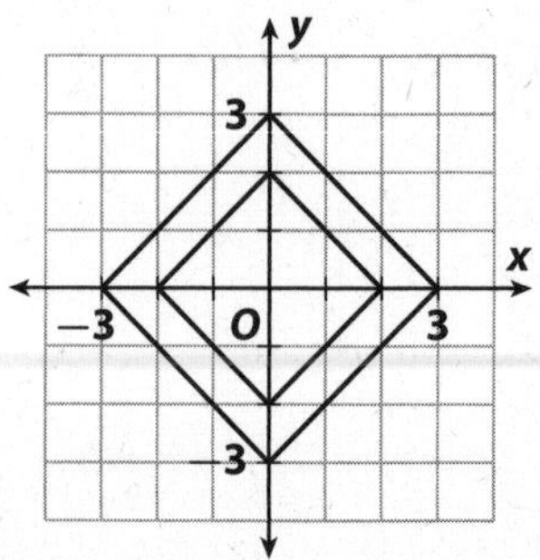

2.

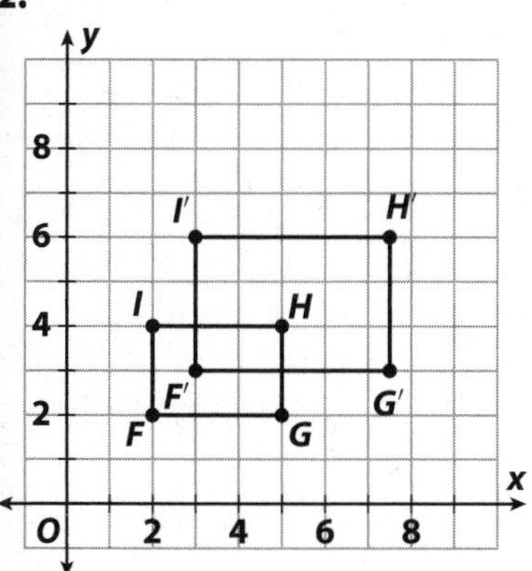

$(x, y) \rightarrow (1.5x, 1.5y)$

3.

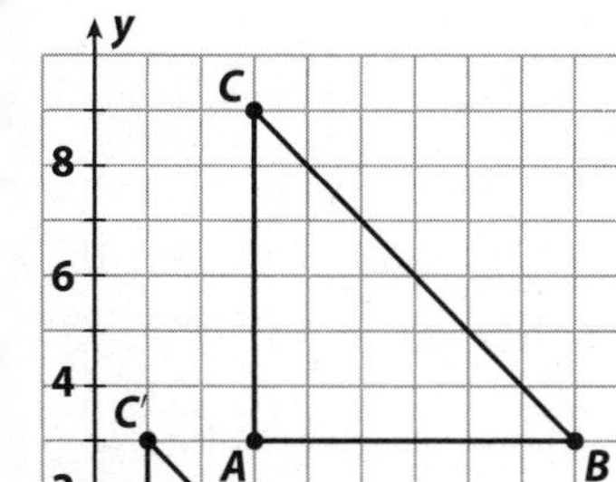

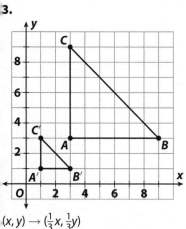

$(x, y) \rightarrow (\frac{1}{3}x, \frac{1}{3}y)$

Independent Practice

5. Green square: $(x, y) \rightarrow (2x, 2y)$; Purple square $(x, y) \rightarrow (\frac{1}{2}x, \frac{1}{2}y)$ **7.** $(x, y) \rightarrow (\frac{2}{3}x, \frac{2}{3}y)$ **9a.** The scale factor is 48. **b.** 48 inches or 4 feet **c.** $(x, y) \rightarrow (48x, 48y)$ **d.** $Q'(2.5, 2.5)$, $R'(8.75, 2.5)$, $S'(8.75, 6.25)$, and $T'(2.5, 6.25)$
e. Dimensions on blueprint: 6.25 in. by 3.75 in. Dimensions in house: 25 ft by 15 ft **11.** The crewmember's calculation is incorrect. The scale factor is $\frac{1}{20}$, not $\frac{1}{12}$. **13.** The figure is dilated by a factor of 2, but the orientation of the figure is rotated 180°.

LESSON 20.3

Your Turn

3. Sample answer: $(x, y) \rightarrow (x + 7, y - 12)$; rotation 90° clockwise about the origin; $(x, y) \rightarrow (x + 5, y + 3)$; $(x, y) \rightarrow (3x, 3y)$

Guided Practice

1.

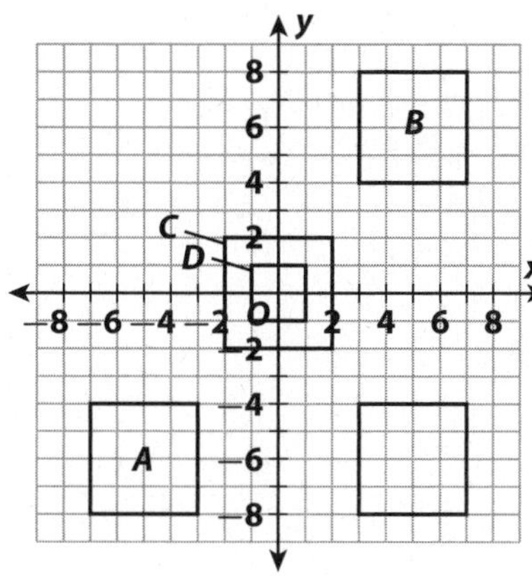

2. $(x, y) \rightarrow (x, -y)$; $(x, y) \rightarrow (x + 5, y - 6)$
3. $(x, y) \rightarrow (x, y + 6)$; rotate 90° counterclockwise
4. $(x, y) \rightarrow (1.5x, 1.5y)$; $(x, y) \rightarrow (x + 3, y + 5)$

Independent Practice

7. Dilate the image by a scale factor of $\frac{1}{3}$ and reflect it back across the x-axis; $(x, y) \rightarrow \left(\frac{1}{3}x, \frac{1}{3}y\right)$, $(x, y) \rightarrow (x, -y)$.
9. Rotate the image 90° counterclockwise and dilate it by a factor of $\frac{1}{5}$; $(x, y) \rightarrow (-y, x)$, $(x, y) \rightarrow \left(\frac{1}{5}x, \frac{1}{5}y\right)$.
11. There must be an even number of dilations and for each dilation applied to the figure, a dilation that has the opposite effect must be applied as well.

UNIT 10 Selected Answers

LESSON 21.1

Your Turn

5. 72° **6.** 108° **7.** 108°

Guided Practice

1. ∠*VWZ* **2.** alternate interior **3.** 80° **4.** 100° **5.** same-side interior

Independent Practice

7. ∠1 and ∠5, ∠2 and ∠6, ∠3 and ∠7, ∠4 and ∠8 **9.** alternate interior angles **11.** 30° **13.** 110° **15.** 78° **17.** 132°; the 48° angle is supplementary to the larger angle because the two angles are same-side interior angles. **19.** ∠6 and ∠2 are corr., so m∠2 = 125°. ∠6 and ∠3 are alt. int., so m∠3 = 125°. ∠3 and ∠7 are corr., so m∠7 = 125°. ∠6 and ∠4 are same-side int., so m∠4 = 180° − 125°, or 55°. ∠4 and ∠8 are corr., so m∠8 = 55°. ∠4 and ∠5 are alt. int., so m∠5 = 55°. ∠1 and ∠5 are corr., so m∠1 = 55°. **21.** 3 angles; 4 angles; no

LESSON 21.2

Your Turn

4. 53° **5.** 90° **8.** 78°; 68°

Guided Practice

1. 71° **2.** 30° **3.** 88°; 29°; 63° **4.** 90°; 45°; 45° **5.** 40°; 76°; 64° **6.** 129°; 32°; 19°

Independent Practice

9. 60°; 30° **11.** 98°; 55°; 27° **13.** 60°; 90°; 30°; 150° **15.** No; the measure of an obtuse angle is greater than 90°. If a triangle had two obtuse angles, the sum of their measures would be greater than 180°, the sum of the angle measures of a triangle. **17a.** 360° **b.** The sum of the angle measures of a quadrilateral is 360°. Any quadrilateral can be divided into two triangles, so the sum of its angle measures is 2 × 180° = 360°.

LESSON 21.3

Your Turn

3. The triangles are not similar, because only one angle is congruent. The angle measures of the triangles are 70°, 58°, and 52° and 70°, 61°, and 49°. **5.** 8 inches **6.** 21 ft

Guided Practice

1. 41°, 109°, and 30°; 41°, 109°, and 30°; two angles; two angles; similar **2.** 7.5; 23.5; 17.2 **3.** congruent; alternate interior angles; congruent; alternate interior angles; AA Similarity; similar

Independent Practice

5. m∠*B* = 42°, m∠*F* = 69°, m∠*H* = 64°, m∠*K* = 53° **7.** ∠*J* ≅ ∠*A*, ∠*L* ≅ ∠*B*, and ∠*K* ≅ ∠*C* **9.** 25 feet **11.** In the first line, Ryan should have added 19.5 and 6.5 to get a denominator of 26 for the expression on the right side to get the correct value of 13.6 cm for *h*.

LESSON 22.1

Your Turn

4. 471 in^3 **5.** 602.9 ft^3 **6.** 452.2 in^3

Guided Practice

1. two congruent circles that lie in parallel planes **2.** Sample answer: 427 in^3; there are 61 cubes on the bottom of the cylinder. The height is 7 cubes. $V = 61 \times 7 = 427$ in^3 **3.** 6; 15; 36; 15; 1695.6; 1695.6 **4.** 1.35; 15.5

Independent Practice

7. 1205.8 in^3 **9.** 942 in^3 **11.** 803.8 m^3 **13.** 6838.9 in^3 **15.** 339,120 m^3 **17.** 57.7 in^3 **19.** Divide the diameter by 2 to find the radius. Substitute the volume and radius in $V = \pi r^2 h$ and solve for *h*.

LESSON 22.2

Your Turn

3. 942 cm^3 **4.** 12.6 ft^3 **5.** 19,286,968.5 m^3

Guided Practice

1. 45; 10; 450; 450; 150; 150 **2.** 54 m^3; the volume of a cylinder is 3

mes the volume of a cone with a ongruent base and height.
. 65.9 ft^3 **4.** 113,982 in^3 **5.** 141.3 in^3
. 13,083.3 m^3

ndependent Practice

. 25.1 in^3 **11.** 94.2 m^3 **13.** 167.5 in^3 **5.** 628 in^3 **17.** 6 cm **19a.** either ne diameter or the radius of the ase **b.** No; the cone is tapered om top to bottom. An equal olume of sand has a smaller adius and a greater height as the and rises. **21.** Since the radius nd height of the cones and ylinder are the same, it will take cones to equal the volume of ne cylinder.

LESSON 22.3

Your Turn

2. 4186.7 cm^3 **3.** 20.6 m^3 **6.** 904.3 in^3

Guided Practice

1. the same distance **2.** radius **3.** 4.2 in^3 **4.** 4,186.7 cm^3 **5.** 14.1 ft^3 **6.** 4.2 yd^3 **7.** 12.8 in^3 **8.** 435 in^3 **9a.** $\frac{1}{3}$; the ball takes up $\frac{2}{3}$ of the space, so $\frac{1}{3}$ is empty. **b.** $(2r)^3 = 8r^3$ **c.** Almost $\frac{1}{2}$; the empty space is $8r^3 - \frac{4}{3}\pi r^3$, or about $3.81r^3$, and $\frac{3.81}{8} \approx 0.48$.

Independent Practice

11. 124.7 m^3 **13.** 904.3 in^3 **15.** 5572.5 cm^3 **17.** 5389 cm^3 **19.** 1766.3 cm^3 **21.** Divide $V = \frac{4}{3}\pi r^3$ by 2 to find the volume of the hemisphere: $V = \frac{2}{3}\pi r^3$. Add the volume of the cylinder, $V = \pi r^2 h = \pi r^3$: $V = \frac{2}{3}\pi r^3 + \pi r^3 = \frac{5}{3}\pi r^3$. **23.** 12.3 in^3 **25.** The cylindrical glass; the cylinder has a volume of πr^3, the hemisphere's volume is $\frac{2}{3}\pi r^3$, and the cone's volume is $\frac{1}{3}\pi r^3$. **27.** About 16 feet; 136 is 8 times 17, so the volume must be 8 times as big. Because $2^3 = 8$, this means the radius, and thus the diameter, must be twice as big.

Glossary/Glosario

ENGLISH	SPANISH	EXAMPLES
absolute value The distance of a number from zero on a number line; shown by | |.	**valor absoluto** Distancia a la que está un número de 0 en una recta numérica. El símbolo del valor absoluto es | |.	$\lvert 5\rvert = 5$ $\lvert -5\rvert = 5$
accuracy The closeness of a given measurement or value to the actual measurement or value.	**exactitud** Cercanía de una medida o un valor a la medida o el valor real.	
acute angle An angle that measures greater than 0° and less than 90°.	**ángulo agudo** Ángulo que mide más de 0° y menos de 90°.	
acute triangle A triangle with all angles measuring less than 90°.	**triángulo acutángulo** Triángulo en el que todos los ángulos miden menos de 90°.	
addend A number added to one or more other numbers to form a sum.	**sumando** Número que se suma a uno o más números para formar una suma.	In the expression $4 + 6 + 7$, the numbers 4, 6, and 7 are addends.
Addition Property of Equality The property that states that if you add the same number to both sides of an equation, the new equation will have the same solution.	**Propiedad de igualdad de la suma** Propiedad que establece que puedes sumar el mismo número a ambos lados de una ecuación y la nueva ecuación tendrá la misma solución.	$\begin{array}{rcr} x - 6 & = & 8 \\ +6 & & +6 \\ \hline x & = & 14 \end{array}$
Addition Property of Opposites The property that states that the sum of a number and its opposite equals zero.	**Propiedad de la suma de los opuestos** Propiedad que establece que la suma de un número y su opuesto es cero.	$12 + (-12) = 0$
additive inverse The opposite of a number; one of two numbers whose sum is 0.	**inverso aditivo** El opuesto de un número; uno de dos números cuya suma es 0.	The additive inverse of 5 is -5.
adjacent angles Angles in the same plane that have a common vertex and a common side.	**ángulos adyacentes** Angulos en el mismo plano que comparten un vértice y un lado.	$\angle 1$ and $\angle 2$ are adjacent angles.
algebraic expression An expression that contains at least one variable.	**expresión algebraica** Expresión que contiene al menos una variable.	$x + 8$ $4(m - b)$

ENGLISH	SPANISH	EXAMPLES

algebraic inequality An inequality that contains at least one variable.

desigualdad algebraica Desigualdad que contiene al menos una variable.

$x + 3 > 10$
$5a > b + 3$

---

alternate exterior angles A pair of angles on the outer side of two lines cut by a transversal that are on opposite sides of the transversal.

ángulos alternos externos Par de ángulos en los lados externos de dos líneas intersecadas por una transversal, que están en lados opuestos de la transversal.

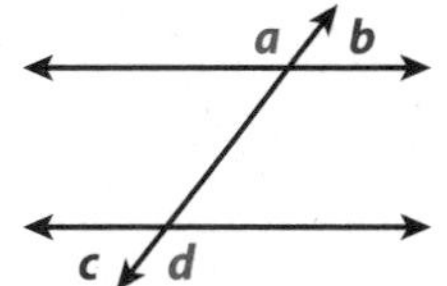

$\angle a$ and $\angle d$ are alternate exterior angles.

---

alternate interior angles A pair of angles on the inner sides of two lines cut by a transversal that are on opposite sides of the transversal.

ángulos alternos internos Par de ángulos en los lados internos de dos líneas intersecadas por una transversal, que están en lados opuestos de la transversal.

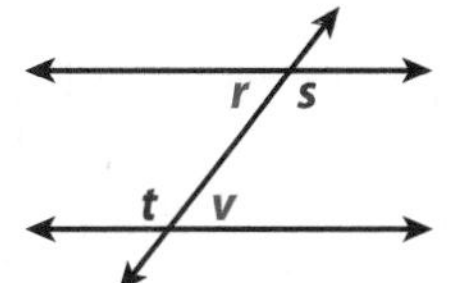

$\angle r$ and $\angle v$ are alternate interior angles.

---

angle A figure formed by two rays with a common endpoint called the vertex.

ángulo Figura formada por dos rayos con un extremo común llamado vértice.

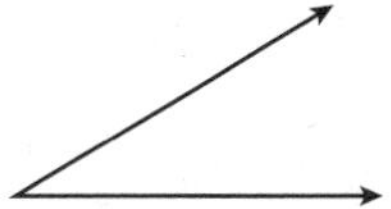

---

angle bisector A line, segment, or ray that divides an angle into two congruent angles.

bisectriz de un ángulo Línea, segmento o rayo que divide un ángulo en dos ángulos congruentes.

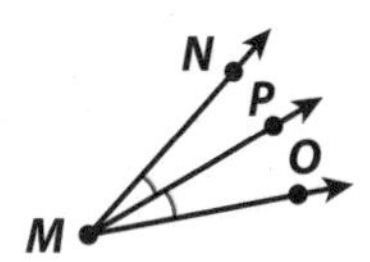

---

arc A part of a circle named by its endpoints.

arco Parte de un círculo que se nombra por sus extremos.

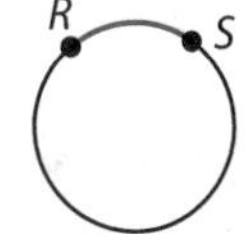

---

area The number of square units needed to cover a given surface.

área El número de unidades cuadradas que se necesitan para cubrir una superficie dada.

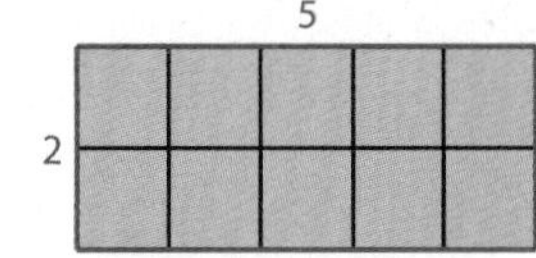

The area is 10 square units.

---

arithmetic sequence A sequence in which the terms change by the same amount each time.

sucesión aritmética Una sucesión en la que los términos cambian la misma cantidad cada vez.

The sequence 2, 5, 8, 11, 14 … is an arithmetic sequence.

---

assets Items a person owns that have monetary value.

activos Cosas que posees y que tienen valor monetario.

Associative Property of Addition The property that states that for all real numbers *a*, *b*, and *c*, the sum is always the same, regardless of their grouping.

Propiedad asociativa de la suma Propiedad que establece que para todos los números reales *a*, *b* y *c*, la suma siempre es la misma sin importar cómo se agrupen.

$2 + 3 + 8 = (2 + 3) + 8 = 2 + (3 + 8)$

Glossary/Glosario

ENGLISH	SPANISH	EXAMPLES
Associative Property of Multiplication The property that states that for all real numbers *a*, *b*, and *c*, their product is always the same, regardless of their grouping.	**Propiedad asociativa de la multiplicación** Propiedad que para todos los números reales *a*, *b* y *c*, el producto siempre es el mismo sin importar cómo se agrupen.	$2 \cdot 3 \cdot 8 = (2 \cdot 3) \cdot 8 = 2 \cdot (3 \cdot 8)$
asymmetry Not identical on either side of a central line; not symmetrical.	**asimetría** Ocurre cuando dos lados separados por una línea central no son idénticos; falta de simetría.	The quadrilateral has asymmetry.
average The sum of a set of data divided by the number of items in the data set; also called *mean*.	**promedio** La suma de los elementos de un conjunto de datos dividida entre el número de elementos del conjunto. También se llama media.	Data set: 4, 6, 7, 8, 10 Average: $\frac{4+6+7+8+10}{5}$ $= \frac{35}{5} = 7$
axes The two perpendicular lines of a coordinate plane that intersect at the origin.	**ejes** Las dos rectas numéricas perpendiculares del plano cartesiano que se intersecan en el origen.	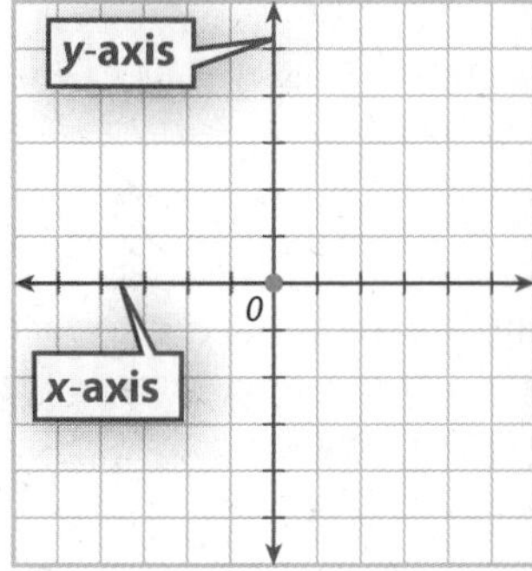

B

ENGLISH	SPANISH	EXAMPLES
bar graph A graph that uses vertical or horizontal bars to display data.	**gráfica de barras** Gráfica en la que se usan barras verticales u horizontales para presentar datos.	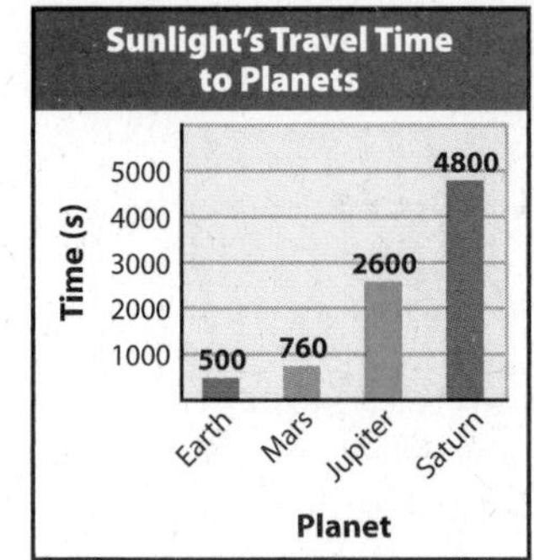
base-10 number system A number system in which all numbers are expressed using the digits 0–9.	**sistema de base 10** Sistema de numeración en el que todos los números se expresan con los dígitos 0–9.	
base (in numeration) When a number is raised to a power, the number that is used as a factor is the base.	**base (en numeración)** Cuando un número es elevado a una potencia, el número que se usa como factor es la base.	$3^5 = 3 \cdot 3 \cdot 3 \cdot 3 \cdot 3$; 3 is the base.
base (of a polygon) A side of a polygon.	**base (de un polígono)** Lado de un polígono.	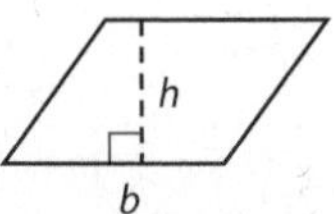

ENGLISH	SPANISH	EXAMPLES

base (of a three-dimensional figure) A face of a three-dimensional figure by which the figure is measured or classified.

base (de una figura tridimensional) Cara de una figura tridimensional a partir de la cual se mide o se clasifica la figura.

Bases of a cylinder

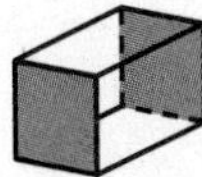
Bases of a prism

Base of a cone

Base of a pyramid

---

biased sample A sample that does not fairly represent the population.

muestra no representativa Muestra que no representa adecuadamente la población.

---

bisect To divide into two congruent parts.

trazar una bisectriz Dividir en dos partes congruentes.

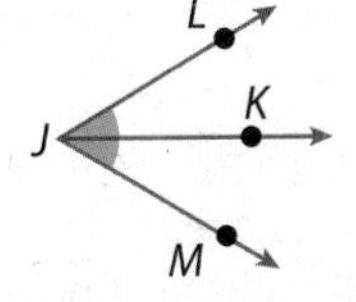

$\overrightarrow{JK}$ bisects $\angle LJM$.

---

box-and-whisker plot A graph that shows how data are distributed by using the median, quartiles, least value, and greatest value; also called a box plot.

gráfica de mediana y rango Gráfica que muestra los valores máximo y mínimo, los cuartiles superior e inferior, así como la mediana de los datos.

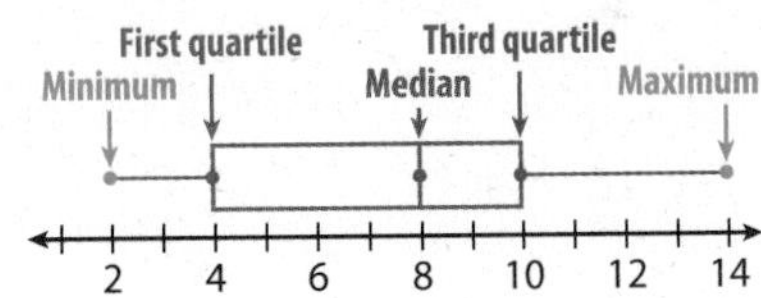

---

break (graph) A zigzag on a horizontal or vertical scale of a graph that indicates that some of the numbers on the scale have been omitted.

discontinuidad (gráfica) Zig-zag en la escala horizontal o vertical de una gráfica que indica la omisión de algunos de los números de la escala.

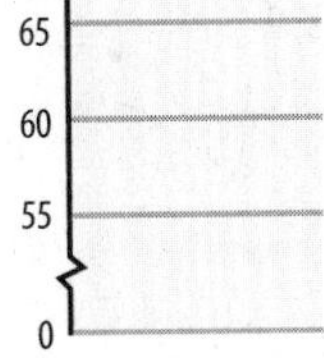

---

budget A plan to help you reach your financial goals.

presupuesto Plan que te ayuda a obtener tus metas financieras.

C

capacity The amount a container can hold when filled.

capacidad Cantidad que cabe en un recipiente cuando se llena.

A large milk container has a capacity of 1 gallon.

Celsius A metric scale for measuring temperature in which 0 °C is the freezing point of water and 100 °C is the boiling point of water; also called *centigrade.*

Celsius Escala métrica para medir la temperatura, en la que 0 °C es el punto de congelación del agua y 100 °C es el punto de ebullición. También se llama *centígrado.*

ENGLISH	SPANISH	EXAMPLES
center (of a circle) The point inside a circle that is the same distance from all the points on the circle.	**centro (de un círculo)** Punto interior de un círculo que se encuentra a la misma distancia de todos los puntos de la circunferencia.	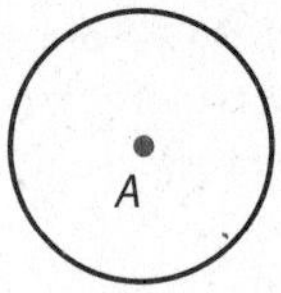 A
center of dilation The point of intersection of lines through each pair of corresponding vertices in a dilation.	**centro de una dilatación** Punto de intersección de las líneas que pasan a través de cada par de vértices correspondientes en una dilatación.	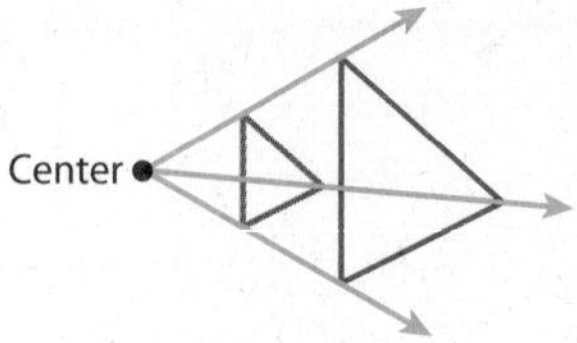 Center

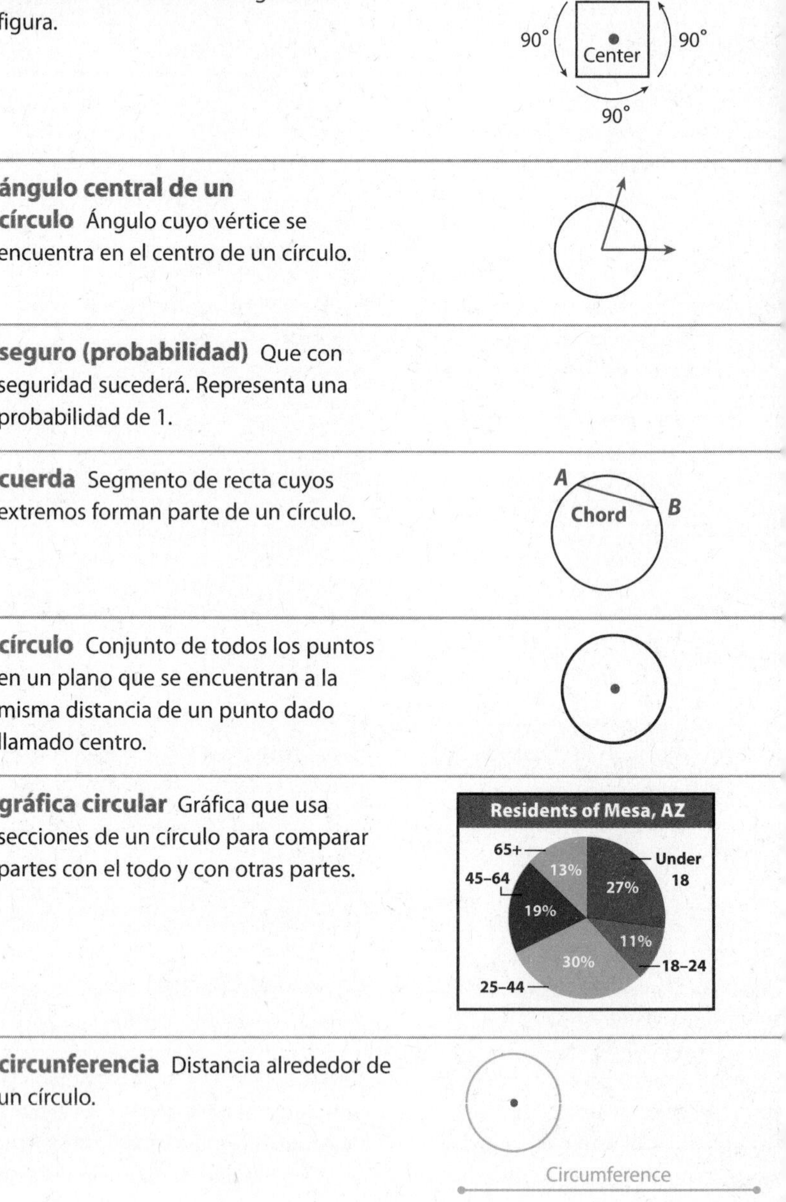

ENGLISH	SPANISH
center of rotation The point about which a figure is rotated.	**centro de una rotación** Punto alrededor del cual se hace girar una figura.
central angle of a circle An angle with its vertex at the center of a circle.	**ángulo central de un círculo** Ángulo cuyo vértice se encuentra en el centro de un círculo.
certain (probability) Sure to happen; having a probability of 1.	**seguro (probabilidad)** Que con seguridad sucederá. Representa una probabilidad de 1.
chord A line segment with endpoints on a circle.	**cuerda** Segmento de recta cuyos extremos forman parte de un círculo.
circle The set of all points in a plane that are the same distance from a given point called the center.	**círculo** Conjunto de todos los puntos en un plano que se encuentran a la misma distancia de un punto dado llamado centro.
circle graph A graph that uses sectors of a circle to compare parts to the whole and parts to other parts.	**gráfica circular** Gráfica que usa secciones de un círculo para comparar partes con el todo y con otras partes.
circumference The distance around a circle.	**circunferencia** Distancia alrededor de un círculo.

ENGLISH	SPANISH	EXAMPLES
lockwise A circular movement in he direction shown.	**en el sentido de las manecillas del reloj** Movimiento circular en la dirección que se indica.	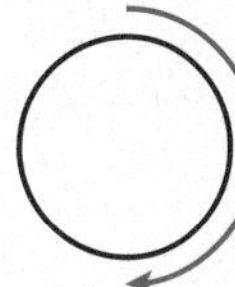
oefficient The number that is nultiplied by the variable in an lgebraic expression.	**coeficiente** Número que se multiplica por la variable en una expresión algebraica.	5 is the coefficient in $5b$.
ombination An arrangement of ems or events in which order does ot matter.	**combinación** Agrupación de objetos o sucesos en la cual el orden no es importante.	For objects A, B, C, and D, there are 6 different combinations of 2 objects: AB, AC, AD, BC, BD, CD.
ommission A fee paid to a person or making a sale.	**comisión** Pago que recibe una persona por realizar una venta.	
ommission rate The fee paid to a erson who makes a sale expressed as percent of the selling price.	**tasa de comisión** Pago que recibe una persona por hacer una venta, expresado como un porcentaje del precio de venta.	A commission rate of 5% and a sale of $10,000 results in a commission of $500.
ommon denominator denominator that is the same in two or more fractions.	**denominador común** Denominador que es común a dos o más fracciones.	The common denominator of $\frac{5}{8}$ and $\frac{2}{8}$ is 8.
ommon difference In an rithmetic sequence, the nonzero onstant difference of any term and he previous term.	**diferencia común** En una sucesión aritmética, diferencia constante distinta de cero entre cualquier término y el término anterior.	In the arithmetic sequence 3, 5, 7, 9, 11, …, the common difference is 2.
ommon factor A number that is a actor of two or more numbers.	**factor común** Número que es factor de dos o más números.	8 is a common factor of 16 and 40.
ommon multiple A number that s a multiple of each of two or more umbers.	**múltiplo común** Número que es múltiplo de dos o más números.	15 is a common multiple of 3 and 5.
ommutative Property of ddition The property that states hat two or more numbers can be dded in any order without changing he sum.	**Propiedad conmutativa de la suma** Propiedad que establece que sumar dos o más números en cualquier orden no altera la suma.	$8 + 20 = 20 + 8$
ommutative Property of ultiplication The property that tates that two or more numbers can e multiplied in any order without hanging the product.	**Propiedad conmutativa de la multiplicación** Propiedad que establece que multiplicar dos o más números en cualquier orden no altera el producto.	$6 \cdot 12 = 12 \cdot 6$
ompatible numbers Numbers hat are close to the given numbers hat make estimation or mental alculation easier.	**números compatibles** Números que están cerca de los números dados y hacen más fácil la estimación o el cálculo mental.	To estimate $7{,}957 + 5{,}009$, use the compatible numbers 8,000 and 5,000: $8{,}000 + 5{,}000 = 13{,}000$.

ENGLISH | **SPANISH** | **EXAMPLES**

complement The set of all outcomes that are not the event.

complemento La serie de resultados que no están en el suceso.

When rolling a number cube, the complement of rolling a 3 is rolling a 1, 2, 4, 5, or 6.

---

complementary angles Two angles whose measures add to 90°.

ángulos complementarios Dos ángulos cuyas medidas suman 90°.

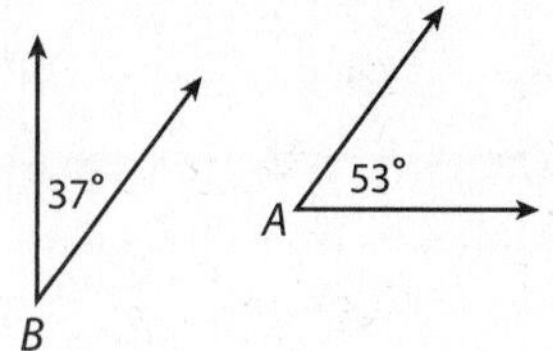

---

complex fraction A fraction that contains one or more fractions in the numerator, the denominator, or both.

fracción compleja Fracción que contiene una o más fracciones en el numerador, en el denominador, o en ambos.

---

composite figure A figure made up of simple geometric shapes.

figura compuesta Figura formada por figuras geométricas simples.

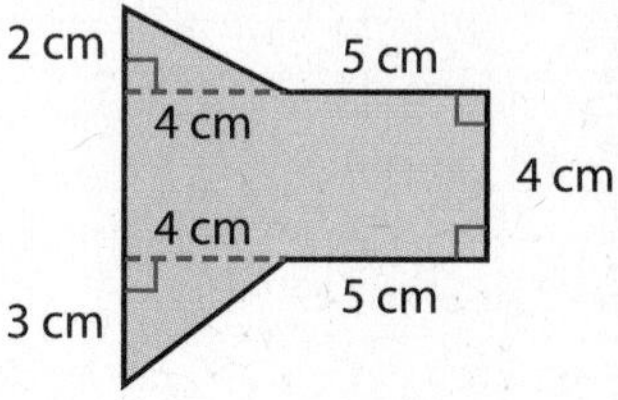

---

composite number A number greater than 1 that has more than two whole-number factors.

número compuesto Número mayor que 1 que tiene más de dos factores que son números cabales.

4, 6, 8, and 9 are composite numbers.

---

compound event An event made up of two or more simple events.

suceso compuesto Suceso que consista de dos o más sucesos simples.

Rolling a 3 on a number cube and spinning a 2 on a spinner is a compound event.

---

compound inequality A combination of more than one inequality.

desigualdad compuesta Combinación de dos o más desigualdades.

$-2 \leq x < 10$

---

cone A three-dimensional figure with one vertex and one circular base.

cono Figura tridimensional con un vértice y una base circular.

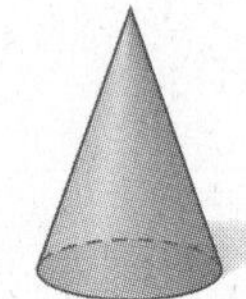

---

congruence transformation A transformation that results in an image that is the same shape and the same size as the original figure.

transformación de congruencia Una transformación que resulta en una imagen que tiene la misma forma y el mismo tamaño como la figura original.

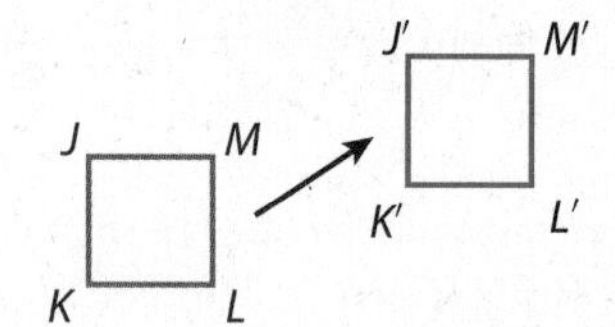

---

congruent Two plane or solid figures are congruent if one can be obtained from the other by rigid motion (a sequence of rotations, reflections, and translations).

congruentes Dos figuras planas o dos cuerpos geométricos son congruentes si de una figura se obtiene la otra mediante un movimiento rígido (una secuencia de rotaciones, reflexiones y traslaciones).

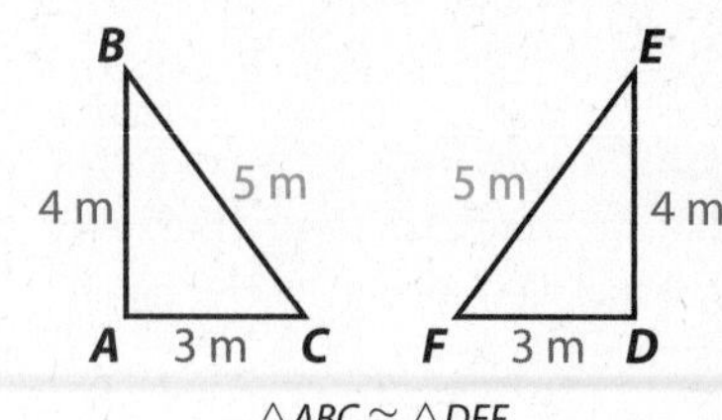

$\triangle ABC \cong \triangle DEF$

ENGLISH	SPANISH	EXAMPLES
congruent angles Angles that have the same measure.	**ángulos congruentes** Ángulos que tienen la misma medida.	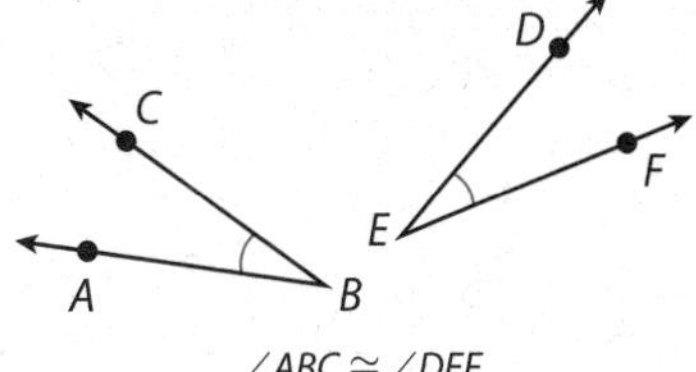 $\angle ABC \cong \angle DEF$
congruent figures See *congruent*.	**figuras congruentes** Vea *congruentes*.	
congruent segments Segments that have the same length.	**segmentos congruentes** Segmentos que tienen la misma longitud.	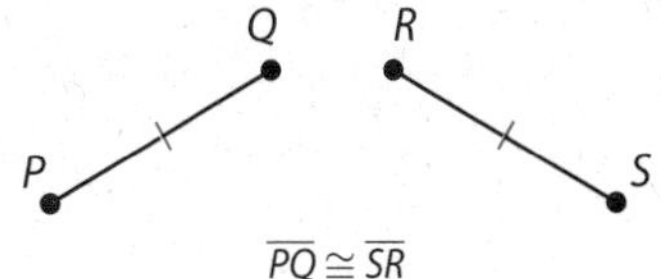 $\overline{PQ} \cong \overline{SR}$
conjecture A statement believed to be true.	**conjetura** Enunciado que se supone verdadero.	
constant A value that does not change.	**constante** Valor que no cambia.	$3, 0, \pi$
constant of proportionality A constant ratio of two variables related proportionally.	**constante de proporcionalidad** Razón constante de dos variables que están relacionadas en forma proporcional.	
constant of variation The constant *k* in direct and inverse variation equations.	**constante de variación** La constante *k* en ecuaciones de variación directa e inversa.	$y = 5x$ ↑ constant of variation
convenience sample A sample based on members of the population that are readily available.	**muestra de conveniencia** Una muestra basada en miembros de la población que están fácilmente disponibles.	
coordinate One of the numbers of an ordered pair that locate a point on a coordinate graph.	**coordenada** Uno de los números de un par ordenado que ubica un punto en una gráfica de coordenadas.	
coordinate plane A plane formed by the intersection of a horizontal number line called the *x*-axis and a vertical number line called the *y*-axis.	**plano cartesiano** Plano formado por la intersección de una recta numérica horizontal llamada eje *x* y otra vertical llamada eje *y*.	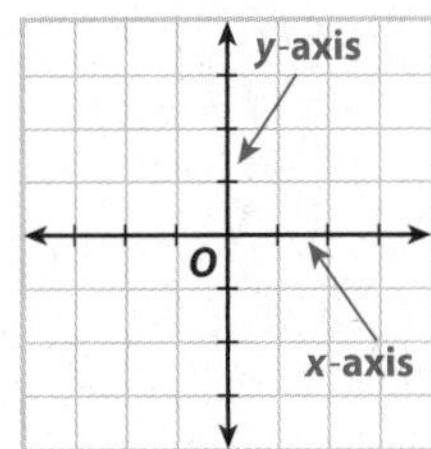
correlation The description of the relationship between two data sets.	**correlación** Descripción de la relación entre dos conjuntos de datos.	
correspondence The relationship between two or more objects that are matched.	**correspondencia** La relación entre dos o más objetos que coinciden.	$\angle A$ and $\angle D$ are corresponding angles. 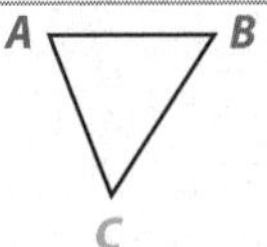 $\overline{AB}$ and $\overline{DE}$ are corresponding sides. 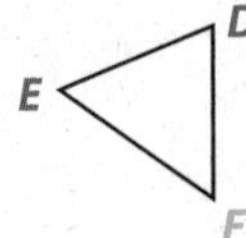

Glossary/Glosario

ENGLISH	SPANISH	EXAMPLES
corresponding angles (for lines) Angles in the same position formed when a third line intersects two lines.	**ángulos correspondientes (en líneas)** Ángulos en la misma posición formaron cuando una tercera línea interseca dos líneas.	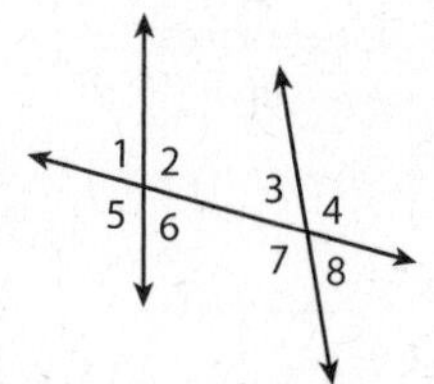 $\angle 1$ and $\angle 3$ are corresponding angles.
corresponding angles (of polygons) Angles in the same relative position in polygons with an equal number of sides.	**ángulos correspondientes (en polígonos)** Ángulos que se ubican en la misma posición relativa en dos o más polígonos.	$\angle A$ and $\angle D$ are corresponding angles.
corresponding sides Matching sides of two or more polygons.	**lados correspondientes** Lados que se ubican en la misma posición relativa en dos o más polígonos.	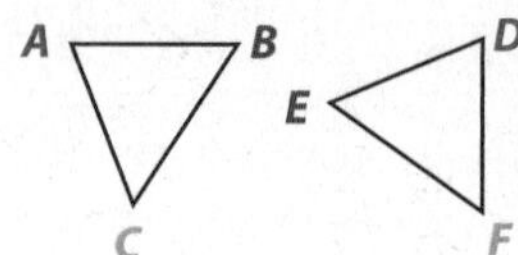 $\overline{AB}$ and $\overline{DE}$ are corresponding sides.
counterclockwise A circular movement in the direction shown.	**en sentido contrario a las manecillas del reloj** Movimiento circular en la dirección que se indica.	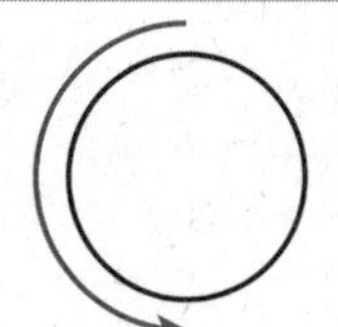
counterexample An example that shows that a statement is false.	**contraejemplo** Ejemplo que demuestra que un enunciado es falso.	
cross product The product of numbers on the diagonal when comparing two ratios.	**producto cruzado** El producto de los números multiplicados en diagonal cuando se comparan dos razones.	 For the proportion $\frac{2}{3} = \frac{4}{6}$, the cross products are $2 \cdot 6 = 12$ and $3 \cdot 4 = 12$.
cross section The intersection of a three-dimensional figure and a plane.	**sección transversal** Intersección de una figura tridimensional y un plano.	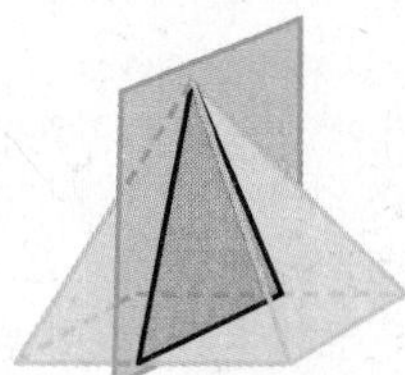
cube (geometric figure) A rectangular prism with six congruent square faces.	**cubo (figura geométrica)** Prisma rectangular con seis caras cuadradas congruentes.	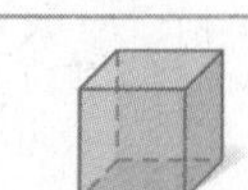
cube (in numeration) A number raised to the third power.	**cubo (en numeración)** Número elevado a la tercera potencia.	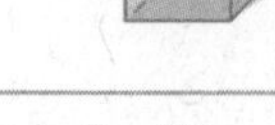 $5^3 = 5 \cdot 5 \cdot 5 = 125$
cube root A number, written as $\sqrt[3]{x}$, whose cube is x.	**raíz cúbica** Número, expresado como $\sqrt[3]{x}$, cuyo cubo es x.	$\sqrt[3]{8} = \sqrt[3]{2 \cdot 2 \cdot 2} = 2$ 2 is the cube root of 8.
cumulative frequency The frequency of all data values that are less than or equal to a given value.	**frecuencia acumulativa** La frecuencia de todos los datos que son menores que o iguales a un valor dado.	

ENGLISH	SPANISH	EXAMPLES
stomary system of easurement The measurement stem often used in the United States.	**sistema usual de medidas** El sistema de medidas que se usa comúnmente en Estados Unidos.	inches, feet, miles, ounces, pounds, tons, cups, quarts, gallons
linder A three-dimensional figure th two parallel, congruent circular ses connected by a curved lateral rface.	**cilindro** Figura tridimensional con dos bases circulares paralelas y congruentes, unidas por una superficie lateral curva.	

D

ENGLISH	SPANISH	EXAMPLES
ecagon A polygon with ten sides.	**decágono** Polígono de 10 lados.	
ecimal system A base-10 place lue system.	**sistema decimal** Sistema de valor posicional de base 10.	
eductive reasoning Using logic show that a statement is true.	**razonamiento deductivo** Uso de la lógica para demostrar que un enunciado es verdadero.	
egree The unit of measure for gles or temperature.	**grado** Unidad de medida para ángulos y temperaturas.	
enominator The bottom number a fraction that tells how many equal rts are in the whole.	**denominador** Número de abajo de una fracción que indica en cuántas partes iguales se divide el entero.	
ensity Property The property at states that between any two real imbers there is always another real imber.	**Propiedad de densidad** Propiedad según la cual entre dos números reales cualesquiera siempre hay otro número real.	
ependent events Events for hich the outcome of one event fects the probability of the second vent.	**sucesos dependientes** Dos sucesos son dependientes si el resultado de uno afecta la probabilidad del otro.	A bag contains 3 red marbles and 2 blue marbles. Drawing a red marble and then drawing a blue marble without replacing the first marble is an example of dependent events.
iagonal A line segment that onnects two nonadjacent vertices of polygon.	**diagonal** Segmento de recta que une dos vértices no adyacentes de un polígono.	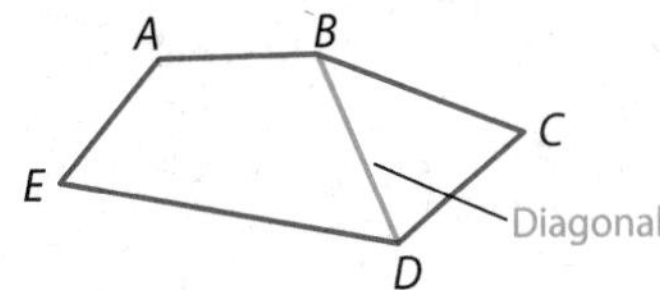
iameter A line segment that passes rough the center of a circle and has ndpoints on the circle, or the length f that segment.	**diámetro** Segmento de recta que pasa por el centro de un círculo y tiene sus extremos en la circunferencia, o bien la longitud de ese segmento.	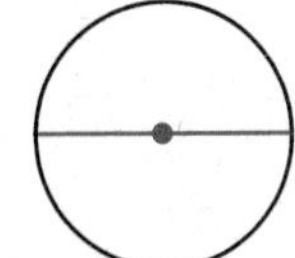

ENGLISH	SPANISH	EXAMPLES
difference The result when one number is subtracted from another.	**diferencia** El resultado de restar un número de otro.	In $16 - 5 = 11$, 11 is the difference
dilation A transformation that moves each point along the ray through the point emanating from a fixed center, and multiplies distances from the center by a common scale factor.	**dilatación** Transformación que agranda o reduce una figura.	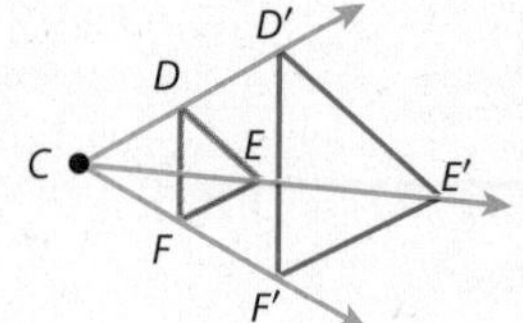
dimension The length, width, or height of a figure.	**dimensión** Longitud, ancho o altura de una figura.	
direct variation A linear relationship between two variables, x and y, that can be written in the form $y = kx$, where k is a nonzero constant.	**variación directa** Relación lineal entre dos variables, x e y, que puede expresarse en la forma $y = kx$, donde k es una constante distinta de cero.	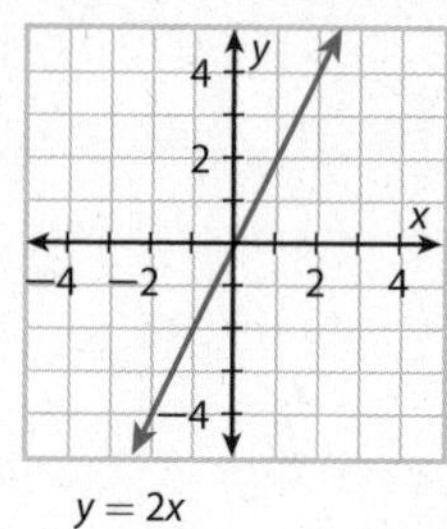 $y = 2x$
Distributive Property For all real numbers, a, b, and c, $a(b + c) = ab + ac$ and $a(b - c) = ab - ac$.	**Propiedad distributiva** Dado números reales a, b, y c, $a(b + c) = ab + ac$ y $a(b - c) = ab - ac$.	$5(20 + 1) = 5 \cdot 20 + 5 \cdot 1$
dividend The number to be divided in a division problem.	**dividendo** Número que se divide en un problema de división.	In $8 \div 4 = 2$, 8 is the dividend.
divisible Can be divided by a number without leaving a remainder.	**divisible** Que se puede dividir entre un número sin dejar residuo.	18 is divisible by 3.
Division Property of Equality The property that states that if you divide both sides of an equation by the same nonzero number, the new equation will have the same solution.	**Propiedad de igualdad de la división** Propiedad que establece que puedes dividir ambos lados de una ecuación entre el mismo número distinto de cero, y la nueva ecuación tendrá la misma solución.	$4x = 12$ $\frac{4x}{4} = \frac{12}{4}$ $x = 3$
divisor The number you are dividing by in a division problem.	**divisor** El número entre el que se divide en un problema de división.	In $8 \div 4 = 2$, 4 is the divisor.
double-bar graph A bar graph that compares two related sets of data.	**gráfica de doble barra** Gráfica de barras que compara dos conjuntos de datos relacionados.	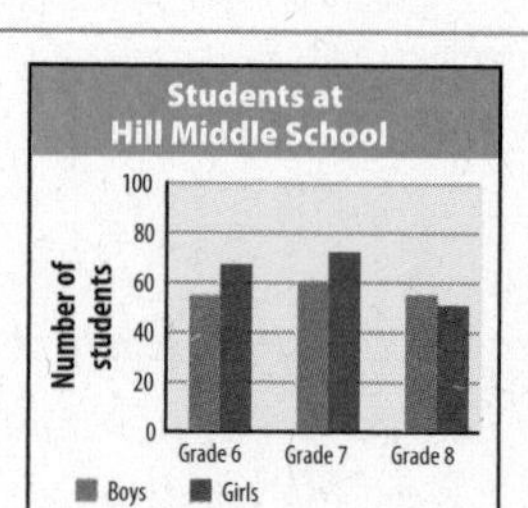

ENGLISH	SPANISH	EXAMPLES
ouble-line graph A line graph at shows how two related sets of ta change over time.	**gráfica de doble línea** Gráfica lineal que muestra cómo cambian con el tiempo dos conjuntos de datos relacionados.	

ENGLISH	SPANISH	EXAMPLES
lge The line segment along which o faces of a polyhedron intersect.	**arista** Segmento de recta donde se intersecan dos caras de un poliedro.	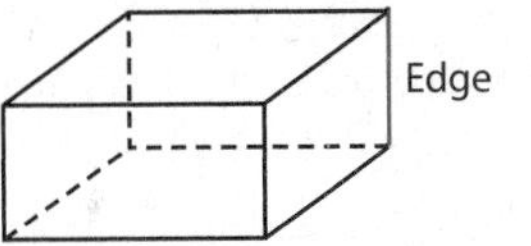
ndpoint A point at the end of a line gment or ray.	**extremo** Un punto ubicado al final de un segmento de recta o rayo.	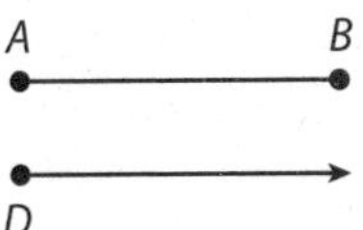
nlargement An increase in ze of all dimensions in the same oportions.	**agrandamiento** Aumento de tamaño de todas las dimensiones en las mismas proporciones.	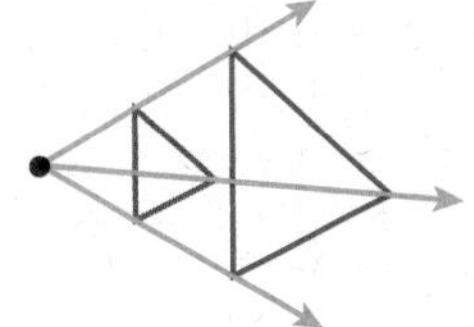
qually likely Outcomes that have e same probability.	**resultados igualmente probables** Resultados que tienen la misma probabilidad de ocurrir.	
quation A mathematical sentence at shows that two expressions are quivalent.	**ecuación** Enunciado matemático que indica que dos expresiones son equivalentes.	$x + 4 = 7$ $6 + 1 = 10 - 3$
quilateral triangle A triangle with ree congruent sides.	**triángulo equilátero** Triángulo con tres lados congruentes.	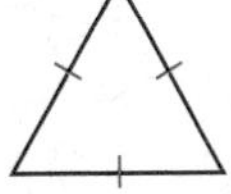
quivalent Having the same value.	**equivalentes** Que tienen el mismo valor.	
quivalent expressions xpressions that have the same value r all values of the variables.	**expresiones equivalentes** Las expresiones equivalentes tienen el mismo valor para todos los valores de las variables.	$4x + 5x$ and $9x$ are equivalent expressions.
quivalent fractions Fractions that ame the same amount or part.	**fracciones equivalentes** Fracciones que representan la misma cantidad o parte.	$\frac{1}{2}$ and $\frac{2}{4}$ are equivalent fractions.

ENGLISH	SPANISH	EXAMPLES
equivalent ratios Ratios that name the same comparison.	**razones equivalentes** Razones que representan la misma comparación.	$\frac{1}{2}$ and $\frac{2}{4}$ are equivalent ratios.
estimate (n) An answer that is close to the exact answer and is found by rounding or other methods.	**estimación** Una solución aproximada a la respuesta exacta que se halla mediante el redondeo u otros métodos.	
estimate (v) To find an answer close to the exact answer by rounding or other methods.	**estimar** Hallar una solución aproximada a la respuesta exacta mediante el redondeo u otros métodos.	
evaluate To find the value of a numerical or algebraic expression.	**evaluar** Hallar el valor de una expresión numérica o algebraica.	Evaluate $2x + 7$ for $x = 3$. $2x + 7$ $2(\mathbf{3}) + 7$ $6 + 7$ 13
even number An integer that is divisible by two.	**número par** Número entero divisible entre 2.	2, 4, 6
event An outcome or set of outcomes of an experiment or situation.	**suceso** Un resultado o una serie de resultados de un experimento o una situación.	When rolling a number cube, the event "an odd number" consists of the outcomes 1, 3, and 5.
expanded form A multi-digit number is expressed in expanded form when it is written as a sum of single-digit multiples of powers of ten.	**forma desarrollada** Número escrito como suma de los valores de sus dígitos.	236,536 written in expanded form is $200{,}000 + 30{,}000 + 6{,}000 + 500 + 30 + 6$.
experiment In probability, any activity based on chance, such as tossing a coin.	**experimento** En probabilidad, cualquier actividad basada en la posibilidad, como lanzar una moneda.	Tossing a coin 10 times and noting the number of "heads"
experimental probability The ratio of the number of times an event occurs to the total number of trials, or times that the activity is performed.	**probabilidad experimental** Razón del número de veces que ocurre un suceso al número total de pruebas o al número de veces que se realiza el experimento.	Kendra attempted 27 free throws and made 16 of them. Her experimental probability of making a free throw is $\frac{\text{number made}}{\text{number attempted}} = \frac{16}{27} \approx 0.59$.
exponent The number that indicates how many times the base is used as a factor.	**exponente** Número que indica cuántas veces se usa la base como factor.	$2^3 = 2 \cdot 2 \cdot 2 = 8$; 3 is the exponent.
exponential form A number is in exponential form when it is written with a base and an exponent.	**forma exponencial** Se dice que un número está en forma exponencial cuando se escribe con una base y un exponente.	4^2 is the exponential form for $4 \cdot 4$.
expression A mathematical phrase that contains operations, numbers, and/or variables.	**expresión** Enunciado matemático que contiene operaciones, números y/o variables.	$6x + 1$
exterior angle (of a polygon) An angle formed by one side of a polygon and the extension of an adjacent side.	**ángulo extreno de un polígono** Ángulo formado por un lado de un polígono y la prolongación del lado adyacente.	

ENGLISH	SPANISH	EXAMPLES
ce A flat surface of a polyhedron.	**cara** Superficie plana de un poliedro.	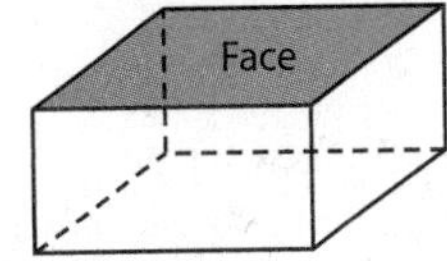
ctor A number that is multiplied by 1other number to get a product.	**factor** Número que se multiplica por otro para hallar un producto.	7 is a factor of 21 since $7 \cdot 3 = 21$.
ctor tree A diagram showing how whole number breaks down into its rime factors.	**árbol de factores** Diagrama que muestra cómo se descompone un número cabal en sus factores primos.	12 $3 \cdot 4$ $2 \cdot 2$ $12 = 3 \cdot 2 \cdot 2$
actorial The product of all whole umbers except zero that are less than r equal to a number.	**factorial** El producto de todos los números cabales, excepto cero que son menores que o iguales a un número.	4 factorial $= 4! = 4 \cdot 3 \cdot 2 \cdot 1$
ahrenheit A temperature scale in which 32 °F is the freezing point of vater and 212 °F is the boiling point of vater.	**Fahrenheit** Escala de temperatura en la que 32 °F es el punto de congelación del agua y 212 °F es el punto de ebullición.	
air When all outcomes of an xperiment are equally likely, the xperiment is said to be fair.	**justo** Se dice de un experimento donde todos los resultados posibles son igualmente probables.	
ederal withholding The mount of an employee's pay that he employer sends to the federal government as partial payment of the employee's yearly income tax.	**retención fiscal federal** Ingresos que descuenta un empleador y que envía al gobierno federal como pago parcial del impuesto sobre el salario anual del empleado.	
first quartile The median of the ower half of a set of data; also called *lower quartile.*	**primer cuartil** La mediana de la mitad inferior de un conjunto de datos. También se llama *cuartil inferior.*	
fixed expenses Expenses that occur regularly and stay the same.	**gastos fijos** Gastos que ocurren con regularidad y se mantienen igual.	
formula A rule showing relationships among quantities.	**fórmula** Regla que muestra relaciones entre cantidades.	$A = lw$ is the formula for the area of a rectangle.
fraction A number expressible in the form $\frac{a}{b}$ where a is a whole number and b is a positive whole number.	**fracción** Número escrito en la forma $\frac{a}{b}$, donde $b \neq 0$.	
frequency The number of times the value appears in the data set.	**frecuencia** Cantidad de veces que aparece el valor en un conjunto de datos.	In the data set 5, 6, 6, 7, 8, 9, the data value 6 has a frequency of 2.

ENGLISH	SPANISH	EXAMPLES
frequency table A table that lists items together according to the number of times, or frequency, that the items occur.	**tabla de frecuencia** Una tabla en la que se organizan los datos de acuerdo con el número de veces que aparece cada valor (o la frecuencia).	Data set: 1, 1, 2, 2, 3, 4, 5, 5, 5, 6, 6, 6, 6 Frequency table: (see table below)
function An input-output relationship that has exactly one output for each input.	**función** Relación de entrada-salida en la que a cada valor de entrada corresponde exactamente un valor de salida.	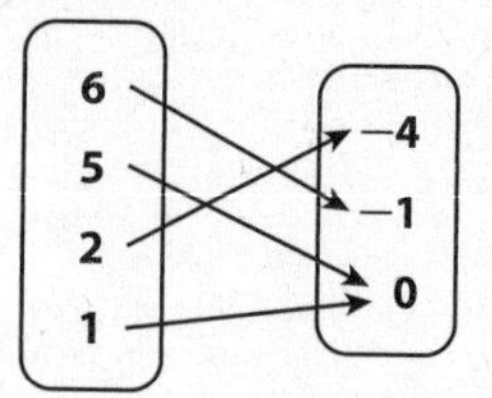
function table A table of ordered pairs that represent solutions of a function.	**tabla de función** Tabla de pares ordenados que representan soluciones de una función.	(see table below)
Fundamental Counting Principle If one event has *m* possible outcomes and a second event has *n* possible outcomes after the first event has occurred, then there are $m \cdot n$ total possible outcomes for the two events.	**Principio fundamental de conteo** Si un suceso tiene *m* resultados posibles y otro suceso tiene *n* resultados posibles después de ocurrido el primer suceso, entonces hay $m \cdot n$ resultados posibles en total para los dos sucesos.	There are 4 colors of shirts and 3 colors of pants. There are $4 \cdot 3 = 12$ possible outfits.

Frequency table example:

Data	1	2	3	4	5
Frequency	2	2	1	1	3

Function table example:

x	3	4	5	6
y	7	9	11	13

ENGLISH	SPANISH	EXAMPLES
geometric sequence A sequence in which each term is multiplied by the same value to get the next term.	**sucesión geométrica** Una sucesión en la que cada término se multiplica por el mismo valor para obtener el siguiente término.	The sequence 2, 4, 8, 16 … is a geometric sequence.
graph of an equation A graph of the set of ordered pairs that are solutions of the equation.	**gráfica de una ecuación** Gráfica del conjunto de pares ordenados que son soluciones de la ecuación.	
greatest common factor (GCF) The largest common factor of two or more given numbers.	**máximo común divisor (MCD)** El mayor de los factores comunes compartidos por dos o más números dados.	The GCF of 27 and 45 is 9.
gross pay An employee's pay before any deductions are taken.	**paga bruta** Paga de un empleado antes de sustraer cualquier deducción.	

ENGLISH	SPANISH	EXAMPLES

eight In a pyramid or cone, the rpendicular distance from the base the opposite vertex.

altura En una pirámide o cono, la distancia perpendicular desde la base al vértice opuesto.

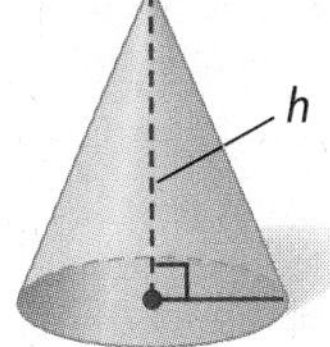

a triangle or quadrilateral, the rpendicular distance from the base the opposite vertex or side.

En un triángulo o cuadrilátero, la distancia perpendicular desde la base de la figura al vértice o lado opuesto.

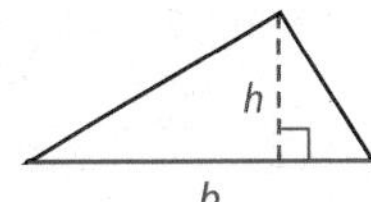

a prism or cylinder, the rpendicular distance between the ses.

En un prisma o cilindro, la distancia perpendicular entre las bases.

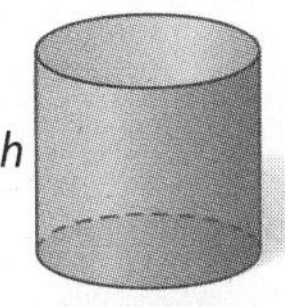

emisphere A half of a sphere.

hemisferio La mitad de una esfera.

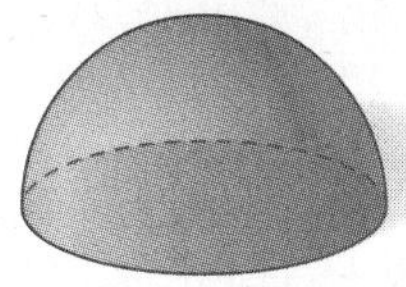

eptagon A seven-sided polygon.

heptágono Polígono de siete lados.

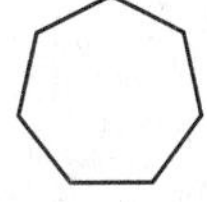

exagon A six-sided polygon.

hexágono Polígono de seis lados.

istogram A bar graph that shows e frequency of data within equal tervals.

histograma Gráfica de barras que muestra la frecuencia de los datos en intervalos iguales.

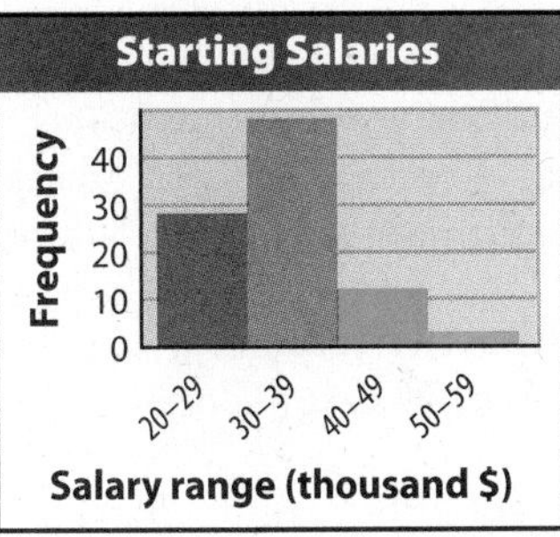

ypotenuse In a right triangle, the de opposite the right angle.

hipotenusa En un triángulo rectángulo, el lado opuesto al ángulo recto.

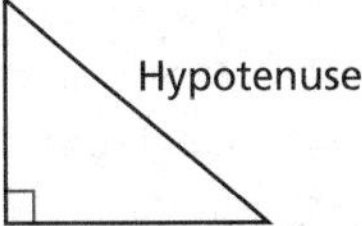

Glossary/Glosario

ENGLISH	SPANISH	EXAMPLES
Identity Property of Addition The property that states that the sum of zero and any number is that number.	**Propiedad de identidad de la suma** Propiedad que establece que la suma de cero y cualquier número es ese número.	$5 + 0 = 5$ $-4 + 0 = -4$
Identity Property of Multiplication The property that states that the product of 1 and any number is that number.	**Propiedad de identidad de la multiplicación** Propiedad que establece que el producto de 1 y cualquier número es ese número.	$3 \cdot 1 = 3$ $-9 \cdot 1 = -9$
image A figure resulting from a transformation.	**imagen** Figura que resulta de una transformación.	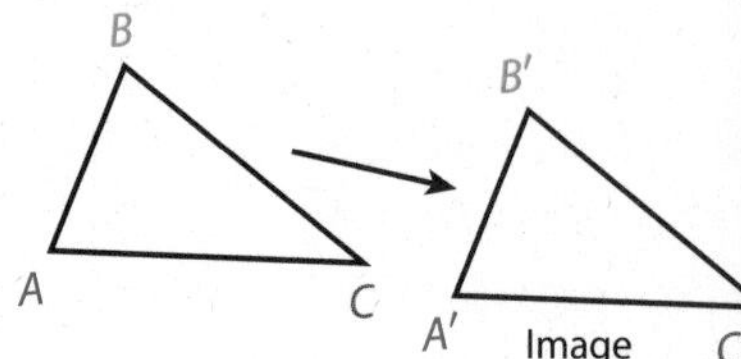
impossible (probability) Can never happen; having a probability of 0.	**imposible (en probabilidad)** Que no puede ocurrir. Suceso cuya probabilidad de ocurrir es 0.	
improper fraction A fraction in which the numerator is greater than or equal to the denominator.	**fracción impropia** Fracción en la que el numerador es mayor que o igual al denominador.	$\frac{5}{5}$ $\frac{7}{4}$
income Money that is paid to a person for goods, services, or investments.	**ingreso** Dinero que se le paga a una persona por bienes, servicios o inversiones.	
independent events Events for which the outcome of one event does not affect the probability of the other.	**sucesos independientes** Dos sucesos son independientes si el resultado de uno no afecta la probabilidad del otro.	A bag contains 3 red marbles and 2 blue marbles. Drawing a red marble, replacing it, and then drawing a blue marble is an example of independent events.
indirect measurement The technique of using similar figures and proportions to find a measure.	**medición indirecta** La técnica de usar figuras semejantes y proporciones para hallar una medida.	
inductive reasoning Using a pattern to make a conclusion.	**razonamiento inductivo** Uso de un patrón para sacar una conclusión.	
inequality A mathematical sentence that shows the relationship between quantities that are not equivalent.	**desigualdad** Enunciado matemático que muestra una relación entre cantidades que no son equivalentes.	$5 < 8$ $5x + 2 \geq 12$
input The value substituted into an expression or function.	**valor de entrada** Valor que se usa para sustituir una variable en una expresión o función.	For the function $y = 6x$, the input 4 produces an output of 24.
integers The set of whole numbers and their opposites.	**enteros** Conjunto de todos los números cabales y sus opuestos.	$\ldots -3, -2, -1, 0, 1, 2, 3, \ldots$

ENGLISH	SPANISH	EXAMPLES
terest The amount of money arged for borrowing or using oney, or the amount of money rned by saving money.	**interés** Cantidad de dinero que se cobra por el préstamo o uso del dinero, o la cantidad que se gana al ahorrar dinero.	
terior angles Angles on the inner les of two lines cut by a transversal.	**ángulos internos** Ángulos en los lados internos de dos líneas intersecadas por una transversal.	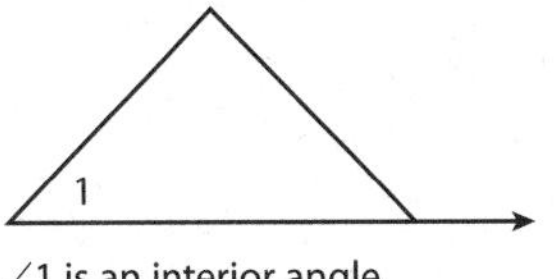 $\angle 1$ is an interior angle.
terquartile range The difference tween the upper and lower quartiles a box-and-whisker plot.	**rango entre cuartiles** La diferencia entre los cuartiles superior e inferior en una gráfica de mediana y rango.	Lower half Upper half 18, (23,) 28, 29, (36,) 42 Lower quartile Upper quartile Interquartile range: $36 - 23 = 13$
tersecting lines Lines that cross exactly one point.	**líneas secantes** Líneas que se cruzan en un solo punto.	
terval The space between marked lues on a number line or the scale of graph.	**intervalo** El espacio entre los valores marcados en una recta numérica o en la escala de una gráfica.	
verse operations Operations at undo each other: addition and btraction, or multiplication and vision.	**operaciones inversas** Operaciones que se cancelan mutuamente: suma y resta, o multiplicación y división.	Addition and subtraction are inverse operations: $5 + 3 = 8; 8 - 3 = 5$ Multiplication and division are inverse operations: $2 \cdot 3 = 6; 6 \div 3 = 2$
verse Property of Addition e sum of a number and its opposite, additive inverse, is 0.	**propiedad inversa de la suma** La suma de un número y su opuesto, o inverso aditivo, es cero.	$3 + (-3) = 0; a + (-a) = 0$
rational number A number at cannot be expressed as a ratio of vo integers or as a repeating or rminating decimal.	**número irracional** Número que no puede expresarse como una razón de dos enteros ni como un decimal periódico o finito.	$\sqrt{2}, \pi$
olate the variable To get a ariable alone on one side of an quation or inequality in order to solve e equation or inequality.	**despejar la variable** Dejar sola la variable en un lado de una ecuación o desigualdad para resolverla.	$x + 7 = 22$ $\underline{-7 \quad -7}$ $x = 15$
osceles triangle A triangle with at ast two congruent sides.	**triángulo isósceles** Triángulo que tiene al menos dos lados congruentes.	

Glossary/Glosario

lateral area The sum of the areas of the lateral faces of a prism or pyramid, or the area of the lateral surface of a cylinder or cone.

área lateral Suma de las áreas de las caras laterales de un prisma o pirámide, o área de la superficie lateral de un cilindro o cono.

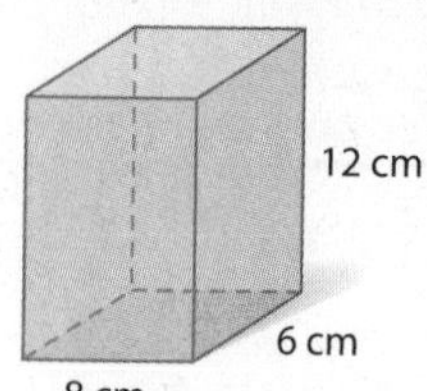

Lateral area $= 12(8)(2) + 12(6)(2)$
$= 336 \text{ cm}^2$

---

lateral face A face of a prism or a pyramid that is not a base.

Cara lateral Cara de un prisma o pirámide que no es una base.

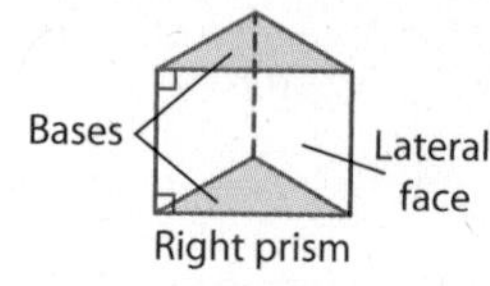

---

least common denominator (LCD) The least common multiple of two or more denominators.

mínimo común denominador (mcd) El mínimo común múltiplo de dos o más denominadores.

The LCD of $\frac{3}{4}$ and $\frac{5}{6}$ is 12.

---

least common multiple (LCM) The least number, other than zero, that is a multiple of two or more given numbers.

mínimo común múltiplo (mcm) El menor de los números, distinto de cero, que es múltiplo de dos o más números.

The LCM of 10 and 18 is 90.

---

legs In a right triangle, the sides that include the right angle; in an isosceles triangle, the pair of congruent sides.

catetos En un triángulo rectángulo, los lados adyacentes al ángulo recto. En un triángulo isósceles, el par de lados congruentes.

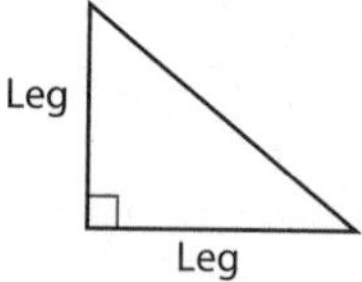

---

liability Money a person owes.

pasivo Dinero que debe una persona.

---

like fractions Fractions that have the same denominator.

fracciones semejantes Fracciones que tienen el mismo denominador.

$\frac{5}{12}$ and $\frac{7}{12}$ are like fractions.

---

like terms Terms with the same variables raised to the same exponents.

términos semejantes Términos que contienen las mismas variables elevada a las mismas exponentes.

In the expression $3a^2 + 5b + 12a^2$, $3a^2$ and $12a^2$ are like terms.

---

line A straight path that has no thickness and extends forever.

línea Trayectoria recta que no tiene ningún grueso y que se extiende por siempre.

ℓ

---

line graph A graph that uses line segments to show how data changes.

gráfica lineal Gráfica que muestra cómo cambian los datos mediante segmentos de recta.

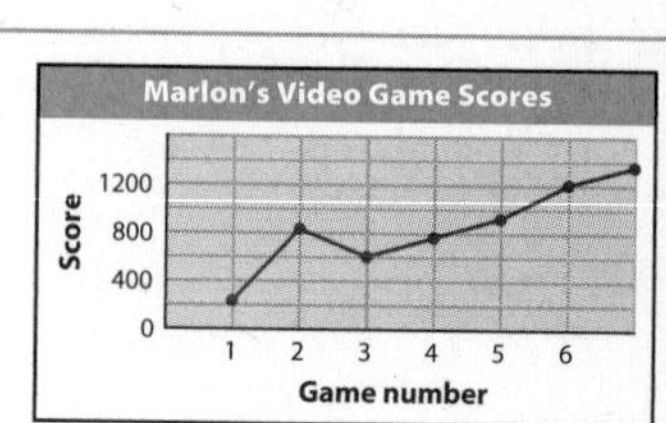

ENGLISH	SPANISH	
ne of best fit A straight line that omes closest to the points on a catter plot.	**línea de mejor ajuste** la línea recta que más se aproxima a los puntos de un diagrama de dispersión.	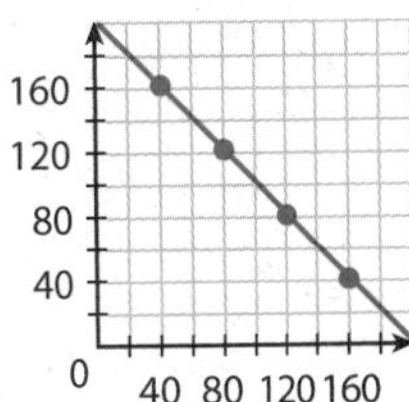
ine of reflection A line that a figure flipped across to create a mirror nage of the original figure.	**línea de reflexión** Línea sobre la cual se invierte una figura para crear una imagen reflejada de la figura original.	Line of reflection
ine of symmetry The imaginary mirror" in line symmetry.	**eje de simetría** El "espejo" imaginario en la simetría axial.	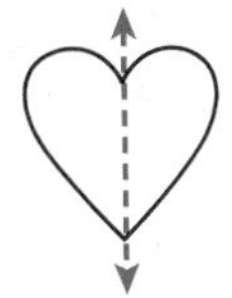
ine plot A number line with marks or dots that show frequency.	**diagrama de acumulación** Recta numérica con marcas o puntos que indican la frecuencia.	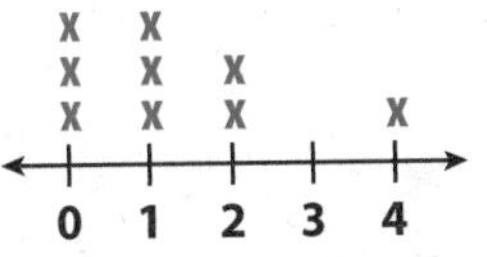
line segment A part of a line made of two endpoints and all points between them.	**segmento de recta** Parte de una línea con dos extremos.	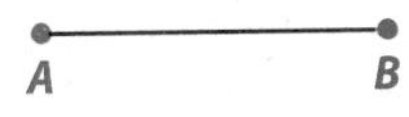
line symmetry A figure has line symmetry if one-half is a mirror-image of the other half.	**simetría axial** Una figura tiene simetría axial si una de sus mitades es la imagen reflejada de la otra.	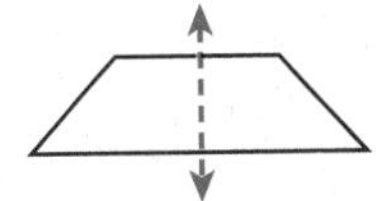
linear equation An equation whose solutions form a straight line on a coordinate plane.	**ecuación lineal** Ecuación cuyas soluciones forman una línea recta en un plano cartesiano.	$y = 2x + 1$
linear function A function whose graph is a straight line.	**función lineal** Función cuya gráfica es una línea recta.	$y = x - 1$ 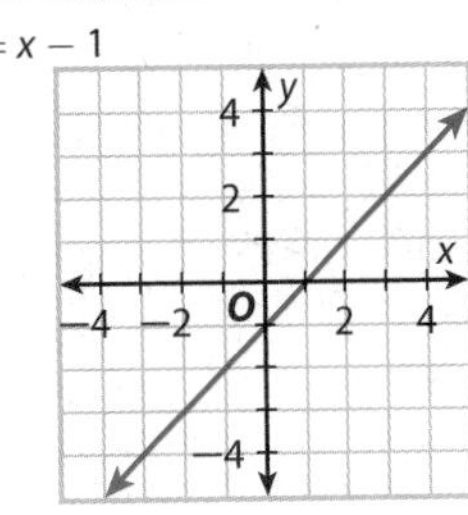
linear inequality A mathematical sentence using <, >, ≤, or ≥ whose graph is a region with a straight-line boundary.	**desigualdad lineal** Enunciado matemático en que se usan los símbolos <, >, ≤, o ≥ y cuya gráfica es una región con una línea de límite recta.	

Glossary/Glosario

ENGLISH	SPANISH	EXAMPLES
linear relationship A relationship between two quantities in which one variable changes by a constant amount as the other variable changes by a constant amount.	**relación lineal** Relación entre dos cantidades en la cual una variable cambia según una cantidad constante y la otra variable también cambia según una cantidad constante.	
lower quartile The median of the lower half of a set of data.	**cuartil inferior** La mediana de la mitad inferior de un conjunto de datos.	Lower half Upper half 18, (23,) 28, 29, 36, 42 ↑ Lower quartile

M

ENGLISH	SPANISH	EXAMPLES
mean The sum of the items in a set of data divided by the number of items in the set; also called *average*.	**media** La suma de todos loselementos de un conjunto de datos dividida entre el número de elementos del conjunto. También se llama *promedio*.	Data set: 4, 6, 7, 8, 10 Mean: $\frac{4+6+7+8+10}{5} = \frac{35}{5} = 7$
mean absolute deviation (MAD) The mean distance between each data value and the mean of the data set.	**desviación absoluta media (DAM)** Distancia media entre cada dato y la media del conjunto de datos.	
measure of central tendency A measure used to describe the middle of a data set; the mean, median, and mode are measures of central tendency.	**medida de tendencia dominante** Medida que describe la parte media de un conjunto de datos; la media, la mediana y la moda son medidas de tendencia dominante.	
median The middle number, or the mean (average) of the two middle numbers, in an ordered set of data.	**mediana** El número intermedio, o la media (el promedio), de los dos números intermedios en un conjunto ordenado de datos.	Data set: 4, 6, 7, 8, 10 Median: 7
metric system of measurement A decimal system of weights and measures that is used universally in science and commonly worldwide.	**sistema métrico de medición** Sistema decimal de pesos y medidas empleado universalmente en las ciencias y comúnmente en todo el mundo.	centimeters, meters, kilometers, grams, kilograms, milliliters, liters
midpoint The point that divides a line segment into two congruent line segments.	**punto medio** El punto que divide un segmento de recta en dos segmentos de recta congruentes.	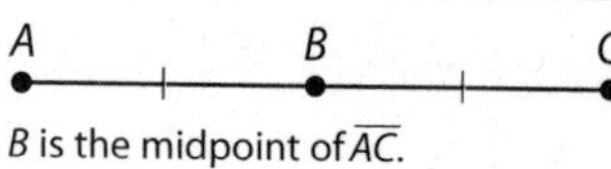 *B* is the midpoint of $\overline{AC}$.
mixed number A number made up of a whole number that is not zero and a fraction.	**número mixto** Número compuesto por un número cabal distinto de cero y una fracción.	$5\frac{1}{8}$
mode The number or numbers that occur most frequently in a set of data; when all numbers occur with the same frequency, we say there is no mode.	**moda** Número o números más frecuentes en un conjunto de datos; si todos los números aparecen con la misma frecuencia, no hay moda.	Data set: 3, 5, 8, 8, 10 Mode: 8
multiple The product of any number and any nonzero whole number is a multiple of that number.	**múltiplo** El producto de un número y cualquier número cabal distinto de cero es un múltiplo de ese número.	30, 40, and 90 are all multiples of 10.

ENGLISH	SPANISH	EXAMPLES
ultiplication Property of quality The property that states at if you multiply both sides of an quation by the same number, the new quation will have the same solution.	**Propiedad de igualdad de la multiplicación** Propiedad que establece que puedes multiplicar ambos lados de una ecuación por el mismo número y la nueva ecuación tendrá la misma solución.	$\frac{1}{3}x = 7$ $(3)(\frac{1}{3}x) = (3)(7)$ $x = 21$
ultiplication Property of Zero e property that states that for all real umbers a, $a \times 0 = 0$ and $0 \times a = 0$.	**Propiedad de multiplicación del cero** Propiedad que establece que para todos los números reales a, $a \times 0 = 0$ y $0 \times a = 0$.	$6 \cdot 0 = 0$ $-5 \cdot 0 = 0$
ultiplicative inverse A number mes its multiplicative inverse is equal 1; also called *reciprocal*.	**inverso multiplicativo** Un número multiplicado por su inverso multiplicativo es igual a 1. También se llama *recíproco*.	The multiplicative inverse of $\frac{4}{5}$ is $\frac{5}{4}$.
ultiplicative Inverse Property e product of a nonzero number and s reciprocal, or multiplicative inverse, one.	**Propiedad inversa de la multiplicación** El producto de un número distinto a cero y su recíproco, o inverso multiplicativo, es uno.	$\frac{2}{3} \cdot \frac{3}{2} = 1; \frac{a}{b} \cdot \frac{b}{a} = 1$
utually exclusive Two events are utually exclusive if they cannot occur the same trial of an experiment.	**mutuamente excluyentes** Dos sucesos son mutuamente excluyentes cuando no pueden ocurrir en la misma prueba de un experimento.	

N

ENGLISH	SPANISH	EXAMPLES
egative correlation Two data ets have a negative correlation, or lationship, if one set of data values creases while the other decreases.	**correlación negativa** Dos conjuntos de datos tienen correlación, o relación, negativa, si los valores de un conjunto aumentan a medida que los valores del otro conjunto disminuyen.	y, x
egative integer An integer less an zero.	**entero negativo** Entero menor que cero.	−4 −3 −2 −1 0 1 2 3 4 −2 is a negative integer.
et An arrangement of two-imensional figures that can be folded form a polyhedron.	**plantilla** Arreglo de figuras bidimensionales que se doblan para formar un poliedro.	10 m, 6 m, 10 m, 6 m
et pay The amount that remains fter all deductions are taken from the ross pay.	**paga neta** Cantidad restante después de restar todas las deducciones de la paga bruta.	

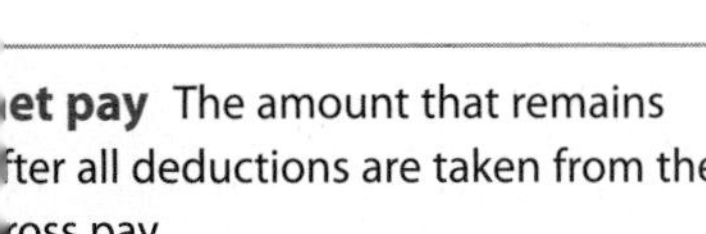

Glossary/Glosario

ENGLISH	SPANISH	EXAMPLES
net worth The difference between the monetary values of a consumer's assets and liabilities.	**patrimonio neto** Diferencia entre el valor monetario de los activos y pasivos de un consumidor.	
no correlation Two data sets have no correlation when there is no relationship between their data values.	**sin correlación** Caso en que los valores de dos conjuntos de datos no muestran ninguna relación.	y, x
nonlinear function A function whose graph is not a straight line.	**función no lineal** Función cuya gráfica no es una línea recta.	
nonterminating decimal A decimal that never ends.	**decimal infinito** Decimal que nunca termina.	
numerator The top number of a fraction that tells how many parts of a whole are being considered.	**numerador** El número de arriba de una fracción; indica cuántas partes de un entero se consideran.	$\frac{4}{5}$ ← Numerator
numerical expression An expression that contains only numbers and operations.	**expresión numérica** Expresión que incluye sólo números y operaciones.	$(2 \cdot 3) + 1$

O

ENGLISH	SPANISH	EXAMPLES
obtuse angle An angle whose measure is greater than 90° but less than 180°.	**ángulo obtuso** Ángulo que mide más de 90° y menos de 180°.	
obtuse triangle A triangle containing one obtuse angle.	**triángulo obtusángulo** Triángulo que tiene un ángulo obtuso.	
octagon An eight-sided polygon.	**octágono** Polígono de ocho lados.	
odd number An integer that is not divisible by two.	**número impar** Entero que no es divisible entre 2.	
odds A comparison of the number of ways an event can occur and the number of ways an event can NOT occur.	**posibilidades** Comparación del número de las maneras que puede ocurrir un suceso y el número de maneras que no puede ocurrir el suceso.	

ENGLISH	SPANISH	EXAMPLES
posites Two numbers that are an ual distance from zero on a number e; also called *additive inverse.*	**opuestos** Dos números que están a la misma distancia de cero en una recta numérica. También se llaman *inversos aditivos.*	5 and −5 are opposites. 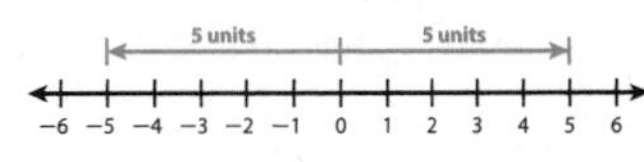
rder of operations A rule for aluating expressions: first perform e operations in parentheses, then mpute powers and roots, then rform all multiplication and division om left to right, and then perform addition and subtraction from left to ght.	**orden de las operaciones** Regla para evaluar expresiones: primero se hacen las operaciones entre paréntesis, luego se hallan las potencias y raíces, después todas las multiplicaciones y divisiones de izquierda a derecha y, por último, todas las sumas y restas de izquierda a derecha.	$3^2 - 12 \div 4$ $9 - 12 \div 4$ Evaluate the power. $9 - 3$ Divide. 6 Subtract.
rdered pair A pair of numbers at can be used to locate a point on a ordinate plane.	**par ordenado** Par de números que sirven para ubicar un punto en un plano cartesiano.	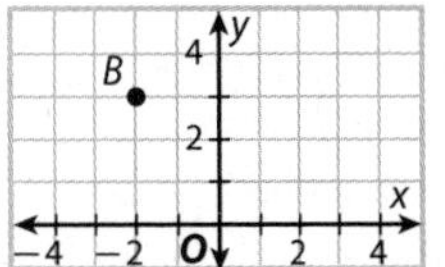 The coordinates of *B* are (−2, 3).
rigin The point where the *x*-axis d *y*-axis intersect on the coordinate ane; (0, 0).	**origen** Punto de intersección entre el eje *x* y el eje *y* en un plano cartesiano: (0, 0).	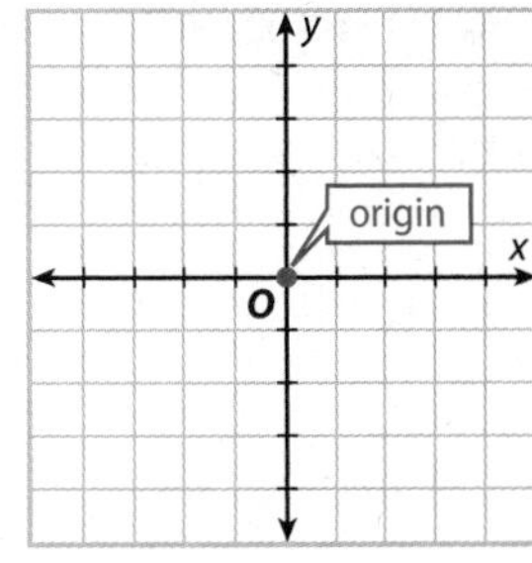
utcome A possible result of a obability experiment.	**resultado** Posible resultado de un experimento de probabilidad.	When rolling a number cube, the possible outcomes are 1, 2, 3, 4, 5, and 6.
utlier A value much greater or uch less than the others in a data set.	**valor extremo** Un valor mucho mayor o menor que los demás de un conjunto de datos.	Most of data Mean Outlier
utput The value that results from e substitution of a given input into expression or function.	**valor de salida** Valor que resulta después de sustituir un valor de entrada determinado en una expresión o función.	For the function $y = 6x$, the input 4 produces an output of 24.
verestimate An estimate that is eater than the exact answer.	**estimación alta** Estimación mayor que la respuesta exacta.	100 is an overestimate for the sum $23 + 24 + 21 + 22$.

arallel lines Lines in a plane that not intersect.	**líneas paralelas** Líneas que se encuentran en el mismo plano pero que nunca se intersecan.	

ENGLISH	SPANISH	EXAMPLES
parallelogram A quadrilateral with two pairs of parallel sides.	**paralelogramo** Cuadrilátero con dos pares de lados paralelos.	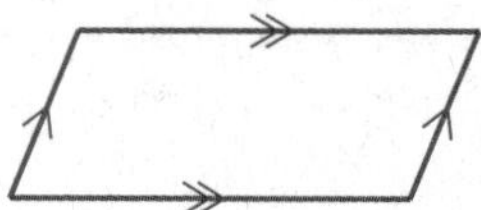
pentagon A five-sided polygon.	**pentágono** Polígono de cinco lados.	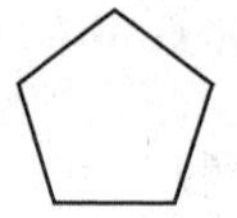
percent A ratio comparing a number to 100.	**porcentaje** Razón que compara un número con el número 100.	$45\% = \frac{45}{100}$
percent of change The amount stated as a percent that a number increases or decreases.	**porcentaje de cambio** Cantidad en que un número aumenta o disminuye, expresada como un porcentaje.	
percent of decrease A percent change describing a decrease in a quantity.	**porcentaje de disminución** Porcentaje de cambio en que una cantidad disminuye.	An item that costs \$8 is marked down to \$6. The amount of the decrease is \$2, and the percent of decrease is $\frac{2}{8} = 0.25 = 25\%$.
percent of increase A percent change describing an increase in a quantity.	**porcentaje de incremento** Porcentaje de cambio en que una cantidad aumenta.	The price of an item increases from \$8 to \$12. The amount of the increase is \$4, and the percent of increase is $\frac{4}{8} = 0.5 = 50\%$.
perfect cube A cube of a whole number.	**cubo perfecto** El cubo de un número cabal.	$2^3 = 8$, so 8 is a perfect cube.
perfect square A square of a whole number.	**cuadrado perfecto** El cuadrado de un número cabal.	$5^2 = 25$, so 25 is a perfect square.
perimeter The distance around a polygon.	**perímetro** Distancia alrededor de un polígono.	18 ft; 6 ft; perimeter = $18 + 6 + 18 + 6 = 48$ ft
permutation An arrangement of items or events in which order is important.	**permutación** Arreglo de objetos o sucesos en el que el orden es importante.	For objects *A*, *B*, and *C*, there are 6 different permutations, *ABC*, *ACB*, *BAC*, *BCA*, *CAB*, and *CBA*.
perpendicular bisector A line that intersects a segment at its midpoint and is perpendicular to the segment.	**mediatriz** Línea que cruza un segmento en su punto medio y es perpendicular al segmento.	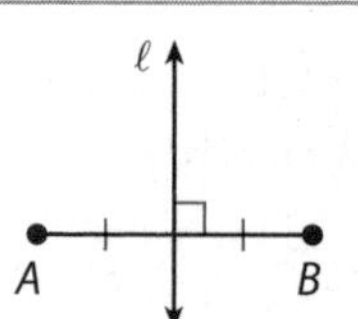
perpendicular lines Lines that intersect to form right angles.	**líneas perpendiculares** Líneas que al intersecarse forman ángulos rectos.	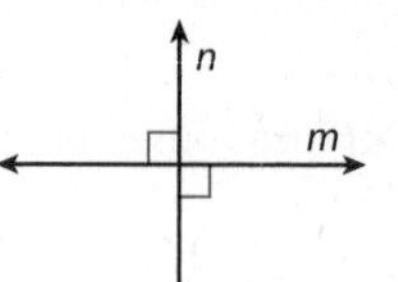

ENGLISH	SPANISH	EXAMPLES
(π) The ratio of the circumference a circle to the length of its diameter; ≈ 3.14 or $\frac{22}{7}$.	**pi (π)** Razón de la circunferencia de un círculo a la longitud de su diámetro; $\pi \approx 3.14$ ó $\frac{22}{7}$.	
ane A flat surface that has no ickness and extends forever.	**plano** Superficie plana que no tiene ningún grueso y que se extiende por siempre.	A • C • $\mathcal{R}$ B • plane *ABC*
oint An exact location that has no ze.	**punto** Ubicación exacta que no tiene ninqún tamaño.	*P* • point *P*
oint-slope form The equation of a e in the form of $y - y_1 = m(x - x_1)$, here *m* is the slope and (x_1, y_1) is a ecific point on the line.	**forma de punto y pendiente** Ecuación lineal del tipo $y - y_1 = m(x - x_1)$, donde *m* es la pendiente y (x_1, y_1) es un punto específico de la línea.	$y - 3 = 2(x - 3)$
olygon A closed plane figure rmed by three or more line segments at intersect only at their endpoints ertices).	**polígono** Figura plana cerrada, formada por tres o más segmentos de recta que se intersecan sólo en sus extremos (vértices).	
olyhedron A three-dimensional ure in which all the surfaces or faces e polygons.	**poliedro** Figura tridimensional cuyas superficies o caras tienen forma de polígonos.	
opulation The entire group of jects or individuals considered for a rvey.	**población** Grupo completo de objetos o individuos que se desea estudiar.	In a survey about the study habits of middle school students, the population is all middle school students.
ositive correlation Two data ts have a positive correlation, or lationship, when their data values crease or decrease together.	**correlación positiva** Dos conjuntos de datos tienen una correlación, o relación, positiva cuando los valores de ambos conjuntos aumentan o disminuyen al mismo tiempo.	*y* *x*
ositive integer An integer greater an zero.	**entero positivo** Entero mayor que cero.	
ower A number produced by ising a base to an exponent.	**potencia** Número que resulta al elevar una base a un exponente.	$2^3 = 8$, so 2 to the 3rd power is 8.
recision The level of detail of a easurement, determined by the unit measure.	**precisión** Detalle de una medición, determinado por la unidad de medida.	A ruler marked in millimeters has a greater level of precision than a ruler marked in centimeters.
rediction Something you can asonably expect to happen in the ture.	**predicción** Algo que se puede razonablemente esperar suceder en el futuro.	

Glossary/Glosario

ENGLISH	SPANISH	EXAMPLES
preimage The original figure in a transformation.	**imagen original** Figura original en una transformación.	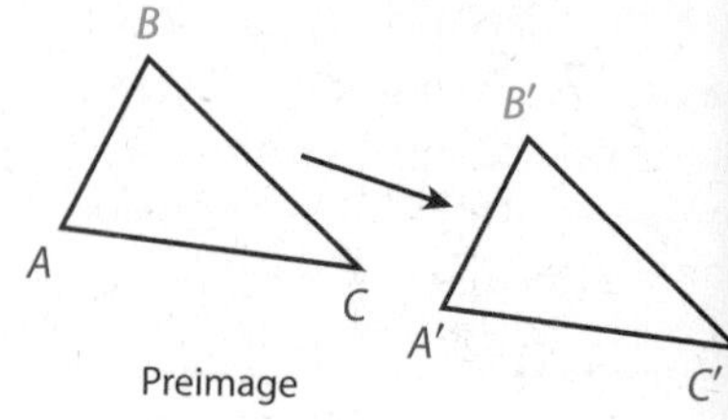
prime factorization A number written as the product of its prime factors.	**factorización prima** Un número escrito como el producto de sus factores primos.	$10 = 2 \cdot 5$ $24 = 2^3 \cdot 3$
prime number A whole number greater than 1 that has exactly two factors, itself and 1.	**número primo** Número cabal mayor que 1 que sólo es divisible entre 1 y él mismo.	5 is prime because its only factors are 5 and 1.
principal The initial amount of money borrowed or saved.	**capital** Cantidad inicial de dinero depositada o recibida en préstamo.	
principal square root The nonnegative square root of a number.	**raíz cuadrada principal** Raíz cuadrada no negativa de un número.	$\sqrt{25} = 5$; the principal square root of 25 is 5.
prism A polyhedron that has two congruent polygon-shaped bases and other faces that are all parallelograms.	**prisma** Poliedro con dos bases congruentes con forma de polígono y caras con forma de paralelogramo.	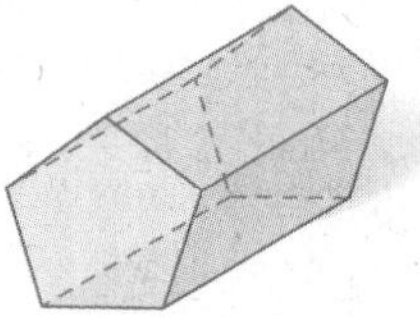
probability A number from 0 to 1 (or 0% to 100%) that describes how likely an event is to occur.	**probabilidad** Un número entre 0 y 1 (ó 0% y 100%) que describe qué tan probable es un suceso.	A bag contains 3 red marbles and 4 blue marbles. The probability of randomly choosing a red marble is $\frac{3}{7}$.
product The result when two or more numbers are multiplied.	**producto** Resultado de multiplicar dos o más números.	The product of 4 and 8 is 32.
proper fraction A fraction in which the numerator is less than the denominator.	**fracción propia** Fracción en la que el numerador es menor que el denominador.	$\frac{3}{4}, \frac{1}{12}, \frac{7}{8}$
proportion An equation that states that two ratios are equivalent.	**proporción** Ecuación que establece que dos razones son equivalentes.	$\frac{2}{3} = \frac{4}{6}$
proportional relationship A relationship between two quantities in which the ratio of one quantity to the other quantity is constant.	**relación proporcional** Relación entre dos cantidades en que la razón de una cantidad a la otra es constante.	
protractor A tool for measuring angles.	**transportador** Instrumento para medir ángulos.	
pyramid A polyhedron with a polygon base and triangular sides that all meet at a common vertex.	**pirámide** Poliedro cuya base es un polígono; tiene caras triangulares que se juntan en un vértice común.	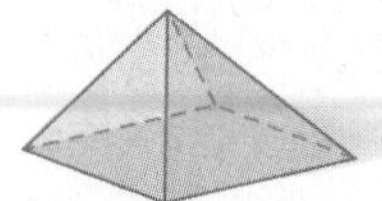

Glossary/Glosario

ENGLISH | SPANISH | 

ythagorean Theorem In a right iangle, the square of the length of ıe hypotenuse is equal to the sum of ıe squares of the lengths of the legs.

Teorema de Pitágoras En un triángulo rectángulo, la suma de los cuadrados de los catetos es igual al cuadrado de la hipotenusa.

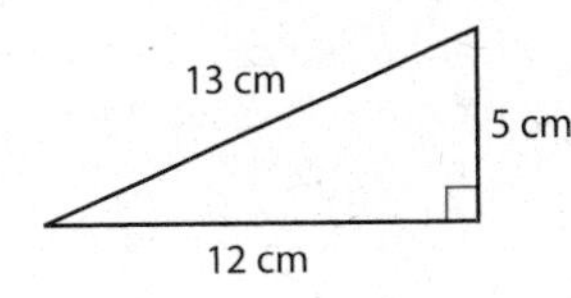

$5^2 + 12^2 = 13^2$
$25 + 144 = 169$

uadrant The *x*- and *y*-axes divide ɦe coordinate plane into four regions. ach region is called a quadrant.

cuadrante El eje *x* y el eje *y* dividen el plano cartesiano en cuatro regiones. Cada región recibe el nombre de cuadrante.

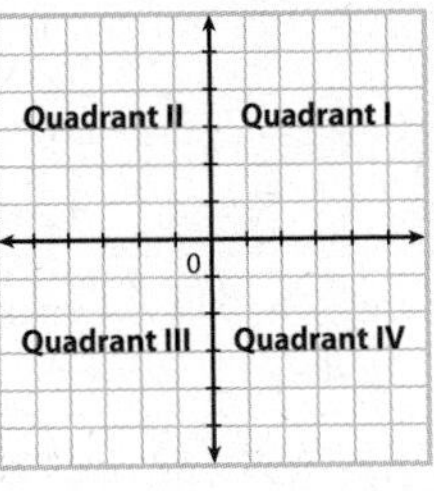

uadratic function A function of he form $y = ax^2 + bx + c$, where $a \neq 0$.

función cuadrática Función del tipo $y = ax^2 + bx + c$, donde $a \neq 0$.

$y = 2x^2 - 12x + 10$,
$y = 3x^2$

quadrilateral A four-sided polygon.

cuadrilátero Polígono de cuatro lados.

quartile Three values, one of which s the median, that divide a data set nto fourths. See also *first quartile, third quartile.*

cuartiles Cada uno de tres valores, uno de los cuales es la mediana, que dividen en cuartos un conjunto de datos. Ver también *primer cuartil, tercer cuartil.*

quotient The result when one number is divided by another.

cociente Resultado de dividir un número entre otro.

In $8 \div 4 = 2$, 2 is the quotient.

radical sign The symbol $\sqrt{\ }$ used to represent the nonnegative square root of a number.

símbolo de radical El símbolo $\sqrt{\ }$ con que se representa la raíz cuadrada no negativa de un número.

$\sqrt{36} = 6$

radius A line segment with one endpoint at the center of a circle and the other endpoint on the circle, or the length of that segment.

radio Segmento de recta con un extremo en el centro de un círculo y el otro en la circunferencia; o bien la longitud de ese segmento.

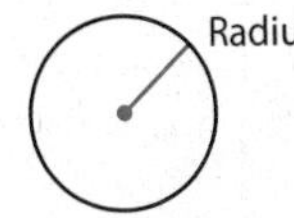

random sample A sample in which each individual or object in the entire population has an equal chance of being selected.

muestra aleatoria Muestra en la que cada individuo u objeto de la población tiene la misma oportunidad de ser elegido.

Mr. Henson chose a random sample of the class by writing each student's name on a slip of paper, mixing up the slips, and drawing five slips without looking.

Glossary/Glosario

ENGLISH	SPANISH	EXAMPLES
range (in statistics) The difference between the greatest and least values in a data set.	**rango (en estadística)** Diferencia entre los valores máximo y mínimo de un conjunto de datos.	Data set: 3, 5, 7, 7, 12 Range: $12 - 3 = 9$
rate A ratio that compares two quantities measured in different units.	**tasa** Una razón que compara dos cantidades medidas en diferentes unidades.	The speed limit is 55 miles per hour, or 55 mi/h.
rate of change A ratio that compares the amount of change in a dependent variable to the amount of change in an independent variable.	**tasa de cambio** Razón que compara la cantidad de cambio de la variable dependiente con la cantidad de combio de la variable independiente.	The cost of mailing a letter increased from 22 cents in 1985 to 25 cents in 1988. During this period, the rate of change was $\frac{\text{change in cost}}{\text{change in year}} = \frac{25 - 22}{1988 - 1985} = \frac{3}{3}$
rate of interest The percent charged or earned on an amount of money; see *simple interest.*	**tasa de interés** Porcentaje que se cobra por una cantidad de dinero prestada o que se gana por una cantidad de dinero ahorrada; ver *interés simple.*	
ratio A comparison of two quantities by division.	**razón** Comparación de dos cantidades mediante una división.	12 to 25, 12:25, $\frac{12}{25}$
rational number Any number that can be expressed as a ratio of two integers.	**número racional** Número que se puede escribir como una razón de dos enteros.	6 can be expressed as $\frac{6}{1}$. 0.5 can be expressed as $\frac{1}{2}$.
ray A part of a line that starts at one endpoint and extends forever in one direction.	**rayo** Parte de una recta que comienza en un extremo y se extiende infinitamente en una dirección.	D
real number A rational or irrational number.	**número real** Número racional o irracional.	
reciprocal One of two numbers whose product is 1; also called *multiplicative inverse.*	**recíproco** Uno de dos números cuyo producto es igual a 1. También se llama *inverso multiplicativo.*	The reciprocal of $\frac{2}{3}$ is $\frac{3}{2}$.
rectangle A parallelogram with four right angles.	**rectángulo** Paralelogramo con cuatro ángulos rectos.	
rectangular prism A polyhedron whose bases are rectangles and whose other faces are parallelograms.	**prisma rectangular** Poliedro cuyas bases son rectángulos y cuyas caras tienen forma de paralelogramo.	
reduction A decrease in the size of all dimensions.	**reducción** Disminución de tamaño en todas las dimensiones de una figura.	
reflection A transformation of a figure that flips the figure across a line.	**reflexión** Transformación que ocurre cuando se invierte una figura sobre una línea.	B B′ A C C′ A′

ENGLISH	SPANISH	EXAMPLES 
egular polygon A polygon with ongruent sides and angles.	**polígono regular** Polígono con lados y ángulos congruentes.	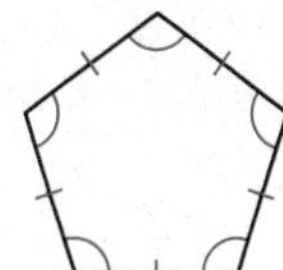
egular pyramid A pyramid whose ase is a regular polygon and whose teral faces are all congruent.	**pirámide regular** Pirámide que tiene un polígono regular como base y caras laterales congruentes.	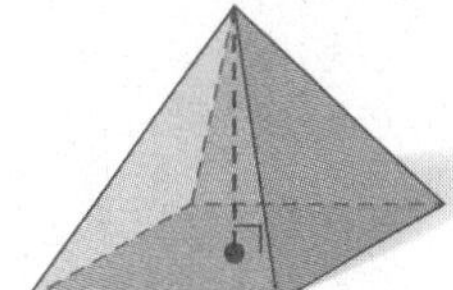
elative frequency The frequency f a data value or range of data values ivided by the total number of data alues in the set.	**frecuencia relativa** La frecuencia de un valor o un rango de valores dividido por el número total de los valores en el conjunto.	
elatively prime Two numbers re relatively prime if their greatest ommon factor (GCF) is 1.	**primo relatívo** Dos números son primos relativos si su máximo común divisor (MCD) es 1.	8 and 15 are relatively prime.
emote interior angle An interior ngle of a polygon that is not adjacent o the exterior angle.	**ángulo interno remoto** Ángulo interno de un polígono que no es adyacente al ángulo externo.	
epeating decimal A decimal which one or more digits repeat finitely.	**decimal periódico** Decimal en el que uno o más dígitos se repiten infinitamente.	$0.757575\ldots = 0.\overline{75}$
hombus A parallelogram with all des congruent.	**rombo** Paralelogramo en el que todos los lados son congruentes.	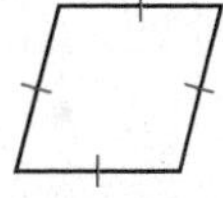
ight angle An angle that easures 90°.	**ángulo recto** Ángulo que mide exactamente 90°.	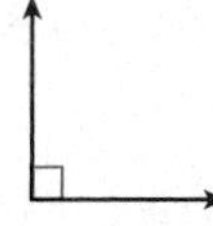
ight cone A cone in which a erpendicular line drawn from the ase to the tip (vertex) passes through e center of the base.	**cono regular** Cono en el que una línea perpendicular trazada de la base a la punta (vértice) pasa por el centro de la base.	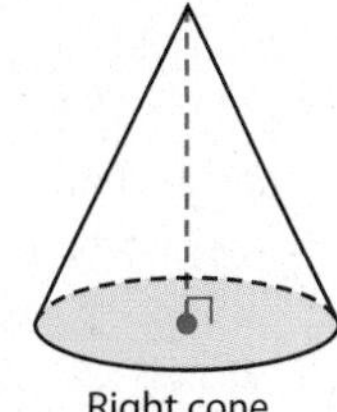 Right cone
ight triangle A triangle containing right angle.	**triángulo rectángulo** Triángulo que tiene un ángulo recto.	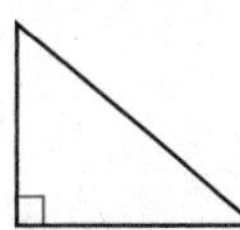
ise The vertical change when the ope of a line is expressed as the tio $\frac{\text{rise}}{\text{run}}$, or "rise over run."	**distancia vertical** El cambio vertical cuando la pendiente de una línea se expresa como la razón $\frac{\text{distancia vertical}}{\text{distancia horizontal}}$, o "distancia vertical sobre distancia horizontal".	For the points $(3, -1)$ and $(6, 5)$, the rise is $5 - (-1) = 6$.

Glossary/Glosario

ENGLISH	SPANISH	EXAMPLES

rotation A transformation in which a figure is turned around a point.

rotación Transformación que ocurre cuando una figura gira alrededor de un punto.

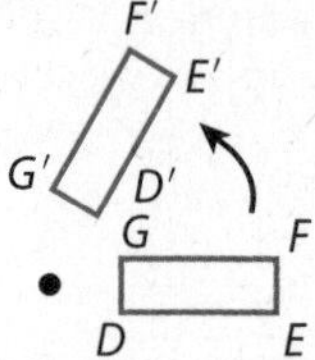

rotational symmetry A figure has rotational symmetry if it can be rotated less than 360° around a central point and coincide with the original figure.

simetría de rotación Ocurre cuando una figura gira menos de 360° alrededor de un punto central sin dejar de ser congruente con la figura original.

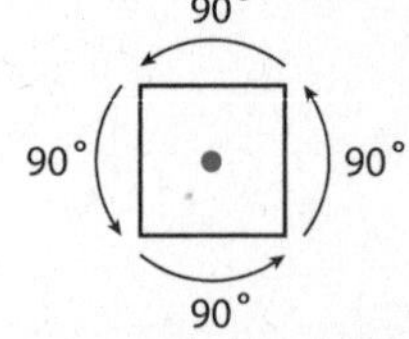

rounding Replacing a number with an estimate of that number to a given place value.

redondear Sustituir un número por una estimación de ese número hasta cierto valor posicional.

2,354 rounded to the nearest thousand is 2,000, and 2,354 rounded to the nearest 100 is 2,400.

run The horizontal change when the slope of a line is expressed as the ratio $\frac{\text{rise}}{\text{run}}$, or "rise over run."

distancia horizontal El cambio horizontal cuando la pendiente de una línea se expresa como la razón $\frac{\text{distancia vertical}}{\text{distancia horizontal}}$, o "distancia vertical sobre distancia horizontal".

For the points (3, −1) and (6, 5), the run is $6 - 3 = 3$.

S

sales tax A percent of the cost of an item that is charged by governments to raise money.

impuesto sobre la venta Porcentaje del costo de un artículo que los gobiernos cobran para recaudar fondos.

same-side interior angles A pair of angles on the same side of a transversal and between two lines intersected by the transversal.

ángulo internos del mismo lado Dadas dos rectas cortadas por una transversal, par de ángulos ubicados en el mismo lado de la transversal y entre las dos rectas.

sample A part of the population.

muestra Una parte de la población.

In a survey about the study habits of middle school students, a sample is a survey of 100 randomly chosen students.

sample space All possible outcomes of an experiment.

espacio muestral Conjunto de todos los resultados posibles de un experimento.

When rolling a number cube, the sample space is 1, 2, 3, 4, 5, 6.

savings Money that is not spent by a consumer currently, but is reserved for later use.

ahorros Dinero que un consumidor no gasta en el presente, pero que reserva para uso futuro.

scale The ratio between two sets of measurements.

escala La razón entre dos conjuntos de medidas.

1 cm:5 mi

ENGLISH	SPANISH	EXAMPLES
cale drawing A drawing that uses a cale to make an object smaller than or rger than the real object.	**dibujo a escala** Dibujo en el que se usa una escala para que un objeto se vea mayor o menor que el objeto real al que representa.	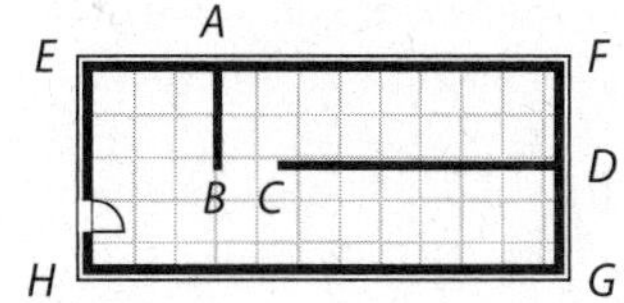 A blueprint is an example of a scale drawing.
cale factor The ratio used to nlarge or reduce similar figures.	**factor de escala** Razón que se usa para agrandar o reducir figuras semejantes.	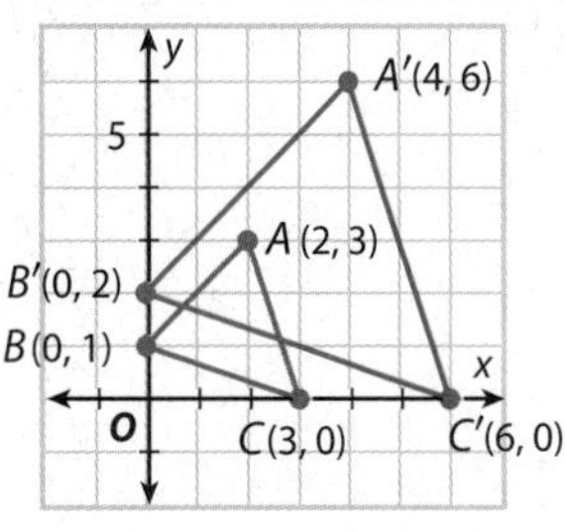 Scale factor: 2
cale model A proportional model f a three-dimensional object.	**modelo a escala** Modelo proporcional de un objeto tridimensional.	
calene triangle A triangle with no ongruent sides.	**triángulo escaleno** Triángulo que no tiene lados congruentes.	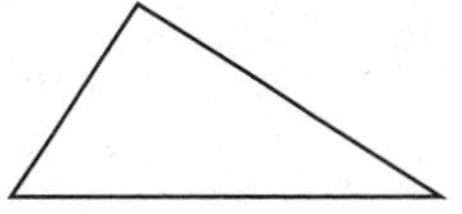
catter plot A graph with points lotted to show a possible relationship etween two sets of data.	**diagrama de dispersión** Gráfica de puntos que se usa para mostrar una posible relación entre dos conjuntos de datos.	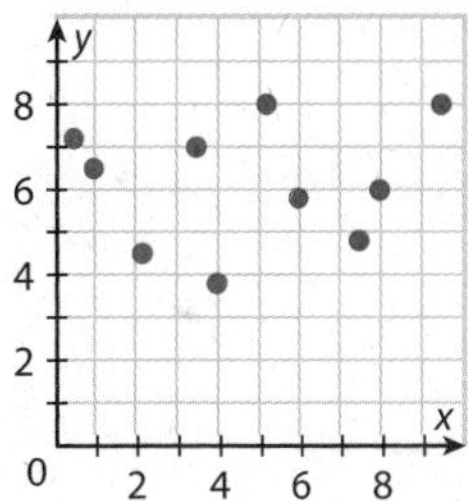
cientific notation A method f writing very large or very small umbers by using powers of 10.	**notación científica** Método que se usa para escribir números muy grandes o muy pequeños mediante potencias de 10.	$12{,}560{,}000{,}000{,}000 = 1.256 \times 10^{13}$
ector A region enclosed by two radii nd the arc joining their endpoints.	**sector** Región encerrada por dos radios y el arco que une sus extremos.	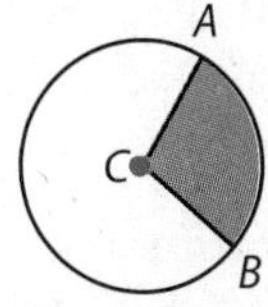
ector (data) A section of a ircle graph representing part f the data set.	**sector (datos)** Sección de una gráfica circular que representa una parte del conjunto de datos.	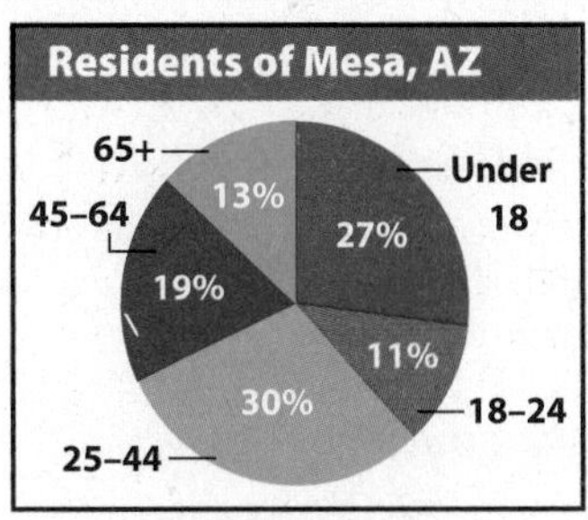 The circle graph has 5 sectors.

ENGLISH	SPANISH	EXAMPLES
segment A part of a line between two endpoints.	**segmento** Parte de una línea entre dos extremos.	
sequence An ordered list of numbers.	**sucesión** Lista ordenada de números.	2, 4, 6, 8, 10, …
set A group of terms.	**conjunto** Un grupo de elementos.	
side A line bounding a geometric figure; one of the faces forming the outside of an object.	**lado** Línea que delimita las figuras geométricas; una de las caras que forman la parte exterior de un objeto.	
Side-Side-Side (SSS) A rule stating that if three sides of one triangle are congruent to three sides of another triangle, then the triangles are congruent.	**Lado-Lado-Lado (LLL)** Regla que establece que dos triángulos son congruentes cuando sus tres lados correspondientes son congruentes.	 $\triangle ABC \cong \triangle DEF$
significant digits The digits used to express the precision of a measurement.	**dígitos significativos** Dígitos usados para expresar la precisión de una medida.	0.048 has 2 significant digits. 5.003 has 4 significant digits.
similar Figures with the same shape but not necessarily the same size are similar.	**semejantes** Figuras que tienen la misma forma, pero no necesariamente el mismo tamaño.	
similarity transformation A transformation that results in an image that is the same shape, but not necessarily the same size, as the original figure.	**transformación de semejanza** Una transformación que resulta en una imagen que tiene la misma forma, pero no necesariamente el mismo tamaño como la figura original.	
simple event An event consisting of only one outcome.	**suceso simple** Suceso que tiene sólo un resultado.	In the experiment of rolling a number cube, the event consisting of the outcome 3 is a simple event.
simple interest A fixed percent of the principal. It is found using the formula $I = Prt$, where P represents the principal, r the rate of interest, and t the time.	**interés simple** Un porcentaje fijo del capital. Se calcula con la fórmula $I = Cit$, donde C representa el capital, i, la tasa de interés y t, el tiempo.	\$100 is put into an account with a simple interest rate of 5%. After 2 years, the account will have earned $I = 100 \cdot 0.05 \cdot 2 = \$10$.
simplest form A fraction is in simplest form when the numerator and denominator have no common factors other than 1.	**mínima expresión** Una fracción está en su mínima expresión cuando el numerador y el denominador no tienen más factor común que 1.	Fraction: $\frac{8}{12}$ Simplest form: $\frac{2}{3}$
simplify To write a fraction or expression in simplest form.	**simplificar** Escribir una fracción o expresión numérica en su mínima expresión.	

ENGLISH	SPANISH	EXAMPLES
imulation A model of an xperiment, often one that would be oo difficult or too time-consuming to ctually perform.	**simulación** Representación de un experimento, por lo regular de uno cuya realización sería demasiado difícil o llevaría mucho tiempo.	
kew lines Lines that lie in different lanes that are neither parallel nor ntersecting.	**líneas oblicuas** Líneas que se encuentran en planos distintos, por eso no se intersecan ni son paralelas.	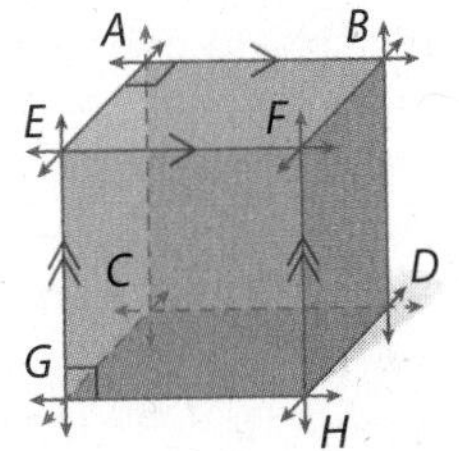$\overleftrightarrow{AB}$ and $\overleftrightarrow{CG}$ are skew lines.
slant height of a cone The distance from the vertex of a cone to a point on the edge of the base.	**altura inclinada de un cono** Distancia desde el vértice de un cono hasta un punto en el borde de la base.	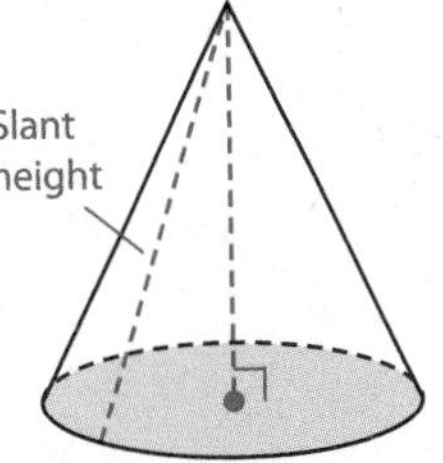
slant height of a pyramid The distance from the vertex of a pyramid to the midpoint of an edge of the base.	**altura inclinada de una pirámide** Distancia desde el vértice de una pirámide hasta el punto medio de una arista de la base.	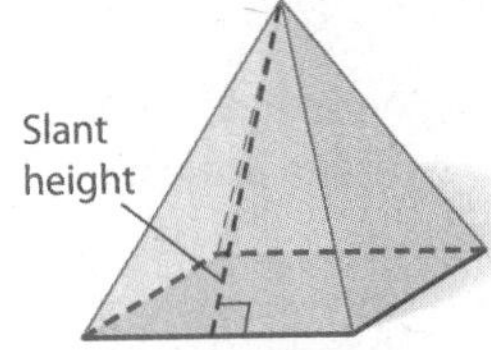
slope A measure of the steepness of a line on a graph; the rise divided by the run.	**pendiente** Medida de la inclinación de una línea en una gráfica. Razón de la distancia vertical a la distancia horizontal.	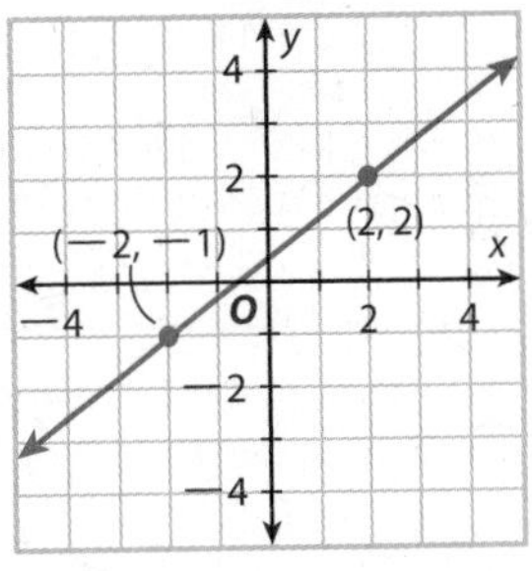Slope $= \frac{\text{rise}}{\text{run}} = \frac{3}{4}$
slope-intercept form A linear equation written in the form $y = mx + b$, where m represents slope and b represents the y-intercept.	**forma de pendiente-interseccíon** Ecuación lineal escrita en la forma $y = mx + b$, donde m es la pendiente y b es la intersección con el eje y.	$y = 6x - 3$
solid figure A three-dimensional figure.	**cuerpo geométrico** Figura tridimensional.	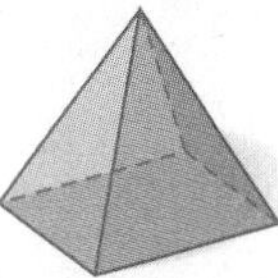
solution of an equation A value or values that make an equation true.	**solución de una ecuación** Valor o valores que hacen verdadera una ecuación.	Equation: $x + 2 = 6$ Solution: $x = 4$

Glossary/Glosario

ENGLISH	SPANISH	EXAMPLES
solution of an inequality A value or values that make an inequality true.	**solución de una desigualdad** Valor o valores que hacen verdadera una desigualdad.	Inequality: $x + 3 \geq 10$ Solution: $x \geq 7$
solution set The set of values that make a statement true.	**conjunto solución** Conjunto de valores que hacen verdadero un enunciado.	Inequality: $x + 3 \geq 5$ Solution set: $x \geq 2$ −4 −3 −2 −1 0 1 2 3 4 5 6
solve To find an answer or a solution.	**resolver** Hallar una respuesta o solución.	
sphere A three-dimensional figure with all points the same distance from the center.	**esfera** Figura tridimensional en la que todos los puntos están a la misma distancia del centro.	
square (geometry) A rectangle with four congruent sides.	**cuadrado** (en geometría) Rectángulo con cuatro lados congruentes.	
square (numeration) A number raised to the second power.	**cuadrado (en numeración)** Número elevado a la segunda potencia.	In 5^2, the number 5 is squared.
square number The product of a number and itself.	**cuadrado de un número** El producto de un número y sí mismo.	25 is a square number. $5 \cdot 5 = 25$
square root A number that is multiplied by itself to form a product is called a square root of that product.	**raíz cuadrada** El número que se multiplica por sí mismo para formar un producto se denomina la raíz cuadrada de ese producto.	$\sqrt{16} = 4$ because $4^2 = 4 \cdot 4 = 16$
standard form (in numeration) A way to write numbers by using digits.	**forma estándar (en numeración)** Una manera de escribir números por medio de dígitos.	Five thousand, two hundred ten in standard form is 5,210.
stem-and-leaf plot A graph used to organize and display data so that the frequencies can be compared.	**diagrama de tallo y hojas** Gráfica que muestra y ordena los datos, y que sirve para comparar las frecuencias.	Stem | Leaves 3 | 2 3 4 4 7 9 4 | 0 1 5 7 7 7 8 5 | 1 2 2 3 *Key: 3|2 means 3.2*
straight angle An angle that measures 180°.	**ángulo llano** Ángulo que mide exactamente 180°.	
subset A set contained within another set.	**subconjunto** Conjunto que pertenece a otro conjunto.	
substitute To replace a variable with a number or another expression in an algebraic expression.	**sustituir** Reemplazar una variable por un número u otra expresión en una expresión algebraica.	

ENGLISH	SPANISH	EXAMPLES
ubtraction Property of quality The property that states hat if you subtract the same number om both sides of an equation, the ew equation will have the same olution.	**Propiedad de igualdad de la resta** Propiedad que establece que puedes restar el mismo número de ambos lados de una ecuación y la nueva ecuación tendrá la misma solución.	$\begin{array}{rcr} x+6 & = & 8 \\ -6 & & -6 \\ \hline x & = & 2 \end{array}$
um The result when two or more umbers are added.	**suma** Resultado de sumar dos o más números.	The sum of $6 + 7 + 1$ is 14.
upplementary angles Two angles vhose measures have a sum of 180°.	**ángulos suplementarios** Dos ángulos cuyas medidas suman 180°.	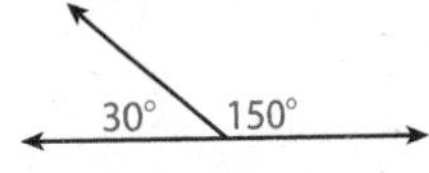
urface area The sum of the areas of the faces, or surfaces, of a three-dimensional figure.	**área total** Suma de las áreas de las caras, o superficies, de una figura tridimensional.	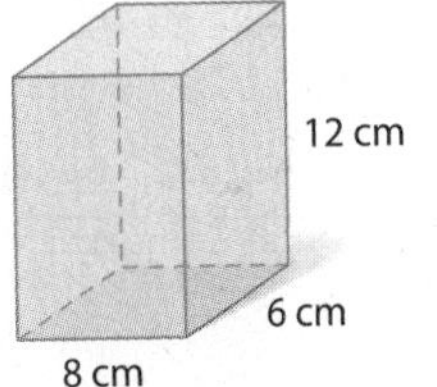 Surface area $= 2(8)(12) + 2(8)(6) + 2(12)(6) = 432\ \text{cm}^2$

T

ENGLISH	SPANISH	EXAMPLES
taxable income The total amount of income minus qualifying deductions.	**ingreso sujeto a impuestos** Cantidad total de ingresos, menos las deducciones aplicables.	
term (in an expression) The parts of an expression that are added or subtracted.	**término (en una expresión)** Las partes de una expresión que se suman o se restan.	$3x^2 + 6x - 8$ Term Term Term
term (in a sequence) An element or number in a sequence.	**término (en una sucesión)** Elemento o número de una sucesión.	5 is the third term in the sequence 1, 3, 5, 7, 9, …
terminating decimal A decimal number whose repeating digit is 0.	**decimal finito** Decimal con un número determinado de posiciones decimales.	$6.75 = 6.75000$
tessellation A repeating pattern of plane figures that completely covers a plane with no gaps or overlaps.	**teselado** Patrón repetido de figuras planas que cubren totalmente un plano sin superponerse ni dejar huecos.	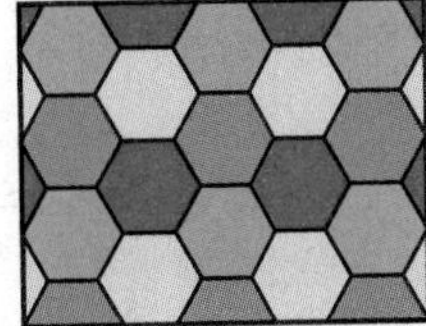
theoretical probability The ratio of the number of ways an event can occur to the total number of equally likely outcomes.	**probabilidad teórica** Razón del número de las maneras que puede ocurrir un suceso al número total de resultados igualmente probables.	When rolling a number cube, the theoretical probability of rolling a 4 is $\frac{1}{6}$.

Glossary/Glosario

ENGLISH	SPANISH	EXAMPLES
third quartile The median of the upper half of a set of data; also called *upper quartile.*	**tercer cuartil** La mediana de la mitad superior de un conjunto de datos. También se llama *cuartil superior.*	
transformation A change in the position or orientation of a figure.	**transformación** Cambio en la posición u orientación de una figura.	
translation A movement (slide) of a figure along a straight line.	**traslación** Desplazamiento de una figura a lo largo de una línea recta.	J M K L → J′ M′ K′ L′
transversal A line that intersects two or more lines.	**transversal** Línea que cruza dos o más líneas.	1 2 5 6 3 4 7 8 Transversal
trapezoid A quadrilateral with exactly one pair of parallel sides.	**trapecio** Cuadrilátero con un par de lados paralelos.	B C A D
tree diagram A branching diagram that shows all possible combinations or outcomes of an event.	**diagrama de árbol** Diagrama ramificado que muestra todas las posibles combinaciones o resultados de un suceso.	
trial Each repetition or observation of an experiment.	**prueba** Una sola repetición u observación de un experimento.	When rolling a number cube, each roll is one trial.
triangle A three-sided polygon.	**triángulo** Polígono de tres lados.	
Triangle Inequality Theorem The theorem that states that the sum of the lengths of any two sides of a triangle is greater than the length of the third side.	**Teorema de desigualdad de triángulos** El teorema dice que la suma de cualquier dos lados de un triangulo es mayor que la longitud del lado tercero.	4 5 7 Can form a triangle; 4 2 7 Cannot form a triangle
Triangle Sum Theorem The theorem that states that the measures of the angles in a triangle add to 180°.	**Teorema de la suma del triángulo** Teorema que establece que las medidas de los ángulos de un triángulo suman 180°.	
triangular prism A polyhedron whose bases are triangles and whose other faces are parallelograms.	**prisma triangular** Poliedro cuyas bases son triángulos y cuyas demás caras tienen forma de paralelogramo.	

ENGLISH	SPANISH	EXAMPLES

nderestimate An estimate that is ss than the exact answer.	**estimación baja** Estimación menor que la respuesta exacta.	
nit conversion The process of hanging one unit of measure to nother.	**conversión de unidades** Proceso que consiste en cambiar una unidad de medida por otra.	
nit conversion factor A fraction sed in unit conversion in which the umerator and denominator represent ne same amount but are in different nits.	**factor de conversión de unidades** Fracción que se usa para la conversión de unidades, donde el numerador y el denominador representan la misma cantidad pero están en unidades distintas.	$\frac{60 \text{ min}}{1\text{h}}$ or $\frac{1\text{h}}{60 \text{ min}}$
nit price A unit rate used to ompare prices.	**precio unitario** Tasa unitaria que sirve para comparar precios.	
nit rate A rate in which the second uantity in the comparison is one unit.	**tasa unitaria** Una tasa en la que la segunda cantidad de la comparación es la unidad.	10 cm per minute
pper quartile The median of the pper half of a set of data.	**cuartil superior** La mediana de la mitad superior de un conjunto de datos.	Lower half Upper half 18, 23, 28, 29, (36,) 42 Upper quartile

ariable A symbol used to represent quantity that can change.	**variable** Símbolo que representa una cantidad que puede cambiar.	In the expression $2x + 3$, x is the variable.
ariable expense Expenses that ccur regularly but may change ecause the consumer has some ontrol over the amount.	**gasto variable** Gasto que ocurre con regularidad y que es necesario para vivir, pero que puede cambiar debido a que el consumidor tiene algún control sobre la cantidad.	
enn diagram A diagram that is ised to show relationships between ets.	**diagrama de Venn** Diagrama que muestra las relaciones entre conjuntos.	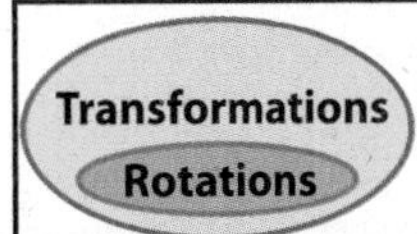
erbal expression A word or hrase.	**expresión verbal** Palabra o frase.	

Glossary/Glosario

ENGLISH	SPANISH	EXAMPLES
vertex On an angle or polygon, the point where two sides intersect.	**vértice** En un ángulo o polígono, el punto de intersección de dos lados.	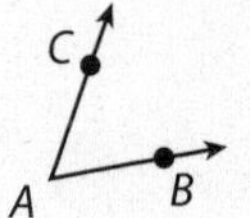 A is the vertex of $\angle CAB$.
vertical angles A pair of opposite congruent angles formed by intersecting lines.	**ángulos opuestos por el vértice** Par de ángulos opuestos congruentes formados por líneas secantes.	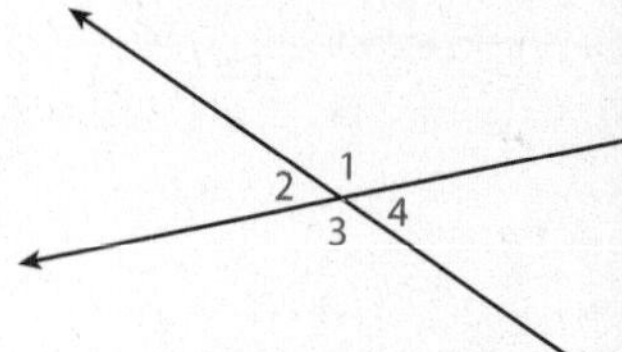 $\angle 1$ and $\angle 3$ are vertical angles. $\angle 2$ and $\angle 4$ are vertical angles.
volume The number of cubic units needed to fill a given space.	**volumen** Número de unidades cúbicas que se necesitan para llenar un espacio.	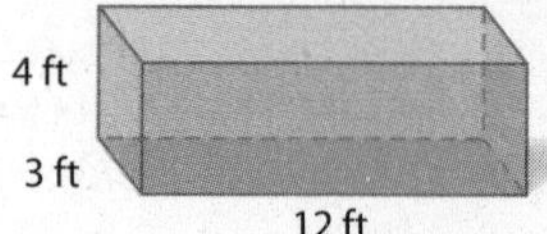 Volume $= 3 \cdot 4 \cdot 12 = 144\text{ ft}^3$

X

ENGLISH	SPANISH	EXAMPLES
***x*-axis** The horizontal axis on a coordinate plane.	**eje *x*** El eje horizontal del plano cartesiano.	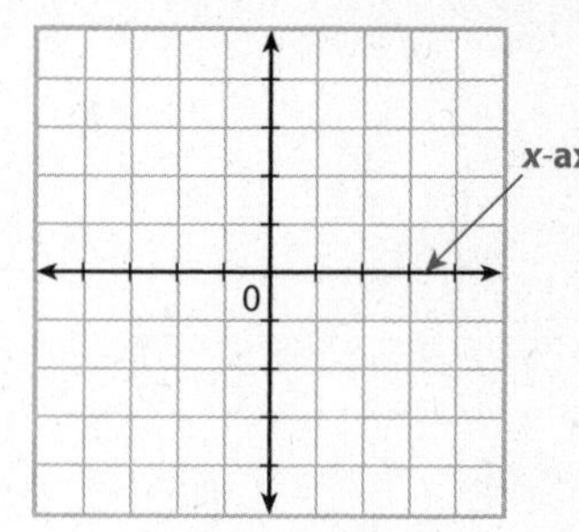
***x*-coordinate** The first number in an ordered pair; it tells the distance to move right or left from the origin, (0, 0).	**coordenada *x*** El primer número en un par ordenado; indica la distancia que debes avanzar hacia la izquierda o hacia la derecha desde el origen, (0, 0).	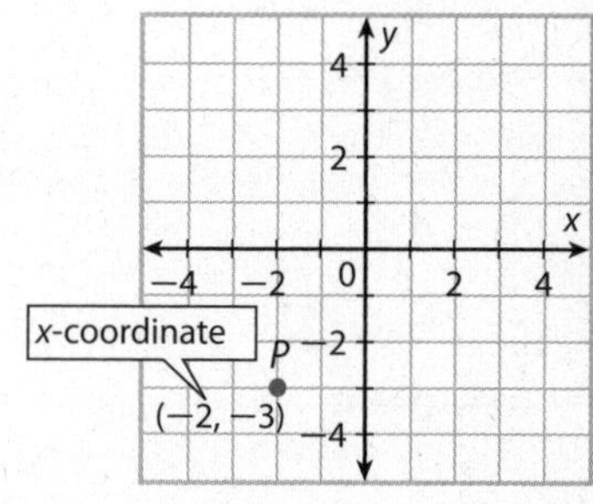
***x*-intercept** The *x*-coordinate of the point where the graph of a line crosses the *x*-axis.	**intersección con el eje *x*** Coordenada *x* del punto donde la gráfica de una línea cruza el eje *x*.	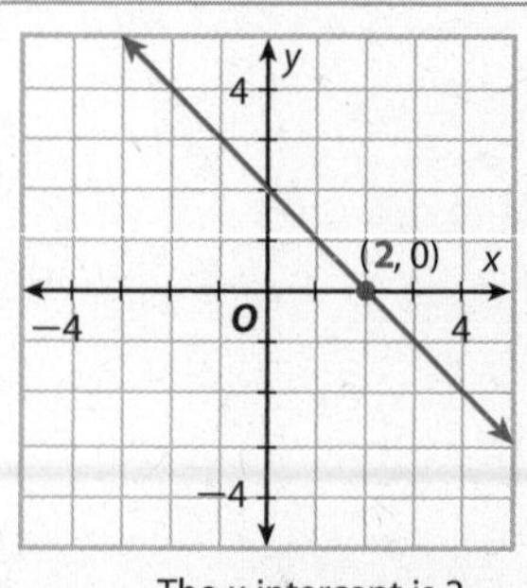 The *x*-intercept is 2.

ENGLISH	SPANISH	EXAMPLES

-axis The vertical axis on a ›ordinate plane.

eje *y* El eje vertical del plano cartesiano.

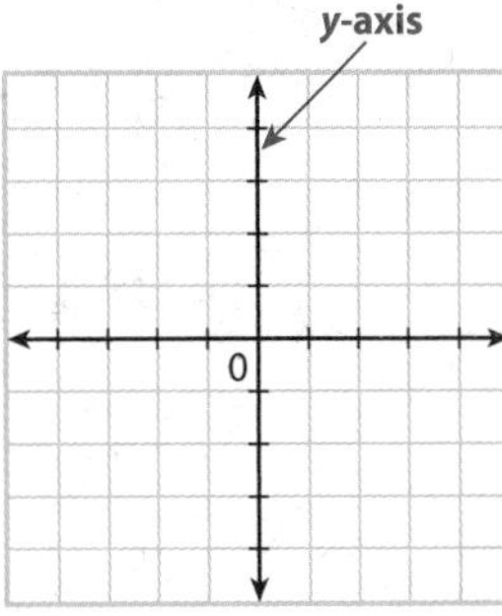

-coordinate The second number ▪ an ordered pair; it tells the distance › move up or down from the origin, ▪, 0).

coordenada *y* El segundo número de un par ordenado; indica la distancia que debes avanzar hacia arriba o hacia abajo desde el origen, (0, 0).

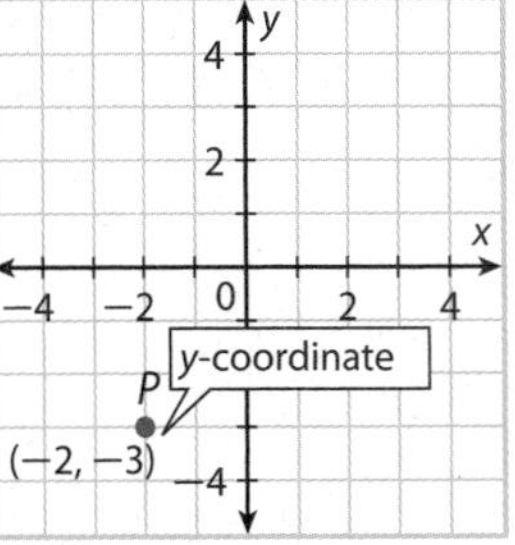

-intercept The *y*-coordinate of the ›oint where the graph of a line crosses ›e *y*-axis.

intersección con el eje *y* Coordenada *y* del punto donde la gráfica de una línea cruza el eje *y*.

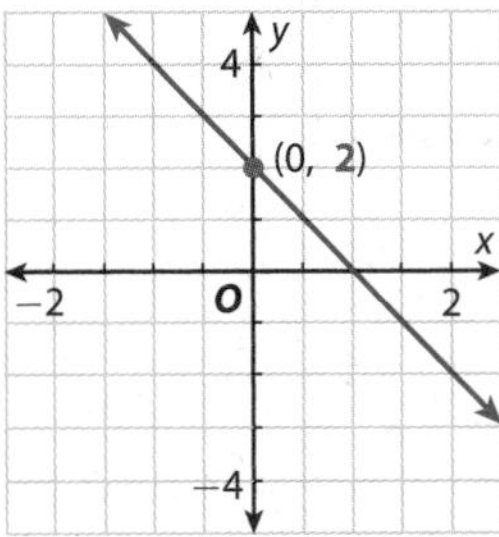

The *y*-intercept is 2.

Z

ero pair A number and its opposite, ›hich add to 0.

par nulo Un número y su opuesto, cuya suma es 0.

18 and −18

Glossary/Glosario

Index

A

B

C

Index

Index

H

I

J

K

Index

Index

N

O

Index

Index

Q

R

S

T

Z

ASSESSMENT REFERENCE SHEET

TABLE OF MEASURES

Length

1 inch = 2.54 centimeters

1 meter ≈ 39.37 inches

1 mile = 5,280 feet

1 mile = 1,760 yards

1 mile ≈ 1.609 kilometers

1 kilometer ≈ 0.62 mile

Mass/Weight

1 pound = 16 ounces

1 pound ≈ 0.454 kilogram

1 kilogram ≈ 2.2 pounds

1 ton = 2,000 pounds

Capacity

1 cup = 8 fluid ounces

1 pint = 2 cups

1 quart = 2 pints

1 gallon = 4 quarts

1 gallon ≈ 3.785 liters

1 liter ≈ 0.264 gallon

1 liter = 1000 cubic centimeters

FORMULAS

Area

Parallelogram	$A = bh$
Circle	$A = \pi r^2$
Triangle	$A = \frac{1}{2}bh$

Volume

General Prisms	$V = Bh$
Cylinder	$V = \pi r^2 h$
Sphere	$V = \frac{4}{3}\pi r^3$
Cone	$V = \frac{1}{3}\pi r^2 h$

Circumference

Circle	$C = \pi d$ or $C = 2\pi r$